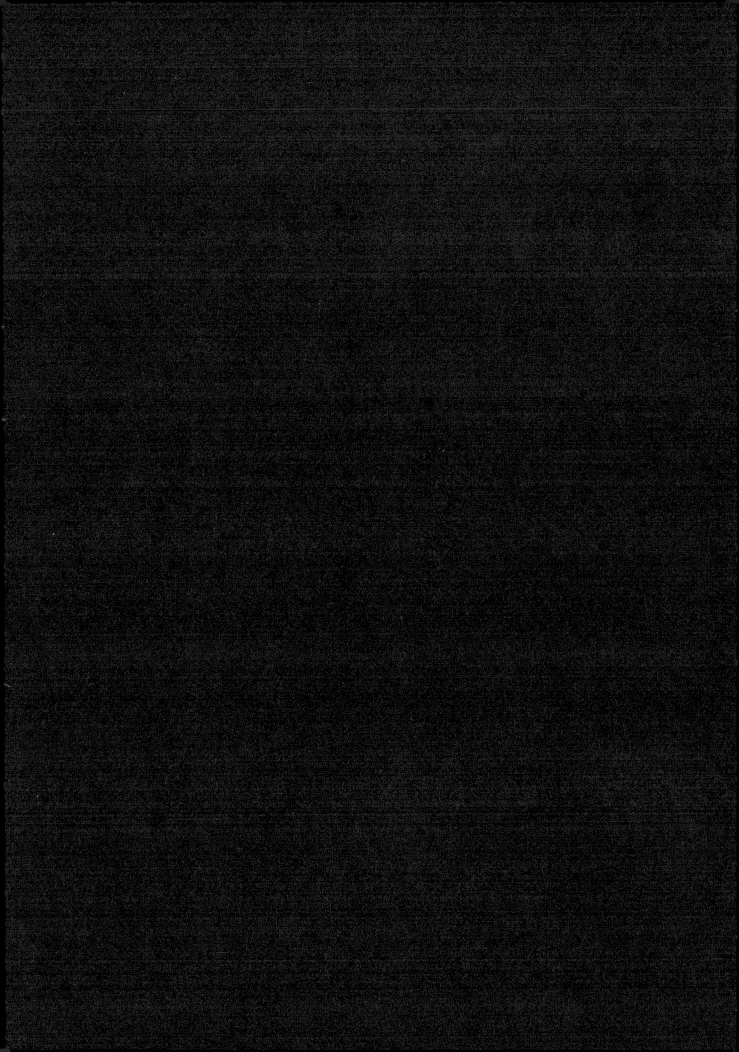

HISTORY OF WOLFEBORO, NH, 1770-1994

VOLUME I

# A CHRONOLOGICAL HISTORY OF THE TOWN AND ITS PEOPLE


BY

Q. DAVID BOWERS

PART I OF A THREE-VOLUME SET

Published by the Wolfeboro Historical Society
Box 1066
Wolfeboro, NH 03894



History of Wolfeboro, NH, 1770-1994, Three Volumes
Volume I—ISBN 0-943161-61-4



**Graphics and layout by Bowers and Merena Galleries, Inc.**

General James Wolfe, namesake of Wolfeboro, who died on September 13, 1759, at the age of 33, while battling the French in Quebec. (Engraving by the American Bank Note Co., New York, for the Wolfeboro National Bank, circa 1930s)

## About the Author

Q. David Bowers, born in 1938, first visited Wolfeboro in the 1970s and became a year-round resident in 1982. A 1960 graduate of the Pennsylvania State University, in 1976 he received that institution's College of Business Administration Distinguished Alumnus Award.

He is the author of over three dozen books and has earned many literary recognitions and awards. Selected titles include *The History of U.S. Coinage* (written for The Johns Hopkins University); *The Encyclopedia of Automatic Musical Instruments* (selected by the American Library Association as one of the most valuable books of the year in 1972 and produced in over 12 printings since that time); *Silver Dollars and Trade Dollars of the United States: A Complete Encyclopedia,* in two volumes; and various biographical, numismatic, and historical texts.

With Raymond N. Merena and a talented staff, he conducts Bowers and Merena Galleries, Inc., in Wolfeboro, a firm that does a worldwide business.

# Table of Contents

## VOLUME I

### History of Wolfeboro, NH, 1770 to 1994

# INTRODUCTION

The idea of writing an updated history of Wolfeboro, a companion to the 1901 *History of Wolfeborough* volume by Benjamin F. Parker, was first broached to me by Marshall K. Ray in the mid-1980s, but I demurred due to other commitments. In 1991 Marshall and I talked again, I offered to begin the research for the project, and he brought the matter before the Wolfeboro Historical Society. This resulted in a November 20, 1991, letter from Joan (Mrs. Gordon S.) Kimball, president of the Society, inviting me to attend a meeting. Additional discussions were held, and by late 1991 the project was begun.

Theodore H. ("Ted") Brigden, who had been interested in Wolfeboro history, particularly that of North Wolfeboro, was named as my contact person and served as such for much of the research stage. From the beginning to the end of the project, I worked closely with Chris (Mrs. John) Fipphen, head of the Publication Committee. Several Society members volunteered to help in research.

What to include and what to omit — these considerations go through the mind of any author endeavoring to write a history of anything. In the case of Wolfeboro, the activities of several thousand people from 1901 to date filled thousands of pages of town reports and the *Granite State News* over the years and could likewise fill thousands of pages of the present book.

In planning the project, I thought it would be best to write and present the history in three volumes, each complementing the others.

Volume I is a narrative time-line of Wolfeboro beginning with an overview of the 1770-1900 years, followed by a decade-by-decade chronicle from 1901 to 1994.

Two separate books have been published as companions to the narrative chronological history:

Volume II is a source book and contains "Wolfeboro Place Names and Origins," "Education and Schools" (by Christine Fipphen), "Churches" (primarily by Theodore H. Brigden), "Civic Organizations and Groups," "Lake Winnipesaukee Boats with a Relationship to Wolfeboro," and "Town Government; Elected and Appointed Officials," "Censuses," and "Statistics." In addition, the Bibliography for Volumes I, II, and III is included in Volume II.

Volume III is the *Business and Professional Directory*.

It is hoped that the three-volume set will provide one of the most comprehensive views ever presented of *any* American town of comparable size.

Parker's *History* devoted over 550 pages to the chronology of the town from the earliest days to 1900 and was published in the following year, 1901. Because reprints of the Parker work are readily available, Volume I devotes relatively little space to this era and places emphasis on happenings from 1901 to date. Volumes II and III each contain much information not hitherto available in any single printed source including Parker.

As this reference work undoubtedly will be used by future generations, and as no comprehensive book covering Wolfeboro has been created since the Parker effort, it became incumbent upon me to detail the early years of the present century, although I was not personally familiar with them, nor were any of my contemporaries. Much of the data had to be taken from town reports and records, copies of the *Granite State News*, Wolfeboro Historical Society archives, directories, and private sources.

As years and decades passed, people and businesses changed so much that important personalities and enterprises showcased in publicity during the 150th anniversary of Wolfeboro celebrated in 1920 for the most part no longer exist. In fact, only a few of the businesses active in 1951 at the century's half-way point were engaged in trade at the concluding year of the present study, 1994. By 1994, only one merchant, Howard Bean, had been continously operating the same business since 1951. Wolfeboro has evolved, and descriptions of life in Wolfeboro show great changes in the cast of characters from decade to decade.

Throughout the years perhaps the most consistent sentiment has been that Wolfeboro is a great place to live, a town that people enjoy, whether they be year-round residents or stay only for the summer. To know Wolfeboro is to love it, it has been said.

Wolfeboro has had numerous industries over the years, beginning with early grist and saw mills, then shoe factories, textile mills, and other enterprises. However, first and foremost its location on two lakes — the wholly contained Lake Wentworth and the town's extensive frontage on Lake Winnipesaukee — has been its greatest attraction. The lakes and surrounding verdant hills gave rise in the mid-nineteenth century to the local tourism and retirement industry, which today is the town's most important source of revenue.

Perhaps more than anything else, the story of

Wolfeboro is the story of its people. On August 24, 1920, in an address given as part of the town's 150th anniversary celebration, Judge Sewall W. Abbott commented:

History has been for the most part a record...of wars, the rise and fall of rulers, the changing of national boundaries, and the different elements of thought, desires, selfishness, greed, love of conquest, and whatnot, which make up the life and character of government. Too little is known, practically nothing in fact, of the lives of the people, the laborers, their homes, their touch with public affairs — all those uncounted things which go to make up human life in the mass.

In addition to recording the lives of the people and the happenings of the near century of time that has passed since 1901, I believe it important to relate much about today — the 1990s — as such information is first hand. In doing this I have endeavored to show Wolfeboro as I and various interviewees know and see it, with emphasis on items important to me and those who have offered assistance, particularly members of the Wolfeboro Historical Society. Undoubtedly, if other authors had been assigned the same task, they each would have approached the project somewhat differently. He who pleases everyone pleases no one, Abraham Lincoln said. While I do not attempt to please everyone, I hope that in the final say the work meets general approval. I thank the many people, each of whom is credited in the acknowledgments section, who have been an important part of this project.

The present book evolved somewhat in the same manner that Benjamin F. Parker's 1901 *History* did, for Parker related:

The town first took action on the matter in 1898, when Messrs. Edwin H. Lord, Albert B. Rust, and Frederick W. Prindle were appointed a committee to confer with the author. As a result of their interest and painstaking labors, this volume, published under an appropriation of the town, is now offered to the public.

Parker, too, had his space limitations, and his book, 557 pages in length, contained relatively few illustrations and was, in Parker's words, "Not particularly rich in genealogy — not because it lacked value, not because it was uninteresting, but for the sole reason that the scope of the work forbade its incorporation therein."

Beginning with a vote at the annual town meeting in 1957, in which the moderator appointed a committee of three (Wilma Paine, Mrs. W. Fred Tuttle, and Prof. Robert F.W. Meader) to examine a manuscript said to have been created by Alta Bailey Meader, forces were set in motion to publish a new history of Wolfeboro. The committee subsequently discovered that Alta B. Meader had not created a text, but had some notes and a desire to write a book.

It fell upon the Wolfeboro Historical Society to create what was hoped to be a sequel to Parker's 1901 work. A committee consisting of Rev. Lewis Coffin, Dolly (Mrs. James) Bovaird, Wilma Paine, and Mrs. W. Fred Tuttle went ahead with the project. Prof. Meader resigned due to other commitments. This Editorial Board of four prepared a subject outline and secured 17 volunteers to each write a chapter on a given subject.

In 1958 the Editorial Board reported at the town meeting and asked for a vote of confidence and an appropriation of $100 for expenses, both of which were granted. Meetings were held in 1958 and 1959 for discussion, but little writing was actually done. Miss Paine had to resign because of ill health, and her place as board chairman was taken over by William C. Krook. Other members were added including Mr. and Mrs. George Fitch, Mr. and Mrs. David Fetzer, Florence Paine, and Roy E. Argersinger.

In 1960 the Board decided to reorganize and call itself the Committee on Wolfeboro History, with a secondary group to act as an editorial board. Roy E. Argersinger was made chairman. The new plan was that articles would be written in preliminary form, and a hired professional editor-in-chief would put them into final copy. By this time the project had expanded to 21 planned subjects, 21 assigned writers, and six assistant writers. Despite all good intentions and a lot of urging and other effort by Chairman Argersinger, only three articles had been completed by early 1961.

Files preserved today by the Society indicate that Florence Paine and Gertrude B. Hamm were among those who performed their assigned tasks admirably. Unfortunately, for each person who completed his or her section, several others let their interest wane. Of the over two dozen writers and assistants who were supposed to have worked together, fewer than six finished what they had set out to do. The history book project lapsed, many files were lost or misplaced, and Mr. Argersinger's efforts ceased.

In the 1970s the book idea was revitalized when Janet E. Macomber took over the project, organized it, interviewed several dozen old-timers, consulted everything relevant she could find at the Wolfeboro Public Library and at the Wolfeboro Historical Society, and expended a truly fantastic amount of energy. Unfortunately, this effort also was not completed.

All was not lost. Even though nothing was published at the time, certain research and writing done from the 1950s through the 1970s survived for my use in the present volume. I had begun keeping notes on local history in the early 1980s. Specific contributions of Hamm, Paine, Macomber, and other dedicated workers from the past are noted in the credits, bibliography, and endnotes.

In recent years major efforts and contributions were made by Dr. Joyce E. Brown, Roberta A. French, and

Dianne Rogers, each of whom spent many hundreds of hours on the project. Special recognition is likewise due to Christine Fipphen and Theodore H. Brigden, both of whom created text used in Volume II. Jennifer Meers helped with and supervised the graphics and production. These people constituted the front-line team for the three volumes.

Sandy Martin (especially) and Cathy Dumont Wilson took many photographs of Wolfeboro people, places, and things in 1994 and 1995. Their efforts illustrate the town as it is today. In keeping with the enlightened society of the 1990s, I have emphasized a wide variety of people, places, events, and subjects for illustration. Volume I in particular covers many subjects of diverse interest. In contrast, the 1889 history of Carroll County and Benjamin Franklin Parker's 1901 *History of Wolfeborough* had illustrations primarily devoted to prominent *men.*

L. Winston Hamm, Harrison D. Moore, and Joseph I. Melanson III, each with a passionate interest in local history, provided much from their files and collections.

The Acknowledgments pages list the names of many others who each played a part. Patrons and contributors who supported the project financially are also noted with appreciation.

During the late nineteenth and early twentieth centuries it was popular to devote large amounts of space in local and county histories to leading citizens who more often than not helped pay for the volume. Of course, many of these same people were indeed important in the community, and such records are valuable. Today, it would be a judgment call to state who is important in Wolfeboro and who isn't — for in my view *everyone* is important, from a baby just born at Huggins Hospital, to a child entering Carpenter School in the kindergarten, to a recent graduate of Kingswood High or Brewster Academy, to someone who has spent 70 years of his or her life within town boundaries, to a summer resident from Massachusetts who spends only July and August here, to someone from a distant state or land passing through Wolfeboro for the first time, and only briefly, eating a meal in one of our restaurants or staying overnight at a local inn. All have contributed to making Wolfeboro what it is. Such names as do appear are those of people who have figured in one notable way or another in the history of the town and whose accomplishments were recorded in newspapers, directories, town records, and other accounts. In particular, Volume III, the *Business and Professional Directory,* records many people who were or still are active in commerce.

As extensive as the three volumes of the present work may be, there is much additional material that could have been included. Indeed, such separate aspects as churches, schools, lake islands, hotels, sports, and industries could have made extensive books in themselves. The same can be said for the biographies of Allen H. Albee, George A. Carpenter and family, Dr. Fred Ellsworth Clow, Mabel Fullerton Hatch, Frank P. Hobbs, Dr. Grace Murray Hopper, Archie A. Horne, Dr. Sarah Jenness, Dr. Henry F. Libby, the Melanson family, Roger F. Murray 2nd, Daniel Pickering, Robert F. Thurrell, and certain other citizens. That the field offers many opportunities for specialized study is illustrated by the current research of S. Paul Jung, Jr., who is completing a book-length manuscript on a Wolfeboro manufacturer, *John Taber and John Taber Jr., Two New England Clay Pipemakers.*

As an apology for any items overlooked, not discovered, or not given their proper due, I quote this from Plato:[1]

*As it is the commendation of a good huntsman to find game in a wide wood, so it is no imputation if he hath not caught all.*

Perhaps the present work will provide a jumping-off spot for anyone wishing to do further research on specific subjects relating to our town.

I moved to New Hampshire in 1980 and lived for a year on Chase Point in Tuftonboro while my home on Wolfeboro Neck was being constructed. My family and I crossed the portal of our Wolfeboro home on January 8, 1982. We have enjoyed living here ever since. We, like so many others who reside in town or who have visited here, consider ourselves fortunate to have discovered this gem among communities of the world — a very special place.

To the past and present citizens of Wolfeboro, to the seasonal residents who pay a good share of our taxes, and to the visitors who have enjoyed our town, these three volumes are respectfully dedicated.

Q. David Bowers
October 21, 1995

Natural resources: Haying scene, probably in Wolfeboro circa 1890s. For nearly 200 years agriculture was an important local industry. (Found among a group of glass negatives depicting Wolfeboro scenes)

Natural resources: Deer abound in Wolfeboro forests and meadows. These two were seen in town in 1994 just off South Main Street behind All Saints' Episcopal Church. (Sandy Martin photograph)

# ACKNOWLEDGMENTS

The following helped in the ways indicated.

In addition to these names, a number of people furnished information about their current businesses and professions (used in Volume III); these are not credited. A special thank you is due, however, to the many Wolfeboro residents and business people who were photographed for possible use in this project or who loaned photographs and illustrations, but whose material could not be used because of space constraints. The author had the pleasant circumstance of having several *thousand* photographs and images from which to choose, and in the absence of making the set of books many times its present size, many fine illustrations had to be excluded.

Photographs and other illustrations are from the collection of the Wolfeboro Historical Society and the research archives of the author unless specifically credited otherwise. When known, images are attributed to the photographer who took them. Thus, the works of Mildred A. Beach, Bruce Bedford, Jack Bickford, Ephraim T. Brigham, Charles E. Brown, Ned Bullock, E. Crawford, David Fetzer, Edson Graham, Charles O. Hodgman, Eleanor and Merwin Horn, Stacy Kendall, Steve Libby, Bruce Lorry, Dane H.G. Malcolm, Sandy Martin, Fred Miller, Arthur H. Sawyer, L.B. Strout, David Wentworth, Cathy Dumont Wilson, Darlene Williams, Ashton R. Woodhouse, H.B. York, and other Wolfeboro and regional lens artists are represented. Certain modern photographs 1993-1995 of merchants and local scenes were taken by Q. David Bowers expressly for this project and are not specifically credited.

**Charles M. Abbott** kept scrapbooks during the 1960s of Wolfeboro and regional news items from New England papers. Now in the Wolfeboro Historical Society's archives, these were reviewed by the author. **Madelyn R. Albee** lent information concerning the Allen "A" Resort. **Jean Allard** provided information concerning local schools. **Rosemary Arctander** provided definitions of certain zoning terminology. **Priscilla ("Pat") Arey** provided information about home schooling. **Howard Avery** wrote an essay on farming and lumbering for the Society in the 1970s; certain of his information has been used in the present text.

**L. Nyoka Babbitt** provided the history of the Hospice of Southern Carroll County and Vicinity and the Visiting Nurse Association. **Mary K. Bagg** furnished a reference book from the Tuftonboro Library. **Allan E. Bailey, Jr.,** and **Julie M. Bailey** reviewed parts of the text, especially Volume III, and made suggestions. **Althea Ballentine** furnished historical details and illustrations pertaining to Camp Kehonka, read part of the text and made comments, and gave several recollections. **Mildred A. Beach** provided extensive information concerning the Lakes Region Association and tourism. **Beverly Bean** answered several inquiries. **Dennis E. Bean** shared information about Mabel Fullerton Hatch. **Evelyn and Lester Bean** furnished a book to the author. **Howard Bean** read sections of the manuscript, made suggestions, and provided several old photographs for study. **Carol Bense** provided the history of the Village Players. **Anne Bentley,** Massachusetts Historical Society, furnished copies of Wolfeboro bank notes. In 1981 **Bradford Bentley** shared recollections and anecdotes about Camp Wyanoke and provided other information to the author. **Edna (Mrs. Bradford) Bentley** provided information and an interview concerning Camp Wyanoke along with information about nearby Camp Ossipee. **Shirley (Mrs. Hayden M.) Bentley** provided the history of the Friends of Music and helped with the Hospice of Southern Carroll County and Vicinity and the Visiting Nurse Association. **Ethel (Mrs. George D.) Black** contributed recollections of Wolfeboro including Huggins Hospital, reviewed sections of the manuscript, and made many suggestions. **Christian Blom** corresponded about Wolfeboro bank notes. **Suzanne Bonin** answered several inquiries and provided copies of her etchings of Wolfeboro scenes. **Mary M. Borckardt** provided the history of local Boy Scout and Cub Scout activities and the Order of the Eastern Star. **Andrew V. Bowers** and **Christine Bowers** provided much encouragement at home during the writing of the three books comprising this work. **Walter P. Bowman,** historian and author on the subject of Lake Wentworth, provided information about the lake and its islands. **Judith Carr Breuninger** lent information from an extensive file kept by her mother, Edith Hoppin Carr, and provided data concerning winter sports and athletic events. **John F. Bridges** shared his recollections of boating on Lake Winnipesaukee from the 1940s to date, discussed various Wolfeboro islands, told of his father Sen. H. Styles Bridges, and answered many questions. **Theodore H. Brigden** of the Wolfeboro Historical Society copy edited much of the text, assisted with the location of material, and helped in many other ways including with publicity. He also created commentaries concerning the Libby Museum, the Rotary Club, certain churches of Wolfeboro, and other subjects (see Volume II). **Jean Brodrick** gave information concerning the Friends of Music and assisted with several picture captions. **Don and Lillian Brookes** answered several inquiries. **Donah L. Brookes** assisted with real estate information. **Deborah A. Brooks,** principal, Kingswood Regional High School, assisted with photographs relating to that institution. **Wanda Brooks** helped with several picture captions. **Dr. Charles E. Brown,** son of Harold F. Brown, furnished historical photographs. **Dr. Joyce E. Brown,** daughter of Harold F. Brown, read the original text, annotated it, and made many important suggestions and corrections; in addition, she furnished information concerning her father's and other Wolfeboro businesses. She was among the most important contributors to the project. **Dorothea (Brummitt) Hayes** contributed several comments. **Robert C. Bryant** sent biographical information concerning Ole H. Bryant, violin maker. **Gloria and Ned Bullock** provided several photographs from 1960s news items as well as from Ned's professional portfolio. **Jack and Ann Burghardt,** publishers of the *Granite State News,* furnished negatives, helped with publicity, and assisted in other ways. **Virginia and Wes Burke** provided information about local Boy Scout activities. **Rev. Lee A. Button** answered an inquiry and provided historical information.

**Douglas H. Cady** provided the history of the Wolfeboro Lions Club. **Jennifer Caldwell** (Mrs. Howie Bean) answered several questions concerning sports. **Don Campbell** publicized the project and published a story in *The Wolfeboro Times.* **Jane Carville** supplied information about the Wolfeboro Nursery School and several businesses. **Ann Caspar** helped with publicity. **Dorothy Caspar** helped with publicity. **Arthur F. Chamberlin** sent information about the Chamberlin (also spelled Chamberlain) family in Wolfeboro, made numerous suggestions concerning listings in "Wolfeboro Place Names and Origins" in Volume II, and helped in other ways. **Marguerite Clarke** was interviewed about the Newcomers Club. **Richard S. Clarke** provided a file of information concerning Clarke Plaza and related businesses. **Stephen E. Clow** reviewed the manuscript and made many suggestions. **William Copeley,** librarian, New Hampshire Historical Society, furnished copies of certain nineteenth century issues of the *Granite State News* and helped in other ways. **Reta Corson** lent a copy of the 1899 *Wolfeborough Directory.* **E. Crawford** took photographs of the 1962 Winter Carnival, copies of which were furnished by Theodore H. Brigden. **Barbara Stackpole Crowley** provided anecdotes concerning her father, Ernest E. Stackpole, and other information and helped with publicity.

**Bridget Daniels** supplied information concerning the Wolfeboro Center Community Church. **Beverly Davis** lent a scrapbook concerning the Sugar Maple Community Playground built in 1991. **Steve Davis** furnished information about John Taber's pipe-making activities, copy-read sections of the manuscript, and made suggestions. **Stephen L. Den Hartog** provided reminiscences of the Varney Islands and furnished copies of real estate sales documents. **Diane K. DeNee,** research and publication coordinator at Brewster Academy, furnished information about the Academy and about John Brewster. **Thomas Denly** corresponded about Wolfeboro bank notes and provided a note for use in Volume III. **Sylvia Gould Denton** provided information about Gould's Dime Store. **Fern Descoteaux** provided information about local Boy Scout activities. **Edith DesMarais** wrote the history of the Wolfeboro Area Children's Center. **Etta I. Drake** furnished the history of the Wolfeboro Woman's Club and information about the Wolfeboro Senior Citizens Club. **Patricia Dugan** proofread part of the text. **Bonnie Dunbar** of the Brook & Bridle guest facility, East Alton, provided information concerning John Taber and his pipe factories and accompanied the author to a Taber factory site on her property. **Penelope Shannon Duncan** discussed historical information. **Father Denys-Martin Du Pont** provided information about the Holy Trinity Mission.

**Denise Earle** provided information concerning the history of public accommodations on Rust Pond and the Cider Press Restaurant. **Kathy and Richard Eaton** lent a large scrapbook of clippings about the Durgin Block. Kathy Eaton granted permission to utilize information appearing in *The Laker* and helped in several other ways. **Elaine Eckhoff** assisted with information about local schools. **Everett Edmunds** proofread certain parts of Volume I with regard to sports events and supplied a photograph. **Nathalie L.A. Erickson** shared reminiscences of her experiences with many facets of life in Wolfeboro over a span of decades and furnished the history of the Kingswood Summer Theatre for Children.

**Dorothy Fabian** sent documentation concerning McKinney Park and helped with publicity. **Stephanie Fairtile** provided information about Scouting. **Doug Fallon** provided a photograph. **Patti Ferber** provided information about the First Church of Christ, Scientist. **Chester Fernald** furnished information concerning Wolfeboro air mail service in the 1920s, when he was 10 years old and helped distribute the mail at Wawbeek in Melvin Village, and furnished a scrapbook of clippings kept years ago by the George A. Carpenter family. **Christine Fipphen** researched and wrote the section on Wolfeboro schools which forms an important section of Volume II. Both she and her husband John read many sections of the manuscript and made many helpful suggestions. **John S. Fipphen** contributed information about Wolfeboro cemeteries and provided a listing of these for cross reference in "Wolfeboro Place Names and Origins" in Volume II; helped with the history of several churches; and as editor of *The Wellsweep,* newsletter of the Wolfeboro Historical Society, encouraged others to submit information; helped with publicity; and assisted his wife Christine with the section in Volume II about Wolfeboro schools. **Arthur Fitts III** corresponded about Wolfeboro bank notes. **Verna Flagg** assisted Roberta A. French with several business questions. **Wes Flierl** provided information about several local businesses. **Frederick L. Foley, Jr.,** furnished the history of the Wolfeboro Wranglers Square Dance Club and the Wentworth House Plantation Association. **John J. Ford, Jr.,** provided a reference book. **Charles ("Zip") Foss** reviewed the manuscript and made suggestions. **Helen Foss** provided the history of Myrtle Rebekah Lodge No. 48. **Robert Fournier** was interviewed about banks including Kingswood Bank & Trust, BankEast, and the Wolfeboro Banking Office of the Farmington National Bank. He also supplied recollections concerning town activities from the 1980s to date. **Bette Frazier** furnished the history of the Hot Peppers Jumprope Club. **Roberta A. French** transcribed much data from the *Granite State News,* made numerous research inquiries, conducted interviews, reviewed Zoning Board of Adjustment files with Larry Keniston at Town Hall, and helped in many other ways over a period of several years; she was one of the most important participants in the project. **Fenton Friend** provided information concerning several businesses. **Dr. Kathy Helgesen Fuller** reviewed sections of the manuscript and made valuable suggestions.

**Philip Ganem** furnished information about certain trust funds he manages. **Shirley E. Ganem,** selectman, helped facilitate research at the Town Hall. **Louise Gehman,** librarian, Wolfeboro Public Library, provided historical directories and references, annual *Town Reports,* and made microfilms of the *Granite State News* available for study. She also furnished a history of the Library. **Kathie Giffin** lent a copy of *Meryl,* a novel set in Wolfeboro. **Bradford W. Gile** provided recollections concerning the Wolfeboro National Bank and the Community Bank & Trust Co. **Arthur Glidden** answered several queries. **Dennis Glidden** answered an inquiry. **Marie Glidden** supplied information concerning several businesses. **Ruth O. Glidden** furnished information concerning an Old Home Week celebration, supplied several photographs, and helped with publicity. **Beverly A. Goodrich** provided information concerning Wolfeboro businesses and local schools. **J. Frank ("Jeff") Goodwin III** provided a file of Wolfeboro memorabilia including a large collection of photographs from the turn of the century. **John A. Graf** shared his reminiscences of the "good old days" of the 1950s and helped with information concerning the so-called Chiang Kai-Shek house (Hopewell summer house) on Wolfeboro Neck. **Wilma Grant** supplied information concerning the Universalist-Union Church. **Priscilla Griffin** furnished information about the Libby Museum.

**Rodney Haines** furnished information to Florence A. Paine in 1972 concerning the East Wolfeboro Post Office; some of this was used in the present work. **Jane Hall** furnished the history of the Wolfeboro Garden Club and made several suggestions. **Donald E.L. Hallock** provided a file of information concerning railroading and fire fighting in Wolfeboro and the rebirth of the Wolfeborough Railroad and shared his recollections. Certain notes, commentaries, and observations of the late **Gertrude Hamm,** written in the 1960s and preserved by the Wolfeboro Historical Society, were utilized. **L. Winston Hamm** reviewed sections of the manuscript, made suggestions, and was interviewed on several subjects. In addition, he shared much information from his computerized historical files and provided a group of nineteenth century issues of the *Granite State News.* **Dr. John J. Hammond** answered an inquiry. **Patricia Hanson** provided information. **Robert L. Hanson** provided much information concerning the Varney Islands, their individual names and their history. **Sumner P. Harris,** principal, Carpenter School, provided information about that institution and helped in other ways. **Paul R. Hatch** discussed his involvement in theatres and other local businesses over the years, provided several photographs, and helped in other ways. **Dorothea (Brummitt) Hayes** reviewed sections of the manuscript and made many suggestions. **Bruce Heald** provided information on Lake Winnipesaukee boats. **John B. Hemenway** furnished information concerning Camp Birchmont. **Warren Henderson** corresponded about Wolfeboro bank notes and provided several images for use in Volume III. **James W. Hill** provided information about local Boy Scout activities. **Barbara Hobbie** granted permission to excerpt information from her numerous articles on local subjects. **Michael J. Hodder** provided information concerning several historical and geographical items. **Patricia M. Hodder** supplied posters for use as illustrations in Volume II. **Ethel Holmes** provided information about Pickering School. **Frank X. Holt** provided information about amateur athletic teams and a description of the Wolfeboro-Tuftonboro Youth Basketball League. **William Hooper** provided two photographs for examination. **Di Hopewell** furnished notes on town history. **Robert Hopewell** furnished historical information concerning Hopewell Point on Wolfeboro Neck and about Parker Island. **Debbie Hopkins** provided histories of the Governor Wentworth Arts Council, the Artists in the Park exhibitions, the Wolfeboro Arts and Crafts Association, and the Wolfeboro League Shop. **Donald G. Hughes** reviewed sections of the manuscript and made suggestions. **George Hutchinson** provided details of certain real estate developments and loaned a set of Sanborn maps.

**Adelbert M. Jakeman, Jr.,** furnished information about Beatrice Maloney (after whom Beatrice Street was named). **Virginia Janik** provided historical information. **Sigrid L. Johannessen-Cameron** was interviewed concerning her observation of the filming of *Once Around* and provided several candid snapshots of the event. **Gwendolyn M. Jones,** town clerk of Alton, provided information concerning the Alton-Wolfeboro boundary changes over the years and answered inquiries about Lake Winnipesaukee islands. **Nancy Jousson** provided notes concerning the Hill School Camp. **S. Paul Jung, Jr.,** provided information and a descriptive text about Wolfeboro pipe maker John Taber and discussed other aspects of nineteenth century commerce.

**Dr. Kathryn Kachovos** corresponded concerning Wolfeboro history. **Chris Karstedt** helped with several research inquiries. **Melissa Karstedt** provided an observation. **Dotti Kay** corresponded about Girl Scouts. **Paul Kemp** discussed Trask Mountain. **Larry Keniston,** code enforcement officer for Wolfeboro, furnished information concerning business permits and helped with inquiries; he assisted Roberta A. French in reviewing several thousand files. **Rev. Matthew Kettler** provided information concerning the Church of the Nazarene. **Joan and Gordon Kimball** helped facilitate the author's research and access to information and supplied several directories and tax listings; they also assisted Christine Fipphen with information about Wolfeboro schools and helped with publicity. **Dr. W. Douglas Kipp** provided four notebooks filled with data pertaining to Wolfeboro fires in recent decades, compiled when he was a member of the Fire Department. **Debbie and Stan Kissell** provided a photograph. **Sarah Kourian** furnished information about the Wolfeboro League Shop. **Guy L. Krapp,** long-time town manager, reviewed several parts of the manuscript.

**Dr. Irene Ladd** provided information about her multi-age classes at Carpenter School. **Bernard Landman,** Wolfeboro postmaster 1960-1965, supplied information to Florence A. Paine in 1972 and corresponded with the author in 1993. **Paul A. Lang** provided information including the history of the Hampshire Chamber Singers. **Brenda LaPointe** assisted with information in the custody of the town of Wolfeboro, including tax and real estate records, suggested sources for additional data, and answered many questions. **Ray LaRocque** provided information about the Wolfeboro Senior Citizens Club. **Alan Laufman,** Organ Clearing House, furnished information on the classic pipe organ once located in the First Christian Church. **Edward R. Laurion,** Alton postmaster, furnished information concerning mail boat service to Wolfeboro. **Betty Laycock** helped with publicity. **Dorothy Leonard** made suggestions concerning sources of research material. **Richard C. Libby** provided information on railroading in Wolfeboro, the Rus Chase Bridge-Falls Path, and the Libby family, and supplied several photographs from the archives of his Remember the Iron Horse Museum and suggested captions. **John M. Loether** provided information about the First Church of Christ, Scientist. **Bonnie Rankin Lord** provided information about sports during the period from the 1980s through 1994.

**Kenneth MacDonald** helped facilitate research at the Town Hall. Certain research notes, articles, and commentaries written by **Janet E. Macomber** in the 1970s were utilized. In addition, Mrs. Macomber conversed and corresponded concerning the present work and made a number of suggestions. **Ralph Malmgren** furnished several publications about postal history and lake steamers and helped with publicity. **Carolyn Malone** gave information concerning Albert George Rollins. **Richard Mancke** made several suggestions. **Richard G. Marden** reviewed portions of the manuscript and made suggestions. **Stefanie C. Marsh** furnished information concerning the Cotton Mountain district. **Sandy Martin** took numerous photographs in 1994, especially of Wolfeboro businesses, printed contact copies from negatives, furnished historical photographs from her own files, and helped in other ways. In addition, many photographs she took for the *Wolfeboro Times* in 1990-1991 have been utilized, as have a number of photographs she took on other occasions. **Betty Maxfield** (Mrs. Henry S. Maxfield) answered several questions. **Henry S. Maxfield** provided information and commentary. **Henry S. ("Chip") Maxfield, Jr.,** discussed the real estate market and helped with several place names. **Mary M. McBride** provided historical data. **Charlotte McDermott** provided information about the George A. Carpenter family, answered several questions about other items, and helped with publicity. **Polly McGee,** librarian, *The Christian Science Monitor,* furnished a 1956 newspaper copy. **David McKenney** supplied details of the *Lady Go-Diva* "dive boat." **Alexander ("Sandy") McKenzie IV,** operator of the *Blue Ghost* mail boat, read several sections of the manuscript and made suggestions for the "Wolfeboro Place Names and Origins" section in Volume II. **Joyce McKnight,** Science and Technology Library, Akron-Summit County Public Library, furnished information concerning the zeppelin *Los Angeles.* **Gail McLeod** furnished a suggestion for further research. Text created in the 1950s by **Alta B. Meader** was utilized. **Robert F.W. Meader,** prominent historian, answered several inquiries and reviewed the manuscript; the latter was one of the final things he did before his death in 1994. **Joseph ("Bucky") Melanson III, Joseph I. Melanson IV,** and **Tim Melanson** provided many early glass plate negatives, several large cartons of records and printed material, plus brochures and other ephemera from their large and impressive collection of historical material; their help was of exceeding importance. **Nancy C. Merrill,** Exeter Historical Society, provided information about Frank Swallow, who issued postcards of Wolfeboro. **Peter Michel**

provided information concerning the exchange program at Kingswood High School. **Gary R. Miller** provided updated information about the Rotary Club. **Barbara Mills** furnished listings of local professionals and merchants as compiled by the Wolfeboro Chamber of Commerce. **Edith Millward** furnished information concerning the First Baptist Church. **Rosalie S. Minnerly,** secretary to the author, helped in many ways including tracking down the answers to many research queries. **Carra Moore** assisted in several ways including providing information about the medical staff and other details from the records of Huggins Hospital and assisting with publicity. **Harrison D. Moore,** prominent local historian and researcher, assisted with historical data and gave information concerning many buildings and landmarks; he also lent a 1907 directory. He read the manuscript and made detailed notes, corrections, and additions. Further, he provided information to Christine Fipphen for use in the section on Wolfeboro schools. **James Morash,** director of marketing for the Winnipesaukee Flagship Corporation, assisted with information about the *Mount Washington.* **Mary Jo Morgan** was interviewed about the Wolfeboro League Shop. **Wilma ("Willie") Mork** provided a magazine copy, photographs, and captions for illustrations of Village Players productions. **Philip H. Morrill, Jr.,** Wolfeboro Fire Department, read several sections of the manuscript and made valuable corrections and additions. **K. Elizabeth Morse** provided information concerning the First Church of Christ, Scientist. **Diantha Moulton,** town of Alton offices, answered an inquiry about town boundaries. **Ruth T. Mowatt** provided information about L. Maude Cate. The **Jack Moyer family** provided a commentary about foreign exchange students at Kingswood High School.

**Patricia R. Nelson** provided information about the Avery family and helped with publicity. **Robert W. Nelson** proofread part of the text. **Wendy Nelson** provided a photograph. **The New Hampshire State Historical Society,** William Copeley, librarian, made its archives available for research. **John R. Nichols** of the Lake Wentworth Association provided much information about the Association and lent a book about the lake. **Rhoda W. Nute,** a member of the Wolfeboro Historical Society Publications Committee, provided the history of the Wolfeboro Chamber of Commerce, furnished notes on children's summer vacation camps, researched the history of All Saints' Episcopal Church, and helped in many other ways including with publicity. **Jane Meader Nye,** secretary of the Meader Family Association, Inc., forwarded the typescript of the present work annotated by Dr. Robert F.W. Meader just before his death.

**John O'Connell** furnished a copy of the *Granite Monthly* for October 1920. **Lawrence A. Ogden** furnished information concerning the New England District, Church of the Nazarene.

Several articles researched and written by **Florence A. Paine** in the 1970s were utilized. **Elissa K. Paquette** granted permission to excerpt information from her published articles on local subjects including Harbor House. **Ronald Paquette** discussed fishing and other sports. **Frances (Brummitt) Parkhurst** reviewed sections of the manuscript and made suggestions. **Richard Parshley** provided information concerning Dr. Burt Parshley and also the Klickety Klack Railroad. **Allyn Perkins** furnished histories of the Wolfeboro Rotary Club and the Cotton Mountain Community Church. **John and Laura Jill Pernokas** read parts of the manuscript and made valuable suggestions. **Alan Pierce** assisted with inquiries about town merchants. **Curtis A. Pike** reviewed sections of the manuscript, made suggestions, and furnished a recollection of a 1937 fire. **Norma Pilkington** provided information concerning the American Red Cross in Wolfeboro. **Ida A. Pineo** reviewed sections of the manuscript and made suggestions; she also provided information about the First Christian Church and Wolfeboro schools. **William Pond** assisted with Lake Winnipesaukee boat information. **Laura Poole** provided information concerning the Evangelical Bible (Advent Christian) Church. **Charles Powell** answered a query. **Kathryn Powell** discussed the history of the *Wolfeboro Times.* **Jesse Putney** provided certain information about the Babson family members who own two of the Varney Islands.

**Jane Quimby** furnished the history of the Caregivers of Wolfeboro Area group and proofread part of Volume I.

**Jean Ray** discussed summer vacation camps and made a suggestion for further research. **Marshall K. Ray** provided information about the Cotton Mountain Community Church and helped in many other ways including with publicity; he also initiated the author's involvement with the project. **David Rich** provided information about local Boy Scout activities. **Gregory Roark** provided information about the Community Bank & Trust Co. **Dorothy Robarts** provided information concerning Wolfeboro schools. **Irving Roberts** was interviewed concerning lake islands and boundaries between Wolfeboro and Alton. **Linda Roeder** suggested a source for information and corresponded about Scouting. **Dianne Rogers** helped with proofreading and copy editing and made many valuable suggestions; her help was central to the success of the project. She also provided information about Brewster Academy to Christine Fipphen for use in Volume II and assisted with publicity. Photographs collected years ago by **Nat Rogers** were given to the Wolfeboro Historical Society by Nancy Stephenson for use in these volumes. **Terrie Rogers** provided pictures of Wolfeboro schools. **Richard Rollins** provided information concerning several town businesses. **Edward K. Roundy** shared information concerning his involvement with the Governor Wentworth Regional School District.

**Jean Rowley** prepared the history of the Clearlakes Chorale.

**Howard Sabin** provided information concerning Wolfeboro schools. **Dianne and Heather Sands** provided information and recollections concerning sports from the 1980s onward. **Dorothy Schafer** of the Street Numbering Committee of the town of Wolfeboro provided much information for the "Wolfeboro Place Names and Origins" section of Volume II, answered inquiries, and helped with publicity. **John Schafer** helped with publicity. **Beatrice Scott** furnished information concerning the Wolfeboro Public Library. **C. Stuart Shannon** was interviewed on several subjects. **Carl Shannon** provided information concerning Harriman-Hale Post No. 18 of the American Legion. **Isabelle Shipman** helped with publicity. **Robert G. Simoneau** provided information about Brewster Academy. **Amanda L. Simpson,** former town planner, provided much information concerning street and place names, street name changes implemented 1992-1993, zoning regulations, and town policies. **Mary Haley Smart** provided information concerning the building occupied in the 1990s by Walker & Varney and also shared a recollection of George A. Carpenter. **David M. Smith,** headmaster of Brewster Academy, facilitated the answering of several inquiries and furnished information. **Hollie Smith** answered an inquiry. **Mark M. Smith,** writer for the *Granite State News* and later editor of the *Lakes Region Courier,* interviewed the author and published information which resulted in the author's receiving several inquiries; he also made several suggestions concerning research and the text. **Patricia Smith** provided information about the Libby Museum. **Senator Robert C. Smith** answered several inquiries, was interviewed, and supplied reminiscences. **Donald Snyder** supplied biographical information concerning Col. Charles H. Cummings, owner of the *Rowena* (discussed in Volume II under Lake Winnipesaukee boats). **Albert ("Duke") Southard** provided information about sports at Kingswood Regional High School and proofread parts of the text. **Carlton W. Spencer** provided information concerning Brewster Academy. **Margaret and Todd Spiller** provided information about local Boy Scout activities. **Joyce Goodwin Stanard** provided a collection of photographs relating to the Goodwin and Stanard families. **Stephany Stanard** provided information. **John Staples** provided information concerning the Masons. **Nancy Stephenson** provided several old photographs for examination and reproduction and furnished historical information. **Allen Stevens** supplied information concerning Point Breeze and helped in other ways. **Norman D. Stevens** lent information about Old Home Week. **Stanley E. Stevens,** Wolfeboro chief of police, provided information about law enforcement, furnished a recollection of Coretta King's stay in town, provided a photograph, reviewed sections of the manuscript, and furnished names of past Police Department chiefs and officers. **Gladys Stinchfield** provided detailed information concerning the business career of Ralph Stinchfield. **Stuart Stinchfield** generously made available at no charge storage facilities at his Ben Franklin store; shipments of the present books were stored and dispersed from that location. **Michael Stith** suggested an avenue of research. **Charles Sturtevant** reviewed part of the manuscript for Volume II. **David Sundman** furnished an 1886 tourist brochure. **William D. Swaffield** provided the history of the Abenaki Water Ski Club. **Richard and Lisa Swasey** answered several inquiries. **Joy Sweeney** supplied a booklet about the Kingswood Golf Club.

**Charles S. Tarr** shared reminiscences of years ago in Wolfeboro, read portions of the text, and helped with publicity. **Dorothy Tarr** provided information concerning the First Congregational Church, lent a copy of *Meryl,* proofread several sections of the manuscript, and helped in other ways including with publicity. **Jeanne Tempest,** editor, the *Granite State News,* published information concerning the author's research inquiries and made available photographs and other items from the files of the *Granite State News.* She also helped with publicizing the project. **Mrs. Jerry Thayer** lent pamphlets on the steamer *Mount Washington* and information about St. Cecilia's Catholic Church. **Betsy Thornton** lent several directories and guides and participated in several discussions about the history of the town. **Louise Irish Tobyne** provided information about the Paper Store, the Irish family, the Furber family, and Wolfeboro businesses. **Dr. Lawrence S. Toms** reviewed several sections of the manuscript and made valuable commentaries, especially concerning the period in which he was a selectman. **Stacy Kendall Trites** supplied information about the Appalachian Mountain Teen Project. The **Tuftonboro Library** lent a copy of Hayley's *History of Tuftonboro.* **Thomas S. Tuthill** provided information about Brewster Academy and the New Hampshire Chamber Singers.

**Frank Van Valen** answered an inquiry and provided a photograph. **Robert Varney** engaged in title searches on behalf of the author and provided an anecdote about Wilma Paine. **Burtis F. Vaughan, Jr.,** provided information about Brewster Academy and education. **Herbert and Anne Vinnicombe** provided information concerning Wolfeboro Home for the Aged, Inc., provided photographs of Clearwater Lodges, and made several suggestions.

**George W. Walker** provided historical information and shared an interview he had with Mary Haley Smart. Photographs collected years ago by **Clayton M. Wallace** were given to the Wolfeboro Historical Society by Nancy Stephenson for use in this project. **Prof. James M. Wallace,** Lewis & Clark College, corresponded about Wolfeboro schools and other historical matters. **Denise Warren** answered an inquiry. **Frederick C. Warren** provided information about the restaurants he operated in town over the years. **Patricia M. Waterman,** Wolfeboro town clerk, provided information concerning the history of various streets and roads, cross-referenced to their authorization or construction in town records. She also read sections of the manuscript, made suggestions, and provided information from town files. **John F. Waters** provided information about Huggins Hospital (for which he was the administrator from June 1965 to October 1980). **Christine Weatherill** provided information about in-home schooling. **Anne Widman** proofread part of the text for Volume I. **Marjorie Wiebe** helped with publicity. **John Wiggin** provided information. **Darlene Williams** provided a file of information about Wolfeborough Historic Productions. **Cathy Dumont Wilson** took many photographs for the book, helped arrange historical pictures, and helped in many other ways. **Elizabeth Ann Wisdom** provided information and photographs pertaining to Camp Owaissa. **Ashton R. Woodhouse** printed negatives photographed by Sandra Martin and some images he took as well. **Lester A. Wright** sent information concerning Lake Winnipesaukee. **Susan Pollini Wright** answered an inquiry.

**Les York** provided recollections of Wolfeboro.

**Paul E. Zimmerman** helped with information about Clarke Plaza. **Barbara and Edward W. Zulauf** read parts of the manuscript and made many valuable suggestions, corrections, and additions; they also provided information about local schools.

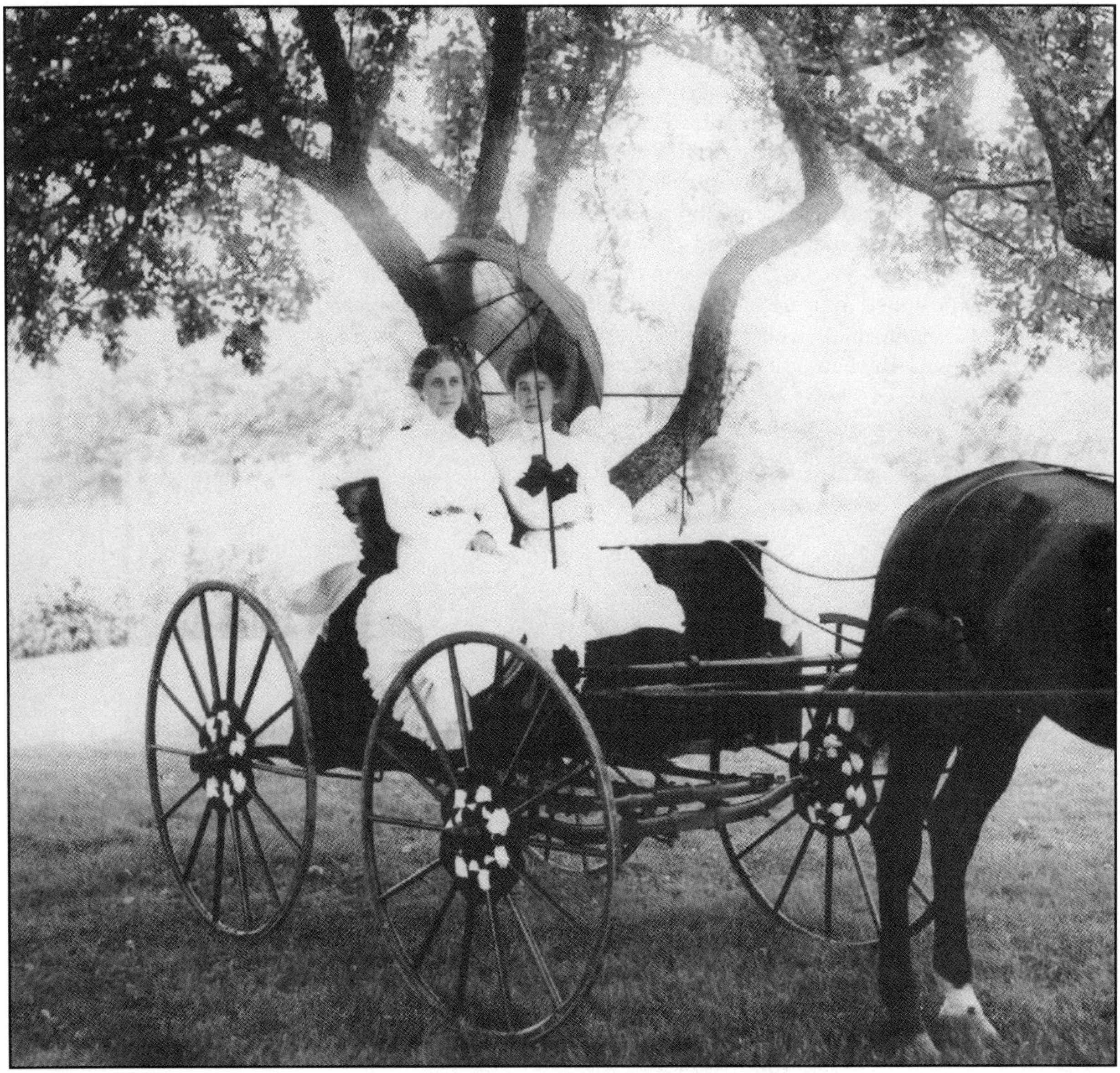

Two young Wolfeboro ladies in a cloth-draped buggy with decorated wheel hubs, parasol attached to the back of the wagon, ready for a parade. (Jeff Goodwin Collection)

# Patrons

The following individuals and organizations are patrons of the three volumes and made financial contributions of $1,000 each or more. The voters of the town of Wolfeboro provided a $10,000 loan-grant.

Mrs. George D. Black
Black's Paper Store
Christine Bowers
Q. David Bowers
Judith Carr Breuninger
Theodore and Carol Brigden
Community Bank & Trust Co.
The Fannie Mae Foundation *(Frederick W. Mowatt)*
J. Frank Goodwin III and Joyce Goodwin Stanard
The Henney Foundation
The Henry C. Hopewell Family
The Family of Dr. Henry F. Libby
Raymond N. and Patricia Roberts Merena
Frederick W. Mowatt
Ruth Tarr Mowatt
Dorothy E. and Charles R. Mulloy, Jr.
Mr. and Mrs. Roger F. Murray 2nd
Marshall K. Ray
Town of Wolfeboro
Wolfeboro Fund-Lakes Region Charitable Foundation
Wolfeboro Historical Society

# Contributors

The following individuals and organizations contributed from $100 to $999 to the project.

Bruce and Nancy Beck, John and Chris Fipphen, Janet E. Hall, Hampshire Pewter, Donald and Elaine Hughes, Mr. and Mrs. William E. Jones, Elizabeth S.L. Kane, Margaret R. Lord, Ralph and Jean Malmgren, Barbara Hobbie and Richard Mancke, Rotary Club of Wolfeboro.

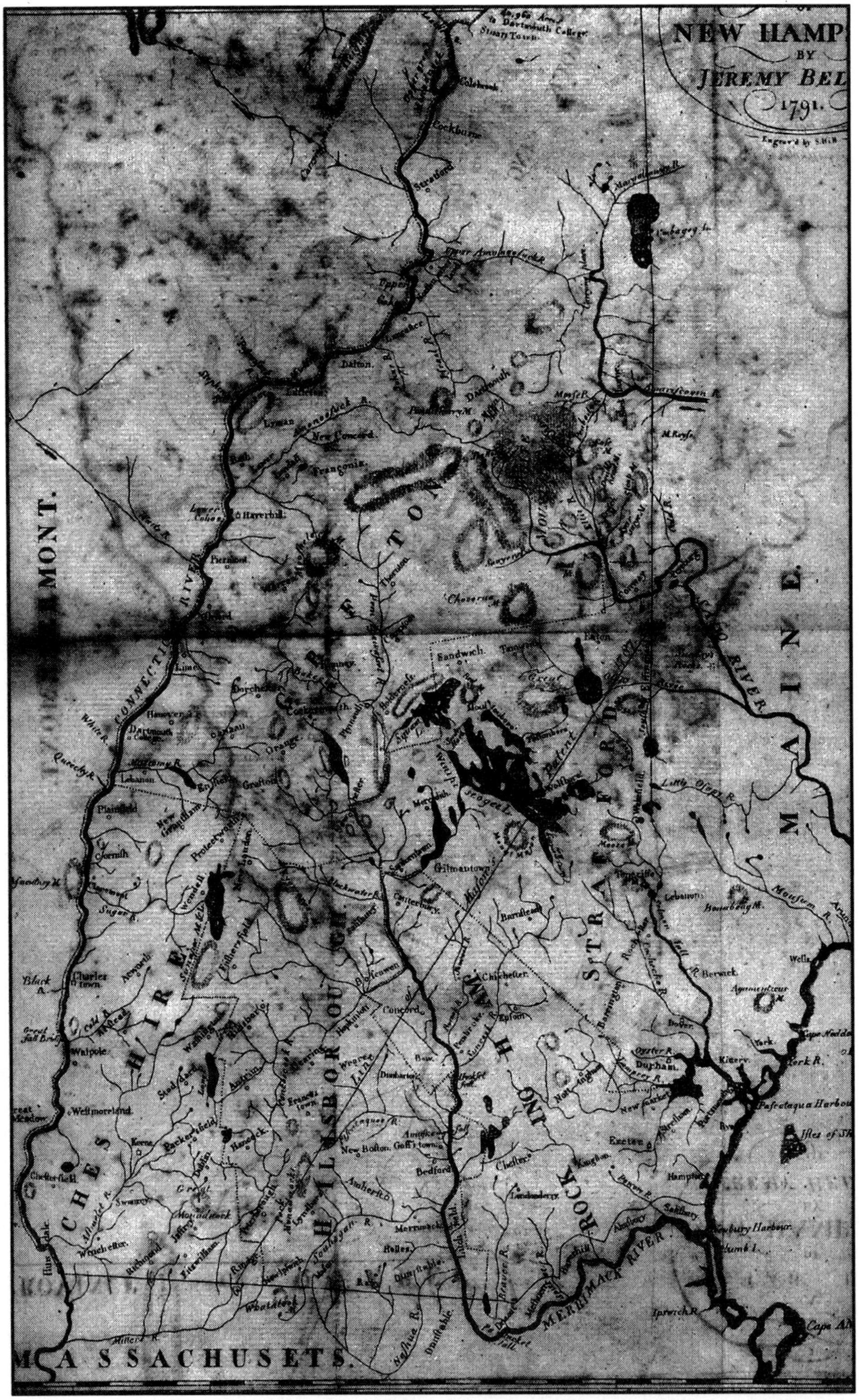


**Map of the state of New Hampshire by historian Jeremy Belknap, 1791, when Wolfeboro and other territories were a part of Strafford County. In 1820 Carroll County would incorporate part of this area. (*The History of New Hampshire,* Volume II, 1891)**

# Use of Sources for Volumes I, II, and III

Many sources of information were utilized during the preparation of the three volumes. I made a number of observations concerning the validity of each of these and weighted them accordingly.

In general, items created at the time something happened are the most reliable sources. Thus, a billhead of a firm dated August 10, 1917, provides reasonable certainty that the company was in business then, the record of the annual town meeting in 1911 describes events that actually happened then, town tax and property records and county records reflect accurately who owned what, and contemporary issues of the *Granite State News* can be relied upon to furnish dates for *current* events reported upon.

Less reliable, but still valuable and certainly interesting, are retrospective accounts published in the *Granite State News* and in essays preserved by the Wolfeboro Historical Society. Time and again while reviewing these, I found numerous dating errors. For example, we know for certain that the Abenaki Outing Club was formed in 1935 and developed in 1936, as week-by-week contemporary issues of the *Granite State News* reported on the situation. However, a retrospective commentary in the same paper, published in the late 1960s, mused that the Abenaki Outing Club was formed in the late teens or early 1920s! In general, the more distant the reporting is from the time it happened, the less reliable it is (unless original source material is used). Obituaries are occasionally unreliable as relatives are called upon to quickly relate (before press time) when the deceased moved to town, the names (and spelling thereof) of surviving relatives, and other data.

Often historical articles would be created by an author without crediting the original source. Thus, a history of Wolfeboro churches written for the Wolfeboro Historical Society in the 1960s used *verbatim* sentences and paragraphs from a 1941 *Granite State News* article, among other articles, without credit to the original sources. Harrison D. Moore related to me that this situation is hardly new; in researching town and county records, he found that Benjamin F. Parker "borrowed" much commentary from original sources and used it as his own work in his 1901 *History of Wolfeborough*, probably with no idea of deception. Further, Parker guessed at many dates and spellings of names and occasionally was wildly inaccurate. The research methodology in use in the 1990s is different from that used decades ago. Very few nineteenth century historical narratives give detailed credits.

The dilemma of the researcher is further illustrated by an situation involving Lorenzo Horn, a manufacturer of wooden piano stools in Mill Village (later known as Wolfeboro Falls) where the Smith River joins Back Bay. Lorenzo spelled his surname as Horn on his piano stools and on certain papers examined by the author. However, on his tombstone (also examined by the author) it is spelled as Horne. Did Horn change the spelling of his name to Horne later in life, or did the person ordering the grave marker spell it incorrectly?

But, that is not all concerning Lorenzo Horn and the aforementioned research dilemma. According to the *Granite State News*, October 19, 1864, Horn's piano stool factory was completely destroyed by fire a few days earlier on October 14, with a loss amounting to $9,000. This *contemporary* account is the one I selected for use in the present work and no doubt gives the correct fire date. However, an account of historical fires published in the same newspaper on January 18, 1913, placed the piano stool factory fire in 1888, another *Granite State News* retrospective account published on February 12, 1932, placed the date as 1867, and in his *History of Wolfeborough*, Benjamin F. Parker said it burned down in 1887! Parker also related that a local factory belonging to John Taber burned in 1850. Never mind that Taber had not moved to Wolfeboro by that time.

The point of this commentary is to issue a *caveat*. If information in the present book is credited to a source contemporary with the event or to government records, it has a higher reliability factor than if it is taken from a retrospective or historical account published years later.

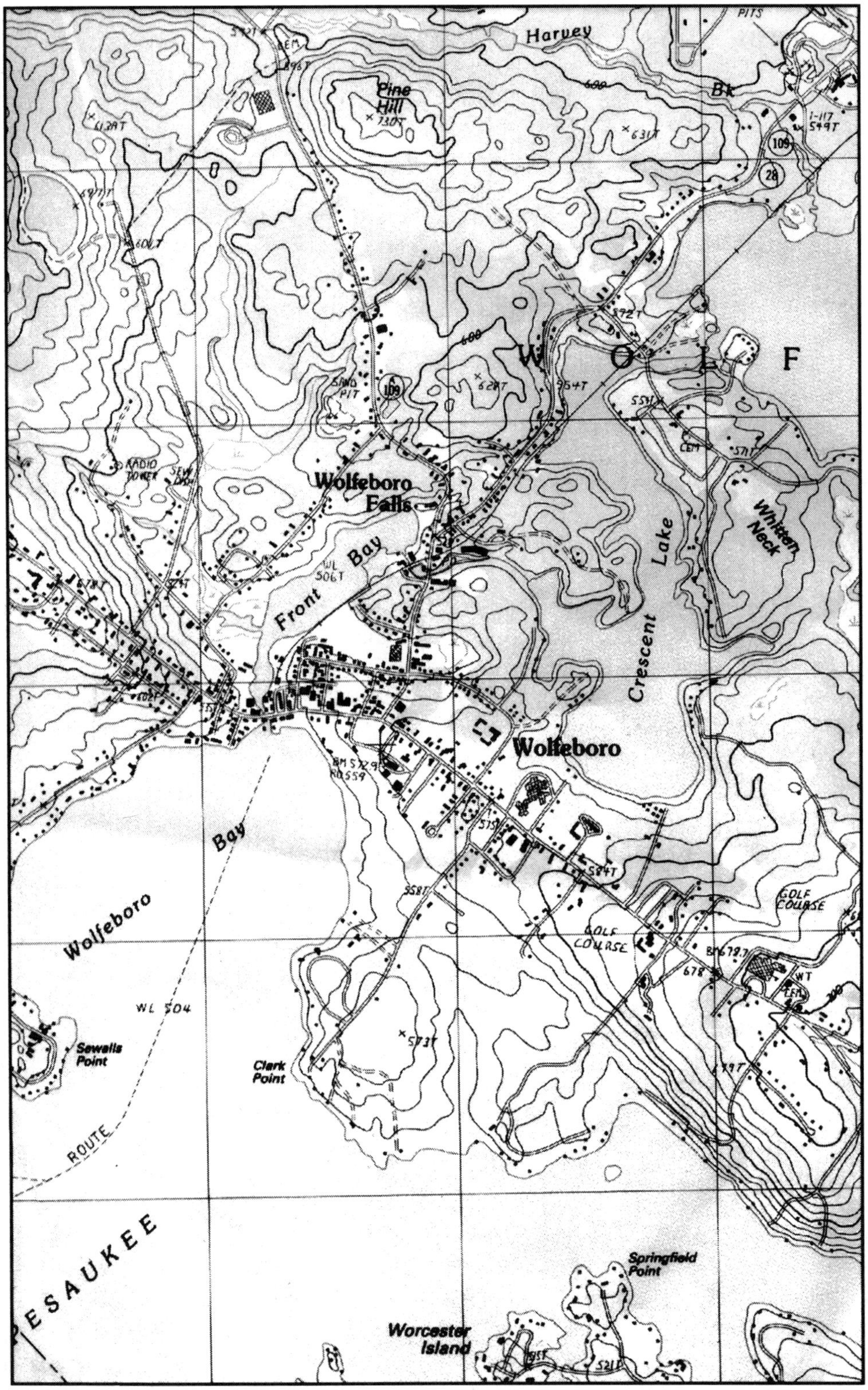


**The downtown district of Wolfeboro is shown between Wolfeboro Bay and Back Bay (here erroneously as *Front* Bay). Orientation: north at top of map. (USGS map, 1987)**

# Style Notes for Volumes I, II, and III

• ABBREVIATIONS: Selected abbreviations, hopefully self-evident, have been used to conserve space. These include modern postal abbreviations for states (MA, NH, etc.), a.k.a. (also known as), d.b.a. (did business as), although some of these — especially postal notations — were not generally used in print until recent times.

•CAMP: In local parlance, *camp* usually refers to a summer cottage, not a summer vacation camp with organized activities for children although such children's camps were also an important part of the scene. Cottage-camps sometimes were very large buildings — George A. Carpenter's elegant Cobham Hall is an example — but were still called camps in many news articles.

•CAPITALIZATION: Original sources sometimes capitalize "state" and "town," as in State of New Hampshire and Town of Wolfeboro, and sometimes do not. Similarly, such constructions as "It is important to follow State (or state) regulations," "The future of the Town (or town) is important," etc., are found. There is no consistency in the historical record. The author has elected not to capitalize these two words in these contexts.

•CONTRACTIONS: In certain business names the word "and" was shortened to "n". The proper punctuation for such shortening should be an apostrophe before "n" and an apostrophe after, as: 'n'. However, in practice there were many variations, especially the use of a single quote before "n" and none after, as: 'n. The name of the Beef 'n' Bun eatery appeared in print with various combinations of punctuation and capitalization including Beef 'N Bun, Beef 'n Bun, Beef 'N' Bun, etc. Wax 'n Facts usually appeared this way, although Wax 'n' Facts would have been better usage. In practice there was no consistency in use of punctuation in contractions in Wolfeboro business names. Thus, variations occur in the present work, especially in Volume III, the *Business and Professional Directory*.

•DATES IN GUIDES AND DIRECTORIES: The typical business and residential directory was compiled the year before the date on its cover. Thus, the 1899 *Wolfeborough Directory* was compiled in 1898 using data from 1897, 1898, and earlier years. Directory compilers were often careless and did not verify listings. Reflecting this, the 1916 edition of *Chisholm's* tourist guide informed its readers that the Kingswood Inn was open for guests; never mind that it was torn down in 1899! In another example the NYNEX telephone directory listing of a man who died in the 1980s was continued into the 1990s because his widow felt that his name in addition to hers would deter unwanted callers. Because of such situations, dates in nearly all such listings must be used only as a general indication for the era, not for precise information pertaining to a specific year. Particularly rife with errors are the dozens of NH state *Register* issues of the nineteenth and early twentieth centuries; such *Registers* were used sparingly in the present work, and an effort was made to verify dates and spelling elsewhere.

•EDITING: In certain quotations from historical sources, the author has corrected misspellings and has lightly edited certain passages. In all instances the original flavor of the text has been preserved.

•ENDNOTES: These are provided at the end of each chapter in Volume I and following specific sections within Volumes II and III. These give further explanations and clarifications, suggest sources for further information, credit sources, etc. Endnotes are not indexed.

• *GSN:* Abbreviation indicating a citation from the *Granite State News,* also referred to as the *News.*

•INDEXING: Volumes I and II are indexed at the end of each. Volume III is not indexed as the entire volume is arranged in alphabetical order and is, in effect, self-indexed. In addition, a separate Index to Illustrations is provided near the end of each volume and identifies subjects shown or mentioned on illustration pages.

The indexing of people's names is much more comprehensive than would be the case if this were a general history work. In that way anyone seeking information about any individual can find it easily. The offset to this is that searching the index and consulting the appropriate text for what constitutes an important vs. an insignificant mention of someone may take more time than if only the important mentions were indexed. Besides, what is important and what is not would have constituted a judgment call.

Endnotes are not indexed, nor are certain sources and credits; for example, with a hypothetical entry such as "Benjamin F. Parker in his *History of Wolfeborough* mentions that the Baptist Church had 97 members," neither Parker nor the name of his book is indexed, but Baptist Church is indexed.

Entries that are not specific are not indexed, as in this example, "pewholders were members of the Smith, Jones, and Brown families." However, the names are indexed if they are specific, as "pewholders included the John A. Smith, Joseph G. Jones, and William Brown families."

Titles, offices, and degrees such as Rev., Hon., Sen., Selectman, Judge, Dr., M.D., Gov., Elder, etc., are not included in the index as such titles varied in their use over a period of time, even among mentions of the same person.

Until recent decades it was common practice in newspapers, club accounts, church rosters, etc., to list married women under their husbands' names, as Mrs. John Smith, even though while married she may have been known also as Mary Alice Smith. Middle initials of married women often vary in citations. Thus, if Mary Alice Brown married and became Mrs. John Smith, she may be referred to as:

Smith, John, Mrs.
Smith, Mary A.
Smith, Mary Alice.
Smith, Mary B.
Smith, Mary Brown

All of the preceding refer to the same person. When the distinction is not clear in original citations or mentions, such names have been separately indexed.

If there are multiple individuals, locations, or items with the same name (for example, there were four Goodwin Blocks and several people named J.A. Chamberlain), they are usually indexed under a single entry such as Goodwin Block.

In general, mentions of "Wolfeboro" are not indexed, as the entire three volumes are largely devoted to Wolfeboro. However, specific Wolfeboro-prefix terms are indexed, Wolfeboro Area Children's Center, Wolfeboro Bay, Wolfeboro Center, etc., being examples.

•LOCAL PAPER: Reference to the *Granite State News.*

•MARRIED NAMES: In most pre-1950 newspaper citations, directory listings, and other in-print mentions of a married woman, she is referred to only as Mrs. John Doe, rather than Jane Doe or Mrs. Jane Doe. As over a period of time John Doe may have had wives Alice and Irene in addition to Jane, a designation such as "Mrs. John Doe" is not as informative as "Jane (Mrs. John) Doe" or "Jane Doe (Mrs. John Doe)." In many instances in which the first name of a married woman is known, it is used in the present work.

• *NEWS:* Reference to the *Granite State News.*

•NON-WOLFEBORO SUBJECTS INCLUDED: While the main emphasis is on Wolfeboro people, places, things, and events, by necessity there are numerous mentions of subjects from other towns. Students at Kingswood Regional High School and Brewster Academy, participants in plays and other civic events, vacationers, club and organization members, and others involved in activities within the town but living elsewhere are mentioned in many instances.

•POSSESSIVE NAMES: Often in advertisements and directories, a building, mountain, or other feature or object would be listed with an apostrophe at the same time that other listings would omit the possessive. Examples include Parker Island and Parker's Island, Goodwin Block and Goodwin's Block, Clow Hill and Clow's Hill, etc. In still other instances, an "s" would be appended to a name, indicating a possessive, but the apostrophe would be omitted, as in Clows Hill. In 1992 the U.S. Post Office advised the Wolfeboro Street Numbering Committee that apostrophes were no longer acceptable in street and other postal delivery names; hence, what used to be Aaron's Road became Aarons Road, etc.

•SPELLING: FAMILY NAMES: Members of some Wolfeboro families varied the spelling of their surnames. Thus, Chamberlain and Chamberlin are often the same family, as are Burleigh and Burley, Clough and Clow, Doe and Dow, Ferber and Ferbur, Fernald and Firnald, Horn, Horne, and Orne, Libbey and Libby, Prindall and Prindle, Tabor and Taber, *et al.* While an effort has been made to utilize the spelling preferred by a particular member of a family when referring to him or her, differences are bound to occur. When cemetery tombstone inscription spelling is available, that form is used. Apropos of the situation, Arthur F. Chamberlin commented as follows:[2]

Here is an explanation of the difference in spelling of our family name: Dudley Chamberlin's father, John, dropped the second "a" from the Chamberlain name. He was married twice; first to Mary Jackson and second to Joanna Banfield. All the children from his first wife spelled it Chamberlin. All the children from his second wife spelled it with the "a" back in again, as Chamberlain. There have been many exceptions, on both sides of the family. I once wrote and asked my father why we spelled it "lin" and his brother, John, used "lain." Dad's answer in 1964 was "I never thought to ask him."

When he started delivering the mail from the East Wolfeboro Post Office shortly after the turn of the century, Ford Smith, according to what he told me, had on his route 17 different people named J. Chamberlain. Of the 17, five were J.A. Chamberlains. If he had a letter for one of those, he simply left it at the first Chamberlain he came to. If they knew to whom it really belonged, they would write on the envelope something like this: Try "Lester's John," or "Begorra John," or "John Jack," or "John, Jr." Then there was "Big John," "Little John," "Jack," "Jack's John," and "John's Jack." Ford said it bothered him until he got used to it. I can remember some of this mess.

In a related vein, this appeared in the *Granite State News,* September 22, 1939, concerning the family name of Frederick E. Clow, M.D.:

The name was originally pronounced "Cluff." This was changed to Clough, pronounced "Clow," and Fred's great-grandfather changed the spelling to Clow. John and Isaac Clow settled in North Wolfeboro in 1810.

As if intended name differences were not enough to cause confusion, town records, directories, the *Granite State News,* and other printed data contain many misspellings, casual uses, etc. Samples: The surname Kalloch was frequently spelled Kallock (probably because it was pronounced that way). Ransom E. Goodrich's first name appeared in print most often as Ransome (somehow, this must have seemed more appropriate than Ransom, which had another meaning). Various people surnamed Hodsdon and Hodgdon were subjected to all sorts of misspellings, Hogsdon being an example. The first names Lewis and Louis were often interchanged. Hansons were called Hansens. In a list of signatures preserved by the Wolfeboro Historical Society the same man signed his last name as Edgerly and Edgerley in different years.

Certainly, anyone researching historical advertisements would be puzzled to find that certain local businesses were owned one month by Joe Brooks, the next month by Henry P. Valley, and then by Joe Brooks again. L. Winston Hamm provided the explanation:[3]

About Joe Brooks: I talked with his widow, "Maggie" Valley, to get the whole story as to why Henry Patrick Valley was known as Joe Brooks. He was also commonly known as Joe Valley. Maggie explained that Joe's correct first name was Henry, his father was Joseph, his uncle was Henry Valley, and there was also a South Wolfeboro resident, not known to be a relative, Joseph Henry Valley. When the new Post Office was built [in the mid-1930s], all four of them worked on the construction crew. When the foreman called for "Henry Valley," he got two answers, and likewise when he called for "Joe Valley." Finally, he got them all together and said that the father was "Joe," the uncle was "Henry," the other man "Joe Henry," and, pointing at young Henry, said: "You're Joe Brooks!"

Of course, situations such as the preceding add a certain element of challenge and enjoyment to research.

• SPELLING: GEOGRAPHICAL AND OTHER NAMES: In text created for this book, modern spelling is used for geographical names including Winnipesaukee and Wolfeboro. Years ago many other styles were employed. Winnipesaukee alone had over 130 different spellings, many of which were used concurrently. The correct spelling (as used originally) for the local seat of learning is Wolfborough and Tuftonborough Academy, and that is the form used in the following text; however, many variations occurred in citations. The local stopping place for trains has been standardized in the text as Wolfeborough Railroad Station, although such variations as B&M Station, Train Depot, Wolfeboro Station, Wolfeboro Rail Road Station, etc., have been used over the years.

# CHAPTER 1
# WOLFEBORO, NEW HAMPSHIRE

*Probably no town in New Hampshire presents a greater variety of attractions than Wolfeboro. This is the universal testimony of those who come within its borders.*
—Benjamin F. Parker, 1900.

## DESCRIPTION OF WOLFEBORO

### Population and Services

Wolfeboro, located in Carroll County, New Hampshire, is in the mid-1990s a community of approximately 4,810 citizens.[1] Known to the outside world as "the oldest summer resort in America"—as proclaimed by signs on roads leading to the town—Wolfeboro's population is augmented by tens of thousands if not even more tourists in the summer months. Many visitors come to occupy summer cottages, popularly called camps, on the shores and islands of lakes Wentworth and Winnipesaukee and among the hills and valleys.

The town is served by the Wolfeboro Post Office, zip code 03894, and the smaller Wolfeboro Falls Post Office, zip code 03896. NYNEX provides telephone service. Wolfeboro's area code is 603, a number that serves all of New Hampshire.

Vehicular access to Wolfeboro is provided by Route 28 leading south to Alton, from which point roads connect to Portsmouth, Concord, Manchester and other cities; by the same Route 28 continuing north to Ossipee, connecting to North Conway and other points; by Middleton Road extending to Middleton and Farmington; by Route 109 east to Maine; and by routes 109 and 109A northwest to Tuftonboro. Within Wolfeboro, state routes have street names. In addition, various local roads connect to adjacent towns.

The nearest large commercial airport is in Manchester, about a 90-minute drive. Boston's Logan Airport, with numerous national and international flights, is 100 miles and two hours distant by automobile. Closer to town are several smaller airports including those at Laconia, Rochester, and Moultonboro. Fifty miles distant is the Pease International Tradeport (formerly the Pease Air Force Base), which in 1993 began offering commercial flights. In town on Wolfeboro Neck the Lakes Region Air Park provides services for private light aircraft.

Seasonal access by boat to Wolfeboro includes scheduled trips by the excursion ship *Mount Washington,* which calls at the Town Docks twice daily during the height of the summer and once daily during transitional times, connecting to docks in Alton Bay, Weirs Beach, and Centre Harbor. Small pleasure craft can land at the public docks in downtown Wolfeboro or at various private docks and marinas.

### Geography of Wolfeboro

The boundaries of the town include Lake Winnipesaukee, Tuftonboro, Ossipee, Wakefield, Brookfield, New Durham, and Alton.

Wolfeboro was incorporated on August 21, 1770, and at first consisted of an original grant. In 1800 the Wolfeboro Addition, a large tract of land bordering Ossipee to the northeast, was officially incorporated into the town by action of the State Legislature. In 1849 a small part of Alton was annexed, followed on June 26, 1858, by the acquisition of part of Tuftonboro beginning with the Benjamin Wiggin (later, Fay) Farm now across from the Clearwater Lodges on North Main Street and extending to what is now the Tuftonboro border in the area of Mirror Lake. In 1895 four large islands and a number of smaller ones were given to the town by Alton. Wolfeboro comprises 37,943 acres, or about 60 square miles of territory, including lake surfaces.[2]

Today, Wolfeboro is defined by a boundary about six miles in length separating it from Tuftonboro on the northwest, a line of about seven miles dividing the town from Ossipee on the northeast, and a boundary of about seven and a quarter miles to the southeast separating it from Brookfield and New Durham. The southwestern bound-

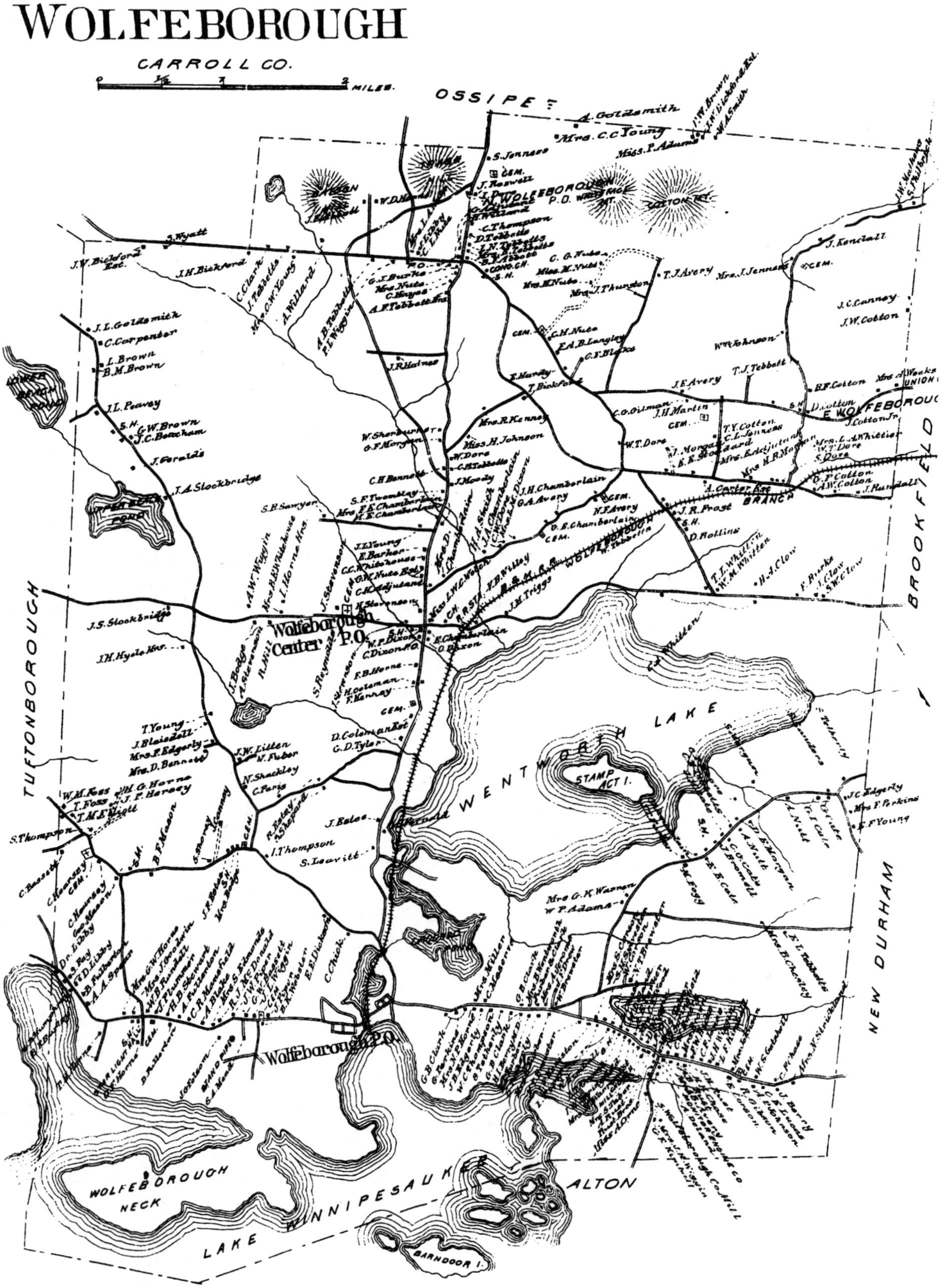


**The town of Wolfeboro in 1892 showing the locations of roads, boundaries, natural features, homes, and businesses. (Hurd's 1892 atlas; there are some inaccuracies including the location of the town line with Alton)**

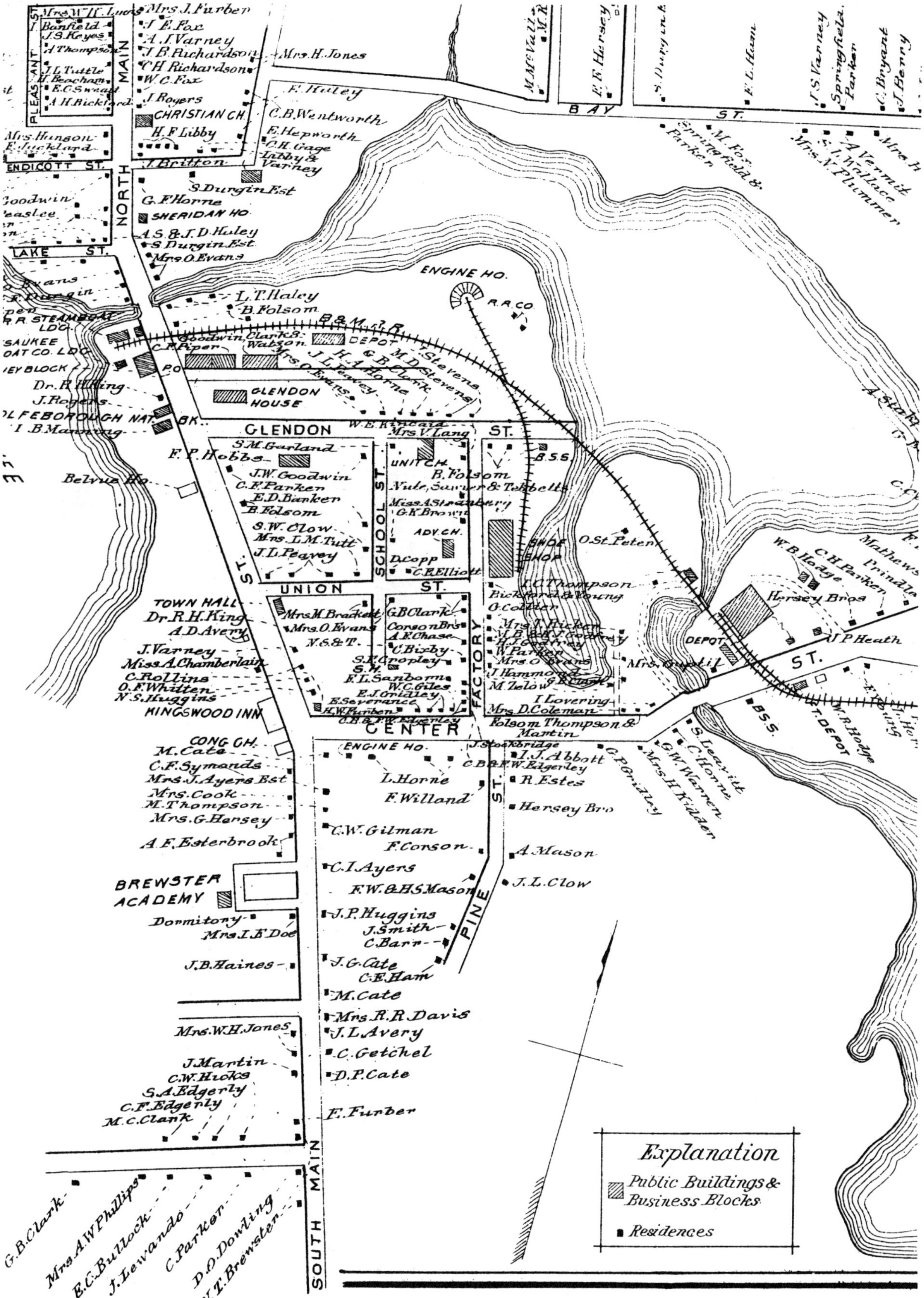


**Details of much of Wolfeboro's downtown district in 1892. (Hurd's 1892 atlas)**

Two loggers dressed in long coats in Wolfeboro at the turn of the century. On the horse-drawn sleigh to the left a large dog rests on a pile of fur robes and blankets. (Jeff Goodwin Collection)

ary defining the separation of Alton and Wolfeboro is largely in Lake Winnipesaukee and is irregular.

Wolfeboro would have a different configuration now if a petition from citizens of a dissenting section of Middleton had been successful in 1785. These individuals, in concert with some disaffected citizens in the section of Wolfeboro bordering Middleton, proposed that both sections separate from their respective towns and form a new community. The petition to the New Hampshire Council and House of Representatives (then located in Exeter) was dismissed. Wolfeboro remained intact, but eight years later the dissident Middleton citizens broke away to form the town of Brookfield.

An 1860 map of Carroll County depicts the town, the name of which was commonly spelled as Wolfborough then, as consisting of several different communities. The main one, what today is downtown Wolfeboro and the surrounding area, was called Smith's Bridge Village or Wolfborough. Nearby, where the Smith River joins Back Bay, was Mill Village, now called Wolfeboro Falls. Outlying districts included (to use today's spelling) Wolfeboro Center, North Wolfeboro (Dimon's Corner), East Wolfeboro, South Wolfeboro, and Pleasant Valley (Raccoonborough).

The main business and residential district of Wolfeboro is situated on Lake Winnipesaukee, 504 feet above sea level, the largest lake in the state. Frontage on Winnipesaukee extends from the Alton town line to Tuftonboro and comprises the shore of Wolfeboro Bay and its islands, Wolfeboro Neck, and much of a bay known as Winter Harbor.

From Lake Winnipesaukee the land rises in a series of hills, sometimes locally called mountains, to the north and east. A notable prominence is Trask Mountain, 1,345 feet high, which at the top offers views of lakes Winnipesaukee, Wentworth, and other local bodies of water, and in the opposite direction, a panorama extending north to the Presidential Range including distant Mount Washington, the highest peak in New Hampshire. In the direction toward and beyond Tuftonboro, the Ossipee Mountains can be seen, known to geologists as the Ossipee Ring Dike (a.k.a. Dyke), the remains of the caldera, seven miles in diameter, of an ancient volcano that is said to have been over 40,000 feet high about 40 million years ago.

### Natural Resources

The town of Wolfeboro is not known for its marketable mineral resources, although in the early days many naturally-occurring substances were used in various manufacturing and commercial processes. Clay exists in a number of areas and in the eighteenth century was exploited for making brick and, possibly, clay smoking pipes (by John Taber). Bog iron ore was found on the northern shore of Lake Wentworth; however, it has never been commercially exploited to any significant extent. Granite is a very common rock and has been used over the years in various construction. At one time granite was quarried commercially in South Wolfeboro, but by 1877 the operation had been discontinued.[3]

In the early 1870s ore was dug near or on the Daniel J. Cotton farm on Cotton Mountain in East Wolfeboro, "which an experienced assayer declared to contain gold, lead, and iron, but uncertainty of the amount and lack of capital prevented development; a few small nuggets of gold were also found."[4]

On Stamp Act Island in Lake Wentworth, chalky earth exists, known as marl (a clay containing calcium carbonate, useful for fertilizer). Deposits of alluvial sand are found in numerous areas—several pits to the left and right of Center Street (Route 28) in the Wolfeboro Center area being examples—but such are sufficiently common that there is more than enough sand for local use, such as in the mixing of concrete. Mica and crystals of quartz and garnet are found in some areas but have no commercial value, although at one time (1895) it was suggested that Stockbridge Mountain might contain worthwhile mica deposits. At one time lead may have been mined on the west shore of Crescent Lake; little is known about this venture.[5]

Field stones have been considered variously as nuisances in farmers' fields and as useful for building foundations. Most stone walls dating from the eighteenth and nineteenth centuries were built as a convenient way of separating fields and delineating boundaries while at the same time clearing impediments to cultivation.

The soil of the town is mostly mixed with rock and over the years has been used for raising hay and other grasses, corn, turnips, and selected vegetables that thrive in northern New England. Relatively few districts have deep, rich, rock-free earth; exceptions are mainly located near ponds, lakes, and marshes.

In 1900 historian Benjamin F. Parker observed: "Pears do fairly well; apples extraordinarily so. Plums and cherries are raised only with difficulty, not due as much to the soil as to insects." By the time the twentieth century arrived and with it pesticides, the many orchards of an earlier era had by and large disappeared or had been left unattended. Today, while the DeVylder farm in Pleasant Valley and several other orchards are functional, the growing of fruit is no longer a major local business.

Contrasting the foregoing, forests have been a major asset of the town virtually from day one. Tall pines constituting part of "King's Wood," suitable for ships' masts and spars, were the attraction this region had to the British crown in the eighteenth century and since then have been a valuable source of building material. Oak, beech, hemlock, maple, and other hardwoods have been suitable fuels for uses ranging from lake steamers in the past to the wood-fired heating stoves so popular in homes today. Poplar trees supplied excelsior factories in Wolfeboro Falls. Maple sugaring has been a small local industry over the years.

A spring on the shore of Upper Beach Pond is said to have been prized for its medicinal value in the last century. Surface and ground water, for the most part of excellent purity, is a valuable asset for drinking. Equally important, and a vital element of the local economy, the water in local ponds and lakes furnishes the opportunity for recreation and scenic beauty. Fresh, clean air is another Wolfeboro asset.

**Commerce and Attractions**

Wolfeboro is well endowed with water. Multiple streams feeding into Lake Wentworth once provided the power for grist and saw mills along their banks, as did Mink Brook in South Wolfeboro and, in particular, Smith River connecting Lake Wentworth to the Back Bay of Lake Winnipesaukee.

The town's primary occupations have changed over a period of two centuries, from farming and lumbering in the early years; to farming, lumbering, and shoe manufacturing in the second half of the nineteenth century; to tourist- and retirement-based businesses today.

In the 1990s Wolfeboro attracts visitors who come to hunt and fish in its woods and lakes, to enjoy boating and water sports, and to savor the atmosphere of a quaint, friendly New England village. In addition, there is sufficient local business that the town has a year-round economy. Huggins Hospital and Brewster Academy are jewels in the community's list of assets and draw patronage from a wide area.

# CHAPTER 2
# WOLFEBORO 1770-1900

*The pleasant location on the lake, the many fine views of natural scenery, the excellent roads, and the extensive provisions made for the accommodations of travelers, together with the varied recreations amid mountain, lake, and country scenery, have caused Wolfeborough to be one of the most important points for summer tourist, in New Hampshire. Those seeking health or pleasure will find this town one of the most beautiful and delightful resorts in the country.*

– *Statistical Gazetteer of New Hampshire*, 1875

## THE COLONIAL PERIOD

### Indians and Early White Settlers

When the land comprising Wolfeboro was granted in 1759, few Indians (today referred to as Native Americans) were in the area.[1] Their numbers had been decimated by disease, war, and famine. After the conclusion of the French and Indian War in 1760, much of the local Indian population moved north to the French settlements on the St. Lawrence River.

Relatively little factual information exists concerning Indians who lived in what is now Wolfeboro. They were known as the Abenakis, a branch of the Pennacooks, who in turn belonged to the Algonquin federation. By 1760 the Abenakis were headquartered on the St. Lawrence River. Other tribes which once frequented the area for hunting and fishing and who may have had settlements here, include the Ossipees and Pequawkets (or Pequakets, also known as the Sokokis) from the Saco River valley.

The so-called Abenaki Trail went through the area, approximately where North and South Main Streets are today. This footpath connected the Pennacook settlement at Concord with the Pequawket community at Fryeburg, Maine. The Nimenabaug Trail went along the north shore of Back Bay where camps were maintained in the summer and continued eastward along the course of present-day Route 109, to what is now Sanbornville, to Great East Lake, where it connected with the Newichannock Trail, which extended from the seacoast to the White Mountains.[2] Today, the Libby Museum in Wolfeboro displays local Indian artifacts including tools, arrowheads, and the remains of two canoes.[3]

During the seventeenth century many hunters and trappers frequented the Wolfeboro area, but none made a settlement here. After the wars between the English and French had ended, and nearly all Indians had withdrawn from the Lakes Region of New Hampshire, the British colonial governors, including Benning Wentworth and his nephew John Wentworth, set about inducing white men, primarily settlers in Portsmouth and other seacoast towns, to establish homes in the area. Large tracts of land were granted to investors who wished to move to the area or influence others to do so.

### Royal Grants

The alleged right to make such grants dated back to the previous century. In 1620 King James of England granted title to what is now New England to 50 men of prominence who became known as the Plymouth Council. Subsequently, John Mason and Ferdinando Gorges received ownership to the territory within 60 miles of the seacoast settlement of Portsmouth and the Piscataqua River. This district was named New Hampshire and included the land which now comprises Wolfeboro.

In 1722 a road was cut from Dover to Alton Bay (earlier called Merrymeeting Bay) on Lake Winnipesaukee. Settlement occurred along the route in the decades thereafter, including at New Durham, which by 1767 had 150 residents.

A town known as Kingswood was chartered by Governor Belcher on October 20, 1737, and included certain areas later within Wolfeboro and comprised all or part of what became Alton, Brookfield, Gilmanton, Middleton, New Durham, and Wakefield. Sixty proprietors were granted title to the land in the town provided that they build houses and settle their families within five years and employ a resident minister within seven years. Although hopes were high at the outset, the charter was annulled in 1739 when Belcher was removed from office. By then, some settlements had been made, but none in what is now Wolfeboro.

The Wolfeboro acreage was not unlike countless other square miles of interior land in Massachusetts, Vermont, New Hampshire, and Maine. It had no unique features which served to attract settlers, nor did any religious faction or other group select it as a retreat. The natural assets of the region—including fur-bearing animals, fish, and trees—existed elsewhere. Further, there were no access roads north of Alton Bay. To reach the Wolfeboro tract, it was necessary either to follow crude paths cut for horses or cross the lake by boat.

### Division of the Township

In the meantime, title to the area was defended by John Mason's descendants and others. Following extensive litigation, a consortium of 12 Portsmouth residents purchased the Mason family rights and were henceforth known as the Masonian Proprietors. Desirous of developing the territory, the proprietors granted numerous townships to prospective settlers and developers on terms which included the improvement of the land and establishment of schools and churches. Fifteen large parcels of land were reserved for themselves.

As part of the distribution, a tract comprising 36 square miles of uninhabited land northeast of the lake known as Winnepesoky Pond was granted in 1759 to a group of four men: Henry Apthorp, Ammi Ruhamah Cutter, David Sewall, and William Treadwell. These pioneers added 20 more investors to their group.

### The Naming of Wolf-borough

On November 14, 1759, a meeting of the 24 proprietors was held in Portsmouth, with Daniel Pierce as moderator and David Sewall as clerk. It was voted "that the township, in honor of the late renowned and illustrious General Wolf [*sic*], deceased, be called Wolfborough."

The error in spelling Wolfe's name passed to the town, was used in the charter subsequently granted in 1770, and remained on various printed material throughout much of the next century and beyond. On the majority of printed material, the "e" was omitted, and Wolfborough became standard. One guide book ventured that the town was named after the wolf—a very ferocious beast—because of the character of its inhabitants!

In 1894 it was agreed among the townspeople to shorten the name and standardize it as Wolfeboro,[4] but the Wolfborough and Wolfeborough spellings were used by many residents and outsiders for much of the next two decades. The State Legislature on February 20, 1907, made the "e" in Wolfeboro official, an action followed by the Post Office in 1908 and generally adopted in 1909.[5] From then on it has been Wolfeboro.

James Wolfe died on September 13, 1759, at the age of 33 while in the front of a victorious army on the Plains of Abraham in Quebec, battling the French. Towns of the same name exist in England and South Carolina, and circa 1840 when a number of Wolfeboro people moved to Stetson, Maine, a district of that community became known as Wolfborough Settlement.

### Improvements Planned

At the November 14, 1759 meeting, Daniel Rindge, George Meserve, and Ammi Ruhamah Cutter were named as a committee to commission a survey and divide Wolfeboro into four parts. The survey was subsequently done by Walter Bryant, Jr., who set up temporary lodging at what later became known as South Wolfeboro, completing the work in 1762. In April of the same year John Wentworth, Paul March, and Ammi Ruhamah Cutter were the members of a committee to settle five families, to grant to each a tract of land not over 1,000 acres, and to give each a bounty not to exceed 250 pounds sterling (£250). On January 19, 1764, the committee authorized the settlement of seven additional families, providing that the total cost did not exceed £1,400.

In May 1764 the committee advertised in newspapers the terms offered to settlers in Wolfeboro. On October 17, 1764, the committee, now also including Daniel Pierce, prepared to make a road in the township, which soon thereafter was surveyed by John McDuffee and cut through by Josiah H. Miles. In 1765 Miles erected bridges spanning several small streams, but not across Smith's River. The new thoroughfare, known as the Miles Road for many years, approximates the route of North and South Main Streets today.

The town proprietors of Wolfeboro were obligated to the Masonian Proprietors under certain rules. To increase their personal involvement, the town proprietors in Wolfeboro on October 1765 voted to divide three quarters of the township then held in common to 24 shares of equal value—reserving some 100 acres of land around the falls of Smith River for a mill and 1,050 acres in the southern part of the town for Elisha Bryant and others who desired to become settlers. It is believed that Bryant and three sons came to what later became known as South Wolfeboro and began cutting trees. They stayed for just a short time after which the land reverted to the proprietors. By this time, nearly a decade of colonization effort had resulted in no permanent settlers.

### Division of Land

On February 19, 1766, a meeting of the proprietors to draw respective lots of land was held at the home of Captain Zachariah Foss in Portsmouth. Various parcels were distributed, and much but not all of the town was assigned to specific owners. Excluded was a parcel in the northeast section known as the Lords' Quarter, which included the so-called Great Lot.

Those drawing lots were mostly from Portsmouth. Exceptions were William Parker of Kingston, NH, Daniel Treadwell of New York, and two commanders of ocean vessels, Thomas Darling and John Long, former residents of Portsmouth. Of the 24 individuals, five were described as gentlemen, eight as merchants, one as an attorney, four as mariners, and two as ships' captains.[6]

The original lots, their acreage, and owners are as follows (comments are from Parker and the present author):

Lot 1: 640 acres; Jotham Rindge. Bordered on Brookfield and also lots 2 and 6, and included Martin's Hill (today known as Clow's Hill) and Mount Delight.

Lot 2: 600 acres; William Parker, Jr. Bounded by lots 1, 3, 7, and Lake Wentworth.

Lot 3: 550 acres; Thomas Darling. Bounded by lots 2, 4, 8, and Lake Wentworth. Probably included the land on which Governor Wentworth's mansion was built.

Lot 4: 560 acres; John Long. Bounded by lots 3, 5, 9, and Lake Wentworth.

Lot 5: 648 acres; Isaac Rindge. Bounded by lots 4, 10, 18, and the Lord's Quarter. The Rindge house was built upon it.

Lot 6: 648 acres; Ammi Ruhamah Cutter. Bounded by lots 3 and 7, the Addition (section of land added to the town in 1800), and Lake Wentworth.

Lot 7: 642 acres; Gov. John Wentworth. Bounded by lots 2, 6, 8, and the Addition. Subsequently, Wentworth acquired five more lots, bordering on Smith's Pond (Lake Wentworth).

Lot 8: 648 acres; Daniel Rindge. Bounded by lots 3, 7, 9, and the Addition. The Cyrus Jenness farm was on this lot in the late 19th century.

Lot 9: 642 acres; Henry Apthorp. Bounded by lots 4, 8, 10, and the Addition, and included Frost's Meadow.

Lot 10: 648 acres; Samuel Moffatt. Bounded by lots 5 and 9, the Addition, and the Lords' Quarter.

Lot 11: 550 acres; Joshua Brackett. Extended from the Bryant Reservation to the Sands, a distance of two miles along the lines of Brookfield and New Durham; the opposite line was along the shore of Lake Wentworth. Brackett's Corner is within its limits.

Lot 12: 550 acres; Thomas Wentworth. Bounded by lots 11, 13, the Bryant Reservation, and Lake Wentworth.

Lot 13: 480 acres; George King. Situated along the Miles Road. Bounded by lots 12, 14, 15, 16, 17, and Lake Wentworth. Included the King's Hill area (where the Windrifter Resort is in the 1990s).

Lot 14: 480 acres; Daniel Treadwell. Situated along the Miles Road. Bounded by lots 13, 15, 16, and Lake Winnipesaukee.

Lot 15: 600 acres; Henry Rust. Part of the Bryant Reservation, including most of Rust Pond and South Wolfeboro.

Lot 16: 440 acres; David Sewall. Situated along the Miles Road. This acreage was on both sides of the Smith River and included much of what later became the main village of Wolfeboro and also Sewall Point.

Lot 17: 600 acres; Robert Odiorne. This lot soon passed to the ownership of William Torey and included much of the remainder of what was to be Wolfeboro (apart from what was in Lot 16) plus Wolfeboro Falls and the outlet to Lake Wentworth.

Lot 18: 600 acres; John Rindge. Bounded by lots 5, 17, 19, 20, the Lords' Quarter, and Lake Wentworth.

Lot 19: 560 acres; Nathaniel P. Sargent. Bounded by lots 18, 20, 21, the Great Lot, and the Lords' Quarter.

Lot 20: 710 acres; William E. Treadwell. This included much of what is now the Pine Hill area. Later became the property of George Meserve.

Lot 21: 650 acres; George Meserve. Northwest of Lot 20, in the Pine Hill area.

Lot 22: Paul March, with the following lot; assigned prior to the drawing for the other lots. Part of tract from Tuftonboro to about Friend Street.

Lot 23: Paul March. Part of tract from Tuftonboro to about Friend Street. Lots 22 and 23 would furnish the acreage for the "seven original farms" of Wolfeboro.

Lot 24: 600 acres; John Parker. Benjamin F. Parker wrote: "At first the Neck was allotted to Henry Rust and John Parker as, before measurement, it was supposed to contain land sufficient for two lots. It was, afterwards, ascertained that it...equaled only 547 acres. The tract was, therefore, given to Parker for his share, and Rust received 600 acres of the Bryant reservation (in the South Wolfeboro area)."

It was intended to have each of the original 24 lots be approximately equal in value. Each of those drawing lots agreed to have a family settled on his property within three years, or else 200 acres would be forfeited.

The Lords' Quarter was later divided into 18 lots averaging about 300 acres each, except for Lot 1, of 450 acres, which was reserved for a school. Lot 18 was for a minister. The others went to individuals and partnerships.

### The First White Settler

During the next several years various lots were sold and traded, and some owners sustained penalties for not meeting the terms of settlement. Despite all of this real estate activity, it was not until the summer of 1767 or in 1768 (accounts differ), or nearly a decade after the proprietors were granted the township, that the first permanent white settler made a home here. Benjamin Blake (1731-1824) constructed a small log cabin on what is now North Main Street on the sixth of the seven original Wolfeboro farms. He and his wife (née Molly Conner) lived there until the cabin burned 18 years later, after which a second home was built on the old foundation.[7]

Parker related that Blake was a hardy and eccentric man and sometimes would remain in his field continuously for several days, sleeping on the ground and eating food brought to him by Molly. He enlisted in the Revolutionary War and was in the campaign that vanquished Burgoyne's army. When he was discharged from service he was in upstate New York. It was his choice to walk home *barefoot* to Wolfeboro. Molly became a popular midwife and is said to have assisted in nearly a thousand births.

### Other Early Inhabitants

As time went by, only a few of the 24 proprietors became settlers. Among those, Governor John Wentworth was the most prominent. George Meserve built a sawmill on the Smith River but did not live up to his contract to have both a sawmill and grist mill in operation by 1768. Ammi Ruhamah Cutter and David Sewall completed their intended work, but neither resided here permanently.

Others who came to live in Wolfeboro in 1768, the same year that Blake pioneered the permanent settlement, included William Fullerton, Joseph Lary, James Lucas, Thomas Taylor, Thomas Piper,[8] and Samuel Tebbetts.

These seven individuals (including Blake) constitute those who took farm lots on the land of proprietor Paul March, comprising about 700 acres totally and extending about from where Friend Street is today, northwest to the Fullerton Farm (in the Goose Corner area), and approximately from North Main Street to the shore of Lake Winnipesaukee. In time, these homesteads became known as "the seven original farms."

Four of these pioneer settlers—Lary, Lucas, Piper, and Fullerton—are remembered in street names today, albeit some of the shortest thoroughfares in the community.

Reuben Libbey was another early settler; one who is mentioned often in town records and in the Parker text. The Libbey name provides an early example of the spelling difficulties that have attended anyone seeking to compile a listing of Wolfeboro residents. In Parker's *History* he is referred to as both Libbey and Libby, and Reuben himself signed his name as Reuben Libbe.

Of all early settlers, excluding Gov. John Wentworth, the one with the greatest influence upon the town may have been Col. Henry Rust, a proprietor who cleared land on his section located in South Wolfeboro. He was also known as Captain Rust from his having made several sea voyages. At first, he and his sons worked mainly in the warmer months and lived in a temporary shelter made of logs. One year, his sons Henry and Richard, ages 12 and 14, spent the winter alone. Eventually, he built a fine home on the north shore of the pond that today bears his name. His wife came to live there circa 1773. His descendants were active in numerous aspects of Wolfeboro commerce, particularly in South Wolfeboro, well into the early twentieth century.

Rust gave this description of early Wolfeboro:[9]

> I Henry Rust of Wolfborough...aged seventy eight years, do testify and say that in the year 1771 I mov'd with my famly into said Town of Wolfborough & have resided until this time and within a small distance of the mills on the stream running from the pond called Smith's pond into the pond or lake called Winnipisiokee, that when I first moved up as aforesaid, there was a sawmill standing thereon, then newly erected, that about the time I moved up as aforesaid, there was also a Corn mill erected thereon.... I also well remember & am knowing to there having had a dam at the foot of crooked pond so called for the purposes of retaining the water in Smith's pond for use of their said mills...

### Shelter, Food, and Clothing

The typical house built in town during the late eighteenth and early nineteenth centuries was quite simply constructed, often of unseasoned "green" wood. "Today it's a tree, tomorrow it's a house," was a local joke with an element of truth. Some residences had but a single room, while others had two or three. The typical house had a small "root cellar" consisting of a stone-lined cellar hole suitable for cool storage of vegetables and other food.

One of the most historically significant buildings in town today, the Clark House, is surrounded by Clark Park off South Main Street. It is believed to have been built by William Kent (probably) or Benjamin Evans, circa 1780. Henry Allard came from New Durham, married the widow of Evans, and lived in the house; Allard sold it to Joseph Clark on March 17, 1817.[10]

Families typically made their own clothes. In the summer, nearly everyone went barefoot. In other seasons people wore shoes. Often a shoemaker would go from house to house and shoe the family—with the host providing the necessary leather.

Most people traveled on foot. Relatively few owned horses. Often two people would ride on the same horse, or two children could be carried at the same time. Carriages were rarer yet. In the winter season, horse-drawn sleds were a frequent sight.

Food was quite simple in the early days. Rye and Indian corn were the principal grains raised and used for bread. Roast potatoes, boiled fish, and butter were popular. A common dinner consisted of boiled meat, turnips and brown bread. Other traditional fare included poultry, bacon and eggs, and puddings.

Local agricultural products included hay for cattle, maple syrup, and flax. Potatoes, wheat, and oats were not often cultivated in Wolfeboro in the early days, although by the end of the nineteenth century potatoes had become popular.

Nearly every house had a spinning wheel for wool, cotton, and flax (the latter requiring a smaller wheel than that used for wool). Women would often gather together and have parties to card these substances into rolls. Many houses had looms made of wood, typically measuring about six feet wide, five feet long, and five feet high.

### Governor John Wentworth

John Wentworth, born in Portsmouth in 1737, the son of merchant Mark Hunking Wentworth, was the last colonial governor of New Hampshire. At the age of 14 he enrolled in Harvard in Cambridge, having traveled there on horseback accompanied by a servant. At the college he met Ammi Ruhamah Cutter, two years ahead of him in school, who was to become a medical doctor and play an important part in the early affairs of Wolfeboro. After graduating in 1755, Wentworth joined his father's business.

In October 1759 he became a proprietor of the township of Wolfeboro and in April 1762 was named, with Paul March and Cutter, to one of the committees charged with settling the area. In 1763 Wentworth went to England where he stayed for four years and was awarded two law degrees. On August 11, 1766, he was appointed by King George II to be governor of New Hampshire and also "surveyor of the King's Woods in North America." At the time, certain tall pine trees in New Hampshire were reserved for use as ships' masts in the Royal Navy, and the district in which they were cut was King's Woods. The name Kingswood in use today is from this context.

Wentworth left England and sailed to Charleston, South Carolina, arriving there in March 1767, from which point he traveled north, arriving in Portsmouth on June 13th. On July 2, he was inaugurated as governor of New Hampshire. In a speech to the council, he declared that his two ambitions were to preserve the honor of the crown and to advance the prosperity of the district.

The *Portsmouth Journal,* September 16, 1767, carried this notice:

> John Wentworth gives notice that the General Court having empowered him to receive in demand 10,000 gallons of West India rum from the several towns in the state in lieu of other taxes, he is ready for it and requests delinquent towns to hand it over.

On November 11, 1769, he married Mrs. Frances Deering Atkinson, the widow of his and her cousin, Theodore Atkinson, Jr. John Wentworth and Frances had been romantically involved earlier in the decade before John went to England. In his absence her allegiance changed, and she married cousin Theodore. Upon his return to New Hampshire, John was a friend of Mr. and Mrs. Atkinson. Whatever else might have gone on between John and Frances was not recorded and has since piqued the imagination of historians. Theodore Atkinson, Jr., died on October 28, 1769, and 13 days later his widow became Mrs. John Wentworth. The union produced one child, Charles, who never married, and who died in England in 1844.

Wentworth, a native son of New Hampshire, was well liked by the citizenry, and under him the colony prospered. However, international events overshadowed his accomplishments, and the fires of American colonial discontent soon ended his governorship. The turning point was in June 1775, when Col. John Fenton, who had been elected to a seat in the Provincial Assembly, was felt by the citizens to be hostile to the American cause and was forbidden from taking office. Angry citizens forced Fenton to flee, and he sought refuge in Governor Wentworth's house in Portsmouth. Fenton was seized and taken in captivity to Exeter.

Fearful for his own safety, Wentworth took his wife and son to Fort William and Mary, where he stayed for a short time. On August 24 he and his family sailed from Portsmouth on the *Scarborough.*

On September 21, 1775, he proclaimed that the assembly of the province should meet in Portsmouth on September 28. The seeds of the American Revolution had been sown, and this would be his last official act. Wentworth, who was still liked by the citizens of New Hampshire, remained in America for the next two years, apparently believing that the war would come to a peaceful conclusion. Finally, on February 7, 1778, he departed for Canada. In 1792 he was named lieutenant governor of Nova Scotia, a position he filled until his death on April 8, 1820, at age 83.

### Wentworth's Legacy

John Wentworth did much to improve New Hampshire. With his enthusiasm and extensive education, he spurred the interests of the colonists. Dartmouth College was established during his tenure as governor, advances were made in agriculture, and the New Hampshire communities prospered. He initiated the Pequawket Road from Wolfeboro over Trask Mountain to the Saco River in Conway and, more important, the College Road passing through Wolfeboro to link Portsmouth on the seacoast with Dartmouth College near the Vermont border. The latter road passed through Wentworth's farm.

Had it not been for the timing of events, and had Wentworth remained in America, no doubt he would be remembered today as one of the country's greatest individuals. As it is, his memory is still honored within his own state, and he is one of the few British colonial officials of the 1770s who is recalled with admiration rather than contempt.

### The Wentworth Farm

By 1768 Governor John Wentworth began to lay out a farm on the north shore of Smith's Pond, today called Lake Wentworth. For the next two years, laborers cleared the forests, arranged and cultivated gardens, planted two large orchards and many ornamental elm trees, built stone walls, and stocked the lake with fish. A spacious two-story mansion, designed by Peter Harrison, was

**Sketch of the Governor John Wentworth mansion drawn by Robert F.W. Meader and G.A. Rollins, and plans of the two floors by Meader, prepared for the booklet, *The Saga of a Palace,* published by the Wolfeboro Historical Society, 1962.**

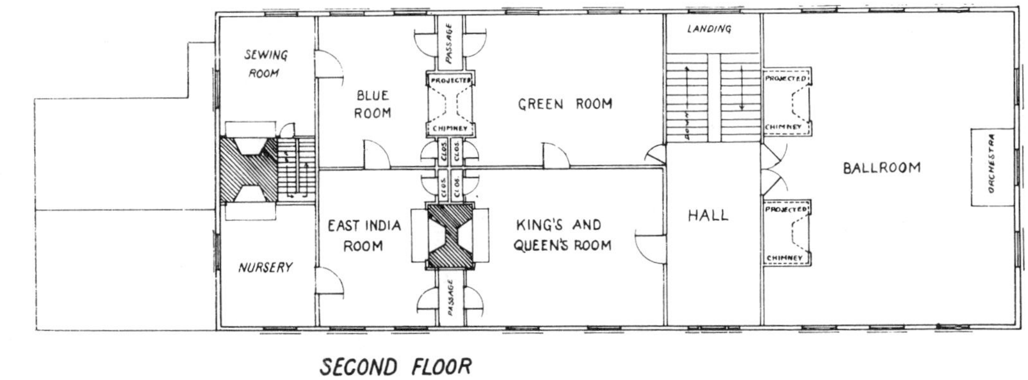


SECOND FLOOR

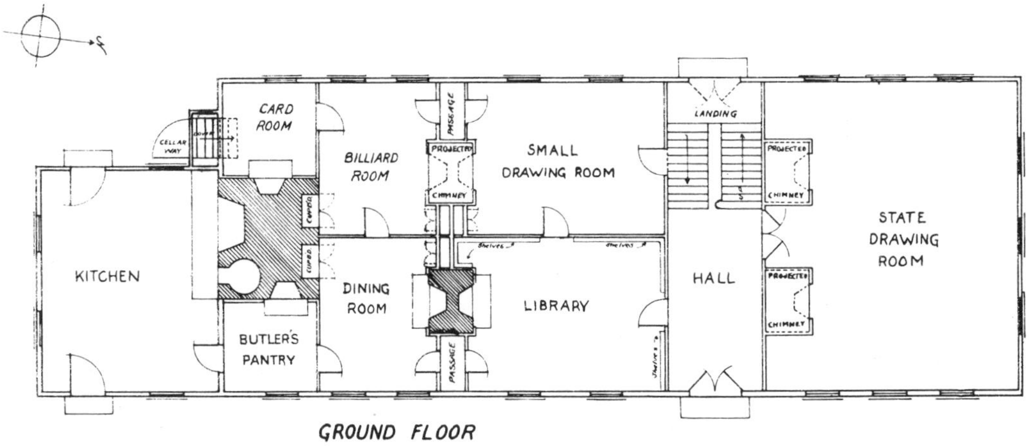


GROUND FLOOR

constructed of wood and was finely decorated. Outbuildings were erected, the largest of which was a barn measuring 100 feet in length. Among other structures were a dairy barn with its own well and fireplace, several other barns, two stables, a smoke house, a blacksmith's shop, a woodworking shop, one or two sawmills, and a grist mill. In its final form the governor's farm was a self-sufficient community, as indeed it had to be, considering its distance from Portsmouth.

The external appearance of the Wentworth mansion has been the subject of several speculative sketches and models.[11] Dr. Robert F.W. Meader, drawing upon his knowledge of history and architecture and upon inspection of the site, determined the dimensions were 99 by 38 feet.[12] The structure was two stories plus attic, the latter probably furnished with dormers to admit light.

In 1770 the governor's house, possibly with portions not completed, was occupied, as noted in an unspecified issue of the *New Hampshire Gazette:* "Last Tuesday, His Excellency our Governor, set out for a country seat on Winnipisogee Pond, and we hear his lady sets out next week for the same place to reside during the summer season." Tradition holds that the governor visited the farm during the summer months from that year through 1775 inclusive, giving rise to the current-day motto, "Wolfeboro: The Oldest Summer Resort in America."

Occasionally the governor and his family would have teas and dinners on a projection known later as Governor's Rock or Tea Rock and on nearby Turtle Island which was connected to the main shore by a small causeway. It is said that the governor's friends from Portsmouth were frequent visitors.

There were two adult black slaves on the Wentworth farm. After the governor fled, they remained. The husband was killed when he was accidentally struck by a rolling log. The widow and her son Remus relocated to New Durham, where they were taken in by a kind family named Willey and adopted the Willey surname.[13]

### The Farm in Later Years

When Governor Wentworth fled from Wolfeboro in 1775, he took only a few possessions including some horses and his silver plate. The state confiscated the farm property. Samuel Gilman eventually became trustee of the governor's land holdings in Wolfeboro. In 1780 he transferred certain furniture, family pictures, and other items to Mark Hunking Wentworth, John's father, who remained in New Hampshire. Library books, "rich and elegant furniture,"[14] two weather glasses, and other items were auctioned in Exeter on June 8, 1780. By this time many other items had been expropriated, scattered, or destroyed.

The state desired to sell the farm, but the market was not favorable. Eventually, in 1782, it was sold to Andrew and John Cabbott (today's spelling: Cabot) of Beverly, Massachusetts. Andrew died soon thereafter, and John died in 1794. In the meantime, the Cabbott interests employed hands to raise horses and cattle under the local management of John Martin, who was succeeded by Deering Stoddard. In 1795 the Cabbott estate sold out. Several transactions later, circa 1805, the property was acquired for $17,000 by Daniel Raynard of Boston, who came to Wolfeboro for several years before moving to Norfolk, Virginia, where he died.

Raynard sold three lots of 100 acres each to George and John Whitton (brothers of his wife) and John Bowker. Other parts of the Wentworth farm were also sold, including 400 acres to James Fernald, who transferred a portion of it to his brother William. Mrs. Raynard remained in the mansion until September 12, 1820, when it was destroyed in a conflagration ignited when a spark set fire to the roof. Other acreage was later sold.

In 1900 Parker described the site of the mansion:

> Sad thoughts may come to the visitor as he looks on the scanty weather-stained debris lying in the old cellar, the dilapidated stone fences, the scraggy apple trees in the decaying orchards, the unkempt pastures where were once odorous gardens and fertile fields.

By the turn of the twentieth century much of the shoreline earlier belonging to the farm had been divided and sold as individual campsites for cottages. At the time, the mansion site was owned by Stephen W. Clow. In the cellar hole of the burned-out mansion, a few hundred yards to the south of the present Route 109, three tall elms grew. Little attention was paid to the history of the area, except for an old well restored by Clow.[15] In 1933 Lawrence S. Mayo, a summer resident from Newton, Massachusetts, and a well-to-do securities broker, deeded the Wentworth mansion site to the state of New Hampshire. In 1935 the Works Progress Administration (WPA) restored the foundation walls[16] and cleared much of the site. In the same decade the state maintained a small seasonal museum nearby which displayed various artifacts.

Beginning in 1985, the State Cooperative Regional Archaeology Plan, or "SCRAP" (isn't that clever?), carefully excavated portions of the site, building upon investigatory work done by professor David Starbuck and Mary Dupre in the early 1980s.[17] The project was directed by Starbuck and Gary Hume, the latter being director of historical resources for the state.

### Town of Wolfeboro Chartered

Governor John Wentworth's building program on his farm and improvements made to the roads leading to the area resulted in the settlement of additional people. By 1770 just one or two years after Benjamin Blake put up his cabin, there were over two dozen families in the

Lady Frances Wentworth, wife of Governor John Wentworth, spent summers in Wolfeboro in the 1770s and is said to have enjoyed parties and social life. (*New Hampshire, A History,* Volume I)

township. The aspirations of the proprietors were being fulfilled at long last.

A committee including Ammi Ruhamah Cutter, Henry Rust, and John Cutter drafted a petition dated Portsmouth, July 9, 1770, seeking a charter for the town, noting in part that:

> There are in the Township of Wolfborough upwards of 30 families settled and more coming to settle there, which makes an incorporation necessary to transact their common affairs with ease & dispatch, and in that case many would be induced to settle there.

On August 21 of the same year, Wentworth granted the charter to Wolfborough (*sic*), which defined the town boundaries enclosing 36 square miles of land, reserved for the British crown certain white pines in the area, and gave residents the right to hold an annual fair or mart on the first Tuesday following the 21st day of September. After the first town meeting, to be held on September 28, 1770, further town meetings were to be held on the last Tuesday of March each year (a schedule later revised).

### 1773 Town Meeting

In the election of 1773 John Sinkler, whom Parker describes as "very illiterate," was named as town clerk. Apparently, Sinkler spelled his name phonetically, for it appears elsewhere as Sinclair. The following is a *verbatim* copy of the minutes by Sinkler for the 1773 meeting:

> Province of New hamsher County of Starford
>
> At the aneuil town meeting of the freeholders and inhabetens of the town of Wolfeborough met at John Sinklers the 30 Day of march 1773.
>
> 1 Voted thomas Lukes moderator 2 John Sinkler town clerk 3 Bengmon folsom 4 thomas tayler 5 James Conner selekmen 6 Joseph Lary Constable 7 thomas Lukes Benjamin folsom sevairs of high ways 8 thomas Piper Bengmon folsom hog Reeves 9 Bengmon Blake Jorge Woodhouse fence viewers 10 thomas Piper Jonathan Harsey Dear Keepers.
>
> 11 Voted to Raise five Pounds Lawfull Money for a scoole.
>
> 12 voted that the Rods Be Repaired By arate.
>
> 13 Voted Cornel henery Rust Capt thomas Lukes Commety men.
>
> 14 that the Seleckmen By A Book to keep their A Counts in.
>
> 15 thomas Piper Culler of Lumber.
>
> 16 Samuel Tebbetts Chose Pound Keeper.
>
> 17 Jacob Scegil Chose Juery men.

Despite shortcomings in orthography, the minutes convey the intent of the voters present. Parker commented as follows after reprinting this and similar early notations:

> The above examples of illiteracy are not inserted as a reproach on the early settlers of Wolfeborough; nor is it to be presumed that the lack of education rendered them deficient in mental caliber. Among them were to be found persons of sound judgment and business tact that would put to the blush some tutored smatterers of the present day. Learning is good, but wisdom is better.

## THE TOWN GROWS

### Population in the Eighteenth Century

A census of the inhabitants of Wolfeboro circa autumn 1773 included the following:

Unmarried men from 16 to 60: 16 people; married men from 16 to 60: 25; boys 16 years and under: 49; men 60 years and upwards: 2; unmarried females: 43; married females: 25; widows: 5. Total: 165 residents.

The paucity of men aged 60 and upwards is probably due more to the pioneer spirit needed to settle the wild territory than to illnesses and other causes of death. As years went on, the young men aged, stayed in town to retire, and the 60 and over population increased sharply.

If it is assumed that the 25 married men represented the fathers of the 49 boys and that an equal number of girls existed, this would give about 100 children for 25 fathers, or an average of four children per family.

The town continued to add residents, and by 1775 a census showed that 211 were in Wolfeboro, including 50 males between 16 and 50 years of age not in the army, 57 males under 16 years of age, four males over 50 years of age, four men in the army, 91 females, and two (on the Wentworth farm) "Negroes and slaves."

The 211 population of Wolfeboro in 1775 was not quite a match for Sandwich with 243 individuals and Moultonboro with 272. The 1790 federal census, the first of the official government decennial enumerations, showed 447 citizens in Wolfeboro per a count as follows:

> Males about 16 years of age or older: 120; males under 16: 110; females of all ages: 217. Total: 447.

### Duties of Town Officials

In the eighteenth century the town of Wolfeboro elected officials to offices that seem strange in today's context, but which at the time were a necessary part of domestic and commercial activities.

The fence-viewer had as his duty the inspection of fences to determine that they were of sufficient height and strength. In that era fences did more than make good neighbors; they were necessary to segregate livestock and to prevent damage to adjoining acreage. If one's fences passed muster, then it would be a violation for the animals of another person to enter the fenced property. If this occurred, the field-driver was summoned to round up stray horses, sheep, cows, and other animals and turn them over to the pound-keeper, who in turn would exact payment from the owner of the trespassing creatures.[18] Nearly every town had its pound—typically a small area enclosed by a stone wall and outfitted with a gate. Wolfeboro had five.

Keeping track of animals—domestic and wild—was no small matter in the early days of the town. In 1810 Wolfeboro residents voted to kill all dogs (presumably, referring to unrestrained ones) in town and to pay a bounty of 10¢ for all crows killed. In terms of buying power today in the 1990s, this reward amounted to several dollars. In 1819 horses, cattle, and other animals could not run at large in the winter time.

The town hog-reeve officer was in charge of seeing that hogs had wires through their snouts to prevent them from rooting up dirt. Another early town officer was the deer keeper, whose specific duties are not known today. Parker suggests that he may have sought to protect this valuable game meat resource from wanton killing.

The town constable's duties consisted not only of keeping law and order, but also collecting taxes. Wolfeboro did not have an organized police department until the twentieth century.

By the 1990s fence-viewers and their like had long since departed from the roster of town officials, although we do have a tree warden in the person of William Swaffield, whose duty it is to supervise trees on town land. He must be doing a good job, for in recent years Wolfeboro has been designated as a "Tree City USA."

### Selectmen

Of all elected officials, the most important in the early days as well as the present era are selectmen, typically three in number. Except for major financial and other decisions subjected to vote on the town ballot or warrant, the selectmen have been charged with running the affairs of the community. Since the early 1970s the town manager form of government has been used, under which the selectmen hire a town manager who takes care of day-to-day operations and relationships among departments.

Over the years the roster of selectmen has included some of the town's most prominent citizens, often professionals or trades people who in the later decades of their lives sought to make a contribution to town government. The first selectmen in 1770-71 were Thomas Lucas, John Sinclair (a.k.a. Sinkler), and Jacob Sceggell. Each year after that point, the composition of the board of selectmen was usually different, although for some periods, the same group remained in office for multiple terms.

Until 1976 all selectmen were indeed males. In that year the first woman selectman (there being no special term for the feminine gender) in the town was elected: Lillian O. Brookes, who served for several years and who has held other offices since. Shirley Ganem was elected in 1985 and has served since that time. Sarah M. Silk served from 1990 through 1993. A roster of selectmen appears as an appendix to this work.

### The Revolutionary War

In 1773 the sum of £5/10s/8d was appropriated by the town for the purpose of buying ammunition to protect the town should any emergency arise. Moses Ham was appointed to effect the purchase. Over 22 pounds weight of powder and 70 of lead were bought in Portsmouth. Upon returning home, Ham cast the lead into bullets. The munitions were held by the town and never used. On November 15, 1777, they were turned over to other authorities. By that time the Revolutionary War was in progress.

On August 7, 1775, Ham was named as the town delegate to the colonial convention, and a Committee of Public Safety was elected to aid the town and help with decisions should war come to the area. Sentiment against British rule was high, and Governor Wentworth was forced to flee the province.

Four Wolfeboro citizens enlisted in the army of the colonists before the Battle of Bunker Hill was fought: Jeremiah Gould, James Lucas, and Ichabod and Moses Tebbetts, who joined Capt. Benjamin Pitman's company in Col. Enoch Poor's regiment. As hostilities increased, more Wolfeboro men were readied to protect the town against possible attack. Parker related that the Wolfeboro militia consisted of four commissioned officers, eight non-commissioned officers, two musicians (drummer and fife player), and 31 privates, for a total of 45 soldiers.

Thirty soldiers left home and joined the Continental Army. Many other citizens who remained in town made contributions of labor or money. When Ebenezer Meader enlisted, the town folk were in a quandary, for he was the only blacksmith in the area. They soon hired a substitute to fight in his stead.

Historian Parker gave many details of the town's participation, concluding with this commentary:

> The demand of the government for men and means to carry on the war were even at first very urgent; but they were met with commendable alacrity, although at great sacrifice, until 1781. At that period the resources of the town, in both particulars had become exhausted, and it could no longer answer its calls. In financial matters a complete collapse occurred. In desperation it offered large bounties for soldiers, but its ability to meet its pledged obligations was discredited, and there were no enlistments. So far as furnishing aid to the state government it was helplessly bankrupt; yet there was hope in the more or less distant future.

With the national economic situation in chaos and Continental Currency paper money notes next to worthless, it would be 16 years before the town paid its debt to the state of New Hampshire.

### The Monetary System

When Wolfeboro was incorporated as a town in 1770, English pounds, shillings, and pence constituted the monetary system. It was not until 1793 that the United

States Mint produced coins for circulation, and even then it would be decades before enough coins were struck to assure an adequate supply.

Locally, the English system was used by nearly everyone in the eighteenth century and by some until at least the 1840s. During the latter decade, some town accounts were still reckoned in English money. Under this system it took 12 pennies (or pence; the penny was abbreviated as "d," after the Roman denarium) to make a shilling, and 20 shillings to make a pound. A notation such as £4/3s/2d (or £4/3/2) meant four pounds, three shillings, and two pence.

During the Revolutionary War, the Continental Congress issued currency in denominations of from $1 to $80, including such unusual (by today's standards) values as $3, $4, $6, $7, and $8. These were payable not in United States dollars, for no such coins existed yet, but in Spanish milled "dollars," the latter consisting primarily of silver coins minted in Mexico and other Central and South American countries under Spanish rule. The Spanish dollar was divided into eight parts called reales or, popularly, "bits." Each bit was worth 121/2¢. The term "two bits," referring to a quarter dollar, comes from this source.

Spanish silver coins were a common sight in Wolfeboro during the early nineteenth century. If you had examined coins in circulation in the town in the early 1850s you would have seen more Spanish silver in use than United States or English coins. Certain foreign coins remained legal tender until the Act of February 21, 1857, was implemented.

In addition to coins many paper notes issued by various privately-owned banks were in circulation. These had no federal or state backing and were apt to vary in value depending upon the issuer. Counterfeits abounded. There was a widespread distrust of paper money, and for this reason very few citizens wanted to hold paper currency for more than a brief time. This situation continued until the early 1860s when the federal government issued its own paper money, after which private notes gradually disappeared.

### The First Financial Crisis

The first financial crisis facing Wolfeboro citizens occurred early in the town's history. After 1776 the paper money issued by the Continental Congress became increasingly valueless. Inflation reared its head, and the prices of commodities rose.

In the summer of 1777 the legislature of New Hampshire enacted a law to regulate the price of certain consumer products and services to prevent inflation due to the war. Among the pegged prices were:[19]

**Clothing:** Cotton yardage, 50¢ to 60¢ per pound.
**Clothing:** Men's leather shoes, $1.33 per pair.
**Clothing:** Men's long yarn stockings, $1 per pair.
**Clothing:** Striped flannel cloth 1 yard wide, 58¢ per yard.
**Commodity:** Bar iron: $6.67 per hundredweight.
**Food:** Beans, $1 per bushel.
**Food:** Beef, 4.5¢ per pound.
**Food:** Butter, 14¢ per pound.
**Food:** Cheese, 8¢ per pound.
**Food:** Corn, 58¢ per bushel.
**Food:** New England rum, 64¢ to 75¢ per gallon.
**Food:** Oats, 33¢ per bushel.
**Food:** Peas, $1.33 per bushel.
**Food:** Pork, 6.5¢ to 7.5¢ per pound.
**Food:** Potatoes, 22¢ to 33¢ per bushel.
**Food:** Rye, 67¢ per bushel.
**Food:** West India rum: $1.11 to $1.28 per gallon.
**Food:** Wheat, $1.25 per bushel.
**Wages:** Farm laborers: 56¢ per day.

Within the year such values were woefully obsolete. Throughout American history the government has attempted many times to regulate the prices of goods and services and the value of money, especially during wartime. The results have always been less than satisfactory.

A primary problem with values during the Revolution was that Continental Currency notes were not backed by gold or silver or, for that matter, by actual examples of the silver Spanish "dollars" they were said to represent. They were issued on the faith and credit of the government, which at times was not very substantial, good intentions notwithstanding. The following synopsis illustrates the depreciation of such notes over a period of time as expressed in the total face value of currency needed to buy $100 worth of Spanish "dollar" coins.

January 1777: $105 in currency needed to buy $100 in coins.
January 1778: $325 in currency needed.
January 1779: $742 in currency needed.
January 1780: $2,934 in currency needed.
January 1781: $7,400 in currency needed.

By 1781 the notes were virtually worthless. Stated another way, it took $74 in Continental paper money to buy a $1 Spanish silver coin. Soon thereafter, the federal government repudiated its currency, and the notes could not be redeemed for *any* price. From this situation arose the terms "not worth a Continental," and "not worth a Continental damn."[20]

With the currency situation in chaos, many if not most transactions were conducted on the barter system. Parker (pp. 258 ff.) gave details of an auction held in Wolfeboro on May 8, 1788, in which numbered church pews were sold to local citizens. A few of the sale prices (in English pounds and shillings) and the method by which the accounts were settled are given below. Virtually all transactions were consummated by barter:

Isaiah Horne: £6/15s. Paid in livestock.
Thomas Piper: £7/3s. Paid in labor and finished lumber.
Reuben Libbey: £6/3s. Paid in labor.
Levi Tibbetts: £4/5s. Paid by Libbey's labor.[21]

Matthew S. Parker: £5/4s. Lumber.
James Lucas, Jr.: £5/13s. His own and Libbey's labor.
John Martin: £4/11s. Lumber and produce.
Joshua Haines: £5/2s. Livestock and cash (one of the few to pay part cash).

### Prominent Families

During the Revolutionary War period, many people came to live in Wolfeboro. By 1790 the census showed a population of 941, more than a four-fold increase from 1775. Other towns in the area experienced similar growth, as the figures of 935 inhabitants in Sandwich and 565 in Moultonboro indicate.

To sketch the histories of prominent settlers and families of the period from 1768 to 1900 would be to duplicate many pages of the Parker work. Suffice it to say that by the end of the nineteenth century the following families had played notable parts in the town's history—and this list could be expanded many times over:

Abbott, Allen, Avery, Banfield, Bassett, Bean, Berry, Bickford, Blake, Brackett, Brewster, Brown, Burke, Canney, Carpenter, Cate, Chamberlain (or Chamberlin), Chase, Clark, Clifford, Clough (or Clow), Coffin, Coleman, Conner (or Connor), Cook, Copp, Cotton, Dame, Davis, Dearborn, DeLand, Doe, Drew, Dudley, Durgin, Eaton, Edgerly, Edmonds (or Edmunds), Estes, Evans (or Evens), Fernald, Fogg, Folsom, Foss, Fox, French, Frost, Fullerton, Furber (or Furbur), Gage, Gilman, Glidden, Goldsmith, Goodwin, Guppy, Haines, Haley, Ham (or Hamm), Hanson, Hardy, Hawkins, Hayes, Hersey, Hide (or Hyde), Hill, Hobbs, Horn (or Horne or Orne), Huggins, Hurd, Jackson, Jenness, Johnson, Jones, Keniston, Kent, Kimball, Lary, Leavitt, Libbey (or Libby), Lord, Lucas, Marden, Martin, Meader (or Meder, the early spelling), Merrill, Mills, Moody, Morgan, Moulton, Neal, Newell, Nudd, Nute, Paris, Parker, Peavey, Perkins, Pickering, Pierce, Pike, Piper, Plummer, Prindle (or Prindall), Remick, Rendall, Rindge, Roberts, Rogers, Rollins, Rust, Sanborn, Sceggel, Sewall, Shorey, Smith, Stevens, Stevenson, Stoddard, Swett, Taber (or Tabor), Taylor, Tebbetts (or Tibbetts), Thompson, Thurston, Towle, Trickey, Triggs, Varney, Warren, Weeks, Wentworth, Whitehouse, Whitten, Whitton,[22] Wiggin, Willey, and Young.

### Changing Counties

On April 19, 1769, the New Hampshire Assembly divided the province into five counties, subject to the approval of the king of England. These were named Cheshire, Grafton, Hillsborough, Rockingham, and Strafford, from the titles of certain English friends of John Wentworth.

In its original form Strafford County was immense and extended as far north as the village of Campton. Within its boundaries were the towns of Alton, Barnstead, Barrington, Brookfield, Chatham, Conway, Dover, Durham, Eaton, Effingham, Farmington, Freedom, Gilford, Gilmanton, Lee, Madbury, Meredith, Milton, Moultonboro, New Durham, New Hampton, Ossipee, Rochester, Sanbornton, Sandwich, Somersworth, Strafford, Tamworth, Tuftonboro, and Wolfeboro.

By action of the State Legislature on December 22, 1840, the northern part of Strafford County was separated from the southern section and divided into two new counties known as Carroll and Belknap, the former from Charles Carroll of Carrollton, famous early American patriot (who never visited the area), and the latter from Rev. Jeremy Belknap, pioneer New Hampshire historian. After the division Strafford County survived to include some of the southern towns.

From that point forward Carroll County included all of the land and water within the following towns: Albany, Brookfield, Chatham, Conway, Eaton, Effingham, Freedom, Moultonboro, Sandwich, Tamworth, Tuftonboro, Ossipee, Wakefield, and Wolfeboro.

Ossipee was named as the seat of Carroll County, a position it holds today. Court is currently conducted in Ossipee Village, close to the Wolfeboro town line in an area off Route 28.

## WARS OF 1812, 1861, AND 1898

### The War of 1812

Few if any soldiers from Wolfeboro voluntarily enlisted in the War of 1812. During this conflict an English fleet was off the harbor of Portsmouth, and New Hampshire men were drafted. Wolfeboro soldiers were enrolled into the 1st and 6th companies of the 27th Regiment of the army, and about two dozen of them spent a month or two at the forts guarding the entrance to Portsmouth Harbor. The town paid them $10 per month for their service, and they later became eligible for government pensions.

### The Civil War

During the 1861-1865 Civil War Wolfeboro citizens in service included 146 enlisted men, 27 draftees, and 15 commissioned officers, for a total of 188. Four men were killed in battle, another four died later of wounds sustained, and 12 died from disease.

Among those who entered the war none was better known than Major James Robert Newell, who came to Wolfeboro as a young man and established the *Granite State News* in 1860. Newell served with distinction in several Civil War campaigns. Wolfeboro Post No. 61 of the Grand Army of the Republic was named in his honor.

Appropriate of matters involving the Civil War, Mrs. Bixby, who is said to have received a handwritten letter from President Lincoln expressing sympathy for the loss of each of her five sons in the Civil War, later lived in Wolfeboro on College Road between the Cotton Valley railroad crossing and the Brookfield town line.[23] Fortunately, the legend was not true, and at least one son survived. A grandson, William Bixby, was a Wolfeboro selectman for several terms beginning in 1914.

First used in 1872 the Wolfeborough Railroad Station, shown here in an 1889 sketch, is still standing today. On hand to meet the train were livery wagons for goods and people. A wooden sidewalk (shown at lower right) connected the facility with the Glendon House (built in 1874) a couple blocks away. (Frederick W. Prindle, *Views of Wolfeboro and Vicinity*, 1889)

The Boston & Maine Railroad locomotive "Ossipee" is shown at the Wolfeboro engine house (located about where the Narrows condominiums are in the 1990s). The turntable in front of the engine was used to assign engines to specific bays in the roundhouse. The building burned on October 3, 1931. (Charles O. Hodgman photograph, late 19th century; collection of the Remember the Iron Horse Museum)

### The Spanish-American War

In contrast to earlier conflicts, the Spanish-American War created little notice among local citizens. On April 26, 1898, the *Granite State News* asked, "Who will be the first to enlist as a volunteer from Wolfeboro?" In the summer Admiral Dewey, the hero of Manila Bay, was commemorated in town by Dewey-brand lead pencils offered for a nickel apiece at the Wolfeboro Drug Store and by a baseball team called the Deweys.

## TRANSPORTATION

### Roads

In the earliest days travel was over crude roads, some of which were little more than Indian trails or footpaths used by settlers, often delineated only by marks on trees. As time went on roads suitable for horse and carriage travel were built to link local farms, stores, and homes. For the most part such thoroughfares were not named and were referred to simply by where they went—from a settlement to a sawmill, for example. Such unofficial and inconsistent names as Mill Road, Old Mill Road, and Willey Mill Road were used.

For travel out of the district in the 1770s, the Pequawket and College roads linked Wolfeboro with Conway and the Saco River Valley to the north; Tuftonboro, Moultonboro, and Sandwich to the west, and to the southeast from the Wentworth farm to Middleton and on to Portsmouth on the coast. For a number of years there was no road to Alton (then called Gore or Alton Gore), and travelers from there and other points on the other side of Lake Winnipesaukee had to reach Wolfeboro by crude trails or by boat.[24] In the winter the trip could be made across the ice. A road was cut to Alton by 1781.

Eventually the Miles Road, North and South, paralleled more or less what are now North and South Main Streets. The Smith River was not bridged until 1791, and those desiring to get from one side to the other had to ford it at a point about 50 feet upstream from the present bridge.[25] Apparently, the first bridge was replaced by a better structure in 1833. The river was much wider then than it is now, as much filling was done later.

During the first half of the nineteenth century, the town's outlying districts such as today's Goose Corner, Wolfeboro Center, East Wolfeboro, Pleasant Valley, and South Wolfeboro, were all linked by dirt roads, often passable in the summer, but rutted and muddy in the spring and snowed shut for periods in the winter. These satellite communities had their own general stores, taverns, schools (usually), and other places of accommodation, and could be self-sufficient for weeks at a time.

By the end of the second half of the century, most of the major roads that we know today had been laid out, all unpaved, often with open drains at their sides and of varying quality. In swampy districts such as along the shore of Lake Wentworth and today's Clarke Plaza, "corduroy" roads were made by placing medium-size logs crossways on the roadbed. These helped to eliminate mud but were bumpy to traverse.

Stagecoaches traveled the main roads. In 1900 there was daily scheduled service in and out of Wolfeboro, Wolfeboro Falls, and South Wolfeboro. In the late nineteenth century, coach driver Stephen Durgin, who built the Durgin Block, sometimes raced the steamboat from Alton to Wolfeboro and beat it. Fine horses were used on the stage run from Sandwich to Dover and were changed at Melvin Village, Wolfeboro, Middleton, and Rochester.

When the Wentworth farm was listed for sale in 1797, the accompanying description advised prospective purchasers that it was situated on Smith's Lake (Lake Wentworth) and that "said pond charges itself into the great Winnipisocky Lake, from thence there will be a canal communication with Boston in a few years." Apparently, the project fell into the category of wishful thinking.

### Railroads

By the time railroad service came to Wolfeboro in 1872, many other Lakes Region towns had long since been connected, including Alton and The Weirs.[26]

The Boston, Concord & Montreal Railroad, the Boston & Maine Railroad, and the Eastern Railroad were active in the Lakes Region and the district to the north. The first two companies had already made connections with Winnipesaukee. The Eastern Railroad branch was more concerned with traffic in the mountains.

It was hoped that the Portsmouth, Great Falls, & Conway Railroad Company would run track south of Lake Wentworth to Wolfeboro. The railroad was finally laid out east of the Wolfeboro hills and 10 miles away from Lake Winnipesaukee, and it was questionable if Wolfeboro would ever be directly served by railroad. However, the Hon. John W. Sanborn recommended that a branch be extended to Wolfeboro if a sum of $35,000 could be raised.

The citizens were impressed and applied for a charter. On July 1, 1868, the Wolfeborough Railroad Company was incorporated to go from Wolfeboro Junction to Wolfeboro, a stretch of 12 miles.[27] On September 20, 1869, the town voted (300 yes, 122 no) to raise the required sum; this vote was ratified on December 2, 1870 (250 yes, 70 no). Work commenced on the railroad in November 1871, when ground was broken near Mast Landing by 87-year-old Lyford Shorey. Service was by the Eastern Railroad (under a 68-year lease dated January 6, 1872), which transferred its interest to the Boston

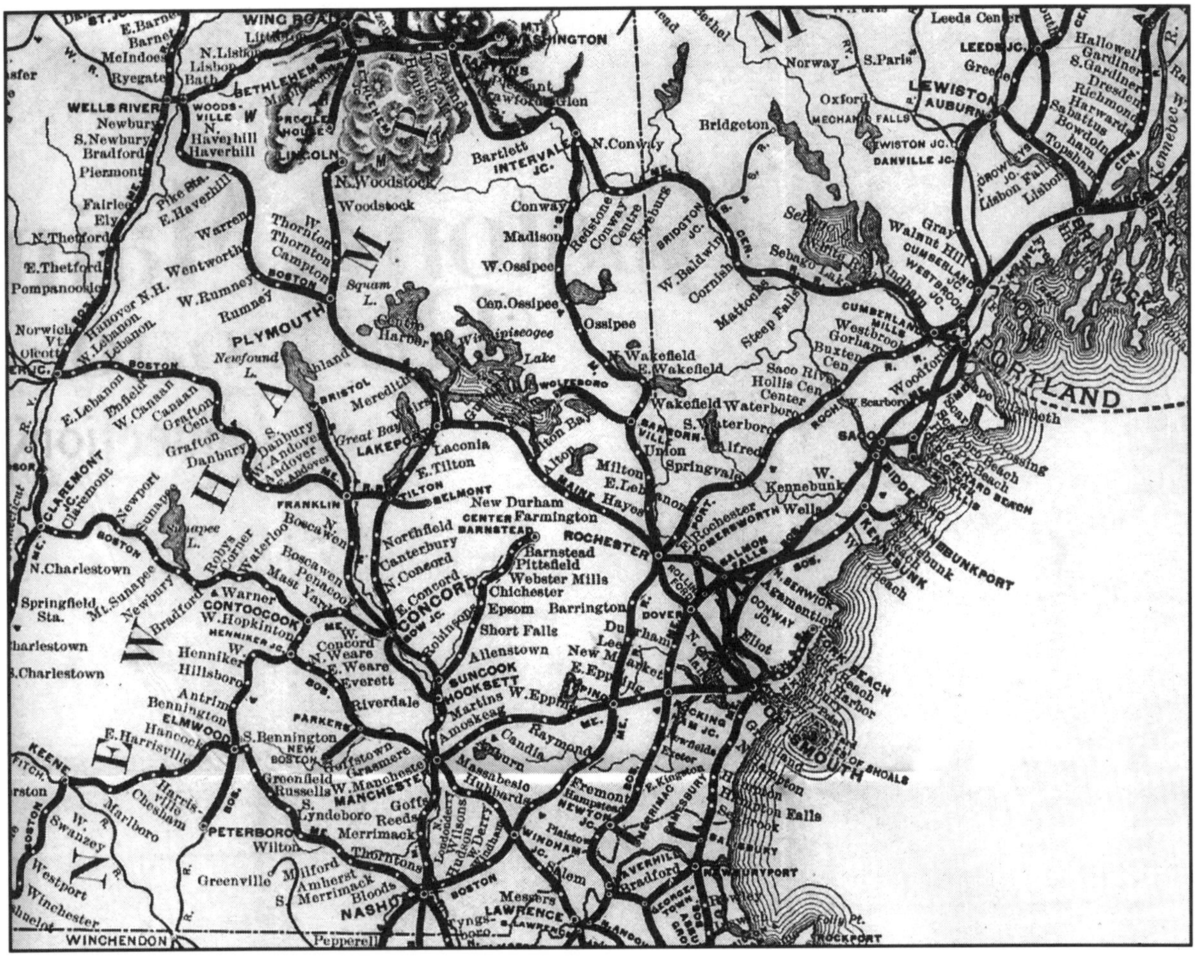

Boston & Maine Railroad connections to Wolfeboro and surrounding areas, 1897. At the time nearly all out-of-state visitors to Wolfeboro came by rail. (Passenger Department, Boston & Maine Railroad)

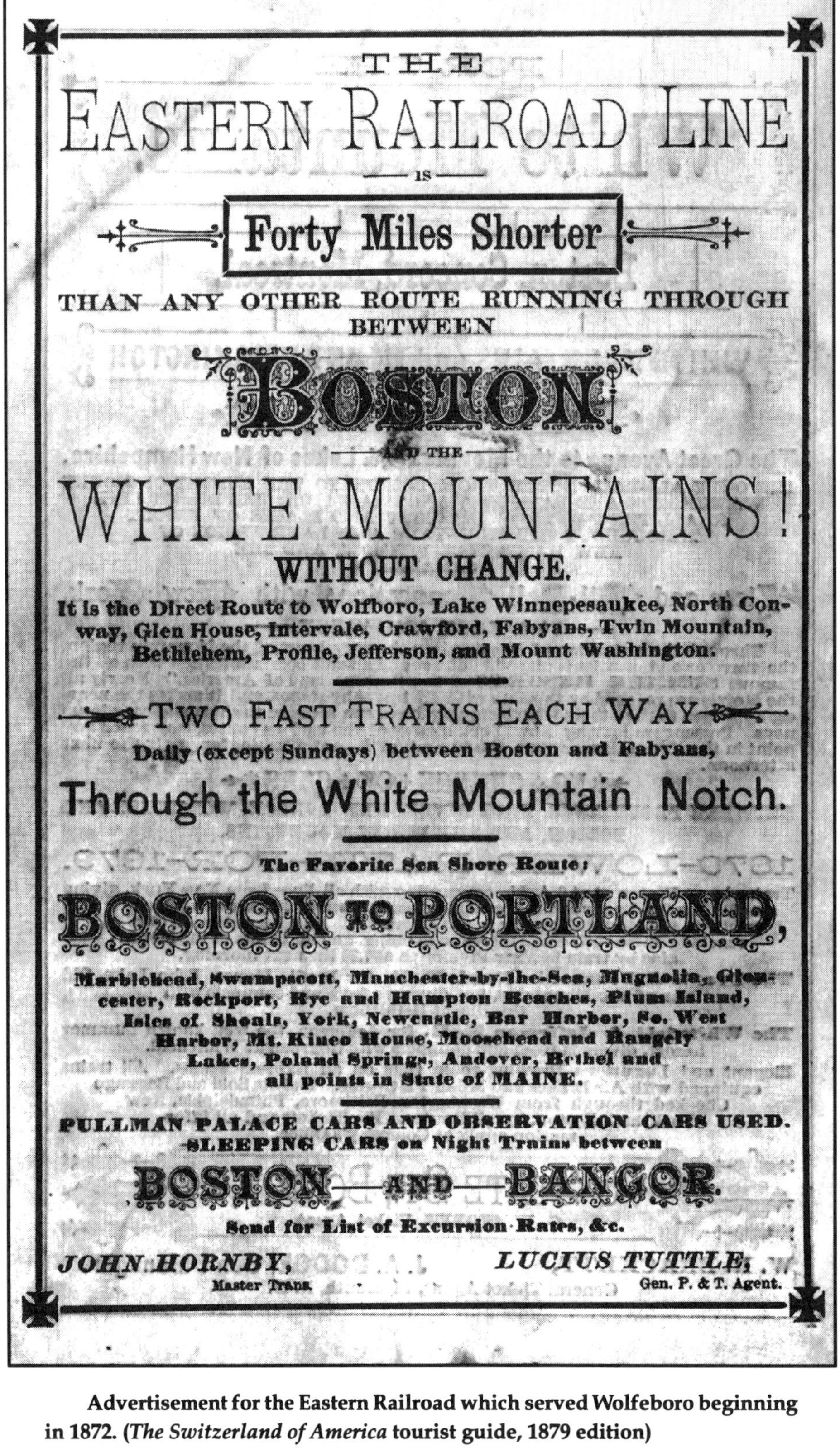


Advertisement for the Eastern Railroad which served Wolfeboro beginning in 1872. (*The Switzerland of America* tourist guide, 1879 edition)

& Maine through a lease followed by a sale effective June 30, 1892.

On August 19, 1872, the first Eastern Railroad locomotive trailing five passenger coaches came into town, with Charles H. Morgan at the throttle.[28] Free rides were given throughout the day between Wolfeboro and Wolfeboro Junction.

The railroad opened new vistas for the town. Now it was a simple matter for vacationers to come from Boston and for local citizens to go from Wolfeboro to Rochester, Boston, and other points for shopping trips and excursions. Factory goods could be shipped by rail to distant points. This sparked a period of growth in the town, best epitomized by the construction soon thereafter of the elegant Glendon House hotel on South Main Street not far from the railroad and connected to the depot by a wooden sidewalk. For many years the Boston & Maine Railroad operated the *Mount Washington* steamship, launched in July 1872, which connected with the railroad at the Town Docks.

Under the Boston & Maine, in the 1890s the line to Wolfeboro was often referred to as the Wolfeboro Branch. A familiar locomotive in local service was the "Great Falls," a.k.a. No. 207, driven by Engineer Randall, which was used through mid-January 1893.[29] Locomotive No. 157, "The North Wind," came into service in 1890 and was used on the Wolfeboro Branch until 1915, when it was consigned to the scrap pile.[30]

At the turn of the century there were trains to and from Boston several times a day in the warmer season. The local facility included a roundhouse and turntable. The Boston & Maine Railroad Depot in downtown Wolfeboro remains a prominent landmark today.

### Boats

Transportation by boat on Lake Winnipesaukee forms a rich part of town history and tradition, linking Wolfeboro with islands and other ports around the lake and, in effect, adding another dimension to the town's assets. Particularly notable was the *Mount Washington* steamship operated by the Boston & Maine Railroad in the late nineteenth and early twentieth centuries, although the *Lady of the Lake* and numerous others each played a part.

### Natural Phenomena

Weather and natural phenomena were popular topics for discussion. Adams, in the *Annals of Portsmouth*, p. 364, told of a remarkable event which must have affected Wolfeboro:

> Monday, November 28, 1814: About 20 minutes after 7 o'clock, there was a severe shock of an earthquake which continued half a minute. It was preceded by a heavy rumbling noise, the convulsion of the earth was violent, several houses were shaken, and persons standing on the ground perceived the agitation. The noise and trembling went off gradually, apparently in a southeasterly direction....

Earthquakes continued to be reported over the years, as in 1871, when the newspaper noted that on September 11 a slight tremor had been felt locally.[31]

Weather forecasting was a primitive science, but from Gov. John Wentworth onward, numerous local citizens kept a barometer on hand to observe highs and lows. This must have been a particularly perplexing problem in 1816, remembered nationally as "the year without a summer." It is said that there was no snow on the ground in Wolfeboro until March, but at that time a memorable fall of four feet occurred. Snow fell on June 6, 1816, and frost was observed during each of the summer months. As a result, crops were poor.

Rain, snow, high winds, ice on the lakes, temperature, and other meteorological topics were fodder for columns in the *Granite State News* and had direct effects upon the local economy.

Representative accounts of natural occurrences include the following from the 1890s:

> 1890, June 16: Report that on the preceding Wednesday afternoon "a young cyclone struck this place. We hear of small damages in several localities." Among the damage was the breaking of a large pane of glass in the Peavey Block.
>
> 1894, October 2: "Wild pigeons are reported seen in this section again, the first in more than 20 years."
>
> 1897, February 2 (Tuesday): "Thursday one of the most severe storms we have experienced since 1888 reached this town and tarried the entire day. It came from the northeast and snow began falling early in the morning, to continue to increase throughout the day, strong wind prevailing, piling the snow in huge drifts, making traveling for pedestrians especially, very difficult and almost impossible.... On the average there was 18 inches on the level." Trains were delayed. In South Wolfeboro it was reported 26 inches deep on the average.
>
> 1897, August 17: "South Wolfeboro. The hailstorm which passed over our village Monday afternoon, the 9th, was the most terrific ever seen in this section. For 15 minutes the hail fell as rain falls in torrents, covering the ground to a depth of an average of one inch and a few places from two to three inches. Nothing like it was ever known in this vicinity, not even by its oldest inhabitant, Mrs. William DeLand. The stones were very large, and several places were found the next morning frozen together in a solid mass. Two and one half inches of rain fell during the storm which lasted but a short time. Fortunately, little damage was done...."

## AROUND THE TOWN

### Commerce and Professions

During the early decades of Wolfeboro's existence, most employment was at or near home. Trees had to be cleared, rocks moved, houses and barns built, and ground plowed. Supporting these activities were saw and grist (flour) mills, which were among the town's earliest businesses.

The town of Wolfeboro as shown on the *Topographical Map of Carroll County,* New Hampshire, Smith and Peavey, 1860. The variant spelling "Wolfborough" is used. The downtown district is labeled as Smith's Bridge Village.

WEST MAIN STREET, OVER THE HILL.
EAST MAIN STR., COPPLE CROWN MT. IN DISTANCE.


**Views of North Main Street (top of page) and South Main Street (below) delineated circa 1889, then called West Main and East Main Streets, seemingly a more accurate reflection of their general orientations. (Frederick W. Prindle, *Views of Wolfeboro and Vicinity*)**

General stores soon opened in Wolfeboro and at various outlying hubs of activity such as South Wolfeboro, Brackett's Corner (now Pleasant Valley), and Dimon's Corner (North Wolfeboro). The typical emporium offered preserved food, dry crackers, baked goods, dairy and poultry products, dried peas and beans, patent medicines, clothing, boots and shoes, yard goods, tinware, nails, hardware, cement, illuminating oil, and other necessities for everyday living. Like as not, the store was a family operation with living quarters on the second floor or in the back.

### Henry Rust's Store

A store ledger kept by Henry Rust for the years 1815 to 1825, for his general store in South Wolfeboro near Mink Brook, reveals that only rarely did his customers pay cash for their purchases.[32] Instead, he kept a ledger reckoned in dollars (frequently in shillings and pence and then converted at the prevailing rate; in 1816, a shilling was converted at 16.7¢), and in the "Contra" column for each he recorded what they exchanged in goods or labor. Below is a representative sample taken from several thousand listings.

ITEMS SOLD (Date, customer, price)

1815, March. John W. Horne. 5,000 shingles. $8.33

1815, May. Nathaniel Rust. Labor (Rust himself, one boy, 1 horse, 4 oxen). $1.50

1815, July 29. Peter Frey. 1 bushel potatoes. $0.33

1815, August 3. Adelphia Ricker. 1 bushel apples. $0.33

1815, November 1. Nathaniel Rust. For pasturing a sheep. $1.50

1817, May 27. Johnathan Gail. 900 feet of planks. $4.90

1819, April 30. Mark Fogg. 1 peck barley. $0.50

1819, July 10. James Johnson. 6 quarts rum. $1

1819, July 22. Nicholas Morrison. 2 quarts molasses. $0.42

1819, October 27. Abigail Martin. Hauling boards and 41/2 days building fence. $4

1819, November 9. Moses Seavey. 1 day, myself, boy and 2 oxen building wall. $1.50

1820, March 27. William Rust. For moving horse to Brookfield, 7 miles. $0.28

1820, May 8. Mark Fogg. 1 bushel corn. $0.50

1820, July 29. George Rendal. Making 1 pair pantaloons. $0.67

1820, May 27. Nicholas Morrison. 1 peck of flax seed. $0.34

1820, August 4. James Langley. 2 quarts rum. $0.34

1820, August 27. George Rendal. Shaving soap. $0.05

1821, May 23. Ebenezer Winget. 1/2 pound of tobacco. $0.125

1821, June 4. Ebenezer Winget. 4 weeks' board of Lizebeth. $2

1821, December 4. James Folsom. 11/2 bushels of turnips. $0.50

1822, January 3. Joseph Ricker. 4 gallons cider. $0.67

1823, May 6. Peter Frey. 4 quarts salt, $0.20

1823, June 31. Peter Frey. 2 lemons. $0.10

1823, December 9. Sarah Wentworth. 1 suit of O.D. [outdoor?] clothes. $2.50

1824, May 10. Joseph Sanborn. 1 pair boots. $1

1825, March 10. Stephen McIntire. Making 1 shirt. $0.50

PAYMENT RECEIVED (Date, payee, value credited)

1815, September 4. Nathaniel Rust. 6 days' work on corn house. $5.

1815, October 14. Adelphia Ricker. One day's work. 3s. $0.50

1815, November 21. Samuel Connor. 1 day framing shop. $1

1816, January 1. Nathaniel Rust. Mending sleigh. $0.83

1816, May 2. Daniel Brewster. 1 gallon molasses. $0.50

1816, November 21. Nathaniel Rust. 2 days' work on house. $1.67

1817, April 17. Peter Frey. 1 day hauling dung. $0.50

1817, April 28. Mark Fogg. 1 calf skin. $0.67

1817, June 13. Johnathan Gail. 28 pounds of fish. $1.12

1817, June 14. Peter Frey. 1 day cutting bushes. $0.50

1817, July 17. Joseph Ricker. 1 day cutting trees. $0.50

1817, November 10. Peter Frey. 3/4 day mowing. $0.33

1819, June 9. Nicholas Morrison. Making 1 pair shoes. $0.50

1819, September 21. Moses Seavey. Reaping 21/2 acr es of rye. $2.50

1819, November 6. Moses Seavey. 1 day cutting stone. $0.50

1820, February 20. Joseph Ricker. 1 day hauling wood. $0.34

1820, March 31. Moses Seavey. Digging well 8 feet, 9 inches, and stoning it. $6.20

1821, June 21. Joseph Ricker. Hire of ox for plowing. $0.17

1821, July 4. Benjamin W. Adams. 3 lemons. $0.10

1822, June 5. Joseph Ricker. 1 day shearing sheep. $0.50

1822, June 10. Joseph Ricker. 1 day hoeing. $0.50

1823, March 23. Benjamin Horne. 10 days' work. $3.07

### Commerce

Many manufacturing businesses, mostly of the single proprietor type, were soon established and by the early nineteenth century included blacksmiths, shoe shops (a particularly popular local industry), furniture shops, and others, in addition to an increased number of saw and grist mills. By 1860 virtually every stream with a decent flow of water had multiple mills and factories on its banks. Certain streams were seasonal, and during dry months they were diminished in effectiveness as power sources.

Small taverns offering food, drink, and overnight accommodations were established in several locations, often being operated by families who lived in the building or nearby. Near the Smith River downtown, the Lake Hotel became a familiar stopping place, was added on to several times and eventually was known as the Sheridan House. As time went on, larger and more pretentious facilities were constructed, including the immense Pavilion Hotel and the French-style Glendon House. In addition, dozens of local residents earned extra money by renting out rooms to lodgers.

The second half of the nineteenth century saw the Steam Mill Company established c.1851 on Back Bay by Moses and Augustus J. Varney, Alpheus Swett, and Benjamin Morrison. Beginning in 1865, this large sawmill and lumber processing facility was operated as the Libbey & Varney Co. (Alvah S. Libbey, Augustus J.

View of the downtown district of Wolfeboro taken from the Lake House (later called the Sheridan House), circa 1865, looking southeast along South Main Street. The Wolfeboro Marketplace is now located on the Sheridan House site. The numbers are identified as follows:

1. Possibly part of the Lake House.

2. Unknown buildings.

3. Possibly the Mason House moved in later years to a site now occupied by the Telephone Exchange on Glendon Street; the Durgin Block was built there in the 1870s.

4. Joseph E. Fox Livery Stable, later a part of Horne's Garage.

5. Unidentified cluster of buildings where Mast Landing and other businesses are today.

6. Levi Haley and Joseph W. Goodwin store, now the Wool Corner in the 1990s.

7. Folsom Block (barely visible), now Black's Paper store in the 1990s.

8. Brackett-Thompson-Walter shoe factory, better known as the Bank Building, built circa 1855.

9. Unknown.

10. Blake Folsom's dwelling, torn down in 1952 to build the A&P grocery store, now where Hunter's IGA is located.

11 and 12. Possibly the Dr. Rufus King home and barn.

13. Cate Block where the Lakeview Service Station is today.

14. Pavilion Hotel.

15. Samuel Avery house built early in the 19th century. The large barn was moved after WW II to the foot of Moody Mountain and Pork Hill Road.

16. Field belonging to the Pickering and Rollins family, now owned by Brewster Academy.

17. Gilman Cooper house, later known as the Belvue House and Ann Inn (among other names), where Town Park and Cate Park are located now.

18. Buildings now on the site used in the 1990s for Hall's Pharmacy and, visible only for a small portion, the present Bridges' Hallmark store.

19. These two buildings stood where the three-story Goodwin Block was later built; it was burned on May 28, 1899, and a smaller Goodwin Block was built on its site.

20. Liberty Pole. Near it is a pile of wood. Later, two buildings were built on the woodpile site (the one to the right of the woodpile may be one of them and in place by this time), but were later removed to make way for the Peavey Block in 1889.

21. Main Street bridge.

Built in 1884 by local capital, the "Big Factory" (as it was known) stood four stories high, was made of wood, and over the years was occupied by various shoe and textile firms, The building burned in 1887 and within a year was rebuilt on the same foundation. The second structure, shown here, is virtually identical to the 1884 building and was made using the same plans. (Melanson Collection)

Members of the Monitor Engine Company and Monitor Hose Co., South Wolfeboro, in the late nineteenth century. Standing in front of the wagon are Fred DeLand, Walter Corson, Rollin Corson, Walter Getchell, and Elwood Corson. Sitting in the wagon are Willie Wiggin, Fred Avery, Horace B. Rust, and Frank York. Standing in the wagon are Jim Corson, Will Piper, and Henry Chase.

Varney, Alonzo Thompson), then Libbey Brothers, then beginning in the late 1890s as S.W. Clow & Co. A large tannery was operated lakeside at the end of Endicott Street by Joseph Varney and associates.

In South Wolfeboro a large blanket mill was set up on Mink Brook in 1861. Over the years the mill was known as the Wolfeborough Woolen Mills, the I.W. Springfield Co., and other names. By the 1890s the facility employed 75 workers and produced 40,000 blankets annually.

John Taber was primarily known as a maker of clay smoking pipes and over a period of time had two factories in South Wolfeboro, one on Endicott Street, and one in East Alton. Taber's pipes were primarily marketed in distant locations, apparently, mostly in England. They were made in several styles, including one with the head of General Grant, another with an eagle claw as part of the bowl design, one with the head of a satyr, and especially popular models with a nubbed motif in imitation of a corn cob. "Taber's Little Washer," pictured as a wooden tub with a hand wringer attached, was patented in 1871 and manufactured in South Wolfeboro.

On Factory Street (now known as Lehner Street), a huge factory was erected through local financing in 1883-84, burned on August 9, 1887, and replaced soon thereafter by a similar building on the old foundation. A.J. McDonald, Wolfeboro's largest contractor at the time, did the construction.[33] Later, Greenleaf B. Clark built a smaller facility on the same street. Over a period of years, tenants included branches of several Massachusetts shoe and textile manufacturing companies.

Wolfeboro Falls, which was nearly always referred to as Mill Village until the early twentieth century, was a beehive of activity, with the main industry being lumber and wood products, including excelsior, building materials, and at one point, Lorenzo Horne's factory which made piano and organ stools. Messrs. Hutchins, Hersey, Berry, and other mill owners prospered.

Beginning in 1834 Wolfeboro was home to several banks and other financial institutions during the nineteenth century, most of which had somewhat checkered histories.[34] These included the Wolfborough Bank (1834-1837), Lake Bank (1854-1865), Carroll County Five Cent Savings Bank (1857-1877), Lake National Bank of Wolfborough (1865-1893), Wolfeborough Savings Bank (1871-1903), and Wolfeborough Loan and Banking Co. (1889-1904)

In 1861 Moses Thompson's emporium near the bridge was a forerunner of a modern department store, except in those days produce was accepted in lieu of cash. Mrs. Israel B. Manning advertised "bonnets, hoods, wool under sleeves, and hoop skirts." She also announced that "grave clothes and mourning goods [are] constantly on hand and made to order."

In 1860 Bennett's Photograph and Jewelry Saloon was situated where Brewster Academy is today. At the time *saloon* usually referred to an elegantly furnished room, not to a depot for alcoholic beverages.

In 1875 Blake Folsom, a prominent dealer in hardware, stoves, crockery, and glassware, and owner of the Folsom Block (where Black's Paper Store is today), employed three peddlers who traveled around the area selling wares. At the time downtown Wolfeboro businesses included clothing, drug, meat, "fancy goods," tack and harness, and other stores, as well as a marble cutter who made fireplace mantels as well as gravestones. "Fancy goods" included luxury items such as stereograph viewers, paintings and art objects, games, binoculars, telescopes, and other desirable items nice to have but not necessary for the basic sustenance of life. Professionals in Wolfeboro included blacksmiths, carpenters, livery stable operators, innkeepers, farmers, cobblers, trainmen, doctors, surveyors, teachers, ministers, and lawyers.

By the 1890s the town was riding a crest of prosperity. Prominent downtown were the three-story Peavey Block, its neighbor the J.W. Goodwin Block, and, across the street the Folsom Block and Bank Building, on Railroad Avenue the Central Block and another Goodwin Block, on North Main Street the elegant Durgin Block (usually called "The Durgin"), the Cate and Pickering blocks at Pickering Corner, and numerous smaller buildings. Indeed, considering the Glendon House, Pavilion, and Sheridan House hotels, and the two large manufacturing establishments on Factory Street, the town had more immense buildings and a more impressive architectural profile in the 1890s than it would a century later.

Wolfeboro also had insurance agencies, barbers, music instructors, boat rental businesses, a steam laundry, a florist, and a dealer in artists' supplies.

Farming was also prospering. For example, Nathaniel Brewster's spread comprised 1,500 acres of pasture, cropland, and woods. In one season he cut 175 tons of hay and had 100 head of livestock. J. Clifton Avery (better known later for his insurance agency) maintained a large farm, as did Blake Folsom and A.W. Wiggin. As can be seen from even a superficial perusal of early town directories, the typical entrepreneur—and Blake Folsom, John Brackett, and Greenleaf B. Clark were prime examples—was apt to have his fingers in many business pies.

The poultry business was sizable. Parker noted that in one instance Wolfeboro "exported" (a term for sending anything beyond town boundaries) 22 tons of Thanksgiving turkeys in a single consignment, shipped by steamer from the town wharf.

Learned professions such as medicine and law attracted many people to Wolfeboro during the nineteenth century. Typically, at any given time in the second half

South Main Street with the Main Street bridge in foreground to left and right, as seen in the 1880s. The two-story building to the left housed C.F. Piper's clothing business for a short time (today the Wool Corner is there), and to its right is seen the Folsom Block (today the location of Black's Paper Store), to the right of it, the Bank Building, and the white fence around the yard of the Glendon House with South Main Street extending to the distance. To the extreme right is the Goodwin Block.

View further down South Main Street (then usually called East Main Street or simply Main Street) circa 1875. The building at the extreme left was owned by Blake Folsom. Immediately to its right is the Bank Building constructed circa 1855 and still standing today, although considerably altered. To the extreme right is one of two structures (the other not visible) where the Avery Building is today. The tall flagpole was known as the Liberty Pole.

of the century the town had two or three doctors and as many lawyers.

### Newspapers

The first newspaper to be published in the town was produced in South Wolfeboro for a short time in the 1850s. The *Carroll County Republican* consisted of four pages, six columns per page, with much advertising. It favored *Democratic* policies and sanctioned slavery.

In January 1856 printer John Roberts launched the *Carroll County Pioneer* in the Bank Building on South Main Street. The periodical was sold in March 1858 to D. Furber, who a few months later moved it to Rochester. Roberts left Wolfeboro and went to Ossipee, where in May 1859 he created the *Carroll County Register* which he published for six years. When he was in Wolfeboro, Roberts maintained a display of popular books from leading publishers for sale.

Activities of the town were best chronicled in the pages of the *Granite State News,* founded by James R. Newell on November 1, 1860, who used a patent lever-press made in 1804 bought second-hand for $50.[35] On December 5, 1861, Newell said farewell to his friends and business associates, left the newspaper in charge of Charles H. Parker, and went off to the Civil War. A steam-driven Fairhaven Power Press was added later. From time to time competing newspapers sprang up, but all proved to be ephemeral. The paper referred to itself simply as the *News* in its columns. On occasion the public called it *The Grunter,* a nickname that currently appears as a subhead on its title page.

Over a period of years the editorial and printing offices of the *News* moved from place to place. Its first headquarters was in the rear of the left side of the Bank Building on South Main Street, then it moved to the attic of the same structure, and later to the second floor. In October 1887 tenants of the Bank Building, including the *News,* suffered extensive water damage when the adjacent Piper Block was burned. The newspaper then moved to the Mount Washington Wharf Building at the Town Docks where everything, including the old 1804 press still in use, was lost in the fire of May 28, 1899. In September 1899 the paper was revived and set up in the Durgin Block. In the twentieth century the *News* moved several more times. All type was set by hand until a Linotype machine was installed in 1920. A Cottrell two-revolution, rear-delivery electric press was first used in 1931.

In some of the early days, the *News* was bought already printed on one side of two of the four pages with patent medicine advertisements and national news. The local editor simply printed the other sides.

### Clippings from the *News*

After the establishment of the *Granite State News,* the interests of Wolfeboro people were recorded in detail, both in news items and from the advertisements.[36]

Selected news items and commentaries:

This from the October 3, 1887 issue:

> Isaac Roberts, the only colored citizen of Wolfeboro, has sold his effects and taken his departure for the sunny clime of Florida. Mr. Roberts has lived in town many years. He was a runaway slave from the neighborhood in which Fred Douglass lived and from which both made their escape north.

On April 9, 1888, three inches of snow on the level plus two or more feet of solid ice prompted this comment: "Indications of an early spring are not apparent!" and "Horrid describes the condition of the roads better than any other word!"

From the frequency of comments in the *Granite State News* about the weather, fishing success, and the condition of roads, one can surmise that these are items of eternal interest in town.

This appeared on March 10, 1896: "There should be a stop put to the fast and reckless driving on the business section of Main Street." The offenders were horses, not Corvettes.

Reports of casualties persisted through the years. A man froze to death on the way to visit his mother; a child drowned in the family well; entire families were wiped out by diphtheria; seven people drowned while crossing the ice; people were injured by kicks from horses or wagons tipping over and from falls from roofs or trees.

Another subject which absorbed townspeople in the 1880s and 1890s was the performance and health of horses. Stephen Durgin had two tracks for exercising his famous trotters. Frank P. Hobbs had horses for his business use and others for recreation, especially trotting.

People always showed great interest in town affairs. Loyal alumni of the Wolfborough (*sic*) and Tuftonborough Academy, disturbed by the prospect of the moving of the building which was the scene of fond memories, petitioned the trustees of the Brewster estate, begging them to select a different site for the proposed town hall. They received a long, courteous, but negative reply.

A "town affair" of a different sort was the subject of this item in the April 18, 1899, issue:

> No little commotion in social circles was created when on Tuesday, April 4, it became known that Mr. Charles H. Peavey and Miss Dora I. Preston of this village have made it convenient and possible to absent themselves from town about the same time. For some time Mr. Peavey had been bestowing considerable attention upon Miss Preston, and Tuesday morning he took his team and drove to Tuftonboro and got his brother to convey it to Ossipee where he took the cars. He told his brother, as reported, to keep the horse until he called for it. The same afternoon Miss Preston took the train for Milton. Both parties were last seen in Rochester, since

Office of the *Granite State News* in the Bank Building, August 1889. The Lake National Bank of Wolfborough (*sic*) and the insurance office of bank official Charles F. Parker were also in the edifice.

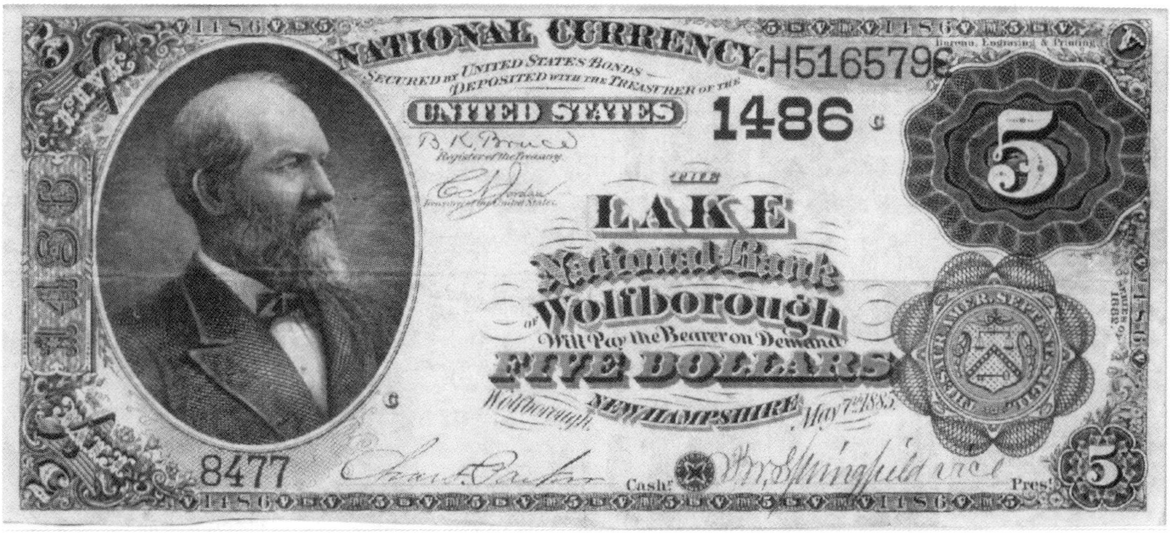


Lake National Bank of Wolfborough $5 note printed by the Bureau of Engraving and Printing, Washington, D.C. This note is hand-signed at the lower left by Charles F. Parker, bank cashier, and I.W. Springfield, vice president. Over a period of years currency notes of the denominations $5, $10, and $20 were placed into circulation for a total face value of $531,100. Most were later redeemed by the Treasury, and only a few are known to exist today. (The detailed history of the Lake National Bank of Wolfborough will be found in Volume III.)

# SPRING ANNOUNCEMENT

OF

## PIPER'S CLOTHING HOUSE!

The manufacturers of the better grade of Clothing have reduced their prices to retailers, and we are enabled to sell Good Clothing for less price than last season. We do not keep cheap clothing, it is poor property at any price. It is a pleasure to sell good clothing. It is economy to buy good clothing.

Spring Overcoats from $6 to $16.
Suits - - from $8 to $20.
Boys Suits - from $4 to $12.
Children's Suits from $1.50 to $7.

**Remember We Deal In Good Clothing.**

We have all the Spring Styles in Hats & Caps, that are desirable. We sell Trunks, Bags, Horse Blankets, Robes, etc, We have the celebrated Gold and Silver Laundered Shirts, a complete and full line of

**GENT'S FURNISHING GOODS.**

**We are situated so we can sell goods at a less profit than formerly and live.**

Wolfeborough, April 21, 1890. C. F. PIPER & CO.

**Advertisement by Charles F. Piper, clothier, financier, and entrepreneur, April 21, 1890.**

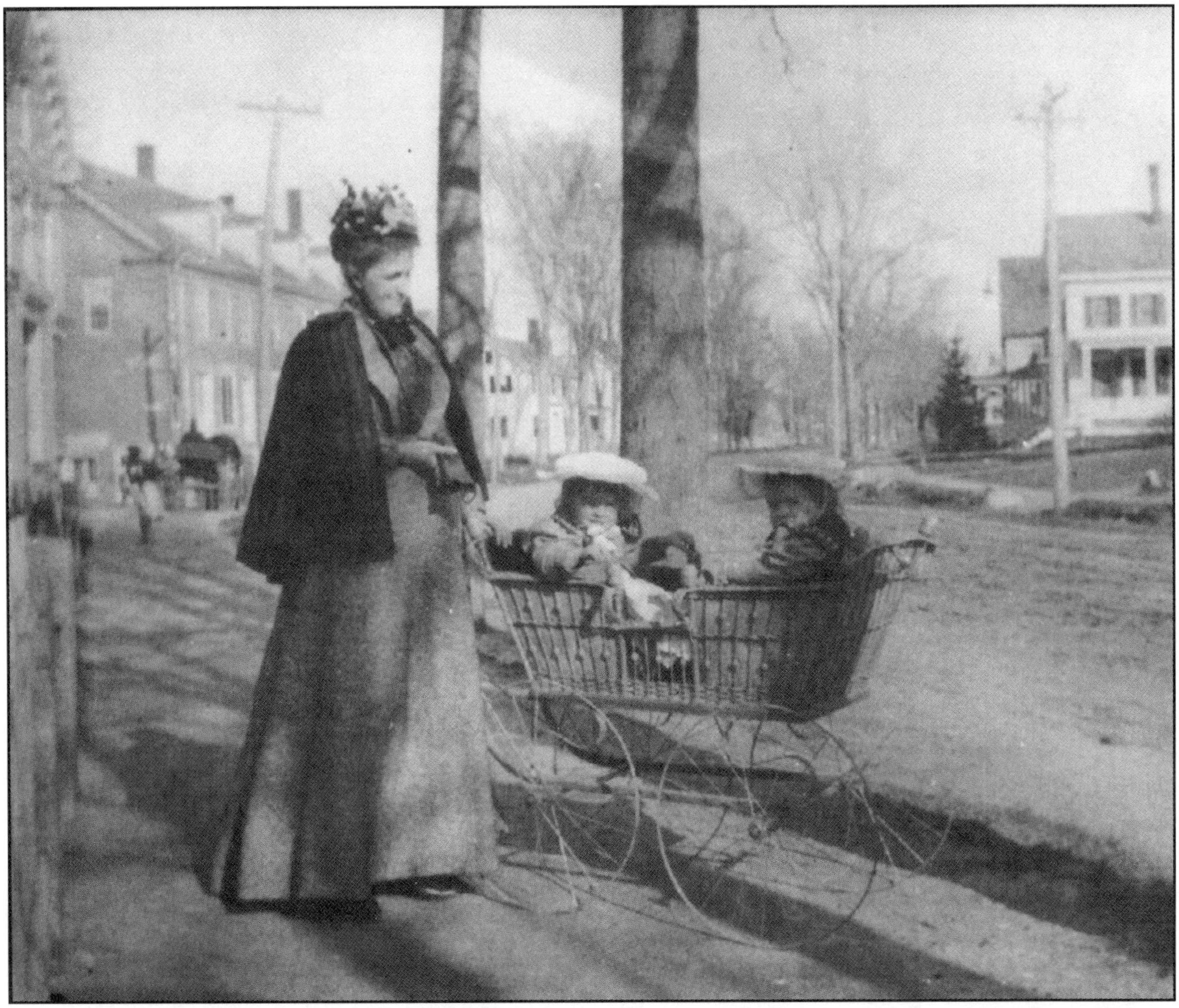

Ethel and Edith Scott, twins born in 1895, go for a baby carriage ride on a late winter day. The Nathaniel Scott house, unseen, is to the left, while at the left in the distance are the Pickering Block and the Cate Block. To the right South Main Street bends at Pickering Corner.

which time no particulars have been heard. Mr. Peavey is a married man, and his wife still resides in town.

In 1886 there was a great deal of agitation about widening Railroad Avenue where traffic was congested when trains and boats arrived. It was finally decided to create a new thoroughfare on the other side of the Bank and Central blocks, between them and the Glendon House; Central Avenue was the result.

One distressing article dated May 9, 1887, pointed out that backyards, pig pens, water closets, and drainage were being neglected. The writer went on to say: "During the entire of the last warm season people passing along some of our streets were obliged to hold their breath because of the intolerable stench proceeding from these places." He pointed out that some of the worst of previous years' typhoid cases and "diphtheria cases this season can be traced directly to these causes." He exhorted citizens to clean up promptly and to "see if we cannot make our village as noted for its excellent sanitary conditions as it is for beauty of location and neatness."

The doings of various ruffians, vandals, scoundrels, and other law-breakers made the news with regularity. In the mid-1880s "plug-uglies" who loitered on the Main Street bridge and annoyed passersby were a problem. History repeats itself, it has been said, and over a century later youth on the Main Street bridge were such a problem in 1994, that public hearings were held on the situation.

Several other law-enforcement topics from the *Granite State News:*

1889, June 10: "Officer C.C. Thompson was called Saturday evening to quell a pugilistic affray between Joseph Kimball and Horace Hasty. Several rounds had been fought, and some discoloration was discernible about the facial portion of Horace before the officer arrived. It was pretty tough, but for the cause ask Lizzie Clough."

1890, September 15: "It has been suggested that when any of our police force wish to exhilarate it would be a good plan to remove their handsome uniform as it—the uniform—might acquire bad habits."

1893, February 14: "Monday, February 6, Eugene A. Sawyer and L. Abra Wentworth, two boys, residents of this village....were charged with larceny. The evidence was mostly in the nature of a confession from one or both boys...." The boys, about 16 years of age, were sent to the New Hampshire Industrial School in Manchester.

1895, August 27, Tuesday: An account was printed of a gang of burglars who had visited Wolfeboro around 4:00 a.m. the preceding Saturday morning. The Post Office (in the Peavey Block) and the Railroad Depot were both burglarized, with the safes in both being blown apart by dynamite in about the same time. It is presumed that the actions were done in concert. No arrests were made and, apparently, there were no specific suspects.

1896, June 18: "Frank Locke and Henry White of this town upon complaint of Alonzo R. Kimball were arraigned yesterday before Justice [Charles O.] Doe for entering his dwelling in the night time with intent to commit fornication with Flossie B. Kimball. They were both convicted and placed under $1,000 bail each for appearance at the October term of the Supreme Court.... Monday morning last, Flossie B. Kimball, daughter of Alonzo Kimball, was brought before Justice C.O. Doe, as a stubborn, willful child, to which she pled guilty and was sentenced to the state industrial school during her minority. Her age is 15...."

## THE DOMESTIC SCENE

### At Home 1850-1900

Until mid-century open fireplaces were used for cooking and baking. Big kettles hung on cranes over the flames, and potatoes were buried in the hot ashes for baking. The invention of the Dutch oven, also known as the reflector oven or "tin kitchen," a three-sided utensil with the open side toward the fire, provided easier baking for small things. Most were equipped with a spit for roasting meat which was turned by hand to assure even cooking. The iron stove with fire brick lining was not popular in Wolfeboro until well after the middle of the century. An 1888 advertisement of an iron range was by a company from Portland, Maine, and was for units priced from $14.25 to $60.

There were no mechanical refrigerators. The common method of keeping foods was by hanging them in the well, in a spring house if available, and in unheated root cellars. By the end of the nineteenth century, insulated ice boxes were popular. Meats were smoked, salted or pickled. Apples, beans, corn, berries and pumpkin rinds were hung to dry from rafters in warm kitchens. In winter poultry, meat and even milk were frozen and stored in snow banks. Home canning in glass jars was introduced toward the end of the century.

Franklin stoves and small living room wood-burning stoves were popular in the early nineteenth century. Coal later became available cheaply and was widely used. No residences had central heat for many years, although most houses had one fireplace larger than the rest. A fire could be kept in it all night.[37] Until the inauguration of the Water Works in 1890, all water was obtained from wells, springs or open streams and lakes. In 1899 the Hobbs-Is-Inn advertised it had "steam heat, electric lights and gas, [and] electric bells." All of these were state of the art in Wolfeboro.

The general style of house furnishings toward the end of the century was "elegant clutter." Horsehair sofas were protected by hand embroidered antimacassars and made comfortable with fringed and tasseled cushions. Pianos and tables, also covered with fringed and tasseled cloths, displayed vases, often hand-painted, and clocks, china dogs, fans, pictures, fancy candles, or oil lamps with ornamented shades. Heavily ornate gilded frames surrounded sentimental pictures of John Alden and Priscilla, or a tempting bowl of strawberries beside

The Webster farm on North Main Street near Forest Road circa 1881. Helen C. Webster, who became Mrs. J. Frank Goodwin, is in the baby carriage to the right of the front door. Her parents, Eliza and Benjamin, are standing to each side of her. The house still stands today and is owned by J.F. ("Jeff") Goodwin III, grandson of Helen and J.F.

Helen Webster Goodwin and J. Frank Goodwin's Christmas card, 1941. Photographed in their home on North Main Street, the same structure as shown in the top photograph. (Jeff Goodwin Collection)

a platter of delectable-looking trout. Ornateness extended to architecture as well. A straight line was never used when a curlicue was available. Even the three-story Peavey Block had a railing around its top and a crest at the center, looking quite like a gigantic china closet.

Wicker rockers invited repose. Sheet music displayed on the piano tended to be sentimental or patriotic. Favorites included *Home, Sweet Home; Annie Laurie,* and other ballads.

The hostesses in these sitting rooms studied *Godey's Ladies' Book* for information about the latest styles and pored over advertisements in the *Granite State News,* which by this time was running columns for women. One could learn that "in bonnets where velvet and fur are combined the fur must match the color of velvet," or that "striped velvets for underskirts are in various charming combinations of colors", or that "English homespun, serge and cheviot gowns prevail — for street and day entertainments." Further, "Young ladies are reviving cadogan braids, and very young girls wear Gretchen braids," and "fluffy bangs are in order."[38] Wolfeboro ladies' clothing had come a long way since the early days! Of course, just a few of the local ladies could afford to be attired in the latest fashions, but without doubt all enjoyed reading about them.

The story of Wolfeboro — whether before 1900 or since that date is not in figures, percentages and quotes — but in the fields and woods, streams and lakes, schools and churches, shops and offices, sitting rooms and kitchens which provided the setting for the most important asset of the town — its people.

## TOURISTS COME AND GO

### John Greenleaf Whittier Visits

John Greenleaf Whittier, born December 17, 1807, in Haverhill, Massachusetts, became well known as an abolitionist and poet. He also developed a strong faith in God and belief in Christianity, following the Quaker religion. Whittier wrote the lyrics for a number of hymns, perhaps the most memorable being *Dear Lord and Father of Mankind.*

Important to the present volume, he spent much time on and about Lake Winnipesaukee, visiting Wolfeboro on occasion. Several of his poems mention Winnipesaukee and nearby towns.

Whittier came to Wolfeboro in August 1853 to attend a convention of the Free Soil Party.[39] Writing to Anson Burlingame from Rochester, on August 17, 1853, Whittier offered this invitation:[40]

> Our friends here are anxious to have thee at their Wolfborough meeting on the 24th. It will be best for thee and others from Boston to come up the day before by the afternoon train which meets the steam boat at Alton and spend the night at Wolfborough. It will be a great gathering beyond question.

Subsequently, Whittier submitted the following report (here excerpted) to the *National Era.*

> Wolfborough, Lake Winnepiseogee, N.H.
>
> August 25, 1853
>
> Will the reader take a seat with me in the cars of the Boston & Maine Railroad, at the Exeter station? It is a dull, foggy, August morning....
>
> We have now reached the end of our land journey — Alton, with its dark hill background. Off to the right, is a glorious reach of blue water — Alton Bay — the southern extremity of Lake Winnepiseogee. We step on board the steamer *Dover,* which lies waiting for us. The strong bracing north-west wind, which breaks down through the gorges of the hills, has swept away the clouds and mists; and, mounting to the hurricane deck, we look forth upon the ever-varying panorama of sparkling waters, green islands, and mountains starting abruptly from the lake, some clothed in the deep verdure of mid-summer, and others bare-browed and slide-scalped.
>
> Ten miles from Alton Bay, gliding between a long projecting headland and a small island,[41] we enter a broad and beautiful bay, at the head of which lies the village of Wolfeboro', its dwellings brilliant in white and green, scattered in their picturesque irregularity along the fertile slopes of the southward trending hills, looking out over crystal clear waters upon long broken ranges of misty mountains on the opposite shore. Nothing finer than its site can be found in New England. It has two large hotels, a flourishing academy, an orthodox and Friends' meeting house.
>
> Two steamboats run regularly between it and Alton, Centre Harbor, and Meredith. The lake itself, some twenty-four miles in length by ten in its widest part, is about 500 feet above tide water and is walled around by mountains from 800 to 2,000 feet high....
>
> The Free Soil Convention, which met here yesterday, was a most spirited and successful demonstration. Early in the morning, the steamboats came in, heavily laden with passengers — a fine representation of the strength and beauty of the Free Democracy of New Hampshire. Large numbers had arrived the night before; and land carriages of all kinds from the neighboring towns, contributed to swell the procession, which moved to a beautiful pine grove, a little distance from the centre of the village. Here a platform had been erected for the speakers in the centre of a sort of natural amphitheatre, well furnished with seats, the ladies occupying the front, with dark masses of men behind and on the right and left. The number present could not have been less than 3,000.
>
> Hon. Amos Tuck, of Exeter, was president of the day, who, after a few pertinent remarks, introduced Moses A. Cartland, of North Weare, who called out the enthusiastic cheers of the multitude by his eloquent and indignant denunciation of the Fugitive Slave Law. He was followed by Ex-Senator Hale, who, on rising, was greeted with cheer after cheer, the waving of handkerchiefs, and every possible demonstration of applause....
>
> From the wharf at Wolfboro' a neat little steamer, the *Lady of the Lake,* runs to Centre Harbor, a distance of twenty miles, through clustering islands, under thick wood-shadows, and in view of the piled mountains looming through every break in the neighboring hills....
>
> But we have lingered overlong by these pleasant waters. The boat bell is ringing, and we must bid farewell to the kind of friends who have freely opened home and hearts to us....
>
> J.G.W.

### An 1875 View of the Town

*Statistical Gazetteer of New Hampshire*, 7th edition, 1875, noted the following:

> Wolfeborough is the largest and most important town in Carroll County, both in wealth and population.... Wolfeborough village is pleasantly situated on two beautiful slopes of land, rising gently from the lake. Between these slopes and nearly in the centre of the village, Smith's River passes into the lake. The river is spanned by a substantial bridge about 25 feet in length, which connects the principal street in the village on either side of the river. On this street are located houses, the academy, banks, hotels, 15 or 20 stores of all kinds, and many dwelling houses....
>
> There are some 20 boarding houses for the purpose of accommodating summer tourists.... Mill Village, about one half mile from the lake, has considerable manufacturing, three stores, one church, and the best school house in the county. At South Wolfeborough is located the Wolfeborough Woolen Manufacturing Company, several stores, one church, a school-house, and a number of dwellings....
>
> Wolfeborough can be reached from Boston by three public routes, viz. direct, by rail, over the Eastern Railroad; by cars on the Boston & Maine railroad to Dover, thence over the Cocheco to Alton Bay, thence (in warm weather) by steamboats, 10 miles, to Wolfeborough; or over the Boston & Lowell, Lowell & Nashua, Nashua & Concord, and Concord & Montreal railroads to The Weirs; thence, by boat on lake, 20 miles, to Wolfeborough.... The estimated number of tourists...last year (1873) is 10,000.
>
> *Employments.* The people are engaged in agriculture, manufacturing, trade, hotel and boarding house keeping. The manufacturing business is very important. The value of woolen blankets annually manufactured is $180,000; value of leather annually tanned $108,700. There are 125,000 pairs of sale shoes manufactured, and 300,000 shingles, and 1,850,000 feet of boards &c., sawed. Sash and blind and various other kinds of mechanical business are carried on. The annual value of manufactured products, of all kinds, is $522,500.
>
> *Resources.* Agricultural products, $146,600; mechanical labor, $71,300; money at interest, $13,014; stocks &c, $42,900; deposits in savings banks, $229,835; estimated amount received from summer tourists, $125,000; professional business, $100,000.
>
> *Churches and Schools.* Congregational, Rev. T.H. Emerson, pastor; 2d Congregational, Christian, Rev. Lewis Philips, pastor; 1st Freewill Baptist, Rev. A.D. Fairbanks, pastor; 2d Freewill Baptist, Christian and Methodist, United; total value of all church property, $20,000. There are 16 schools in town; average length, for the year, 20 weeks; total amount of money appropriated annually for school purposes, $2,505.14.
>
> *Literary Institution.* Wolfborough [*sic*] Christian Institute is a prosperous Institution and has a fund of $10,000, J.W. Simonds, A.M., is the principal.
>
> *Libraries.* Wolfeborough Public Library, 750 volumes; Charles H. Parker, private library, 500 volumes.
>
> *Banks.* Lake National Bank, Carroll County Savings Bank, and Wolfeborough Savings Bank.
>
> *Hotels.* Pavilion, Glendon, Belvue, Lake, and Franklin houses. Value of hotel property, $175,000.

## FOUR NOTABLE HOTELS

When tourists came to town they had to have places to stay. Over the years dozens of different facilities sprang up—ranging from private homes with a spare room or two for lodgers, to the immense Pavilion Hotel.

If there is one constant among the larger hotel facilities in Wolfeboro in the nineteenth and early twentieth centuries, it is that they changed management and ownership almost as frequently as the country changed presidents. Apparently, owning a sizable hostelry in town has never been a sure road to financial success.

Four of the more notable caravansaries are discussed below. It is perhaps ironic, certainly sad, to note that these centerpieces in Wolfeboro history were eventually demolished to make way for two gas stations, an athletic field, and a post office.

### The Sheridan House (1795-1941)

One of the longest-lived local lodging places was the Sheridan House on North Main Street between the Colonial Arms and Durgin Block. The large, rambling wooden structure ranged in sections from two to four stories in height, was simply furnished, and catered to travelers on restricted budgets. Built by Andrew Jewett in 1795, the facility was expanded over the years and was known under several different names including the Lake Hotel and finally the Sheridan House. On the second floor of an ell, Union Hall (a.k.a. Sheridan Hall) was the site of numerous public meetings and events. On the extreme left of the hotel there was a stable (known as the V.B. Wentworth Livery in 1887).[42]

The 1887 Sanborn map shows a brick wall 25 feet high immediately to the right of the Lake House. Popular Wolfeboro folklore has it that hotel proprietor George Keniston resented the elegance of the Stephen Durgin mansion next door and emptied the hotel chamber pots in a manner that invited repercussions.[43] This durable legend has been repeated in other articles and publications over the years. The wall was built beginning May 12, 1875, while the Durgin mansion is said not to have been completed by builder Charles Prindall II until autumn or winter 1876. While this may discredit the story, it could be that Durgin erected the so-called "spite wall" before his house was finished. The wall was torn down in October 1914. In the 1920s Mrs. Elizabeth M. Tarpy was owner. Her clerk was Isaac Allbee, whom she later married.

In 1941 the Sheridan House was sold to the Standard Oil Company, which demolished the structure and erected on the site what became known as Harold Fournier's service station. In the 1980s the Hamel Realty Co. built the Wolfeboro Marketplace complex where the gas station once stood.

### The Pavilion Hotel (1849-1899)

The *grande dame* of Wolfeboro accommodations was the Pavilion Hotel at Pickering Corner with a command-

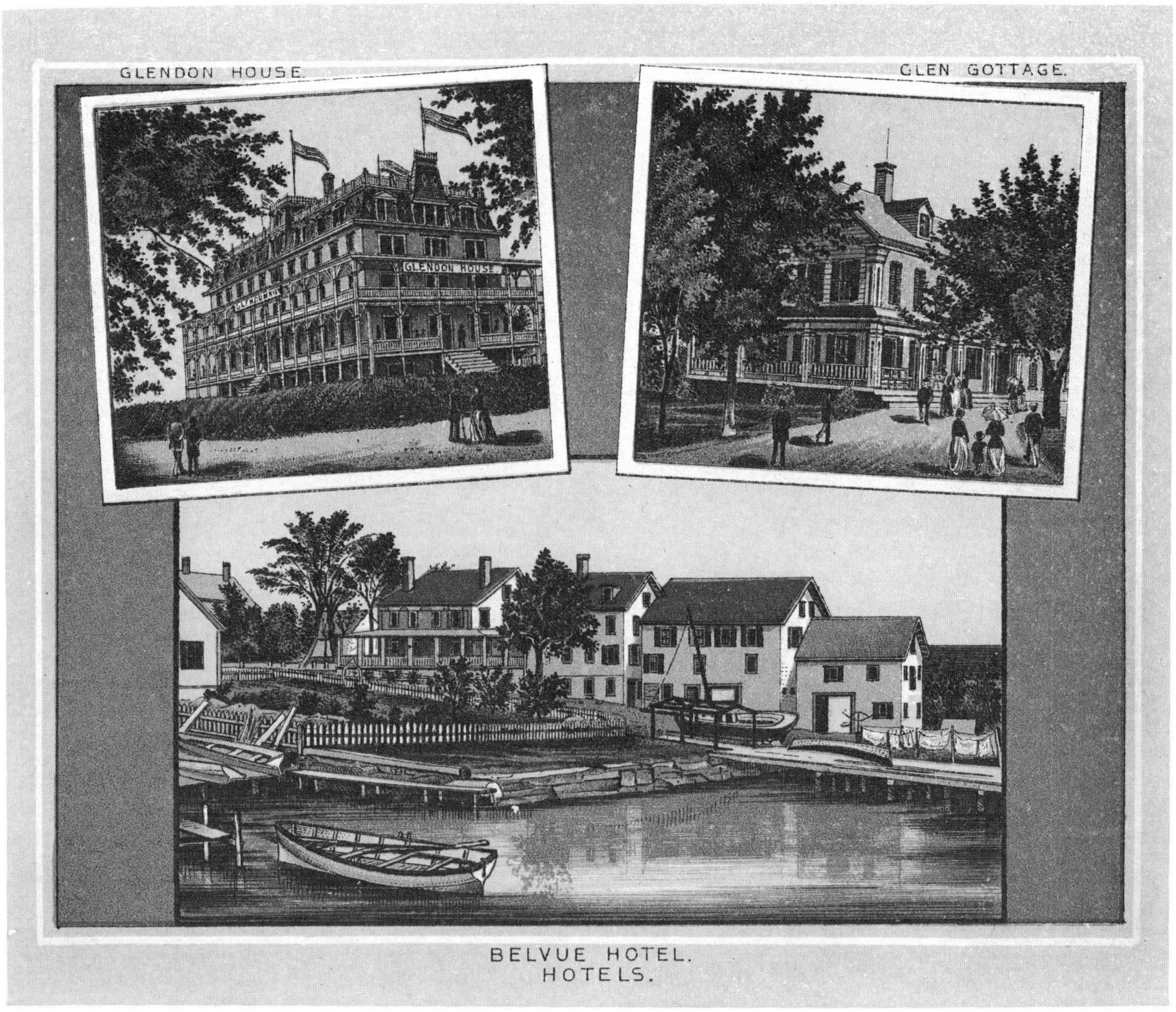


Three important hotels in Wolfeboro during the closing decades of the nineteenth century were the Glendon House (located on South Main Street where the Post Office is today), Glen Cottage (where the white marble First NH Bank is today), and the Belvue House with its attached buildings (where Town and Cate Parks are today). The rowboat in the foreground of the lower picture is moored where the Town Docks are today. (Frederick W. Prindle, *Views of Wolfeboro and Vicinity,* 1889)

Stereograph card by Kilburn Brothers (of Littleton, NH) depicting the Pavilion Hotel. During the 1880s and 1890s many such cards depicting Wolfeboro and regional scenes were produced by several different makers. The Pavilion, known in the 1890s as the Kingswood Inn, was Wolfeboro's largest place of public accommodation. The structure was razed in 1899. Today, the Brewster Academy soccer field is on the site.

Built in 1849 with money supplied by Daniel Pickering and many investors, the immense Pavilion Hotel was added on to several times, and during the second half of the nineteenth century was a magnet for visitors. John Greenleaf Whittier stayed there in 1853. (Frederick W. Prindle, *Views of Wolfeboro and Vicinity,* 1889)

ing view of Wolfeboro Bay.[44] The facility was built in 1849-1850 by Daniel Pickering and his son-in-law Charles Rollins (who was in charge of the project), together with E.P. Evans of Boston.

*Eastman's White Mountain Guide*, 1863, commented:

> The village of Wolfborough is delightfully situated on two beautiful slopes of land rising from a bay of the lake. The Pavilion, which is one of the largest and most comfortable houses in the region, is admirably situated.... Mr. A.H. Dunton is landlord of this hotel and has placed it in the rank of first class summer houses.[45] Visitors will be sure of receiving every attention they can desire and will find the tables supplied with all the delicacies of the season and the rooms neat and airy....

Although the Pavilion became widely known and praised as a premier resort, the financial aspects of the hotel must have been uncertain, for the ownership and management changed a half dozen or more times.

An advertisement, circa the 1880s, noted the following:

> The Pavilion...is the finest located and largest first-class hotel on Lake Winnipesaukee.... The house has been painted, new carpets and furniture added, and after a most thorough renovation, is now complete in all its departments.... Music, billiards, bowling, bathing, boating, and all the usual amusements found at summer resorts. The black bass fishing has no equal in this country. A fine lot of new boats connected with the house, and every comfort and facility for the pleasure seeker may be found.
>
> Transient rates: $3 per day. Board by the week: $10 to $17.50. Free coach on arrival of all boats and trains.

Beginning in 1890 the hotel was known as the Kingswood Inn. By that time a wooden *port cochere* had been added to the front center of the building. Despite this and other improvements, the hotel fell into disuse, and the structure and land became the property of Brewster Free Academy. A half century after it was built, the wooden structure was razed in 1899.[46]

### The Glendon House (1872-1935)

Wolfeboro's second largest hotel was the Glendon House on South Main Street where the red brick United States Post Office would be erected in 1936.

Construction began in December 1872 following the design of Henry Philips, who also was the master builder. John L. Peavey, Charles W. Thurston, and Charles H. Hersey were the primary investors. Opened at a cost of $29,000 in June 1874, the Glendon House was the most elegant tourist facility ever constructed in the town. Four stories in height with a French mansard roof, the wooden Glendon House faced the lake and was just a few hundred feet from the water's edge. The lower two floors had wide verandas extending around the building. There were 91 guest rooms and several parlors for functions. About 125 to 150 tourists could be accommodated. For most of its history it was open only in the summer, but some years it accommodated year-round lodgers.

Ownership and management of the Glendon House changed every few years. Finally, it closed. On May 5, 1899, Frank P. Hobbs, who in the same year leased the Lake Shore House (earlier known as the Belvue House) diagonally across the street, bought the defunct Glendon House. He reopened it to the public on June 20, 1899, and changed its name to the Hobbs-Is-Inn. The lakefront diagonally across the street was called Hobbs' Landing.

In 1902 rates were $2 to $3 per day, $10 to $20 per week. The facility accommodated 200 guests and was open year-round. An advertisement noted:

> Hobbs-Is-Inn grounds extend to the lake, with nice lawn and shade, and is surrounded by broad piazzas affording fine view of the lake and surrounding mountains. Is equipped with all the modern furnishings and conveniences, [including] long distance telephone, bath rooms, pure spring water and perfect drainage. Fine orchestra. Good livery of 25 horses; also steamboats, sailboats and rowboats connected.... The tables are presided over by a fine chef and are supplied with the best the market affords, with fresh vegetables and pure Jersey milk and cream furnished from our own farm and garden.

The Hobbs-Is-Inn certainly out-horsed the Sheridan House up the street, which reported ownership of only 12 steeds. Hobbs was a horse fancier and had one personal mount for in-town trips and a matched pair for longer rides.[47]

The *Granite State News*, June 8, 1907, told of a change:

> T.L. Thurston is now manager of the Hobbs-Is-Inn Hotel, having leased the same June 1. Mr. Thurston is a hotel man of experience and intends to conduct as fine a public house as can be found in this section. Already he has made many improvements and will make his house up-to-date.

Thomas L. Thurston, a well-known local personality, had been in the hardware trade at the turn of the century, having bought Blake Folsom's business. Tiring of this, he sold out and entered the harness and wagon trade which he gave up soon thereafter. Unfortunately, Thurston's turn at the helm of the Hobbs-Is-Inn (he never changed the name) was brief. He died in his hotel on February 19, 1908. For about two months L.S. Haley managed the property for the Thurston estate before it was sold to Michael and Annie Cronin of Boston. Michael had been a chef at the Parker House and had been associated with other fine hotels. For the first time in many seasons, it was announced the facility would be open all year.

On June 1, 1909, the name was changed to the Hotel Elmwood. During the next several years the business operated seasonally, before reverting to year-round operation in 1915-1916. The Cronins owned the hotel for the rest of its existence, with their sons Franc and John Leon participating in the management.

In June 1921 the Belvue House diagonally across the street was acquired from Hobbs by the Cronins and renamed the Ann Inn. The Hotel Elmwood was razed in 1935, and the present-day red brick Post Office was constructed on the site.

Family life. The Stevenson family of Wolfeboro Center with others in a group scene in the late nineteenth century. Seated, left to right: Mrs. Clara Stevenson Day (in black dress), Albert Stevenson (young lad), Mrs. James Stevenson, unidentified (black dress), Henry Stevenson (young lad), Mrs. Eldredge Fletcher (patterned dark dress), unidentified (white dress, dark skirt), Grace Day (white dress), and John L. Peavey (seated at end in rocker; builder of the Peavey Block in 1889). Top row: Helen Stevenson (in hammock on porch), Inez Day, Kitty (Mrs. Paul) Brown (seated on railing), Mrs. Alvah H. Bickford (standing against post), Estelle Stevenson, James Stevenson, Paul Brown (standing against post), and Mrs. John L. Peavey.

Lynn Camp, built in 1884 for the Goldthwait family of Lynn, MA, is said to have been the first summer vacation lodge on Lake Wentworth. (R.P. Goldthwait archives)

**The Belvue House (1868-1940)**

Best known as the Belvue House, this stopping place had several other names during the course of its operation. Located diagonally across South Main Street from the four-story Glendon House, the two-story (plus attic) structure was built in the 1840s. In the mid-nineteenth century it was the private home of Gilman Cooper, a local dry goods merchant who traded as Gilman Cooper & Co. It later was owned and used as a private residence by W.H. Jones,[48] who sold it in October 1868 to Daniel A. Horn. Subsequently, it was known as Horn's-on-the-Lake. In 1872 two structures were added to the rear, a wide piazza was built on the main house, and 50 to 75 guests could be accommodated.

A lady boarder is said to have renamed it the Belvue, meaning "pretty view." In the late 1880s and early 1890s the Belvue House name was used concurrently with Horn's-on-the-Lake. Bacon's 1890 directory described the facility:

> Horn's on the Lake has become the best-known public house in the Lakes Region, especially among sportsmen, for Mr. Horn...gives careful attention to the wants of parties camping out and is prepared to furnish fishing tackle, bait and guides, besides boats, these latter being let by the hour, day or week. The Belvue Hotel...can accommodate 50 guests.... The chambers are comfortably furnished, the table is supplied with an abundant variety of the best the market affords....

By 1892 another building was added to the rear, at lakeside. On June 1, 1898, the hotel was leased to Frank P. Hobbs, who renamed it the Lake Shore House. On August 5, 1901, Hobbs took title to the property. He encountered financial difficulties and was bankrupt in 1903. He lost part of his equity in the hotel but regained all or part by January 1, 1908, when he sold out but continued to live there. During the early part of the present century the facility was also known as the Hobbs-Is-Inn Annex, reflective of Hobbs' ownership of the nearby Hobbs-Is-Inn (earlier known as the Glendon House).

Behind the Lake Shore House was a dock area variously known (circa 1906) as Lake Shore and Hobbs' Wharves, which accommodated a dozen or more rowboats and canoes and several steam and gasoline launches.

On July 5, 1921, the hotel was bought by Michael and Annie J. Cronin, owners of the Hotel Elmwood (the latest name for the Glendon House), and was renamed the Ann Inn, after Annie. The Cronins made the Ann Inn their residence in November of the same year. In 1924 a new gift shop was opened in the hotel, followed by the Lakeview Tea Room in 1925.

In June 1930 it was announced that the Onthank-Rich Company, a Boston dealer in motorboats, oil burners, etc., had acquired the property and intended to convert it for use as its headquarters for the state of New Hampshire.[49] Flower beds were to be planted, surroundings landscaped, and premises illuminated by decorative lighting. Frank McHugh, widely known locally, was tapped to be manager.

In the 1930s the Ann Inn was back in the tourist business, after having been a showroom briefly. In 1936 the Ann Inn advertised as follows:

> Rooms of real charm. Dining room overlooking the lake. Sandwich to a banquet. Beer and ale. M. Cronin, chef, formerly of the Parker House, Boston. The Beatrice Beauty Shop in the Ann Inn; a modern shop of beauty culture.

In November 1940 the Ann Inn was sold and demolished. The upper part of the property was used for a gas station (the Esso Servicenter), and the lakeside part eventually became Cate Park through a donation by Mr. and Mrs. Philip Sidney Smith and assistance from others.

## JOHN BREWSTER AND THE LIBRARY

**John Brewster**

From the 1880s to the present day, the Brewster name has been an integral part of Wolfeboro life. The Brewster Memorial Hall is the Town Hall, Brewster Academy is the local (and now private) preparatory school, and there are other remembrances.

John Brewster traced his lineage to William Brewster who arrived in America aboard the *Mayflower* in 1620. Although in his youth he spent only a year or two at the Wolfborough and Tuftonborough Academy, the memories of the experience were strong enough that in later years he referred to Wolfeboro as his home town. In the autumn of 1828 John, then 15 years of age, taught school in West Milton, but soon sought employment with his uncle, Jonathan Torr, who owned a general store in Rochester. Torr became ill, and Brewster took charge. Beginning at age 18, Brewster worked during the daytime for William Hale in a hardware store at Dover Landing while spending evenings in the dry goods trade. Having saved $2,500 by the time he was 23, Brewster went to Boston to become a dry goods merchant. He secured an additional $10,000 in loans and became a partner in Williams & Brewster on Hanover Street. The new arrangement lasted but a year. However, in that brief time, Brewster was able to repay his indebtedness.

A new firm, John Brewster & Co., was organized with two partners and was a success from the start. The company successfully weathered the Panic of 1837, a financial crisis which disrupted the American currency system and saw many businesses fail. In 1845 the enterprise restricted its business to the wholesale trade. Prosperity continued. In 1850 Brewster sold his shares to Alfred H. Otis of Dover and retired a relatively wealthy man.

Retirement was brief, and after living in Wakefield, NH, for slightly over a year, he returned to Boston to

Enjoying the summer place: Members of the Mino Club at Harry Jones' Camp Comfort on Sewall Point in the third week of August, 1895. The group of single young men and women with chaperones met annually to sail, hike, play music, dance, and otherwise enjoy each other and their surroundings. The club is said to have been named after its mascot, a talkative "parrot" (mynah bird?). Among the members in 1895 were Misses E.B. Edgerly, M.M. Johnson, S.M. Whitton, Z. Furber, E.C. Whitton, and C.L. Rendall, and the following men: E. Goodwin, H.B. Furber, William J. Britton, P.S. Davis, R.S. Parker, H.B. Peavey, and G.R. Britton. Mr. and Mrs. Harry Jones of Roxbury, MA, were chaperones. Later, Jones' camp was called Monhegan Lodge. (L.B. Strout photograph)

Col. Edward B. Dickinson's summer place, Ferncliffe, the first seasonal residence accessed by Rogers Street (today known as Sewall Road). Built by Alexander McDonald and J.A. Warren, it was completed in spring 1890.

form Brewster, Sweet & Company, a banking firm. Once again success was his, and the firm grew rapidly. The company soon was one of the leading financial institutions in New England. During the Civil War, Brewster, Sweet & Co. was the leading fiscal agent in New England for the U.S. Treasury Department.

When Sweet retired in 1874, the company was dissolved. Brewster soon formed a new firm, Brewster, Bassett & Company, with William Bassett, Henry E. Cobb, and Arthur F. Estabrook as partners. Brewster remained active until February 1883, when he retired at the age of 70. During the same month he wrote his will.

Brewster died on January 13, 1886. In the same year his will was probated, with assets totaling over $1 million. He left the sum of $10,000 annually to the Academy, provided that its name be changed to the Brewster Free School or Academy, and that "no restriction should be placed upon any person desiring to attend and receive instruction from said school or academy on account of age, sex, or color, provided only he or she is of good moral character."

Further, he stipulated that not more than 25% should be spent in erecting buildings or alterations, improvements and repairs, and that the remaining income be used for salaries of teachers and educational purposes, "so near as possible to make instruction and education therein free."

A further amount of the estate was set aside to, in his words:

> Erect in my native town of Wolfeboro, New Hampshire, a plain brick building, as nearly as possible, from the plan of and like the public building or town hall erected by W.S. Sargent in and for the town of Merrimack in Massachusetts; said building shall be held by my trustees forever for the use and benefit of the inhabitants of the town of Wolfeborough, as and for the town as a public library. The stores and such buildings on the lower floor shall be rented by my trustees and all the rent income over and above the expense and charges therefrom used and appropriated for the necessary care and repairs of said building, and for the care, support, and purchase of books for said public library to be in said building.

Further, insurance was to be maintained on the building, and if destruction should occur, a new building should be erected "in as nearly possible the same manner and style as the same plan as was before erected."

He willed that if additional funds became available from the estate, that among the uses of the income was to be the "support and maintenance of the deserving poor and persons needing aid in said towns of Wolfeborough and Tuftonborough."

### Libraries

In the early nineteenth century, relatively few Wolfeboro residents were interested in books and reading. However, as the school system developed, literacy became more widespread, and the use of printed materials increased.

The Republican Social Library in Wolfeborough, as it was called, was established in 1804 by Isaiah Horne whom Parker describes as the most scholarly citizen of the town at the time.[50] By 1888 interest faded, and the library, which had received very few additions in recent years and had been little used, was sold at public auction.

A separate public library was owned by citizens of North Wolfeboro and the nearby part of Ossipee. At one time or another several private businesses had rental book libraries. An example is furnished by Israel B. Manning, who enjoyed a good trade in this regard from his South Main Street store in the 1880s. Books were also loaned by J.C. Watson, who maintained a news agency and confectionery shop on Railroad Avenue in the same decade.

The Brewster Library established by John Brewster's will was opened in March 1890. In 1900 the town of Wolfeboro voted to set up a library commission. Housed in the Town Hall the library contained 1,750 "well selected volumes plus pamphlets, periodicals, and newspapers." Of the books on hand in 1900, 1,426 were purchased using funds from the Brewster will and 324 by the town.

The original Brewster Library facilities were used for the best part of a century thereafter, until the town constructed a new building on South Main Street which opened in 1979. Today the part of the Town Hall that was earlier given over to the library is used by the Planning Department.

## LEISURE TIME

### Recreation

Recreation ranging from outdoor sports to indoor games and hobbies has always been a part of Wolfeboro culture. In the early days of the town, popular pursuits included card games, dancing, foot and horse races, wrestling, and horsemanship.

Traveling stock companies regularly visited town and presented melodramas such as *Uncle Tom's Cabin, East Lynne, Lady Audley's Secret,* and other favorites. In 1894 a Wolfeboro entrepreneur, Larkin D. Hobbs, in partnership with George Wentworth of Dover, founded Wentworth, Hobbs & Rothwell's Uncle Tom's Cabin Co., which performed at the Pavilion Hotel in town and then went on the road briefly before folding.[51] Musical groups as well as soloists, minstrel shows, and traveling circuses all played a part in local entertainment. In addition to professional actors, speakers, and musicians who came to town, numerous Wolfeboro residents were on stage as part of events and functions conducted by many societies and organizations.

Samples of the hundreds of entertainment notices appearing in the *Granite State News:*

September 24, 1862:

Prof. Harrington, ventriloquist and prestidigitator, gave an entertainment on Saturday evening last, Union Hall, which fully sustained the great reputation which he has acquired and sustained during the last 34 years.

This account of August 13, 1888, concerns Wallace & Co.'s Great World's Menagerie, which arrived on a train of 17 cars pulled by two engines, comprising 125 horses and 200 employees and performers, and set up on August 10 under canvas on the Avery field in South Wolfeboro:

The music was fine in quality and abundant in quantity. The calliope excited much interest. The specimens of the African and Asiatic elephants and Bactrian camel were very good, of the latter there were four of large size. Not less than 3,500 people visited the show during the afternoon, and from 1,200 to 1,500 in the evening. The attendance was highly satisfactory to the management, netting them a handsome sum over and above the $1,400 to $1,600 which is the average daily cost of the show to the company.... The entire premises showed the utmost care, neatness and order. The management, actors and musicians live on the train. The exhibition closed at 10:00 p.m., and a few minutes before 12:00 the train started for its next place of destination. Thus, within the space of two hours, taking down and loading upon the cars the entire property and people, belonging to this really big show.

The lyceum was popular in the nineteenth century. This basically comprised one or more speaking activities conducted from a stage. Presentations were given to audiences on various subjects, and debates were conducted. One lyceum was affiliated with the local Academy, and another was held at the Brick School House as early as the 1850s.

The Mill Village Lyceum in 1889-1890 debated such interesting topics as: "Is machinery beneficial to the laboring class?" and "Ought females be allowed to exercise the right of suffrage?" Both questions "after interesting discussion [were] decided on [their] merits in the negative." In addition to lively debates, the lyceums sometimes presented artistic entertainment, piano selections, tableaux, and singing. From biographical remarks in obituaries of those days it appears that many Wolfeboro citizens were accomplished public speakers and able debaters.[52]

In the 1890s Dartmouth Hall, on the second floor of the Boston & Maine Railroad Wharf Building, offered roller skating and dancing. A baseball team was formed at Brewster Academy in its opening year, but it had been a popular local sport long before then.

On December 11, 1891, this was printed in the local paper:

If you have never heard a phonograph, you will now have an opportunity, and if you have, we know you'll be pleased to hear it again. This Friday evening Mr. W.G. Rollins will be at the Unitarian Church with one of Edison's phonographs, which will talk to you, sing for you, and produce the finest musical selections from popular bands, etc. Admission: Adults, 15 cents, Children, 10 cents.

In a related vein was this report of an instrument played during the choir's rest periods at the Harvest Sunday School Concert held on November 11, 1894, at the South Wolfeboro Church:[53]

One of the most interesting and delightful features of this concert was the music furnished by wonderful music box owned by Mr. Gerish of South Wolfeboro. At intervals during the exercises it played the old tunes such as *Rock of Ages, Nearer My God to Thee,* etc. The air was played in rich sweet tones like those of an organ, while a delicate running accompaniment went all through the theme as if hundreds of fairy bells were sweetly chiming. All present surely enjoyed the rich musical treat afforded them by Mr. Gerish and feel grateful to him for the loan of his music box for the occasion.

The World's Columbian Exposition opened a year late in 1893 to observe the 400th anniversary of Columbus' 1492 landing in the New World. Many Wolfeboro citizens went by train to Chicago during the summer and autumn to attend the event. The October 23, 1893 issue of the local paper carried this:

Mr. and Mrs. G.B. Clark are seriously contemplating a visit to the Columbian Fair at Chicago, expecting to go the latter part of this present week or the early part of next week.... Mr. John H. Beacham and wife have returned from the Columbian exhibit.... Mr. John Goodhue likes to see what is going on, so he takes in the World's Fair with the rest of the folks this past week.

In August 1894 local merchant John Rogers returned from Rattlesnake Island in Lake Winnipesaukee with a live rattlesnake, "Sweet Marie," which he subsequently exhibited around downtown Wolfeboro.[54] In the autumn the venomous reptile was placed in a cool cellar where it hibernated, but occasionally she (?) was checked on, and reports appeared in the local paper, this December 25, 1895, example being representative:

"Sweet Marie," the captive rattlesnake, is taking his [*sic*] cold weather snooze. The boys have warmed him up once just to see where he was at. He was there, and make no mistake about it.

And this on April 23, 1895:

The captive rattlesnake is still sleeping in the darkness of the cellar, but shows by occasional slight nervous drawing that he is getting well towards the end of his half-early snooze.

In September 1896 the Kickapoo Indian Show was a featured attraction at Sheridan Hall. Between skits and antics staged by "Indians," the sponsors of the show sold Kickapoo patent medicine to the audience.[55]

Feature films were not yet a reality in Wolfeboro, but motion pictures began to be shown locally by itinerant projectionists in the late 1890s. One of the earliest took place in 1898 and was billed as follows:[56]

Brewster Memorial Hall, April 8. Don't miss it! The wonderful Lumiere Cinematographe.[57] Direction of John T. Morrison. The marvel of the age. Life motion reproduced.

Ice boating on Wolfeboro Bay circa 1890s. The craft bore such names as *Fleetwing* (second from left), *Spider,* and *Arrow.* In the background at the extreme left is part of the old Brewster Free Academy building (burned in 1903), while between the third and fourth boats may be seen the shore buildings of the Kingswood Inn (the erstwhile Pavilion Hotel).

Local baseball players in the 1890s, youth and adults, some with bats, gloves, and other equipment. Seated, left to right: Arthur Edgerly, Ed Geary, Fred Avery, Harry Johnson, Si Wentworth, Mel Wadley, and Will Mattison. Standing: Herbert Champaigne, John Gilson, Hartley Johnson, Charles Kimball, George Kimball, Fred Hodgdon, Percy Kimball, Charles York, Nat Hicks, Scott Garland, and Willis Corson.

Each view presented with accompaniment by the Edison phonograph. Remember: This is no stereopticon or magic lantern show, but exhibition of the most wonderful achievement of the electrical age, which reproduces scenes from real life and depicts all the natural movements of the objects. This exhibition is startling and so true to nature as to almost force the observer to believe they are viewing the reality and not its photographic reproduction. Come and see the Empire State Express running 70 miles an hour. The Queen's Jubilee procession, pillow fight, czar and French president entering Paris, camel parade in Egypt, inauguration of President McKinley, New York Fire Department, Niagara Falls, lone fisherman, burning stable, dead man's curve, gardener, bad boy and hose, cuirassiers charging, Mr. Edison at work at his chemical laboratory, Negroes diving scene in African village, and many others. Extra! Special films of *U.S.S. Maine* taken just before the big battleship left Key West for Havana. The picture shows the ship in motion. All our views are genuine Edison and Lumiere subjects. No duplicate films. Admission 25 cents. Children 15 cents. Reserved seats 35 cents. Entertainment begins at 8:00 p.m. sharp.

Swimming in lakes, ponds, and streams was a popular sport with local citizens and visitors alike. Certain local residents apparently enjoyed swimming without the restriction of clothing, as evidenced by this item in the August 5, 1892, number of the *Granite State News:*

A petition has been presented to our selectmen by the summer guests to have nude bathing in the near vicinity prohibited.

A contemporary newspaper article describes the bowling party given by Mr. and Mrs. Gilman L. Martin in September 1887 at the lakeside facility owned by the Pavilion Hotel:

The alleys were tastefully decorated with lovely-hued fall flowers and foliage and were made gay with brilliantly illuminated Chinese lanterns. The little card room upstairs was laid with rugs, and after a dainty supper served there, whist and bowling were enjoyed till the wee sma' hours.

Music was an important part of community life. Lessons were given on the piano, reed organ, and other instruments, and public recitals were held at appropriate times. Choirs and orchestras, often from other towns, performed to the delight of Wolfeboro audiences.

In the last two decades of the nineteenth century, church suppers were well patronized and sometimes followed by entertainment. According to an account in the *News,* Mrs. Tarley presented her "famous wax figurines" after a church supper in 1899.

Concerts were enjoyed at the wooden bandstand to the left of the Glendon House. The Original Norfolk Jubilee Singers, billed as "A Genuine Slave Band," presented a "Sacred Grand Concert" in 1882.

What might have been considered work was sometimes changed into a pleasurable pursuit. For example, volunteer crews packing down snow on the roads in winter would be rewarded with rum or ale at various houses along the way. In spring, maple sugaring was often turned into a group activity, participants gathering around the blazing fire in the sap house to exchange stories, drink, and have a jolly good time. Barn raising, hay gathering, and corn husking were often shared with neighbors. The Woman's Christian Temperance Union (WCTU) and Sons of Temperance members notwithstanding, most Wolfeboro men enjoyed lifting a mug, and even at the annual town meetings West Indies rum was often served and was an item in the town budget.

### Gatherings and Holidays

Town meetings were usually day-long affairs with a few hours devoted to the business at hand and the rest to renewing acquaintances, sharing snacks and lunches, playing games, and in other ways making merry. Reaching the site of the annual meeting was not an easy task, especially for those who had to travel several miles. Once there, citizens wanted to enjoy themselves. Sometimes the town meeting could drag on to seemingly interminable length. For example, in 1845 there were nine candidates for representative, 14 for first selectman, 12 for second selectman, and 40 for third selectman. The latter was not chosen until ballots from eight separate rounds of voting were tallied.

For many years the Town House was located between Wolfeboro Falls and Wolfeboro Center, not far from where the Bittersweet Restaurant is today. Meetings were held there until the Brewster Memorial Hall (Town Hall) was ready in 1890. The Town House was later sold, dismantled, and moved to Factory Street to be used for industrial purposes; the remains still stand today and were adapted in 1993 to a facility known as Antiques on Lehner Street.

On the quaint New Hampshire holiday, Fast Day, most commercial and laboring activities would cease, and the order would be fun and games.[58] Weather permitting, the first baseball game of the year would be played. Lawn tennis was another popular pursuit.

Independence Day furnished the occasion for all sorts of patriotic activities, including a parade in the center of town, a band concert, orations, and fireworks.

In addition to Town Meeting Day, Fast Day, and the Fourth of July, two other holidays observed with festivities were Muster Day and Thanksgiving. Muster Day marked the time that the members of the 27th Regiment of the New Hampshire Militia gathered from several towns at a spot in Ossipee to practice, parade, and have a good time. Historian Benjamin F. Parker related that as many soldiers were felled by drink as by "enemy" action in the exercises.[59]

Christmas was generally overlooked as a major holiday by the early citizens of Wolfeboro, who in the main considered it to be little more than a Catholic festival favored by the Pope. This would not change until well into the nineteenth century, when Santa Claus and gift-giving became popular.

In addition to the officially recognized holidays, Saturday afternoons were often set aside as a time to lay down the saw, plow, or knitting needle, and gather at the nearest commercial center to make purchases, exchange news and gossip, and partake of refreshment.

Hunting and fishing were popular Wolfeboro recreations which had a useful purpose as well. Fish were taken from the lakes, and deer were shot for food. Bears were a nuisance to agriculture and would often be hunted. In the autumn their flesh was considered desirable to eat; less so at other times of year when it was gamier in taste. Deer and bear were also useful for their hides. Trapping, while not particularly a sport, yielded fur from foxes, beavers, and other small mammals. Apparently, the national bird was considered a desirable target as well, as this item from the *Granite State News*, August 8, 1893, indicates:

> John Hackett, a farmer residing on the southerly shore of Lake Wentworth, is probably the champion eagle slayer of the state, having killed 13 of the noble birds in the vicinity of his farm.

The outdoors offered other recreational activities. Numerous tourist guides suggested that visitors to Wolfeboro cross the town boundary to the east and ascend Tumble Down Dick or Copple Crown mountains, both of which overlooked much of the Wolfeboro area, or go in the other direction to Ossipee Mountain Park in Moultonboro.

Many social and civic organizations were active and often specialized in a specific aspect of life such as religion, temperance, past military service, or fire fighting. The Village Improvement Society and the Mill Village (Wolfeboro Falls) Benevolent Society offered still other opportunities.

### Churches

Although early citizens of Wolfeboro cannot be characterized as being fervently religious, early selectmen desired to attract a clergyman.[60] The contract with the Masonian Proprietors stipulated that a lot should be set aside for the "first minister of the Gospel who shall settle there." In 1781 Andrew Collins was hired as both a preacher and teacher for a one-year term. His contract was not renewed. In the meantime some families held services in their homes. In 1792 Ebenezer Allen became the town minister, adding to the services of Isaac Townsend who had come to Wolfeboro a couple years earlier. Allen's position was controversial, and there was a vocal and litigious group of citizens who vigorously opposed the town's paying for religious services. Upon Allen's death in 1806 the town lost the only minister ever on the public payroll. For the next 30 years Townsend is said to have been the only ordained local minister.

The First Free Will (also spelled Freewill) Baptist Church, established by the followers of Isaac Townsend on October 19, 1792, was the first house of worship in the town. Eventually other denominations followed, and the next two centuries would see the Christian Scientists, Quakers, Episcopalians, Adventists, Catholics, Congregationalists, Mormons, Jehovah's Witnesses, Unitarians, and others establish sanctuaries. (Volume II gives detailed histories.)

## CIVIC IMPROVEMENTS

### Fires, Fire Engines, and Water

Although there were many conflagrations in the town in the early days, fire fighting was not done on an organized basis until the 1860s. In 1862 the Monitor No. 1 company was formed in South Wolfeboro, and its two-story hall stood until the 1980s. Residents of the western district of Wolfeboro formed the Village Fire Precinct in 1866 and appropriated $1,075 to buy a used Hunneman pumper, Strafford Engine No. 1 of Dover, the name of which was changed to Carroll No. 2. A building to house it was erected on land leased from Moses T. Cate. This pumper was used until 1889. The Rollins Hose Co. was set up at Pickering Corner in 1867 and was also known as the Carroll Engine Co. Village Fire Precinct meetings were held there.

Until the late 1880s water was obtained from local streams and wells. In 1887 the Wolfeborough Aqueduct & Water Company was privately incorporated under rights granted by the town. However, citizens felt that the operation of a water system should be a community responsibility. The newly-formed company waived its rights, and in June 1888 the town voted to establish a local water works fed by gravity from Beach Pond. Experienced contractors from as far away as New Jersey were hired to plan and lay out the mains. Financing was provided by two bond issues totaling $57,000. On November 18, 1889, the first customer, Samuel A. Meader, received service.[61] By early 1890 nearly 70 families were connected to the system. By 1900 there were 400 private customers, 57 hydrants, and three public fountains connected to 18 miles of pipe fed from a holding reservoir of 300,000 gallons. By that time mains extended to South Wolfeboro, Goose Corner, and Wolfeboro Falls. In 1890 and 1891 the Precinct purchased three hose wagons. One of these was operated by the Eagle Hose Co. and housed in Horn's barn near the Baptist Church in Wolfeboro Falls. A fire station was later established on River Street.

By the turn of the century, fire fighters could attach hoses to hydrants in most downtown points. In other districts water was sucked from streams and ponds by pumpers. In 1900 the hose companies, as they were called, were Rollins No. 1, A.W. Wiggin No. 2, Eagle No. 3, and Monitor No. 1 (of South Wolfeboro).

Notable fires of the nineteenth century included:[62]

**1811 Town Meeting House:** Struck by lightning, burned.

**1813 (circa). Samuel Nudd house:** North Wolfeboro Burned, and Nudd's two sons, ages 10 and 12, were killed.

**1820, September 12. Gov. Wentworth mansion:** Burned to the ground after a spark ignited the roof.

**1823 Avery store:** Samuel Avery's store burned (a later *Granite State News* historical account says 1820).

**1826 Whitton house:** Daniel Whitton's house burned (*Granite State News* account says 1836).

**1829 Isaac Poor house.** North Wolfeboro. Burned.

**1830 David Blake house.** Burned.

**1841, December 15. Woolen factory:** Woolen factory built in 1816 in Wolfeboro Falls burned (in 1836 it had been acquired by the Pickering Factory Co.: Stephen and Daniel Pickering, Nathaniel Rogers, and Samuel Avery). Loss on buildings and machinery, $5,000; on inventory (owned by Stephen Durgin), $1,500.

**1845 Moses Varney tannery:** Burned. Loss: $10,000.

**1845, November 1. Nathaniel Rogers barn:** Struck by lightning; burned.

**1846, December 5. South Wolfeboro:** A large fire destroyed a chair factory, a wool-carding and cloth-dressing mill, a tannery, a shingle mill, a carriage shop, and a vacant store. Owners affected were Henry B. Rust, Nathaniel Banfield, John C. Corliss, and William DeLand. Loss: $5,000.

**1850 Boyle woolen factory:** South Wolfeboro. Burned.

**1850(?). Taber factory:** John Taber's small factory for making smoking pipes burned (cf. Parker; validity now questioned).[63]

**1850. John Haines' house:** North Wolfeboro. Burned.[64].

**1861, March 7. Colby mill:** Grist mill owned by Mrs. Alphonso G. Colby burned. Loss: $3,500.

**1862, January 21. William Clark buildings.** Burned.

**1864, October 14. Lorenzo Horne (a.k.a. Horn) piano stool factory:** Mill Village. Completely destroyed. Loss, $9,000; insurance, $2,000.[65]

**1864 Paul Varney house.** Burned.

**1868, July 11. John A. Chamberlain barn:** New barn, part of house, and $200 worth of goods burned.

**1871, June 24. Libbey & Varney mill:** Steam lumber mill on Back Bay; loss: $12,000.

**1875, March 29. Samuel Jenness house:** Trask Mountain. Burned.

**1877, July 4. Moses Varney tannery:** Tannery, shed, barn, and a large inventory were burned. Loss: $15,000.

**1877, December 7. Parker house:** South Wolfeboro. The former residence of Col. Henry Rust, now known as the Parker house, burned.

**1878, August 10. Clow buildings:** Buildings on John Clow's farm burned.

**1878, September 9. Paul D. Rand house.** Burned.

**1878, November 9. Libbey buildings:** Buildings owned by Alvah S. Libbey burned; loss: $1,500.

**1881, October 11. Capt. Jasper H. Warren house.** Mill Village. Estimated loss $1,200; insured for $800.[66]

**1885, January 21. Brewster-Piper house:** House owned by Nathaniel T. Brewster and occupied by Isaiah Piper burned.

**1887, February 2. Goodwin and Piper blocks:** Two wooden store buildings were burned on the site of what was later known as the Central Block. The Post Office was located in one structure, but no mail was destroyed. One building was known as the Joseph Goodwin Block (different from the Joseph W. Goodwin Block on South Main Street). The adjacent Piper Block (Bank Building) suffered minor damage. Loss: $8,000.

**1887, August 9. Spectacular shoe factory fire:** Large shoe factory at west end of Factory Street, occupied by the Cropley and Monroe companies, was destroyed by fire, along with eight residences (three dwellings owned by Blake Folsom, Lucern Ham's carpenter's shop, a double house owned by Sawyer & Tibbetts, three houses owned by William C. Thompson, and one house belonging to Greenleaf B. Clark) and a large amount of finished lumber owned by Libbey & Varney. Loss: $140,000. The factory had been built in 1884 by the Wolfeborough Steam Power Company to be leased for the manufacture of shoes. The building was 200 feet long and four stories high. After the fire many citizens and businesses contributed to a fund to guarantee the construction of a new building on the old foundation, which was ready for operation within a year.[67]

**1887, October, 14. Piper Block:** The Piper Block, a wooden structure attached to the back of the Bank Building, was destroyed by fire. October 17, 1887, *Granite State News* account: "A big blaze! Valuable property destroyed in the flames! Piper's Block a smoldering heap! The *News* office seriously damaged by water! Friday morning, about 5:00 an alarm of fire was sounded, making the fourth time this year our firemen have been summoned to fight the fiery element in our village.... The fire was found to be in Piper's Block, so-called, Railroad Avenue, being the wooden portion of the old Lake Boot & Shoe Factory. When discovered, it was breaking out in several places. The new Central Block, not yet quite completed, was within a few feet of the northerly end of this block, while the brick Bank Building adjoined it on the south. The [Piper] block burned and was occupied as follows: The lower story by John B. Waldron as a saloon and Henry W. Furber as a meat market. The second story was used by the Peavey Rifles, Company K, for an armory. The third story was very finely fitted up by the GAR Post and used by them and also by the Sons of Temperance, Knights of Labor, Royal Arcanum and Ladies Relief Corps. The brick [Bank] Building was occupied by Lake National Bank, C.H. Hersey's Store (dry goods and groceries) and the Hon. J.M. Brackett's office on first floor. Three fourths of the second story was occupied by the *Granite State News* office, the other fourth is lodging rooms. On the third floor was a hall occupied by the Knights of Honor.... The damage to the Central Block was slight. Piper and Brackett own both buildings and were insured for $4,500. Mr. Waldron was fully insured, saving portions of the stock. C.H. Hersey's was damaged slightly. His goods were moved out in good condition. H.W. Furber was not insured but saved his stock in good condition. The Society lost most of their effects with little insurance. The *News* office was very much demoralized by water and hasty removal. Damage serious, insurance sufficient to cover loss. The cause of the fire was, undoubtedly, the careless use of a cigar stub or a spent match in Armory Hall the evening previous...."

**1887, November 2. Gould and Manning stables:** Jesse Gould's stable on North Main Street burned, the work of arsonist L.C. Holton, who also set afire the stable of Israel B. Manning, Gould's neighbor, by spreading kerosene over flammable articles.[68]

**1888, June.[69] Baptist Church:** The Free Will Baptist Church was damaged by fire, and horse sheds were destroyed.

**1888, June.[70] B.F. Garland house:** Pine Hill district. Loss: $1,000.

**1889, December 24. Libbey & Varney Co. mill:** Lumber mill on Back Bay burned; started by spark in engine room. Loss, $12,000 to $15,000; insurance, $6,000.[71]

**1891, March 5. Glendon House:** A fire was discovered in the basement, having been set in a barrel containing straw. It was quickly extinguished. William B. Nason, a hotel guest, was charged with arson. Apparently, Nason was angered at having been assaulted by William Fleming at the hotel about the same time (Fleming was later fined $10 for this). Nason was found in Farmington by police.[72]

**1891, November 10. Train fire:** Baggage car No. 53 on the Boston & Maine Railroad, the car in daily service to Wolfeboro, was found on fire. The blaze was extinguished quickly by A.W. Wiggin Hose Co. No. 2.[73]

**1891. Frank B. Hutchins' mill:** Excelsior mill on Centre Street destroyed. Loss: $6,000.

**1891. Mrs. Lowell's house:** Pleasant Valley. Burned.

**1893, April 9. Daniel Colman's house:** Near Wolfeboro Center. Burned. Occupied by Geo. E. Danforth at the time. Loss: $200.[74]

**1893, June 1. Brush fire out of control:** A small fire started by C.S. Paris in Wolfeboro Falls to burn brush raged out of control, burned over neighboring lots, and blackened about 100 acres.[75]

**1894, January.[76] F.W. Mason's clothing store:** Stock damaged.

**1894, March 3. Frank B. Hutchins' mill:** Excelsior mill (and nearby equipment belonging to William B. Hodge) were burned in a conflagration that threatened to destroy much of the Wolfeboro Falls business district. Loss: $6,000 to Hutchins and $1,900 to Hodge.[77]

**1894, July 19. Robert W. Hill's house and barn:** Fernald Road, Fire spread over 10 acres. What remained was auctioned a week later.[78] (Hill had another fire on January 1, 1896; see below.)

**1894, October 18. Arthur F. Hasty farm buildings:** Whitten Neck. Fire believed to have been set by an arsonist. Loss: $1,000.[79]

**1895, October 24. Three cottages:** Harmony Grove. Nathaniel Copp's cottage tenanted by a family named Copp was destroyed, as was the adjacent cottage (owned by Charles E. Ham). The nearby cottage owned by Mrs. Sleeper was damaged beyond repair. First fire alarm in the village since October 18, 1894.[80]

**1896, January 1. Robert W. Hill barn:** "Barn of Robert W. Hill of Wolfeboro Highlands was burned together with a horse, hay, hens, etc. A controversy erupted between Mr. Hill and his housekeeper, who was to receive the deed to the property if she would take care of him during his life. Forgery was detected in certain documents prepared by Mr. Hill, and he was called to account for it, and after a sequence of events, attempted suicide."[81]

**1896, February 20. Fred E. Hersey's house:** Center Street, Wolfeboro Falls. Badly damaged by fire. Loss: $2,000.

**1896, February 23. N.T. Brewster's farm:** Large barn (150 x 36 feet), a cider mill 40 x 30 feet), and 20 tons of hay were burned. Loss: $5,000. George L. Brewster lived there; owned by the estate of Nathaniel T. Brewster.[82]

**1896, September 22.[83] Jones' Drug Store:** Damage: $2,000.[84]

**1897, February 24. Estabrook dormitory:** Brewster Academy dormitory was gutted by fire (but was later restored).[85]

**1897, November 16. Charles Clark's Fair View Farm:** North Wolfeboro. The former Thomas Nute place, purchased by Clark in 1891 and thereafter operated as a tourist facility in addition to the farm. House and buildings destroyed. Insurance: $2,500.[86]

**1898, July 14: George I. Cate property:** Pleasant Valley. House, stable, and shop destroyed. No insurance.[87]

**1899, May 28. Goodwin Block, B&M Wharf Building, etc.:**[88] "Wolfeboro was visited on Saturday night by a fire that will be remembered by our townspeople for many years.... At 9:00 that evening, fire was discovered at the portion of the Mount Washington Wharf Building occupied as a waiting room by the B&M Railroad. The fire spread very rapidly. The alarm was quickly given, and the Fire Department responded with the usual commendable promptness. It was quickly comprehended that the fire was to be one that could not be quickly mastered. The building on the 'Lady' Wharf was soon ablaze. The building wherein the fire originated was soon completely enwrapped in flames. A stiff breeze from the lake scattered the embers for a long distance. It was soon apparent that the Peavey Block was in great danger of destruction. For its saving the firemen made most heroic efforts, aided by willing workers upon the roof. Soon, further danger was feared. The blazing embers alighting upon the roof of the building owned by the Wolfeboro Loan and Banking Company quickly ignited, and as every line of hose was engaged in other work, the flames soon gained headway. Willing work by the students at Brewster Academy with lines of small hose, aided by one line from Rollins Hose Company No. 1 and, later, one from Eagle Hose Company No. 3, prevented the total destruction of the building. Fortunately, when the danger to the Peavey Block seemed greatest, the wind veered somewhat and also lessened. The great heat from the fire raging on the Mount Washington Wharf Building indicated that the Goodwin Block was to be soon doomed for destruction. Never did firemen fight braver. No retreat was made until it was impossible to withstand the intense heat emanating from the burning building. The water source was at its best from first to last, notwithstanding six hydrant streams in use at one time, with many smaller ones, no lessening of power was at any time perceptible. In spite of all endeavors the Goodwin Block was ablaze, and a long and strong fight to prevent further spread was made. The firemen fought from behind wooden barricades and many vantage spots, and after hours of hard and severe work became the master of the old and ever vengeful foe. The many blistered, weary men of the department gave thankful voice that the hard work was now apparently at an end. The destruction of the Goodwin Block was nearly complete, only the end next to the Peavey Block remaining. The firemen would not allow its destruction. With that destroyed, the doom of the Peavey Block would be recorded. While the wind was at its highest the blazing embers were quickly carried to the roof of many buildings. Hobbs-Is-Inn, the residence of Sheriff [Frank P.] Hobbs, and that of William S. Doak, James I. Allard, and the block owned by Edwin L. Furber were afire quite a number of times. Willing workers aided by lines with a small hose and a stream from the hydrant near the [photographic] studio on Glendon Street were the means of preventing further spreading. Hasty removal of household effects were made by many in this neighborhood, no hope being entertained for the saving of the residences.... Several firemen reported burns and other injuries.... In Goodwin's Block were six safes. A safe of Charles F. Parker had a time and combination lock. This being located over the drugstore was enwrapped for hours with flames of the most intense severity. It was removed from the ruins Monday morning. In its descent it fell upon its base, bending the spindle. It could not be opened. It will be sent to Boston to be worked on by an expert. The safe of the Wolfeboro Drug Store was opened Monday afternoon, and its contents were found to be in the best of condition. The safe of Everett S. Albee had not been opened Wednesday morning. The contents of the

After the fire of May 28, 1899, little usable structure remained behind the Peavey Block (three-story top-railinged building at right). To the left at lakeside are charred remains of the Lady Wharf, while the former Lewando & Mattison building is a wreck with skeletal roof supports and a gutted interior. Behind the building, not visible in this view, is the site of where the Mount Washington Wharf Building once stood, it also reduced to a heap of debris.

The formerly elegant Goodwin Block in ruins after the catastrophic fire of May 28, 1899. This was one of four structures destroyed in the largest conflagration the town has ever known. The other buildings were on the waterfront nearby and included the Boston & Maine Railroad Wharf Building, the building at the adjacent Lady Wharf, and a structure earlier used as the Lewando & Mattison grocery store and moved behind the Peavey Block in 1889.

safe of Sylvester A. Edgerly came out in the best of condition. The contents of value of the safe of Judge Sewall W. Abbott were removed before the flames reached his office. The examination on Monday showed that the safe underwent the baptism in great shape. The safe of Morning Star Lodge No. 17, A.F. & A.M., fell from the third to the second story. It was pulled from the ruins Sunday morning. Upon being opened the records of the lodge and those of Carroll County Chapter No. 23, R.A.M., were found to be in good condition, other than the charred bindings.... Where the businesses relocated: Everett S. Albee, jewelry, etc., may be found at Brewster Memorial building, in the store formerly occupied by the Wolfeboro Loan and Banking Company. The Wolfeboro Drug Store may be found at the first store from Main Street in the Central Block, Railroad Avenue. Sylvester A. Edgerly, boots and shoes, may be found in the second store in Central Block, Railroad Avenue. Charles H. Johnson, dry goods, may be found in the third store in Central Block, Railroad Avenue. Dr. F.E. Meader, dentist, may be found in the store at Brewster Memorial building occupied by Everett S. Albee. Judge Sewall W. Abbott may be found in Peavey's Block in the store formerly occupied by James Welton. Charles F. Parker, insurance agent, may be found at Room No. 10, Central Block, Railroad Avenue. George H. Clough, electrician and bicycle repair, may be found in Folsom's Block, South Main Street. *Granite State News,* for a few days anywhere and everywhere about town. Losses: Wolfeboro Drug Store, drugs and stock, $4,500, insurance $3,000; Mrs. M.A. Goodwin, Goodwin Block, $12,000, insurance $7,000; Charles H. Johnson, dry goods, stock $5,000, insurance $3,000; Sylvester A. Edgerly, boots and shoes, stock $6,000, insurance $6,000; Everett S. Albee, jewelry and stock, $2,500; insurance $1,500; Dr. F.A. Meader, dentist, fixtures, $1,000, insurance $500; Judge Sewall W. Abbott $1,000, insurance unknown; Charles F. Parker, insurance $300; Morning Star Lodge No. 17, A.F. & A.M., inventory $1,000, insurance $500; Carroll County Chapter No. 23. R.A.M. inventory $1,000, insurance $400; Boston & Maine Wharf Building $12,000; *Granite State News,* $4,000, insurance $1,200; Wolfeboro Cornet Band, loss $500, no insurance; John McHugh, laundry, inventory, $400, no insurance; Mrs. G.H. Chamberlain, laundry machinery, estimated value $750, insurance $350; George H. Clough, electrician, estimated value $200, no insurance; Frank B. Hutchins, owned poplar wood stored on wharf, $200, no insurance; John Goodhue, pictures, etc., $300, insurance $300.... Wolfeboro Loan & Banking Company, building and fixtures, valued at $6,000, insurance $2,000; Charles H. Hersey, water damage, stock valued at $2,500; Charles W. Hoyt, water damage to furniture, $200, insurance none.... Work was commenced Wednesday morning on the repairing of the roof of the building owned by the Wolfeboro Loan & Banking Company. Mrs. M.A. Goodwin is considering the feasibility of rebuilding on the lot which Goodwin Block was located. The fire of Saturday night is generally thought to be of incendiary origin."

**1899, September 10. Stable:** Owned by Joseph A. Stockbridge, Factory Street. Destroyed.[89]

### Electricity, Telegraph, and Telephone

Telegraph service was instituted in Wolfeboro in 1872 with the coming of the railroad.

Although there had been a private line from the Glendon House hotel to Frank Cook's livery stable on Center Street as early as 1887-1888, it was not until 1896 that the New England Telephone and Telegraph Company began telephone service in Wolfeboro from a trunk line extending from South Wolfeboro. In the first year there were 20 subscribers served by one operator. The office was within a fruit and confectionery store on the corner of Lake Avenue and South Main Street to the left of the Peavey Block. Early instruments were of the wall-mounted, hand-cranked type and contained large dry cells that had to be changed yearly. Early telephone subscriber lists were published in the *Granite State News.* In 1897 a competing firm—the Wolfeboro Telephone Company—announced its formation and accepted applications for connections. Its rate was $12 to $15 per year, compared to New England's $24 to $64. However, on October 12 at a Precinct meeting, the idea of granting a new local franchise was rejected by the citizenry.[90]

A steam-operated electric generating plant was first operated by the town of Wolfeboro in 1897 and used power from the Libbey & Varney Co. sawmill on Back Bay. In 1898 the business was sold to Stephen W. Clow, who continued to furnish power. After the Electric Department was established, the newspaper regularly noted which citizens were installing electric service. In homes, room lights usually hung from the center of the ceiling and were turned on at the pendant fixture. For years all bulbs were exposed. Wiring was often bare, particularly in basements and attics, and was strung between porcelain posts or spacers. Woe to anyone who inadvertently touched them!

Earlier, candles, oil lamps, and kerosene lamps were used for illumination. In 1889 there were 50 or more oil lamps in town to illuminate the streets. The town lamplighter would ignite these every evening except when the moon was full or nearly so. It was determined not to have street lighting the year 1892, as citizens "are weary and no longer desiring to gaze at the mute sentinels whose oil-burning illuminating flickerings have been so unsatisfactory to all." The annual cost of $250 was saved.[91]

On January 5, 1897, the editor of the local paper stated that as electricity had passed the novelty stage, it was about time that Wolfeboro had electric street lights. Certain downtown residences were wired that summer. On August 14, 1897, electric street lights were switched on for the first time. Power was provided by a steam-powered generator at the Libbey Brothers mill on Back Bay under a contract to the town.[92] By 1900 there were 100 incandescent street lamps in Wolfeboro and an estimated 1,700 bulbs in private homes.

## THE ECONOMY AND MONEY

### Industry

In the earliest years the town's economy was primarily based upon agriculture and limited manufacturing. Most of the cows and corn raised, lumber sawed, and other products were used locally.

General stores kept records for each customer or family and settled them at intervals. Accounts would often be settled by bartering. The owner of a sawmill would be paid in chickens or milk by a farmer seeking boards to build a shed. In September 1873 Orin Dixon, dealer in dry goods and groceries at Wolfeboro Center, advertised thus: "Eggs and beans taken in exchange for goods."

As time went on, areas with water power—especially Wolfeboro Falls and South Wolfeboro—furnished the sites for manufacturing enterprises such as lumber processing (into boards, shooks, or excelsior), shoe making, and textiles, the products of which were shipped far beyond town borders. With the advent of the railroad to Wolfeboro in 1872, which connected Wolfeboro Falls (but not South Wolfeboro) with the outside world, manufacturing increased sharply. In time, blocks of ice taken in the winter from Crescent Lake and Wolfeboro Bay were added to the list of products shipped to Boston and elsewhere.

By the end of the nineteenth century Wolfeboro was known primarily as a seasonal tourist town, with manufacturing and limited agriculture; however, in terms of dollar volume, the factories did more business than tourist accommodations.

### Business Trends

From the earliest days of the Union the economy of America has experienced well-defined trends and cycles. The inflationary times of the Revolution, the Panic of 1837, the inflation during the Civil War era, and other events all impacted Wolfeboro. As an example, the Panic of '37 and the consequent Hard Times era (as it was called) spelled the end of the town's first financial institution, the Wolfborough Bank.

During most ups and downs in the economy during the eighteenth and nineteenth centuries, Wolfeboro took care of its own inhabitants. To a large extent the community was self-sufficient with its agriculture and lumber activities. In the financial depression of 1893, conditions were better in Wolfeboro than to the south, as reflected by this account dated October 3, 1893, in the *Granite State News:*

> Word received from some of our people who have gone to Massachusetts to work this fall, report that the people in our town do not fully realize what hard times are in other places. Application has been already by upwards of 40 for work who offer to labor for simply their board.

After the 1870s outside financial interests invested in the town, particularly in industries on Factory Street where they leased buildings put up by local investors. During the 1880s and 1890s the shoe and textile businesses housed in a huge building known as the "Big Factory" (years later as the Bell Shop) and in a later, smaller one called the Clark Shop experienced difficulties ranging from fires to poor financial planning. It seemed that the more Wolfeboro depended upon out-of-town ownership of businesses, the more economic difficulties it experienced. In 1894 the "Big Factory" building was vacant; the Massachusetts-based manufacturers had decamped. Residents tried to help:[93]

> The citizens' meeting in Sheridan Hall, Thursday evening, was well attended, and was an assuring hope that something must, shall, and will be done to establish some desirable and permanent business in the Wolfeboro Shoe Factory building...."

Prayers were answered by Coburn, Gauss & Co., an "old, reliable firm," which began making shoes locally in early 1895. However, joy was short-lived, and a few months later the "Big Factory" was vacant once again.[94]

At the turn of the twentieth century the two large buildings stood empty, several hundred townspeople were looking for work, and the future of this aspect of the local economy seemed uncertain.

## THE CENTURY ENDS

### Old Home Week, 1900

Beginning in 1899 Old Home Week celebrations became popular in the state. The typical event featured a parade, decorated stores and public facilities, concerts and lectures, and a special welcome for old-time residents who had moved elsewhere, but returned for the occasion.[95] From August 11 to 18, 1900, Wolfeboro held its second annual Old Home Week.

The following is extracted from *Second Annual Report of Old Home Week in New Hampshire, August 11 to 18, 1900,* by N.J. Batchelder:[96]

> Wolfeborough's celebration...was excelled by none of all the Old Home Day observances in the two years. Five thousand spectators witnessed the best parade of 1900.... A bonfire 50 feet high ushered in the week on Saturday night. Sunday morning a union religious service was held in Brewster Memorial Hall.... Monday night a brilliant ball was given.
>
> Tuesday morning at 6 o'clock the booming of cannon ushered in the great day and summoned the people to view a beautifully decorated town. Nearly every residence and place of business on the line of march of the parade was covered with flags and bunting.... Rare old china and Indian relics figured appropriately in some of the store window displays.
>
> Public exercises were held in a large tent on the grounds of Brewster Academy at 2 p.m. Hon. Sewall W. Abbott presided. Prayer was offered by Rev. W.O. Hornbaker, and Miss Mabel E. Fullerton gave the address of welcome. Hon. Fred E. Hurd of Boston, assistant attorney general of the state of Massachusetts, gave the principal address.... [Numerous sports events were staged.] The day closed with extensive illuminations on the shore and inland.

**Looking to the Future**

By the time the nineteenth century ended, Wolfeboro had earned its place on the map. From a few scattered farms in the 1770s the community had grown to support 2,390 permanent citizens (1900 census) and several dozen stores and commercial enterprises. The town hosted thousands of visitors in the summer, many of whom stayed at an ever-growing number of cottages on Lake Wentworth, along the shore of Lake Winnipesaukee, and on scattered islands.

Education, commerce, religion, town services, and other aspects of Wolfeboro had matured, and in sharp contrast to the uncertainties of pioneer days, the village was an attractive, highly civilized, and very enjoyable place in which to live.

The citizens of Wolfeboro looked to the future with anticipation.

# CHAPTER 3
# WOLFEBORO 1901-1910

*God might have made a prettier place than Wolfeboro, but doubtless He never did.*
– *Granite State News,* May 23, 1903.[1]

## INTRODUCTION

Although celebrations for the "new century" were held in 1900, the first day of the twentieth century was technically January 1, 1901. For the purposes of the present book this dovetails nicely with Benjamin F. Parker's study, *The History of Wolfeborough,* mostly completed by the end of 1900.

The first decade of the twentieth century brought many changes to Wolfeboro. Perhaps the most dramatic was wrought by the automobile, a curiosity in 1901 which became a standard fixture by 1910. Many areas of commerce, religion, politics, and other activities changed as well.

In 1901 most local residents were content to stay in or around Wolfeboro. Such distant states as Florida and California were places to read about, not to visit. If a trip were taken, like as not it would be by railroad connecting to Boston, a favorite destination. Some of the more affluent citizens of the town enjoyed going farther away, again by railroad, or, rarely, by ship out of Boston, but in the year 1901 probably not one person in 10 had ever been outside of the boundaries of New England.

While it is popular to think of the "good old days," in reality there were as many problems then as there are now, if not more. By today's standards, medicine and nutrition were primitive, and life expectancy was considerably shorter, although numerous Wolfeboro residents lived to their eighties or nineties. Advantages we take for granted in preventive medical care, mental health, surgical procedures, and diagnosis were largely unknown then.

Houses were often uncomfortably cold in the winter. Factories had little in the way of safety devices. Social Security was decades away, and unless one had a caring family—and many citizens did not—the primary option for old age was poverty and a bed at the poor farm.

Social classes were stratified into the "haves" and "have nots." While perhaps two or three dozen local manufacturers, merchants, and professionals were in the wealthy category and could afford such amenities as fancy clothes, player pianos, and train trips to visit Boston, the vast majority of Wolfeboro residents had all they could do to earn enough money to keep their children clothed and to put food on the table.

Despite trials and tribulations the average local citizen of 1901 seemed to be content with his or her station in life. There was a warm camaraderie among the populace, and in an age before computers, television, and the depersonalization of individuals, people probably enjoyed each other's company more. Certainly, the turnouts for local concerts, plays, school events, picnics, and the like were, on the average, greater then than now.

The spirit that we know in the 1990s—the emotion that prompts many of us to fire letters off to the *Granite State News* and the *Lakes Region Courier* whenever a change in the status quo is contemplated—is, I like to think, directly descended from the spirit of years ago. We will probably always have social, political, financial, and other problems, but somehow the pleasures always more than balance the pains. The result is that Wolfeboro was in 1901, and is today, a very special section of the world.

## COMMUNICATIONS

### The *Granite State News*

In the 1901-1910 decade, the weekly *Granite State News* was four pages in size. Occasionally, a supplement would be issued, as in cases when copies of the current laws of New Hampshire were sent to subscribers. The newspaper cost $1.25 per year in 1903, but a special deal in effect in October of that year offered a full subscription for 1904 plus the balance of 1903 for just $1, available to new subscribers only.

Editor Frederick W. Prindle and others in front of the *Granite State News* office in the Durgin Block, June 20, 1903. Left to right: Prindle, Parry T. Hersey, Charles H. Warren, Herbert J. Horne, Clara Sawyer Sanborn, and Lydia E. Sawyer.

On March 22, 1908, the George A. Smith residence on Center Street was gutted by fire, but was soon rebuilt on the original foundation. Decades later the facility housed Bill's Auto Service. (William Hooper Collection)

Church news dominated the front page for much of the decade. Lengthy extracts from religious texts, reprinted sermons from periodicals, and numerous other spiritual messages faced the reader.

Beginning on January 3, 1903, the *Granite State News* adopted a new format. Henceforth, it was declared, local news would be on the front page instead of the interior pages. Earlier, the front page was devoted to fillers from out-of-town newspapers, patent medicine advertisements, and other items of non-local origin including religious dissertations. Despite all good intentions, by April 1903 most front page news was anything but local—and had to do with international, national, or state events, plus more religious articles. Local news was back where it had been before—primarily on pages 2 and 3. The first and last page—pages 1 and 4—were of a less timely nature, permitting the paper to be "made up" with pages 1 and 4 during the week, and then as deadline approached, interior pages 2 and 3 containing late-breaking local news. In 1903 the average weekly circulation was 1,345 copies.

Among the items appearing in 1903 is this poignant commentary from the July 18 issue, reprinted from *The Wall Street Journal:*

> HISTORY IN SIX WORDS: War, poverty, peace, prosperity, pride, war.

The newspaper's emphasis on religion had diminished somewhat by 1905. However, much space was given to details of the bitter feud between two different factions of the First Congregational Church, involving a move from their old wooden structure at Pickering Corner to a new location. At one point in the contretemps, each group contracted to buy a different piece of land for the new building! The acrimony became so bitter and the arguments so repetitive that the editor finally stated that no more on the subject would be printed.

### "The Goose"

If one local newspaper writer had to be singled out for the human interest aspect of his or her words, a favorite choice would be Mabel E. Fullerton. In 1903 she adopted the *nom de plume* of "The Goose" and proceeded to chronicle the happenings at Goose Corner. Coming under her watchful eye was not only the general district of Wolfeboro today located at the intersection of North Main Street and Waumbeck Road and called Goose Corner, but in Mabel's view, much of the rest of the town as well, at least the part from the Tuftonboro line to Wolfeboro Neck.

The Goose became very popular over time. Born in 1874, Miss Fullerton possessed a seemingly unlimited knowledge of and interest in various historical, philosophical, and literary subjects, many of which she interwove in her column. Other times her words were simply whimsical as:

> Not long ago when The Goose was particularly afflicted by the lack of news, a wise citizen suggested lying one week and taking it back the next. "Thus," said he, "you have two paragraphs, whereas if you tell the truth you have but one."

Every now and then she would take her pen name seriously, sort of, and would cast herself in the fanciful form of a goose and talk about her "feathers," etc.—all in a pleasing, modest, humorous way.

Readers undoubtedly shared the joy when they scanned this:[2]

> On Tuesday, June 4, 1907, at the home of the bride, Mr. Alvan T. Hatch of St. Louis, Missouri, and Miss Mabel Fullerton of this town were united in marriage. A few friends and neighbors attended the ceremony, which was performed by the Rev. Allen C. Keith.

Less enthusiasm probably greeted this notice of September 14, 1907:

> *News* readers will regret the absence from our columns hereafter of the items of The Goose, who has gone this week to join her husband in the West. We shall expect however, an occasional letter from the quill of this brilliant writer.... May success attend her in her new home.

Husband Alvan was a traveling jewelry salesman based in St. Louis, and he took his bride with him on his train trips throughout the Midwest. Over the next few years, Mabel Hatch's dispatches datelined Texas, Kentucky, Kansas, Colorado, and elsewhere were published in the *Granite State News*. For example, the January 29, 1910, issue contained a missive sent from the St. Anthony Hotel, San Antonio. Mabel had been traveling around the Midwest with her husband, who had "striven to persuade a somewhat reluctant public that it was in great need of his wares."

### Place Names

Spelling of place names was a recurrent subject in the *Granite State News*. On July 29, 1905, this appeared: "The United States Board on Geographic Names has passed upon the orthography of the name of the lake on whose shore Wolfeboro stands; the board's decision is in favor of 'Winnepesaukee.'" However, come hell or high water on the lake, the local paper had no intention of swerving from its preferred Winnipesaukee spelling, as unofficial as it might have been. Nearly all townspeople followed suit. A few weeks later on September 9, 1905, the newspaper reported that the same omniscient Board declared that "Wolfboro" was the correct spelling of our town's name. However, the editor said that "the town was named from General James Wolfe, not, as one would naturally infer from 'Wolfboro', because this region was formerly infested by wolves."

The spellings of many other local names were discussed in print. For example, an item published on December 26, 1908, treated a particular railroad crossing

Photograph taken circa 1901 from the Thompson House on the hill, looking southeast toward the main section of the town. A long string of boxcars is at the Wolfeborough Railroad Station. In the distance at the right and above the center is the Brewster Free Academy building. Slightly to the left of the center a white plume of steam rises from the S.W. Clow & Co. sawmill, while to its left are piles of lumber. Copple Crown mountain in New Durham rises in the distance at the right.

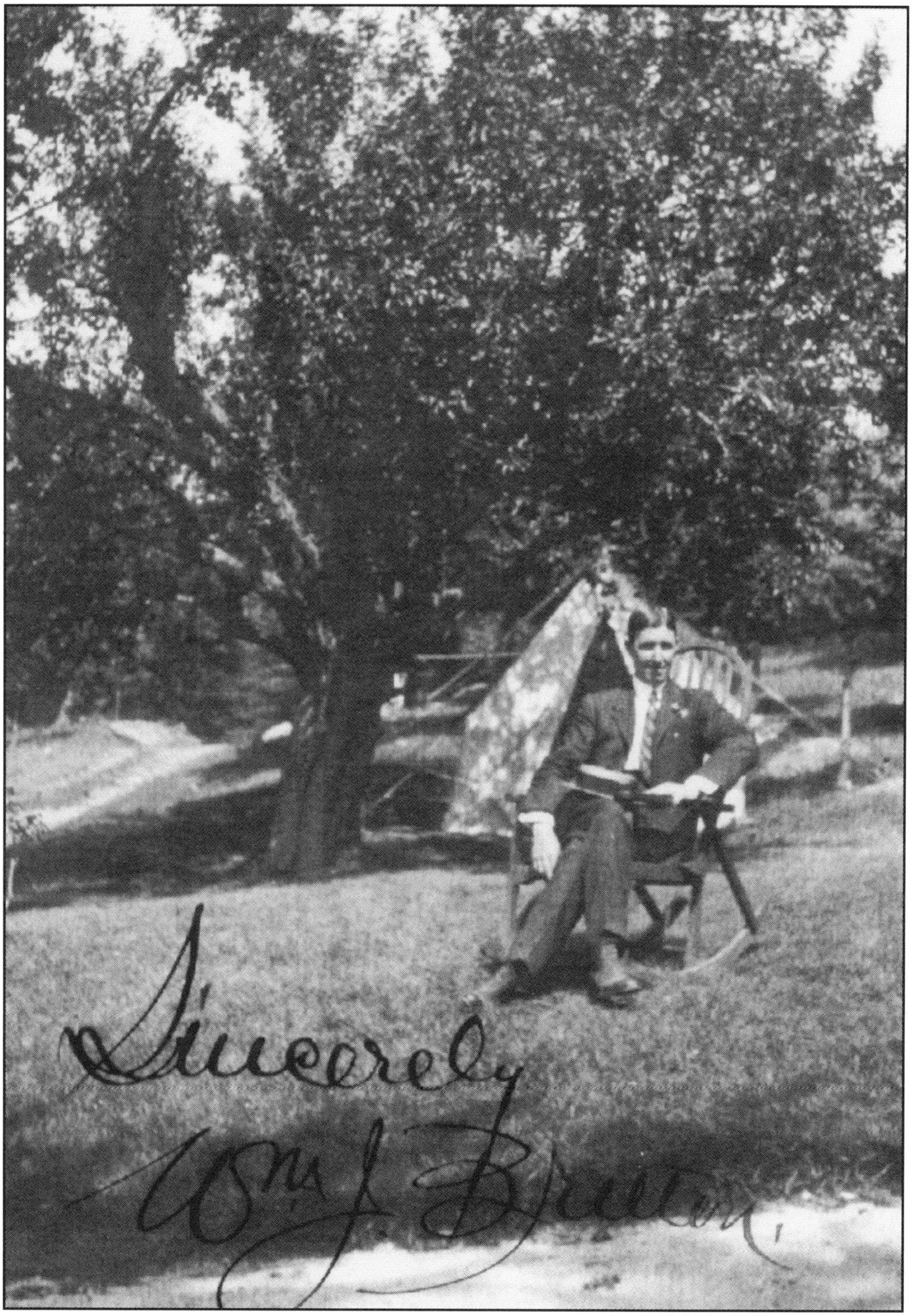


William J. Britton (1872-1943) lived in Wolfeboro all of his life. He became an attorney in 1905 and later entered the insurance business as well. Judge Britton, as he became known, lived on North Main Street at the corner of Mill Street. A sportsman and outdoorsman, he is shown in a coat and tie sitting in front of a tent.

Two teams of horses and eight teams of oxen scraping snow on North Main Street near Lucas Street at the turn of the century. More often the snow was packed down by the use of horse-drawn rollers.

in Wolfeboro Center, noting that it was spelled Fernald, Fernald's, and Fernalds, with no particular agreement as to which was right. (As a further complication, this crossing was considered by some to be in Wolfeboro Center and others to be in East Wolfeboro; boundaries of districts were not defined.)

In April 1910 the spelling of the town's name came up again—as it often did. By that time the official government spelling was Wolfeboro for the main section of town, and for certain other places it was East Wolfeboro, South Wolfeboro, and Wolfeboro Center. However, two other places were officially spelled North Wolfboro and Wolfboro Falls! By this time, local citizens did not much care what was official and what wasn't; Wolfeboro was preferred. Residents often ignored pronouncements emanating from Washington. Yankee cussedness and independence, it was called.

### Advice to Women

It was a man's world in the first decade of the present century. Women could not vote, were very rarely involved in organizations in the community except those having to do with churches, schools or music, and were expected to defer to men in matters of importance. An editorial signed H.R.D. in the *Granite State News,* May 18, 1907, reflected this:

> Women's lives are narrower than men's, and they are more liable to fall into the way of looking downward, hence this appeal is to women. Don't gossip, don't hate, don't get envious of your neighbor, don't tell every ache and pain you have. Read more and talk about what you read, only be careful about the selection of the reading matter.... Love everybody and everything....

By 1910 the front page of the *Granite State News* was apt to contain a scattered patent medicine ads, stories reprinted from out-of-town papers, selected reports of national news events, but only a relatively small percentage of church matter. To be sure, there were exceptions, and religious items did appear occasionally on the front page and elsewhere, including this unbelievable (from today's standpoint) item in the issue of December 17, 1910:

> Clifford Sargent, who was expelled from Brewster Free Academy some weeks ago by the acting principal because of his refusal to act as a spy and report such of the students as elected to attend Sunday services at the Free Baptist Church, but who neglected to comply, has this week been reinstated with the full privileges of a student by the Trustees.

### Oops!

As might be expected from the strain and urgency of turning out a weekly paper, typographical errors—some quite funny—appeared now and then. Usually they were ignored, but sometimes they were corrected, as in this item in the July 31, 1909, issue: "Last week...we were made to say that Agnes Robinson was 70 years of age, when we should have said 11."

Arguably, the most humorous filler of the decade was this, appearing on December 25, 1909:

> We apologize for all mistakes made in former issues and say they were inexcusable, as all our editor has to do is hunt news and clean the rollers and set type, sweep the floor, fold papers, write wrappers, make paste, mail the papers, talk to visitors, distribute type, carry water, saw wood, read proofs, hunt shears to write editorials, dodge the bills, dun delinquents, take cussing from the whole force, and tell our subscribers that we must have money. We say that we have no business to make mistakes while attending to these little matters. [Further, the editor has to] turn a smiling countenance to the man who tells us our paper ain't worth a dollar subscription anyhow, and that he could make a better one with his eyes shut.

### Telephone and Telegraph

Although the New England Telephone & Telegraph Company had a local office downtown in 1901, across the street to the left of the Peavey Block, most distant communications were sent by letter, or if the sender was in a hurry, by telegraph. Either the New England Telegraph or the Boston & Maine Railroad Telegraph (the latter at the train station) wires could be utilized.

In Wolfeboro during the early years of the century, the telephone slowly became increasingly popular. However, the number of local and area telephone subscribers and stations as of June 13, 1903, per the *Granite State News* of that date, were still few and far between. Most of the nearly three dozen places with telephones in Wolfeboro were businesses or professional offices:

> Public pay stations in the greater Wolfeboro area: Melvin Village; Bonnie Doon Golf Grounds, Center Tuftonboro; J.A. Edgerly, Mirror Lake; B.F. Burleigh, Wolfeboro Falls; Cotton Valley; South Wolfeboro.
>
> Private subscribers in the town of Wolfeboro: Sewall W. Abbott, H.B. Furber, Frank P. Hobbs, Elmer R. Durgin, Frank B. Hutchins, Charles F. Piper, Herbert E. Haines, Stephen W. Clow, Edwin H. Lord, F.E. Hurd, George A. Carpenter,
>
> Sheridan House, C.W. Hutchinson, Jesse Gould, C.P. Berry, Samuel A. Meader, Dr. Herman I. Berry, G.W. Berry, B&M Railroad Station, American Express, F.C. Meacham, J.J. Herrick, Dr. Nathaniel H. Scott, Isaac W. Springfield, F.P. Cox, G.W. Moses, Wolfeboro Drug Store, Charles E. Rendall, J.E. Fox, Dr. S.P. Getchell, and Dr. Fred C. Tobey.

This published directory was not even in alphabetical order—so few were the names.

In the summer of 1905 the New England Telephone & Telegraph Company offered "for a limited period, trial telephones in the residences of those who have never before had telephone service." This campaign must have borne fruit, for the January 1906 issue of the New England Telephone directory listed 86 names for Wolfeboro—a new high. Installations were mentioned in the paper as social news.

The July 14, 1906, issue of the local paper printed this item:

A Wolfeboro living room in the early twentieth century. Mabel (Mrs. E.J.) Davis is shown in her home on Pleasant Street. The room is wired for electricity including a ceiling fixture and two sconces on the fireplace mantel. The fireplace seems decorative, rather than functional, as the interior bricks and birch logs are pristine.

The Davis house. (Arthur H. Sawyer photographs; Melanson Collection)

> Miss Leila Jenness, our popular girl at "Central," was married last Saturday to Carl P. Eastman, the night operator at the office. We wish them both much happiness.

In June 1908 residential telephone service cost 55 cents a month, while business phones were 70 cents.[3]

### Parker's *History* (1901)

Benjamin F. Parker commenced writing *The History of Wolfeborough* in 1898, employing to a large extent material prepared earlier, including much data included in his *Granite State News* column, "The History of Wolfborough," begun in the early 1860s, and several chapters he wrote for *The History of Carroll County* published in 1889. Parker died on December 30, 1900, one day short of the end of the nineteenth century. He did not live to see his book in print, nor was he able to finish the manuscript, which was completed by his son, Bert W. Parker.[4]

At the annual town meeting held in Wolfeboro on March 12, 1901, among the items voted was $1,500 to publish the Parker history, an amount equal in purchasing power to about $60,000 to $80,000 today. In addition, the author was paid by the town for his labor on the book.[5]

While Parker's *History* was not primarily a vanity piece, for many weeks the *Granite State News* carried this notice: "Those who wish cuts of individuals or residences inserted in the History of the Town will please consult with the History Committee at once." Those who wanted to pay for the privilege could have favorite photographs included. Nevertheless, among the pictures were numerous illustrations of churches and geographical features as well as other images probably selected by Parker earlier. The book was printed by Caustic & Claflin of Cambridge, Massachusetts.

On October 5, 1901, an item in the local paper advised:

> Some copies of the history of the town of Wolfeboro have been received, and the whole number are promised in the coming week. This is a work that every native will surely want and take pride in. As a history it is very creditable work. Any parties wishing copies should address E.H. Lord, A.B. Rust, or F.W. Prindle.[6] Price, $2.75, $3.25, $3.75 according to the bindings.

The town report of February 15, 1902, under Assets, listed 817 copies of the town history at $2,400 the group, which equals $2.94 each; there were also 200 unbound copies valued at $1 each.

## INDOORS AND OUT

### Pastimes

In an era when home radio and television were years away, reading was one of the most popular indoor pastimes for those with a literary bent. The latest novels, poems, and magazine articles were apt to be topics of conversation. Most citizens who had completed a high-school education had a working knowledge of the classics, could recite popular lines from Shakespeare, and identify selections from Burns, Shelley, Whittier, Longfellow, and other poets. The more ambitious school students strove to memorize lines from great plays and poems—the longer, the more impressive. To recite Edgar Allan Poe's *The Raven* was much more of an accomplishment than to memorize John Greenleaf Whittier's *Maud Muller,* although the latter was not to be taken lightly.

Debates, orations, and talks were popular activities not only at home but in meeting halls. Those with a religious orientation—and in Wolfeboro in 1901 this included many people—were expected to have at least a working knowledge of familiar Bible verses such as the Ten Commandments and to readily suggest what Jesus might have done if confronted by a particular moral dilemma. For the typical child in a religious family, attending Sunday school or church was not an option, it was a parental requirement. Many activities in the big, wide world were classified as being "good" or "bad." In actuality, morality was not that much different in 1901 than it is today. However, our forebears were less open-minded about it.

Most homes with any pretension of "culture," always an admirable goal to attain (prestige was in vogue then as now), had a foot-pumped parlor reed organ or a piano or better yet, one of each. Hymns, classical numbers, and popular tunes would be played for hours on end. Little Mary might play *Yankee Doodle* on the reed organ for her own pleasure, but a folio boldly lettered "BACH" on the cover would be kept on the music rack for visitors to see.

Just becoming available on the market in 1901 were organs and pianos using perforated paper rolls. Particularly in demand was the Aeolian Pianola, a foot-pumped device that played a 65-note paper roll and cost about $250. The Pianola pushed up to the keyboard of a regular piano and played it with small felt-tipped wooden fingers. Next to the price paid for a house, the second largest expenditure in 1901 was often a piano.[7]

Reproduced music could be played on a Swiss-made cylinder music box, such as those imported by Hermann A. Ockel, of Providence, Rhode Island, from Mermod Frères of St. Croix, Switzerland, and sold for prices ranging from about $20 to well over $1,000. More popular were Regina music boxes made in Rahway, New Jersey, which used interchangeable steel discs of varying diameters. In that way, one could buy discs of favorite tunes, and as new melodies were published, a music library could be updated, much as a cassette or compact disc collection can be added to today.

Favorite tunes included Stephen Foster songs, popular melodies such as *Grandfather's Clock, Old Oaken*

Ice-skimming automobile built by George F. Brewster in 1908, powered by a one-cylinder, four horsepower motor taken from a 1901 Crestmobile. Shown on Wolfeboro Bay.

This device, built in 1903 by George F. and Robert C. Brewster, was described as a "two-boy powered automobile."

"Steam Ice Auto" built in 1907 by George F. Brewster. In action on Wolfeboro Bay.

The John L. Peavey mansion at the corner of South Main and Union Streets was a Wolfeboro landmark, as seen here about the turn of the century. In 1934 the current owner of the Peavey mansion, Charles F. Pinkham, installed gas pumps in front of the Peavey house. In 1938 he sold out to Texaco, which tore the building down and put up a service station.

The Pinkham farm on South Main Street in the early twentieth century. Today the facility, vastly altered and expanded, is known as the Windrifter Resort. (Arthur H. Sawyer photograph; Melanson Collection)

**House built circa the 1850s on South Main Street for Blake Folsom, who became one of the town's leading merchants and benefactors. Today Hunter's IGA store is on the site. (Photograph taken circa 1906-1907)**

**Huggins Sanitarium, founded by local physicians and others in 1907 and established in the former Rev. Theodore Jerome residence on South Main Street, is shown here in an early view. Known today as Huggins Hospital, the institution is vastly larger and is at a different location on the same street. (Melanson Collection)**

Blake and Ruth (Mr. and Mrs.) Folsom. Blake Folsom, born in Wolfeboro on October 25, 1824, remained a resident until his death on October 11, 1911. The owner of a local hardware business and other enterprises, he was one of the most generous benefactors the town has ever had. (Edson Graham photograph, circa 1901-1902)

*Bucket, When You and I Were Young Maggie,* etc., as well as new marches (often composed by John Philip Sousa), and that up-and-coming music form, ragtime, as exemplified by *At a Georgia Camp Meeting, Smokey Mokes,* and, especially, *The Maple Leaf Rag.* In 1901 ragtime was said to corrupt the morals of youth, a reputation later inherited, in turn, by jazz, rock and roll, and acid rock. As has been said, the more things change, the more they stay the same.

Although Emile Berliner had invented the disc phonograph the preceding decade, the typical record-player in use in Wolfeboro in the early 1900s was of the cylinder type, most likely bearing the Edison trademark, which provided a selection of two minutes in length. With a few turns of a hand crank, one could hear Teddy Roosevelt give an oration (again, limited to just two minutes) or a talk by William Jennings Bryan, known as the Silver-Tongued Orator of the Platte, who in the 1896 presidential contest electrified listeners with his "Cross of Gold" speech. During the next several years the local paper made frequent mention of social gatherings enlivened by a phonograph.

The November 28, 1903, the *Granite State News* contained an advertisement from The Paper Store, noting that the following newspapers were on hand (presumably, these constituted the journals most preferred by local readers):

> *Boston Daily Globe, Boston Daily Herald, Boston Post, Boston Journal, Boston Evening News, Boston Record, Boston Evening Transcript, Boston Sunday Globe, Boston Herald, Manchester Union, Utica Saturday Globe,* and the indigenous *Granite State News.*

The following magazines were available:

> *Ainslee's, Argosy, Beauty and Health, Century, Elite Styles, Everybody's Magazine, Frank Leslie's Popular Magazine, Household Ledger, Harper's, Ladies' World, Le BonTon, Ladies Home Journal, McCall's Magazine, Munsey's, McClure's, New Idea Women's Magazine, Outing, Pearson's, Pictorial Review, Popular Magazine, Physical Culture, Something To Read, Success, Scribner's, Smart Set, The Strand, Toilettes, The Delineator, The Designer, The Black Cat, The Nickel,* and *Woman's Home Companion.*

Books could be bought at several stores in town, could be rented from at least two shops, or could be borrowed free of charge from the Brewster Memorial Library then located in the back part of the Town Hall. Included was a novel titled *Meryl* which was offered by the Paper Store and billed as "the book about Wolfeboro." Written by William Tillinghast Eldridge and published by Dodd, Mead & Co. in April 1908, it was quite popular in its time.[8]

Among popular distaff pastimes were sewing, knitting, crocheting, weaving, quilting, gardening, and lawn sports.

Men and women, boys and girls could all enjoy the parlor pastime of looking at three-dimensional stereograph cards (sometimes called stereopticon cards) with a hand-held viewing device. These cards depicted thousands of topics ranging from local views of the Pavilion Hotel and Wolfeboro Bay, to mining scenes in the Colorado Rockies, to Chinese opium dens. Before the decade was over, stereograph cards would be replaced in popularity by picture postcards.

Coin and stamp collecting were enjoyed by many.[9] Indian arrowheads (which could be found along the shores of Back Bay or Winter Harbor if you were lucky), birds' eggs, and mineral specimens were popular items to acquire and display. Solving jigsaw puzzles, anagrams, and quizzes were other pursuits, as were card games.

In 1901 residents could view short film subjects (usually only a few minutes in length) projected on a sheet, sometimes under a tent set up in a field in the summertime. Motion pictures as part of a stage program of vaudeville acts, skits, and orations furnished interesting fillers and were shown at Sheridan Hall and Brewster Memorial Hall among other venues. By means of this new medium, viewers could see an express train rushing toward them, the wonders of Coney Island at night with its seeming millions of electric bulbs, or laugh at slapstick such as an unwary gardener being sprayed by a hose or a baker being covered with flour from head to foot. William McKinley was the first president whose activities were captured by a movie camera, and after that, things would never be the same.

For casual entertainment, men enjoyed playing chess, checkers, or a round of poker. The relatively new game of Pit soon became such a fad that numerous Pit parties were held in town.

Photography was a popular pastime. "Kodaks are the order of the day, and hiding in the corn does not prevent one from having his picture 'took'," the *Granite State News* commented on August 28, 1909. Each year, or so it seemed, a new professional photographer would arrive in town, set up in the north-lighted studio established in 1889 by E.T. Brigham on the corner of Depot and Glendon Streets, and then leave after the summer season. Apparently there was not enough studio trade to make a year-round business successful. Amateur photography was another thing entirely, and local jeweler and optician Everett S. Albee, who had been open since 1883, kept busy selling cameras and film to those who wanted to try their hand.

Painting in watercolor and oil was also enjoyable for many local residents, some of whom took lessons, especially in the summer. A few painters achieved at least passing notice in the press, as evidenced by this representative comment, July 1, 1905:

> Mrs. James Kimball is an artist of more than ordinary note. Her home is filled with choice oil paintings, the work of her hands.

### Sports

Hunting and fishing were two popular local sports, and all general stores sold equipment for their pursuit. Of the two, fishing received the most press coverage. Typically, the captain of a yacht would take a fishing party out in Lake Winnipesaukee and report the results to the local paper. This 1903 notice is representative:

> Charles W. Hoyt's party in his steamer *Crystal E. Goodwin* have caught over 800 pounds of trout out of Lake Winnipesaukee this season and are after more.[10]

Deer hunting was another popular pastime. On October 10, 1903, this was reported:

> The most successful hunter this far in this section [South Wolfeboro] seems to be Charles Kimball, who succeeded in killing the first deer he ever saw. It was a young buck about 150 pounds, which was shot in the Mooney field last Saturday. A more excited and delighted young man than Charlie would have been hard to find.

However, of all sports, it was athletic contests—particularly baseball—which garnered most attention in newspaper columns. An example is provided by this colorful, irreverent, humorous—even breathtaking—August 9, 1905, account:

> SATURDAY'S GAME MOST EXCITING THIS SEASON. Idlewild vs. Wolfeboro drew a large crowd....
>
> Players from Camp Idlewild[11] arrived on Saturday after a slight accident to the steamer *Belle of the Isles* on which they had embarked. They arrived at our port bringing with them a large following, after which they were escorted to the campus of the Brewster Free Academy....
>
> When lined up the Idlewilds showed to fine advantage, large, splendid, cultured athletic fellows, the man from Michigan being a magnificent specimen of the genus *Homo*, the man from Illinois as the brilliant young gentleman with eyes worth a fortune for another's use after his decease, the gentleman from Indiana has opposed the king's guardsmen, the man from New York a model of perfection, while others representing Cincinnati, Washington, Cambridge, Boston, and Utica were worthy of all the sly glances cast upon them by the natty up-to-date summer girls domiciling in our village, whom we consider absolutely irresistible. The Idlewilds were accompanied by umpire "Joe" whose face we know as we have saluted him for several years; the giant Michigander caught; the flaxen-haired Magnolia of Washington pitched; the bag and plates were their natural heritage.
>
> The Wolfeboros served under the red pennants of the "archiehorne."[12] The event was arranged by Barrett of Lynn. Smythe, the Brewster daisy, whose shoulder was lamed by exercise, and the superb Foote were in possession of the boxes. Horne, Rickerson, Hoxie, and Carpenter, young yeomen of Wolfeboro, with Donohoe of Boston, Burnham of Malden, and Ingalls of Alton constituted the home nine.
>
> The young Massachusetts man by the name of Whorf, chum and guest of Ralph Carpenter, was called to umpire the Wolfeboro end of the game, and both Mr. Whorf and Idlewild's Joe did fine work, they were just, sure and positive.
>
> As the game progressed Wolfeboro made *three* runs, the Idlewilds *one*.
>
> Wolfeboros now make *two* more, while the Idlewilds score *three*. From here the game laid until the seventh inning, when the Idlewilds *again* scored *one*, and on the eighth *tied*, the billboard showing 5 to 5. Then came the tug-of-war, every nerve of both nine was strained to the limit, rooters were too anxious to holler, every neck was craned, every move was watched. The celebrated Dr. Greene[13] fought for a better position and in his excitement shouted for both nines, Professor Lord [Edwin H. Lord, headmaster of Brewster] engaged in silent prayer, Harry Pettingill was carried from the field in a state of coma.
>
> The ninth inning and no score.
>
> The tenth inning came and passed, both nines retired, still no score, the eleventh inning and the hearse was ordered, yet the Idlewilds made several bases but never found the home plate, the home nine went to the bat, off goes the ball one, two, three, and the man rested; another man left third dying 10 inches from home plate, next man at bat, one, two, three and out. Up steps Carpenter, grim and determined, off flies the ball, and off goes Ralph, reaches first, up comes another one, two, strikes and three balls. Carpenter had reached third, three strikes and out, the next batman comes up, one strike, one ball, a bunt and a go—megaphones were not in it, steam whistles were nowhere, *viva voce* did it all. Legs and arms filled the air, gyrating like Sancho Panza's mill wing, or a la cuttlefish, Ralph sat down on the home plate and wept, umpire Whorf shouted safe, Idlewild was beaten, and the red banner of archiehorne is still there.

In 1906 tickets to baseball games were 25¢ each. During the season the home team under the management of Archie A. Horne won a large majority of its contests, its opponents including Sandy Island (Tuftonboro island), Camp Buena Vista (also on Sandy Island), YMCA Camp, Camp Idlewild (Cow Island), South Wolfeboro, Alton Cycle Club (this contest saw a 31 to 0 shutout), Union (NH town), Donohoes (summer team led by a Bostonian who had played on the Wolfeboro team the year before), and Camp Tecumseh (Moultonboro).

Football was the second most reported-upon sport in local news columns. Detailed stories about particular Brewster Academy contests would often be given, together with line-ups of players (usually with surnames only—a source of annoyance to modern-day historians).

### Entertainment

Downtown Wolfeboro was the site of many events such as parades, annual (which proved to be not-so-annual) Old Home Day celebrations, stage shows by traveling vaudeville or repertory groups, concerts, dances, church gatherings, carnivals and circuses, political forums, and more. Typically, the more important of these would be announced weeks in advance by handbills or posters put up on walls, fences, and poles. Scarcely a week went by without a show to entertain Wolfeboro residents and visitors. Most were held in Sheridan Hall or Brewster Memorial Hall.

A sampling of *Granite State News* clippings gives an idea of the variety of events:

> **1901, August 15. Stage play:** Witherall & Doud's Uncle Tom's Cabin Company.[14] At the time, *Uncle Tom's Cabin* was the most popular American stage melodrama, as it had been for years.

**Amateur theatricals on the stage on the second floor of the Town Hall, circa 1900s. Seated, left to right: Bertha May Stevens (with fan behind her head, banjo near her knee), Harry Moulton Lee, Clara Luella Whitton (in rocker), Maude May Freeman, Emma Chesley Tobin, Ida Louise Sanborn, and Clara May Pitman. Standing, left to right: Austin Phelps Christy, Jr., James Nelson Cooke, Fred C. Tobey, Edwin Harris Mattison, Frank Leon Mattison, and Carl Samuel Dorr.**

**Brewster Memorial Hall, a.k.a. Town Hall, opened in 1890, included space for the town offices, library (in the rear), theatre (on the second floor), and at the front of the first floor, several retail stores. (Circa 1914 view)**

Horsepower in action at the turn of the century. Shown is a team and wagon owned by Bickford & Young (Alvah H. Bickford and Obed S. Young). The driver is Frank Connor, and the location is in front of the Nathaniel Rogers homestead on North Main Street.

Panoramic view of downtown Wolfeboro looking northwest from the Brewster Memorial Hall tower. In the foreground are the Parker, Folsom, and Peavey houses that were part of "Bankers' Row" situated between Glendon and Union Streets. The large structure with the French mansard roof to the right of center is the Hobbs-Is-Inn. To its left the Bank Building, with two rounded-top windows on the ground floor, was home to the Wolfeboro National Bank opened in 1906. (Photograph taken circa 1900s)

**1902, November 3.**[15] **Corn-husking party:** "Frank B. Horne held a husking at his place [in Wolfeboro Center] Monday evening to which some 75 or 80 responded to invitations, and in short order farmer Horne had his excellent crop of corn husked and stored away, when his good wife invited the company to the house to partake of clam chowder, hot coffee, etc., which she had spread for them. It was a good time enjoyed by all."

**1903, February 7. Piano-playing device:** "W.P. Marshall of Boston, representing M. Steinert Company, is stopping in town at Hobbs-Is-Inn. He is a very skillful player on the Pianola and has recently given recitals in Concord and other cities."

**1903, March 21. Traveling medicine show:** "The German Medicine Company of Cincinnati was here last week, and we can say it was the best of its kind that had ever visited our village.... After the show was over, free dances were given until 12:00. The show consisted of Irish and Negro specialties which were most pleasing, also a contortionist who was simply great. Each and every night was different and the audience was just kept in a laughing humor the entire evening."

**1903, April 20. Minstrel show:** Lucier's Consolidated Minstrels appeared at Brewster Memorial Hall. "Mr. J.M. Lucier, theatrical director, is the only blind interlocutor and cornet soloist before the public.... The hall was completely filled while the gallery was crowded."

**1903, May 23. Trained animal show:** "Hammett's Trained Animals exhibited in Sheridan Hall Wednesday afternoon and evening. Those who failed to go know not what they missed, the tricks of the canaries and cockatoos alone being well worth the price of admission."

**1903, July 25. Circus:** This issue of the local paper contained a publicity announcement for a troupe set to appear in town on July 30, Sig Sautell's rather gradiosely-named New Big Three-Ring Railroad Circus, Menagerie, Royal Roman Hippodrome and Wild West. The performances were to be heralded by a free parade ending on South Main Street, where the tents were set up.

**1903, August 10. Motion pictures and vaudeville:** Sheridan Hall Monday evening: "Moving pictures, illustrated songs and other vaudeville specialties, combining wonder and fascination, sentiment and mirth which old and young will enjoy."

**1903, September 2. Stage play:**[16] *The Real Widow Brown* was presented at Sheridan Hall. Prices for seats were 25¢, 35¢, and 50¢.

**1903, December 12. Birthday party:** It was reported that a party with 75 guests was held to celebrate the 54th birthday of Herman I. Berry, M.D. A speech was given by H.S. Roberts, superintendent of schools. Entertainment was provided by Mrs. Charles Corser, who brought a phonograph.

**1903, December 19. Card party:** "Several rather noisy people were the guests of Alice Brown Tuesday evening. The noise is easily accounted for by the fact that they played Pit in the most earnest and strenuous fashion. Music and dancing rounded out the thoroughly pleasant evening."

**1904, July 30. Motion pictures, etc.:** "Mills & Kenneth Company were here and gave a first class show to a full house [at Sheridan Hall] three evenings this week. The singing, moving pictures, and hypnotism were great attractions.... Each appearance showed large increase in numbers over the former...."

**1904, December 10. Piano-playing device:** "Mrs. M.R. Beacham has purchased a fine 'Angelus' for a piano, having bought it from Mr. Beddell. It is a beauty and is the first 'Angelus' in town."[17]

**1905, February 4. Phonograph news:** "Last Tuesday evening a phonograph party, small and select, was held at the home of Parry T. Hersey on North Main Street. The Edison phonograph furnished the principal entertainment of the evening. Refreshments were served." In the same issue: "A company has been organized in Boston to send music to its subscribers by telephone, but it is an accomplished fact at present in Wolfeboro. A certain private telephone line has six stations, and one of the stations has a phonograph, and it has been rigged so that the phonograph will talk into the telephone transmitter. The different stations are then called and the music proceeds for a time to the delight of all on the line."

**1905, July 15. Annie Oakley visits:** "The first of a series of the A.A. Babb summer dances held last Thursday evening at Woldcroft Hall was voted a howling success. The picturesque hall was brilliantly lighted, floor was good and the music excellent. Annie Oakley, the world renowned crack rifle shot, a guest at one of the Woldcroft camps, gave two delightful recitations."[18]

**1905, October 21. Roller skating:** "A roller skating rink is soon to be opened in town." This was followed on October 28 by: "The roller skating rink started up last Saturday evening and was well patronized, but someone would fall down occasionally." [Location of rink not given.]

**1906, March 24. Phonograph parties:** "There was a phonograph social held at the vestry of the Christian Church last Saturday at which ice cream and cake were served, and a fairly good crowd of young people enjoyed the affair. Wednesday evening last, Edgar Abbott, who resides on Pleasant Street, who has recently become the owner of a Victor Graphophone, invited a number of his friends to spend the evening in listening to his sweet lullabies.... You should hear it. It has a morning glory-shaped horn, finely nickel plated. It can't be outdone. Ask Ed about it."

**1907, March 2. Player piano:** "Fidelity Lodge I.O.O.F. have installed a Pianola, which will be of great assistance in their work."

**1907, July 8. Trained animal show:**[19] Washburn's Trained Animal Show, Museum and Menagerie exhibited at Wolfeboro with two shows at the lot on South Main Street. Included were a herd of performing elephants, the "untamable lion Nero," a laughing hyena, a "den of performing teddy bears," and other attractions. Teddy bears were the latest sensation.

**1908, May 2. Motion pictures:** "The moving picture company at Sheridan Hall is all right. Views of the Chelsea [near Boston] conflagration were shown. The singing, harp and violin solos can't be beat. The same company shows again tonight. Everything new."

**1908, July 4. Phonograph orations:** "William Jennings Bryan's talk at the Lake Shore House last night was a success. He talks again tonight at eight. The subjects are swollen fortunes, the labor question, the railroad question, the trust question, the tariff question, popular election of senators, imperialism, guaranty of bank deposits, an ideal republic, and immortality. By calling on F.P. Hobbs at any time you can hear Mr. Bryan talk on these subjects."

**1908, August 22. Organ grinder:** "A hand organ grinder and monkey entertained the people this week. The monkey had a lively scrap with a dog and came out winner."

**1908, August 22. Motion pictures:** "The New York Amusement Company's moving picture show at Sheridan Hall, Thursday evening, drew a good audience and gave excellent satisfaction. Everybody was pleased. Will return next week, Thursday, with new pictures."

**1909, February 13. Children's party:** "The following composition was written as a part of the regular schoolwork of Miss Maude Cate's room at the Pickering School, the writer being Miss Theodora E. Hayes in the fourth grade, 'The Party. I went to a party last night. It was at Louise Hersey's house. I wore a plaid dress, at the party. We played post-office, telephone, and sang *The Kansas Emigrants*, played on the piano, and drop the handkerchief. Now I will tell you who was there. Marion Folsom Edith Horne Hazel Harthone Luella Durgin.... This is all I can think of. I do not think there was any more anyway.'"

**1909, March 25. Motion pictures and vaudeville:** The Superba Amusement Company from Concord, offering "incomparable moving pictures, illustrated songs, and vaudeville," appeared at the Brewster Memorial Hall. Another attraction was Mr. F.O. Perkins, who performed "the great box mystery" in which he was handcuffed and placed into an ordinary packing case, and the box was nailed up by prominent citizens.

**1910, June 4. Phonograph:** "Pine Hill news. Mr. Jenness has purchased an Edison improved phonograph."

**1910, July 9. Motion pictures:** "The Stevens & Conant Moving Picture Company gave a fine entertainment Friday night at Sheridan Hall. Full house. Are to be here once a week during the summer. See bills."[20]

## Wolfeboro Bands

Almost as certain as spring following winter was the regular notice in the *Granite State News* that a village band was being formed. It seemed that no sooner did a musical group get together, than it split apart. Then the town would be without a band for a few months or a year or two, and another announcement would be made.

On March 31, 1902, interested musicians, including members of the defunct Wolfeboro Cornet Band,[21] were invited to meet at the G.A.R. Hall to organize a new Wolfeboro Cornet Band. Agreement was reached, and the group, best known as the Wolfeboro Band, was active the following summer. The band practiced in a vacant store rented from furniture dealer Mrs. Sarah M. Hodge.

The Wolfeboro Band apparently dissolved soon thereafter, for on April 27, 1907, the local paper carried this notice:

> Efforts are being made to organize a village band. A good idea and it is hoped it may prove a success. We miss our band very much and surely a village the size of ours ought to be able to support a band.

This item in the May 18, 1907, issue explained what happened:

> An effort was made to organize a band in this village Thursday night, but only five men responded to the call for a meeting, and it was decided that as there seemed to be such a lack of interest in the matter it was better to abandon the project until a little later.

All was not lost, for about a year later a new group, the Wolfeboro Cadet Band, emerged on the local scene. The musicians' first public performance was for the Grand Army of the Republic veterans' ceremony on Memorial Day, 1908. On May 23, the *Granite State News* reported:

> Over three quarters of the members are new men, and this will be their first appearance on the street, but they hope to make a credible showing.

## Old Home Days

On Old Home Day, Tuesday, August 20, 1901, it was predicted the town would see "the greatest holiday in its history." For a week or two previous, Fred Clow, a 19-year-old Harvard medical student and son of local lumberman Stephen W. Clow, had been building a huge stack of dry wood on top of Martin's Hill in East Wolfeboro. In the meantime, a parade with four divisions was scheduled, and the various hose companies, boys from Camp Idlewild, and town organizations were scheduled to participate. At the time, there were no local summer camps for children, and the Idlewild boys were welcomed as visitors from across the lake.[22]

The Kingswood Club, a group organized in Massachusetts on the preceding February first and which was dedicated to improving local facilities such as roads, train schedules, and dock facilities, erected an arch over South Main Street at Glendon Street consisting of a wooden framework three feet deep, a span of 16 feet, and an arch measuring 24 feet high at the center—illuminated by 80 electric lights.

All went as planned. An estimated 8,000 people—a number more than triple the town's year-round population—turned out to witness the events. The parade started on time and was directed by Col. Edward B. Dickinson, best known for his "Ferncliffe" summer camp, the first to be built on Sewall Street.[23] The local paper reported that he had his hands full moving a "long column of mixed teams and undisciplined paraders over the line of march," but all turned out well.

It was noted that steamers in Wolfeboro Bay for the occasion included the *Spartan, Greyhound, Lynn, Spray, Belknap, Waterwitch, Irene, Queen, Scud, Mohawk, Iroquois, Farmington, Paugus, Rochester, Brookline, Waveland,*[24] *Eudora,* and *Della Osburn,* accompanied by 10 launches of unknown names and 53 rowboats.

At night high on Martin's Hill, Clow's huge bonfire reached to the sky and was reflected in the waters of nearby Lake Wentworth, while on another hill closer to town a 50-foot pyre gave it competition.

Alas for tradition the Old Home Week momentum that launched the twentieth century was not to be a permanent festival. In the next year, 1902, there was no celebration although many people were eager to have one.[25] In 1903 things were better, and Tuesday, August 18, was selected as Old Home Day. The 1904 observance was skipped.

In 1905 Old Home Day took place on Tuesday, August 22. There was quite a bit of dissension surround-

The Hobbs-Is-Inn decorated with bunting and lanterns for a celebration at the turn of the century. The U.S. Post Office is on the site today. (Jeff Goodwin Collection)

The Sheridan House, owned and operated by W.E. Wiggin, as shown in a circa 1910 view. The structure stood where the Wolfeboro Marketplace was built in the 1980s.

Double team of horses pulling a wagon full of young girls in a parade in front of the Sheridan House.

Hobbs-Is-Inn as shown in a 1906 view by the Detroit Publishing Co. Earlier known as the Elmwood House (1874-1895) and the Wolfeboro Hotel (1895-1899) and then as the Hobbs-Is-Inn (1899-1909), the edifice was later named the Hotel Elmwood.

Lobby and registration desk of the Hobbs-Is-Inn, June 1903. On a rack against the left wall are railroad timetables. To the right of the clock on the wall, behind the desk, is a calendar from Thompson's Pharmacy showing the date June 1903. To the lower right is a public telephone. Frank P. Hobbs, local entrepreneur, owned the facility.

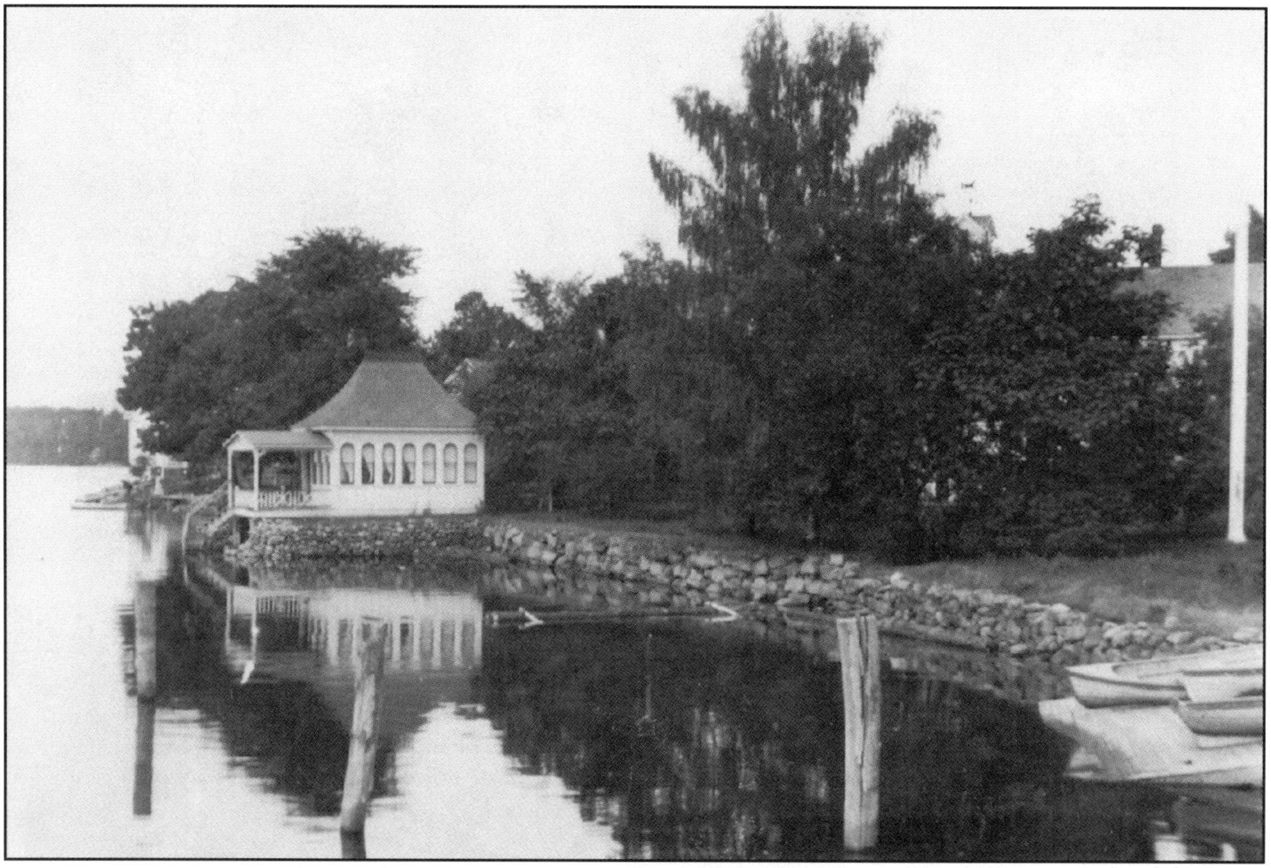

The Carroll Piper boathouse on Wolfeboro Bay, circa 1905. The rock retaining wall to the right is behind where the Yum Yum bakery and Yankee Pedlar real estate office are in the 1990s.

Photograph captioned "From G.B. Clark's House" with penned greetings and news from Greenleaf B. Clark sent on November 14, 1906, to Emma (Mrs. George A.) Carpenter at her Boston address. Clark says he looks forward to a ride with her next year, has unsuccessfully searched for three of his missing colts in the Huggins pasture, and that the snow measures nine inches on the ground. He closed with, "Mr. [Prof. E.H.] Terrill [of Brewster Free Academy] said there were 9 at J.W. Goodwin's rooms last Fri. to see to maintaining temperance. Love, Green."

ing the celebration, and planning for it did not begin until July. Apparently, everyone enjoyed watching the festivities, but few wanted to do the necessary work to make the Old Home Day celebration a reality. According to onlookers, Old Home Day 1905 was a non-event. This caused a visitor to write to the *Granite State News* complaining that he had traveled 125 miles expecting to enjoy a welcoming address, greetings, parades, clambakes, and other celebrations, but found only a band concert and ball game (with Camp Idlewild).

In 1913 it was voted to give long-unused, accumulated funds for Old Home Day to the Pine Hill Cemetery for use toward the construction of a receiving tomb.

## ASPECTS OF TOURISM

### On the Water

Recreational activities on lakes Wentworth and Winnipesaukee were popular subjects for local newspaper articles. A boom in cottage building occurred on Lake Wentworth, with Sherman D. Brummitt, J. Frank Goodwin, and others erecting camps along the shore and on islands. The Loon Island House furnished a popular destination for boating parties and served meals and drinks.

The following account from the *Granite State News*, June 10, 1905, discusses the expansion of boating:

> The fleets upon New Hampshire's lakes will be larger in number and more varied in character this summer than ever before. The comparatively new motorboats [powered by small gasoline engines] will add greatly to the variety, while other accessions range from large passenger steamers down through every variety of craft. In a few weeks the *Mount Washington* will begin her season's work under Captain Wentworth's direction.
>
> Among the powerboats on Lake Winnipesaukee is the *Scamp*, owned by A.H. Whitney of Newton, Mass., who has a fine summer residence on Pine Island, Lake Winnipesaukee. The new craft was built by Lawley of Boston, is 75 feet long and equipped with 25 h.p. Buffalo engines. Fourteen large new pleasure craft are to be launched on Lake Winnipesaukee this season, some of them quite elegant yachts. Mr. Goodrich, who has a summer place near Centre Harbor, expects to have the fastest power boat on the lake this season and will soon launch a boat which is calculated to make 22 miles an hour, or fast enough to run around the *Mount Washington* or in fact, anything else on the lake. Congressman Powers of Massachusetts will also have a new boat, a 40-foot cabin launch of 40 h.p. capable of attaining a speed of 18 miles an hour.

Unlike the situation a decade earlier, by 1910 pleasure boating was now a widespread popular sport on the lake due in large part to the availability of inexpensive engines which could be fitted to just about any medium-sized boat. Powered by gasoline, they were cheaper to buy and less expensive to operate than the turn-of-the-century steam launches, although the latter were still used by those who could afford them.

### Enjoying the Out-of-Doors

In season, adults and children enjoyed berry picking. Out-of-town tourists from Boston and other cities enjoyed this pursuit as well and were also entertained by activities that were more mundane to the locals, such as watching hay being cut, cows being milked, and other aspects of farm life. Historian Robert F.W. Meader told of a city-bred lady who visited his family's boarding house around the turn of the century, watched a bull in action in the pasture behind the house, and referred to the animal as a "gentleman cow."

Happiness for a young boy or girl could be something as simple as walking across a sunny hillside field with a pet dog, or skipping rocks across the mirror surface of a small pond, or trying to catch a chipmunk.

### Naming the Camp

The decade of 1901-1910 was one of great expansion in the number of private summer camps located in the town of Wolfeboro, especially on the shores of lakes Wentworth and Winnipesaukee. More likely than not, the owner was from Massachusetts or New York and used the lakeside retreat as a place to get away from the rigors of city life. Although summer residents were tourists in one sense, they were also a permanent and vital part of the community in that the taxes they paid helped to fund Wolfeboro services and activities year-round.

It was a common practice for seasonal visitors to name their summer camps, a tradition which started toward the end of the preceding century. Some of these appellations survive today, an example being Wiscasset on Sewall Road. Not everyone wanted to name his or her camp, and others were slow in doing so. For example, Henry W. Greer's summer refuge was marked as "Camp unnamed" in the 1907 town directory. However, he was in the minority.

The same directory offered the following camp names (partial list). Commentary has been added by the author:

**Allherne:** Pleasant Valley. Allherne, the summer residence of Judge Robert F. Tilney, received its name as after construction it was presented in its entirety to Mrs. Tilney and was therefore "All Her'n." In 1907 Judge Tilney, brother of Albert A. Tilney (who owned the Pioneer camp), lived in Brooklyn, NY. The camp was demolished in 1922 to make way for scenic planting.

**Almahton Lodge:** Sewall Road. George W. and Percy L. Moses, Brookline, MA. President of the First Ward National Bank, Boston, and electrical engineer respectively. The Moses camp was near the present-day Goodhue & Hawkins Navy Yard.

**Ari-Anna:** East Wolfeboro. E.H. Hall, Reading, MA. Principal of Allen Hall & Co., interior decorators, Boston.

**Beth-Shan:** On an unspecified Wentworth island. Rev. Sherman F. Ellis, Brockton, MA. Pastor, Methodist Episcopal Church. "Beth" means *house of* in Hebrew.

Exterior and interior of Laurallan, a summer camp on the Townsend Shore of Lake Wentworth owned by A.V. Healey of Plainfield, NJ, president of the Farmers Loan & Trust Company. The camp name was derived from his two sons, Laurence and Allan.

**Birch Camp:** Wentworth Park, Wolfeboro Center. Frank W. Rice, Portsmouth, NH. Retired merchant.

**Birches, The:** East Wolfeboro. Harriet S. and Caroline C. Hammond.

**Brewster's Rest:** Pleasant Valley. Henry D. Brewster, New York City. Employed with Brokaw Brothers, clothiers, 34 Astor Place, New York. Charles H. Stevens of Point Breeze also worked for Brokaw Brothers in the winter months.

**Burnbrae:** Pleasant Valley. John W. Murray, Plainfield, NJ. Retired.

**Camp Comfort:** Waveland (Keniston) Island. Lynn, MA.

**Camp Mayo:** East Wolfeboro. Harry A., Lawrence S., and Lawrence S. Mayo, Jr., all of Newton, MA, clerk, broker, and clerk respectively.

**Camp Narrowneath:** South Wolfeboro. Eben P. and Starr Parsons, Lynn, MA. The latter was a lawyer.

**Camp Roxbury:** Wolfeboro Neck. Charles F. Riley, Boston deputy sheriff.

**Camp Tudor:** Wolfeboro Neck. Charles F. and John G. Dolan, Boston. Counselors at law. William A. McDevitt, Jr., Boston deputy sheriff, also summered there.

**Camp Wollaston:** South Wolfeboro. Albert and Ernest Armstrong, Wollaston, MA. Bank clerks. Adelaide Armstrong of the same city also summered there.

**Camp Woodhaven:** Sewall Road. Granville and L.F. Hovey. Lowell, MA. Occupation of former unstated; latter retired. L.F., Jr., New York City, salesman, also summered there, as did M.M. Hovey of Nashua (occupation not given), and W.T. Hovey of San Francisco, bank clerk.

**Castle Constantine:** South Wolfeboro. George H. Swazey, Malden, MA. Electrical contractor.

**Cobham Hall:** Green Street. Mr. and Mrs. George A. and Mr. and Mrs. Ralph G. Carpenter, 636 Beacon Street, Boston. Note: This rambling wooden structure, begun in 1892, was far from being a "camp" and is now Bearce Hall of Brewster Academy.

**Eagle Camp:** East Wolfeboro. E.A. Robbins, Newton, MA. Bookkeeper.

**Edgemere:** Sewall Road. Fred C. Meacham, Brooklyn, NY. With the firm of L.L. Benedict & Co., bankers and brokers, 27 William Street, New York City.

**Edgewater:** Louis S. Clunet, Baltimore. Assistant auditor of the Consolidated Gas, Electric, Light & Power Co. of Baltimore.

**Eyrie:** Miss Lydia J. Cousins, Boston; Emily M. Meader, Boston.

**Fair View:** Pork Hill Road. Mr. and Mrs. C.A. Bachellor and their daughter, Isabel, of Boston, MA. Mr. Bachellor was listed as "proprietor of dyehouse."

**Ferncliffe:** Sewall Road. Col. Edward B. Dickinson, Brooklyn, NY. Official stenographer, Hall of Records, Brooklyn.

**Freba:** Keewaydin area of Winter Harbor. Frederick D. Barstow and Fannie Barstow, M.D., New York City.

**Great Pine, The:** East Wolfeboro. Cora L. Stebbens, Allegheny, PA.

**Hazelmere:** Andrew Schlehuber, Lynn, MA. Caterer.

**Hillside:** Wolfeboro Center. J. Henry and Albert F. Stevenson, East Boston. Mason-builder and student respectively.

**Interbetulas:** Waveland (Keniston Island). Fred A. and Carrie Broad, Lynn, MA. City claim agent. Miss Hattie S. Aymar also summered there.

**Kenniston:** Waveland (Keniston) Island. Benjamin, Daniel, Esmond, and Napoleon Crowley, all of Danvers, MA., along with Catherine (married) and Miss Gladys Crowley.

**Kittiewink:** Wentworth Park. E.L. Hall, Dorchester, MA. Representative for the National Blank Book Co., Boston.

**Lakeside Camp:** Wentworth Park, Wolfeboro Center. I.G., Lyman W., and Orwin Griffin, Portsmouth, NH. Postal clerk, druggist, and "collector" respectively.

**Lakeside:** Wolfeboro Neck. Stephen A. Potter, Providence, RI. Scannevin & Potter, electrical contractors.

**Laurallan:** Pleasant Valley. A.V. Healey, Plainfield, NJ. President, Farmers Loan & Trust Co., New York City. From the names of two of his sons, Laurence and Allan.

**Lynn Camp:** East Wolfeboro. James E. Jenkins, Lynn, MA. Cashier, Lynn National Bank. E. Thomas Mahoney, Salem, MA, clerk of the Middlesex Court, also summered there, as did Edwin J. Thompson, Lynn dentist. This camp was established in 1884. A century later the current owners published a booklet on its history (see Goldthwait listing in Bibliography).

**Mandalay:** Keewaydin camps. Dr. F.W. Halsey, Boston. Physician.

**Manhaut Lodge:** Elbridge S. Young, Lynn, MA. Grocer.

**Maple-hurst:** Wolfeboro Neck. Charles T. Glines, Providence, RI. Dealer in groceries and provisions.

**Milton's:** Sewall Road. E.T. Milton, Arlington Heights, MA. Representative for James A. McDougal & Co., Boston.

**Minnehaha:** Pleasant Valley. Joseph W. Sanford, Plainfield, NJ. President of Sanford Realty Co., New York City. His wife's first name was Minnie. The camp is said to have had one of the finest stone fireplaces in the state.

**Monhegan Lodge:** Harry Jones, Roxbury, MA. Daniel E. Page of Roxbury also summered there, as did F.B. Washburn, of Worcester, MA.

**Mount Vernon:** Mr. and Mrs. Ezra B. Baily, New York City. Principal of Baily, Green & Elger, importers.

**Onaway Camp:** Wentworth Park. Mr. and Mrs. John M. Bradford, Peabody, MA. Horse trainer. George A. Griffin of the same town, bookkeeper, also summered there, as did Bessie C. Allen of Salem, MA.

**Oswego:** Waveland (Keniston) Island. George B. Grant, Lynn, MA. Reporter. Allen G. Shepard, Lynn grocer, also summered here.

**Pine Camp:** Wentworth Park. John T. Folsom, Salem, MA. Elbridge T. Philbrook, of Portsmouth, NH, also summered there, as did Frank Pryor, Portsmouth, of Pryor & Matthews, dealers in hardware; and Frank A., Philip W., and Albert Vanderhoof, Concord, MA, the last-named a hardware dealer; and others

**Pine Needles:** East Wolfeboro. Mr. and Mrs. William T. Coppins, West Newton, MA. Clerk.

**Pioneer:** Pleasant Valley. Albert A. Tilney, Plainfield, NJ. With the firm of Harry Fish & Sons, bankers and brokers, New York City.

**Point Pleasant:** Triggs Island, Lake Wentworth. Rev. Francis H. Spear, Woonsocket, RI. Pastor of First Methodist Episcopal Church. Note: He literally spearheaded a movement of ministers to establish summer camps on and around Triggs Island.

**Pomeka Camp:** Wentworth Park. Mr. and Mrs. Fred B. Coleman, Portsmouth, NH. Druggist. Fred W. Coleman of the same city, a drug clerk, also summered there.

**Roxmere:** "Wentworth Island" (otherwise unidentified). Edward H. Walter, Lakewood, RI. Tool manufacturer. Note: Did "Roxmere" represent "rocks view"?

**Rusticana:** Keewaydin camps. Charles L. Edgar, Brookline, MA. President, Electric Illuminating Co., Boston. Leavitt L.

Exterior view of the summer lodge of Frank W. Rice, Birch Cottage (a.k.a. Birch Camp), on Lake Wentworth. Rice was a retired merchant from Portsmouth.

Interior of Joseph W. Sanford's "Minnehaha" summer home on Lake Wentworth off Pleasant Valley Road. The stone fireplace of this lodge was said to be one of the finest in New Hampshire. Lighting was by kerosene lamps and candles.

Maple-hurst, the summer camp of Providence, RI, grocer Charles T. Glines on Wolfeboro Neck. His launch *Alfarata* and a canoe are moored at the shore.

Busy times at the Lake Station at the Boston & Maine Railroad Wharf on Wolfeboro Bay. In the foreground is the front deck of the steamer *Mount Washington* with passengers and baggage, while waiting on land are dozens of tourists. Lake Station was a favorite departure point for campers going to Lake Winnipesaukee islands. (1906 photograph by the Detroit Publishing Co.)

Edgar of Brookline, student at Harvard, also summered there.

**Sunset Cottage:** Turtle Island, Lake Wentworth. George W. Ellis, Hamilton, MA. Shoe manufacturer.

**Sunset Lodge:** "Wentworth Island" (not otherwise identified). Rev. and Mrs. F.W. Coleman, Fall River, MA. Pastor, St. Paul's Methodist Church.

**Thrushland Camp:** Governor's Shore, East Wolfeboro. E.W. Otis, Needham, MA. Retired.

**Turtle Island Cottage:** Turtle Island, Lake Wentworth. R.F. Wiley, West Somerville, MA. Traveling salesman.

**Wabeek:** Triggs Island, Lake Wentworth. Harlie E. and Maude S. Buckey and their daughter Hazel M., Central Falls, RI. Clerk. John H. Buckey of the same town, clergyman, also summered there.

**Wastena:** Wentworth Park. W.A. Miller, West Somerville, MA. Candy manufacturer.

**Weironthemap:** Waveland (Keniston) Island. Fred C. and Fred H. Eastman, Swampscott, MA. The former was a student, the latter a civil engineer.

**Wentworth Lodge:** Wentworth Park. Carl DeWitt. Dover, NH. J.E. Everingham of Dover, a clergyman, also summered there, as did Joseph W. Coleman, a Portsmouth contractor.

**Wiscasset:** Sewall Road. This lakeside structure was home to Albert N. Keigwin, D.D., 139 West 103rd Street, New York City, pastor emeritus of the West Presbyterian Church, Wilmington, DE, and his son, A. Edwin Keigwin, D.D., same New York City address, pastor of the West End Presbyterian Church, New York City. Hugh Alexander, 166 West 105th Street, New York City. Private secretary to A. Edwin Keigwin, D.D.

As has been seen, the names run the gamut from descriptive to fanciful. No doubt, Birch Camp and The Birches both were nestled among white-bark trees, and Pine Camp, Great Pine, and Pine Needles each were beneath trees of the specified kind.

Apparently, some campers did not want to completely get away from it all and kept a tie with home by naming their places after the places from whence they came. Camp Wollaston was host to visitors from Wollaston, MA, while Lynn Camp was enjoyed by visitors from Lynn in the same state. Other towns are reflected in names such as Monhegan Lodge (Monhegan is an island off the Maine coast), Oswego (town in upstate New York), Roxbury (Massachusetts town near Boston), and Wiscasset (Maine coastal town). Mandalay evoked the mysterious, exotic Far East.

Somewhat lyrical is Ari-Anna, named for Abbie Anna Hall (Mrs. E.H. Hall) and her kid sister, Ari-Etta.[26] What can be said about Kittiewink other than it sounds cute?

Family names were an easy way for Henry D. Brewster to name Brewster's Rest; the members of the Mayo clan from Newton, MA, to name Camp Mayo; and E.T. Milton to create Milton's. More inventive was FREderick BArstow, who used letters of his name to create Freba.

One can presume that in 1907 Camp Comfort offered easy relaxation, Camp Woodhaven was a refuge in the forest, the Lakeside Camp was indeed a shorefront camp as was Edgewater, and that Weironthemap was truly to be found on a chart of some sort. Sunset Cottage and Sunset Lodge both may have faced to the west, and Hillside may have been built on an incline. Rusticana surely offered its inhabitants the opportunity to rusticate.

Seemingly the most pretentious of all was Castle Constantine. One can envision a huge, crenellated structure guarding South Wolfeboro against attack. Reality was probably quite different.

Sometimes it is nice to leave something to the imagination. And the coiners of the Interbetulas camp did exactly that. Who knows what it means? The "etulas" part is "salute" backwards. But, where to from here?

Successful businessmen and professionals constituted the main categories of summer camp owners. However, the typical visitor to Wolfeboro during 1907 had no such luxury as a cabin or house to come back to each summer. Rather, he or she was apt to rent a room or two in the Hobbs-Is-Inn, Sheridan House, or one of the many boarding houses in the area.

### Children's Camps

The first long-term summer camps for children were established in Wolfeboro in the 1901-1910 decade.[27] A group of girls from Massachusetts under the direction of Laura I. Mattoon began summer camping at Point Breeze Farm on Lake Wentworth in 1902 and in 1907 established Camp Kehonka on the lakefront just across the town border in East Alton. In the late 1920s additional facilities were acquired in Wolfeboro on what is now known as Kehonka Hill. In 1907 Camp Birchmont for girls began on Mount Delight on the shore of Lake Wentworth. Camp Wyanoke, established for boys by Walter Bentley on Wolfeboro Neck in 1909, was another early summer gathering spot. Founded in 1910, the Hill School Camp for boys is operating today as the co-educational Wolfeboro Camp School.

### The Postcard Craze

In the first decade of the present century, all of America was in a dither about picture postcards. Reflective of the passion, the *Granite State News* went into the postcard business and used its job press to print black and white scenes on stiff white paper stock. On June 20, 1903, the following editorial was published:

> Last year the summer people who visited Wolfeboro felt the need of some kind of an inexpensive souvenir that they could send to their friends, but were unable to secure a really desirable article at a low price. This fact set some of our townsmen thinking. The result is that the *News* has put on the market a line of souvenir postal cards, with views of Wolfeboro and vicinity thereon, at the low price of 3 cents each or two for five cents. They can be secured at the *News* office or the store of J.L. Young, who has the exclusive agency for them.

The same issue included this advertisement:

> Souvenir postal cards. Views of Wolfeboro Bay, South Main

Cobham Hall, George A. Carpenter's summer home at the end of Green Street. Turn of the century view. In the background is Wolfeboro Bay with Sewall Point visible to the left of the main house. Later, Cobham Hall was the year-round home of Ralph and Connie Carpenter. Today it is known as Bearce Hall on the campus of Brewster Academy.

George A. Carpenter seated on the left, holding a cane, and his family on the front porch of Cobham Hall. Turn of the century view. (Jeff Goodwin Collection)

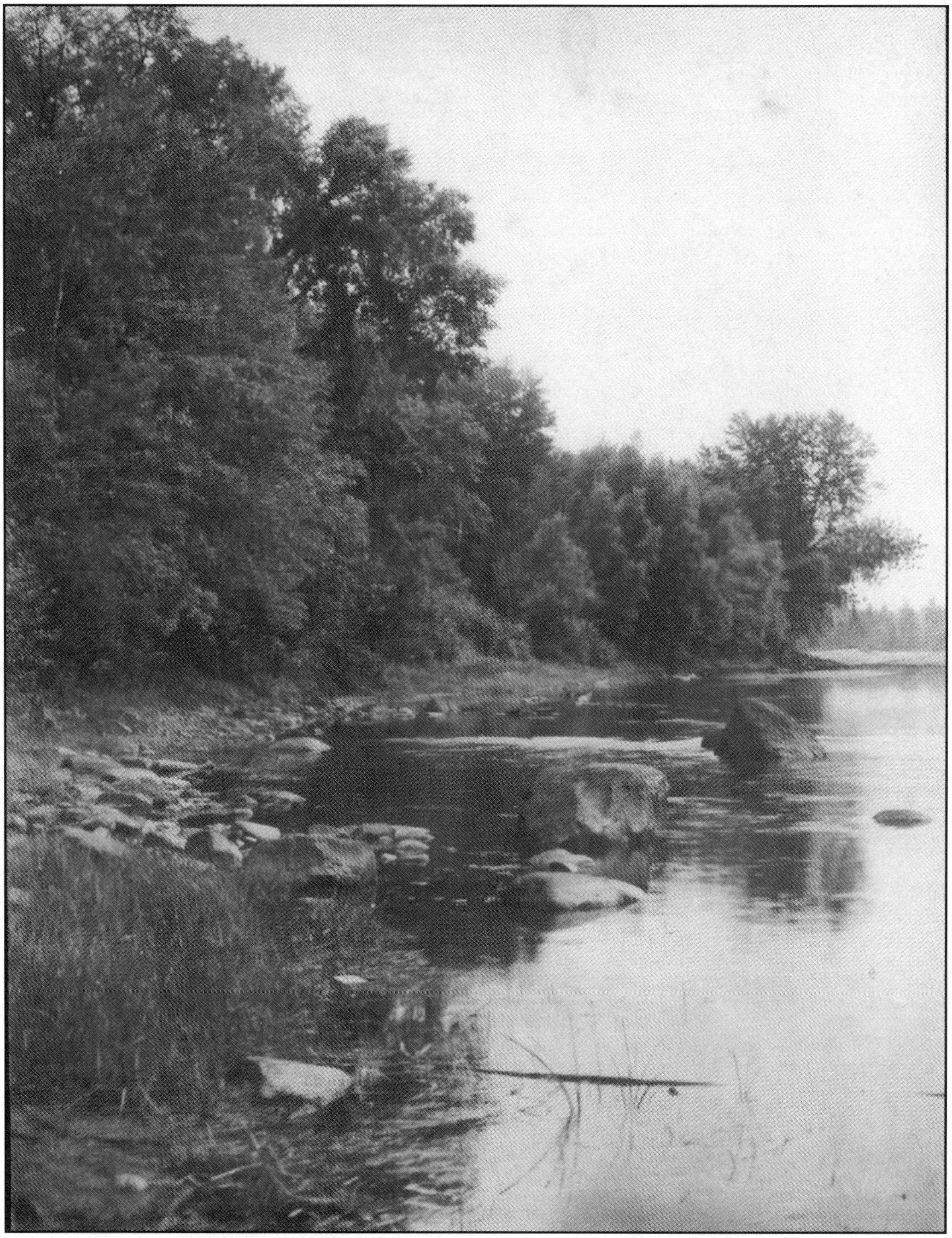

A local postcard in the making. Scenic snapshot taken during the early 1900s, retouched with oil paints at the center right to eliminate a bridge (the distant treescape at the far right is fictitious). This picture was taken to the order of Wolfeboro merchants Wallace & Rogers circa 1908 or later. There were no bridges near the lake shore in any forested area of Wolfeboro. Thus, the location may have been elsewhere, but *near* Wolfeboro (see next page).

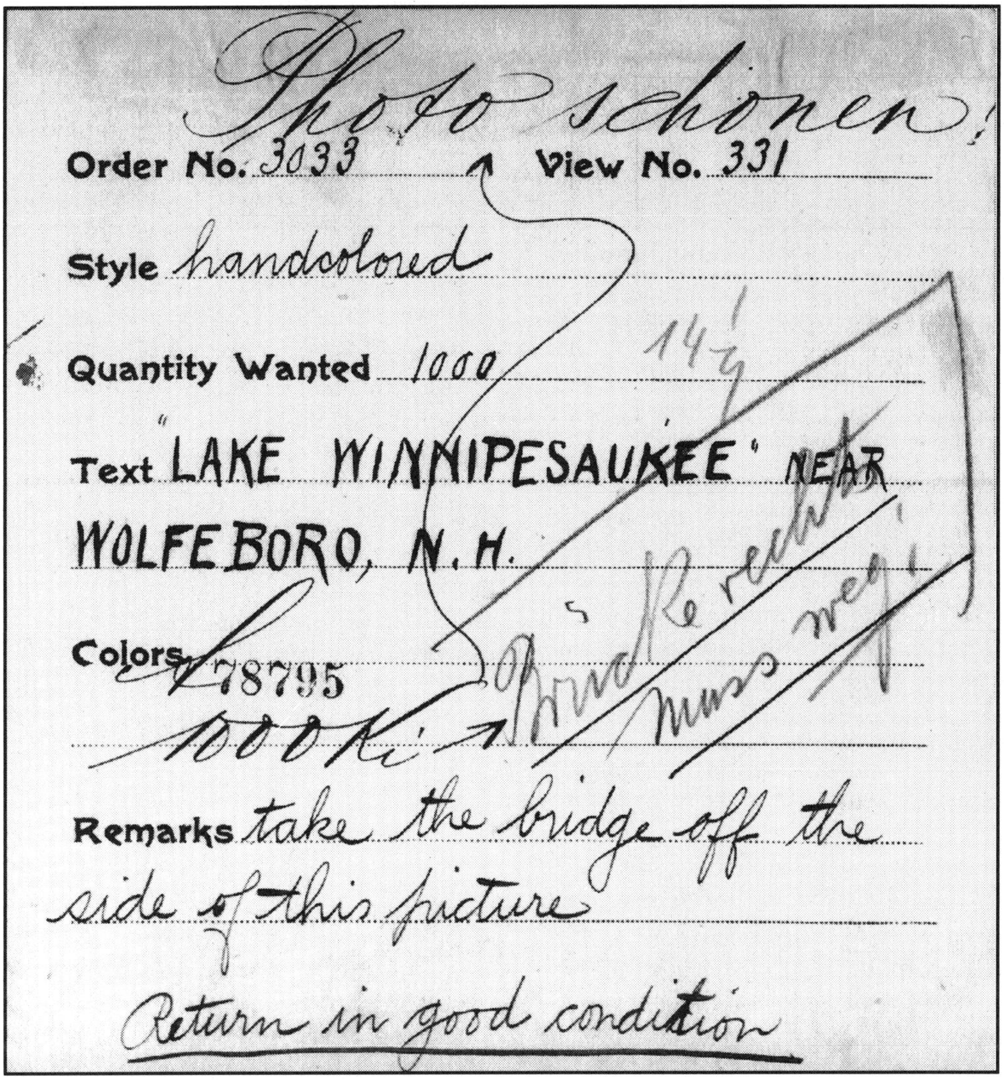
Photo schonen!

Order No. 3033 View No. 331

Style handcolored

Quantity Wanted 1000

Text "LAKE WINNIPESAUKEE" NEAR WOLFEBORO, N.H.

Colors 78795

1000 Ki

Brucke rechts muss weg!

Remarks take the bridge off the side of this picture

Return in good condition

Label from the back of the photograph on the facing page. The label was filled out and sent to a German maker of cards. The recipient has written in ink at the top, *Photo schonen!* (Beautiful photograph!). This is order No. 3033, View No. 331, ordered in a quantity of 1,000 hand-colored cards to have the inscription, "Lake Winnipesaukee near Wolfeboro, N.H." Wallace & Rogers gave these instructions: "Take the bridge off the side of this picture. Return in good condition."

Street, steamer *Mount Washington,* and Brewster Free Academy, on private mailing cards, just the thing to mail to your friends. On sale at J.L. Young's store or the *News* office. 2 for 5 cents.

This was followed the next week by this note: "'Just what we wanted' is the comment about the souvenir mailing cards. Two new ones out this week, Glen Cottage and Smith's River." Other local subjects included Wolfeboro Bay, Brewster Academy, Lake Winnipesaukee, Upper Smith's River, and multiple views of the Old Brick School House.

On September 5, 1903, the newspaper published this:

The souvenir postals put on the market this spring have had such a good sale that the series will be materially enlarged next year by the addition of several new views. One store sold as many as 866 in one month, which is quite a record.

In a notice dated June 15, 1905, these were offered: "Colored postal cards of Wolfeboro, N.H., and Lake Winnipesaukee, set of 12, 25 cents at J.L. Young's souvenir store, Railroad Avenue." Unlike the issues of 1903, these were printed in Germany. So far as is known, the *Granite State News* printed only black and white views.

On June 24, 1905, a competitor made this offer:

Come in and see our handsome new line of souvenir postals. 38 views of Wolfeboro and Lake Winnipesaukee on postal cards, 60¢ a set. Postal card album, holds 100 cards, cover in colors, price 25¢. Album and complete set of our postals, only 75¢. The Paper Store

In 1905 George H. Mason's variety store in the Central Block offered a selection of Wolfeboro views on finely printed postcards published in England by Raphael Tuck. From this point on, there was a rash of local scenes mostly published in Germany by color lithography. In addition, the Detroit Publishing Company issued color-tinted views of the town.

The summer of 1905 saw tourists sending record numbers of postcards, each of which required a one-cent stamp. On a typical August in the early 1900s the Wolfeboro Post Office sold 2,500 stamps of this denomination, but in August 1905 the quantity jumped more than five-fold to a record 13,500.

In July 1906 J.L. Young advertised: "Postcards. 10 subjects of local views in colors."

While the vast majority of Wolfeboro postcards of the era were printed on presses, many photographic cards were issued as well. In 1908 the destruction of the new one-story commercial building on South Main Street furnished the occasion for Young to issue a series of such cards, advertised as follows on November 7:

Ruins of the fire! Six postcard views of the destructive effects of October 13, which destroyed Goodwin's Block and the entire stock of its occupants: complete set 50¢; 1—Front view. Goodwin's Block. 2—Interior (front view) C.H. Johnson's; 3—Interior—(back view) C.H. Johnson's; 4—Interior view (front). S.A. Edgerly's; 5—Interior view (front) S.P. Morrill's; 6—Interior view (front) J.W. Robins. Orders promptly filled. Samples on exhibition.

In 1909 Walter G. Colbath manufactured over 14,500 photographic postcards at his studio on the corner of Glendon and Depot Streets. Probably more than 200,000 printed postcards of Wolfeboro scenes were sold by local merchants that year.

The January 2, 1909 issue of the *Granite State News* carried this item:

"Wolfeboro of the Future" is having a great run at the store of J.L. Young. This is a postal showing the town's condition 50 years hence, with its elevated to Wolfeboro Falls, surface line to Pleasant Valley, subway to Goose Corner, automatic parcel delivery tube, etc. They are cute and very taking.[28]

For the 10-year period beginning in 1903, postcards were a form of mass communication, and the scenic virtues of Wolfeboro and vicinity were made known to recipients of mail all over the United States, indeed the world. The favorite local topics for depiction were the new Brewster Academy building (completed in 1905), Brewster Memorial Hall (Town Hall), the steamer *Mount Washington,* the Hobbs-Is-Inn (but not the Sheridan House), panoramic views of Wolfeboro Bay, and the downtown business district including the Peavey Block.

## TRANSPORTATION

### The Railroad

Citizens of Wolfeboro had a love-hate relationship with the Boston & Maine Railroad. On one hand, the railroad, which also owned the steamer *Mount Washington,* was the primary deliverer of tourists to local hotels and boarding houses and conveyor of local products including excelsior, lumber, farm produce, and blocks of ice to distant markets.

On the other hand, the Boston & Maine set its schedules and rates without either the advice or consent of its customers. Regarding this "taxation without representation," the *Granite State News,* March 17, 1906, commented:

Beginning April 1 the railroads are to advance the freight rate on ice 25 cents per ton, which is practically equivalent to five dollars a car. This may seem a small matter, but it means a great deal to such a town as Wolfeboro, where the ice industry might be carried on extensively if this prohibitive rate was not exacted. While the 25 cents per ton applies to all [local] stations, it must be borne in mind that the rate from Wolfeboro is 25 cents above the established rate elsewhere.... Today our town in groaning under a debt contracted in bygone days so that we might have railroad facilities and all advantages that other places are entitled to on the line of its road, and for such gave to the railroad $35,000, which now shows it gratitude by discriminating in freight rates....

The editorial went on to say that the railroad was doing "what it can to injure our national industries."

During the decade 1901-1910, most mentions of the local rail line were simply news items. Samples:

1901, October 1, 1901: As of this date 6,515 pieces of baggage had been received at the railroad station during the

The S.W. Clow & Co. sawmill as seen in a circa 1909 view across Back Bay. Except for a small passageway kept open for boats, the bay was clogged with logs. For many years the Clow mill dumped sawdust and other refuse into Back Bay, much of which remains on the bottom of the bay today.

"Wolfboro, N.H., in the Future," a fanciful postcard published by J.L. Young in 1909 and sold widely at the time. This was the era in which electric trolleys and interurban railways were becoming very popular in America. However, tracks such as shown here never ran down North and South Main Streets. Note the bird-winged aircraft perched on top of the Peavey Block and marked "Waveland," a name for Keniston Island at the time.

The Wolfeborough Railroad Station circa 1910 was a busy place with passenger coaches and freight cars arriving and departing daily.

Locals pose as a photographer records on film the Boston & Maine Railroad Station at Wolfeboro Falls. Although it was just 6/10ths of a mile east of the Wolfeborough Railroad Station, the little depot had a full crew. (Collection of the Remember the Iron Horse Museum)

preceding nine months, an increase of 488 from the year before.

1903, October 10: "The mile posts on the Boston & Maine Railroad have been repainted, the markings changed, the posts being numbered from Boston instead of from Sanbornville. The one in town now reads 'B. 109.'"

1903, November 14: "The B&M Depot has been painted a bright green this week by the railroad painters."

1905, August 12: Report that over 5,000 patrons had arrived so far during the summer at the Railroad Station.

The Boston & Maine Railroad owned the best-known ship on Lake Winnipesaukee, the *Mount Washington*. On July 11, 1903, she was in a contest with the *Gilnockie* owned by Mrs. George Armstrong, who with her husband lived on a 500-acre spread on Moultonboro Neck. This account was published in the *Granite State News*:[29]

> Saturday afternoon there was a race between the steamers *Mount Washington* and *Gilnockie*, in which the *Gilnockie* had the best of the race. The steamers started from Centre Harbor and raced to Wolfeboro. At the start the *Mount* got by the *Gilnockie* about two lengths, on account of the fires on the latter boat burning hard coal. In short time the *Gilnockie* began to gain on the *Mount* as the engineer, Nathaniel Goodhue, pushed things for all they were worth. The *Mount* was passed somewhere up the lake, and the *Gilnockie* came into the bay about a quarter of a mile ahead. Captain John Goodhue was pilot, and Mrs. Armstrong and her son and daughter and some friends were on board to enjoy the defeat of the *Mount Washington*. A very large crowd gathered at the wharf, and in a very short time many were the congratulations and praises showered upon Captain John and Nat. This was the first time that the *Mount Washington* was ever beaten.

As an owner of both land and lake transportation, the Boston & Maine Railroad was the most active promoter of tourism to Wolfeboro and the Lake Winnipesaukee area in the early twentieth century. A brochure, *Vacation Days in Southern New Hampshire*, issued in 1907 noted that a delightful train trip could be made from Massachusetts north to New Hampshire through Manchester, Hooksett, Concord, Tilton, and Laconia. Wolfeboro could be reached by disembarking at The Weirs and boarding the steamer *Mount Washington*.

For those who wanted to come by land, this Boston & Maine Railroad schedule was in effect from August 5, 1908, through the winter:

> Trains left Wolfeboro at 6:10 a.m., 8:30 a.m., and 4:00 p.m. daily except Sunday for Sanbornville, Rochester, Somersworth, Portsmouth, Newburyport, Salem, Lynn, and Boston. Trains arrived in Boston at 10:07 a.m., 12:40 p.m. and 7:55 p.m.
>
> Trains left Boston for Wolfeboro by the Eastern Division at 7:30 a.m., 12:30 and 3:30 p.m., and by the Western Division at 8:45 a.m., 11:15 and 4:30 p.m. connecting at Rochester. Arrived at Wolfeboro at 12:28, 5:05 and 7:45 p.m.

Thus, a trip by rail from Wolfeboro to Boston took about four hours. The fastest return trip, the 4:30 p.m. train out of Boston, took three hours and 15 minutes.

### Automobiles

1901-1910 was the decade of the automobile. At the beginning of the era, the horse was the primary means of local transportation. By the end of the decade, motorized vehicles were familiar sights on local roads, although horses remained in everyday use.

It is not known who owned the first "horseless carriage" in Wolfeboro. In the *Granite State News*, October 21, 1897, is what may be the earliest local account:

> Saturday a steam carriage passed through the streets of our village, the first ever seen on our streets. It was the property of and made by Mr. George Whitney, of Boston, who will be remembered as the gentleman who built the steamer *Mohawk* and chime whistle for Dr. Libby. Mr. Whitney is stopping with Mr. Libby. He made the trip from Boston with his carriage in nine hours.[30]

However, the Libby intended as driver was John H. Libby, brother of Dr. Henry F. Libby (who owned the *Mohawk*).[31]

Automobiles were still a novelty a year later as evidenced by this clipping dated September 13, 1898:

> South Wolfeboro. Quite a crowd was seen on the square last Sunday. The attraction was a "horseless carriage."

When Florence Paine was researching the subject circa 1960, it was suggested to her that honors for the first car ownership in Wolfeboro went to Dr. Henry F. Libby (later of Libby Museum fame), or per another recollection, to Parry T. Hersey. Still another historian stated that Harry E. Libby (of laundry renown) had the first car. In 1901 the *Granite State News* reported that Harry Bickford possessed a runabout. By 1903 at least 15 automobiles were owned locally.[32]

Sorting out the above, it seems likely that John H. Libby may have *driven* the first car locally, but who *owned* the first car in town is not known today.

Selected clippings from the local paper give first-hand impressions of the effect that automobiles had on the town:

1902, September 27: "The gasoline automobile from Boston attracted considerable attention Wednesday and Thursday. Wednesday evening, while standing in front of the store of W.H. Swett, one of the men tried to light the acetylene headlight on the machine, and the water that makes the gas failing to flow freely, he deliberately spit into the cylinder and thus got the gas to generating, much to the amusement of the spectators."[33]

1903, May 9: "An automobile in town this week caused a number of horses to feel quite frisky. We understand that Nathaniel Brewster's horse ran away and that not much was left of the buggy. Another horse attempted to climb a stone wall in posthaste, and even old Ned, usually sedate, concluded it was a fine chance to get his name in the *Granite State News* and accordingly did his best to attract attention."

1903, May 16: "George W. Jepson and family [summer visitors], and Walter Furber, made a trip to Boston in an automobile Monday. They made the trip of 107 miles in 61/2 hours."

1903, May 23: "Blake Folsom is sporting a handsome roadster which he has recently purchased."

1903, May 30: "There were three automobiles in town over Sunday. Two of them were gasoline machines and very pretty running. They had come a long distance and stopped here to rest and clean the mechanism."

1903, July 11: "The supply of gasoline in town has been inadequate to supply the demand some days, lately. Two automobiles were in town over Sunday. Some of the horses of dignified age resent the arrival of modern conveyances."

1904, May 7: Mabel E. Fullerton's "Goose Corner" column: "We [at Goose Corner] claim the honor of having the first automobile in town for the season of 1904. Henry Libby arrived with a steam Locomobile Tuesday afternoon. In it he traveled the whole distance from Bridgeport, Connecticut, where the Locomobiles are manufactured, without a single mishap and over the very heavy roads caused by last week's rain."

1904, June 4: "A large automobile touring car passed through town Saturday afternoon. It was the property of Charles L. Edgar of Keewaydin Camps."

1904, June 11: "W.H. Swett is in the gasoline business for good, and with four or five autos to draw on him regularly, and any number of boats coming in, has quite a little to do drawing and delivering it."

By 1905 there were at least two local automobile "agencies." However, the term *agency* was not well defined. In several instances, Wolfeboro residents went to Boston or another metropolitan area, bought a car for their own use, returned with it to Wolfeboro, showed it to their friends, and announced they were taking orders for similar vehicles. Certain Crestmobile, Cadillac, Reo, and Rambler vehicles were sold this way. It would be a number of years before a traditional dealership with an inventory of cars on display would be set up in town.

More *Granite State News* clippings:

1905, May 20: "It looks now as if there are to be quite a lot of automobiles stopping in town this summer, so see that your horse gets accustomed to them."

1905, June 10: "Almon W. Eaton has been driving around the village this week in his brand new White steam touring car, undoubtedly the best car owned by any of the Wolfeboro automobilists."

1905, July 8: "The speed limit seems to be strained a little by our autoists, which is attracting some attention and comment.... Speed limits are as follows: No automobile or motorcycle should be operated...in the compactly built sections of city or town at a speed greater than eight miles an hour."

1905, September 16: "Percy Moses made a trip around Lake Winnipesaukee Thursday in an automobile. He reports a very enjoyable time and says the scenery is magnificent."

After about 1905 automobiles ceased being a novelty, but reports of them continued to appear regularly in the newspaper. Judging from advertising commentaries, the Buick may have been the most popular local model in the years just prior to 1910.

The automobile was a boon to local tourism. In the decade previous to the coming of gasoline-powered vehicles, nearly all tourists and boarders arrived by train with a lesser number coming across Lake Winnipesaukee by steamer. Travelers to the town were hampered by having to carry luggage aboard the train and were subject to the railroad timetables. In addition, transportation had to be arranged from the train station or steamer dock to a lodging place. The automobile permitted travelers to leave Boston, Providence, or other home city at any hour, stop at will along the way, arrive in town whenever they pleased, and park right at the front door of their destinations. Still, there were no gasoline stations. In 1905 one had to buy fuel at a hardware store.

By the same year, most "men about town" either owned an automobile or were seriously considering buying one. George A. Carpenter, summer occupant of Cobham Hall at the end of Green Street and Wolfeboro's wealthiest summer resident, had "a whole outfit of several automobiles" in which he could take his family and guests on excursions around town, including to baseball games.[34]

By 1906 automobiles were commonplace, and there was a competition among brands for price, endurance, and speed. The local paper commented on June 16:

> W.S. Lord, agent for the Reo car, is wearing a satisfied smile nowadays, as all of the Reo cars owned in town have climbed the Brickyard Hill lately in the high gear, something that various people have said was impossible for a car of their size. Dr. Tobey, who recently purchased a car, ran his up over the hill in high before he had it two hours, and Mr. Lord ran up twice in succession one day.[35]

About 3,000 New Hampshire residents owned automobiles in 1909. At least a few hundred were seen in and around the Lakes Region. For the area's businesses, automobiles were a godsend. No longer was it necessary to be within easy reach of a railroad station or stage line. Now inns and hotels could be located just about anywhere served by roads.

### Aircraft

Following the Wright brothers' powered flight at Kitty Hawk, NC, in 1903, America became interested in aircraft. However, it would be many years until aviation had a direct impact upon Wolfeboro.

On July 25, 1910, this item was in the local paper:

> Some of our townsmen report seeing an airship pass over Lake Wentworth Thursday night. They feel confident it was none other than Warren Canney's of this town.

In 1910 there were several other mentions in the *Granite State News* of heavier-than-air craft, but none had landed in Wolfeboro.

### Roads

The condition and appearance of town roads, docks, and other facilities of transportation were of public concern and mentioned often in the local press. This comment about Forest Road appeared June 22, 1901:

> One thing is very essential and that is a better means for reaching Camp Ossipee by land. The accommodations are something terrible and a disgrace to a town which is sup-

posed to be catering for summer residents. They don't ask for macadam road, but they certainly are entitled to a passable one.

The road linking Wolfeboro and Tuftonboro was one of the most intensely used in the area. In the spring months in particular the thoroughfare was often muddy, especially in low areas, and rutted wherever there was a slope. In 1906 the selectmen of Wolfeboro debated whether the road should be covered with gravel at a cost of $2,000 per mile, or paved with macadam for twice that price. "Macadam road is admitted the best but not considered by some as a practical proposition for the entire town," an editorial in the *Granite State News,* July 14, 1906, noted. It was many years before it was paved.

In the meantime the wretched condition of the Shields' Hill section of the road between downtown Wolfeboro and Tuftonboro was a frequent subject of discussion by Mabel Fullerton in her "Goose Corner" column. The loose rocks, sand, and other impediments to horse and automobile travel were ignored by the town. In 1907 Blake Folsom personally contributed $1,000 to have the necessary repairs made to this small stretch.

Sewall Street along Wolfeboro Bay was primitive and rutted. Anyone wanting to go to Ferncliffe or one or another of the summer lodges encountered mud (in season), rocks, and tree roots.

The warrant for the town meeting of 1906 contained a provision to replace the wooden bridge on Main Street with a steel one, following years of complaints about the old structure. In due course a new span was built.

The first substantial piece of self-powered road equipment acquired by the town of Wolfeboro was discussed in the *Granite State News* on May 30, 1908:

> The Buffalo-Pitts steam roller which arrived last week has been tested this week on the piece of state road above the village to the apparent satisfaction of the committee chosen to purchase a steam roller for our town.

### Docks

In 1906 the lack of suitable wharfage at the Town Docks caused many complaints. Of all Wolfeboro transportation problems, this is one that never to this day has been resolved to the satisfaction of everyone. It seems that as more docks are built, more boats arrive to fill them, in a never-ending cycle. Until 1906 docks were privately owned by the Boston & Maine Railroad, the Concord & Montreal Railroad, lakefront hotels (such as the Belvue House), and residents with shore frontage. There was no town-owned facility. "This is a matter that our Board of Trade should look into and give its influence in securing prompt action," an article in the *Granite State News* suggested on March 3, 1906.

Frank P. Hobbs, manager of the Belvue House hotel which owned the shorefront of what today is Cate Park, advised the public that boats could dock at his landing, but that stays there should be brief so that all could be accommodated.

## NATURAL PHENOMENA

### Weather Conditions

On Sunday, March 1, 1903, an unusual sight greeted residents along the Winnipesaukee shore. It had rained extensively, and so much water had accumulated on top of the lake ice, that winds whipped up whitecaps on The Broads off Wolfeboro Neck.[36]

In the winter of 1906-1907 the expansion of lake ice caused great destruction to docks. In April 1908 high winds racing along Winnipesaukee caused ice chunks, many of them quite large, to pile up as high as 10 to 12 feet on some unprotected areas of the shore, causing much damage to waterfront structures.

The summer of 1909 was dry, creating hazardous fire conditions. The water level of Lake Winnipesaukee was so low that near the far end of the lake the wreck of the old steamer *Belknap* was exposed. It was also reported that the water on Lake Wentworth was at the lowest autumn level in many years. Despite the drought, it was anticipated that the local corn crop would be the largest ever, due to more acreage being placed into use.

1910 was another year of insufficient rainfall. During the summer months the roads became very dry and dusty. In the downtown Wolfeboro area, a group of merchants and public-minded citizens put up their own funds to acquire a horse-drawn water tank and sprinkler that spread about 20,000 gallons of water daily over the main traveled thoroughfares. On October 22, the local paper reported: "The water in our lake is extremely low, absolutely stopping navigation on the bay and also obliging one of the Clow mills to suspend business. It is the lowest ever."

### The Great Comet

The once-every-76-years arrival of Halley's Comet in early 1910 was the cause for intense local interest. On April 9, 1910, this question appeared in the local paper: "Have you seen Halley's Comet? Don't fail to get up early and see it."

The opportunity to view the celestial apparition lingered on. A Saturday, May 7, 1910, column about doings in Wolfeboro Falls noted:

> Several of our people felt rewarded for their early rising Friday morning as they had a fine view of Halley's Comet. It was clearly visible at 2:50.

### Tornado!

On September 24, 1910, between two and three in the afternoon, a tornado ripped through Wolfeboro and

Damage from the tornado of September 24, 1910: At the Hooper homestead an outbuilding is turned on its side, and wreckage is strewn about.

At the McDonald home on North Main Street structures behind the residence have been reduced to flinders.

Turn of the century view taken from Hobbs-Is-Inn looking to the northwest. In the foreground is Back Bay with the Wolfeborough Railroad Station spire at lower right. On the other side of the water is the steam-powered mill of S.W. Clow & Co. with its large stockpile of lumber.

North Main Street looking northwest from a vantage point a few hundred yards past Forest Road. In the distance on the left is the homestead on the fifth lot of the original seven farms established in Wolfeboro in the eighteenth century.

caused much damage, particularly to farm buildings and crops. The loss was estimated at $25,000 to $35,000.

The twister touched down in the southwestern section of town near Goose Corner. In that district the violent wind damaged several homes and other buildings and destroyed many trees including 200 in Arthur Blake's maple sugar grove. The George Folsom farm and residence, adjacent to the Blake place, had all the chimneys of the house destroyed and much roof damage done, a large flock of hens killed, and an apple orchard ruined. From there the tornado went in more or less a straight line cutting a swath a half-mile wide to the shore of Lake Wentworth at the Clay Pit bridge.

In the Lake View Cemetery on North Main Street, nearly all the trees were uprooted and much damage was done to monuments and headstones. The *Granite State News* reported:

> Everything that stood in its path was removed, without form and little ceremony, and all done within the space of two minutes' time or less. There was no time for planning or escape. You could hear its roar, see it coming, and feel its power, and then all was over. Roads were blockaded by massive trees and treetops, travel suspended, telephone poles and tangled wires down, communications with the inner and outer world stopped, electric light put off commission for several days.

## NOTABLE FIRES

### Fire Fighting

The volunteer corps of Wolfeboro fire fighters were located at several stations and served various districts. The local firemen relied upon hand-pumped "tubs" and water under pressure from municipal fire hydrants.

As of February 15, 1901, the fire companies in Wolfeboro were as follows: Pequawket Hook and Ladder Co. No. 1, Rollins Hose Co. No 1, A.W. Wiggin Hose Co. No. 2, Eagle Hose Co. No. 3, and Monitor Hose Co. No. 1.

During the decade 1901-1910 the following notable fires were reported. In addition, there were numerous brush fires, chimney fires, and other small blazes.

**1901, January 27. Charles Stevens building:**[37] Pleasant Valley. Damaged by fire. Loss: $400.

**1901, February 2. Isaac Allbee house:** Pleasant Valley. Loss: $2,000.

**1901, April 16. Church:** South Wolfeboro. Damaged by fire, caused by burning brush.

**1902, January 24. H.B. Furber's slaughterhouse:** On the shore of Crescent Lake. Burned.

**1902, September 30. Samuel A. Meader barn:** North Main Street. Barn, shed, ice house, hen house, grain, and tools were destroyed. Barn included a bowling alley in the loft, a full crop of dried oats, the autumn crop of potatoes, and two fine carriages. A tramp may have set it. Among the firefighters were Brewster students who worked a bucket brigade.

**1902, October 15. Granville grist mill:** At the foot of Glendon Street on ground leased from the Boston & Maine Railroad. The loss also included a fine pair of horses, a carload of corn, and other property. A freight car on the track was also destroyed. Loss: $3,500.

**1903, May 3. James M. Cate barn:** Pleasant Valley. Loss: $600.

**1903, first week in June. Forest fires:** Several raged in the area.

**1903, October 7. Roswell buildings:**[38] "Our little village [North Wolfeboro] was badly frightened by the fire which occurred at James Roswell's at about 3:00 one morning last week. The house and barn were saved, but the other buildings were burned to the ground. It is doubtful if either the house or barn could have been saved had there been any wind, because all the water had to be carried from Sherburne's well." (In the 1990s the Berkowitz family lived there.)

**November 2, 1903. Brewster Academy:** The most serious fire of the decade was discovered at 3:40 a.m. in the Brewster Academy building off South Main Street. *The News* reported: "The building was a brick structure. The fire was wholly confined to the interior, which was a mass of flames when discovered.... By 5:00 the cruel flames had accomplished their work and reduced to a heap of ruins a building which was the pride of the village." The loss was estimated at $45,000, of which about $30,000 was covered by insurance. Principal Edwin H. Lord took the first train to Boston to consult with the Academy trustees and to obtain books and other supplies. Classes were transferred to temporary quarters in the Town Hall, and not a single session was missed.

**1903, July 23. Melvin O. Morgan house and barn:**[39] Pine Street.

**1904, October 2. Central Block:** On Railroad Avenue, owned by Joseph Goodwin and Greenleaf B. Clark. By the time firemen arrived the rooms of the K.N.H. and insurance broker Charles F. Parker were in flames, and fire was reaching into the Odd Fellows Hall on the third floor. The flames seemed to be extinguished, but later the blaze flared up again at the eaves of the building. There was extensive damage to the interior, not only of the upstairs rooms, but by water on the ground floor to the vacant store earlier occupied by Almon W. Eaton and to the Crockery Department of George H. Mason's variety store.

**1904, November 1. Addison Getchell building:** South Main Street.

**1905, September 11. William Thompson house:** In Harmony Grove. Destroyed in a blaze believed to have originated with an overturned or exploding kerosene stove. He and an overnight visitor, Mrs. Lydia A. Perkins, were killed. Thompson, a bachelor, was 59, and Perkins, twice married and the mother of three children, was 49. Loss: $300.

**1905, November 8. Wiggin house:** Pleasant Street. Occupied by Albert W. Wiggin and his daughter-in-law Mary Wiggin. Loss: $2,500.

**1906, January 14. Hersey Brothers' mill:** Planing mill caught fire.

**1906, January 30. O.P. Berry excelsior mill:** The roof of this mill in Wolfeboro Falls caught fire. Firemen were on the scene promptly, and damage, estimated at $3,000, was confined to the roof and water damage to the interior.

**1906, January 30. Cate Block:** Chimney fire caused damage.

**1906, June 11. Hersey Brothers mill:** Loss: $5,000.

**1907, June 17. Alice Haines house and barn:** Barn struck by lightning, set afire, and destroyed. Two horses and three hogs were killed. The flames spread to her house, which was also consumed. The contents of her home were saved, however. The insurance amounted to $4,000. Later, Edwin Chamberlain rebuilt the house and outbuildings.[40]

**1906, November 17. Charles Earle house.** Burned.

**1908, March 22. George A. Smith residence:** Center Street. Fire caused by the accidental overturning of a small kerosene stove. Mrs. Smith sustained serious burns when her clothing caught fire, and Mr. Smith was likewise burned when he tried to subdue the flames. Most household furniture was saved, but the house and outbuildings were totally consumed.

**1908, September 23. Brummitt-Colbath house:** A fire that started in a nearby woodshed spread to a Pleasant Valley house owned by Sherman D. Brummitt and rented by Henry Colbath, who was not at home. Neighbors removed most contents.

**1908, September 23. Edgerly wood supply:** In East Wolfeboro a passing train set fire to underbrush on the property of Sylvester A. Edgerly. The flames spread rapidly and destroyed several hundred cords of wood and almost burned the nearby Avery farm.

**1908, October 13. Goodwin Block:** The *News* reported: "Goodwin's Block, South Main Street, was seriously damaged by fire, incurring a loss to the building of $10,000 to $12,000.... Owned by Mrs. Martha A. Goodwin, occupied by C.H. Johnson, dry goods; S.A. Edgerly, boots and shoes; F.T. Morrill, restaurant; J. Robins as the Wolfeboro Drug Store; all of whom had their stocks more or less injured by smoke and water. The drug store was totally destroyed, whose stock is estimated at $7,500; Frank T. Morrill, $2,500; S.A. Edgerly, $4,500; C.H. Johnson $4,000." Total damage: $30,500. "Mr. Edgerly is the only one able to secure an apartment to continue his business as soon as matters can be adjusted with the insurance company, which is in Central Block. Mr. Morrill had just closed his restaurant for the winter and left town."

**1908, November 17. Obed S. Young's woodshed:** Burned. Loss: $600.

**1909, March 15. John Allen house:** South Wolfeboro. Burned.

**1909, July 20. Alice Stevens property:** Barns and ell of the summer residence of Mrs. Alice Stevens on South Main Street were burned to the ground. "The main building was slightly damaged.... The barn was well filled with hay, property of C.L. Grant, who that day had just completed haying on the place."

## RUM, RELIGION, AND POLITICS

### Wet or Dry?

Religion and politics were the two most popular subjects for discussion in town particularly during the middle of the decade. If space in the *Granite State News* is any indication, coming in a strong third was the debate on liquor. Should Wolfeboro license the sale of alcoholic beverages, or should liquor sales be prohibited?

After the turn of the century, William Rogers, meat dealer on South Main Street, was the town liquor agent. At the time, towns could vote to establish what amounted to their own liquor store.[41]

In addition to Rogers' sales, liquor was unofficially purveyed by several local stores and restaurants. If need be, a supply could also be bought through the mail. This advertisement appeared in the *Granite State News*, January 27, 1901:

> Take advantage of our special offer and send $3 by money order express and we will deliver at once, by express, free of charge, right to your home, four full quart bottles of Schwarz XXX Old Family Rye Whiskey in a plain box. Nothing on box to indicate what the contents are. Sold by A.L. Schwarz Company, Paterson, N.J.

On May 12, 1903, towns around the state conducted referendums to determine local policies on the subject of licensing alcohol. Under the proposal, licensing meant that liquor sales could take place, but that a license would be required. A no vote meant that liquor could not be sold ("prohibition"). Within Wolfeboro, 179 voters (all men; women would not have the franchise until 1920) said yea to licensing and 177 said nay. Only 356 of the 732 registered voters in town cast a ballot. Statewide, 131 towns voted for licensing, and 59 voted against it.

The subject would not go away, and in 1904 there were 270 votes in favor of licensing and 256 against. Those against licensing were very vocal and were backed up by several regional and national anti-alcohol groups. Those in favor of licensing were not organized.

Numerous "sermons" against alcohol appeared in the local paper. A particularly fervent disciple of prohibition was local do-gooder Charles O. Doe, whose letter appeared in the local press on October 13, 1906:

> In Wolfeboro there are upward of 50 common tipplers and 75 more occasional tipplers. Knowing the temperament of these neighbors of ours, as a man of intelligence will your judgment prompt you to remove all legal restraint and control of intoxicants?

Doe seemed to have no tolerance at all for anyone who had views different from his. An example of this is provided by this god-like comment in the *Granite State News*, February 29, 1908:

> In 1864 I was insulted by an officer of the U.S. Army, and in 20 days he had been embalmed. Eight years later I was insulted in print by an alderman of Boston, and 60 days an autopsy, then burial at Forest Hills. Seven years later I was insulted by a former editor of the *Granite State News* by an article in this paper, and in four months he lay with his father. Last November I was insulted by its editor of a neighboring journal in print, in 60 days I had written his eulogy....

In autumn 1906 the advocates of prohibition went into high gear. Numerous articles against alcohol appeared in the *Granite State News*, and a large unsigned advertisement with the title "No-License" appeared on the front page of the October 27 issue. As the November 6 election drew nearer, articles, advertisements, and even a poem appeared in the local paper urging people to vote no against a liquor license. Perhaps the only objective commentary was made by Mabel E. Fullerton:

> The Goose noticed with some amusement the big NO LICENSE placard in the *Granite State News*.... In all the discussion she has heard, she has been moved to joy by the naive

On October 13, 1908, a fire swept through the one-story Goodwin Block on South Main Street between the bridge and the Peavey Block and ruined all of the businesses within including, left to right: C.H. Johnson (dry goods), Sylvester A. Edgerly (shoes), F.T. Morrill (restaurant), and the Wolfeboro Drug Store. In 1909 the structure was rebuilt and reopened with new businesses as tenants.

C.H. Johnson's dry goods store after the October 13, 1908, fire. Damage to this shop amounted to $4,000.

Interior view of the Wolfeboro Drug Store, owned and operated by Joseph W. Robins, after the October 13 1908, fire.

> assumption on the part of the no-license people that no license was synonymous with no liquor. If that were the case the problem would be greatly simplified. The Goose has not yet forgotten all the years when the state had a strong prohibition law, and remembering conditions then she cannot feel very optimistic about the result of changing to no license in this town. She believes it would not decrease the consumption of liquor one pint while at the same time it would encourage hypocrisy and evasion of the law.

Wolfeboro voted to go no-license at the election, 319 for licensing and 330 against.

### A Puzzling Outcome

As time went on, alcoholism in Wolfeboro did not seem to either decrease or increase. Crime increased. This state of affairs surprised and puzzled Charles O. Doe, who wrote that if anyone had knowledge of any illegal sales, they should contact him, and he would personally be sure that the law prosecuted the offender.

Something had to be blamed for the increased vandalism, thefts, and the like. Aha! A new culprit was found. Several articles now cited lack of religious upbringing and good training in the home. Overlooked was the fact that although alcohol was no longer openly sold locally, it was still available in unmarked cartons by mail order or simply by going to a nearby town where liquor was still available.

This advertisement by a New York distiller appeared in the *Granite State News* on January 15, 1910, and was rerun in other issues of the time, indicating that it must have brought in quite a few orders from Wolfeboro locals:

> CONVALESCENCE after typhoid or other wasting diseases or fevers requires a pure, gentle, and invigorating stimulant to aid digestion, stimulate and enrich the blood and to give new strength to body and brain. Duffy's Pure Malt Whiskey is invaluable as a tonic when you are run down and depressed, when the heart is weak and the blood is sluggish. It builds new tissue. It aids failing nature to resume its functions, and assures refreshing sleep and imparts vim and energy to every part of the body. It invigorates the brain.
>
> Thousands of doctors prescribe it, and leading hospitals use it. The standard of purity and excellence for 50 years, Duffy's Pure Malt Whiskey has brought health and happiness to many thousands of homes during the last half century. Virtues have been endorsed by temperance advocates [!!!], clergymen, scientists, and men and women in all walks of life, who cannot say too much in praise of the world's greatest medicine, available by mail prepaid.
>
> If you are unable to secure Duffy's Pure Malt Whiskey from the local druggist or dealer we have made special arrangements and will have shipped direct, in plain case, express prepaid, one bottle for $1, four bottles for $3.80, six bottles for $5.50, and 12 bottles for $10.

### Religion

Religion was an integral part of Wolfeboro activities in the early years of the present century. Many parents read the Bible to their children at home, and on the walls were samplers or lithographs with such sentiments as "God Bless Our Home" and "Give Us This Day Our Daily Bread." A substantial portion of the typical 1901 issue of the *Granite State News* was devoted to reprinting sermons and relating news of religious groups. This emphasis in the local paper extended for many years. For example, in 1907, more space by far was devoted to the legal difficulties of Mary Baker Eddy, the founder of Christian Science, than to what Theodore Roosevelt, president of the United States, was doing.

Places of worship in town included the First Congregational Church on the lake side of Pickering Corner, with Rev. Edgar L. Warren officiating. Groups affiliated with the church included the Helping Hand Society, Young People's Society Christian Endeavor, and, apparently, to forestall some terrible eventuality, the Society for the Preservation of the First Congregational Church.

On North Main Street was and is the Christian Church. Organized c.1812, it was going strong in 1901. Affiliated groups included Young People's Society Christian Endeavor and the Ladies' Aid Society. The church had been built at Rendall's Corner in 1838 and lumber from it used to build a new structure at its present location about 20 years later.

The First Free Will Baptist Church, located on Center Street in Wolfeboro Falls, was very active. Groups connected with the Baptist Church included the Associates of Christian Fidelity and the Ladies' Benevolent Society. Rev. Allen M. Freeman was the pastor at the turn of the century. The church used several different names over the years.

Other religious groups in Wolfeboro in 1901 included the Advent Church on Union Street and the First Unitarian Church on Glendon Street. In South Wolfeboro the Union Church, organized in 1844, had no resident pastor, nor did churches in most other outlying districts such as Wolfeboro Center and North Wolfeboro, the Cotton Mountain church being an exception for a time.

In 1906 and 1907 a wave of religious fervor swept over Wolfeboro, especially during the liquor debate of 1906 and the subsequent victory it gave those who were against intoxicating beverages. Many columns in the *Granite State News* were devoted to revival meetings, the unique benefits of Christianity, and details of religious services. In January and February, 1907, revival gatherings called "Union meetings" were held at the Town Hall and were organized by several of the local churches.

Chronicled in print at regular intervals were the activities of Rev. A. Edwin Keigwin, pastor of the Park Presbyterian Church in New York City, who in autumn 1904 received a call to minister to the West End Presbyterian Church of Amsterdam Avenue in the same city. Rev. Edwin and his father, Rev. Albert N. Keigwin, spent their summers at "Wiscasset," their cottage on Sewall Street, where they enjoyed speedboating on Lake

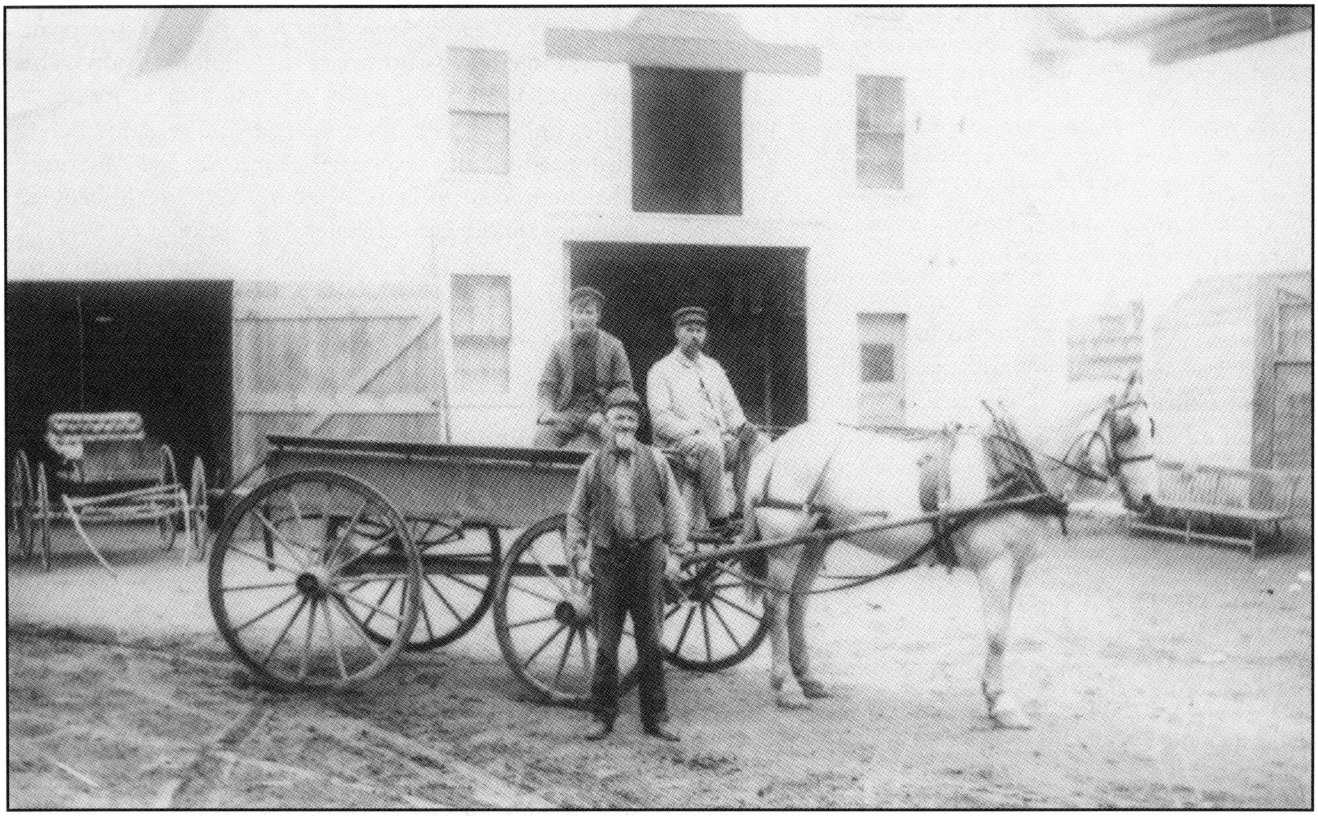

Bickford & Young delivery wagon and teamsters in front of the Joseph E. Fox livery stable (formerly the Durgin stable) on North Main Street. Horne's Ford garage was there years later. (Circa early 1900s photograph)

Willey's Mill on Willey Brook leading into Lake Wentworth as shown circa 1904. This water-powered facility was built by Jonathan Lary and was first known as Lary's Mill, then Trigg's Mill, finally Willey's Mill.

Winnipesaukee, but not without a modicum of work (the younger Rev. Keigwin brought his male secretary along). In 1906-1907 he helped organize local revival meetings and select speakers.

The front page of the June 15, 1907, newspaper was dominated by a large article telling about the Winnipesaukee Summer Assembly, a conference set up by Christian ministers, supervised by Rev. A. Edwin Keigwin and others, to be held in Wolfeboro July 16-28. Special train fares were announced and local hotels and boarding houses had special reductions for the event.

### Societies

Anyone with the urge to belong to a church or society in 1901 had many options from which to choose. The list of local lodges and societies was lengthy and included these:

> Morning Star Lodge No. 17, A.F. & A.M.; Carroll Chapter No. 13, R.A.M.; Warren Chapter No. 10, Order of the Eastern Star; Fidelity Lodge No. 71, Independent Order of Odd Fellows; Kingswood Encampment No. 31, I.O.O.F.; Myrtle Rebekah Lodge No. 48, D. of R.; Wahawa Tribe No. 19, Improved Order of Red Men; Tecumseh Council No. 11, D. of P.; James R. Newell Post No. 61 G.A.R.; James R. Newell W.R.C. No. 44; Capt. A.S. Libbey Camp No. 19, S. of Y.; Carroll Lodge No. 7, A.O.U.W.; Lake Council No. 247, R.A.; Winnepesaukee (*sic*) Lodge No. 64, N.E.O.F.; and Lake Shore Grange.

As can be seen, exotic-sounding names and unexplained initials abounded.

### Politics

The *Granite State News* usually concentrated upon local, county, and state politics, and ignored the national scene. Exceptions were provided by quadrennial presidential elections.

In the contest of November 1904, Wolfeboro registered 401 votes for Theodore Roosevelt, the Republican candidate, and just 183 for Alton Parker, his Democratic opponent.

In 1900 Wolfeboro had cast 439 votes for Republican William McKinley and only 196 for Democrat William Jennings Bryan. Unsuccessful in 1896 and 1900, Bryan tried again in 1908. To put it mildly, the editor of the *Granite State News* did not like Bryan. Throughout October 1908 many anti-Bryan cartoons and articles were run. Not at any other time during the century was so much disfavor heaped upon any candidate for any office. The count was 405 for Republican candidate William Howard Taft and his running mate James S. Sherman, and 209 for Bryan and Kern, with 13 stray votes for Prohibition party candidates Chafan and Watson.

Bryan, defeated once again at the polls, did what retired politicians have done before and since: he was prominently featured in advertisements for patent medicines, land promotions, and the like, and lent his name whenever a buck was in the offing.

## LAW ENFORCEMENT

### A Youthful Runaway

Charles O. Doe often made the news in other contexts besides prohibition and religion, such as in this notice dated October 14, 1905, in relation to his capacity as a deputy sheriff and justice of the peace:

> Lizzie St. Peter, age 16 years, of this town, and Leonard Y. Stanley, age 17 years, of Alton, were married about midnight by [justice of the peace and constable] Charles O. Doe in the Town Hall at Alton, October 10. Doe's errand to Alton was to arrest the girl on the charge of being a stubborn child and return with her to Wolfeboro.
>
> For the last week the girl has been missing from her home here, and her folks had about given up hope of seeing her again, when they learned that she was in Alton with Stanley, with whom, it was said, she has been keeping company for some time. One of the reasons the girl left home, it is said, is because she did not want to attend school. When it was learned that the girl was in Alton, Doe sent word to Officer Place of that town to arrest and hold her until he arrived. The girl was found by the officer, and when she was taken young Stanley accompanied her, and when Mr. Doe arrived to take her back home he found them together in the same cell.

This was one "crime" with a happy ending.

### Crime and Punishment

During the first decade of the present century, most crimes were of a non-violent nature. Malicious mischief and disturbing the peace were common incidents, as were petty thefts. Civil legal proceedings often involved such matters as boundary disputes, non-payment of debts, non-fulfillment of contracts, divorce (virtually always either for adultery or desertion), and water rights.

An editorial in the September 23, 1905, issue of the *Granite State News* suggested that Wolfeboro should have a police court, especially since it had been voted at the town meeting the preceding March to establish one, after which Edward F. Cate was appointed judge.

A November 14, 1908, editorial suggested that Wolfeboro was of sufficient size that it needed a regular police department or service. At the time the town had neither a formally-organized police department nor a jail. Arrests were made by a local constable or a deputy sheriff. During the decade most Wolfeboro cases of significance were tried in the Carroll County Court House in Ossipee. Selected cases are described herewith:

### A Greedy Thief

In late December 1902 and the first few days of January 1903, Wolfeboro Falls grocer Perley E. Young was perplexed that his inventory was diminishing quite rapidly without a commensurate accumulation of money in his cash drawer. The proprietor played detective, and early on Sunday morning, January 4, he discovered Howard W. Burroughs in his store.

Young went to Judge Sewall Abbott, and papers were granted which permitted Officer Kimball to search Burroughs' home, where a vast amount of Young's merchandise was found. Burroughs was arrested and held against $300 bail. It took four wagon trips to remove all of the stolen goods. The crook received a two- to three-year prison term.

### Malice and Mischief

On October 15, 1901, Judge Sewall W. Abbott's summer cottage on Sewall Point was broken into, and the interior was vandalized. The local paper commented:[42] "Such a malicious act has not occurred in this locality for several years. The community was considerably stirred about the matter and are determined to make strenuous efforts to stop such vandalism."

The January 31, 1903, issue carried this advertisement: "$10 reward. I will give to convict the person or persons who broke into my camp on Waveland or Kenniston's [*sic*] Island. Starr Parsons, Lynn, Mass."

The June 3, 1905, *Granite State News* included:

> Wednesday night about 11:30 some hoodlums for some unknown cause saw fit to destroy several of the electric globes and demolish the fenders by stoning same, also smashing the signal lamps of the Boston & Maine Railroad. At different times the lamps on Bay Street and North Main Street have been broken, while on Sewall Street last fall nearly every lamp below the residence of Harry Roberts and the woods was shot off, which up to the present time have not been replaced. If there is any way to bring these culprits to justice it should be done.... It has come to a pretty pass if property may be wantonly destroyed at will of offenders and there be no redress.

Another report dealt with a mysterious man who on several occasions emerged from behind bushes or walls, gave unwanted hugs to women, and then disappeared.

### The Celebrated Case of Charles F. Piper

Of all crimes allegedly committed in Wolfeboro during the early years of the twentieth century, none received more attention than the case of Charles F. Piper, cashier of the Wolfeboro Loan and Banking Company.

Founded in 1889, the bank had a board of directors and slate of officers consisting of prominent local citizens. Charles F. Piper, a widely respected gentleman who had served as treasurer of the town of Wolfeboro and in other positions of public trust, was appointed cashier.

Seemingly, the financial institution went from one success to another, until on February 8, 1904, it abruptly closed its doors. Businessmen with commercial deposits, school children with savings accounts, and others were left wondering what had happened, as all accounts were frozen. Suddenly, Wolfeboro had no bank! Then followed the most sensational local scandal of the early twentieth century.

The *Granite State News* reported this in a story datelined February 8:

> Wolfeboro Bank Closed for a Time.
>
> Irregularity is Found in the Accounts of the Cashier, Hon. Charles F. Piper.
>
> It was a surprise to the public when it found that the Savings Department of the Wolfeboro Loan and Banking Company was closed today, that no deposits would be received or any moneys paid from this department. The cause for this action being that special auditor James E. French of Moultonboro, who had been appointed at the annual meeting to make special examinations of the books of cashier Charles F. Piper, preparatory to the election of a new cashier, and justice to his successor, had found inaccuracies to the amount of some $41,000. From information which we have learned since, the officers of the bank were informed of the trouble before they commenced any investigation.
>
> There was a meeting of the directors this afternoon, which was adjourned to await Alpheus W. Baker, of Lebanon, savings bank commissioner, who came on the evening train with President Albert O. Robinson of Sanbornville. The directors assembled in Judge Sewall W. Abbott's office. The Hon. James E. French of Moultonboro said that a meeting of those directors was held January 26 to choose officers, and after the election of president and vice president, it was decided that on account of Mr. Piper's mental and physical condition, he was not to be continued longer in the service of the bank and that in justice to his successor there should be an examination of the books.

The account went on to say that it was deemed "necessary for the public safety that said corporation should not continue to transact business" as "the accounts were badly muddled."

Throughout most of the remainder of the year, the curious doings of Charles F. Piper were recounted and discussed in the columns of the *Granite State News*. Piper, a highly respected citizen, had served in various town and state offices and positions of public trust.

On March 5, 1904, the paper reported that investigations were still being made, but

> upon information, lately received from good authority, the shortage in the Loan and Banking department will be $15,000 or more, and the Savings Department will be $35,000 or more.... The principal topic for discussion this week is the shortage in the accounts of the Wolfeboro Loan and Banking Company. Little knots of men are gathered in various stores and on the streets, and all have some theory for the state of affairs which now exists, but are greatly surprised as to the efficiency is reported constantly on the increase. Of course, no one knows positively the amount, as no official report has been made, but enough has leaked out so the public feel well satisfied that the shortage far beyond expectations. Those who heretofore have been considered uncharitable in their expressions are becoming emphatic in their statements and have lost confidence in the conduct of the one in whom a short time ago they had such profound respect.

A report of bank auditor James E. French, dated March 9, 1904, showed a shortage of $41,404.01 in the Savings Department of the Wolfeboro Loan and Banking Company and $18,309.95 in the Trust and Banking Department, for a total shortage of $59,713.96.

He reported that since January 1, 1898, a steady stream of unauthorized withdrawals had been taken from the savings departments ranging from a few dollars to $5,000 at a time. Many erasures, alterations, and falsifications were found on the books. As an example, one depositor's passbook showed that the depositor withdrew the sum of $100, but bank records were falsified to show that $500 had been paid him. Transfers had been made without authority from one account to another to cover up existing conditions and to mislead bank examiners and directors.

An appended statement showed liabilities of the bank of $128,047.43, and assets of $109,737.48 in the Trust and Banking Department, for a deficit of $18,309.95. In the Savings Department liabilities amounted to $200,599.01, whereas assets amounted to $159,195.03. This showed a deficit of $41,403.98. The shortfalls for both departments totaled $59,713.93, thus in effect wiping out the capital stock of $50,000. Further:

> Upon report of special auditor James E. French, a meeting of the directors of the bank was held in the banking room Thursday afternoon, March 4, which has continued until late in the evening. It was decided to begin action against cashier Charles F. Piper and his son Carroll D. Piper, assistant cashier, and state attorney general Eastman was asked by the directors to cause an arrest of each to be made. The directors also decided to close the institution, as the capital stock being practically wiped out. The capital stock of $50,000 is partially secured by a bond of $20,000, and it is estimated that under favorable conditions Piper's property along the lake shore will bring $10,000. The deficit covers a period of six years.

However, Piper was never to explain his defalcations. A team of doctors judged him legally insane and incapable of reason. As if that were not enough, on Saturday, April 23, 1904, the *Granite State News* reported:

> Thursday morning at 7:15 the trials and sufferings of Charles F. Piper terminated. The cause of death was paresis. A loving wife, dutiful son, three brothers and a sister besides a host of friends are left to mourn.
>
> Piper was born at Lee, N.H., May 22, 1849. He came to Wolfeboro while young and received his education at the Wolfborough and Tuftonborough Academy. From 1868 to 1872 he was a clerk in a country store. He was on the mail route from Boston to Bangor, Maine, 1872-1876. He served as town clerk and representative in legislature in 1887, was town treasurer for 17 years, member of the Republican state committee since 1880, and treasurer of the Wolfeboro Loan and Banking Company since its organization.
>
> The late affairs to be regretted, but still time will efface much, and he must be remembered as one of Wolfeboro's public spirited citizens.

**Carroll D. Piper**

The brunt of the investigation fell upon his son, Carroll D. Piper. In Superior Court which convened in Ossipee on June 14, 1904, the younger Piper was indicted for falsifying bank records. The prosecution of the case of the younger Piper was continued until December, and a bond of $5,000 was posted. On March 25, 1905, a detailed discussion of the indictment and court case involving the State vs. Carroll D. Piper was printed in the local paper. Sentiment against Piper ran high, not only for his own misdeeds, but those of his deceased father.

On June 29, 1905, Carroll D. Piper had his day in court. After months of waiting, and following numerous news reports, the public was eager that justice be done. It was believed by many that Piper would be sentenced to a long term in jail. On trial day, the jurors were all present, as were most witnesses. However, State Attorney Eastman informed surprised onlookers that the state of New Hampshire had nol-prossed the case and dropped its action against Piper, as it was not clear that he had benefited personally. However, Eastman believed Carroll D. Piper to be guilty and said:

> Now, then, there are other indictments for making false entries on the books of the bank. Now I don't imagine there is much defense to those charges, but in view of the fact that the bank has not suffered any loss and money on account of Mr. Piper's connection to that transaction, and in view of the fact that Mr. Piper is a young man who has never had any business experience until he was put in the bank by his father, and was put in the bank with those conditions existing, and he was undoubtedly made acquainted with those facts to some extent by his father; that those entries were made not for his own interests, but in the interests of his father, not for the purpose of obtaining money from the bank, but for the purpose of protecting his father and with the hope that the shortage would be made up, and that Mr. Carroll D. Piper made effort to interest people to contribute money so it might be made up.... I have concluded it would not be useful to prosecute that case.

It was further stated by Eastman, on behalf of the state, that Carroll D. Piper was a recent graduate of Harvard, "a young man without business experience, but has some future before him," and:

> He now has some chance to go to work and be somebody; he is only 24 years old. If we see fit to enforce these claims on account of false entries, then of course I cannot see but in the long run he must be guilty of some of them, and that would be the end of his undertaking to do business, for the offense is one of such a nature that he would have to go to state prison for a year or more. I cannot see the public good would be served by any course of this kind. The young man was not put in the bank on account of any fault of his own, but by force of circumstances, and he was there and undertaking to help out his father.

The court granted the nol-pros motion, and the judge stated: "I understand that this explanation is the opinion of all the parties that are connected to this matter, and I certainly hope that Mr. Piper will undertake to go on and do what is right."

For young Carroll D. Piper there was, indeed, a heaven. He went on to become a prominent and well-respected businessman (insurance) and teacher.

Apparently, his father, the late Charles F. Piper, had used his ill-gotten gains to finance a real estate deal involving Lake Winnipesaukee property on Little Bear Island, to invest in S.W. Clow & Co., and to participate in numerous other ventures. Many of his assets were sold at public auction on August 19, 1905, and the proceeds paid toward bank losses. His property on Little Bear Island fetched $3,025 to Robert Lamprey's high bid.[43] His interest in the Belvue House brought $6,950 to William Coburn of Manchester. The bank's furniture and fixtures were sold to Henry D. Cotton, owner of the Bank Building.

Eventually, all depositors were paid in full from the realization of bank assets. However, the equity of the shareholders was completely wiped out.

### Other Items

The August 12, 1905, edition of the local paper commented that burglars recently struck several Wolfeboro homes within the past week. Petty thefts continued for the remainder of the year.

On March 2, 1906, Sheriff Johnson arrested Joseph McDonald and Jasper Hoyt, both of Rochester, and charged them with looting summer cottages on Lake Wentworth. They confessed to the crime, and each was sentenced to state prison.

On September 21, 1909, George H. Kimball was arrested for stealing goods from Harvey C. Kalloch. In Carroll County Court he pleaded *nolo contendere*. The judge sentenced him to state prison for not less than two nor more than five years.

The *Granite State News* printed this item on Saturday, May 1, 1909:

> Tuesday evening Bessie B. Swett and Herbert Hill of this town were apprehended by Sheriff Myron L. Johnson and police officer [Ervin] Godfrey and arrested. Wednesday morning they were brought into court and arraigned, Mrs. Swett, for concealing the birth, death and burial of a child on August 25, 1907, and Hill as accessory. Both pleaded not guilty....

On May 4, 1910, Rollin W. Haines was arraigned in Wolfeboro Police Court for polygamy upon the complaint of May Haines, wife number two. Found guilty, he was given a sentence of one year in jail.

### 21 Ways to Go to Jail

In 1905 a list of 21 offenses which could, if one were convicted, result in fines and jail sentences, was published as part of Chapter 264 of the General Statutes. Today's reader will find some of them quite amusing. A synopsis follows:

Section 1: "No person shall make a brawl or tumult, nor in any street, lane, alley, or other public place, be guilty of rude, indecent, or disorderly contact, nor shall insult or wantonly impede a person passing therein, nor throw any stones, bricks, snowballs, or dirt, nor play at any game in which a ball is used."

Section 2: "No person shall address any offensive, derisive, or annoying word to any person who is lawful in any street or public place, nor call him by any offensive or derisive name, nor make any noise or exclamation in his presence and hearing with intent to deride, offend, or annoy him, or to prevent him from pursuing his lawful business and occupation."

Section 3 forbade the use of obscenities and profanity in public places.

Section 4 warned against the injury or defacement of buildings, fences, gardens, etc.

Section 5 prohibited unlawful gains, including any in which money or other property was at stake.

Section 6 disallowed the use within the business district of town a cannon, gun, pistol, or other firearms, beating of a drum "except by command of a military officer having authority therefore," the discharging of rockets, etc.

Section 7 addressed indecent exposure.

Section 8 forbade the leaving of any sled, wheelbarrow, cart, or other impediment in a public way for more than two hours during the day or one hour at night.

Section 9 provided for the granting of a license for people to occupy a portion of a street to lay lumber thereon or other materials for building purposes, for a time not to exceed four months.

Section 10 directed anyone whose activities required a license to conform to the provisions of such license.

Section 11 prohibited the unnecessary use of wheeled carriages, sleds, or wheelbarrows on sidewalks and certain other areas.

Section 12 prohibited coasting and sliding on sleds or other vehicles in public ways in a manner to endanger travelers.

Section 13: "No person shall exhibit or lead a bear in or upon any public highway."

Section 14 prohibited drunkenness in any public place or in a private place if it disturbed his family or others.

Section 15 prohibited prostitution.

Section 16 forbade the furnishing of spirituous liquors to certain individuals, especially those under guardianship or in houses of correction.

Section 17 stated this: "No person shall purchase or receive, in exchange or otherwise, from a pauper supported in an alms house or poor house without permission of the overseers of the poor, any properties whatever."

Section 18 was worded thus: "No person shall ride through a street or lane, in the compact [business district] of a town, at a swifter pace than the rate of five miles an hour."

Section 19 provided that owners or drivers control horses or oxen in public areas.

Section 20 stated that any person convicted of any of the preceding 19 sections "shall be fined not exceeding $20 or be imprisoned not exceeding six months."

Section 21 read as follows: "A rogue, vagabond, lewd, idle, or disorderly person, person going about begging, a person using any subtle craft, juggling or unlawful gain or play, a person pretending to have knowledge in physiognomy or palmistry, a person pretending, for money, to tell destinies or fortunes, or to discover by any spell or secret art where lost or stolen property may be found, common piper, fid-

Morrison & Chamberlain clothing store in the 1900s. Interior view showing Charles Morrison (left) and Ed Chamberlain. The partnership lasted from 1903 until 1910. Today Miltner's shoe store is in the same building on South Main Street next to the bridge.

Sylvester A. Edgerly's shoe store, interior view circa 1908. This was located in the one-story Goodwin Block which burned that year.

dler, runaway, stubborn servant or child, common drunkard, pilferer, person wanton and lascivious in speech or behavior, common railer or brawler, person who so neglects his employment or misspends his earnings as to not provide properly for the support of himself and family, shall be imprisoned not exceeding six months."

One can imagine how crowded the jails would be today in the 1990s if being a "common piper or fiddler" were a crime, or if anyone who misspent his earnings so as not to be able to support himself were imprisoned! Woe to anyone in 1905 who received money for writing a newspaper column on astrology or investment advice or attempted to forecast the outcome of the World Series! Further, if a servant was *stubborn,* into prison he or she went!

## SANITATION AND CLEANLINESS

### Ecology and Sanitation

The word *ecology* was unknown in Wolfeboro in the early 1900s. Little thought was given to the preservation of natural resources. Occasionally, items concerning pollution or unsightly objects would appear in the local paper, but little was done to correct such problems.

In Wolfeboro in the early 1900s animals played a very important part in everyday life. Numerous articles in the *Granite State News* pertained to the care and feeding of horses, attention to their injuries, and other aspects. From children to adults, just about everyone was familiar with the habits and peculiarities of barnyard pigs, cows, and other livestock. It was not at all uncommon to see cows and sheep herded through town streets or a drover to bring several dozen cattle over the roads from Vermont to be sold and fattened in Wolfeboro and then slaughtered for use in local as well as Boston markets.

Horses, the primary means of transportation for those who could afford to own one, were kept in many locations in town, typically in a stable, often filthy, attached to the kitchen end of the house, with little thought for the principles of sanitation. Children and adults would usually bathe once a week, typically on Saturday.

### Condition of the Streets

Some town streets had open drains or sewers along their edges. In 1904 the *Granite State News* commented that the stench was so intense along a half-mile stretch of Mill Street that people had the choice of either holding their noses or taking an alternate route. It was common for sink and bath drains to run into the ditch alongside roads, including North Main Street. Sewage was drained into cesspools (now called septic systems), but these often overflowed into yards and streets. Gutters along the roads in town were filled with trash, animal excretions, decaying matter, carcasses, and other refuse, often causing a great stench.

On July 18, 1904, the Wolfeboro Board of Health was organized, with Nathaniel H. Scott, M.D., as president, Fred C. Tobey, M.D., as secretary, and Charles O. Doe as executive officer. Although such topics as open drains and deposits of animal matter in public places were discussed, little if anything changed.

### The Back Bay Problem

Back Bay and the Smith River were repositories for sewage, garbage, and other refuse. During this era, millions of board feet of lumber were cut by the S.W. Clow & Co. mill on Back Bay, with much of the bark, sawdust, etc., being dumped into the water. Even today in the 1990s it is several feet deep in areas. A stench arose from the decomposing wood mass. On occasion in the 1901-1910 decade, there were so many logs and bark scraps jammed into Back Bay that it was impossible for even small boats to navigate.

On May 9, 1903, the local paper commented as follows:

We always feel pain when we see anybody using either the lake or river as a dumping ground for old rubbish of any kind. The lake is not made for a dumping ground for anything. Our townspeople should take care of their waste by burning it or dumping it in some swamp. A townsman (whose name we will not mention) threw in the river this week a lot of old, dry waste, and it floated down to the lake, there to remain as an eyesore to everybody. But another citizen, more thoughtful than the first, set fire to the floating mass and thus destroyed a greater part of the rubbish. Thanks, Charlie.

This was followed on May 23, 1903, by:

It is too bad, and may prove expensive to the town, unless our people desist. We allude to the foolish habit which too many nearby residents and traders have, of depositing their garbage, old paper boxes, wastepaper, empty bottles, etc. into our bay or tributary thereto. It is uncalled for, unnecessary, and uncomely, as well as unlawful, making our harbor, which is the handsomest and largest on the lake, an eyesore to lovers of beauty and cleanliness, thereby losing, to many, much of its charm.... To see the shores covered with all kinds of refuse...is a source of much unfavorable comment.

The editor went on to say that on the other side of the lake there were spotters who prevented such things, and that the Wolfeboro Board of Trade should see that no trash was dumped this way in our town.

The body of water between the railroad tracks and Centre Street, was nothing less than a trash dump. (Later filled in, this is the site of today's Foss Field and the Wolfeboro Shopping Center.) The *Granite State News* had this to say on May 7, 1904:

The town has a reputation of being a neatly kept and well-painted town, and that is true in most cases. But in one case and that a *very public place,* is kept in such condition that it should shame our people every time they pass it. We refer to that part of Centre Street known as the Causeway. On the side next to the bay it is a custom of many to dump any old rubbish they do not know what else to do with, and in consequence the place is covered up with tin cans, kettles, broken crockery, clothing, and most every namable thing that a man or woman could throw away.

Now and then, efforts were made to rectify the mess. The April 16, 1910, issue of the *News* noted:

> The job which Herbert Kimball and crew have been doing in cleaning up the shore of Back Bay is a good one, not only in that it improves the appearance, but sanitary condition as well. Now the Board of Health should see that it is kept so.

Much of the Back Bay remained a public nuisance for decades thereafter. The part between the railroad tracks and Center (as it was later spelled) Street was filled in, beginning in a large way in the 1930s as a WPA (Works Progress Administration) project. The rest of Back Bay remained a waste dump for sawdust and other products. In fact, it was not until the 1980s that it could be called scenic or beautiful.

In 1907 the State Board of Health implemented regulations to protect the waters of Lake Winnipesaukee. The December 5, 1908, issue of the local paper told readers of the Sewage Bill which was to become effective January 1, 1909, "prohibiting the discharge of sink, cellar, urinal drains and other polluting matters into the waters of the lake. Many cesspools must be built by the cottages and others or a general clearing-up of the lakeshore will be in order." However, around this time the town got a ruling that Back Bay and Smith River were not part of the lake.

## HOMES AND LIVING

### Residential Districts

Private homes were located in all areas of the town, much as they are now. In or near the downtown districts, residences such as the Augustine D. Avery house and its South Main Street neighbors owned by John L. Peavey, Dr. R.H. King (whose house-store was where Carpenter School is now), Blake Folsom (where the IGA is now), Joseph Varney, and others were among the finest in Wolfeboro.

Numerous homes, some pretentious in their aspect and others modest, were on North Main Street. Houses along Glendon, Factory, Clark, Green, and other streets, provided their inhabitants easy access to local stores and factories. Farther away, Pleasant Street boasted a particularly impressive Victorian-style residence part way up the hill on the side toward the lake. Many large residences along recently-built Sewall Street (now called Sewall Road), most of which had been constructed in the 1890s, were occupied only in the summer. Unlike the situation today, the area was relatively treeless, except close to the shore.

One of the most striking of all Wolfeboro homes was the Victorian mansion completed by contractor J. Frank Goodwin in Wolfeboro Falls in 1900 for Frank B. Hutchins, whose mill was just a short walk away. This house stands today and is every bit as imposing as it was nearly a century ago.

Where was Paugus Street? Apparently, it was intended to be a duplicate of Pleasant Street and parallel to it in the direction opposite from North Main Street. Connecting roadways to Paugus Street included Adams, Mohawk, and Belknap Streets. Since they no longer exist, they were probably planned but never developed. Only Adams Street, not marked by a sign, survives as a short, dead-end passage on which there are two residences.

Some areas in which there are many houses today were not built upon in 1901. Not a single year-round home was on Forest Street (now Forest Road; the Frederick E. Meader house, a.k.a. Vinecroft, was not built until c.1902), Cricket Hill, or Wolfeboro Neck.[44] Much of the land in the area was devoted to apple orchards.

Most homes in outlying districts were two-story farmhouses with connecting buildings to facilitate tending livestock during the winter.

An easy way for the typical Wolfeboroite[45] to earn a few extra dollars was to take in summer boarders by the day or week. Those intending to do so registered with the Boston & Maine Railroad office which posted a listing of accommodations. Typical boarding house rates were $5 to $7 per week including breakfast, lunch, and dinner. Almost every large house in town had rooms for rent at one time or another in its history. Even citizens who had lots of money took in boarders including John L. Peavey in his home on South Main Street.

Rental units were found primarily near factories—on Factory Street, in Wolfeboro Falls, and in South Wolfeboro. Greenleaf B. Clark was the primary landlord. Most tenements, as they were called, were homes which housed two or three families.

### At Home

In 1901 the typical Wolfeboro in-town residence was a two-story wooden structure, often with a one-story addition on the back to serve as a food pantry and wood storage facility. While most houses in town had indoor plumbing, many homes on smaller streets and in rural districts used wooden privies in the backyard. These "outhouses" would be moved around the yard and new holes dug under them.

The typical rural home had a well with a hand pump. Many downtown residences were hooked to the municipal water mains which then, as now, were fed by gravity from Beach Pond. According to a contemporary account, "water rental is only $6 per faucet per year."

Living quarters, usually on the first floor, consisted of a living room, dining room, and kitchen. Bedrooms were upstairs. Interior construction was plain with plastered walls covered with paint or paper, and with plastered ceilings. Some of the more expensive homes on North and South Main Streets, Pleasant Street, and

**Interior of a local drugstore, June 1903, with soda fountain to the left and a cigar stand to the right. On the wall behind are various drugs and compounds packaged generically, apparently from which prescriptions could be made up. To the right and dimly visible is a case of books, part of the drugstore's circulating rental library.**

The Wolfeboro Post Office at the left side of the Peavey Block, June 1903. At the right is seen part of the store front of the neighboring business, John I. Sanborn, with men's shirts on display. Sitting in front of the Post Office are, left to right: Forrest Peavey, (postmaster), Henry P. Corliss, and Arthur Copp.

Sewall Street had such accouterments as libraries, art glass windows, and ornate wood or plaster moldings, but these were exceptions. The Stephen Durgin house even had its own gas-generating plant for interior illumination.

Electricity generated by steam at the lumber mill of S.W. Clow & Co. on Back Bay was wired to many houses and nearly all businesses in town, but in outlying areas, light was furnished by lanterns, oil lamps, and candles. From time to time, electric power would be interrupted, as per this notice in the local paper, July 6, 1901: "On account of repairs to the boiler at the steam mill of S.W. Clow & Company, the electric light plant will not run on Sunday evening, July 7."

Heat was usually generated by burning wood and sometimes by coke or coal furnished by several dealers in town. In winter a house was allowed to cool down at night. To keep warm, a heavy layer of blankets and flannel sheets was in order, plus flannel or wool night clothes. A lady who spent her youth in the Piper residence on North Main Street (on the right side past the Lake View Cemetery) related that there was no heat at all in the bedrooms at night, and that hot bricks or soapstone wrapped in thick blankets were put at the bottom of each bed upon retiring. Of course, a few hours later the bricks were cold, but by that time the children were supposed to be in slumberland. During the first decade of the twentieth century, many heating stoves in larger homes were replaced by central hot water or steam heat units.

Interior walls were decorated by paintings or, more usually, by inexpensive colored lithographs. Currier & Ives prints were especially popular and included pretty girls, views of Lake Winnipesaukee, domestic scenes, sporting motifs, and other topics including cats and dogs—then as now, the most popular household pets. Framed photographic portraits of past and present relatives were also in vogue as well as depictions of far-off places such as Niagara Falls, the Colosseum in Rome, and the pyramids of Egypt.

Inexpensive, mass-produced Rogers statuary groups, cast in plaster and painted off-white or gray, were popular decorations. Many Rogers subjects were available, including children engaging in amateur theatricals, Abe Lincoln, two rivals playing chess, and an organ grinder.

### Eating and Drinking

Diets were probably healthier in 1901 than today, as staples such as mutton, beef, pork, vegetables, and bread were emphasized, although lard and sugar were used in quantity in baking. One of a wife's finest accomplishments was to be a good cook and baker, often making pies and cookies for the entire neighborhood.

In the days before mechanical refrigeration for residential use, nearly every home had an ice box stocked more than likely with a block cut from Crescent Lake or another nearby pond the winter before and stored in sawdust insulation. Ice deliveries were made weekly by horse-drawn wagon. Milk and eggs were delivered daily by the same method. Meat and groceries were purchased two or three times a week, although many in-town residents bought their food on a daily basis. The firm of Lewando & Tilton, among others, offered home and, in season, island cottage delivery of groceries.

Quality standards were non-existent in the grocery business. It was not unusual for canned or bottled products to contain harmful substances or be misrepresented on their labels. Meat could be old, tainted, or of doubtful attribution. The Pure Food and Drug Act did not become a reality until 1906 and was not enforced until January 1, 1907.

Cocaine, opium, and other drugs considered harmful today were not regulated then and could be obtained without prescription at any local drug store. Abuse of these substances was rare in Wolfeboro. A bigger problem was alcoholism. Cigarettes and cigars existed in a great proliferation of brands, many of which advertised on colorful placards and posters. While most men smoked, most women did not. Tobacco chewing was popular with men, and all taverns and hotels were equipped with brass or porcelain spittoons.

Among the most popular soft drinks in Wolfeboro were Moxie (first sold in 1885), Coca-Cola (1886), and Hires Root Beer, as well as regional brands bottled in Concord and Manchester. Beer and ale were very popular and were mostly state or regional brews, as beer could not be shipped long distances without deteriorating. Wine was sold in taverns and restaurants but, unlike today, was used somewhat sparingly in the home. Mixed drinks were simple and usually involved combining whisky with some flavoring. Vodka was virtually if not completely unknown, and such fashionable mixed drinks of today as daiquiris, bloody marys, and screwdrivers awaited liquor promotions still decades away.

Mail order shopping was very popular, with Sears, Roebuck & Co. of Chicago being the leading purveyor. Sears offered everything from gravestones to kit-form houses. Larkin was another leading mail-order firm. Magazines were crammed with advertisements offering merchandise from liver pills to hair restorers to parlor reed organs. Larger items would be delivered by railroad shipment and smaller items by mail carrier.

## COMMERCE

### The Downtown Area

An article in the May 23, 1903, *Granite State News* de-

The Wolfeboro National Bank as seen in a view from the first decade of the twentieth century. Founded in 1906, the facility remained in the same building until June 1963. (Melanson Collection)

Principals of the Wolfeboro National Bank. Shown here (left to right) are Ella Swett, Wilbra H. Swett (cashier), Joseph Lewando, Fred L. Melcher (who lived in Butte, Montana; his wife was from Wolfeboro), Almon W. Eaton (vice-president) and James H. Martin (president), all of whom were among the first stockholders.

scribed the Wolfeboro commercial district:

> Riding down Main Street this summer with a friend who was visiting me, I was asked the question, "Why is it that you have no trees or grass in the compact, or business portion of the town?" What was I to say in answer to this query?... The center of the town, near the stores, Post Office, bank and railroad station, was bare of verdure....

The article went on to say that in downtown there was no place for people to sit down and enjoy the surroundings. Boston had its Common, and other towns had their parks and squares, "but Wolfeboro in its business portion hasn't even a shade tree." Further:

> This plain, unvarnished tale has doubtless made you exclaim, "I thought Wolfeboro was a pretty place!" I will hasten to assure you that Wolfeboro *is* a pretty place. Don't forget that. To alter the words of the familiar quotation, "God *might* have made a prettier place than Wolfeboro, but doubtless He never did."

In downtown Wolfeboro at the turn of the century there were several large buildings. The Peavey Block (known today as the Avery Building), put up by wealthy local resident John L. Peavey in 1889 (for some reason it bore the date 1890 across its facade) and had three floors of activity. Along the top and extending to the sides was a railing resembling a fence, and at the front center was a crest. In its day the Peavey Block was an ideal representative of Victorian architecture. Today the "gingerbread" is long gone.

At ground level were three businesses facing Main Street, among which were the Post Office on the left side, a men's store in the center, and Lewando & Tilton on the right. Run by Joseph Lewando, the latter establishment billed itself as a high-class grocery store, but also sold paints, oils, and hardware items. Among the tenants in the two upstairs floors was Clarence Kent, who resided there and gave piano lessons. Kent was in the building from at least the 1890s through 1936 and was a local institution.

For nearly a decade the Peavey Block had a companion to its right on South Main Street, the three-story Goodwin Block (also called Masonic Hall), also a prime example of the Victorian style and also a business center housing many enterprises. After it was destroyed by fire on May 28, 1899, a new Goodwin Block, a rather plain-appearing one-story structure known in the 1990s as the Roarton Building, rose on the site. In 1908 it suffered a serious fire but was rebuilt. Beginning in 1909, it housed Tobey's Drug Store which remained there until it ceased business in June 1995. In addition to these two Goodwin Blocks successively on the same site, there was the Elijah Goodwin Block on Railroad Avenue; that one burned in 1958. Still *another* Goodwin Block on Railroad Avenue had burned in 1887.

Directly across the street from the Peavey Block was the Bank Building, built in 1856, which had been headquarters for at least two financial institutions. In 1906 it became the first home of the Wolfeboro National Bank. At one time the *Granite State News* was printed there. There were two front doors, and on the right side only, a semi-circular window. Later, the front entrance was made just one door, and a matching semi-circular window was added to the left. The upper two levels were apartments.

In 1901 the Wolfeborough Loan and Banking Company, established 12 years earlier, occupied the front right of the Bank Building next to Harry Piper's general store (which sold everything from groceries to ladies' dresses). The bank did a lively business and handled nearly all of the private and commercial accounts in town.

Occasionally, a $5 or $10 bill bearing the imprint of the Lake National Bank of Wolfborough *(sic)* would be seen, and residents would recall the scandal that forced the bank's closing back in 1893 and sent its perpetrator, William S. Jewett of Lawrence, MA, to jail.

The two-story wooden building housing Black's Paper Store in the 1990s was known as the Folsom Block at the turn of the century. At the end of Railroad Avenue was the Boston & Maine Railroad Depot, which looked then much as it does today (thanks to restoration efforts spearheaded by Donald L. Hallock in the 1970s).

The Durgin Block, still in existence on North Main Street and still beautiful (Richard Eaton and Gorham Humphrey restored it in the 1980s), offered a combination of retail stores in the lower levels and professional offices and apartments above. In the preceding century it had been used as the private residence of Stephen Durgin. To the left was the not-so-beautiful Sheridan House, which by the turn of the twentieth century was a low-budget hotel operation (the Wolfeboro Marketplace is on the site today).

The Glendon House hotel, in 1901 owned by Frank Hobbs (who renamed it the Hobbs-Is-Inn and put a big sign to this effect across the front, after people stumbled at calling it Hobbses' Inn, Hobbs's Inn, and other variations), was by then somewhat faded in glory, but in the summer was often fully booked.

Up and down North and South Main Streets were numerous other business buildings, mostly of one- or two-story height, made of wood, and mostly painted white, this being by far the most common exterior color used in the town. Along the thoroughfare just about any needed item or service could be obtained, ranging from hardware, coal, and wood, to fancy hats, picture frames, ice cream, and the latest Boston papers.

At several places around town were public fountains from which water constantly flowed. One was in Wolfeboro Falls where Elm Street split off to the left from Center Street. Another was in the center of the road at the end of South Main Street in South Wolfeboro, just as it turned right toward Alton. Still another was on Cen-

The four-story wooden shoe factory, popularly known as the Clark Shop, built by Greenleaf Clark and others in 1895. With a front 18 windows wide and sides 9 windows deep, it was a smaller version of the "Big Factory" (a.k.a. Bell Shop) which was 36 windows wide by 18 deep. In this circa 1906 view the Clark Shop was occupied by the C.K. Fox shoe company.

August 1905 view from a postcard captioned "Summer residence of C.K. Fox, Wolfeboro, N.H." This particular card bore the handwritten invitation "Come over on my veranda" and was addressed by shoe manufacturer Fox to Miss Grace B. Lake in his home town of Haverhill, MA. The Fox mansion stands today on North Main Street.

tral Avenue, and a further fountain was at Goose Corner. Horses drank from a bowl-shaped receptacle, and a metal cup on a chain was provided for humans. Little thought was given to germs or the transmission of diseases.[46]

The intersection of Center and South Main Streets was known as Pickering Corner. Facing Center Street, the block on the left was the old Pickering Block, now called the Rollins Block (from Charles Rollins, who inherited it from his father-in-law Daniel Pickering). The Cate Block was on the right and was a large, rambling structure with five or more doors for boarders. According to one historian, it was a rather decrepit place.[47]

### Vacant Shoe Factories

In May 1901 Spaulding & Swett announced it would be vacating its leased four-story building on Factory Street where it had been operating since 1895 and would move its machinery to Lowell, MA. Following the shutdown, out-of-work citizens drifted away, primarily to Massachusetts and Maine, to seek positions at mills there.

Many of the boarding houses up and down Factory Street were soon vacant, and there were empty rooms in the Cate Block. Reflective of this downturn, a brochure published by the Wolfeboro Loan and Banking Company noted the following:[48]

> Our intent...is to try and induce some manufacturer,...particularly a shoe business, because this town from its earliest has always been more or less acquainted with that particular line of work. The town bears, and rightfully, too, the reputation of having the best and most thorough shoemakers in New England.... You can scarcely find a poor workman among them....
>
> Another ever favorable condition in the past was the fact that the help could at all times be relied upon for steadiness.... There were no strikes or labor difficulties. No foreign element in the town. All American workmen.... There can be no trouble in procuring from 500 to 700 employees upon the shortest notice and all of the best.

In an era in which women could not vote, when black people in the South had a second-class citizenship (if even that), and when foreigners were often discriminated against and crowded into ghettos in Boston, New York, and other cities, the Wolfeboro financial institution's boast that the town had *no foreign element* was not necessarily different from the outlook of numerous other Yankee villages. Today, this sentiment cannot be excused, any more than the "Gentiles only" signs posted at hotels and vacation spots around Wolfeboro in the 1930s and 1940s can be; they are at once historical facts and embarrassments. However, we all learn from the past, and today discrimination is no longer tolerated.

Actually, the statement of Wolfeboro having no immigrants in 1901 was patently false. There were many of the *foreign element* in town, especially those of French descent who had come across the border from Nova Scotia and elsewhere in Canada to seek work.

The brochure continued its plea:

> There are now two idle factory buildings that have heretofore been occupied in the manufacture of shoes.... One of these shops, known as the "big shop," is 200 feet long by 36 feet wide, four stories high, having a wing at each end 78 feet long by 36 feet wide, and each is also four stories high.... There is also another "big shop"[49] that was recently built. It is four stories high and equipped with power, etc. This shop is 100 feet long by 44 feet wide with basement. The boiler house is a separate structure of brick, and the motive power is generated by a 45 h.p. engine and 60 h.p. boiler.

On November 1, 1902, the newspaper reported that a meeting of the citizens of the town had been held two days earlier at Sheridan Hall, and that a committee reported that it had communicated with and had seen 20 or more firms, but none had agreed to settle in Wolfeboro. It was agreed to form the Wolfeboro Board of Trade consisting of prominent local merchants and citizens.

Weeks passed, and still no new businesses had been attracted to town. Finally, on April 25, 1903, came some good news:

> It is practically settled that Wolfeboro is to have one of its vacant factories occupied for the manufacture of shoes.... One of the most reputable and responsible manufacturers of Haverhill has agreed to lease our small factory (or the Greenleaf B. Clark Shop).... We have every reason to believe that in a few weeks the hum of shoe machinery will again be heard in our village, and that many of our absent ones may return to us again.

More on this subject was printed on May 2, 1903:

> Mr. Charles K. Fox of Haverhill, Mass. has entered into an agreement to put into operation at once the Clark factory, and it will begin the shipment of machinery early next week. The factory is being put into condition. The boiler and its dynamo have been tested...and the shop is to be wired at once for lighting. Our people feel proud to think that they, by waiting, have been so fortunate as to secure a firm of such excellent reputation.

On June 13, 1903, the *Granite State News* printed this item:

> Our new shoe firm is doing a fine little business already, giving employment to some 30 or more hands. They are constantly adding new machinery, all of the most approved patterns, and expect to be able to have some stitchers at work next week, which will be followed by the cutters as feasibly as possible.... It looks now from present indications and prospects that the intention of Mr. Fox to have employed from 200 to 250 hands this fall may be fully realized. All of the machinery in what is known as the second factory is to be moved here as promptly as is consistent with good business measures.

In September 1903 the Board of Trade reported that all was going well with the C.K. Fox Company in the Small Factory (as it was called, a.k.a. Little Factory), but that a tenant was still needed for the Big Factory. By February 1904 Fox employed 110 people.

Interior of the Lewando & Tilton store in the Peavey Block, June 1903. Among the items that can be seen are Moxie bottles, canned vegetables, crackers, decorative prints, pickles, baking powder, salad dressing, fresh fruit and vegetables, watermelons (to the left on the floor in front of counter), flour, rice, smoked meat, cheese, and candy. Lakes Region Sport & Photo shop is located there in the 1990s.

In March 1905 the Big Factory was offered for sale by Nathaniel T. Brewster. At the annual meeting of the Village Fire Precinct,[50] March 31, 1908, it was voted that the building be purchased for use in establishing a municipal electric plant, the price not to exceed $4,000. Nearly two years later, on January 29, 1910, the *News* commented that nothing definite had been done toward refitting it to be the Electric Light Plant. "Voters are becoming restless."

At the Village Fire Precinct meeting, March 29, 1910, it was voted to raise an additional $2,000 by bonded debt to repair and preserve the Big Factory. Public opinion was divided. Some citizens thought the building should be demolished. Others believed that the town never should have bought it in the first place. The local paper reported this on May 14, 1910:

> Our shoe shop 200 feet long, 40 feet wide, four stories high, with two wings 80 by 40 is destined to remain as is, with occasional repairs indefinitely, such as was decided at the recent Precinct meeting.

**Local Merchants**

Wolfeboro was a town of shops in the early years of the present century. General stores and specialty shops stocking everything from groceries to stoves, from fishing tackle to horse saddles, held forth not only in the downtown district, but in East Wolfeboro, South Wolfeboro, Wolfeboro Falls, and other outlying areas.

Similarly, barber shops sold fishing tackle, restaurants sold cigars, and grain dealers sold boat engines. Perhaps the amount of money spent in town was too small to permit the typical store to have but a single line of merchandise or goods except for popular products such as shoes or fish. Surely, one of the most diverse enterprises in Wolfeboro was that of George H. Clough, M.D. A medical doctor and oculist by training, Clough was also an electrician, a repairer of marine engines, and seller of automobiles.

During the 1901-1910 decade Frank P. Hobbs was a hotel operator, auctioneer, steamer captain, real estate agent, and livery stable operator, among other things. On August 5, 1901, he purchased the Belvue House, also known as the Lake Shore House, which he had been leasing for several years. This was used as an annex to his Hobbs-Is-Inn located diagonally across South Main Street. Hobbs, despite his local prominence and multiple business interests, went bankrupt in 1903. Apparently, he was back on his feet again a few years later. Hobbs is said to have had a photographic memory and a capacity for recalling details unequaled by any townsman of his era.

In 1903 local grocer Herbert E. Haines filed for voluntary bankruptcy. Business times were tough, especially following a couple years with vacant shoe factories. Retailers felt the pinch most of all. Although the C.K. Fox Company came to town in the summer of 1903, it was many months before workers were employed in quantity. By that time much economic damage had been done. Good times did not return locally in a significant way until 1904.

In October 1903 student desks, "made in birch, finished to resemble mahogany, fitted with lock and key," were a "big value" for just $3.75 at the S.M. Hodge Furniture Store in the Town Hall. Following the death of William B. Hodge in June 1901, his widow Sarah Hodge took the business reins. The success of the enterprise continued under her management.

At the shop of Everett S. Albee, jeweler, Kodak Brownie cameras cost $1 to $2. Almon W. Eaton, grocer and one of the most prosperous local merchants, offered Chase & Sanborn's Seal brand coffee put up in a one-pound can for 23¢. Charles O. Doe, "sole agent for Carroll County for American Woolen Mills Co., who manufactures their goods from raw material and makes custom garments individual measure only," offered measured-to-fit men's suits for $7 to $30 in his 15th season of business. P.S. Marden advertised that $50 "buys a nice boathouse, thoroughly built and painted."

Another vignette is furnished by Fred W. Mildon, who came to Wolfeboro from Biddeford, ME, in spring 1904 and bought the general store operated by Harry R. Leavitt. With his partner G.H. Morrill, of Portland, ME, Mildon anticipated doing a lively trade. Unfortunately, by autumn 1905, Morrill had decamped for parts unknown, leaving no forwarding address. Mildon petitioned the court to schedule the Morrill & Mildon firm into bankruptcy so that finances could be reorganized. This done, Mildon rented a store in the Central Block on Railroad Avenue, and opened a grocery and variety store in March 1906. In spring 1908 Mildon was bankrupt again. This time he moved back to Maine from whence he had come.

The Paper Store, as it was called in the 1900s, was earlier owned by Israel B. Manning. During the early part of the century it served as a depot for paper goods such as stationery, blank books, office supplies, daily papers, magazines, toys, games, postcards, greeting cards, and novelties. This is one of the few turn-of-the-century business names still familiar today (as Black's Paper Store) although it has gone through multiple ownership changes over the years.

John I. Sanborn, who came to Wolfeboro in 1898, in 1903 purchased Frank L. Ham's men's clothing store in the center front section of the Peavey Block. As a sideline, he rented rowboats from the back of his store and maintained the steamer *Katrina* for lease.

Among the several local entrepreneurs at the time was J. Frank Goodwin, who arrived in town in 1893 and promptly set about getting his fingers in as many business pies as possible. By the turn of the century he operated an ice cream parlor, fruit and confectionery store, and tobacco counter all in a small wooden building to the left of the Peavey Block. At the same time he ran a contracting and building business. He later became a prominent landholder and owned all of the property immediately to the east of Forest Road from North Main Street to Lake Winnipesaukee, some of which has been developed in recent decades by his grandson, Jeff Goodwin.

When the Wolfeboro economy recovered in 1904-1905, real estate began to trade at a brisk pace, S.W. Clow, J. Frank Goodwin, and other contractors had many commissions to build houses and summer cottages, and there seemed to be a general air of prosperity. Boat sales increased sharply, and Goodhue & Hawkins on Sewall Street did a banner business. Several local merchants moved into new stores or remodeled old ones. Lewando & Tilton, with headquarters on the right side of the ground floor of the Peavey Block, bought a boat to permit them to deliver groceries to camps on Lake Winnipesaukee.

The local economy remained robust for the next several years, even in 1907 when Wall Street suffered a setback and there were troubles on the national scene. About the only negative registered in town in 1907 was the closing in December of the blanket mill in South Wolfeboro, with no announcement as to when it would reopen.

A large lawsuit involving O.P. Berry and others versus Frank B. Hutchins concerning the use of water in the Smith River dragged through the courts for years beginning in the 1890s. Finally, each litigant was assigned a specific amount of runoff, and James E. Gridley of the town (who also measured the rainfall, acted as a weatherman, and operated a greenhouse) was hired to take charge of monitoring the water given to each of the adversaries.

From the time of the Wolfeboro Loan and Banking Company's collapse in 1904 to the founding of the Wolfeboro National Bank in 1906, there was no local financial institution. In the meantime merchants and other citizens did their banking in Rochester, Laconia, Dover, and elsewhere. In 1908 the Wolfeboro National Bank, scarcely two years old, reported record profits, the Wolfeboro Post Office did a record mailing and receiving of Christmas packages, and there was much new construction and remodeling. It was a time of local prosperity.

Toward the end of the 1901-1910 decade, cooking ranges were all the rage. H.M. Bickford, whose hardware store in the Folsom Block carried just about everything including kitchen sinks, ran large advertisements in the *Granite State News* for Glenwood, Herald, and other brands of ranges which burned wood or coal or both.

Here today and gone tomorrow. Over the years, many local businesses fit this syndrome. Typical is the story of Howe & French, who in the summer of 1908 set up a showroom in the Central Block and sold stoves and lamps that operated with denatured alcohol as fuel. Demonstrations were conducted daily. Early in September the premises in the Central Block were vacated, and a scaled-down version of the stove and lamp exhibit was moved to Tobey's Drug Store where it was soon taken down.

Effective April 1, 1908, the blacksmiths in town—Walter F. Pickering, Elbridge G. Copp, Larkin D. Hobbs, Herbert L. Bruce, and Fred Hurd—united to announce new rates. Four new shoes for a horse now cost $1.25, resetting four existing shoes cost 60 cents. By 1920 the automobile forced most blacksmith shops and livery stables to curtail or discontinue their business.

Local painters banded together to announce that on and after January 1, 1908, rates for their labor would be $2.50 per day.

### Shopping Out of Town

Then as now, Wolfeboro merchants preferred that local citizens spend their money in town. In practice, the typical buyer often thought that the merchandise was more attractive and cheaper elsewhere, whether or not it actually was.

Once or more each year, merchants of Laconia banded together to charter the steamship *Governor Endicott* to bring potential buyers across the lake from Wolfeboro. In October 1907 they sponsored an excursion, suggesting that Laconia offered a larger selection and lower prices than hometown stores. This prompted "Peter" (surname not given) to write to the *Granite State News* to remind readers that merchants of Laconia never donated to Wolfeboro schools, churches, public improvement projects, or anything else. They were takers, not givers.

Throughout and beyond the next decade, the local paper printed many negative stories and editorials about buying out of town and through the mail. A dollar spent with Sears in Chicago or across the lake in Laconia was a dollar not spent in downtown Wolfeboro.

### Some Fleecing Was Done

No account would be complete without mention of the biggest stock promotion in Wolfeboro in the early part of the century. The story begins about July 1909, when Charles C. Witham came to Wolfeboro and opened up a tourist home called The Oaks on the shore of Crescent Lake. Apparently a satisfactory number of patrons crossed the threshold, and business was good. In the meantime, Witham had bigger things in mind.

With Col. George A. Emery and a group of Massachusetts entrepreneurs, Witham created the Crescent

**View circa 1903-1904 of Morrison & Chamberlain's clothing store (which was undergoing ownership transition and may have lacked a sign for this reason) and M.R. Beacham's clothing and millinery shop, North Main Street near the bridge. These two buildings were later moved apart and a brick building constructed between them. In the 1990s Miltner's Shoes is in one and Rumors Café in the other, while Dive Winnipesaukee is in the later brick structure.**

**Interior of N.L. Horne's dry goods shop on North Main Street 1905 or later. Charles A. and Nellie L. Horne are shown toward the back of the store. "Terms Cash, Please Do Not Ask For Credit" proclaims a sign at the center. The reflection of the camera tripod legs can be seen in the glass on the front of the display case. Rumors Café is in the building today.**

Lake Land & Livestock Company, capitalized at $200,000, with a like number of shares having a par value of $1 each, plus some preferred stock paying 7%. Pronouncements were made to the effect that the company had excellent financing and that no local capital was needed. "The company specializes in fine grade sheep for wool and meat products, as well as the finest first-rate males for the improvement of the breeder's flock," the *Granite State News* noted on April 15, 1910.

E.C. Hatstat of Leominster, MA, was president; A.L. Walker of Leominster was secretary and treasurer, Witham was a director, George A. Emery of Wolfeboro Falls was the directing general manager, Ralph A. Lupton of Wilmington, DE, was a director, and Clinton Goudy of Springfield, MA, was legal counsel.

While Witham was taking care of things in Wolfeboro, Col. Emery was in Maine buying sheep to stock the spread.

"The organizers of this company are not only hustlers, but practical businessmen, well and favorably known in the community in which they live and enjoy the confidence and esteem of all who know them," the editor of the local paper enthused. Further, Wolfeboro citizens were urged to welcome the entrepreneurs to town and encourage their success. So far, so good.

The Oaks, Witham's boarding house, was selected for the company's headquarters due to its nearness to shipping facilities and its large grounds and stables. In the issue of April 23, 1910, the editor of the *News* exhorted citizens as follows:

> Now is the opportunity for our farmer friends, if interested in the upbuilding of agriculture and also a safe investment, to secure an interest in this company.... There can be no safer investment for idle capital than in sheep husbandry.

Apparently the well-heeled investors from out of state could, indeed, use a few local dollars, too. The enthusiasm of the *Granite State News* was repaid by the Crescent Lake Land & Livestock Company which bought advertising space amounting to half of the *front page* of the very next issue to show a picture of The Oaks (the new headquarters of the Crescent Lake Club "composed of those interested in the company" and where it "entertains its guests"), accompanied by this text:

> To the end that you may be induced to come and see for yourself, we have instituted what we are pleased to call the Crescent Lake Club. Every stockholder, large or small, has issued to him with his certificate of stock a membership card stating that he as a stockholder is a member of this club and entitled to all the privileges thereof.

Information concerning how to invest in stock was given at the bottom of the advertisement.

On May 14 the newspaper informed readers that the company had already secured 800 sheep.

The issue of June 4, 1910, included an enthusiastic report about a visit to Wolfeboro the previous Saturday by many stockholders and the officials of the enterprise. "The company is in a prosperous condition, while the prospect for success is very flattering," President E.C. Hatstat was quoted as saying. "Already we have secured 600 to 800 acres with promises of as much more when needed. The sheep at the home place, now some 150 [*sic*], are in good condition while several hundred more have been bought. Monday the first fleeces were taken from the home flock."[51]

The *Granite State News*, September 17, 1910, carried this advertisement:

> SHERIFF SALE! The sheriff, Myron L. Johnson, will sell at public auction on Thursday, September 22, 1910, at 10:00 in the forenoon the following goods and chattels on writ in favor of Charles C. Witham and against Crescent Lake Land & Livestock Company. 76 sheep and lambs, 51 fleeces of wool, one horse, one harness.

What happened to the perpetrators of the fraud was not stated.

*Sic transit gloria mundi.*

## KEEPING HEALTHY

### Drug Stores

Drug stores were social centers in addition to being dispensaries of medicine. The typical pharmacy had a soda fountain, medicines and remedies, and a selection of gifts and novelties for sale. Among the businesses in this category in operation 1901-1910 were: Wolfeboro Drug Store (owned by C.H. Ferguson; sold to Joseph W. Robins in 1902), Town Hall Drug Store (went out of business in 1901 after the death of its owner, Ernest H. Goodsoe), Thompson's Drug Store (owned by Dr. Edward H. Thompson; sold to Delmar U. Hobbs in 1903 and operated as D.U. Hobbs & Co.), and Tobey's Pharmacy (founded as such in 1907, although Dr. Fred C. Tobey, owner, had dispensed his own prescriptions as early as 1903). Tobey's continued to attract a wide clientele until its closing in 1995.

The June 12, 1909, edition of the *Granite State News* printed this:

> Dr. Tobey has a new and one of the handsomest drug stores in New England. The store was formally opened to the public at noon Saturday, and until midnight five clerks were kept on the jump dispensing the choicest ice cream, soda, confections, and 7-20-4 cigars,[52] besides hundreds of pinks and perfumes to the ladies. Everyone was in the best of spirits. Over 1,000 were served. In the evening this store with its numerous plate glass mirrors, glass showcases set in mahogany, the onyx counters, and silver fittings sparkled under the electrics and displayed a charming scene of animation.

Earlier, Tobey's Pharmacy had been located across South Main Street from the Hobbs-Is-Inn. After the drug store opened in the Goodwin Block next to the bridge,

Dr. Tobey operated Tobey's Spa in the old store, which stayed open less than a year.

### Patent Medicines

During the first six years of the present century, patent medicine advertising dominated the pages of the *Granite State News*. There were two ways to buy these remedies—by mail or over the counter. In 1901 Thompson's Pharmacy was the leading emporium for patent medicines in Wolfeboro and the leading advertiser, although the Wolfeboro Drug Store came in a close second. Later, D.U. Hobbs & Co. and Tobey's Pharmacy got into the game. In addition, most general stores had a shelf or two of patent medicines for sale.

There were no holds barred in the hawking of cures. Why visit a doctor, when 25¢, 50¢, or $1 spent for a patent medicine was a guaranteed way to good health? Among the many medicines locally advertised in 1901 were:

> Dewitt's Little Early Risers, which were said to "compel your liver and bowels to do their duty."
>
> Lydia E. Pinkham's Vegetable Compound stood "prepared to meet the needs of woman's system at this trying period of her life."
>
> Carter's Little Liver Pills were the best way to "cure sick headache and relieve all the troubles incident to a bilious state of the system."
>
> Laxakola was "the great tonic laxative."

Dr. Williams' Pink Pills for Pale People, an alliterative product title that sounds silly today, was meant to be taken seriously. Moreover, if a reader of the *Granite State News* was skeptical of its glorious benefits, Dr. Williams stood ready with a $1,000 reward for "evidence of fraud in testimonials."

A Wolfeboro physician decided to increase his profits by making his own patent medicine. The local paper printed this on November 1, 1902:

> Dr. E.H. Thompson has fitted up over his pharmacy a workroom for the purpose of manufacturing his specialty, "Thompson's Toothache Drops." He has a large amount of printed material, vials, etc., and is making preparations to begin at once putting this preparation on the market. Already he has created a large demand for the preparation. When it gets down to working business it will require several hands to supply orders.

In 1905 a series of reports by Samuel Hopkins Adams appeared in *Collier's* magazine. Titled "The Great American Fraud," the articles exposed patent medicines and revealed that they were medically worthless concoctions laced in many instances with alcohol, opium extracts, poisons, and flavoring. A great hue and cry arose from the public, and as a result, Congress passed the Pure Food and Drug Act which took effect on January 1, 1907.

Some products continued in the marketplace, although those that depended upon opium or alcohol to "cure" the afflicted, or at least sedate them into insensibility, no longer worked. Nevertheless, their advertising rolled merrily along.

A latecomer to the patent medicine field was the Balm-Elixir Corporation of Sanbornville, conducted by A. Judson Hamm just across the Wolfeboro town line. The company took out large advertisements in the *Granite State News* in 1907 and 1908. Their product was Balm-Elixir, good for "family or stable"—apparently equally efficacious for man or horse—which sold at 50 cents per bottle. Testimonials from regional people were reprinted in an effort to persuade others to buy the nostrum.

The *Granite State News* published an article which encouraged local people to buy stock in the Balm-Elixir Corporation, noting:

> It seems probable from the present demand for their goods from old customers that the earnings will double in the next year.... This is certainly a desirable opportunity for anyone with money to invest to put it where it will bring them double what the savings banks pay, and at the same time the original investment will rapidly increase in value, for no doubt their stock will be worth several times what it is selling for today when the business is in full swing.... We hope that those who are nearby and able will encourage as long as possible this business in our county and town by the personal investment of whatever amount they can spare.

### Health and Wellness

"Early to bed and early to rise" may have helped to make Wolfeboro citizens healthy. Whether they were wealthy or wise is another matter. The 10-hour work day was common, and the self-employed often worked from sun-up to sunset. Hard work made strong bodies and promoted longevity. However, not all was ideal.

Children were often expected to work when not attending school. Child labor laws were not yet in effect. The January 5, 1902, number of the *Granite State News* carried this advertisement: "Wanted: Position in good family for boy eight years old. Capable and willing to work." Chances are good that the boy's parents wanted him to earn money not for himself but for them.

In 1903 a Mrs. Johnson, who worked in the house of James and Mary Martin, called upon Dr. Nathaniel H. Scott and displayed symptoms of what seemed to be typhoid fever. It was not, and Scott consulted other physicians who were all puzzled. Eventually, Scott learned that Mrs. Martin had a parrot from New York City, and it had died. It was finally determined that the lady had a case of parrot fever or psittacosis—the first ever reported in the United States and thus a medical landmark.[53]

According to records kept by the Board of Health, 32 people died in Wolfeboro in 1907. Most frequent causes of death were cardiac diseases (nine cases), cancer (six), apoplexy (five), and senility (four).

Each year the *Boston Post* newspaper awarded the Post Cane to the oldest citizen of each town in its greater circulation area. In response to a query as to whether women were eligible for the honor, the "Canes Department" of the *Boston Post* informed the *Granite State News*,

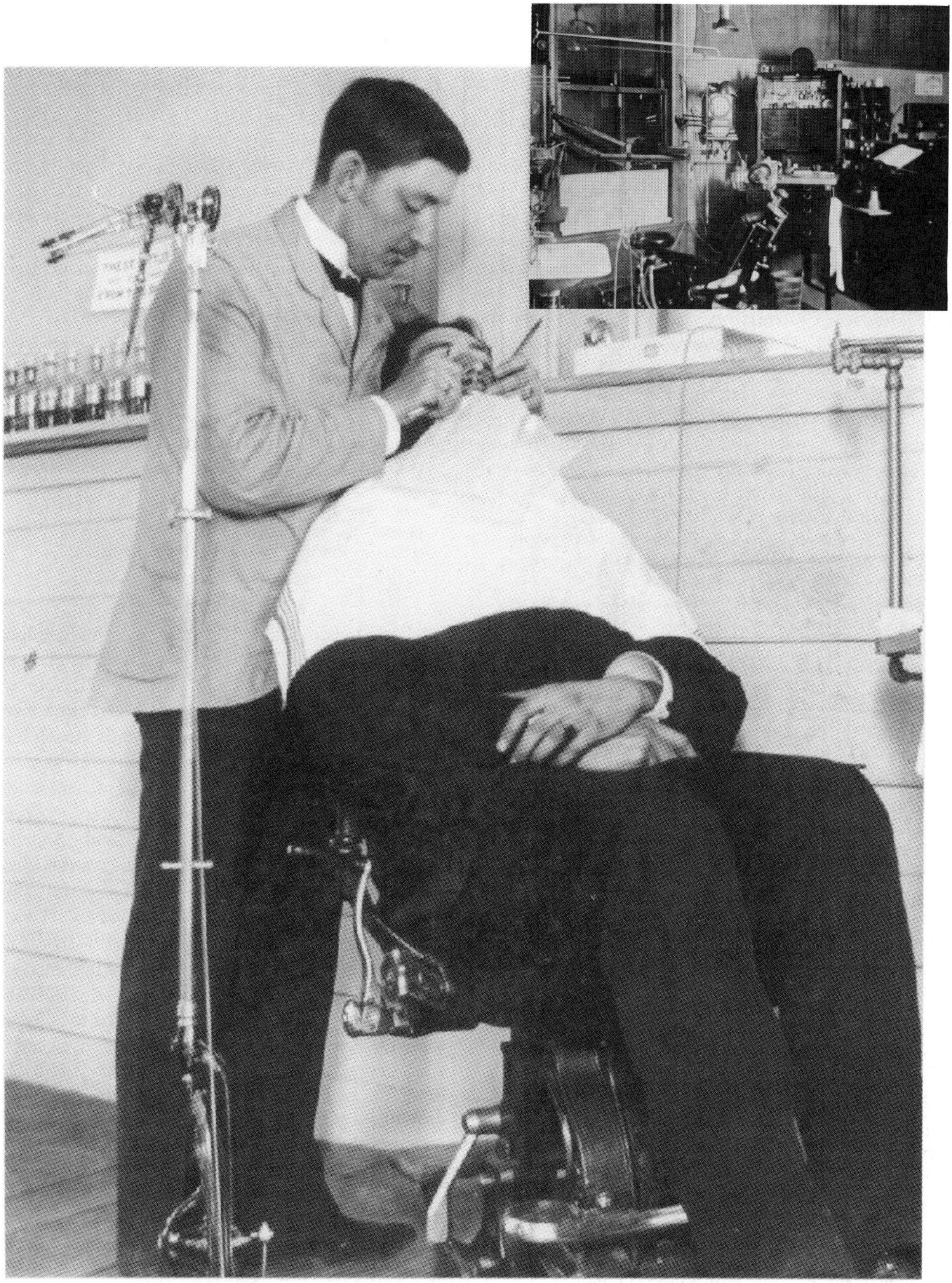

Dentistry: Dr. Frederick E. Meader (shown here at Harvard) graduated from Harvard Medical School in 1894 and by 1895 had dental offices in Boston and Wolfeboro in the Goodwin Block. In 1899 he installed an electric light in his office, being one of the first local businesses to do so.

Inset at upper right: Dental office of Dr. Burt W. Parshley in his residence on North Main Street in the early part of the present century. His home was built in 1905-06.

in a reply published on September 18, 1909, that the "oldest citizen" meant "the oldest *male* citizen who is a voter."

Physicians in Wolfeboro standardized their fees, as did painters, blacksmiths, and certain other classes of professionals. On January 1, 1908, doctors' charges were as follows:

> Office consultations 75¢. Visits in the central section of Wolfeboro, $1; visits outside the section $1 plus 25¢ per mile. Anesthetic for minor surgery, $5, anesthetic for major surgery, $10. Obstetric cases (normal) $10.

There were few health or food quality regulations in effect, and even fewer that were enforced. Apparently, Wolfeboro rated a blue ribbon for its milk quality, as this sad commentary on conditions elsewhere noted on July 21, 1906:

> Of 25 different samples of milk from different towns in the state, taken for the State Board of Health and analyzed, the four samples from Wolfeboro were regarded as being of legal quality, out of six samples [statewide] reported legal. The other 19 samples were below standard, or watered. Take off your hat to the Wolfeboro milkmen.

Perhaps in response to this acclaim, the local sellers of milk raised the price on October 1, 1906, from 5¢ a quart to 6¢.

In 1910 town medical doctors included Fred E. Clow, a Harvard graduate who started practice in Wolfeboro in 1905; S.P. Getchell, who began his practice in 1899; Fred C. Tobey, who was as well known for his drug store as for his doctoring and, on occasion, his veterinary practice;[54] Curtis B. Cotton, who sold his practice to young Dr. Tobey in 1903, but who a few months later started in practice again; and Nathaniel H. Scott, whose clientele was one of the largest in town.

Dr. Oliver Dowlin had been practicing dentistry since the 1860s. His office was on the ground floor of the Pickering Block. A relatively new dentist on the local scene was Dr. Burt W. Parshley, who had come to town from Dorchester, MA in 1905 and who had an office on the first floor of his beautiful home on South Main Street in 1910. Ephemeral was the local dental practice of F.A. Charles, who was in town only for a few weeks in the summer of 1910. Dr. Frederick E. Meader saw most of his dental patients at his office in Boston and during the decade was usually in Wolfeboro for two days each week.

### Huggins Hospital

The inception of what would become one of the town's greatest assets (although it was not municipally owned) and sources of pride began on the evening of January 9, 1907, at the office of S.P. Getchell, M.D., upstairs in the Peavey Block. Getchell was viewed as a gentleman of learning and culture. Meeting with him on that date was Fred E. Clow, M.D. At least one account states that Curtis B. Cotton, M.D. was in attendance as well.[55] Getchell and Clow (and possibly Cotton) discussed the current unsatisfactory situation of having major surgery done in private residences and contemplated renting or buying a modest house for use as a hospital and putting a nurse in charge.

An early history of Huggins Hospital noted:[56]

> A second meeting was held on January 14, attended by doctors Getchell, Cotton, Clow, and Messrs. James H. Martin [president of the Wolfeboro National Bank], Joseph W. Robins [druggist], Wilbra H. Swett [banker], Parry T. Hersey [merchant], Edwin Chamberlain [clothier], and Kent.
>
> The following morning James Martin convened a meeting and suggested that the matter be put on a business basis. Incorporators were Sewall W. Abbott, James H. Martin, and Stephen W. Clow, Edwin Chamberlain, Parry T. Hersey, Wilbra H. Swett, Blake Folsom, Joseph W. Chadwick, and Allen C. Keith. The Ladies' Aid Association was formed on September 8, 1907, at the First Congregational Church.

Interviewed by *Granite State News* editor Frederick W. Prindle after the get-together, the doctors noted that a new hospital would cost them money, because "a poor laboring man now pays a dollar for a house call, but he would go to the hospital for free treatment. For a field to draw from, the county around would furnish many patients, and one of our doctors thinks that in Wolfeboro alone at least one patient would be in the hospital all the time, and perhaps more than one." The financial outlook was uncertain.

Wolfeboro National Bank President James H. Martin and his wife, Mary (daughter of Mr. and Mrs. John Huggins of Wolfeboro), agreed to make an initial contribution of $10,000 toward the project. Apparently, Blake Folsom was also involved in the early stages, and the name Folsom Hospital was proposed but not adopted.

The *Granite State News*, February 2, 1907, printed this:

> A hospital is as good as assured for this town. Already $20,000 has been pledged, one of our most influential men offering $15,000 if a like sum could be raised. It is intended to call it the Huggins Hospital.

On April 23, 1907, a board of trustees of 15 was elected.[57] From the start the venture had a wide base of community support. It was announced in June that the Furber homestead comprising about 14 acres had been acquired, with possession to be after September 1 when remodeling began. The two-story wooden house was located where Kingswood Regional High School is today.[58]

Huggins Hospital was dedicated on December 31, 1907. On January 1, 1908, the 12-bed facility was opened to the public, and the first patient was admitted on January 4. In the early years, it was popularly called the Huggins Sanitarium, but, eventually, the Huggins Hospital name prevailed.

Joseph W. Robins was named as the official supplier of medicine for the institution. The first superintendent of the hospital was Miss Lona A. Westover, of Manchester, a graduate of the Elliot Hospital and the Boston Floating Hospital.

Mrs. Sherman D. Parsons was named president of the Ladies' Aid Association, and Mrs. S.P. Getchell, vice-president. Bake sales and other events were held to raise money.

## AROUND THE TOWN

### Short Takes

The 1901-1910 decade included many events of a varied nature including the following, as reported in the *Granite State News* on the dates indicated.

**1902, June 7. Carpenter's palatial home:** "George A. Carpenter, Esq., is the possessor of the largest private residence in town. When completed it will be with its landscape embellishment classed with Massachusetts' best." The reference is to Cobham Hall, built at the end of Green Street and now known as Bearce Hall at Brewster Academy. Several years later, in 1905, Carpenter succeeded in having the town close off the end of Green Street, which portion then reverted to his private use. Greenleaf B. Clark acquired numerous structures on that section of Green Street and moved them elsewhere in town.

**1902, September 20. Old silver dollar displayed:** "N.C. Frost, our barber, is sporting one of the dollars of our daddies bearing date 1799."

**1903, January 3. Helen Keller visits:** Reported that Miss Helen Keller, deaf and blind, registered at the Sheridan Hotel on December 31, 1902. She and two others came here to consult with Henry W. Bradford, M.D., local oculist.[59]

**1903, May 23. Pigs, snakes:** Center Wolfeboro: "Elder J.F. Chamberlain is the owner of seven young pigs. Monroe Smith killed a black snake in his woodshed this morning [May 14] which measured four feet 11 inches long."

**1903, May 30. Livestock:** The yearly town inventory showed 436 horses, one mule, 167 oxen, 603 cows, 224 neat stock [cattle other than milk-producing cows], 187 sheep.

**1904. Potatoes:** Records were set for potatoes harvested in Wolfeboro. Nathaniel B. Horne of Lakeview Farm harvested from 9/20th of an acre 175 bushels.

**1904, August 6. Brewster Academy news:** "The contract for the building of the Brewster School Building has been let to E.C. Cummings & Co. of Boston, and the work is to commence immediately. The building is to be covered in by November 15 and finished for occupancy April 1, 1905."

**1904, August 27. Ex-president Cleveland visits:** "Monday the steamer *Gilnockie* was in port and had on board ex-president Grover Cleveland and family, who are spending the summer at Sandwich."

**1905, October 14. Fauna:** "C.H. Davis, while visiting at central Wolfeboro this week, went down beside the railroad track near the brook and seeing a hole in the sand started to dig and in a few minutes unearthed 27 young turtles, just hatched out."

**1905, October 24. Tuftonboro forges ahead:** "We hear that the town of Tuftonboro is to have a receiving tomb built immediately.... Are we going to let a town like Tuftonboro go ahead of us?"

**1905, November 4. Brewster dedication:** "The dedication of the new Brewster Free Academy took place in the assembly hall Wednesday afternoon [November 1], with trustees, faculty, students, and alumni and invited guests present...."

**1907, June 1. Public benefactor:** The paper contained an account of the will of Josiah W. Brown of Boston, who gave the town of Wolfeboro $20,000 for a high school. The residue from his estate was to be invested, and the net income thereof was to be given to the selectmen of Wolfeboro "to be by them used for the education of poor and worthy young ladies and men residents of such town."

**1907, July 27. Accomplishments:** Progress in 1907 as listed in an editorial: The establishment of the YMCA in Wolfeboro, repairs and expansion of the Christian Church above the bridge, the starting of Huggins Hospital, the setting up of Camp Birchmont on Mount Delight, the securing of the old Joseph Varney tannery by the Kingswood Club on the shore of Lake Winnipesaukee, and the Winnipesaukee Summer Assembly of religious meetings.

**1909, January 30. Electricity:** A feature titled "Electrical Definitions" told readers what such terms as alternating current, ampere, armature, circuit, circuit-breaker, electromagnet, fuse, etc., meant. Electricity was just coming into widespread use.

**1909 March 6. Local inventor:** "One of the attractions of our village is a 'motor sled' owned and operated by Fred Brewster and Palmer Pinkham. The motor power of the steam engine development is about one horsepower. When seen on our streets it attracts a crowd."

**1909, June 5. Visitors:** The *Granite State News* printed items concerning visitors from out of town. Sample: "Mr. and Mrs. Arthur W. Fitts of Boston are stopping for a few days with Mrs. Fitts' parents, Mr. and Mrs. Newman Hayford of Mill Street."

**1910: November 19. Musical talent:** Wolfeboro merchant Joseph Lewando was a juror from Wolfeboro in the court at Ossipee and during recesses gave piano selections for guests and other jurors at the nearby Carroll Inn.

## PRICES IN 1910

The following prices and related items are from advertisements and notices in the *Granite State News*, 1910.

**Appliance:** Sewing machine, White brand, $19.50 to $29.50.

**Automobiles:** Buicks, 18 h.p. four passenger touring car, $1,150; 24 h.p. five passenger, $1,400; 30 h.p. roadster, $1,750; Reo, 30 h.p., $1,250.

**Beverages:** Coffee, pound, 17¢. Moxie, glass, 5¢. Coca-Cola, glass, 5¢.

**Clothing:** Boy's shoes, pair, $2 to $2.50. Fur coat for ladies, $25 to $85. Gloves, cotton, per pair, 10¢ to 20¢. Ladies' suit, $7.50 to $15. Lady's long winter coat (on sale), $5. Men's shoes, pair, $3 to $4. Underwear, lamb's down fleece, per pair, 65¢. Underwear, union suits, 85¢.

**Engine:** 8 1/2 h.p., single cylinder marine, $55.

**Entertainment:** Ticket for three-act stage comedy, 25¢.

**Flowers:** Per dozen: Carnations $1.50 to $2, daffodils 50¢, Easter lilies $3 to $4, narcissus 50¢, roses $1 to $4, tulips 75¢ to $1.50; violets, 75¢ to $5 per bunch. Molasses, choice, gallon, 30¢. Quaker Oats, package, 5¢. Raisins, Daisy brand, seeded, package, 9¢. Sugar, 18 pounds for $1. Sweet potatoes, 10 pounds, 25¢.

**Food:** Meat: Beef, round steak, pound, $0.13. Corned beef, pound, 6¢ to 12¢. Salmon, can, 13¢. Ham, pound, 18¢. Sausage, pound, 16¢. Steak, sirloin, untrimmed, pound, 15¢.

**Food:** Various: Butter, pound, 30¢. Cocoa, Baker's, pound, 22¢. Flour, barrel, $6.50.

**Fuel:** Kerosene, gallon, 11¢.

**Fur:** *Buying* price for prime fox skin, $6.

**Medicine:** Doan's Regulets Constipation Pills, supply for 25¢.

**Real estate:** 7 acres of undeveloped land, $100. Cottage and boathouse on Clark's Point, $500. Cottage on Keniston Island (assessed valuation), $300.

**Soap powder:** Gold Dust brand, 4-pound package, $0.17.

**Soap:** Santa Claus brand, eight bars, 25¢; Swift's Naphtha, eight bars, 25¢.

**Tuition:** Peaslee's Commercial School in Rochester, day school, per week, $2.50; night school, per week, $1.

**Wages:** Farm worker in Wolfeboro, per day, $1 to $1.50.

# CHAPTER 4
# WOLFEBORO 1911-1920

*Wolfeboro grows in grace as a vacation center year by year, and its glory is never likely to be dimmed by any of the other Winnipesaukee resorts.*

—Boston & Maine Railroad brochure, 1917

## INTRODUCTION

The decade 1911-1920 was one of many changes and evolutions in Wolfeboro. Such topics as the high cost of living, movies, the Spanish flu, still more automobiles, and, especially, the World War were each pivotal and influential.

## NEWS IN PRINT

### Reporting the News

The *Granite State News,* Frederick W. Prindle, editor, continued to be the newspaper of record for local activities. Charles O. Doe was one of the most frequent outside commentators.

In 1914 the unmarried Sawyer sisters sold the Paper Store, and the editorial office of the *News* had to vacate its long-time premises within the establishment. The editor's desk was moved to quarters up the street in the Durgin Block, where Frederick W. Prindle was to spend his afternoons from 2:00 to 5:00. In the morning he worked at his home in Wolfeboro Falls. As before, the paper came out on Saturday afternoon each week.

The January 25, 1919, issue was the first printed on a press driven by an electric motor. Earlier numbers had been produced on a steam-driven press. On July 12, 1919, the paper was not printed, due to a broken press—the first omission since the plant burned down in 1899. Beginning with the issue of January 23, 1920, the *News* was eight pages in size, or double what it was earlier. News, fillers, and advertising readily expanded to use the space.

The editor was capable of humor, sometimes inadvertent, as in this September 30, 1911 item. Perhaps, today we would say that here is "some bad news, some good news":

> Friday afternoon, September 22, George Manuel, employed at the box factory of S.W. & J.L. Clow, sustained a severe accident involving the loss of all the fingers on his right hand.... Fortunately, he is left-handed.

Typographical errors occurred with regularity, as they did in every other newspaper ever printed. Sometimes they were funny, as in this correction in the December 1, 1917 issue:

> Last week in "Stray Shots" we made an error saying "Do not believe what prohibitionists tell you," when we intended and should have used the word "politicians." Please so read.

### Space Fillers

From time immemorial, newspaper editors have relied upon "fillers" to amuse readers and complete the empty spaces before press time. Thousands of fillers appeared in the local paper. Some were of a local nature, but most were not. Samples from the 1911-1920 decade:

**1911, July 29. A puzzle:** "Take the number of your living brothers, double the amount, add to it three, multiply by five, add to it the number of your living sisters, multiply the result by 10, add the number of deaths of brothers, and subtract 150 from the result. The right figure will be the number of deaths, the middle will be the number of living sisters, and the left will show the number of living brothers. Try it and see."

**1912, July 6. Let's hear it for snakes:** "It has been suggested by a French professor that every household have its snakes instead of its cats or dogs for the purpose of keeping rats or mice away. It is not new, for in the days of the Romans many snakes were kept by the housekeepers for precisely this purpose. Since those early times, however, the household reptile has been supplanted by the cat or dog, and the modern housewife has nothing but revulsion of feeling for every species of snake, harmful and harmless.... The snake is much cleaner than either of the other household pets."

**1913, September 27. It's true:** "Tell a man that there are 270,169,825,481 stars and he will believe you. But if a sign says 'Fresh paint' he will have to make a personal investigation."

**1914, May 30. Come to think of it:** "You never hear of a face powder factory being forced to shut down on account of poor business."

**1914, October 3. Now or never:** "When a marriage is put off, the probability is that it will never occur. The fine burst of courage which enables a man to face a marriage service comes to him only once or twice in his lifetime."

**1914, December 5. Then, don't do it:** "The highbrows claim that the use of a medicated tissue screen will make kissing 'safe and sanitary.' It may make it sanitary, but there isn't any way to make kissing safe."

**1916, February 26. A point to ponder:** "At a recent address, Mr. Bodine, superintendent of compulsory education for Chicago, said that in more than 10,000 cases of delinquency only one Boy Scout's name appears."

**1916, February 26. Laugh your way to good health:** "There is not the remotest corner or little inlet of the minute blood vessels of the human body that does not feel some wavelet from the convulsion occasioned by good hearty laughter. The central man is shaken to the innermost depth, sending new tides of life and strength to the surface, thus materially tending to insure good health to the persons who indulge therein."

**1919, September 20. Political prediction:** "It is a 10-to-1 shot that Russian Bolshevism will blow up and blow out as suddenly as French terrorism vanished a century and a quarter ago."

**1919, November 22. Local beauty:** "East Wolfeboro. If you want a pretty sight call and see Maude Dore's guinea pig."

## ENTERTAINMENT AND SPORTS

### The Masonic Temple

During the second decade of the twentieth century there was never lack of entertainment. With frequent church group and lodge meetings, motion pictures three nights a week, and a steady parade of plays, concerts, vaudeville acts, and other events at Brewster Memorial Hall, Sheridan Hall, the Masonic Temple, and Brewster Academy, anyone desiring to fill up evenings with activities had no trouble in doing so.

On January 1, 1912, the Masonic Temple opened on Glendon Street. Previously known as the Unitarian Church, it had been acquired by a local group of Masons who had issued shares to finance the acquisition and extensive remodeling. By opening day, a temporary projection booth, stage, curtains, and other theatre accouterments were in place. During the first year or so, the structure was known by several different names, including Masonic Hall (the most popular designation), New Masonic Hall, Temple Auditorium, and in late 1911 and early 1912, Opera House. After the opening of this facility in 1912, the importance of Sheridan Hall, in an antiquated hotel, diminished.

### Fun at Home

The phonograph continued to be a prime entertainment device at home, at parties, and in public gatherings. Player pianos were likewise in vogue, but fewer in number as they typically cost $500 to $1,000 each. Card games were an ideal entertainment on rainy or cold days. Particularly popular were Flinch and, with the older folks, whist. Then as now, parties were fun. This account is of a 1912 gathering:

> Saturday evening, January 20, Miss Edith Horne was agreeably surprised, when on responding to a knock at the door, to find 12 of her schoolmates, led by her teacher, Miss Douglass. It dawned on Edith that the 21st was her 12th birthday. Wraps were taken off, the usual greetings were given by members of the family, piano solos and duets were enjoyed, another knock on the door and Master Carroll Lucas appeared on the scene, carrying a mysterious small package, which was handed to Delphine Ames, and was given to Miss Edith, which proved to be a very handsome opal ring which showed the esteem of Edith held by her teacher and schoolmates.
>
> A hearty "thank you" was given by Edith. An exciting game of Flinch was played, also Logomachy, a peanut hunt was then indulged in, then button-button was played. The children were called to the dining room to find goodies of all kinds, and a very handsome birthday cake lighted by 12 candles.

### In Public Places

In July 1911 the DeRue Brothers Ideal Minstrels, "beyond a question of doubt the premier musical experts of the 20th century," appeared at Town Hall. "Their work consists of both popular and classic masterpieces, rendered upon 25 different instruments of both novelty and standard makes."

During the summer months, the boys from Camp Wyanoke often came into town and presented minstrel shows, gave skits, and marched in parades. Other local and regional campers did likewise.

Year after year, the Guy Brothers Minstrels came to town and, in fact, were the most often seen performers in this category. Singing, orchestra numbers, and comic routines were favorably reviewed. As Wolfeboro citizens had come to know the troupe performers by name, occasional reports of their health, family situations, and other personal notes were printed.

Amateur stage productions were very popular. An example is furnished by *Sisterhood of Bridgit* given at the Temple Auditorium. This three-act farce by Robert Edwin Ford drew 400 people on February 16, 1912.

On August 19, 1912, Howe's Great London Shows arrived in town. Advance billing gave the impression that hundreds of performers and others were in the troupe, but in actuality the number was probably far fewer than that.

Whenever a circus arrived in town, certain procedures would be followed: Several weeks beforehand, an "advance man" would come to the village, stay at the Sheridan House (usually), and paper Wolfeboro with posters. At the designated time, the circus would arrive in town in one or several railroad cars. After unloading, the circus would parade through town. About three or four hours later, the first afternoon show would be held under a pitched tent, followed by an evening show. Then, the circus would move on.

Each Independence Day local and regional people would turn out to watch an array of floats, marching groups, bands, and other attractions. The July 4, 1913, parade had two divisions, the first being decorated automobiles and the second being decorated floats and horse-drawn vehicles. The lineup march formed at South Main Street, and the parade went to North Main Street, Sewall Road, Pleasant Street, Oak Street, back down South Main Street to the Town Hall, where it disbanded. An estimated 5,000 people were in attendance. Later in the day a boat race held in connection with the celebration was won by Ezra Bailey in the *Scud II* which posted the remarkable speed of 35 miles an hour.

On October 26, 1913, the 12th New Hampshire Regiment from the Civil War staged a gala reunion and celebration in Wolfeboro with eight hours of festivities, including receptions at the Hotel Elmwood and the Sheridan House, a tour of the Libby Museum, a musical serenade, and greetings from Governor S.B. Felker. "These heroes...were made to feel perfectly at home. Wolfeboro did itself proud," noted the local paper.

On March 24, 1914, the Fourth Annual Concert of the Ladies Club was presented at the Temple Auditorium to a large audience. The feature number on the program was an operetta, *The Japanese Girl.*

On the evening of May 12, 1914, Dixie's Comedians performed at the Temple Auditorium to benefit the newly reorganized Wolfeboro Band. "Bess, the high-diving dog, will dive at a height of 50 feet into a tank of water in front of the theatre."[1]

After the July 15, 1914 appearance of LaTena's Big Three-Ring Wild Animal Circus, two writers wrote reviews.[2] One said:

> The circus was one of the best which have exhibited in our town. Every act was carried out as advertised. The animals were in prime condition, trappings and costumes were rich. The circus members were gentlemanly and civil, devoid of unsavory language. In fact, the circus was good.

However, in another section of the same paper, the circus parade was reviewed somewhat differently:

> The most pathetic spectacle that Wolfeboro has witnessed of late is that of the circus parade on Wednesday last. A mediocre band, few heart-sick, weary-looking women in cheap, tawdry apparel, and a few cages of broken-spirited, subdued animals, men with women dragging poor, tired, frightened little bits of humanity, rushing after them to the suffocating, pestilence-breeding tents....
>
> Shall we as true loyal citizens allow such things to come into our midst to attract the attention of our young people, or shall we endeavor to bring them clean worthwhile amusements?

The preceding points up the role of the journalist in recording history, for later generations often know of the past only by what has appeared in print. Was LaTena's Circus a great event or a poor one? Were the animals "in prime condition" or "broken-spirited"? We may never know the truth.

Many public events were staged on behalf of local charities and worthwhile causes of which none has been more popular over the years than Huggins Hospital. One such event for Huggins was a suite of three one-act plays performed in the Temple Auditorium on January 15, 1915, *In Search of a Wife, The Picture of Dorian Gray,* and *The Old and the New,* interspersed with musical numbers and a minstrel act.

On June 30, 1915, the Christian Church on North Main Street held a dedication ceremony for its newly installed Hook & Hastings pipe organ. This was the second pipe organ in Wolfeboro and was more elaborate than the one in the First Congregational Church. Several public concerts were played upon it during the first several years of its operation. Among these was a performance on July 28, 1915, showcasing the talents of Dr. Minor C. Baldwin of New York City who was billed as "the world's greatest concert organist."[3]

Church socials continued to be a popular way to entertain and to raise funds. Typical is the November 12, 1915, chicken pie supper held by the ladies of the Christian Church. The cost was 25¢ for a repast that included chicken pie, mashed potatoes, cranberry sauce, celery, hot rolls, cake, bread, and coffee.

Contrary to what might be expected, during 1917, when America was involved in the World War in Europe, the Fourth of July celebration was subdued. Selectmen prohibited the use of fireworks.[4]

Beginning on August 12, 1917, Swafford's Pavilion Theatre Stock Company performed a different play on each of seven nights in a tent seating 300 behind the Town Hall. Tickets for adults were 25¢, children 15¢.

### The Wolfeboro Band

The Wolfeboro Band (one of several groups to be designated as such over the years) was exceedingly popular circa 1911-1912 and played in parades, gave concerts on the steps of the Masonic Temple, and was seen and heard with regularity during its brief existence. One of its star members was Primo Pollini, an immigrant who had played with the Royal Italian Band. From time to time he rendered solos on the euphonium. During the decade several different musical groups formed and later dissolved, as had been true the decade before.

Under the direction of J.E. Alcide Bilodeau from Rochester, yet another Wolfeboro Band, alternatively called the Wolfeboro Brass Band, was formed. On October 28, 1913, it gave its first concert at the Temple Auditorium.[5] The group performed many times during the next couple of years, often outdoors just before the evening motion picture show. In front of Temple Auditorium and Brewster Memorial Hall were favorite venues.

A few years later Leslie Anderson organized a small musical group of three to four pieces, which played in many events up to the end of 1917.

### Dances

Dances were among the most popular local events during the decade, as they had been for many years and would continue to be. This March 15, 1913, account is illustrative:

> In South Wolfeboro the Annual Masquerade Ball was held in the Engine Hall. Nineteen couples entered the grand march, after which everybody joined and one of the best times for the year was enjoyed. Refreshments consisting of frankfurts, cake and coffee were served.

And this account April 26, 1913:

> The second and last dance for the benefit of the Dayton, Ohio, flood sufferers, given by Winnipesaukee Lodge 70, Knights of Pythias, will be held at Masonic Hall May 1, at which time the beautiful chafing dish which has been offered as a prize to the holder of the lucky ticket will be awarded.

On April 3, 1915, the Poverty Ball was held in South Wolfeboro. This type of dance was held at intervals in the community, with prizes given to those who came dressed with the most poverty-stricken appearance. Poverty balls and parties of one sort or another continued to be held for many years.[6]

There were occasional problems at dances, as related in this notice dated May 22, 1915:

> I wish to announce that the next dance in South Wolfeboro, four weeks from the last one (which took place last Saturday night, May 15), will be postponed until the dances can be carried on in a proper way. —Earl H. Davis.

Davis was a local musician and band leader. Left unsaid was what the problem at the event was. However, dancing in bare feet and dancing to certain types of music had annoyed many observers in recent years, and some considered dancing to be immoral. Whatever the improper conduct was, it was soon corrected or forgotten, for the dances in South Wolfeboro soon continued.

### Chautauquas

On April 24, 1915, an article in the newspaper observed that Chautauquas, once educational, had become the equivalent of vaudeville shows. Chautauquas were booked by program bureaus and traveled from town to town. It was suggested that larger audiences would attend if some timely subjects were debated, such as "Unionism vs. the Open Shop," "Should Women Vote?," "Socialism vs. Democracy," "Prohibition vs. Regulation," "Armament or Peace," "High Tariff vs. Low Tariff."

In April 1916 the Wolfeboro Chautauqua was organized, with Sewall W. Abbott as its president, F.U. Landman as first vice-president and Mabel Fullerton Hatch as second vice-president.[7] It was announced Wolfeboro would be part of a Chautauqua circuit that included 71 towns, among which was New York City, "thus assuring a series not to be excelled."

On July 21 the event began with a lecture by Lee Francis Lybarger, a Philadelphia attorney, who declaimed about waste and "pork barrel" methods in politics. On the program during the next several days were Ole Theobaldi (a Norwegian who played on a $25,000 violin made in 1592 in Milan, Italy), Geoffrey O'Hara (Irish tenor and songwriter), W.T. Wetmore (impersonator), Victor's Florentine Band and Neapolitan Troubadours, and the Dunbar Southern Singers, featuring Charles Frink, stated to "delight you with a number of old darky melodies sung to the accompaniment of the banjo."

The programs were held in a large waterproof tent on the Brewster Academy grounds near the site of the old Pavilion Hotel. The tent accommodated 1,000, and most seats were filled.

In the summer of 1917 an epidemic of infantile paralysis in Vermont had resulted in the cancellation of 14 shows in that state. At the last minute the Chautauqua was booked into Wolfeboro for five days beginning August 4. Attractions included the Saxophone Singing Band, a talk by Dr. Lincoln L. Wirt, the Schubert Concert Party, a lecture by Dr. Frederick Poole (authority on things Chinese), Hawaiian singers and players, a declamation by Byron Piatt (an appeal for individual and community efficiency), Robert O. Bowman (impersonator), the Royal Marine Band, Wilfred ("the world's foremost lute player"), Dr. T. Alex Cairns (Irish orator and humorist), and the Manhattan Grand Opera Quartet presenting the second act of *Martha* and other operatic numbers.

In 1918 the Chautauqua began on Tuesday, July 23, closed on the following Sunday, and offered a wide variety of presentations.

### Wolfeboro's Sesquicentennial (1920)

The year 1920 saw the celebration of the 150th anniversary, or sesquicentennial, of Wolfeboro's founding in 1770.[8] Subsequently the *Granite Monthly* reported:

> August 24 proved to be a beautiful summer day. The church bells were rung for 15 minutes at sunrise, noon and sunset. As early as 8:00, a beautifully decorated street began to present an animated appearance. Crowds had begun to arrive from all directions by automobile, carriages and boats, and continued to arrive until estimates placed the number of people at over 10,000, and 1,000 automobiles.
>
> Every lawn was smooth and green. Flowers were everywhere. Flags waved in the breeze, and public buildings and private residences were elaborately draped and decorated with bunting, flags and every device known to add to the gay and brilliant effect. The sun shone brightly from a cloudless sky, and the beautiful elm trees waved their long, droop-

ing branches to welcome the gathering crowds....

The Harriman Post of the American Legion, led by Lieutenant Gordon A. Meader and the Cornet Band, led floats, marchers, and automobiles on a route through Glendon Street to South Main Street, where the parade position began. The procession included the Civil War veterans, 60 girls from Camp Kubeyan (led by Elizabeth B. Embler), 175 boys from Camp Wyanoke (Walter H. Bentley, leader), 60 boys from Camp Winnipesaukee (led by Charles L. Olds), Hanson's American Band from Rochester, and decorated automobiles and floats, the entire over three quarters of a mile in length....

In front of the Hotel Elmwood Governor Bartlett and other distinguished guests reviewed the paraders. Following the parade, about 70 boys from Camp Wyanoke gave an exhibition drill at Brewster campus. The fine marching and evolutions of these little fellows evoked round after round of applause.

On the campus under the elms a tent with a capacity of 2,000 was erected, but far more than that crowded the area. The ceremonies were presided over by Frederick U. Landman, superintendent of schools. Community singing began the program, led by Mr. F.D. Carter, a former football cheerleader at Yale. Rev. A. Edwin Keigwin, D.D., gave a prayer.

In the afternoon a ball game between the Legion boys and Meredith was held, with Meredith's one run in the first inning being the only score. Later, canoe and swimming races were done.

The Hanson American Band gave concerts twice in the afternoon, and in the evening from 7:30 to 9:00 the Wolfeboro Band played on Brewster campus. At 9:00 in the evening Harry L. Miles supervised a spectacular fireworks display. After the fireworks, the crowd returned to Railroad Avenue, where a band held forth at each end of the street, with bunting and Japanese flags along the sides, with music and dancing until midnight.

### The Movie Craze

This was the decade of the popularity of motion pictures—or movies, as they gradually became called. Although short films had been shown earlier on numerous occasions in Sheridan Hall and in Brewster Memorial Hall, nearly always these had been in connection with vaudeville shows or other stage entertainment.

Beginning with the opening of the Masonic Temple (which became better known as Temple Auditorium) in January 1912, motion pictures became an integral part of the local entertainment scene.[9] By year's end, probably more tickets had been sold to the movies than to all other types of auditorium entertainment combined. The nation was experiencing a movie craze, and Wolfeboro was caught up in it.

Leon Yeaton was in charge of the local motion picture enterprise. Typically, films were shown on Monday, Wednesday, and Saturday evenings or on Wednesdays and two shows on Saturday. After the Wednesday film there was a dance. At other times the Temple Auditorium was used for recitals, stage programs, and numerous other events. Occasionally, the doors would be thrown open for a special picture show, such as for children in connection with a holiday or picnic. Typical admission was 10¢ for children under 12 and 15¢ for adults. Seats were offered on a first-come, first-served basis. In some instances a concert or other musical performance would be given before the show, often on the wide steps in front of the building.

The pictures were said to have been of "excellent character being passed by the National Censor Bureau" and to have drawn large, enthusiastic audiences.

This success was not without its opposition. Many old-timers felt that motion pictures were immoral, and local lodges and organizations resented competition for entertainment. From 1912 to the early 1920s movies were the whipping boy for do-gooders, the temperance set, evangelists, *et al.* (the notice of April 19, 1913, below, hints at the situation).

### Local Film Chronology

A selection of film notices and advertisements from the *Granite State News* indicates the subjects shown and practices of the period:

**1912, April 13:** "At new Masonic Hall, *David Copperfield*, an educational picture, in three reels, will be the feature at the motion picture entertainment this Saturday night." This film, with each reel lasting about 15 minutes, was produced by the Thanhouser Company in New Rochelle, NY.

**1912, May 23:** *The Texas Cattle King*, "a thrilling romantic drama," accompanied by the famous Cow Boy Band, with special scenery, up-to-date specialties, etc.

**1912, July 1:** "*Buffalo Bill's Wild West Shows* and *Pawnee Bill's Far East* in moving pictures." Buffalo Bill and his entourage had been a drawing card all across America in the late nineteenth century. Now in the twentieth century the great buffalo slayer was portrayed on the screen.

**1912, July 13:** "Special attraction Monday evening [July 15] at Masonic Hall will be *The Call of Woman*, three reels, drama depicting the curse of drink. This intensely interesting feature will be augmented by the Hampton Glee Club."

**1912, December 14:** "*The Passion Play* will be the feature Monday evening, as the motion picture entertainment." The Passion Play illustrating the life of Christ had been filmed by multiple companies and always served to illustrate how "good" motion pictures could be for the public.

**1913, April 19:** "Mr. Alexander has established a new innovation at the 'picture' dances in the form of an ice cream and lunch room. This is indeed a much appreciated novelty by those who attend. Mr. Yeaton richly deserves the good crowds he has been drawing lately, for despite great opposition and numerous reverses, he has persisted in giving the public a regular Wednesday night dance."

**1913, September 27:** "Talking pictures Monday night at Masonic Temple." At the time, motion pictures accompanied by sound were quite popular, with a device made by Thomas Edison receiving the most attention, although it was not stated what was being used locally. These took several forms, most commonly that of a picture on the screen synchronized by the means of gears and shafts to a phonograph record.

**1914, January 24:** *His Hour of Triumph*, two reels, produced by the Imp Company. On January 26, 1914, *Uncle Tom's Cabin*, by the Imp Company, three parts, was shown.

**1914, February 28:** "Coming soon, *Quincy Adams Sawyer,* the best story of New England life ever told. Produced in motion pictures and talked by Theodore Holman." This four-reel film was to be shown on March 11, 1914. It was stated that Holman would introduce 4,000 feet of motion picture "talking for the pictures in consonance when he acted." These were "talkie" films in the most literal sense.

**1914, October 5:** The second episode of *The Trey O' Hearts,* a serial adopted from a novel by Louis Joseph Vance and produced by Universal Moving Pictures, starring Cleo Madison and George Larkin. Episodes were screened each Monday. In accordance with a popular promotional plan of the era, local interest was generated by running the novel serially in the *Granite State News* several episodes ("chapters") in advance.

**1914, October 14:** The first episode of *The Perils of Pauline,* a serial starring Pearl White, distributed by Universal, was shown, the first of many Wednesday presentations. Serials served to "lock in" patrons, who wanted to be sure not to miss a single thrill. Every Wednesday was described as "bargain day" with eight reels equal to about two hours of entertainment.

**1915, July 10:** The 20th episode of *The Million Dollar Mystery* was scheduled for the preceding Wednesday, July 7th, but the film did not arrive on time, and was postponed to July 10. Starring James Cruze and Florence LaBadie, this melodramatic serial lived up to its name and earned its producer, Thanhouser, a million dollars. As sometimes happens, its sequel *Zudora* was an unmitigated flop.

**1916, February 9-10:** Producer D.W. Griffith's highly publicized film, *The Birth of a Nation,* was shown. "Various novelties are introduced on the stage in conjunction with the production, and a symphony orchestra of 10 men offers a musical backing for the masterpiece that makes it truly effective." Posters heralding the event were plastered around town.

**1918, July 6:** Monday, Wednesday and Saturday night shows this summer. Leon Yeaton secured a Miss Lancaster of New York City for the season as pianist to accompany the action on the screen.

**1918, autumn:** Theatre closed for a time due to the Spanish Flu epidemic.

**1918, November 23:** "Monday, November 18, Ansel N. Sanborn of Sanbornville closed a deal whereby he succeeds Leon Yeaton as manager of the motion picture business.... He is to continue the business at the Auditorium weekly. Mr. Sanborn is a manager of experience and controls theatres at Manchester-by-the-Sea, Massachusetts, Sanbornville, and [now] Wolfeboro, and promises the best in his line."

**1918, December 7:** First day that films shown at the Temple Auditorium were under the management of Sanborn, who said that for the most part Paramount and Artcraft features would be shown.[10] He decided to have only one show each week during the winter, that being on Saturday.

### Hunting and Fishing

Hunting and fishing continued to be popular. Shad, trout, and bass were favorites with anglers. There were many boats on the local lakes in the spring and summer. In Wolfeboro Falls several fishing guides were kept busy during the summer, primarily on Lake Wentworth.

In April and May 1912, records were kept of trout caught in Lake Winnipesaukee, and as of May 18 there was a three-way tie among T.M. Elliott, Ray Hersey, and Leon Roberts, who had each caught a six-pounder.

In 1915 one of the largest fish in *Field and Stream's* annual prize contest was a five and one-half pound smallmouth bass taken in Lake Winnipesaukee with a fly by E.H. Coutlis of New Bedford, MA.

On February 5, 1916, this notice was printed:

> On Tuesday last, Ed. Kimball, Ervin Godfrey and John Whitehouse succeeded in capturing 80 shad and one trout. Mr. Whitehouse being the lucky one, he having caught alone 68 shad and the lone trout. Who can beat it?

While shad were among the most popular and tasty of local game fish at the time, salmon eventually took their place. When a new fish screen was installed at Lakeport in 1916, salmon were stocked. Cusk, once common, were becoming scarce.

Deer were bagged with regularity, and an occasional bear was taken, but there was no mention of moose in accounts of local sportsmen.

On October 12, 1916, Henry F. Libby held an organizational meeting at the Hotel Elmwood for a local fish and game club, but the group did not attract widespread interest.[11]

### Boating and Swimming

Boating on local lakes attracted more adherents each year. Licenses were first required in 1916, and documents reveal that on Lake Winnipesaukee there were 191 registered utility, work, and commercial boats and 635 private boats that year. Lake Wentworth had two utility boats and 28 private boats. To aid in navigation, an acetylene gas post was installed on Little Mark Island in Alton and generated a light that could be seen five miles away. It was proposed that more be put in place.[12]

The C.H. Ray Company on the shore of Lake Winnipesaukee near Clark's Point was a well-known builder of wooden boats up to 40 feet in length, until the facility burned on January 7, 1918. Goodhue & Hawkins on Sewall Road did much marine work, but during the decade the firm emphasized tooling, machining, and automobiles.

Swimming was a popular activity in local ponds and lakes. Bathing attire became more revealing to the enjoyment of many and to the consternation of others. A note in the *Granite State News,* June 26, 1920, advised: "As for this year's bathing suit, let conscience be your guide, girls."

### "Ski-ing" and Hiking

Many engaged in snowshoeing in the winter. However, skiing was virtually unknown in New Hampshire. In the February 5, 1916 issue of the local paper, a native of Norway who was in Wolfeboro at the time suggested that ski-ing (as it was spelled) could be as popular in

New England as it was in Norway. "We have the hillsides, we don't have to import the snow. The young people would really enjoy ski-ing, when they first get a real taste of that invigorating sport."

Hiking continued to be a popular summer pastime. Hills and trails in nearby towns were often visited by Wolfeboro citizens and tourists. Scouting gained a foothold. On September 30, 1911, this was reported:

> The patrol of Boy Scouts in Wolfeboro are an energetic lot of boys. They have already passed the requirements of the tenderfoot and are well along in the second class scout work.

The Boy Scouts had been organized at the First Christian Church whose pastor, George E. Dorman, was leader of the group. Scouting continued in town for many years thereafter, but intermittently.[13]

Ornithology had a few advocates during the era. The local paper reported this on May 29, 1920: "A new bird is seen in Pleasant Valley this year. It is very handsome and it is the American Redstart. There are other strange birds, too."

**Baseball**

Without a doubt, baseball was the most popular local team sport in the 1911-1920 decade. At one time or another there were teams fielded by Brewster Academy, the American Legion (and a breakaway team of Independents), Camp Wyanoke, and the local merchants (the latter sponsored the Wolfeboro Baseball Team). Contests were held in the warmer months against opponents from around the state and the northern part of Massachusetts.

On September 23, 1911, under the title of "Dragging the National Game in the Mud," an account was printed in the *News* of a September 19 contest between Wolfeboro and Meredith in which two rowdy players from Meredith became involved in a brawl, and one struck an umpire from Wolfeboro. The writer noted that a Meredith umpire called someone safe even "after being blocked off from third base over 12 feet." The score of the baseball game was 2-1 in favor of Wolfeboro.

Among the more ambitious ideas of the era was the Wolfeboro Improvement Association's plan to have a local professional baseball team with volunteer as well as hired talent.[14] It was announced that colleges in New England were being scoured to find exceptional players. The plan did not come to fruition, and an examination of professional baseball encyclopedias and record books today will not reveal accounts of our town.

This May 23, 1914, account tells of a Wolfeboro win:

> For the first time in four years Brewster Academy has defeated its greatest rival, Tilton, 13-5. The whole town celebrated. On receipt of the news of the victory, preparations were made for a fitting reception of the victorious team of Wolfeboro. Fireworks were purchased and the student body granted the evening off from studies to celebrate. Shortly after 10 p.m. the headlight of the *Dolphin* rounded Sewall's Point, and immediately the noise broke loose. Skyrockets, Roman candles, and red fire were set off, and cannon crackers made an incessant din while the students on the wharves joined with cheers. As the *Dolphin* made fast, the Wolfeboro Band marched down to meet the team, and eager hands grabbed the players and hoisted them onto their shoulders and danced about the square.

In the second week of August 1915 Prof. C.W. Haley of the Brewster Free Academy issued an edict that no further baseball games were to be played by any local teams on Brewster Field, which was the only public baseball facility in town.[15] This decision was received with anger and regret by citizens and visitors alike. Walter Bentley, owner of Camp Wyanoke on Wolfeboro Neck, offered the camp's baseball diamond. Local games were played there for the rest of the 1915 season including an August 25 contest in which the Camp Wyanoke counselors bested the Wolfeboro Baseball Team by a score of 7-3. By September, Brewster Academy relented, and Brewster Field was used again.

**Football and Basketball**

Football was the second most popular local team sport. In 1911 Brewster Free Academy squad played Holderness (twice), New Hampton (twice), Portsmouth High School, and Tilton (twice).[16]

Basketball games were played in the colder months at Brewster Academy as well as on the top floor of the Durgin Block. This account appeared in the local paper on February 12, 1916:

> The Winnipesaukee Club, second team, beat the Fast Fox Five team to the score of 19 to 4 on Saturday evening, February 5. The game was played in Durgin Hall and was witnessed by a large crowd. On Tuesday evening, February 8, the Winnipesaukee Club, second team, was defeated by the Fast Fox Five team in Durgin Hall. The score was 19-2. Attendance was very large.

In November 1920 it was announced that Wolfeboro was going to have a strong professional basketball team.[17] The Masonic Temple was to be the site of a game each week, to be followed by a dance. Frank Flynn was brought from Dover to serve as one of the guards, while the other guard was Archie A. Horne, local automobile dealer. "This is the first time that Wolfeboro has ever had a professional team," the local paper noted, "and the lover of good clean sports, both male and female, should see that the game is properly supported by their regular attendance."

On Wednesday, November 24, the opening game was scheduled, but was called off as the local team had not practiced enough. The first game was finally played on Friday night, December 3, 1920. This account was published:

> Talk about excitement! Last evening, Wolfeboro in its first professional basketball game ever played here, defeated the Dover All Stars at the Masonic Hall by a score of 40 to 16. To those who expected to witness a tea party the game would

prove to be a bitter disappointment, for from the first toss-up until the finish there was surely something doing all the time. Owing to the very slippery condition of the floor and the uncertain footing, both teams agreed to the elimination of all fouls so as not to spoil the game....

Wolfeboro proved their superiority right off the bat, and at the end of the first half the score was 20 to 4 in their favor. In the second half they allowed their opponents more leeway and scored 20 to 12, but would have been much larger but for their inability to cage the ball after many tries. This was the first game of the season and judging from the excitement of the crowd it was really a success.

On Tuesday, December 7, the Wolfeboro team trampled Ossipee 66 to 10. The victory was not as merited as the score indicated, as the Wolfeboro ball players were to have played Portsmouth, but a last-minute cancellation forced them to look for other partners. In good spirit, the Ossipee YMCA team, which was composed of amateurs who had never played away from their home court, stated they would give the contest a try and do the best they could.

On Tuesday, December 21, 1920, Wolfeboro bested the Pittsfield team 48 to 12.

### The Kingswood (Golf) Club

The Kingswood Club (known later as the Kingswood Golf Club) was organized on February 1, 1901, as a social organization composed of seasonal visitors from Massachusetts. Few local residents were involved. Original aims included the improvement of roads and tourist facilities. A clubhouse was maintained on Forest Road at what today is the intersection of Bassett Road. In May 1907 the group bought the old Varney tannery at the end of Endicott Street. On August 16, 1907, Judge Sewall W. Abbott represented a group of 15 out-of-towners who incorporated the club. The tannery was removed and replaced by a beautiful new clubhouse built by J. Frank Goodwin. Years later this building was known as the Wolfeboro Casino.

This newspaper item of August 5, 1911, reflects activities of the time:

The Kingswood Club prepares and carries out a regular program of exercises, having some special feature each week. This week, Saturday is the beginning of the tennis tournament for the Jones' cup—the annual meeting—piazza lunch—triangular meet for the President's Cups—cards and dancing in the evening. The Jones Cups are two solid silver cups of considerable value given by Mr. and Mrs. Rollin Jones to be contested for annually at the tennis tournament.... President Charles L. Edgar gives two valuable cups for first and second prizes to be competed for in Annual Field Day, August 5. The events will include both field and water sports and will be open to teams of eight men from Kingswood Club, Hill School, and Camp Wyanoke.

On August 3, 1912, the *Granite State News* posed this question: "Where are the Wolfeboro golf links? Such a worldwide game should not escape us." Where there was an inclination there would soon be activity. During the summer of 1914, Henry Lucas and a crew of 20 Italian immigrants kept busy laying out a golf course. The site was between South Main Street and the shore of Lake Winnipesaukee.[18]

On July 5, 1915, five holes of the nine-hole Kingswood Club course opened officially, but rain postponed play until the 10th. On July 17 the first tournament held on these few holes was won by F.H. Stephens, who had a handicap of 18 and turned in a card of 83 for 18 holes, netting him 65. The lowest net score for playing 18 holes—by repetitive play over the five holes that were open—was 78 by John G. Anderson.

The prime mover behind the new course was Francis McDonald Sinclair, a wealthy manufacturer of printing ink from New York City, who with his wife Jennie built a beautiful summer home, Winneconnett, on Wolfeboro Bay.[19] In 1915 he was president of the Kingswood Club. In the same year, Frank Butler was engaged as the course pro, a position he would maintain until his retirement in 1963.

On August 5, 1916, this account reached print:

For the first time in the history of Wolfeboro a real moving picture comedy was staged in the [Post Office] Square last Monday afternoon. Members of the Kingswood Club were filmed in a two-reel comedy entitled *The Mystery of the Satchel*, which will be presented at the club's annual minstrel show this month.

The scenario of the comedies worked out by members of the club and contained many interesting scenes. The scene of the Wolfeboro National Bank, Post Office, the fight on the telephone pole at Tobey's Pharmacy, the auto chase, mob scenes, and the fight in the lake were especially well acted. The players were assisted by a small mob of camp boys in sailor suits who have put a great deal of enthusiasm in their work, especially in the chase over the freight cars at the depot.

The play was filmed by George Armstrong of Centre Harbor.[20] The leading characters of the comedy were Ralph Carpenter and Harold Whitney, desperate robbers, Merrill Delano, a real hero (?), and Miss Grace Meacham, heroine. The acting of this comedy was witnessed by a large gathering of townspeople who were anxious to witness the presentation at the annual minstrel show August 17 and 18.

The Kingswood Club House at the end of Endicott Street was a beautiful facility, but it was distant from the golf course. Soon, a temporary golf facility was set up in a former chicken coop leased from the Pinkham Farm (which at the time was also a year-round tourist facility; the Windrifter is there today). The structure was at the club's first tee located not far behind the big Pinkham barn. The building was expanded greatly circa 1922.

Land was purchased over a long period of time beginning in 1919, with the final parcel being acquired in 1959. In its completed form, the golf course land comprised 18 holes and stretched from the shore of Lake Winnipesaukee to the shore of Crescent Lake.

The original Kingswood Golf Club house, also called the Bonnie Doon Club (a small golf course in Tuftonboro bore a similar name), on Forest Road at what is today the left corner of Bassett Road. Early twentieth century. (Jeff Goodwin Collection)

Forest Road near the corner of North Main Street as photographed early in the twentieth century. The land to the left belonged to J. Frank Goodwin and stretched down to the shore of Lake Winnipesaukee. The trees are mostly elms. (Jeff Goodwin Collection)

## TRANSPORTATION

### Automobiles

During the 1911-1920 decade automobiles were still enough of a novelty that the local paper carried numerous mentions of even small trips, including an account of motoring from East Wolfeboro to the downtown district. Horses continued to be used by many, especially for commercial hauling and deliveries. By 1915 many merchants were using cars or small trucks.

If the frequency of news items is an indication, Ford was the most popular make. Until near the end of the decade, there was no showroom where a potential buyer could see models on display. Finally in 1917, Archie Horne had a selection of Fords on view.

There were only a few rules governing conduct of drivers on the road. As of July 1, 1914, all moving vehicles at night—motorized as well as horsedrawn—had to carry lamps unless they were within 500 feet of a street light. In 1915 it was decreed that drivers in Post Office Square should keep to the right side of the road. Speed in the downtown district had been limited to 15 miles per hour since 1912, an increase from the earlier restriction of 8 miles per hour and the prior 5 miles per hour. There were very few road signs, nearly all streets were unmarked, and accidents became increasingly frequent.

Wolfeboro excursionists ranged farther abroad than they did a few years earlier. It became common to drive to Boston to an automobile show, pure food fair, or other event. Trips through the White Mountains were popular, where the "grand hotels" all had facilities for autoists.

By 1920 there were several automobile repair shops in town, and the local paper printed numerous advertisements for accessories such as batteries.

Selected clippings from the local paper give first-hand impressions:[21]

**1911, April 29:** "Automobiles are beginning to appear. The road is cleared of snow and ice. Arrangements have been completed this week for the opening of a garage early in May, near the stable of Joseph E. Fox on North Main Street, just above bridge. The promoters are Archie A. Horne and Parry T. Hersey. Besides having room for housing several cars they will carry gasoline, oil and a small line of supplies and have arrangements for securing tires on short notice, as well as doing light repairing and adjusting of automobiles, vulcanizing tubes, etc."

**1911, May 13:** "Dr. [Fred E.] Clow has recently purchased a Hupmobile runabout. Otis Sargent drove it up from Portsmouth Monday. H.E. Libby has appeared on our streets this week with his automobile delivery car. It looks good and serviceable."

**1911, June 2:** "Archie Horne has purchased a new automobile of the Abbott-Detroit make."[22]

**1911, June 10:** "Ye poor editor had the good fortune Tuesday morning to enjoy an auto trip through the courtesy of our respected townsman, James H. Martin....We enjoyed every mile of the distance to Rochester and then, oh! my! This trip was in Mr. Martin's new Pierce-Arrow, which he has just received, and when you talk about comfort combined in a car it certainly must mean a Pierce-Arrow."[23]

**1911, July 29:** "Pine Hill. A neighbor with a carriage, and another with a load of hay, barely escaped a serious collision with an auto one day this week. What are the horns for, anyway? We seldom hear one."

**1911, September 9:** "Tuesday afternoon, while cranking an automobile, Parry T. Hersey had the misfortune to break a large bone in his right forearm, close to the wrist joint."

**1911, September 16:** "A number of the 1912 model automobiles will be equipped with the electric alarm horns and electric lights."

**1912, February 10:** "W.J. Tilton has placed his order for a new 'Reo the Fifth', a four-passenger touring car, thus making the second 'Reo the Fifth' to come to town, E.R. Durgin having ordered the first one."

**1912, February 24:** "E.R. Durgin, agent for the Reo cars in this section, has this week placed an order for a carload of cars to be delivered very soon."

**1912, March 2:** "Ford automobiles for 1912: The car of low-running expense. Touring car, five passenger, 22 h.p., four cylinder engine, with magneto, equipped with windshield, top, speedometer, gas lights, etc. Price $690. Runabout, two passenger, fully equipped. Price $590. Call and see them. Joseph E. Fox, agent, Wolfeboro."

**1912, May 11:** "Herbert E. Haines has purchased an E.M.F. auto and soon will be seen running around the streets. Steven Valla's new Overland delivery car arrived in town Tuesday p.m. and has been seen on the streets lately every day. It is a neat-looking car, too. He will use it for conveying his fruit this summer to the surrounding towns and villages."

**1912, July 6:** "Archie Horne and wife went to Sanford Tuesday and returned Wednesday with a new car, the Marion. J. Frank Goodwin has a new Ford car."

**1912, July 13:** "Our fish vendor Joseph King is now supplying his customers by the aid of an auto. It is easier and he can cover a larger territory."

**1912, July 27:** "It's a beauty. We of course refer to the new Marion touring car which George W. Berry has purchased. He drove the car from Dover Tuesday. She behaves beautifully and is one of the fine cars of the town. Has all modern appliances."

**1912, September 28:** "Archie A. Horne has this week sold and delivered to Rob O'Brien of Wakefield one of his well-known, four-passenger Ford cars. This makes 13 he has sold this season."

**1913, April 19:** "E.R. Durgin last week brought a new Reo over the road from Boston, and despite the wretched condition of the roads reported that he encountered no difficulties. He negotiated the entire distance in six hours, the greater part of which was used up between Dover and Wolfeboro."

**1913, May 24:** "The proposed plan for an automobile parade for the G.A.R. and a march from the wharf to the burial grounds on Memorial Day has been abandoned at the request of the old veterans themselves owing to the fact that many of them, while appreciative of the generous offers by auto owners, much prefer to continue as heretofore in the use of carriages."[24]

**1913, July 19:** "Abel Haley is the proud possessor of a new Buick touring car which arrived Wednesday."

**1913, October 4:** "Still they come! What? Why the Overland touring cars. Harry L. Miles has purchased a fine looker of the agent, Archie A. Horne."

**1913, November 8:** "J.C. Avery has purchased a Ford car this week."

**1913, November 29:** "J. Frank Goodwin is the proud possessor of a new Overland car."

**1914, March 14:** "The Metz automobile is to be represented in this town by Harry E. Libby and Dr. F.E. Clow."[25]

**1914, March 21:** "The first 1914 auto to arrive in town this year was a Ford which was driven in by Archie A. Horne, February 23."

**1914, June 27:** "Archie A. Horne returned from Boston one day this week driving a new Chalmers car."

**1915, April 10:** "Archie Horne is adding to his already large garage a 3,000-foot additional capacity, which will make his the largest in Carroll County."

**1916, May 6:** "Friday morning Walter D. Bartlett of South Tamworth was seen in our village demonstrating the Studebaker car, and the ease of which it climbed the hill on North Main Street was very noticeable. G.W. Berry is sporting a new car which arrived last week. It's a beauty and the first of this make in town, Scripps-Booth. Hoyt Jackson is the representative for Moultonboro, Alton, New Durham, the Ossipees, and Wolfeboro."

**1916, May 20:** "Judge Sewall W. Abbott has yielded to temptation and now is the proud and happy possessor of a Willys Knight auto."

**1916, May 27:** "Albert Brown has purchased a new Selden auto truck, two-ton capacity."

**1916, July 8:** "The trains continue to daily bring large numbers of new arrivals and additions to our summer colonies. Saturday night 24 autos were waiting at the station for parties."

**1917, May 12:** "C.H. Stevens of Point Breeze fame has purchased an automobile for the transportation of passengers and baggage. Archie Horne, the Ford agent of this town, delivered the car this week."

**1919, April 19:** "J. Frank Goodwin has bought himself a new Ford runabout this week. The much talked about Nash car, will, according to reports, soon be on exhibition at Horne's Garage."

**1919, May 10:** "J.W. Tilton, our prosperous merchant, has purchased a new Briscoe automobile."

**1919, August 9:** "The large number of autos on our Main Street, at times four deep stopped along the sidewalk, makes it inconvenient for parties to get away. Would it not be a wise plan for Chief Thompson to insist that drivers should 'nose-in' and thus make it possible to back out while the same time it would relieve congestion on the Square?"

**1920, July 31:** "Judge Abbott had his new Stearns-Knight five-passenger touring car delivered last week. Some car, Judge."

### Roads

As cars became more popular, the condition of local roads became increasingly important. By mid-decade most if not all of the surface of North and South Main Streets had been macadamized, as had much of the Lake Winnipesaukee waterfront area near the Boston & Maine wharf and the access to the old *Lady of the Lake* dock behind the Peavey Block, the shore work having been done in 1911. Other roads were dirt covered. At first, the unpaved thoroughfares in town were watered in the summer to keep down the dust, but eventually large quantities of oil were spread to accomplish the same thing, but in a more lasting manner.

In the autumn of 1910 the new bridge over the Smith River in Wolfeboro Falls was completed. Made of reinforced concrete, it replaced an ancient span and was widely acclaimed as an excellent piece of construction.

In March and early April 1913 the town road crew filled in muddy low sections of North and South Main, Glendon, and Factory Streets. A cheap, red-colored material was used, and the result was more mud—this time of a reddish hue.[26] Enough of the new surface washed off of Factory Street that the editor of the local paper said that nearby Back Bay "looks like a dye kettle." At the same time, the condition of the road between downtown Wolfeboro and Melvin Village was said to have resulted in "extremely bad traveling."

Indeed, it seems that even during the summer when conditions were not as wet as the spring, travel was apt to be uncertain on the primary roads. The *Granite State News* reported this on August 23, 1913:

> The wretched condition of our main road from Wolfeboro to Ossipee, especially in the Wolfeboro Center section, is a disgrace to the town as well as a danger to safe transportation. It is rumored that this piece of road is to be made a state highway. Being a direct avenue of communication between Wolfeboro and the county seat at Ossipee, as well as the mail route, its proper maintenance is warranted.

The contemplated state highway became a lively topic of discussion in 1914 and 1915. As a rule of thumb, the state suggested that grades of important roads not be greater than 7.5%, equivalent to a seven and one-half foot rise in 100 lateral feet of roadway. However, several local thoroughfares exceeded this. A portion of Haines Hill Road was said to be over 15%, a fatal flaw which precluded it from being seriously considered as part of the state route finalized in 1915. Slightly over 11 miles of the so-called Ossipee-Suncook Road went through the town of Wolfeboro and included what is known as Route 28 today.

In June 1914 tarvia, a petroleum-based substance, was spread on Railroad Avenue in an effort to lay the dust. It was reported that if this experiment were successful, tarvia would be used on other routes.[27] Tarvia and oil were soon spread over most well-used roads.

In response to complaints from motorists and a growing awareness of the need for better roads, the road between South Wolfeboro and the Wolfeboro business district was redone in the summer and autumn of 1914. Curves were straightened, grades reduced, and the road bed widened. As soon as that was completed, the town road crew, superintended by C.A. Wiggin, started to improve the stretch between downtown and the Tuftonboro line.[28]

Increased attention began to be paid to signage. Joseph T. Meader noted that it would cost very little to create an informative system of roadside guides.[29] There were no signs at all on the several roads going toward

Ossipee, nor were there any at the intersection at Wolfeboro Center. Meader reported that while in the 1890s there were signs for local street names, *not a single sign* existed in 1915.

While automobiles dominated the roads, many horses were still seen. Accidents and ill-tempered incidents involving horses being frightened by cars were reported frequently.

In an earlier era of horses only, the winter snow was compacted by rollers to permit the passage of sleighs. As the automobile came of age, roads were plowed. In January 1918 for the first time snow was scraped off the streets and dumped into Lake Winnipesaukee.[30]

On June 26, 1920, this appeared in the paper: "Road Agent Carr is preparing to use 18,000 gallons of oil on our highways. Some oil!"[31] Over the years countless tens of thousands of gallons of petroleum, including used crankcase oil, were used to keep down the dust and harden road surfaces.

### The Railroad

Time was when the railroad was the great hope for Wolfeboro's future. It will be recalled that in 1872 the tracks laid into town were first used, and that local citizens had been eager to go $35,000 into debt so that the trains would come here, rather than elsewhere. The history of America is strewn with accounts of ghost towns caused by railroad tracks being laid "somewhere else."

However, by the 1911-1920 decade the Boston & Maine had become a monster, at least in the view of many Wolfeboro residents. Anti-B&M sentiments filled columns of many state newspapers, and candidates for public office would often adopt a platform against the railroad as a way of seeking votes. It was alleged that in the olden days, the Boston & Maine "owned" the New Hampshire State Legislature, and more than a few people thought that it still did.

Finally, the line sought to defend itself with its own publicity campaign. The February 11, 1911, issue of the *Granite State News* printed as an advertisement a letter sent by Boston & Maine President Charles S. Mellen to New Hampshire Governor Henry C. Quinby, complaining of actions pending in the courts of New Hampshire against the railroad, brought "to restrain the railroad from continuing to effect certain rates which it had alleged are in violation of statutes." It was stated that the Boston & Maine Railroad wanted its legal rights determined.

In March 1911 Frank P. Hobbs, well-known former hotelier and now Wolfeboro's representative to the State Legislature in Concord, spent much effort to get the Boston & Maine to adjust schedules and rates to the satisfaction of his constituency. All too often, if the railroad thought that an industry was making a nice profit, it would arbitrarily raise rates on ice, lumber, or another commodity, sometimes selectively so as to affect a specific business or town. Local merchants and factories were powerless, as there was just one railroad serving the town, and other methods of transportation were neither economical nor efficient.

Hope came in 1912 when the Grand Trunk Railroad sought to expand its route to comprise much of New Hampshire, possibly including Wolfeboro. The Boston & Maine Railroad took out large advertisements stating that this would result in unnecessary duplication and many other problems, and that railroad service would be more expensive if the Grand Trunk were given rights. In response, a local editorial suggested that nearly all Wolfeboro citizens wanted competition in railroad service and freight rates, and that the Boston & Maine had long since outlived its welcome.[32]

Perhaps to build good will, the Boston & Maine began improving the local line. A spur track was laid to expand capacity in Wolfeboro Falls, and in November 1914 construction began on a 60-foot turntable capable of accommodating larger engines. It was anticipated that this would make longer trains possible, including Pullman cars running through service from New York City.[33] The following was realized, as reported on August 5, 1916:

> Through the efforts of the Retail Merchants' Association the Boston & Maine Railroad has decided to inaugurate weekend parlor car service between Boston and Wolfeboro commencing Saturday, August 5. The car will leave Boston every Saturday for the remainder of the summer season at 1:35 p.m. arriving in Wolfeboro at 5:13. Returning on Sundays it will leave Wolfeboro at 5:45 p.m. and arriving in Boston at 9:05.
>
> This is the first time that regular parlor car services have been given at Wolfeboro, and it is hoped that it will be so profitable to the railroad that we may have daily service next year. Wolfeboro is one of the very few summer resorts of prominence which has not had parlor car accommodations.

While it was not the hoped-for Pullman car service through to New York City, the facilities were better than before.

### Aviation

The aviation age was slow in coming to Wolfeboro. One of the earlier local mentions of aviators in the local paper was printed on November 4, 1911, but was primarily about an *automobile:*

> Harry N. Atwood, the well-known aviator, and family were in town Monday, stopping overnight at the Sheridan House, and his auto, the official car, drew the attention of many who pronounced it a great machine.

Closer to the mark is this account datelined February 21, 1914:

> Harry M. Jones, a noted aviator, who has the distinction of being the first United States Parcel Post aviator, the first aviator to land on Boston Common, the first to fly over New York City by moonlight, is now making arrangements for a flight,

which he expects to begin in the middle of April, starting from Buffalo, New York to Lake Winnipesaukee.... This will be the first opportunity for people in this town and vicinity to see a real aviator. His machine is capable, he claims, to carry two passengers, and arrangements may be made for some of our people to enjoy a short flight.

What happened if or when Jones was in the Wolfeboro area was not reported.

On August 12, 1919, an unusual sight greeted citizens in the downtown area:[34]

Tuesday afternoon quite an interest was manifested, and a large number gathered at the wharf and around the Square to witness the arrival of a hydroplane from The Weirs. This was the first exhibition of this nature in our village. When the airplane was first discerned approaching from the southwest flying high, it had the appearance of a mammoth bird sailing majestically. It was but a few minutes before it began to spiral over the housetops, when it commenced to lower and glided smoothly on the waters of the bay to the delight of the spectators as well as the astonishment, as for many this was the first they ever witnessed.

An "airplane exhibit" was among the attractions scheduled for Welcome Home Day for soldiers in August 1919. During this period, spelling was not standardized, and such variations as air-plane, aeroplane, and even aireoplane were seen in articles.

During the town's 150th anniversary celebration in August 1920, a hydroplane was in Wolfeboro Bay and made 10 to 12 flights carrying paying passengers.

## COMMERCE AND ECONOMICS

### More Tourists Arrive

From 1911 to 1920 tourism continued to be an important and growing part of the local economy. The increasing popularity of the automobile made it possible for middle- and upper-income people from Concord, Manchester, and other areas in southern New Hampshire, and from Massachusetts, to easily visit Wolfeboro for a few days or longer. Others took the train.

In the days before mechanical air conditioning, even the finest homes in Boston, New York City, Providence, and elsewhere were apt to be sweltering and stuffy in the summer. A pleasant alternative was for the family who could afford it to come to Wolfeboro for a week or two, or, better yet, for the entire summer. In a guest house on Cotton Mountain, or at a cottage near the water at Point Breeze Camp on Lake Wentworth, or on Keniston Island in Wolfeboro Bay, the days and months passed quickly, as visitors from the south enjoyed everything from berry-picking to canoeing, from dancing to fishing. For many families, summering in Wolfeboro was a tradition continued from one generation to another.

The sentiment "Wish you were here," and its variants, continued to be expressed on thousands of postcards mailed from Wolfeboro. The Paper Store, local drug stores, variety stores, and just about every other place catering to tourists had racks of local views for sale. In 1911 Joseph W. Robins' Wolfeboro Drug Store charged 1¢ a card or 10¢ a dozen. On November 21, 1914, the local paper noted that "McFadden & Libbey, druggists, have on display 30 new views of Wolfeboro penny postcards that are beauties."

### Good Times

The 10 years from 1911 to 1920 were relatively prosperous for the town. For the first part of the decade, employment was quite steady at the local factories and mills, with the C.K. Fox Shoe Factory on Factory Street being the biggest of the group.

Charles K. Fox lived in Haverhill, MA, and summered on North Main Street in Wolfeboro in an elegant Victorian-style residence. After he died in Haverhill on July 31, 1912, his widow continued to visit Wolfeboro in season, and the Fox factory remained open for the balance of the decade.

In the downtown section new businesses opened, old ones closed, and others changed hands as time marched on. John I. Sanborn's store in the center of the Peavey Block went out of business at the end of 1911, and unsold inventory was auctioned the following January by Frank P. Hobbs at the Old Brick Store on North Main Street. The Wolfeboro Drug Store moved into the former Sanborn facility. On the right side of the first floor of the Peavey Block, dry goods merchants and grocers Lewando & Tilton continued to do a lively trade. On February 14, 1913, Wilbur J. Tilton bought out Joseph Lewando's interest and became sole owner.

The early years of the decade were boom times for builders. J. Frank Goodwin was pre-eminent in his trade and obtained the lion's share of major projects. Fred E. Hersey, young Andrew Doe, and others obtained many construction contracts as well. There was an acute shortage of both year-round and vacation homes, and many felt that this prevented people from coming to town and gaining employment.[35] For a time, there were more jobs than people to fill them.

In 1912 Back Bay was jammed with poplar logs awaiting conversion into excelsior, about 2,000 pairs of shoes were being made each day at the Fox factory, and hay was selling for a record $24 a ton, and at that price there was little to be had.[36]

So far as is known, the first mental health therapist to have an office in town was Mrs. B.M. Weed, who set up in June 1912 and specialized in "mental healing." A quarter century earlier, circa 1885, when the floor of the G.A.R. Hall collapsed and the audience fell with it, she was on the scene. "Her successful treatment then will be remembered by many, and it is a pleasure to know she treats such patients as may desire her assistance."[37]

Early in 1913 there was an ice shortage throughout

New England, which worsened as the year went on. William D. Herbert and other local ice dealers were kept busy during the winter months cutting all the ice they could produce and shipping it to the Boston market by the railcar full.

In the spring of the same year local lumber mill owner and selectman Stephen W. Clow purchased acreage on and near the site of the old tannery and announced plans to erect a large number of modern cottages, tenements and apartments. It was hoped this would end the housing shortage. In the meantime, it was hoped that some new businesses would move into town. In April 1913 rumors circulated that a small factory for making cigars would set up in Wolfeboro, but nothing further happened.[38]

In 1913 Harold F. Ricker opened up a variety store in the Central Block on Railroad Avenue, kept shop briefly, and closed in 1915.

The "Big Factory" at the western end of Factory Street had been purchased by the Village Precinct earlier and was vacant in 1911. At the Precinct meeting on March 28, 1911, a sum not to exceed $1,000 was voted for the demolition of the building, except for the west wing which was to be preserved. It was recommended that the spared wing be reduced in height. In May, Samuel Leavitt, wood products dealer of Wolfeboro Falls, purchased the top two stories and removed them.[39]

### National Change, Local Status Quo

In 1914 the American economy suffered a setback. The editor of the *News* noted that when the Democrats came into power in 1913, business conditions were excellent and there was general prosperity and full employment. However, the record for the first six months of 1914 showed "business stagnation, idle freight, and more than a million men without work." Banking failures had increased, while earnings of corporations had decreased. Some factories that once boasted full employment and offered overtime pay were now idle. The local paper suggested that while President Woodrow Wilson might be ignorant of conditions in the United States, the people were not.[40]

Fortunately, Wolfeboro was not dependent upon manufacturing to feed the mouths of its citizens. The excelsior and wood factories kept fairly busy, and the C.K. Fox Shoe Factory hummed right along. Tourists kept coming.

### Onward and Upward

With the onset of the World War in Europe in August 1914, rampant inflation began to pervade the domestic scene. The high cost of living soon became such a frequent topic of discussion that in articles and cartoons it was simply referred to as h.c.l. or HCL. From 1914 to 1920, prices of consumer goods and services rose sharply.

Appetites for household and other goods increased. Automobiles became very popular, home appliances were the fad of the day, and more money was being spent on items that would have been considered frivolous a decade or two earlier. Typical was this offering:[41]

> On August 18 and 19 the ladies and gentlemen of our town will be given a wonderful demonstration of the Arco Wand Vacuum cleaner at John D. McHugh's store on Main Street. It is built in the home like a radiator heating plant, to last as long as the building itself.

During the 1911-1920 decade, several new business-promoting groups sprang up including the Retail Merchants Association, the Wolfeboro Commercial Club, and the Wolfeboro Improvement Association. In 1916 the last-named group had among its objectives the securing of a business to move into the shortened, reroofed remaining west wing of the "Big Factory" on Factory Street, and to reactivate the woolen mill in South Wolfeboro which had been idle for a year or two.[42] An out-of-town manufacturer, a Mr. Picard, had seen the latter facility, commented that it was woefully obsolete, and that he would not give even $5,000 for it, although it was valued by the owners at tens of thousands of dollars.

Finally, in the autumn of 1917 Fred E. Hersey and a crew of workmen began refurbishing the South Wolfeboro mill.[43] In December the Village Precinct extended electrical service to the building. Early in 1918, the Racine Woolen Company, Harold H. Hart, president, began operations there.[44] During the first week of April 1918, downtown merchant Harry D. Piper exhibited in his store the first blanket made at the newly reopened mill. "It is a beauty and of various colors and stripes," it was reported.

The Wolfeboro Improvement Association suggested that signs identifying town streets would be helpful. Further, if the three wooden buildings to the left of the Peavey Block could be torn down, a small square could be fashioned there with a bandstand in the center and with sanitation facilities beneath it. What a boon this would be to tourists. The idea was never actualized.

The price of coal doubled and doubled again. In December 1916 the Standard Oil Company of New York ran advertisements stating that due to the current high price of coal, consumers might wish to consider using a smokeless kerosene heater which for 10¢ to 15¢ would provide 10 hours of clean, odorless heat, more than enough to warm an ordinary room.

This advertisement appeared in 1917: "Chesterfields hit the smoke-spot, they let you know you are smoking—they satisfy! Yet, they're mild!"[45] A pack of 20 cigarettes cost 10¢.

Inflation continued relentlessly. On January 1, 1918, local painters raised their standard wage scale to $3 per day, and after May 1 barbers charged an all-time high price of 15¢ per shave.

Toward the end of 1918, after hostilities in Europe had ceased, the American economy paused to catch its breath. Many prices fell, and by year's end, coal, lumber, and many other commodities were selling for less than they were a year before, although in most instances still more than they brought five years earlier.[46] Some wages also fell, as in this December, 21 1918, note in the *Granite State News:* "Lumber manufacturers have been obliged owing to the decline in price of lumber to reduce the wages of the laborers."

### The Economy in 1920

The local paper commented on June 5, 1920, that the cost of living in Wolfeboro had doubled since December 1914. The cost of turning out the *Granite State News* had nearly tripled. However, for the preceding year or two many large national companies, Swift & Company meat packers being prominent among them, advertised that they were making very little profit. It seemed everyone wanted to blame the increased prices on someone else! The editor of the *News* was more realistic:[47]

> Millions of people are waiting with such patience as they can muster for the time when prices will come down. They have faith that the time will not be long deferred. But we fear that they will be disappointed. Before any great reduction can be expected in the retail markets there first must be a readjustment of the price of labor, raw materials, etc. Can you imagine the laborer voluntarily reducing his wage, the manufacturer the prices of his products?

The national census showed Wolfeboro had 2,178 residents in 1920, a decrease from 2,224 in 1910, which, in turn, was lower than the 2,390 number for 1900. The decline was caused by smaller employment on farms and in factories.

Attracting new commercial entities seemed to be a permanent goal, an objective of decades past and a hope for generations to come, the Holy Grail for town spokesmen and office-seekers. "Bigger is better," it was said.

The Racine Woolen Mill in South Wolfeboro was a shining star in the constellation of local businesses in 1920, and everyone was happy to have it humming with activity. Beginning on August 3, 1920, the factory had a special sale of cloth, suitings, and overcoatings and polo cloth—all wool:[48]

> Suits will be tailored if desired by a New York tailor. $26.50 to $33.50; overcoats with high-grade linings and workmanship, satisfaction guaranteed, $25.50 to $32.50. Here is an opportunity to get some fine suits at low price.

Meanwhile, the tourist business continued its strength. More out-of-state residents had automobiles, and Wolfeboro's attractions became more enticing than ever. At the close of the 1920 season the *News* observed:[49] "Local authorities say there have never been as many summer people in this section of the town for years, if there have ever been, as there were here the past summer."

Notwithstanding this heartening assessment, not all was well. On December 18, 1920, the local economic news of the decade closed out with this editorial comment:

> Business, generally speaking, is quiet, the box factory being idle and the woolen mill quiet, making everything seem quiet. The labor supply is equal to the demand.

### Electricity

The decade saw great expansion of electric service in Wolfeboro. In 1911 power was often interrupted, never for a longer time than for the span beginning on January 3, when an engine at the generating station became disabled until January 30.[50]

During the next several years, street lighting was expanded, and wires were extended to many outlying districts. Demand increased, and by February 1912 there were an estimated 3,000 light bulbs glowing within town limits. In the same year it was voted to install an electric plant on Factory Street on the site of the former main part of the "Big Factory." The sum of $15,000 was appropriated.

In the summer of 1915 electric service reached Pleasant Valley. In the first week of January 1917, power was connected to South Wolfeboro, and the current was turned on in Horace Rust's general store there. John McHugh, local electrician, supervised the crew that did most of the installations. By March 1917 there were 354 customers for electricity within the town.

In late 1918 and early 1919 electric motors were installed in many factories to replace steam and water power systems. Mark Blaisdell's grain mill, Fred Hersey's lumber mill, and others made the change. The Electric Department sought to increase demand for its product by getting into the appliance business, and for a period of years it sold and rented flat irons, toasters, grills, heaters, and vacuum cleaners at prices claimed to be a discount from those in retail stores.

In keeping with the inflationary trend, electric rates increased during the decade. However, it was announced that on December 1, 1920, the price of current would be reduced from 25¢ per kilowatt hour to 20¢ for yearly customers and from 30¢ to 25¢ for seasonal users. Rates dropped sharply in later years.

### Radio

A December 9, 1911, account related:

> Leonel Copp has this week been installing at his home on North Main Street the first wireless station in town. The mast stand is 30 feet high, and he says it will be receiving in a radius of 150 miles.

In the next 15 years, dozens of local citizens hooked up radios. It was not until the 1920s that the first commercial broadcasting station (KDKA in Pittsburgh) became a reality and decades later when Wolfeboro had its own commercial broadcasting station, WASR 1420 AM on the dial, in April 1970.[51]

### Telephone Service

Although telephones had been in use locally since the late nineteenth century, the greatest advance in service was made during the 1911-1920 decade. In January 1911 it was announced that henceforth telephone connections would be bundled in cables, rather than in a myriad of separate lines to various subscribers. Strands were being extended to outlying areas, and soon campers at Point Breeze would be able to say, "Hello, Central."

On May 1, 1911, the method of short-distance toll calls was simplified. Henceforth, if the number answered, the calling party would be charged. Earlier, the operator had to record the specific directions of the person making the call. This made possible a reduction in some rates. For example, to call Milton Mills from Wolfeboro cost 10¢ for five minutes, as opposed to 15¢ for three minutes under the old system. In August 1911 linemen were busy running telephone cables to North Wolfeboro.

In the spring of 1914 a large crew of out-of-town telephone workers came to Wolfeboro to upgrade the local service, install a larger switchboard in the exchange, and make modifications. The New England Telephone & Telegraph Co. placed frequent advertisements to answer patrons' questions. Readers were advised that to place a call the receiver should be lifted, and the caller should wait to hear the operator from Central say, "Number, please." About 100 words per minute could be spoken in a normal telephone conversation.

In July 1914 a three-minute call from Wolfeboro cost 35¢ to Portland, ME; 20¢ to Rochester; $5.50 to Chicago; and $3.25 to Washington, DC. The company provided personal service that, in hindsight, seems almost unbelievable, as per this June 1915 announcement:

> Give the toll operator a clue to the supposed whereabouts of the salesman, touring automobile party, possible customer or client you want to talk to, and she'll try to connect you. The toll operator does extraordinarily clever work in following up these clues. Tell her the name of the person you want, where he is likely to be or where normally he ought to be, and there's more than an even chance she will put you in communication with them—and quickly, too.[52]

## AROUND TOWN

### The Municipality

On March 11, 1911, to protect the town water supply, the selectmen purchased shore rights and property around Beach Pond from seven land owners, generally paying more than the assessed valuations. The most money went to C.S. Paris, $1,750 for property assessed at $600. A strip measuring 100 feet or more around the shore was thus acquired for sanitary reasons.

The Back Bay area of Wolfeboro continued to be a problem. The area near the Clow sawmill and the O.P. Berry excelsior mill was usually jammed with logs, making navigation inconvenient or impossible. In particular, the arm of Back Bay extending along Factory Street to the causeway (on Center Street) was a mess. On April 29, 1911, this was printed:

> If ever "Little Back Bay" needed the attention of our Board of Health, now is that time. It resembles the Red Sea and is certainly Dead, if not Dread Sea; even fish are unable to escape alive.

On April 24, 1915, the *Granite State News* commented:

> The spirit of clean-up and paint-up is strongly manifested throughout our village. The fever seems to have struck everybody. Result: this ever-beautiful village looks more beautiful. There is one thing, however, which seems to be overlooked, and that is the dumping ground around Back Bay. The rubbish could be covered with sawdust or earth and it would present a much nicer appearance to our visitors when they arrive.

Beginning in September 1911 the first municipal septic basin was completed on Lake Street at a cost of $200 and accommodated 120 residents. The septic system was expanded to comply with state regulations, and the next two basins were built on Factory and Glendon Streets in the autumn of 1913.

The annual town inventory of July 1, 1912, showed 665 registered voters, $1,752,386 real estate assessment, 424 horses, two mules, 42 oxen, 472 cows, 162 neat stock, 67 sheep, 29 hogs, 91 vehicles (including autos), two portable sawmills, and 102 boats.

### At Home

On the home scene spare time was becoming more precious. On July 29, 1911, Frederick W. Prindle editorialized:

> We have been thinking about the present day hobbies and how they create within us a longing for the return of the good old days of our forefathers—days when calloused hands warmly clasped each other and kid gloves were unknown, days when at eventide the family gathered at the old place and enjoyed the pleasures of home.
>
> How different now. Take the average family today, and the servant girl is usually the only one home after the evening meal.[53] The father is gone to lodge, the mother to her club, and Jane to the music circle, Kate to the card party, Robert has gone downtown for a game of billiards, Peter to the reading room. Verily, we live in a progressive age.

In winter more homes were being heated by central furnaces. Coal was the fuel of choice in the downtown district, while wood was still popular in rural areas.

### Blake Folsom

On October 11, 1911, Blake Folsom passed away at the age of 87.[54] In the hardware business for many years until his retirement in the late nineteenth century, he was widely admired as an enlightened citizen and benefactor to numerous town projects. He had started several young men in business and had helped with many charities—often anonymously.

His will, probated in November 1911, contained a number of public bequests. He gave in trust to Wolfeboro $15,000 "to be used by the said town forever for the keeping and repair annually so much of North and South Main Streets as lie within the present Fire Precinct. The above funds shall be invested in bonds of state, county, city or towns in the New England states."[55] Numerous other bequests were made, including $12,000 to the Blake Folsom Charitable Fund "for aiding and assisting in the support and maintenance of the worthy poor of said Wolfeboro."

### A "Modern Utopia"

An April 12, 1912, article by Charles O. Doe, often a critic of the local scene, but now laudatory, noted:

> Wolfeboro was born in honor, mantled with fame, and set in a frame of beauty. It is the setting of the town that strangers are solicited to visit, observe and enjoy. The scenic landscape cannot be destroyed. So long as the world lasts Wolfeboro will be a garden of God.
>
> We are English today, we have neither Hebrew, Chinese, African nor Turk;[56] we are all comfortable and frugal; our children are well groomed and educated free. Our school system takes and prepares him for Harvard or Yale.
>
> Our water system is good, any up-to-date town may say that, yet while they pump, we have 500 feet dead fall and the natural reservoir is eternal. Our electric light plant is okay.... Our telegraph, telephone and railroad conveniences are ample and satisfactory, and concrete sidewalks and good roads are common, houses are neat, convenient and well kept, stores sufficient, and nearly every trade is covered. Fraternal societies fill each hall each night, churches are well attended. People are law abiding. Gentlemen of leisure and wealth find ample plots and scenic locations on which to be built either palace or bungalow.
>
> Our factories are ever ready to employ men or women of character and good deportment. Wolfeboro will neither employ nor harbor rowdies nor hoodlums. Five heavy steam whistles give signals, five fire companies are ready to respond at the fire signal. We have lawyers, doctors, dentists, blacksmiths, and all the professional luxuries of an up-to-date city. We raise our garden stuff, make our own butter, raise our own swine, lamb and poultry, and pay our bills promptly. When we want fish we just take our line and catch them, shad, trout, bass, or pickerel as we prefer. If we want game we take the rifle, run out a mile or so and bag a deer, partridge or woodcock as we may choose.
>
> The town is full of beautiful women yet unmarried, and the man who could not satisfy himself with the material on hand has yet to be born, over 50 buxom maids controlling $200,000 or more are mostly willing subjects for matrimony, while marriageable men will not exceed a baker's dozen.
>
> We have automobiles and motor boats galore, and in winter the ice boats glide over the smooth frozen "Smile of the Great Spirit." Then there is brotherly, neighborly, fraternity or social life, that pleases the sentimentality of the inhabitants. Scandal, criminal gossip, and professional mischief makers are unknown,[57] and the "Golden Rule" is the accepted law of the corporation....
>
> Wolfeboro is a modern Utopia. What it requires it promptly secures for spot cash. Its bank account is steadily increasing as are its corporation assets, with the Huggins Hospital and Libby Museum still absolutely sound. We advertise the above facts, and can make good by full delivery of guaranteed collateral. Come to us stranger, we will show you 50 miles of mountains, 30 miles of Winnipesaukee, 300 islands, two superb mineral springs, and rest for weary souls.

Immediately following the conclusion of the preceding article, titled "Wolfeboro a Modern Utopia," was this local news item, obviously by a different author:

> Considerable excitement was caused in the vicinity of Masonic Hall by two very tough-looking men who were begging money from those who passed into the hall to attend the Fireman's Ball. Several of our citizens who met them earlier in the evening said that they were the toughest looking customers who have visited Wolfeboro in a long time. It was reported that during the evening John Fernald was held up and solicited for funds, and on his refusal they followed him down the street.

Many townspeople were somewhat xenophobic, and the passing through Wolfeboro of Gypsies (in particular), tramps, and other non-residents was reported in the *News* upon occasion.[58]

Despite its occasionally perceived shortcomings, Wolfeboro continued to be admired and appreciated far and wide. On August 9, 1913, this comment appeared in the local paper:

> Mr. H.M. Mayo, former camper on Lake Wentworth, now engaged in the timber business in Eugene, Oregon, spent Sunday in Wolfeboro. Although he has traveled abroad in the 46 states of the Union, Mr. Mayo says he has seen nothing more satisfying to the eye than the view across Winnipesaukee from Wolfeboro Bay. He hopes sometime to make his permanent residence in Wolfeboro.

### Of Young Men, Girls, and Fashions

An editorial in the *Granite State News,* July 20, 1912, noted:

> Boys with hats on the back of their heads and long hair hanging down over their foreheads and cigarettes and very smutty stories and foul mouths are cheaper than old worn out workhorses. Nobody wants them at any price. Men don't employ them, and sensible girls won't marry them. They are not worth their keeping to anybody, and it is not likely that they will be able to keep themselves. If anybody should happen to read this who answers to the above description, let him look at himself and jump in a well and say, "Here goes nothing."

A reader signing as M.I.B. contributed this to the October 4, 1913 edition:

> With the editor's permission I would like to put a few lines in the *News* in regard to one of the latest styles of dress, that being the slit skirt. Of course, we have heard quite a good deal about it in the papers, and we know that these skirts are worn in large cities, but we hope that the little town of Wolfeboro is above anything like that, and would have thought they cared more for their reputation than to be seen in anything so ridiculous....

George A. Carpenter, born in Boston in 1857, began business as a jeweler in Wolfeboro in the 1870s. He later moved to Boston and made a fortune in real estate and other ventures, but continued to spend much time in his native town. Carpenter lavished many gifts upon Wolfeboro including funding for Carpenter School (named for his mother Lavonia Carpenter), Huggins Hospital, gifts and medical care for children, and shoes and clothing for the needy. At one time the selectmen quipped that Wolfeboro should be renamed "Georgetown" in view of his benefactions. Carpenter died in 1934.

> No modest woman will appear in one of these above mentioned skirts. I have seen only one person with one of these skirts, a naughty young girl.... I read...where the officers were planning to arrest anyone seen on the street wearing a slit skirt. I think that would be a good idea.

In 1919 Abel Haley, who billed himself as Haley the Outfitter, whose shop was on the bridge in Wolfeboro (where the Wool Corner is in the 1990s), was selling men's collars at 15¢ each. At the time it was customary to buy a starched white collar and affix it around the neck and wear a shirt underneath. During the same era it was virtually mandatory that men wear hats at social occasions and at such activities as watching a parade in the hot summer. Men, particularly those of the professional and business class, were usually dressed in suits and hats.

### Among the Citizens

Alvan T. Hatch, husband of Mabel Fullerton Hatch ("The Goose" of newspaper commentary fame), moved from the Midwest, where for 11 years he had been a traveling representative for jewelry manufacturers, and settled on the Fullerton family farm near Goose Corner. There he set up a facility for repairing clocks, watches, and jewelry, although he continued to travel occasionally.

Frank P. Hobbs, who in the preceding decade had been well known as the owner of the Hobbs-Is-Inn and the Belvue House, was busy selling real estate and politicking. On June 30, 1915, one of his two daughters, Shuah M., "married well" and took as a mate Benjamin E. Sanborn, a Deerfield physician. Earlier, Benjamin and Shuah had been president and vice president respectively of their graduating class at Brewster Free Academy.

J. Clifton Avery straddled two active businesses—an insurance agency in town and what seemed to be a larger enterprise, a dairy farm on South Main Street. Almon W. Eaton, erstwhile grocer, "retired" and became well known as a poultry fancier after becoming interested in chickens during a vacation visit to Southern California. Before long, his local breeding enterprise was widely known.

On December 25, 1917, Greenleaf B. Clark, Wolfeboro's primary owner of rental properties, gave the town a plot of land valued at $5,000 on South Main Street, to be developed into a public park in celebration of the 100th anniversary of his family's arrival in Wolfeboro in 1817. Today it is known as Clark Park.

On April 30, 1920, Col. Edward Brown Dickinson died at his home in Brooklyn, NY. He was remembered as being the pioneer Wolfeboro summer resident along the Winnipesaukee shore, the first to build (in 1889-1890) a summer villa on what later became Sewall Road.[59]

### The Carpenter Family

George A. Carpenter was one of the greatest benefactors the town ever had. Each year during the second decade of the twentieth century he gave thousands of dollars to aid the poor, put on Thanksgiving dinners for children, and provided holiday gifts. He was constantly on hand to help mitigate disasters—such as helping when a family's home was burned and paying hospital expenses for illnesses and accidents. Carpenter, who began trade as a jeweler in Wolfeboro in the 1870s, made his fortune in Boston real estate and by 1916 owned several large commercial structures in that city including the Shoe & Leather, Blake, and Winter buildings.

Every summer he and his wife Emma would come from their Boston home and set up residence in Cobham Hall, which was acknowledged as the most palatial house in Wolfeboro.[60] His prime hobby was farming, despite his being crippled and able to walk only with support. Each year he would raise vegetables and keep the local newspaper posted on his output. In the autumn of 1914 he harvested 500 bushels of potatoes.

Their son Ralph stayed nearby on South Main Street in a home that later became known as the Goodwin House. Unfortunately, Ralph's personal life was not a happy one during the decade. The most sensational court action of the era involved the drawn-out and very acrimonious divorce case between Ralph and his wife Marguerite. For a time, week-by-week installments were carried in the local paper, although the trial was out of town. Their only child, Ralph, Jr., was a pawn in the proceedings, as each parent endeavored to obtain custody.

In addition, Marguerite Paul Carpenter brought separate suit against her father-in-law, George A. Carpenter, alleging that since her marriage to Ralph on April 30, 1906, and the birth of Ralph, Jr., on February 13, 1907, he had "contrived to destroy and alienate the affections of her husband from her, and finally his persuasion resulted in his son's leaving her in May 1915 and continuing to remain absent from her house."[61]

The matter was settled eventually, and in the following decade, Ralph Carpenter remarried. He and his new wife Rita spent summers in Wolfeboro, while his first wife Marguerite, also remarried and now known as Mrs. John B. Elliman, was likewise in town often and had a summer residence on Sewall Road.

## HEALTH AND MEDICINE

### Patent Medicines (Again)

Although preposterous, unfounded claims for medicines and cures were supposed to have disappeared after implementation of the Pure Food and Drug Act in 1907, promises of miracle cures still proliferated.

In the September 16, 1911, issue of the *Granite State News* the editor indicated that he personally took certain advertising claims at face value; to wit, this editorial comment: "Those who have purchased the electric belts are loud in their praises of them. All ailments disappear at their magic touch." A consistent advertiser was the Kickapoo Indian Medicine Company, which offered the Kickapoo Worm Killer, "a pleasant candy lozenge which expels worms, regulates the bowels, and tones the system, makes children well and happy."

From all seen in print, one might gather than the average reader of the *Granite State News* had tired or impure blood, falling hair, malfunctioning kidneys, worm infestation, and was at death's door!

On the front page of the *Granite State News,* April 3, 1915, was an article, "Fighting the Quacks," which began as follows:

> The majority of patent medicines not only rob deluded people of thousands of dollars, but what is even worse, will lead to vicious drug habits. The ethics of newspaper advertising would ban them to such an extent that most reputable newspapers have closed their columns to patent medicines, exceedingly profitable as such advertising is....

One can only assume that the person who set the "Fighting the Quacks" article in print was not the same person who set up the numerous weekly patent medicine ads that continued to appear. In the very same issue were advertisements for Parker's Hair Balsam, which "promotes a luxuriant growth" and "never fails to restore gray hair to its youthful color; prevents hair falling;" Lydia E. Pinkham's Vegetable Compound guaranteed to take care of organic inflammation, female weakness, pain and irregularities; S.S. Kidney and Bladder Pills, and more. Today, doctors might be surprised to learn that the common cold was indeed cured in 1915, when Mother Gray's Sweet Powders For Children were said not only to cure colds in just 24 hours, but also to end teething disorders, and destroy worms. Kilmer's Swamp Root offered wonderful results where eminent physicians failed.

Doan's Pills ran numerous advertisements featuring the testimonies of local merchants and officials, as in this notice of May 15, 1915:

> E.W. Godfrey, chief of police, Wolfeboro, says; "For some time my kidneys were disordered and I suffered from backache and sharp pains through my loins.... I tried serveral remedies, but got no relief until a friend told me about Doan's Kidney Pills. I got a supply from Tobey's Pharmacy and three boxes removed the backache and pains. I haven't had a bit of trouble since...."

### Among the Citizenry

The Anti-Fat Club met regularly in 1911. On April 13, 1911, a meeting was held at the home of Mrs. Charles Ellis. The to-be-beautiful-be-slim movement was just beginning in America. Many models and movie stars of the decade—including Mack Sennett's famous Hollywood "bathing beauties"—were solidly built or even a bit plump by the media standards of a later era.

Wolfeboro continued to be a healthy place to live. There were very few childhood deaths, and, in fact, deaths below the age of 50 were the exception. Records of longevity were mentioned frequently in the local news, as when on November 14, 1911, Mrs. Mary Stackpole celebrated her 102nd birthday at the home of her daughter, Mrs. John L. Wiggin, on North Main Street.[62]

Sanitation continued to be emphasized, and it is probable that the average Wolfeboro citizen of 1915 bathed more often and came into contact with fewer harmful germs than did his or her counterpart a quarter century earlier. Still, it was customary to go many days, often a week or more, without a bath, particularly in the winter. Many homes lacked bathtubs or shower facilities, prompting the local paper to suggest on May 22, 1920, "Wolfeboro ought to have a public bath house." Personal deodorants for men were virtually unknown, although many women utilized perfumes.

Milk was widely recognized as being good for one's health and was sold in embossed glass bottles delivered to residences. In 1920 paper cartons were tried, after which the *Granite State News* commented: "Paper milk bottles are not a success. There is too much danger of drinking the bottle."

### The Cost of Being Sick

Local physicians Nathaniel H. Scott, S.P. Getchell, Curtis B. Cotton, Fred C. Tobey, and Fred E. Clow set up a new table of charges to take effect on March 15, 1913. Among the tariffs an office visit cost $1, but preparing insurance papers cost an additional $1.50. Then, as now, doctors would rather tend to the sick than fill out forms.

Discussing ailments over the telephone cost the caller 50¢ each time. Vaccinations were $1 each. In-town house calls were $1.50 each, but $1.75 was charged if the doctor had to travel to South Wolfeboro. Other places merited a surcharge of 25¢ per mile above the basic rate. If the doctor had to visit a home between 9 p.m. and 7 a.m., double the day rates were assessed. In the case of contagious diseases, in-home visits cost $3 to $10 each while office consultations were $2.

### Huggins Hospital

Founded in 1907, Huggins Hospital continued to expand during the 1911-1920 decade. A report dated September 5, 1911, showed that for the preceding year, 96 patients were treated including 54 in wards and 38 in private rooms. Days of treatment totaled 1,672. There were five free patients who obtained a total of 78 days of care. Fifty-one surgical cases were treated and 49 medical cases, and there were 9 maternity stays. Twenty-one patients were discharged as being well, 59 as improved, and 5 were not treated. Nine operative cases were "not remaining." Eight deaths were reported. Total amount of revenue for the year came to $2,924.67, while expenditures added up to $4,167.47. In the same year, the building was expanded.

On May 1, 1915, this account was carried in the local paper:

> One of the most delicate operations ever performed at the Huggins Hospital and the only one of the kind, was performed Wednesday on a child, 16 months old, for an abscess of the brain. The operation was done by Dr. C.B. Cotton, assisted by doctors Tobey and Scott. The child is doing well, and if no complications arrive it will make a complete recovery.

Likewise memorable is this notice dated December 1, 1917:

> Mrs. Otis Hersey [of Center Tuftonboro] and her baby son, John Leander, returned home from the Huggins Hospital Monday, November 26, 1917. Mrs. Hersey is the first woman in Carroll County to give birth to a living child by Cesarean section. The operation was done November 3 at the hospital by Dr. F.E. Clow with the assistance of Dr. N.H. Scott and Dr. H. Leon Clow.

### Flu Epidemics

In December 1916 and January 1917, an influenza epidemic swept through town, prompting the paper to report on January 27 that "the village streets are not absolutely deserted, yet there is scarcely a home but that is more or less afflicted with illness." Editor Frederick Prindle of the *Granite State News* was confined to bed, as were numerous merchants and other local people.

This epidemic, whatever its nature may have been, paled into insignificance in comparison to the so-called Spanish influenza epidemic that pervaded America in the autumn of 1918, halting travel in many areas, forcing cancellations of events, and causing 548,000 deaths in the United States and 20 million worldwide. Nothing like it had been seen before or has been seen since.[63] In early October all Wolfeboro churches, lodges, schools, and public gathering places were shuttered. Many local and regional deaths, especially of older people, were registered during the next several months.

Ever seeking to turn a profit on human misfortune, patent medicine peddlers took advantage of the epidemic, although in reality there was no known cure. For example, Dr. True's Elixir was advertised with the headline "Save yourself from influenza."[64]

## NATURE IN ACTION

### Temperature and Precipitation

The winter of 1910-1911 was extremely cold, and the ice in Lake Winnipesaukee was reported as being 30 inches thick. By the third week of March, North Wolfeboro had four feet of snow on the ground.

In the first week of July, 1911, temperatures were extremely hot, with the mercury touching the 104° mark on at least four days. The editor of the paper suggested that it might be a record-breaker, but as no accurate records had been kept earlier, there was no way to prove it. On Monday, July 10, 1911, a new peak of 105° was recorded.

In the summer of 1913 there was little precipitation in Wolfeboro. Hay was stunted and in short supply, and apples were small. However, in the second week of September there was a torrential downpour that dumped nearly three inches of water in a short time, including nearly an inch "in a very few minutes." This heralded a spate of storms during the next two months.

On October 20, 1913, there was a very heavy downpour accompanied by extremely high winds. In Wolfeboro Bay several power boats were wrenched from their moorings and smashed, Eli Hall's boathouse was destroyed, the steamer *Ellen* was sunk, and many other vessels went to the bottom. Damage was particularly heavy in the Clark's Point area.

The heaviest deluge in several years occurred on Sunday, June 17, 1917. Almost incessant rain washed out many roads, especially in hilly areas, and covered Pond Road (today known as the Gov. Wentworth Highway, along the north shore of Lake Wentworth) with 15 inches of water. Many cellars were flooded, and local damage was estimated at $5,000.

While the editor of the local paper had earlier lamented the lack of town temperature records and also apparently forgot what had been printed about hot weather in the summer of 1911, this did not deter him from stating on August 4, 1917:

> Not since 1875 has such a long continued spell of extreme hot weather been experienced in this section as of the present week. Since Sunday it has been one continued hot wave, each day increasing in intensity, until Thursday it was almost unbearable.... From 92° on Sunday the mercury rose to 102° in the shade on Thursday. It certainly has been a record breaker.

In contrast, cold weather caused problems too. About 10 in the evening on January 8, 1918, accumulated snow caused the collapse of the Wolfeboro Garage owned by Albert F. Auderer on Center Street. The structure, not yet a year old, contained 15 to 20 motor vehicles which were damaged to the extent of about $1,500 to $2,000, plus $1,500 to the building.

In early 1920 snowfall was very heavy in Wolfeboro. On February 15 a storm added about 10 inches to snow already on the ground, giving an accumulation of up to 28 inches. By February 28 snowfall during that month alone totaled 43 inches. Roads were closed, and the Boston & Maine Railroad was inoperative. Stalled trains were vandalized along the line to Boston, and merchandise, especially foodstuffs, was stolen. Fuel supplies ran out, and the Electrical Department was forced to cut power to street lights and certain other services so that homes and businesses could be supplied. The editor of the paper stated that the snow reminded him of the storms of 1876 and 1893, but curiously did not mention the Blizzard of 1888—the greatest snowfall of the nineteenth century when trains and telegraph lines were out of commission for seven days.[65]

As if this were not enough, the region was hit by another storm on March 6, 1920, a blizzard described by the Editor Prindle as being far beyond anything that had ever blanketed the town—even exceeding the storm of 1873, which had not been mentioned in other recollections![66] Further:

> This storm really began about midnight of the 5th with a heavy rainfall, towards morning this turned to snow, not considered very bad but making traveling horrid, sort of slush; it continued, the storm all the forenoon increasing in severity, the wind increased to a small hurricane, making it impossible for pedestrians on the street, even traffic was stopped as teamsters, livery men and express companies could not make use of their teams. Those who tried the trick were most willing to abandon it as the driving sleet and strong winds in spite of extra urging could turn the teams about on their own and they could not make headway. Treetops were broken off like pipe stems and drifts piled like Himalayas on the highways, one-story buildings in many instances were buried to the eaves. And, in some cases the occupants were obliged to escape from second story windows. It was a great storm without question....
>
> No mail was received from Saturday noon until Tuesday night. At Cotton Valley about two feet of water covering the rails formed ice; also the same condition near Wolfeboro Center Sunday, Monday, and Tuesday....

On March 27, 1920, it was reported that residents of Pork Hill had been snowed in for *nearly six weeks* and only now were able to get their mail.

### Winds

January 28, 1911, saw freak winds in town, and many trees, signs, and other objects were blown down or tossed about, causing several thousand dollars in damage.

On December 1, 1912, it was extremely windy, and a large raft of logs being towed off Sewall Point in Wolfeboro Bay broke up. It took three days to corral all of the errant logs and take them to Clow's Mill on Back Bay.

At about 2:00 in the afternoon of Sunday, September 25, 1915, the wind began to increase in strength, building up to gale force by midnight, blowing continuously at an estimated 60 miles per hour. Trees were uprooted, apple orchards damaged, telephone and power lines snapped, and many boats destroyed.[67]

### Phenomena

On the evening of February 1, 1912, a double circle around the moon attracted the attention of many observers. The cause was refraction by ice crystals high in the atmosphere.

On July 29, 1916, the sky was yellow from horizon to horizon, and the atmosphere had an eerie glow, probably caused by smoke from distant fires. Not since 1881 had this occurred, noted the local paper.

On March 22, 1920, a fantastic display of northern lights (aurora borealis) shimmered:[68]

> It appeared as a great, transparent and illuminated drapery, constantly changing and swaying, extending clear across the sky from east to west with various hints, making it almost as light as any moonlight evening.

### Invasion of the Gypsy Moths

Gypsy moths and, to a lesser extent, brown-tail moths, have been the bane of Wolfeboro shrubbery and tree owners for years. On occasion, such as the summer of 1981, the infestation of gypsy moths has reached scorched-earth proportions as whole neighborhoods were stripped of every vestige of foliage.

The March 1917 town meeting voted $350 for the suppression of these pests. A bit of history on the subject was provided on March 17, 1917, in an article by J.W. Chadwick. Excerpts:

> Just before leaving Wolfeboro last November I discovered in our orchard several clusters of the eggs of the gypsy moth. I had been looking for the appearance of the pest in that locality because of my unfortunate experience on my place in Malden, Massachusetts. This may justify me in giving a brief account of the origin of gypsy moths in New England....
>
> Nearly 40 years ago a Frenchman named Trouvelot, a sort of amateur scientist, conceived the idea that the caterpillar of the gypsy moth could be utilized to spin silk after feeding upon the foliage of the oak, much as the silkworm has done by feeding on the mulberry. Provided with a quantity of moths, Professor Trouvelot made his first venture in this country, located at the experiment station at little more than a rifle shot from my house; consequently my experience with the varmints came first-hand.
>
> He confined his pets in a small grove of white oaks enclosed within a fine wire fence and waited for results. The larvae multiplied with marvelous rapidity for two or three seasons, but without any visible results producing silk or anything else useful. Trouvelot soon grew tired of this experiment, gave up his plan, and it was reported that he became a professor of French at Harvard College. He left his pets to hunt for themselves, which they promptly proceeded to do with complete success, to the discomfort of us who chanced to be near them. In a very few years they multiplied so rapidly that all the fruit trees for miles around were literally swept clean of their foliage to the dismay of their owners....

As they say, the rest is history.

## FIRES

### Fires and Fire Fighting

The decade 1911 to 1920 saw its share of local conflagrations. A summary of notable fires and items relating to fire fighting follows:[69]

**1911, March. Alarm boxes installed:** John McHugh, local electrician, did the work.

**1911, May 11. Hutchins excelsior mill:** Wolfeboro Falls. Totally destroyed by fire, at a loss of about $2,000. At the time it was operated by William Lord of Union.

**1911, July 10. Barn destroyed.** On the former Triggs property now owned by Frank Fields.

**1911, July 1. Alarm system:** Fire alarms as of July 1, 1911, consisted of nine different signals, all issued by steam whistle blasts from the lumber mill of S.W. & J.L. Clow on Back Bay.

**1911, September. New alarm boxes:** New alarm boxes made in Stonington, CT, by the Loper Fire Company Alarm Company were installed, replacing boxes bought earlier from a Baltimore firm. Certain sections of the previous system had been inoperative. The Baltimore company denied responsibility, but tests showed that the fire alarm boxes were poorly and improperly constructed. A legal action ensued.

**1912, May 18. Fire company organized:** *Granite State News* report: "A cooperative fire company has been organized at Goose Corner with Luke Fay as foreman and William Fullerton as secretary. This company is without expense or pay from the town of Wolfeboro." (Also see November 1914 note.)

**1912, July 4. Roberts' store, Veazie Hotel:** Major fire in North Wolfeboro destroyed Capt. Roberts' store (owned by Ernest Avery), the historic Veazie Hotel (occupied by Mrs. Mary Nute), and almost burned the nearby residence of selectman Arthur J. Willand.

**1912, December 11. Maple sugar house:** Owned by Charles F. Hersey. Destroyed.

**1913, February 6. Mrs. J. Langille's house:** Wolfeboro Falls. Suffered extensive fire damage.

**1913, December 11. Barn.** Large structure on Main Street owned by A.C. Kennett was burned including 160 *tons* of hay.

**1914, January 5. Moody House:** The house occupied by Daniel Moody and owned by C.H. Tebbetts, Wolfeboro Center, was destroyed, with its contents.

**1914, April 21. Walter Clifford's camp:** Seasonal camp and its contents in Pine Hill were destroyed.

**1914, September 22. Davis barns:** Two barns owned by the Walter Davis estate of Newton, MA, and occupied by Charles A. Whitton in East Wolfeboro, were destroyed by fire, as were the contents, for a loss of $2,000 to $3,000. Fire believed to have been started by a tramp who fell asleep while smoking; charred bones believed to be his were found in the ruins.

**1914, October 2. John Leavitt's barn:** Barn and contents at the corner of North Main and Mill Streets were burned, with damage estimated at up to $5,000. Lost were 18 tons of hay, three horses, carriages, tools, and an automobile. Cows in the basement, hens, and a hog were saved. It was said that the three horses that perished were suffocated by lack of oxygen, and "not even the hair was singed."

**1914, November. Goose Corner Volunteer Fire Company:** Organized with about 15 local members under Gorham B. Humphrey as foreman. A hose carriage was to be kept near the top of Fay's Hill and additional fire apparatus placed around the Goose Corner neighborhood.

**1914, November 18. Wiggin house:** The house of Mrs. Annette L. Wiggin near the Lake View Cemetery burned to the ground.

**1915, January 28. Alonzo Bickford's house:** High Street. Gutted.

**1915, February 20. S.W. Clow building:** A residential rental building on Bay Street owned by Stephen W. Clow was burned.

**1915, March 15. Dr. F.E. Clow residence:** Dr. Fred E. Clow's house on the corner of School and Union Streets caught on fire on the roof. The blaze was subdued, but much water damage was sustained.

**1915, June 10. Berry house:** The property of Hosea C. Berry occupied by Ralph Colby of Center Street near Mast Landing was heavily damaged by fire.

**1915, June 23. Huge Ossipee fire:** A major fire in Ossipee destroyed the Carroll County Court House (but two vaults of records were saved), a funeral parlor, a store, and several residences. Wolfeboro firemen responded, but were hampered by lack of water. For a time, major Wolfeboro-related Carroll County Court cases were moved elsewhere including to Dover.

**1916, May 8. Vehicle:** Large motorized truck burned at the side of the road linking Wolfeboro Center to Ossipee.

**1916, May 12. Keigwin camp:** Summer cottage on Sewall Road, "Wiscasset," owned by Rev. A. Edwin Keigwin of New York City was totally destroyed by fire. Later rebuilt.

**1916, August 3. Dale mills:** Rendering plant, sawmill, cider mill, and shingle mill owned by P.D. Dale, Cotton Valley Road, burned. Loss: $3,000.

**1916, November 28: Clark cottage:** Small unfinished cottage owned by Oscar Clark, Bay Street, was destroyed. Loss: $200.

**1917, October. Fire station locations:** Center Street, Factory Street, Libby Street, South Wolfeboro, and Wolfeboro Falls.

**1917, July 8. Log cabin:** Sewall Point. Owned by James Smythe of Chicago. Burned. Loss: $3,000.

**1917, August 16. Leavitt farmhouse:** In Pleasant Valley the Harry R. Leavitt farmhouse was struck by lightning and destroyed.

**1917, September 17. Wolfeboro Laundry:** Large building on Center Street destroyed by fire. 20 people were employed there. Rebuilding soon commenced. Loss: $5,000.

**1918, January 7. Ray boat factory:** "E.C. Ray's boat-building plant located on the shore of Lake Winnipesaukee near Clark's Point was totally destroyed by fire, resulting in a loss of up to $6,000. Destroyed were three boats being built, two of which were nearly completed, plus four powerboats in storage for the winter."

**1918, January 22. Mason store:** The store of junk dealer A.L. Mason on Center Street was afire, but firemen quickly put out the blaze. For years the Mason place, littered with unsightly clutter, was considered a nuisance.

**1918, May 16. Lumber camp:** Ames' lumber camp on the Mooney Farm near the Hill Camp at Rust Pond was destroyed by fire. John Bordeau of Sanford, ME, caretaker of the portable sawmill there, was killed.

**1919, September 8. Melanson (Meader) farm.** The Joseph I. Melanson barn was struck by lightning, and it, a wood shop, and ell were destroyed in a blaze causing a loss of $12,000. Cattle and many tons of hay were lost. The residence was saved. An earlier Meader barn had burned on September 30, 1902, and this was its replacement. The Meader farm had been sold in 1919 to Melanson of Lynn, MA.

**1919, September 2. Congregational Church:** Fire in the church was estimated to have caused $2,000 damage, but was later "admitted to be much in excess" of that figure. Few details were publicized.[70]

**1919, September. Excelsior mill:** Excelsior mill in Wolfeboro Falls owned by Lord & Cobb (earlier the Frank B. Hutchins mill) was destroyed by fire.

**1919, November 19. Burke barn.** In East Wolfeboro, Ethel Burke lost her barn by fire.[71]

**1920, January 3. Perry house:** Arthur Perry's home in East Wolfeboro was destroyed. A landmark, the building was known as the Cotton Homestead.

**1920, April 20. Morgan barn:** In Pleasant Valley a barn on the estate of the late Samuel Morgan was burned to the ground when fire spread from nearby brush and grass.

**1920, April 26. Clow mill:** Henry Clow's sawmill in East Wolfeboro was destroyed by fire.

**1920, June 10. Durgin block:** Tires, supplies, and other contents of the vulcanizing room operated by Archie A. Horne in the basement were destroyed by fire. $8,000 damage.

## LAW ENFORCEMENT

### Disturbing the Local Scene

Crimes and misdemeanors committed from 1911 to 1920 were mainly of a minor nature, such as disturbing the peace, stealing garden vegetables, illegal sale of alcohol, petty thievery, vandalism, and drunkenness. Typical of petty crimes are these newspaper accounts:

> August 2, 1919: "Some seven of our townsmen are complaining, and justly, too, against the criminal action of some unknown party for the poisoning of their dogs."
>
> July 10, 1920: "One of the meanest acts is to steal flowers and plants from graves in a cemetery, which is being done at Pine Hill."

Ervin W. Godfrey was police chief for much of the period and was assisted by officer Charles E. Kimball. Minor crimes were usually adjudicated at the Wolfeboro Police Court in the Town Hall. Major cases went to the Carroll County Court in Ossipee.

What might have been a major fire by arson, but was stopped in time, was reported on February 10, 1912:

> On the evening of February 2 an attempt was made to burn at least the fish house of Eddie Howard and possibly to start a big conflagration. Kerosene was used liberally and the blaze well started. Fortunately, Arthur Rickard happened along in season to extinguish the flames. This event occurred a little after 9:00 in the evening. It was a fortunate termination for had it gained a little headway, the destruction of property might have been extensive, from the fact that this fish house is stored back of Sheridan and the Durgin and near the livery stable of Joseph E. Fox....

On March 9, 1912, Postmaster Charles O. Dixon of Wolfeboro Center was brought before the Police Court and charged with the assault on a minor child. Bond was posted in the amount of $500, and he was scheduled to appear in the Carroll County Court in May. At the time, crimes within the home or involving minor children were rarely reported.

### The Welch Mystery

The Welch mystery was the most celebrated case of the decade.[72] On the morning of April 23, 1912, Captain Godfrey and Officer Kimball, in the company of Sheriff John H. Burke (of Madison) and Deputy Sheriff Myron L. Johnson (of Union), began a search for Gilbert Welch of Wolfeboro who had been missing for over two weeks. He had last been seen under the influence of liquor at Frank E. Hersey's shop on Mill Street. The newspaper reported:

> On the evening of April 4, about 7:30 o'clock, an outcry was heard by a few of the residents as follows, "For God's sake, can't you help me?" Leon Yeaton, who at the time was near the bridge, heard this shout and judged the outcry had come from a point in the rear of Joseph E. Fox's livery stable near the steam mill, and he immediately started for assistance and proceeded with dispatch to the supposed spot, but the search proved to no avail. Others heard the outcry but considered it came from a different quarter.
>
> Mr. Welch is reported to have been an honest, hard working man, but had the habit of periodically leaving home and being absent for a couple of weeks without his folks hearing from him. Consequently, his absence did not excite suspicions earlier. He had been making his home with his sister, Mrs. Edgar Thomas, who not hearing or learning of his whereabouts, reported to the authorities. The circumstances of the night of the fourth brought vividly to mind the cry for help, and on this basis the officers commenced their search, dragging the river and doing everything to find the body....
>
> Wednesday afternoon the body was accidentally discovered by James Clough, a millhand, who was poling a log raft along the shore near the mill, when his pick pole struck something that "felt peculiar" to him.... Clough succeeded in bringing to the surface the body, which so startled him that he nearly fell in himself. Regaining himself he shouted to the police, "I've got him! I've got him!"
>
> The body was conveyed to the undertaking rooms of Joseph L. Young and an autopsy was conducted.... This showed that there was no water in the lungs. There was an abrasion in the neck which indicated that he may have been strangled or have been kicked on the neck, or had pressure downward while his body was on a floor. All that remained of the large sum of money Welch was reported to have had about his person were two nickels. His watch was stopped at 2:20. The facts were sufficient to indicate a probable cause of murder.

The case became the talk of the town. It has been said that every cloud has a silver lining, and seizing an unexpected opportunity for profit, the Paper Store offered for 5¢ each, "postal cards showing the spot and surroundings of the finding of the body of Gilbert Welch, lately supposed to have met death by a foul play." The mystery remained unsolved.

### Other Cases

In May 1913 Mrs. Thomas Heath, wife of an itinerant lumberman, was charged with deserting her nine-month-old baby, who was found to be emaciated. Subsequently, she was sentenced to 90 days of confinement in the House of Correction at Ossipee. Her husband was fined $20 and sentenced to six months in jail for neglect; these were suspended if he would pay $3.50 per week to support the baby and a three-year-old child.

In December 1913 John Malloy and Charles Harris, both from Boston, were arrested for breaking and entering a large number of cottages along the Wolfeboro and Tuftonboro shore of Lake Winnipesaukee.

In October 1914 the cottage of G.M. Ellis on Turtle Island in Lake Wentworth was entered and ransacked, after which the local paper suggested:

> If Wolfeboro is to cater to summer visitors the town must make a more determined effort to protect property. Almost every season some cottage is broken into. The law is strict on this, and the authorities ought to give this subject attention.

Shortly after 1:00 a.m. Wednesday, November 9, 1914, downtown buildings were shaken by three blasts, as thieves attempted to blow the safe in the Post Office on the ground floor of the Peavey Block. Shots were fired at two fleeing bandits who managed to escape.

In July 1915 police officer Charles E. Kimball resigned after 26 years of service, to become a prosecuting liquor agent. Lester Thompson was appointed as an officer in his stead. Chief Ervin Godfrey had resigned earlier and in the same month was succeeded in the post by Lucern R. Ham, a well-known local carpenter who in his off hours was a poultry fancier and raised Rhode Island Reds.[73] Ham remained chief only for a short time and resigned effective April 25, 1916.

In September 1915 Charles H. Drew was arraigned in the local court on a charge of "assault with intent to carnally know" a woman—equivalent to what would later be called rape.

On September 23, 1915, Joseph Sylvain of Wolfeboro was found guilty of operating his automobile while under the influence of alcohol, was fined $100, and had his license suspended. The fine was the largest ever levied by the Dover Court (where Carroll County Court sessions were held after the devastating Ossipee Court House fire of the preceding June 23).

In September 1915 Mrs. Gertrude Watson of New Durham was charged with theft of $42 worth of goods from the store of John K. Chase, a blind man of Wolfeboro Falls who let his patrons operate on the honor system. The circumstances of the crime outraged many local citizens, and the proceedings leading to her conviction were closely watched.[74]

On December 6, 1919, it was reported that the summer home of Mrs. F.M. Sinclair had been broken into during the preceding week and the interior ransacked.

On January 10, 1920, a report stated that earlier in the week Constable Ralph C. Mitchell of Wolfeboro apprehended and brought before the Municipal Court Jake Hammon, who had been arrested in a summer cottage in Wolfeboro and admitted to "breaking into nearly every camp from Melvin Village to Wolfeboro, some 20 in all." He was one of a gang of rowdies that had been breaking into cottages seeking liquor and smashing dishes and causing destruction. Hammon could not make bail and was sent to jail in Ossipee to await the May court term.

## POLITICS AND POPULAR MOVEMENTS

### Rise of the Democrats

Politics and the two popular causes of the decade—women's suffrage and temperance—were closely intertwined. However, many other movements and causes came up as well.

In 1912 there was a great national division when Theodore Roosevelt, who had not sought re-election as president in 1908, challenged the president elected from his own party, Republican William Howard Taft. Finding that Taft was firmly ensconced in the White House and intended to run again under the Republican banner, Roosevelt split with tradition and formed the renegade Bull Moose Party. The main objective of Roosevelt from this point onward was to criticize Taft's actions. On March 16, 1912, Editor Frederick W. Prindle made this statement about the situation:

> The *News* can and does favorably endorse and admit it is in hearty accord with many and most of the expressed sentiments of Theodore Roosevelt. It has always been a supporter in the past, but at present can see no good reason for a recall of President Taft, whose administration has been so satisfactory.

In the November election Roosevelt succeeded in dividing the Republican vote, and Democratic candidate Woodrow Wilson was elected in a landslide. In Wolfeboro, 179 votes were cast for Taft, 126 for Roosevelt, and 281 for Wilson, effectively illustrating the Republican split.

The national success of the Democrats, who had been out of office for years, cast its glow on Wolfeboro. At the time, candidates for town offices had to declare whether they were running on the Republican or Democratic ticket. Democrats had previously been a rare species in and around Post Office Square and other local haunts. Not so now. In the March 10, 1914, town election, the Democrats were successful for the first time in decades. Charles R. Grant, who straddled both Democratic and Republican tickets, swept the field with 445 votes. The other two selectmen positions were captured by Democrats Arthur J. Willand (239) and William A. Bixby (243). In contrast, Republican Stephen W. Clow, local lumberman, garnered only 228 votes for selectman, while on the same ticket Cyrus L. Jenness brought home just 211.

### The State Election of 1914

In the statewide election of November 3, 1914, local citizens voted 390 no and 171 yes for licensing the sale of alcoholic beverages.

There had been a spirited contest for state representative. Winners were Republicans J. Frank Goodwin and Henry F. Libby (of Libby Museum fame) and Democrats Arthur J. Willand and Perley E. Young. Charles O. Doe, who ran as an independent after losing the Republican

Front of the Libby Museum as photographed shortly after its opening in 1912. From the beginning the facility, located on North Main Street near the town line with Tuftonboro, became a prime drawing card for tourists. Visitors over the years included Calvin Coolidge, who stopped by in the early 1920s. Exhibits emphasize natural history (founder Libby's main interest) but also include art and local history.

Interior view of the Libby Museum circa 1912. Opened in that year by Dr. Henry F. Libby, a Massachusetts dentist whose primary hobby interest was nature, the institution has been a focal point for local citizens and tourists ever since.

nomination, trailed. Doe was a brilliant man. While few questioned his stand that women should be allowed to vote, his inflexible statements concerning religion, morality, and other personal matters alienated many citizens.

### Woodrow Wilson

In the eyes of the *Granite State News* editor, President Woodrow Wilson, who served beginning in 1913, could do nothing right. In a situation reminiscent of that involving Democratic presidential candidate William Jennings Bryan who lost the 1908 election to Taft, the local paper reprinted anti-Wilson articles, cartoons, and sentiments whenever they could be found. According to the local news sheets, a more befuddled, insincere, and naive president than Wilson never walked the corridors of the White House.

In November 1916 the Republicans pitted Charles Evans Hughes against incumbent Wilson. The *News* listed many arguments why one should vote for Hughes and numerous reasons why Wilson should be thrown out of office. When the ballots were counted, Wolfeboro had voted 355 for Hughes and 284 for Wilson; however, the rest of the nation felt differently, and Wilson was reelected.

### Who Pays for Water Service?

Should all taxpayers bear the burden of new mains and outlets, or, keeping in mind that numerous citizens had their own private wells, should the public water system be paid for only by those who used it? Annual *Town Reports* show that the debate has gone on for years. For example, in the March 1917 town election, Rev. A. Edwin Keigwin, who had a summer place, "Wiscasset," on Sewall Road but as a citizen of New York could not vote in Wolfeboro, suggested that all town voters pitch in to pay for an extension of the water main on Sewall Road. Starr Parsons, a registered local voter, suggested that $1,200 be raised for this purpose. The idea was voted down. In the meantime Sewall Road, which dead ended and which in the off-season had many vacant driveways, gained a reputation with automobilists as the local lovers' lane.[76]

### The 1920 Election

In September and October 1920, after the Democratic party had nominated Governor James M. Cox for president and the Republicans had named Warren G. Harding, the local paper began running many anti-Cox and pro-Harding items.

In the issue of October 2, 1920, a picture of a banner hung in a saloon in Chicago was printed, which read as follows: "IF YOU WANT BEER AND WINE VOTE FOR GOV. COX FOR PRESIDENT." Adjacent to this, and in sharp contrast, was a photograph of Senator Warren G. Harding, appearing distinguished in a business suit, holding a paper, with this caption: "The newspaper holds much interest for Senator Harding these days. In the few moments of leisure that are left to him, the senator, a newspaper editor and publisher himself, reads his newspapers carefully."

The November 1920 election was the first in which women could vote in New Hampshire. Appeals were made to ladies as "first-time voters" in various advertisements and invitations to hear lectures. In Wolfeboro for the Harding ticket 680 votes were cast, and for Cox 332 votes were registered.

### Women's Suffrage

Women's suffrage was the most hotly debated topic of the decade. In Wolfeboro the majority of printed opinions seemed to be in favor of it, although most citizens, particularly men, remained silent. In 1914 the question was brought to the fore by Charles O. Doe, who suggested that women had the right to vote and that exercising this prerogative was long overdue. He invited anyone with a contrary opinion to state it, but the only person who felt moved to do so at first was Mrs. Abbie Scates Ames in a letter printed on February 14, 1914.[77] Writing from Massachusetts, Ames suggested that a woman's duty was to act as a mother, and that nature endowed men with the desire and ability to act as their protectors.

Mabel Fullerton Hatch, who was living in St. Louis at the time, sent a letter to the *News,* taking exception to the statement that males "instinctively care, support and protect" females, noting that never "in all her 39 years on the farm, in all of her observation of 'oodles' of cats and kittens, has she ever beheld a gallant tomcat toting mice to the mother of his progeny."

### The Libby Museum

Playing the most controversial part in the suffrage debate was Dr. Henry F. Libby who was best known as a naturalist. Born in Tuftonboro, April 7, 1850, Libby lived in Reading, MA, in 1912 and practiced dentistry at 366 Commonwealth Avenue, Boston. Libby spent his summers in Wolfeboro, which he declared as his legal residence. He also owned property in Wolfeboro and held the deed to Rattlesnake Island in Alton. Libby Street, laid out in 1893, was named for him, as he owned four houses on the short thoroughfare. Tradition has it that Dr. Libby was not mentioned in Parker's *History* due to animus, reason unrecorded, between Libby and Parker. No matter, Libby was quite prominent on the local scene.

His pride and joy was the Libby Museum. Located near the Tuftonboro town line, the rectangular structure

**Crew in the beginning stages of work on the Libby Museum. Left to right: Frank Bradley, H. Sleeper, Isaac Burke, Fred Gould, Gilbert Welch, John Gould, Joe King, unidentified, Charles Libby, J.C. Blake, and George W. Hersey.**

**Front view of the Libby Museum shortly after its opening.**

displayed a marvelous group of stuffed, mounted, and preserved animals; Indian relics, and other artifacts collected since 1890 (when, according to popular accounts, he acquired his first major prize, a caribou in the Maine woods).[78] In addition, a collection of flowers formed by H.E. Sargent, botany professor at Brewster Academy, was shown.

During the previous decade, Libby's frequent excursions aboard the steam yacht *West Wind* resulted in many newspaper notices. An account related this concerning the museum's first few days:[79]

> On Saturday, August 17, 1912, the Libby Museum was opened to the public.... Residents of ours and nearby villages showed their appreciation of the doctor's undertaking by visiting in large numbers and continued to do so throughout the interval. To say that they feel well repaid is stating it mildly, for people feel proud of this institution, and recognize it too as a monument to the doctor and of more enduring nature than a shaft of crumbling marble.

During the first year of operation, the museum attracted 3,700 visitors, a number that rose to over 7,000 annually by the end of the 1919 season.

Soon after opening the facility, Dr. Libby announced his desire to create an arboretum nearby to show specimens of all trees indigenous to New Hampshire. The project was begun, never received much publicity, and was later abandoned.[80]

### ...And the Libby Furor

In the 1990s, decades after its founding, the Libby Museum was recognized as one of the town's most important cultural assets. Largely forgotten was an inflammatory speech made to the New Hampshire State Legislature in early March 1917, when Henry F. Libby was serving as representative from Wolfeboro. Libby was personally responsible for the Legislature's voting against women's suffrage in the state of New Hampshire. This was one of the most controversial actions taken by any local citizen during the decade and ignited a firestorm of protest.

On March 24, 1917, the *Granite State News* ran a lengthy article on the subject. Excerpts:

> The address of Representative Henry F. Libby of Wolfeboro, delivered a week ago during the debate of the women's suffrage, continues to be a topic much discussed by the solons. The speech was a strong card for the anti-suffragists and helped carry the day for them. The facts it presented were the result of a scientific study by Dr. Libby....
>
> Libby's speech said the following:
>
> "We are seeking qualification. If we are seeking for facts, and if we are seeking for truth, we should go to Father and Mother Nature for instructions. In the suffrage movement are we upsetting nature's plan of rights while we are trying to adjust equal rights? Do you find equal rights displayed in any of the lower form of life between the sexes? To be equal is to be completely and absolutely adjusted to an equilibrium. Nature never instituted such a law....
>
> "Is the suffrage plan nature's plan? Yes and no. There are vastly more nays than ayes....
>
> "You can observe the process and minor details of the vegetable world by cross-fertilization, and in the animal as well, by intelligent mating. Is it consistent with nature's plan to have one individual physically unlike another, and expect them to be co-equal?... Are there not innumerable examples in the insect animal world where the male predominates in structural strength and leadership? Why do the males of some species of animals have horns while other species have other weapons to give battle to the adversary in times of mating, this time of the greatest need for evolving the best in all things?...
>
> "If we are heirs of these laws of nature and are living under them (which we have every evidence to show we are by scientific research), why are we in such haste to give women every voting power? Why not let them prove that they are capable of making laws, by becoming law students in the same proportion of men? There seems to be a distaste for this heroic law-making by women. They seem likewise to have a distaste for doing the things men do, yet they want the vote!..."

Libby went on to say that 11 states with an aggregate population of less than eight million had adopted women's suffrage while 37 states with populations of about 36 million had rejected it. Thus:

> "This enormous proportion unfavorable to suffrage protects our present welfare. Have we not discovered there is always danger in introducing in any country new and untried plant or animal life? This proposed ballot is something like introducing a plant into our garden. An untried plant, it may be a weed bearing a seed that looks like a grain of wheat. Have not botanists discovered errors when it is too late? Have we not suffered untold misfortune by the introduction of that beautiful gypsy moth?..."

In conclusion Libby said:

> "If I were privileged, I would like to ask these 404 representatives and some 430,000 people of New Hampshire this question: If each one had a very important question to decide, how many do you propose would go to a woman for counsel? And these women we are voting for today are to help make our laws!"

Once again Mabel Fullerton Hatch came to the fore. On March 17, 1917, she suggested, peppery tongue in cheek, that it was too bad that the 15 states which had already given the ballot to adult females, hadn't known about "the status of women as fixed by nature and defined by the representative from Wolfeboro," for then "all of this passing out of ballots to people unfit to use them wouldn't have occurred." Further: "The Goose wishes while nature had been about it, she had interposed a barrier between women and the paying of taxes."

As the controversy raged, The Goose penned still another article against Libby.[81] She suggested that his science was bogus, and that if the ability to make laws was essential to the intelligent use of the voting franchise, "Do you suppose that they would send a dentist such as Libby to Concord to legislate for them?" The Goose also mused that "since more men than women occupy prison cells, women should be allowed more liberty than men," and that "since there are more men drunkards than women drunkards, women have greater self restraint than men."

On April 7, 1917, Charles O. Doe fired off a long letter to the *Granite State News* criticizing Libby, stating that he "misrepresented the majority of the people of Wolfeboro." Concerning Libby's contentions that very few women enter law schools, Doe retorted by saying "You men who legislate prohibit the privilege by refusing women to qualify as justice or magistrate."

Doe then took closer aim: "What kind of dentist would you make if you were enjoined from pulling or filling a tooth, brushing a plate, or looking at the patient's mouth?" Moreover, "Who has determined that man is above the peerage of woman? MEN THEMSELVES."

In conclusion Doe stated that Libby's actions were "reprehensible" and that "to add voluntarily insult to injury warrants the anathema of every true and intelligent woman."

By decade's end women did indeed obtain the long overdue right to vote. At once they became accepted, and candidates for office now had to present platforms with planks appealing to the distaff members of the electorate.

### Prohibition and Temperance

By all rights, the local temperance movement should have withered after the November 6, 1906, town vote against alcohol. However, the Woman's Christian Temperance Union (universally referred to simply as W.C.T.U.) held regular meetings during the period as it would for decades thereafter.

The license vs. no-license question came up again on the ballot at two-year intervals, and each time the no-license advocates prevailed with majorities much greater than in 1906. Still, campaigns against alcohol were waged at each biennial election.

On January 16, 1920, Prohibition under the Constitution began nationwide. On February 21, 1920, the Bureau of Internal Revenue issued a statement which included the following:

> Any physician duly licensed to practice medicine and actively engage in the practice of this profession may obtain a permit to prescribe intoxicating liquor and may then issue a prescription for distilled spirits, wines, or certain alcoholic medicinal preparations for medicinal purposes for persons upon whom he is in attendance or in cases where he believes the use of liquor as medicine is necessary. In no case may spirituous liquor be prescribed by one or more physicians in excess of one pint for the same person within a period of 10 days. No specific limitation is placed upon the quantity of wines which may be prescribed for medicinal purposes.

Many local residents made for themselves what they could not readily buy in stores. Basic ingredients for a batch of one popular type of home brew consisted of a pound of raisins and a cake of yeast.[82] The sale of these two items increased dramatically in grocery stores. In addition, large quantities of liquor and illicit "moonshine" were shipped into the state, and apple cider was fermented in local basements in unprecedented quantities.[83]

## WAR

### The Soldiers' Monument

During the first decade of the twentieth century, several "entertainments," as they were called, were held to raise money to finance a monument to Civil War veterans. Despite much publicity, apparently only about $700 to $800 had been raised toward the memorial, which was estimated to cost several times that much.

On November 5, 1913, the Women's Relief Corps held a quilting bee followed by a picnic dinner to raise funds for the now-revived project.[75] The editor of the local paper found it to be "a lamentable if not a humiliating fact that good old Wolfeboro does not seem to appreciate the sacrifices made by her boys in blue as much as almost every other town of equal size in the state."

At the March 1914 town meeting voters solidly backed the memorial by pledging $2,000 against an interest-bearing note. The Soldiers' Monument was soon erected at Pickering Corner, opposite Center Street, where the First Congregational Church had recently stood. On Columbus Day, Monday, October 12, 1914, at 2:00 p.m. Judge Sewall W. Abbott was the master of ceremonies for the dedication program.

### Prelude to Involvement

In August of 1914 war erupted in Europe. The first year of conflict had little impact upon Wolfeboro, about the only exception being the gathering of food, gifts, and supplies in late autumn of 1914 to furnish relief to war-torn Belgium.

From time to time, accounts of hostilities reached print, as did essays and philosophical dissertations on the subject. Although other nations were drawn into the vortex of war, the leading belligerents were Germany and England. Most sympathy seemed to be on the British side, but to be fair, the *Granite State News* published a lengthy commentary advancing the German point of view, which was that the industrial empire of Great Britain sought to vanquish Germany in order to eliminate competition.[84] Much was made of the fact that the English cut German lines of communications and were trying to manage the news. As time went on, most Americans took the British interpretation that the Germans were trampling over Europe and mistreating the inhabitants of the countries they conquered.

In 1914 and most of 1915, the average Wolfeboro citizen considered this to be a foreign war, somebody else's conflict. However, most American factories were eager to furnish supplies and munitions for anyone who wanted to buy them. The plants of the Bethlehem Steel Co., which extended six miles along the Delaware River in Pennsylvania, were running day and night. Industrialists were rubbing their hands with glee as unprecedented profits rolled in.[85]

By autumn 1915 this was hotly debated: Should America arm for war? "Preparedness" was the watchword for many, and it was said with some foundation that this philosophy was agitated by suppliers of war munitions and materiel, many of whom were making vast fortunes. A new battleship cost $18 million, and not only did each war vessel provide employment at home, but also contributed to the American arsenal. Amid all of this, our country remained neutral. It was an uneasy indifference.

Local ministers got into the discussion. Rev. Carlyle Summerbell of the Christian Church; Rev. William Hathaway Pound, who held forth in the First Congregational Church pulpit; and Rev. T.H. Scammon of the Free Will (a.k.a. First) Baptist Church quoted scriptures and advocated peace. Rev. Summerbell reminded listeners of the words of Jesus as recorded in the book of Matthew, "All they that take the sword shall perish with the sword"[86] and went on to say:

> All the nations of antiquity that have depended upon the sword have been relegated to the scrap heap of ancient history. Only one great nation still exists, the Chinese, who witnessed the infallible teachings of history, that war and great preparation for war bring destruction. Shall we choose destruction for our beloved America?

By the end of 1915 over five million people had died in Europe, hardship had descended upon millions of other innocent citizens, and just about every European nation had been caught up in the conflict in some way.

America continued to prosper from war activities. "With these huge expansions in industries due to the war, the stimulus thrills every artery of the country's trade. What wonder is it that times are looking up?"[87] While trade arteries were being "thrilled" in America, the slaughter of humanity in Europe continued unabated.

In early 1916 there continued to be much talk in the local paper about the policy of "preparedness" and much criticism against President Woodrow Wilson and other alarmists, who were said to have been leading America toward an unwanted war, stirring up unrest, and causing problems just for political reasons. Wilson's fellow Democrats in Congress were just as bad in the eyes of the *News*.[88] On May 13, 1916, Charles O. Doe editorialized that Germany was justified in establishing its own war policies and that Wilson and others may well be "harnessed to 'frenzied finance', preparedness, duty bound to promote the interests of the food, munitions, clothing, etc., trusts in order to secure the gold of Europe."

The situation continued to heat up. On July 5, 1916, NH Governor R.H. Spaulding issued a draft call for 1,100 fit single men of the state, between the ages of 18 and 35, to serve in military duty.[89] Wolfeboro's quota was 11 "enlistees," with any unfilled positions to be subject to draft. There was excitement in the air, and the required men stepped forward. However, only four passed requirements and were assigned to companies: Fred Richardson, Clifford Smith, LeRoy P. Mansfield, and Earl Leonard Walsh.

### Getting Ready

On February 3, 1917, the United States suspended diplomatic relations with Germany, and on April 6 declared war against it. Now, there were no longer two schools of opinion. Germany was the enemy and was to be defeated at any cost. News articles about war being fought in the trenches, at sea, and in the air filled the columns of the local paper. Nearly all businesses in town displayed patriotic flags and in some instances posters and bunting, and many residents did likewise. There was a flag in every window of the C.K. Fox Shoe Co. factory.

Next came a wave of pro-war, anti-German propaganda. Typical is an article printed on April 7, 1917, "Must Prepare for War," in which an unnamed spokesman for the NH League for National Defense told of the evils of Germany, of various plots that were being hatched, how Germany was making a deal with Mexico to attack the United States, how Mexico and Japan were to seize the West Coast and Germany the East Coast. As if to drive the point home to Wolfeboro, the writer stated that Germany was going to seize all property in New England and colonize the area with Germans.

Beginning in April, conservation measures were instituted. As time went on, restrictions were made on the consumption of sugar, the use of fuel, and the purchase of certain other domestic goods and supplies. Prices rose.

Patriotic local citizens wanted to become involved. Statewide membership in the Red Cross increased from 800 people in 1916 to 12,000 in April 1917. Mass meetings and rallies were held in the Temple Auditorium and elsewhere. Parades were formed, displays were mounted, and just about everyone joined in supporting the Allies (as they were called) in Europe.

An editorial by Frederick W. Prindle exhorted local citizens to join the ranks of farmers and to plant a garden. It required four people at home to supply one person on the front. Increasing food production was a town-wide goal, and even seasonal visitors were heard to remark that they would like to get into the act and help as much as they could at their summer camps. In May the first Liberty Loan drive started, with the Wolfeboro

National Bank contributing its facilities as a clearing house without profit or commission.

On June 5, 1917, every male between the ages of 21 and 30 was required to register for possible military service. Failure to do so meant one year imprisonment if convicted.

On July 28, 1917, this account was printed:

> Wolfeboro sent its first quota of young men to join the New Hampshire troops, Wednesday morning, July 25, at which time the wharf and Post Office Square was filled by townsmen to do them honor. Fathers, mothers, sisters, and sweethearts gathered to bid them farewell and good luck to these young men as they boarded the steamer *Gilnockie,* Captain John Goodhue, to be conveyed to The Weirs where they were to take the train.... There were 25 in the party which left Wednesday morning, while five left Tuesday by train, making it a total of 30.... Of these, 28 were from Wolfeboro....

In the beginning, most soldiers from NH were sent to Camp Greene near Charlotte, NC. An article in the local paper told of the fine scenery in and about Charlotte, and how the citizens there were eager to welcome soldiers into their homes. The situation seemed idyllic. Reality was somewhat different, and it was later disclosed that the training camp was unsanitary and muddy, rifles were in short supply, and that many soldiers simply sat around with little to do.

### Wolfeboro Sets National Record

The *Granite State News* carried much news from the European battlefields and other theatres of war. Typical is this notice dated September 8, 1917:

> British shipping losses for the week show an increase over the seven days previous, a total of 23 vessels being reported torpedoed. Trieste refugees are fleeing into the interior. An entire Russian division flees in disorder and face of Austro-German attack on Southern Rumanian line. Foe advances unopposed. President Wilson places an embargo on virtually every commercial export of America and formally prohibits the export of any article to Germany or her allies, thus to a great extent relieving Great Britain of the work of directing the blockades. It goes into effect at once.

Throughout the autumn the front page of the paper was dominated by lists of men called up for service, schedules of draft numbers, relief efforts, and other war news, especially as it related to the town and state. In due course, the Second, Third, and Fourth Liberty Loan drives were initiated, and in each instance the town went over the top of its quota. For the First Liberty Loan, Wolfeboro held the *national* record at $68 per person, a remarkable accomplishment.[90]

### Harry A. Harriman

On November 3, 1917, American forces had their first armed clash with German troops.[91] This report and others did not mention if Wolfeboro men were involved, as the whereabouts of specific soldiers was secret. This letter datelined October 25, 1917, from "Somewhere in France" was published locally on November 24:

> I can write only a line to show I have not forgotten those who are dear to me at home, and I wish to be remembered to everybody but I cannot write to everyone, but wish you to tell them that they are not forgotten. I am well as also is my chum Smith. We had a long, hard, and tiresome trip. A short stop in England. I was glad when we left for France. Cannot write much what I am wishing all good luck and am hoping to get a speedy return and be with you all again.
>
> Faithfully yours, Harry A. Harriman.
>
> Company H, 103d, Inf. U.S.A.
>
> American Expeditionary Forces.

Another Harriman letter from "Somewhere in France," dated December 20, 1917, contained this message:[92]

> It is just after a good snowstorm I am writing this. It is quite cold, when we came here they called it sunny France, but now the boys call it stormy France. When anyone says they do not have any winter here they are fooling themselves. We had a very good Christmas, having good old American turkey, and in a short time we won our battle over turkey by the good work of cook Richardson and his assistants. All the boys are well and in the game the same as ever. The great talk of the day is that canning the Kaiser, and you can sure bet that the 103rd will come back with colors high. The roar of the guns sound "We will win." May this find everybody at home in good cheer, and here's to the good winter sports we used to have and hope to enjoy later on. Good luck and good cheer to all at home.
>
> "Here's to the U.S. Army rifle, That never vary but a trifle,
> As for old Kaiser Bill, We will bounce him off his sill."
>
> Sincerely,
>
> Harry A. Harriman

As fate would have it, Harriman became the first Wolfeboro soldier to be killed in action, when on July 17, 1918, in France, at Belleau Wood, Chateau-Thierry, he was felled by a German machine gun bullet.[93] His name was given to the local American Legion Post, and today is remembered as part of the Harriman-Hale Post (Clayton Hale being the first local resident killed in World War II).

### Wartime

One of the best ways to help the boys on the battlefield was to send them cigarettes. In November 1917 the *Granite State News* set up a tobacco fund whereby anyone sending a quarter could get 50¢ worth of tobacco delivered to the troops.

Prices continued to rise, and industrialists raked in record profits, prompting many scare stories about the government taking control of prices and regulating industries. Communism and socialism were just around the corner, many suggested.

Effective December 21, 1917, restrictions on the use of electricity went into effect in town. Sundays and Thursdays were to be "lightless nights," with households burning as few bulbs as possible and with no commercial signs illuminated. In January 1918 the U.S. Department of Justice announced that all people of German birth who were not naturalized American citizens had to register as "alien enemies."

The C.K. Fox Shoe Co. was closed for five days beginning on Friday morning, January 18, 1918, to conserve coal. Further, on each Monday for the next 10 weeks there was to be no work performed in the factory. This was the only steam-powered Wolfeboro business using coal for fuel. All others used waste wood products to generate steam or operated on water power. The Fox shutdown "was not accepted with good grace," as it meant no income for those employed there.[94] The government proposed other ideas, including closing all stores on Mondays after the noon hour and substituting cornstarch and other products for wheat. Over a period of time new regulations were added, and certain old ones found to be unworkable were dropped. The Monday closing rule lasted less than a month.

Many Wolfeboro and regional boys were in training in Massachusetts at Camp Devens in January and February 1918.

In April it was announced that citizens had to furnish reports as to how much flour and sugar they had on hand.[95] By that time coal rationing had been in effect for several months. As a commentary of the time noted, there were meatless, wheatless, heatless, and sweetless days. A new term became popular: those who complained about conservation or who did not contribute to the war effort were called "slackers."

### Peace

On November 11, 1918, a truce was declared. Headlines in the November 23 *Granite State News* read as follows, whimsically perhaps, but perhaps not: "Nation is wholly unprepared for peace arrival. Industry is thrown almost in panic at sudden armistice."

By March of 1919 soldiers were returning one-by-one from training camps and Europe. In April the Fifth Victory Loan was launched to pay for reconstruction after the war. A poster titled *Victory Liberty Loan, Americans All,* by Howard Chandler Christy, was illustrated in the paper in connection with the drive.

Wolfeboro was tired of war. On July 19, 1919, the editor of the local paper commented on the recent July 4th celebration, noting that only a few United States flags or regimental flags were in evidence, clearly an oversight. Further:

> Usually Wolfeboro keeps in the forefront, but appears at the present to be lagging insofar as public demonstration is concerned relative to our homecoming soldiers. Of course, all rejoice to see these boys come home again and thankful they have returned in such prime condition, but why stifle our sentiment? Why not let the world know how glad we are and rejoice with us? Let's explode so the echo may be heard around the world, for that matter. Give the boys a rousing, cheery welcome.

An appropriate celebration was held Friday, August 22, with an estimated 10,000 people participating. In the parade was a banner with two gold stars honoring Harry A. Harriman and Samuel Valley, two local soldiers who had made the supreme sacrifice.[96]

The Harry Harriman American Legion Post No. 18 received its charter on August 4, 1919. Elected chairman of the Executive Committee of the group was Dr. Fred E. Clow. Any man who was in the military between April 1917 and November 11, 1918, was eligible to join. This applied to Wolfeboro residents as well as those from neighboring towns. The 1919 observance set the stage for the American Legion Post to sponsor Independence Day celebrations, a tradition that has continued intermittently to the present time.

### Those Who Served

These 110 men of Wolfeboro who served are listed on the World War I memorial plaque which was erected in 1941 near the Soldiers' Monument:

Curtis E. Abbott, Everett E. Abbott, Tracy L. Abbott, Floyd E. Adjutant, Leslie N. Anderson, Merton E. Aspinwall, George J. Barry, Herbert M. Beacham, Edgar L. Bean, George Fred Brewster, Henry W. Britton, Edwin M. Brown, Ashton R. Chamberlain, Leslie M. Chamberlain, Joseph A. Chamberlain, Thomas W. Charles, Arthur S. Clow, Fred E. Clow, M.D., John E. Colbath, Guy W. Corson, Curtis B. Cotton, M.D., Edwin R. Craigue, Berthold F. Cropley, Leaman E. Cunningham.

Chester T.C. Davis, Joseph Demars, Frank Dore, Wilbur C. Drew, Harry C. Dunfield, Adelbert S. Fisher, Austin F. Fogg, Elbridge N. Furber, Arthur E. Goodrich, Ransom E. Goodrich, William F. Goodrich, Henry N. Hale, Howard E. Hammond, Harry A. Harriman, John B. Harvey, Carl D. Hayes, Robert J. Irish, Morrell A. Jackson, George B. Jenkinson, 3rd, Perley J. Jones, Harlan B. Kelley, Herbert B. Kendall, Percy M. Kenney, Edward Kimball.

Wilfred L. Lampron, John S. Langille, Samuel W. Leighton, James W. Locke, Curtis N. McDaniel, Frank S. McHugh, Thomas R. McHugh, Lawrence McIntire, LeRoy P. Mansfield, Guy Marden, Gordon A. Meader, Edwin V. Moody, Carl L. Morgan, Noyes V. Moore, Harry Dean Morgan, Luigi Paolucci, Eben Parsons, Fred Pearson,[97] Perley C. Perkins, George L. Philbrick, Henry P. Pinkham, Chester M. Ray, Addison R. Reed, Sumner H. Reynolds, Percy B. Rhodes, Frederick A. Richardson, Leon F. Roberts, Oliver M. Roberts, Harlan P. Sanborn, Francis H. Sargent, Natt Harlan Scott, Clifton Simms, Clifford A. Smith, Warren E. Snitcher, Fred A. Stackpole, Harold T. Stitt, Rev. Carlyle Summerbell, Ernest H. Swift, Edgar O. Tetherly, Herbert D. Tinker, Auguste P. Valley, Eugene Valley, Joseph B. Valley, Samuel Valley, Samuel F. Walcott, Clayton M. Wallace, Wallace Webb, Guy H. Wentworth, Llewellyn H. Wentworth, James Guy Whittier, Scott Wilbur Whittier, Albert W. Wiggin, Pierce C. Wiggin, Earl F. Willand, Howard Willand, Harry E. Woodman, Henry Wright, Guy M. Wyman.

Noyes V. Moore was the only man from Wolfeboro who served in the Marine Corps in World War I, where

Parade in downtown Wolfeboro, August 22, 1919, honoring soldiers returning from the World War in Europe. A "Welcome Home" banner extends across the street. The photograph was taken from near where Bridges' Hallmark store is today.

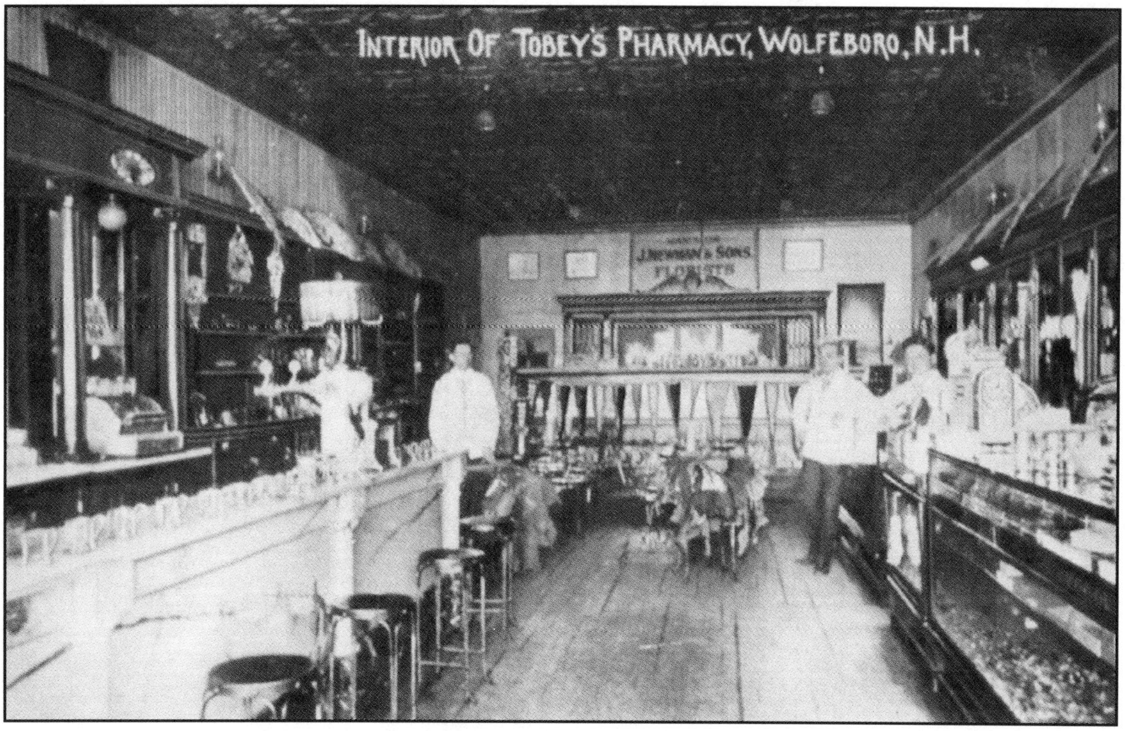


Tobey's Pharmacy as it appeared circa 1911. Along the left is a long marble counter and soda fountain with stools with twisted-wire legs. A sign above the National cash register offers "Milk Shakes 10¢." Farther along the left wall are shelves with merchandise. Triangular pennants around the store bear the names of local lodging places. A sign reading "Agents for J. Newman & Sons, Florists" is high on the back wall just under the pressed tin ceiling. Along the right is a counter for cigars, candy, and the dispensing of prescriptions.

his tour of duty included action in the Battle of Belleau Wood. Several of his sons and a daughter served in the Marines in World War II.

## PRICES IN 1920

The following prices and related items are from advertisements and notices in the *Granite State News:*

**Automobile repair:** Pinhole in inner tube, 30¢.

**Automobile supplies:** Tires for Ford cars, guaranteed for 3,000 miles, $7.50 and $8.50.

**Automobiles:** Ford Coupelet (with starter), $745; Ford Runabout $395, with starter, $465, chassis alone, $360.

**Barber service:** Shampoo, 35¢; hair tonic, 15¢; razors honed, 35¢; massage, 35¢; haircuts, 35¢, pompadours 45¢.

**Boats and canoes:** Small, wooden, $77.50 to $105.

**Broom:** 50¢.

**Clothing:** Men's: Ties, 39¢ to 79¢. Cotton socks, pair, 18¢. B.V.D. shirts and drawers, pair, 79¢. Black oxford shoes, pair, $3 to $7. Shirts, 98¢ to $1.69. Suits by Nash, $24 to $29. Topcoats, $20.98 to $37.48. Work overalls, $1.25 up.

**Clothing:** Women's: Bathing suits, one-piece, $1.25 to $6.25. Hosiery, black, cordovan, and white, various sizes, made of luxite, per pair, $1.75. White canvas oxford shoes and pumps, pair, $2.45.

**Dogs:** Coonhound pups 10 weeks old, each $5; 10-week old collie pups, small, each, $5, large, $10.

**Entertainment:** Movie ticket, evening, adult, 30¢ plus 3¢ war tax; children, 15¢ plus 2¢ war tax.

**Food:** Beverages: Cocoa, pound, 13¢. Coffee, pound, 29¢. Milk, evaporated, 1-pound can, 15¢. Tea, pound, 40¢.

**Food:** Meat: Bacon, pound, 32¢. Beef, round and rump, per pound, 35¢. Chicken, pound, 40¢. Pork, fresh, steak and roast, pound, 35¢. Fish, haddock, pound, 15¢; pollock, pound, 10¢; salmon, can, 19¢.

**Food:** Various: Dried beans, pound, 11¢. Flour, barrel, $13.75. Molasses, extra fancy, gallon, $1.10; common grade, 80¢. Peas, can, 15¢. Potatoes, bushel, $4 (considered to be an extremely high price due to recent inflation). Raisins (used in home brew), per pound, 22¢. Rice, two pounds, 15¢. Wheat flour sold from government stock amassed during the World War, 24.5-pound bag, $1.50.

**Fuel:** Birch, per cord, delivered in Wolfeboro, $7.50. Coal for town electric generating plant (had cost $8.25 per ton in summer 1919), summer 1920, per ton, $17

**Fur:** Pelts, *buying price,* depending upon size, color, and quality: Mink, $4 to $35; muskrat, $1.25 to $6; red fox, $8 to $40.

**Hay:** Ton, $30.

**Money:** Bank interest charged for mortgage, 6%.

**Motorboat license:** $3.

**Pails:** Ten-quart galvanized maple syrup pails, per dozen, $4.50.

**Soap:** American Family brand, full-size bar, 7¢.

**Stud service:** Moore brothers' farm, Pleasant Valley, stud fee for Berkshire boars: Faithful Duke, $3, Artful Baron's Majesty, $5. From another farm: registered thoroughbred Devon bull, per time, $2.

**Tractor:** Ford tractor, $790.

**Truck:** Ford truck with pneumatic tires, $545.

**Typewriter:** Corona brand, $50.

**Wages:** Bottle washer and helper's wages, hour, 25¢. Cow milker at dairy, hour, 40¢. Delivery man, hour, 40¢. Painter, day, $4.50. Team of two large horses plus a dump cart, for 9-hour work day: $8.50.

**Wrist watches:** Ladies', solid gold, $37.50 to $75.

# CHAPTER 5

# WOLFEBORO 1921-1930

*Of course we believe in Wolfeboro.*

—Tag line placed in advertising by over a dozen Wolfeboro merchants in the summer of 1930 when the national Depression was just beginning to take effect.

## INTRODUCTION

The 1921-1930 decade saw many changes in town. While shoe manufacturers came and went on Factory Street, businesses elsewhere generally flourished. By 1930 Wolfeboro was one of New England's foremost poultry centers. With the ever-increasing popularity of the automobile there were more tourists than ever before; indeed, so many that at least three separate proposals were made to build new "grand" hotels to house the influx.

Radio was the latest fad. Sound and even color were experienced at the movies. Airplanes landed on Wolfeboro Bay and Winter Harbor, and there was a municipal dock for hydroplanes (as such aircraft were called).

## WOLFEBORO IN PRINT

### News of the "News"

As in every decade since its founding in 1860, the *Granite State News* continued to be the journal of record for local happenings. The editor during the decade was still Frederick W. Prindle, who had been part of the staff ever since 1873 or 1874.[1] Thus, 1923 may have marked his 50th anniversary in the editor's chair, and for certain he had been there for a half-century by 1924.

In late December 1920 the newspaper moved its office and printing press to new premises on Railroad Avenue over Barry's Meat Market, not far from the rear of the Bank Building where the *News* had been founded in November 1860. The editor was old-fashioned in his ways (or else did not want the distraction), and it was not until October 1921 that a telephone was installed in the office.[2]

During the 1920s the *News* vastly expanded its national and international coverage. Arthur Brisbane's syndicated commentary column ran for years. Cartoons included a few by Rube Goldberg. Radio, farming, beekeeping and poultry were subjects of numerous features. Each issue contained "Autocaster" news photographs transmitted to the paper by wire.

On January 5, 1924, Mabel Fullerton Hatch's new column, "Goose Quills," made its debut. Mrs. Hatch ("The Goose") and her husband Alvan were dairy farmers on North Main Street, who lived amid numerous cats, dogs, chickens, and, of course, cows. Their Ford automobiles were given names such as Cordelia and Praise Be and were often mentioned in print.

In one column Mrs. Hatch commented that she had read Sinclair Lewis' new and somewhat controversial novel, *Elmer Gantry,* prompting a correspondent to complain to the editor. Hatch dismissed such prudery, noting that "the writer did not allow anyone to read 'indecent' literature after he had perused it himself."[3]

On January 1, 1927, a new decorated title made its debut at the top of page one. The name of the paper was presented in ornately shaded letters against a background of Wolfeboro Bay as viewed from the water, showing buildings along the shore.

Effective July 5, 1929, the publication changed from its long-standing Saturday publication day to Friday—a schedule it was to maintain for decades. In the summer of 1930 a new printing plant was set up in Wolfeboro Falls, and the first issue on the new press was dated May 23, 1930.

### *Photo-Era Magazine*

Every so often throughout Wolfeboro's history, someone would "discover" the town and move his or her business here—lock, stock, and barrel. Indeed, this has continued down to recent times.

Representative of this is the experience of Alonzo Hawes Beardsley, Boston publisher of *Photo-Era Magazine,* a journal of photography founded in 1899. The August and September 1921 issues contained an illustrated article, "A Pilgrimage to Wolfeboro, New Hampshire." The preceding January 20, Beardsley and his father had moved their personal and business effects to rooms in the home of Ella Sanborn on South Main Street.[4] Edna B. Castle accompanied them as office manager.

Beardsley soon became well known on the local scene. An indefatigable camera buff, he took pictures of children at parties, boats on Lake Winnipesaukee, and civic events, among many other things. He prepared a series of glass slides and projected them at various club meetings. A favorite show depicted what Wolfeboro looked like in the wintertime and was shown to summer visitors.

On December 23, 1925, he married a local girl, Dorothy Abbott Goodhue, in a ceremony at the First Congregational Church. In 1926 he moved the *Photo-Era* office from South Main Street to the building behind the Wolfeboro National Bank.[5] Beardsley, one of the greatest boosters the town had during the era, died in 1933 after a long illness.

## ENTERTAINMENT

### Books, Puzzles, and Games

Reading continued to be a popular local activity. The widespread availability of electric lighting encouraged reading on dark days and evenings. The local library reported great activity.

Crossword puzzles became a national fad in 1924 and launched the New York publishing firm of Simon & Schuster on the road to fortune. Before long, racks in the Paper Store, grocery outlets, and elsewhere displayed booklets of crosswords for sale. On December 30, 1924, Mabel Fullerton Hatch's column contained this commentary:

> One of the town merchants was somewhat discouraged about the languid shopping this Christmas season. What do people expect? It does take so long to work out your daily crossword puzzles!
>
> After you've sat up half the night listening to the radio and the other half wondering what four-letter word beginning with F you are going to insert in a given space, why naturally you can't put your undivided attention on picking a 50-cent present for your third cousin more or less removed. The papers that run Christmas ads should declare a closed season on crosswords, don't you think?

Dominoes was a very popular table game, and especially nice sets were made of ivory. Then there was mah jongg, with its Oriental tiles, not to overlook the Ouija Board, by which one could make all sorts of predictions.[6]

### Social Notes

On November 13, 1922, the organizing meeting of the Winnipesaukee Chapter of the Daughters of the American Revolution was held at the First Congregational Church with over 20 in attendance, two of whom were members in other states. "We may not care for the distinction for ourselves so much, but it will be of increasing interest to succeeding generations to know what families were of Revolutionary descent; it is also valuable to band together those of old colonial stock."[7]

On March 15, 1925, the marriage of Violet Thurston, one of Wolfeboro's most popular young ladies, to Lt. Carroll D. Crossman, a World War flying ace, of Los Angeles, took place in an airplane 1,500 feet over Glendale, California:

> The bride left Wolfeboro after being graduated from Brewster Free Academy in 1920, and some 10 months ago went to the big West in search of the great adventure.[8]

In February 1929 the Wolfeboro Social Club formed with headquarters in a room in the Central Block. Facilities included tables for cards and checkers and an area for reading. A monthly supper was furnished to the membership which totaled 60 by March 1929.[9]

### Auld Lang Syne

In the January 3, 1925, issue of the *Granite State News,* a new year's editorial took stock of the American scene:

> Today! 1925. Everybody rides in automobiles or flies, plays golf, shoots craps, plays the piano with their feet, goes to the movies nightly, smokes cigarettes, drinks Rukus juice, and blames the high cost of living on their neighbors, never goes to bed the same day they get up, and thinks they are having a hell of a time.
>
> These are the days of suffragetting, profiteering, rent hogs, excess taxes, and prohibition. But it's a pretty good old world after all. We thank you for our share of the good of 1924. At the close of 1925 we hope you will have missed all of the bad and have had some of the good.

### Radio

Just as the period 1911-1920 saw the rise of movies as a popular entertainment medium in Wolfeboro, the next 10 years witnessed the radio changing from a novelty to a staple item.

Early in the decade radios were primarily used by hobbyists, who put up long antennas to receive signals from distant locations, often with home-built sets. By the end of the period, factory-made radios, often in fancy consoles costing several hundred dollars or more each, were found in many homes.

Estimates as of January 1, 1928, tell of the rise of the radio's popularity, although it still had a long way to go. Quantities are totals for the United States:[10]

Number of homes in the U.S.: 27,850,000
Homes wired for electricity: 17,596,000
Telephone receivers: 18,250,000

Automobiles.: 16,100,000
Phonographs.: 12,500,000
Radio sets sold to date: 13,250,000
Homes with radios: 7,500,000
Retail value of 1922-1927 radio sales: $1,936,550,000
Radio manufacturers 1922-1927: 1,200
Radio retailers, total through 1927: 28,000

Items from the *Granite State News* (day dated and in quotation marks), a reminiscence by Stephen E. Clow, and the author's commentaries trace the rise of this popular form of entertainment:

**1921:** Recollection by Stephen E. Clow:[11] "Prior to the time when the radio was so popular, and sets owned by so many, Allen H. Albee performed a service for the townspeople. His father operated a jewelry store on South Main Street. Allen tinkered a lot with radios, loudspeakers, and amplifiers. On the nights of outstanding professional boxing matches, he would set up amplifiers outside of his father's store to broadcast the fights. The street and sidewalk in front would be filled with people listening. The first fight I can remember hearing on a set that we owned at home was the Dempsey-Carpentier fight."

**1922, January 28:** "Jimmy Collins has recently installed a wireless telephone, and this week he had the pleasure of hearing some fine addresses as well as instrumental music miles away. One was chime bells at Springfield; Henry Cabot Lodge's address before a club meeting, and others as far off as Washington, D.C., all could be distinctly heard. Will wonders never cease?"

**1922, June 10:** An article stated that the height of an antenna for short-wave reception used with a small receiver should be 30 feet, and the length should be not less than 50 feet or longer than 200 feet. "A simple radiophone receiver capable of picking up stations similar to KDKA at East Pittsburgh can be assembled by a novice for from $4 to $15, depending upon the builder's ability to use his hands...." Alternatively, a basic "crystal set" tuner with no refinements could be purchased already assembled for about $3.50 to $4.

**1922, December 16:** "Clarence Stinchfield has this week succumbed to the radio bug and has had an instrument installed in his residence."

**1923, January 20:** The Radio Club was formed by residents of Pleasant Valley, and in the Pleasant Valley schoolhouse a receiver was installed by W.C. Paris. The building soon became known as Radio Hall.

**1923, February 23:** "Nat Rogers with his jitney conveyed a happy dozen to Radio Hall, Pleasant Valley, Wednesday evening to participate in the radio concert. Delicious refreshments and hot coffee were served. We left at a late hour, well pleased with our entertainment."

**1923, June 16:** A syndicated column devoted to the radio made its appearance. There were no stations in the Wolfeboro area, and all reception was from distant transmissions.

**1923, October:** T.S. Marshall set up a radio shop in Room 10 of the Central Block and advertised: "Entertainment tonight. Pick your own program at will from Schenectady, Pittsburgh, Chicago, New York, and other large cities while sitting by your own fireside." A complete single tube set, brand not specified, was available for $48, a Radiola V with loudspeaker, installed, for $150, and the "C.R.-12, Grebe's latest, with loudspeaker, installed, $265."

**1924, January:** The only broadcasting station in New Hampshire was in Laconia. The Winnipesaukee Lake Region Association[12] suggested in December 1923 that a transmitter called the Lake Winnipesaukee Station be set up.

**1924, March 1:** Pleasant Valley. "Mrs. Mattie Burroughs entertained at her home Thursday morning a party of friends and neighbors to 'listen in' and enjoy the fine radio concert and was much enjoyed.... Refreshments...were served. It was a good time for all."

**1924, October 4:** Mabel Fullerton Hatch commented in reference to radio broadcasts: "It seems like according to the campaign speeches there are a powerful lot of villains looking for public office this year!"

**1924, December 20:** It was noted that in Seattle the government wanted to dismantle an innocent-looking broadcast station because every evening the wife of the proprietor sent through the air a beautiful children's tale. "The government says...the bedtime story sent out contains code information for bootleggers."

**1925, March 28:** "Radio fans of Wolfeboro will be pleased to know that Ray Alexander and his Brewster Academy Orchestra will broadcast from station WEEI of Boston, Thursday, April 2.... This will be the first time that Brewster Academy has been so well represented or advertised."

**1925, November 14:** "It looks as though the Pleasant Valley Radio Club will cease existing with so many of the members' homes radio equipped."

**1926, March 13:** It was reported that Allen H. Albee had installed a fine radio set for Perley E. Young, Wolfeboro Falls grocer.

**1926:** Radios were the sales item of the year, and even Horne's Garage, local Ford dealer, advertised a line of radios for sale. Everett S. Albee, who had been a jeweler in town since 1883, offered the largest selection, and his son Allen did much of the installation and service work for him.

**1927, October 22:** The Radio Shoppe, conducted by automobile dealer Archie A. Horne and radio sales specialist T.S. Marshall, opened for business on October 22, 1927.

**1928, February 25:** "Misses Wilma and Florence Paine had supper with Mr. and Mrs. Percy Clark Sunday. They were entertained in the evening by the radio and phonograph."

**1928, November 6:** On election day Miss Josephine Rust had T.S. Marshall set up her radio in the fire station in South Wolfeboro. "We were able to get a few election returns but annoying 'grounds' and static made reception rather poor."

**1928, November 10:** Mabel Fullerton Hatch: "The Goose remembers in the so-called good old days walking to the [Main Street] Bridge election night eager to hear the scant and meager tidings which percolated to this region.... This memory exercise makes a wonderful background to the Goose's experience Tuesday night when score card in hand she heard the radio reports. It was a curiously moving piece of business to stand up to the strains of the *Star Spangled Banner* played in Palo Alto, Cal., at one o'clock in the morning. The Goose would change places with no flapper on earth to whom electric lights, telephone, automobiles, radios are just the standard equipment of living. It is great fun to have lived in the beginning and development of these things, to have experienced the before and after taking of these particular 'elixirs.' Living in November 1928 is certainly great fun."

### A Ticket to the Picture Show

While the main entertainment in the home was the radio, the most popular form of community amusement continued to be the movies. For most of the decade films continued to be shown by Ansel N. Sanborn at the Auditorium Theatre (the Masonic Temple; a.k.a. Temple Auditorium) on Glendon Street.

In contrast to the one-reel subjects of the preceding decade, the typical 1920s program featured a multiple-reel film lasting 90 minutes or more. Occasionally, a grand production would be heralded by extensive advance advertising, such as for this film projected to Wolfeboro audiences on July 25, 1922:[13]

> At the Temple Auditorium next Tuesday afternoon and evening the famous D.W. Griffith picturization of the delightful New England play, *Way Down East,* with Lillian Gish in an all-star cast, is to be shown to the accompaniment of a special orchestra which travels with the production.

On June 6, 1923, *The Toll of the Sea,* "in perfect natural colors; it is as full of color as a flower garden in the morning sunshine," filled the screen. The technology was developed over a period of seven years by two scientists from the Massachusetts Institute of Technology.

Week in and week out, important feature films as well as lesser productions were shown to local audiences. Stars such as Gloria Swanson, William S. Hart, Charlie Chaplin, Lionel Barrymore, Tom Mix, Ethel Clayton, Mary Miles Minter, Buster Keaton, Bebe Daniels, Harold Lloyd, Rudolph Valentino, Marion Davies, and Mary Pickford each had a following.

In May and June 1926 the trustees of the Brewster estate, working with Sanborn, remodeled the second floor of the Town Hall. An account noted:[14]

> The building has been painted inside and out, a dormer window put on the balcony, and a new maple floor laid, all new electric light fixtures, new lavatory fixtures, additional lights placed and new seats installed. Mr. Sanborn has equipped his booth with two new Power's [made by the Nicholas Power Co. of New York City] motion picture projectors with General Electric Mazda lighting outfits, the latest type, and is to use the latest projection lenses that is possible to buy.

The first show in the new venue was *Madame Behave,* starring female impersonator Julian Eltinge and dancer Ann Pennington. In addition, Misses Noreen Dynan and Myrtle Farnham appeared on stage in person in costume. Admission was 50¢ for adults and 15¢ for children. For several decades thereafter, Brewster Memorial Theatre (a.k.a. Memorial Theatre) was Wolfeboro's home-town movie house.

In October 1927 audiences thrilled to the world's heavyweight championship film showing the fight between Gene Tunney (new champion) and Jack Dempsey (ex-champion). "You can see this battle much better in the movies than you could have at Chicago, unless you had a ringside seat."

Cecil B. DeMille's film, *King of Kings,* was "presented with sound on the Syncrophone with a perfect musical score" on November 14-15, 1928. The sound was on phonograph records, more or less synchronized with action on the screen. In June 1929 Ansel N. Sanborn installed speakers and amplifiers as part of a new film industry system in which a sound track was recorded directly on the 35 mm film.

On June 25-26, 1929, *Close Harmony,* "our first 100% singing, talking, and dancing picture," with Charles ("Buddy") Rogers and Nancy Carroll, was shown. On August 1-2, 1929, *On With the Show,* with Vitaphone sound, "100% natural color—talking, singing, and dancing hit" was the first all-color, all-sound film to be shown in town.

In May 1930 it was announced that motion pictures consisting of nine reels of "educational and home comedies" would be shown in Wolfeboro at the Pythian Hall every Tuesday night at 7:30. Admission for adults was 20¢, children 5¢. Shown were 16 mm films on a Kodascope projector. The quality of the projection and subjects in this new "theatre" fell far short of what was being offered by Sanborn.

### Entertainment Indoors and Out

Many other entertainment features were offered in Wolfeboro during the decade. Churches, fraternal lodges, schools, civic groups, and others presented countless plays and stage performances. Outdoors there were many parades, carnivals, and other activities for participation or watching. Each winter, Fisherville—a collection of temporary wooden huts on Wolfeboro Bay—attracted many fishermen and visitors.

A sample follows:[15]

**1920s. Dances:** Arthur Moody's barn in Wolfeboro Center was the location of numerous barn dances and social events.

**1921, June 21. Minstrel show:** Hi Henry's All-Star Minstrels at the Temple Auditorium, with 10 vocalists, four comedians, eight vaudeville acts. A street parade for the event was held at noon, and a band concert in front of the theatre at 7:15 p.m. Tickets were 55¢ and 85¢.

**1921, July 22. Passion Play:** "Temple Auditorium. One night only. Boston Community Forum presents the original Passion Play of Oberammergau, as given by Anton Lang and his famous associates. Photographs on the spot by special arrangement. Pictures projected by the new and novel Delineascope. The story is graphically and dramatically told by the well-known traveler and author Axel Gerhardt Dehly." Prices: 20¢ and 30¢.

**1921, September 26. Chautauqua starts:** First of a series of six Chautauqua programs at the Temple Auditorium sponsored by the Swarthmore Chautauqua, a traveling group. This entertainment was underwritten by 26 Wolfeboro residents. Programs included the Fara Groves Sextet, advice and criticism in a talk by Walfred Lindstrom, and the Unique Opera Company.

**1922, February 22. The first Winter Carnival:** Opened at 9:00 a.m. when about 100 people gathered at the Post Office where Alonzo H. Beardsley, Dr. Burt W. Parshley, and Roy S. Haggard led them in a hike on snowshoes to Clark's Point, where a campfire was blazing and refreshments were served. At noon there were dog races on the lake and a prize for the person who ate the most hot dogs. At 2:00 p.m. near the wharf there were ski races, dashes, a potato race, and a tug-of-war.

Sled dog races in the 1920s. The photographer was standing in North Main Street opposite the Durgin Block. Horne's Ford showroom is shown at the left. In the distance the outline of the Town Hall tower can be seen against the horizon. (Jeff Goodwin and Joyce Goodwin Stanard Collections)

Clearing roads the hard way. A crew with shovels removes snow on North Main Street opposite the Lakeview Cemetery. J. Frank Goodwin's barn is in the distance at the right of the road. (Jeff Goodwin and Joyce Goodwin Stanard Collections)

At 3:00 p.m. there was a hockey game. Skijoring (being towed on skis behind a horse or car) was very popular. All day long there were skating, sliding and skiing activities.

**1922, May 20. Popular song.** A note in the paper stated that the most popular recording was the song *Tell Her at Twilight* and that quantities had been ordered by the Music Store.

**1922, June 4. Excursion:** "To Old Orchard Beach, Sunday, June 4. Reo Speed Wagon leaves the Post Office at 8:00 a.m., arrives at Old Orchard at 10:30.... $3.50 round trip. Tickets at Horne's Garage."

**1922, August 9. Vaudeville:** Boys from Camp Wyanoke appeared at Brewster Memorial Hall in a vaudeville review. It had been 10 years since the boys from this camp had appeared on a local stage.

**1922, October 4-6. Chautauqua:** Three-day series of lectures.

**1923, February 22. Winter Carnival:** A toboggan slide and ski jump made of wood in a manner providing that it could be disassembled and stored during the summer was being constructed on the property of P.A. Horne on Main Street. The toboggan slide was about 250 feet in length, while the ski jump was such that a jump of nearly 30 feet could be made from it. Participants enjoyed skiing, coasting, skijoring, and even a baseball game on skis. Events were culminated by the showing of the film, *The Prisoner of Zenda,* at the Temple Auditorium.

**1923, July 4. Festivities:** The largest Independence Day celebration in the town's history began on the night of July 3 with movies and a huge bonfire lighted in Wolfeboro Bay. On July 4 activities began at 9:00 a.m. and ended at midnight under the supervision of the American Legion. Attractions in the parade included the "Horribles," a name given to people in unusual garb. At noon there was a band concert in front of the Hotel Elmwood. A baseball game between Wolfeboro and Manchester was won by the latter, 7 to 1. Races and athletic contests came next. In the evening there was a concert and a carnival midway. A spectacular fireworks display capped off the event, together with dancing in Post Office Square. An estimated 10,000 people and 1,300 automobiles were in town for the occasion.

**1923, August 3. Cottonboro Church sale:** The Ladies' Aid group of the Cottonboro Church on Cotton Mountain held its annual sale, packing the little building to overflowing.

**1923, August 18. Melodrama:** The Sterling Brothers Troupe presented *Uncle Tom's Cabin* under canvas at Avery's field. The cast consisted of 25 people and horses. On hand to attract attention was a device called an "electric calliope," details of which were not described.[16]

**1923, August 15. Headstand caper:** "Wednesday evening a public exhibition was given on Post Office Square when someone needlessly and foolishly climbed the Peavey Block and on its highest part, stood on his head. It was a daring deed it is true, but it seems to be a needless and foolish trick."

**1923, October 1-3. Chautauqua:** The Swarthmore Chautauqua consisting of stage entertainment appeared in town for three days at the Temple Auditorium.

**1923, November 26. Redpath Bureau Lyceum:** The Maitlands, first of the entertainment groups booked through the Redpath Agency, was slated to appear in Wolfeboro, but was canceled. As a substitute the Corine Jessop Company, a trio of young ladies, was scheduled to play on December 4.

**1924, February 21-23. Winter Carnival:** Many events. The ski jump contest was won by E.B. Bruce who soared 58 feet 4 inches.

**1924, July 4. Independence Day:** Festivities included a parade, band concert, races and athletic contests, boat race, band concert, and fireworks. The night before on July 3, a dance was held at the Temple Auditorium, and a large bonfire was set on a raft in Wolfeboro Bay. In the morning Wolfeboro played baseball with Farmington with the latter winning 4 to 1; in the afternoon there was a return engagement in which Wolfeboro won 7 to 6. It was estimated that 13,000 people attended.

**1924, August 12. Street music:** A hand-organ man visited town and played selections to a crowd.

**1924, November, 14. Concert:** The Wolfeboro Community Center announced its winter series of entertainment beginning with the Metropolitan Grand Quartet at the Temple Auditorium.

**1925, March 21. Winter Carnival:** Postponed from a rainy February 23. Usual events, with about a foot of snow on the ground.

**1925, September 2. Circus:** Walter L. Main Shows arrived in town on double length railroad cars. Advertisements noted there were upward of 500 men and women and 200 horses and almost 10 acres of tents, a herd of elephants, and a caravan of camels.

**1926, February 25. Sled dog race:** The first international sled dog race to be held in NH since 1922 was run by teams from Canada and the United States with the route passing through Wolfeboro.

**1926, April 29. Operetta:** *Pickles* was presented by Brewster Academy. "Was very interesting from many points of view. It has more plots than most operettas, clever dialogue, catchy music and many laughs. In addition there were beautiful costumes, beautiful scenery, and a good orchestra."

**1926, August 14. Circus:** Gentry Bros. Famous Shows, with lions, tigers, acrobats, and other attractions.

**1926, August 8. Boat races:** Motorboat races were held in Lake Winnipesaukee under the auspices of the newly-formed Chamber of Commerce. The boats began just off the town wharf, continued along the Sewall Road shore to a buoy off Dr. Keigwin's "Wiscasset" cottage, then to a marker off Jones' Ledge, and then home by way of Clark's Point and Sandy (Brewster) Beach. The first two classes were sent around the course four times for a total of nine miles. The first race was between Hacker-Dolphin runabouts, and was won by the *RAM* owned by Richard A. Mesters and driven by George Childs. The second boat to finish was *Velmo II* owned by Frank Hopewell and driven by John Hopewell. Both achieved 32 miles an hour and finished just 20 seconds apart. This inaugurated an era of organized boat racing on the lake.

**1926, August 17. Minstrels:** John R. VanArnam's Minstrels, "Sweet singers, funny comedians, nimble dancers, 35 all-white stars.[17] 50¢, 75¢, $1.10. Big street parade at noon."

**1926, August 20. Canoe races:** Held at Point Breeze on Lake Wentworth. The first race was the men's double. Five canoes were entered. In the second race of mixed doubles, eight canoes were entered, and the winners were Christine Saddler and Roger Murray, and Grace Murray and Vincent Hopper.[18]

**1926, December 17. Whist games:** Popular community card game, and numerous parties were held. On December 17 a whist game was held at the Community House at East Wolfeboro, with a $2.50 gold piece given to the person having the largest cumulative score for the preceding four weeks.

**1927, February 10-12. New England Sled Dog Race:** This was the first such race ever scheduled to begin and end in Wolfeboro; three days were needed to complete the circuit. The contest began in front of the Post Office on Main Street at 11:00 a.m. The first day's run was to Ashland, 36.5 miles away. Each of the 10 teams was started at five-minute intervals. On February 12 various sports events were held in connection with the last day of the race, these as part of the Winter Carnival. The race was won by Leonhard Seppala, a 50-year-old Alaskan, who did the course in 11 hours, 57 minutes and 45 seconds. Meanwhile, in Wolfeboro many people were enjoying rides on vehicles made on Ford chassis by The Snowmobile Company, Inc., of West Ossipee (which became nationally known).

**1927, May 3. Melodrama:** *East Lynne* played on the stage at the Temple Auditorium. By this time, melodramas were a scarce type of entertainment, having given way to the movies. Admission 50¢ and 25¢.

**1927, May 13. Stage comedy:** "The comedy, *Aaron Slick from Punkin Crick,* was staged at the Temple Auditorium by the Baptist Church Choir. "The whole cast showed the excellent work done by the coach, and the players themselves took their characters admirably. Miss Rena Piper as Miss Rose Berry, an Oklahoma widow, catered to the audience's attention from the first, and a round of applause greeted her."

**1927, July 4. Independence Day:** For days in advance the American Legion manned a booth at the corner of the Bank Building on South Main Street offering fireworks for sale, "large assortment, reasonable prices." An estimated 10,000 people were in town on the 4th. Events included a baseball game (Wolfeboro 11, U.S. Marines 1), and boat races featuring new Hacker Craft Express Runabouts.

**1927, July 5. Songs:** "Songs of the American Red, White and Black Man" rendered by George B. Hernandez, "Negro tenor soloist," a member of the Jubilee Singers.

**1929, April 15.**[19] **Recorded music:** At the monthly meeting of the Wolfeboro Chamber of Commerce the special feature of the evening was provided by Miss Laura I. Mattoon of Camp Kehonka fame, who "had brought down her beautiful 'Electrola', a new and wonderful musical instrument, a sort of glorified and magnified Victrola, which gave great pleasure to everybody."

**1929, April 25. Dance:** The grand opening for the season of the Wolfeboro Casino was celebrated with a dance featuring music by Fogg's Doctors of Rhythm, of Brockton, MA. Admission 50¢.

**1929, April 28. Stereopticon slide show:** At the Baptist Church. Subject: "Africa Awakening."

**1929, May 2. Stage comedy:** The Gladys Klark Stock Company presented *Lovers – and How!* Billed as "a comedy with a big love story everybody will like; played on Broadway five solid months."

**1929, June 5. Indian show:** Chief Toma, "a direct descendant of the great chiefs of the Algonquin tribe which inhabited this section of New England when the pale-face first landed," went on stage at Town Hall, singing songs of the American Indians and telling of their lore, together with a description of the making of the film, *The First American,* which was also shown.

**1929, July 4. No celebration:** For the first time in memory, Wolfeboro did not have a patriotic demonstration on Independence Day.

**1929, August 9. Downie Brothers Circus:** Arrived in town on 75 trucks.

**1930, February 10. Poverty Ball:** Held at the I.O.O.F. Hall.

**1930, July 4. Independence Day:** Parade, baseball game (Wolfeboro vs. Farmington; 6-0 Wolfeboro), boat race, carnival midway, and fireworks. An estimated 4,000-5,000 people attended.

**1930, August 4. Melodrama:** *Ten Nights in a Bar Room* stage production at the Temple Auditorium. Tickets 50¢ and 25¢.

**1930, August 13. Melodrama:** *Uncle Tom's Cabin* was given by a traveling group consisting of 20 actors and others under canvas at the corner of North Main and Friend Streets.

**1930, September. Rides:** During the third week of September a Ferris wheel and merry-go-round were set up on the corner of North Main and Friend Streets and were well patronized.

**1930, October 6. On stage:** *Mock Court Trial.* A farcical breach of promise case involving J. Clifton Avery, defendant, and Mrs. Martha Lucke, plaintiff, with many local citizens taking part.

## SPORTS AND RECREATION

### Hook, Line, and Sinker

Sure to increase the pulse rate of any fisherman was this item in the *Granite State News,* September 9, 1922:

> The black bass in Wolfeboro waters are so anxious to be caught that they don't wait for the hook and line but will jump right out of the water into your boat, if you happen to be in the right place. Recently, while fishing for bass in Lake Wentworth, Forrest Clough was thunderstruck when a two-pounder made a leap for him,...landing in the bottom of the boat.... If you don't have luck anywhere else, come to Wolfeboro and get a boatload of bass while you wait.

During the era the state stocked Lake Winnipesaukee with thousands of Atlantic salmon fingerlings and Chinook salmon. In September 1926 the state Fish and Game Commission established what became known as the Fish Rearing Station in South Wolfeboro, under the sponsorship of the local Chamber of Commerce.

To encourage the slaughter of suckers in Wolfeboro streams, a fish said to eat the eggs of game fish, a bounty of one cent was presented for every sucker tail brought into Clarence W. Estabrook's sporting goods store during the month of April 1929. Over 2,000 bass fingerlings were released into Wentworth in June of the same year.[20]

### On the Lakes

Lake Wentworth continued to be the prime focus of organized summertime activity. Point Breeze Camp, managed by the Stevens family, saw the yearly return of visitors from New Jersey, New York, and elsewhere. Birchmont Camps, as they were called, operated by the Hemenways, likewise attracted a share of vacationers.

Sherman D. Brummitt and others continued to build cottages around the lake shore and on the islands. The amount of undeveloped shoreline steadily diminished. The water level of Wentworth remained a vexation to cottagers, as it had been ever since the 1880s when the first seasonal camps were constructed. The demands of factories on Smith River, including the O.P. Berry and Gardner Pad Company mills, took precedence over recreational uses. By late summer much water had been drained, and many docks and boathouses were high, dry, and useless.

Summer residents along the shore of Lake Winnipesaukee became increasingly interested in power boating. In 1922 the Elto Outboard Motor Company was marketing the Elto Light Twin, developed by Ole Evinrude. "It weighs only 48 pounds, yet it's a twin cylinder with a full three horsepower." The availability of outboard motors gradually changed the boating scene on the "Big Lake" and made it possible for the average vacationer to travel fairly long distances inexpensively.

During the decade many high-powered craft were launched, most often at the Goodhue & Hawkins Navy Yard on Sewall Road, and hitherto unheard of speeds of well over 50 miles per hour were registered. In January 1927 the Winnipesaukee Power Boat Association was formed in New York City during a boat show. Standard speedboat race courses were subsequently laid out at Wolfeboro, The Weirs and Alton Bay. There were many weekend competitions the following summer.

On September 1, 1928, an outboard motorboat marathon beginning at Wolfeboro, going to The Weirs and Alton Bay and returning to Wolfeboro, attracted 34 entrants, 17 of whom actually started. Race day was very windy, and lake conditions were rough, forcing numerous boaters to cancel. Others, upon seeing the competition, realized they were outclassed and withdrew. Elbridge Robie in an Elto-powered Pigeon boat started out in ninth place at the beginning of the race, but at three miles had gained first place and then tried his best to hold it. He went from Wolfeboro to The Weirs in 22 minutes. An account noted:

> Upon reaching Diamond Island, the steamer *Mount Washington* hove in sight and created swells which forced Mr. Robie's boat to leave the water 30 inches or more several times, and on the last time his boat hit the water at such an angle as to force the bow deep into the water so that it poured over the bow to a depth of approximately eight inches.
>
> Robie persevered and came in first.[21]

In July 1929 it was reported that 1,000 motorboats were in use on the lake. The *Jeyee II*, equipped with an incredible 880 h.p. marine engine and said to be capable of 80 miles per hour, attracted a lot of attention. Such formidable power in a private craft had not been seen before on local water.[22]

Swimming at the town-sponsored Sandy Beach, also called Bathing Beach, was very popular (today this spot is known as Brewster Beach). In 1928 average daily attendance was 121, of which 51 were children. A lifeguard taught 41 children to swim that summer.[23]

## TEAM SPORTS

### Baseball

The most popular local team sport continued to be baseball. This excerpt from a report printed June 4, 1921, is representative:

> The ball game Memorial Day on the Brewster campus between the Brewsters and Concord High was one of the best of the season and was witnessed by a large audience. It was exciting and interesting from start to finish, the score being 2 to 1 in favor of Brewster.

Even when the local team did not win, there was usually something nice to say anyway.

In sharp contrast, in early 1929 there were a number of accounts in the local paper that the Brewster baseball team lacked spunk. Typical was this condemning note in the issue of July 8, 1929:

> The fault with Brewster this year could not be charged to the coach, for no one can build a brick house out of loose sand, but is directly due to the fact that there are not more than four men on the team who care enough about the game to give any time or effort to it. The team lacks weight, baseball sense, and courage. This situation is due to the lack of a real school spirit on the part of the faculty and student body to back and encourage any sport other than girl's field hockey and possibly tiddley-winks. There is a vast difference in the sports of the school 20 years ago and today. It's enough to make a real man weep, and the poor grad hasn't a chance to open his mouth in protest.

### Bowling

In July 1921 the Wolfeboro Casino opened for business under the management of Frederick Riley in the structure earlier used for the Kingswood Club. In the basement four regulation bowling alleys were installed by the Brunswick, Balke, Collender Company and became a local attraction. The fee per game (one line in the scoresheet) was 15¢.

After its formation in 1926, the Wolfeboro Chamber of Commerce maintained a bowling league at the Casino, and scores were printed regularly in the local paper.

### Football

Every autumn the Brewster team took to the turf and challenged regional schools. This account appeared on November 7, 1925:

> Brewster-Tilton game...greatest gridiron battle in Brewster's athletic history:
>
> Monday witnessed a phenomenon such as never before been seen in our community. Over 50 autos loaded with Wolfeboro residents went to Tilton for the big event of the football season.... For many years the spirit of friendly rivalry has grown until it has spilled over at the students and alumni bodies to the general public....
>
> The Brewster girls met Tilton on the hockey field and they emerged after an hour of thrilling action with a 4-2 victory.... Just as the hockey game ended, the pigskin was kicked off. The first half ended in a stalemate with Tilton apparently having the moral if not the physical advantage. Brewster's friends were defiant but anxious. The team had been on the defensive too much for any feeling of confidence.
>
> In the third quarter Tilton scored her only tally by a cleverly placed field goal. Menard tried the same tactics but failed. A position on the extreme right of the field was responsible for the failure of his gallant attempt. Brewster had played brilliant football from the start, holding Tilton for downs in-

side the 10-yard line, using the punt to keep Tilton from becoming too dangerous—and abiding the time when a break would give Brewster a chance to score. Her sons and daughters were earnestly pleading for just one touchdown.

After a series of line-bucking plays brought the ball to Tilton's 20-yard line, Menard threw a forward pass that will be long remembered. Captain Nelson, old faithful that he is, snuggled the pigskin to his side and fought his way, two tacklers holding him over the goal line. Such a cheer as went up from the Brewster stands has not echoed about the Tilton hills in many a day. Kearns, as usual, calm, self-reliant, kicked as clean a goal as ever sailed between the rival's goal post. This was the climax and such a climax it was!

Tilton by a series of brilliant forward passes and smashing line plays could not force the Brewster line. Menard intercepted one forward pass and ran 50 yards before being downed....

After the game Tilton hosts sorrowfully left the field while a snake dance across the field of victory was staged by the red and blue.... Sure it was a great day. It was Brewster's day....

### Basketball

Basketball attracted many fans during the winter months. In earlier times, games had been played in a number of places around town, including in the top floor of the Durgin Block on North Main Street. In 1928 Greenleaf B. Clark purchased the century-old Wolfborough and Tuftonborough Academy building, which had been moved when Carpenter School was built. Now situated not far from its original site, the old structure was partially remodeled by Clark and made available to the town as a community center. Clark *Memorial* Hall was the name used in several press accounts, although the title of the building remained with Clark himself, and Clark was still very much alive.[24]

The hall was dedicated on Tuesday evening, January 22, 1929, after which the Wolfeboro Basketball Club played its initial game of the season.[25] A newspaper account noted that the contest, which was with the Durham Celtics, drew many people who had never seen a basketball game before.

### Golf

The Kingswood Club continued to be the local center for golf, as it had been since 1915. On August 6, 1921, the group held its annual meeting. The club was experiencing some difficulty, and it was suggested that "to make the club all that it was a few years ago, each member must realize that he is responsible for its success or failure."

Summer dances held in members' homes were part of the Club's activities until July 1922, when the first such event was held in its new dance hall. In September 1925 the golf course was doubled in size to 18 holes with the acquisition of the old Huggins Hospital property and the Harry Morgan homestead. With the new purchases, the Club owned 70 acres of cleared land and another 12 acres in woodland and shore areas.[26]

In the 1920s Mr. and Mrs. J. Ernest Mann of Salem, MA, maintained a summer home on Trask Mountain, known as "The Manor" (a.k.a. "The Mannor"), which had its own private golf course.

## TRANSPORTATION

### On the Road

By 1921 the automobile was firmly entrenched as the transportation method of choice in Wolfeboro. Horses were mainly used as draft animals on farms and in logging projects and were seen only rarely on primary roads. In the same year the local paper suggested that police haul into court the numerous automobile owners who roared up the hill between the Town Hall and the Soldiers' Monument with their muffler cut-outs wide open.[27] At the time New Hampshire had 42,500 cars registered or one car for every 10.4 persons (in comparison, California had a car for every 5.2 persons).

Many Wolfeboro residents participated in the second annual automobile show held in Ossipee beginning June 13, 1922. Events included the first cross-country run from Wolfeboro to Ossipee, stunts for Ford cars, baseball game, foot race, stage show, and "wireless telephone concert" (radio programs played publicly).

In January 1923 it was reported that downtown traffic in Wolfeboro had increased 250% in the past four years. Around the same time it was stated that 70% of the cars in town had Hood tires on them, many purchased from the Quality Tire Shop operated by Clarence W. Estabrook in the Folsom Block. Success knocked on Estabrook's door, and by decade's end he was profitably involved in several other ventures around the village, including selling real estate.

News of accidents, mostly of a minor nature, was reported with frequency. Typical is this 1923 account:

> Linley Moore and James Melrose were in an automobile collision Wednesday at the corner of Lake and North Main Streets; both windshields were broken and fenders dented. George Britton was busy sweeping up the broken glass.

In 1923 the town posted new guideboards (as they were called) at various intersections and in other prominent locations, directing travelers to different areas. Previously, such signs had been deficient or non-existent. In earlier days an automobilist going from Wolfeboro to Ossipee encountered an old guideboard directing him over Trask Mountain. Upon achieving the summit, the traveler would find that the road down the back side of the hill was impassable and would have to go back to his starting point and ask directions of passers by.[28]

A visitor to Wolfeboro in the spring of 1924 could buy the following cars locally: C.A. Short, South Wolfeboro, was the dealer for the Oakland marque. Harry E. Libby, best known for his "Libby Laundered Linen Lasts Longest," was selling Chandler vehicles. Goodhue & Hawkins sold Chevrolets in addition to boats. The South Wolfeboro Garage, owned by Clarence W. Estabrook, offered Dodge Brothers, Rickenbacker, and Graham Brothers cars. Horne's Garage probably had the most active dealership in town and brought Ford cars in from Detroit by the boxcar load.

In 1925 and 1926 there were many calls for the town to buy a motorized snow plow, as entire areas of Wolfeboro would sometimes be cut off from the downtown district during snowstorms. At the March 1926 town meeting, $6,000 was voted for this purpose. Beginning in 1927 roads were plowed regularly.[29]

In the summer of 1928 the first stretch of concrete road was laid beginning at the Soldiers' Monument in Wolfeboro and was 18 to 24 feet wide. Such construction helped reduce the need to spread many thousands of gallons of oil on town roads each year.

The H.H. Hart Motor Company was established in 1925 by Harold H. Hart, who arrived in town in 1918 as general manager for the Racine Woolen Mills in South Wolfeboro. The firm sold Buicks (later, Chevrolets and Cadillacs as well) on Glendon Street, where the old Glendon House stables used to be—tangible evidence of the supremacy of motorcar over horse (today Rite-Aid Pharmacy is on the site).

In 1929 William B. Herbert operated the Wolfeboro Bus with several rows of seats and an extension on the back for holding luggage. The vehicle was offered for hire, but bookings proved less than hoped for, and the venture was short-lived.

In June 1930 the Wolfeboro selectmen went to the square in South Wolfeboro where the road turns sharply toward Alton "in anticipation of the placing of the long looked for blinker; [the] traffic problem demands practical demonstration for a happy solution."[30] In September Harry V. Perry was appointed as a policeman for South Wolfeboro, with one of his prime duties being to control traffic rounding the corner "thus avoiding what might otherwise have been bad crashes."

General Motors regularly placed local advertisements to describe each of its brands, which in March 1927 included Chevrolet, Pontiac, Oldsmobile, Oakland, Buick, La Salle, and Cadillac.

Without doubt the greatest automotive event of the decade was the introduction on December 2, 1927, of the new Model A Ford, the replacement for the Model T, America's best-selling car. Doors of Horne's Garage opened promptly at eight in the morning. Curiosity seekers packed the showroom all day long. There were no Model A's on hand for sale, but orders were taken for spring delivery. By early February 1928 sixty-eight of the new Fords had been reserved.[31]

### Selling a Car the Hard Way

On March 4, 1928, Rochester clothing merchant Solomon Feineman and John Richardson went for a drive across frozen Wolfeboro Bay in Feineman's new Buick. All went well until they were opposite Sewall Point when they saw a ridge of ice ahead. Down went the gas pedal, and the car charged ahead, only to break through the ice and sink in 90 feet of water. Fortunately, the occupants escaped unharmed, albeit a bit scared.

Enter laundryman and automobile vendor Harry E. Libby, who heard of the accident and offered the careless and now carless Feineman a new Chandler, taking the submerged Buick, present condition unknown, in part trade. A diver was hired, who found the hapless vehicle buried nose-down in mud on the lake bottom. After several days of effort and frustration, the soggy vehicle was raised, apparently little damaged once it was dried out. Alonzo H. Beardsley, local publisher, turned the incident to his advantage and prepared photographic postcards of the rescue and sold them for 8¢ each.[32]

### The Railroad

The Boston & Maine Railroad's passenger business declined during the decade. Time was when the steamer *Mount Washington,* owned by the railroad, tied in with passenger service from Boston and other points. A tourist could board a passenger car in Boston, come to Wolfeboro and alight at the Lake Station next to the Town Docks, and board the boat for connections to other points around the lake. Alternatively, tourists could alight at the Wolfeboro Station at the end of Railroad Avenue and be whisked by carriage or car to one of the hotels or cottages. By the early 1920s the widespread use of automobiles bode well for local tourist businesses, but not for the Boston & Maine.

Throughout the 1920s, as in the decade before, there was much local antagonism toward the railroad. Many felt that decisions made by the Boston & Maine were inimical to the interests of Wolfeboro. For example, protests arose in 1924 when the railroad discontinued one of the trains in and out of town, again when the Walter L. Main Circus had to be canceled because the railroad refused to haul its cars, and once again when it was announced that the branch station at Wolfeboro Falls was to be closed.[33] Concerning the latter, a mass meeting was held, protests were made, and the state Public Service Commission denied the railroad the station closing.

It became increasingly evident that the management of the Boston & Maine cared little for what was happening in Wolfeboro. There was one public relations gaffe

On March 4, 1928, Solomon Feineman, a Rochester clothing merchant who advertised extensively in the *Granite State News,* decided to take his new Buick for a drive on the frozen surface of Wolfeboro Bay with John Richardson as a passenger. All did not go as planned, the car broke through the ice and soon was under 90 feet of icy water. Local automobile dealer and laundryman Harry E. Libby viewed this as a challenge and took the submarine Buick in trade sight-unseen against a new Chandler. Libby hired a diver and crew, and before long the soggy vehicle was hoisted to the surface, apparently little the worse for its lake-bottom experience.

Lt. Robert Fogg's modified Curtiss MF flying boat used in 1925 under a contract to deliver air mail from The Weirs to points on the other side of the lake including Camp Ossipee and Camp Wyanoke on Wolfeboro Neck. Fogg also gave tourist rides from Wolfeboro Bay and Lake Wentworth. In this view the craft is moored in Wolfeboro Bay with the Town Docks in the background.

A match in progress at the Kingswood Golf Course. (*Lake Winnipesaukee,* a travel guide issued by the Boston & Maine Railroad, 1917)

after another. An example is furnished by this item dated May 1, 1926:

The new train service is quite disappointing to the traveling public. The connections are so poor it is not possible to reach Dover by rail. In some instances one minute's delay would make it possible, the train leaving Rochester one minute before the arrival of the train from North Conway. It doesn't take long to wait a minute, and the accommodation would be great, allowing patrons to reach Boston via Dover.

To be sure, there were a *few* favorable comments about the trains in and out of town, as this on August 20, 1927:

The public have good reason, so far as Wolfeboro is concerned, to be grateful to the B&M management for the excellent service we are now enjoying to reach Boston and return daily, having opportunity to leave here and arrive in Boston at 9:25 a.m., 1:04 and 8:10 p.m. It is a service the public surely appreciates.

### The *Mount Washington*

By the early 1920s travelers using the steamer *Mount Washington* became fewer in number. The Boston & Maine put the boat up for sale, much against the wishes of Wolfeboro business interests, who felt that this would spell the end of the tourist industry.

After much controversy, the vessel was sold to Capt. Leander Lavallee, who continued his position at the helm. Most business aboard the steamer in the 1920s was from day-trippers who enjoyed seeing the islands and other scenery. The ship was not used to any extent to carry baggage or freight.

### Aviation

In the mid-1920s there was great interest in hydroplanes (as they were called at the time) which were based at The Weirs or Lakeport and which landed frequently in Wolfeboro Bay and in the western arm of Winter Harbor near the Libby Museum. Five dollars was the usual price for a ride aloft for about 15 minutes to see the town and lake from the air. The most famous of these was Lt. Bob Fogg's craft described below.

### Air Mail to Winter Harbor

On July 18, 1925, the *News* announced: "There is a possibility that Wolfeboro may have mail delivery around the lake region by airplane." More details were forthcoming on August 8:

Through the efforts of the Winnipesaukee Lake Region Associates in connection with the Post Office Department, Wolfeboro received and dispatched its first airmail August 1, 1925, 6:00 a.m., by Robert S. Fogg's seaplane. First ever attempted on a country route in the United States was made this morning by Lieutenant Fogg of Concord, who left The Weirs in a seaplane shortly after 6:00 loaded with 150 pounds of first-class mail and newspapers to deliver to summer residents on the northeast shore of Lake Winnipesaukee.

From Wolfeboro the plane delivers and takes mail at nine of the principal places on the northeast side of Winnipesaukee Lake, namely Camp Wyanoke, Camp Ossipee, Philip Smith's landing, YMCA Camp Belknap, Chester Campbell's, Hotel Wawbeek, Camp Idlewild, Long Island, and Sandy Island, reaching The Weirs in time for the 9:00 a.m. mail south....

Officials said this would be the first Lake Star Route Air Mail Service established in the United States. The round trip this morning from The Weirs and return, making the 10 stops, was made in one hour and 10 minutes, 43 miles....

The new route is designated by the Post Office authority as the Emergency Star Route, and the contract was awarded to Lieutenant Fogg for the period August 1 to September 1.... Only first-class mail and newspapers were handled by the hydroplane....

A related article stated that no special stamps or extra expense were necessary. The most important thing was that the mail be addressed correctly. Further:

The Concord postmaster suggests that Wolfeboro be designated after the name of the camp to which the letter is going, thereby incurring delivery at any time, the railway mail clerks coming to The Weirs on the early morning train. There is but one air mail a day, the plane connecting with the train that arrives at The Weirs at 6:00 in the morning. The train leaves Concord at 4:30 o'clock. Letters mailed in the Concord office late in the afternoon and early in the evening will be delivered by plane. Letters mailed in the morning or early afternoon would be routed to Wolfeboro by train. From then to midnight, the mail would go by plane. The mail for these points is being made up on the train going north and put up in separate sacks to be taken by the seaplane pilot at The Weirs. The 16-mile trip from The Weirs to Wolfeboro takes the plane about 10 minutes. To that point Tuesday Lieutenant Fogg carried about 200 pounds of mail and newspapers.

The August 29 issue noted that Fogg had visited Birchmont Camps to give scenic rides and that the air mail service would be continued until September 8.

### Chester C. Fernald Remembers

Chester C. Fernald, who was 10 years old in 1925 and helped load and unload the mail when Lt. Fogg came to Wawbeek in Melvin Village, researched the landmark air service and wrote about it for the July 1970 issue of *New Hampshire Profiles*.

He related that Fogg, born in Brookline, MA, was commissioned a lieutenant in the U.S. Army Flying Corps at Kelly Field in Texas and learned to fly in a Curtis JN-4 "Jenny." In 1920 he came to Concord and opened the first airport in New Hampshire, earning most of his money by "barnstorming"—taking novices aloft at $5 per head. In 1924 he bought for $750 a war-surplus Curtiss MF flying boat, lacking its 90 h.p. engine. He installed a 150 h.p. Hispano-Suiza engine in its place and created a better-performing craft. The boat-type hull was altered to accommodate four passengers plus the pilot. In 1925 he signed up for the aforementioned air service to Wolfeboro and other points across the lake from The Weirs and was paid $35 per day for his service. In addition, he earned money giving scenic flights.[34]

### Stephen E. Clow Remembers

Stephen E. Clow, son of Dr. Fred E. Clow, recalled the air mail service and noted that people with summer homes on the lakefront objected strenuously to the early-morning noise of the craft's unmuffled engine. Concerning Clow's involvement:

> I was delivering Special Delivery letters from the Wolfeboro Post Office and had to be present at the plane's arrival. However, very seldom was there anything for me to do. At that time, the cost for a Special Delivery letter was ten cents; I was paid eight cents for the delivery.[35]

### Local Airport Planned

Local interest in aviation continued apace. One of the main objectives of the Chamber of Commerce (founded in 1926) was the establishment of a flying field in town. The May 26, 1928, issue of the *News* commented:

> The report from the Chamber's Aviation Committee is awaited with eagerness. A New Hampshire map about to be issued by the Publicity Bureau lists four airports—Manchester, Concord, Keene and Claremont. Let's hope Wolfeboro will soon have joined her enterprising predecessors.

In June, Alonzo H. Beardsley, chairman of the Aviation Committee, advised that Robert Brewster offered the use of a field on Brewster Farm on South Main Street until permanent premises could be acquired.

In September it was stated that the Hart & Hart Transportation Company of New Haven, CT, "is using the W.A. Lawrence farm at Wolfeboro Center as a flying field for a short time, where they will take passengers who wish to obtain a bird's eye view of our beautiful lake and mountain scenery." The charge was $5 per person. In September Lawrence leveled several rises, filled gullies, cut down trees, and made other improvements. Unfortunately, the resultant landing strip was not considered to be safe, and the idea was abandoned.[36]

### Wolfeboro Bay

In the summer months and on the frozen ice of the winter too, Wolfeboro Bay was rapidly becoming an aviation center. In 1930 the town paid Goodwin & Doe to build a hydroplane landing platform using lumber sawed by S.W. Clow & Co.[37] On August 8, the newspaper reported:

> The airport landing at the foot of Lake Street makes a fine place for the landing of the hydroplanes, and it is but an easy distance from the business section. Wolfeboro is bound to keep the good work going.

Meanwhile, to guide an ever-increasing number of aviators, Harry E. Libby of laundry fame painted "WOLFEBORO" in large letters on the roof of his plant on Center Street. "No aviator need be at a loss as to his whereabouts in this vicinity," commented the *Granite State News*.[38]

## TRAVEL AND TOURISM

### Guest Facilities

In the literal sense, a true "cottage industry" in Wolfeboro was the renting of rooms and camps for the use of summer tourists. Just about everyone with a few rooms to spare made them available in season to earn extra income.

The venerable Hotel Elmwood opened in 1874, the Ann Inn also dating from the preceding century, and the Sheridan House which traced its founding to 1795 were the main stopping places.

It was reported in 1923 that many American tourists were going to Europe in the warm months, where Prohibition was not in effect. During that summer, tourist baggage aboard American trains was lighter than at any other time in recent memory.[39] While local hotels could not *officially* serve liquor, there was usually enough on hand under the counter to quickly fill a customer's order.

### Record Years

The summer of 1925 saw "more summer visitors in the village this year than for many years."[40] Business was excellent, and local merchants prospered. A local sentiment arose to build one or more "grand" hotels. Fred Riley, proprietor of the Wolfeboro Casino for the preceding five years, announced that his property would make a fine site for such a project. Another proposal was to construct a hotel on Winter Harbor, and still another idea involved putting one up on Clark's Point. Despite much discussion, none of these hopes was translated into wood or bricks.[41]

Local trade was even better in 1926. "Every train brings welcome visitors, and traffic requires an additional car for the express, while many are arriving with autos which makes business quite lively and our Main Street is well filled with cars," the newspaper noted in mid-July. Crowds were even greater on the Labor Day weekend: "Saturday and Sunday new arrivals were a capacity test for our hotels, parties coming mostly by autos.... Chief of Police Thompson said it was a record breaker."[42]

In autumn of 1927 the old Glen Cottage near Pickering Corner reopened as the Wolfeboro Tavern after extensive remodeling by the new owner, Lester Wiggin. This became the meeting spot of choice for the year-old Chamber of Commerce and various other civic organizations. Tourist business maintained its strength in 1928.

### The Libby Museum

In the 1920s the Libby Museum continued to be a prominent attraction. In July 1922 Vice-President Calvin A. Coolidge signed the guest register but did not make his presence known while there. Later, museum-keeper

Dr. Henry F. Libby found his name and had his signature verified.[43]

The museum was a repository for curiosa gathered by local residents. For example, in the summer of 1923 teenager Ralph Carpenter, Jr., donated a specimen of the rare red ibis, a member of the heron family. Charles S. Paris gave his collection of Indian relics, primarily unearthed on his own property in Wolfeboro Falls.[44]

An indication of the drawing power of the Libby Museum is furnished by statistics for Sunday, August 21, 1927. Over 650 visitors filed through the massive front doors, 119 cars parked in the area, and two motorboats tied up out front. Visitors came from nine different states. A count of traffic on the road out front showed that from 9:00 in the morning until 6:00 at the end of the afternoon 483 cars passed.

### Jungalow Camps

A front page article in the *News*, July 15, 1922, noted that "Wolfeboro was probably never better able to really entertain its summer visitors than it is this year, for its many diversities are surely able to amuse the most fastidious."

It was suggested that autoists call at the new Jungalow Tea Room at the Jungalow Camps on the Alton Road in South Wolfeboro. Offered were tea, light refreshments, books from a lending library, and even a self-improvement course. The Jungalow Camps were a private venture of Rev. Fred P. Haggard, minister of the First Congregational Church, and his son Roy. Financial results fell short of expectations, and Rev. Haggard was forced to file bankruptcy in February 1924.

Another Wolfeboro attraction, quoting the same 1922 article, was the new Ye Rose Garden Gift Shop on Railroad Avenue, which not only had a fine collection of souvenirs, but offered "cuddle corner" booths where ice cream and soft drinks were served. "One visit to this place surely means another."

### As a Visitor Saw Us

A *cause célèbre* of the decade of the 1920s was the reaction to an article published in the local paper on January 27, 1923. Titled "Complacent Wolfeboro," it was signed by "a visitor and a friend," not otherwise identified, who stated that he had visited the town in summer and winter for several years and had been impressed with "the basic spirit of goodwill and friendliness." However, he felt moved to point out some problems confronting the town:

> As the steamer *Mount Washington* turns into Wolfeboro Bay, the panorama is delightful; but what an unpleasant awakening as we near the pier.... Old boxes and barrels, old lumber, a smoldering fire on a refuse heap, ice cream containers, and other rubbish greet the eye. A yellow tonic and ice cream parlor, a lunch wagon, and the back of a store completed the disillusionment.
>
> Perhaps, the first impression of the visitor as he arrives by train is a little better, but not very much, as the shore of the Back Bay is a regular dump. But, then, is there really anything attractive about the right-hand [west] side of Railroad Avenue, with its lunch room and tumble-down sheds?

The scribe went on to say that the Hotel Elmwood

> looks more like a hospital or sanitorium as compared to modern ideas of a cozy country inn.... If the traveler arrives in wintertime this hotel offers no warmth or cheer.

The locals were split by petty jealousies and fancied wrongs and had no spirit of bigness, he continued, stating that he had listened to long discourses of what Wolfeboro needs for improvement, by the very same gentlemen who are narrow-minded and self-satisfied and who weren't willing to do anything to help. Hundreds of words later, the writer stated this:

> The crying need is for a real leader, a man of education, broad-minded, sincere and friendly, who at the head of an energetic body of townspeople will convince even the individual community millstones that Wolfeboro is awake and determined to make the most of present opportunities. Let there be a strong, thoughtful, but progressive spirit that will meet every obstacle with quiet assurance and confidence.

### Citizens React

In quick response, on February 3, 1923, an open forum was held at the First Congregational Church to discuss these questions: Is there anything the matter with Wolfeboro? If so, what is it and what are the remedies?[45] Speaking on the subjects were Hugh H. Wallace, Alonzo H. Beardsley, Frederick U. Landman, Perley E. Young, Mabel Fullerton Hatch, Dr. Fred P. Haggard, Ernest H. Trickey, Parry T. Hersey, Dr. Fred E. Clow, Frank P. Hobbs, H.T. Merritt, and Frank Cronin. Many valuable suggestions were made.

The Wolfeboro Community Association was formed the next month. Mrs. Hatch was designated as publicity chairman.[46] The group remained active. In the same year, 1923, the Winnipesaukee Lake Region Associates was formed in Laconia to promote tourism in the area.

On January 11, 1926, the Wolfeboro Chamber of Commerce was organized. Harold H. Hart was chosen as president. Clayton M. Wallace as treasurer, and Mildred B. Avery as secretary. After this time nearly all efforts to increase business and industry in town were coordinated by this group.

In September 1929 Professor James W. Goldthwait of Dartmouth College, who had been a summer resident for 45 years, gave a talk to the Rotary Club and said one of the great charms of the town was its people, "and to city residents there is an irresistible appeal of New Hampshire men and women *as they are*, without trying to copy city ways and manners and fashions."[47]

## COMMERCE AND ECONOMICS

### Items of the Decade

The economic climate of the 1920s consisted of good times sandwiched between slow and uncertain conditions. In 1921 the country was in a recession. At the end of the decade in 1930, the nation was headed toward the great Depression, in fact was already in it, but this was not yet fully recognized. In between, times were generally good.

The Wolfeboro National Bank remained the only financial institution in town and was used by nearly all local business people. Throughout the decade its assets increased. About $60,000 face-value worth of federal paper money, including the new small-size $10 and $20 notes introduced in 1929, with the WOLFEBORO NATIONAL BANK inscription, were in circulation.

### Chickens and Cows

Although Almon W. Eaton, for one, had established a large poultry business in town earlier, and turkeys had been mentioned by Parker in 1900 as being an important local export, it was not until the 1920s that this industry became one of the most prominent in Wolfeboro.

The pioneer in the new wave of interest was Robert F. Thurrell, who came to town in 1922 to operate the Cotton Mountain Farm owned by his brother-in-law, J. Ellison Morse. Thurrell, a graduate of the University of Maine, was a go-getter, and within a few years he had established a mammoth chicken breeding and raising emporium in East Wolfeboro, complete with a two-story building measuring 252 feet long.

Other active participants in the poultry trade included Linley and Noyes Moore, who operated the Pleasant Valley Stock Farm (which also raised cattle and pigs); and, in South Wolfeboro, Roy Foster. In addition, several dozen other farmers kept from a few dozen to a few hundred breeders on hand. Products of these enterprises included newly-hatched chicks and mature fryers.[48]

The dairy and livestock business was also a vital part of the local scene in the 1920s. Producers included Goose Acres (Mr. and Mrs. Alvan T. Hatch), the Pleasant Valley Stock Farm, and Brewster Brothers, the last-named being located on South Main Street. Alfalfa was an important local crop for cattle feed.

During the decade groups of visiting farmers occasionally toured Wolfeboro facilities to learn techniques.

### The Early Twenties

In the early 1920s the shoe operations on Factory Street and the wood industries on Back Bay and Wolfeboro Falls, which depended on the health of distant markets, were erratic in their performance and profitability. There were many layoffs and temporary closings.

An account dated January 15, 1921, noted: "George Thompson has been in town selling autos this week and had good luck in spite of the times." This encouraging note was printed on April 2 of the same year: "The whistle at Clow's Mill is being heard daily now, which we hope is a sign of returning prosperity." On the other hand, there was this item in the paper on August 27: "Our shoe workers are not employed as constantly as they desire, somewhat impatient with winter approaching." Many workers moved out of town or talked of doing so. Despite this, rental housing accommodations were scarce. Few builders had the confidence to put up new structures.

The most popular non-alcoholic beverage in town in the early 1920s was probably Moxie, displays of which were featured from time to time in store windows. In June 1921 the Moxie Horsemobile passed through town and created attention.[49]

In 1922 it was reported on several occasions that business was erratic. By early summer 1923 the local economy had strengthened. Laborers were in short supply, and nearly all tenements and rental properties were under contract.

Commercial trucks were becoming popular. The decade saw an expansion of delivery facilities by local businesses and of vehicles making the rounds of downtown streets and outlying districts to sell fish, meat, fruit, and baked goods.[50]

### The Good Years

The mid-1920s were prosperous. In 1923 plans were underway to build a new schoolhouse (which became known as Carpenter School), a new facility for Huggins Hospital, and an old people's home.

Although George A. Carpenter had bought property on South Main Street to erect a charity retirement home, this never came to pass. However, the school (largely financed by Carpenter) and hospital were soon under construction.[51]

Many Christmas gift items were advertised in the local paper in December 1923. Haley the Outfitter offered selections from flannel shirts to jewelry. G.E. Thompson displayed clothing for sale. Low & McDuffee, furniture dealers, announced that they had just opened a Wolfeboro branch in J.L. Young's store and featured telephone stands, kitchen tables, dining tables and chairs, smoking sets, and other items.

Harry C. Doe suggested that typewriters make a useful and practical gift. Harry D. Piper's store in the Bank Building offered clothing and dry goods. Tobey's Pharmacy, known as The Rexall Store, sold Christmas cards, booklets and stationery, pipes, cigars, cigarettes, flashlights, clocks, baskets, Thermos bottles, shaving sets, candies, cameras, fountain pens, pencils, pocketbooks, folders, bags, and toiletry articles in addition to medicine. The Elliott Beauty Shoppe at the lake end of Endicott Street offered hand-painted articles, baskets made from armadillo shells, California beads, plaques, and other articles. H.H. Wallace sold hardware and utensils.

Everett S. Albee had a fine selection of jewelry and radios on display. The Music Store offered typewriters, phonographs, and phonograph records. The Paper Store next to the Main Street bridge had a wide selection of gifts.

Robust business continued in 1924 and 1925. In the latter year local painters united to state that after March 25 they would charge $5 per day. This amounted to about $1,500 per year. Wages of other tradesmen and professionals rose during the period. Factories hummed with activity in Wolfeboro Falls and along Back Bay.

### Later Years

In April 1927 the Gardner Pad Company, with its head office in Gardner, MA, took over the old Hutchins mill and announced it would employ 20 workers in the manufacture of excelsior-filled wrapping pads. The Gardner operation flourished for several years and even added to its plant which produced about 300 boxcars of excelsior each year. However, problems continued with the supply of water power. In 1930 the Boston & Maine Railroad and the town of Whitefield jointly formulated a plan to move the company to that village.[52] However, the firm remained in Wolfeboro.

On November 19, 1927, Savard's Market on South Main Street—dealer in meats, groceries, and other foods—announced it would give S&H (Sperry & Hutchinson) Green Stamps on all sales, at the rate of one stamp for each 10¢ spent.

Business signals were becoming mixed. On March 31, 1928, the local paper, commenting on M. Roberts and family moving away, said: "We are sorry to have them leave us but we hope some will move in, for there are enough closed buildings now." However, in the autumn it was reported that labor was scarce in Wolfeboro, and comments were made that finding people to do haying of fields was not an easy task unless advance arrangements had been made. The lumber mills were going full tilt, and retailers seemed to be enjoying the economic climate.

The Chamber of Commerce had as its main objective the attracting of new industries to Wolfeboro. Many meetings, forums, and programs were held on the subject in 1928 and 1929.

### Decade's End

On December 13, 1929, an editorial noted that the factory known as Clark Shop on Factory Street, given to the town by the recently deceased Greenleaf B. Clark, had been reconditioned and was waiting for lease if a new manufacturer could be found to locate there. In the meantime, no one knew that the great Depression had already taken a strong foothold. On January 3, 1930, Editor Frederick W. Prindle commented on recent happenings:

> In American life the stock market smash of October-November might be considered the most distinctive event. Though many losses were caused, a fantastic speculation was checked before it reached too dizzy heights. We have seen a notable movement of business executives to equalize the waves of prosperity and adversity, and keep business running regularly... Thus, though the year has troubles, we enter 1930 with a brighter outlook than that of January 1, 1929.

In January 1930 Sherman D. Brummitt began tearing down the venerable Cate Block at Pickering Corner, to be replaced by a Socony gas station under the management of Harold H. Hart.

In June of the same year the Ann Inn—earlier known as the Belvue House—was acquired by the Onthank-Rich Company of Boston and designated as New Hampshire headquarters for a large sales operation involving motorboats, appliances, and other mechanical devices. In the same month the 1930 federal census showed 95 people unemployed in Wolfeboro (such being defined as being without a job, able to work, and looking for a job). In contrast, there were 3 in Tuftonboro, 10 in Tamworth, 21 in Sandwich, 22 in Ossipee, and 153 in Conway. The same survey showed that there were 2,348 people living in Wolfeboro, as compared to 2,178 on January 1, 1920.

### Home Prices in 1922

Early in the decade, on August 26, 1922, Frank P. Hobbs, erstwhile hotel operator and presently a leading real estate dealer, advertised several local properties for sale in the high-end category. Typical in-town houses of modest proportions were apt to cost much less, usually in the $500 to $1,000 range. Samples:

**Camp:** On Lake Winnipesaukee, completely furnished, four sleeping rooms, living room, fireplace, dining room, kitchen, pantry, mission-style furniture, nice beach and pine grove. $3,000.

**Farm:** 50 acres, on Lake Winnipesaukee, 500 feet of lake frontage, farmhouse with 13 rooms, barn 40 x 50 feet, ice house, woodshed, fruit trees. $5,000.

**House:** 11 rooms and baths, three fireplaces, 38 x 16 foot living room, hot and cold water, piazza 8 feet by 160 feet, barn 24 by 30 feet, $400 player piano, garage, large lawn, shrubs, five minutes from Post Office, seven acres of land bordering Lake Winnipesaukee. $10,000.

**House:** On high elevation overlooking lakes Wentworth and Winnipesaukee, 12 rooms and bath, fireplace, hardwood floors, 40 x 50 foot stable, two acres of land, suitable for summer or winter, 1/2 mile to Lake Wentworth, three miles to Lake Winnipesaukee. $3,500.

## FACTORIES

### The C.K. Fox Shoe Co.

In 1921 the C.K. Fox Shoe Co. on Factory Street was busy most of the time. By November orders were coming in at a satisfactory rate, giving promise for a busy winter.[53] Meanwhile, the local paper was filled with stories of New England manufacturers of leather and textiles who were moving to the South to secure cheaper labor and longer working hours. On Monday, July 16, 1923, employees of the Fox plant were stunned when they were told that Fox would close down its Wolfeboro factory on or about September first, would close a similar plant in Northwood, and transfer all operations to Haverhill, MA.[54]

Ida L. Fox, widow of Charles K. Fox (who had died July 31, 1912), continued coming to Wolfeboro each summer to occupy her home, "a pride of the village," on North Main Street, although by 1925 she had been an invalid for several years. Mrs. Fox died on August 4, 1926.

### The Jenkins Caper

On April 11, 1922, a mass meeting was held at the Masonic Temple. The get-together was called by Frank P. Hobbs and Ernest Rickey, who reported that J.A. Jenkins, a Massachusetts shoe manufacturer, had expressed interest in renting the vacant wing representing the remaining portion of the "old factory" purchased years earlier by the Village Precinct. The firm's Massachusetts plant employed 100 or more and turned out 1,200 to 1,500 pairs of shoes daily, certainly a heartwarming prospect if it relocated its operations to Wolfeboro. It was stated that the 100 workers would provide employment for another 300 people in town to provide them with food, clothing, shelter, etc. Surely, good times were ahead as soon as the Hampshire Shoe Company (as it was to be called) began hiring!

Near the end of the same month, nine large trucks arrived in town and began unloading. In May overhead shafting was installed to drive stitching machines.[55] July and August came and went.

This appeared on September 20, 1922: "Our new shoe firm seems to be rather slow in beginning operation." October and November passed on the calendar.

On December 2 this was published:

> The indications are very promising that the Jenkins shoe shop is about to start at an early date. Already shipments of stock have been received and word received to have heat turned on at the shop. It sounds good and looks good and is to be trusted that work is about to begin.

Still no shoes.

On April 7, 1923, the story ended:

> The Hampshire Shoe Company, leased from the Precinct last year what was known as the "Little Shop," for the manufacture of shoes, was served last week a writ alleging a breach of contract, and its property, consisting of such machinery as therein contained, placed under attachment.

The Precinct had the machinery carefully removed and stored.

### Wolfeboro Shoe Company (Bell Brothers)

There was more news on the shoe factory front in 1923. The remaining "Little Factory" wing of the former "Big Factory" owned by the Village Precinct might just come alive again despite the Jenkins fiasco. Items in the *Granite State News* tell the tale:

> **1923, April 14:** It was announced that the town commissioners completed a deal with Bell Brothers, of Salem, MA, on April 12, 1923, to lease the factory building. Bell Brothers already operated four factories elsewhere and planned to make McKay brand men's slippers. Local work was expected to begin on June 1 with Frank E. Merrill, formerly of Sanbornville, as superintendent.
>
> **1923, May 5:** "The shafting has been ordered and also machinery which will be shipped the 12th."
>
> **1923, June 16:** "Cutters began operation this week at the new shoe factory, and indications now are very favorable for a nice little business and operation at our 'Little Factory.'"
>
> **1923, August 11:** "The cutters at the new factory, being dissatisfied with prices for their labor, quit work." (Labor unrest of this nature was a rarity in Wolfeboro.)
>
> **1924, September 13:** "Work in the Bell Shoe Factory has been quite steady this summer and fall."
>
> **1925, April 4:** It was a good prospect to enlarge the factory for the increasing business at the Bell Shop. The Precinct recently had voted up to $8,000 for this purpose.
>
> **1925, July 18:** Announced that Goodwin & Doe had been awarded the contract for adding a third story to be ready for occupancy by September 1.

The Bell Brothers' Wolfeboro Shoe Company factory remained in business until the late 1930s.

### The Paris Shoe Company

Another chapter in the history of shoe businesses in Wolfeboro is related by these *Granite State News* accounts of an enterprise that set up in the Clark Shop formerly occupied by the C.K. Fox Shoe Co.:

> **1923, August 25:** "The Paris Shoe Company, of Haverhill, which succeeds the C.K. Fox Company, began work in the cutting room Wednesday, August 22 with George E. Libby at the bench. Additional cutters are expected to be added at once, and thus the good work goes on with only a short interruption between the two firms, which is very gratifying, and it is to be hoped that business will be good this winter."
>
> **1923, September 22:** "The Paris Shoe Company is steadily increasing its output. After being in operation but three weeks it is turning out seven cases a day."
>
> **1924, March 29:** "Wednesday afternoon 30 employees of

the stitching room at the Paris Shoe Factory, owing to a misunderstanding or misconstruction of orders, left their machines and walked out. This is the first act of the kind which has occurred in this town in many years by Wolfeboro operatives.[56] There have been several conferences held, and it is to be hoped and evidence seems favorable for a timely adjustment and a better understanding."

**1926, February 20:** "The personal property of the Paris Shoe Company was disposed of by auction at the factory, Thursday. Many bidders from out of town were in attendance."

### The Wolfeboro Mills

The Wolfeboro Mills, formerly the Racine Woolen Mills, and under different names before that, was very active in South Wolfeboro in the early 1920s. Local people were given the opportunity to buy "seconds in all grades" at discount prices.

For most of the twentieth century the property had been bandied about from one owner to another, punctuated by numerous closings due to lack of business and vacancies between operators. In 1923 the mill property was on the market but continued in operation. In November the Wolfeboro Mills opened a factory outlet store on South Main Street opposite Brewster Academy. Offered were Profile bed blankets (marked with a logotype showing the Great Stone Face) from $5 to $20 per pair, crib blankets $3.50 and $5.50, automobile robes $5.50 to $14.50, and Indian robes and woolen couch covers at $9 to $14.

By September 1924 the factory had been closed for some time, and remodeling was taking place in preparation for a "new line of work." The plant was then owned by Springer & Co., of Connecticut, who also maintained a boarding house across the street. Fred and Nelson Springer supervised 58 employees, whose total wages amounted to about $1,200 per week; or less than an average of $20 per worker.

The next month, this news item appeared:

> The familiar sound of the old whistle once again tells us there will be work for us at home this winter and we won't have to go to neighboring towns for employment. We hear over a hundred have already signed for work. The Springer Company will make cloth a specialty and a few blankets.

Alas, only a few months later it was reported that on Thursday evening, April 9, 1925, the Wolfeboro Mills facilities were totally destroyed by fire, with a loss of $150,000 or more.[57]

The factory outlet on South Main Street remained open after the fire and continued to sell Wolfeboro Mills products still on hand, plus wooden toys made in a factory in South Tamworth, Christmas gifts embroidered by hand by local artisans, and a group of automobile accessories consigned by Harold H. Hart, whose recently established automobile showroom was not yet ready for occupancy.

## TECHNOLOGY

### Municipal Electricity

In 1922 this question was posed in a Brewster Academy civics examination: "What is meant by the municipal ownership of public utilities? What are the arguments in favor of it? Against it? Give an example in your own town or a neighboring town, if possible." A woman in the senior class answered:

> Municipal ownership means that a business is owned and run by the town or city instead of by a man or a group of men. The argument for it is that even if it did not make money it will keep going, while if it were owned by an individual it would have to stop business. Against it is the fact that when a thing is run by the government, either of city, town, state, or country, it costs more than if private business. In our own town we have the electric lighting station owned by the town, and we pay more for electricity than any of our neighboring towns do.

Frederick W. Prindle, editor of the paper, then commented:

> If all our young people understood things as well as this, we should have much more common sense in our public operations and smaller material on which demagogues at campaign time could expect to get away with their sophistries.

By 1926 most houses in downtown Wolfeboro and many outlying homes and farms were wired for electricity from the municipal system. Those without municipal electricity either had their own generating plants, which was quite rare, or illuminated their homes with kerosene lamps. Radios and some other small appliances could be operated by batteries.

In December 1927 Mabel Fullerton Hatch observed that from the Tuftonboro line to the top of Quaker Meeting House Hill in Wolfeboro (about where the Lakeview Inn is today), "I believe only three houses depend on kerosene for lighting."

In the summer of 1927 Charles T. Glines of Providence, RI, a seasonal visitor to the town since 1897 and the owner of a camp on Wolfeboro Neck, received an electrical shock at his cottage. In January 1928 he filed suit against the Wolfeboro Precinct seeking to recover $15,000 in alleged damages.[58]

### Service Extended

Electrical service was extended to most of the far outlying districts of Wolfeboro during the decade. For a time, property owners in East Wolfeboro, united under the leadership of Robert Thurrell, chicken mogul of Cotton Mountain Farm, threatened to make an arrangement with an outside supplier, Electric Utilities of the White Mountains. This spurred the Wolfeboro Precinct into action, and in 1929 town electric service reached the eastern section of Pleasant Valley, the Cotton Mountain district, and adjacent areas.

Electro-mechanical refrigeration became very popular, and in the late 1920s many different Frigidaire, General Electric, and other units were installed in homes, often accompanied by a mention in the local paper. Point Breeze Camp put in an especially large commercial unit. This foretold the decline of the local ice-cutting and delivery business.

On May 1, 1929, new electric rates went into effect. Year-round customers were charged 18¢ per kilowatt hour, less 5¢ for prompt payment. A special rate for electric heating and cooking was set up at 10¢ for the first 10 KWH, and 3¢ per KWH after that time, with a minimum charge of $2 per month.

A report of the Electric Light Commissioners for the year 1929 stated that there were 611 yearly and 167 summer light customers, as well as 142 yearly and 41 summer power users. On the new extension in eastern Wolfeboro there were 97 light and 7 power customers and a gain for the year of 182 accounts.[59]

## AROUND TOWN

### Odds and Ends

A public restroom was opened at the *Mount Washington* wharf in June 1924. The need for such a facility had been expressed for many years. The ownership of the wharf was in dispute. The town claimed title under a gift from pioneer settler Judge David Sewall's widow, but the Boston & Maine Railroad stated that it owned the facility. In April 1925 the selectmen finally closed a deal with the B&M, and the town obtained a warranty deed.

Toward the end of the decade there were frequent suggestions that Wolfeboro adopt the town manager system of government. On March 14, 1928, the proposal was defeated at the polls by a two-to-one margin. The next year, March 11, 1929, this question was on the ballot again and was knocked down 360 to 114.[60]

### Requiem for Harmony Grove

Ever since the middle of the nineteenth century, Harmony Grove—a stately stand of pine trees near the northern shore of Back Bay to the west off Center Street—had been a gathering place for picnics, outdoor concerts, religious revival or "union" meetings, and camping.

In 1922 its future was unsettled. Althea Berry and the estates of Frank B. Hutchins and James H. Martin owned the property jointly, wanted to sell, and hoped that the town would buy and preserve it. They were not in a financial position to donate the tract to the community. A local committee was formed to learn more, but it was slow in functioning, and the property was sold in the meantime. The new owners announced that they were going to sell the timber, prompting this comment from the local paper:[61]

> The old adage, "You'll never miss the water till the well goes dry," is as true today as ever, until the woodman has completed his work, which he intends to commence next week. You will have a long time to be sorry, and sorry you'll be. Commercialism is king, public spirit and home loyalty today is a waning element.

### Treeless Prospect

In January and February 1926 several articles in the local paper discussed the desirability of forests and remarked that few tourists wanted to see a treeless landscape. Certain communities in New Hampshire were setting up town forests, and it was suggested that Wolfeboro might benefit from having one.[62]

Portable sawmills were stripping the area, and very few stands of tall pines remained, as special taxes were levied on standing forests. It was said that the taxes amounted to about double the value of the growth accomplished by the trees each year. Thus, forests could not grow fast enough on an annual basis to keep up with tax payments.

In her January 9, 1926 column Mabel Fullerton Hatch took up the subject and suggested that those advertising New Hampshire as a nice place to visit "might well consider to try to correct the devastating work of the portable mills in the state. They raise more particular hell with the scenery which we are trying to sell to out-of-town folks than any other one factor." Under current taxation, "it's a luxury to own timber lots—only rich folks can afford to keep them."

### Greenleaf B. Clark

Greenleaf B. Clark, who was born in Wolfeboro and spent his entire life here, continued to be well known on the local scene. His benefactions were several and included the remodeling of the old Wolfborough and Tuftonboro Academy building as the new Community Hall which the town was invited to use free of charge. He gave many small cash gifts—$10 and $20 were typical amounts—as prizes for church, scholastic, and other activities.

In 1917 he had presented the town with several acres of land on South Main Street, his family homestead where he had spent much of his life. First known as Village Park and later as Clark Park, the premises were neglected by the community for the first several years which caused him to become quite upset. The 1924 town warrant asked the voters to determine if the park should be returned to the donor. The vote was in the negative, but the proposal goaded the town into action, and improvements began shortly thereafter.

In July 1924 Clark was in a benevolent frame of mind and built a 50′ by 75′ wooden dance platform on his South Main Street property not far from the old homestead he had given the town, opening it to the public on August 1. A band from Farmington played a concert, dancing was enjoyed, and an estimated one thousand automobiles were parked around the grounds.[63]

On November 30, 1925, "Green" Clark, as he was known, celebrated his 80th birthday by giving his 48 tenants a free oyster supper with donuts, cheese, pickles and coffee, in the banquet rooms of the Temple Auditorium. As part of a special program chaired by Frank P. Hobbs, he was acknowledged as being a prime mover in the acquisition and remodeling of the Temple Auditorium and in building the shoe shop years earlier. He mortgaged his home in 1895 in order to raise funds to build a factory, which he leased to Spaulding & Swett.

A special Precinct meeting was held at Memorial Hall on July 1, 1929, to consider the matter of accepting the gift offered by Greenleaf B. Clark of his shoe-factory building and also to discuss if the Precinct would raise by bonds or notes a sum not to exceed $10,000 to repair it. The vote was 559 yes to 2 no. The factory was vacant at the time.

### Wolfeboro Historical Society

On September 1, 1925, the Wolfeboro Historical Society was established. One of its first missions was the gathering of local artifacts and mementos and the arranging of the former Clark homestead as a museum and tourist attraction.

The 1926 town meeting appropriated the sum of $2,000 to improve the Clark property and make it available for use for the Historical Society. Annual membership in the Society was fixed at $1.[64] Stephen W. Clow was president. Mrs. Ernest H. Trickey was in charge of receiving membership payments and gifts. By August 1927 the group had over 100 members. On July 10, 1929, the Clark house was opened for the first time to visitors, displaying articles lent or given by townspeople. Admission of 25¢ was charged.

On Saturday, August 3, 1929, the Wolfeboro Historical Society held a costume party at the Clark House, with about 80 in attendance. Apparently, this "wasteful outlay" and other uses of his ancestral home irritated Greenleaf B. Clark, who had become somewhat of a curmudgeon in his advanced years, being generous one moment and annoyed another. On August 23, 1929, this was published in the *Granite State News:*

> I wish to state through your paper the beautiful lot of land on South Main Street, my homestead, which I sacrificed over 12 years ago for ornamental, quiet and restful purposes, and a few other small demands, for a public park to Wolfeboro, and was accepted by the town, have not been complied with by the latter. My future interest is much blighted...
>
> Unless Wolfeboro gives me evidence of something more than the wasteful outlay of the past week, my future interest will be very light to Wolfeboro.
>
> G.B. Clark.

Whatever his ill feelings may have been, they were not translated to changing his will, which, indeed, had been written in 1911.

On November 30, 1929, at age 84, Clark died at his home after a brief illness. Twice married, he left no children. He was buried in Lake View Cemetery. Most of his assets, consisting primarily of rental properties in poor repair, were bequeathed to local churches.

### "Georgetown"

George A. Carpenter continued to be an important benefactor to the town and its residents, a generous contributor to local charities and events. At one time he stocked a building near his Cobham Hall residence on Green Street with pairs of new shoes and unused clothing and invited those in need to help themselves.[65] On June 30, 1923, the editor of the local paper noted: "Unless friend Carpenter has a limit on his benefactions to his native town it may be we shall feel the duty as a mark of appreciation to change the name to Georgetown."

Meanwhile frequent items in the local paper told of Carpenter's burgeoning real estate empire in Boston.[66] Behind the scenes he was furnishing much of the financing in Wolfeboro to build what would later be named Carpenter School after his mother, Lavonia[67] Carpenter. In addition, he was a major benefactor of Huggins Hospital.

On July 6, 1928, Mr. and Mrs. George A. Carpenter celebrated their 50th wedding anniversary in Wolfeboro, observing the day quietly with their son Ralph G. and their grandchildren.

Ralph was frequently mentioned in the local news, such as this item which appeared on October 24, 1925: "The spacious estate on Sewall Road, formerly the Burton property, has recently been purchased by Ralph Carpenter for his summer home."

On February 23, 1921, Ralph married Rita B. Klinck, age 32, of Tuftonboro, the second marriage for both. The couple became the parents of a son, John, on November 28, 1921.[68]

## HEALTH AND MEDICINE

### Chiropractors Popular

In the April 15, 1922, issue of the *Granite State News,* a letter from an "observant citizen" praised certain cures accomplished locally by chiropractors, noting that Mrs. Ellwood Corson, who for many years had been invalid, could now move about freely and that her neck, the main source of her complaints, no longer bothered her.

In September local chiropractors R.G. and L.G. Brown paid for a full-page advertisement stating in part that 95% of all diseases are due to pressure upon nerves along the side of the vertebral column. "It is a business of the chiropractor to release this pressure with the hands."

On December 31, 1927, a lengthy article in the local paper suggested that chiropractors could cure just about every known disease. An alphabetical list was given, noting that of acne cases 85.4% were considered to be cured, adenoids 75.8%, appendicitis 90.2%, arterial hardening 66.6%, etc., down to typhoid fever 96.4% and whooping cough 95.4%. It seemed that with chiropractors in town, one would not need the services of physicians or even the remarkable Shattuck system described below.

### The Marvelous Oxygen Vapor Bath

Sensing a greener pasture in Wolfeboro, in December 1926 Joseph E. Shattuck packed up his Oxygen Vapor Bath apparatus in Rochester and moved it to Room 17 in the Central Block on Railroad Avenue. Advertisements in the *Granite State News* informed readers that his system would cure gangrene, diabetes, rheumatism, high blood pressure, nervous troubles, cancer, and more.

Before long these painless and apparently pleasant treatments were all the rage. Not everyone agreed with the claims made by Shattuck, and in March 1927 the State Board of Health issued a cease and desist order for practicing medicine without a license. The focal point of the case was the claim that since January 20, 1927, Herbert E. Foss of Wolfeboro, who had been suffering from cancer for three years or more, had "showed improvement so astonishing to himself and friends that his hope of a complete recovery buoyed up his spirits." The State Board would buy none of this. Wolfeboro citizens came to the rescue of Shattuck and patient Foss, circulated a lengthy petition, and the State Board relented. Shattuck was back in business.

Editor Frederick W. Prindle must have been inhaling the vapors and liking it, for on September 3 he recommended the treatment to his readers, stating, "A trial will convince the efficacy of these baths." Thus emboldened, on October 8 Shattuck advertised that his Oxygen Vapor Bath was also good for "all skin troubles, scalds, burns, growths." Apparently, there was nothing it could not cure.

Unfortunately for Shattuck and still more unfortunately for his patient, cancer-ridden Herbert E. Foss took a turn for the worse. Shattuck blithely stated it was because "the public has failed to provide suitable care of said Foss. There is and has been marked improvement, which would result in the complete cure of the monster menace." Shattuck stated he would provide no more treatments. Foss died on November 15. In 1928 Shattuck moved on, possibly to still other green pastures.[69]

### New Hospital Building

Meanwhile, Huggins Hospital and the well-trained physicians and nurses on its staff were doing excellent work treating many cases. In July 1921 Mrs. Robert Crabb donated funds to buy an International X-Ray outfit, the latest in medical technology. As the patient load increased, it became evident that more space was needed. In September of 1922 a call for a new structure was made.

George A. and Emma Carpenter donated a site for a new hospital building, land on South Main Street formerly owned by J. Clifton Avery and used for dairy farming. Once again, James H. Martin came to the fore, donating $25,000 provided that funds would be forthcoming from others. Albert H. Dow of Boston was named as architect. The first spade of earth was turned on October 23, 1923. The estimated cost of the project was $60,000 (actual cost amounted to $70,000).

The local contracting team of J. Frank Goodwin and Andrew F. Doe constructed a 24-bed building of red brick. On November 11, 1924, the new Huggins Hospital was dedicated. This formed the nucleus of a facility that would expand greatly over the years. The old wooden structure stood until April 1935, when it "terminated its existence in an unsightly heap of debris."[70]

The first direct transfusion of blood at Huggins took place on November 15, 1927. Harry Jones of Alton was the donor, and the recipient was his mother Mrs. George Jones.[71]

### A Tour of the Hospital

On February 19, 1927, the local paper gave readers a tour of the facility:

> The building is of red brick and is a plain and simple, but impressive structure. The interior is most admirably and effectively designed. Mr. Dow gave his personal attention to the convenient arrangement of the wards, offices and sun-parlors, and to the deadening of all floors from one sub-division wall to another, making the building practically fireproof, to the ventilation, plumbing, and drainage of the entire building, resulting in what the trustees, doctors and patients consider the safest, most healthy and most comfortable hospital in this section.
>
> Entering the main hall, the ceiling is in carton pierre, a composition which is fireproof and waterproof. The transparency of the colors of the rooms opening out of the corridor has a pleasing effect. The sun-parlor at one end is flooded with sunlight. Adding to the cozy, well-heated, cheerful atmosphere, are pedestals bearing ferns and boxes of bright geraniums. The delivery room is approached by a fireproof alcove. All of the trimmings and wainscoting are of immaculate white. This room is well equipped and well lighted. Outside are white cases filled with surgeons' instruments.
>
> The idea of the hospital physician is introduced in a favorable manner in the operating room, with its violet ray, Baker X-ray machines, and dark room adjoining. The entire furnishings are new and much praised by authorities from larger hospitals. Easily accessible to these rooms are the sterilizing room and the doctor's "scrub-up" room. The former is a

model of sanitary convenience as to instruments and bandages, thoroughly arranged for cleanliness, comfort, and convenience as to care of patients. The great extent of patronage at the hospital depends upon the minor operations. The room given over for these purposes is fortunate in having a Sorensen pump, which is one of the latest inventions whereby ether may be administered.

Camp Kuwiyan has a room with tiny beds and furnishings for the baby visitor and mother. The frieze and walls show the idea of the artist was to produce something new in juvenile good taste. The effect is in harmony with infant equipment. Another room is furnished and endowed in memory of Frank McD. Sinclair. The doors, as of other rooms, are a close resemblance to San Domingo mahogany. Across the hall and overlooking beautiful Lake Wentworth is a room supported by the American Legion boys. Another room is the Women's Ward, a semi-private ward with four beds and lighted by two large windows. Before one reaches the apartment of Henry S. Mason is the Utility room.

A pleasant room opposite the entrance door is for the office of the superintendent, with a convenient pharmacy and linen closet. The latter room has been well stocked by the local Ladies' Aid. A room is given over to dietetics. Here a study of food and reference to its use in the body is prepared by the doctors, male attendants, and nurses. This includes practice in weighing and measuring standard portions and in calculating dietaries. Model diets are prepared for persons of diverse occupations. The diet in disease is studied. Special attention is given to the feeding of children.

Other rooms are those of the Eastern Star, Mrs. Bailey, and Mrs. Crabb. The latter room has amongst its furnishings, solid silverware, china, and choice bed and table linen.... The sunparlor at this end of the building is now only made possible for summer use.

### Other Medical News

In 1923 an anonymous donor made it possible to buy a "lung motor," which was placed at the Wolfeboro Electric plant where it was available anytime for use in "cases of drowning, asphyxia from gas inhalation, electric shock from lightning or contact with high tension electrical currents."[72]

In 1928 two proposals for health care units were made. In July the George C. Avery homestead was sold to a Miss Clark, who "will conduct a country home for invalid children." In December newspaper readers were informed that the former Jungalow Camps in South Wolfeboro on the road to Alton had been sold to a doctor "who intends to put it into a sanitarium."[73] Neither proposal came to pass.

In January 1929 a nationwide wave of severe colds and influenza reached Wolfeboro. During the first week of February, social and public events for the next week were canceled including motion pictures, sports, and meetings. The schools were closed from late January through early February because so many teachers and students were absent.

### Shadows

Several tragedies occurred during the decade and left long-lasting scars on the community.

About 11:00 in the evening of June 23, 1924, Homer Young, age 20, son of Perley E. and Lillian Young, well-known grocers in Wolfeboro Falls, attended the movies, then went to the Wolfeboro Casino. There he met a lady friend, Isabell Horne, and offered her a canoe ride across the lower part of Wolfeboro Bay to Sandy Beach near the Brewster campus. The short crossing was rough due to a high wind, but the couple arrived safely.

On the way back they hit a large wave which threw Homer into the water. Then came another crest, and Isabell was tossed overboard. While she was able to cling to the canoe and eventually make it to shore in a dazed condition, Homer slipped beneath the waves and was not seen again. Later in the evening, Chief of Police Lester E. Thompson took charge of searchers in nearly 20 boats supplied with grapples. The body was found a short distance from shore.

On the afternoon of December 17, 1927, the only two children of Dr. and Mrs. Leon Clow—Henry Leon Clow, Jr., and Elizabeth Shipley Clow, ages 15 and 12—broke through the snow-covered thin ice near the shore of Crescent Lake. Those coming on the scene later saw that tracks led to a hole in the ice, where there were signs of a struggle and a broken snowshoe. Inspection revealed that Betty had first fallen victim and that Henry's heroic effort to save his little sister brought his end as well.

A few months later Dr. and Mrs. Clow moved to Danvers, MA, to try to start a new life. Dr. Clow had been born and educated in Wolfeboro.

In the 1920s one of the most familiar people on the local scene was Archie A. Horne. A graduate of Brewster Free Academy, he had distinguished himself in field sports while there, and later as a team coach. In 1909 he became one of Wolfeboro's first automobile dealers. His business grew, and in the 1910s and early 1920s he achieved prominence as the local outlet for the Model T Ford, America's best-selling car. On March 15, 1912, he married Ethel Bartlett of Springvale, ME. The couple had four children—Archie, Jr., Paul, Maurice, and Beatrice Leota.[74] In 1919 he bought all of the real estate between the Durgin Block and the Smith River. By 1928 he had several successful enterprises including a radio sales company in addition to his Ford dealership. While in Boston on business in the same year, at the height of his career, Horne became ill, was hospitalized, and died of a heart attack on February 21.

In December 1929 Merwin Horn and Reginald Wiggin demonstrated a propeller-driven ice boat on Lake Winnipesaukee which zipped along at 60 miles an hour. Merwin, 16 years old, quickly sold the unit and by January was building another. On February 19, 1930, Maurice Horne, son of the late Archie, was killed when his head was struck by the unprotected revolving blade of one of these devices.

## THE EFFECTS OF NATURE

### Storms and Weather

On March 28, 1921, Lake Winnipesaukee was free from ice, being the earliest recorded date in history, the previous record being April 3, 1902. On September 22 of the same year high winds damaged a number of buildings and boats along the shore.

The year 1922 was marked by heavy rains in April and May which raised the waters of lakes and ponds six to eight inches and made roads muddy. On June 16 a notable thunderstorm occurred with much rain. Lightning struck several places and set fire to the Elliott summer cottage on Wolfeboro Neck, many limbs were torn from trees, and the Lord & Cobb excelsior mill in Wolfeboro Falls was put out of commission temporarily.

January 1923 was the snowiest winter anyone could remember, possibly outranked only by the blizzard of 1873 it was said.[75] By January 13 East Wolfeboro was closed off from the rest of the town. An outbreak of colds and other illnesses occurred, but as many roads were drifted shut, doctors had to make their rounds on foot. Along the western side of Railroad Avenue, snowbanks were nearly six feet high.

On August 22, 1923, very high winds buffeted the Wolfeboro region. The steamer *Mount Washington* had her paddle box damaged and arrived late on its afternoon trip. A few weeks later on September 16 an intense thunderstorm was accompanied by so much hail that some ice pellets remained on the ground until the next morning.

A flash downpour of two inches on July 7, 1925, accompanied by almost incessant lightning was called one of the most severe in many years. Catch basins were unable to contain the torrents. On South Main Street water was up to the hubs of automobiles. The *Mount Washington,* due in Wolfeboro at about the time of the downpour, made three unsuccessful attempts before finally landing.

This thunderstorm was apparently eclipsed by one that occurred a month later on August 9 and was called the heaviest of the season. Between two and three inches of rain fell in the downtown area in a very short time. Curiously, at the other end of town at the Libby Museum there was hardly any rain at all. Lightning struck the house of E.L. Stackpole on Elm Street, and in Pleasant Valley the house of Harry R. Leavitt was hit, dazing the owner.[76]

Residents awakened on February 26, 1927, to find three feet of snow and a raging gale, the worst day of the winter. The train due in Wolfeboro shortly after noon did not arrive until 10:15 in the evening. Telephone wires and electric wires were down, and on North Main Street the drifts were over 10 feet high. Unfortunately, the town's new snowplow was out of commission. However, Horne's Garage had a Fordson tractor equipped with a plow on hand, and by 6:00 Saturday evening it had cleared a path through all the streets in the village. On Sunday it cut through the road to the Libby Museum.

A heavy electrical storm wracked Wolfeboro on the afternoon on July 6, 1929, causing much damage to trees, buildings, and wires.

### Destructive Tornadoes

The decade of the 1920s had more than its share of tornadoes, popularly called "cyclones" at the time.

High winds and a tornado caused damage in the Center Square district and along the Pond Road near Wolfeboro Center on June 10, 1927, breaking trees, scattering wood, and moving the barn of Cyrus Jenness six feet off its foundation.

On July 7, 1927, a severe thunderstorm with hail and high winds spawned a tornado said to be second in destructiveness only to that of 1910. "Its course was from southwest to northeast, cutting a swath from a quarter to half mile in width, passing over the property of Mrs. F.M. Sinclair bordering Lake Winnipesaukee, and laying waste to the handsome and extensive growth on her estate." The adjacent property of Roy Foster had its timber demolished, and nine of his 10 hen houses and 1,500 chickens were lost. One hen house was carried across the main highway, where it struck and damaged Walter Hale's house and then was carried aloft and dropped into Rust Pond. About two dozen telephone poles were broken off, and numerous maple and apple trees were twisted and destroyed. Hill Camp in South Wolfeboro was seriously damaged. The overall loss from the storm was estimated to be about $10,000, including $5,000 to Foster.

On April 30, 1928, a small tornado touched down on South Main Street near the Brewster and Prescott farms. Trees were blown down and "one car on the road was almost wrecked by encountering a lawn swing coming through the air."

On January 6, 1929, high winds (possibly a tornado) in the North Main Street area near the Libby Museum uprooted and broke off many large pine trees on land mainly owned by Luke Fay. Salvaging the downed timber took many months.

About four o'clock on Tuesday afternoon, September 9, 1929, a thunderstorm struck the town. A tornado touched down in Wolfeboro Center and continued across several miles of land, increasing in force, to Jockey Cove and the eastern side of Wolfeboro Neck. It caused over $30,000 worth of damage along a strip of destruction 600 to 800 feet wide. Mary Shaw's cottage was lifted off its foundation and moved several feet, the piazza demolished, and one end of the building destroyed. Curiously, dishes set on a table remained in position! The nearby Charles T. Glines cottage was extensively damaged. The greatest damage was done to the Helen Hopewell summer place on Tips Cove. The garage was demolished and numerous trees torn up, amounting to a loss of about $20,000.[77]

### Earthquakes

The ground shook perceptibly several times during the decade. On Saturday evening, February 28, 1925, at about 9:20 an earthquake was felt throughout Wolfeboro. Apparently, no damage was done. The paper noted: "The direction was east and west; duration about two minutes seems to be the general report." It was said to be the most severe in Wolfeboro since 1870.[78] On October 9 of the same year a small earthquake was felt in Wolfeboro about 8:55 a.m. Dishes and stoves rattled. The tremor moved from east to west.[79]

On November 18, 1929, a mild earthquake was felt in town, but no damage was done. The shock was stronger along the New England coast. Still another earthquake occurred the evening of February 19, 1930, when tremors were felt in Wolfeboro, but the shock was considerably stronger in Laconia.

### Look to the Skies

On Sunday morning, November 15, 1925, a large meteor passed over Wolfeboro. According to an account:

> William Alexander, going to ring the church bell for the morning service, had his attention arrested by a hissing sound above and saw a brilliant ball of fire about the size of a big water pail with a long tail of shooting stars going in the direction of the Wolfeboro Laundry, and describes it as the most beautiful spectacle he has witnessed.

Several other residents reported seeing the apparition and thought it hit the ground locally, but no one was able to determine where.

On the evening of April 13, 1926, Wolfeboro citizens were treated to a remarkably vivid display of northern lights described as "a wonderfully handsome sight."

What must have been an especially brilliant rainbow was seen by many people on Tuesday morning, September 16, 1930, and was the subject of two separate accounts in the local paper. It was observed in the west and was said to have been "a wonderful sight."[80]

## FIRES

### Fires and Fire Fighting

As of January 21, 1920, the fire companies in Wolfeboro were as follows: Monitor Engine Co., Pequawket Hook and Ladder Co. No. 1, Rollins Hose Co. No 1 (disbanded on December 3, 1929), A.W. Wiggin Hose Co. No. 1, and Eagle Hose Co. No. 1.

In the autumn of 1922 work commenced on the Fire Department Building on Factory Street near the Municipal Power Station, to house a hook and ladder truck. In 1923 a new chemical fire engine was purchased. As fire fighting became more centralized with motorized equipment, the need for district companies lessened.

In 1926 Herbert E. Davis was fire chief and was paid $30 for his work during the year, and Abel Haley was assistant chief and received $20. These were part-time positions.[81]

The 1920s saw improved response to alarms, with the result that the following list is much shorter than it would have been if numerous small blazes had erupted into conflagrations. Among the notable fires and events making the *Granite State News* columns were these:

**1921, May 28. Wiggin place:** At 3:00 a.m. the stable of Dr. George Wiggin at the corner of Glendon and School Streets was discovered ablaze. Firemen saved most of the barn. An automobile and household goods were destroyed. The Masonic Temple located eight feet away had a narrow escape. Damage: $1,800.

**1921, September 10. Wolfeboro Falls Post Office:** About 4:00 a.m. fire was discovered on the roof of the building. Firemen responded promptly, and the flames were brought under control, but there was extensive water damage to the interior.

**1922, June 13. Joseph I. Melanson farm:** North Main Street. Completely destroyed by fire. The structure was said to have been built in 1802 and for many years was known as The Elms and the Meader Retreat, a tourist facility.

**1922, August 23. Nute buildings:** The buildings of the Matilda Nute farm in North Wolfeboro were burned to the ground, the result of an oil stove apparently lighted by children. There was no well on the premises, just a small cistern for collecting rainwater from the eaves. Thus, it was not possible to douse the fire with water.

**1922, October 17. Richardson buildings:** Late in the evening the unoccupied house and buildings of Miss Mattie Richardson at Pine Hill were burned. Loss: $2,000 to $2,500.

**1923, August 20. Mason building:** Building on Spring Street owned by A.L. Mason caught fire. Assistant Fire Chief Thompson had a crew on the job quickly, and damage was limited mainly to water.

**1923, December 6. Old Town Meetinghouse:** Factory Street. The old structure, moved to the site by Greenleaf B. Clark in 1890 and now used for storage by the Paris Shoe Co., caught fire during the noon hour. Firemen quickly subdued the blaze, but there was extensive smoke damage.

**1924, July 21. Birch Café:** Seriously damaged by fire and smoke as a result of a defective oil stove. Railroad Avenue.

**1924, September 19. Peasley building:** Double tenement building owned by George W. Peasley and estate of the late Hattie Ames was destroyed by fire. It was occupied by Peasley, Edwin Perry and family, Charles J. Ames, and Lawrence Reynolds. About 2:45 in the morning Mrs. Perry was awakened by her child's crying and discovered the room filled with smoke. She escaped but lost all her clothing and money. Peasley, over 80 years of age, was taken down a ladder by firemen. Reynolds escaped by running along the eaves and jumping 15 feet into a large elm. Ames, age 70, whose sleeping room was in the attic, suffocated and was found near the window.

**1924, September 21. Mark Blaisdell's barn:** Damaged by fire to the extent of about $800.

**1924, December 19. Boiler explosion at Wolfeboro Laundry:** At about 6:45 a.m. the steam boiler at the Wolfeboro Laundry on Center Street exploded with such terrific force that the entire plant was demolished and was left a heap of ruins. Fortunately, no one was there at the time.

**1925, April 9. Wolfeboro Mills:** Old factory in South Wolfeboro was totally destroyed on Thursday evening with a loss of not less than $150,000. It was believed that spontaneous combustion in a storeroom was the cause. Although the Fire Department was prompt in response and saved adjoining property, the building was a pile of ashes two hours later. Much of what the firemen were able to accomplish was due to the hand-truck, Monitor No. 1. The conflagration was so intense that firebrands were carried through the air to as far as the shore of Lake Wentworth.

**1925, June 22. J.W. Pettee house:** On School Street. Extensively damaged by a fire caused by a defective kerosene stove.

**1926, April 14. Dana W. Emery house:** Pine Hill Road. Totally destroyed by fire around 9:00 a.m., with damage of $1,500 to $2,000. The cause was believed to be an explosion of the parlor coal stove.

**1926, October 15. Louis Herbert barn:** Bay Street. Burned.

**1927, July 7. Libby Lodge:** The Lodge, a facility owned by Dr. Henry F. Libby and located behind the Libby Museum, was severely damaged by fire, with a loss of furniture and personal belongings.

**1928, July 28. Day building:** A.W. Day's building used as an ice cream parlor near the railroad station at Wolfeboro Center was totally destroyed by fire caused by an exploding kerosene lamp.

**1929, April 5. Wolfeboro National Bank Building:** Seriously damaged by fire on the roof which was gutted.

**1929, May 16. Horne's Garage:** Fire started by an emery wheel flared up but was quickly extinguished by the Fire Department. Three new cars were seriously damaged.

**1930, February 17. Cotton Mountain Farm:** Barn and small brooder house burned. Several hundred chickens were prematurely roasted.

**1930, April 8. Harley homestead:** Buildings owned by Samuel Harley on the highway leading to Ossipee were totally destroyed by a fire caused by a spark lodging upon the roof from a bonfire in the front yard.

**1930, June 30:** "The new fire apparatus which the Precinct has purchased is expected to arrive this Friday."

**1930, July 11. Alice Sanborn cottage:** Wentworth Park Shore on Lake Wentworth. Destroyed. Two men, not professional firemen, fighting the fire were burned, one seriously. Loss about $4,000.

**1930, August 22. Boston Branch Store:** Boston Branch Store on the Causeway, Center Street, owned by Albert L. Mason, was totally destroyed by fire, and his dwelling and antique shop nearby were seriously damaged; this structure was the former kitchen of the Pavilion Hotel. The blaze originated by the overturning of a kettle of tar that was boiling on a stove. Mason was severely burned.

**1930, August 29. Murray camp:** The buildings of James Murray on Goss Island, Lake Wentworth, were struck by lightning and totally destroyed.

## LAW ENFORCEMENT

### Around Town

The vast majority of crimes during the decade consisted of misdemeanors such as public drunkenness, vandalism, and petty theft. Lester E. Thompson was chief of police for much of the decade, in an era when there was no town police department. The several officers who helped did so on a part-time basis.

In June 1930 Thompson, who had served as chief for 18 years, filed his resignation due to illness. Constable Ralph C. Mitchell took his place, apparently on an acting basis,[82] and Captain James H. Lolley became traffic officer. Part-time police officers were Harry V. Perry, Charles H. Tulley, and Winfield S. Nichols.

### The Chicken Mystery

In 1921 the town was abuzz with news of chicken thieves who struck farms in East Wolfeboro. Their method consisted of breaking into coops at night and diffusing chloroform fumes in the roosts. The insensible fowl were then tossed into bags and hauled away.

Mrs. Helen Bryant, whose well-known chicken and pig farm on Whitton Road was victimized at least twice, posted a $25 reward for the apprehension and conviction of those responsible. While conducting a heist on another farm, the hoodlums decamped quickly amid a hail of buckshot. The chicken-nappings remained unsolved.[83]

### Brief Accounts

On July 26, 1923, a recent visitor at the Sheridan House, a Mr. Brown, was arrested in Boston and charged with stealing registered packages from the mail. The evidence had been found in his Wolfeboro hotel room.

On June 7, 1924, it was reported that Arthur Keenan of Wolfeboro, drunk and traveling at high speed in his automobile, was chased 145 miles over country roads by State Inspector Jonas R. Welcome, who finally captured him in Sanbornton. He was haled into Police Court in Concord, pleaded guilty, and was sentenced to 60 days and costs.[84]

In October 1924 Francis Rogers, the young son of Nathaniel Rogers, was brought before Judge Trickey at the Wolfeboro Police Court, charged as an incorrigible child, and sentenced to two years at the state industrial school, plus costs; suspended on the condition of good behavior. Two weeks before, he had fired a high-powered rifle from a half-mile away and accidentally killed Cornelius Courtley, age 70, who was picking apples in an orchard.

Vandalism of summer cottages continued to be a problem during the off seasons, especially along the shores of Lake Wentworth. A.R. Webb, a concerned reader of the local paper, suggested that the town set up a full-time police department to deal with such matters.

Early Wednesday morning, June 21, 1925, four downtown Wolfeboro businesses were burglarized: S.A. Edgerly's shoe store, Tobey's Pharmacy, Abel Haley's (men's clothing), and Charles A. Horne's (dry goods). About $550 worth of loot was taken.

On July 27, 1930, two youths came to the area, stole New York plates from a car at Alton Bay and put them on their own high-powered vehicle, ransacked the home of Mrs. Grace in East Alton, then came to Wolfeboro. They sneaked into S.A. Edgerly's shoe store and Tobey's Pharmacy on South Main Street, and the Wolfeboro Falls Garage of H.H. Hart. Police theorized the pair then fled north to cross the border to Canada.[85]

### A Local "Cowboy"

In July 19, 1924, this account was printed:

> Lester Nute of North Wolfeboro, whose particular hobby is to represent and imitate the Western cowboy, has by his actions in the past caused no little comment, as well as uneasiness, in the community by his recklessness, dressed in costume and cowboy hat, and displaying revolvers from his belt, riding his ponies and performing, but of late he has caused much uneasiness, and his business conduct has been questionable, being charged with bootlegging.
>
> Not long since at Freedom he was apprehended and some excitement was caused by his too free use of firearms, where Sheriff Leavitt attempted to arrest, and Nute fired shots and succeeded to make his escape.

It was further related that Chief of Police Lester E. Thompson succeeded in arresting him on Saturday, July 12, "after much strategy." He was discovered in East Wolfeboro when he walked into the Danvers Camp "armed to the teeth."

> Nute refused upon command of Chief Thompson to surrender, but went back to his waiting automobile to make his stand. Shots were exchanged, Nute, giving orders with a .245 calibre revolver. Great excitement prevailed, but finally Chief Thompson succeeded in capturing his man and conveyed him to the Ossipee Jail, where he will serve out his suspended sentence of 60 days for peddling booze. Nute, while in jail, has been acting strangely, possibly faking as demented, and has made attempts to injure the keeper.

It was noted that Lester Nute had broken out of his cell, had attacked the jailer, and had been put in solitary confinement. It was planned to arraign him on additional counts once his 60 days were completed. In early September Nute was brought before Judge Reed at the Carroll County Court and charged with assault upon an officer. The judge considered it best for public good that Nute remain in jail another month.[86]

Arthur F. Chamberlin commented as follows:[87]

> Lester Nute, son of A.J. and Mary (Avery) Nute, went to school with my dad at the turn of the century at the Dimon's Corner School. When he was about 16 he went west and got as far as Ohio. He came home with "cowboy" ideas. He was pretty good with a six-gun, but most of the local boys could outdo him with a rope. He wasn't really very dangerous. He had long, shoulder-length auburn hair which my grandmother said any girl would be proud to have. Lester could play most any stringed instrument left-handed. He ended up in Center Ossipee and was always a character.

## POLITICS AND POPULAR MOVEMENTS

### National Election Notes

On February 22, 1921, mill owner Stephen W. Clow and his son, Dr. Fred E. Clow, left Wolfeboro and headed to Washington to be on hand at the inauguration of Warren G. Harding.

After years of anti-Wilson invective, the editor of the local paper finally approved of a president. From Harding's election in 1920 until his death in the summer of 1923, nearly all articles about him in the *Granite State News* were of a favorable nature. When Vice President Coolidge was installed as Harding's successor, the local paper reprinted an item stating that all should have confidence in his ability.

In the 1924 presidential election Republican candidate Calvin Coolidge and his running mate Charles G. Dawes received 716 votes in Wolfeboro, compared to 301 for their Democratic opponents. The editor of the *Granite State News* commented that the Republican ticket had a clean sweep. "Let the good work continue."

Four years later, in October and early November 1928, the presidential campaign was discussed avidly in town and throughout New Hampshire. Thirty thousand photographs of Republican candidate Herbert Hoover were distributed within the state.

In the month before the election there was much publicity about Herbert Hoover and the work that he had done in the world including feeding starving citizens of Europe. For a time a serialized cartoon strip appeared showing great events in his life. Virtually nothing appeared about his opponent, Al Smith. On November 6, Wolfeboro voters cast 890 votes for Hoover and just 214 for Smith. Beginning at 7:00 p.m. nationwide election returns were aired by the National Broadcasting Company.

### Local Politics

In March 1921 a selectman was elected for the first time to a three-year term, initiating a procedure of staggered three-year tenures for each of the three officials. Each of the three seats had previously been up for grabs at the annual election.

In October 1924 Mabel Fullerton Hatch switched her party affiliation and threw her hat in the ring as the Democratic contender for Wolfeboro's representative to the General Court in Concord. In the November election she was roundly trounced and received just 345 votes, compared to 674 for Harold H. Hart, Jr. This was her first and last foray into politics.[88]

### The Ku Klux Klan

On April 5, 1924, the *Granite State News* printed this:

> The K.K.K. held its first meeting in Wolfeboro Thursday evening, April 3. Dr. Wilson of Ohio, a lecturer for the Klan, addressed a representative gathering of the residents of our town on the motives and objects of the Klan. There was a goodly number of members present at this meeting, who listened with rapt attention for nearly two hours.
>
> From his talk and explanation of method and desire, one was led to believe that every true-blooded virile American should rather favor than fear the work which this organization is endeavoring to accomplish. It is expected that in the near future there will be another general meeting in the village. If the American Constitution is correct, and the Klan is based upon it, then the Klan must be correct. If the Bible is true and it is one of the basic principles, then the Klan must be correct.

The preceding article provoked a response by David H. Harrington of West Newfield, ME, who suggested that all people read his letter "and think about it before they sound again the praises of the hooded brethren." He pointed out the KKK endeavored to harm Catholic, Jewish, and Negro citizens, committed murders in Louisiana, and recently had brutally assaulted a man in Claremont, NH, when he was investigating a fiery cross at night. He concluded by saying "there is no place in the 'land of the free and the home of the brave'—the land of Washington, Lincoln, Roosevelt and Harding—for such scurrilous bigotry."

Local interest in the KKK grew apace, and cross-burnings were reported. To advertise meetings during this era, notices reading "K.K.K. TONITE" were painted on Wolfeboro pavements.[89] On August 30, 1924, the local paper printed this:

> Last Friday evening the knights of the Ku Klux Klan held a very interesting and enthusiastic meeting at the Goodrich Farm, Center Wolfeboro. Nearly 1,000 Americans were present. King Kleagle Gayer of Rochester was the speaker of the evening. He carried the audience by storm by his statements which can be proved....
>
> A few of Dr. Gayer's statements deserve special mention. He said that the Ku Klux Klan is a truly great national organization. "It is truly American. Although we have been accused of several wrongs we have yet to be proven guilty of crime.... Truly this country needs this organization as much as it did George Washington or Abraham Lincoln," he concluded.
>
> He said that a fiery cross indicates a large number of new members. The meeting proved successful, for on the following evening a cross was burned on Wolfeboro Bay.

In January 1925 the Wolfeboro chapter of the Klan went on record approving the idea of a full-time police department.[90] On September 27, 1925, a regional meeting of the KKK was held in Lakeport and drew a large crowd.[91] In November 1928 the United States Supreme Court upheld a New York law declaring the Ku Klux Klan to be an undesirable organization.

Arthur F. Chamberlin recalled:[92]

> The Ku Klux Klan continued to meet in the Wolfeboro Center area quite a few times in the early 1930s. Most of the members wouldn't admit to belonging to the group, even in later years.

### Prohibition In Force

In the 1920s while Prohibition was in effect the Woman's Christian Temperance Union and the New Hampshire Anti-Saloon League remained very active. Meetings were often more devoted to social and entertainment aspects than to denouncing demon rum. Newspaper reports gave mixed messages as to the effectiveness of the no-alcohol amendment to the national Constitution.

One account related that in Washington, DC, arrests for drunkenness were significantly higher during the first year of Prohibition than in the year before it was adopted. Many people became drunk on medicines, hair tonics, and other items containing alcohol. In Wolfeboro, many people formulated their own spirits, prompting a notice in the paper which reminded citizens that this was illegal.

Another article noted: "A lot of reckless driving of autos are chargeable to 'home brew' in our village, and several narrow escapes are reported." And: "If stories or reports are to be relied upon, the Prohibition times, insofar as our village is concerned, cannot boast an improvement over former days. The condition is nothing to be proud of."

The state of New Hampshire set up detailed regulations involving the production and sale of apple cider, noting that quantities that could be possessed by an individual were limited, and that cider should be "sweet," not fermented. Alcohol abuse was said to be on the increase, not only locally but nationally.[93]

The fact that Prohibition had been in effect in Wolfeboro for many years did not deter certain townspeople from trafficking in liquor. This account appeared on August 28, 1926:

> Sheriff Dinsmore and his deputies, assisted by state law enforcement agent Mr. Caswell, swooped down on the Sheridan House Thursday evening and raided for intoxicating liquor. About 10 gallons of hooch were found. Mr. [Isaac] Allbee was haled into court at 11:00 p.m. and upon a plea of guilty to sale of intoxicating liquor was fined $200 and costs and given a jail sentence of 60 days, suspended. Perley Abbott, upon a like plea, was fined $200 and costs of $23 and given a suspended jail sentence.

## PRICES IN 1930

The following prices and related items are from advertisements and notices in the *Granite State News.*

**Appliance:** Frigidaire electric refrigerator, $157.50 f.o.b. factory in Dayton.

**Automobiles:** Chevrolet roadster, $495; sport roadster, $525. Buick, $1,260 to $2,070. Marquette (made by Buick), $990 to $1,060. Ford roadster, $435; DeLuxe Coupe, $550; DeLuxe Sedan $650.

**Cigarettes:** Old Gold, "Not a cough in a carload," carton, $1.15.

**Clothesline:** 50 feet, 35¢.

**Clothing:** Men's: Golf hose, pair, 20¢. Shirt, Arrow brand, white $1.95, colors, $2.15.

**Entertainment:** 65-mile cruise aboard the *Mt. Washington,* adults, $1; children, 50¢. Movie tickets, evening: adults, 40¢; children, 20¢.

**Food:** Beverages: Cocoa, Hershey's, 2.5 pounds, 25¢. Milk, quart, 16¢.

**Food:** Various: Bread flour, 24.5-pound bag, 99¢. Bread, large loaf, 10¢. Cereal, Kellogg's Corn Flakes, box, 8¢. Crisco shortening, 1-pound can, 25¢. Gingersnaps, 2 pounds, 25¢. Honey, 5-ounce jar, 14¢. Jell-O, three packages, 25¢. Mincemeat, Nonesuch brand, 18-ounce can, 19¢. Mother's Oats with a piece of china inside (a popular promotion), large 55-ounce package, 33¢. Pickles, sour or dill, quart, 31¢. Rice cereal, 2 packages, 27¢. Sardines, three cans, 29¢. Soup, Campbell's Tomato, can, 7¢. Spaghetti noodles, large package, 27¢. Sugar, 10 pounds, 53¢.

**Fuel:** Cordwood, maple, oak and birch, cord, delivered, $12.50. Gasoline, Socony brand, gallon, 18.1¢.

**Haircuts:** Ladies' and children's, 25¢.

**Horse rental:** Saddle horse rental at Birchmont Camps, per hour, $1.25.

**Paint:** Quart of flat, wall, 90¢; quart of floor enamel, $1.

**Soap:** Camay, per cake, 5¢; Palmolive, 3 bars, 19¢.

**Telephone:** Cost for connecting an extension in house, $2.

**Toilet paper:** Roll, 7¢.

**Truck:** Chevrolet 1 1/2 ton with cab $625.

# CHAPTER 6

# WOLFEBORO 1931-1940

*[Wolfeboro is] the best place under the sun to live and the poorest place to die; because, whatever happiness we might find in the next world, we cannot help thinking how pleasant it would be to walk down Main Street a fine spring morning and greet all the neighbors and friends, hear the birds sing in the trees, glance at the flowers growing in the yards, and see the fine old New England houses....*

– *Granite State News*, February 11, 1938.

## INTRODUCTION

The decade of the 1930s began with optimism. It was widely felt that the Depression, as it came to be called, was just temporary and that prosperity was literally "just around the corner." Recovery did not happen, however, and by 1933 the local economy touched its low spot. Notwithstanding, conditions in Wolfeboro, with its tourist-based businesses, were much better than in many other New England towns, especially those which depended upon manufacturing.

Toward the end of the decade growth started again. However, enthusiasm was dampened by the specter of Hitler on the horizon, as Nazi troops rolled through Poland, Czechoslovakia, and other European countries. By 1940 the inevitability of America's involvement in World War II was the main topic of concern.

## WITH THE NEWSPAPER

### The *Granite State News*

In August 1931 Gertrude B. (Mrs. Lloyd) Hamm joined the staff of the *Granite State News* as a bookkeeper and assistant to the editor.[1] She wrote much during the 1930s including the "Personalagraphs" column of local news.

Mabel Fullerton Hatch's "Goose Quills" column continued its popularity, as did columns ranging from stamps, agriculture, and the Garden Club, to the doings at Carpenter School as written by L. Winston Hamm, son of Gertrude. Beginning in 1931 a new feature, "The Retrospector's Column," discussed local history and appeared intermittently. Charles E. Stevens, owner of the Point Breeze Camps on Lake Wentworth, was a prolific letter-writer to the paper, especially during the winter when he was at his home in Queens Village, NY, or on vacation in Florida.

Poems were often published, not only in this decade, but in others, and rhapsodized on diverse subjects including Lake Winnipesaukee, summertime, and New England, or specialized topics such as Camp Wyanoke, the demolition of the Sheridan House stable, and memories of leading citizens.

In March 1933 the *Granite State News* business office rented for 5¢ a day Jo-Jig brand jigsaw puzzles cut from wood. There was a nationwide craze for assembling puzzles at the time, and over 200 firms turned them out.[2]

In 1935 the paper had about 1,200 out-of-town subscribers in addition to its local readers.

On August 30, 1937, Frederick W. Prindle, who had been editor since the death of his father-in-law, Charles H. Parker, on November 24, 1876, passed away at his home in Wolfeboro Falls, thus closing an era.

In the October 15, 1937, issue Rev. Orman T. Headley, minister at the First Christian Church for the preceding eight years, gave his greetings as new editor. Born on a cotton plantation in Alabama, Headley founded a newspaper in West Virginia years later and was editor of another paper in the same state. Victor W. Hodge, son-in-law of Prindle, became owner and publisher. A new Model 8 Blue Streak Linotype machine was used for the first time to set the December 25 edition.

Reverend-Editor Headley did not take kindly to a religious group whose members came to town in autumn 1938, as reflected by this comment in the November 11 issue:

> Jehovah's Witnesses are beginning to conduct a campaign here. They are traveling in a red car with amplifiers to help

Downtown Wolfeboro from the air in the 1930s. In both views the steamer *Mount Washington* is seen near the Town Docks.

throw their voices. This is the sect that teaches their children not to salute the flag. This fact and traveling in a red car and making loud noises are three facts that make them look like communists.

Headley resigned with the issue of December 30, 1938, having been in the editor's chair for slightly more than a year.[3]

The ownership and editorship then passed to Ralph G. Carpenter, 2nd (a.k.a. Jr. and II), grandson of the late George A. Carpenter. The plant of the *Carroll County Independent* in Center Ossipee, now partly owned by Carpenter, was utilized for printing. More news photos began to be published. In April the editorial offices were moved from Wolfeboro Falls to downtown, overlooking the town wharf. For the next three decades, Parker M. Merrow of Ossipee wrote most of the editorials.

### A Marvelous Discovery

One of the most interesting items to appear in the *News* in the 1930s was this article about the history of the area:

> What is believed to be part of the British Man-o-War *Fearless* that nearly 200 years ago patrolled the waters of Lake Winnipesaukee has been found on Alpine Island, located about five miles west of Wolfeboro.... Captain Edward Lavallee of the mailboat *Marshall Foch* and a crew of men were at work driving piling for a new wharf at Old Wrecks Harbor, when near the shoreline they unearthed the skeleton of this submerged old derelict with the nameplate FEARLESS across its prow.
>
> Further investigation revealed several old muskets and cutlasses and a large cannon deeply imbedded in the sand. The small vessel, history says, patrolled the waters of the lake under the command of Sir Alton Wolfeborough. The craft mysteriously disappeared shortly after the colonists declared their independence from the mother country. The lake towns of Alton and Wolfeborough, it is said, derived their names from Sir Alton Wolfeborough.

Apparently, this "history" had appeared as a factual item in the *Boston Globe*. The editor of the *Granite State News* suggested that perhaps there would be an account next week in the *Globe* telling of the finding of Caesar's flagship in Roberts Cove in Lake Winnipesaukee, and it would be disclosed that The Weirs, Centre Harbor, and Meredith were really named after the commodore's wife and two children![4]

Somewhat related was this note of levity in the July 28, 1939 issue:

> Great excitement when a car drove on Main Street with a number plate purporting to be from Cairo, Egypt, complete with hieroglyphics and a picture of the Sphinx. Great disappointment when the driver said he bought the plate in Maine for 19¢. Such is life for a newshawk.

## ECONOMICS AND POLITICS

### The Economy, 1931-1932

The economic condition of America was the number one topic on everyone's mind during the 1930s. In 1931 Herbert Hoover was in the White House and made frequent statements that the business slump was just temporary. Nationally syndicated columnist Arthur Brisbane had this to say in the *Granite State News* on May 22, 1931:

> If in search of encouraging thoughts, try this: In 1929 our great minds assured us that the Depression wouldn't last; everything would be going sweetly in the spring of 1930. They were wrong. Now some change from excessive optimism to excessive pessimism, predicting a long depression. perhaps they are wrong again. Once wrong, twice wrong is often the rule.

In 1931 the Depression was mentioned rarely, if at all, in local context. Life and business went on as usual in Wolfeboro. Most people who wanted work found it and for six days a week. Orville F. Porter, local hardware merchant in the Folsom Block, was doing a land office business installing Williams Oil-O-Matic furnaces, 20 units by mid-October. The Paper Store, Tobey's Pharmacy, and other local enterprises did well. Electricity use was a measure of economic well-being, and in 1931 the Electric Department increased its assets by $12,500.

On the national scene, however, it was a different story. Millions were thrown out of work, and there was vast suffering. This came home to Wolfeboro shortly thereafter. The town took care of its own, so to speak, and in December this was reported in the local paper:

> In order to relieve the unemployment condition to some extent, many have been given work upon our highways such as cleaning gutters and roadsides and several instances widening curves and recoating our gravel sidewalks.

With markets declining, prices also fell. Locally, new Fords and Chevys were cheaper in 1931 than they had been a couple years earlier. On June 15 First National Stores stated that average retail grocery prices had dropped 36% since 1927.

In March 1932 the American Legion reported good success in "finding jobs for men and men for jobs." Post Commander Ted Sturgis urged local citizens and businesses to contact him if they had work to be done. In June the local paper discussed the advantages of planting "subsistence gardens" to help with food, particularly items that could be stored for future use.

On June 17, 1932, this was printed:

> Not very large crews are working anywhere, but a few local men working here and there means a great many in the aggregate. We looked into a few offices a day or two ago and learned that Horne's Garage had nine men at work as well as one young lady; at H.H. Wallace's there are two men employed the year 'round and three extra in the summer; Harry Graham employs seven men in the summer and three in the winter—they have just unloaded a carload of Star cement. There are 12 East Wolfeboro men and some women at Birchmont. The Wolfeboro Lumber Company has four employees at present.

This on August 5, 1932:

Plummer Eldridge is picking blueberries for a living. Plummer says that he has got to get a living some way. We wish that there was more work in our town. What are men with large families going to do this winter?

Enter the rabbit. Well known for its prolific powers of multiplication, it could well mean prosperity for anyone lucky enough to possess a pair. In January 1932 E.H. Leonard and Harry Cotton (a Wolfeboro native) were in town representing the Lehigh Packing Company of Esmus, PA, to establish a district branch for the sale of these creatures to prospective investors, who could then reap up to $200 in monthly profits from their meat and fur. Not just any rabbit, mind you, but the Cloverdell White offered by Lehigh. A special exhibit was set up on North Main Street at the Estabrook sporting goods store. Unfortunately, financial paradise was lost. In May the local paper revealed that the proposition was simply a "gold brick scheme of promoters."[5]

This upbeat item appeared on August 19:

Cotton Valley: We seem to have heard that there is a world-wide lack of jobs, but we are glad to say that the conditions do not apply here. We counted 14 men at the chicken factory at Cotton Mountain Farm, not to mention the others who were engaged in carrying the birds to the slaughter house. A sawmill has started cutting up the trees blown down by the recent tornado so that some of our men have found jobs there. Berries of all kinds are waiting in the fields for the pickers. Red Farm has found the fruit business needs an extra man, and the Magouns are starting a rock garden in the near future.

At a special town meeting in September, voters accepted a loan of $4,431 from the state for road construction, which was utilized to improve the route leading from Wolfeboro to Tuftonboro via Pine Hill (called 109A today).[6]

### The Local Economy, 1933-1940

The year 1933 was the low point for business nationally and also in town. Nothing like it had ever been seen before in Wolfeboro. Hundreds were out of work, and many more were idle at least part of the week. Local businesses folded. This January 20 news item is typical: "South Wolfeboro: The garage has closed for an indefinite period due to lack of business." In February the editor of the *News* suggested that in the absence of finding work, his readers go fishing.

On March 6, 1933, recently-inaugurated President Franklin Delano Roosevelt ordered all banks in the United States to close. The Wolfeboro National Bank complied. Then this happened:

The Chamber of Commerce swiftly went into action and at its regular meeting Monday evening arranged the use of scrip [privately printed paper "currency" notes] among the townspeople. Early Tuesday morning it was ready for distribution, and approximately $150 worth was exchanged for checks, this amount being divided among many persons.

Wolfeboro was the first town in the state to put such a system in operation during this emergency. When the bank is authorized to open for business again, the checks in the hands of the Chamber of Commerce will be exchanged for cash, which they in turn will use to retire this scrip.

E.H. Trickey was appointed conservator of the local bank, which was found to have an insufficient amount of capital in relation to its deposits, although there was no danger of insolvency. The Boston office of the Comptroller of the Currency reviewed the bond portfolio, which had diminished in value, and stated at first that $25,000 additional capital was needed, after which the requirement was ratcheted upward until it reached $278,000. The bank raised $145,000 locally and sold $123,000 worth of preferred stock to the Reconstruction Finance Corporation, a government agency started by President Herbert Hoover.[7] Finally, with adequate capital the Wolfeboro National Bank reopened on March 22. In order to prevent a "run" by scared depositors, withdrawals from savings accounts were for a time restricted to $10 per transaction with a maximum of $50 per month.[8]

Continuing to help its own citizens, the town placed this advertisement on April 7, 1933:

Attention: Free seeds, fertilizer and land to plant on. Head of the family needing seeds, fertilizer or land on which to plant may obtain them free by communicating with the selectmen. Stephen W. Clow, Ralph S. Parker, Sherman D. Brummitt.

Subsequently, it was stated that no record would be kept of the people applying for assistance, and the *Town Report* would only carry the cost of seeds and fertilizer—thus preserving anonymity.

This cheery note was printed on October 20, 1933: "It seems good to hear the familiar sounds of the excelsior machines operating at the Berry Excelsior Mill these days." By the waning months of the year, federal money was helping the local economy, as per this notice of December 22:

There are two crews of 11 men each picking browntail moth nests along the roadways of Wolfeboro. This is a federal project for benefit of the unemployed. The state is giving Wolfeboro $1,250 for work between the Hersey Cemetery and the Tuftonboro line, and 30 men are at work there.

For those who did not have cash to spend, barter was available. In January 1934 the Used Furniture Shop at Ellis Farm, North Main Street, advertised, "We'll exchange for potatoes."[9]

By the end of 1934 the local economy had improved greatly. In the summer there was actually *prosperity*. In winter, jobs remained scarce, but things were looking up. Nationally, in March and April 1935 it was reported that the car industry was doing well.

In 1936 work on the new Post Office was underway downtown, there was a demand for new homes and lake cottages, and local business in the winter was nearly as good as in "the good old days," and in the summer was better than ever. Still, most Wolfeboro residents fixed

Cobham Hall on Green Street was the palatial summer residence of George A. Carpenter and, later, his descendants. Built in 1892, at one time it was considered to be the most luxurious residence in Wolfeboro. In 1905 Carpenter convinced the town of Wolfeboro to grant him possession of the right-of-way of the end of Green Street, but the town reserved the right to get it back should it ever wish to do so; as of the 1990s this option has not been exercised.

House-moving Wolfeboro style: a residence being moved across the water of Lake Winnipesaukee, early twentieth century. (Melanson Collection)

up their old cars instead of buying new ones, bought used furniture, and scrimped and saved. The demand for old rags and junk was so great "that women can't find enough cloth to patch their husbands' pants," the paper commented in May 1936.

On June 12, 1936, the *News* reported that all of the men in South Wolfeboro were employed. Nevertheless, there continued to be ups and downs on the business scene. In 1937 the Wolfeboro National Bank threatened to sell the Goodhue & Hawkins Navy Yard at auction unless Nathaniel Goodhue and Chester E. Hawkins could honor mortgage commitments. Apparently, the situation was resolved privately.

In February 1938 it was reported that the town's 1937 fiscal year was improved over the preceding period. In the private sector many new homes and cottages were being built by Andrew F. Doe, Fred Varney, and others. The O.P. Berry Co. and Gardner Pad Co. excelsior mills were running full bore, and the local lumber industry was booming.

Rev. Orman T. Headley, editor of the *Granite State News*, recommended that growing drug plants could become a profitable local enterprise. "There are 178 plants that produce drugs in one form or another, while it is found that most if not all of these can be grown right here.... Three of the most common of these plants have been grown here for generations: peppermint, sage, and horehound." In addition, he suggested that lemon balm, hemp (marijuana), hyssop, catnip, basil, chamomile, thyme, lavender, sweet marjoram, caraway, and burnet could be raised with ease.

Whether marijuana was allowed to be cultivated in the Town Gardens was not stated, but it was noted that in recent years about two dozen people had been raising vegetables there, and in the previous summer about 500 bushels of potatoes had been harvested. This facility had been instituted during World War I.

In 1938 the government reported that 17 out of 20 families in New England had a refrigerator, and that 60% of these units were cooled by block ice, although mechanical refrigeration was becoming increasingly popular.

In December 1938 the *Granite State News* reported: "Merchants are saying that judging from the holiday trade this Christmas season has been much better than for many years now.... The children's stockings were filled."[10]

The Chamber of Commerce was very active. In 1931, in the face of the national Depression that was becoming increasingly real at home, the slogan, "Help build Wolfeboro" was used by members in advertising. Early in 1933 the group changed its name to the Wolfeboro Development Association.[11] It was felt that in this year, at the depth of the now very real Depression, the town needed development.

In January 1935 both Harold H. Hart, founding president of the group, and Miss Mildred Avery, founding secretary, retired after nine years of service. Hardware dealer Clayton M. Wallace was named president.

### The Factory Street Headache

The town continued to own two large and often vacant wooden structures on Factory Street. The one at the western end was known as the Bell Shop (occasionally as the Little Shop or Little Factory now that it was just a fraction of its former size), and the one near the middle of the street was referred to as the Clark Shop, although it, too, was sometimes called the Little Factory, especially in the earlier years of the century. In a game resembling musical chairs, businesses with out-of-town ownership would be wooed by the townspeople and the Chamber of Commerce, would demand concessions, promise much, but eventually renege, and businesses would mysteriously close or go bankrupt. The view of many citizens was expressed in this comment in the local paper in 1933:[12]

> The general impatience of the town with a long succession of shoe firms that has filed through the local shops, each demanding concessions and remaining hardly more than long enough to get them, was expressed by Tracy Abbott and highly endorsed by many others who feel that the expense of the concessions is hardly compensated by added prosperity.

In 1931 the Chamber of Commerce and the town met with officials of the Holland Brothers Shoe Co. of Derry, offered incentives, and helped them raise money. The firm stated it would be in operation in the second week of February in the Clark Shop, but by August no shoes were being turned out. It is believed that the company finally operated, but only briefly.

In November 1931 the Bell Brothers' Wolfeboro Shoe Company, which had been operating since 1923 in the Bell Shop, served notice to the town that it was going to close and move its equipment to Maine. Nearly 100 employees would be thrown out of work. The Chamber and Precinct officials came up with a financial package, and the doors stayed open. In early 1933 the Bell Shop received a boost at the expense of several towns in Maine, when the firm closed down three plants in that state and gave the orders to the Wolfeboro factory. By March 1933 one hundred and forty shoe workers were employed there.

The Wolfeboro Shoe Company prospered during most of the rest of the decade. In June 1934 it employed 130 workers who drew a payroll totaling $2,000 per week and turned out McKay brand shoes. Sales were through Sears, Roebuck & Co. and other outlets, some as far away as South America. On April 21, 1938, manager Harvey Vincent Bell died. Scarcely a week before, the enterprise had been sold to Samuel S. Shapiro of Boston. The factory under Shapiro stayed open until March of the next year when it suddenly shut down "for the taking of inventory." Employees were told that the Bell Shop would reopen, but it did not. Year in and year out, veracity was not a common attribute of Wolfeboro shoe company owners and managers.

Meanwhile, the Clark Shop remained vacant. A special Precinct meeting was called on April 28, 1933, to discuss shoe firms which were considering moving into it. One contender demanded free rent, light, heat and power from the town for a period of three years. Meanwhile, the town offered no such concessions to any potential or existing tourist or mercantile businesses.

In early April of 1938 representatives of a cotton sheet factory were in town to inquire about buying the still vacant Clark Shop. Nothing came of the idea. On January 8, 1940, the Wolfeboro Development Association held an open meeting to address the problem of finding tenants for both empty shoe factories. On October 28, 1940, over 400 people turned out to hear a presentation by the newly-formed Lyons-Patch Company, composed of John E. Lyons, a former shoe salesman for the Endicott-Johnson Company, and Roy Patch, an experienced manufacturing manager.[13] Nothing happened.

In March 15, 1940, a tenant finally was found for two floors of the four-story Clark Shop. The New Hampshire Fibercraft Company, based in Center Ossipee, hired 150 men and 15 trucks and made the move of equipment in one day. The firm employed eight men and made children's furnishings including hampers, bassinets, and chairs.

## ENTERTAINMENT

### At Home

Just about every home had a radio set to furnish instant entertainment day and evening. Early in the decade several local shops sold "cathedral" type sets in fancy consoles, costing several hundred dollars each or more. However, by 1933-1934, the realities of the national economy intervened, and most radios cost from $25 to $75 and were of simple design.

The majority of Wolfeboro residents probably had their RCA, Philco, or other set turned on every evening. Static and poor reception were problems discussed frequently in the local paper, and it was suggested that electric motors and other devices that caused interference should be banned by law.

Among regular programs, *Amos and Andy* was undoubtedly the most popular. The autumn brought mixed blessings, with many local listeners protesting against the seemingly endless babble of political candidates.

Phonographs continued their popularity but played second fiddle to the radio. By the 1930s phonograph cylinders were no longer being made, and all records were of the disc type. Several local stores sold the latest tunes. Wurlitzer, Mills, and Seeburg jukeboxes were just beginning to become popular in a big way, at 5¢ a play.

In July 1940 Gould's Dime Store published the latest list of hits on Bluebird Records, with *Fools Rush In*, by Glenn Miller, being number one. Other titles were *The Breeze and I, Make Believe Island, Playmates, Where Was I?, The Woodpecker's Song, Sierra Sue, Imagination,* and *I'll Never Smile Again.*

Popular card games included whist and, in particular, contract bridge, with several local citizens, Joseph I. Melanson, Jr., Frederick A. Richardson, and Roland L. Murray, achieving statewide recognition in bridge.

### Join the Club

In the 1930s there was no lack of civic, scholastic, fraternal, and religious societies and clubs to attend.

In May of 1937 the following met regularly, as per a notice in the paper:

> Wolfeboro Development Association; Wolfeboro Group, Arts and Crafts; Lake Shore Grange; Woman's Christian Temperance Union; American Legion and Auxiliary; Order of the Eastern Star; Rotary Club; Myrtle Rebekah Lodge No. 48; Morning Star AF & AM No. 17; Carroll Chapter R.A.M.; Knights of Pythias; Boy Scouts; Cub Scouts; International Order of Odd Fellows; Order of the Rainbow; Winnipesaukee Chapter Order of De Molay; and Woman's Club.

This list omitted numerous church groups, the Wolfeboro Historical Society, groups at the Brewster Free Academy, the Model Railroad Club, the Village Players, and others.

Among these was the Panology Club for those interested in medicine, archaeology, and other intellectual pursuits. In the spring of 1938 business and professional women in town organized a club, name not given in the local paper, with Miss Frances Puffer (superintendent of Huggins Hospital) as president, and, among various other designations, Mabel Fullerton Hatch as chairman of the Committee on International Relations. Wide-ranging activities were contemplated.[14]

### On the Screen

Throughout the decade Ansel N. Sanborn continued to show films on the second floor of the Brewster Memorial Hall (Town Hall). Programs changed weekly, and scheduling depended upon the season with more shown in the summer than in the winter. In mid-January 1931 shows were cut to one a week on Saturday, due to reduced attendance. However, a few months later, the standard two-per-week schedule was resumed, followed by shows three days a week in the summer.

A typical program included a feature film accompanied by a short or two or a serial episode. For much of the middle and late 1930s Wednesday was Bank Night,

Elvira Avery, her husband Howard Clifton Avery, their children Mary and Katherine, and their dog Nippy in their new home on South Main Street, 1937. For many years Howard was with the family business, the J. Clifton Avery Insurance Agency. Elvira (née Zulauf) was active in many local organizations and projects.

when movie patrons could register for a drawing to win cash, typically $25 to $100. This was so popular that Wednesday evenings were often standing room only. On January 15, 1936, the second largest audience ever gathered in the theatre (largest was for a Will Rogers picture earlier) was on hand to see Robert Tutt win $85.

In May 1931 an RCA Photophone sound system was installed to replace the earlier apparatus.[15] For much of the decade, Sanborn made numerous pleas to show movies on Sunday, but local ministers (in particular) objected.[16] Finally, in March 1937 Sunday films were allowed.

Sample movie news items:

**1932, summer. Another theatre:** Sound motion pictures were shown in Clark Memorial Hall (the remodeled Wolfborough and Tuftonborough Academy building). However, Brewster Memorial Hall continued to be the primary local screening place.

**1933, March 10-11. "Technivision":** New process projected images on the screen at the Town Hall, featuring action and sounds photographed and instantly transmitted to a projector by wire. Shown were local people. "It is possible for the artists to remain at any convenient point and transmit the program to whatever location the spectators choose—another public hall, or even to individual firesides, as radio." Technical details were not given.

**1933, November 11. Mae West:** On the screen at Memorial Hall in *I'm No Angel,* said to be "direct from its big city showings where it has been breaking more box office records than any other picture ever made."

**1934, January 6. Program:** Stan Laurel and Oliver Hardy in *Sons of the Desert,* seven reels. Also *The Three Little Pigs,* and *Who's Afraid of the Big Bad Wolf?* —the latter said to be Walt Disney's most popular Silly Symphony.

**1935, May. Program:** Mid-month program included on May 18, Mae West in *Goin' to Town;* on May 22, Rudy Vallee in *Sweet Music;* and on May 25, Shirley Temple in *Our Little Girl.*

**1935, July 17. Overflow:** The Temple Auditorium, used as a movie theatre years earlier, before Memorial Hall Theatre had been set up, was again pressed into service to handle overflow crowds and was now called The Little Theatre. In addition, it had its own film program on some days.[17] The arrangement was continued intermittently for many years.

**1936, July 13 and 14. Program:** Clark Gable and Jeanette MacDonald in *San Francisco.* Next, Shirley Temple appeared in *The Poor Little Rich Girl.*

**1937, June 11. Air cooling:** Four blowers had been installed to throw 20,000 cubic feet of fresh air into the Memorial Hall Theatre each minute.

**1938, June 11 and 12. Hi-yo Silver!:** *The Adventures of Robin Hood* with Erroll Flynn was on the screen. *The Lone Ranger* and his horse Silver appeared as a weekly serial.

**1938, September 2. Wolfeboro first:** "The Boston city editor of the *Globe,* in conversation with Mrs. Gertrude Hamm last Friday evening, stated that a picture now showing in Wolfeboro had not yet been shown in Boston. He stated that such was often the case."

**1939, November 29-30. Local "stars":** A short film, *World's Fair Junior,* featured "Wolfeboro stars Barbara Harvey and Maurice Wilkinson, Jr.... See these kiddies perform in the movies as you have seen them in person. They will win your heart again."

**1940, January 27-28. Newsreel:** *Republic of Finland,* the latest *March of Time* newsreel, "the pictorial story of the brave and unyielding people of Finland—today desperately fighting for their lives!" As the war ravaged in Europe, film dispatches were screened weekly.

Nathalie Erickson remembered the motion picture theatre in the Town Hall as it was in the 1930s:[18]

> As kids, we used to tramp up the stairs to the theatre. There was a balcony to the theatre, too. We did have a fire up in there one time. It wasn't too serious. The balcony was very hot. Sometimes, those in the balcony would throw popcorn on those in the seats below.
>
> We had movies all summer long, and the theatre was very popular. There were two shows, 7 and 9 in the evening. This schedule went on for years and years. Often, there would be long lines in front of the Town Hall, of people waiting to get in. I guess that today it would be considered a firetrap, but then we did not think about this.
>
> The seats were permanently fixed to the floor and were covered with red leather or similar material. They were very comfortable. The screen was up on the stage. The stage itself was used for many other purposes, such as shows. Merrill Rich presented ballets there, for example. It is sad that the movies are not there anymore, as we all enjoyed them a lot.

Films would sometimes be shown at other Wolfeboro locations, but none on a steady basis or with first-run features. Other in-town projection facilities included the Wolfeboro Casino, Clark Memorial Hall, Ann Inn, Temple Auditorium, and Brewster Academy. Outside Wolfeboro the nearest movie houses were Pineland in Center Ossipee, the Opera House in Alton, and the Opera House in Sanbornville, all managed by Ansel Sanborn.

### Before the Footlights

Brewster Academy students, church groups, and lodges continued to give plays, orations, concerts, and other programs. Due to the increasing popularity of movies at Memorial Hall, radio programs, and the financial constraints of the economy, stage presentations were fewer in the 1930s than before.

Among popular attractions were plays staged at the Temple Auditorium by The Barnstormers, a touring summer repertory theatre group under the direction of Francis G. Cleveland, son of President Grover Cleveland. Each summer a half-dozen different productions would be given in Wolfeboro on as many different weeks. Beginning in 1931, the troupe also played at its own headquarters theatre in Tamworth. Years later the shows were presented only in Tamworth.

### Entertainment Chronicle

Minstrel shows, circuses, and other traveling companies occasionally came to town but not as frequently as in earlier years. Circuses arrived by truck motorcade (no longer by railroad) were usually set up under canvas in a field off South Main Street, and contained fewer animals and performers than in years past.

The Wolfeboro Casino, billed as "a beauty spot on Lake Winnipesaukee," was a focal point for young and old alike. Owned by Ansel N. Sanborn and managed by Norris R. Sanborn, it offered dancing during the summer, four bowling alleys in operation all year long, and occasional movies.

Below is a cross-section of entertainment in Wolfeboro during the decade:

**1931, February 23. Winter Carnival:** Included a film, basketball game, hike, costume ball, and sports events. Limited events were held, but slush made it difficult for winter sports to be enjoyed.

**1931, June 2. Cowboys and Indians:** Allen Brothers Wild West Show exhibited on Stephen W. Clow's lot.

**1931, July 4. Celebration:** The American Legion staged its eighth annual Fourth of July celebration. Events included a baseball game (First National Stores of Boston vs. the Harry Harriman Post of the American Legion; 2 to 1 in favor of the visitors), band concert, motorboat races, and parade.[19]

**1931, July 14. Circus:** The Walter L. Main Circus returned to Wolfeboro for the first time in several seasons.

**1931, July 24. Stage show:** The Barnstormers were on the boards at the Temple Auditorium with *Ghost Train*. "The same trains and the same bodies will roar and fall, while equally green and horrid faces will look and see that all is well."

**1931, July. First art exhibit claim:** An art exhibit billed as the first ever held in Wolfeboro was staged at the Hotel Elmwood and featured 16 watercolors by Aaron Burkman and landscapes and portraits in oils by Micheal (*sic*) Gerard.

**1931, November 24. Frolic:** Wolfeboro teachers held a Depression Party at Carpenter School. Guests wore old clothes. Games included Murder, crossword puzzles, charades, and a blindfold jumping contest. Sandwiches were served in brown paper bags, coffee in tin cups.

**1932, January. Wolfeboro Band:** New group using the old Wolfeboro Band name was formed, with Alcide Bilodeau of Rochester as consultant. Otis Sargent, local electrician, was president. By July 1932 there were 30 members. Concerts were held regularly, including one on the roof of the Goodwin Block on South Main Street, under the leadership of Charles Downs, earlier of the Barnum & Bailey and U.S. Fifth Infantry bands. In August 1933 Otto Fritzsche, who lived on Cotton Mountain, was leader and continued for the next year or two, after which he was succeeded by C.M. Wilkinson of Lakeport.[20]

**1932, August 14. Afloat:** An excursion aboard the *Mount Washington* took place in the late afternoon and early evening from the Town Docks, representative of many lake trips of the era.

**1932, September 10. Circus:** The Wheeler & Sautelle Circus was scheduled to exhibit on the Clark Estate lot on South Main Street. "Reduced admission price of 35¢ for adults and 25¢ for children. The largest motorized circus in America."

**1932, October 13. Magic show:** Daigle, a magician billed as the "greatest since Houdini," gave a three-hour performance featuring ropes, chains, handcuffs, shackles, cages, boxes, etc., heralded by this attraction: "See Daigle escape from straight-jacket while suspended from roof of the Peavey Block at 12:45 p.m." Tickets to the stage show were 25¢ and 35¢ for adults, children 15¢. While in town, Daigle was clapped into the town jail cell by Chief of Police Sturgis while 100 people crowded around to watch. He was free in moments, to the amazement of all, as no prisoner had ever escaped before.[21]

**1933, January 1. Band concert:** Marches, overtures, waltzes, and familiar melodies were played by 80 men from bands in Freedom, Farmington, Conway, Barnstead, Laconia, Wolfeboro, and elsewhere.

**1933, January 26. Show and dance:** At the Temple Auditorium the musical comedy, *The Count of Unoware,* and a dance were held for the benefit of the Knights of Pythias. Admission: 40¢.

**1933, February 20. Minstrel show:** Temple Auditorium under the auspices of the American Legion. Done in blackface with Southern comedy routines.

**1933, February 23. "Depression Supper":** Congregational Church. Roast pork, cold boiled ham, mashed potatoes, gravy, applesauce, coffee and baked Indian pudding. "Those of us who attended did not seem to mind the Depression so much that night," a review noted.

**1933, August 29. Gilbert & Sullivan musical:** *Pirates of Penzance* on stage at the Temple Auditorium with a local cast under the direction of Leopold Damrosch from Newark, NJ, who with members of his musically-talented family lived on Little Mud Island in Lake Winnipesaukee during the summer.

**1933, December 30 to January 1, 1934. New Year's celebration:** Three-day festival with many events. A mock town meeting on January 1, moderated by Mabel Fullerton Hatch, offered a "town warrant" including these items: Article 6: "To see if the town will vote to raise $200 for the purpose of consolidating the Public Bathing Beach with the water trough at Goose Corner." Article 11: "To see if the town will vote to extend the official summer season from April 1 to December 31 annually."

**1934, December 28. Firemen's evening:** Firemen's New Year's supper and dance on the second floor of the Engine Hall in South Wolfeboro. Admission 50¢.

**1935, February 6. Merwin Horn:** Gave a talk titled "Stroboscopic Light and High-Speed Motion Picture Photography" at the Christian Church. Horn, a talented technician and aviator, worked as a projectionist at the Massachusetts Institute of Technology.

**1935, April. Hobby show:** During the last week of April the first hobby show in Wolfeboro took place at the Christian Church. Exhibits included Indian relics (including "the largest collection of Indian pottery ever found in New Hampshire," recently found locally), figures of elephants, old photographs, historical glass flasks, woven goods, camping and sports goods, model trains and airplanes, and political memorabilia.[22]

**1935, June 10. Stage play:** The stage comedy *Oh, Doctor!* was presented at the Temple Auditorium by the Combined Glee Clubs of Brewster Free Academy.

**1935, August 3. Theremin concert:** Demonstrated at the Baptist Church by Pearl Young, earlier with the Pryor Band, the electronic Theremin "produces a delightful music at the will of the player without any mechanical means or any personal contact, simply by the gestures of the artist's hands in the air."

**1935, August 19.** Kay Brothers Circus.

**1935, August. Organ grinder:** A hand-cranked organ was played in downtown Wolfeboro. "Familiar tunes were heard on the streets, and everyone cried."[23]

**1935, August 31. Lake Wentworth Water Carnival:** Diving, swimming, rowing, and other events.

**1935, December 6. Wolfeboro Band:** Concert in Temple Auditorium. Admission 35¢.

**1936, January. Fortunes told:** At the Lake View Cabins,

Ladies at an Auxiliary dance at the American Legion Hall, 1940. Left to right: Mrs. Nellie Graves (7th grade teacher), Mary Roberts, Belle Dore, Ms. Kelley, Marylyn Moore, Louise Irish (president of the Auxiliary), Ellen (Mrs. Ed) Craigue, Eleanor Moore, Mrs. Harold Harvey, Janet Swift, and Margery Swift.

This illustration appeared in *The National Geographic Magazine,* September 1931, as part of an article by George Higgins Moses (U.S. senator from NH), "New Hampshire, the Granite State." The caption noted: "One of the projects of the Wolfeboro Historical Society is the restoration and preservation of the Clark House, built about 1790, to its original colonial style in furniture and fittings. This set of old pewter and tableware, with horn handles, is of the Revolutionary period. The hostess's fichu is more than 100 years old and belonged to her great-grandmother." The picture was by *National Geographic* staff photographer Clifton Adams, who was a house guest of Mr. and Mrs. Alonzo H. Beardsley in Wolfeboro in May 1931 while on his photographic mission.

Madam Jeroe was in residence giving card readings.

**1936, January 17. Radio talent:** "Our local boys, Earl Davis and Charles Piper, of whom we are justly proud, are making rapid strides on the road to fame with their musical radio programs. They are on the air in Laconia as 'Jack and Frost' every Tuesday night at 8:30. Last Saturday they were on a vaudeville program at the State Theatre in Manchester."[24]

**1936, January 20. Brewster on the air:** A one-act play presented by the Dramatic Club of Brewster Academy was aired over WLNH in Laconia.

**1936, February 20 and 21. Minstrel show:** Temple Auditorium. Sponsored by the American Legion.

**1936, July 4. Celebration:** Parade, etc. Gov. H. Styles Bridges gave a speech on the Brewster campus, followed by lunch at the Carr House; he came to town from Alton Bay in the *Legionnaire* speedboat.

**1936, August 9-16. Old Home Week:** Sponsored by the Wolfeboro Rotary Club. Included an amateur open golf tournament, indoor sports, beano games, hobby show, arts and crafts exhibits and sale, excursions on the *Mount Washington,* movies, sales conducted by merchants, recreation at the Wolfeboro Casino, beach activities, Libby Museum exhibits, seaplane trips, speedboat rides, special church services, picnics, baseball games, band concerts, pet show, garden parties, wrestling matches, tea party, carnival, dance, aquaplaning, and more. On August 11 Gov. H. Styles Bridges spoke at Carpenter School and dedicated a historical marker on the road near the Governor Wentworth mansion site.[25]

**1937, May 9. Concert:** The Community Chorale Society presented *The Holy City* under the direction of Mrs. Leaman E. Cunningham.

**1937, May 14. Talent show:** The Miserable Minstrels, a blackface troupe, consisted of Mrs. Ralph Horn with trombone, Leslie Brock with banjo, and Walter Hood with accordion. Harlan Kelly, Jr., entertained with harmonica, guitar, and songs. John Pollini sang songs with a "beautiful voice." Young violinists performed under Mrs. Otto Fritzsche. Melba Griffin gave a violin solo. Kenneth Craigue performed a piano solo, and Corrinne McBride danced a solo number: "The latter...was notable for the courage with which she made her appearance, with a fractured elbow held tightly to her body. The show was badly in need of a dance number, and Miss McBride came smilin' thru." Herbert Beane [also spelled as Bean] gave the *Yodeling Ranger* and other requests; he was well known as a performer on the Laconia radio station. Over a dozen others participated.[26]

**1937, July 6. Technology show:** "Previews of Progress, the World's Fair of the Future," sponsored by the General Motors Research Laboratories and earlier on view at the Century of Progress Exposition in Chicago, demonstrated electrical and other phenomena and devices at the Town Hall Theatre.

**1937, August 9. Entertainers of the airwaves:** Uncle Ezra and his Radio Barn Dance Gang came to town.

**1938, February 19-20. Winter Carnival:** Sponsored by the Abenaki Outing Club, the first such event in several years. There was little snow, thus most outdoor events were canceled.

**1938, May 15. Apple Blossom Festival:** At J. Frank Goodwin's orchard off North Main Street. Picnic lunches followed by a talk on the apple industry, planting ceremonies, local 4-H club events, singing by Wolfeboro schoolchildren and adults, and a tour of the orchard.

**1938, July 16. Circus:** Barnett Brothers Three-Ring Circus & Trained Animal Shows. Advertised to include 400 people, 35 horses, and three herds of performing elephants.

**1938, November 11. American Legion dance:** 20th Annual Armistice Ball held at the Temple Auditorium.

**1938, December 1. Village Players:** First production of the season, *The Newspaper Bride.*

**1939, March 10. Concert:** New Hampshire Federal Orchestra played at Carpenter School Auditorium, sponsored by the Cate Trust Fund Committee. This orchestra was beginning its fourth season and had been established under the New Hampshire Federal Music project, under the WPA.

**1939, July 5-7. Antiques show:** First annual Wolfeboro Antiques Exhibition and Sale was held at the Wolfeboro Casino; 20 dealers.

**1939, July 25. Circus:** Eddy Brothers Circus. Three rings including elephants, lions, bears, dogs, horses, ponies, and aerial acts.

**1939, August 25. Street music:** "One of the few things left remind us of 'the dear dead days beyond recall' is the hand organ which makes the rounds of the town each year. Children still follow the man around, just as their parents did, as he grinds out *The Sidewalks of New York."*

**1939, August 31. Bridge:** Duplicate Bridge Tournament held at the Kingswood Country Club. $2 per couple, proceeds to Huggins Hospital.

**1940, February 2-4. Winter Carnival**: Sponsored by the Abenaki Outing Club. Over 400 people participated despite poor snow conditions.

**1940, July 4. Celebration:** Parade, moving pictures, dance, concerts, fireworks, and a midway. Fireworks were on sale by the American Legion. There was local sentiment against fireworks, but a contract had been signed: "It seems best to carry on the plans that were formulated long before the tragic events of Europe had grown to such alarming proportions," a Legion spokesman noted.

**1940, July 5. Stage play:** The Barnstormers presented *The Weak Link,* a gangster farce with Allen Wood.

**1940, August 1. Refugee concert:** Viennese musicians who had fled Adolf Hitler and the Nazis presented their first American concert in Wolfeboro.

**1940, August 15. Choir concert:** The Bretton Woods Boys' Choir featured 12 youngsters. Their opening number was Sibelius' *Finlandia* in observance of the recent tragic conquest of Finland by Russia.

**1940, August 20. Flower show:** Held at the Wolfeboro Casino by the Wolfeboro Garden Club.

**1940, November 25 to December 1. Art exhibit:** Held at the Wolfeboro Library. Featured these area artists: Helen H. White, Isabelle Rector, Mildred Doe, Marion Cowan, Rev. Harry E. Shattuck, Mrs. Harry E. Shattuck, Lillian E. Hooghkirk, Norman P. Hooghkirk, Oliver E. Shattuck, Mrs. Elbridge Robie, Harold A. Harvey, Ellen H. Craigue, Harlan B. Kelley, Jr., and Donald Roberts.

## SPORTS AND RECREATION

### Abenaki Outing Club

Interest in wintertime activities grew apace in the 1930s. In the autumn of 1936 at a meeting of the Wolfeboro Development Association, Roland Peabody, a guest speaker from Franconia, related that only six years earlier there were just a couple of professional skiers and a few amateurs in that part of the White Mountains, but since then skiing had developed into a major business.

In 1935 the Abenaki Outing Club was formed "to stimulate interest in outdoor sports," and as of February 4, 1936, it had 87 charter members. Ralph G. Carpenter, 2nd, was elected president, Harold Harvey vice-president, Norman Davis secretary, and Edgar Tetherly treasurer. Lacking extensive facilities in Wolfeboro, the members often went to nearby towns. In 1936 at the Alton Winter Carnival they earned three first-place awards. As its first order of business, the Abenaki group laid out two ski trails on Poor Farm Hill (not far from the intersection of Waumbeck Road and Route 109A, which today in the 1990s still serves as the focal point for Wolfeboro winter sports). Each was about a quarter mile long—one straight and gentle and the other with curves, very fast, and requiring considerable skill. A small ski jump and a toboggan slide were planned.

On Copple Crown in New Durham a 1.2-mile downhill ski slope with a vertical drop of 1,200 feet was completed by the club in December 1963. In January 1938 the club expanded the skiing facilities on Poor Farm Hill. A new ski slope was opened for the season of 1939-1940 with an 800-foot rope tow powered from a tractor supplied by Elbridge Robie. Materials salvaged from the razing of the Ann Inn were used to build a ski hut for warmth and refreshment and was dedicated on December 20, 1940. In its annual meeting on October 5, 1940, the group changed its name to the Wolfeboro Abenaki Outing Club, to call attention to its location in the town and to popularize local events. Meanwhile, the club sponsored several Winter Carnivals.[27]

### Other Winter Activities

Downtown off Center Street the Municipal Skating Rink, sponsored by the Wolfeboro Development Association, was formed by flooding a rectangular area 200 by 58 feet and surrounding it with a board fence.[28] On February 25, 1937, hockey fans of Wolfeboro saw their first game when the Wolfeboro Wolverines competed with the North Conway Granites at the new rink. North Conway won 8 to 4.

In 1939 the renamed hockey team made the news with regularity, as in this account dated March 10:

> The Abenaki Indians played 17 games in a very full and fast schedule this past season. The team started under many handicaps. Some of the men had not played organized team hockey, relying solely upon their experience in shinny games on the lake.... By keeping their heads and cooperating all the time, centering their whole attention upon team work and organization, the team came along rapidly. From mid-season on they won half the games they played.
>
> The best game the team played all season was against the Manchester Hockey Club, the last time they met. The Abenakis had suffered many defeats at the hands of this team in the previous two seasons, and it was a great satisfaction to everyone to see our team out-skate, out-pass, and out-fight such a strong opponent for a 5-1 victory. This was a wider margin than was won at any other game played this season, whether for or against the local team.

In 1939 the Wolfeboro hockey squad included Archie Horne, Arnie Spencer, Wendy Carr,[29] Johnny Ayers, Charles ("Zip") Foss, Paul Glidden, Jimmy Clough, Nazaire ("Onion") Jutras, Carl Massey, Guy Foss, Bob Page, Joe Melanson, Freddie Fraser, Hugh ("Scottie") Wootton, Howard Smith, and Neal Morgan. Norman Turner was the coach, and Joe Melanson scheduled the games.

The *Granite State News*, March 17, 1939, mentioned another winter sport:

> Ice boating is gradually coming into its own on Lake Winnipesaukee. Last weekend nine boats had a very exciting time at the head of Wolfeboro Bay. Local boat owners were Furber Jewett, George Glidden, Fred Tuttle, Joe Melanson, and Ralph Carpenter, 2nd.

However, the sport was hardly new, as evidenced by this item appearing in the same publication nearly a half century earlier:[30]

> Ice boating is growing in favor quite rapidly, and almost every day a new boat puts in an appearance. On a good day the handsomest bay on the lake is full of "white wings that never grow weary."

### Fisherville

Fisherville, a community of portable ice houses in Wolfeboro Bay, continued to be popular with sportsmen each winter, as it had been since its formation in 1888. In the winter of 1938-1939 and again in the winter of 1939-1940, frivolity was at an unprecedented pace. Streets were laid out, "precincts" were established, officials were elected, and municipal buildings (town hall, courthouse, jail) were set up.

"Dusty" Rhodes was elected mayor in the winter of '39-'40 in an election in which both candidates had this identical platform:[31]

> If elected I will erect a building in which the residents may store free of charge their fishholes through the summer months. This will save a great deal of confusion when winter comes, as the holes will be ready to use and no ice cutting will be necessary.

The *Granite State News* carried many other farcical accounts, this excerpt from "news" published on January 5, 1940 being typical:

> Fisherville is rapidly being rehabilitated after the great flood that dissolved its very foundations in May and continued until December 29. Mayor "Dusty" (Pullemup) Rhodes is to hold a Fisherville caucus.... Roy (Coalandeggs) Foster,[32] campaign manager of Mayor Rhodes, is likely to receive a lucrative appointment....
>
> Many new buildings have been erected during the past season. "Yankeemont" Dunham, architect, builder and janitor of the Court House, has given other Fisherville builders a high standard of architecture to follow.... Precinct Two seems at present to be the main center of Fisherville. The Municipal Jail, in charge of Sheriff [J. Frank] Goodwin, has been erected close to the Court House, while "The Palace"

has been taken over as City Hall until a more suitable building is ready. The population of Precinct Two is at present 12 houses....

Sam White of Swampscott ran a nice boat taxi service from the public wharf to Precinct Two practically all day long. Precinct One's political boss, Tommy Charles, has already got together quite a following. Eight buildings have been erected in his precinct. Mayor Rhodes opened his office out in the exclusive Precinct Three, where at present there are but three houses. As the mayor controls most of the available lots in the precinct, it appears that he is going to be very careful whom he allows in his section.

In December 1940 the "official ballot" for mayor for the 1940-1941 season included this pivotal question: "Will Fisherville be wet in July?" At the bottom of the sheet was the tag line "Vote early and often!" The winner was Harry Perkins, who bested his opponent, Ike Allbee (owner of the Sheridan House hotel), and went on to serve for many years thereafter. There were 135 registered voters who cast 1,156 votes for Perkins and 979 for Allbee. Indeed, participants must have voted often![33]

In some years, there were branches of Fisherville elsewhere on Lake Winnipesaukee including Little Fisherville off Keewaydin Point in Winter Harbor and another near Barndoor Island. In some years, an "airport" was maintained on the ice, and local aviator Merwin Horn and others flew in and out.

### Rod and Reel

A contest held on Saturday, February 21, 1931, offered $10 in gold as first prize and $5 in gold as second prize for the largest fish caught in Lake Winnipesaukee on that day. Fishing for bass, trout, salmon, and shad was pursued with vigor. The federal government and state Fish and Game Commission stocked local lakes.[34]

In June 17, 1932, this was printed:

The pickerel, bass, pout, and brook trout fishermen are enjoying fishing better than for years.... Estabrook's Sporting Goods Store reports the sale of over 300 fishing licenses to date.

And this on May 24, 1935:

P.H. Gilford of Lynn, Massachusetts, was exhibiting at Wolfeboro Landing Thursday morning a Chinook salmon he had just caught. Four pounds, 14 ounces, just a pound lighter than the one reported by L.E. Sawyer last week. This is a beautiful fish with a silvery back, white belly, and platinum sides.... Fishermen who know their salmon say there are plenty of them in Lake Winnipesaukee for those who know how to catch them....

Followed by this on June 2, 1939:

Harry Perkins is spending this trout season bringing in catches which are a challenge to all Winnipesaukee fishermen. He reported a catch of an 111/2 pound tr out on May 19. This promises to be the largest trout of the season caught in local waters.

Finally, this on May 17, 1940:

Willey Brook, which flows into Lake Wentworth, has been the scene of great activity during the past week. The smelt have been running up that brook in large numbers, and fishermen from all parts of the state have congregated there nightly. Some nights there have more than 200 men lining the brook 10 deep on a side. Many of those have got their limit in from one to three dips. Three conservation officers...have been kept busy most of each night weighing smelt.

### Hunting

Hunting deer in season continued its popularity. Moose were occasionally seen, but they existed only in small numbers and could not be hunted. Woodchucks were popular targets, and the town paid a bounty of 20¢ each for them. However, on one occasion, the local newspaper praised an automobilist for having the kindness to stop on the road in South Wolfeboro to allow a baby woodchuck to cross safely.

On June 16, 1934, the Sporting Pasture, a commercial venture, was opened for business off Pine Hill Road by Clarence W. Estabrook. Offered were skeet shooting and membership in the Spitfire Skeet Club, small-bore rifle and revolver shooting, archery, and fly casting.

### Indoor and Field Sports

Clark Memorial Hall was a center for many local boxing matches, basketball games, wrestling contests, and other sports events until June 12, 1933, when the Wolfeboro Arena, a new building off Pine Street, opened with a seating capacity of over 600.

In January 1931 a new local basketball team, the Wolfeboro Wolverines, was formed, with Daniel L. Hirth as manager. This name was later used for a hockey team.[35] Accounts of baseball, football, and basketball were carried with regularity, with Brewster Academy fielding teams in several of these sports along with other organizations such as the DeMolay and Chamber of Commerce. Bowling at the Wolfeboro Casino included several teams under the sponsorship of the Chamber. New, improved lanes were installed at the Casino in the summer of 1937.

Baseball was a popular seasonal sport, and several teams were organized locally, including those formed by the town, Brewster, and Camp Wyanoke. Numerous relevant items were published, including these:

June 23, 1939: The Wolfeboro Baseball Team, organized by the Rev. J.F. Morin [priest at St. Cecilia's Church], played and won its first game Sunday afternoon, when they defeated Tilton by the close score of 6-5 in 12 innings. The Wolfeboro battery was made up of "Red" Simpson and Johnny Keenan. Albert Garnels is manager of the club....

July 19, 1940: The best ball game of the year was made at Brewster Field, Sunday, July 14. The local team played the strong Durkee-Moore team of Lynn, Massachusetts. The Wolfeboro aggregation, behind the airtight pitching of Bradbury Hunter, shut out the Lynn boys by a score of 6 to nothing, the first shut-out of the year....

The re-dedication of the Governor Wentworth Road connecting Portsmouth and Wentworth's summer home on Lake Wentworth took place on August 11, 1936, and was sponsored by the Wolfeboro Historical Society and the Wolfeboro Development Association. Shown standing, left to right: Fred Stackpole, Maj. Leigh A. Harvey (Old Home Week chairman), Robert Merritt, Harold H. Hart (local automobile dealer and booster of the town), Governor H. Styles Bridges (hat in hand next to sign), Josephine Rust (who unveiled the marker), Jasper Palmer (who suggested the placement and dedication of the marker), and Dr. Frederick E. Meader. Within a few months the sign was shot apart with bullets by an unknown vandal. (Relevant articles appeared in the *Granite State News,* August 14 and 21, 1936)

Gray Rock, a turreted mansion overlooking the northern arm of Winter Harbor, was built in the 1890s near where the Clearwater Lodges resort is today. For many years it was owned by Gorham Humphrey, who rented it to sportsmen and vacationers. On March 8, 1932, by which time it had been owned for about two years by W.A. Brophy, it burned to the ground. The land was once part of the historic Samuel W. Fay Farm.

One of the greatest sports figures in Wolfeboro history was Archie A. Horne, Jr., son of the late local Ford dealer. On March 10, 1939, the *Granite State News* informed readers that Horne was to report for baseball training in Winter Haven, Florida on March 20, and added this:

> Archie is to join the Rochester Red Wings, a farm team of the St. Louis Cardinals.... He started his baseball training as a boy, under the tutelage of his father who is still remembered in Wolfeboro as the finest athlete this town has ever known. Junior, as he is called here, played on the Brewster Academy team during his three years there and captained it last year. He played baseball four years at Wesleyan University, being captain his senior year, and was graduated in 1938.

This follow-up appeared in print on May 19, 1939:

> Archie Horne is back in Portsmouth, Ohio, after playing a few games with the Columbus Redbirds as a utility infielder, in place of a man who was hurt. In his first professional game he got three hits out of four times at bat.

In the summer of 1932 the Cotton Mountain Country Club was organized and intended to use land donated by Robert Thurrell. Double tennis courts, a badminton court, and a miniature golf course were planned.

In 1932 William Tatem Tilden II, seven times national tennis champion of the United States and the world's professional titleist, announced that he would play exhibition matches in three different courts in NH, including one on August 12, 1932, at Brewster Academy. He had been here the year before and had drawn large crowds.

### Tennis and Golf at Kingswood

On December 9, 1932, the *Granite State News* printed this:

> Mr. and Mrs. A.P. Saunders of Wolfeboro were victors in the tennis tournament held under the auspices of the Kingswood Club.... There were 64 entries. Charles P. Phinney of Newton, Massachusetts, and Wolfeboro, conceived the idea of the tournament. He realized that the Kingswood Club needed tennis courts, for the Brewster courts had been filled every day this summer.... They are being installed back of the old hospital. There will be two courts next summer and in time two more will be added.

In the early 1930s the Kingswood Club experienced extreme financial difficulties, and for a time it was feared that the Wolfeboro National Bank would foreclose on its mortgage. However, a number of members came to the rescue to guarantee the debt via ownership certificates, and a new mortgage was floated. At the time, the membership policies were largely controlled by visitors from Massachusetts. "Townies" from Wolfeboro were in the minority and often felt uncomfortable.[36]

No account of golf in Wolfeboro in the 1930s would be complete without mentioning Joseph I. Melanson, Jr., who excelled at the sport and was a bridge champion as well. The local paper printed this on June 23, 1939:

> Joe Melanson, former state champion, while playing with Frank Butler [Kingswood golf pro] and Freddy Richardson, June 19, turned in the lowest official score ever recorded on the Kingswood Golf Course. His score for 18 holes was 65, six under par.

And this on July 26, 1940:

> For the second time in 39 years of competition a tournament medalist came through at Dixville Notch last week to win the State Amateur Golf Crown, breaking a long-established jinx. Joe Melanson turned the trick... It was Melanson's third conquest of the amateur title and places him in a tie with Henry Ekstrom of Concord, who copped top honors in 1929, 1932, and 1933. Melanson's former victories were in 1936 and 1937.

## TRANSPORTATION

### Even a Rolls Royce

Although the national economy was poor, in the summer in Wolfeboro it seemed that just about everyone had a car. On Sunday, July 31, 1932, a count was kept of the number of automobiles passing through Wolfeboro Falls for one hour in the afternoon; 208 were seen.[37]

The Hart Motor Company sold many Chevrolets and Buicks and a few Cadillacs during the decade. Horne's Garage did a land-office business with the Model A and later versions of the Ford. On Center Street in the same building that housed the Wolfeboro Laundry, Libby Motor Sales displayed Chandler automobiles. For a time, Harry E. Graham, local trucker, was agent for Plymouth and Dodge models.

In 1937 there were 997 automobiles registered in town, the most expensive of which was a Rolls Royce.[38] Meanwhile, the horse had become an anachronism, and while a few were kept on farms or for hauling logs, they were rarely seen in the downtown district. By 1931 there was no longer a full-time blacksmith in Wolfeboro. In 1940 there were only 53 horses within Wolfeboro limits, and some of these were for summer pleasure riding. By contrast, 30 years earlier there were more than 400.[39]

The need to care for automobiles caused major changes in the appearance of the town. On April 1, 1938, an article titled "March of Progress" in the *Granite State News* noted that another fine old-time Wolfeboro residence had been claimed for a gas station. The Glidden manse (a.k.a. the John L. Peavey house, from its earlier owner) to the left of Town Hall on the corner of South Main and Union Streets, the front part of which had been used by Charles Pinkham for a service station, was to be torn down in the name of "progress," to provide space for a modern Texaco station. At Pickering Corner the old Cate Block on the right side of Center Street and the Pickering Block on the left had already suffered the same fate.

The Ann Inn was sold in 1940 to make way for yet another gas station, this one of the Esso brand. The

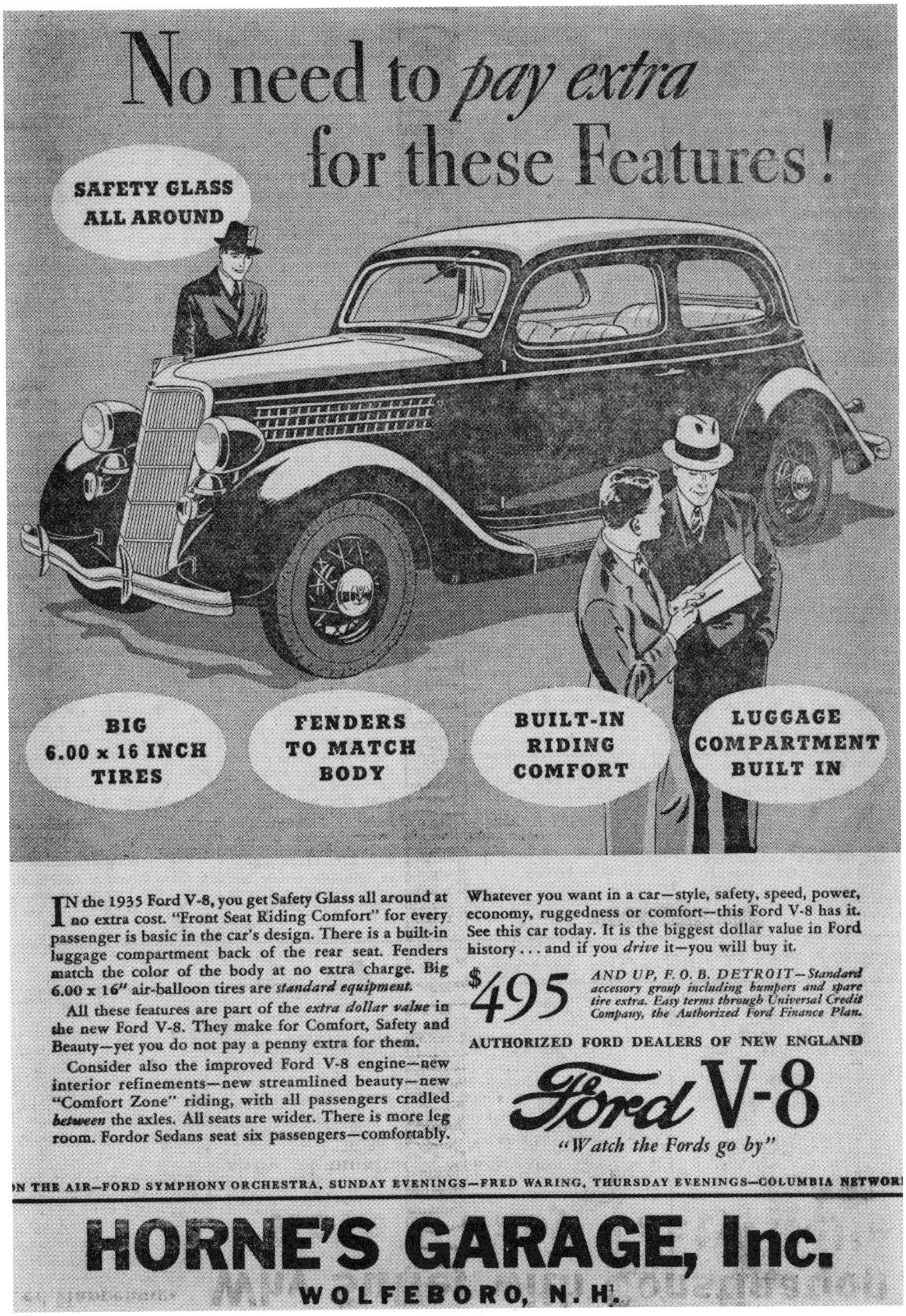


The 1935 Ford automobile offered many features and was available for $495 up (f.o.b. Detroit). Horne's Garage, Inc., on North Main Street was the local dealership. (*Granite State News,* April 12, 1935)

It is a hot day, August 19, 1940, and the crew of Boston & Maine Railroad locomotive 1468 is taking a break at a local eatery. The 2-6-0 engine, its tender, and cars wait in the middle of Railroad Avenue on tracks which once continued across South Main Street, down the alley on the right side of the Avery Building, and to the Lake Station (where P.J.'s Dockside Restaurant is in the 1990s). (Collection of the Remember the Iron Horse Museum)

Boston & Maine Railroad Sykes railbus pauses at the Wolfeborough Railroad Station before returning to Sanbornville. In the early 1930s these rail vehicles served the branch as passenger train, baggage truck, and school bus. The unit was not popular with riders, most of whom preferred the larger engine-drawn coaches. (Collection of the Remember the Iron Horse Museum)

lakeside portion of the property was acquired by funds left to the town by the late Edward Cate. The shorefront was extended up to 114 feet by an estimated 6,088 cubic yards of fill. The site today is known as Cate Park.[40] The Esso station property was purchased by Wolfeboro years later and became Town Park. Today, Cate and Town parks adjoin and are often collectively referred to as Cate Park. In 1941 the Sheridan House, which had been catering to travelers since 1795, came tumbling down to provide space for another gasoline dispensary.

Existing auto repair facilities prospered, prominent among them being Elbridge Robie's garage, Horne's Garage, Wolfeboro Garage Co. (Albert F. Auderer), and several garages on Center Street. In 1938 McBride & Weston was founded in South Wolfeboro (today known as Weston's Body Shop).

### No Love Lost Here

In the 1930s whatever little warmth some local citizens may have had for the Boston & Maine Railroad earlier, changed to downright dislike. Many columns of print were devoted to the B&M's threatening to curtail or end various phases of service. Meanwhile, the railroad sought to diversify and in 1931 set up a bus line between Concord and Boston with connections by bus to New York City.

Around this time a gasoline-powered rail car, nicknamed "Dinky" from the *Toonerville Trolley* cartoon strip, was used to carry passengers to and from Sanbornville. Riders preferred the larger locomotive-drawn coaches.

In September 1935 the Boston & Maine Railroad served notice to Wolfeboro citizens that effective September 30 all passenger trains to the town would be discontinued. The editor of the local paper remonstrated:

> This is unwelcome information. Public sentiment is being aroused regarding the management's attitude.... In 1868 this branch line, now under lease from the Eastern Railroad, was chartered to operate for 68 years from the completion of the road; this lease will terminate August 1940.
>
> We admit that in recent years the public has failed to patronize as well as formerly, owing to the introduction of the automobile and the further fact that the road has continued its high rates of fares, heavy freight tariffs, rather discouraging than attracting patronage. It sells tickets by the "bus" to the same destination much more cheaply than by train. People prefer to ride by train and doubtless would at a more reasonable rate.... Why not call a citizens' meeting and not let the matter go by default?... Go with our protest before the Public Service Commission, asking the road to continue to live up to its contract, at least. The railroad never permits a breach in *its* contracts to the public.

September 30, 1935, came and went, and the railroad continued its service, albeit reluctantly. A public hearing was held at Town Hall on December 4 with many people present. Testimony overflowed into the next day and was continued in Concord on the third day. Protests, accusations, counter-charges of misleading information, and other turmoil continued, as did the rail service. Passengers continued to be carried in and out of the Wolfeboro station by gasoline railcar, pending review of petitions.

Meanwhile, separate protests erupted over the Boston & Maine's declaration of intent to shut down the Wolfeboro Falls station completely, thus ending freight as well as passenger service.

The Public Service Commission in early May ordered the Boston & Maine to continue passenger service to Wolfeboro, but it could be part of the freight service and on freight train schedules, which were not specified. In other words a freight train was to include a passenger car. On May 16, 1936, at 3:05 in the afternoon, the last regularly scheduled passenger train left the Wolfeboro station.

While local residents foretold economic doom, decline of local agriculture and business, and even the deprivation of some children's high school education if the Boston & Maine stopped bringing tourists and commuters to town, facts presented to the Public Service Commission revealed a different story. A local hotel owner stated that fewer than 1% of his guests arrived by rail. No one could be found who claimed substantial use of the Boston & Maine for carrying dairy or agricultural products. In fact, only two milk cans per day were hauled on the train, producing revenue of just $200 per *year* to the line. Twelve high school students—locally known as "train kids"—used rail service, but other transportation was possible for them.

From August 4 through September 12, 1936, during the height of the tourist season, a bus service was operated by the Boston & Maine to connect the town with Sanbornville, a 37-minute trip for a fare of 25¢. After Labor Day buses were discontinued, and "sedan service" took its place for a short time on a twice-daily schedule connecting with trains at Sanbornville, stopping anywhere along the way on signal. The sedans were less than satisfactory, and in November a committee of Wolfeboro citizens went to Concord to plead that buses be restored, which they were until January 8, 1938.

Perhaps foreseeing the day when there would be no trains at all *anywhere,* the Boston & Maine in 1937 began to advertise as "Boston & Maine Modern Transportation," with a logotype featuring an airplane, bus and train. The text noted: "Boston to Portland in 35 minutes? No, not by train—but Boston & Maine Airways. The newest, fastest planes we could buy." Such air service was not run out of Wolfeboro, however.

Meantime during the decade, Interstate Lines, an unrelated company, offered bus service from Wolfeboro to Boston and other points, and stopped in town at McFadden & Libbey's Drug Store.

**"The Goose" Comments**

Mabel Fullerton Hatch in her "Goose Quills" column took a "what-did-you-expect?" view of the matter:

> When the Boston & Maine Railroad indulges in its daily glorification of the joys of railroad travel, it might suitably preface its splurge with "Wolfeboro folks turn off your radios, please. This invitation to travel relaxed and happy in our luxurious air conditioned trains doesn't include you."
>
> The Goose listens with grim amusement. For eight years she spent a good deal of the time traveling on railroads in the Midwest and Southwest and has been profoundly suspicious of railroads ever since.[41] There were plenty of experiences to make the most generous and unsuspecting of us cynical as the deuce.
>
> So, to her there has always been something phony sounding about B&M's protestations of the desire to serve the public. Maybe she is all wrong. However, there is nothing about the way in which this town has been "served" (in reverse) to counteract that impression. Needless, you regard it a very conciliatory attitude to couple reduced "service" with threats of doing worse if the cut isn't accepted gracefully.... So, the Goose listens to the radio-advertised delights of train travel and wonders if the B&M Railroad possesses a cheek to put its tongue in as it speaks.

What remained of freight service worsened, and on August 8, 1938, the editor of the *Granite State News* mused that "the day may soon come when Wolfeboro has no railroad."[42]

**Aircraft**

On Monday morning, May 25, 1931, Wolfeboro townspeople were getting ready to go about their day's business when a "weird sound" was heard from the southwest. Gradually increasing its volume, it became a full roar. Then:

> As the townspeople hurried to points of vantage, they saw what residents of the Granite State never saw before: nearly 40 airplanes of the United States Air Corps flying in formation.... Without question it was the most beautiful and spectacular display of modern aviation thus far witnessed in the vicinity....

Less noisy, in fact, silent, was what Elbridge Robie witnessed on October 1, 1931, when driving near Lake Wentworth: "A balloon with crew, which crossed the road so low that he was able to converse with them. He understood it to be a Navy balloon."

On Wednesday morning, April 20, 1932, the two operators on duty at telephone exchange in Wolfeboro were overwhelmed with a flood of calls as friends tried to call each other to tell them to look at the sky to witness an awesome sight. Passing overhead was the gigantic zeppelin *Los Angeles*.[43]

Each summer during the decade, Lt. Robert S. Fogg, whose seaplane was based at The Weirs, came to Wolfeboro to offer passenger rides from the town Seaplane Base in Wolfeboro Bay, to vacationers at Point Breeze and Camp Birchmont on Lake Wentworth, and to anyone else caring to part with the necessary fare. Typically, two passengers were carried on each trip.

The warm months of 1938 buzzed with aviation activity in Wolfeboro Bay. At 2 p.m. Thursday, May 19, a large Sikorsky amphibian air mail plane landed some distance from the wharf and was greeted by Postmaster Frank B. Hutchins, members of the press, and a delegation from the Wolfeboro Development Association. "The coming of this huge bird of the air...was of particular interest to Wolfeboro people," the newspaper noted. The occasion was the celebration of National Air Mail Week. Dentist Burt W. Parshley, representing the Carroll Philatelic Club, gave the pilot, Lt. Fogg, a bouquet, as 703 pieces of mail—most of which consisted of envelopes with a commemorative cachet—were loaded aboard. The kids at Carpenter School were given an hour's leave so they could watch from the shore. It was truly a week for aviation spectacles, for on the Saturday before, two Army bombers passed over the town "low enough as to be clearly identified."

During the same summer, Lt. Fogg had his own new four-passenger Beechcraft hydroplane which he tied up at the Town Docks behind the Peavey Block. On August 28, a record was set with 53 flights carrying a total of 207 passengers.[44]

**Airport Locations**

In January 1934 Wolfeboro citizens were informed that the government was going to build an airport in town, one of 15 in the state to be constructed as federal work projects. A site in back of the Brewster farm off South Main Street was considered to be ideal. However, it was soon announced that the government had approved a different location on the east side of Clark Road. A special town meeting was held, and the idea of having an airport was approved. Not everyone was in favor, however. Elizabeth B. Corwin, who had been a summer visitor for 17 years on Sewall Road, protested any airport being established within five miles of Wolfeboro Bay, stating that "the sound of motors would drive people from homes they so dearly love and would also drive birds away." However, summer residents had no voting power. The discussion was moot, for the government dropped the proposal.

In 1940 Merwin Horn, prominent local aviator, addressed local businessmen and told of the advantages of having a Wolfeboro airport. An average new plane cost less than $1,000, he said, and a "very deluxe" model cost about $2,000. A trip from Wolfeboro to Boston would use just four gallons of gas. Horn noted that there were two large farms (one of which was owned by his family) for suitable sites at the end of Wolfeboro Neck. This elicited a number of letters on the subject in the local paper, most of which were against the idea. Hilda P. Hopewell's sentiments were representative:

The Allen "A" Camp, later called the Allen "A" Resort, was operated by Allen H. Albee on Route 28 beginning in the mid-1930s. It grew rapidly, and from the late 1940s through about the 1960s it was a focal point for local tourists, especially for families who would come to stay for a week or two each summer. (*Where to— In The Lakes Region*, 1940 edition, Lakes Region Association).

> I have no legal vote in New Hampshire and your town meeting. However, as a property owner of Wolfeboro Neck for more than 25 years I want to send you my hard and vigorous protest to such a proposal. I am very much opposed to it from all angles. A very large proportion of Wolfeboro Neck consists of property holders who go there for rest and a vacation from just such things as noises of cities and airplanes and also to have rest and peace....

Walter H. Bentley, proprietor of Camp Wyanoke, commented in a similar vein. Soon thereafter, Ralph Horn (Merwin's father and the owner of the Lakeview Cabins on North Main Street) offered Wolfeboro Neck land free of charge to the town if an airport would be built there.

This aroused a new round of letter writing. Most were negative to the proposal, but P. Blake Wilkins of Beverly, MA, stated:

> I should say it was a perfect location as there are practically no inhabitants there...and it would entail very little expense to complete a road. Also it is so situated as to cause no noise or bother to the town of Wolfeboro proper. I do not anticipate any depreciation in my location at Wolfeboro Point as it will not be as busy as some of the larger airports.

There was no municipal action. In November 1940 Merwin Horn and his wife Eleanor took matters into their own hands and began to build their own private airport on Wolfeboro Neck. In the same month the State Aeronautics Commission reported that another survey for a government-owned airport was to be made in town. After proposals for Pleasant Valley and Wolfeboro Neck were given, nothing further was done.[45]

## TRAVEL AND TOURISM

### Depression? Is There One?

Throughout the 1930s Wolfeboro continued to be a premier tourist attraction. Had an economist been on the local scene to study the tourist industry, he or she would have asked, "What Depression?" On many summer weekends all local accommodations were fully booked. However, in off-season months there was local unemployment, and Wolfeboro was more in step with the rest of the nation.

In June 1931 Camp Birchmont, operated by the Hemenway family on Mt. Delight overlooking Lake Wentworth, expected to have every lodge occupied by July 4. "In spite of the Depression, this June has been a better month for them than the corresponding month last year, and there are more reservations made for the summer. It is a pleasure to hear such good news in the midst of the general gloom among businessmen," the editor of the newspaper commented.

In May 1931 Clifton Adams of the *National Geographic Magazine* was the weekend guest of Mr. and Mrs. Alonzo H. Beardsley. "Mr. Adams is making photographs of New Hampshire for his publication and is especially interested in Wolfeboro and vicinity."

In the summer of 1932 the *Granite State News* printed this commentary:

> In spite of the fact that last year was one of widespread depression, Wolfeboro's summer business was admitted by most of the merchants to have been above normal for the season, which is a significant indication that Wolfeboro has steadily grown in popularity with our summer visitors.

Such euphoria was not present in 1933, however, and for the first time in recent memory, some facilities had numerous vacancies. This year proved to be just a temporary dip in the statistics. At the close of the next season, 1934, this appeared in the local paper:

> The summer business season is now drawing to a close and proves to have been quite prosperous, considering the times, owing to the fact, no doubt, that Wolfeboro is one of the most attractive spots of God's own country. Nearly or quite every available cottage bordering Lakes Wentworth and Winnipesaukee was occupied for the entire season....

In 1935 the Point Breeze resort on Lake Wentworth had its most successful season in over 45 years of being in business.

The Allen "A" Camps, later known as the Allen "A" Resort, opened in 1935.[46] It was the brainchild of Allen H. Albee and his wife Lillian, who purchased land between Wolfeboro Falls and Wolfeboro Center in 1933. The first building of note to be erected had a peaked roof and prominent shingles. As years went by, small cabins and cottages were added, as were a theatre and several other facilities. Over a period of time, guests were offered a full program of summer events ranging from rodeos to boating events to hayrides. Most visitors came from Massachusetts to spend from one to several weeks. Allen Albee was a showman and enjoyed entertaining his guests.

In 1936 the local tourist business remained in rosy health, and at the end of the summer it was reported that on one weekend, "there was hardly a vacant room or cot."

During the summer of 1936, in its second year of operation, the Wolfeboro Tourist Information Booth set up at Pickering Corner served 5,692 people, plus telephone and mail inquiries. Thirty-four states were represented. Most inquired about routes, local directions, places to eat or stay, but some questions were different, including the submitting of a matchbox filled with small amphibians and the inquiry, "Can you tell us whether these are toads or frogs?" (They were toads.)

It is said records are made to be broken, and in 1937 Point Breeze attendance topped all previous figures. The Allen "A" planned to add 3,000 square feet of additional floor space, including a main hotel.

A round-up of business results after the 1939 season related that the Allen "A," with a capacity of between

75 and 85 guests, had no vacancies from June 20 to Labor Day, and over 16,000 meals were served. The Lakeview Cabins with a capacity of 60 were full from July 1 to Labor Day, and 12,000 meals were served. Ruth Thompson at Rust Pond Cabins had 18 cabins including six built that year and was to add two or three more.[47]

On South Main Street the Hotel Prescott was a popular stopping place and charged $4 per day and up. It would be sold in 1940 to Mr. and Mrs. Alvan M. Anderson and renamed the King's Hill Inn (today, we know it as the Windrifter).

The Ann Inn, located on Main Street on the site of today's Town and Cate parks, offered "rooms of real charm." Local cabins and boarding houses included the Wentworth Hillside Cabins, Willey Farm, Green Gables, Stonelodge, Colonial Arms, and the Ethel B. Horne home ($1 up per day), among many others.

However, the welcome mat was not out for everyone. Camp Birchmont advertised a "restricted clientele," which meant no Jews need apply. In an unenlightened age, this discrimination existed at many lodgings in the Wolfeboro and Lake Winnipesaukee area, as it did in much of America.[48] Rust Pond Cabins limited its visitors to "Christian clientele." Point Breeze was open to "Gentiles only" as was the Tumble Brook Inn (the Isaac Springfield House) in South Wolfeboro.

Several facilities in the area catered to a Jewish clientele (but to their credit, Gentiles were not excluded). Camp Wunnishaunta in South Wolfeboro offered Jewish-American cuisine under the supervision of Sadie Brickman. Her husband, Dr. Charles Brickman, a chiropodist, had summer offices in the Peavey Block.

Relative to tourism and restrictions of the era, Mildred A. Beach, long-time head of the Lakes Region Association, commented:[49]

> It is true that many properties made reference to "restricted" and "selected clientele" in the 1930s and prior to the end of WWII. In a like manner resorts in Bethlehem, NH, advertised in Jewish periodicals for "Jewish clientele only." But as WWII ended, the world became smaller and people became more open minded, and those words were dropped from advertising. Laws also were passed prohibiting clientele preferences....

### A Bite to Eat

Allan E. Bailey came to town in 1935 and set up the Bailey Woodworking Co. in Wolfeboro Falls. Three years later, on May 28, 1938, he held the grand opening for another business: Bailey's Ice Cream Shop on South Main Street, later known as Bailey's Restaurant. The restaurant became (and continues to be) a local tradition, and its ice cream gained great fame.

The Wolfeboro Café and Grill on Railroad Avenue offered steaks, chops, fried clams and sandwiches—"all home cooked food." McBride's Lunch was on the wharf where the *Mount Washington* docked and had this slogan: "The food is great, the price is right, so try McBride's, day or night."

The Village Inn, operated by Grace Berry on Center Street, featured "excellent beds" and "delicious home cooked food" at $3 per day or $18 per week. Charlie's Restaurant and the adjacent Diner, "anything from a sandwich to a boiled live lobster," were operated by Charles Rowse and billed as "two of the finest eating places in New Hampshire."

Scotty's Restaurant on the wharf was a popular stopping spot in the 1930s and early 1940s. Years later it would be known as Dockside, then Bailey's Dockside, and, beginning in 1992, P.J.'s Dockside. The Barn Dining Room at the Colonial Arms on the corner of North Main and Mill Streets was well patronized, including by the Rotary Club for its meetings. The Wolfeboro Tavern (where the First NH Bank is now) was likewise popular, as was the Carr House (today, the Wolfeboro Inn). Out on Route 28, the Goldthwaite Manor (today, the Bittersweet) offered food and lodging.

### "Semi-Residents"

In 1931 the paper referred to people who lived in Wolfeboro only in the summer as "semi-residents" and for a time had a special column with information for them. News was given for those who owned summer camps on the lakes or who went to Cotton Mountain, Moody Mountain, or other scenic spots, and spent several or more weeks during the warm months. Certain areas of the town could be quite lonely when the summer folks were away. The *Granite State News* correspondent from North Wolfeboro wrote this on a March day:[50]

> There are no personal items. There are only three houses occupied in this section, the other two more than a mile away, and no telephone connection. It is a very wintry world and we hope there will be a break soon. The ground has been covered with snow continuously since before Christmas.

In the 1930s contractor Andrew F. Doe noted that building cottages was a specialty. The Diamond Match Company, with a sales yard and facility in Wolfeboro Falls, offered to erect summer homes or winter cabins which could be financed at $20 per month. The building business was excellent for much of the decade.

In early 1935 it was announced that Dr. Isaiah Bowman, who summered on Turtle Island in Lake Wentworth, had been elected president of The Johns Hopkins University in Baltimore.[51] William O. Douglas, a summer resident of the same lake, was stepping up the political ladder:[52]

> Carroll County folks are pointing with pardonable pride to the nomination of William O. Douglas, chairman of the Securities and Exchange Commission, to the Supreme Court by President Roosevelt. Mr. Douglas was born in Washington.... In recent years Professor Douglas has had a summer home on an island in Lake Wentworth and has taken a prominent part in the life of the summer colony there.

# ROY W. FOSTER

**COAL - WOOD**

Baggage and Freight
Delivery Service
**PHILGAS SERVICE**

---

**LAKELAND ORCHARDS**

Fresh Eggs Dressed Poultry

Phone 125 or 123

WOLFEBORO

# Stonelodge

ON LAKE SHORE
WOLFEBORO, N. H.

**The Best and Coolest Location on**
Lake Winnipesaukee
**No Charge for Boats, Canoes, Badminton, Ping Pong and Shuffleboard**
PLEASE WRITE FOR RATES

---

**BAILEY'S DELICIOUS ICE CREAM**

SUNDAES, SANDWICHES, SODAS
SILEX COFFEE

The Finest Food Served the Way YOU Like It
AFTERNOON TEA

SO. MAIN ST. WOLFEBORO

---

**Union St. Service Station**
**"TEXACO"**

**Let Us "MARFAK" Your Car**
Willard Battery Service Armstrong Tires
Bowes Tire Repairs
REGISTERED REST ROOMS
We offer to our customers the free use of parking space at all times
Cor. So. Main and Union Sts.,
WOLFEBORO, NEW HAMPSHIRE
Phone 8371 C. F. Pinkham, Dealer

When writing Advertisers please mention the book, "Where to . . . . in the Lakes Region."

**Wolfeboro businesses in 1939:**

**Top: Roy W. Foster was involved in multiple businesses and was a prominent figure on the local scene for many years. Stonelodge was located on Sewall Road and catered to guests for many years.**

**Middle: Bailey's Ice Cream shop, founded in 1938, was popular from the start. Today, Bailey's Restaurant is its successor in about the same location on South Main Street.**

**Bottom: Texaco gasoline was and still is dispensed at the corner of Union and South Main Streets. (*Where to— In The Lakes Region,* 1940 edition, Lakes Region Association)**

# POINT BREEZE

**ON THE SHORE OF LAKE WENTWORTH**

PHONE 163-R2 WOLFEBORO, N. H.

**A Family Resort in a 40-Acre Pine Grove—Established in 1889**

Home Cooking, All Fresh Vegetables, Canoeing, Boating, Bathing at Your Door, Social Hall, Bass Fishing, Tennis, Modern Sanitation, Running Water in All Rooms, Golf Nearby.

C. E. and M. H. STEVENS, Ownership Management

Gentiles Only Rates, $17.00 to $19.00 per week Write for Booklet

---

# LAKE VIEW FARM
# CABINS AND RESTAURANT

**CABINS**

Modern De Luxe Cabins equipped to give you the maximum of comfort. Heated, with cold and hot water, showers, toilets, and baths.

**RESTAURANT**

The Restaurant is equipped to give you the finest foods possible, all home cooked. Milk, cream and all vegetables furnished from our own farm.

RATES, $1.00 to $1.50—OVERLOOKING BEAUTIFUL LAKE WINNIPESAUKEE

WOLFEBORO, N. H. WRITE FOR BOOKLET TELS., 250-2; RES. 8547

When writing Advertisers please mention the book, "Where to . . . . in the Lakes Region."

**Wolfeboro businesses in 1939:**

**Top: Point Breeze resort operated by the Stevens family. "Gentiles only" were welcome there.**

**Bottom: The Lake View Farm Cabins and Restaurant was the forerunner of today's Lakeview Inn on North Main Street. (*Where to— In The Lakes Region,* 1940 edition, Lakes Region Association)**

## THE BROOK AND BRIDLE INN Wolfeboro, N. H.

A View of Lake Winnipesaukee From the Inn

One of Our Bathing Beaches for Use of Guests Only

Lodges for Family Groups. Guest privileges for Golf and Tennis nearby. Stable of well-trained saddle horses. Riding instructor (Red) Mullen.

---

Draughting and Designing

Estimates Cheerfully Given

Old Farm House Remodeling One of Our Specialties

Plumbing, Heating and Electric Wiring

Ruberoid Roofing Materials

Iron Clad Cement

One of the Many Beautiful Cottages on the Shore of Lake Winnipesaukee

Designed and Built by

# ANDREW F. DOE

**CONTRACTOR AND BUILDER**

WOLFEBORO, NEW HAMPSHIRE TEL. 85

When writing Advertisers please mention the book, "Where to . . . . in the Lakes Region."

**Local businesses in 1939:**

**Top: The Brook & Bridle Inn, located in East Alton not far from the Wolfeboro town line, was one of numerous business which advertised a Wolfeboro address. Bonney Dunbar, proprietor, once served as president of the Wolfeboro Chamber of Commerce. Today her granddaughter Bonnie (*sic*) Dunbar is the owner.**

**Bottom: Andrew F. Doe, formerly a partner in Goodwin & Doe, built many structures in and about town. (*Where to— In The Lakes Region,* 1940 edition, Lakes Region Association).**

# THE WOLFEBORO CASINO

A BEAUTY SPOT ON LAKE WINNIPESAUKEE

DANCING (Summer Season)

BOWLING (all year) 4 Regulation Alleys

Ansel N. Sanborn, Owner — Norris R. Sanborn, Manager

## MOBILGAS - MOBILOIL

## STANDARD OIL OF NEW YORK

**Division of Socony-Vacuum Oil Company, Inc.**

**Wolfeboro businesses in 1939:**

**Top: The Wolfeboro Casino at the end of Endicott Street was a popular gathering place from 1921 until its demolition in 1959.**

**Bottom: Standard Oil Co. of New York operated the Mobilgas station on the east side of Pickering Corner where French's Lakeview Station is today. (*Where to— In The Lakes Region,* 1940 edition, Lakes Region Association)**

# HOTEL PRESCOTT

A Hotel Famed for Its Homey Atmosphere, Agreeable Surroundings and Gracious Hospitality

AN UNEQUALLED PANORAMA OF LAKE AND MOUNTAINS

Kingswood Golf (18-hole) Course at the Door. Running Water or Private Bath with Every Room. Rates, American Plan, $4.00 and Up.

Wolfeboro Offers All Summer and Winter Sports Activities

FOR RESERVATIONS WRITE OR TELEPHONE

**HOTEL PRESCOTT** **WOLFEBORO, N. H.**

MR. AND MRS. E. WENTWORTH PRESCOTT, Proprietors

One of Our Many Plantings Illustrated

Landscape Gardening Tree Surgery

**RAYMOND & TUTTLE**

**Registered Arborists**

TEL. 250-3, WOLFEBORO, N. H.

Spraying, Stump Pulling, Landscape Forestry

**Wolfeboro businesses in 1939:**

**Top: Hotel Prescott, owned by Mr. and Mrs. E. Wentworth Prescott, later was altered dramatically and became known as today's Windrifter Resort.**

**Bottom: Raymond & Tuttle, operated by Marcus L. Raymond and W. Fred Tuttle, offered landscaping and related services. (*Where to— In The Lakes Region,* 1940 edition, Lakes Region Association).**

**(On facing page):**

**Top: The Village Inn was located on Center Street and like many tourist homes offered food and lodging. Upper middle: Charlie's Restaurant and Diner were on North Main Street next to the bridge. The Christian Science Reading room is located in the 1990s in the restaurant building. Lower middle: Camp Wunnishaunta was located not far from the Alton town line where East of Suez restaurant is in the 1990s.**

**Bottom: The Abenaki Outing Club was very popular in the late 1930s and 1940s. Hart Motor Company (Harold H. Hart) was the largest automobile dealership in town. (*Where to— In The Lakes Region,* 1940 edition, Lakes Region Association).**

## THE VILLAGE INN

Catering to Summer Tourists and Winter Sports Enthusiasts

AS MODERN AS TOMORROW

EXCELLENT BEDS

DELICIOUS HOME COOKED FOOD

Vegetables from Our Own Garden

**Rates: $3.00 per day, $18.00 per week**

Grace Berry — Phone 4

Wolfeboro, N. H. — Route 28

---

## Charlie's Restaurant and Diner

All Home Cooked Foods

ANYTHING FROM A SANDWICH TO A BROILED LIVE LOBSTER

Two of the Finest Eating Places in New Hampshire—Our Restaurant and Diner is Equipped to Give You the Finest Foods Possible, North, East, South or West.

Charlie's Foods Are Always Best!

Charles Rowse, Prop. Tel. Conn.

WOLFEBORO, N. H.

---

MOUNTAINS LAKES WOODS

Splendid Food
Sports Galore
Snappy Staff
Sandy Beach
Scenery Supreme
Superb Accommodations
Social Activities

Is More Than a Vacation

**EVERY HOUR FILLED WITH PLEASURE AT**

## CAMP WUNNISHAUNTA

**On Beautiful Lake Winnipesaukee Wolfeboro, N. H.**

**New England's Finest Camp for Young Men and Women**

Sadie Brickman, Hostess

Write for Free Booklet Jewish-American Cuisine

---

## Abenaki Outing Club

OF WOLFEBORO, N. H.

Offers

**WINTER SPORTS**

**Ski Trails, Tobogganing, Skating Rinks Ice Boating**

Excellent accommodations for winter guests are available at reasonable rates

---

## HART MOTOR CO., INC.

BUICK and CHEVROLET
Sales and Service

**EXPERT REPAIR SERVICE**
**On All Makes of Cars**

Pleasing You Means Success to Us

TEL. 537 WOLFEBORO, N. H.

During the decade of the 1930s the John U. Lemmon family summered on Sewall Road with their son, Jack, a student at Andover. Beginning in the 1950s Jack would achieve worldwide fame as a comedian on the screen. Arthur Fiedler, conductor of the Boston Pops Orchestra, regularly vacationed with his family at Moody Mountain Farm on Pork Hill Road in the late 1930s and early 1940s.[53]

In the summer of 1935 J.C. Penney, merchandising magnate from New York City, leased a Lake Winnipesaukee waterfront cottage in Wolfeboro. Soon thereafter, several other executives from the Penney firm leased or bought cottages in the area, primarily on Tuftonboro Neck.[54]

Graham Harris, a prominent musician, summered on Sewall Point. In the autumn of 1935 he was invited to conduct the Houston Symphony Orchestra, but declined. An outstanding violinist, Harris went from Radio City in New York City to Hollywood with Leslie Howard, a film star, to provide musical interludes on radio and film programs.[55]

H.E. Harris, no kin to the above, who became known as the world's largest-volume stamp dealer, rented a cottage on Jockey Cove on Wolfeboro Neck in the 1930s. His wife and children Billy and Betty enjoyed summertime activities.[56]

Among the summer visitors at the Ann Inn in June 1938 was Luise Rainer, an Oscar-winning MGM movie star who wore sunglasses while she was here, "but was immediately recognized."[57]

### On the Lakes

Power boating continued to increase in popularity during the 1930s, Depression notwithstanding. On Lake Wentworth there were eight motorboats registered in 1934, a figure which nearly doubled to 15 in 1936. On Lake Winnipesaukee, the respective figures were 610 followed by a modest increase to 644.[58] By 1937 there were nearly 1,400 power craft on the big lake. However, most vacationers and local residents were apt to have just a rowboat or two.

The steamer *Mount Washington* was completely destroyed in a fire at its home dock at Weirs Beach on Friday night, December 22, 1939, when a blaze in the railroad station spread to adjacent areas. All that remained was a useless skeleton of charred, twisted steel. Launched on July 4, 1872, the *Mount* had been familiar to most local residents from their childhood. Each summer it stopped daily at the Wolfeboro Town Wharf, discharging and loading throngs of happy tourists. Now it was gone.

However, scarcely a few weeks had passed when Capt. Leander Lavallee announced that he had gone to Lake Champlain and had found another steamer, the iron-hulled *Chateaugay,* built in 1888 and now relegated to use as a clubhouse for boaters. In due course it was cut apart, hauled to Lake Winnipesaukee by rail, and reassembled. Known as the *Mount Washington II,* it was powered by an oil-fired steam engine. The same boat, extensively remodeled and expanded and with diesel engines installed after World War II, still serves the town in the 1990s.[59]

### Tourist Stops

On South Main Street the Clark House, a museum maintained by the Wolfeboro Historical Society, was open during the summer. In June 1932 a white picket fence was put up to enclose the grounds. During Old Home Week in August 1936 the Society presented a special display of antiques at the Clark House, with additional open houses hosted by Society members at Cobham Hall and the Maurice A. Shea home on Middleton Road.[60]

In the same summer a major exhibit of "Wolfeiana," covering the life and times of the town's namesake, Gen. James Wolfe, was held at the Libby Museum and featured 265 items. On view throughout the decade was a wide selection of local fauna, stuffed and mounted, as well as Indian artifacts, pioneer tools, and other relics. By the time Dr. Henry Forrest Libby died on August 1, 1933, he must have had great satisfaction in knowing that the museum he created had become one of Wolfeboro's, indeed the state of New Hampshire's, most admired facilities of this type.[61]

From the start of improvements in 1933 until completion in 1936, the former Gov. Wentworth estate site and nearby Clow's Beach on Lake Wentworth were sites of much activity. In August 1931 Stephen W. Clow had given the town of Wolfeboro 1,510 feet of shoreline, a gift augmented by 145 feet from Joseph A. Parant and 175 feet from Sherman and Frances Brummitt. In autumn 1933 the federal government expressed interest in acquiring the land as part of a plan to develop state recreational areas. In December of the same year, Prof. Lawrence S. Mayo, of the Harvard Graduate School and a lifelong summer resident of Wolfeboro, donated 78 acres of land to the state, including the site of the Gov. John Wentworth house. In June 1934 twenty-eight men and four trucks were busy on the grounds. By autumn the cellar of the Wentworth house, excavated under the foremanship of Guy Whittier, yielded a coffee mill, a coin, blue willow ware, several ox shoes, pottery, and other items. It was suggested that a museum might be erected in the area to display these. On February 15, 1936, in the middle of the winter, workers finished the Wentworth Beach project, and on August 11 it was dedicated.

In the autumn of 1936 the state mounted a campaign to attract visitors to observe the brilliant fall foliage. An official map suggested that ideal places to go in Wolfeboro were Wentworth Beach and the Gov. Wentworth farm site.[62]

### Extending Weekends

This editorial in the July 7, 1939, issue of the *Granite State News* was ahead of its time. It would be many years until the basic idea was accepted:

> More and more people are coming to the conclusion that it would be wise to observe all national holidays on Monday, no matter what day of the week they happen to fall on. Ten and 15 years ago, before both auto and railroad transportation became both fast and economical, it did not make much difference whether a holiday came on Monday or Thursday. But today, with the Saturday half-holiday universally observed and fast cars and fast roads making the industrial cities and recreation areas but two to four hours distant, it makes a very real difference. When Armistice Day, Fourth of July, Memorial Day, and Washington's Birthday fall in the middle of the week, neither city dweller nor the man in the recreation business receive any benefit from the holiday....

## AROUND WOLFEBORO

### Improving the Town

In July 1931 Thomas Dreier, in his *Granite State News* column, "Sunny Meadows Farm Philosophy," stated that Wolfeboro was in need of a town planner, and to do without would be similar to building a house without an architect. Moreover, he suggested that all unsightly (not otherwise defined) buildings be demolished and replaced with buildings copying colonial architecture for that is what people in Wolfeboro wanted.

Soon thereafter the same writer stated that Wolfeboro without zoning was similar to the situation "if the great art museums permitted artists to hang what pictures they pleased, or turned over each to a different individual to fill it with such sculpture or art objects as appealed to him." During this time there was much discussion as to what Wolfeboro should be. Did it need more industry, should tourism be expanded, or what should be done? Many people wanted to do an unspecified *something*. However, there was no consensus as to direction. Or, could it be that Wolfeboro is okay as it is? This same grasping for goals was to continue for decades thereafter.

On November 2, 1931, John Nolen, "internationally famous town planner and landscape architect," spoke on a town plan for Wolfeboro at the Temple Auditorium, noting this, among other concerns:

> Wolfeboro needs a street system to take care of moving vehicles and parking vehicles. It is now absolutely without a parking space. It is not primarily a question of beauty, but a question of efficient functioning. Wolfeboro needs a general cleaning up. You can approach it by water, rail, and roadway, but you do not give the impression to visitors or to your own citizens that the sights along these approaches represent the ideals of Wolfeboro as a town.

Considerable effort was expended to develop a zoning plan in 1932, and by August, five different districts were proposed, some of which had multiple zones. Various regulations and building requirements were outlined for each. In September the editor of the local paper commented when the proposals came to naught after four attempts to have them passed: "The outstanding lesson in the zoning fiasco was that two radical factions, each bent on unqualified victory, impede progress." Townspeople wanted zoning but could not agree on how to accomplish it.

The matter was debated for the rest of the decade. In March 1940 regulations, primarily involving the commercial district, were placed in front of the voters at town meeting and adopted.[63]

The Back Bay area on both sides of Center Street and east of Factory Street had been a stagnant, trash-ridden eyesore for decades and, in fact, was the primary town dump. In January 1932 the Chamber of Commerce called the situation "shocking" and called for action. Four years later in February 1936, when WPA (Works Progress Administration)[64] workers finished the Wentworth Beach project, their next order of business was to fill in Back Bay. Work started on Center Street next to the Wolfeboro Laundry. During the remainder of the decade, countless tons of fill were placed there and smoothed over.[65]

### Roads and Traffic

During the 1930s the maintenance of roads and parking areas (as limited as they were) was a prime concern of the town government. Many thoroughfares were improved by filling low spots and cutting away embankments. In Wolfeboro Falls two houses on Center Street were removed so a curve could be straightened.[66]

Parking spaces were at a premium, especially in summer months. In January 1933 the town hauled many loads of rocks to the area behind the Peavey Block, filling in what for years had been known as the "Lady Wharf" because the *Lady of the Lake* docked there in the preceding century. By the summer the parking area there had been expanded considerably. In August 1938 a protective canopy was built along the edge of the same area.

In the summer of 1935 the bridge on Main Street over the Smith River was rebuilt. In 1933 the newspaper commented that the town's "odious reputation as the hardest town in the state in which to drive, for lack of street signs" was being changed, and "smart, white arrow-shaped signs, printed in black, and at the level of the eye," made it impossible to become lost.

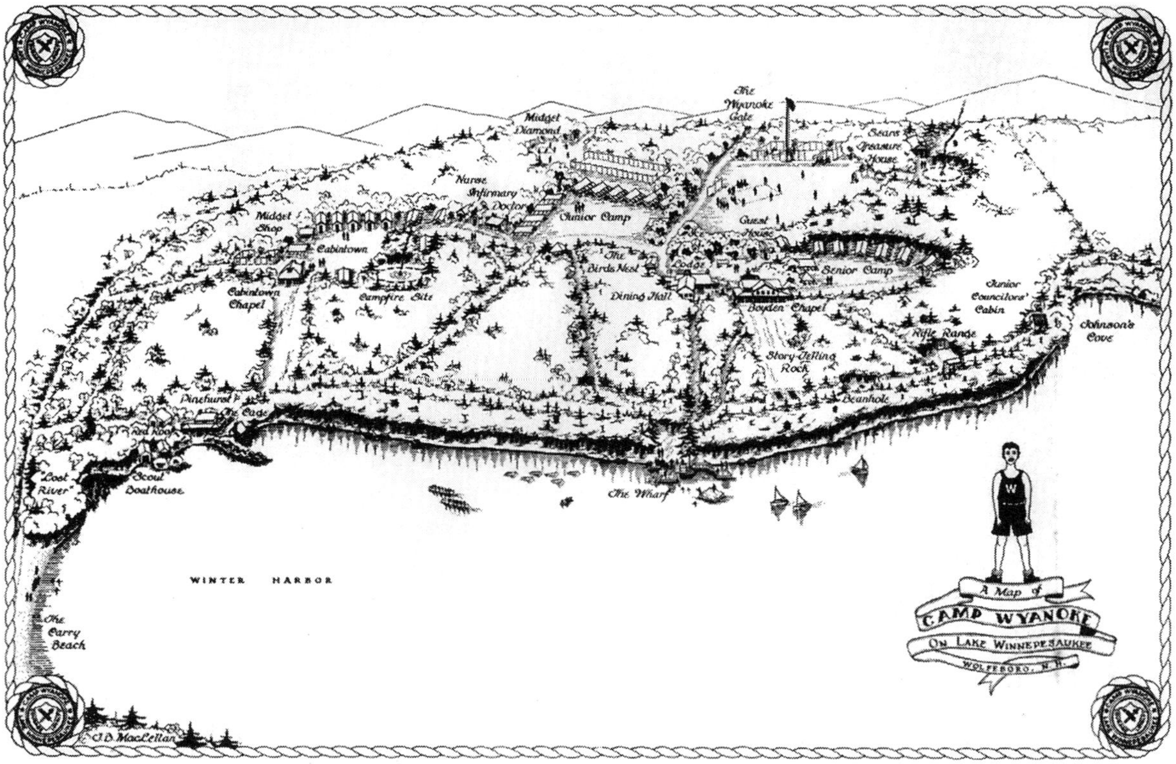


Camp Wyanoke, a nice place to spend the summer: Bird's-eye view and map of Camp Wyanoke on Wolfeboro Neck drawn by J.B. MacLellan in the 1930s. To the extreme left is Carry Beach, while near the top of the map is Wyanoke Gate (Wyanoke Gate Lane is there today).

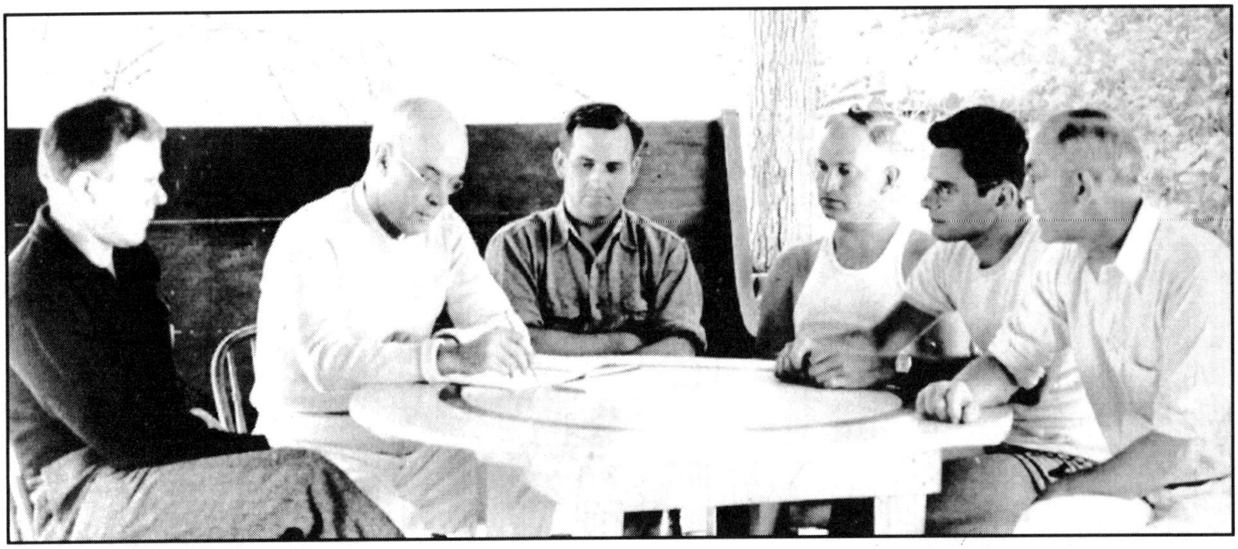

A planning session at Camp Wyanoke, 1938. Left to right: William F. Aitken, head councilor of the Senior Camp (from Hartford, CT; his 5th season at Camp Wyanoke); Walter H. Bentley, director and founder (Boston, MA; 30th season); Irving L. Vaughan, assistant director (Newton Centre, MA; 14th season); L. Arthur Walton, head councilor of the Midget Camp (Pitman, NJ; 17th season); Bradford Bentley, assistant director, son of Walter Bentley (16th season); and B. Reed Henderson, head councilor of the Junior Camp (West Chester, PA; 17th season). These men were part of a 42-person council who managed the camp. (Photographs taken in 1938 and published in a brochure titled *Wyanoke 1939*).

Camp Wyanoke, a nice place to spend the summer: Campers examining specimens on display at the Sears Treasure House (sited on the left corner of today's Forest Road and Chapel Lane; building no longer standing). "Treasures" included items collected from nature, crafts, artwork, and models made by boys at Camp Wyanoke.

Campers on a rainy night gather in the Boyden Chapel for movies, a songfest, story telling, and other activities. Banners around the upper railing bear the names of Ivy League colleges.

Camp Wyanoke, a nice place to spend the summer: Herb Pennock, pitching coach for the Boston Red Sox, was on hand at Camp Wyanoke in 1938 and is shown giving a camper instruction on how to pitch a curve ball.

Boys from Camp Wyanoke and girls from the related Camp Winnemont engage in races on Winnemont Day, 1938, at Camp Wyanoke's waterside facility on Winter Harbor.

Speeding and drunken driving resulted in numerous arrests. At the intersection in South Wolfeboro a "dummy policeman" was set up to help slow automobilists who enjoyed careening around the bend in the road to Alton. In August 1936 a truckload of STOP signs was distributed around town, and the speed limit was fixed at 20 miles per hour in the downtown area. The word SLOW was painted on the road at points considered to be dangerous.

In 1939 the *News* printed this editorial:

> Each summer the pleasure of driving is lessened by the presence of a few irresponsible young reptiles who make the night hideous by racing around in old rattletrap cars. With no business to do except to see how much gasoline they can burn, they go tearing up and down the roads, driving pedestrians into the gutter, scaring parents whose children are at play, making other drivers dive into the ditch and, in general, making fools of themselves.... If sheriffs and state police recommended that a few driving licenses were suspended for three months, life would be both pleasanter and safer.

In 1937 and 1938 the section of North and South Main Streets in the business district was rebuilt by the firm of Thibodeau & Hagan. The roadbed was excavated down to depths of up to 12 feet, revealing that about 80 years earlier, the terrain had been from eight to 10 or more feet lower and had been filled in by placing logs crisscross two feet apart on the base, then filling in with stumps, rocks, and dirt. A pine log 36 inches in diameter was found in perfect preservation as if recently cut. Evidence suggested that in the early 1800s the Smith River was very wide and extended to what is now the Post Office side of Central Avenue, and that much of the central business district had been constructed on fill. Where the Bank Building was erected in 1855, the water had been nine feet deep at an earlier time—following the raising of the level of Lake Winnipesaukee in the early nineteenth century.

In the summer of 1938 five "The First Summer Resort in America" signs were put up on roads leading into town. The wrought-iron frames were crafted by Allan Crosby (formerly of Wolfeboro, then living in Concord), and the lettering was done by Ivan E. Weston, following a design created by Walter Dorwin Teague, a nationally-known artist who lived in New York City and summered in Tuftonboro. Signs were erected on Route 28 at the Alton and Ossipee lines, near the Libby Museum, on the Tuftonboro Center Road (Route 109A today), and on the Brookfield line on the road to Sanbornville.

It was soon realized the "First Summer Resort" could mean many things, such as leading, largest, or oldest. To avoid ambiguity, the signs were repainted to read "Oldest Summer Resort...."[67]

### Sewage System

On April 30, 1932, Charles D. Howard of the State Board of Health reported on the necessity of Wolfeboro's installing a sewage disposal system to prevent polluting Lake Winnipesaukee. It was estimated that this would cost about $52,000, or $21.50 per capita, to build, plus upkeep. There were no comparable systems in Tuftonboro, Moultonboro, or Meredith, prompting the question, why Wolfeboro?

A public meeting was planned for October 28 to discuss the question. The editor of the *News* found fault with the idea, noting: "Of the 600 families in town 550 now take care of their own sewage but are being asked to pay for the remaining 50, which does not seem reasonable or just."

The situation turned more serious in November when it was realized that a sewage system was not optional, it was mandatory. Frederick E. Meader, chairman of the local Committee on Sewage Disposal, was quoted as saying that the law "states that a sewer system shall be *self-liquidating*—like a water system—paid for by all those are connected with it."[68] A town meeting was held on November 28, but a motion to appropriate funds was not passed. In March 1934 the state of New Hampshire sued the town for polluting the lake. At a special meeting held on August 27, it was finally voted in the affirmative (92 in favor, 34 against).

On May 26, 1938, $100,000 was appropriated by the town. On June 1 the Wolfeboro plan was approved as a federal WPA project with a grant of $42,412 plus a loan authorization for $41,848—the amount considered necessary for completion. The new sewer was laid by October 1939, by which time the pumping station, treatment plant, and disposal plant had all been installed.[69]

### 1932 Town Meeting

The town of Wolfeboro held its annual town meeting each March. Typically, there was little debate, and business was transacted in a straightforward manner, although there were notable exceptions.

The March 8, 1932, polls and town meeting saw 522 ballots cast from a base of 1,200 registered voters. What type of activities could be conducted on Sunday was a burning issue. It was decided by a narrow margin (221 yes, 215 no) that amateur sports could be played if no admission were charged, if events did not begin until 1 p.m., and "provided peace and quiet are not to be unreasonably disturbed thereby." However, public dancing, horse racing, prize fighting, wrestling, pool, billiards, motion picture viewing, and bowling were strictly forbidden. Only certain products could be sold in town on Sunday (vote 249 yes, 84 no), among which were newspapers, periodicals, ice cream, fruit, cigars, cigarettes, gasoline, and oil.

### 1935 and 1936 Town Meetings

The editor of the local paper reported on the March 12, 1935, meeting which, apparently, was remarkable for its illogic and inefficiency:[70]

> The annual farce-comedy, appropriately held during the windy month and called "Town Meeting" because anyone in town may grab a speaking role for himself or herself, has once more passed into history with the usual result.
>
> The great majority appeared at the Town Hall with little idea what many of the articles in the warrant meant. A few clever ones with silver tongues sang their favorite interpretations with lyric beauty surprising even to themselves, the loudest shouters knew least what they were shouting for, and the series of adjourned and special meetings to do it all over will begin at 7:30 on Monday evening April 1. (Honest!)....[71]
>
> All the town's financial problems were solved at one fell swoop, by voting to adopt the provisions of the hastily concocted Municipal Budget Act, with a committee of six to be appointed by the moderator....
>
> In spite of copious figures offered by John McHugh,[72] who had measured the early spring slop in several places between his home and the Town Hall and could tell exactly how much mud every pedestrian must expect to have splashed on his clothes while walking in the street, the requested appropriation of $2,500 for sidewalk construction and repair was cut to $1,000 by request of those who always ride wherever they are going—and possibly do some of the splashing....
>
> Frightened almost into jitters at thought of Bob Thurrell getting a little benefit in case the Cotton Valley Road (which does *not* pass his farm) were improved, a standing, sitting, and somewhat undecided squatting vote cut the proposed appropriation of $1,500 for that purpose, to $1,000.[73]
>
> Quite some fireworks introduced by a lyric tenor solo by Clayton M. Wallace[74] entitled "Harmonee, Eeconomee, Deeplomacee," attended the disposition of Articles 10 and 11. One hardly knew from one moment to the next what motion was before the house, or why he was standing up or sitting down, or what difference it made.... Wallace skated out confidently on slippery ground, nonchalantly cut a few figure eights and pigeon wings on the proposed skating rink, quite reversing a former judgment of some years ago that Wolfeboro did not want snow trains and winter sportsmen. It seems now she does. Mr. Wallace had it all figured out, also how the money could be provided without any appropriation, adding legerdemain to his repertoire of accomplishments. Cyrus Jenness, not being born yesterday nor being in the habit of going around with his eyes closed, saw just how the rabbit got into the hat and exposed the whole thing, with the result that the proposed skating rink is to remain just that—or even less.

In sharp contrast, the March 10, 1936, town meeting elicited this editorial comment: "No heated debate, no names called, no dire threats, just love and harmony."

### Beach Pond

In the summer of 1934 the outflow of the town water supply from Beach Pond dried up to a trickle. Pumps were installed, and water from Rust Pond in South Wolfeboro was utilized. The New Hampshire State Board of Health soon took exception to the quality of the liquid and forbade its use. Local residents went back to Beach Pond water, but in restricted amounts for essentials only (no lawn sprinkling, for example). In April 1935 at an adjourned town meeting, $60,000 was voted to run a new line from Beach Pond and otherwise improve the system.[75]

### New Post Office

In September 1922 it was reported that Uncle Sam had decided to invest in land in town for a new Post Office, on the theory that this would save the rent being paid for facilities in the Peavey Block. However, it was not until 15 years later in 1935 that anything definite was done and when land offers were considered. The venerable and somewhat dilapidated Hotel Elmwood (open for business intermittently since 1874) was bought for $10,000 and torn down to make way for a new, red-brick U.S. Post Office. Ground was broken in July 1936, and the cornerstone was laid on October 28. On May 1, 1937, the facility was dedicated.[76]

The interior murals by accomplished artist Andrew Winter featured a maple sugaring scene said to be typical of New Hampshire in the early days. As part of the Federal Artists' Project, murals were created for many Post Offices built during the era.[77] Door-to-door delivery service of mail was instituted to numerous in-town addresses in 1938.

### What Time Is It?

Should Wolfeboro adopt Daylight Savings Time in the summer? This was a burning question in 1935 when about 40% of the state's population was on the plan. Wolfeboro was officially in the other 60%, although many summer residents used it in their cottages as did all of the area children's camps including Wyanoke.

In 1936 many stores and offices in town took the matter into their own hands and declared that beginning on Monday, May 4, and ending Sunday, September 27, Daylight Savings Time would be used for the first time on a widespread basis in the commercial district. Apparently, this turned out to be the horological equivalent of the Tower of Babel, as reported in the local press:

> Confusion reigned supreme in Wolfeboro this week due to the varieties of "time" kept by different individuals, organizations, and business houses. Houses have been divided against themselves, with each timepiece keeping a different time and the radio disagreeing with all. Employees have insisted upon going to work in the morning by Standard Time and quitting in the afternoon by Daylight Savings Time.... People get up an hour earlier because the clock says they must, and then they stay up an hour later because they don't take any stock in clocks that tell lies....

The account went on to say that stores that opened on Daylight Savings Time on Monday were mostly back on Standard Time on Tuesday. The next year, beginning April 25, 1937, nearly all the businesses in town, the schools, the town offices, and most others adopted Daylight Savings Time.[78]

### George A. Carpenter

On November 19, 1934, George A. Carpenter passed to his reward at his winter home in Brookline, MA, leaving a son, Ralph G., two grandsons, Ralph G. II and John, and two great-grandchildren, Ralph George III and William Benbow Carpenter, all of Wolfeboro. His sister, Mrs. Emma Frost, resided in Portland, ME, at the time.

The funeral was held in Cobham Hall, the Carpenter home in Wolfeboro. Pallbearers included William J. Britton, Dr. Burt W. Parshley, Ivan J. Piper, J. Clifton Avery, and Sherman D. Parsons, all of Wolfeboro, and William H. Smart of Boston. Carpenter School and the Wolfeboro stores closed during his funeral. Interment was in the Lake View Cemetery.

Over the years Carpenter's benefactions to the town had been many and were estimated by the School Board to have been well over $100,000 in gifts to needy families, $25,000 for Carpenter School, and countless other donations.

Two years before his death, Carpenter was quoted as follows:

> When I was a boy I remember that I was deprived of many comforts. Experience is a great teacher, and it has made me more considerate of the little folks. Changing time and conditions permit me in some measure to relieve want and distress of the young, which I am pleased to do.

His son Ralph moved into a large white wooden house, the former Burton place, on Sewall Road, which was called Oakleigh (name later changed to Oaklee). Grandson Ralph, Jr., became proprietor of Cobham Hall, but spent most of his summers on Barndoor Island in the 1930s and 1940s.[79]

### The Clows

On December 19, 1935, Stephen Whitton Clow died at the age of 80. He was best remembered for the Clow Mill on Back Bay which he and fellow investors acquired in 1901 (as successor to Libbey Brothers). His private residence was atop Clow's Hill, formerly known as Martin's Hill, with a commanding view of Lake Wentworth. In 1931 he gave the town what today is known as Clow's Beach, part of Wentworth State Park. He served a remarkable 28 terms as selectman, more than anyone else before or since.

One of his children, Fred Ellsworth Clow, M.D., became one of the town's most loved citizens. In 1905 he opened a medical office in the Durgin Block and over a period of time came to practice what he referred to as "the *science* of medicine and also the *art* of medicine." He passed away on January 4, 1941. During his funeral, flags flew at half-mast, and the town schools and stores were closed. Poignantly, the 1941 Town Report was dedicated to him, two years following a dedication to his father.

### Electrical and Telephone Service

The Wolfeboro Fire Precinct Electric Light Department, as it was officially called, sought to change its name to something simpler and clearer, inasmuch as it no longer dealt with fires. In 1937 it became known as the Municipal Electric Department.

In March 1936 electric rates were 50¢ per month basic charge, plus 8¢ per kilowatt hour for the first 30 KWH, 5¢ per KWH for the next 30 KWH, 3¢ each for the following 40, and 2.5¢ per KWH for all electricity in excess of 100. In 1937 the expansion of the power plant on Factory Street, authorized two years earlier, began. Wiring of outlying districts of the town continued, and by June 1937 only about 10 houses in Wolfeboro were without service.

In 1925 street lights were kept on all night for the first time, at an annual cost to the town of about $5,000. With many more lights but with improved efficiency, the cost had dropped to $2,000 by 1938.

In March 1939 monthly electrical rates were reduced. The first 30 KWH cost 8¢ each, declining to as low 1.5¢ per KWH over 300. At the time there were 1,335 electrical meters in town (an increase from just 350 in 1919) and over 40 miles of line.[80]

In October 1939 the New England Telephone & Telegraph Co. announced the impending installation of modern equipment. "Customers will not have to use a hand crank to call the operator. They will simply lift the receiver and the operator will answer, 'Number, please.'"

By a year later, new equipment had been installed in a new exchange building, a one-story wooden structure built on the site of the late Frank P. Hobbs burned-out house on Glendon Street. The first call made on the new lines was by Dr. Fred E. Clow at the new telephone office, who telephoned Sherman D. Brummitt in the Town Hall.[81]

### Popular Family Names

The 1934-35 Wolfeboro Directory listed the following family surnames having four or more separate businesses or residences. While some surnames are common throughout America, certain others such as Avery, Berry, *et al.*, indicate interrelated Wolfeboro families. The number of individuals listed is given in parentheses:

> Kimball (14; the most popular surname), Glidden (11), Corson (10), Horne (10), Abbott (8), Berry (8), Clark (8), Davis (8), Libby (8), Moody (8), Sargent (8), Smith (8), Clow (7), Dore (7), Moore (7), Piper (7), Tibbetts (7), Adjutant (6), Chick (6), Clough (6), Cotton (6), Jones (6), Morgan, (6) Parker (6), Roberts (6), Thompson ( 6), Young ( 6), Avery (5), Brewster (5), Britton (5), Brown (5), Carpenter (5), Chamberlain (5),

Edgerly (5), Griffin (5), Herbert (5), Hersey (5), McHugh (5), Meader (5), Nichols (5), Drew (4), Durgin (4), Gould (4), Graham (4), Grant (4), Harvey (4), Kenney (4), Leavitt (4), Lord (4), Merrill (4), Potter (4), Sawyer (4), Varney (4), and Willey (4).

## HEALTH AND MEDICINE

### The Medical Scene

In 1931 Wolfeboro was selected to be the summer headquarters of President Herbert Hoover's "Committee on the Cost of Medical Care," organized to study the economic aspects and adequacy of treatment. For several summers thereafter, the group held meetings at Brewster Academy. About 50 people, including families of staff members, boarded at Kehonka Hill and elsewhere around town.[82]

Effective April 26, 1932, local doctors Curtis B. Cotton, Fred E. Clow, W.J. Paul Dye, John S. Wheeler, and Francis J.C. Dube united to give the following fee structure: Minimum charge for a house call from the settled part of the community $2, for a visit up to one hour. Night calls between 8:00 p.m. and 8:00 a.m., double the day charge. Telephone consultations $1. Preparing insurance papers $1. Prescriptions for alcoholic liquor $2 each, unless it was a regular patient *really* needing alcohol for medicinal purposes, in which case there would be no charge.[83]

In the 1930s Ferncliffe, the summer home of the late Col. Dickinson, the first cottage built on Sewall Road (in 1889-1890), was used by the Pomeroy Home of Newton, MA, as a summer facility for orphan girls.

In 1940 the editor of the *News* commented that Carroll County was well-known for the longevity of its citizens, noting that living in a rural area resulted in less tension. Further:

> The proof is rather definite. Folks who live easily and take each day's work as it comes, and who are not forever dashing from one meeting to the next and dodging cars and answering telephones, do live a few years longer than folks who are so foolish as to bother with these things.

In the summer of 1940 Dr. Harry B. Luke, who had come to Wolfeboro from Utica, NY, in December 1937 to take the place of Dr. Wheeler on the Huggins staff, had Goodhue & Hawkins Navy Yard construct for him what was called a "floating hospital."[84]

On the local dental scene, this was reported on April 2, 1937:

> Dr. Fred E. Meader has purchased a new device to kill all pain while leaving the patient conscious. It is regulated by the patient, who holds a rubber bulb in his hand which he presses when he begins to feel pain, inhaling at the same time through a nosepiece connected with a tank of hydrogenous gas. Plain air enters through valves in the tube, except when the bulb is pressed. The effect wears off in a few minutes.

### Huggins Hospital

From 1932 onward, nurses lived across the street from Huggins Hospital in a building acquired from the Greenleaf B. Clark estate. In February 1933 the hospital announced that through a gift from Mrs. Jennie H. Sinclair an electrocardiograph from France had been installed, only the second such instrument in the state.[85] By November 1934 the hospital had treated over 7,000 patients since it opened its doors in 1908. In 1933 admissions were over 300.[86]

In 1935 Huggins was accredited by the American College of Surgeons, a certification it has maintained since that time. In the same decade the hospital became associated with Tufts Medical School as a teaching facility for fourth-year students. This arrangement lasted until 1949, after which Boston University Medical School sent students to Huggins for clinical work.[87]

In 1938 the Huggins Hospital Street Fair was started as an experiment to raise money. About $900 was taken in, and thus was started what would become an annual event.[88] On August 18, 1939, the second annual one-day fair on Brewster field lasted until 10 p.m. and featured home-cooked food and candy, a white elephant table, refreshments, fortune telling, beano, and games. In the afternoon, the band from Camp Wyanoke played a concert. Close to $1,200 was realized, an increase from the year before. In 1940 $1,241 was raised.[89]

On March 10, 1939, this was reported:

> The great need that is being met by this hospital is clearly shown by the fact that patients have had to sit in the hall, waiting until beds could be vacated by patients ready to leave for home. The hospital has been filled beyond official capacity continually since the second week in December. The hospital is equipped to have 35 patients and has had from 38 to 46.

An August 4, 1939, article stated:

> There is an operating cost of $5.14 per patient per day and an average income of $3.61 per patient per day. This leaves an operating deficit of $1.53 per patient-day. However, when the income from trust funds and from gifts is added, this deficit is wiped out and a surplus of 7¢ per day per patient is created.

In 1939 Huggins recorded 11,516 patient hours (compared to 5,524 in 1931), 123 babies were born, 252 major and 394 minor operations were performed, and there were more than 8,000 laboratory examinations. Nearly half this work was done free of charge.[90]

## NATURAL PHENOMENA

### A Roaring Tornado

When one thinks of tornadoes, one usually thinks of the Midwest, not New Hampshire. However, by July 17, 1932, the typical Wolfeboro resident had heard a lot about them and could probably recite a tale or two from personal experience. On this date, a Sunday afternoon, a twister ripped through East Wolfeboro "removing and dislocating all of the buildings and sturdy trees, while geraniums and hen pens were untouched. Accompanied by a darkness and a deafening roar, the storm demon struck and was gone within five minutes' time, carrying with it the patient growth or labor of years." In nearby Wolfeboro Center "a number of buildings were torn off their foundations, and others had their roofs destroyed."[91]

**Water, Water Everywhere**

In March and April 1933 a heavy snow cover plus much rain caused Lake Wentworth to rise to a level hitherto unknown. Many roads were washed out. Muddy conditions lasted for weeks.

Tuesday, July 3, 1934, an intense thunderstorm accompanied by hail and high winds swept through town. The steeple of the Christian Church on North Main Street was splintered by a lightning bolt, the electric system was disabled in Wolfeboro Falls, lightning ignited the Furber Jewett home, a Ford automobile being delivered to a new owner was turned turtle, countless trees were devastated, and along Wolfeboro Bay there was great damage to boats.[92]

Late winter and early spring 1936 brought torrential rains. All told, 8.91 inches of rain fell on top of about three feet of snow in March and resulted in about a foot of water runoff into lakes Winnipesaukee and Wentworth, raising both to high levels and inundating the first floor of some cottages. At one point the flow of water over the upper dam at Wolfeboro Falls was 22 inches, a veritable Niagara, while the dam on Rust Pond had 18 inches of water rushing over it.

Basements of nearly all downtown buildings on the lower parts of South Main Street, including the adjacent Peavey and Goodwin blocks, were awash with flood water. On March 18 no trains operated. Mink Brook went on a rampage in South Wolfeboro, and residents lined its banks with sandbags to prevent extensive damage to low-lying buildings at the intersection. Despite all efforts, Hamel's store was flooded.[93]

**The Great Hurricane of '38**

September 21, 1938, is a date that will forever live in the memory of those who witnessed the greatest hurricane in recorded New England history. For several days, torrential rains had fallen over much of the territory. In the days before accurate predictions were possible, no one realized what was coming next. There was a hurricane in the Atlantic Ocean, but no indication that the United States was endangered by it. When the downpour ceased on the 21st, clear weather seemed to be approaching.

However, what happened next was just the opposite. High winds slammed into the Outer Banks of North Carolina, went up along the seaboard, crossed Long Island, then raked the New England coast and continuing northward, ravaged the landscape. When all was finished, about 700 people had been killed, primarily in coastal areas hit by monstrous waves; there were more than 2,000 injured; over 60,000 homeless; and about 6,000 boats and 26,000 automobiles wrecked. Gusts up to 186 miles per hour were recorded.

The next edition of the *Granite State News* reported:

> [The hurricane] exceeds anything known during the more than 400 years history of this section since the colonists first landed. From one end of this section, southern Connecticut, to northern New Hampshire and Maine, the people are engaged in the cleaning up of debris, taking care of the injured and burying the dead. The property damage is well nigh incalculable, though early Thursday morning after the storm, advance estimates were set at a figure of $200 million. Houses without number have been blown to pieces, boats and sea craft have been battered, driven ashore, or sent to the bottom, and the fine old elm trees of New England, the pride of this section, by the millions are lying prostrate today.... Wolfeboro felt the full intensity of the storm for several hours.

While there were no local deaths or serious injuries, trees amounting to many millions of feet of timber were blown over as entire forests were flattened. The Peavey Block, the Advent Church, and many other buildings and private residences were damaged, but none destroyed.

In early October the federal government stated that 39,000 WPA workers would be sent to New England, with 12,000 of these destined for New Hampshire to join with local men to attempt to salvage fallen timber. If there was a silver lining to the hurricane cloud, it was this:

> In Wolfeboro laboring men are coming into their own during this autumn season after the storm. The old saying goes that it is an ill wind that does no one any good, so the hurricane, according to this saying, was not all bad. It certainly has given labor a break at a time when it was needed. And, if present plans are carried out, need not but be little lost in this section from the storm.... The federal government will buy all of this timber to place in lakes and ponds, where not used generally, and gradually work this timber into the market in the next few years without disarranging the market. This is a very sensible thing to do, and people with woodlots and downed timber should cooperate with the plan.

The WPA set up log-buying depots, first filling Back Bay, then Johnson Cove (then called Wolfeboro Cove) in Winter Harbor, and, finally, much of Crescent Lake. It was found that by immersing logs in water they could be preserved to await later sawing into lumber. Left on land, the logs would soon be infested with beetles and start to decay. In April 1941 all of the "hurricane timber" stored in Wolfeboro waters was purchased by the New England Box Company, and operators of two portable sawmills were hired to process the logs. The last log went through the mill at 2:15 p.m. on October 24.

The September 21, 1938, hurricane downed untold thousands of trees in Wolfeboro and caused great devastation throughout New England. Fortunately, Wolfeboro was spared human casualties. These views are of a fallen telephone pole near Vinecroft on Forest Road and downed trees at a residence near the Baptist Church on Center Street.

Notwithstanding salvage operations, there are still many "1938 logs" on the bottom of Johnson Cove today.[94]

### Earthquakes

On October 16, 1932, "about 10:00 Sunday afternoon, a slight earthquake shock was felt in this vicinity, sufficient force to rock dishes on the cupboard shelves. Its duration was nearly a minute."

Early Thursday morning, October 25, 1939, the third earthquake to be felt in New Hampshire in a week caused but slight local tremors and awakened a few people, but was intense in towns to the south from Manchester to Keene.[95]

In December 1940 earthquakes on December 20 and 24 and other days prompted the editor of the local paper to comment as follows:

> The shocks that came in the night made people think their stoves or furnaces had blown up.
>
> Being in an earthquake affords a good opportunity to find out about yourself. In a fire or flood or hurricane—and Carroll County folks have had literal experience with all three—there is always a place of safety to be found. But an earthquake is another matter entirely. There is the shaking, the rumbling. The house begins to vibrate. Dishes rattle on the shelf, tables begin to walk around the room. A few bricks rain down the chimney...then it is over and the earth is quiet again, and you are busy telling your family and friends just what you saw and how you felt. Right here in Carroll County we have been at the center of two minor earthquakes and a good number of slight tremors within the past week.

Damage in Wolfeboro was light. The shaking was much more intense in Ossipee in particular. Robert F.W. Meader and Robert F. Thurrell, Jr., made a survey of the earthquake damage and on December 27 visited afflicted areas, reporting their findings to the *News*. One man told of a wide crack in the ground, large enough to receive a man's fist, which slowly closed as the witnesses stood by watching.

In January 1941 the area swarmed with seismologists and journalists who took measurements and interviewed local residents, many of whom delighted in regaling the out-of-towners with exaggerated tales. "The shocks built up a fine store of lore and legend. Mountains flamed, lakes leaked, tombstones spun like tops, and roads grew waves like ribbon candy."[96]

### Curiosa

The ever-changing program of natural events brought a number of interesting and curious things to Wolfeboro.

On Wednesday afternoon, August 31, 1932, there was a total eclipse of the sun. In advance of the event, hardware dealer Hugh H. Wallace had a special Eclipse Sale. The *Granite State News* passed out cardboard spectacles with dark film eyepieces bearing an advertisement for the paper. These observations were subsequently printed:

> At 3:00 it was becoming noticeably darker, but at no time was it necessary indoors or out to use lights to get about. At 3:20 the sky was stippled with clouds such as we see in the winter when snow is expected. At 3:37 this effect was gone, although the sky was still full of clouds. After totality, the sun burst forth suddenly and blindingly.... The only wild things here were a little flock of birds which flew across the yard as though in search of a resting place.... Only one of the planets could be seen from here, as it was rather cloudy during totality.
>
> Mr. Thurrell, who owns Cotton Mountain Farm, reports that his enormous brood of chickens all went to roost at the disappearance of Old Sol and then crowed lustily as "dawn" broke.
>
> Kehonka Hill was very fortunate inasmuch as the clouds did not interfere with the visibility.... The moon shadow was seen rushing across the lake afterwards."[97]

In the autumn of 1935 two gigantic sunflowers at the home of Charles A. Horne on Pleasant Street attracted attention. The larger was 14 feet 2-1/2 inches tall and had a flower 20 inches in diameter.

During the last week of February 1936 the atmosphere in Wolfeboro was choked with dust which blew in from vast storms in Kansas, Colorado, and other western areas. This mixed with falling snow and was so thick on February 24 that snowplows had great difficulty operating. The official estimate was that 10 tons of dust per square mile fell on the town. Professor J.W. Goldthwait, of Dartmouth, who summered on Lake Wentworth, commented that it was "the most marked phenomenon of its kind" he had witnessed in 28 years of teaching.

An aurora borealis said to have been the most brilliant viewed in Europe and North America for many decades was seen in the northern skies by local residents late Tuesday evening, January 25, 1938.

In early February 1938 ice 12 to 18 inches thick on Lake Wentworth expanded due to a warm spell and caused folds buckling in some cases eight feet high. "Fog-horn type of noises" were heard as tremendous pressures were exerted.

In September 1939 Dr. Frank C. Baker, known as "the Snail Man," made the Allen "A" his headquarters while he studied snails, small fish, and parasites in local lakes and ponds. "In Harvey Brook, that runs through the grounds of the Allen 'A', Dr. Baker has found a species of snail so small and so numerous that he obtains 500 or 600 in a dipper full of water."[98]

## FIRES

### Fires and Fire Fighting

A perspective of the era is provided by the report of Chief LeRoy P. Mansfield for the Fire Department's fiscal year ended January 31, 1937.[99] Ninety-one alarms were answered, over half of which were caused by dirty smoke pipes and chimneys. During the year an estimated $18,735.70 was lost by fire happening to property valued at $340,050. Of this amount, $17,085.70 was repaid by insurance, resulting in a net loss of only $1,650. In April 1937 Mansfield was elected president of the New Hampshire Association of Fire Chiefs.

In the summer of 1939 the men of the Wolfeboro Fire Department were trained in using a diving helmet for rescues in Lake Winnipesaukee and sought to develop new equipment and techniques in this line.[100]

In March 1940 a new fire truck arrived and consisted of a Ford chassis purchased locally, to which a custom body and equipment, including 150-gallon booster tank, were added. Carried on board were 1,900 feet of hose and a booster pump with a capacity of 100 gallons per minute.

Chief Mansfield and a number of other firemen, including Norman Davis and Leonel Copp, on October 10, 1939, organized the Wolfeboro Radio Club at the Fire Department headquarters. Copp was named president and Earl L. Walsh vice president. Mansfield received his broadcasting license in May 1940, being the first in town to do so. Others followed soon thereafter.[101]

In 1940 these divisions of the Fire Department were active: Engine Co. No. 1, Engine Co. No. 2, Hose Co. 2, and Ladder Company No. 1. As in previous times, the fire fighters were volunteers.

Below is a listing of notable fires as well as events concerning the Wolfeboro Fire Department. The dates given are those the fires occurred (unless stated otherwise); typically, these were reported in the next following issue of the *Granite State News*. In addition, there were dozens of fires of a minor nature.

**1931, February 15. Frank P. Hobbs house:** Glendon Street. Destroyed. Loss: $15,000.

**1931. New ladder truck:** March 24, 1931: $8,000 was voted for a service ladder truck. May 22, 1931: Perley E. Young took issue with the authorization, stating that the Committee did not have enough time to consider it, and the main decision was made by just a few people. A *Granite State News* editorial suggested a smaller truck would do. July 3, 1931: "'Wolfeboro's Folly' reached town Saturday, and beautifully painted in shiny red, a thing of beauty and (we trust it will prove) a joy forever. It cost enough so that it should be. Not every town would lavish so much on the drawing of nine ladders to a fire."

**1931, October 3. Roundhouse:** The Boston & Maine Railroad roundhouse within which was stored a gas-electric motor rail car caught fire. The motor car was virtually destroyed, the roof of the building collapsed, and the interior of the structure was badly charred. Loss: $30,000.

**1931, October 10. Boat:** Blaze erupted from a gas explosion on a Chris Craft motorboat moored at the wharf of Goodhue & Hawkins and owned by Charles French, who had a cottage on the lake. The boat was sunk to quell the blaze. Damage: $3,000.

**1931, October 13. Arthur Moody's buildings:** Two barns, woodshed, and part of house (all connected) were burned.[102] Damage: several thousand dollars.

**1932, March 8. Gray Rock:** The large, turreted wooden house belonging to W.A. Brophy, bought by him from Gorham Humphrey about two years earlier and known as Gray Rock, was reduced to ashes. "The imposing set of buildings are said to have been erected 40 years ago. The cause of the fire is as yet undetermined, although rats are strongly suspected, as it is known that a great many of them inhabited the building. In fact, they were plentiful underfoot when the firemen were at work." (Located where the Piping Rock Lodges are in the 1990s.)

**1932, April 25. Point Breeze:** Seven camp buildings were burned including the old Henry D. Brewster camp, social hall, dining hall and kitchen, and large adjacent building, plus boats and equipment. Owner Stevens was in New York. A tramp had been seen in the area earlier.

**1932, May 10. Bickford house:** The house and buildings of Newell Bickford on Park Avenue burned.

**1932, June 7. Hayes farm:** Farm buildings owned by Seth Hayes in South Wolfeboro were destroyed.

**1932, July 28. Oliver homestead:** The Lillian Oliver home and farm in Pleasant Valley were destroyed by a fire believed to have been caused by a cigarette.[103] There was no water with which to fight it.

**1932, October 28. Tobey's Pharmacy:** A fire in a partition was discovered at 3:40 a.m. There was smoke and water damage to the extent of $10,000 including to the business of George B. Thompson next door. "Tobey's store will have to be entirely redecorated, refurnished and restocked."

**1932, November 9. Peterson Express:** The Wolfeboro garage and office of the Peterson Motor Express of Rochester were destroyed by fire. Also lost were two trucks, a car, a motorcycle and a large quantity of supplies, and a house owned by Mr. Peterson and occupied by Mr. and Mrs. Wallace Cole.

**1933, August 15. B.G.D. Tutt barn:** Wolfeboro Center. Destroyed by fire of unknown origin.

**1933, November 1. John Lampron's barn:** Off Bay Street. Destroyed when his young son wanted to burn some hay, but not the barn, but the best laid plans....

**1933, November 12. Roberts house and print shop:** At 1:00 a.m. on Sunday the home and contents of Myron G.F. Roberts on Center Street were destroyed by fire. The printing plant connected to the house was severely damaged, mainly by water. His stock, accounts, and jobs in progress were destroyed.

**1934, May 10. Hamel house:** The home of Mrs. Albert Hamel in South Wolfeboro was slightly damaged by fire—but more problems were caused when sightseers and gawkers were said to have crowded a fire department truck off the road, and two firefighters, Joseph Corson and Charles Bombard, were thrown to the pavement. Warrants were sworn out against eight people including two juveniles, some of them being prominent citizens. The adults were Franklin Champaigne, Benjamin Earle, Walter Hood, Ralph Herbert, Edwin Moody, and Harold Thompson, who were charged with obstructing the firemen and almost causing the death of two of them.[104]

**1934, Early June. Norris Cate house:** Destroyed by fire; Cotton Valley.

**1935, March 12. Gunpowder:** Two children playing with gunpowder caused an explosion which ignited a fire and destroyed a barn. No serious injuries.

**1935, May 26. Forest fire:** On the Haines place in North Wolfeboro, consuming about 30 acres.[105]

**1935, May 27. Cotton Valley store:** The unoccupied old store, filled with stored furniture, at the depot was destroyed by fire. Known as Bill Dore's Store, owned by John L. Prindall of Brookfield.[106]

**1935, October 25. Earl Adjutant's shop:** Shop and henhouse in East Wolfeboro burned. "It seems that there must be a fire bug near Cotton Valley, as this is the third fire here within a short time."[107]

**1936, April 22. Mildram house:** Wolfeboro Center. One of the finest homes in the area burned.

**1936, August 21. Careless campers:** The director of Camp Mascoma (Enfield, NH) and two of his counselors were convicted this date of violating forest fire laws. Earlier, they led 12 people on a canoe trip and landed at the Hopewell property on Wolfeboro Neck, went into the woods, built a fire and cooked their meals, thought they had put out a fire, and went on. However, the fire blazed up and caused "heavy damage."[108]

**1936, October 14. Adjutant house:** House and contents of Mrs. Ethel Ayers Adjutant and her three sons on Keewaydin Road burned. In the finest local tradition the Red Cross, Rotary Club, American Legion, and the Wolfeboro Development Association helped the family. By a *week later,* Goodwin & Doe had built a new house for them, using donated help and materials.[109]

**1936, November 18. Fred Glidden's auto:** Destroyed by fire at Wolfeboro Center.

**1936, December. Wolfeboro Tavern:** Small fire; closed dining room for two or three weeks, including on Christmas.

**1937, January 9. Folsom Block:** Fire erupted in Robinson's Store in the basement, spread quickly due to lack of fire-stops in the partitions, and caused $10,000 damage before firemen extinguished it.

**1937, January 13. Movie theatre:** Film broke in the projector, touched a carbon-arc lamp, and caught fire in projection booth on the second floor of Town Hall. Explosive flames blew the ventilator off the projection booth and scorched the balcony. The incident caused little damage, but much excitement.[110]

**1937, January 16. Chimney fires:** Three chimney fires occurred this date.

**1937, April 24. Office explosion:** In the office of dentist Dr. J.E. Dunham; brought the Fire Department in a hurry, but the damage was slight.

**1937, May 1. Gardner Pad Co.:** Plant in Wolfeboro Falls caught fire from an electrical spark. A room full of excelsior became an inferno, but the structure was prevented from being a total loss by 35 sprinkler heads and five hose lines manned by firemen. Damage: $4,000.

**1937, July 16. Truck.** A truck carrying rubbish from Camp Wyanoke to the town dump had its load catch on fire. The Fire Department (alerted by J. Frank Goodwin) quickly extinguished the blaze. Two motorists who illegally passed two pieces of Wolfeboro fire apparatus were haled into court and fined.[111]

**1937, September 25. Claudius D. Pendill house:** North Main Street. Ell and the roof of the main house, built c.1790, damaged by fire. Known as the old Folsom Farm.[112]

**1938, June 2-3. Cotton Mountain:** Fire raged over 145 acres, threatened houses, and destroyed an oil truck owned by H.E. Graham and a car.[113] 175 firefighters were on the scene.

**1938, July 3. Automobile:** A Packard sedan belonging to George Grant on Sewall Road burned due to an electrical short.

**1939, May 8. Cobham Hall:** Fire broke out in the walls of the Carpenter house on Green Street, apparently caused by a spark from a torch used to remove paint. Firemen ripped holes in walls and ceilings and safely carried outside many valuable antiques. Bedding was pitched out of the windows.

**1939, June 27. Wolfeboro Laundry:** Small fire on outside of building caused by boiler ashes being dumped too close to structure.

**1939, July 18. Crowley speedboat:** Arthur Hanson, Jr., and Lorraine ("Rainey") Crowley, both summer residents of Keniston Island, were aboard Crowley's speedboat, *Dixie,* when it caught fire. Quickly put out by an extinguisher from the municipal Seaplane Base nearby.[114]

**1939, August 22. Swaffield boat:** In the evening, Rev. W. Douglas Swaffield of East Alton was having his gas tank filled at the Wolfeboro public wharf. Fumes crept to a kerosene lantern and flared into a "very spectacular blaze." The Fire Department was on the scene quickly, and little damage was done. However, his son Bud received painful burns on his hands.[115]

**1939, September 15. Price boat:** While Mr. and Mrs. William Carlyle of Sewall Road were out on Elliot Price's boat about 7:30 in the evening, about halfway between the Navy Yard and Sewall Point, the boat caught fire. The two were rescued by Nathaniel and Richard Goodhue. The Fire Department was notified, and the flames were quelled. $450 in damage.

**1940, March 17. Beaupre's Fruit Store:** Pickering Corner. Basement fire. Few flames, but much smoke damage. Loss: $1,800.

**1940, July 9. Herbert house:** Friend Street. Lighting set fire to the attic, but firemen put the blaze out quickly. "Several people saw the bolt which struck the house, describing it as 'a ball of fire dropping out of the clouds.'"[116]

**1940, November 30. Clubhouse:** Wooden clubhouse of the boys' Goose Corner Hockey Club was burned. In the next week it was replaced by donations and volunteer help.

**1940, December 14. Drew furnishings.** Contents of the home of Mr. and Mrs. Earl Drew on Factory Street were destroyed by fire started by an overheated stove, but the structure received little damage. Local residents donated furniture, clothing, and other items to help.

## LAW ENFORCEMENT

### Break-Ins

Local crimes of the 1930s primarily consisted of off-season vandalism of unoccupied cottages. The situation was so bad at Lake Wentworth that William O. Douglas, secretary of the Lake Wentworth Association, offered a $100 reward for the arrest and conviction of anyone stealing from the property of any summer resident.[117]

The following news clippings are in a similar vein:

**1932, September 23:** "The unoccupied C.D. Hersey buildings on Center Street were broken into recently and several articles taken. The culprits, who proved to be two local burglars who had not yet reached their majority, were arrested, haled before the court, given suspended sentences, and ordered to attend church services during the probation. It was the second similar offense for one of these juveniles."

**1932, November 11:** Comment from Charles E. Stevens: "Each season when we return to Point Breeze we find evidence of breaking, entering and pilfering, windows shot through, and even the kitchen range perforated with rifle shot."

**1933, January 6:** Report published that a number of East Alton camps on Lake Winnipesaukee had been broken into and ransacked and also Camp Wunnishaunta in Wolfeboro near the Alton border.

**1933, July 25:** Fred Griffin and Kenneth Bailey were arrested on a complaint of breaking into an unoccupied farmhouse in Cottonboro. Griffin was proprietor of the Center Square Lunch; he later went into the bakery business.

### A Multipurpose Bank

In April 1932 Theodore Sturgis was appointed chief of police by the selectmen, replacing Ralph C. Mitchell who had been on the force for 20 years and acting chief since 1930. By 1937 Sturgis received an annual salary of $1,300 plus overtime and expenses.

In November 1932 concern was expressed about the local seat of justice:

> The Police Court: what about it?.... At the present time, court is held, as it has for some time been, in the conference rooms of the Wolfeboro National Bank. This has manifest disadvantages. In the first place, it annoys the employees and customers of the bank to have the justice, court officers, and culprit walk through the banking rooms and behind the banking partition to reach the "court room."... The auditorium of the Town Hall may be obtained for gatherings free of charge.... Cannot such an arrangement be made? There is everything to gain and nothing to lose.

In August 1933 a Police Court facility was set up in a remodeled office formerly occupied by the *Granite State News* on Railroad Avenue.[118]

### Other Happenings

Roving Gypsies made regular unwelcome visits to town. Over the years numerous of their kind had been summarily "deported," although not charged with any particular offense. This notice in the April 17, 1931, *News* is typical: "Several cars with Gypsies have been escorted through and out of town by Constable Ralph C. Mitchell."

On Thanksgiving Day, 1932, Mrs. Everett S. Albee, wife of the town's longest-established jeweler, was robbed when two men came to her home. While one engaged her in conversation, the other took two pocketbooks and money. The culprits, Lester Rouleau and Adilon Bellmore, both of Maine, were apprehended and sentenced to jail. Earlier, Rouleau had been an employee at the jewelry shop. Allen H. Albee, son of Mrs. Albee, met the two on the street and was surprised to see Rouleau, who had not been in town for quite some time, and became suspicious when he tried to hide his face. The loot was recovered.

On January 26, 1933, two automobilists stopped at Albert Hamel's store in South Wolfeboro, obtained gasoline, and drove off toward Alton without paying. Hamel telephoned ahead and then gave chase. Two juveniles from Somersworth were arrested in Meredith. The car had been stolen in Maine, where the boys were sent for prosecution.

Harry V. Perry, who had served as a part-time officer on the police force in the 1920s, was arrested at his home in South Wolfeboro on February 7, 1933, and charged with stealing firearms four years earlier from local sports dealer Clarence W. Estabrook. The guns had changed hands several times since 1929, but police traced them back to Perry.

On May 3, 1933, Arthur H. Copp, postmaster for more than 30 years, attempted suicide. Authorities had been investigating a series of irregularities at the Wolfeboro Post Office and had found sufficient evidence to arrest Copp. On the prior evening, Copp had been arrested and on Wednesday morning was being taken by Officer Hugh Tulley to Concord for a hearing. Tully stepped away from Copp briefly, heard a gunshot, and witnessed the attempt. Copp was taken to Huggins Hospital, where he recovered. On September 12, 1933, in the U.S. Court in Concord, Copp was found guilty of stealing from the mail, fined, and given a one-year and one-day jail sentence at the federal penitentiary in Lewisburg, WV. The sentence was suspended in lieu of three years' probation.[119]

In 1935 someone had a grudge against Gould's Dime Store on Railroad Avenue and threw bleach on the large, expensive awning out front and later destroyed it with acid. On July 25, 1935, burglars entered the Wolfeboro Laundry, dynamited a safe, and fled with about $300 in cash plus valuable papers. On December 12 of the same year, John Murray broke into the Irving Rollins house and stole a watch. Arrested five days later, he was sentenced to six months in jail. In late December, Auderer's Garage was broken into. The thief cut himself on window glass, leaving a bloody trail across the snow; this for a take of 19¢ from the cash register.[120]

In February and March 1936, in a South Wolfeboro crime wave, over a dozen camps on Rust Pond were burgled, the Knowlton home was broken into, and the Hill Camp was illegally entered. Two state detectives were called to assist Chief Sturgis in the investigation. However, it was Charles Rines, a local caretaker, who followed tracks in the snow leading from a break-in, found two culprits, and called the police to make arrests. A juvenile from Massachusetts was subsequently convicted.

In June 1936 brothers William and Raymond Baker, who lived in Rochester, NH, and Berwick, ME, respectively, and who had criminal records, were arraigned for pilfering automobile accessories from Point Breeze. Apparently, they had been stealing things around town for a month under the guise of "collecting junk."

On August 5, 1936, Leaman E. Cunningham was sworn in as the new justice of the Wolfeboro Municipal Court, succeeding Augustus M. Fowler, who retired due to age. Cunningham, a Brewster graduate, was employed by local hardware dealer Hugh H. Wallace and was an authority on Frigidaire installation and service. One of his first actions was to try Ira Lovingheart, who must have acted in a manner contrary to the implication of his surname, and who was found guilty of assault and given a six-month suspended sentence with the provision that he leave Wolfeboro and never come back.

During July and August 1936 there were two police officers in Wolfeboro, one working days and the other nights. In the winter there was one officer in town—the only person in Carroll County to be employed in law enforcement year-round.

A feud of three years' standing, aggravated by intoxication, resulted in Lewis Herbert's being brought to court on a complaint by Bert Clough, his neighbor on Bay Street. The case aroused great interest, and the court room was packed. Herbert pleaded guilty, was fined $20 and costs, and given a suspended sentence. "Chief Sturgis was instructed to notify sellers of beer to place the names of both men on the forbidden list, and the men were advised to control their mutual animosity and avoid further trouble," the paper reported.

One of the toughest sentences meted out for a local crime was that handed down on January 3, 1937, against Michael Rabin, former president of the R.E. Granath Company, a New York City securities firm, for not being registered in NH and for selling stocks to Mrs. A.H. Willey of Wolfeboro Falls. He was given a sentence of not less than two or more than four years at hard labor and a fine of $1,000 on the first count, and a later court date for sentencing on the second.[121]

On March 3, 1937, Deputy Sheriff Harry M. Leavitt of Carroll County announced that there had been 22 break-ins to summer residences in and around Beach Pond in Wolfeboro and Water Village in Ossipee and that two Center Ossipee youths had been arrested and had confessed their misdeeds. Other offenses of the year included a car theft in front of the Wolfeboro National Bank (recovered in Bangor, ME, and the youth brought to Wolfeboro to face charges), a noontime burglary of Richard C. Connor's electrical shop, and theft of Henry Davis' automobile (recovered in Laconia).[122]

In early 1938 Ralph V. Gould was hired as a Wolfeboro patrolman. For most of that year there was little in the way of criminal activity. However, on December 16, 1938, this was reported:

> A character around town has been annoying young children in various places. The police have been on the trail for some time, and after a particularly disgusting episode in the rear of the Durgin Block, this character is now safely locked in the County Jail. Chief Sturgis did a terrific job in rounding him up. He will be tried soon and perhaps put safely away.

In April 1939 burglars struck the Allen A. Libby, Jr., camp near the Libby Museum and stole silverware, guns, and clothing. "This is the first break that has been discovered in Wolfeboro for some time," the *Granite State News* commented. That month two or more people broke into Perley E. Young's store in Wolfeboro Falls and stole cigarettes and small change. The same store was hit several times between then and July. A rash of other thefts and break-ins occurred including one at the Diamond Match Co. A rowboat was stolen from Dolph Lewando on Clark's Point.

Percy A. Shannon's poultry business in Wolfeboro Falls was broken into on three successive nights in November 1939, and hens were killed by stomping on their heads. On other occasions the Perley Young family was harassed and their garage set afire. On November 10, Willard S. Flanders, one of Shannon's employees, admitted the crimes. He waived examination and at his request was committed to the State Hospital for observation. He had received two severe head injuries in the preceding year. "If examination under the X-ray, with other tests, prove him to have been temporarily insane because of these injuries, no prosecution will be made, and all efforts will be made to restore his physical and mental health."

On November 24, 1939, the editor of the *Granite State News* reviewed a talk given at the Ossipee Rotary Club by Philip Caswell, a state probation officer. Discussing criminal activity, Caswell stated that the main cause was broken homes. He observed that church-going was the best thing for young people and "not more than one out of 50" who did so ever got into trouble.

At about 11:15 on the cold Tuesday evening of February 13, 1940, a group of 15 men and women were in a "free-for-all with no holds barred" brawl near the Ann Inn. The police arrested two out-of-towners. Crimes that year were mostly minor, such as a break-in at Harold H. Hart's garage ($87 taken) and the theft of a $1,000 Oriental rug from a cottage.[123]

## PROHIBITION, POLITICS, WAR

### Prohibition Ends

The 18th Amendment, passed in 1919, and the Volstead Act that enforced it made nationwide Prohibition a reality. However, Wolfeboro had been "dry" since shortly after the turn of the century, although there had never been any difficulty obtaining alcohol from out of town including by mail order. During the 1920s commercial liquor was harder to find locally, more expensive, and of uncertain quality, but was available to anyone with a thirst and a pocketbook to match.

Many Wolfeboro citizens believed Prohibition to be ridiculous, Mabel Fullerton Hatch being among the most vocal in this regard. Meanwhile, bootleggers and other gangsters found it to be enormously profitable. In 1931

Charles E. Stevens, owner of Point Breeze, reported that while driving to Wolfeboro from his home in New York, he was stopped outside Portsmouth at 2 a.m. by hijackers who suspected that he might have some valuable liquor in his car. The bandits let him proceed after he convinced them that he was but a peaceful vacationist. On another trip Stevens and his friends were stopped in North Athol, MA, and rudely and roughly searched by federal officers who suspected he had alcohol aboard. "They were much disgusted at finding only household goods and wearing apparel." So much for "the noble experiment," as Stevens called Prohibition, using a popular term.[124]

By the early 1930s Prohibition was widely regarded as a failure. Alcohol was increasingly available. This advertisement appeared locally and was typical of the times:[125]

> Prescriptions for medicinal liquors written by doctors practicing in the state of New Hampshire can be filled at McFadden & Libbey.

However, there is no doubt that on a national or even local basis, many of the evils of the excessive use of alcohol were now past. In 1932 Nathaniel H. Scott, M.D., who had been practicing medicine in Wolfeboro for over a half century, shared these reminiscences:[126]

> When I came here in 1880, liquor was sold at the hotels, at drug stores on prescriptions (and sometimes without), at saloons, and kitchen barrooms. At one time there was said to have been 17 places in town where liquor could be bought. Boston papers advertised whiskey at $2.50 a gallon, and a good many sent there for it. Some who received it would do no work until that was gone.... A large amount of cider was sold by farmers, and some put in a surprisingly large amount in the cellar for home use.... On summer nights men could be found in a drunken sleep in back of the Goodwin Block and on the platform of the Wolfeborough Railroad Station. We always expected drunks at town meetings and at Fourth of July celebrations....
>
> Drinking was common among the boys and young men. Brewster students were expelled for drinking. Some of the brightest boys I knew when I first came here died from the effects of drinking.... For years I have not seen an intoxicated man pass the house, and men who ride in the cars [railroad coaches] a great deal say that they never see one. The younger generation cannot imagine the conditions of a quarter of a century or more ago.

In May 1933 there was a great debate in print in the local paper as to whether Prohibition should be repealed. Against the idea, an earlier issue of the *Journal of the American Medical Association* was quoted that nationwide there were only eight hospitals with a total of 183 beds exclusively devoted to inebriety. Before Prohibition the Keeley Institute alone treated an average of 8,000 patients a year for alcoholism.

In the meantime, permits were granted by the State of New Hampshire to sell 3.2% beer. Locally, Hamel's Store in South Wolfeboro was the first to offer the brew. Business boomed, and beer advertisements proliferated in the *Granite State News*.

"While the *News* advocates and favors repeal, it nevertheless opens its columns to its opponents to express their strongest arguments for ratification, feeling confident of the outcome," the editor stated. In June 1933 a statewide referendum revealed that 75,969 were in favor of repealing Prohibition, while less than half that number, or 30,337, wanted it to be retained. In Wolfeboro the vote was extremely close: 297 for repeal and 286 against it.

On December 5, 1933, the 21st Amendment, repealing Prohibition, was ratified by the 36th state, thus making it effective. In May 1934 a bill in the State Legislature provided for the sale of alcoholic beverages through state-operated stores in towns of more than 3,000 population. A town could be "wet" or "dry" by local option. Hotels would be permitted to serve liquor with meals, but if the town were "dry," only residents could be served with alcohol. Local drugstores could continue to sell liquor by prescription.[127]

Sentiment for Prohibition still remained. In 1936 Clayton M. Wallace, local hardware merchant, was reelected president of the New Hampshire Anti-Saloon League. The Woman's Christian Temperance Union was active in town and remained so for many years.

### The Roosevelt Era

The presidential election of 1932 pitted incumbent Herbert Hoover against Franklin D. Roosevelt, a New Yorker and a *Democrat,* the latter being the ultimate sin in the eyes of many Wolfeboro locals. The Republican slant of the *Granite State News,* long in evidence and especially strong during the quadrennial presidential contests, was in full force in 1932. In the September 30 issue, a caption beneath a photograph of Hoover read as follows: "For four years has worked untiringly against tremendous odds without thought of party or himself. He reveals a man who is carrying on with patience, wisdom and courage." In the same issue, it was stated that candidate Franklin D. Roosevelt was not qualified in any way to preach economy "when the records reveal that he has been the most reckless spender of any New York governor." As the election approached, Hoover's leadership was glorified. He blocked waste, killed pork-barrel projects, and defended taxpayers.[128] There was just one problem, however: the economy continued to worsen under his administration.

In the November 7 election the United States went for Roosevelt. The state of New Hampshire voted 100,777 for the winner, but even more, 103,557, for the loser, Hoover. In Wolfeboro, Hoover swept the polls with 901 votes vs. a measly 339 for Roosevelt.[129]

Editor Frederick W. Prindle softened on the Roosevelt issue, especially after the president-elect made it clear that his major goal was to put America back to work again. In the March 24, 1933, edition, the *News* printed a picture of President Roosevelt with this caption: "The man of the hour endeavors to make the country safe for democracy and his pledge is good. He is daily becoming more popular with his countrymen." Meanwhile, the Harry Harriman Post No. 18 of the American Legion adopted a resolution to pledge to support the president's economic program.

On April 7 the local paper printed this:

> Our National Skipper Roosevelt is ordering full steam ahead, and the old U.S.A. is quivering along her keel as she heads out into the stream of new and better days. Only the date of reaching port now seems in doubt. For who can say when?

President Roosevelt's so-called New Deal for the American public involved subsidies, payments for not working, and other techniques that offended many New Englanders who basically felt that a dollar should be paid for a dollar's worth of work, and nothing should be paid for idleness. Now, in effect, Roosevelt said that down was up, and white was black. Along the way, many new agencies and programs, called WPA, CCC, NRA, FDIC, CWA, SEC, etc., were created, popularly called "alphabet soup."

The sentiments of many were perhaps reflected in Ogden Nash's "New Deal Nursery Rhymes," printed in the local paper on September 28, 1934. Excerpt:

> Higgledy, piggledy, my black hen,
> She lays eggs for gentlemen.
> Gentlemen come every day,
> To count what my black hen doth lay.
> If perchance she lays too many,
> They fine my hen a pretty penny;
> If perchance she fails to lay,
> The gentlemen a bonus pay....
> Abracadabra, thus we learn,
> The more you create, the less you earn,
> The less you earn, the more you're given,
> The less you lead, the more you're driven.
> The more destroyed, the more they feed,
> The more you pay, the more they need,
> The more you earn, the less you keep,
> And now I lay me down to sleep.

Many of Roosevelt's ideas and programs met with public resistance, but most were implemented. On February 18, 1935, the United States Supreme Court handed down a 5 to 4 decision favorable to President Roosevelt on his abrogation of the "gold clause" in contracts, which hitherto promised payment in gold for bonds, etc., thus giving a solidity unmatched by paper money. The editor of the *News* commented: "It now becomes lawful for the government to repudiate its contract. What reliance can now be placed in the government's promise to pay?"[130]

On July 5, 1935, the editor reminded readers of Roosevelt's campaign speech of October 19, 1932: "I regard reduction in federal spending as one of the most important issues of the campaign. In my opinion, it is the most direct and effective contribution that the government can make to business." Editor Prindle then pointed out what actually happened: From the administrations of George Washington to Woodrow Wilson, 1793 to 1913, a total of 124 years, the government spent $24 billion. This was just about the same amount of money spent by Roosevelt in 1934, plus his anticipated spending for the next two years. Roosevelt's New Deal and numerous make-work programs served their purpose, however, and within two years of the time he took office, optimism was beginning to spread through the country.

### Coughlin and Townsend

Rev. Charles Edward Coughlin, known as "The Radio Priest," was the first man of the cloth to use the national airwaves to mold public opinion. In the mid-1930s he was the nemesis of Roosevelt and opposed him at every turn, stating, for example, that the so-called New Deal "tends towards bureaucracy, dictatorship and extreme socialism." Locally, radio listeners considered Coughlin to be either a saint or a raving heretic. After a time, he turned anti-Semitic. The Catholic church finally pulled the plug on his microphone.

Likewise controversial was the Townsend Old Age Pension Plan, which originated in California and spread nationwide. It took as its premise that wealth was concentrated in the hands of just a few, and millions of citizens had no money. Those who desired to do so should be able to retire at age 60 with an income of $200 per month, to be paid for by a tax of 2% on all transactions in America. This money would in turn be spent and would generate employment and help the economy, thus ending the Depression. By 1940 there was a local Townsend Club with an enrollment of 50 members. The movement became so intense, especially circa 1936-1938, that candidates in state and national elections were compelled to state their positions on the plan.[131]

### State and National Elections

In the 1936 presidential campaign the local paper endorsed the Republican ticket as usual and predicted that contender Alf Landon would triumph over incumbent Roosevelt. In fact, it was almost a sure thing, for a poll taken in Illinois gave Landon a 2 to 1 lead.

On the state scene the 1936 political battle involved two prominent candidates in the Republican party vying for the U.S. Senate nomination—long-time incumbent George H. Moses and Governor H. Styles Bridges. Both were well known in Wolfeboro. Moses had been a guest of the Carpenter family numerous times at Cobham Hall. Bridges had been in town at least twice during the summer, for a dedication and an oration. The *Granite State News* preferred Moses and printed a large front page article favoring him, while Gov. Bridges had to use paid advertising to extol his advantages. In the September primary, Bridges trampled Moses locally, 365 votes to 201, and statewide results were in similar proportion. On November 3, 1936, Bridges carried Wolfeboro with 849 votes, as opposed to his Democratic opponent William N. Rogers, who straggled in with 430 following the statewide trend.

In the race for president, Roosevelt was re-elected in the greatest electoral college majority in modern history, even carrying the home and native states of his opponent, Alf Landon, and the home, native, and adopted states of Landon's running mate, Col. Frank Knox. However, Landon was the strong local favorite.

During the course of being senator, Bridges developed closer ties with Wolfeboro and eventually bought a local home on Lake Winnipesaukee. In 1938 one of his sons, H. Styles, Jr., went to Brewster Academy and in the summer worked at the McFadden & Libbey drug store.

Senator Bridges made the news in April and May 1939 when he expressed interest in being a candidate for president, and a "boom or boomlet" (as the local paper put it) was started, including a nationwide postcard campaign. Syndicated columnist Mark M. Sullivan stated, "Styles Bridges, senior senator from New Hampshire and former governor of the Granite State, stands in the top group of 1940 Republican presidential possibilities." It was hoped to pair Bridges with Alf Landon, the unsuccessful 1936 candidate, but a wag coined the phrase, "Landon-Bridges falling down." End of campaign.[132]

In his third-term try, Roosevelt was an anathema locally once again. In July 1940 the editor of the *News* expressed his support for the Republican presidential challenger, "the political phenomenon that is Wendell L. Willkie. "Further:

> Here is a man who has never been interested in politics, and yet without any formal organization, without a long campaign, stampedes the Republican convention and walks away with the nomination.... One thing is certain, the United States is going to see the most dramatic presidential election it has known since the reelection of Lincoln.

On October 11, 1940, a few weeks before the election, this item appeared in the *News:* "One plucky recent visitor to Wolfeboro had the courage of his convictions. He had a Roosevelt sticker on his car—about the only one seen here this fall."

The Tuesday, November 5, 1940, contest saw the Republicans win heavily locally, but lose nationally. Willkie garnered 964 votes in Wolfeboro, while Roosevelt mustered only 454. The editor bowed to the inevitable and acknowledged that the nation should continue "to follow the leadership of the president and face the common foe in Europe." However, this was printed for good measure: "Considerable interest was shown by the Republicans of Wolfeboro in the flag which appeared on South Main Street last Wednesday morning, which was placed at half mast and upside down."[133]

Communists were very much in the news in the 1930s and were suspected of disrupting certain government programs. On March 12, 1937, Mabel Fullerton Hatch wrote:

> There appears to be a fashion in epithets. Right now if the other fellow disagrees with us we call him a Communist. A few years ago we up and labeled him a Bolshevist. That was stylish at the time.

### The Dawn of War

After World War hostilities ended in 1918, America and most of the rest of the world hoped that peace would prevail around the globe. Such expectations proved short-lived, however, when by the early 1920s most of the former belligerents were engaged in a new arms race of unprecedented proportions.

By the early 1930s Japan and Italy had overrun certain weaker countries, and Germany was an armed military camp under the rule of Adolph Hitler and the Nazi party. Although the increasing militarization of world powers had been described widely in city newspapers, one of the first specific accounts in the *Granite State News* was by way of an April 27, 1934, review of Leon Feuchtwanger's novel, *The Oppermans,* a work of fiction set against an all too real Nazi background. The author described the muzzled German press, noting that not only foreign observers, but residents of Germany itself, had been misled and that "no one comprehends the full enormity of the crimes against civilization committed in the name of a 'reawakened Germany.'" The persecution of the Jewish people in Germany was then detailed.[134]

Beginning around 1937 and 1938 the tide of public opinion in America seemed to go against the Nazis, with a few well-publicized exceptions. Among the latter, aviation hero Charles Lindbergh went to Germany and was photographed with high-ranking officials of the Hitler regime and gave glowing reports of Nazism.[135] Increasingly, Hitler was condemned as a rascal, liar, and worse. Japan, too, was denounced, and the editor of the *Granite State News* suggested that readers not buy "a single square inch of Japanese silk until that nation comes to her proper senses."[136]

In March 1938 Germany annexed Austria. A few months later the Nazis dismembered Czechoslovakia. Poland fell to Germany in the blitzkrieg ("lightning war") of September 1939, and it was only a matter of time until Hitler's forces overpowered France, Belgium, Holland, and the Scandinavian countries. Russia got into the act and in 1940 overpowered Latvia, Lithuania, Estonia, the eastern section of Poland, and Finland. Italy was having a free-for-all in North Africa, where dictator Benito Mussolini's son commented with seeming delight that anti-personnel bombs dropped among native horsemen caused them to be flattened like so many rose petals.

In the United States, opinion as to what, if anything, America should do was mixed. Should we join the arms race? Or was the war in Europe out of our jurisdiction and interest? Did it really matter in New York and Los Angeles—or Wolfeboro—if Paris was occupied by Nazi troops?

Meanwhile, American military units were being activated. On August 11 and 12, 1938, a detachment of the 197th Coast Artillery Anti-Aircraft Division camped at the Gov. Wentworth farm site in Wolfeboro and practiced military maneuvers. The group consisted of 35 transport trucks, an ambulance, radio truck, two searchlight trucks, one eight-ton truck towing a three-inch anti-aircraft gun, and 550 men and officers from various New Hampshire towns.[137]

By 1940, with much of the world under the dominance of the totalitarian powers of Germany, Japan, Russia, and Italy, the American people nearly all agreed with President Roosevelt that action was needed, and soon. Ships and munitions were sent to England in the Lend-Lease Program, men were required to register for military draft, and work was rushed on new military aircraft and weapons. In Wolfeboro, the Red Cross and other organizations set up facilities to provide clothing, food, and supplies. "Relief gardens" were planted. United States involvement in the war seemed to be inevitable.

In the November 1, 1940, edition of the *Granite State News,* a list of draft-pick numbers for Carroll County men was published, from 1 through 1,728. The plan was that certain numbers within that group would be called at random from Washington, and in Carroll County, as well as other locales across the nation, men whose numbers were identical would be drafted subject to medical acceptability. The first Wolfeboro man to be called was Gordon Glidden, who lived on Varney Road with his wife Isabelle and daughter Sally.

## TRANSITION

### Ten Years in Review

On September 8, 1939, Orman T. Headley, editor of the *Granite State News,* reflected upon the "Depression and Progress of 10 Years":

> The face of Main Street in Wolfeboro has made an almost complete change during the past 10 years. So much so that a man passing through then and now again, the first time since then, would have some trouble recognizing the place. Both chain stores were then just holes in the wall.... The Post Office was then in what would now be considered very cramped quarters....
>
> The old Glendon Hotel then towered high, while now it is listed among the things that were. Several fine old mansions have been converted into modern gas stations. A weird section known as Mason's Second-Hand Store has been revolutionized during the past 10 years—now gas stations galore with conveniences for winter sports, not even dreamed of in 1929. Besides these, numerous fine summer and year round dwellings have been built....
>
> In 1929 when coming into Wolfeboro, a caravan traveled over miles of dirt road in order to reach the town. At that time there was only one completed hard surface road leading all the way in and out of Wolfeboro—this was the road to Ossipee.... At that time the road to Sanbornville had not been hard surfaced, Clow's Hill being a test for many of the Fords of the time to go up in high, while the road to Alton was just in the "being discussed" stage.... The road west to Moultonboro was hard surfaced through the town and through Tuftonboro, but was only dirt road through Moultonboro, so someone going west had to leave hard surfaced roads. The road then to Farmington was through a wilderness, with hardly a modern home in the 17 mile route....
>
> At that time the Carr House and Colonial Arms were private residences, Ralph Horn was just beginning to experiment with overnight cabins, while the Allen "A" was an unclaimed swamp. Now these two camps are almost villages in themselves in the summertime. If they continue to grow as they have in the past few years, the village of Wolfeboro may just become suburbs of these two camps.
>
> Now, if all this took place during a Depression, what might have been the status of the Wolfeboro section, had Coolidge prosperity prevailed, during all of this time? One hesitates to guess....

## PRICES IN 1940

The following prices are from the *Granite State News,* 1940. A year-by-year analysis would reveal prices beginning to weaken about 1931, falling through 1933-1934, and inching upward from that point to 1940.

**Appliance:** Frigidaire refrigerator, 6 cubic feet, $114.75.

**Automobile tire:** Goodyear, $10.

**Automobiles:** Buick four-door Special 6 sedan, 1941 model sold in autumn 1940, $1,052 plus shipping. Buick Business Coupe, $895. Chevrolet Master 85 Business Coupe, $659. All f.o.b. Michigan.

**Boat charter:** Gar-Wood speedboat, hour, $9.

**Clothing:** Men's: Shirts, Arrow, $2. Suits, $23.50 up. Shoes, Thom McAn, pair, $3.35. Ties, Botany brand, $1.

**Clothing:** Women's: Dark sheer and print dresses, $4.95, $7.95, $10.95. Silk dresses, sizes 14 to 50, each, $3.98. Silk hose, pair, 79¢. Fur coats, muskrat dyed to look like mink, $98; dyed skunk, $128; natural Chinese kidskin, $118; raccoon, $98; Persian lamb, $148. Slip, rayon with lace brassiere top, $1.

**Food:** Beverages: Coffee, pound, 25¢. Coca-Cola, bottle, 5¢.

**Food:** Meat: Frankfurts, pound, 19¢. Halibut, pound, 23¢. Hamburger, pound, 27¢. Sugar-cured bacon squares, pound, 15¢. Top round rump sirloin, pound, 25¢. Turkey, pound, 27¢.

**Food:** Various: Bananas, pound, 7¢. Bread, 1 1/4-pound loaf, 9¢. Butter, pound, 32¢. Donuts, dozen, 14¢. Ice cream, pint, maple walnut, 20¢. Iceberg lettuce, head, 8¢. Lard, pound, 9¢. Macaroni, 8-ounce package, 5¢. Mustard, 17-ounce jar, 10¢. Oranges, dozen, 15¢. Pea beans, New York state, pound,

5¢. Peanut butter, 2-pound jar, 25¢. Raisins 15-ounce package, 9¢. Rice, pound, 5¢. Rolled oats, 5-pound package, 25¢. Soup, Campbell's chicken or mushroom, can, 11¢. Sugar, granulated, 10 pounds, 49¢.

**Garden hose:** 50 feet with couplings, $3.98.

**Golf ball:** 25¢.

**Interest charged for money:** 18-year home mortgage, 5% per year.

**Paint:** Gallon, Sherwin-Williams flat-tone, $2.70; semi-lustre, $3.70, floor enamel and porch paint, $3.85.

**Phonograph records:** Each, 35¢.

**Real estate:** Cottage on Lake Winnipesaukee, 8 rooms plus guest house, $8,500.

**Restaurant food:** Art's Lunch: Soup, main course and dessert, 35¢ to 50¢.

**Soap:** Oxydol washing powder, large package, 22¢. Palmolive, bar, 6¢.

**Sports equipment:** Skis, children's, $1.10; adults, $3.50 to $20; ski poles, pair, $1 to $6.

**Telephone:** Day rate for three minutes, Wolfeboro to Hanover, 50¢ (25¢ night and Sunday).

**Toilet paper:** Scott tissue, roll, 10¢.

**Transportation:** Railroad fare, Sanbornville (closest stop to Wolfeboro) to Boston, coach round trip, $4.88.

**Wages:** Employee of portable sawmill, per day, $3.

**Watch:** 17 jewels, $37.50.

# CHAPTER 7
# WOLFEBORO 1941-1950

*I am leaving. Very soon I shall be on active duty with the Army Air Corps. I didn't want to pack my bags and slip away without first expressing my thoughts about you. I have grown to love you. I have worked in your hay fields; climbed your mountains; swam in your lakes; and tramped through your woods and pastures; and with each new experience, I've grown to love you more.... I'm sorry I can't stay.... I don't know when I have enjoyed life so much before. After viewing your beautiful countryside, and knowing intimately your friendly, worthy inhabitants, I'm sure I now have a better understanding of what I am going to fight for.*

—Excerpt from open letter to New Hampshire, in the *Granite State News,* November 6, 1942, from Paul Sanborn Brown, about to go overseas to war.

## INTRODUCTION

Perhaps more than any decade of the century, the years 1941-1950 were ones of suffering, of joy, of hardship, of plenty, of war, of peace. The period can be summed up briefly: War, peace (curiously, bringing with it more frustration than happiness), and then war again.

## WOLFEBORO AT WAR

### Getting Ready

In 1941 the United States was at war, not officially, but in actuality. The bombing of Britain, the capture of European countries by the Nazis, the conquests by the Japanese, and other events foretold that the involvement of America was inevitable.

The *Granite State News,* January 3, 1941, portended the future with publication of a list of potential draftees. Meanwhile, numerous local recruits were at military training camps.

Women, too, were doing their part, and while a few eventually signed up for duty in the armed forces, most were kept busy stateside working in factories, acting as aircraft observers, manning civil defense stations, and helping with clothing and supplies. In the Durgin Block the Red Cross outfitted a special room for the use of women who wanted to sew. In March 1941 a local branch of Bundles for Britain, Inc., was organized with Mrs. Leaman E. Cunningham as chairman, to provide war-stricken people with needed supplies.[1]

Dr. Herbert A. Miller, born in Tuftonboro and a graduate of Brewster Academy, collaborated with Thomas Masaryk in writing the Constitution of Czechoslovakia after World War I. In 1938 with Brewster as headquarters, Miller brought together an extraordinary group of talented refugees from Germany, Austria, and Czechoslovakia. Every man and woman of them held a Ph.D. degree. These artists, scientists, and musicians contributed richly to the cultural life of Wolfeboro while learning to be Americans.[2]

### Getting Set

To finance continuing aid to England and to strengthen what President Franklin D. Roosevelt called "the arsenal of democracy," billions of dollars had to be raised. In 1941 citizens were implored to buy U.S. Defense Savings Bonds which paid 2.9% interest if held 10 years to maturity.

In July the United Service Organizations drive was started, with Clayton M. Wallace of Wolfeboro as county chairman, and in Wolfeboro with Edmund A. Jewett and Mrs. E.S. Parke as co-chairmen. The group sought to help with entertainment of soldiers in their spare time and with welfare, religious, educational, and social services.

As the defense effort grew, shortages arose. One of the first was gasoline. In August the state commissioner of motor vehicles limited automobile speed to 35 miles per hour to conserve fuel. Meanwhile, more local men went to military training camps.

Wolfeboro residents were invited to attend a demonstration at the Brewster Academy field on November 23, 1941, of how to douse incendiary bombs, which might rain down from the skies if German bombers were

**FREE FREE FREE**

**THURSDAY, JANUARY 8TH**

**8:00 P. M.**

**Brewster Memorial Hall**

# DEFENSE RALLY

**WITH MOVING PICTURES**

**OF AN ACTUAL BOMBING OF LONDON**

There will also be the following speaker:

**Governor Robert O. Blood**

**Prof. T. V. Kalijarvi of New Hampshire University**

**J. Watson Flett, Chief Air Raid Warden of Belmont, Mass.**

The Report Center at Brown Hall will be open from 7:00 to 7:45 P. M. for public inspection. During this period several demonstrations of the method of operation will be given.

**FREE FREE FREE**

**On January 8, 1942, with memories of Pearl Harbor scarcely a month old, Wolfeboro residents were encouraged to attend the Defense Rally held at the Town Hall. Brown Hall (behind the First Congregational Church), which served as the local Civil Defense center during much of World War II, also was open to visitors. (January 2, 1942 advertisement)**

to attack the East Coast. LeRoy P. Mansfield, chief of the Fire Department, had five bombs on hand, apparently made of magnesium, and was quoted as saying:

> I may burn my pants off, but I'm going to do my best to show folks how to handle the things. Some people seem to think that to study how to extinguish incendiary bombs is far-fetched. The one answer to this objection is that a great many people in Europe thought it foolish to study how to put out incendiary bombs. Those people have no homes today.[3]

### War!

News was carried about people in the military service, and the local paper printed numerous letters. One dated December 19, 1941, was from Emily Sargent, of Wolfeboro, who was in Honolulu during the Pearl Harbor raid on December 7 which brought America into the war. Excerpts:

> It was terrible, the ease with which the enemy bombed our ships. They were all huddled together in the harbor and so vulnerable to attack. They also bombed the flying field and the army posts. The brother of a very good friend of mine was killed just as he was about to get into his airplane....
>
> This morning a big squadron of airplanes came over to help us. I still can't believe it. It seems like a dream. I don't know whether I was supposed to go to work this morning or not, but I didn't.... Our boys are all fighting mad, and they are doing all they can. I know a lot of them—or did. Some of the women at my hotel have just left for their Red Cross duties. There were many wounded in yesterday's attack. Don't worry, we are well protected. But I don't like it.

The December 12, 1941, edition of the *News* listed rules for local air raid blackouts, including covering windows and turning out lights. Gould's Dime Store advertised on January 30:

> Blackout window shades, 65¢, 89¢, and $1. Pick one room in your house and black it out so you can live as usual with lights. Be ready when the blackout or air raid signal is given.

One Wolfeboro listening post had heard unidentified aircraft overhead and reported the incident to Boston civil defense headquarters. "The Army regulation is that all planes are considered enemy planes until proved otherwise." Soon teams of aircraft spotters were stationed around town.

On December 12 instruction of volunteer air raid wardens began at Carpenter School. Brown Hall on Brewster campus was put into service as headquarters of the Wolfeboro Civilian Defense Committee and was equipped with telephones and other apparatus. Major Leigh Harvey was in charge.[4]

### "German Planes Will Hit Boston"

In December 1941 Wolfeboro was headquarters for the only dog sled rescue patrol in the United States registered for disaster work under the Red Cross. Pulled by Siberian huskies, each sled carried a first aid kit, blankets, and supplies.

By January 1942 Carpenter School, the Post Office, and the Masonic Temple had been set up as potential emergency hospitals in case of enemy attack. On January 8 a defense rally held at Brewster Memorial Hall featured films of the bombing of London. It was announced that the town of Wolfeboro would deliver sand free to householders to keep on hand to extinguish incendiary bombs. Pictures of aircraft markings were published so that townspeople could tell the difference between United States planes and those of hostile Germany, Italy, and Japan.

American citizens were forbidden to write about or discuss ships, troops, defense preparations, war production, damage by attacks, or other information until details were officially printed by the government. However, the right of individuals to criticize the government was not limited.

Meanwhile, increased shortages were being felt. Soon it was announced that rationing was going into effect for motor vehicle tires and tubes. The editor of the local paper commented:

> We Americans have run up against a brand new situation. For the first time in our lives we have money in our pockets and can't buy exactly what we want. It's a brand new feeling for folks who want tires and autos, to look at them and then finger their folding money and not be able to put that money on the counter and take possession of the desired vehicle.[5]

The Japanese controlled many rubber-producing areas, and there was as yet no satisfactory synthetic substitute. Automobile assembly lines had been ripped out and put into storage, and Detroit factories had been converted to war work. Sugar and other foods were rationed.[6]

On March 12, 1942, H.H. Wallace Hardware advertised that production of civilian radios in the United States was going to stop on April 22, but in the meantime some were available for $18.75 to $184.50 each. Beginning in March filling stations were not allowed to be open more than 12 hours per day or 72 hours each week. The speed limit was revised slightly upward to 40 miles per hour. With gasoline rationed, bicycles enjoyed a new wave of popularity.

On April 16, 1942, the first local blackout was held from 9:30 to 9:50 in the evening. Signals were blown by the fire whistle. The test was a success. Howard C. Avery was the chief air raid warden, Jesse H. Gould was the town chairman, and Roy W. Foster held the post of blackout officer.

Local residents were advised to register for ration coupons issued by the OPA (Office of Price Administration).[7] On May 15 this was printed:

> No one really knows yet what is going to be the true impact of gasoline rationing upon the recreation industry. There are many schools of thought on the matter. It is argued that the summer people will come and stay in their homes. The family will keep the car here and the breadwinner will go

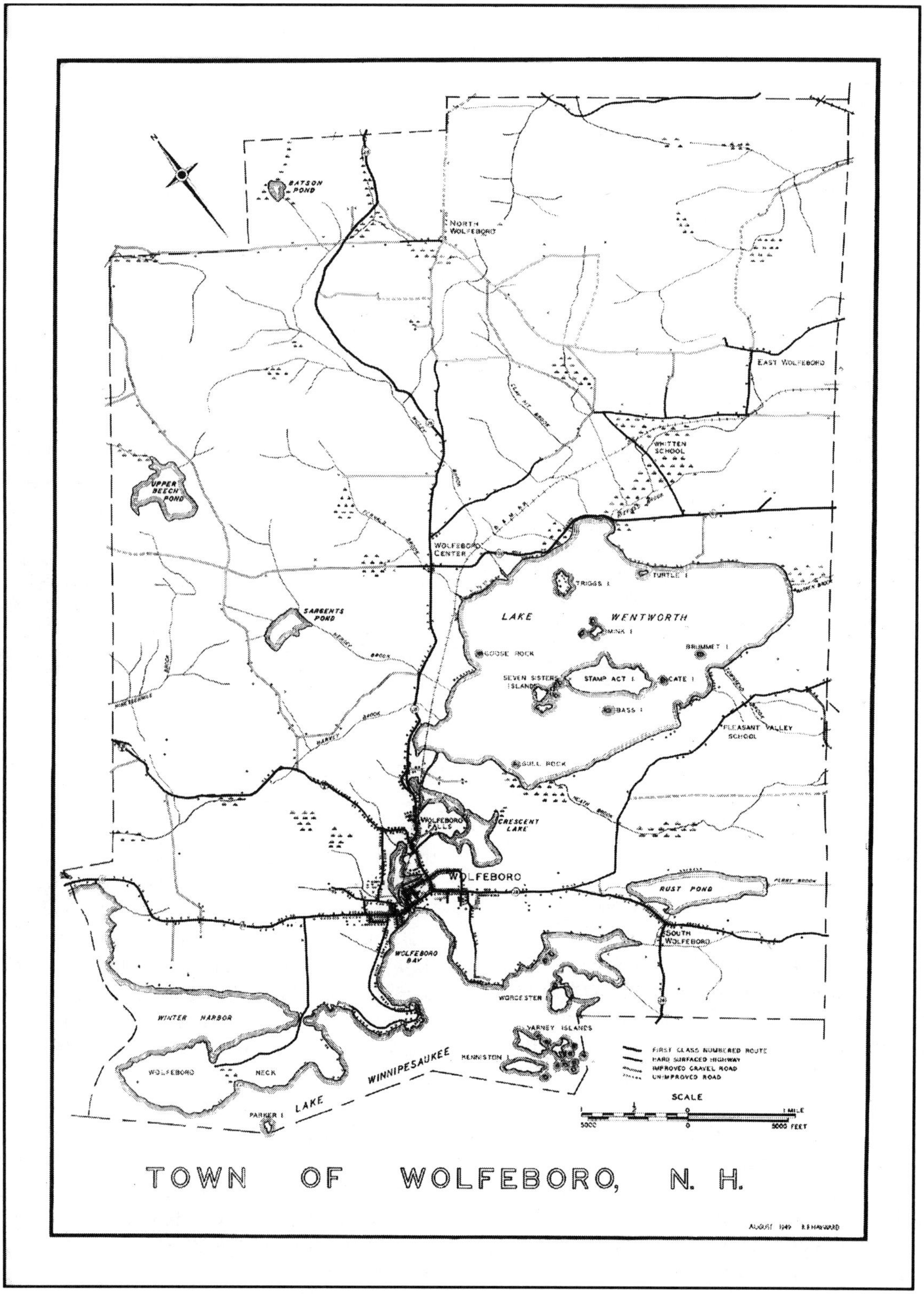


**Map of the town of Wolfeboro. (R.B. Hayward, August 1949)**

> back and forth weekends by train. [Trains at that time came as close as Sanbornville.] The counter argument to this is that the railroads will not be able to handle the extra weekend traffic of tired husbands, so the whole family will stay at home....
>
> Some people say that about the middle of June German planes will hit New York and Boston. As a result, we will enjoy the greatest summer business we have ever known. People will flock to the country no matter what the obstacle, and the families will not return to the city until their raiding season is over.

For those worried about Nazi bombers flying over Wolfeboro, good news came from the Ossipee Insurance Agency: "War damage insurance expected to be available through this office after June 20."

By summer coffee was becoming scarce. In East Wolfeboro Mrs. Helen Bryant, for one, was raising chicory to be used as a substitute. Scrap metal drives were initiated, and in September it was announced that the local goal of 20 tons had been far exceeded by a collection of triple that amount. Among the relics salvaged was a horse-drawn mowing machine that had been used by Stephen W. Clow in the nineteenth century.[8]

On September 10, 1942, Clayton E. Hale, son of Walter L. Hale of South Wolfeboro, became the town's first mortal casualty of the war. Later, the local American Legion was renamed the Harriman-Hale Post.[9]

### On the Home Front

As months passed the war continued with no end in sight. Rationing spread to include fuel oil, electrical wire, building supplies, and even beans. Tires wore out and could not be replaced. The hoped-for civilian supplies of synthetic rubber were delayed. Citizens were urged to plant Victory Gardens, and to this end, free use of land was offered by the town. To provide for emergencies, canning of food was encouraged. Mrs. Ralph Horn, of the Lakeview Cabins on North Main Street, put up 1,100 jars of vegetables.

In its drive to enlist or draft, the government depopulated the area of strong-bodied men capable of harvesting crops, prompting the *News* to suggest that high school girls be pressed into service to do the work. In the summer many boys from local vacation camps volunteered to do farm duties. Wolfeboro and area citizens pitched in to do their part with the war effort including rationing, buying savings bonds, and everything else.

Sometimes there was disillusionment, as when it was reported that a local garage operator visited California and spent some time in various service stations. "He was first amazed, then shocked, then just plain angry watching the manner in which gasoline rationing regulations were being flaunted. Favored customers were not being asked for coupons. They simply gassed up and drove off." The editor mused that here in New England people were being very careful about the regulations, but because of waste in California, local citizens were being forced to go without.

In early 1943 sliced bread could not be sold, as this "saves the steel that replacement machines and parts would be made of." A cartoon published by the New Hampshire Christian Civic League showed that while telephones, sewing machines, tires, automobiles, office equipment, washing machines, refrigerators, household appliances, fuel, razors, and many other things were rationed, beer, wine, and whisky were not. Washington was hard to figure out.

A black market arose for rationed goods. Local poultry breeder Robert Thurrell estimated that 75% of the chickens sold in America were illegally peddled at prices above those set by regulators. Separately, an editorial said that "trucks go around the countryside paying fantastic prices for hens. It is hard to blame the poultryman for yielding to the temptation of cold cash and selling his flock for fantastic profit."[10]

### The Tide Turns

In the spring of 1943 the Allies scored impressive victories in Tunisia and elsewhere, driving the Axis (Germany and Italy) from all lands on the south side of the Mediterranean Sea. The shoe was on the other foot for the first time since the war started. On May 14 Editor Parker M. Merrow wrote:

> Hitler can no longer play a skillful war of nerves. Now he and the people speculate where the next attack will come. The English no longer wonder, at sunset, which of their cities will be blasted before the sun rises. Now it is the Germans that dread the going down of the sun, for they well know that death and destruction can await them during darkness.

While Germany continued the war aggressively, the Italians were at the point of surrender.

An easing of restrictions took place in 1943. Pleasure driving, heretofore banned, was allowed as of September 1. Now Wolfeboro residents could go fishing, to the movies, and visit autumn agricultural fairs.[11] The prohibition of the use of pleasure boats was lifted. By the end of the year the Civil Defense office in Brown Hall on the Brewster campus had been disbanded. No longer was it feared that German bombers would rain incendiary bombs on the town. However, local Red Cross facilities were continued.[12]

Still, many items remained rationed, and conservation was the order of the day. The war was still going on. This editorial appeared on December 10, 1943:

> We plain folks back here in New Hampshire have not been able to find out that Washington is making a real effort.... The number of men and women employed in the various bureaus does not seem to have been cut down, releasing these people for more important work....

Earlier, the editor wryly observed that while newspapers such as the *Granite State News* were ordered to save paper, the bureaucrats in Washington were using it with reckless abandon, making unnecessary mailings and printing needless notices—as if there had been no emergency going on.

**The Year 1944**

On January 24, 1944, the War Production Board released restrictions on copper tubing, enabling the Wolfeboro Water Department to add new customers and replace obsolete lines, if there had been local manpower to do so.

Beginning in 1944 there was much talk about the end of the war and what would happen stateside. In particular, would there be enough employment for the returning soldiers, and would prices spiral upward out of control? By this time Americans had vast amounts of money tucked away in savings accounts, war bonds, and other financial instruments. Most time payments for automobiles, refrigerators, washing machines, and sometimes even homes, had long since been liquidated, and cash was piling up. There was a great pent-up demand for goods and services.

In the meantime Germany and Japan were fighting to their death, and American forces continued to suffer heavy casualties. Writing to soldiers overseas helped ease their loneliness and pain, and each outbound mail from Wolfeboro contained many such letters. Sometimes correspondence was delivered late, as when Walter Nary, a local lad in the Navy, was delighted to receive a hoard of 67 letters "in one avalanche of good cheer."

On March 31, 1944, about 11 a.m., a Grumman Avenger torpedo bomber on a training mission crash-landed on the ice in Jockey Cove in Lake Winnipesaukee. The gunner, of the British Royal Navy but stationed at a Maine air base, was taken to Huggins Hospital with a spine fracture. The pilot escaped without injury. Ivan Piper and Edwin Moody dragged the plane to nearby Carry Beach, where a dozen or more people from the Royal Navy dismantled the craft and packed it aboard two trucks.

The event had a bright side: Wolfeboro "was drained of men by the armed forces, so much that it had thought of incorporating itself as an all-girl town." The visiting soldiers, United States and British, were thus given a warm welcome. Among the popular unmarried young ladies helping to make the troops feel at home were Beatrice Horne, Lillian Osgood, Barbara Lewando, and Helen Adams.[13]

While optimism was expressed that the war would soon be over, shortages continued in some areas and even worsened. Citizens were advised that supplies of sugar would be 6% lower in 1944 than in the previous year. No civilian cars were to be produced, and if there were cars made in 1945, they would go to law enforcement agencies and other essential users. The average person was not likely to get a vehicle until 1946 or 1947, it was predicted.

By early June 1944 tires were being advertised locally, the first time in several years. However, Grade 1 tires of the best quality were strictly rationed, and even poor Grade 3 tires remained in short supply. Synthetic rubber was available, but there was a shortage of people to process it into tires.[14]

Meanwhile, the war with Germany seemed to be drawing to a conclusion. Crews of B-17 and B-24 bombers over the skies of the Fatherland were no longer met with swarms of enemy fighter planes. One by one, German cities were flattened into rubble. By this time several hundred Wolfeboro men and a number of women had gone to war. The front page of the May 26, 1944, issue of the *News* showed five Wolfeboro brothers in the armed forces, the sons of Mr. and Mrs. Bernard Tutt: Richard N., Delmar L., James G., Leon H., and Allan C. The William Massey family also had five sons in the service.

The status of the conflict was provided by an editorial of July 28, 1944:

> The war is working...toward the climax we have all been striving for, not the climax that the Axis had planned. What a long, long road has been traveled since the Germans smashed the Maginot Line and rounded up two million French prisoners; since the British fled France at Dunkirk in their thousands of small boats; since the Germans flooded into Russia sweeping all before them; since Pearl Harbor was left a great funeral pyre of our fighting ships; since Rommel was pounding at the gates of Cairo....
>
> The German people, who were members of the "Master Race," gladly accepted and used the loot of Russia, France, Belgium, Holland, Greece, Poland, and Norway, but now tremble for the wrath to come.... The Japanese, firm believers in the ruthless old saying "Might makes right," and who seized a vast empire, now see their ships sunk day by day, their planes shot out of the sky, and their island garrisons cut off one at a time. The Japs, who once mocked us for our inability to relieve our men at Bataan, now know what it means to be forced to stand helpless while garrison after garrison of their soldiers are wiped from the face of the earth.
>
> Slowly but surely the pattern of things to come is making itself shown in blazing clarity. Now the terrific impact of our great fleets of ships and planes, of our great armies, of our ordnance, are making themselves felt in a manner that shakes the world....

During the conflict, a large flag was stretched over South Main Street between the Bank Building and the Peavey Block. It displayed a gold star with the number of Wolfeboro military personnel deaths recorded below it and a blue star with the number of people in service. By war's end, the totals had increased to 14 gold stars and 293 blue, the former including two sons each from the Archer Tebbetts and Amedee Spadone families.

When a person died in military service, advice of this was made by telegram delivered by special messenger.

The arrival of a taxi with only a driver was an omen of death. This was printed on December 8, 1944:

> This morning a passengerless taxi drove to the door. The driver hung his head as he delivered the telegram: "The Secretary of War regrets your son, Robert H. Ballentine, was killed in action in France on November 16." His mother struggled against the cruel reality of this message.... The details of the action in France may never be known, but it was not in Bob's nature to hold back when there was a job to be done. The chances are he advanced with determination toward an objective—as he had all his life.

As the year progressed and America continued on a course toward victory, domestic problems came to the fore. Strikes, race riots, anti-Semitism, and other incidents made the news. Editor Merrow stated that national leaders had to take clear-cut, decisive actions to prevent racial problems after the war.

As the conflict with Germany and Japan continued, children at Carpenter School did their part in the war effort and collected 162 bushels of milkweed floss for packing into life jackets. Manpower shortages remained widespread. A circuit of lights on South Main Street was blacked out for several nights, as there were only two linemen left to keep the entire municipal system in order. Use of electricity was restricted. No outdoor advertising or show window lighting was allowed, and marquees, such as for a movie theatre, could not use more than 60 watts, the same limit imposed for signs directing the public to doctors and hotels.

In November, 301 Christmas gift boxes were sent to Wolfeboro service people. In the same month it was announced that New Hampshire's quota in the Sixth War Loan was $33 million in bonds, which was enough to build 55 Superfortress bombers. "The giant B-29s now striking Japan cost $600,000." Further:

> The vapor trail from a bomber on a practice flight, so high the plane itself can be neither seen nor heard, makes something new and interesting to watch. Sometimes they streak rapidly across a brilliant blue sky leaving a straight white line behind them as though God were drawing a mark across the heavens. Or, one circles the lake, leaving a halo over the head of our good Saint Winnipesaukee.[15]

### The Year 1945

In late 1944 and early 1945, hopes for a quick peace in Europe were dashed when the Germans mounted a strong counter-offensive. Easing of civilian rationing was curtailed. However, the German action proved temporary. As victory after victory piled up for the Allies, Editor Parker M. Merrow reflected on the situation.

> There is a deep and abiding sense of satisfaction that comes from reading the detailed accounts of the raids on Tokyo. Think back to the days of December 1941. On the morning of December 7, the Japs made their treacherous dawn attack on Pearl Harbor. Their planes bombed our fleet at anchor, like shooting fish in a barrel. They bombed and burned our men in their beds. They struck without warning.... The Japs struck when and where they chose and they struck in the manner that they chose.
>
> Now, just a little over three years later, it is we who strike when and where we choose and in the manner we choose. To the Japanese living in Tokyo, Nagoya, and Osaka, the rumble of the great fleet of B-29s coming over the city must have been like the Day of Doom. The great planes rained down freight car loads of incendiary bombs that no device yet known to man can extinguish. The closely packed houses and factories, where Japs live and work 75,000 per square mile, turned into furnaces. Demolition bombs spread death and destruction ahead of the flames. If a true hell on earth could be created, the American air crews made it in parts of Tokyo, Nagoya, and Osaka.
>
> That is just the beginning.... After Germany collapses, the great air fleets of the Americans will be flown out from Europe. The day is coming when more airpower will be assembled to strike at the island of Japan and the Japanese possessions than has ever been gathered anywhere in the world. No living man can foretell how long the war with Japan will last. But one thing is certain, from now on the Japanese are going to pay, day by day, tenfold and more, for the crime they committed at Pearl Harbor and the days that followed.[16]

On March 30, 1945 this was printed:

> A special short subject on the U.S. Marines landing at Iwo Jima showing at Memorial Hall, Wolfeboro, on Saturday and Sunday, March 31 and April 1.... Not only does the picture show the landing of the U.S. Marines, but the naval battle which was preliminary to the Marines landing. It is said that several local boys are shown in the picture.

In early August, 1945, two atomic bombs dropped on Japan ended World War II. In the several months before then, ships and trains were crowded with soldiers returning from Europe. There was much joy in Wolfeboro, although formal celebration of the conquest of the Nazis was postponed until Japan, too, had fallen. Then this:[17]

> The announcement from the White House of Japan's acceptance of surrender terms and the end of the greatest war in the world's history had not been completed, at 7 o'clock Tuesday night, when Wolfeboro's celebration began.
>
> While we were still listening, the bells of our churches could all be heard ringing out their joy that peace had come at last. Then automobile horns began to be heard, rising steadily into an ear-splitting crescendo, as one and another took their place in a great parade which gathered strength from every section of the town, and continued for hours. One of the Fire Department's trucks joined in with one of the boys ringing a huge bell mounted amidships. As the parade continued, all kinds of noise-makers appeared—horns, cowbells, dinner bells, sleigh bells, trumpets, gongs of different sorts—and pails, old water-tanks etc., dangled and jangled on the ground behind the cars. Then paper streamers of all colors were let loose on the air. Shotguns and rifle fire were heard. Five-inch crackers saved from a Fourth of July celebration of years back began to pop. And believe it or not, a few rockets and aerial bombs even put in their appearance.
>
> The celebration had hardly begun when a parade of boats of all descriptions came across the bay from the general direction of Keniston Island, horns blaring full blast announcing the coming of our summer friends to join with us in a grand good time. A little later, two hayracks full of guests from the Allen "A" came to town with all kinds of noisemakers to help out.

Around eight o'clock an impromptu snake dance, joined in by hundreds—veterans of World War One, old folks and young boys and girls—began through the center of town up one side and back up the other side and back continuing for hours. Torches had popped up from somewhere, red flares that lasted for many minutes, carried by the marchers as they weaved and shouted and sung.

Men went 'round slapping each other on the back and shaking hands; women hugged one another; all congratulated each other that their boys and girls would not have to fight anymore and would soon be home again.

In the midst of the fun, the fire alarm sounded, calling the crew to the campus, to quell a bonfire that was getting out of hand. Oh yes! Of course, there were several false alarms as were to be expected, but everyone was glad that they were false, and even the firefighters were not too disturbed.

As the evening wore on and the marchers began to tire, Harry Harriman Post 18, American Legion, through Commander Marcus Raymond and with the help of Past Commander Fred Tuttle, set up its loudspeaker system in front of Wallace's store and furnished music for square dancing in the street.

Then came community singing, with some especially stirring solos, and some hillbilly numbers, sounded out through the mike.

Amazingly enough there were no accidents and no disorder. Just a grand celebration with only one thing missing to make it perfect. Yes—you guessed it, the boys! But one and all were with us, we know in spirit as our thoughts were with them.

Wolfeboro did itself proud!

After the war, the Harriman-Hale American Legion Post served as a focal point for local service people. On January 16, 1947, Wolfeboro Memorial Post No. 8836, Veterans of Foreign Wars of the United States (VFW), was founded at the Wolfeboro Grange Hall, opening additional social possibilities for those who had served.[18]

### World War II Honor Roll

The following list includes Wolfeboro people who served in the war:[19]

Harold M. Adjutant, Norman L. Adjutant, Owen S. Adjutant, Lee A. Albee, Kenneth M. Alexander, Charles E. Aspinall [Aspinwall in some listings], Albert F. Auderer, Jr.

Robert H. Ballentine,* Hazel L. Bean, Herbert A. Bean, Howard E. Bean, Jr., Hildreth F. Beaulieu, Ludger H. Beaulieu, Jr., Hugh C. Bell, Francis S. Berry, Frank C. Berry, Fred W. Berry, Leonard F. Berry, Raymond J. Berry, Everett J. Bickford, Maurice R. Bickford, Frederick K. Bierweiler, Romeo E. Bilodeau, Lewis P. Bissell, Walter C. Bodwell, James E. Bovaird, M.D., Francis Douglas Bowles, Evelyn M. Brewster, Lloyd F. Brewster, John N. Brewster, Mary C. Brewster, N. Blair Brewster, Charles Brickman, Fred J. Britton, Napoleon Britton, Jr., Harold E. Brock, Clifford R. Brown.

Gordon Carlisle, John G. Carpenter,* James W. Carr, John A. Chamberlain, Mary L. Chamberlain, Arthur F. Chamberlin, Albert J. Champagne, Leodore J. Champagne, Henry J. Champagne, Oliver F. Champagne, Leonard Charles, Chester E. Chellman, Jr., George E. Chick, Jr., Marguerite J. Chick, Russell G. Claflin, John E. Clark, Loring T. Clark, Oscar F. Clark, Jr., Stanley R. Clark, Walter H. Clifford, Jr., Erwin L. Clifford, Lewis W. Clifford, Fred Clough, James L. Clough, Jr., Jesse W. Clow, Earl W. Colby, Gordon P. Colby, Walter B. Colby, Kenneth E. Corliss, Charles F. Corson,* Joseph R. Corson, Eric N. Courtney, Daniel B. Craigue, Jr.,* Donald E. Craigue.

Thomas W. Danforth, Homer W. Davis, Jr., Howard E. Davis, Allan B. Detscher, Richard W. Detscher, Jr., Howard F. Dore, Jesse V. Dore, Lyford W. Dore, Roland F. Dore, Roswell L. Dore, Charles N. Doty, Bruce C. Douglas, James R. Douglas, Leroy E. Dow, Earl W. Drew, Elwyn T. Drew, James E.S. Dunham, DMD.

Elliott Earl, Gilbert H. Edgerly, Sherman Eldridge, Albert Elliott, Robert B. Emerson.

Harlan E. Feyler, Forrest G. Flanders, Charles E. Foss, Jr., Guy L. Foss, Ruth F. Foster, Harold L. Fournier, Edward G. Fraser, Lyle E. Frost.

Alfred J. Gagne, Robert J. Gilman, Ella White Glidden, Donald E. Glidden, George E. Glidden, Gordon E. Glidden, Gordon S. Glidden, Lawrence W. Glidden, Nelson Glidden, Paul V. Glidden, George Glines, Richard Y. Goodhue, Barbara L. Goodrich, Philip F. Gorman, Roger H. Grant, Charles O. Graves, Roger W. Gregory, Alcide J. Grenier, Alonzo J. Grenier,* Leonel V. Grenier, Paul H. Gridley, Asahel M. Guild.

Roger S. Haines, Robert G. Hale, Clayton E. Hale,* Lloyd Winston Hamm, Jr., Arthur W. Hanson, Jr., Robert L. Hanson, Richard M. Hart, Stella L. Hart, Richard Haven, Carleen M. Hayes, Eugene M. Head, William A. Head, Fenner G. Headley, Francis E. Headley, R. Ferrell Headley, Gene L. Herbert, Merland Herbert, Woodrow W. Herbert, Carroll F. Hersey, John W. Hildreth, William W. Hildreth, Sr., William W. Hildreth, Jr., Calvin J. Hill, Howard A. Hooper, Russell R. Hooper, Beatrice L. Horne, Archie A. Horne, Jr., Paul E. Horne, Ralph Merwin Horn, Elmer C. Hurlburt, Albert A. Hutchins, Lyford Hutchins, Russell E. Hutchins, Walter A. Hutchins.

Edwin R. Irish, Louise H. Irish, Robert J. Irish.

Dean M. Jackson, John F. Jarvis, Bernard W. Jewell, Edmund A. Jewell, Martha E. Jewell, Elmore H. Johnson, Kenneth G. Jones, Willard R. Jones, Leon L. Jutras.

Charles W. Kelley, Jr., Harlan B. Kelley, Jr., Willis E. Kelley, Herbert B. Kendall, Jr., Robert E. Kenneson, Alden L. Kimball, Ernest W. Kimball, Gordon S. Kimball, Harold P. Kimball, Robert W. Kimball, Katherine V. Kirkland, M. Priscilla Kirkland.

Leo Lampron, Francis L. Lavertu, Robert N. Leighton, Carl F. Lemery, George Lemery, Frank L. Long, Jr., Fred W. Long, Arnold G. Lord, Charles L. Lord, Orion Lord, Jefferson C. Lovering, Jr., Willard F. Lozon, Carroll L. Lucas, Louis R. Lumbar, Mary A. Luxford.

Leslie W. MacDonald, G. Douglas MacFarlane, David E. MacMartin, Donald E. MacMartin, Edward B. MacMartin, Frank MacMartin, Warren J. MacMartin, Alfred S. Manson, Leon Marden, Jr., Richard G. Marden, Kenneth P. Massey, Richard N. Massey, Roland I. Massey, Warren A. Massey, Ralph W. Mastern, Roger W. Mattison, Frank P. McBride, Maurice F. McBride, William J. McDonald, Arthur L. McHugh, Jr., John D. McHugh II, John D. McHugh III, Lawrence M. McHugh, Robert J. McHugh, Thomas L. McHugh, Thomas R. McHugh, Lawrence McIntyre, Avon W. Miliner, Grover L. Moody, Vilene M. Moody, Walter L. Moody, Clair B. Moore, David B. Moore, Eleanor D. Moore, Harrison D. Moore, Kenneth E. Moore, Marilyn J. Moore, Fred H. Morgan, Kenneth H. Morgan, Lloyd C. Morgan, Lowell C. Morgan, Maynard A. Morgan, Robert E. Mulvey.

George W. Nary, Jr., Lawrence A. Newhall, Frederick A. Nichols, Samuel Niblett, Jr.

Bernard F. Osgood, Howard F. Osgood.

Robert R. Page, Emilio J. Paolucci, Stephen [Sylvester] M. Parshley, Russell Q. Pecunies, Edwin M. Pennell, Sarah Pennell, Henry W. Perry, Raymond E. Perry, Charles C. Piper, Clinton T. Piper, Elmer C. Piper, John Pollini, Raymond F. Pollini, Samuel E. Pollini, Wendell E. Pratt, Frances B. Puffer.

Basil L. Reed, Norman E. Reed, Charles W. Rines, Frank A. Rico, Harry H. Rines, Edward L. Roberge, Robert P. Roberge, Donald O. Roberts, Richard H. Rogers, Lester K. Rouleau, Donald P. Russell, George D. Russell, Kenneth M. Russell.

Howard B. Sabin, John A. Sandstrom, Bernard J. Sargent, Harry A. Sargent, John A. Sargent, R. Mitchell Sherlock, Frank W. Sinclair, Clarence G. Shannon, Lawrence A. Smart, Joseph Howard Smith, Warren A. Smith, Amedee Spadone, Sr., Amedee Spadone, Jr.,* Donald Spadone, Mitchell S. Spadone,* Richard F. Sterling, Vincent R. Stevens, Janet H. Swift, Marguerite Swift.

Charles E. Tebbetts, Harry A. Tebbetts,* Harvey E. Tebbetts,* Carroll E. Thibeau, George E. Thibodeau, Donald C. Thomas, Alvah George Tibbetts, Donald W. Tibbetts, Dorothy B. Tibbetts, Ernest H. Tibbetts, Robert J. Tibbetts, Joseph W. Tinker, Philip E. Thurrell, Robert F. Thurrell, Jr., Roger F. Thurrell, Robert D. Thurston, Wilbur D. Tracy, Joseph F. Turner, Norman W. Turner, Delmar L. Tutt, James G. Tutt, Leon H. Tutt, Richard N. Tutt, Raymond C. Tuttle.

William J. Valley, Jr.,* Henry P. Valley, Joseph Valley, Burtis F. Vaughan, Jr., Irving L. Vaughan.

Hugh S. Wallace, Earl Leonard Walsh, Jr., Donald E. Walter, William G. Welch, J. Arthur Wheeler, Jr., John L. Wentworth, Albert E. White, Alvin R. White, Joseph W. White, Jr., Harold T. Whittum, Jr., Ernest H. Wilkes, Ernest B. Wilshire, Frederick I. Wood, Lawrence J. Wood.

Frank H. York, Wallace York.

Elwin H. Young, Lloyd W. Young.*

## ECONOMICS AND TOURISM

### Just Before the War

Prices in 1941 were higher than in the depth of the Depression in 1933. In July a wage of 40¢ per hour was offered for a man willing to clerk in a local store. The Allen "A" Camps paid $25 per week (plus noon meals) for housekeepers. New Fords were on display at Horne's Garage, and at the Hart Motor Company a selection of Buicks was on view. Sales were brisk. Downtown stores were busy in 1941, and all was well with commerce.

The 20-acre Furst tract on Clark Point was divided into lots:[20]

> Although Wolfeboro for some time has been enjoying a healthy real estate business, the sale of this property represents the largest group of new homes to be planned in any section for several years. The Municipal Electric Department and the Water Department are cooperating by extending their facilities to this tract.

### Factory Street

In January 1941 a new company opened at the Clark Shop on Factory Street. Known as B.H. Wilson Fisheries, the firm sought to employ 35 women and 15 men. The payroll was anticipated to be $1,000 per week. The operation lasted for just a short time.

Trying to find tenants for the two town-owned buildings on Factory Street (the Bell Shop at the west end and the Clark Shop in the middle) continued to be a prime objective of local officials as well as a group of businessmen known as the Wolfeboro Industrial Committee. "Hope springs eternal" must have been the motto of those involved, or "If at first you don't succeed, try, try again." In any event, a parade of business candidates demanded concessions from the town and in return usually paid minimum wages, provided little or no employee benefits, and operated for just a short time.[21] Disregarding the lessons of history, local merchants continued to believe that if out-of-town manufacturers could be brought to Wolfeboro, business conditions would somehow be ideal. As before, few if any incentives were offered to merchants and tourist-based businesses which, in fact, were the true backbone of the local economy.

The chronicle of yet another hopeful situation began in the *Granite State News,* April 25, 1941:

> The Wolfeboro Industrial Committee is negotiating with a high class established shoe firm to open the Bell Factory within a short time....

More on June 20, 1941:

> The Wentworth Shoe Company, which is setting up its equipment in the Bell Shop, expects to be ready to begin operations the first of July.

July 11, 1941:

> Howard Webber, superintendent at the Wentworth Shoe Shop, intends to hire between 75 and 100 men and women.... The company manufactures lounging slippers.... The stitching room went into operation Thursday morning, and all indications are that orders will be steady and plentiful.

February 27, 1942:

> The Wentworth Shoe Company reports that they are manufacturing about 30 cases of shoes per day. There are plenty of orders on hand and full-time work is expected to continue indefinitely. At present there are about 40 employees.

May 22, 1942:

> Three of the "treers" at the shoe shop walked out Tuesday morning for more pay, but the shop was on regular schedule Wednesday morning.

Like many of its Factory Street predecessors, the Wentworth firm lasted but a short time, probably not past 1942.

### Local Commerce in Wartime

From 1941 through 1945 commerce in Wolfeboro was subdued. A number of businesses reduced their operations or closed their doors. Eventually, nearly all eligible men ages 18 through 45 were in the military service, resulting in a shortage of manpower. It became difficult to have crops harvested, and children pitched in, as did women and older folks. In downtown stores the owners were often absent, having set up caretaker arrangements with friends, employees, or family members, often to the detriment of profits. New inventory was diffi-

Alvan T. Hatch and his wife Mabel Fullerton Hatch on the steps of their home, "Goose Acres," on North Main Street, circa early 1940s. Alvan, earlier in the jewelry trade, became a local dairy farmer. His wife styled herself as "The Goose" and wrote a popular column for the *Granite State News.* Alvan passed away in 1945, Mabel in 1956.

"Goose Acres." (Photograph taken years later when the home was owned by Lester E. and Evelyn Y. Bean.)

cult to obtain, particularly for anything crafted in wood or metal. Imports of gifts and novelties were virtually halted. The local economy was "on hold."

### Will Anyone Come?

In 1941 before the war, the local tourist business was flying high. The Independence Day weekend was reported as "the most successful our state's recreation industry has ever seen."

By 1942 optimism had turned to worry. America was deep in war, and the future was unknown. In February the editor of the local paper expressed concern that rationing of tires and gasoline might precipitate "the worst [season the] recreation industry has ever known" plunging many people "deep in the red.... Grass will start to sprout on our express highways and the tourist business will be a thing of the past."

However, there was also the possibility of a silver lining. As the coastal areas were under threat of German raids, it was foreseen that "vacationists will flock to the mountains and inland lakes." Further: "If the Germans should give Boston or New York a token bombing in the middle of June, the rush to the country for the summer would make a gold rush seem like an old ladies' home out for a Sunday afternoon stroll by comparison." However, in retrospect it seems difficult to envision families from nearby states enjoying themselves boating in Wolfeboro Bay while bombs were falling on Times Square or the Massachusetts State House.

On the lighter side, on June 12, 1942, a well-known local restaurant and tourist stop placed this front-page advertisement:

> Something new at Bailey's: Marion and Allan E. Bailey wish to announce the birth of a son, Allan E. Bailey, Jr., June 11, 1942.

As it turned out, the tourist business was satisfactory for just about everyone in the summer of 1942. Summer camps were filled to capacity with arrivals by train, bus, and boat, "by almost any form of transportation, in fact, except automobile." On Lake Wentworth "Point Breeze camps are filled to overflowing with vacationists." More factual were the numbers of automobiles and tourists stopping at the Information Booth manned by the Chamber of Commerce on Brewster field:

> Summer 1940: 2,153 cars and 8,005 people.
> Summer 1941: 3,724 cars and 10,815 people.
> Summer 1942: 1,972 cars and 6,383 people.

Although absolute numbers were reduced in 1942, it seems that all local restaurants and lodging places were very grateful for the business they did get. Many hotels were closed on the New England seacoast during this summer.

In November the oil-fired steam power plant on the *Mount Washington* boat was removed and sent off to the Navy. The next two tourist seasons would see virtually no power boating on the lake. The summers of 1943 and 1944 can best be described as slow. There were tourists in town, but the entire industry was in low gear due to shortages of gasoline and tires, men being in the service, and other aspects of the war effort.

In early August, 1945, public cruises on Lake Winnipesaukee were resumed with the launching of the 65-foot diesel powered *Sophie C.*, which accommodated 100.[22]

### Wartime Hardships

Effective April 9, 1942, no new residential construction in excess of $500 (later, $200) could be started. However, farm buildings costing up to $1,000 could be built. Lumber was needed in other quarters, as noted on April 24:

> With the strong and steady demand for box boards to make ammunition and gun shipping cases, the crash of the falling tree and the whine of the sawmills are heard throughout the county of Carroll. Not since the days of the First World War has so much lumber been sawed and chipped.

The farm trade prospered in 1942. Cotton Mountain Farm enjoyed a strong market for its chickens. Not far away, Earl Adjutant in East Wolfeboro sold his corn crop to two canning factories. Apples, maple syrup, and dairy products were also in great demand.

Horne's Garage and the Hart Motor Co. no longer had new Fords, Buicks, or Chevrolets for sale. Instead, they concentrated in keeping old vehicles rolling and selling what used cars they could find.

There were many dollars chasing fewer goods and, as a result, nearly all available products rose in price. The OPA slapped new price controls and rations on many items. For example, the retail price of a quart of milk was pegged at 14¢ to 16¢ in Wolfeboro. Producers were caught in a price squeeze. Labor and supplies cost more, but no higher prices could be charged to customers. Black markets arose, but not as much (if at all) locally as in distant areas. Some stores closed due to lack of merchandise. For a time Porter's Hardware and the store next to it were shuttered.

In 1944 the Quick Freeze Locker Service was set up on Railroad Avenue. Produce from Victory Gardens could be stored in refrigerated drawers, and withdrawals could be made at will. However, within a decade or so home freezers were all the rage, and the local plant became redundant.

Several private kindergartens sprang up during World War II and later years, freeing mothers to do work elsewhere.[23]

### Me-First-Itis

In the autumn of 1945, with the war now part of history, consumer confidence soared. Returning servicemen

**An Osgood family get-together in 1949. The Osgoods have been prominent in town activities for many years. Front row, left to right: JoAnn T. Osgood with Johnnie, Esther D. Osgood with Laurie, Ruth Osgood, Barbara O. de Bruyn with Karen Osgood, Lillian O. Brookes with Chip, and Phyllis Osgood. Back row: Len de Bruyn, Bernard Osgood, Fred Osgood, Donald Brookes, and Mary Osgood. (Ruth Osgood Glidden Collection)**

Activities in the cold season: Dockside in late winter or early spring. At the left a dump truck discharges a load of snow into Wolfeboro Bay. In the distance wooden "bob houses" await removal and storage for the season.

Activities in the warm season: Happy campers at Camp Kehonka in the 1940s. Girls gather in a lodge to knit, read, and talk.

FAMILY ALBUM:

Top left: Ruth Goodwin (daughter-in-law of Helen and Frank Goodwin) with her two children, Joyce and J. Frank ("Jeff") III, August 1, 1948.

Top right: J. Frank and Ruth Goodwin's daughter Joyce and her two children, Stephany and Scott, in the 1960s.

Bottom left: Peter J. Stanard at his Mobil station on North Main Street (on the site where the Wolfeboro Marketplace is today) passing out Hallowe'en candy to school children, an annual tradition at his business. Circa early 1970s.

Bottom right: J. Frank Goodwin, Jr., and his wife Ruth, September 14, 1941. (Jeff Goodwin and Joyce Goodwin Stanard Collections)

and others who had been outside of the community, plus local people who were feeling optimistic, bought many properties that had been on the market. Labor was in short supply. Wages rose.

Labor unrest pervaded America. During the war John L. Lewis had been criticized by millions when he led his United Mine Workers out on strike; after all, wasn't winning the war more important? Apparently not.

After the war all hell broke loose. In January 1946 any prospect of getting a new car soon was dashed by automobile workers on picket lines. Mabel Fullerton Hatch opined that "We are suffering from an acute seizure of me-first-itis. It is a bad malady, only to be cured by the steady application of the Golden Rule, we reckon." Alas, Hatch was an idealist. Reality was different, and strikes continued in many industries.

Editor Parker M. Merrow had this to say:

> Unrest on the part of labor, dissatisfaction on the part of the manufacturer, disgust on the part of the consumer, fear on the part of the farmer, are all widespread. Each day that goes by without the production of durable goods in appreciable quantities brings major inflation nearer. Labor wants more money for less work. That is only natural. The manufacturer demands more money for his product because he is paying higher wages. The farmer wants subsidies to keep crop prices from dropping. The Administration wants no rise in the price of manufactured goods or foodstuffs. Goods are not coming up in the market. Money is plentiful and cheap.
>
> Without goods to take up the extra money the spread of inflation mounts from day to day. The consumer, who had been promised a flood of fine new merchandise as soon as the war was finished, is still making his worn-out equipment do and now cannot even buy parts to patch it up. A series of strikes and a series of arguments over price ceilings tie up industry after industry. As soon as one production bottleneck is cleared up, another one develops. Financially, the country is in a bad way. No one thinks of this because he has a pocketful of cheap money. But the truth of the matter is that we are mortgaged to the hilt by the Second World War. Our national debt is tremendous, and we are making no effort to reduce it....

Internationally, world peace was now threatened by communism. Optimism was replaced by disgust and a sense of futility. Finishing last in the race was the average American citizen.[24]

On September 27, 1946, a columnist in the local paper mused, "When do you suppose we will get some meat?" In the meantime, meat was abundant north of the border in Canada but could not be readily imported. Butter remained scarce in the United States, but large quantities of butter were being shipped by the United States government as relief to people in Japan, although people there had never seen butter before and didn't know what it was, nor did they want it; they had only used oil for cooking.

New cars remained rare. Through August 1946 the production of Chevrolets was at a rate of only 22.6% of what it had been before the war in 1941.

**Postwar Tourism**

In the summer of 1946 the local tourist business was hectic, prompting the paper to print this in July:[25]

> Right now our recreation industry is enjoying the greatest season in its history. Every available bit of housing, down to a hen coop, is rented. Roads are jammed with cars on the weekends. Merchants report record sales. Over the long holiday weekend, the shelves of the average grocery looked as if a swarm of locusts moved in, fed, and moved out.
>
> With abundant business and with a shortage of goods and housing, it is a real temptation for anyone in the recreation business to use a take-it-or-leave-it attitude. After explaining to the 300th customer that there is only vanilla ice cream, no meat, no soda pop, no butter, the bread is all gone, and that the *Boston Heralds* never did show up anyway, there is a very understandable temptation to get a bit short of tongue and temper. But it is well to remember that other summers are coming. Next year the quick hot money will have all been spent. The recreation business will be back on a highly competitive basis once more....

"Restricted clientele" signs continued to be posted on a number of local tourist accommodations including the General Wolfe Inn (today known as the Windrifter) and a new facility opened on Whitten Neck by Edward Zulauf. Jews were still discriminated against, but not to the extent of pre-war times.

During the same era the most popular local facility was the Allen "A" Camps (later called the Allen "A" Resort) on Route 28, operated by Mr. and Mrs. Allen H. Albee. Each summer, notable entertainers from New York City and elsewhere would hold shows. While the Allen "A" allowed Jewish patrons (having changed its earlier policy), there were other restrictions. Mildred A. Beach commented:[26]

> Still in my memory is seeing a large sign behind the registration desk that read "If alcohol is a major part of your vacation, please do not bother to register."

**The Tourist Trade (1946)**

The burgeoning tourist industry of 1946, with its "No Vacancy" signs, attracted a number of business people to town. At the September 9 gathering of the Chamber of Commerce, "Howard Avery, president, after a short business meeting, introduced many who have recently come to town as proprietors of hotels and lodges."[27]

Among the newcomers to the trade was Wendell Emery Carr, who had been a prominent visitor in the 1930s and a resident after that. He enjoyed sports and figured prominently in the activities of the Abenaki Outing Club. In October 1945 he purchased Charlie's Diner from Charles E. Rowse, followed in December by the acquisition of the Museum Lodges in Tuftonboro (resold in May 1946), and in the summer of 1946 the venerable General Wolfe Inn (resold in spring 1947). Wendy Carr, as he was known, had a trading instinct and enjoyed buying properties, improving them, and

The Carr House, Mr. and Mrs. James W. Carr, proprietors, at the corner of North Main Street and Sewall Road was built as a private residence in 1812 and first opened as a guest facility in 1931. By the 1940s it was a well-known local stopping place. Years later it was vastly altered and expanded, and today it is known as the Wolfeboro Inn.

The Brightwaters Inn on the shore of Wolfeboro Bay at the end of Lake Street. Owned by Mr. and Mrs. Herman Wallenfels, the facility opened under the Brightwaters name in May 1946. Today the structure still stands and is part of the Windrifter Yacht Club.

then selling for a profit.[28] Meanwhile, he and his family lived in several different houses during the decade.

Mr. and Mrs. Herman G. Wallenfels bought Shaw's-on-the-Lake at the end of Lake Street, renamed it the Brightwaters Inn, and did a lively trade, later adding the Terrace Dining Room.

### The Economy (1947-1948)

Restrictions and shortages eased in 1947. Household appliances such as refrigerators, tools, and space heaters became readily available. All the rage was the front-loading Bendix Automatic Home Laundry, a departure from the tub-and-wringer models sold before the war. Cars were being delivered slowly, and there were long waiting lists. Surprisingly, pleasure boats were in generous supply, including new plastic-hull models. Most people felt there was enough unfulfilled demand for goods that prosperity would continue through at least 1949. Cash remained plentiful.

In 1948 meat and butter continued to be scarce and expensive. In April the latter was 93¢ a pound. Sawyer's Sales Shed on Varney Road did a lively business selling used goods plus occasional parcels of real estate, and each week ran humorous classified advertisements. The latest fad in building was concrete blocks, which took the place of brick and stone in many applications.

In June the Belknap Corporation, recently located in the town-owned Clark Shop on Factory Street, wanted to hire "at least 50 girls," presumably at cheap wages, to work on textiles. There was a lot of hoopla, and the town obligingly put up $7,000 cash to repair the factory. In due course, the business folded.

In the same year, the first innovative postwar automobile designs made their appearance. A new entry was the Kaiser-Frazer, which was sold through local Texaco gas station dealer Howard E. Keith at the corner of South Main and Union Streets. He advertised "deliveries daily," although such a sales rate is highly doubtful. New styling on Hudsons and Fords attracted a lot of attention, mostly window shopping, as quantities were not at hand.[29]

### The Tourist Trade (1947-1949)

In 1947 the tourist trade continued its boom. Witness this account dated July 6:

If you had bed or board to sell or give away over the holiday you found it snapped up. The story was the same in all the tourist lodges and restaurants. They were not only full, they overflowed.

In the same summer, the Aeromarina was opened by the Northeast Equipment Co. on the shore off North Main Street. Forty feet of lakefront was filled in to expand the facility which served both boats and seaplanes. Around the same time, the Brightwaters Inn at the end of Lake Street expanded its acreage by dumping rocks into the water. Lest a present-day reader find this violation of the lake to be unusual, it should be mentioned that a new master plan for the town, unveiled in 1949, proposed that much of Back Bay be filled in, so that the water would run in a narrow channel. However, this never came to pass. Had it not been for the time-honored practice of augmenting one's real estate holdings by filling in Lake Winnipesaukee, much of what is now known as the downtown Wolfeboro business district would be underwater today. There would be no Avery Building, no Latchaw Building, Black's Paper Store, no Railroad Station, no Post Office, no central shopping district.

Increased numbers of tourists meant more problems, not the least of which was parking congestion, sometimes with two or three cars deep along North and South Main Streets. Should parking meters be installed? Should there be town parking lots? These and other questions were considered. At the September 8 meeting of the Chamber of Commerce, gripes of summer visitors were aired, including poor fishing (rebuttal: it will improve), stream pollution, scarcity of public bathing beaches, noisy airplanes, and high taxes. In season, 2,476 cars and 8,017 people stopped at the Information Booth.

In 1948 it happened. Business slowed. Visitors still came to town, but they spent less money. The cause seemed to be the diversion of cash elsewhere, due to the high cost of food and clothing, plus new deliveries of automobiles, washing machines, radios and refrigerators that had been awaited for years. Finally, the tourist business was becoming competitive.[30] In the same year, Clearwater Lodges opened on North Main Street on a section of shorefront once a part of the old Fay farm. This attractive colony of lakeside cabins proved to have great longevity and is still going strong today.

On March 8, 1949, the townspeople voted to take over the maintenance and upkeep of the Libby Museum. It was estimated that 8,000 to 10,000 people went through its doors each season, except when it was closed during the war. In the summer of the same year, local tourism spending was subdued, continuing the 1948 trend.

### 1949: Slow Times

"A mild depression, recession or technical corrective has set in," the *News* commented in January 1949. Except for automobiles, nearly all consumer demand had been filled, and in some areas of the market there was a glut. By May, business conditions in Wolfeboro were slow. The rush for erecting houses and summer camps was over, and many local tradesmen contented themselves with repairs and odd jobs.

Once again the Chamber of Commerce stated that the cure to all local economic ills was to bring new indus-

Equestrian activities at the Allen "A" Resort in the 1940s. Located on Route 28, the popular stopping place offered many forms of entertainment to families who typically came from Massachusetts or Rhode Island to stay a week or two in the facility's cottages during the summer.

Main Dining Hall of the Allen "A" Resort in the 1940s. From a postcard sent by a visitor, postmarked July 16, 1946, and inscribed on the reverse as follows: "I am having week vacation here at the Allen A Camp and it is a beautiful place & lots of fun."

tries into town. A committee named Wolfeboro Industries was set up, and, by gosh, if out-of-town businessmen wouldn't rent the vacant Clark Shop on Factory Street, then Wolfeboro Industries would turn the economic tide on its own by making wood products! Great profits were envisioned but did not materialize.

Local merchants banded together to stimulate holiday sales by staying open evenings. Santa Claus (played by Matt Brendel, owner of Clearwater Lodges) was in town, with headquarters at Orville Porter's hardware store. Other events included caroling by the boys' and girls' chorus of Carpenter School and the Girl Scouts.[31]

**1950: Decade's End**

According to the State Constitution, business in New Hampshire in 1950 still should have been conducted in British pounds, shillings, and pence, as it had been when the state was founded. The politicos in Concord decided that it was about time the state recognized dollars and cents, and on December 1, 1950, the Constitutional Convention made the necessary revision.

In 1950 new automobiles were readily available at long last on the market. To stimulate sales, Ford suggested that families would do well to own two cars, a sedan and a station wagon, available locally at Horne's Garage. At the intersection of Routes 28 and 109 in Wolfeboro Center, the Lakes Region Motor Co., owned by Stanley N. Juthe (earlier by Elbridge Robie), featured 1950 Austins, including the Atlantic convertible, the Countryman station wagon, a panel delivery truck, and a half-ton pickup. Juthe had come to town from Massachusetts in 1942 and purchased the Stephen W. Clow estate atop Clow's Hill, renaming it Hillsbaron.

A visitor to Wolfeboro in 1949 or 1950 would have been able to patronize the following businesses and professional services, among many others:

Insurance firms included the J. Clifton Avery Agency, the John M. Mixer Agency, the Brummitt Agency, Clinton T. Piper (successor to the business of his father, Carroll D. Piper), Wayne L. Parkhurst (successor to his father-in-law, Sherman D. Brummitt), and the Norman Turner Agency.

Also prominent on the insurance scene was the William J. Britton Agency. Britton died on November 11, 1949. Upon his death, W. LeRoy Haven, minister of the First Congregational Church, suggested that if a survey had been taken asking, "Who is Wolfeboro's first citizen?" the winner would have been Britton, who had been a lawyer and judge, moderator of town meetings, and a trustee of Huggins Hospital and Brewster Academy, among other accomplishments. His insurance agency on Railroad Avenue continued under the management of Carlotta Kimball.[32]

There were nearly half a dozen cars for hire in town, the most active service being Roy's Taxi, operated by Francis Roy assisted by John Lyman and Fred Long. Roy's used three cabs, two of which had radio telephones.

On North Main Street the Dorothy Ann Store sold women's fashions under the management of Richard W. Detscher. Next door to the right, in a small building put up on the front lawn of Carroll D. Piper, was the real estate office of Clarence M. Mixer & Son (John), which had moved from Tuftonboro to Wolfeboro in February 1947. Another local realtor, established in town in 1919, was Clarence W. Estabrook, who in 1950 had as an associate John R. Lovering. In the same profession was Norman Turner, with Wendell Carr as his partner. Joseph I. Melanson, Jr., was a real estate seller and developer on a very large scale and by April 1949 owned over 44,000 feet of Lake Winnipesaukee shore frontage in Alton (Black Point Estates), Meredith (Col. Cummings estate), and Moultonboro (Castle Shores). In 1950 he bought Rattlesnake Island which he developed, assuring potential buyers, "There are no rattlesnakes on Rattlesnake Island."

Corkum's Men's Shop, operated by Cecil ("Steve") Corkum, did a lively trade, as did the Harmony Gift Shop and Gould's Dime Store. Manning's Jewelry, owned by Mr. and Mrs. Horace D. Manning, sold watches, rings, and other goods. In 1948 Harry W. May joined the firm as a clock repairer.

Haskins Hardware had been operating since 1946 as the successor to the old-time H.H. Wallace Hardware business. For a time it seemed that Clayton M. Wallace would continue the store, but his career interest turned to temperance, and he moved to Indianapolis to lead the Anti-Saloon League. Wayside Appliances, owned by Roy G. Nelson, was located on the corner of Lake and North Main Streets. Brocky's, Inc. (Harold E. Brock), a West Ossipee appliance dealer, had a Wolfeboro outlet for a short time and offered radios, washers, ranges, and other goods.

The venerable Paper Store, now under the ownership of George D. Black, who bought it from the Irish (surname) family, continued to be a popular local depot for newspapers, magazines, and gifts. Footwear was sold by the Pollini Shoe Store (Primo Pollini) and Harold F. Brown. Leon Robinson sold dry goods.

Various service stations of the era dispensed Atlantic, Tydol, Gulf, Socony (Mobil), Amoco, Texaco, and Esso products.

Groceries of the decade of the 1940s included Clark's, Nation-Wide Store, Lamprey's, Kent's, Stockbridge's, the new Market Basket (opened by Ralph Stinchfield in 1949), A&P, Bowman's, Bourdon's General Store, and Carl Young's.

The Lakeview Oil Company, Roy W. Foster, and Wood's Wolfeboro Oil took care of local heating and other fuel needs. The Diamond Match Co. in Wolfeboro Falls advertised a complete line of building supplies. Andrew F. Doe and Fred E. Varney were among a dozen or more local contractors.

Emerson's Dry Cleaning Service and the nearby Wolfeboro Laundry (Libby Laundry) enjoyed an active business. Drugs and notions were purveyed by Tobey's Drug Store, Hall's Pharmacy, and McFadden & Libbey (a Walgreen Agency store since 1949).

James J. Kalled, who had come to town in 1948, was fast building his career in the legal profession and had recently purchased the former Henry F. Libby (of museum fame) home on Winter Harbor. In the same year, Jerry L. Thayer became associated with the local law practice of Eliot U. Wyman.

In the printing trade, the Kingswood Press, managed since 1948 by Gordon D. Swaffield, was the leading local firm, although there were several others in town during the decade, including Creative Printing (L. Winston Hamm, 1947).

Local restaurants, mostly seasonal, included Bailey's on South Main Street, the Dockside at the *Mount Washington* wharf, the Barn Dining Room at the Colonial Arms, the Terrace Dining Room (part of the Brightwaters Inn), the Lakeview Cabins and Restaurant, the diner and adjoining restaurant near the Main Street bridge (operated under several different names, including Charlie's, Wendy's, and White's), and the Carr House.

As had been the case since its founding in 1906, the Wolfeboro National Bank was the only financial institution in town.

## TRANSPORTATION

### Cars, Buses, and Trains

The automobile continued to be the main method of transportation locally, despite great shortages of equipment, fuel, and supplies during the war. In July 1942 the editor of the local paper observed that with lower speed limits and fewer cars on the roads there were fewer accidents. In fact, there had not been a serious accident to report so far that year. Sometimes a driver could go five miles on a main road without meeting a car coming in the other direction!

The Boston & Maine Railroad passenger service came only as close as Sanbornville. Beginning on June 18, 1942, connecting bus service to Wolfeboro was instituted. In the same year, a bus route from Wolfeboro to Melvin Village was set up under the direction of Roscoe Adjutant. The first schedule called for trips on Wednesdays and Saturdays. Mabel Fullerton Hatch, who lived on the road to Melvin Village, commented that "there has been no public conveyance available here since stagecoach days."

The gasoline shortage didn't bother Oscar York, of Sewall Road, who took an old Stanley Steamer and converted it to use wood and coal, so that he "passes gasoline pumps without even a glance to the right or left. A pound of coal carries him about a mile, with the heavily loaded trailer attached to the car." He loaded about 200 to 300 pounds of coal aboard.

In the 1940s Wolfeboro was served by Interstate Lines bus to Alton Bay and Sanbornville, connecting to Boston, Manchester, and other points.[33]

By 1950 automobiles became widely available once again, and dependence on bus and rail transportation diminished.

### Aviation

Aviation facilities grew apace in town after the war. On May 31, 1946, the Northeast Equipment Co. announced a new service for summer residents—a seaplane base on the lake shore behind the company's office on North Main Street. A new Piper Cub pontoon plane was available for charter trips, and a Republic Seabee amphibian accommodating four persons was on order. Manager James A. Wales, Jr., had been in the aviation business since 1933 in New York.

The leading lights of local aviation were Ralph Merwin Horn and his wife Eleanor, who before the war and again beginning in 1944, operated the Lakes Region Flying Service. During the war Merwin Horn was a flight instructor for two years for the Army Air Corps. In September 1944 the Horns had a Piper Cub on floats and a Taylor Craft on wheels, and had about 20 students in their flying school. It was expected that their airport on Wolfeboro Neck would be completed the following spring and have a 3,500-foot main runway and a secondary 2,500-foot strip.

In the summer of 1947 the airport was approved by the Civil Aeronautics Board. On June 16, 1950, the first twin-engine craft, a Cessna, landed there. Aboard were Mr. and Mrs. Bradley Frankum, who owned a summer home on Johnson Cove next to the airport.

Meanwhile other aircraft made the news. In September 1947 low-level flying over land and Lake Winnipesaukee was being done with P-51 Mustang fighter aircraft of the 82nd Fighter Group from Grenier Field, in groups of four, cruising at 280 miles an hour.

On November 21, 1949, Wolfeboro residents were subjected to a new type of advertising. A twin Cessna from New York made several passes over town advertising 1950-model Hudson automobiles. "The music was easily heard, and in the downtown district the descriptive speech was fairly well understood."[34]

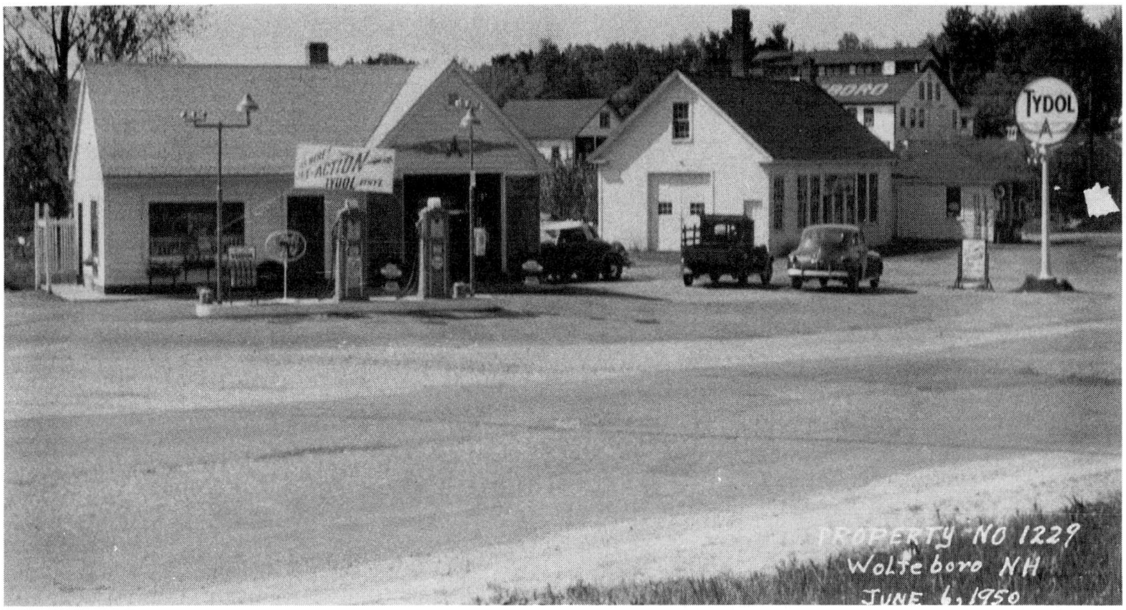


Flying "A" Tydol gasoline station near the corner of Lehner and Center Streets. Later in the decade the Wolfeboro Shopping Center was built on the site to the right of the station. In the distance part of WOLFEBORO lettered on the Wolfeboro Laundry building can be seen. (June 6, 1950 photograph; Howard Bean Collection)

Flying "A" station a few years later with Wolfeboro Oil Co. sign on the roof. (November 1957 photograph; Howard Bean Collection)

## THE LOCAL PAPER

### Wartime

During World War II the *Granite State News* experienced a sharp reduction in advertising. With food being rationed and manufactured goods being scarce if not non-existent, there was little need to advertise for customers, many of whom were serving overseas anyway. This, combined with paper shortages, resulted in the *News* occasionally having four-page issues.

Accounts of the war pervaded the paper, with overseas letters and dispatches from local servicemen (and a few servicewomen) being published. During the height of the conflict, virtually every issue had a service person pictured on the front page.

Complimentary subscriptions to the local paper were given to Wolfeboro servicemen by the Chamber of Commerce. In one instance, a local soldier stationed in North Africa spied a white object in the distance on the sand of a forlorn desert, drew closer, and found it was a copy of the *Granite State News*.

### Business Items

In March 1942 the office of the newspaper moved to new premises in the building formerly occupied by the Hutchins Hat Shoppe on North Main Street.

Throughout the period, Ralph G. Carpenter II continued as owner and publisher, and Norman W. Turner as business manager. The pair also owned the Carpenter & Turner real estate and insurance agency. Carpenter spent most of his time as fish and game commissioner for the state of New Hampshire. Writing was not his forte.

Printing was done in Ossipee by the Independent Press. Editor Parker M. Merrow, who lived in Ossipee and also wrote the very popular "Hank" column, which in dialect gave a country hick's view of goings-on, a sharp contrast to Merrow's erudite commentaries on the editorial page.

The November 29, 1946, issue was the last to come off the old Cottrell printing press used in Center Ossipee since 1924. Years earlier, it had been employed in Boston to print *The Youth's Companion*. Replacing it was a used Miehle press bought in Portland. The superannuated Cottrell was smashed into bits and melted by Kenneth Berry of Wolfeboro Falls, who poured the metal into castings at his Berry Machine Shop.[35]

Beginning with the issue of July 29, 1949, the *News* went to eight columns per page rather than seven, to bring "this paper into conformity with about 90% of all weeklies in the nation." This made it easier to use stock advertising plates.

### Columns

During the decade many regular columns appeared in the local paper. "The Quiet Hour," written by a Maine contributor, gave Christian religion information. "Brewster Briefs" told of school news (in 1947, Warren Thompson was editor of the column). "Wolfeboro Personals," written by Gertrude B. Hamm and others, told of local happenings.

Hamm wrote many feature articles as well. That she was a mainstay of the paper is evidenced by this commentary in the issue of March 26, 1946, in which she responded to criticism that the paper had carried no coverage of a recent event: "Sorry about town meeting, but they have no accommodations in the Town Hall for 'mattress voters', mattresses and all." She had been home in bed sick for the preceding five weeks. Apparently there was no backup!

In autumn and early winter 1947, Gertrude B. Hamm was editor of *News of Our Town*, a tabloid newspaper published for a short time. Her son L. Winston Hamm was publisher.

The December 31, 1948, issue of the *Granite State News* told of another local newspaper launched by a young entrepreneur:

> Among the budding businessmen of Wolfeboro is Paul Hatch of Union Street, age 11. He is doing both letterpress and multigraphing work in a credible manner, though in a small way, and is planning to try to publish a neighborhood newspaper. He says the toughest problem is to get reporters. Among his Christmas gifts were a paper cutter and a cash register for his shop. Until recently, he and Danny Haskins have been in partnership, but Paul has bought Danny out.

A year and a half later, on July 21, 1950, this notice appeared:

> Hatch's Printing Company, Wolfeboro, wishes to announce the starting of *The Enterprise News*, published weekly, on sale Monday, 5¢, brought to your door.

## POLITICS AND MOVEMENTS

### H. Styles Bridges

H. Styles Bridges won a second term as U.S. senator on November 3, 1942, and a third term on November 2, 1948. By the latter year he was one of the most influential people in Washington and served as chairman of the Senate Committee on Appropriations, ranking member of the Senate Armed Services Committee, chairman of the Joint Committee of the Senate and House Representative on Foreign Aid, chairman of the Joint Committee of the Senate and House of Representatives on the Federal Budget, and a member of the National Forest Reservation Commission.

In January 1946 it was announced that Senator. and Mrs. Bridges had acquired the Ralph Y. Scott property on Sewall Road, an eight-room house with about 100 feet of shorefront.[36] In 1952 Senator and Mrs. Bridges built a log-cabin style cottage off Forest Road on Wolfeboro Neck.[37]

### Presidential Contests

In 1944 President Franklin Delano Roosevelt, seeking a fourth term, opposed Thomas E. Dewey, the Republican contender. The *Granite State News* made token objections to Roosevelt's continuation and faintly (from the standpoint of space used) endorsed Dewey. However, by this time the war was drawing to a definite conclusion, victory over Germany seemed imminent and very few people were willing to change horses in midstream, so to speak. Despite Roosevelt's overwhelming win nationally on November 7, 1944, on the local scene Dewey had a strong majority, with 884 votes to the incumbent's 398. Thus it can be said that none of Roosevelt's four presidential wins was helped by local ballots.

On April 20, 1945, this appeared in the *Granite State News:*

> The death of President Roosevelt [on April 12] came at a particularly inopportune time.... Men who opposed him bitterly in the conflict of politics during the days of peace supported him staunchly in time of war, for they knew that in Franklin Roosevelt there lived one of the great leaders of true democracy, both in spirit and in practice. Why he should be taken at this critical hour no man can say. We simply know that the great and gallant leader has gone from the scene of conflict and the nation is much the poorer for his passing.

After Roosevelt's death Vice-President Harry S Truman ascended to the presidency. Truman's actions were often ridiculed in the local paper, an expected situation in view of its long-time Republican bias.

In 1948 the contest between incumbent Truman and challenger Thomas E. Dewey caused relatively little local attention. Dewey, it was said, had compiled an impressive record as governor of New York state, and it was expected he would trample Truman, who was considered responsible for allowing strikes, inflation and the spread of communism to occur.

Indeed, if Wolfeboro results had been representative of the nation, Dewey would have won in a landslide. The local tally was 1,045 votes for Dewey and a paltry 249 for Truman. However, the rest of the country felt differently, and Truman was elected.

### Sherman Adams

Sherman Adams entered the national political scene in 1944 when he was named to Congress to represent the Second District of New Hampshire. In 1948 he was elected governor of the state, and in 1950 he was voted in for a second term. In the 1950s Adams became influential in the Eisenhower administration until he succumbed to a patronage scandal, after which he returned to New Hampshire and founded the Loon Mountain ski resort in Lincoln. During the 1940s he was a frequent visitor to Wolfeboro.

### Also in Politics

The Townsend Plan movement, such a vital part of national and local politics during the Depression, came to an end in Wolfeboro in 1941.

The "liquor question" was always good for a debate and the 1940s decade was no exception. The Woman's Christian Temperance Union remained active locally, but it was more of a social group than a destroy-the-saloons movement.

Time after time, alcohol came up on the local ballot. In the November 7, 1944 election, the town voted 547 for and 448 against state liquor stores and 678 for and 387 against beer sales. By 1948 state liquor stores had become popular, and in the November 2 election Wolfeboro voted 722 yes and only 291 no on the subject. The yeas and nays for beer remained about the same as four years earlier, now 651 yes and 329 no.

One of the most popular politicians in the region was Ansel N. Sanborn, chairman of the Republican State Committee, known locally as the operator of the Memorial Hall (Town Hall) Theatre and Little Theatre (Temple Auditorium) and as the owner of the Wolfeboro Casino.

Among the social and political issues of 1950 were whether a doctor should assist in the death of a terminally-ill patient and whether the government should set up a compulsory health insurance program. The American Medical Association vehemently opposed the latter.

Wolfeboro continued to be governed by three selectmen. The town manager concept was discussed from time to time, but was not adopted. Selectmen of the decade were Howard C. Avery, George R. Britton, Sherman D. Brummitt, J. Frank Goodwin, John C. Kimball, Noyes V. Moore, Wayne L. Parkhurst and Earl F. Willand.[38]

## HAVING FUN

### Hobbies

Hobbies flourished during the 1940s. The Carroll Philatelic Association, named after the county, was reorganized on November 14, 1941, and became known as the Wolfeboro Stamp Club. Monthly meetings were held at the home of club president Mrs. Ralph Horn on North Main Street.

Coin collecting was also popular. For several summers, K.H. Ways, a seasonal visitor, advertised to buy, this being a typical notice: "Old coins wanted, high prices paid. I am not a dealer but a private collector."

In 1941 the local paper reported that three local young men were antique car buffs. The collection of Harry Hopewell on Wolfeboro Neck included a 1921 Dodge town car, a 1905 Grout steamer, and the remains of a 1908 Reo. He also had a Model T Ford and was negotiating for a Stanley Steamer once owned by the late Thomas G. Plant of "Castle in the Clouds" fame. Lewis Bissell of Cotton Mountain had a 1909 Franklin touring car and a 1911 Maxwell. John Nutter of North Wolfeboro was proud of his Model T Ford.[39]

### Indoor Pastimes

Music appreciation was a popular avocation in the 1940s. The continuing popularity of the radio brought with it an increased awareness of music, from country to classical, from big bands to vocal solos. Late in the decade, the phonograph industry was revolutionized by 45 rpm and 33 rpm long-playing records. The days of the old 78 rpm discs were numbered. The Amy Cheney Beach Club, with Mrs. Ella Lord Gilbert as its leading light, was very active during the 1940s. Numerous concerts were presented in the Carpenter auditorium and elsewhere.

By the beginning of the decade nearly every home in Wolfeboro had one or more radios, tuned to the closest station (WLKZ in Laconia) or to Boston, New York, or elsewhere. By 1950 television were installed in a few local homes, although there were no stations in the state, and the black-and-white reception was fuzzy at best.

A 1950 map titled *Where to Find It in Wolfeboro* noted that indoor activities in wintertime included beano games, minstrel shows, baked bean suppers, and local stage plays, along with movies, dancing, and bowling. The Wolfeboro Casino continued to be a prime spot for conviviality.

Films were shown year round at the Memorial Hall Theatre and occasionally at the Little Theatre, the latter having been remodeled in 1946 to include new, comfortable chairs, a new screen, and an improved RCA sound system.[40]

On July 15, 1949, this notice concerning a film and TV star with local connections appeared in the *Granite State News:*

> Miss Estelle Parsons, daughter of Attorney and Mrs. Eben Parsons of Marblehead, Massachusetts and Wolfeboro, was received by President Truman in the Oval Room of the White House on Wednesday, July 29, in company with a group of members of the Washington Students Citizenship seminar.... Miss Parsons is well known in Wolfeboro. Her parents and grandparents have been summer residents for the past 50 years.[41]

Parlor games included Monopoly, Parcheesi, chess, and checkers (regular as well as Chinese). Popular card games were Flinch, Pit, bridge, whist, and on Saturday nights out with the boys, a few rounds of poker. Old Maid, fish, and "war" were popular card pastimes with the younger set.

The following "approved" (by *Parents Magazine*) comic books were offered for sale at Gould's Dime Store in 1950: *Mutt and Jeff, Peter Porkchops, Superman, Leading, Buzzy, Funny Stuff, Action, Wonder Woman, Girls Love, Miss Beverly Hills, Teen, Funny Folks,* and *Ha Ha.*[42] Boys and girls wanting somewhat more substantial but still entertaining fare could buy Hardy Boys, Bobbsey Twins, Nancy Drew, and Honey Bunch adventure books. Popular magazines included *Life, Look, Saturday Evening Post, Collier's,* and *Reader's Digest.*[43]

As in earlier decades, there were enough lodges, social clubs, church groups, and other organizations to satisfy just about everyone. A partial list from the 1949-1950 years includes these:

> Abenaki Outing Club; American Legion; American Legion Auxiliary; Amy Cheney Beach Club; Boy Scouts; Brownie Scouts; Carroll County Pomona Grange; Cub Scouts; Fidelity Lodge No. 71 IOOF; Girl Scouts; Fireside Club; Hospital Aid Association; Lakeshore Dramatic Club (part of the Lakeshore Grange); Lakeshore Grange (whist party and dance every Saturday night); Lakeshore Juvenile Grange; the Morning Star Lodge AF & AM; Myrtle Rebekah Lodge No. 48; Rugged Hookers (made hooked rugs); Veterans of Foreign Wars, Post Number 8836, South Wolfeboro, and the VFW Auxiliary; Warren Chapter No. 10, Order of Eastern Star; Winnipesaukee Chapter Daughters of the American Revolution; Wolfeboro Firemen's Relief Association; Wolfeboro Garden Club; Wolfeboro Stamp Club; Wolfeboro Woman's Club; Wolfeboro Historical Society; Women's Auxiliary of All Saints' Church; and Attorney and Mrs. Eben .

If all church and school societies and clubs were included, the list could probably be doubled in size.

### Entertainment and Events

The following are some of the many events, programs, and other entertainment activities held in Wolfeboro during the decade. In general, activities were diminished during the 1942-1945 war years.

Events that were annual, or nearly so, included the Fisherville gathering on Wolfeboro Bay, the Winter Carnival, the Water Carnival (beginning in 1947), the Huggins Hospital Street Fair, and the Independence Day celebration.

**1941, January 17. Fisherville:** The usual winter community of wooden shacks and other buildings on the ice on Wolfeboro Bay was a beehive of activity.

**1941, January 24-26. Winter Carnival:** Conducted by the Wolfeboro Abenaki Outing Club. Skiing, skating, bowling, pool, ping-pong, dancing, and films. Mud buggy races were held in the snow on Wolfeboro Bay

**1941, February 20. Village Players:** *Candle-Light* was presented in the Temple Auditorium. "A light-hearted comedy in three acts." The 1941 year promised three different shows for a $1.60 season pass.

**1941, May 6. Concert:** The WPA Symphony Orchestra, organized five years earlier as a government sponsored unit, gave a concert at Carpenter School.

**1941, May 19. Play:** A three-act comedy, *Andy Has the Answer,* was presented at the Temple Auditorium by the Baptist Young People. Admission 35¢.

**1941, July 4. Independence Day:** Festivities included a parade with the Wolfeboro Band and different floats, with the Wolfeboro Abenaki Outing Club float winning first prize in its class. However, due to the war in Europe the evening display of fireworks was omitted at the request of numerous citizens.[44]

**1941, July 16. Circus:** Mills Brothers circus played at Clark's field on South Main Street. A few days later on July 22, Hunt's Three-Ring Motorized Circus set up on the same spot.

**1941, August 3. Magician:** Mystic Kirma, "famed hypnotist and dealer in matters occult," appeared on the stage of Memorial Hall for a week beginning August 3 and also performed stunts at local stores. Sample: At noon on Monday, "blindfolded, the great Kirma will drive General Motors' new creation, the new Buick. See the bandage applied to Kirma's eyes directly in front of our [Hart Motor Co.] showrooms. See Kirma in the new Buick and the daring death-defying blindfold drive through the streets of Wolfeboro." It wasn't stated whose deaths were being defied—the pedestrians' or his![45]

**1941, August 6. Pageant:** Governor Wentworth Historical Pageant on Lake Wentworth Beach.

**1942, February 6. Fisherville forest:** A new attraction consisting of used Christmas trees put out on the ice. Earlier, the paper reported that Fisherville and Wolfeboro had formed a mutual assistance pact in case of enemy attack. After all, it was a time of war.

**1942, June 6-7. Films:** Gary Cooper and Barbara Stanwyck in *Ball of Fire,* at the Memorial Hall Theatre, plus a short, *Soldiers in White,* telling of the Army Medical Corps. Next on the bill, June 10, were Edward G. Robinson, Jane Wyman, and Broderick Crawford in *Larceny, Inc.,* and a short, *Our Russian Front.*

**1942, July 4. Muted observance:** Citizens were warned not to ring church bells, blow horns and whistles, beat gongs, discharge firearms or fireworks or build large fires during Independence Day. "When peace is returned there will be ample opportunity to celebrate. Until then, let us refrain from making any disturbance that might possibly be construed as an air raid alarm." No parade was held (and none would be held until 1946). Events included the dedication of the World War I Memorial plaque on the front lawn of Carpenter School, a band concert, and a carnival midway.[46]

**1942, August 25. Excursion:** Moonlight sail on the ship *Swallow* under Captain Nat Goodhue, who picked up a crowd of Rotarians and Rotary Anns (women's auxiliary) at the public dock at 6:00 p.m. The boat went past Little Barndoor Island, circled Big Barndoor Island, and landed on Keniston Island at Daniel Crowley's dock. Crowley offered his front porch for a picnic supper. After the meal, the celebrants reboarded the *Swallow* and went on a cruise with hearty singing while enjoying an eclipse of the moon.[47]

**1942, September 4. Indians:**[48] Forty Indians from Oklahoma and New Mexico who were soldiers at Fort Devens in Massachusetts came to the Allen "A" Resort. On two evenings they gave Indian dances and other exhibitions to promote the sale of war bonds.

**1943, August 18. Concert:** At Carpenter School. Benefiting the National War Fund. Featured performers from the Boston Symphony Orchestra and elsewhere.

**1943, August 27-29. Cigarette mascot:** "Johnny," the mascot of Philip Morris cigarettes, and his entourage were at the Allen "A" Camp.[49]

**1944, January 7. Music appreciation:** The MacDowell Piano Club held its meeting at Harmony Cottage on Pleasant Street, the home of Ella Lord Gilbert.[50]

**1944, May 12. On stage:** The operetta *Treasure Island* was presented by seventh and eighth grade pupils at Carpenter School.

**1944, October 9. Mentalist:** Henry Gerald's "Psychology in Action" stage show, featuring a Scandinavian psychologist and physician who demonstrated mental telepathy, clairvoyance, and magic. $1.

**1944, December 2. Teenagers:** Dance held at Carpenter School, first event of the new "Wolfeboro Teen-Age Canteen," which was formed on October 20 with local parents advising, to provide monthly events for teenagers. Dancing was to a juke box lent by Joseph I. Melanson. There was a grand march and conga line, and, in addition to dancing, games were provided.[51]

**1945, March 10, 11. Film:** Errol Flynn in *Objective, Burma!*

**1945, July 26. Concert:** At the First Congregational Church; featured talented singers and musicians from different parts of the country "who happened to be spending the summer in Wolfeboro."[52]

**1945, August 17. Hillbillies:** In tent on the Avery field on Clark Road. "In person, America's greatest hillbilly jamboree. John Lair's Original Renfro Valley Folks. Barn Dance Show, with those great hillbilly funmakers from the hills of old Kentucky. Heard every day on CBS network." 50¢ adults, 25¢ children.

**1945, November 12. Armistice Ball:** Held at the American Legion.

**1946, February 15.**[53] **New device:** "Roy Nelson took his new Wilson-Gay Recordio up to Brewster Academy Tuesday afternoon so that the Swingsters [local musical group] could make about 30 recordings for future enjoyment. This marvelous gadget can record to perfection anything in anybody's voice. Nice to know there is a machine such as this in town. Think of the fun of hearing yourself as others hear you."

**1946, March 5: Cate Concert:** Arranged by Mrs. Marjorie R. Hatch. Grace Cunningham, a 1945 graduate of Brewster, played a medley of Victor Herbert numbers on bells. Other soloists included Robert Bishop, Eugene Levy, Joan Melanson, Mary Dye, and Warren Thompson. Sponsored by funds provided from the will of the late Edward F. Cate, such concerts were held regularly.

**1946, June 22. Theatres:** On this date the new "voice of the theatre" sound system and new projection machines were used for the first time at the Memorial Hall Theatre in Wolfeboro, said to be "the second theatre in the United States to have such modern equipment." The Temple Auditorium (called the Little Theatre) was also open in the summer.[54]

**1946, July 4. Independence Day:** The parade, the first held since the war began, was a great success. Antique cars and floats lent interest. A double header baseball game resulted in two victories for the Abenaki Indians over the Farmington team. The Wolfeboro Historical Society opened the Clark House, and various antique items and crafts were on exhibit.[55]

**1946, August 7. Circus:** The King Brothers Combined Shows had two performances on Brewster campus. Advertised a cast of 600 people, a herd of elephants, and 250 animals.

**1946, September 3. Rotary outing:** The Wolfeboro Rotary Club and its auxiliary, the Rotary Anns, held a clambake at Boyden Chapel at Camp Wyanoke, with catering by Charles E. Rowse. "Sixty people sat down to steamed clams, hard-boiled eggs, corn steamed in the husk, sweet potatoes, white potatoes, lobster, ice cream, and coffee.... Following the din-

## Wolfeboro MEMORIAL HALL

**Matinees at 3:00 — Except Sat. at 2:30 EVENINGS at 7:15 (Everything Repeated after 9:00) Saturdays (only) Two Complete Evening Shows at 6:45 and 9:00**

**SATURDAY & SUNDAY** **April 15 & 16**

**GREGORY PECK, GARY MERRILL, HUGH MARLOW in**

**"Twelve O'Clock High"**

A Popular Novel About The Air Force, Transferred To The Screen As QUALITY ENTERTAINMENT. You'll Regret Missing It!

**Plus — Selected Colored Short Reels**

**WEDNESDAY (at 3:00 & 7:15)** **April 19**

**RONALD REAGAN, PATRICIA NEAL, and introducing RICHARD TODD in**

**"The Hasty Heart"**

From the Stage Play by JOHN PATRICK

A Tale Of A Man Who Had No Friends Until He Needed Them; It Will Touch Your Heart

**Plus — GARY COOPER with Mrs. Cooper,** Dog teams, Outstanding Ski Races and Many Other Sport Events in The TECHNICOLOR FEATURETTE

"SNOW CARNIVAL"

Filmed at ASPEN, COLORADO

## ● Center Ossipee (Pineland)

**Evening Shows at 7:15 — Patrons May See A Complete Show by arriving by 9:00**

**FRIDAY (at 7:15)** **April 14**

**GREGORY PECK, GARY MERRILL, HUGH MARLOW in**

**"Twelve O'Clock High"**

A Popular Novel About The Air Force, Transferred To The Screen As QUALITY ENTERTAINMENT. You'll Regret Missing It!

**Plus — "TINY TERRORS MAKE TROUBLE" "Green Harvest," Others**

## ● Sanbornville (Opera House

**SATURDAYS 7:30 followed by DANCING**

**SATURDAY (at 7:30)** **April 15**

**Spencer TRACY, Katharine HEPBURN in**

**"ADAM'S RIB"**

The Comedy Riot Of The Year!

# THE WOLFEBORO CASINO — YOUR FUN HOUSE

**BOWLING DAILY —— IT KEEPS YOU "FIT"**

ARRANGE SPECIAL PARTIES —— AFTERNOONS OR EVENINGS

# EVERYBODY'S DANCING

# SATURDAY NITES AT SANBORNVILLE

**9:30 TO MIDNIGHT — 52 WEEKS IN THE YEAR**

ALWAYS MORE FUN FOR LESS MONEY

**CONTINUOUS DANCING — NO INTERMISSION**

**Entertainment program for the movie theatre at Wolfeboro Memorial Hall (second floor of Town Hall), Pineland in Center Ossipee, and the Wolfeboro Casino, all operated by the Ansel Sanborn family. (*Granite State News*, April 14, 1950)**

ner everyone enjoyed singing and entertainment before a roaring fire in the large fieldstone fireplace. Mr. and Mrs. Bentley were hosts to one of the most successful Rotary meetings held in recent years."[56]

**1946, September 20. Movie stars:** The *Granite State News* of this date featured 10 movie personalities who were candidates for being the top favorites of 1946: Ingrid Bergman, Gary Cooper, Bing Crosby, Bette Davis, Clark Gable, Judy Garland, Greer Garson, Betty Grable, Van Johnson, and Spencer Tracy.

**1947, February 11. On stage:** Two one-act plays, *The Weird Sisters* and *The Man Upstairs,* were presented at the Temple Auditorium and were sponsored by the Wolfeboro Garden Club. Actors and actresses included Barbara Lewando, Mrs. Norman Hale, Pauline Colia, Mr. and Mrs. Richard W. Detscher, Mr. and Mrs. H.E. Erickson, and Mrs. Theodora Whitten.

**1947, March 10. School play:** Brewster senior class gave the play, *Our Town,* by Thornton Wilder. Participants included Barbara Lewando (director of the play and organist), Roger Tracy, Marbra and Alice Doe, Ruth Wallenfels, Marguerite Jutras, Roger Selier, Isaac Osgood, and Ellis Ring.

**1947, March 17. Dance:** The Abenaki Outing Club staged its St. Patrick's Day Dance for about 100 couples.

**1947, July 25. Island melodies:** Concert at Carpenter School sponsored by the Amy Cheney Beach Club. "The three young performers who are studying at the summer school of the Institute of Modern Piano Technique on Varney Island brought to Wolfeboro one of its rarest musical treats. They played to a small but rapt audience who made the rafters ring with their applause.... There are already a number of practice cabins on the largest of the Varney Islands, and it is rumored that a concert hall was to be built there. If all the signs are right, Wolfeboro is to be more and more greatly blessed musically."[57]

**1947, August 1.[58] Donald Duck:** "Harry Foster Welch, who supplies not only the voice of Popeye, Donald Duck, and various other cartoon characters when they appear in the movies, but also imitates the sound of airplanes, ferry whistles and band instruments entirely with his mouth, nose and throat, recently entertained the guests at the Allen 'A'."

**1947, August 25-28. Sex film:** Film titled *Mom and Dad* was shown at the Little Theatre and included Elliott Forbes, "famous radio commentator discussing secrets of sensible sex," in person on stage. "Can be shown to segregated audiences only! Women only at 2:00 and 7:00 p.m., men only at 9:00 p.m." Further account in the *Granite State News,* August 22, 1947: "Shocking are the truths it tells and fearless are the facts it presents.... It's the story of a fine, pretty young girl who made 'just one' mistake. It points out the idiocy of parents today trying to keep their growing boys and girls innocent through ignorance.... The vital subjects of conception, birth, and venereal diseases are openly and frankly portrayed and discussed. Nothing is left to the imagination...."

**1947, October 3. Hit Parade:** Gould's Dime Store advertised the top hit tunes, including nos. 1 to 5: *Near You, Peg O' My Heart, I Wonder Who's Kissing Her Now, That's My Desire,* and *Smoke, Smoke, Smoke.*

**1948, January 30-February 1. Winter Carnival:** Sponsored by the Abenaki Outing Club. Skiing, skating, snowshoeing, ice hockey, aircraft landings, carnival ball.

**1948, April 13. Brewster on the air:** The Boys' Glee Club and Girls' Glee Club at Brewster Academy, under the direction of Burtis F. Vaughan, Jr., were broadcast over station WLNH, Laconia, on a half-hour program beginning at 4:00 p.m. Musical selections included *Shenandoah, The Reaper Song, Think On Me, The Wiffenpoof Song,* and *Stout-Hearted Men,* among others.

**1948, July 3-5. Extended Independence Day celebration:** Included band concert, midway, baseball games against Meredith and Laconia, parade, and carnival midway where the greatest attraction was the new Chevrolet automobile on display.

**1948, July 7. All Saints' Church Fair:** Baby contest, white elephant sale, thrift shop, fortune telling, food, children's activities. The prettiest girl baby was Patricia A. Peard, the handsomest boy was Kenneth Jones, the best personalities were Margaret Randall and Leigh Harvey Turner, the healthiest were Betty Ann Hutchins and Rufus W. Bly, Jr., and the curliest hair honors went to Beverly Ann Griffin and Malcolm G. Young.[59]

**1948, August 7. Water Carnival:** The *Granite State News,* July 23, 1948, told of preparations being made for the boat race: "The most enthusiastic racer in the outboard class is teenager Billy Marriott, who is spending most of his time getting the boat and motor in tip-top shape." Account in the *Granite State News,* August 13, 1948, stated that the boat parade prize was won by Nathaniel Goodhue for the *Swallow,* "which was the oldest steamboat with typical costume, topped off with a hand-organ man." Entry blanks for the boat program had been signed by a number of prominent businessmen, including Henry J. Kaiser (president of the Commonwealth Chevrolet Company), Joseph Maguire (president of the American Tar Company), E.P. Sams and George Bushnell (president and vice president, respectively, of the J.C. Penney Company), and J. Willard Marriott (president of the Hot Shoppes, Washington, DC).

**1948, December 3.[60] Among the first:** "Television is in Wolfeboro. Dr. Ed Dunham is an enthusiastic owner of one of the new sets."

**1949, January 28-30. Winter Carnival:** Square dances, movies, and more. Albert F. Auderer as "Chief Abenaki" presided over the events.

**1949, July 29-30. Horse show:** The first annual Lakes Region Fair and Horse Show was held at the Allen "A" Resort and featured Morgan show horses. Entertainment included vaudeville acts, acrobats, a band, and other festivities. Sponsored by the American Legion and the Veterans of Foreign Wars.

**1949, July 9. Circus:** Biller Brothers Three-Ring Wild Animal Circus. Brewster Field. 60¢.

**1949, July 4. Independence Day:** Parade included the following outstanding entries: Lakeshore Grange, Northeastern Equipment Company, "Horribles" (people in unusual dress), Wolfeboro Fire Department, local camps, Myrtle Rebekah Lodge, American Legion Auxiliary, Veterans of Foreign Wars, VFW Auxiliary, Wolfeboro Garden Club, Abenaki Outing Club, Woman's Christian Temperance Union, Dockside Restaurant, Hart Motor Company, Mr. and Mrs. Parker Merrow and Mr. and Mrs. Norton Leighton in antique costumes and old cars, "Amos and Ruby" in blackface, Lakeview Oil, Wolfeboro Oil, Haskins Hardware, and the Alton Fire Department. Music was furnished by the paper-roll-operated Allen "A" calliope[61] and the Farm and Trades School Band of Boston.

**1950, February 15. Minstrel show:** Temple Auditorium under the sponsorship of the Lakeshore Grange.

**1950, July 14. Governor speaks:** Gov. Sherman Adams spoke to the combined meeting of the Winnipesaukee Chapter of the Daughters of the American Revolution and the Wolfeboro Historical Society.

## SPORTS

### In and On the Lakes

In summer the Bathing Beach (Brewster Beach) was a popular spot. Attendance in 1943 was 3,268, under supervision of lifeguards Beatrice Horne and Merton Rumrill. In the 1948 season, 8,651 youngsters and adults visited; lifeguards were Douglas Bowles and Eleanor Johnson.

After the war, power boating came to the fore once again. By 1947 craft were readily available. Leading local retailers included the Northeast Equipment Company and Goodhue & Hawkins Navy Yard.

The popular new sport of the time was waterskiing. On June 7, 1946, this was printed:

> Ned Bullock, star skier of the Abenaki Outing Club, was seen on Memorial Day in training for next year's ski season as he tried out a new pair of water skis in Wolfeboro Bay. By the end of the afternoon he had worked out some snappy turns and had figured out how to start and stop without getting wet. According to Ned, waterskiing is just as much fun as snow skiing.

On August 2, 1947, the first annual Water Carnival was held in Wolfeboro Bay and included water skiing, boat racing, and about 200 entries in a boat parade. A squadron of Navy planes flew overhead, a performance arranged by Senator H. Styles Bridges. The Camp Wyanoke band gave a concert.[62]

### Fishing

Fishing in lakes Wentworth and Winnipesaukee continued to be popular pursuits, even in wartime, although during most of the conflict no power boats were available. A few news clippings:

> **1941, May 2. Salmon:** "Harry Moore caught a 6 3/4-pound salmon early this week in Winter Harbor. The fish is 27 inches long and one of the best specimens of land-locked salmon caught in Winnipesaukee in recent years."
>
> **1941, August 15. Eel:** "Harlan B. Kelley reports catching an eel 31/2 feet long and weighing 41/2 pounds at the outlet to Crescent Lake. Unfortunately, their physical resemblance to a snake prejudices many people against them, so their meat is wasted."
>
> **1942, May 1. Salmon:** "Mr. and Mrs. Joseph I. Melanson's son, Bucky, caught a two-pound salmon off the bridge last Friday. To say that Bucky was thrilled is putting it mildly."
>
> **1943, April 16. Whitefish:** Lake Winnipesaukee had been stocked with whitefish fry (known in New Hampshire as shad or bluefins) which had been obtained at Put-In Bay on Lake Erie. When adult, the average shad is 13 to 15 inches in length.

### William O. Douglas on Fishing

In 1950 Harper & Brothers published *Of Men and Mountains*, by Supreme Court Justice William O. Douglas, who in the 1930s had spent much time on Lake Wentworth. Excerpts:

> Lakes, like people, have personalities. It takes time and patience, but if one goes about it the right way he can get on intimate terms with a lake. Lake Wentworth in New Hampshire was such a lake to me. I discovered on my own every good bass pool that it harbors. Some are near points of islands, some are in unsuspected spots offshore where a ledge is concealed 30 or 40 feet below the surface. Others are in sandy stretches where the bass like to cruise. One is in the least likely place of all—three feet of water a few yards beyond a marshy shore. Here at sunset I would anchor both bow and stern, cast out a live minnow hooked lightly through the lips, and watch for the dorsal fin of a bass as he came viciously for the bait in the shallow water.
>
> I knew the ledges and rocks of Wentworth as one knows his own property. I could safely feel my way across it in darkness as one would navigate his living room or work his way across his pasture without a light. I swam off its shore; and I swam great distances between its islands, two miles or more. I felt the warm surface water and the chill of a current coming from some spring in the middle. I knew the winds and what to expect of them. I knew the wet east wind and the three-day blows out of the west. And I knew where the bass were feeding at those times....
>
> I remember a case when I was...anchored in thirty feet of water off Turtle Island in a pool where I seldom failed to take bass. For bait I was using crayfish that are native to the lake and which I caught with my hands. This day the lake was mirrorlike. There was no breath of air, and the sunlight fell with the full intensity of July.
>
> For several hours I had been unable to interest any small-mouthed bass in the crayfish. I peered over the edge of the boat and saw a bass poised directly below. I lowered a fresh crayfish until it hung suspended in front of the bass's nose. The crayfish, hooked through the tail, was waving his claws menacingly at the bass. The bass did not move. That went on for five minutes or more. Then the bass lunged at the crayfish. He seized it from the side and slowly turned it in his mouth so as to swallow it tail first. When the tip of the tail was in his mouth, I set the hook. The bass was transformed into a mass of energy. He came straight up from the bottom of the lake as if he had been shot out of a cannon. He came so fast I could not begin to take the line in on the reel. He hit the surface about a foot from the boat and jumped. the force of his jump carried him some three feet in the air; he gave a side twist, shook his head, and landed in the boat—a pound and a half of fightin-mad bass flesh....

### Hunting

Deer hunting was one of the most popular and, at the same time, most controversial sports. Typically, about 550 to 750 would be killed annually in Carroll County. While deer hunting was primarily a recreation in earlier years, in 1946 the local paper commented that it "isn't a question of bagging a trophy, it's a matter of steaks, chops, roast and mincemeat." At the time meat was in short supply.

The 1947 deer season was fraught with problems. Hunters from the southern part of the state, traveling in large bands and roving through local farmlands, committed vandalism and caused much damage. Many farmers began posting their land to prevent such happenings.[63]

# *Runners-up in Central N. H. League*

Back Row, left to right: James Pollini, Albert Auderer, Jr., Archie A. Horne, Bradbury Hunter, Gordon Harris, Delmar Tutt
Front row, left to right: Norman Hale, Robert Mulvey, Thomas Hunter, Edward Fraser, William Shea, Herbert Kendall, Jr.

**Local baseball team: The front page of the first edition, October 9, 1947, of the short-lived paper, *The News of Our Town,* published by L. Winston Hamm, who also printed *The Shopper,* a give-away periodical. Shown is the Wolfeboro baseball team sponsored by the Harriman-Hale American Legion Post No. 18. Archie A. Horne, Jr., shown in the back row, followed his father's footsteps as a local sports star. (Melanson Collection)**

In 1950 it was reported that outside of town a hunter from the city shot a goat and carried it off, thinking it was a deer, over the loud protests of the farmer who owned it! Other domestic animals would be often shot as well. The suggestion was made in the *Granite State News* that farmers would do well to shroud their livestock in bright garments and identify them with large letters on their sides, such as COW or HORSE.

Other animals besides deer were hunted. The newspaper carried this account on October 21, 1949:

> Middie Goodrow of the Wolfeboro Highlands Road shot a bear Tuesday night near Rock Point. The animal weighed 280 pounds.... Within a few minutes he had sold the carcass where it lay for $25. Goodrow has shot about two dozen bear during his lifetime of approximately 40 years.

### Winter Sports

The following appeared in the *Granite State News*, January 24, 1941:

> With a large hole in its lineup on account of illness, the local hockey club executed a blackout of the Plymouth club here Sunday evening. Score, 8-0. More than balancing the absence [from the Wolfeboro team] of Norman Hale, Archie Horne, Art Spencer, and Joe Melanson, was the lack of practice which handicapped the visitors.
>
> Leon Jutras made a goal for the Abenaki Indians in the first period, which on the whole was rather tame. In the second period, Nazaire Jutras netted one and assisted Jimmie Clough in scoring another. Immediately afterward, Leon Jutras came across with another goal. In the opening minute of the third period "Zip" Foss scored. The other three goals were made by Nazaire Jutras, Hugh Wootton, and Foss obliging with an encore.

In January 1941 the Municipal Skating Rink off Factory Street near Center Street was wired for sound by connecting a Victrola with three speakers. During the decade another rink was maintained behind Carpenter School. As it turned out, the winter of 1940-1941 was to be the only normal sporting season in the early 1940s. Winter sports were restricted during the war. The Abenaki Outing Club suspended its activities. There was no hockey team after the 1941-1942 season (which was short of players), and few people went skiing.

In the winter of 1945-1946 the Abenaki Outing Club was reactivated. During the first week of January, the rope tow on Poor Farm Hill was put back in service. An old Buick automobile motor (replaced by a new outfit in 1950) furnished the power to haul skiers up the hill.

By this time the Abenaki Indians hockey team had been formed. Members, including alternates, were Stan Sikorsky, Wendy Carr, Eric Courtenay, Zip Foss, Norman Hale, Bob Hale, Nazaire Jutras, Carley Massey, Jimmy Clough, and Leon Jutras.

During the 1947-1948 winter season, the town of Wolfeboro leased the Wolfeboro Ski Area (as it was called) on Poor Farm Hill to H.G. Wallenfels and Ernest E. Grueter, "with the understanding that the use of the slope and trails will be free to anyone, they only to charge for the use of the ski tow and food at the lodge." Residents could buy season tow tickets for $8 to $10; nonresidents were charged $15.

Gail Macomber, daughter of Clark and Janet E. Macomber of East Wolfeboro, and a student at Smith College, became a championship skier and took eighth place in the Eastern Women's Championship Races. Her brother George, who was at M.I.T., was on the United States Olympic Ski Team in Switzerland in 1948.

Ice boating was a popular winter sport, and local devotees included Norman W. Turner, Ralph G. Carpenter II, and H. Furber Jewett. Conditions permitting, tours were taken over Lake Winnipesaukee to as far away as Meredith.[64]

### Baseball

Baseball was inactive during the war, as most potential adult players were in the service. In the spring of 1946 the Abenaki Outing Club stated it would sponsor the first club since 1940. Enthusiasm was immediate. In 1947 the local team made it to the semifinals.

In 1948 the players, by then sponsored by Harriman-Hale Post No. 18, were New Hampshire Central League champions, winning eight games and losing five. On the team were Albert Auderer, Lawrence Bartnick, Edwin Fraser, Roger Grant, Norman Hale, Rayburn Hodgdon, Archie Horne, Bradbury Hunter, Thomas Hunter, Herbert Kendall, Mel Massucco, Thomas Mitchell, Robert Mulvey, James Pollini, Delmar Tutt, and Henry Valley (manager).[65]

### Football

Throughout the decade football was played by Brewster Academy. One of the outstanding games was the November 1, 1942, win over Holderness 12-0, an exciting score, as earlier Holderness had beaten Kennett which in turn had beaten Wolfeboro. Outstanding players from Brewster that year included Alfred Nichols, Herbert Kendal, Raymond Perry, David Deegan, Roger Thurrell, Lyndon Moody, Harrison D. Moore, Lawrence McHugh, and Hayes Sawyer.

Brewster ended the 1949 football season with six victories and no defeats. Wins under coaches Larry Bartnick and Tom Hurst included the first in 50 years over Phillips Exeter Academy and a triumph over the UNH freshmen. On December 13 Governor Sherman Adams attended a testimonial dinner for the team. Radio station WLNH of Laconia covered the event through sportscaster Bill Allen. Decorations were placed up and down North and South Main Streets.[66]

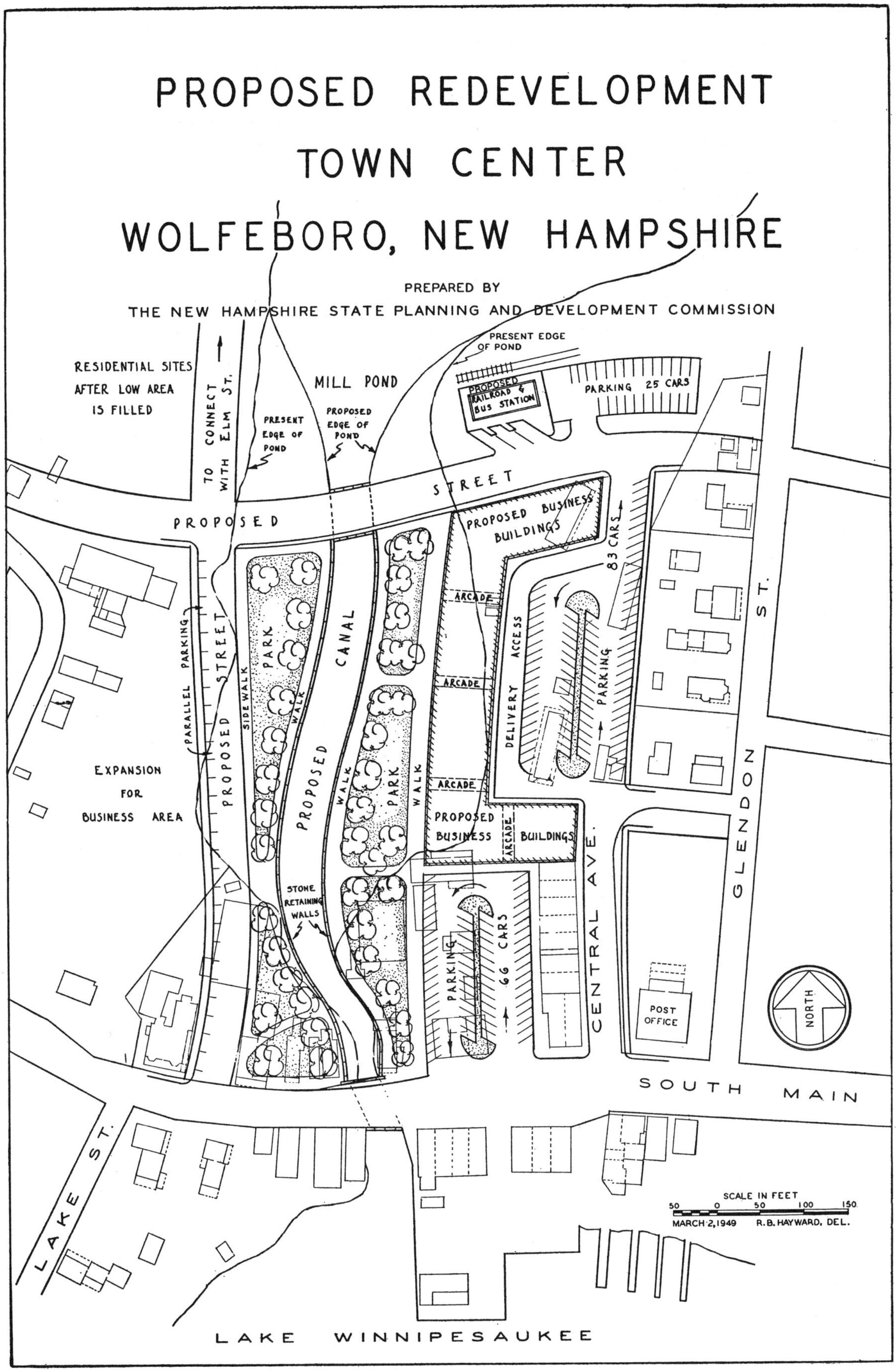


**Things have changed since 1949 when the New Hampshire State Planning and Development Commission recommended filling in nearly all of Back Bay and converting open water areas to a narrow stone-lined canal for drainage. The Wolfeborough Railroad Station was to be demolished. This plan never got beyond the discussion stage (fortunately, most would say). (Melanson Collection)**

### Other Sports

On August 2-3, 1941, a PGA golf tournament was held at the Kingswood Club for the benefit of British war relief. The July 24, 1942, edition of the local paper carried this account of the same sport: "Living up to his reputation as golf champion, Joe Melanson of our neighborhood for the third time won the Manchester Union Trophy thus securing it for keeps."

Candlepin bowling at the Wolfeboro Casino made the news columns regularly. Several teams of local women sponsored by town businesses played during the autumn and winter months.[67]

## TOWN GOVERNMENT

### Regulations and Policies

In the spring of 1941, members were appointed to the Planning and Building Commission which was charged with carrying out protective regulations and the zoning ordinances adopted at the 1940 town meeting covering the business district and a small part of the residential area. Years later in 1947 it was reported that the zoning regulations had been working well.

Labor for town projects was scarce during the war. On June 30, 1944, this was published:

> Back to the old-fashioned system of working "bees" have gone the towns of Wolfeboro, Wakefield, Brookfield, and Milton, exchanging work on a town-wide scale.... No town having a sufficient crew to finish its road oiling and sanding within reasonable time, all crews of all the towns have combined with their equipment, and the State Highway Department has furnished supervision and additional equipment. Almost all the men are over draft age, and at least one is over 70.

During the 1940s, as in previous years, town meetings were held in daylight hours, a tradition remaining from the early days when satisfactory lighting was not always available, and travel at night was apt to be uncertain. In 1946 L. Winston Hamm, who worked at the Kingswood Press, arranged to take part of the day off in order to attend the March event. When there, he noticed that the audience was small, as most people were busy elsewhere at their jobs. After the town warrant had been taken care of and the moderator called for "other business," Hamm proposed changing the meeting time to the evening so that more people could participate. Beginning with the March 1947 town meeting, attendance was much larger.[68]

On June 17, 1946, municipal collection of rubbish began on an experimental basis and lasted until September 6, 1947, after which the job was done by private individuals. Until 1947 garbage and other refuse had been dumped at several spots around town, including in the bay off Factory Street, at the Pine Hill Dump, and illegally at Mast Landing. In May of that year, disposal was limited by the State Board of Health to the Pine Hill Dump and dry trash only at Factory Street.

In 1947 parking spaces in the downtown area were marked with yellow lines, and time regulations were adopted. Central Avenue, Glendon Street, Wharf Avenue, and Lake Avenue were set up as one-way streets.[69]

The 1950 town meeting voted to purchase the Wolfeborough Railroad Station building from the Boston & Maine for $5,000 and tear it down. Fortunately for posterity, the demolition was postponed (as it turned out, permanently).[70]

## HEALTH AND WELL-BEING

### Illnesses

On Tuesday, January 21, 1941, Carpenter School was closed for the balance of the week as a precautionary measure against the spread of grippe and influenza. Within the month, there were so many local cases that Huggins Hospital was filled to overflowing, with a waiting list.

At the time, infantile paralysis—better known as polio—was a primary health concern, particularly among children. The State Board of Health continually recommended that in the summer months youngsters should pay attention to cleanliness, stay away from people who had polio, and not swim in polluted water. The March of Dimes was held yearly to raise funds to combat the scourge, a cure for which was not known.

In 1946 there were two cases of polio in Wolfeboro, both of whom recovered.

In 1949 a measles epidemic swept through town and involved most of the students at Carpenter School plus a few older people. There was a higher incidence of polio, and children under the age of 16 were once again advised to stay away from crowded places. In September 1949 there were 17 confirmed cases in Carroll County. Hydrotherapy for polio was available at the local hospital.[71]

### At Huggins Hospital

Throughout the decade the annual Huggins Hospital Street Fair was held in August to raise money for the facility. Under the supervision of Mrs. W.J. Paul Dye (née Ethel Clow) and others, receipts continued to mount.

Miss Frances Puffer was superintendent of the hospital in the early 1940s. She later went into the Army, and Miss Nettie L. Fisher became her substitute, to be followed on September 15, 1945, by the appointment of Mrs. Dorothy Rounds. She was succeeded by Miss Gladys Siefert, then for two years by Myron Burton, who on August 1, 1949, was replaced by Clarence B. Murphy. On occasion, Mrs. W.J. Paul Dye was temporarily in charge, as in January 1947, when she was acting superintendent following the resignation of Miss Siefert.

In 1946 the "baby boom" began. Huggins ran short of diapers and invited anyone locally who had some to spare to bring them in.

In the summer of 1947 a campaign to raise funds for an addition to the hospital began under the chairmanship of Trustee Ernest Gile, owner of Horne's Garage and other businesses. The old facility had been designed for about 23 beds, but in recent times occupancy had been increased to 36 by using hallways. On some days, up to 42 patients were taken in, a violation of good practice as there was no margin of safety for emergencies. Upon completion, the hospital had 66 beds. The first patients were accommodated in the new addition on March 3, 1950, while construction was still underway. After the addition was completed, the original building was remodeled. The total cost came to $530,401.20 (including $55,410.82 for new equipment), of which $169,598.93 was federal aid under the Hill-Burton Act. By December 31, 1950, a total of 24,507 patients had been admitted since the hospital's opening in 1908.

On December 13, 1950, the medical staff of Huggins voted that the doctors serving the Wolfeboro area would each charge a standard minimum fee of $3 for an office visit and $4 for a house call.[72]

### Mental Health

On December 3, 1948, the *Granite State News* printed a commentary under the title "No Mental Rehabilitation Costs Too Great." Editor Merrow noted that from time to time he had served as a municipal court justice and was "impressed more and more with the very great need for adequate mental care and guidance for people who find it hard to live in present day society." He questioned the practice of simply sending people to jail, stating:

> In many cases such treatment is like pouring water on a gasoline fire.... Only after a careful study has been made to find out why the individual transgressed the rules laid down by the community for living, is it possible to deal with the individual man and make certain the offense will not be repeated. No price is too high to pay to secure the services of psychiatrists or mental workers who can do a really effective job.... In securing the services of doctors who work with the mentally ill and emotionally unbalanced, the state should never ask, "How cheap can we hire them?" but rather "How good are they?" A doctor who can take people from a hospital for those who are mentally ill, from our jails, and from our reform schools, and return them to society as sound useful members is worth almost any price paid to him.

### Dr. N.H. Scott

Born in 1851, Nathaniel Harvey Scott earned a medical degree from Bowdoin College in Maine. In July 1880 Dr. Scott visited Wolfeboro on business and was detained over Sunday. In his own words, this is what happened next, per a recollection voiced decades later in 1946:

> I was shown over the town and thought it the most desirable one in which to live that I had ever seen. I still think so. A week from that Sunday we were here bag and baggage. All but three years of the time since have been in a now more than century old brick house, overlooking the lake and wooded mountains beyond. Our six living children have been born here, there has been no year in which every child and grandchild (there are 11 grandchildren) has not been here. It is home to all of them.

In 1930 Scott reduced his practice due to failing eyesight, and in 1934, with a hearing loss, retired. He remained active locally and engaged in hobbies including vegetable gardening, weather, and Wolfeboro history. Among his observations was that weather and temperature conditions in Wolfeboro were often identical to those in Chicago a day earlier. When Dr. Scott died on January 25, 1946, the town mourned one of its leading citizens.[73]

### Dr. W.J. Paul Dye

Born in Sistersville, WV, in 1902, Dye graduated from Harvard Medical School in 1925 and came to Wolfeboro in 1931. For several years he had been the protégé of Dr. Fred E. Clow, and on June 7, 1930, married his daughter, Ethel Alma. The couple had two children, Paula and Mary.

Dr. Dye became chief of the surgical staff at Huggins Hospital and for many years was one of the most prominent physicians in the area. Active in town affairs and serving as town health officer, he was well liked and respected. On October 17, 1950, he passed away following a brief illness.

An editorial noted that Dr. Dye did not follow the famous biblical quotation, "Physician, heal thyself," and that he had joined "that illustrious list of Carroll County physicians who shortened their days through zealous devotion to duty." Memorial services were held on October 20. Governor Sherman Adams, Senator Styles Bridges, and numerous doctors, among many others, were in attendance. The 1950 Town Report was dedicated to him.[74]

### Other Health News

On October 22, 1941, Dr. Burt Wilbur Parshley died after an illness of less than 48 hours. In 1906 he had set up his dentistry practice in town, soon moving into his oak-paneled residence on South Main Street (to the left of where Town and Cate parks are today) where he remained for the rest of his life. He was survived by his wife, the former Juliette Mansfield of Meredith, a daughter Virginia, and a son Sylvester (a.k.a. Stephen). Mrs. Parshley remained in the family home and conducted

Huggins Hospital on South Main Street in the 1950s. Over a period of time the facility became widely known for the quality of its medical service and patient care.

WOLFEBORO, N. H., FRIDAY, JANUARY 27, 1950

Will He Be Forgotten?



Polio was a nationwide health threat, particularly to youngsters, in the 1940s and early 1950s. Its best-known victim was President Franklin D. Roosevelt who as an adult could not walk unassisted. Roosevelt was a key figure in the annual March of Dimes fund-raising effort for polio, and because of this, after his 1945 death the U.S. dime was redesigned to feature his portrait (the new dime made its debut in 1946). In Wolfeboro public facilities such as beaches were closed from time to time because of the polio threat. In 1955 the first clinic was set up in Carroll County for the administration of the Salk vaccine for polio. (*Granite State News*, January 27, 1950)

Edgelake Gardens until 1942, a plant and garden business she had started in 1938. On August 11 and 12, 1944, the house and contents were sold at auction, by her order.[75]

In July 1944 John Hildreth Clow, D.M.D., of Rochester, purchased the Joseph T. Meader house, an ornate Victorian structure on Pleasant Street, and subsequently moved to town. Wolfeboro had no other dentists, as Drs. Parshley and Frederick E. Meader had died, and J.E. Dunham was in the military service. Clow had been coming to town three days a week, practicing in the office of his late father, Fred E. Clow, M.D.

In April 1946 Dr. Rockwood M. Batchelder, a chiropractor, moved into the Parshley house and advertised the use of a "neurocalometer" and X-rays.

On January 7, 1944, Frederick E. Meader, D.M.D., passed away. Born in 1872 at the old Meader homestead on North Main Street, he earned his dental degree from Harvard Medical School. Until 1914 he practiced in Boston and made regular visits to his office in the Durgin Block in Wolfeboro. In that year he bought Vinecroft on Forest Road, the home of his uncle, George Meader, and became a permanent resident. He and his first wife, née Sarah Morse Whitton, had a son, Robert Frederick Whitton Meader, who became a well-known teacher and historian. After his wife's death in 1927, he married Alta Bailey in 1928. Alta Bailey Meader also achieved renown as a local historian and in the 1950s contemplated writing a history of the town.

On May 8, 1950, Dr. Sushila Nayar, former personal physician to Mahatma Gandhi (life dates: 1869-1948) of India, spoke at the Carpenter School auditorium about Gandhi. She was working at the time at The Johns Hopkins University as part of an American visit and tour.

## FIRE FIGHTING

### News of the Department

On September 30, 1942, two-way radio equipment was put into service by Chief LeRoy P. Mansfield, thus making Wolfeboro the first town in the state to have constant communication with its fire fighters. In September 1946 Mansfield retired, and fireman Guy Foss was named chief.

In the summer of 1948 Wolfeboro fire equipment included a 1948 Buffalo pumper of 750 gallons per minute capacity, a Buffalo ladder truck with 252 feet of ladders, a Buffalo pumper acquired in 1930 with 600 gallons per minute capacity, a Buffalo hose truck built on a 1941 Ford chassis, and a 1931 Chevrolet truck used to transport men and forest fire fighting equipment.

Guy Foss was chief of the department. Assistant chiefs were Gordon Durgin and Tracy Abbott, and Hugh Tulley served as station man. Drivers were Carl Massey, Kenneth Massey, Charles Foss, Jr., Roger Gregory, Thaddeus Berry, Fred Bierweiler, and Eugene Lehner.[76]

### Notable Fires

**1941, January 24. Guy Whitten car:** Fire caused by a short circuit destroyed vehicle and garage in East Wolfeboro.

**1941, March 12. Theodore Champaign house:** The upper story and other parts of house destroyed by fire.

**1941, May 18-19. Trask Mountain:** Intense brush fire lasted for two days.

**1941, June 1. George Robbins camp:** Rust Pond. Destroyed.

**1941, June 14. Walter L. Hale farm:** South Wolfeboro. Building in which poultry was dressed was completely destroyed, including a wax tank and a set of scales. The tank was kept hot 24 hours a day for plucking feathers, and it was believed that the fire started there.[77]

**1941, September 20. Camp Wunnishaunta:** Unoccupied dining and recreation building and several other structures in South Wolfeboro were burned, with all contents. Fire fighters were hampered and delayed in reaching the scene by persistent spectators crowding the entry road.[78]

**1942, July 16. Ivan Piper farm:** Barns and the ell of his house burned. Coffee and sandwiches were served to the firefighters by Allan E. Bailey.[79]

**1942, September 6. Gardner Pad Company:** Wolfeboro Falls. Blaze started in a pile of baled excelsior outside on bank of Smith River, traveled through the factory, and spread to an adjoining storehouse full of excelsior. Fire Department quickly brought the fire under control. Damage: $8,000.

**1942, September 7. Henhouse:** Homer Davis' henhouse in Wolfeboro Falls destroyed.

**1942, November 19. King's Hill Dairy Farm:** Fire destroyed the barn, 24 milk cows, three or four calves, one bull, and about 80 tons of hay.[80]

**1943, November 27. Diner:** Small fire at rear of Diner on North Main Street.[81]

**1943, December 22. Dudley Holden house:** Green Street. Gutted. The Holdens and their daughter Shirley, age 12, barely escaped in their nightclothes.

**1944, August 1.[82] South Wolfeboro:** "Mr. and Mrs. Samuel Niblett have the sympathy of this community in their loss by fire of nearly all they possessed."

**1944, September 19. Hart Motor Co.:** Service department gutted; six cars destroyed. Started by car motor backfiring.

**1945, November 11. William L. Fletcher house:** House on Pine Hill Road destroyed.[83]

**1946, March 15.[84] Walter L. Hale farm:** Chicken broiler house in South Wolfeboro was burned, and 200 chickens were lost. No one saw the fire, although the farm was on a state highway.

**1946, March 15. Charles W. Bryant home:** Contents of home on Bay Street ruined by smoke and water when a rubbish fire spread from the outside.[85]

**1946, September 6.[86] Allen "A":** Lodging building for employees burned.

**1946, November 19. Convalescent home:** Mrs. Leah Herbert's convalescent home on Waumbeck Road caught fire from an overheated furnace. Flames rushed up between partitions and into the roof, which was cut open by firemen. Considerable fire and water damage.[87]

**1947, January 9. W.H. Flickinger cottage:** Cottage, with eight rooms and many conveniences, valued at $25,000, on Sewall Road, destroyed by fire. It was beyond the town water supply, and the firemen attempted to go through the ice to get water. "One of the most finest and most valuable cottages in the Wolfeboro area."[88]

**1947, January 19. Moore Brothers Farm:** Pleasant Valley. Chicken house and 800 chicks destroyed by fire.

**1947, March 25. Sugar house:** Sap house and contents (maple syrup, firewood) of John Will destroyed.[89]

**1947, May 12. Airplane crash and fire:** Richard Forestal, 23, of Peabody, MA, was found about 3:00 a.m. on April 13, wandering in the woods, clothing covered with soot, near the wrecked and burned airplane from which he had escaped a few hours earlier, and was taken to Huggins Hospital. A student pilot, Stephen Lefavor, was found near the home of Roy Nelson. The pair had been on the way from Beverly, MA, to Portland, Maine, and had lost their way, and thought they were at The Weirs or Alton Bay. The plane failed, and the two jumped out. About an acre was burned before the fire was put out by 2:00 a.m. Apparently, both men had parachutes, but it wasn't certain that either parachute was deployed; it was known for sure that the student pilot's wasn't.[90]

**1947, May 23.[91] A. Cooper Ballentine camp:** Private camp (not Kehonka) in South Wolfeboro and contents, temporarily occupied by Mr. and Mrs. Lowell Morgan, who had been married three weeks earlier, destroyed by fire. All wedding gifts, clothing, and a hope chest were lost.

**1947, August 23. Seaplane fire:** A Taylorcraft seaplane owned by Howard Maxim of Sewall Road was destroyed by fire, from ashes dropped in the cabin of the craft from a cigarette. The owner was showing the plane to another pilot and both were standing on the pontoons. It took less than five minutes to destroy the craft.[92]

**1948, July 23.[93] Ernest Jones house:** Fire broke out in the upper story of house in Wolfeboro Falls, but was quickly controlled by the Fire Department.

**1948, November 14. Bowling alley:** Fire started about 90 minutes after the afternoon closing in a pit in one of four alleys in the Wolfeboro Casino. Several thousand dollars' worth of damage. Fire Department prevented even greater loss.[94]

**1949, November 5. Allard cabin:** Owned by Mr. and Mrs. Preston Allard. River Street. Destroyed by fire.[95]

**1950, April 22. Marine fire:** Paul S. Strang of Pleasant Street and a friend, Dr. T. Carlson, were fishing in Wolfeboro Bay when their boat and engine caught fire. Rescued by Mr. Chamberlain, who saw the fire from the Town Docks and went out in his boat.

## OBEYING THE LAW

### The Early 1940s

On February 6, 1941, Chief of Police Ted Sturgis joined other Carroll County law enforcement officials for an area-wide hunt for slot machines:

> After a day spent in driving hither and thither, sometimes with success and sometimes without, the sheriff and troopers had bagged 13 machines, an elaborate horse-racing machine, two punchboards, and one penny machine. The seized equipment totaled a small truckload.

In July of the same year, Carroll County officers cracked a crime ring responsible for many break-ins during a three-year period, including a number in Wolfeboro. The solution began when two sisters living together with their husbands had an argument. Then this happened:

> One couple moved out, and the husband who left sent a sheriff to recover his clothes. His mother-in-law, so it is said, told the sheriff that the man had been driving without a license. When the sheriff questioned the man, he is alleged to have replied that he might have been driving without a license, but his brother-in-law had been doing a whole lot worse. With this as a starting point, questions, denials, more questions, then a series of alleged confessions clearing up about 100 breaks....

In January 1942 Hans Rossman, age 39, a native of Germany, was arrested in Lynn, MA, as a fugitive from justice from Wolfeboro, where Chief Sturgis had sworn out a warrant for his arrest for "illegal surgery" (abortion?).

In the same month it was reported that the deputy sheriff had just finished wrecking 45 confiscated slot machines taken at various places in the area. "It was pointed out by a Carroll County official that while most of them were confiscated in the northern part of the county, the largest amount of money was taken from machines confiscated in and around Wolfeboro."

During the war local men were either employed or off to battle. There was little idle time, and the few local crimes were limited primarily to petty thefts, vandalism, and break-ins. Beginning in 1942, tires, which had become scarce and expensive due to the war effort, were sometimes stripped from cars. Citizens were advised to keep their cars in lighted parking areas or, better yet, in locked garages. Unattended summer camps were tempting to hunters in the autumn and to juveniles year-round. There was a break-in at the Wolfeboro Rationing Board office in 1945.

In August 1944 Harry Wilson, a vagrant with police records in four states, was arrested for breaking into Gould's Dime Store and stealing $44.36. Mrs. Carroll D. Piper, who lived across the street, saw him hanging around the store late in the evening and later heard breaking glass. Chief Sturgis was called to the scene, along with Fred Copp, who went around to the back. Wilson broke through a front window to escape and was captured by Sturgis, assisted by Bradford Bentley of Camp Wyanoke who happened to be nearby.[96]

### After the War

After World War II Wolfeboro experienced its share of increased crime, still mostly of a petty nature.

In February 1947 Mr. and Mrs. Herbert Johnson of Needham, MA, checked on their summer home, Maple Crest, in Cotton Valley, only to learn that it had been ransacked. On February 24, 1947, Richard Lillie, age 25, was extradited from Natick, MA, to Wolfeboro and confessed to a string of area burglaries including the Helen Stephenson summer home.

In spring 1947 Chief Sturgis resigned to become deputy sheriff of Carroll County.[97] Albert K. Elliott, night patrolman for a year, was named by the selectmen to fill the post. In July 1947 Harrison D. Moore, who had served with the Marines during the war, was appointed as a policeman for the summer season.

On July 23, 1947, Lawrence Shaw Mayo, age 59, of West Newton, MA, at one time assistant dean at Harvard University, shot himself at his summer home on Lake Wentworth. His wife found the body and two written notes. Mayo, a distinguished historian, had written a biography of Gov. John Wentworth. In the 1930s he had given the site of the Wentworth mansion to the state for use as a park.

The body of Homer W. Davis, age 57, was found on September 14, 1947, in his home on Grove Street, where he lived alone. The discovery was made by his son, Homer, Jr., who was paying a weekly call. The possibility of foul play was to be investigated.[98]

### Gunfight on Railroad Avenue

On the night of October 4, 1947, Chief Albert K. Elliott was almost killed by a shotgun blast from Gene Herbert, age 21. It started when Arthur L. McHugh, Jr., tried to break up a fight on Railroad Avenue between Gene Herbert and his father Ralph, a local restaurateur. It was alleged that the younger Herbert stabbed McHugh in the shoulder with a knife. Chief Elliott was contacted and came on the scene. Meanwhile, Herbert had gone home, fetched a 12-gauge shotgun and a revolver, and went back to Railroad Avenue, where he told three patrons to step back into a lunch room, backing up his demand with a shotgun blast. Chief Elliott ordered Herbert to come to the side of the town's Chevrolet police car. The gunman then fired at the car and came close to hitting Elliott, who then gave chase, firing five shots at Herbert, who was later halted and arrested by Deputy Sheriff Ted Sturgis and Sergeant Ernest Swift. On December 11 he was sentenced to two to three years in state prison.[99]

A bit of detective work was needed to unravel a theft of Christmas trees grown by Wolfeboro resident Ralph Carpenter on land in Alton. Ax marks found on some of 135 trees suspected of having been stolen were matched with marks on Carpenter's remaining stumps. Five people from Dorchester, MA—Michael, Edward, Henry, Walter, and Alexander Jondartz—were arrested and charged.

In May 1948 a stranger walked into the Paper Store, and while saleslady Junia Irish was otherwise occupied, took money from the safe and drove away. In August of the same year, four counselors from a local boys' camp defaced signs in Wolfeboro for which they were found guilty and assessed $84 in repairs and $25 in court costs.

On October 12, 1949, Chief Albert K. Elliott was stricken with a severe heart attack, which landed him in Huggins Hospital for more than 10 weeks, thus ending his service. He was succeeded as chief by Harold Thompson, who became known as "Thompy."[100] In retirement in 1950, Elliott caned and reseated chairs. He died February 27, 1955.

## NATURE AROUND US

### The Weather

During the last week of June, 1941, the worst hailstorm in many years, accompanied by torrential rain, damaged apples, strawberries, and other crops. The road from Route 28 over the hill to Water Village "washed badly and was like a river."

In late summer and autumn 1942, wells were low or dry. The situation was not relieved until November when steady rain fell.

On July 16, 1944, a severe thunderstorm swept through East Wolfeboro. Lightning strikes caused power outages, and Jesse Clow's barn was hit. A month later, from about 1:00 a.m. to 3:00 a.m. on September 15, hurricane winds, the residue of a tropical storm, accompanied by 3.43 inches of rain, did much damage. Tons of apples were ripped from their branches, electrical service was out in many areas, and numerous trees were blown down. The area on North Main Street between Mill and Friend Streets was a scene of devastation, the worst in the entire state; a tornado must have touched down.

On October 14, 1944, at about 9:30 in the evening, a thunderstorm accompanied by hail struck the region. The hailstones were said to be as big as golf balls in Center Tuftonboro. The size of the pellets in Wolfeboro was not recorded.

During the first half of February, 1945, large amounts of snow fell on the town. Drifts 12 feet deep blocked the road on Whitten Neck, a building or two collapsed, and in Cotton Valley the snow was so deep that the plow could not clear the roads.

On April 22, 1945, high winds ruptured a restraining boom at Moultonboro Neck on Lake Winnipesaukee, releasing thousands of logs, which floated downwind to Wolfeboro and other points, making navigation hazardous.

On May 10, 1945, a freak storm ripped through the area, dropped nearly two feet of snow, and downed many power lines and trees. Transportation was snarled and schools closed.

The autumn of 1947 was exceedingly dry. Forest fires raged in the area, and many outdoor events were canceled. On October 21, Principal Vincent Rogers, of Brewster Free Academy, called upon 21 boys to help lo-

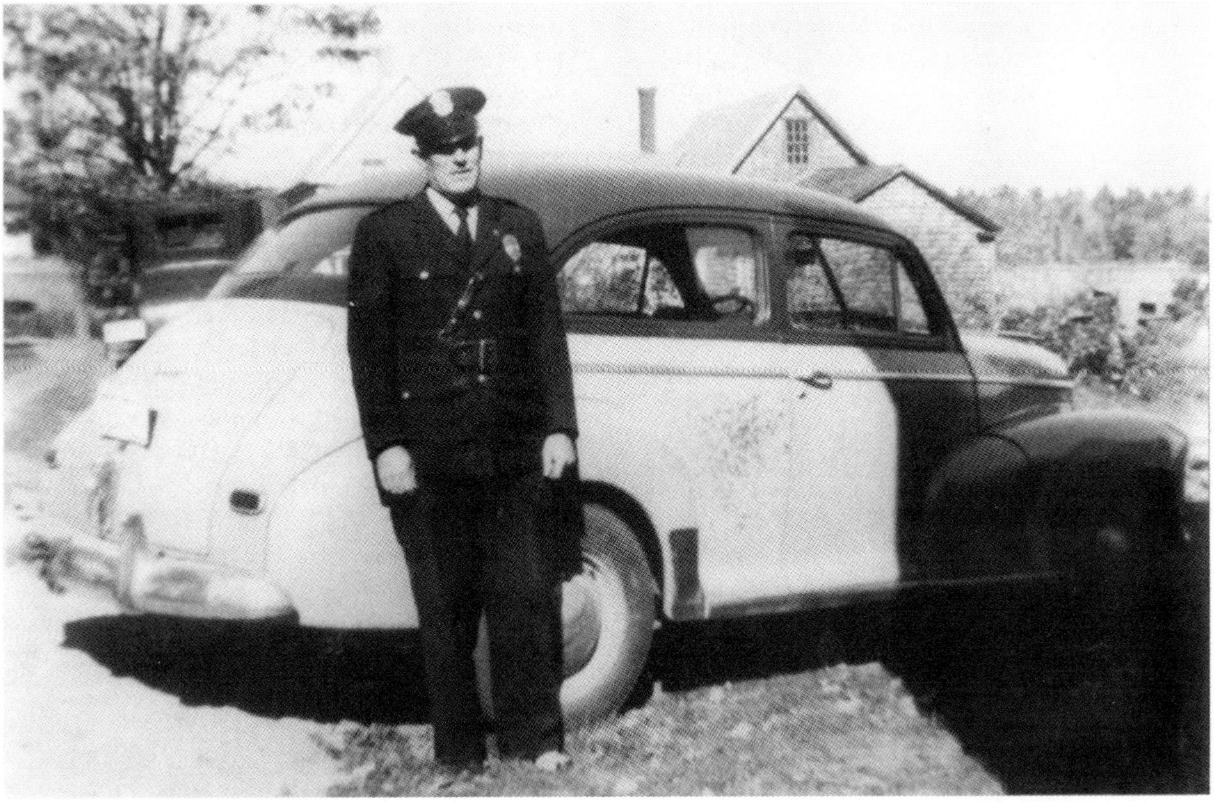

Law enforcement: Police Chief Albert K. Elliott in front of his car which was sprayed with 12-gauge shotgun pellets (see panel to the left of the door latch) after he tried to break up a fight on Railroad Avenue on October 4, 1947. (Photograph courtesy of Chief Stanley E. Stevens)

Town government: Selectmen of Wolfeboro who served from 1947 to 1950. Left to right: Noyes V. Moore, Wayne L. Parkhurst, and Earl F. Willand.

cal crews fight a large forest fire in Wakefield. "At night the flames could be seen on the horizon from the Lake View Cemetery as a red glow fading to pink at the top." A thousand men worked on the fire lines. In the Wakefield-Sanbornville area two observers counted 55 homes that had been burned out. Joseph I. Melanson lost two sawmills and two lumber mills valued at about $35,000. There were many fires elsewhere in New England, and at Bar Harbor, ME, many mansions and other buildings were destroyed. Water levels in the lakes went to very low levels. On November 8, high winds and rain swept through the area, trees and power lines were destroyed, but less than a half inch of rain fell.

Drought continued through the summers of 1948, 1949, and 1950. Many wells went dry, and crops were reduced or lost. The fire hazard continued, but no major damage occurred within town limits.

During the last week of August, 1950, heavy rain finally fell, but too late to save garden and farm crops. On November 25 and 26, hurricane force winds dumped nearly four inches of rain on the town, washing out many roads. Pork Hill and Cotton Valley roads were especially hard hit. Several buildings were destroyed, and many trees were blown down.[101]

### Other Events

Shortly after supper on March 7, 1944, many Wolfeboro residents heard a fire alarm. However, none was being rung in Wolfeboro at the time. Solution to the mystery:

> Weatherman Kenneth Berry makes the following explanation: At the time the alarm was heard there was a low-hanging solid cloud bank over the lake. The sound of the alarm bounced from the lake to the cloud bank and, carried on by a light westerly breeze, reached Wolfeboro.

On April 14, 1944, an undated account from the Cotton Valley correspondent to the local paper noted: "I didn't hear the earthquake we had here yesterday around 4:30 p.m. Mrs. Thurrell said the house shook and she could hear the tinkle of glass."[102]

On Monday evening, November 13, 1944, a large meteor blazed through the sky, traveling in an east-to-south direction.

In the summer of 1946 Robert F.W. Meader raised some curious peas, using four ancient seeds that had been taken in the 1920s from the tomb of Tut Ankh-amen in Egypt. "From that modest beginning, he now has a real crop. They differ quite a bit from the peas with which we are familiar—something like a cross between peas and string beans in flavor."

At about eight in the evening of November 19, 1948, Orman T. Headley of Wakefield reported "the biggest, brightest meteor he has ever seen in four years of meteor observing." Headley, an amateur astronomer, estimated it must have fallen to the ground between Wakefield and Rochester.[103]

### Birds Observed or Heard

On several occasions during the 1940s Mrs. C.H. Pratt of North Wolfeboro, an amateur ornithologist, reported the species of birds she had seen or heard during the year. Here is the 1943 list:[104]

> Bank swallow, barn swallow, black and white warbler, black billed cuckoo, black throated green warbler, blue headed vireo, blue jay, bluebird, bobolink, brown creeper, catbird, cedar waxwing, chickadee, chimney swift, chipping sparrow, Cooper's hawk, crested flycatcher, crow, field sparrow, flicker, golden and ruby crowned kinglets, goldfinch, towhee, great blue heron, great horned owl (heard), hairy and downy woodpecker, hermit thrush, hummingbird, indigo bunting, junco, kingbird, least flycatcher, marsh hawk, myrtle warbler, Nashville warbler, nighthawk, northern yellow throat, oriole, ovenbird, phoebe, pileated woodpecker (heard), pine grosbeak, purple finch, red breasted nuthatch, red eyed vireo, red tailed and red shouldered hawk, red wing blackbird, redstart, robin, rose breasted grosbeak, sapsucker, scarlet tanager, sharp shinned hawk, snow bunting, sparrow hawk, starling, tree sparrow, tree swallow, vesper sparrow, whippoorwill (heard), white breasted nuthatch, white crowned sparrow, white throated sparrow, song sparrow, wood peewee, wood thrush, woodcock, yellow palm warbler, and yellow warbler.

## BACK TO THE BATTLEFIELD

### Korea

If there were one thing that Americans did not need or want, it was another war. And yet no sooner had World War II ended in 1945 than talk of World War III started. Mainly to blame were the communists, particularly in Russia and China.

In 1949 it was learned that Russia had developed the atomic bomb. Now the American continent, largely immune from attack during the other two great wars, was no longer sacrosanct. However, the editor of the *Granite State News* did find *something* favorable to say:

> We who live in rural areas can be thankful that our destruction is not worth a single bomb, whereas our friends who live in Lynn, Boston, Portsmouth, Springfield, Worcester, Hartford, New Haven, Bridgeport, and New York can begin to sleep uneasy at night. The wise man, if he can possibly do so, will now move his business from the city to the country.

Thus began a decade of national preparation against atomic attack, eventually including the building of bomb shelters and the forming of Civil Defense networks. In November 1949 the Rotary Club and others proposed that a National Guard company be set up in Wolfeboro and that it be an anti-aircraft unit equipped with 90 mm. guns. This idea was translated into reality, and at long last it was announced that the best-known municipal headache, the empty Clark Shop on Factory Street, would be occupied by a unit with the seemingly clumsy name of Battery BD, 744th Antiaircraft Gun Battalion, 197th Antiaircraft group, National Guard of New Hampshire. The battalion was activated on June 13 after 13 soldiers had signed up, the minimum required.

Gifts at The Harmony Shop

*We cordially invite you* TO INSPECT OUR CHRISTMAS LINE OF UNUSUAL GIFTS. THIS YEAR WE ARE OFFERING THOSE HARD-TO-FIND GIFTS TO FIT EVERY BUDGET . . . MANY OUTSTANDING ITEMS FROM $1.00 TO $3.00

PICTURED ABOVE ARE A FEW OF OUR MANY GIFT ITEMS FROM

WESTMORELAND GLASS

MAKERS OF THE FAMOUS HAND-MADE CRYSTAL AND MILK GLASS

SEEN IN THE SHOPS

For the ladies, Harold Brown is displaying some attractive fur-topped overshoes, cloth and sheep skin lined.

Leon Robinson has a nice item for the girls and women in the "White Stag" nylon parkas and ski pants.

Haskins Hardware has many items of interest, but our attention was taken by the Burgess Vibro Sprayer, a completely self-contained unit. It has no hose, compressor or motor: just plug in, pull trigger and spray, paint or other materials. It is priced at $12.95.

In the Harmony Shop we found a new collection of miniature figurines, from England and France.

AS BEAUTIFUL AS Christmas . . OUTSIDE

AS ENDURING AS Christmas INSIDE...

A BRAND NEW

Hamilton

AT A NEW LOW PRICE!

NEW!

17 Jewel

CLINTON

Only

$49.50

Stainless steel case, black figure dial. 17-jewel movement.

HORACE D. MANNING

Wolfeboro Market

OPPOSITE THE POST OFFICE

Carroll A. Lamprey

Fancy Meats and Groceries

Tel. 392

*The Best Christmas Anyone Can Have is A New Home.*

THE DIAMOND MATCH CO.

Building Material

Lumber Paints Hardware

Operating Yards Throughout Maine, New Hampshire, Massachusetts, Rhode Is.

Wolfeboro Falls - Tel. 73

Walgreen Agency Drug Store

McFADDEN & LIBBEY

YOUR DRUGGISTS

ROGER MATTISON, Reg. Pharm.

Fresh VITAMINS

Multiple Vitamins OLAFSEN AYTINAL Bottle 100 tablets for . . 2.69

Koller Analgesic BALM 59c

100 Tablets WALGREEN ASPIRIN 43c

High Potency—50-mg. OLAFSEN VITAMIN E Bottle 100 capsules for 2.69

Good Health Insurance

"Glolite" Multiple 7 Light Set Each burns independent . . 1.79 Add-on connector, for indoor use.

"Glolite" Indoor 8 Light Set Tri-plug connector . . 98c With open outlet for additional sets.

WE ARE HEADQUARTERS *for* Domestic SEWMACHINES

*On Display At Our Store*

Desk Model 729-151 $234.95

End Table Model 735-153 $191.95

Table Model 723-151 $164.95

PLUS: OTHER FURNITURE AND PORTABLE MODELS

**LADIES --- These machines on display at our showroom are waiting for you to come in to use, and see for yourself why the name DOMESTIC has been famous for seventy years. Now for the first time electric sewing machines are sold and serviced by your local dealer. We carry parts and accessories for all standard makes of machines. Come in and let us show you how beautifully tailored buttonholes are made in just a few seconds.**

CHECK THESE FEATURES:

- DIAL TENSION CONTROL easily adjusted for loose machine basting or regular sewing by numbers.
- HINGED PRESSER FOOT eliminates hand basting by enabling you to sew right over pins and heavy seams.
- 4 POINT FEED assures straight stitching by gripping material evenly at the front, back and sides of the needle.
- FINGERTIP RELEASE releases pressure on the foot so that darning and mending may be done quickly.
- SIMPLIFIED THREADING...no hole to thread except the eye of the needle, thread other guides with one hand.
- FORWARD AND REVERSE SEWING---a quick way to back tack seam ends, reinforce corners without stopping the machine.

PRICES BEGIN AT $139.95 TERMS LOW AS $1.75 wk.

Sold Exclusively In This Area by

THE WAYSIDE

*Appliances and Equipment*

ROY G. NELSON

CORNER LAKE & NO. MAIN STS. TEL. 276-W

**Page of advertisements (shown reduced) from *The Shopper,* December 9, 1949. This short-lived free paper was produced by L. Winston Hamm and his Creative Printing Company, Bay Street.**

In June 1950 American troops were ordered to Korea, and the country was once again at war. In some areas hoarders bought all of the sugar they could find. This time, they didn't want to be caught short. Mabel Fullerton Hatch suggested that a brand new epidemic of the distressing malady me-first-itis might be occurring.

In August the editor of the local paper commented on a puzzling situation: "One significant item comes through in the stories filed by the war correspondents in Korea—that the American men never received proper indoctrination as to why they were in Korea, or what they are fighting for." Congress never formally declared war, and thousands of Americans died in what was called the "Korean Conflict."

A report soon came that a Wolfeboro soldier, Private Winfield S. House, was missing, later modified to killed in action; his was the first local life to be lost.

In October 1950 this was published: "Business sage Roger W. Babson advises Boston firms to store vital records and to establish small branches in New Hampshire." Babson was no stranger to the area, as he owned two Wolfeboro islands in Lake Winnipesaukee. In the same month the Civil Defense group in Wolfeboro held its first meeting, under the leadership of Fred Miller, who had served with the rank of major in World War II. "In the event that military and industrial centers should be attacked, and large numbers of civilians move to Wolfeboro for shelter, urgent problems would be feeding, housing and sanitation." It seemed like World War II all over again.

In the meantime, during a realignment the National Guard unit changed its name to the 210th AAA Gun Battalion. At a special town meeting on November 14, 1950, it was voted to purchase 27 acres of land in South Wolfeboro on which a National Guard armory would be built. The cost of the land was $5,000, plus an additional $9,000 to run a town water line to the site.[105]

## PRICES IN 1950

The following prices and related items are from the *Granite State News*, 1950. In general, prices are sharply higher than they were a decade earlier, primarily due to wartime inflation and the scarcity of consumer goods.

**Appliances:** Bendix Economat automatic washer, front-loading, $189.95. Frigidaire refrigerator, 9 cubic feet, $309.75; 7.6 cubic feet, $234.75. Iron, electric, General Electric, $8.95. Kitchen range, combination gas or oil (or both), Glenwood, $199.95. Sewing machine, Singer, electric portable, $39.50. Water heater, electric, 30 gallons, $109.50.

**Automobiles:** Buick, 1950, three-passenger coupe $1,910; super 4-door, 6-passenger sedan, $2,165. Hudson, 1950, 6-cylinder, four-door sedan, demonstrator in as-new condition, $2,175. Pontiac, 1950, Chieftain Business Coupe, $1,673; Chieftain Deluxe 4-door sedan, $1,942. Willys Jeepster "with sensational new Hurricane engine. America's lowest-priced open car," $1,589.07.

**Baby powder:** 1-pound tin, Rexall, 59¢.

**Beverages:** Coca-Cola, bottle, 5¢. Moxie, eight 7-ounce bottles, plus deposit, 25¢. Orange juice, frozen, Minute Maid, 6-oz can, 28¢.

**Boats:** Correct Craft Dart, 75 h.p., $1,794; Correct Craft, Jr., 45 h.p., $1,590. Penn Yan, 16-20 feet, 45 to 160 h.p., $1,675 upward.

**Cigarettes:** Popular brands, carton, $1.80.

**Clock:** Electric, Telechron, 9" square, $7.50.

**Clothing:** Boy's ski jacket, $8.75. Men's socks, pair, 25¢ Men's sweatshirt, $2.25. Men's wool plaid shirt, $7.95. Men's pants, wool, $6.75. Ladies' nylon stockings, pair, 89¢.

**Drinking glasses:** Fruit juice, dozen, $7.50.

**Food:** Meat: Chicken, pound, 39¢. Beef chuck roll, boneless, pound, 55¢. Corned beef, pound, 55¢. Frankfurts, skinless, pound, 39¢. Hamburger meat, pound, 55¢. Tuna, can, 37¢.

**Food:** Various: Apples, Baldwins, pound, 6¢. Baby food, Gerber's, jar, 10¢. Broccoli, bunch, 20¢. Butter, Swift's, pound, 69¢. Cabbage, pound, 7¢. Catsup, 14-ounce bottle, 15¢. Cheese, old-fashioned sharp, pound, 69¢. Corn flakes, Kellogg's, 13-ounce package, 20¢. Cranberry sauce, 1-pound can, 10¢. Grapefruit, each, 8¢. Ice cream, Hood's, pint, 28¢. Jell-O package, 9¢. Lettuce, large head, 17¢. Margarine, colored, pound, 39¢. Onions, pound, 7¢; 10-pound bag, 33¢. Oranges, Florida, dozen, 39¢. Peanut butter, Skippy, 1-pound jar, 39¢. Potatoes, 15-pound bag, 39¢. Soup, Campbell's chicken, can, 17¢; vegetable, can, 13¢. Spaghetti, Franco-American, 15-1/2-ounce can, 14¢. Sugar, 10-pound bag, 87¢

**Fuel:** Bottled gas, two cylinders, 20 pounds each, installed, $23.75. Gasoline, gallon, 17¢.

**Greeting cards:** Hallmark, dozen, 29¢.

**Hair styling:** Woman's permanent with haircut and finger wave, $7.50.

**Key:** Made to order, 20¢.

**Lawn mower:** Granite State brand, hand-pushed, $14.95.

**Medical care:** Blue Cross compensation for appendicitis operation and hospital stay, seven benefit days, $136.70.

**Paint:** DuPont house, outside white, gallon, $4.99.

**Pen:** Ball-point, 59¢.

**Phonograph:** RCA Victor 45 RPM record changer with amplification system, including $10 worth of records, $39.95

**Radio:** RCA Victor table model, 8" speaker, $29.95.

**Real Estate:** 165-acre farm, 8-room colonial house with all modern conveniences, large barn, beautiful view, $7,700. Guest home on Main Street, Wolfeboro, 17 rooms, 3 baths, all-year business location. $14,000. Winnipesaukee shore lots, large shade pines, road, electricity, per front foot on lake, $9.50. Land on Route 28 with 600 feet of highway frontage, $1,300. North Wolfeboro home, antique Cape Cod colonial, six large rooms and two fireplaces, just off Route 28, $5,900. One acre of land on north side of Kingswood Golf Course off South Main Street, $250.

**Restaurant food:** Businessman's lunch, $1; cheese omelet, 70¢; dinner special, $1.50; frankfurts and potato salad, 65¢; fried clams or chicken with French fries, 75¢; hamburger steak, 75¢; T-bone steak, $1.50.

**Skates:** Men's hockey, pair, $9.95.

**Ski boots:** $11.50 to $25.

**Tennis balls:** Can of 3, $1.95.

**Toilet seat:** Hardwood, $4.95.

**Tool:** Electric drill, 1/4-inch portable, Home-Utility brand, $18.95.

**Towel:** Turkish, 20 x 40 inches, 43¢.

**Utensils:** Saucepan, stainless steel, 4 quart, $6.95. Silverplate table service for six, Gorham, $45.75.

**Watches:** 17-jewel, men's, $49.50 to $59.50; 17-jewel, nurse's, $33.75 to $43.75; Mickey Mouse, $6.95.

# CHAPTER 8
# WOLFEBORO 1951-1960

*I think I may be a little prejudiced because I was born here.... But, just the other day a friend from New York who has been coming here for many years [told] me that Wolfeboro was somehow in her blood and she always wanted to be associated with it. And, this attraction is not just for summer time, but it lasts 12 months in the year. And it's a right-size town. Big enough so you can find plenty of congenial friends and neighbors, and small enough so that you feel you have a real stake in the community.*

—Mabel Fullerton Hatch, *Granite State News,* July 29, 1955.

## INTRODUCTION

The decade 1951-1960 commenced with the Korean Conflict entering its second year. While the war was a matter of concern to local residents, the patriotic fervor that supported the troops on the front in World War II was largely missing now. This was a new kind of war, one without fixed objectives or strategies.

On the economic scene, *inflation* was the key word. By hindsight in 1960, prices of 1951 would prove to be incredibly cheap in many instances, and prices of the 1930s might as well have been from ancient history. To paraphrase an old saying, the only constant in local commerce was change. There were many transitions, not the least significant of which was the transformation of a formerly foul area of Back Bay into the site for the new Wolfeboro Shopping Center, which threw open its doors in July 1958. The Chamber of Commerce continued its perennial effort to increase the town's industrial base, with little in the way of results.

Inflation and growth went hand-in-hand. By the end of the 10-year period, many new houses had been built, the number of boats on lakes Wentworth and Winnipesaukee had increased dramatically. In general, Wolfeboro escaped much of the economic ups and downs on the national scene in the 1950s, probably because the main local activity was tourism, and in good markets and bad, people wanted to visit a nice place.

## WAR AND CIVIL DEFENSE

### America at War

While thousands of American soldiers were losing their lives in far-off Korea, on the home front there was relatively little concern for safety. Citizens were told of air-raid warning signals, but, unlike the situation in World War II a few years earlier, this time there were no frightening predictions of bombs dropping on Boston or New York City or of incendiary bombs raining down upon Wolfeboro itself. This was someone else's war, in a distant place. Not even the enemy was well defined—was the enemy China or possibly even Russia, or was the opponent solely North Korea? No one seemed quite sure. From time to time, local service people would be depicted on the front page of the *Granite State News.* Perhaps, the most attention-getting news was the controversy that swirled around the firing of General Douglas MacArthur by President Harry Truman.

Wolfeboro residents supported the activities of Battery D, 210th AAA Gun Battalion, stationed at the Wolfeboro Armory on Middleton Road, a National Guard unit whose happenings were chronicled nearly every week in the paper and which functioned as an effective training facility.[1]

### A High Platform in a Low Spot

In January 1952 the Air Force announced it would train volunteer civilians to serve in the Ground Observer Corps to help spot enemy planes. In June the town Civil Defense Committee built an observation tower on the roof of the derelict Wolfeborough Railroad Station.

Enemy bombers were likely to fly 30,000 feet or higher and could not be identified by civilians lacking sophisticated optical equipment. Perhaps low-level fighter planes might be a threat, but, if so, why was the observation post not put on a hill, rather than in one of the lowest spots in town? As it was, the platform was a high spot in a low part of town. Many other questions were raised.

# MUSTER DAYS FEB. 22 – 23

90MM AA GUN CREW training in loading and firing drill, with dummy ammo, under the command of SFC Herbert W. Barter.

**PROGRAM — SATURDAY**

8:00 AM — Volunteers of Battery B will muster for roll call.

9:00 AM — Recruiting Teams, each with a jeep, will fan out over Carroll County, to visit prospects.

4:00 PM — Teams will return to Armory.

**PROGRAM — SUNDAY**

1:30 PM — Volunteers of Battery B will muster for roll call.

2:00 PM — OPEN HOUSE at Armory. All equipment will be demonstrated. Movies. Refreshments. Program to continue into evening as long as people are present.

See Page 1 Story for Further Details

SAME 90MM GUN CREW firing the gun at a radio controlled aerial target, at Camp Wellfleet, Mass., during 1957 field training.

**WHO ARE YOUR GUARDSMEN NEIGHBORS?**

They are young men you know well. Some of them are veterans of WWII and Korea, some have only National Guard service, but they work for a common cause: to immediately defend the United States against any enemy attack, and to serve the local communities in any emergency that might arise.

**WHAT KIND OF A UNIT IS BATTERY B?**

It is one of the four gun batteries in the 744th Antiaircraft Artillery Battalion, of the N. H. National Guard. Its primary function is to destroy enemy aircraft in any attempted attack upon this country. Its secondary function, in its State status, is to help the community in any emergency. The week-long service rendered at the Mt. Shaw fire in 1953 is a good example of community service.

**IS THERE A PLACE FOR YOU IN BATTERY B?**

YES, whether you are a veteran with 10 years service or a younger man with no military service. This Battery will soon receive more modern equipment, so that it can better carry out its assigned military mission. About forty more men are needed to fill up the sections to efficiently carry out the mission. Every man, whether veteran or not, progresses on his own merit, and there are many NCO positions still open in the Battery. Visit the Armory, to find out if there is a place for you.

## *Keep Your Guard Up*

SUPPORT AND JOIN YOUR NEIGHBORS IN

## BATTERY B, 744th AAA BN.

**STATE ARMORY, WOLFEBORO TEL. WOLFEBORO 369**

Located on New Durham Road, South Wolfeboro: Watch for Sign at the overhead blinker on Route 28 at South Wolfeboro.

**Announcement for Muster Days, February 22-23, 1958, featuring the Wolfeboro unit of the New Hampshire National Guard.**

Ellis F. Miller, director of Civil Defense, hastened to assure naysayers that the operation was logical, despite appearances to the contrary. The Air Force wanted to:

> cut the observation radius to approximately two miles to avoid the confusion of overlapping.... This comes about when observers have unlimited view of the surrounding territory, and report planes that are seen and reported at the same time by observers in other communities....

Anyone wishing to enroll for three hours a week in the crow's nest atop the train station was urged to sign up with Selectman Noyes V. Moore, who was supervising the project locally.[2]

On July 27, 1953, an armistice was signed in Korea. Peace was a reality, but no one believed it would last. The continuing threat of atomic war with Russia overshadowed much of the enthusiasm which might have otherwise occurred.

### Korean War Honor Roll

Two Wolfeboro men died in the Korean War, Winfield Scott House and Leon H. Tutt.[3] The following Honor Roll lists men and women from Wolfeboro who were in the armed services, including active duty in Korea, between June 25, 1950, and July 27, 1953:[4]

> Bradley Barker, Charlton Beach, Herbert A. Bean, Bruce L. Beaulieu, Sheldon A. Beaulieu, Raymond J. Berry, Newell H. Bickford, Jr., Romeo E. Bilodeau, William B. Carpenter, Andre J. Champagne, Richard H. Charles, Paul Clifford, William Coppins, 2nd, Franklin W. Dore, Homer W. Eatock, George H. Elliott, Keith A. Elliot, Neil S. Fogg, Richard A. Fogg, Francis B. Foss, Robert L. Foss, Bruna D. Fusi, Fred Gassett, Chester F. Gilman, Lawrence Glidden, John L. Hamlin, Robert L. Hanson, Charles A. Hatch, Stephen B. Hatch, Robert B. Hawkes, Eugene M. Head, Ellis Herbert, Paul G. Herbert, Carroll F. Hersey, 2nd, Winfield House,* Lyford Hutchins, Richard L. Hutchins, H. Furber Jewett, Jr., John Paul Jones, Gordon Keenan, Ernest Franklin Kenney, William H. Kenney, Robert A. Lampron, Eugene F. Lehner, Jr., Charles L. Lord, Jr., Donald C. Lord, Myron S. Lord.
>
> Herbert C. MacMartin, James C. McBride, William A. McBride, William A. McDonald, H. George Moody, Robert E. Moody, Roger Moody, Bernard Moore, Courtney Moore, Harrison D. Moore, Donald M. Morgan, Sr., Wayne A. Morgan, David S. Morrill, John L. Morrill, Jr., Paul F. O'Leary, Stephen (Sylvester) M. Parshley, Edwin M. Pennell, Roy G. Parkhurst, Jr., Stephen M. Parkhurst, Chester H. Pike, Clinton T. Piper, Norman Piper, John C. Rico, Paul A. Rico, Richard A. Ridlon, Charles R. Robarts, Edward L. Roberge, Richard Y. Robbins, Rodney H. Roome, Howard B. Sabin, James R. Sanborn, Helen A. Stead, Harold A. Taylor, Irving L. Thomas, Roger F. Thurrell, Robert D. Thurston, Warren D. Thompson, Jr., Alvah G. Tibbetts, Scott M. Tinker, Daniel S. Tucker, Leon H. Tutt,* George R. Valley, Arthur F. Waite, Alvin R. White, Paul G. Whitney, and Kenneth B. Wilkinson.

### On Guard

Although the Korean Conflict (as it was officially called; *war* had not been declared) had come to an end, the threat of Communist expansion and nuclear proliferation dictated that America remain on alert. In Wolfeboro, National Guard Battery D, 210th AAA Bn (Gun, 90mm) announced "Operation Expansion" to increase its strength from approximately 40 men to about 70. Its 28-acre facility off Middleton Road in South Wolfeboro was renamed the Hart Military Reservation, for the late Col. Harold H. Hart, prominent Wolfeboro automobile dealer, military reserve officer, and founding president of the Chamber of Commerce.

In 1954 there was much discussion of the hydrogen bomb, a super-weapon possessed by America and also Russia. The only reasonable defense against overflights of bomb-laden Russian planes was the dispersal of American population and industry. In this regard Wolfeboro had reason to feel safer than metropolitan areas. Preparation for nuclear fallout was advised, and the government recommended that every family have a month's supply of dry foods and canned goods, to be drawn upon daily and rotated for freshness. In a scenario reminiscent of World War II predictions, it was envisioned that an atomic attack on Boston or New York City would bring millions of people to rural areas such as Wolfeboro, where grocery stores did not have enough food on hand to last long if supplies were cut.

In 1959 Battery B, 744th AA Battalion (Gn. 90 mm.) was renamed Battery B, 2nd Howitzer Battalion, 197th Combat Arms Regiment, again hardly a cognomen that a soldier's sweetheart could easily remember while addressing mail. The unit's new weapon was a self-propelled, 45-ton, 8-inch howitzer.[5]

## THE POLITICAL SCENE

### Wanted: A National Direction

Politics and war went hand-in-hand early in the decade of the 1950s. At times it seemed that there was more bickering in Washington than there was concern for the welfare of American troops in Korea. Every politician had a view as to whether we should stay in Korea or withdraw and as to whether American bombers and fighters should cross the Yalu River and strike at China (which backed the North Korean enemy efforts). Seemingly, the Korean war had no direction or stated objective.

On November 6, 1951, Senator H. Styles Bridges, who had close connections to the town, gave a speech to the Wolfeboro Rotary Club, urging that "this country take definite action in Korea, and either fight and clean up the mess, or get out."[6]

On December 28, 1951, *Granite State News* editor Parker M. Merrow reflected on the state of affairs, noting that Russia had strengthened itself with many satellite states, and for all practical purposes had recently annexed China. "We have been sucked into a war in Korea that has cost us over 100,000 casualties and untold billions of dollars." The national debt was rising, and inflation continued to be out of hand. "Worst of all there has been a steady deterioration of our ethics, and a growing feeling that it is legal to make a fast buck as long as it is done within the letter of the law. There is an aimless drifting of purpose of our entire nation..."

In 1953 and 1954 America was caught up in the "Communist scare." Dossiers of public officials, entertainment industry personalities, and others were searched to learn if they had ever belonged to a Communist organization, or had read *The Daily Worker,* or, for that matter, had ever been associated with someone purported to be a Communist. It became popular to call one's enemies and political opponents Communists, regardless of the facts.

Not only were there many alleged Communists, a.k.a. "reds," but there were also numerous people called "pinks" or "pinkos," who were said to have had a tinge of "red." All of this was on the national scene, not in Wolfeboro, although Mabel Fullerton Hatch stated that she had even heard complaints that Robin Hood was subversive and should be taken off children's reading lists. In 1954 the congressional hearings conducted by Sen. Joseph McCarthy in Washington created a national sensation. Eventually, New Hampshire was "searched" for suspected Communists.[7]

### Presidential Contests

In 1951 the state law was changed, and voters in presidential elections could henceforth make direct choices for candidates in the primary contests in March. This early primary should focus national attention on New Hampshire during each presidential election, it was stated. Perhaps Sen. Robert A. Taft of Ohio and Gen. Dwight D. Eisenhower would have tests of strength in the state in 1952, the editor of the local paper mused.

The March 11, 1952, primary saw these results in Wolfeboro: Dwight Eisenhower received 312 votes, Robert Taft 298, Estes Kefauver 23, Harry Truman 16, Harold Stassen 15, and Gen. Douglas MacArthur 12. The November race narrowed to Eisenhower for the Republican ticket and Adlai Stevenson for the Democrats. "Ike" Eisenhower was considered a shoo-in. At the November 4 election, this proved to be the case.[8] For the first time since Herbert Hoover was elected in 1928, the majority of Wolfeboro voters were on the side of the winner.

In the same month, President-Elect Eisenhower announced that Sherman Adams, governor of New Hampshire, would be his personal assistant. In January 1953 in Ike's inauguration parade several past and present Wolfeboro residents were aboard the New Hampshire float: Connie (Mrs. Ralph, Jr.) Carpenter, Martha Corkum, and Peg McDonald.[9]

At the next presidential go-round, November 6, 1956, there was hardly a contest. In Wolfeboro Eisenhower was re-elected with 1,310 votes, and Adlai Stevenson was left in the dust with 116.

Then came the 1960 election. In September of that year, Editor Parker M. Merrow commented:

> At the head of the ticket there is Kennedy, a brilliant mind, engaging personality, a notable war record, and backed by a family fortune reputed to be in the neighborhood of a quarter of a billion dollars... If Kennedy should win the presidency, thrifty New Hampshire folks with a good part of their savings in government bonds and savings bonds and annuities can make up their minds that the buying power of their money will depreciate between 10% and 25% when Kennedy is in office... If the Republicans want to win this election, they must organize and get out and work. The opposition is smart and it is able...

Of 1,950 registered local voters, 1,596 (or 82%) turned up at Town Hall to cast ballots. If Wolfeboro had been representative of the nation, John F. Kennedy wouldn't have had a chance with his meager 257 local supporters to Republican Richard Nixon's overwhelming 1,329. However, across America it went the other way, and Kennedy won. Republican Senator H. Styles Bridges, seeking reelection, garnered 1,364 votes, against a trifling 196 for his opponent.[10]

### State and Local Politics

For years New Hampshire had financed much if not most of its activities by levying property taxes. On June 8, 1951, the editor of the *Granite State News* suggested that a 2% statewide sales tax, with one-half of the net proceeds being returned to the town, would be an excellent idea and would contribute to the relief of real estate taxes. Nothing came of the idea, then or later.

For many years Wolfeboro Republicans and Democrats held their own caucuses prior to the March annual town meeting in order to put forth candidates for local posts. In 1959 this policy was abolished. From 1960 onward, local office-seekers did not state their party affiliation on the ballot.[11]

Selectmen serving during the 1951-1960 decade included Earl F. Willand, Noyes V. Moore, Weare Fred Tuttle, Charles L. French, Sr., Edward W. Zulauf, and Norman A. Hale.

## THE ECONOMY AND TOURISM

### Inflation and Employment

In 1951 a government price freeze was applied to many goods in an effort to curb rampant inflation spurred by the Korean Conflict. As it turned out, prices would continue to escalate, even after the war ended. Although there were ups and downs during the decade, most who wanted to work found jobs. In the winter,

DEMOCRATS & INDEPENDENTS!
VOTE
FOR SENATOR JOHN F.
KENNEDY
FOR
PRESIDENT
A Time For Greatness
Proven Leader
Proven Statesman
Proven Courage
Vote for Senator Kennedy for President and for the Delegates pledged to him
Signed:
Roger E. Brassard
Chairman:
Kennedy For President Committee
VOTE MARCH 8th

The 1960 presidential campaign was one of the most closely followed in recent times and pitted Richard M. Nixon against John F. Kennedy. In the November election Nixon captured the most votes locally, but Kennedy was the winner nationwide. (*Granite State News*, March 4, 1960, advertisement for presidential primary)

Linemen of the Municipal Electrical Department in the early 1950s. Lower left, upper left, and upper right: Gordon E. Glidden, Edward Fraser (tentative), and Edwin R. Craigue. (David Fetzer photograph)

employment slipped somewhat, due to lack of work in the farming and tourist industries. For example, in February 1951 about 100 local citizens reported weekly to the unemployment office.[12]

**Focus on Tourism**

A great deal of effort was made during the 1950s by the Chamber of Commerce to support Wolfeboro's primary business—tourism.

In 1951 the Festival of Fairs was conceived whereby local summer businesses agreed to extend their operations until October 15, thus adding six weeks to the tourist season. Package vacation trips to Wolfeboro were offered for three, four, and five days. Each special deal included a trip to a country fair (such as Fryeburg, Rochester, and Sandwich), an excursion around the White Mountains, a boat trip on Lake Winnipesaukee, a country dance, films at the Memorial Theatre, and admission to arts and crafts exhibits and antiques shows, as well as room and breakfast. Dozens of events were on the calendar. The promotion was a smash success.

Local merchants and innkeepers repeated the Festival of Fairs in 1952. Among visitors was a group of 300 amateur photographers. A massive advertising campaign included large notices in Boston, Springfield, Worcester, and Hartford papers and an 80-page booklet about Wolfeboro.

A tourist coming to town in the summer of 1953 and staying at the General Wolfe Inn (in the 1990s known as the Windrifter) could partake of entrées including fried Ipswich clams for $1.45, whole roast stuffed baby capons $2.45, broiled center cut pork chops $1.65, sautéed chicken livers on toast en brochette $1.75, fried fresh jumbo shrimp $1.85, chopped sirloin steak $1.85, fried Maryland soft-shell clams $1.80, broiled live lobster $2.75, two lamb chops $2.45, filet mignon $2.45, and golden brown chicken $2.10. Prices included vegetables, potato, rolls and relish.

Other popular stopping places included Bailey's Restaurant, the Lake Motel, the Colonial Arms (with its Barn Dining Room), the Carr House (renamed the Wolfeboro Inn after it was sold in 1959), the Lakeview Inn, and Dockside Restaurant, as well as several restaurants on Railroad Avenue and South Main Street.

In the summer of 1954 over 11,000 people visited the Information Booth on South Main Street. Despite this turnout, not all was well with local trade. New businesses set up in town diluted the profits of the older ones in a season which was below expectations. In mid-August, Matthew H. Brendel, owner of Clearwater Lodges, estimated that business volume had dropped 10% to 15%, while taxes, labor, and other costs had increased 10% to 25%. During the Christmas season, 15,500 "cheers" coupons were given out and prizes were awarded by merchants in an effort to stimulate sales.

In May 1956 a new tourist facility was opened by Norman E. Langdon at the old Meader (later, Melanson) farm on North Main Street. "The Highway Robber" sign out front "has created no end of discussion in Wolfeboro circles," according to the paper.[13]

**Déjà Vu**

What Wolfeboro *really* needed, certain local businessmen said, was new industry. Apparently, it would be great if Wolfeboro became a miniature version of Manchester or Lowell.

In March 1952 the Chamber of Commerce Industrial Committee stated that it had been busy trying to attract new industries to Wolfeboro. Overlooked were the lessons of history, that such efforts in the past had been largely a waste of time and money. "Old-timers and town fathers" who discouraged such efforts were accused of impeding progress. Rarely were ancillary costs considered—such as the expense of sending workers' children through the local school system (supported nearly in its entirety by property taxes) and municipal services.

Success at last! In May 1952 the Merit Products Corporation of Brooklyn, NY, moved to Wolfeboro and occupied the old Gardner Pad Co. mill on River Street. A $10,000 loan backed by local Chamber members helped grease the skids. Merit intended to hire 100 workers in the manufacture of excelsior-stuffed hassocks and related products.

As usual, reality proved to be different from expectations. Only about 30 people were ever employed. Worse, without warning the Merit firm closed up shop in October 1952 and dismissed its workers. A reporter commented: "It followed an anti-climax to months of conscientious effort on the part of businessmen and state and local officials to keep the business operating in Wolfeboro." As Yogi Berra is alleged to have said, it was "déjà vu all over again."[14]

The following appeared in print simultaneously with the news of the plant's closing. The writer was James A. Wales, Jr., president of the Chamber of Commerce. In part:

> After months and months of painstaking effort which went into the location of a plant here and to the ironing out of its very large number of small problems, it seems almost impossible that any such move [as the closing] was made....
>
> It seems to me that Wolfeboro now has to make a choice between two courses of action. We can forget the hassock business and any other new business and allow an impression to exist that we cannot be even lightly industrialized, or we can swallow this experience with a hard-earned lesson and will go out after a business that will provide jobs and opportunity to make it succeed. From what I have seen, it seems more than satisfactory that a good solid light industry can and would succeed... Preliminary work has already begun attempting to locate another industry here...

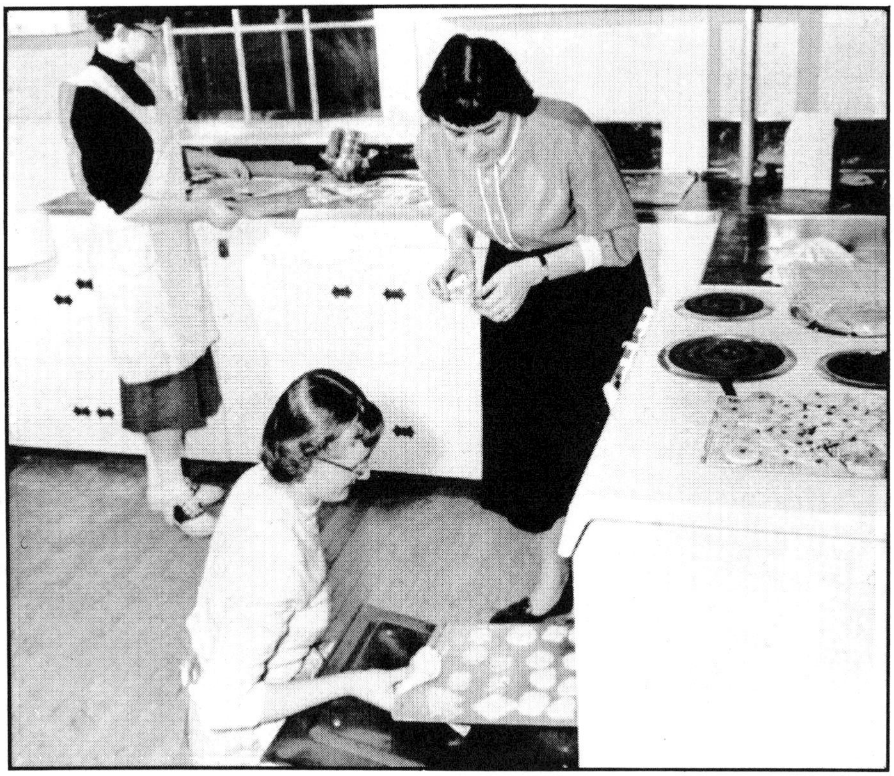

Life at Brewster Academy in the 1950s:

Top: Art classes moved to the basement of the new gym in 1954 and were taught by Mr. Rupert Brown. On the far right among the students is Lee Gridley who later became a well known local artist.

Left: Home economics (sewing and cooking) were part of the curriculum for many years. Baking cookies in the Kimball House classroom are, left to right: Nellie Piper and Joan McBride with teacher Jean (Mrs. Thomas P.) Hurst.

Life at Brewster Academy in the 1950s: Reviewing prom gowns and knitting are dormitory students (left to right) Millie Parker (from Cuba), Ellie Child, and Betty Ann Clark.

Glee Club was the most widely participated-in extracurricular activity due to the talented and inspired leadership of Burtis F. Vaughan, and the accompaniment of his wife Virginia (shown at the far right of the 1955 Girls' Glee Club photograph).

Life at Brewster Academy in the 1950s: Football was a big sport enthusiastically supported by students and townspeople. Postgraduate enrollment factored into successful seasons including playing some college teams.

The 1954 soccer team went undefeated for the first time since the sport's inception at Brewster in 1948. The team also won the New Hampshire Prep School Championship the second year in a row. First row (left to right): Alan Stevens, Jack Cleary, Ron Sinclair, Ron Ridlon, Richard Lampron, Dave Ross, co-captains Arthur Dalphond and Ralph Stevens, Dave Pollini, Roger Kent, Ken Bickford, Willis Manson, and mascot Stewart Brown. Second row: John McDermott, Rodney Haines, David Goodwin, Eliot Wyman, Bruce Bierweiler, John Kimball, Ken Gould, Jim Rogers, Bill Lord, Lee Gridley, Dave Rich, goalie Don Roberge, and coach Burtis Vaughan.

Life at Brewster Academy in the 1950s:

Commencement traditionally took place in front of the main Academy building, surrounded by magnificent elm trees which would, sadly, all eventually succumb to Dutch Elm disease.

(Brewster campus illustrations in this chapter are from a booklet, *Brewster Academy*, and the captions for the present work are from the identifications and suggestions of Dianne Rogers)

On October 7, 1957, a meeting sponsored by the Chamber was held in the Carpenter School auditorium to tell about an electronics firm that wanted to move to town and offer about 400 jobs, if the town could provide incentives. Observing the proceedings, the editor of the *Granite State News* observed dryly:

> Although there has never been much success in bringing industry to Wolfeboro, many men have spent a large amount of time trying to accomplish this.

To be sure, there were industries in town. The Malone Knitting Company had been on Factory Street (now Lehner Street) since the early 1940s, the latest of a long parade of businesses in the old Bell Shop. In 1960 a small outfit called Furniture Petites opened up shop in the old Hutchins excelsior mill in Wolfeboro Falls. However, the typical industry paid very low wages and usually cost the town more in services than it generated in taxes.

Whether or not Wolfeboro should "modernize" and industrialize continued to be a matter of debate. A letter signed "Progressive" was printed in the paper. He (or she) suggested that a large and beautiful elm tree in the downtown district should be "cut down immediately" and that more telephone poles, television antennas, and neon signs should be installed. "Finally, it is obvious that Wolfeboro needs more filling stations and hardware stores. By what other landmarks can a vacationer tell really whether or not he is in a really up and coming town?"[15]

### Business Marches On

The tourist business, faint of heart in 1954, revived. July 1955 saw record numbers of vacationers, and there would have been even more had it not been for the polio outbreak and much rainy weather. A boom was taking place nationwide. People had a lot of money to spend. In 1955 the average income of a *man* was $3,400 (up from $1,900 in 1945). In Wolfeboro it was a seller's market for real estate.

At the January 23, 1956, meeting of the Chamber of Commerce, President Henry S. Maxfield, local real estate man and entrepreneur, posed this challenge:[16]

> The question is not what can the Chamber of Commerce do for you, but what you can do through this organization for the town.

In the spring of 1957 there were three accredited realtors in town: Richard I. Bowe, Joseph I. Melanson, Jr., and Clarence M. Mixer. In addition, there were numerous sales agents and dealers.

### Commercial Miscellany

On December 9, 1951, Primo Pollini, well-known local shoe repairer and store operator for several decades, passed away. He was survived by four sons and a daughter, several of whom became prominent in the community.

Beginning in 1952, John Johnson's Quick Freeze Locker Service on Railroad Avenue made a big splash by promoting its smoked meats. A division called Country Smokehouse subsequently placed advertisements in the *New York Times, Gourmet* magazine, and elsewhere. This was reported on February 8, 1952:

> Volume has now reached the point where large shipments of uncured hams are made from the Midwest to Wolfeboro, smoked, and then sold. Wolfeboro's pheasant and ham business is slowly but steadily increasing and seems to be headed toward a good-sized volume.

Elsewhere in town, realtor Richard I. Bowe's pheasant pens on South Main Street, stocked with 600 or more birds, were making people sit up and take notice. Bowe's fowl are said to have been delicacies in Boston restaurants.

Meanwhile, farming as a local enterprise was on the decline. On August 7, 1953, this was published in the *Granite State News:*

> Driving over the back roads of Carroll County, every year we are more and more impressed with the complete collapse of farming, except in exceptionally favored areas. The small self-sustaining farm, as we once knew it, is gone. The fields...are now coming back into gray birch, pine and ground hemlock. Some barns are still standing, but they are used to house summer furniture, automobiles, or old farming machinery for which there is now no market...

The chicken-and-egg business remained active in the 1950s, but the number of birds was reduced from what it had been the decade before. Particularly notable in the trade in 1952 were Robert F. Thurrell (whose Cotton Mountain Farm had 4,000 chickens), Walter Hale, Robert G. and Candace Hale (who in the decade diversified by purchasing Robinson's Store and renaming it the Toggery Shop), Roy Foster, and Raymond Moody.[17]

Out on Sewall Road the venerable firm of Goodhue & Hawkins turned out a stream of wooden craft. In November 1953 the Falls Boat Shop was started in Wolfeboro Falls, changing its name to New Hampshire SportsCraft in 1960. The firm produced several models of inboard and outboard boats. The Northeast Marina, with facilities on Wolfeboro Bay as well as Back Bay, was a leading seller of equipment and boats including new fiberglass models. The hand-crafted wooden boat was going the way of the passenger pigeon and dodo (but would enjoy a revival several decades later).

In January 1955 the Wool Corner opened on Railroad Avenue. Like many other Wolfeboro shops, it would have several locations over the years, finally moving into the Haley Building where it still enjoys a lively trade today. On May 26-29 of the same year, the Wolfeboro Rotary Exposition was held at Brewster Academy to showcase local businesses. About the same time, Bailey's Restaurant on South Main Street announced a new specialty—pizza—perhaps being the first local business to serve it.

Another eatery printed this notice:

> Gentlemen: If your wife can't cook, don't shoot her. Keep her for a pet and eat at Dockside Restaurant.

From 1900 until 1955 the minimum charge for a local call from a pay phone was a nickel. On September 7 the New England Telephone and Telegraph Co. filed a new rate schedule doubling the fee to a dime (a tariff which was still in effect in the 1990s). During the same era, dial telephone service was being installed in Carroll County. By decade's end, Wolfeboro was one of the few towns still remaining without it.[18]

### The Wolfeboro Shopping Center

Henry S. Maxfield of Maxfield Real Estate, having convinced the First National Store (grocery, a.k.a. Finast) to move to a site on Center Street and become the nucleus of a shopping center, sold the land to Henry C. Hopewell of Wolfeboro and Frank Whipple of Tamworth.[19]

In March of 1958 construction began on the Wolfeboro Shopping Center on fill where a town dump had been earlier. The plaza was a success, and within a year or so of its July 1958 opening, the tenants in addition to the First National Store included Lampron's Grocery, Western Auto Associate Store, Samaha's (clothing), and the Wolfeboro Oil Co. A prefabricated building was set up on the right side of the center, and in early 1960 housed Lake & Village (real estate) and the offices of the *Granite State News.*

S&H Green Stamps had been around since 1896,[20] but they were never more popular than in the late 1950s and early 1960s, when they became a nationwide fad. To remain competitive, most merchants felt they had to sign up with S&H or some other trading stamp company and offer a stamp for each 10¢ worth of purchases. The stamps could be redeemed for premiums once enough were accumulated.

On Crescent Lake, Edwin V. Moody was one of the few local people still in the ice business. In 1956 he sold 1,600 tons, a figure that dropped to 1,000 tons by 1960. In addition, Moody did much work chipping ice from around docks in order to prevent damage to the pilings. This came to an end after 1960 when air bubblers became popular and automatically kept the water open. "The melting process is so effective that power from a small half-horsepower electric motor can melt more than 100 tons of two-foot thick ice in 24 hours."[21]

In the Chamber of Commerce Christmas promotion in December 1960, the following businesses participated: The Album Shop (owned by Paul R. Hatch, records and recordings), Bickford's (grocery), Harold F. Brown (shoes and men's clothing), Black's Gift Shop, The Ballard Store (clothing), Bradley's Hardware and Marine, Corkum's (men's clothing, sporting supplies), Diamond National (building supplies), Family Footwear, Gene's Hardware, Gould's Dime Store, Hall's Pharmacy, Hill's Jewelry, Jack Frost Shop (gifts), Lakeview Oil and Service Station, Market Basket (groceries), Parsons' Furniture, Samaha's (women's clothing), Stationery Shop, Tobey's Pharmacy, Villager (men's clothing), Wolfeboro National Bank, Wolfeboro Oil, Wood's Florist Shop, Wool Corner, and Western Auto.

### Local Attractions

For a time during the mid-1950s the Libby Museum was dark due to lack of operating funds. Meanwhile, the Clark House offered a constant stream of exhibits under the sponsorship of the Wolfeboro Historical Society. For example, in 1955, displays were changed each Wednesday and over a period of time included dolls, scrapbooks and family albums, samplers, old bottles, old costumes, and other specialties.

On May 28, 1956, by action of the Probate Court the Libby Museum was placed under the supervision of the selectmen. "The physical condition of the grounds and the building had seriously deteriorated. The lawns had grown up into hay..." Up to $5,000 was needed for restoration. Temporary repairs were made. On July 1 the doors were opened to the public once again.

Professor Robert F.W. Meader, formerly of Wolfeboro, who was then teaching at the Susquehanna University in Pennsylvania, was curator in the summer. Great strides were made under his management. In 1957 the museum's coin collection was catalogued, rearranged, and enhanced by new acquisitions including gifts from Robert Fonteyn and Harold Bodge. Among the exhibits were examples of nineteenth century currency issued by the Wolfborough (*sic*) Bank and the Lake Bank. By summer's end, 3,645 people had passed through the doors, an increase of 529 over the like 1956 period. Meader continued as curator through the end of the 1958 season.

In 1959 attendance jumped to 5,394 due to the museum staying open later in the season and having better signage. In 1960 William Carpenter was curator. Attendance was 4,668. An exhibit of the works of local artists drew wide attention.

The *Mount Washington* excursion boat continued to be a great local attraction in the summer. Charles "Pop" Davis of Wolfeboro was in charge of tying up the vessel when it arrived twice each day. Among the most popular questions asked by tourists were these: "When does the tide go out?" "Does this boat run all winter?" and "Is this salt water?" One man got off the boat and complained that someone had stolen his car. He thought he was at The Weirs![22]

### Famous Visitors

Over the years Wolfeboro has attracted its share of well-known personalities, many of whom rated mentions in the local paper. Samples from the 1950s:

In the 1950s and 1960s Paul R. Hatch, who operated the Memorial Theatre on the second floor of the Town Hall, greeted many screen stars who came to town. On this page are several snapshots from his collection. To the left is shown Franchot Tone shaking hands with Paul.

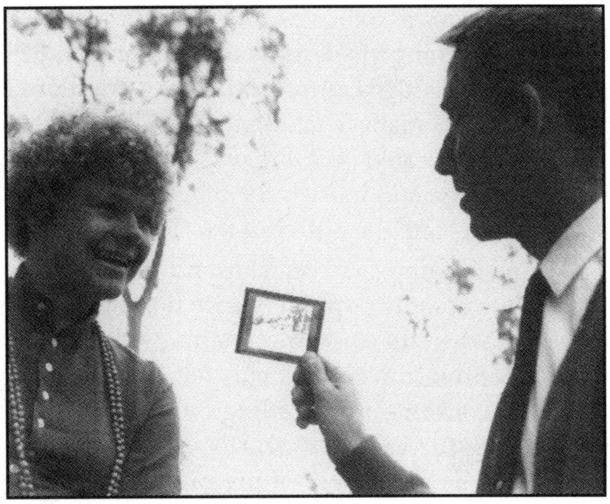

Estelle Parsons, star of television and screen, a frequent visitor to Wolfeboro as her family had lived here for many years, discusses a photograph with Paul Hatch.

Movie actor Kirk Douglas with his arm around the shoulder of young Paul Hatch in the 1950s. Over the years many prominent personalities from the stage and screen visited Wolfeboro.

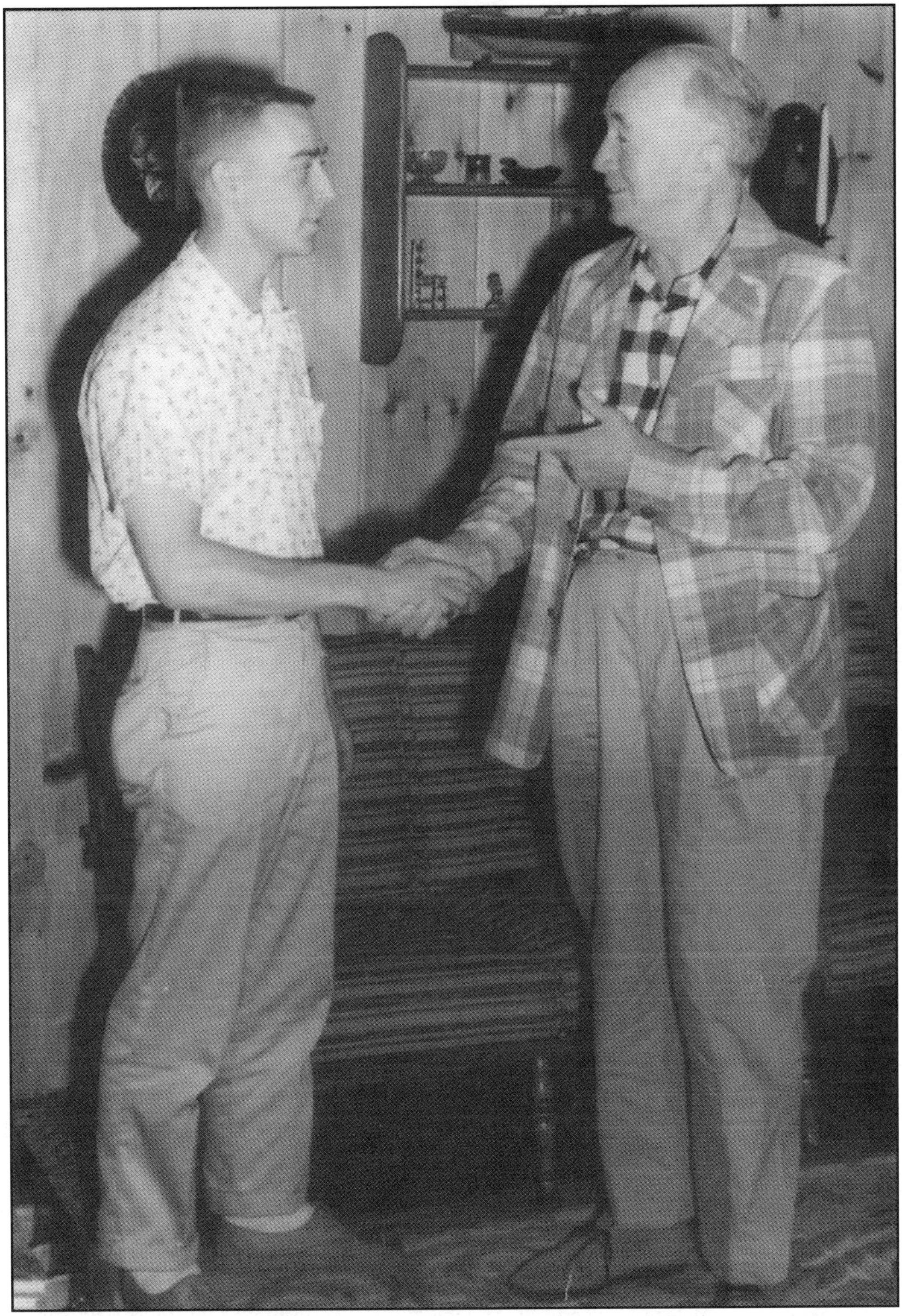

Wolfeboro motion picture theatre operator Paul Hatch (left) with three-time Academy Award winner Walter Brennan during one of the latter's visits to town, circa 1957. Brennan often stayed at Rust Pond Cabins operated by the Durkee family in South Wolfeboro. (Paul R. Hatch Collection)

Lakes Region Motor Co. advertisement, January 18, 1952, featured new Hudson automobiles, a popular make at the time. The dealership was located at the corner of Route 28 and North Line Road where Christy's convenience store is in the mid-1990s.

**Mme. Chiang Kai-Shek and Debra Paget:** In the 1950s the Hopewell summer estate on Wolfeboro Neck was sold to the Chinese legation. From the 1950s through the 1970s Col. Lin Chi Kung and his wife, American movie star Debra Paget, spent time there. Mme. Kai-Shek, wife of the leader of Nationalist China and father of Col. Kung, is believed to have visited once or twice.[23] Local stories and legends concerning the place abounded, but hard facts were scarce.

Dr. Lawrence S. Toms, former Wolfeboro selectman, commented in April 1995 after reading the preceding and other commentaries:[24] "I believe the Kung-Paget-Chiang Kai-Shek part of the Wolfeboro history is somewhat downplayed. I have had many talks over the years with 'Red' Berry who was the caretaker of the estate at various times. He told of soldiers guarding the roads with rifles, gate posts with soldiers, boats arriving at night, and in later years helicopters in the dark."

**Claude Rains:** 1951, August 17: "Mr. and Mrs. Claude Rains of Hollywood movie fame...were recent guests for a few days with Mrs. Pike at Island View Lodge, Lake Wentworth. They visited with their daughter Jennifer, summering at nearby Valley Camp. This is Jennifer's second season at least with the girls comprising this delightful dance-drama camp conducted by Miss Etta W. Johnson of Richmond, Virginia. I should have had a camera last summer when I spied Mr. Rains, hat in hand, coat on arm, in deep reverie as he emerged from the camp road..."[25]

**Marjorie Mills:** 1951, September 14: "Marjorie Mills of radio fame was a recent visitor in Wolfeboro."

**Estelle Parsons:** 1950s. Estelle Parsons, daughter of Mr. and Mrs. Eben Parsons of Wolfeboro, became a prominent television personality on Dave Garroway's NBC *Today* show when it was launched in 1952. Estelle had been in Wolfeboro almost every weekend during the summer of 1952, "finding it much more pleasant than New York City."[26] On June 18, 1954, the local paper noted that she and her husband, Richard Gehman (magazine writer and book author), hoped to spend part of their summer in town. She was here on many other occasions as well.

**Les Brown:** 1954, July 23: "Les Brown and members of his 'Band of Renown', players on the Bob Hope show, were personal guests of Mr. and Mrs. Norman Hill.... Mr. Hill was a member of the band at the time he became acquainted with Mrs. Hill." The Hills operated the Lakeview Inn on North Main Street.[27]

**Brian Donlevy:** 1955, September 2: "Doubtless there are many famous people in town during the course of the year.... Mrs. Ruth Moore waited on Brian Donlevy of movie and TV fame, at the Paper Store."[28]

**Walter Brennan:** 1957, May 24: "Many pleasant people come into the Wool Corner and the *Granite State News* office. Among those recently was Walter Brennan, the movie and TV star and three-time Academy Award winner. With him were Mrs. Brennan and the Durkees, whose guests they were last weekend. While Mr. Brennan ordered some slacks from the Hattons, he told us that in the fall he would have his own weekly TV show, *The Real McCoys*.... We had seen him the previous Sunday night on *What's My Line*, and he told us to look for him in the audience last Sunday night in a spot in Ed Sullivan's show, which we did. A warm personality and full of fun."[29]

**Franchot Tone:** 1958, August 8: "Actor Franchot Tone was here for the weekend visiting a son at Hill School Camp on Rust Pond. Pat was the third generation in his family to attend Hill School, and Franchot, his brother and his father were also students there... He plans to hunt deer in the Wolfeboro area in the fall."[30] While in town he enjoyed the Huggins Hospital Street Fair.

**Kirk Douglas:** 1959, August 28: "Among the New York and Hollywood personages recently seen on our streets was Kirk Douglas, Academy Award winner, and his son Joel, who came to visit the other one, Michael, at Wolfeboro Camp [formerly the Hill School Camp] on Rust Pond. Mr. Douglas recently finished the movie version of *Spartacus*, and is also remembered for his work in *The Champion* and *20,000 Leagues Under the Sea*."[31]

## TRANSPORTATION

### Speed and Power

On September 14, 1951, readers of the local paper were advised that two notable cars had been acquired by Wolfeboro citizens. Joseph I. Melanson, Jr., was seen driving around town in a new Mark VII Jaguar sedan, while in East Wolfeboro, Stanley Juthe, already the owner of a classic Mercer Raceabout, was busy rebuilding a 1923 Cadillac.

In the early 1950s the Lakes Region Motor Co., on Route 28 at the intersection with North Line Road, offered Hudsons made in America and Austin and MG autos imported from England. Horne's Garage on North Main Street sold Fords as it had for decades, while the Hart Motor Company offered the latest Chevrolets and Buicks. In 1956 Bud's Service Station, located where Lakes Region Motor Co. used to be, displayed new Pontiacs.

In the mid-1950s two trends developed:

Tail fins, which had first sprouted on the 1948 Cadillac, soon appeared on nearly every American brand.[32] So proud was Detroit of its new posteriors that many car advertisements c.1957 showed the vehicles from the rear!

The second emphasis was on horsepower. A 1955 advertisement for the Hart Motor Company boasted: "Nothing in its field can match the Chevrolet for acceleration!... When you need a quick sprint for safer passing, this V-8 delivers! Pure dynamite..." Results were given from a recent Daytona Beach race.

As time went on, accidents became more frequent and injuries more severe. Perhaps the most unfortunate single-car crash was that illustrated on the front page of the August 21, 1959, issue of the paper, showing the crumpled remains of the 300-h.p. Chrysler driven by William W. Cusumano, 16, who had carried a driver's license for only a month. Racing on twisting Route 109 in Tuftonboro near the Wolfeboro line, tires screaming, he failed to make a curve and crashed—the speedometer frozen at 90. The engine was ripped from the vehicle and thrown 36 feet. It took three hours to cut his corpse out of the tangled mass. Meanwhile, on Route 16 in Ossipee, Patricia A. Reed, 25, was driving a new Chevy Impala so fast that she could not hold to her lane,

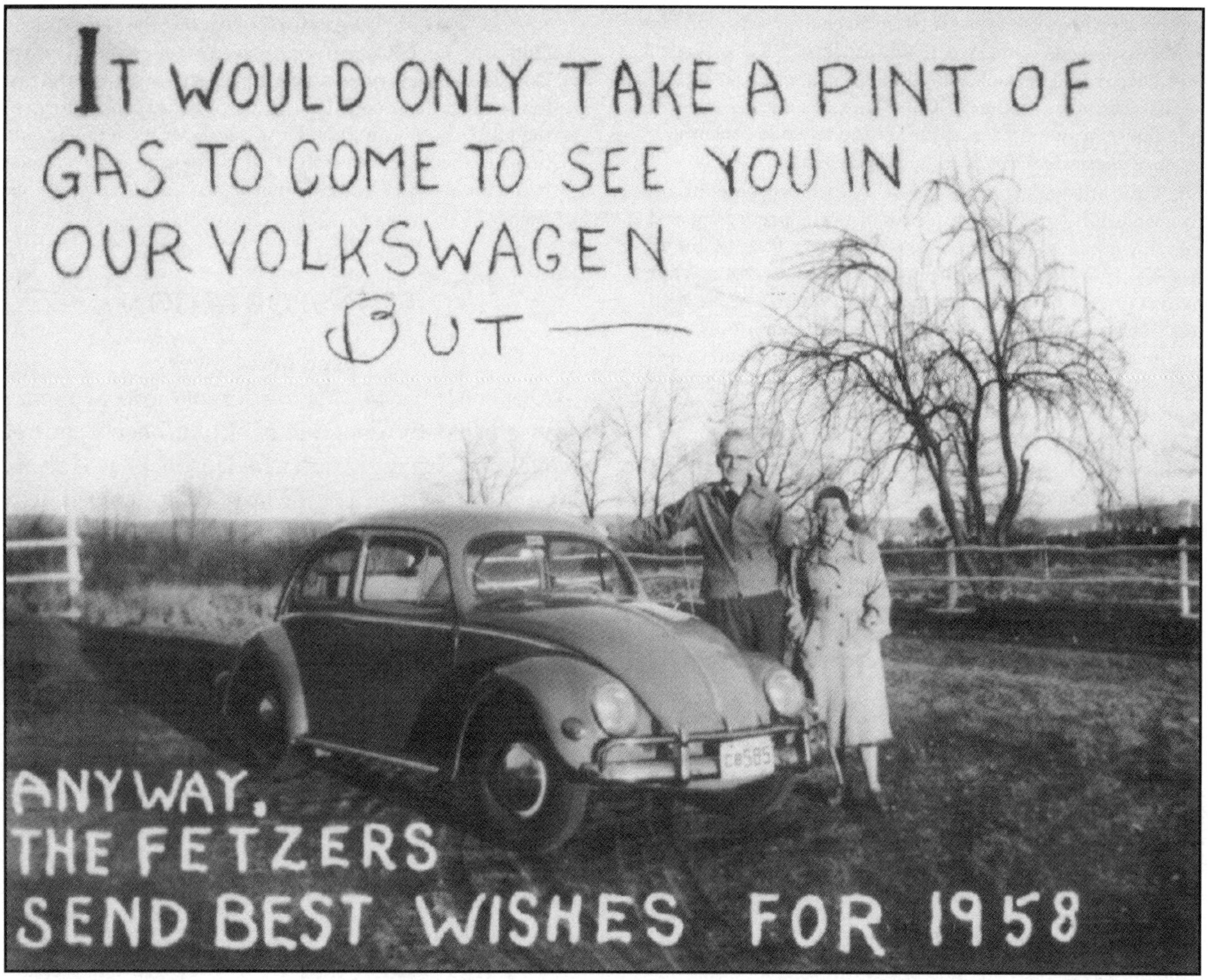

IT WOULD ONLY TAKE A PINT OF
GAS TO COME TO SEE YOU IN
OUR VOLKSWAGEN
BUT —
ANYWAY,
THE FETZERS
SEND BEST WISHES FOR 1958


**David and Helen Fetzer and their Volkswagen as photographed in 1957 for a 1958 greeting card. David was a prominent local photographer, and Helen was a writer for the *Granite State News*. In the 1950s the Volkswagen "Beetle" (as it was fondly called) was the first best-selling imported car, the first serious foreign threat to automobile makers in Detroit. There was no Volkswagen agency in Wolfeboro, however.**

**The downtown area circa early 1950s. In the left foreground is a Gulf service station beyond which is the original location of the Yum Yum Shop. The brick building at the extreme right was home to the First National Stores grocery (Dive Winnipesaukee is there today).**

crossed the divider, and was killed instantly in a crash involving three other cars. The local paper printed an editorial including these words:

> Advice to children:
>
> The years have taught me that too much speed in the wrong place kills. The 70 miles an hour that is a legal lullaby on the main pike is plain suicide on Route 109 and some sections of Route 16. The 50 miles an hour that is legal on most of Route 16 is an invitation to death on many town roads. You young folks have absolutely no right to risk foolishly your precious lives. You are just entering upon all that is worthwhile in life... Your family has invested untold money and love and care and prayer and worry in your safety and your future. And if you kill yourself you leave wounds of grief that no words of comfort or rationalization or sympathy can ever assuage. Just for the sake of hearing the squeal of the tires and the rush of the wind and the drumming of a wide-open motor for a quick 10 minutes, you can toss away all that has gone before and all that is to come. It is a poor deal—a lousy one.

Compact cars became very popular in 1959. The new Ford Falcon was on view at Horne's Garage, while at Hart's the new Chevy Corvair, billed as a six-passenger compact with engine in the rear, was said to be "astonishingly different" from anything ever built in this country.[33]

**Roads and Tracks**

Local roads continued to be improved. In the summer of 1952 a large section of Route 28 near a structure that in the 1990s is known as the Bittersweet was straightened, with this result:[34]

> It cannot be denied that the posterior view of the Goldthwaite Manor which is now shamelessly exposed through no fault of its own to the touring population is less enticing than the front of the house which remains on the old road.

On July 14, 1956, Leslie M. Chamberlain, Sr., retired after 33 years as supervisor of town roads and was succeeded by Linley L. Moore. On August 9, 1957, the Everett and Spaulding turnpikes were opened, bringing people into the Lakes Region faster than ever and helping to spur the tourist trade.[35]

During the 1950s Boston & Maine freight trains came in and out of Wolfeboro to service the factories, especially at Wolfeboro Falls, but, as had been the case since the 1930s, there was no regularly scheduled passenger service.[36] The Interstate Bus Service had long since taken up the slack with regular arrivals and departures from town. In April 1959 the Trailways Bus System took over the Interstate franchise and announced that it would be running clean, modern $3,000 buses seven days a week. The terminal was located at Charles L. French's Mobil Station at the intersection of Center and South Main Streets. The trip to Boston took less than three hours.[37] A one-way ticket cost $3.80, plus tax.

**Aviation**

The focal point of local aviation continued to be the Lakes Region Airport operated at the end of Wolfeboro Neck by Merwin and Eleanor Horn. It was not unusual for a dozen or more private craft to arrive there on a busy summer day. The Horns maintained a seaplane facility nearby in Winter Harbor. In 1951 Fred W. Long sought permission to open a seaplane base on Rust Pond, but little more was heard of the project. In 1957 the Aeromarina (as it was called) was set up in Wolfeboro Bay off North Main Street and serviced planes and boats.

On January 13, 1951, "everyone but the telephone operator was watching a flock of B-36s with jet escorts, dog-fighting over Lake Winnipesaukee Saturday morning and then flying off toward Portland so high that only the vapor trail could be seen..." It was revealed that six of these mammoth bombers had overflown the town on a direct air route from Fort Sherman, TX, to Europe.

In the summer of 1955 a twin-engine PBY "Catalina" flying boat was used by the Navy for seaplane practice, taking off and landing in Winter Harbor with eight crew members aboard.

Increasingly, Wolfeboro residents were flying to far-away places, usually from the airport at Boston. In 1955 Northeast Airlines proudly announced that it had just ordered 10 four-engine DC-6B planes for $1.4 million each. On various carriers tourists could fly from Boston or New York non-stop to Los Angeles, or fly to Europe (often with intermediate stops at Gander, Newfoundland and Shannon, Ireland). In 1957 Merwin Horn instituted the Air Taxi at his airport at the end of Wolfeboro Neck to connect with Boston flights.

**Not So Naive**

At the time, certain visitors to Wolfeboro were inclined to view the locals as yokels. However, as Parker M. Merrow pointed out:

> Residents of the area will not be dazzled by tourists telling of the wonders of Miami, New York, and other places, as most have been there and are quite familiar with such.... Just because you pay with a $20 bill, do not expect people to turn somersaults. $20 bills are no novelty up this way. Chances are that the native in logging clothes...has more folding money in his pocket than you have.

Indeed, Wolfeboro citizens had been well-traveled for quite some time, and the air age made them more so. As one of many examples, in September 1953 Mr. and Mrs. Norman Hale visited Southern California "where they witnessed the operation of an electronic digital computer."[38]

## WOLFEBORO IN PRINT

### Reporting the News

During the fifties the *Granite State News* continued under the ownership of Ralph G. Carpenter, 2nd, in partnership with Parker M. Merrow. The paper was printed in Ossipee.

The June 5, 1959, edition offered "A Tour In Type Of Today's Granite" and detailed every step needed to turn out the weekly journal. It was noted that the Wolfeboro editorial staff included one full-time and two part-time employees. Gloria Bullock had been managing editor for two years and worked on a daily basis, Monday through Friday. Her husband Ned worked part time as staff photographer with his Deluxe Polaroid Press Camera and wrote three columns on sports. From her home on Bay Street, Gertrude B. Hamm turned out a constant stream of news, personal items, and nostalgic articles, as she had since 1931.

As always, news items ranged from the urbane to the arcane with much in between. Sample social tidbits selected for their quaintness:

> **Life of the party:** 1954, July 23: Unsigned note under personal items: "My wife's frosty comments suggest that I was the life of the party last night at the Frank Bradfords. I didn't mean to be. It is just that Mr. Bradford is a quiet, scholarly type, and his bubbly, young wife obviously needed someone to dance and cut up with."
>
> **No cat:** 1954, February 5: "East Wolfeboro. The Ray Hoopers have enjoyed watching as many as five gray squirrels at a time in and around the oak trees by their house; also six pigeons and many other birds, as they hadn't any cats to scare them away."
>
> **What happened there?:** 1955, January 28: "Cotton Valley: Last Thursday it was Susan Thurrell's fourth birthday, and I have been trying to contact Pat to find about the party they had Saturday—but no luck, so I guess I'll have to skip the rest of the story. I'm sure Susan had a lively party, though."

The editorial office moved in May 1954 from the Folsom Block (in the 1990s, Black's) to Brocky's appliance store across the street. At the same time, Norman Turner, who had been local news coordinator and business manager for a long time, resigned to devote more attention to his real estate and insurance business. Moving into the chair was John C. Fuller, a summer resident recently discharged from the Army, who was called "copy control editor." The average number of copies distributed each week in 1954 was 1,653. A year's mail subscription cost $2.50.

In January 1955 the office moved to the newly-opened Wool Corner in the Central Block on Railroad Avenue where Manning's jewelry shop had been before it moved to South Main Street.

In August 1955 Fuller moved to Boston.[39] "Mr. and Mrs. John C. Prescott, who recently moved to Wolfeboro from Grafton, Mass., will take over the office of the *Granite State News*. Mrs. Prescott will handle the editorial and copy control, while Mr. Prescott will handle the business end of the office." Mr. Prescott had been a banker.

Occasionally a rival to the paper would spring up, as per this July 27, 1956 item:

> The *Granite State News* has a small competitor in town, *The Neighborhood Citizen*, with a very neat mimeograph job, and it tells the story of Pleasant Street and upper Sewall Road.

On December 19, 1956, columnist Mabel Fullerton Hatch, fondly known as "The Goose" of Goose Corner, passed away. She had been a local literary institution for over half a century.

On January 1, 1958, the Central Block offices of the *Granite State News* were burned out. The office of the paper was then set up in the home of Gloria and Ned Bullock at the corner of North Main and Oak Streets, where it remained until March 3, when it and the Wool Corner moved to the Hampshire Apartments (the former Carroll Piper house). In early 1960 the office was moved to the Lake & Village real estate building on the right-hand side of the Wolfeboro Shopping Center.

The September 13, 1960, issue of *Look* magazine had a special 60-page section devoted to New England, including six pages about life around Wolfeboro. Appearing on the cover was Betsy Fernald, who was scheduled to be a senior at Brewster Academy.[40]

### Tempest in a Beer Bottle

On May 20, 1955, a letter was published from Ella P. Swett, a former Wolfeboro resident now living in Santa Rosa, CA, stating she had faithfully read the *Granite State News* since 1888,

> and never saw a liquor ad before. I implore you to cease the advertisement for liquor... Our nation is trying to defend its children from disease but the taste for liquor is more harmful.

This stirred up a commotion, and the May 27 issue contained this notice from the local temperance group:

> To those who have asked what the Wolfeboro WCTU is doing about alcoholic beverage advertising in the *Granite State News*: In the temporary absence of our president, the undersigned officers hasten to assure you that we disapprove...

Completely forgotten was the fact that alcoholic beverages had been advertised in the *Granite State News* for many years including before Prohibition, ale and beer in the 1930s, and numerous other instances. In addition, much space was bought by patent medicines of the nineteenth and early twentieth centuries, which were laced with much more alcohol than the currently offered Heffenreffer beer (brewed in Boston). One must presume that whatever Mrs. Swett had been reading since 1888 did not include the advertisements!

Early American Living Museum complex on South Main Street, July 1960. A sign notes that the Clark House (on the right) is operated by the Wolfeboro Historical Society, and another notice states that it is open 2:00 to 4:30 p.m. daily except Sunday and Monday. On the left, set back from the road, is the Pleasant Valley Schoolhouse moved to South Main Street and dedicated on its new site in 1959.

Gladys Tuttle and Wilma Paine at the Public Library in the Wolfeboro Town Hall, circa 1950s. (Polaroid snapshot taken in the era when this type of instant camera was beginning to achieve wide popularity)

## ENTERTAINMENT

### Television

Early in the decade, the installation of a TV set was sufficiently newsworthy to catch a line or two in the local paper. On February 9, 1951, readers were told that "Will Rollins of Wolfeboro Falls is one of the latest to install television in his home." On January 18, 1952, they were informed that Mr. and Mrs. Norman Turner had succumbed to the temptation.

There were no nearby stations. "If you want to try your luck with television, there is only one way to find out how it will work in your home—put in a set on trial. It may be good and it may be horrible." Answering this problem, Richard Connor, Haskins Appliances, and other sellers offered sets on approval.[41]

On March 28, 1954, WMUR-TV, New Hampshire's first television station, went on the air. Meanwhile, local viewers had been enjoying fairly good reception of WCSH-TV in Portland via large rooftop antennas. In the summer of 1954 station WGAN-TV, also of Portland, increased its power. Beginning on September 25, 1954, a new station, WMTW, broadcast from the top of Mt. Washington. After opening ceremonies, the first program was a baseball game between the Cleveland Indians and the Detroit Tigers with Dizzy Dean doing the dialogue.

In October 1954 the weekly WMTV program schedule included the following evening features: *I Lived Three Lives, Ozzie and Harriet, Schlitz Playhouse, Sammie Kay, Jackie Gleason Show, Life With Father, You Asked for It, The Original Topper, Gene Autry, John Daly and the News, Cavalcade of America, Voice of Firestone, I Love Lucy, My Little Margie, Charlie Chan, Stu Erwin Show, Lone Ranger,* and *Victory at Sea,* among many others. The program for much of the rest of the day simply read "Test Pattern."[42]

### At the Movies

Throughout the 1951-1960 period, motion picture films continued to be shown at the Memorial Theatre on the second floor of the Town Hall. Sample billings:

1951, December 15-16: *Across the Wide Missouri.* Clark Gable.

1953, March 28-29: *The Road to Bali.* Bob Hope, Bing Crosby, and Dorothy Lamour.

1953, July 12-13: *Gentlemen Prefer Blondes.* Jane Russell and Marilyn Monroe.

1954, January 2-3: Walt Disney's *Peter Pan.*

1954, February 6-7: *Shane.* Alan Ladd, Jean Arthur, Van Heflin, and Jack Palance.

1954, May 22-23: *Hondo.* John Wayne.

1954, May 26: *Abbott & Costello Meet Dr. Jekyll and Mr. Hyde.*

1955, July 1: *20,000 Leagues Under the Sea.* Kirk Douglas, James Mason, Paul Lucas, and Peter Lorre.

1955, August 21-22: *Davy Crockett.* Fess Parker and Buddy Ebsen.

1955, August 23-24: *Marty.* Ernest Borgnine and Betsy Blair.

1956, October 10: *Annie Get Your Gun.* Betty Hutton.

1957, March 16: *High Society.* Bing Crosby, Grace Kelly, Frank Sinatra, and Celeste Holm.

1957, June 22: *I Was a Teenage Werewolf* and *Invasion of the Saucer Men.*

1958, March 8: *Jailhouse Rock.* Elvis Presley.

1958, March 22: *April Love.* Pat Boone and Shirley Jones.

1958, July 4-5: *Old Yeller.* Dorothy McGuire and Fess Parker.

1959, November 8: *How to Marry a Millionaire.* Marilyn Monroe.

1960, March 26-27: *Jack the Ripper.* "This show restricted to adults only (high school age and over); children admitted only when accompanied by a parent."

1960, July 15: *The Mouse That Roared.* Peter Sellers and Jean Seberg.

1960, December 30: *Psycho.* Directed by Alfred Hitchcock.

In the meantime, there were several changes at the theatre. Ansel N. Sanborn, who had managed the business for several decades, died on December 26, 1953, and ownership passed to his heirs. In keeping with new methods of film photography and projection, in December 1954 a wide screen was installed, measuring 20 feet from left to right and 10 from top to bottom.[43]

On January 1, 1959, Paul R. Hatch, who had worked at the theatre since his boyhood days, took title to the operation, which became known as Hatch Theatres and included Pineland in Ossipee. The first film shown in town under the Hatch ownership was *A Nice Little Bank That Should Be Robbed,* with Tom Ewell and Dianna Merrill.

### Melody Island: "Pride and Joy of Wolfeboro"

In the summer of 1947 Hedy Spielter and her husband, Jules Epailly, opened the Institute of Modern Piano Technique, a branch of their New York City school. Selected as the site was Mud Island facing Wolfeboro Bay. Its hardly euphonious name was changed to Melody Island, a designation it retains to the present time. Eventually, nearly 20 cabins plus a main lodge were erected there, together with a wooden band shell seating 300.[44]

For the first five years, activities were not publicized. However, music would waft on the breeze across the lake each summer, and those with a romantic turn of mind would draw their boats close to the shore of Melody Island to listen to the students who always enjoyed an audience. Beginning about 1952, Ella Lord Gilbert, director of the Amy Cheney Beach Club, a local group devoted to music appreciation, took a strong interest in Mme. Spielter and her protégés. On July 20, 1952, members of the club went across Wolfeboro Bay for a special concert.

In the summer of 1953, Melody Island played host to the New Symphony Orchestra of New York conducted by Maurice Bonney. Several concerts were presented under the auspices of the Amy Cheney Beach Club. The

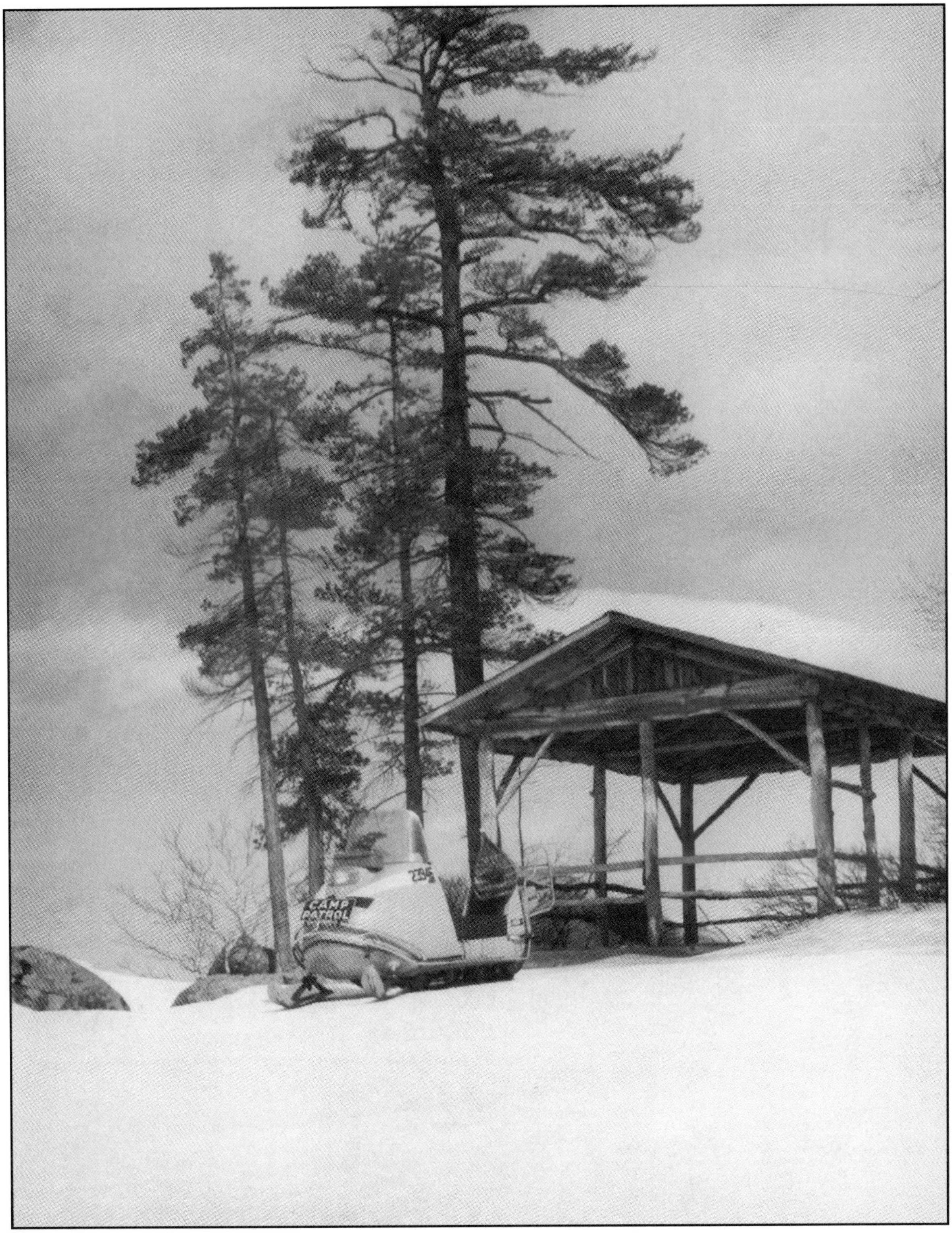


Snowmobile operated by Ned Bullock of the Camp Patrol as seen on a wintry day near Lake Wentworth. Bullock also achieved recognition over the years as a master photographer. (Gloria and Ned Bullock Collection)

Independence Day parade in the early 1950s with the V.F.W. Auxiliary float in the foreground. In the Folsom Block (a.k.a. Porter Block; Black's Paper Store is there today) were these businesses, left to right, The Toggery Shop, Carpenter & Turner real estate agency, and O.F. Porter hardware.

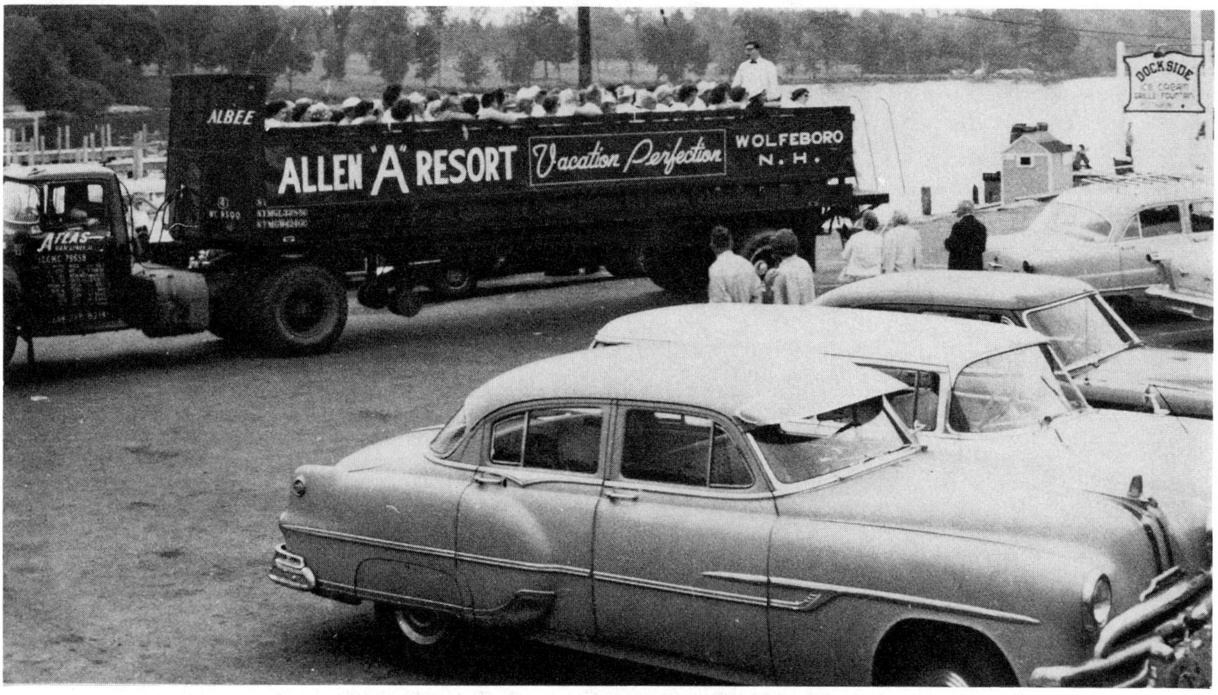


A trailer full of Allen "A" Resort guests waits at the Town Docks for the motor vessel *Mount Washington* in this photograph taken from the loading platform of Harold E. Brown's shoe and clothing store. (Photograph by Charles E. Brown, late 1950s)

first, on Monday evening, July 20, included a picnic supper. Capt. Nat Goodhue and his yacht, *Swallow,* ferried patrons from the Town Docks to the island. Every seat in the band shell was occupied. Unfortunately, a downpour began as the concert commenced. The musicians played Beethoven's *Eighth Symphony,* after which the balance of the program was canceled. Rain checks were exercised the following Friday, and Schubert's *Fifth Symphony* and other works were presented.[45]

The success of the summer concerts prompted the formation of the New Hampshire Music Festival. On September 20, 1953, an organizational meeting was held for patrons who responded to this invitation:

> All who are interested are invited to go to the island Sunday afternoon and learn all the details of the effort. All will have an opportunity to inspect the island, where a number of new buildings will be erected before the beginning of next season—and where they will be permitted to enjoy a piano program by some of Miss Spielter's gifted pupils.

In the summer of 1954 the New Hampshire Musical Festival, Inc., held three concerts on Melody Island and one at the Town Hall. In August, Rudolph Elie, a reviewer from the *Boston Herald,* commented:[46]

> This New Hampshire resort on the north shore of Winnipesaukee, has a treasurable legacy in the recent residence on nearby Melody Island of a musical organization calling itself the New Symphony Orchestra of New York...an exceedingly competent ensemble...competent enough to handle the most advanced repertoire.

Although the 40-piece orchestra attracted garnered favorable reviews, it was felt that future concerts should be held on the mainland in order to attract a larger audience.[47] A new schedule was implemented in 1955, and although Melody Island thronged with musicians in residence, concerts were staged in Wolfeboro and Gilford. It was estimated that 2,000 people had enjoyed them by the third week of July.[48]

During the summer of 1955 noted conductor Leopold Stokowski and his family spent 10 days on Melody Island. Upon leaving, he handed this letter to Hedy Spielter:[49]

> We, all four of us, cannot thank you enough for thousands of kindnesses from you, and Mr. Epailly, and everyone on the Island. I have been deeply impressed by your two piano students that I heard recently. I feel that they are talent of the highest order, and that you have recognized that talent and developed it in a wonderful way.
>
> I am equally impressed by what you and Maestro Bonney are doing on this island for symphonic music of all periods and styles. Maestro has known how to select young talented players of remarkable musical quality and rapidly to fuse them into an ensemble capable of every kind of music. I feel you are both doing a wonderful thing for American music, with the concerts of the New Hampshire Music Festival, Inc. I would like to make a small contribution to the Melody Island School of Music if you will permit.
>
> With deep-felt thanks from the two boys and Trudi and myself, and with the best wishes from us all,
>
> Leopold Stokowski.

On June 22, 1956, this appeared in the *Granite State News:*

> Within the next two weeks, people living in and around Wolfeboro points blessed with unusual natural acoustics will be hearing faint notes of flutes, oboes, trumpets, violins and cellos. Folks skimming gaily over Lake Winnipesaukee in their boats will hear not only the delightful sounds, but also, if you circle around, the dramatic chords and arpeggios of piano concerti and instrumental chorus of a complete orchestra earnestly rehearsing. The source of this enchantment as nearly everyone in this region knows, is Melody Island, rapidly becoming one of the Lakes Region's most treasured assets and the particular pride and joy of Wolfeboro....

In 1956 there were 42 musicians on the island drawn from 20 symphony orchestras around America. One of them was Yvonne Bizet, concertmistress, a great granddaughter of French composer Georges Bizet. Chamber music concerts were presented on the island every Sunday evening, admission free. Nine adult and two children's concerts were held on the mainland.[50]

While Melody Island was a success musically, the school operated at a loss. By 1959 the island was vacant, and the headquarters of the New Hampshire Festival had been relocated to the four-story Garnet Inn in Centre Harbor.

### Have You Read It?

In the February 8, 1957, issue of the local paper, Editor Parker M. Merrow reviewed a new book written by Grace Metalious and set in Gilmanton Iron Works. Excerpts:

> We have skimmed through *Peyton Place,* the book that has busted into the best seller list and is supposed to be life in a small New Hampshire town. It seems to be loaded with sex and alcohol and is basically a poor job of writing. We feel that the reason the book has gone into the best seller list is that it is a straight dose of sensationalism, and people buy it to get a quick, cheap thrill.
>
> Our principal quarrel with the book is its basic lopsidedness. True it is that sex (legitimate and illegitimate) and alcohol (legitimate and illegitimate) have been important factors in the life of our New Hampshire townspeople ever since the last Indian was run up over the hill. But there are equally strong factors in the life of all New England towns. What the author has missed completely are the other factors of small town life...

### Other Entertainment

Wolfeboro offered many forms of entertainment. In fact, often there were too many things going on, as per this commentary:[51]

> It is nothing new for hearts to break and tears to flow over conflicting dates in Wolfeboro, where there are more than 30 organizations and never more than 31 days in the month.

A sampling of events of the decade:

**1951, August 4. Water Carnival:** Wolfeboro Bay. Waterskiing, boat racing, and other events.

**1951, August 16. Allen "A" Resort open house:** About 1,200 cars full of people came to enjoy aerial acrobats, a German

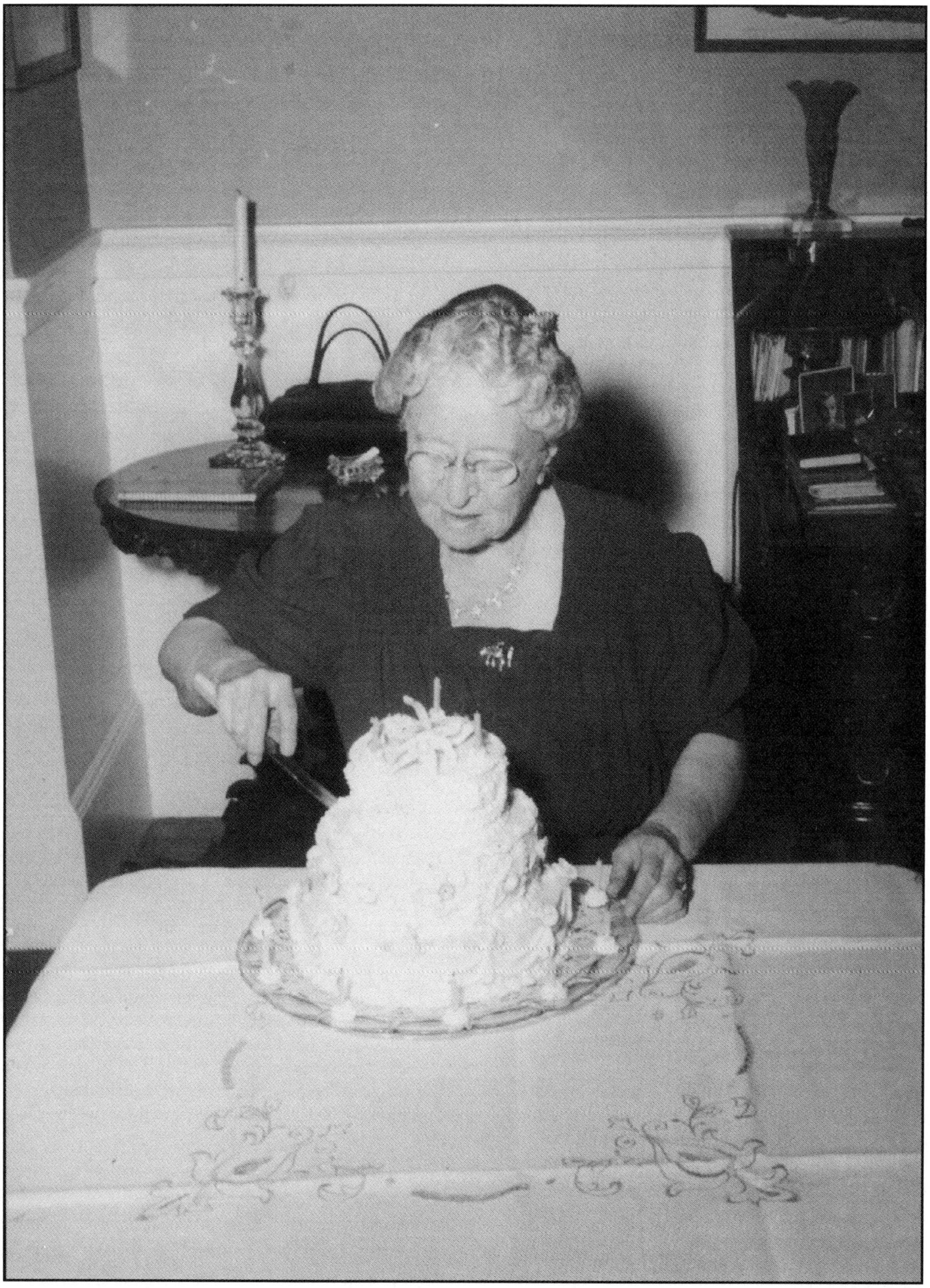

Ella Lord Gilbert celebrates her 80th birthday, November 17, 1958. Mrs. Gilbert founded the Amy Cheney Beach Club, today known as the Friends of Music. This group brought many noted performers to town over a long period of years. Mrs. Gilbert gave music lessons at her Pleasant Street home known as Harmony Cottage. (David Fetzer photograph)

musical troupe, and a concert on the calliope.[52]

**1951, November 12. Armistice Ball.** American Legion.

**1951, December 17. Opera:** *Pagliacci,* by Leoncavallo, at the Carpenter School auditorium under the auspices of the Amy Cheney Beach Club. About 250 attended.

**1951-1952. Canasta:** This card game was all the rage at parties.

**1952, February 7-8. Wolfeboro Follies of 1952:** Music, comedy, and other acts by local talent. Nearly 1,000 people enjoyed a cast of over 40 people young and old.

**1952, January 31. Disney animator:** Ken Walker appeared at Carpenter School and Brewster Academy and demonstrated animation. He had developed characters in almost all Disney's top features including *Fantasia* and the newest film, *Peter Pan.*

**1952, March 21. Stage play:** *Blithe Spirit,* Noel Coward's famous comedy, was presented at the Masonic Temple under the direction of Nathalie Erickson.[53]

**1952, July 4. Parade:** Floats included those of the Lakeshore Grange, Malone Knitting Company, Allen "A," Richard Bowe (caged pheasants), and more.[54]

**1952, August 3. College race centennial:** "The Harvard and Yale crews marched down through the middle of Wolfeboro stopping all the traffic to get their shells around the corner and into the water by the Town Docks. They were celebrating the centennial of their first boat race which was on Lake Winnipesaukee. Following the race both crews enjoyed a chicken barbecue at Camp Kehonka. Campers and crew members had a great time together."[55]

**1952, August 4-7. Antiques show:** At Carpenter School.

**1952, September 23. Drama Workshop organized:** John Ballentine presided. By mid-October over 50 had joined[56]

**1952, October 11-13. Arts and crafts exhibit:** Aboard the *Mount Washington* docked at Wolfeboro. Over 1,000 attended.

**1952, November 5. Stage play:** *Goodbye, My Fancy* at the Temple Auditorium, the first performance of the Drama Workshop. Admission 85¢. Cast included Patricia Quinlan, William Farrington, Connie Hale, Harriet Hawes, Jane Baker, Louise Dodge, Rebecca Dodge, Thelma Chamberlain, Ellen Bowe, Virginia Edwards, Patricia Stenberg, Dawn Brookes, Tony Robbins, Jim Kalled, Norma Bowe, Arthur Glidden, Jr., Joanne Marden, and Jack Piper. Margaret Emerson was director.[57]

**1953, April 3: Popular tunes:** Available at Gould's Dime Store were these 45 r.p.m. phonograph records, 49¢ each: *Doggie in the Window, Side by Side, Anywhere I Wander, Gal Who Invented Kissin, Till I Waltz Again With You, Why Don't You Believe Me, Don't Let the Stars Get In Your Eyes, Glow Worm, You Belong to Me, Jambalaya, It Wasn't God Who Made Honkytonk Angels, Your Cheating Heart,* and *Tell Me A Story.*

**1953, July 31: Beers-Barnes Trained Wild Animal Circus:** Brewster campus. Forty animals plus tightrope acts and other attractions.

**1953, September 1. Barbecue:** Rotary Club. More than 600 people came to the Brewster campus to enjoy entertainment including music on the xylophone, accordion, and cathedral chimes.

**1953, November 6. Memory wizard:** William Wallace appeared at Brewster Academy. He had memorized the entire 1953 Sears, Roebuck catalogue and could state on what page any item was listed. Audience was invited to bring Sears catalogues.[58] (In 1954 did he have to start his memorizing all over again?)

**1953, November 14. Sadie Hawkins Dance:** Brewster Academy. Local boys were being snapped up quickly, an account in the *Granite State News,* November 13, 1953, noted.

**1954, June 26. United Nations Town Meeting of the World:** Sponsored by the Lakes Region Association. Statewide event at Brewster Academy; estimated 1,000 attended. Emphasized were Greece, Indonesia, and Panama—each of which sent representatives. NH senators Styles Bridges and Richard William Upton and congressmen Norris Cotton and Chester Merrow were on hand.[59]

**1954, July 15. Teenage dance:** Kingswood Club. 75¢.

**1954, July 17. Recording celebrity:** Muriel White, "the blonde bombshell singing star of Sheraton Records," made a big hit in concert at the Wolfeboro Casino.[60]

**1954. Scrabble:** Especially popular board game.

**1954, April 9. Carpenter School 8th grade play:** *Rest Assured.*

**1954, October 2. Brewster Academy Homecoming Day:** Parade, soccer and football games (both vs. Holderness), supper at the First Congregational Church, dance.

**1954, October 30. Hallowe'en party:** American Legion Hall; 127 children came.[61]

**1955, February 12. Lincoln Day dinner:** Congregational Church. Address by Sen. Norris Cotton.[62]

**1955, March 24-25. Minstrel and variety show:** Masonic Temple. Harry Beane at the Hammond organ, the Carpenter School band, songs by Harry May, Scotty Tinker, John Pollini and others, skits and jokes, etc. Sponsored by the Sportsmen's Club of Wolfeboro.[63]

**1956, May 9. Stage play:** *Petticoat Fever.* Temple Auditorium. Cast included Russell Claflin, Frank C. Berry, Connie Hale, Nathalie Erickson, John W. McDermott, Jr., Helen Fetzer, and Louise Dodge.

**1956, July 16. Pipe organ concert:** Congregational Church, sponsored by the Amy Cheney Beach Club. David C. Johnson, organist (from MIT), Mary Fraley Johnson, cellist.[64]

**1956, July 24. Governor's Day:** Allen "A" Resort: "Probably the largest, most dramatic and best run spectacle in the history of entertainment and mass meetings in Carroll County." From 5,000 to 8,000 people attended, and an estimated 2,000 people were turned away. Stage performers, speech by Gov. Lane Dwinell, fireworks display.[65] Entrepreneur and impresario Allen H. Albee was in his glory.

**1957, February 10: Sports car gymkhana on ice:** Obstacle course on Lake Wentworth near Clow Beach. Sponsored by the NH Sports Car Club and the Portsmouth Air Force Sports Car Club.[66]

**1957, May 10. Ned Bullock on the air:** The *Granite State News* announced that every afternoon from 2:00 to 2:30 a program about Wolfeboro would be broadcast over radio station WWNH in Rochester. Its creator was Charles Edwin ("Ned") Bullock, Jr.[67]

**1957, August 9. New technology:** The editor of the *Granite State News* discussed FM broadcasting and stereo sound, both relatively new to the Wolfeboro area.

**1957, October 31. Hallowe'en parade:** Children in 1st through 4th grades of Carpenter School dressed in costumes and walked up and down Main Street.[68]

**1957, December 31. New Year's Eve dance:** American Legion Hall.

**1958, February 14. Teen Hop:** Odd Fellows Lodge. 35 attended. Dancing to a phonograph, ping-pong, darts, and cards. Smoking was permitted downstairs only.[69]

**1958, February 21. Firemen's Ball:** Firemen's Relief Association. Held at the Wolfeboro Casino. 75¢.

**1958, July 19: All Saints' Mission Fair:** Children's attractions, cooked food, luncheon, handicraft items, etc. Annual event.

Grace Marion Reynolds Paris (left) and Wilma M. Paine in Cobham Hall on Green Street, July 1960. Miss Paine was town librarian from 1943 to 1966. The violin she is holding was made by her father, Smith H. Paine of Pleasant Valley, who completed work on it in early 1932. (David Fetzer photograph)

**1958, August 23. Community Day:** Wentworth State Park. Swimming races, costume parade for children, rowboat races, beauty contest, etc.

**1959, April 16-17. Stage play:** *Just Ducky,* a three-act comedy by Brewster seniors. Cast included Wenda Thompson, Joyce Goodwin, Jane Clow, Henry Tutt, Kilburn Culley, and Arthur Manzer.

**1959, August 7-8. Huggins Hospital Street Fair:** Fun, games, booths, prizes, contests. Treasurer Charlotte McDermott reported a profit of about $12,000. A pet show was run by Dr. Lawrence Toms.[70] First prize for the most unusual pet was given to Ellen Cutler for two long-haired guinea pigs. Second prizes went to Marion Hamm for two kids (goats) and to William Bowe for his goat Wimpy. Third prize went to Stephen Jones for his snail named George Washington Jones.

**1960, July 20. Tom Sawyer party:** Held at Clark Park by the Wolfeboro Historical Society. People were invited to come in old clothes and bring paintbrushes to paint fence pickets for one hour. Those allergic to paint were invited to serve donuts and coffee.[71]

## RECREATION AND SPORTS

### Boating

Boats on lakes Wentworth and Winnipesaukee increased in number, horsepower, and speed. On a typical day the afternoon air hummed with inboard and outboard (mostly) noise. Most everything went well, but there were occasional accidents, including these notable mishaps:

On Monday evening, July 20, 1951, a Chris Craft run by Carleton Klinck collided in Wolfeboro Bay with a speedboat, *The Wild Duck,* owned by the Crowley family. Both craft sank. Judge George Sweeney, a shore resident, rescued the 10 people aboard.[72] Around midnight, August 18, of the same year, Warren Treanor, age 17, lost control of a 24-ft. Chris Craft. Traveling at high speed in a stiff wind and across waves, it jumped a sea wall and landed 46 feet from the water's edge on the lawn of the Frederick H. Fuller cottage on Sewall Road.[73]

In September 1957 the editor of the *Granite State News* called for development of private or state-owned marinas around Lake Winnipesaukee to alleviate the congestion caused by trailers backing into the water. This evoked a letter from island resident Arthur C. Hardy, who stated that although he paid taxes, he received no police protection. He observed that those who owned cottages on or near the lake were law-abiding and respected the property rights of others, but that day-trippers—such as those with boat trailers—who simply used the lake caused most of the problems.[74]

On July 4, 1954, the Aqua Lung scuba (also spelled all capitals as SCUBA) device was demonstrated at the Town Docks. In time, scuba diving would become a popular sport on the lake.[75]

Ice boating continued to attract local aficionados. On one January day in 1955, six craft were seen skimming over Wolfeboro Bay. Furber Jewett, Frank Redding, Fred Miller, and Eric Erickson were among those aboard. The local paper printed several pictures and noted that "contrary to some opinions, ice boating is not a dangerous sport. It is proven to be safe, fast and thrilling." This provoked a letter from Tracy L. Abbott, who said that an ice boat had recently collided with his bob house, "breaking both runners and doing considerable other damage." He wished that someone had taken a picture of the accident so that it, too, could be published.[76]

### Water Skiing

The Wolfeboro Water Ski Club was formed on July 10, 1959, at a meeting at the Grange Hall initiated by George Greer of the Northeast Marina Ski School. Soon thereafter the 23-member group sought Public Utilities Commission permission to anchor a ski jump in Wolfeboro Bay.[77]

On August 21, 1960, a water-skiing exhibition was held in South Wolfeboro Bay. The Achievement Trophy was won by Peter Brewitt. One event of the afternoon was:

> A demonstration of trick skiing: Dave Senecal circled the bay with Jeanette Smith upon his shoulders, followed by Staff King and Donna Hackman doing the same feat. Next was a pyramid built by Dave Senecal, Staff King, and Peter Brewitt. The climax of the afternoon was Peter Brewitt riding a saucer...[78]

### Hunting and Fishing

Deer hunting attracted many devotees each autumn. Moose, rarely seen in Wolfeboro earlier, were spotted on several occasions in 1952, but could not be taken. A pair of adult bobcats and two kittens were said to be on the loose in Wolfeboro Neck and were a danger to deer. A bounty of $20 per animal was currently being paid, although, in actuality, dogs did much more damage to deer than did large cats.

The trapping of beavers was more a commercial activity than a sport. In early 1953 Frank Sinclair of Bay Street harvested 32. Other animals that could be hunted or trapped included the ruffed grouse, male pheasant, woodcock, rabbit or hare, and raccoon.[79]

In 1951 the fishing season began with uncertainty, as there were so many smelt in the lake that the larger fish were well fed and might not be enticed by anglers' bait. In fact, the channel at the Main Street bridge was black with them. In August of the same year a 5-pound, 12-ounce bass, one of the largest of the era, was caught in Wolfeboro Bay by Howard Pett. Local attorney Elliot U. Wyman captured first prize in the 1952 Fishing Derby with a 7-pound, 3-ounce salmon.

Ice fishing was popular, especially at the Fisherville community of bob houses set up in Wolfeboro Bay. In February 1952 Rudolph Elie of the *Boston Herald* spent a

Miss Virginia Jackson (in far corner), music and band teacher at Carpenter School, with some of her pupils at a performance held in July 1960 in Cobham Hall, the home of Ralph J. Carpenter 2nd on Green Street.

John Vanderpool, age 93, photographed October 5, 1951, just after being presented with the Boston Post Cane by the Wolfeboro selectmen for being the oldest male resident voter (women were not included in nominations for the honor). Vanderpool was born in 1858 and died at the age of 98 in 1957. Shown left to right are four old-timers: Samuel Buxton, honoree Vanderpool, Luther Elliott, and Isaac L. Allbee.

Allen "A" Tigers Little League baseball team in the late 1950s. For many years baseball has been Wolfeboro's most popular summer team sport.

weekend indulging in the sport and upon his return wrote about the fun he had. As a direct result local accommodations were crowded with visiting Bostonians for the next several weekends.[80]

### Outdoor Team Sports

Each summer saw several baseball teams take to the local fields. Beginning in 1953 the American Legion sponsored the Junior League set up by Fred Long. It had been many years since there had been organized youth baseball in town.

The 1954 Junior League included these players: Art Dalphond, Bruce Hatton, Gerry Cate, Dick Lampron, Dave Pollini, Billy Lord, Sam Pollini, Tim Long, John Pollini, Bill Pollini, Rod Haines, Norman Black, Nathan Stevens, Ralph Stevens, John Hamlin, and Ron Ridlon.

The Lions Club (which had been chartered locally in 1954) sponsored a team of older players. This account was carried in the *Granite State News*, September 28, 1956:

> Last Sunday the Wolfeboro Lions defeated Ashland in the final playoff game 16 to 1 to win the Central N.H. League championship for 1956.
>
> The Lions scored 1 run in the first inning and for the following four it was a close pitchers' duel. Wolfeboro, however, started a rally that sewed the game up by scoring 15 runs in the sixth. Fifteen runs for a single inning established a new league record...
>
> The Lions' top sluggers for this season in order are Dick Robbins, Jimmy Sanborn, Paul Whalen and Brad Hunter. Due credit should be given to coach Roger "Pinky" Grant and especially to Kenny Wilkinson who produced fine pitching throughout the season, also to Paul Whalen who took over the catching job after the regular catcher became injured. Wolfeboro has not had a team for five years and thanks to the new team sponsor, the Wolfeboro Lions Club, baseball in this town has made an outstanding recovery and record in winning the league championship.... This is only the second time Wolfeboro has ever won the title.

In 1958 there were six sponsored Little League baseball teams: Bankers (Wolfeboro National Bank), Wildcats (Fred Varney Co.), Bears (Wolfeboro Hardware), Tigers (Allen "A" Resort), Cubs (American Legion), and Lions (Market Basket). Each sponsor bought a set of uniforms. In the summer of 1959 George Black (Paper Store owner) outfitted the Black Panthers, and the American Legion set up another team called Post 18.[81]

In 1953 the Brewster Academy soccer team became NH state prep school champions, finishing the best season since the sport was introduced six years earlier. On December 1, 1953, the Rotary Club hosted coach Burtis F. Vaughan, Jr., and 22 members of the Varsity and Junior Varsity teams. In 1954 history repeated itself, and the state championship was brought home to Wolfeboro. Rivals included Holderness, Pittsfield High, New Hampton, Tilton, and Phillips Andover.

In August 1960 a town soccer team was organized under coach Jack Ellis. Members included Jay Durkee, goalie; Jack Pollini, fullback; Jim Clough, fullback; Charles and Sam Niblett, and Rick Hale, halfbacks; Wilbur Ford and Buzzy Dore, wings; Dave Garner and Bob Penney, insides; and Bob Pollini, center. Miles Niblett was the team's substitute.[82]

Golf was popular during warm months at the Kingswood Club. On September 5-6, 1959, the organization held Frank Butler Days in observance of Butler's 45th year as the golf pro there. He was said to have started in 1914, but in actuality, Butler did not begin his Wolfeboro activities until 1915.[83]

### Indoor Team Sports

Basketball was popular in the schools during the decade. On October 5, 1958, local citizens were treated to an exhibition professional game at the Brewster Gymnasium by the Boston Celtics under the auspices of the Lions Club. The entire team of 15 men and their dynamic coach, Red Auerbach, were on hand, including Bob Cousy, who was billed as "the world's greatest basketball player."

In 1959 under Coach Bob Becker, the Carpenter School boys' basketball team had an undefeated 13-game season. The first team consisted of Wilbur Ford, Jay Durkee, Fred Antonucci, R. ("Buzzy") Dore, and David Garner. The remaining six boys were H. ("Mike") Morgan, Dennis Dodier, Mike Niblett, Bob Penny, Jerry York, and Everett Edmunds. High points of the season included Fred Antonucci's 29 points against Sacred Heart and Wilbur Ford's 20 points against Gilford.

Bowling at the Wolfeboro Casino attracted many men and women fans, who formed such teams as the Castoffs, Casino Cubs, Hot Pops. Malco Guys, Zeros, Village Squaws, Merry Bowlers, Penny Pinchers, Polecats, Market Basket, and Mixers. The sport ended locally in January 1959 when the Casino was closed due to plumbing problems. The structure was demolished in March. Subsequently, a facility opened in Melvin Village.[84]

### Winter Sports

During the 1950s the Abenaki Ski Slope on Poor Farm Hill operated intermittently. In December 1956 the facility, which had been closed by apathy and vandalism for two winters, was reopened with a 1,200-foot rope tow. However, most serious local followers of the sport went north to commercial slopes, which offered more trails and *après ski* amenities.

In January 1959 Ned Bullock, who wrote a column on skiing for the local paper, traced the history of the Abenaki Outing Club, concluding with this:

> You have read the shortest history of the Abenaki Outing Club you will ever read. Today there are no ice boats, no town hockey team, no mud buggy races, no ski jumps, and but a few hardworking men under Rupert Brown, We have almost let skiing come to an end in Wolfeboro.

Bullock went on to note that "skiing, like the cowboy and gold prospector, have been taken over by organizations who run areas as a business not as a sport." He noted that the Mount Whittier Ski Area was under construction and would be a large commercial enterprise. However, he expressed this desire: "In our own backyard I look forward to the day when the Abenaki will again be Wolfeboro's ski center, under the management of the Parks and Recreation Committee."

During the winter of 1959-1960 the ski slope was, indeed, put under the Parks and Recreation Committee with Forrest Durkee and Bob Hale in charge. By late January the facility was operating nicely. Free ski instruction was given to youngsters by Paul Glidden, Wayne Shipman, and Rev. Roy Chamberlin.

At the end of the season, Ned Bullock reported that the tow had run 211 hours and had pulled about 4,000 people up the slope for about 152,000 rides. The largest daily attendance was 150, and the second largest was 125. Of nine major injuries, there were four broken bones and five sprains.

During the decade the younger set enjoyed sledding and skating. There were many excellent slopes in town, to which another was added in January 1956 through the generosity of Merwin and Eleanor Horn:

> The marine roadway at the Wolfeboro Airport has been made available to children for weekend coasting. The sloping hill with Winter Harbor at the base should be ideal for this purpose. Coffee and hot chocolate will be furnished free of charge at the Airport Cottage.[85]

## AROUND TOWN

### Zoning and Real Estate

There were many zoning disputes in the fifties. One of the most spirited was in 1951, when realtor Joseph I. Melanson, Jr., desired to open an office on South Main Street next to Bailey's Restaurant. He received approval of the neighbors, submitted detailed plans of his building, and was granted permission by the clerk of the Zoning Committee. Subsequently, Harold H. Hart, chairman of the committee, who was out of town when the approval was granted, returned and revoked it. So angered was Melanson that he took a large advertisement in the newspaper to protest that current regulations made it difficult to do business in Wolfeboro.

In late 1955 and early 1956 "a case which has caused more comment and discussion than any similar zoning problem in all the years since the enactment of the current zoning regulations in 1950" erupted. The Sun Oil Company wanted to tear down a venerable home at the southwest corner of Main and Endicott Streets and erect a blue-colored gas station. Sunoco won, and traditionalists lost. Ironically, after the controversial station was built it stood vacant for over a year as Sunoco tried in vain to find someone to lease it.

In 1954 Joseph I. Melanson, Jr., spearheaded a campaign to have Wolfeboro reassessed, a proposal that was passed at the March town meeting. However, Matthew Lahti led a counter-movement, and at a subsequent adjourned meeting, "the state tax assessors were voted out of Wolfeboro."

At the town meeting of March 14, 1955, voters rescinded the 1950 mandate to tear down the Boston & Maine Station which was now being used by Girl Scouts, Boy Scouts, and others, and was known as the Wolfeboro Youth Center.

As of July 5, 1955, state law prohibited the filling in of "great ponds" below the high water mark, unless permission was obtained from the governor and his council. Previously, the time-honored way to increase one's acreage bordering lakes Winnipesaukee and Wentworth was simply to extend the shoreline by dumping fill. The Brightwaters Inn, for one, had increased the size of its premises substantially in this manner.

In July 1960 Selectman Charles L. French made the suggestion to the Rotary Club that as 50% of the town taxes were paid by summer visitors who owned property, it might be desirable to hold a model town meeting in the summer so that suggestions could be taken from seasonal residents.[86]

### Electricity and Water

In February 1955 the changeover from incandescent to the more economical mercury vapor street lamps began, with the first of the new lights installed on the Brewster campus.

On March 1, 1955, the town was without power for much of the day. Schools were closed. Manager H.E. Erickson explained that a short circuit in lines buried under concrete within the plant had caused the first mechanical failure of the plant in over 27 years. Other outages had been due to hurricanes, ice, and diverse natural causes. Around the same time, there was a movement to sell the local facilities to the Public Service Co. of New Hampshire, but the idea was defeated at the Precinct meeting on March 22, 1955.

In September 1955 town water was chlorinated for the first time.[87]

### Downtown

In 1955 merchants petitioned to have parking meters installed for operation during 14 weeks of the summer to alleviate congestion and prevent loss of retail trade. Research suggested that business would increase 12%, time spent in looking for parking spaces would be cut 50%, and the meters would bring the town $13,800 annually. On June 10, 1957, a special meeting was held. Voters rejected the idea, 187 to 57.

During this era there was much discussion of traffic flow. Several one-way streets were instituted. In the summer of 1957 blinking yellow caution lights were installed in several places. In 1958 two-way radio communication, including mobile units, first linked various town departments 24 hours a day.[88]

### Bicentennial Celebration

In the summer of 1959 the Wolfeboro Bicentennial celebration was held to observe the anniversary of the granting of the land on which most of the town is situated. Events included dedication of the Pleasant Valley Schoolhouse at its new Clark Park site (July 1), carnival and midway (July 3-4), parade (July 4; seven bands, 54 parade entries), Strawberry Festival (July 5), sale at Baptist Church (July 10), Masonic Temple bazaar and supper (July 17), Christian Church baked bean supper and sale (July 18), NH Music Festival concert (July 23), street dance and historical pageant (July 24; about 1,000 attended the pageant which featured 200 players), St. Cecilia's bazaar and luncheon (July 25), All Saints' bridge and canasta party at Kehonka Hill (July 31), street dance (August 1), Old Home Sunday at the Christian Church (August 2), local history tour hosted by Mr. and Mrs. Clark Macomber (August 5), concert (August 6), Huggins Hospital Street Fair (August 7-8), and many more.

*The Bicentennial Banner,* a tabloid telling about the older days, was distributed for free. The Wolfeboro Historical Society had its own agenda with exhibits and lectures at Clark Park on numerous occasions from July 1 through August 26.[89]

## HEALTH AND WELLNESS

### Epidemics

Polio continued to be the number one health concern of the 1950s. By the autumn of 1951 there were eight local residents with the disease, four of whom had become afflicted during the year. By 1953 the vaccine developed by Dr. Jonas E. Salk was a reality, although local distribution had not yet taken place. Many people felt that the polio problem was over, and contributions to the March of Dimes dropped. However, there were still many people suffering.

On May 25, 1955, the first clinic in the county for the administering of the Salk vaccine was set up at Town Hall. First to receive shots were first- and second-grade children. Meanwhile, polio continued to be a scourge. In August of the same year, all public beaches were closed in town, and James E. Bovaird, M.D., town health officer, recommended that children 14 years or under should avoid public places. At the annual Huggins Hospital Street Fair, pony rides and other children's attractions were canceled. It was reported that as of August 24, there were 17 new cases of polio, including one fatality, in the Wolfeboro area. Gamma globulin shots were offered to all people from infants to age 20 and to anyone (up to age 50) who had been near someone with the disease. School openings were postponed for two weeks. There was a bright side: Of the 19 local cases, "practically all have recovered with a minimum of ill effects and are continuing steadily toward complete recovery."

Local polio sufferer Richard C. Libby met Dr. Salk as part of a ceremony at the Georgia Warm Springs Foundation and also appeared on national television.[90] In later years, as inoculations became widespread, polio was no longer a threat.

Epidemics of a less serious nature included measles and chicken pox, which recurred with regularity. In March 1952 many Wolfeboro children had measles, including "most all the young people" living on North Main Street.[91]

On June 27, 1952, this appeared in the local paper:

> Chicken pox is still mopping up all the children who have not had whooping cough and measles, and even some of those who have had both. After all the epidemics that have swept Wolfeboro during the past spring, it would seem as though no one should be ill again for at least 10 years.

Ticks were a menace in the summer of 1954. A local account stated they were unknown locally until after the hurricane of 1938. If the situation got worse, the town might ask for government aid, it was noted.[92]

### Huggins Hospital

The town's local facility received many commendations during the decade. In 1951 this was printed:

> If rumor is correct, there are only three general hospitals in New Hampshire with completely equipped physiotherapy departments. One of these is Huggins Hospital in Wolfeboro.

On December 4, 1953, Dr. Ralph Adams, whose work with human heart surgery had achieved international renown, worked as part of a six-person team to perform a difficult operation on a patient suffering from mitral stenosis, only the second time it had been done in the state. (The first was at Mary Hitchcock Hospital in Hanover.)

In March 1954 Ralph W. Tuttle, M.D., chief of staff at Huggins Hospital, was honored for 50 years of medical service in the state. He came to Barnstead to practice in 1914, moved to Alton in 1924, and joined the staff of Huggins soon thereafter.

The year 1956 produced these statistics: Admissions 1,497; personnel, 96; births, 160; emergencies, 983; operations, 709; meals served, 66,267.

In September 1957 a drive was launched to raise over $100,000 for a new hospital wing, with $22,100 to come

Prominent local medical personalities of the decade: Dr. Ralph Tuttle (left), who in 1954 was honored for 50 years of medical service; Dr. Ralph Adams is at the microphone; to the right are Dolly (Mrs. James) and Dr. James Bovaird.

from the Ford Foundation, $40,000 from federal grants and the balance from the public. By mid-May 1958 the new facility was a reality. Featured was a new piece of X-ray equipment which had been purchased by the Hospital Aid Association for $18,500. Each August the annual Street Fair raised money for various Huggins Hospital projects. In 1958 the fair made over $11,000.

In April 1959 Huggins was recognized as one of only two state institutions with radioisotope facilities. Hitchcock was the other.

In early October 1959 it was reported that the current issue of *Time* Magazine devoted a column—with a picture of Dr. Ralph Adams and Miss Virginia Bayer— to the excellent procedures in effect at Huggins Hospital. It was noted that staphylococcus infections at Huggins, since new routines (developed in part by Dr. Adams) had been in force, had dropped to just two cases out of 1,000 patients (0.2%). Nationally, infections ranged up to 5% in operations, and 2% was acceptable. Before the new procedures were installed at Huggins, the rate was 1.4%. The accomplishment was highlighted in a convention of the American College of Surgeons held in Atlantic City, attended by 7,000 registrants.

Later in the month the local paper noted that Dr. Adams was working with Dr. Robert W. Correll (of the Engineering Department of UNH) to use the electrical principle of capacitance to measure blood pressure within an artery. "The name Huggins Hospital is fast becoming known throughout the country because of the outstanding work performed by those who staff it."[93]

On May 4, 1960, the first cataract removal operation took place at Huggins under Dr. Edwin B. Goodall, an ophthalmologist and graduate of Harvard Medical School who had come to Wolfeboro to set up practice that year.

### Other Medical Notes

The American Red Cross Bloodmobile made its first scheduled visit to town in December 1951, with the First Congregational Church being the donor center, thus initiating a tradition that is still going on.

In 1954 the McFadden & Libbey drug store, founded in 1913, closed, leaving just two competitors in town: Tobey's Pharmacy and Hall's Pharmacy.

On April 12, 1955, Dr. Louise Bates Ames, co-founder in 1950 of the Gesell Institute of Child Development, spoke at Carpenter School under the auspices of the Cate Fund Committee. Her subject was child behavior, an increasingly popular area of research.[94]

The first page of the May 1, 1959, issue of the *Granite State News* showed Mrs. Charlotte McDermott being honored for her long services as volunteer chairman of the Blue Cross-Blue Shield community enrollment. Mrs. McDermott was also active with Huggins Hospital, Girl Scouts, and other civic affairs.

## FIRE FIGHTING

### News of the Department

During the decade chimney and brush fires commanded the greatest share of attention by the Fire Department. Nearly all of these were extinguished promptly and without serious damage.

The largest fire of the era was not in Wolfeboro, but claimed 1,800 acres on Mt. Shaw in Moultonboro. The woodland conflagration started on June 22, 1953. *A month later* there were still hot spots. Members of Wolfeboro's National Guard battalion were ordered to the lines by Gov. Hugh Gregg and joined other firefighters including many local volunteers and 400 soldiers from Camp Devens. The town of Wolfeboro served as a command post and central dispatch spot for the sustained effort.[95]

For the best part of a century, the Monitor Hose Co. firehouse in South Wolfeboro served the town, not only as part of the Fire Department, but, on the second floor, as a social hall for public suppers, dances, wedding receptions, club meetings, and other events. In April 1956 the roof collapsed under a heavy snow load. It was announced immediately that the structure would be restored because of its historical significance, as it was believed to be the last remaining district firehouse in town.[96]

In November 1957 the Wolfeboro Fire Department took possession of a new 750 gallon-per-minute pumper which cost $14,800. Painted white, it was called Engine No. 2.[97]

### The "Tuftonboro Problem"

During the evening of October 19, 1956, the barn and much of the main house on the Keith Benson farm at Mirror Lake in Tuftonboro were destroyed by fire. Tuftonboro issued a call for help to the Wolfeboro Fire Department. At the time Wolfeboro had well-trained and equipped fire-fighting facilities while those of its neighboring town were modest. The Benson fire set in motion a long-simmering controversy as to whether Wolfeboro should expend men, money, and effort assisting its neighbor, while Tuftonboro taxpayers elected not to upgrade their own department. "Let Wolfeboro take care of us," seemed to be the prevailing feeling.

On April 4, 1960, the Wolfeboro fire commissioner directed Chief Guy Foss not to respond in the future to any building fires in Tuftonboro. Mutual aid was allowed only in the case of brush and forest fires. "The reasons behind this decision are long and involved," noted the *Granite State News.* In response, Tuftonboro served notice that it would not be able to help Wolfeboro if asked to do so. The situation deteriorated from that point.[98]

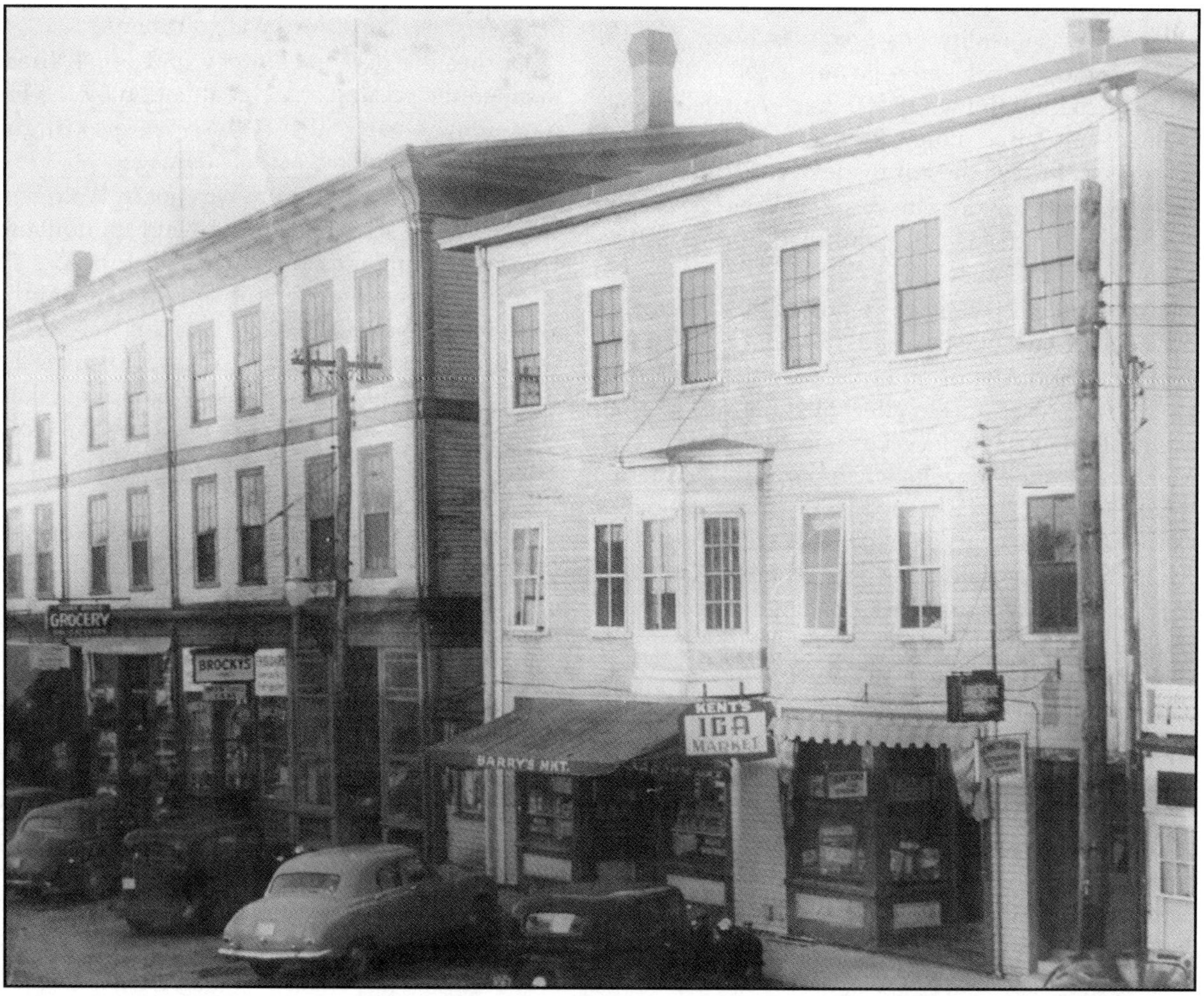


View along the east side of Railroad Avenue, March 12, 1951. In the Goodwin Block at the left are signs for Jerry L. Thayer, attorney; Wm. Britton insurance agency; Gray Brothers grocery and delicatessen, and Brocky's appliances (which also offered bus ticket sales and a taxi stop).

In the building to the right are signs for Barry's Market (Kent's IGA Market, successor; both names were used simultaneously), Thompson's shoe repair (Walter Thompson); Lake Shore Grange; and Bennett & Berry accountants. (Photograph by Elgar St. Clair)

View along the east side of Railroad Avenue, January 1, 1958, showing the Goodwin Block as it was being gutted by fire that started in the Beef 'n Bun restaurant. The structure was razed later in the same year. Today the Central Square building is on the site. (Photograph by Charles E. Brown, a spectator upon the scene who snapped photographs that were subsequently printed in several newspapers)

## Notable Fires

**1951, February 10. Eva Hayford house:** Fire began in chimney and progressed to a general alarm. Damage: $1,200.

**1951, October 29. Wolfeboro Tavern:** Fire at the back end of the buildings did much damage before being extinguished by firemen. In earlier years this facility was known as Glen Cottage.

**1952, February 1. Brewster Dairy:** Building ablaze, but was put out quickly. Damage: $1,000.

**1952, February 9. Philip Thurrell house:** Chimney fire spread to ell; house gutted.[99]

**1952, April 18. Pleasant Valley barn:** Total loss.[100]

**1952, April 20. Mount Delight; lots of sixes:** Six-acre brush fire destroyed six cabins at Birchmont Camps. Local firefighters spent six hours on scene.[101]

**1952, April 25. Harry Leavitt barn:**[102] Old barn on New Garden Road burned.

**1952, June 20. Dudley Holden place:** A barn on Whitten Neck, which had been converted into a lounge and a suite of bedrooms, burned flat. Damage: $10,500.

**1952, August 17. Camp Wunnishaunta bath house:** South Wolfeboro. Loss: $1,000.

**1952, December 17. Mrs. Andrew J. Melanson house:** House ell and attached shed burned.

**1953, March 9. Oil furnace explosion:** A new oil burner in the Charles L. French home exploded setting timbers afire. Firemen prevented further spreading.[103]

**1953, March 18. Bee Hive apartments:** Structure on Union Street owned by the Advent Christian Church had raging fire in attic and roof area. Loss: $2,000.

**1953, June 19. General Wolfe Inn:** Kitchen wall and ceiling.[104]

**1953, July 20. Morris Camp:** Rust Pond. Gutted.[105]

**1953, August 3. Hutchins boat fire:** Robert Hutchins was burned when an explosion took place on a power launch he was working on at Camp Bernadette on Lake Wentworth. He dived overboard and saved his life, but was hospitalized with second-degree burns.[106]

**1953, August 14. Boat fire:**[107] Vessel with six occupants (who jumped overboard; treated for burns by Dr. Ralph Tuttle) caught fire off Winnipesaukee Motor Craft docks after a fuel leak. Boat sank.

**1953, September 6. George Rockwell place:** Garage and shed destroyed. Pleasant Valley.[108]

**1954, April 18. Bennett homestead:** A fire in Cotton Valley destroyed much valuable "botanical growth." Apparently, no structures were affected.

**1954, August 11. Hill School Camp:** Two tents a total loss.[109]

**1954, September 8. Gardner Pad mill:** Ceiling, walls, equipment damaged.[110]

**1954, September 20. Whitman camp:** Camp of the Courtney S. Whitman, Jr., family on Sunset Point on Lake Wentworth, one of the nicest in the area, was destroyed, save for the kitchen.[111]

**1954, November 1. Mrs. O.H. Bryant's cottage:** Varney Road structure extensively damaged by fire caused by an overheated chimney from a fire too large for the fireplace.

**1955, February 18. Ray Dow's garage:** Destroyed, with tractor. No attempt to extinguish.[112]

**1955, May 19. Wolfeboro Hardware:** Flash fire on platform behind store destroyed merchandise. Believed to have been caused by a glass jug of lacquer thinner overheating in the sun and exploding.[113]

**1955, August 5. Fred Nichols family house:** Bay Street. Lightning struck a bottled gas container; home destroyed. Mrs. Nichols was slightly injured.[114]

**1955, September 17. Frank Dodier's barn:** Pleasant Valley. Destroyed by fire. Loss: Over $1,000.

**1955, December 14. Althea and Walter Sweet house:** Pine Hill district on Route 109. Extensively damaged by fire.[115]

**1956, April 11. Bernard W. Pineo. greenhouse:** South Main Street. Damage: $500 to $600.

**1956, August 19. Town jail:** Mattress fire; prisoner unconscious.[116]

**1957, June 8. Edgar H. Glidden residence:** Factory Street. Gutted. Glidden, age 22 and head of a family, subsequently moved to Varney Road.[117]

**1957, June 30: Edwin Chamberlin house:** Route 109. House and contents a total loss by fire.[118]

**1957, August 20. Boat explosion:**. Edward Desrosier, who had a summer home on Lake Wentworth, took his Evinrude outboard-powered boat for a spin, accompanied by his younger sister and her friend. They were 10 to 15 yards offshore when a gas leak apparently ignited by the engine started a fire. He threw both children in the water and dived in himself, after which the boat exploded.

**1957, November 9: Goodrow camp:** Beach Pond Road. Burned to the ground.

**1957, November 11. C.E. Campbell, Jr., barn:** Fire destroyed a barn and part of the house at the C.E. Campbell, Jr., place (an old stage inn) in the Brown's Ridge section.[119]

**1957, December 14. The Little Diner:** Completely gutted.[120]

**1958, January 1. Goodwin Block on Railroad Avenue:** Three-story wooden commercial block gutted by fire that started in the refrigerator of the Beef 'n' Bun Restaurant. Eight tenants were affected, including the office of the *Granite State News*, Wool Corner, Gene's Hardware, Britton Insurance Agency.[121] The building was later razed.

**1958, May 11. French cottage:** Lightning ignited fire that destroyed the cottage of Mr. and Mrs. Charles L. French, Jr., on South Wolfeboro Bay.[122]

**1958, November 25. Rust house:** The "old Rust place" (Morris house) in South Wolfeboro was severely damaged by fire, despite firemen pumping 113,500 gallons of water on the blaze.[123]

**1958, December 28. Alvin Donovan's camp:** Lake Wentworth. Destroyed.[124]

**1959, January 8. Allard cabin:** Mr. and Mrs. Preston Allard were killed when their two-room cabin on River Street burned to the ground. In 1949 their earlier cabin on the same site was burned.[125]

**1959, February 1. Al Stock house:** On road to Sanbornville. Quick action by the Fire Department limited damage to the interior.

**1959, April 10. Pleasant Valley Schoolhouse:** Situated in Pleasant Valley and scheduled to be moved to Clark Park. Slightly damaged by fire at its rear right corner.[126]

**1959, May 8. Varney lumber yard:** A fire in Mrs. Fred Varney's lumber yard in South Wolfeboro started in a pile of dry boards "by the sun shining through a glass jug containing water." The fire threatened three nearby residences, but the Fire Department quickly extinguished it.

**1959, May 9. Elbridge Snow's barn:** Waumbeck Road. Barn leveled; fire raging in house ell was put out by firemen.[127]

**1960, January 21. Clarke's Shell Station:** Center Street. Explosion and small fire.[128]

**1960, March 9. Malone Knitting Co.:** Bell Shop at west end of Factory Street. Finished clothing extensively water-damaged in fire on ground floor; 20 sprinkler heads were activated and prevented further destruction. Building was evacuated safely.[129]

**1960, March 26. Clyde Kimball home heater explosion:** Oil-burning water heater in Kimball residence occupied by Raymond Pollini on Pine Street exploded in basement. Four fire trucks responded, and the house was saved.

**1960, July 2. Willard Jones mobile home:** River Street. Burned to the ground.[130]

**1960, November 12. Masonic Temple oil furnace explosion:** Doors were blown off the furnace, and much smoke issued forth. Firemen arrived quickly, and no further damage occurred.[131]

**1960, December 11. Rogers buildings:** North Main Street opposite Wolfeboro Inn. Barn and small buildings owned by Mrs. Nathaniel Rogers burned; house was damaged. A heart attack took the life of Deputy Fire Chief Lyle Colby, age 49, who collapsed at the fire station.[132]

## LAW ENFORCEMENT

### About the Department

The Wolfeboro Police Department was busier than ever during the 1950s. In particular, young men with fast automobiles brought a new level of mobility to thievery. As in earlier times, most of the more serious local property crimes were committed by out-of-towners, while local youngsters and young adults accounted for most vandalism and petty theft.

In 1958 citizen Fred A. Goodwin commented that the Police Department needed to be upgraded. He observed that it did not have a board of commissioners and was run only by the selectmen. Further:[133]

> No other department is called out more than the police. Lost children, pocketbooks, keys, etc., are just a few of the things the officer is asked to be on the lookout for. Miscellaneous disturbances are all in a night's work. Motor vehicle violations and minor accidents are too numerous to mention. What the working conditions of this department are remain a matter of record. To list a few:
>
> The chief's salary is $65 per week. From late September to early June the chief is on duty 24 hours a day with one day off in eight. At least eight of the 24 hours he must be on the beat; the other 16 he must be near a telephone waiting for the inevitable call to come in....
>
> Where is the police station? The answer has to be: "I am sorry, we have none...."
>
> Where can the police take a person he wishes to question or detain while he is running a check? Up to the Court Room, which serves as a courthouse, an office for the Highway Department, an office for the Town Employment Board, and an examination room for the motor vehicle inspector, which is only a few of the services it is used for.
>
> Where does he go to answer a red light? Usually, if it is not too late and he looks long enough, he will find a store open, where he may use the phone. There is always the public booth, which is generally occupied by somebody making a long distance call. A FINE system!...
>
> I would like to ask the voters to keep in mind these situations....

In the summer of 1955 there was a four-man crew on duty, including Chief Harold E. Thompson, Officer Fred Long, newly-appointed Officer Fred Richardson, and another new person, C.E. ("Ched") Bullock, who was tapped to be a day police officer.[134]

On June 13, 1958, this was reported in the *Granite State News:*

> The Wolfeboro Police Department has been reorganized under the direction of Chief Harold E. Thompson with the complete approval of the selectmen. Police headquarters are now at the selectmen's office where the new radio system is being installed. Two new full-time officers have been added for the summer, and the town will have protection 24 hours a day. Also, another police cruiser will be available for use.

### Crime Bulletin

Newspaper accounts of local problems included these representative examples:

**1951, May 30. Harmony Shop:** Gift shop entered at night by breaking glass. Over $300 cash stolen, primarily New England Telephone Co. receipts, for which the shop was a collection agent.[135]

**1953, March 3. Paper Store:** Break-in by three youths (subsequently arrested) yielded two fountain pens, cash, a watch, cigarettes and a cigarette lighter. The culprits threw part of their loot in Lake Winnipesaukee when they feared arrest.[136]

**1954, June 4.[137] White collar crime:** Louis Berube and Clarence Herbert pleaded guilty to counts of falsifying claims for unemployment compensation. Each was fined, given a suspended prison sentence, and made ineligible to receive any further benefits for one year.

**1955, autumn. Breaking and entering:** Many reports. A trained dog was put on duty at the airport hangar during the night "to take care of prowlers."[138]

**1956, August 9. Car theft:** A 19-year-old counselor at a local camp "borrowed" Allan E. Bailey's Lincoln to visit his girlfriend. Passing through Moultonboro at high speed, he was arrested by a state trooper. The car was returned, and the joy rider paid a $50 fine.[139]

**1957, March 21. Store break:** Bourdon's Store at Wolfeboro Center was burgled. Chief Harold E. Thompson and Ernest Swift picked up Alfred P. Heald and Harry Abbott, both age 20, who pleaded guilty and were sentenced to six months in jail, plus restitution.[140]

**1957, March 30. Boat motor thefts:** Three were swiped at two locations.[141]

**1957, July 30.[142] Crime wave:** Multiple thefts from local stores, including a break-in at Gould's Dime Store ($800 taken) and shoplifting at Corkum's men's shop and Black's Gift Shop.

**1958, January 13: Raids:** "Wolfeboro was hit hard and fast by two daring raids." A car stopped in front of the Sportsmen's Center, and the occupants rushed out, smashed glass, and stole firearms and ammunition. A few minutes later the same gang broke into Nick's Esso Station and stole money. Later, four young men were arrested in Haverhill, MA, after a gunfight. One was a resident of East Wolfeboro.[143]

**1958, October 24.[144] Cottage thefts:** Frank Caswell, 21, of Dover, was arrested for stealing from the cottages of Dr. and Mrs. Jansen K. Hoornbeck, Mr. and Mrs. A. Cooper Ballentine, and others. The case was broken by local realtor Richard I. Bowe, who jotted down the license number on a suspicious car.

Law enforcement: In September 1959 Police Chief Harold E. Thompson and Officer Elywn Drew sought to reach to an ever-increasing amount of local crime by setting up an auxiliary police force. For about a half year the group was kept secret, until its existence was revealed in the *Granite State News,* February 6, 1960. Shown here are most of the members of the auxiliary force.

Bottom row, left to right: Eric Erickson, R.B. Emerson, Chief Harold Thompson, Officer Elwyn Drew, Norman Hale, and Raymond Berry.

Top row: Unidentified, John Corson, Alvin White, Charles Foss, Jr., Fred Goodwin, and Lawrence Glidden. Also named to the special force were Everett Albee, Roswell Dore, Roger Gregory, E. Fred Miller, Clinton Piper, Ralph Stinchfield, and Raymond Tuttle. (David Fetzer photograph)

**1958, November 16. Shoot-and-run:** Herman Young was hunting on Whiteface Mountain when an unseen hunter fired a shot which hit him in the leg and then fled. A ballistics investigation and interviews determined that the culprit was Lewis Dow, 23, of New Durham, who was in Young's hunting party, but who concealed his deed. Dow was given a six-month jail sentence, fined $100, and lost his right to hunt in the state for 10 years.[145]

**1958, December 19. Auto chase:** Officer Linley L. Moore spotted a car traveling at high speed at night on South Main Street and gave chase in his cruiser. The speedster put out his lights, accelerated, and disappeared down Middleton Road. Officer Linley ran the cruiser up on a dirt bank while trying to make a curve. The culprit escaped.[146]

**1959, April 9. Burglaries:** Night break-ins at Horne's Garage, White's Restaurant, and the Western Auto Store. Total take was about $100.[147]

**1959, July 17.[148] Island break-ins:** 16 small camps and the main dining room of the abandoned music camp on Melody Island were vandalized, and a break-in was reported on Parker Island.

**1959, July 20. Theft:** James Smith of RI took over $1,000 from a local resort owner, was subsequently identified by a tip, and was arrested in Los Angeles. In August he was extradited to NH and clapped into the Carroll County Jail.[149]

## A Controversial Move

Reacting to what seemed to be an ever-increasing amount of crime, Chief Harold E. Thompson and Officer Elwyn Drew devised plans in September 1959 for an auxiliary police force. It was hoped to curb the rash of break-ins, vandalism, and reckless driving, particularly by the younger set. However, nothing further was said publicly about the proposed augmentation of the Police Department.

Underscoring the situation was the recent break-out by five Carroll County Jail inmates, who were believed to be at large in Wolfeboro. In another incident, on an October afternoon two nine-year-old girls were molested while riding their bicycles. An area-wide hunt was instituted, and based upon a description of a 1951 Chevrolet with a customized grill and broken tailpipe, David St. George was arrested in his Barnstead home. He pleaded guilty and was fined and sentenced. In the meantime, numerous business and residence break-ins occurred within town limits.[150]

On February 5, 1960, the *Granite State News* revealed that in the previous August, the Board of Selectmen secretly gave appointments to 16 men to serve as special officers in the Auxiliary Police Force. What Wolfeboro residents thought *might* happen someday, actually had occurred a half year earlier.

> Because of security reasons this is the first time the roster has been made public... All auxiliary police force officers are volunteers and serve at no cost to the town 24 hours a day.

For six months Wolfeboro citizens had been infiltrated, so to speak, by well-intentioned citizens who had secret police powers.

Among those serving were Everett Albee, Raymond Berry, John Corson, Roswell Dore, Elwyn Drew (also on the regular force), R.B. Emerson, H.E. Erickson, Charles Foss, Jr., Lawrence Glidden, Fred Goodwin, Roger Gregory, Norman Hale, E. Fred Miller, Clinton Piper, Ralph Stinchfield, Chief Thompson (on the regular force as well), Raymond Tuttle, and Alvin White.

## Changes

In February 1960 the Police Department moved into renovated quarters in the basement of the Brewster Memorial Hall. The selectmen's appointment of the formerly secret Auxiliary Police Force did not sit well with many citizens. For this and other reasons, on March 29, 1960, some 540 voters turned out to elect three police commissioners and to strip the supervision powers from the selectmen. Elected as commissioners were Norris R. Sanborn, Joseph I. Melanson, Jr., and Theodore J. Sturgis.[151]

A list of "police responsibilities surrendered by the selectmen" included parking ordinances, the control of water skiing off Town Docks, and the restraining of activities involving narcotics, alcohol, gambling, prostitution, obscene literature, and more. Selectman Charles L. French, "in summing up the responsibilities surrendered by the selectmen, stated that the new commission is personally responsible for the safety and protection of life and property in the town of Wolfeboro on a 24-hours-a-day basis."

Before long a serious rift developed between the power-shorn selectmen and the new police commissioners. This was brought into sharp focus on June 10, 1960, when selectmen Charles L. French, Jr., Edward W. Zulauf, and Norman A. Hale wrote an open letter of apology in the *Granite State News* to Col. Ralph W. Caswell, Department of State Police, Concord, concerning "the recent action by Police Commissioner Joseph I. Melanson in regard to State Police radar checks in Wolfeboro," noting, in part:

> As the Board of Selectmen we will want you to know that we exceedingly regret the incident that took place a week ago, when one of our police commissioners was instrumental in interfering with the safety check your police were operating in Wolfeboro. We consider this action not only poor judgment but poor taste...

In the same issue the three police commissioners wrote a letter to the State Attorney General Louis Wyman with their diametrically opposed view of the situation, stating in part:

> Several times recently the state police have set up speed traps in our town. This controversial method of apprehending motor vehicle violators, conducted by the state police so close to the center of our town, is not to our approval. We feel that this annoyance and embarrassment to our citizens and summer guests is unnecessary and unwanted...

In response, a letter from Wyman contained this:

> In fairness to all parties concerned, I must advise that an investigation of the incident discloses that Commissioner Melanson did not order the state police out of Wolfeboro. On the contrary, Trooper Forsyth's report confirms Melanson's version of the incident to the effect that he expressed the conviction that the operation of the unit within the compact area of the town was an unsatisfactory location, and the wish that such operations be conducted outside of the compact area of the town, upon the public highway, but indicated that he recognized he had no authority to order the state police to leave. Further, Trooper Forsyth's report indicates that the decision to leave was made by Forsyth...

### Here and There in Law Enforcement

Donald Joy led a double life. In the daytime he was foreman of the Furniture Petites factory in Wolfeboro Falls. In his off hours he was a burglar. A routine stop on Middleton Road of Joy's car by Deputy Sheriff Fred Long raised suspicion. Joy's temporary residence on River Street was searched, and many stolen items were found. He and accomplice Milo Maynard went to jail.[152]

In June and July 1960 numerous private and business signs were stolen from Wolfeboro locations. Finally, a cache of them was discovered by the Sheriff's Department. Included were signs for the Libby Museum, Maple Rock House, local real estate firms, Canopache Lodge, and others.

Obscenity, elusive of definition, reared its head in 1957. The local police were alerted "to eliminate the sale and distribution of obscene books and magazines in our town, which other law enforcement agencies say contribute to juvenile delinquency."

In 1958 "we had for the first time complete police protection 24 hours a day throughout the year."[153]

In June 1960 a team of five magazine hucksters and their crew manager swept through town, using unpleasant sales pitches, resulting in numerous complaints to the police.[154]

At decade's end in 1960, Leaman E. Cunningham was justice of the Municipal Court, and local attorney Jerry Thayer was associate judge. In the Police Department, Harold E. Thompson was chief, Elwyn Drew and Laurence Nihan were officers, and part-time officers included Frederick Picard, Donald Nason, Forrest Anderson, and Wilbert Freethy.

## NATURAL PHENOMENA

### Wind and Snow

On Sunday, April 15, 1951, a freak windstorm, possibly accompanied by a tornado, raked through town for about 10 minutes, flattening trees, knocking down utility poles between the General Wolfe Inn and the top of King's Hill, and causing telephone and power outages for over eight hours.

On Sunday, February 17, 1952, a fall of about 10 to 15 inches of snow closed several roads and isolated residents in distant areas. Many streets were still closed on Monday, and there was no mail in or out of town. During the next several weeks, additional storms added to the accumulation, and by mid-March numerous camps and small structures had been flattened by the snow load. The Camp Patrol, operated by "Ched" Bullock (father of Ned, who took over the business in 1959), helped prevent much damage by spotting overburdened roofs.

On Friday morning, September 19, 1952, a storm accompanied by high winds lashed Wolfeboro, resulting in the downing of power lines in many areas. Within a short period of time 2.57 inches of rain fell. An old-time resident on the Lake Winnipesaukee shore reported that she had never seen waves so high.

### High Water

In March 1953 there was heavy flooding throughout Carroll County, but damage to the inland parts of Wolfeboro was limited. Lake Winnipesaukee was a different story, however. In order to prevent flood damage downstream, the Public Service Company of New Hampshire kept the outlet dam high, resulting in the water rising to extraordinary levels. At Carry Beach water was even with the top of Forest Road. Nearly all beaches and docks in the town were submerged.

Freak winds were the order of the day on December 14, 1953. In some areas there was damage to trees and buildings, the Town Docks were harmed, and at the airport, hangar doors were ripped off. However, in other locations the winds were scarcely noticed.

In the spring of 1954 the high lake water scenario of 1953 was repeated with a vengeance. "The wettest season in years," the local paper commented. Every dock along Sewall Road was underwater, as was the yard at the Brightwaters Inn at the end of Lake Street. Downtown cellars were awash. Water covered part of Bay Street. At the Allen "A" Resort, Lake Wentworth expanded to cover Route 28. On the Gov. Wentworth Highway on the north side of the lake, fish swam where automobiles normally rolled along. To the east a veritable torrent of water rushed downhill from Ford Smith's pasture and washed out Cotton Valley Road to a depth of up to five feet. Debris was scattered everywhere.

### High Winds

On July 31, 1954, a tornado ripped through the Sewall Point area. "Branches and trees were snapped as one might snap raw spaghetti." Fortunately, no one was injured, but a group of children was narrowly missed by a large falling limb.

Hurricane Carol rammed Wolfeboro on Tuesday afternoon, August 31, 1954. The storm was warned of in ad-

Record high lake levels in March 1953 completely submerged the decking on the Wolfeboro Town Docks. Only the posts remained above water. Docks and low-lying areas were flooded all around Lake Winnipesaukee.

The Main Street bridge during the high water of March 1953. Water came within a foot or so of the top of the bridge arch, and basements of local businesses were flooded. This was a man-made disaster as Public Service of New Hampshire kept lake levels artificially high by damming the outlet to prevent flooding downstream.

vance, and residents were prepared. High winds from this huge spiral weather system approached from the northeast, then shifted direction to the south. Electricity was knocked out in many areas, and Huggins Hospital used emergency power for seven hours. The *Mount Washington* boat canceled its daily run. Captain Lawrence P. Beck of the *Tonimar* mail boat determined that the mail must go through, but the rapidly falling barometer prompted him to change his mind, and he returned all the sacks to the Post Office. Meanwhile, numerous private boats in Wolfeboro were battered and trees were flattened, but there were no injuries. H.E. Erickson and his Municipal Electric Department worked 16-hour days for the next week. Mabel Fullerton Hatch commented:

> There have been protests from all over about giving these devastating hurricanes feminine names. Obviously, whoever so named them agreed with Kipling (was it?) who declared the female species is more deadly than the male!

### Lightning and Wind

On August 7, 1955, Judge William E. Fuller, age 57, a graduate of Harvard Law School who had spent every summer of his life at Camp Ossipee at the end of Wolfeboro Neck, was struck and killed by a bolt of lightning. During the same storm many trees were downed on Sewall Point and Wolfeboro Neck, and power was cut off to the airport.

The September 2, 1955, issue of the *Granite State News* carried a report of high winds on Lake Winnipesaukee. William Flickinger rescued seven boys and girls whose 22-foot Higgins boat had sunk off Rattlesnake Island. Included among those saved was Richard Marriott (son of Willard Marriott of restaurant and hotel fame). Soon thereafter, Merwin Horn, owner of the Lakes Region Airport, was flying in a seaplane when he saw two boys thrown out of an aluminum boat at the entrance to Winter Harbor. With great courage Horn landed the plane on the rough water and took them aboard. The plane could not take off and awaited a rescue boat from nearby Camp Ossipee.[155]

### Too Much Snow; Too Little Water

Late winter and early spring of 1956 was a time of heavy snow. By March 17 the average depth on the ground was estimated at 39 inches. Many houses in outlying areas were isolated. Moody's old ice house on Crescent Lake collapsed, the Allen "A" Resort recreation building caved in, and the roof of the Monitor Hose Co. building in South Wolfeboro was crushed (and soon restored).

A problem of the opposite sort occurred at Lake Wentworth in the late summer of 1957 when water receded to very low levels, exposing the lake bottom up to 450 feet from the shore. Low rainfall coupled with a leak in the old (built in 1854) dam contributed. The level was reduced even more by letting water through the dam, after which repairs commenced.

### Snow

On January 7, 1958, a snowstorm began. Intermittently throughout the month there was additional accumulation. As roads were cleared, the Highway Department dumped countless tons of snow off the Main Street bridge into the river. However, there was not enough flow to wash the white stuff away. The Berry brothers in Wolfeboro Falls opened the dam on the Smith River, water cascaded into Back Bay, and the mass of snow broke apart and surged into Lake Winnipesaukee. Three weeks later the paper issued this plea:

> Special appeal to our Florida subscribers. Come home—we need you! There are excellent snow shoveling opportunities available to ambitious people who are interested in outdoor work in an invigorating climate!

From Thursday, March 12, 1959, through Saturday, March 14, local activities were at a standstill due to a heavy snowfall.

On March 11, 1960, this item was printed in the *Granite State News:*

> When W.J. Butts on South Main Street was shoveling his walk and minding his own business...a town snowplow came along and buried him in a drift. Fortunately, the crew realized what had happened and disinterred Mr. Butts, for he was unable to help himself.

### Mysterious Yellow Houses

On October 24, 1959, a heavy storm dumped over two inches of rain on the town. From the clouds came a dirty substance which clung to building exteriors, causing white houses to become yellow. A few weeks later it was learned that a similar situation had happened in East Orange, NJ, and that it was due to hydrogen sulfide gas. Eventually, the houses reverted to white.[156]

### Waves and Wind

How high do waves get on Lake Winnipesaukee? This age-old question has never been answered with certainty. When six-footers are seen, which is rarely, this is occasion for editorial comment. In mid-December 1959 there was a blow-out which may have shattered all records. Capt. Nat Goodhue, aboard the *Swallow* with his helper, Otto Pecunies, estimated the wave height at an amazing 10 feet. Certainly, Goodhue was as expert as anyone in lake statistics.

On September 12, 1960, most local residents remembered what had happened in 1954 when Hurricane Carol paid a visit. Now Hurricane Donna was due to arrive, and it did. However, unlike the situation in many other areas, local damage was light.[157]

### Heavenly Sights

On September 25, 1951, what was described as one of the most vivid displays on record of northern lights was seen in the night sky.

Orman T. Headley, erstwhile Wolfeboro minister and avid amateur astronomer, gave this account of another heavenly phenomenon, this on November 19, 1952:

> Last Wednesday evening at 8:06 by the clock, the third largest meteor that was ever my experience to witness fell just west of North Wakefield, somewhere between Wolfeboro and Ossipee. This meteor in falling on a dark, cloudy night, lighted up the sky like the noonday sun. It was the closest of any meteor I had ever seen fall, though it burned out just before reaching the ground. Accustomed as I am to these things, this was the first ever to frighten me, it being so close.

On November 20, 1957, a balloon carrying a radiosonde weather transmitter package burst when it reached the altitude of 16 miles. The package dropped by parachute and landed in the yard of the Lakeview Inn on North Main Street.[158]

### And the Ground Shook

The *Granite State News* reported this on October 31, 1952:

> A series of noisy happenings took place between 9:00 Saturday evening and 6:00 Sunday morning, interpreted by various Wolfeboro people as:
>
> 1. Their furnace is blowing up.
> 2. Night blasting on a highway.
> 3. The falling of a meteor.
> 4. Bomb raid.
> 5. Earthquakes.
>
> Everybody agreed that there was vibration, crashing and banging, rumbling and rolling. Some slept right through the night and didn't see, hear or feel anything, while others sat up all night wearing out the telephone system. The operators didn't know either.

Scientists at the Harvard Geological Laboratory reported sensing temblors at 2:45 and 4:07 on Sunday morning and a third at 3:46 on Monday morning.[159]

### Miscellany

In June 1954 a rare albino porcupine was spotted in Pleasant Valley. A few months earlier an albino deer had been seen locally. A month later eggs were the subject of this account:

> A great deal of interest was manifested by the chef and pastry chef at Hill School Camp when they recently opened several triple-yolk eggs. They opened many a double-yolk egg in the past, and even one with no yolk, but a triple-yolk was a first for these two experienced men. The Hale farm supplies the eggs.

In the same month much local foliage was laid bare by an infestation of gypsy moths, which had been a bane for decades, with some summers being worse than others.

Bears were a frequent sight around Wolfeboro and furnished the subject for much editorial copy as their novelty never faded. Typically, a bear would be spotted, and within a matter of minutes it would be punctured by rifle fire. On October 29, 1954, William W. Ayre took an opposing view, writing to the newspaper to protest the "kill-all-the-bears" game laws of the state.

Meanwhile, the hens at the Hale farm in South Wolfeboro kept laying surprises. In October 1954 one hen produced two eggs on the same day, contrary to accepted avian custom. Further:

> An egg found in an anonymous biddy's nest weighed six ounces and measured almost three inches in length. Broken for use, it was found to contain another egg, complete with shell, which was graded as "large."

For decades, beautiful elm trees arched over Wolfeboro streets and the Brewster Academy campus and shaded many drives and pathways. By the mid-1950s Dutch elm disease was on the way to making the species extinct. Eventually, all local elm trees succumbed.

Heretofore, objects circling the earth were of celestial origin. Now in 1957 came the Soviet satellite Sputnik. All of the sudden, watching the skies became a popular pastime. For example, on the evening of October 24, Cotton Mountain Road was bustling with automobiles filled with Sputnik-spotters seeking good observation points, but few saw the tiny orb.

On the afternoon of June 6, 1959, a swarm of honeybees stopped at a tree on North Main Street in front of the *Granite State News* office and the Wool Corner. As the bees showed no sign of moving on, a number of citizens offered sure-fire theories on how to remove them. Tom Morrison and George Moody finally sawed off the bee-laden limb at night. No sooner had this been done, than a new swarm came into town and took up position in another branch of the same tree![160]

### Wolfeboro in the 1950s

*A reminiscence by*
*John A. Graf*

During the 1950s I was a high school and college student with the good fortune to spend my summer vacation living on Wolfeboro Neck and working in the village. Many things were the same in the 1950s as in the 1990s, but there were some dramatic differences.

A filling station was where the Wolfeboro Marketplace is now. The Yum Yum Shop was a filling station. Uphill from Cate Park was another filling station.

The Miltner's Shoe Store building was owned by Cecil ("Steve") Corkum, but looked the same as it does today. Winnipesaukee Motors in its strong brick building on Main Street was actually the First National Store and the site of one of my first summer jobs. The A&P Market operated in downtown across from the Post Office. This was long before the new shopping center out toward Wolfeboro Falls.

**Past commanders of American Legion Harriman (later Harriman-Hale) Post No. 18 as photographed in the American Legion Hall on Center Street circa 1950.**

**Front row, seated, left to right: Edwin Craigue, Noyes V. Moore, Ransom Goodrich, Theodore Sturgis, Percy ("Dusty") Rhodes, and Percy Kenney.**

**Standing: Lloyd W. Hamm, Howard Smith, Robert Straw (of Tuftonboro), Leaman Cunningham, Earl Willand, George Campbell (of Ossipee), and Fred Goodwin. (Identification by Harrison Moore)**

The Massey brothers ran their barber shop on the west side of the Avery Building with a view of the bay. They later moved across the street. The Avery Building stood looming as a beacon in 1950 as the pre-eminent structure in the village. The Avery building mirrored Black's Paper Store as the dominant buildings and business locations in downtown Wolfeboro.

Community events were as important in the 1950s as they are now in the 1990s. The annual Memorial Day presentation of a wreath in honor of the Unknown Soldier was delivered to Wolfeboro Bay, followed by the magnificent Fourth of July parade meandering down the hill, through the village, up toward the Huggins Hospital, to turn around and retrace the route through the village and up the hill.

The parade always featured a magnificent float from the Allen "A" Resort. Square dancers, old cars, youngsters, flags and bunting were the touchstones of the parade in the 1950s as they are in the 1990s. The Huggins Hospital Street Fair dominated summer activities during this 40-years-ago period, with stale cigars, chuck-a-chuck, the pungent smell of food and the noise and excitement of camp kids watching rides and other events. The *Mount Washington* continues to be a fixture as it still travels to Dockside today as it did in the 1950s.

Brewster Academy was smaller and less prominent from an architectural standpoint in the 1950s. Of course, this was before Kingswood Regional High School began. Kingswood Golf Club was truly a country course with only 14 *good* holes rather than the reconstructed and redesigned 18 holes that exist today.

In the 1950s Wolfeboro sponsored a baseball team in a summer league in which players competed against Lancaster, Groveton, Hebron, Groton, Plymouth, Tilton, and other communities in central New Hampshire. Home games played at the ball field at Brewster every Saturday and Sunday brought a crowd of 100 to 200 people usually led by Carley and Dickie Massey and, occasionally, Harry Hopewell. Carley Massey's black Cadillac was able to refrigerate sufficient quantities of cold beverages to support the 15 or 20 local athletes.

The names of the players included locals and summer folk. People like Brad Hunter, the Lord family, Jimmy Sanborn, Ken Wilkerson, "Bucket" Robbins, Chan DeMille, "Needles" Taylor, and Jackie Piper were resplendent in their gray and green uniforms. Our leader, coach, and manager was Roger Grant. Many of us had our uniforms sponsored by local merchants and trades people. Our team drew rave reviews when we traveled to our remote competition. I recall a hot summer Fourth of July day catching a double header in Lancaster. As I rushed back toward the stands to catch a pop-up, I still remember a loud voice yelling, "If you catch this one, you really are a highway robber!" I did not catch the ball. Baseball in the summer was a fun game for all of us — fans, players, and revelers.

Since any town is a composite of its people, a few names come clearly to mind. When I worked at the A&P Store, the assistant manager was Ed Gridley, of Gridley's Green Thumb Greenhouse. These were the days when prices were somewhat different. We wore wooden fruit baskets on our head and hawked peaches singing, "Four pounds for forty-nine cents." Gridley made selling produce an art. Our baseball manager Roger Grant worked full time in the liquor store in Wolfeboro Falls. A strict taskmaster, he would not permit his athletes to imbibe his products. Fortunately, luminaries such as Carley Massey and Harry Hopewell were able to find alternatives to the restrictions imposed by our coach, manager and leader.

Traffic and people in Wolfeboro are now managed by officers in fancy blue complete with electronic devices, walkie talkies, night sticks, and other important physical attributes of law enforcement. In the 1950s we had Harold E. Thompson, also known as "Thompy" [pronounced "Tompy"], who was able to keep not only the youth of Wolfeboro but local traffic under control. His wife's ability to sell earthworms picked off the golf course at night allowed his income to be effectively supplemented.

The village of Wolfeboro is physically more beautiful today than in the 1950s. It has preserved and protected and improved its wonderful buildings. It has maintained many of its historical events and continues to be overrun by "summer folk." Its uniqueness and its character still remain because of its people and its sense of history. It remains not only "The Oldest Summer Resort in America" but the finest one, too.[161]

## PRICES IN 1960

The following prices are from the *Granite State News*. Prices continued their upward march from the decade before.

**Appliances:** Electric shaver, Remington, rechargeable, $35.95. Frigidaire 10-cubic-foot freezer, $198.96. Garbage disposal unit, $39.95 to $49.95. Slide projector, Kodak Cavalcade, $159.50. Stove, electric, Hotpoint, four burners and automatic oven, $239.95.

**Automobiles:** English-made Ford station wagon, $1,669. Ford Fairlane, 1961, 4-door, $2,315, with automatic transmission, radio and heater, $2,628.40; Ford Special, 4-door, fully equipped, $2,712.88; Ford F-85, fully equipped, $2,712.88. Morris 1000, compact car made by the British Motor Corp., $1,495.

**Battery:** Automobile, 12 volt, $31.95.

**Beverages:** Coffee, Maxwell House, 1-pound can, 65¢.

**Boat:** 18' Thompson with Evinrude 75 h.p. motor, $2,295.75.

**Clothing:** Bathing trunks, men's, $2.95 to $8.95. Snowsuits, boys and girls, sizes 2 to 7, $10.95 to $19.95. Nylon stockings, pair, $1.75. Shirt, men's, Van Heusen, $4.25. Shirts, Pendleton, wool, $13.95 to $17.50. Sweaters, $5.95 to $17.98.

**Electricity:** Average cost per KWH for home heating, 1.5¢.

**Entertainment:** Ticket to feature film, adult, $1.

**Food:** Meat: Bacon, sliced, pound, 49¢. Frankfurts, skinless, pound, 55¢. Ground beef, pound, 45¢. Pork chops, center cut, pound, 59¢. Swordfish, pound, 69¢. Turkey, 16-18 pounds, per pound, 45¢.

**Food:** Various: Bread, 16-ounce loaf, 15¢. Broccoli, bunch, 29¢. Carrots, 1 pound, 10¢. Cheddar cheese, pound, 59¢. Flour, Pillsbury's Best, 25-pound bag, $1.89. Ice cream, half gallon, 69¢. Ketchup, Heinz, 14-ounce bottle, 23¢. Oranges, California navel, 5 pounds, 59¢. Potatoes, 50-pound bag, $1.39. Raisin bread, 1-pound loaf, 23.

**Fuel:** Cord of hardwood cut for stove, $20. Outboard motor oil, quart, 40¢.

**Furniture:** Serta Posture mattress, springs, headboard, four-piece set, $99.95 (mattress alone, $44.88).

**Lodging:** Double room with double bed in lodging house, per day $8, week $50.

**Real Estate:** Cottage: New, 3 bedrooms; Lake Winnipesaukee, 250′ frontage, two sandy beaches, $16,500. Cottage: Two-stories, to be removed from site in Pleasant Valley, $2,000. House: Three bedrooms, with garage, at the corner of North Main Street and Keewaydin Road, $14,000. House: Two-bedrooms, water frontage, $11,000. Winnipesaukee shore frontage, per front foot, $35 and up. Mobile home, 10 x 50 feet, $6,000.

**Restaurant food:** Smorgasbörd at the Huggins Hospital Street Fair, lobster salad, cold turkey and ham, casseroles, hot rolls, desserts, and beverages, $2.

**Tools:** McCulloch chain saw, One/40 model, $154.95. Stanley saber saw, $44.95.

**Toys:** High-Flier paper kite, 10¢. Ping pong table with legs, $22.50.

**Transportation:** Bus ticket from Wolfeboro to Portsmouth, one way, $2.20, Boston $3.80, New York $10.55, Washington, DC, $17.05 (each plus tax).

**Trucks:** Dump truck, Chevrolet, with three-yard dump body, $4,800. Volkswagen pickup truck, $1,980.

# CHAPTER 9
# WOLFEBORO 1961-1970

*It is indeed a pleasure to write of our wonderful vacation taken this year (for the first time) in the Wolfeboro and Mirror Lake area of New Hampshire.... We were most courteously greeted and treated well in Wolfeboro, by the merchants in their stores, by the Wolfeboro chief of police, by other vacationers, by everybody. Much congratulations are in order for the cleanliness and beautiful appearance of the downtown area of Wolfeboro itself. Yes, we had a wonderful vacation in Wolfeboro this year and will return in future years.*

– *Granite State News,* July 28, 1961. Letter from Bill Jones, WIBG Radio, Lafayette Hill, PA.

## INTRODUCTION

The decade of the 1960s was characterized by social changes including widespread domestic resistance to government policies in the Vietnam War from about 1965 onward. On the home front, rising prices were a concern. Meanwhile, growth continued in Wolfeboro, including the development of more real estate tracts than in any 10-year period before or since.

## POLITICS AND VIETNAM

### Prelude to War

In 1961 National Guard Battery D of Wolfeboro was reorganized as Service Battery D, 1st Howitzer Battalion, 197th Artillery, and assumed the ordnance functions previously carried out from the Laconia Armory. First Lieutenant Curtis A. Pike was commander.

In the early 1960s fallout shelters were the order of the day, as there was a perceived threat of atomic attack from Russia. In addition, North Korea, North Vietnam, Laos, and Cuba were solidly Communist, and recently Cambodia had become Communist as well, not to overlook numerous Communist Bloc countries in Europe. By the autumn of 1964 two local public shelters had been stocked with food and supplies. The Wolfeboro National Bank had a capacity for 167 during an emergency, and the Wolfeboro Post Office could accommodate 54. Presumably, other citizens were well advised to take advantage of loans advertised by the bank for the construction of home shelters.

At the end of October 1962 the so-called Cuban crisis – which involved the confrontation of Russia and the United States over Russia stocking Cuba with missiles – caused nationwide concern. Local churches held prayer vigils and were kept heated and open around the clock.

On November 22, 1963, President John Fitzgerald Kennedy was assassinated in Dallas, TX. The *Granite State News* told of the tragedy's effect locally:[1]

> Shock and sorrow were the emotional common denominators of all people during this past tragic weekend.... A hush settled over Wolfeboro's business community Friday afternoon, as most people deserted the streets to stay close to their radios and televisions.... The usual friendly exchanges of smiles and hellos were conspicuously absent from the trickle of traffic at the Wolfeboro Post Office. Shortly after 3:00 the stillness was broken when schools were dismissed and the youngsters made their way along the streets discussing in shrill, excited voices the news which their teachers had given them....
>
> All stores were closed all or part of the day on Monday in keeping with the national day of mourning proclaimed by President Lyndon Johnson. Schools were also closed. Attendance figures compiled from Wolfeboro and Tuftonboro churches showed that approximately 1,500 people worshipped on Sunday morning. All clergymen reported a higher than normal attendance....

### Senator Goldwater in Wolfeboro

On Thursday, January 23, 1964, Senator Barry Goldwater, a contender for the Republican nomination for president of the United States, visited town. At the Town Hall the candidate, Mrs. Goldwater, and Sen. Norris Cotton were greeted by an estimated 500 well-wishers.

Sen. Goldwater gave his views on such topics as the possible Communist threat to the Panama Canal, admitting Red China to the United Nations, and the situation with Cuba. In an interview with local theatre operator Paul R. Hatch, Goldwater told of his interest in ham radio. On hand were representatives from city newspapers, *Newsweek*, NBC, ABC, CBS, and even the British Broadcasting System. Howard K. Smith, ABC-TV news commentator, made a filmed report while on the sidewalk on South Main Street between the Bovaird and Avery houses (second and third houses east of Town Park) and interviewed hardware store owner Joe Bradley as a typical citizen.

When the presidential primary was held on March 10, Wolfeboro gave Goldwater 160 votes, Nelson Rockefeller 92, Richard M. Nixon 135, and Henry Cabot Lodge 288. In the same election Wolfeboro supported the statewide acceptance of the lottery sweepstakes with 272 yes votes and 229 opposed.[2]

### The Vietnam War

In 1964 serious involvement of the United States in the Vietnam War began with the Tonkin Resolution passed by Congress on August 7, following an alleged attack on two U.S. destroyers by North Vietnam vessels. Within the year, American troops by the tens of thousands had been sent to South Vietnam. On August 6, 1965, an editorial in the *Granite State News* commented:

> In South Vietnam Uncle Sam finds himself in a predicament similar to that of a pig caught in a hole in a fence—he isn't getting ahead, and he can't very well back out. Certainly, this Vietnam business is getting worse by the hour. Defeat has followed defeat in policy and in the field. There is something wrong somewhere....

In Wolfeboro and elsewhere in America, citizens were perplexed. It was Korea all over again. There were no clearly defined objectives, no goals for either civilians or the military. Various politicians campaigned for the war, or against it, with equal fervor. Congress was hardly united on the subject. Were we at war with the Vietnamese people, were we at war with China (who some thought was backing Vietnam), or what were we doing? No one was really sure.

By the end of 1965 a number of Wolfeboro citizens were serving in Vietnam. However, unlike the situation a quarter century earlier in World War II, there were no campaigns, rallies, or special support for them on the home front. Meanwhile, soldiers on the front were dying. On February 4, 1966, the paper printed this from Tim Morrill of North Chichester:

> We are constantly looking for the peaceful way out and are refusing our boys the weapons and strategy that is needed to win. To allow American boys to die, without taking every possible means to prevent it, is immoral. I wonder how our mothers are told that their sons have died at the hands of those who a few well-placed bombs would have incapacitated. If we want to win, why aren't we bombing Hanoi and strategic power plants and levees in North Vietnam? Isn't it about time the president told us that we are going to win?[3]

### Politics in 1967 and 1968

During the first week of July, 1967, Governor George Romney of Michigan spent four days as the guest of Mr. and Mrs. J. Willard Marriott at their home on Tuftonboro Neck, where a public reception was held to advance Romney's ambition to be the candidate for president on the Republican ticket. Crews from CBS and ABC news, *Time* magazine, the *Washington Post*, the *Boston Globe*, the *New York Times*, and other media were lodged in 20 rooms at the Lake Motel on South Main Street. Further:

> Two of the Bailey dining rooms have been converted to newsrooms where telephones and typewriters have been busy round the clock since Romney arrived. Allan Bailey comments that the day and night activity of the nationwide communications center is a sharp contrast to the usual relaxing and leisurely atmosphere of a vacation resort.

Louis Wyman, Wolfeboro's congressman, was in town on October 27, 1967, to share his opinions, noting that the federal fiscal crisis, the Vietnam War, and crime were the three major concerns of his constituents. Wyman gave his view on Vietnam:

> Congress itself is not involved in Vietnam, as you know. This [the branch actually involved] is the executive branch of the government.... I do not think it is fair or right to ask the boys to go over there and fight to die, or to be shot at, if you are not doing everything to destroy both the enemies that are shooting at them and the materiel and the supplies that are reaching the enemy. We are not doing this and have not done this ever since this foolish, intolerable war started, and it's a shame.

At home in the United States, young people, potential draftees in particular, felt that they were being swept up in a situation beyond their control. While there were no demonstrations or civil disturbances locally, there were numerous discussions, including one held at Brewster Academy in January 1968 by First Sergeant John T. Oliver. The speaker, a Vietnam veteran, said, "I have laid my life on the line many times for this flag of ours. I don't appreciate people who go around burning it, and neither does any other soldier."

While soldiers and most citizens continued to honor the flag, the Vietnam struggle continued to divide America. The local paper carried this talk given on February 5, 1968, by a visitor to town (who stayed at the Lakeview Inn):

> William W. Evans, Jr., Republican presidential candidate in the coming primary election, strongly advocated the United States disengage itself from the Vietnam conflict when he spoke Tuesday evening to the Wolfeboro Rotary Club. The Paterson, New Jersey, trial lawyer was the first announced Republican candidate for the New Hampshire primaries and was a supporter of Nixon in 1960 and Goldwater in 1964.

In the November 1968 election, Wolfeboro voters cast 1,226 ballots for the Republican candidates for president and vice president, Richard M. Nixon and Spiro T. Agnew, and just 328 for Democrats Hubert H. Humphrey and Edmund S. Muskie. George C. Wallace and S. Marvin Griffin came in a distant third with 40 votes. By this time, 1.5 million American troops were in Vietnam.[4]

CONSERVATIVES
REPUBLICANS
and
DEMOCRATS
WE CAN CLIMB TO NEW HEIGHTS ABOVE THE POLLUTION OF POWER POLITICS
STAND HIGH FOR YOUR PRINCIPLES
VOTE YOUR CONVICTIONS
VOTE THE AMERICAN PARTY CHOICE
TV
Thursday Oct. 22 Channel 9 9-9:15 p.m.
Friday Oct. 23 Channel 9 8-8:15 p.m.
Saturday Oct. 24 Channel 9 7-7:15 p.m.
Saturday Oct. 24 Channel 8 11:15-11:30 p.m.
RADIO
Thursday Oct. 22 WGIR Manchester 6:30 p.m.
Monday Oct. 26 WKXL Concord 8:40 a.m.
Monday Oct. 26 WSMN Nashua 6:30 p.m.
Tuesday Oct. 27 WKBR Manchester 6:30 p.m.
Wednesday Oct. 28 WGIR Manchester 9:20 a.m.
Thursday Oct. 29 WKXL Concord 7:35 p.m.
Friday Oct. 30 WKBK Keene 8:30 a.m.
VOTE - MEL THOMSON X
FOR GOVERNOR
Send Contributions to: Henry C. Waldo, Lincoln, N. H., Fiscal Agent

October 22, 1970, *Granite State News* advertisement advancing the gubernatorial candidacy of Meldrim Thomson of Orford. His 1970 campaign and his earlier 1968 effort were both unsuccessful, but he was the winner in 1972, 1974, and 1976. At one time he considered running for the United States presidency. Thomson had a special connection with Wolfeboro after his son Robb married local girl Andrea Flagg (daughter of Calvin and Verna Flagg, owners of the Nordic Skier) on July 26, 1975.

### Decade's End

In October 1969 the Wolfeboro Chapter of the American Red Cross shipped 100 "ditty bags," each filled with $3 worth of Christmas gifts, to boys in service in Vietnam. This was one of the few local manifestations of support for war troops. In the following month, the American Citizens Fund placed a large advertisement in the *Granite State News,* addressed "Dear Mr. President," stating that the chief executive should choose between two alternatives and either:

> (A) Win the war in Vietnam by all appropriate and necessary means generally accepted among nations at war including blockade of enemies and destruction of industrial facilities, or
>
> (B) Get our men out of Vietnam without further procrastination and delay.

However, the war went on and on, without any announcement of definite goals or policies.

In May 1970 Meldrim Thomson, Jr., of Orford, NH, was guest speaker at the Rotary Club meeting held at the First Congregational Church. Thomson had unsuccessfully sought the Republic gubernatorial nomination in 1968 and again in 1970, but was determined to be heard. He discussed campus disorders all over America, noting that law and order must prevail, that the "hullaballo about infringement of free speech" and the "desperate beating of drums by the Civil Liberties Union" should be ignored, and that so-called radicals such as Abie Hoffman should not be permitted to speak to student audiences at state centers of learning. In response to a question as to the desirability of having an income or sales tax in New Hampshire, Thomson replied that he was not in favor of either and noted that in neighboring Vermont the imposition of a sales tax had done nothing to reduce real estate taxes.

In August of the same year the editor of the *Granite State News* commented as follows:[5]

> The three years of the Kennedy administration completely reversed the gloomy climate [of former presidential terms], and laughter swept the country—laughter *with* the president, not *at* him.... And now we're in the '70's, but right back in the 50's. Any attempt at humor by Nixon comes out like cooked apples going through a sieve, forced and strained. End-man Spiro [Agnew] adds some comic relief, but most of our officialdom seems afraid to acknowledge humor—they represent the people—the people of that certainly silent non laughing majority.

## LOCAL BUSINESS AND TRENDS

### Trading Stamps

During the early years of the 1960s many local merchants joined in the nationwide fad of issuing trading stamps. Although S&H (Sperry & Hutchinson) Green Stamps were seen here and there around town as early as the 1890s, in the 1961-1963 era merchant and consumer interest became especially widespread. Soon the old-time S&H stamps were joined by such brands as Gold Bond, Top Value, MacDonald Plaid, and Discount stamps. A local grocery store's advertisement was headlined, "What's a Diamond Bracelet doing in the A&P?" and showed jewels among the groceries, with this text:

> Diamond bracelet? Oh, you get 'em when you shop at A&P, along with the bread and bananas. Of course, you've got to save Plaid Stamps—quite a few. Perhaps you would rather save for something more practical. Plaid Stamps offer you...3,076 gifts to choose from.

By mid-1963 one could obtain trading stamps at restaurants, grocery stores, gas stations, and just about every other type of business. However, trading stamps then began to fizzle, as they no longer offered a competitive advantage or sales incentive. On July 22, 1968, A&P discontinued them.[6]

### Credit Cards

Purchases were nearly always made on the spot with cash or check, although some stores kept monthly accounts for established customers. By decade's end, the consumer credit card had gained a small toehold. First to advertise was MasterCharge (name later changed to MasterCard), billed as "the interbank card." Acceptance by local merchants was slow in coming, as the card issuers charged a fee to sellers.

The editor of the *Granite State News* did not have a charge card, if this September 11, 1969, commentary is an indication:

> We may be old-fashioned, but frankly we don't like the way the banks across the nation are going into the credit card business. If you're on a list, you probably received a letter from your bank saying you'll soon be receiving a credit card, and then the letter goes on to extol the joys that will come to you with credit spending....

In 1970 Diamond National, a lumber and building supply company located in Wolfeboro Falls, advertised it was accepting MasterCharge as well as Uni-Card and was one of the first Wolfeboro businesses to do so.

### Should Wolfeboro Join Megalopolis?

The Malone Knitting Company, which had been active in Wolfeboro since 1942, had 15 men and 75 women on its payroll in 1961 and occupied the town-owned Bell Shop on Factory Street. Soon thereafter, operations were moved to River Street, followed by a return to Factory Street. In 1967 management transferred most work to the firm's Statesville, SC, plant, where wages were even lower than the modest rates paid to Wolfeboro workers. What remained of the firm locally was put in charge of Mrs. Ida Z. Biehl, who changed the name to the Biehl Manufacturing Co., an enterprise that proved short-lived. Meanwhile, Theodore Malone, who had been associated with Malone Knitting for many years, formed a new company, the Wolfeboro Products Corporation.

In 1963 the other town-owned factory building on Lehner Street—the Clark Shop—was deeded to the Albee Moving & Storage Company for the sum of $1. This put the structure back on the tax rolls and ended the town's continuing frustration in keeping the premises occupied.[7]

In May 1965 there was some enthusiasm when it was stated that the Guttman-Kesslen Shoe Manufacturing Co. might establish a branch here. However, Farmington was selected as the site instead.[8]

Opinion on the industrialization of Wolfeboro was divided, and numerous old-time residents who had witnessed a long series of futile efforts felt that the town was fine just as it was. On the other hand, the local Chamber of Commerce continued to insist that more manufacturing industries in Wolfeboro would mean great prosperity. On May 26, 1967, an editorial titled "Let's Leave 'Megalopolis' Where It Is" told of a seminar held by the federal Small Business Administration in Concord, which was attended by many businessmen who eagerly greeted the news that Megalopolis—the great East Coast industrial complex—now extended from Portland, ME, to Richmond, VA. However, the writer of the editorial, A.H. Chapman, was not a believer:

> The implication was that efforts should be made to extend this unbroken belt of feverish activity up to the north country.... Now it is suggested that the great East Coast industrial complex is bursting at its seams and must expand into the north country for pure lack of any other place to go. It is further suggested that this was good luck for us.

The writer said that if this were done we would soon be on a collision course between industrial expansion and Wolfeboro's current recreational business and high quality of life. Indeed, numerous citizens had come to Wolfeboro specifically to avoid industry they had experienced in "Megalopolis" and elsewhere—and valued Wolfeboro for its quiet, tree-shaded streets, its relative lack of major crime, its beautiful lakes and hills, and non-industrial surroundings. All throughout the twentieth century, these opposing forces met repeatedly in town meetings, in the pages of the *Granite State News,* and elsewhere.

The town-owned Bell Shop found a new tenant in 1969 when Techcraft set up business to make plastic packaging material, padding for football practice machines, and pontoons.[9] In 1970 there was a flurry of excitement in certain quarters when Mrs. Rita Giniewicz of Tyngsboro, MA, treasurer and general manager of Hampshire Enterprise, proposed to set up a clothing manufacturing business in vacant quarters in the mill on River Street. This was accomplished in the same year and was called Hewd Manufacturing Company.[10]

**Business Notes**

In the early 1960s the poultry business was prospering in Wolfeboro although not at the levels seen in the 1930s and 1940s. The 1963 town inventory noted there were 10,000 fowl. As had been the case for many years, local operations ranged from a dozen or two birds to thousands.

In 1963 Harry Hopewell and Douglas Parsons began developing Wentworth Meadows, a tract on Route 28 that in April 1964 became the site of Parsons Furniture, which moved from its long-time quarters in Town Hall to a new showroom of "rustic design."

In 1965 and 1966, following a spate of vandalism, a number of security services sprang up in addition to the long-established Camp Patrol operated by the Bullock family. Norman and Don French advertised "reliable camp patrolling," and Ralph J. Herbert was in the business, as was S. Michael Hickey (Winter Watch).

Inflation was rampant during the decade. In the autumn of 1966 Ernest Roberge, Jr., carpenter and the father of three, organized a demonstration against rising food prices, to take place at noon, Friday, November 4, in front of the First National and A&P grocery stores. Fifty protesters showed up, some with signs such as JUST THE MILK, NOT THE COW and STAMP OUT STAMPS—the latter referring to trading stamps which increased the cost of doing business. A related editorial in the *Granite State News* written by A.H. Chapman suggested that throwing Democrats out of office and replacing them with Republicans would solve the problem.

In March 1967 Gile's Dairy Products announced that it had withdrawn milk and other items from the local A&P store, explaining:

> We feel that this is necessary because the retail price charged on Gile's Dairy gallons sold through this store was 6¢ above prices charged by other stores in this area. We...were not responsible for the retail price.

The March 10, 1967, issue of the newspaper was filled with advertisements from hopefuls seeking local offices. This humorous advertisement appeared in another context: "Vote for Paul Kimball at Hillside Lumber for Plywood Commissioner of Carroll County. I promise to give you the best value on all plywood sold."

In 1970 a business tax was passed by the State Legislature. Although the deadline for filing for most firms was November 15, only about a third of New Hampshire enterprises responded by that time.[11]

By decade's end, T-shirts displaying advertisements, political sentiments, and ecology commentaries were popular sales items in local stores. Bumper stickers were likewise purchased in large quantities.

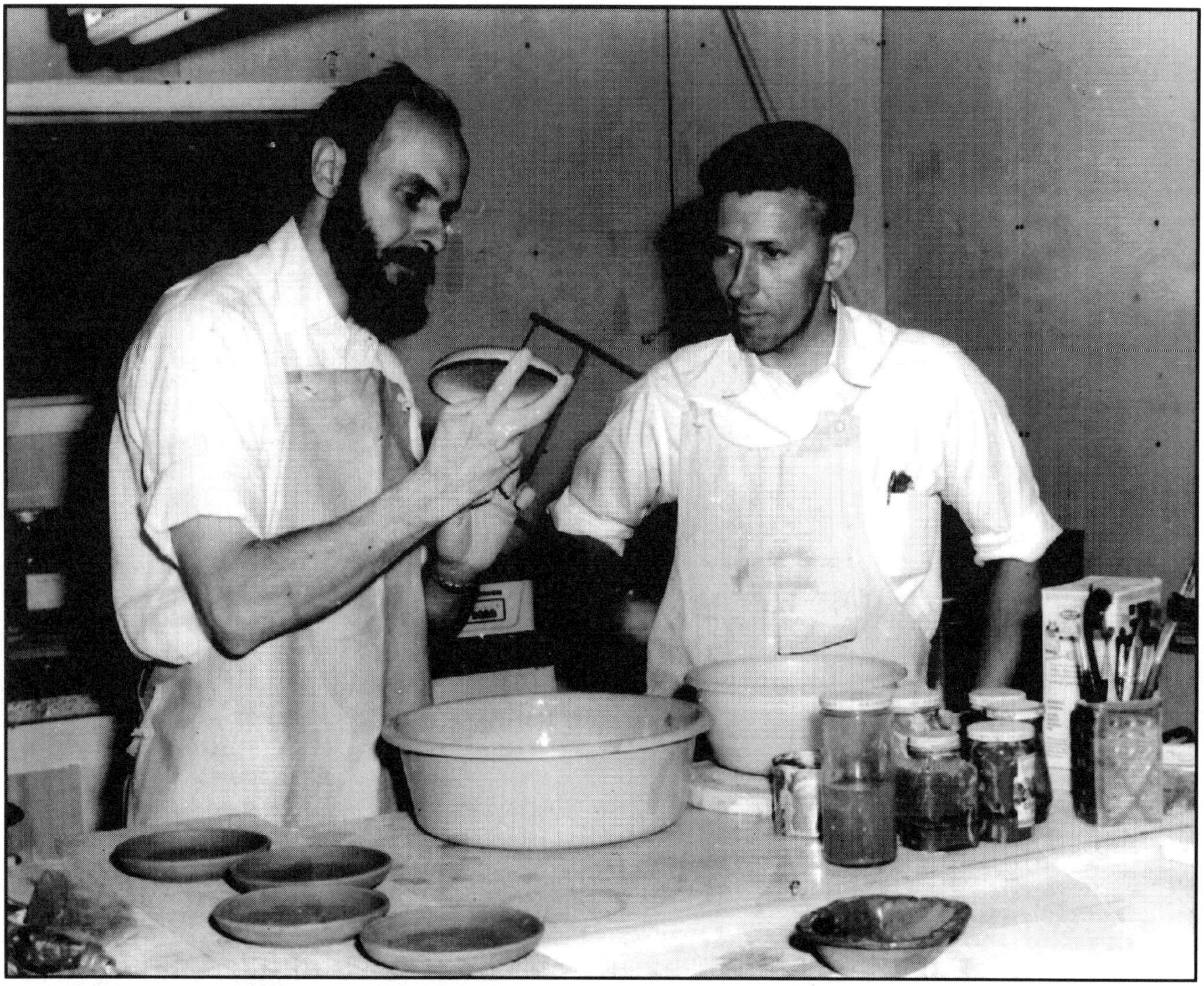

Instructor John P. Emery (left) of Springvale, Maine, inspects the work of his Wolfeboro student Nelson R. Glidden. In 1961 Glidden opened a pottery shop in his residence on South Main Street, Wolfeboro, and sold hand-made items including bowls, platters, and ashtrays. Some of his products were offered through the League of New Hampshire Craftsmen shops. (Jack Bickford photograph)

## PLACES TO STAY, THINGS TO DO

### Tourism Thrives

Tourism remained strong each summer season, despite ups and downs in the national economy. Local accommodations often were filled during the height of the season in July and August. In 1961 from July 4 through Labor Day, 8,338 visitors to town were assisted by Mrs. Catherine Ford and Mrs. Isabel Shipman at the Information Booth on the edge of the Brewster Academy campus at Pickering Corner on South Main Street. Records showed that 32 states were represented including Massachusetts (2,319 tourists), followed by New York (926), Connecticut (658), New Jersey (525), Pennsylvania (299), and Rhode Island (237).

Wolfeboro hospitality received many accolades from visitors, including when an out-of-stater saw a sign displayed at the Sunoco station on North Main Street, reading "You are welcome to turn in this driveway." The tourist remarked, "Imagine that! The first time in all my travels."[12]

### Stopping Places

In the mid-1960s the Allen "A" Resort on Route 28 and Point Breeze on Lake Wentworth were the two main destinations for tourists who desired to rent cabins and spend a week or two in town. Various smaller accommodations also offered pleasant stays. On North Main Street the Colonial Arms, Wolfeboro Inn, Lakeview Inn, Clearwater Lodges, and Piping Rock Lodges were popular during the summer season, as were the Berry Motel on Center Street and the Lake Motel on South Main Street. Ample lodging for transients resulted in town businesses having a steady turnover of new faces eager to spend their money at restaurants, antique shops, gift stores, clothiers, and other stores.

In 1966 there were numerous restaurants and snack bars from which to choose.[13] Warren's Delicatessen (Frederick C. Warren) in the Wolfeboro Shopping Center specialized in submarine sandwiches. The Bubble, in a small wooden shed attached to the Railroad Avenue side of the Bank Building and also operated by Warren, likewise offered sandwiches. In the following year, The Bubble was run by the Moore Brothers, farmers in Pleasant Valley, who offered home-grown fruit and vegetables.

The Pirates' Den at the end of Lake Street advertised "Fine food and fine music at low, low prices," with dancing on Wednesdays, Fridays and Saturdays during the summer. Patrons could come by foot, car, or boat.

The Barn Dining Room at the Colonial Arms on North Main Street was popular, and the Rotary Club had its dinner meetings there. Owner Rhea Colburn had the facility on the market for several years at an asking price of $125,000, and in 1967 it would be sold.[14]

The Wolfeboro Inn on North Main Street, owned by Paul and Mary McBride, was becoming exceptionally popular in view of its attentive management and excellent menu. Recently, the Redcoat Lounge had been opened at the General Wolfe Inn & Motel. Also in vogue was the Liberty Room at the Lakeview Inn.

Bailey's Restaurant on South Main Street continued to attract crowds. The municipally-owned Dockside Restaurant at the Town Wharf was likewise popular. Operators of Dockside during the decade included Philip Stevens and Richard White, the former at one time associated with the Lakeview Inn, and the latter a well-known local restaurateur since the 1940s.

Helmer and Mary Leppanen of Malden, MA, purchased the Open Door Restaurant from Don and Lillian Brookes in August 1966. This popular eatery was located on Center Street in the area that would later be known as Clarke Plaza.

The Bittersweet Restaurant out on Route 28 featured The Inn Lounge, advertised as "the most unusual antiquated place beknown!" and had been recently restored from a rather decrepit condition. Years earlier it was known as the Goldthwaite Manor.

In South Wolfeboro near the top of the hill on the way to Alton was Nelson's Hilltop Drive-In Restaurant, "featuring Mrs. Nelson's famous pizza, 27 varieties," as well as fried chicken, clams, scallops and other specialties.

### Cottages and Cottagers

The many cottage owners around the shores and islands of lakes Wentworth and Winnipesaukee added to the vacation atmosphere. In 1961 "choice island lots only a six-minute boat ride to Wolfeboro" were offered for sale by local realtor C.M. Mixer. "These are on Melody (sometimes known as Varney) Island. This island of nearly 18 acres and more than 4,000 feet of shore frontage on Winnipesaukee commands an unsurpassed view of the lake and its mountains...." This was the second of the two large Wolfeboro islands (Keniston was developed c.1899) in Lake Winnipesaukee to be subdivided.

In August 1964 *Popular Boating* magazine featured an article written by Ned Bullock about cruising on Lake Winnipesaukee. A number of local businesses were mentioned, including the Pirates' Den, Northeast Marina, and Goodhue & Hawkins.

Among the visitors to town in the 1960s was the wife of the leader of Nationalist China, whose government was exiled on Formosa (Taiwan). Gertrude B. Hamm wrote this in a retrospective on events of 1965: "Madame Chiang Kai-Shek and her daughter-in-law, film star Debra Paget, slipped in and out of Wolfeboro almost without notice." While in Wolfeboro, Mme. Kai-Shek stayed at the former Helen Hopewell residence on Tips

**Local snapshots:**

Otto Pecunies, well-known local boat builder, practicing his craft.

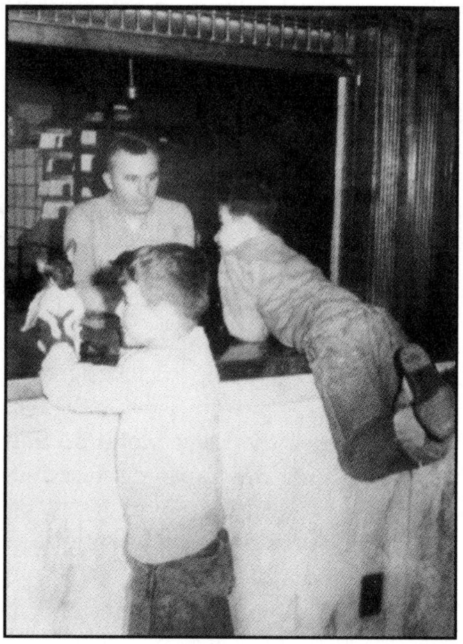

Fred Bierweiler behind the window counter at the Wolfeboro Post Office window with two young patrons.

Colorful local character Sampson Bickford, who used to spend much time in the downtown district. (Photographs by Ned Bullock, circa 1960s; Gloria and Ned Bullock Collection)

Cove on Wolfeboro Neck, an area later (in the 1980s) subdivided as Embassy Estates.[15] The August 1, 1968, number of the *Granite State News* printed a photograph of Debra Paget getting a lesson from Paul R. Hatch, operator of the Memorial Theatre, in the operation of an antique hand-cranked 1904 Power's Cameragraph film projector, a part of his display of old-time movie artifacts.[16] It was noted that Paget was "spending part of each summer at her home on Lake Winnipesaukee."

### Two New Museums

Two new museums opened during the decade and joined the Early American Living Museum (at Clark Park) and the Libby Museum as local attractions.

The William Brewster Museum made its debut on May 17, 1962, in the Brewster Academy Gymnasium. Featured was a collection of stuffed birds indigenous to New Hampshire formed by William Brewster, a well-known ornithologist of his day and one of the original Brewster Academy trustees.

On July 2, 1966, a private attraction—The Big W Wolfeboro-Winnipesaukee Outboard Motor Museum—opened its doors in a section of the Hilltop Restaurant on top of Old Perk (Perkins Hill) close to the Alton town line. A commentary noted:

> In the collection are shown such motors as the 1907 Waterman (the oldest), the 1912 Joymotor, 1913 Gray Gearless, 1914 Evinrude, 1914 Koban, 1915 Caille, 1919 Johnson bicycle motor, 1922 Johnson outboard, and many others. The museum is under the direction of Dr. John W. Hunt, practicing dentist in Sanford, Maine, and a summer resident in Wolfeboro for 24 years. His youngest son, Jeffrey, a student, is assisting him.... There is a small admission charge.

Financing was provided in part by local investors, who had been offered a 10% or more return on money "in a speculative venture with good prospects."

In 1967 the collection's name was shortened to The Big W Outboard Motor Museum and relocated to the second floor of the newly-built Kingswood Marina at the end of Endicott Street. To assure that boaters in Wolfeboro Bay would not overlook it, a zoning variance was sought to erect a sign 26 feet wide on the roof. In 1969 the museum was in still another location, in part of David McGee's auto shop and junkyard on Route 28 in North Wolfeboro.[17]

### The Libby Museum

The Libby Museum retained its popularity, with about 5,000 to 7,000 signing the guest book each summer. In 1964 an art show featuring 54 works by 15 artists drew additional visitors who might not have come otherwise to the nature and history displays.[18] During the decade several regional artists gave lessons *in situ* for a fee. In 1966 the building was repainted inside and out. Attractions that year included 87 works by 20 different artists. Jackson H. Emery served as director for much of the decade.

In 1968 the selectmen disclosed that the dock in front of the Libby Museum had been constructed at a time when there was a strong need for a facility for visitors who came by boat, but when funds were not available. A nearby landowner with no frontage on Lake Winnipesaukee made an arrangement with the selectmen to erect a dock with the express provision that the "north side of the dock would be for the landowner's exclusive use, while the south side would be used exclusively for the use of museum visitors arriving by boat."

In 1970 the bicentennial of the town of Wolfeboro was celebrated, but activities were not as numerous as in 1959 when local citizens observed the bicentennial of the 1759 land grant. In 1970 special commemorative medals made of bronze, silver, gold-filled metal, and gold were offered for sale by the Chamber of Commerce and the Wolfeboro National Bank. One side showed the steamer *Lady of the Lake* at dock in town in the 19th century, and the reverse showed a view of Lake Winnipesaukee. Lead proof impressions and a framed copy of the original design were given to the Libby Museum.[19]

## REPORTING THE NEWS

### Transition

Beginning in 1961 and continuing through 1964, Alan N. Pope, owner of an advertising agency in Concord, was a columnist in the *Granite State News*. In 1964 he put his hat in the ring for the gubernatorial nomination but soon withdrew it in view of the demands placed upon him by his business. Years later in the 1990s Pope wrote editorials for the *Wolfeboro Times* (name changed to *Lakes Region Courier* in 1994).

On April 18, 1964, Parker McLauthlin Merrow, longtime co-owner of the newspaper, died following emergency surgery. Born in Malden, MA, October 9, 1903, Merrow graduated from Dartmouth in 1925, and in 1927 married Grace Wooley of Malden. He moved to Ossipee, where he became prominent in many areas, including as judge of the Ossipee Municipal Court. He was survived by his wife and two children, Lyford A. Merrow II of Center Ossipee and Ann Merrow Burghardt (Mrs. Jacob J. Burghardt) of Athens, Greece.

In May attorney Richard F. Cooper, executor of the Merrow estate, and Ralph G. Carpenter II, co-owner of the *Granite State News* (and also of the *Carroll County Independent*), announced that the newspapers would be continued. Mrs. Gloria Bullock, who had edited the *News* for several years, would be managing editor of the *Granite State News* and editorial assistant for the *Carroll County Independent*. Meanwhile, her husband Ned was the pre-eminent local photographer as well as operator of the Camp Patrol security service. For news shots, Polaroid cameras with ultra-fast film had been used since 1960.

### Short Takes

In 1964 as in earlier years it was nearly always the practice of the *Granite State News* to identify women by their husbands' names. For example, the general chairman of Huggins Hospital Street Fair was identified as Mrs. Lloyd Thomas and co-chairmen as Mrs. John Lillis and Mrs. Harold Morse. The secretary was Mrs. Harry Hopewell, and the treasurer was Mrs. John W. McDermott, and so on.

John Noyes and A.H. Chapman of Ossipee wrote most of the editorials in 1965 and 1966. Mrs. Gertrude B. Hamm, who had worked with the paper for more than 35 years and who had been responsible for numerous local news, business, and social notes, passed away on August 5, 1967. Her successor in compiling local items was Helen L. Fetzer.

On August 1, 1966, Dr. Walter Bowman, summer resident of Lake Wentworth, presented a program to the Wolfeboro Historical Society about the history of the *Granite State News.*

On August 1, 1969, "Glo" Bullock, who had been with the newspaper since 1957, resigned in order to help her husband in his businesses. She was replaced by Mrs. Norman (Jeanne) Tempest of Alton, a journalism major in college and mother of eight children, who had been employed formerly by the West Haven, CT, *Town Courier* and the *New Haven Journal.* Mrs. Tempest was assisted in her new Wolfeboro post by Mrs. Norman (Constance, known as Connie) Hale. Jacob J. Burghardt of Ossipee—son-in-law of the late Parker Merrow—was editor and owner. Mrs. Tempest remained until November 1970, when she moved to Somersworth, where her husband was employed by the school district. (Years later in the 1990s she was to become editor of the *Granite State News.*) Connie Hale was her successor.[20]

Effective with the January 29, 1970 issue, the newspaper was redesigned, with new headline type, with the first line of certain articles in boldface type to explain the content, and other innovations.

Amidst disturbing national and international news of war, drugs, increasing crime, and more, the *Granite State News* always had space for local events, such as in the issue of November 26, 1970: "Dog Wanders Away While on Walk," a 14-line story about a German shepherd that had been lost the preceding Monday and hadn't been seen since.

## ENTERTAINMENT

### Hobbies and Crafts Popular

The 1960s saw a boom in hobbies. The number of enthusiasts collecting rare coins and stamps multiplied. Wolfeboro pharmacist Louis A. Soucey, owner of Tobey's Drug Store, published buying prices for gold coins and other items in the *Granite State News.* Tobey's had special sales departments devoted to coins and stamps. Responding to the interest, in 1968 the local paper had a syndicated column, "Heads N' Tails," by Dick Sullivan, who discussed various aspects of rare coins.

Collecting old bottles was another area of interest, and for a time the Bencliff Bottle Shop did business in town. Numerous 1967 and 1968 issues of the *Granite State News* carried information about regional bottle clubs and growing interest in excavating old pieces of glass.

Arts and crafts were very popular, and up and down North and South Main Streets and on Railroad Avenue, several shops catered to the interest, including The Retired Bovine leather goods shop, which a year after its opening changed its name to Schillereff's Bovine. The Governor Wentworth Arts Council had its beginnings by staging exhibitions on the grounds of Brewster Academy.

In 1967 the Hobby Craft Shop was set up in the former Arts and Crafts Building near the Town Docks. Featured were items made by retired senior citizens. Russell C. Chase, a former executive of Shell Oil who had recently moved to town, was named business manager.[21] In 1969 the shop moved to the Wolfeborough Railroad Station. From selling home-made candy at this store, "Rus" Chase developed a thriving seasonal business called Oh Fudge.

### Television

The 1960s represented the first full decade in which children in Wolfeboro grew up with television in their homes. In 1970 it was noted that the average American child watched the screen from 15 to 20 hours a week and saw an act of violence on the average of every 14 minutes. Whether this "desensitized" them and offered unfavorable role models was a matter of debate which has continued ever since.[22]

Meanwhile, hobbies, board games, reading, and other activities continued their popularity.

### Paul R. Hatch

Throughout the period, the Memorial Theatre conducted on the second floor of the Town Hall continued to be a popular gathering place. Paul R. Hatch, who had purchased the enterprise from the heirs of Ansel N. Sanborn on January 1, 1959, maintained the policy of bringing a varied program to town, including first-run films.[23]

The new Hatch Theatre opened on May 1, 1970, on Depot Street to the right of the Wolfeborough Railroad Station. The first film shown was *Funny Girl,* starring Barbra Streisand, through May 4th, followed by *Bob & Carol & Ted & Alice* with Natalie Wood and Robert Culp. Coming attractions included *Cactus Flower* (Goldie

Movie actress Debra Paget, who summered in town on Wolfeboro Neck, is shown with Paul R. Hatch, operator of the Memorial Theatre. In the foreground is an antique 1904 Power's Cameragraph projector made in New York by Nicholas Power. (*Granite State News* photograph, August 1, 1968; Paul R. Hatch Collection)

Mother and daughter act: In February 1961 Miss Freda ("Keli") Smith (seated) was crowned queen of the Lions Club Winter Carnival. She later became Mrs. Kenneth Douglass.

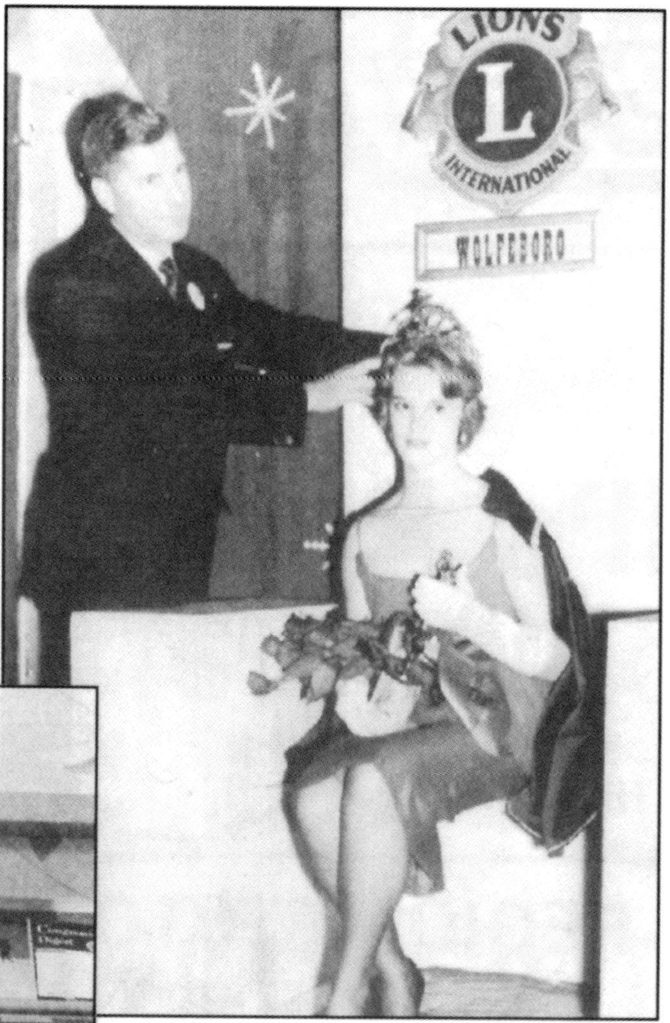

In February 1979 her daughter Jennifer Douglass (standing with ribbon, photograph taken in the Wolfeboro Public Library) was crowned queen of the same event. (Lions Club program photographs)

Hawn and Walter Matthau), *Marooned* (Gregory Peck), *Butch Cassidy* (Paul Newman), *On Her Majesty's Secret Service, Airport,* and *Topaz.*

A newspaper account told of the facility:[24]

> The new theatre was built with an accent on patron comfort. In the previous Hatch theatre [in the Town Hall] seats were 29 inches back to back. The new theatre features seats which are 36 inches back to back with a special section spaced 41 inches back to back for extra tall people. The interior decor of the theatre is of colonial design. The walls and carpeting are done in shades of blue and red, and accents are wrought iron and milk glass. Mr. Hatch intends to continue to present a program geared to family entertainment.

Facilities included a lobby area (with box office and concession stand), restrooms, and a projection room. The facade of the theatre was of brick. Proprietor Hatch hoped to keep the theatre open on a five-day schedule from Wednesday through Sunday during autumn and winter months. Capacity was 350 patrons, as compared to 385 in the Town Hall facilities.[25]

### WASR Radio

The town's radio station, WASR, AM 1420 on the dial, sunrise to sunset, had its inception in 1967, when Alan Severy conducted a local survey and determined that there would be an enthusiastic audience. A corporation was formed in 1969 with Alan Severy as president and treasurer, Sharon J. Severy as vice president, and Mildred A. Beach as clerk. On Sunday, April 5, 1970, at 11:09 a.m., WASR (for "Wolfeboro All Seasons Radio") signed on. For a time, it operated just three hours a day to test the facilities, with formal broadcasting starting on Saturday, April 11, at 6:30 a.m.

The first broadcast personalities were Don McMaster (Music with McMaster Show), Del Olney (Del-O-Show with "finger-snapping, familiar tunes"), and Ron McArthur (Sounds of the Seventies). It fell to Alan Severy to handle most of the news, weather, and special features, while his wife Sharon was sales and office manager. Rick Davis handled the afternoon news and was station engineer.

Initially, the power was 1,000 watts, increased as years went by to 2,500 and then to 5,000. Over the years Alan and Sharon Severy were to receive many honors.[26]

### In and Around Town

The following listing is a cross-section of the varied entertainment and amusement items of the decade. Some events were yearly, the Huggins Hospital Street Fair and the Independence Day parade being but two examples. Many other entertainments were one-of-a-kind.

**1961, February 2-4. Winter Carnival:** Sponsored by the Lions Club. The first such event held in a number of years. Governor Wesley Powell attended. Miss Freda ("Keli") Smith was the carnival queen. She had been a registered nurse in her native town of Glen and had moved to Wolfeboro the preceding autumn to accept a position at Huggins Hospital.[27]

**1961, April 8. Stage play:** Brewster seniors presented *The Many Loves of Dobie Gillis,* featuring the talents of Joyce E. Brown, John Coyne, Emery Trowbridge, Dorothy Johnson, Tony Leitner, James R. Wales, Betsy Fernald, Mary Ann Leavitt, Rick Hale, Donna Wagenfeld, and others.

**1961, May 5. Interesting advertisement:** "Rumor: Contrary to current popular opinion, John J. Hoppin wishes to announce that he has NOT taken on the bonds of matrimony. (As a matter of fact, he would hate to disappoint all the lovely ladies in Wolfeboro)."

**1961, May 20. 11th Anniversary Military Ball:** By the local National Guard unit. American Legion Hall. Music by Gordon Dunkley & the Pick Ups.

**1961, June 30-July 1. Film and music:** Memorial Hall. *The Big Show* with Esther Williams, Cliff Robertson, and David Nelson was featured. "Plus extra added attraction at theatre—at 6:30 to 7. *Big Show* music played on the big Allen 'A' calliope. Come early!"

**1961, July 26. King Brothers Circus:** On Brewster Field under canvas.

**1962, April 7-8. Film:** Memorial Theatre. *Blue Hawaii,* with Elvis Presley.

**1962, April. The twist:** The latest dance fad. At least two movies of the month featured "twist" in their titles.

**1962, July. Antique shows:** July 12: Antique sale held at Clark Park under the auspices of the Wolfeboro Historical Society. July 11-14, at the Brewster Gym, the Ninth Annual Wolfeboro Antiques Fair & Sale was held under the private sponsorship of E.M.C. French.

**1962, July 6. Local films:** Advertisement: "*The Story of Winter in Wolfeboro* in a one-half-hour color movie. The film takes you from the season's first snowstorm through watching the ice go out of the lake and includes skiing, skating, fishing, and the Lions Club Winter Carnival. This is a film of special entertainment to resort guests. Cost for the program is only $10. Contact Ned Bullock." This was one of three local films produced by this well-known photographer.

**1963, April 5-6. "Kissing" film:** *Splendor in the Grass,* with Natalie Wood and Warren Beatty. "Adult entertainment. No one under 16 will be admitted unless accompanied by an adult!... Whether you live in a small town the way they do, or a city, maybe this has happened to you right now—maybe (if you are older) you remember when suddenly the kissing isn't a kid's game anymore. Suddenly it's wide-eyed, scary and dangerous!"

**1963, July 6. Sells & Gray Circus:** Brewster field. Under the auspices of the Lions Club. 50 artists and performers, giant menagerie.

**1963, August 13. Concert:** New Hampshire Festival Symphony Orchestra drew a large crowd.

**1963, August 31. Rock dance:** Twist & Shout! Dance featuring The Crossfires (Strand recording artists). Masonic Temple.

**1963, November 9. Hawaiian Night:** Sponsored by the Catholic Youth Organization. American Legion Hall. Singing, skits, pantomime, refreshments.[28]

**1963, December 21. Movies while parents shop:** *The Snow Queen* at the Memorial Theatre, tickets free to children. Sponsored by local merchants.

**1964, February 1. Record hop:** At Brewster Gymnasium, sponsored by the Wolfeboro Lions Club. David Maynard of WBZ Radio in Boston was disc jockey.

**1964, January 31 to February 2. Winter Carnival:** Angela

The Lions Club Winter Carnival, February 2-4, 1962.

Top of page: Banner across South Main Street with Pickering Corner in the distance.

Middle: Ice skating on the Brewster Academy soccer field; First Congregational Church and Town Hall in the background.

Bottom: Happy kids being towed by a Polaris Sno Traveler snowmobile. (E. Crawford photographs; Ted Brigden Collection)

Piper was named Carnival Queen. Activities included carnival ball (400 attended), ski races, sled dog races, girls' basketball, travelogue film, sports car racing on ice in Wolfeboro Bay, skating races, and a hockey game. Dr. and Mrs. W. Douglas Kipp and their children, Nancy and Jonathan, won a prize for their snow sculpture of an Olympic torch.[29]

**1964, August 7-8. 27th annual Huggins Hospital Street Fair:** Included balloons, beano games, books, candy, children's games, rides, Christmas booth, chuck-a-luck gambling, clothes, home-cooked food sale, ice cream and tonics, popcorn, refreshments, barbecue, smorgasbörd, garden booth, grabs, hats, handicrafts, jewelry, major prize drawing, pet show, pony rides, punchboards, white elephants, country store, toy booth, Huggins Hospital booth, and makeup booth. The general chairman was Mrs. Lloyd Thomas, and the co-chairmen were Mrs. John Lillis and Mrs. Harold Morse.[30]

**1964, August 17. Concert:** The Festival Symphony presented a string quartet program for the Amy Cheney Beach Club at the First Christian Church.[31]

**1964, September 11. Folk music record:** Announced that "an album of Wolfeboro folk music featuring the Rye Cove Singers" was planned. "The tapes were made at Monday night hootenannies held this summer at the Music & Sound Center." The Rye Cove Singers were from out of town. The album, titled *Wolfeboro Folk Sing,* was released in January and featured a jacket designed by local artist David MacKinnon with photography by Ned Bullock.[32]

**1965, January 16. Beach party film:** *Bikini Beach,* with Frankie Avalon, Annette Funicello, Little Stevie Wonder, The Pyramids, The Exciters, Keenan Wynn, and others. Also Tom & Jerry cartoon. Memorial Theatre.

**1965, March 19-20. Stage play:** *The Miracle Worker* at Kingswood Regional High School. Carol Dunn played the role of the young teacher Anne Sullivan, and Ruth Woodworth took the part of Helen Keller.

**1965, summer. Too much entertainment on Lake Street:** The South Market Street Jazz Band of San Diego was contracted to play Dixieland jazz all summer long at the Pirates' Den, a restaurant at the end of Lake Street owned by Lawrence V. Grover, a Californian. What started as innocent fun developed into a *cause célèbre.* On August 20 neighbors and other citizens packed the Wolfeboro District Court to vent their displeasure at the ruckus said to last up to three o' clock in the morning. Patrons of the Pirates' Den were described as acting in an obscene manner in view of neighbors. Alleged offenses included abusive language, drunkenness, trespassing, and frequent incidents of urinating on nearby lawns. In one instance when a house owner asked a urinating man to get off his property, the reveler smashed his front door. Among the complainants were such well-known citizens as Dr. Ralph Adams, Ernest Bainton, Mr. and Mrs. John Dickinson, Mrs. Howard Avery, Mrs. Harold Morse, Mrs. James E. Bovaird, and Mrs. E.W. Carr. "Mr. Grover's attorney, Frederic L. Cox, suggested that those who disliked the Den might buy it out, setting a figure of $135,000...." There were more charges and counter-charges. The affair became a stand-off, and in 1966, Grover reopened what he billed as "The action spot of Wolfeboro." After closing on September 4, 1966, the facility was sold to Leonard Adrien, who operated it in a more peaceful manner.[33]

**1965, July 2-5. Film:** *Goldfinger,* with Sean Connery. Memorial Theatre.

**1965, July 17. Teen dance:** Featuring The Vistas. Brewster Gymnasium..

**1965, July 20. N.H. Music Festival Symphony Orchestra concert:** First of three programs of the season. The first number played was Brahms' *Fourth Symphony.* Kingswood High School Auditorium.

**1965, December. Money exhibit:** The Federal Reserve Bank of Boston had an exhibit in the lobby of the Wolfeboro National Bank. John W. McDermott, vice president, explained details of the display to numerous local students and other visitors.[34]

**1966, March 10-11. Theatre organist:** George Epstein, who had been playing silent film and vaudeville accompaniment on the piano and organ since 1916 including in such popular New York City theatres as the Rialto, Rivoli, Criterion, Capitol, and Roxy, appeared at the Music & Sound Center and entertained about 300 listeners on an electronic organ. Selections ranged from Rossini's *William Tell Overture* (billed as the Lone Ranger theme song), to Grofé's *Grand Canyon Suite,* to the title song from *Hello, Dolly!*[35]

**1966, July 30. Dance:** Music by the Luv Lace Lads. Brewster Gym. Sponsored by the Wolfeboro Water Ski Club.

**1966, August 4-6. Huggins Hospital Street Fair:** Grossed over $25,500, a record.

**1966, August 30. Rotary Club clam bake:** Held at Camp Wyanoke on Wolfeboro Neck. Brad and Edna Bentley, hosts.

**1966, December 17. Christmas party for children:** American Legion Hall.

**1966, December 31. New Year's Eve party:** Wolfeboro Masonic Temple. Organizers included Cy Moody, Ken Douglass, and Joseph Long.

**1967, February 3-5. Winter Carnival:** This year's event was held at the Copple Crown Ski Area which had opened in New Durham in December 1965. Events staged there included a record hop, night skiing, races, and a torchlight parade. Carnival queen was Jane Glidden. "A talented seamstress as well as a pretty young lady, Janie made the stunning blue and white velvet gown she wore to the ball. Before a record attendance of nearly 500 people, Queen Janie was presented with a trophy and a bouquet of roses. The crown was placed upon her head by beautiful Bette Hutchins, queen of the 1966 Winter Carnival. Queen Janie, a member of the junior class at Kingswood, was escorted by Walter Goes of Chicago, a student at Brewster Academy."[36]

**1967, March 3. Ace Gorham, magician:** Sponsored by the Wolfeboro Rotary Club. Kingswood Auditorium.

**1967, March 17-18. Stage play:** *Brigadoon,* at Kingswood Auditorium, staged by students. Players included Roger Tice, Jim Merrill, Kristen Jones, Steve Dow, Steve Hale, Lynn Parsons, Lee Hale, and Nancy Hodgdon.[37]

**1967, April 7. Talent show:** Sponsored by the Rotary Club. Featured 16 acts at the Kingswood Auditorium. The winners were the Back Bay Singers, a trio composed of Kirk Titus, Carol Sprague, and John Whiting. "The folk singing group combined Kirk's versatility on guitar and harmonica, Carol's fine voice, and John's polished guitar playing to win the $100 savings bond presented by Rotary president Willard Whiting."[38]

**1967, April 9. Dog show:** Brewster Academy Gym. American Kennel Club sanctioned match sponsored by the Carroll County Kennel Club.

**1967, May 27. New Hampshire Bandstand:** Traveling show brought to Wolfeboro by the Lions Club. Featured five musical groups including The Morning After and the Come Tomorrows (all-girl folk group including Diane Dickinson, Carolyn Bowe, and Alex McFarlane) from town. Brewster Gym.

**1967, July 1. Teen dance:** At Nelson's Hilltop Restaurant. Music live by The Trolls.[39]

Barbara Titus (left) presents a trophy to Angela Piper, crowned Winter Carnival queen in 1964. (Jack Bickford photograph)

**1967, August 6. Old cars:** NH chapter of the Antique Car Club, on tour, stopped Sunday morning at about 10:45, parked in the A&P lot, and walked to the Town Docks to watch the *Mount Washington* arrive and depart.[40]

**1967, December 8-9. Stage play:** *The Diary of Anne Frank.* Kingswood students. Marianne Gooding was Anne Frank, Barbara Quimby played her mother, and Kim Roundy took the role of her father.

**1967, December 9. Stage play:** *Waiting for Godot.* Brewster Academy Drama Club.

**1968, January 20. Barber Shop quartette concert:** Kingswood Auditorium. Sponsored by the Wolfeboro Police Department in cooperation with the West Ossipee Fire Department.

**1968, April 22: Local writer's novel screened:** At the Memorial Theatre the Warner Brothers film, *The Double Man,* based on the book *The Legacy of a Spy,* by Wolfeboro entrepreneur and real estate agent Henry S. Maxfield, had a special preview showing before its regular opening at the Orpheum Theatre in Boston on May 8. The picture starred Yul Brynner, Britt Eklund, and Clive Revill. After the preview, guests went to the Wolfeboro Inn to talk with author Maxfield and have copies of his book autographed. It was reported that his second novel, *A Country Affair,* dealing with a small New Hampshire town, had been completed, but not released for publication. Meanwhile, he was completing a sequel to *The Legacy of a Spy,* and was working on another book involving Air Force desertion in World War II.[41]

**1968, May 31. Wolfeboro Rotary Club Talent Show:** Kingswood Auditorium. Bradford Jackson, folk singer-guitarist, took first prize by performing *All Around Blues, Unicorn,* and *Meadowland.* Second prize went to the Back Bay Singers. Third place went to the Come Tomorrows.

**1968, July 4. Book of poetry published:** "The Village Press of Wolfeboro has completed a book by Dorothy Louise Brown entitled *Out of My Heart,* a collection of 100 poems. Half of the poems included were written by Mrs. Brown.... [who] works as bookkeeper at the Country Smokehouse in Wolfeboro."

**1968, July. Autograph party:** *Northwater,* a new novel by Cecily Crowe of Tuftonboro, was to be available at the Camelot Bookstore in Wolfeboro after July 8, with an autograph party to follow. "I haven't named a specific town or even state for the location of the story, but I am sure that both will be recognizable to anyone who lives in Wolfeboro," the author stated.

**1968, July 15-16. Governor Wentworth Art Festival:** 45 exhibitors set up on the Brewster Academy soccer field.[42] This was the forerunner of what would become known as the Artists in the Park event.

**1968, August 25. Carillon concert:** First Christian Church. Given by Paul Bartholomew of Pennsylvania, who worked with the firm that installed the instrument.

**1968, November 1. Cate Lecture Fund program:** Stanton Waterman, famous underwater photographer, told of his techniques. Made possible by the bequest of Edward Cate (who also endowed Cate Park).

**1968, November 1. Film ratings:** Effective this date, the Motion Picture Association of America instituted a voluntary national film rating program with G (general audiences), M (mature audiences), R (restricted—persons under 18 not admitted unless accompanied by a parent or adult guardian), and X (persons under 16 not admitted). Subsequent local film advertisements carried this information.

**1968, December 13-14. Stage play:** *Bad Seed.* Kingswood Auditorium. Players included Merry Lester, Monica Breedlove, Laura Kennard, David Tibbetts, Betsy Fahlman, Janet Waldron, Bob McKenzie, David Rines, Marshall Hewitt, Phil Valley, Bob Buehler, and Chip Albee. Lyn Parsons was student director and Bonnie Hylander was house manager.

**1969, January 18. Baked bean supper:** Carpenter School.

**1969, March 15. Musical entertainment:** "Not Quite a Coffee House" was the name of a regular get-together at the Wolfeboro Grange Hall featuring "live folk entertainment." A non-profit venture intended as a gathering spot for teenagers and others, with no alcohol served.

**1969, April 23-24. Stage play:** *Peter Pan* presented by students at Carpenter School. Players included Susan Reade, Scott Titus, Jeff Newcomb, Denise Burnham, Cindy Rouleau, Billy Todesco, Madison Toms, Tinker Curtis, and Diane Poisson, among others.

**1970, January 24. Musical review:** Sixth Annual Carnival of Harmony, Kingswood Auditorium.

**1970, April 22-23. Stage play:** *Tom Sawyer,* by Carpenter School students. Tom was played by Mike Lovett and Becky Thatcher by Carolyn Cossette.

**1970, May 2. Clown:** Ring-A-Ding, a TV circus clown, appeared at Kingswood High School.[43]

**1970, July 14. Mozart Opera:** First of five summer concerts of the New Hampshire Music Festival.

**1970, July 18. All Saints' Episcopal Church Fair:** Luncheon: lobster $2, turkey salad $2.15. Booths, attractions, etc. Annual event.

**1970, August 22. Rodeo:** At Allen "A" Resort featuring Tom Bishop's Fabulous Four B Ranch Rodeo and Wild West Show. $2 admission.[44]

**1970, October 24. United Nations Day:** Buffet and dance at the Masonic Temple, with proceeds to UNICEF.[45]

**1970, October 30. Hallowe'en party:** Hatch Theatre. Sponsored by the Rotary Club, Lions Club, and many merchants. 350 children attended.[46]

**1970, December 11-12. Stage play:** *The Spiral Staircase,* presented by Kingswood High School students. Players included Cindy Curdo, Dorothy McGuire, Vicky Hansen, Caroline Carpenter, David Tibbetts, John Quimby, Phil Valley, Charlene Dubel, and Marshall Hewitt. Ray Lord was the director.[47]

## RECREATION AND SPORTS

### On the Field

Throughout the decade, baseball was one of the most popular field sports, especially for children and young adults. In the spring of 1967 the lineup for the Major League division of the Wolfeboro Little League included the following teams: Allen "A," Black's Panthers, Market Basket, Varney's, Bankers, Legion Cubs, Albee Movers, and White's Construction.

The new (opened autumn 1964) Kingswood Regional High School organized a girls' field hockey team in 1966, which finished its first season undefeated. Participants included Susan Miliner, Patsy Hersey, co-captains Linda Smith and Polly Stimpson, Susan Zulauf, Holly Swaffield, Jill Spates, Andy Flagg, Mardi Mixer, Karen Erickson, Mary Croteau, Judy and Susan Thurrell, Nancy Hodges, Barbara Montieth, Mary Hunter, Judy Cardinal, Patty Bean, and Natalie Peterson (coach).

In 1961 the Brewster Academy football team had an excellent season following a shaky start. Scores (Brewster listed first) and competitors were: Bridgton (14-14), Phillips Exeter (6-7), Cheshire (14-13), Dartmouth Frosh "B" Team (32-0), Bowdoin Frosh (32-0), Bridgton (41-18), University of Massachusetts Frosh (28-7), Harvard Frosh "B" (14-0), for a total of 181 points for the Brewster team during the season in contrast to just 59 for their opponents.

In October 1964 Kingswood High fielded its first football team—the Knights—under Captain Ken Jones, coached by Paul Fairfield, Phil Decelle, and Ed Tetreault. The first match resulted in a victory for the Plymouth Bobcats.

In November 1966 the Brewster Academy varsity football squad (the Bobcats) ended the season undefeated with 6 wins, 0 losses, and 1 tie. Brewster racked up 182 points against 96 by its opponents. Competing teams included Berwick, New Hampton, Winchendon, Hebron, Kent's Hill, Proctor, and Tilton academies. Coaches and members of the local squad included Neal Abeles (coach), Fred Alford, Clifford Ambrose, Ross Army, Jeffrey Berry, Robert Black, David Boyajian, Robert Carnes, Richard Cullen, James Demetri, Roger DiStefano, John Eberhart, Steven Fremont-Smith, Patterson Gannett, David Golden, J. Goyette, Frank Harris, Paul Hogan, Paul Jernberg, Richard MacKenzie, Edward Mantenuto, John Mercer, Robert Richardson, Jeffrey Ross, John Schoenrock, Carl Schweinshaut, David Siegel, Stephen Smith, John Staples (coach), Robert Tarbell, Jeffrey Wingate, James Wright (head coach), Harry Wright, and Bruce Wyatt. Leading scorer was Cliff Ambrose with 8 touchdowns and 4 extra points.[48]

The Brewster Academy soccer team also played many notable games during the decade.

### On the Links

The Kingswood Golf Club continued its popularity throughout the decade. Frequent accounts of activities there appeared in the local paper including this item dated August 31, 1962 (excerpt):

> Jim Pollini Wins Championship at Kingswood: Playing some of the finest golf that has been seen in this area in a long time, Jim Pollini defeated his son Dave in the final 36-hole match of the Men's Championship at Kingswood on Saturday, August 25.... There was only a one stroke difference between father and son in total medal play as Jim scored 72 and 74, and Dave scored 74 and 73. It was indeed a very fine contest.

On September 1, 1963, Ralph Stinchfield, owner of the local Market Basket grocery, claimed the $500 prize on a special 125-yard hole to win the club's hole-in-one contest.[49]

### Tennis, Anyone?

In 1968 Jack Corbin and Henry S. Maxfield offered to refurbish two clay tennis courts owned by the Kingswood Golf Club. Others involved included Alan Skelley and George Walker. Subsequently, the Wolfeboro Racquet Club was formed and signed a 10-year lease with the golf club, renewable for an additional 10 years. "The club hopes to make tennis even more popular in Wolfeboro and to promote the game at its most recreational and competitive levels." Courts were made available to the public at $4 per hour, and lessons were $8 per hour. In 1988 at the expiration of the 20-year lease, the courts were bulldozed; this action spawned a new three-court facility built behind Parsons' Furniture on Route 28 on 3.1 acres of land donated by Henry and Betty Maxfield; today this is known as the Wolfeboro Tennis Club.

Don Brookes, director of recreation for the town of Wolfeboro, announced the formation of the Junior Tennis Association. In the summer of 1970 boys and girls ages 10 through 18 played on the Brewster Academy courts.[50]

### Indoor Sports

In the 1962-1963 winter season, the Brewster Academy junior varsity basketball team was undefeated. Opponents included North Yarmouth, Kennett, Laconia, New Hampton, Bridgton, Hebron, and Berwick. High scorers included Dennis Appleby (average 23.7 points per game), Bob Penney (11.2), Woody Elliott (8.6), Terry Tewksbury (5.7), Tad Hale (4.7), and B. Dore (4.3).

On September 18, 1965, Richard S. and Marge Clarke opened a candlepin bowling alley on Center Street in what would later be known as Clarke Plaza. Designated PJ Lanes, the facility was named in memory of the Clarkes' daughter, Pamela Jean, a victim of cystic fibrosis. During the decade, Mr. and Mrs. Clarke did much to advance local fund-raising to help with research on the affliction. Included were airplane rides at the strip operated by Merwin and Eleanor Horn on Wolfeboro Neck.

Bowling had been absent in town since the Wolfeboro Casino closed in January 1959. In the interim, most local bowlers had pursued the sport at Strikers Haven in Melvin Village. By 1967 PJ Lanes was firmly established as a local entertainment spot with several leagues and numerous teams. Anyone who got three strikes in a row earned a special award, as the feat was very difficult with candlepins. The facility was continued through the mid-1980s, by which time it was known as Fuller's.[51]

### On the Lakes

On July 7 and 8, 1962, the New England Open Water Ski Tournament sponsored by the Wolfeboro Water Ski Club was held on Rust Pond in connection with the statewide Thirteen Hundred Lakes Festival promotion.

**Independence Day parade, 1964. View down South Main Street toward the main business district.**

Headquarters were at Rust Pond Cottages. Many other competitions were held throughout the era.

In July 1962 a picture of a red and white dive flag under the title "What Is It?" appeared in the local paper. Readers were informed that this identified a diver below the surface. Scuba diving was becoming an increasingly popular sport on Lake Winnipesaukee, and many enthusiasts were taking part.

On August 2, 1964, about 500 people were on hand in Wolfeboro Bay to welcome Harry Briggs, a college professor from Alaska, at the end of his 25-hour and 25-minute, 22-mile swim from Centre Harbor.

Boating on lakes Wentworth and Winnipesaukee continued its popularity. The Kingswood Boat Club, founded on June 23, 1966, was organized by Herb Sommers, Dick Sommers, and Charlie French for the purpose of enjoying cruising and sailing on the lake.

On November 11, 1966, a 62-foot racing shell donated by the Dartmouth College Athletic Council was delivered to Brewster Academy, the first eight-man shell ever used locally.

The Sea-Doo aquascooter, a new water craft by Bombardier, Canadian maker of Ski-Doo snowmobiles, achieved popularity in 1969 and was described as having a speed of up to 35 miles per hour and to be "virtually untippable."[52]

### Fishing and Hunting

In April 1961 George C. Waugh, owner of a section of Willey's Brook in East Wolfeboro, under authority of the Fish and Game Department, consented to allow his stream to be:

> open on a trial basis to New Hampshire smelt fishermen who would like the enjoyment of fishing...under the following conditions:
> 1. No fires.
> 2. No drunken brawls or fights.
> 3. No unnecessary loud noise and swearing after 8:00 p.m.
> 4. No throwing empty bottles and trash in the brook or on the property....

During a typical night in 1961 about 200 fishermen responded to the invitation and lined the banks of Willey and Tyler brooks. In 1962 it was noted concerning Willey Brook that:

> Hundreds of fishermen have crowded the brook night after night.... This year the Wolfeboro Lions Club is also on hand with their snack wagon and hot dogs, coffee, and hot cocoa for the fishermen. As usual, local police were directing traffic while the conservation officers kept an eye on the number of fish taken by the smelters.

On May 18, 1964, thousands of salmon were dropped by plane from a height of about 75 feet into Lake Winnipesaukee. This was the first time that salmon had been stocked aerially there, although aircraft had been used to drop trout in remote ponds in the state since 1947.

Hunting of deer and other game in season continued to be a popular local sport. Moose, hitherto rare in Carroll County, increased in number, although they could not be legally hunted. The fine for doing so was up to $300. It was estimated that several dozen moose roamed the local woods.[53]

### Skiing at Abenaki

During the 1960s the Abenaki Ski Slope (also called the Wolfeboro Town Ski Slope) continued to be well patronized, so much so that in February 1964 the Parks and Recreation Department noted that beginning the next December, only town *taxpayers* would be allowed to use it. Left unresolved was how people renting properties would fare or how children would fit in. This ignited a far-ranging controversy in which people in Tuftonboro in particular became upset at insinuations that Wolfeboro did not want to provide facilities for them. Writing in the *Granite State News,* Ned Bullock suggested that Tuftonboro, for example, build its own facilities; otherwise, Wolfeboro people would be crowded out of the Abenaki slope. As the situation became more tense he suggested that the two towns should work out a mutually agreeable arrangement. In the interim, Tuftonboro students and citizens, excluded from Abenaki, finished out the season at the Mt. Whittier ski area.

The contretemps was concluded at the end of March by this statement from Mr. and Mrs. Carroll Hersey:

> As owners of the ski slope land in Wolfeboro we would like to make a statement concerning the future of this recreation area. This land is and has been made available for use by Tuftonboro and Wolfeboro children. We cannot approve any other use or arrangement....

In December 1964 new policies were announced including these:

> In case of overcrowding, adults from towns other than Wolfeboro will be asked to leave the slope. If the slope is still crowded, Wolfeboro adults will be asked to stop skiing. Finally, if there are too many children on the slope to ski safely, the manager will have to stop the tow. The schools of this area have agreed to cooperate in the plan to organize skiing programs so they will not interfere with individual skiing....

In early 1966, other popular skiing facilities included the Copple Crown, Moose Mountain, and Mt. Whittier slopes out of town. The abundance of slopes served to multiply the number of those interested in the sport and, contrary to expectations, put even greater pressure upon the Abenaki area. Don Brookes managed the Abenaki slope during the last part of the decade.

On February 9 and 10, 1968, the Kingswood Boys Ski Team (the Knights) won the State B-3 chamionship for the third consecutive year. Competition to the local lads included Inter-Lakes, Groveton, Gorham, Lisbon, Plymouth, and Newfound Lake schools. Scorers for Kingswood included William Swaffield, Larry Riley,

Glenn Roundy, John and William Stockman, Roland LaPlante, Albert Dow, Richard LaPlante, Bruce Van Dyke, and James Huston.[54]

### Snowmobiling

The second most publicized winter sport of the 1960s was snowmobiling. A December 28, 1962, announcement that Bradley's Hardware was a local dealer included this statement:

> The Ski-Doo and its prototypes are vehicles that allow the operator a safe way to travel or play over snow with considerable zest. As they have heavy endless rubber and steel tracks they can climb over hill and dale at speeds around 25 miles per hour, carrying several passengers and towing loads on a toboggan.... For the hot rod and the go-kart enthusiast, the Ski-Doo makes winter snow an exciting playground, whether it be a joy ride, casual trip through the woods, or a fast wild race.

The February 1963 Winter Carnival featured a half-dozen snowmobiles provided by Bradley's:

> Everyone will have an opportunity to ride on a Ski-Doo to see how it feels to forget about getting stuck in the snow and just skim over the lake, through the woods, and over snow-covered fields. [Joe Bradley] reports that if there is a lull in the Carnival activities, action will spring up quickly as drivers of the Ski-Doos stage impromptu races on Wolfeboro Bay.

In the winter of 1964-1965 Northeast Marina featured the Arctic Cat snowmobile. At Shore Acres on Chase Point in Tuftonboro, Russ Whitten acquired the Ski-Doo dealership and had a display at the Wolfeboro Shopping Center after Bradley's picked up the Moto-Ski line. Thomas Chain Saw & Marine of Melvin Village offered the 14-h.p. Evinrude Snow Skeeter that could go 30 to 40 miles per hour. In March 1967 the General Wolfe Inn (in the 1990s known as the Windrifter) had a snowmobile outing with trail riding followed by "warming up" at the inn. The Lions Club sponsored the first Lakes Region Championship Snowmobile Race as part of that year's Winter Carnival.

On December 5, 1967, the Wolfeboro Snowmobile Club, Inc., was formed and had as its objective safe and enjoyable snowmobiling. On January 25-26, 1969, the New Hampshire snowmobile championships were hosted by the local club. An estimated 3,500 people were on hand to watch Bob Fortin of Lancaster earn the first "Wolfeboro Cup." In 1969 new snowmobiles typically cost from about $750 to $1,500 and had engines from about 12 to 30 h.p. On February 21-22, 1970, the second annual state championships were held on an elliptical track at Kingswood Regional High School. In December of the same year, the *Granite State News* ran an editorial on the sport, noting that it was extremely popular, but that there had been many complaints about excessive speed, loud noise, and late-night operation. "Safety commandments" were listed.[55]

## GOINGS ON AROUND TOWN

### Town Government

For the first several years of the decade, the town continued to operate its own school system, as it had for well over a century. There was relatively little public interest in the financial aspects of education. In January 1961 two public hearings were held for public input on plans and appropriations, and in each instance just one person was in the audience. In 1963-1964 the Governor Wentworth Regional School District assumed control of area schools including those in Wolfeboro.

The 1961 annual town meeting treated the subject of revising the manner in which the town was governed. As the town grew in population, it was realized that full-time professional management might be preferable to having most work and major decisions made by the selectmen who were often too busy with other duties to devote extensive time to the town. The vote to change the present system was 339 no and 280 yes. Years later, at the March 10, 1970, annual town meeting, 546 voted yes for a change to the town manager system, and 203 were opposed. The system became effective as of the 1971 town meeting.

On July 22, 1961, the Chamber of Commerce conducted the first Summer Town Meeting. "The purpose of such a gathering is to give the non-resident taxpayer an opportunity to express his views...." Although no voting would or could take place, it was anticipated that non-residents could be asked to suggest articles for the town warrant, and town officials would be on hand to answer questions. At the time, out-of-towners paid about half of the taxes collected by Wolfeboro. The event was a success, and in some later years, additional summer meetings were held. In November 1970, of the 2,568 property tax bills mailed, 1,236 went to non-residents (48% of the total), and the actual amount of dollars billed to non-residents came to 44% of the total. Reflecting upon this, the selectmen, Gerald F. Briggeman, John G. Metcalf, and Raymond F. Pollini, commented:

> These friends of Wolfeboro do not send their children to our schools. We do not have to plow any of the roads they use for their summer homes. Their stay in town on the average is less than 20% of the year. They do not come to town meeting and if they did, the law does not permit them to vote. However, they place many dollars in our business economy. Let's face the facts, they make a major financial contribution to Wolfeboro for which we should all be grateful.

At the March 1964 annual town meeting, Wolfeboro residents voted that sweepstakes tickets could be sold locally.[56]

### Town Areas, Facilities, and Zoning

In 1961 docks accommodating 32 small boats were built on Back Bay near the Wolfeborough Railroad Sta-

Auctioneer Robert Thurrell stands before a microphone and tries to find a new home for a rail-back chair (missing two rails) at a charity auction sponsored by the Rotary Club, circa 1960s. Thurrell (1891-1981), for years a highly successful poultry breeder on Cotton Mountain and moderator at town meetings, made handicrafts in the final years of his life.

tion (which at the time was called the Wolfeboro Youth Center, a focal point for scout groups, club meetings, and other gatherings).

Causing quite a stir in 1962 and 1963 was the practice by Cotton Mountain Farm of dumping quantities of dead birds and "unusable hatching eggs" at the town dump, after which numerous of the eggs would hatch, chicks would run around the town dump and would be eaten by rats or otherwise killed. It was intended that such eggs be covered by dirt, but this could not be done because the egg farm truck arrived after the hours town employees were on duty. Dr. Lawrence S. Toms, selectman for many years, recalled:[57]

> The hatching trays were dumped every 21 days, usually on a Thursday evening. People would go to the dump and collect the chicks and raise them for the pot or for their eggs. Quite a few people built up small flocks. Later the Thurrells (leading poultry raisers located on Cotton Mountain) buried the eggs on their farm.

During the era there were several town dumps, including one behind the Wolfeboro Shopping Center, the Wakefield Pit Dump (and Area C near it), and the Pine Hill Dump. By decade's end, facilities had been consolidated into a single facility, the Hyde Hill Dump.

By 1963 nearly all of the stately elms that once arched North and South Main Streets and certain other areas had fallen victim to Dutch elm disease. By the end of April, 50 Norway maple trees had been planted at a cost of $7 each, under the direction of town tree warden W. Fred Tuttle. Many more trees were planned.

On July 1, 1963, the postal zip code system went into effect. "Postmaster Bernard Landman reported that Wolfeboro's zip code will be 03894. The Wolfeboro Falls digits will be 03896, according to postmaster Reginald Stevens."

In 1964 town-owned or operated facilities for public recreation included the Town Docks, Carry Beach, Brewster Beach (leased from Brewster Academy for $1 per year, later raised to $2), Cate Park, Pleasant Valley Park, Rust Park, Wolfeboro Falls Park, Abenaki Ski Area, and benches maintained on Brewster campus near the Information Booth.

In 1964 a plan to build a Route 28 bypass at decade's end was discussed. It was suggested that a limited-access highway begin at the Wolfeboro-Alton town line, swing west of South Wolfeboro, cross South Main Street near the Hale Farm, cross Pleasant Valley Road, go north of the Kingswood Regional High School between Crescent Lake and Lake Wentworth, and emerge on the existing Route 28 near Parsons Furniture.

Using the *Granite State News* and radio station WASR local realtor Henry S. Maxfield spearheaded a drive for citizens to express their views. At a meeting said to have been the largest turnout ever for a Highway Department hearing, winter and summer residents voiced fear that the bisecting of Wolfeboro by a superhighway would change the character of the town. After much discussion, the idea was eventually abandoned—at least for the time being. Even though the law was on the side of the Highway Department, it refused to buck such overwhelming public sentiment. (In 1973 the idea resurfaced; see next chapter.)

At the March 1965 annual town meeting, the most discussed item was Article X, which appropriated $5,000 in town money to add to $15,000 in federal funds to participate in Economic Development Program No. 701. By the autumn of 1969 a tremendous amount of time and money had been spent to create a 350-page report containing suggestions for Wolfeboro's future. Leonard Hubbard, chairman of the Board of Selectmen, commented that Edwards & Kelsey, the Boston firm that had compiled the report, had done a "fair job" of gathering information, but that the report offered no solutions to existing problems. Further, there were "glaring inconsistencies." Ultimately, the findings of the study were ignored.[58]

In 1966 and 1967 the town developed Back Bay Park (now known as Foss Field) behind the Wolfeboro Shopping Center in an area earlier used as a dump. New facilities included a baseball diamond and skating rink.

Following a fund-raising effort spearheaded by Dolly Bovaird and a generous donation from Mr. and Mrs. Philip Sidney Smith, Town Park, located adjacent to Cate Park on South Main Street, became a reality. Some local wags referred to it as "Cate Smith Park" for a while, *Kate* Smith being the name of a well-known singer.[59] Dedicated on August 13, 1967, the park was on land used earlier for an Esso station and before that, the Ann Inn.

In 1968 and 1969 the newspaper contained much discussion about zoning regulations. It was stated that growth was getting out of control. Part of the concern as to what might happen to Wolfeboro was sparked by the finalization in Meredith of plans for a 10-story modern apartment building complex on Meredith Bay, and a pending proposal to fill in part of Lake Winnipesaukee there. Apparently, there were no zoning regulations prohibiting this.

### Electricity and Water

Two employees of the Municipal Electric Department were injured in August 1954 when the pole on which they were working crashed to the ground. On February 28, 1963, local attorneys James Kalled and Frederic L. Cox, of Kalled, Ganem & Cox, won a verdict in court against the New England Telephone and Telegraph Co. in favor of Basil L. Read ($75,000) and Gordon E. Glidden ($30,000). The telephone company later sued the town, and Wolfeboro was held liable.

At 2:00 p.m. on September 25, 1963, the town began receiving electricity from the Public Service Company of New Hampshire transmission lines via the "high line" on a right-of-way cut through the woods from the base of the Ossipee Mountains, continuing to cross Back Bay.

In 1964 the Municipal Electric Department had 19 employees who serviced 2,435 customers, of whom 38 used electric heat. The average kilowatt hour was sold for $0.0268 and cost $0.0216 to manufacture and distribute. In the past 10 years, electricity usage in town had increased 116%. In 1965 a big flap arose when the American Telephone & Telegraph Co. proposed to build a microwave relay facility on Moody Mountain, but obtain power directly from Public Service and bypass the Municipal Electric Department. To the dismay of citizens, the Public Service Commission ruled that as Public Service had *two* customers in Wolfeboro earlier (two isolated homes on Brown's Ridge, with electricity run from Ossipee), Public Service could now impinge upon the local department's franchise.

In May 1968 the Wolfeboro paper carried news of a $150 million nuclear power generating facility to be constructed at Newington by the Public Service Company of New Hampshire and its partners, to be operational in 1974. "We know from involvement in other nuclear projects that nuclear generating plants make excellent neighbors in the community. They operate in a quiet, clean and safe manner and bring substantial economic benefits to the area in which they are located," stated William C. Tallman, Public Service president. As it turned out, the project, the site for which was changed to Seabrook in December 1968, would drag on for many years amid much controversy, fighting, financial problems, escalating costs, protests of local and area residents, and more. It was probably the most single disruptive influence to the seacoast of New Hampshire in the present century.

By March 1967 the Wolfeboro Water & Sewer Department had nearly completed its program of installing meters in local homes. Earlier, flat rates were charged depending upon the number of faucets, toilets, and other facilities.

Pollution of Lake Winnipesaukee and other water areas continued as it had for decades, although septic systems and holding basins alleviated the problem somewhat. Roger F. Murray II commented in an article in the newspaper that a number of water samples had been taken in and near Back Bay, and with the exception of a single area on Smith River above the Wolfeboro Products plant, no area was suitable for bathing. All downstream sites including the bay were heavily infested with harmful bacteria. In 1970 plans for a new municipal sewage treatment plant were announced, with 1972 scheduled as the completion date.[60]

### Dial Phones at Last

In 1963 the New England Telephone Co. announced that a new dial-system office would be erected in town and would be in service by the autumn of 1964. Wolfeboro was one of only a few remaining towns in New Hampshire in which patrons had to use an operator to place local calls. On September 20, 1964, Sunday at 7:00 a.m., "a cold impersonal dial tone will obliterate the 'number please'-ing voice of the 15 unseen friends when automation takes over." Wolfeboro numbers were given the prefix 569. The first dial call in town was made as a test four days earlier by two selectmen when Edward W. Zulauf dialed Norman Hale.

In December 1966 there were 2,800 telephones in Wolfeboro. In January 1968 the Bell System noted it was going to offer three-digit 911 emergency service in the communities it served. However, Wolfeboro nearly always lagged in telephone innovations, and it was not until *1993* that the 911 service was adopted.[61]

### Getting There

In the 1960s regularly scheduled public transportation in and out of town consisted of two daily visits by Trailways buses. The local "station" was in various locations; in 1961 at the corner of South Main and Center Streets at the Lakeview Service Station; in 1969 at PJ Lanes on Center Street. In the latter year, daily departures were at 9:54 a.m. and 5:54 p.m. One-way fare to Boston was $4.45 or, connecting to New York City, $12.

The local rail line had not been used for regular passenger service since the late 1930s. Occasionally, an excursion would be run, as on June 26, 1961, when five aluminum Buddliner cars from Haverhill, MA, pulled into the station and discharged 400 children, who walked down Railroad Avenue to the Town Docks to board the *Mount Washington*. In 1970 the Boston & Maine Railroad petitioned the state to completely abandon the line between Sanbornville and Wolfeboro, which in recent years had been used only for freight.

This appeared in the *Granite State News* in 1962:

> The helicopter that landed on Wolfeboro Bay on September 26 was a 28-passenger Sikorsky S-61 two-engined jet-powered craft. The brief Wolfeboro stop was part of a 500-mile tour of New Hampshire by Sikorsky executives and the NH Department of Resources and the Economic Development Department. The flight was designed to demonstrate the turboprop's potential for feeder air service in New Hampshire. Miss Mildred A. Beach, executive secretary of the Lakes Region Association, was...aboard.

During the decade, Merwin and Eleanor Horn continued to operate their airport on Wolfeboro Neck. In July 1966 ten students were taking flight instruction there. In the summer of 1970 the Hart Memorial Airport Development Committee sought to purchase runway lights and a beacon, the latter to be furnished with a plaque in memory of the late Harold H. Hart "whose

This Hart Motor Company advertisement in the *Carroll County Independent,* May 6, 1966, mentions several fads in its headline. Telstar II was a communications satellite. The twist dance faded in a few years, but electric toothbrushes have remained on the scene.

lifelong public service to the town, state, and New England have never been properly honored." Scrip notes were sold for $3 each to raise money.[62]

The jet age was a reality, and Wolfeboro residents were just as apt to fly to Europe or the Caribbean as to take traditional trips to New York or Boston. Similarly, many tourists who came to town in earlier years, often went to far-flung locations instead. Homes in Boston and other large cities were often equipped with air conditioning, lessening the attraction for a urban family to get away from summer heat by spending a week or two at the Allen "A" or another local lodging place. Private homes which rented rooms to vacationers became fewer in number.

### Keeping Up Appearances

In the autumn of 1965 there was much discussion as to whether the town should grant David McGee a permit to operate an automobile junkyard and salvage shop on Route 28 in North Wolfeboro. McGee won out, but was required to set up a screen of vegetation to keep scrap out of view from the main road. During the next several years, the town sought to remove hundreds of junked vehicles which littered various roads. In 1968 alone, 568 cars were taken to the Wakefield Pit Dump (off Beach Pond Road) and other sites as part of a clean-up program.

In June 1967 a group of residents signed a protest asking the selectmen to direct Dr. John H. Clow, of Lebanon, absentee owner of a structure at the corner of School and Union Streets, to clean up his property which was derelict and rubbish-strewn. The building, once "one of Wolfeboro's finest homes," was "now an apartment house [with] three families totaling 24 people, 17 of them children."[63]

### Modern Architecture

The traditional "colonial" (as it was often referred to) architecture of the town was abandoned in several large commercial projects of the late 1950s and the 1960s, starting with the Wolfeboro Shopping Center in 1958. The Wolfeboro National Bank, a two-story structure of rectangular outlines faced with Italian marble, was opened on Center Street on June 10, 1963, replacing the Bank Building facility on South Main Street in use since the institution's founding in 1906. The new "mausoleum" (as some called it) had been the brainchild of Joseph I. Melanson, Jr., bank president, until his death—ruled a suicide—on the bank premises on December, 24, 1962.

During the 1960s other examples of modern architecture, sometimes built with economy rather than appearance in mind, included the New England Telephone building on Glendon Street, Clarke Plaza on Center Street, and, in particular, the Governor Wentworth Regional High School on South Main Street. The flat roof on the last-named required frequent repairs.

### Islanders Ignored

For many years, continuing to the present time, islanders, most of whom have no voting privilege, sought better service from the town. In the *Granite State News,* September, 1, 1967, an editorial by A.H. Chapman suggested that Wolfeboro make more effort to help island residents who paid taxes year-round and who were customers of local merchants. Suggestions included providing more moorings and "perhaps even making deliveries."

The August 28, 1969, issue of the paper printed this letter signed by island residents:

> We islanders wonder if you are aware of the unfair treatment we receive from you in Wolfeboro. For our tax money, which is the same as that paid in the center of the town of Wolfeboro, we are not given the ordinary services one would expect. As we believe you are not aware of this, we should like to make some suggestions to you:
>
> 1. Give islanders stickers to place on their car windshields so they may park on the wharf beyond the two-hour limit. (Those of us who have parked at the Youth Center [current use of the Wolfeborough Railroad Station] or behind the Post Office have had their cars damaged.)
>
> 2. Adequate lighting on town wharf so it can be found on dark, stormy nights, and people won't break their necks on any night.
>
> 3. Limit cruiser parking to 24 hours. As it is now they get free water and electricity and unusual amounts of wharf space. We do our shopping in Wolfeboro but most of these people don't!
>
> 4. Consider reserving a town wharf for islanders as the Back Bay area parking is unsafe.
>
> Very truly yours,
>
> Jean Hanson, John W. Hill, F. McGloin, Barbara L. McGloin, Cynthia Soll, Dorothy K. Allison, Therese M. McKillop, Leo D. McKillop, Dr. Richmond W. Allison, Mrs. Thomas C. Spence, Donald E. Legro, Bernice K. Legro, Margaret I. McKillop, Clyde F. Roberts, Jr., Irene R. Roberts, Mr. and Mrs. Peter H. Flood.

The October 2, 1969, issue of the *Granite State News* furnished the reply by the selectmen, who said, in effect, that nothing was going to be done for the islanders, noting in part:

> In short, we fully appreciate the islanders' difficulties, but you have voluntarily selected an off-shore location which, you forget, does relieve you of some equally bad headaches suffered by the mainlanders.

### Rapid Development

In the late 1960s especially, entrepreneurs laid out parcels of land and offered them for sale to the public. While they were usually real estate only, they were sometimes combined with building proposals (as in the case of Old Mill Estates and Robin Acres, for example).

Such developments included Rusty Shores (Rust Pond), Osseo (Winter Harbor), Port Wedeln (Winter Harbor), Robin Acres (near the Libby Museum), Hardwood Estates (Route 109A), Museum Shores (near the

Libby Museum), Nelson Subdivision (Crescent Lake), Alpine Meadows (off Middleton Road), McCarthy Subdivision (near the Libby Museum), Old Mill Estates (off South Main Street), Wentworth Estates (off Pleasant Valley Road), Chestnut Hill Mobile Home Park (Beach Pond Road), Penn Air Estates (North Wolfeboro), and others.

On June 9, 1967, Norman R. Poisson, builder, advertised lots and houses for sale on Lakeview Drive. For $20,000 one could buy a white cedar and brick split-level 1,528-square-foot house on a lot 140 feet on the front by 227 deep. The interior included a living room with bow-front window and fireplace, kitchen with French provincial cabinets, electric range and hood, dining area, three bedrooms, 1 1/2 baths, family room with fireplace, laundry room, office or hobby room, garage with workbench space, combination storm windows, hot water heat, and 220-volt electricity.

The Osseo tract at the end of Keewaydin Road ignited the first major real estate development controversy in town history. Mr. and Mrs. Frank A. Richardson (of Yankee Pedlar Real Estate) and Mr. and Mrs. Leonard Eckblom (of Quincy, MA) pooled their interests and bought 300 feet of Lake Winnipesaukee shoreline connected to 15 back-land acres off Winter Harbor. Their plan was to divide the shore into three lots, sell two of them, and keep only the remaining 100-foot lot to serve as a beach and dock area for 24 small interior lots. This "funnel development," as it came to be called, brought forth vigorous protests from nearby residents, one of whom wondered if someone might take 1,000 interior acres and develop them to feed into just 100 feet of shoreline.

Making matters worse, apparently the developers did a poor job of checking rights of way and easements. The Wolfeboro selectmen accused them of carelessness and "substandard planning."[64] Commenting on the preceding, Donald G. Hughes recalled:[65]

> The Port Wedeln development was even more of a wake-up call than Osseo, to the changes that might occur if funnel development continued. Two hundred 1/4-acre lots were initially approved, each with rights to 600 feet of common shore line. The plan was scaled back a little after a few years, but the relationship to water frontage for each home remained less than five feet per lot, vs. regulations of three decades later in the 1990s of 150 feet per building lot.

The 1950s and especially the 1960s saw nearly a half-dozen local agents for prefabricated and mobile homes hang out their shingles for such brands as Westville Homes, Assembled Homes, Stanmar, U.S. Steel Homes, and Swift Homes, as well as unspecified brands sold by such vendors as James Wales, Jr., and the Pettengill Construction Co. In an era of rapidly rising costs, factory-made buildings made it possible to acquire a home at a lower price than would have been possible otherwise.

**Social Changes**

Wolfeboro was depersonalized to an extent during the decade. Sweeping social changes pervaded America, engendered in part by widespread use of drugs, permissive sex, and student rebellion fostered largely by uncertainties over the Vietnam War. Wolfeboro, although it was not a focal point of any of these activities, was not immune either.

The new Kingswood Regional School District seemed to have a very disorienting effect upon Wolfeboro residents, although it is difficult to separate reaction to the new school district from the changes being made on the social scene. What seemed to once be a fairly tranquil local educational system erupted in the mid-1960s into a lot of bickering as to budgets, curricula, salaries, student behavior, and more, and the dissension has continued, more or less, ever since.

**The Historical Society**

The Wolfeboro Historical Society, founded in 1925, continued to provide a link between modern progress and the traditions of bygone times. The Clark House and the nearby Pleasant Valley Schoolhouse, owned by the town and managed by the Society, offered postcards and stationery to visitors in the summer of 1961. These featured new pen-and-ink drawings by Norman Hooghkirk (of Tuftonboro), and were put on sale alongside postcards made from photographs taken by David Fetzer. For summer tourists the two buildings in Clark Park, together known as the Early American Living Museum (name changed on February 7, 1966, to the Wolfeboro Historical Museum), offered a glimpse of local history. In 1963 there were over 1,200 visitors to the site, the largest attendance up to that time.

Research and preservation efforts included the purchase of photographic negatives from the Arthur Sawyer estate, the cleaning and marking (once again; this had been done in the 1930s) of the site of Governor John Wentworth's summer home, and the publication of a booklet written by Robert F.W. Meader, *The Saga of a Palace,* about the Wentworth mansion. By 1964 the town and the Historical Society had each run out of original copies of Benjamin F. Parker's 1901 book, *History of Wolfeborough.* The Society made a plea to acquire used copies.

Meanwhile, work on what was called Volume II of the *History of Wolfeboro* continued by a committee of over 20 writers-to-be. An advisor was called in to give a pep talk to the group and said, "Keep the narrative flowing." As of mid-November, 1962, only four chapters had been completed out of a planned 20. The project was scheduled for completion on April 1, 1963. The deadline was missed and the project ultimately abandoned.

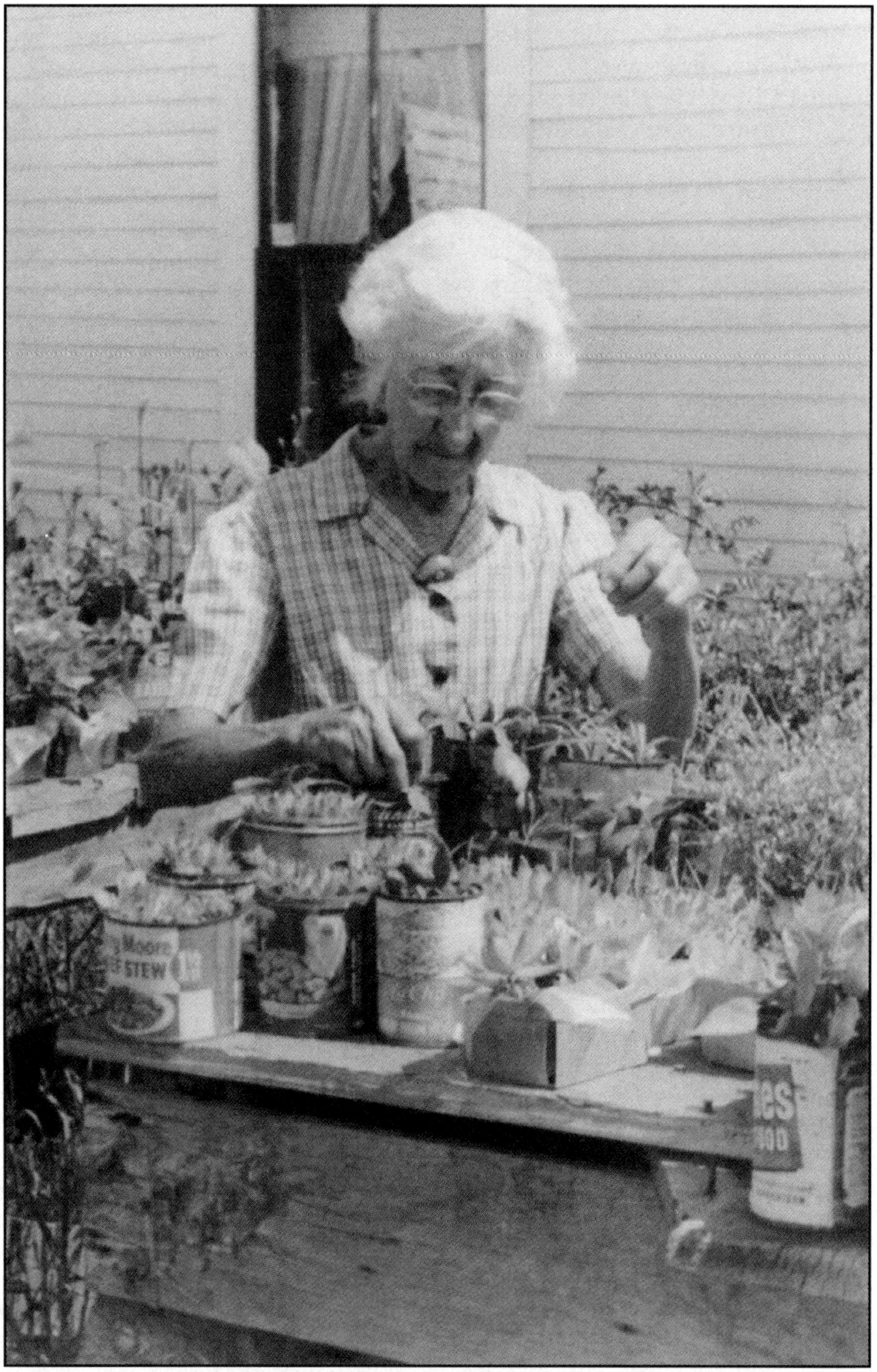

Mrs. Alison Rines prepares seedlings to be sold in the garden booth at the annual Huggins Hospital Street Fair. Many local people contributed their garden produce, crafts, talents, and time to this popular event. (Jack Bickford photograph, circa early 1960s)

In 1967 John W. McDermott of the Wolfeboro National Bank presented the Wolfeboro Historical Society with the ledger from the first bank in Wolfeboro, which in the 1830s was located in what is now the Scott House to the left of the Corner Store. "These records of transactions dating from 1837 to 1861 are a welcome addition to the Society's library," a spokesperson commented.[66]

## HEALTH SERVICES

### Health Notes

At the March 1962 annual town meeting, citizens voted to purchase a water chlorinator for the municipal system at a cost of about $15,000, after a mandate by the State Board of Health. On June 1 of the same year, Sabin oral vaccine against polio was first administered in a local clinic to children age six weeks to five years. Two additional vaccinations were given at subsequent six-week intervals. New cases of polio had all but disappeared.

On March 28, 1964, Thomas Spence, a 15-year-old sophomore at Brewster Academy, was hurt, but no bones were broken, when a rope broke during his descent down an 80-foot cliff near the top of Mt. Longstack on the Wolfeboro-Alton town line. Lawrence Hamm, 16, who with his dog Jasper was climbing an easier slope on the same mountain, saw the injured Spence and ran for help. Dr. Frank Allen treated the victim.

In July 1966 attorney George Walker of Wolfeboro spoke on behalf of community leaders and supported the concept of a local mental health clinic and psychiatric counseling service, noting in part:

> Doctors, ministers, attorneys, teachers, and social workers do what they can on individual cases coming to their attention, but, generally speaking, this is only on a sporadic and hit or miss basis and far inadequate to the actual need. All too frequently those most in need of professional counseling receive no assistance until it is too late, and as taxpayers we are paying for the lack of it....
>
> The sad part is to observe the disturbed and maladjusted children — all teachers are familiar with them — who are products of their upset and unhappy family and environmental backgrounds, and who, while potentially salvageable, perpetuate the same maladjustments and disturbances in the classroom and among their playmates. These problems can be coped with under a comprehensive counseling program designed to reach first the adults and parents and, second, the following and younger generation, by providing a healthier environment. If this is done perhaps...more of our children can be helped toward a happier and more useful life.

In October 1966 the dream became a reality, and the Carroll County Community Service opened an office in the Nelson Building on the corner of North Main and Lake Streets.

On March 13, 1968, Sherman D. Parsons passed away at the age of 107. For a number of years he had received much publicity as the town's oldest citizen.

In November 1968 there was much ado about a new 80-bed nursing home to be called Wolfeboro Knoll, to be constructed the following year on the site of the Flying Eagle Farm (earlier known as the Pineo Farm on South Main Street and the location of Joseph I. Melanson III's real estate and antiques business). Joseph M. Flynn, a summer resident, stated that he would spend $750,000 on the project and create 100 new jobs. The facility was never built.

In December 1968 Drs. Austen and Lorna Damm, both graduates of the Palmer College of Chiropractic in Davenport, IA, opened their offices in the Wolfeboro Shopping Center. "Dr. Austen Damm is a native of Sweden and received his pre-professional education in Sweden and Norway.... He became interested in chiropractic after being restored to health by a Norwegian chiropractor." In 1969 the office was advertised in part as follows: "When you want to enjoy better health consult your doctor of chiropractic FIRST."

On July 23, 1969, at the All Saints' Episcopal Church the Wolfeboro contingent of Weight Watchers International held its first weekly Wednesday night meeting.

In December of the same year, an unidentified 6th grade Carpenter School student submitted this letter to the paper:[67]

> Everyone is taking too many pills, take pills to stay awake, pills to put them to sleep, pills to quiet themselves down, and then they are called junkies. Instead of using their brains to control themselves, they take pills, pills, and more pills. After a while the brain loses all control and pills take over. Pills distort the vision, and no one should drive a car that takes pills or alcoholic drinks. Death is a pretty final thing, but loss of one's mind is a long trip to hell, and for many there is no return.

### At Huggins Hospital

In the early 1960s Huggins Hospital experienced financial difficulties. Norman Brown, administrator of the Concord Hospital, came to Wolfeboro to conduct a survey and make recommendations. The Hospital board of trustees passed a resolution to follow much of Brown's advice and to seek a mature *male* as a new administrator. In June 1965 John F. Waters was named to the post, a position he filled with distinction until his retirement in October 1980.

In the 1950s and early 1960s Dr. Ralph Adams had brought international recognition to Huggins Hospital with his highly-acclaimed procedures of surgical cleanliness and the reduction of noscomial (hospital-acquired) staph infections. In November 1965 the *Granite State News* reported that a majority of the members of the board of directors "and a minority of the medical staff" had prompted his resignation by their apparent unwillingness to cope with certain issues stated in a letter recently received from the surgeon. Details were not given at the time. However, later interviews and commentaries by the present writer brought to light an uncomfortable situation under which Dr. Adams was said to have had certain privileges not accorded to other physicians on the active staff.[68] As examples, he had his medical office in the hospital, while other doctors used their homes for this purpose. The pay scale for certain of his employees was about twice that paid similar people on the Huggins staff, although Huggins was billed for his employees' service. While he was recognized as a brilliant surgeon, his interpersonal relationships and practices caused problems with others on the staff.

Dr. Adams announced the removal of his offices to his home. However, before this took place, Dr. Adams died of a heart attack on November 23, 1965, while meeting with the medical staff at the hospital. Subsequently, the *Granite State News* printed one of the most laudatory eulogies ever to appear in its pages, titled "Death of Dr. Ralph Adams Is Loss To Community, Medical Science."

Details of the controversy between Dr. Adams and the hospital were never made public, despite a call from some area citizens (Attorney Philip Ganem among them) to do so. The doctor's death laid to rest the conflict, and hospital staff members saw no point in engaging in public debate.

The Adams controversy would not go away, despite the hospital staff and administration not engaging in further public discussion. In September 1972 it was announced that Mrs. Heidi King, chairman of the Ralph Adams Memorial Fund, had acquired a portrait of the doctor, to be hung at Huggins, in view of his "having done so much for the hospital and the community."[69] The picture was hung in a prominent location. A year later in September 1973 Heidi King and other committee members (including Rev. Edward Cantwell, Dr. Edwin Goodall, and attorney James Kalled) protested the removal of Dr. Adams' painting from its previous location "which we and everyone else thought a proper place" to a "corridor or alley" where, apparently, it couldn't be seen readily. In protest, Heidi King took the painting down and took it home with her. "I will present it to the hospital again and they can make up their minds to select the proper place to hang the painting, for it properly belongs in the hospital. However, this painting is not going to hang in an alley!"[70] The painting remained outside of the hospital.

In May 1966 Huggins Hospital was informed by the federal government that it had been approved as a provider of services under the Medicare program and fully met all the requirements for the Health Insurance Benefits Program for the aged.

The Huggins annual report for 1966 showed an income of $6,000 over expenses, as opposed to a deficit of nearly $35,000 the preceding year. The cost of providing service to one patient for one day rose to $52.68, as compared to $47.90 a year earlier. This compared to a 1966 national average of $54.05.

New amenities included the installation of television sets in patient rooms in 1967 and 16 all-electric beds purchased by the Hospital Aid Association in 1968. As in years past, the Association raised money by conducting the Huggins Hospital Street Fair each August.

In May 1969 Dr. Edwin B. Goodall performed the first complete corneal transplant at the hospital on a young woman, Anne Goodwin, of North Haverhill, MA, who had been waiting seven months for a donor. Merwin and Eleanor Horn made an emergency flight to Boston to bring the cornea to Wolfeboro, and Lt. Stanley E. Stevens delivered it to the hospital from the airport on Wolfeboro Neck.

In 1969 Huggins Hospital began a capital fund drive to raise a minimum of $750,000 toward a modernization program estimated to cost $2.25 million, but which reached $3 million. Sources of money included $400,000 from the Hill-Burton Fund, proceeds from a $1 million endowment from the estate of Jennie H. Sinclair, a gift of $40,000 by J. Willard Marriott, public contributions of about $1 million, and a mortgage loan of $834,000. The facility was named the Sinclair Patient Care Center and opened in May 1972. It included three wings, 82 new beds, a new kitchen, and new dining facilities.[71]

## THE FIRE DEPARTMENT

### Activities

Typical activity for the Wolfeboro Fire Department is reflected in the report for the year ended December 31, 1961:[72] The firemen answered 81 calls consisting of 16 box alarms, 2 brush alarms, 1 engineer's call, and 62 still alarms. The emergency calls were for 34 residential fires, one place of public assembly, 2 mercantile buildings, 18 grass and dump fires, 8 automobile fires, 2 false alarms, 7 smoke scares, 8 first aid and rescue calls, and 1 out-of-town fire.

During the decade there was cooperation between Wolfeboro and neighboring Tuftonboro fire fighters. Past disagreements had faded. Residents of the latter town were advised as follows:[73]

> To report fire [in Tuftonboro], dial or call Wolfeboro operator and ask for 182 which is the Wolfeboro Fire Station number. They will activate the siren in Melvin Village and Mirror Lake and also call the firemen by radio.

In 1967 Eleanor Horn pointed out the need for a modern headquarters for the Fire Department, noting that at the existing station, which had been in use for more than a quarter of a century, "the ingenious crew manages to house the major pieces of equipment at the Factory Street location with the aid of a shoe horn and a long handled wooden spoon."[74] At the time, there was a permanent staff of four men assisted by 44 volunteers.

In the same year, Dr. Herbert W. Drury, a resident of Tuftonboro Neck, commissioned Nat Goodhue of Goodhue & Hawkins to convert a 22-foot fiberglass vessel into a fireboat—the first ever on Lake Winnipesaukee. Two pumps were installed that could pump 310 gallons per minute through four outlets, spraying a distance of about 150 feet.[75] Dr. Drury kept the boat at his home, on call for use by local firemen. When he was out of town it was berthed at Goodhue & Hawkins. Two years later, on October 10, 1969, he gave the vessel to the Wolfeboro Fire Department.

### Notable Fires

The following listing includes notable fires of the decade. Much information is from the records kept by Dr. W. Douglas Kipp, prominent local dentist who served with the Fire Department as a volunteer. Other data are from the *Granite State News*. In addition to the conflagrations noted, there were dozens of minor blazes including chimney, brush, and oil-burner fires.

**1961, January 4. Ernest Roberge, Jr., house:** Dining room and living room gutted, other areas damaged.

**1961, January 19. George Woodman residence:** Park Avenue. Blaze in bedroom closet.

**1961, February 13. Old Chamberlain tavern:** College Road. Fire between kitchen and adjoining room. Minor damage.[76]

**1961, February 14. Otto Pecunies' home:** Wolfeboro Center. Chimney fire spread to studs.[77]

**1961, July 24. Car burned:** E.P. Berry of Varney Road lost his 1952 Buick.

**1961, August 6. Archer Tibbetts house:** North Wolfeboro. Back wall and attic gutted. Started when he tried to burn a hornets' nest on the back of his home, and the fire got out of control.

**1962, March 31. Fred Baker house:** Beach Pond Road. Owned by Ada and Flora Crosby, Cambridge, MA. Destroyed except for ell.[78]

**1962, August 16. Allen "A" Resort:** Upstairs of office and dining building gutted.

**1963, January 24. Dr. Daniel Postance's residence:** House gutted, garage and two cars destroyed.

**1963, April 10. Walter Bodwell's house:** Fire damage to roof and attic. Some of the firemen were criticized for extinguishing the fire, as the interior of the house was very unsanitary as for a long time the family had used the cellar as a latrine.[79]

**1963, April 14. Alvin Donovan's camp:** Wentworth Pines. Total loss, estimated at $15,000. Donovan had lost an earlier camp to fire on December 28, 1958, and had kept the road plowed in winter since that time as a precaution should another occur.[80]

**1963, August 1. Albert Berry's barn:** River Street. One end and ridge of building burned.

**1963, September 26. Ralph Barnes' camp:** Beach Pond Road. Owned by Arthur Wheeler. Destroyed.[81]

**1963, November 1. Shattuck camp:** Sewall Road. Wall and loft burned.

**1964, July 10. Allen "A" Resort:** Fire in boiler room caused by flooded oil burner.

**1964, November 1. Tumblebrook Inn:** South Wolfeboro. 2:30 a.m. fire. Snack bar and recreation facility operated by John L. Dalton and his wife Lilo. Inside gutted. This was a major loss to the community, as it had been a favorite place for young people. The Tumble Brook Fund was set up to help, but the facility did not reopen.[82]

**1965, May 2. "Hillsbaron" estate:** At top of Clow's Hill. Two barns, a four-car garage, an outbuilding, part of house, and 20 acres burned. Firemen were on the scene for six hours. Formerly owned by Mr. and Mrs. Stanley N. Juthe. Now owned by Harry P. Curtis. Six volunteer firemen (Charles Foss, Bob Hale, Eddie Morgan, George Moody, Ken Weeks, and Richard Charles) were hurt when they were blown out of the house by an explosion.[83]

**1965, May 18. Gordon A. Reade's barn:** Wolfeboro Falls. Gutted.

**1965, July 26. Hill School Camp:** Rust Pond. Building gutted and small area of woods burned.

**1965, July 29. Island fires:** On Parker Island, a blaze in underbrush was caused by "the stupidity of some unknown person who had built a campfire on the ground when a fireplace was nearby. The camper left the fire without putting it out." On the same day, on Keniston Island a fire in decayed vegetable matter and pine needles was burning. "Occasionally the fire smolders along underground and will pop up many yards away from the original fire."[84]

**1965, August 1. Hill School Camp:** Classroom tent a total loss by fire; platform damaged.

**1965, August 7. Dot Willey's house:** Kitchen gutted.

**1965, August 22. Dr. James Bovaird's garage:** South Main Street. Burned.

**1966, January 11. Bickford residence:** Park Avenue. Partition and ceiling burned.

**1966, May 23. Bridges cottage:** Fire extensively damaged the summer cottage owned by Mrs. Deloris Bridges on Rocky Shore Road.[85]

**1966, October 11. Earl camp:** Totally destroyed.

**1966, December 7. David Moore's chicken house:** Pleasant Valley. One and one-half floors scorched by fire.

**1967, January. Paul Ashford house:** "More news of the Paul Ashford family. They are still temporarily in Sanbornville after having their home in Stoneham Road destroyed by fire.... The mother and the daughter need shoes...."[86]

**1967, February 11. Garry shack:** Middleton Road. Totally destroyed.

**1967, February 18. Ride's camp:** Varney Road. One end of building and all of roof burned.

**1967, April 20. Robert Snow family house:** Varney Road. Gutted. Fire started in the living room furniture. House owned by Inez Kimball of Wolfeboro Falls.

**1967, June 21. Horne's Garage:** Fire in service pit.

**1967, July 18. Terrific dynamite explosion:** Eight-ton tugboat owned by Garrett Construction of Wolfeboro and used as a work boat by Donald C. Stanley, 35, of Mirror Lake, was blown to splinters in The Broads off Rattlesnake Island while en route to Wolfeboro Bay. Stanley was killed instantly. "Exactly what caused the dynamite to explode has not been established.... The largest pieces of floating debris were described as about half the size of a chair seat."[87]

**1967, August 17. John N. Dyer camp:** Rocky Shore Road, Wolfeboro Neck. Extensive fire damage and injury. Mrs. Catherine Deguire tried to start a charcoal fire by putting a flammable liquid (Solex, a household solvent made by National Distillers & Chemicals Corp.) on the "dead" briquettes. Unseen embers ignited a flash explosion, throwing fire on Mrs. Deguire and her four-year-old daughter Louise. The former suffered burns on 30% of her body, the little girl, 60%. The husband and father, Dr. William Deguire, head of the Music Department at Upsala College, East Orange, NJ, suffered minor burns when carrying Louise to the lake to extinguish the flames. In 1971 Mrs. Deguire and her daughter accepted $625,000 in settlement from National Distillers.[88]

**1967, September 2. Dorothy Glidden house:** Cotton Valley. One end gutted. Fire started in the living room.[89]

**1967, December 8. Mr. and Mrs. Harold Abbott's house:** North Wolfeboro Road. Gutted. Fire started by a flooded floor furnace.[90]

**1968, February 6. Camp Birchmont:** Garage destroyed.

**1968, March 6. Penn Air Estates:** House destroyed.

**1968, March 15. William Meffert's rented house:** Gutted. Meffert was later charged with arson, pleaded guilty, and was convicted.[91]

**1968, April 27. Bernard Pineo, Jr., accident:** Gas heater in a barn owned by Pineo exploded, throwing him across the floor and inflicting several burns, none severe.[92]

**1968, June 12. Allen "A" Resort:** Workers' cabin gutted.

**1968, November 2. Thayer camp:** Gutted.

**1968, November 27. Paul Kimball's garage and shop:** Gutted.

**1969, January 28. Wolfeboro Café:** Factory Street. Rear end gutted. Starting in the cellar, the fire spread through the building.[93]

**1969, January 28. Rust Pond Inn:** Main building a total loss; kitchen, lounge, dining room. Fire started at 10 p.m. when grease in the kitchen ignited. Owned by Forrest Durkee, Sr. The all-out was sounded at 7:16 a.m. on the 29th. While storing hose after the fire, Eugene F. Lehner, Sr., suffered a heart attack and died. At the March town meeting, it was voted to change the name of Factory Street to Lehner Street in his honor; this was effected in 1970.[94]

**1969, July 2. Bud Swaffield's garage:** Gutted.

**1969, December 16. Furber house:** "Minor damage. Rather hush-hush."[95]

**1970, February 11. Joe Bradley's Repair Shop:** South Main Street. 3:55 a.m. Many boats and much equipment were saved; the building was a total loss.[96]

**1970, May 2. Luke Travis house:** South Wolfeboro. Gutted.

**1970, June 11. Oscar York house:** Porch gutted.

**1970, August 19. Murray house:** Clark Road. Wall and ceiling burned.

**1970, September 7. Allen "A" Resort.** Hot water tank exploded.

**1970, September 28. Lakeview Inn:** North Main Street. Kitchen ceiling and wall burned.

**1970, December 4. Colonel Hamlin's house:** Springfield Point. Partitions burned.

## LAW ENFORCEMENT

### Vandalism Epidemic

On December 1, 1961, the *Granite State News* printed an article, "Local Law Enforcement Officers Report a Rash of Problems Involving Juveniles and Young Adults." An example was the case of Paul R. Elliott, age 18, of Wolfeboro, who was found guilty of procuring and delivering alcohol to a 14-year-old boy. Oscar Michaud, age 28, was identified as Elliott's source. It was noted that about 15 to 20 local juveniles were involved in breaking and entering, malicious damage, possession of alcohol, disturbing the peace, and motor vehicle violations.

In particular, vandalism was a problem, as it had been for many decades. In 1962 it was reported that 25% of the town's budget to maintain facilities (leased from Brewster Academy) at Brewster Beach went toward repairing damage caused by vandals. (Damage at this beach continued for years, and in 1970, following the recent destruction of the toilet facilities, lights, and telephone, the town threatened to close the facility unless it was stopped.)

On August 30, 1963, the local paper reported:

> Local police solved the early summer rash of breaks recently when they apprehended two male juvenile Wolfeboro residents. Police were surprised when they found that the boys had successfully entered nine buildings and tried to enter two others. The only reported breaks were the Wolfeboro Garage, White's Restaurant, Gould's Dime Store, and Horne's Garage. Also entered were two Sewall Road homes, North Main Street homes, and Hart's Garage....

And this on November 1, 1963:

> Vandalism at the Town Ski Slope last Saturday night resulted in a massive smashing of windows in the base hut.... Police are working with photographic evidence and are conducting their investigation....

And on December 20 of the same year:

> Two young men with more beer in their bellies than charity in their hearts destroyed Christmas decorations, overturned a window box, and tore down the overhead door lighting at Gould's Dime Store during the late night hours last week. The men have made their peace with Mrs. Gould, local police authorities, and hopefully with themselves.

In June 1964 several local youths thought it great sport to drive automobiles over the Kingswood Golf Course greens and flatten the flags. Arrests were made. Shortly thereafter came this report:

> The Fourth of July weekend was not all fun and festivities. A few people have warped ways of celebrating Independence Day. Sixteen windows were smashed with rocks at the Kingswood Regional High School under construction. Two 28 x 4' wall sections were also damaged. Residents of the six-town regional school district whose tax dollars are paying for the $2 million school will be keenly interested in knowing the names of the vandals when they are apprehended by the police.

More on wanton destruction early the following year:

> The inexcusable, willful and malicious destruction and defacing of government owned property makes it imperative to close the Wolfeboro Post Office lobby on Sunday, Postmaster Bernard Landman said this week....

Vandalism continued to be the number one crime problem in Wolfeboro. A number of accounts in the paper noted that this was mostly due to beer being consumed by underage people. At one particular time, seven people were awaiting court hearings for selling beer to minors.

Of course, there were other types of incidents. On February 10, 1964, police officer Bill Freethy identified Richard A. Valley of Laconia in a stolen Oldsmobile parked near Huggins Hospital. "Valley took off with the Olds and was clocked at 70 to 75 miles an hour going through Wolfeboro's Main Street. Freethy reported him as topping North Main Street Hill at about 100 miles an hour...." The chase continued out of town, after which Valley skidded onto Tuftonboro Neck Road and crashed into a snowbank. He was arrested on the spot.[97]

### A Solution?

On February 17, 1965, the second of two public forums was held and was titled "Youth Speaks—Adults Listen."

It was stated that challenges for Wolfeboro youth included opportunities for recreation, weekend needs of Brewster dormitory students, teenage drinking, fair treatment by the police, need for adults to set a better example, and job opportunities. Among specific needs were accessible public tennis courts, a bowling alley not monopolized by adult teams, a rink for roller skating, a youth center, and student field trips to museums, art exhibits, and cultural centers. However, it was also noted that a certain contingent of local youth simply didn't want to do anything in the way of recreation or legitimate entertainment.

In December 1965, at the request of the Wolfeboro Recreation Advisory Council, Mr. and Mrs. Donald K. Brookes kept their Open Door Restaurant on Center Street open two evenings during the school vacation. During the same decade, the Tumble Brook Lodge (burned on November 1, 1964) and Not Quite a Coffee House were among the other places the younger set could gather and talk.

Despite much discussion and effort, vandalism (including a rash of sign stealing) and teen-age drinking continued to be major problems throughout the decade. Beginning about 1967, the use of marijuana and other narcotics became popular with certain segments of the teenage population, although Wolfeboro citizens seem to have had minimal involvement in comparison with metropolitan areas. In February 1968 attorney George W. Walker of Wolfeboro was part of a panel at a New Hampshire Bar Association in Manchester titled "New Legislation to Combat the Growing Problems of Narcotics Use."

Burglaries were committed frequently in the 1960s. A typical incident occurred on October 25, 1968, when the Lakes Region Sports Shop, owned by James Warner, was broken into, and guns valued at $1,500 or more were stolen. Daniel H. Fuller, age 23, of Wolfeboro and Baltimore, MD, and an accomplice were charged with the crime. Fuller was found guilty.

On August 25, 1969, two break-ins took place at the Wolfeboro Shopping Center. The First National Store reported a loss of $6,390.71, and Lampron's Grocery Store had $1,556.71 in cash and some old coins taken. "Entry in each instance was made by forcing the back doors with heavy instruments. The thieves opened the safe in each establishment by peeling or tearing off the front door."

On October 1 and 2, 1969, two telephone calls were placed to the Kingswood Regional High School, alerting school officials to bombs on the premises. The affair was a hoax, and a Kingswood High pupil and a Brewster Academy student were arrested and subsequently found guilty.

In November of the same year it was reported that "a man has reportedly called school-aged children to his car on some pretext and then exposed himself." He was identified as David Bunnell, 23, of Manchester, who was found guilty in court.

On February 20, 1970, vandals entered the Abenaki Ski Area, stole candy and soft drinks, "and then walked to the top of the hill and proceeded to tear all the wires to the motor, the cable from the coil and distributor, the wires from the spark plugs and the rotor from the distributor." In March, Chief Arnold H. Wentworth reported that the department had solved about 20 cases of breaking and entering and malicious mischief, with the arrest of six juveniles. On March 25, 1970, over a dozen antique firearms and the "Thomas Downing powder horn," most items dating back to the Revolutionary War, were stolen from a local exhibit. On March 27 equipment was stolen from the Lakes Region Survey Service, a local firm that was in the process of completing work for the town.

On September 10, 1970, Wolfeboro police arrested Arnold Van Amburgh, 20, of Waltham, MA, and Paul Cilley, 23, of Rochester, and stated that this had solved 30 burglaries in the area. Both were later convicted. In November 1970 three television sets valued at $450 each were stolen from Huggins Hospital. Christmas lights were swiped from downtown trees "faster than they can replace them!"[98]

Reflective of the general disrespect for authority, trash and garbage thrown along town streets and state highways reached unprecedented proportions during the 1960s, to the extent that one survey disclosed that a truckload of trash could be collected per running mile on one route. Usually the melting of the spring snow would reveal hundreds of beer cans thrown along Carry Beach, Forest Road, and other places where youngsters parked and drove.

However, many if not most citizens, including the much-discussed younger set, were law abiding. This letter from Nathalie Erickson appeared in the *Granite State News,* August 20, 1970:

> Recently during the Huggins Hospital Street Fair it was a pleasure to work with 14 young people between the ages of 11 and 16 in our make-up booth. They were dependable, co-operative, dignified and fun! I was impressed by their desire to help a good cause and their respect for each other and those around them while they worked. Shows me that if we provide interesting and constructive opportunities for our youth, they usually respond accordingly. They, too, need a vote of confidence. Should this town fail them?

### Facilities and Personnel

In August 1962 Troop E of the State Police moved into the Wolfeboro Town Hall, next to the town offices, where it remained until September 1968, when facilities were relocated to an old schoolhouse on Route 25 in Moultonboro.

Arnold H. Wentworth was sworn in as chief of police on July 13, 1964, replacing Harold E. Thompson, who had held the post for 13 years and who now became deputy chief.[99] At the time there was no 24-hour police coverage. To answer after-hours calls, off-duty policemen were telephoned at their homes. In 1965, officer Bruce Beaulieu was the target of one or more vandals who dumped sugar into the gas tank of his personal car, and on another occasion deflated the tires.

On October 26, 1965, the Wolfeboro Police Rescue Squad was organized by Peter D. Hayes with the assistance of H.E. Erickson and Stanley E. Stevens. Members sought to provide quick response to any situation involving potential injury, including accidents and fires. "The main function is to remove a person from a dangerous situation he is present in and prepare him for an ambulance...." In June 1966 Rescue Squad members included Joseph E. Bradley, Bradley Fournier, John Goddard, Larry Hamm, Peter D. Hayes, Benjamin Ladd, James McBride, John Rines, David A. Senecal, Garland Sprague, and Stanley E. Stevens.

In November 1965 personnel of the Wolfeboro Police Department remodeled a two-room headquarters at the east end of the Town Hall. A move was soon made from the existing facilities in the basement at the west end of the building under the town offices.

In 1967 Chief Wentworth attracted a reporter's notice when he stopped traffic one day in front of Carpenter School, so that he could pick up a pocketful of change which had been dropped by a young girl while making the crossing.

On November 17, 1967, the Wolfeboro District Court room was dedicated in the Town Hall.

In 1969 certain State Highway Patrol cars were equipped with Sony videotape recorders to record the actions of motorists, including drunken drivers. In 1970 the Wolfeboro Police Department had three cruisers: a 1968 Plymouth which registered 22,585 miles, a 1969 Plymouth which was driven 69,038 miles, and a 1970 Ford which ran up 4,801 miles, for a total of 96,424 miles for the year.[100]

### Mrs. Coretta King in Seclusion

On July 11, 1968, this was printed in the *Granite State News:*

> Late last week other news media proclaimed...that Mrs. Martin Luther King, widow of the slain civil rights leader, was seeking seclusion in the Lakes Region in order to complete the book she is writing on her life and the life of her husband.... At the request of her associates, we elected not to print the story and to respect Mrs. King's wish for complete anonymity during her stay.
>
> Since the assassination of her husband in Memphis last April, Mrs. King has been very much in the limelight. Her decision to come to Wolfeboro for seclusion and relief from the glare of national and international publicity was an understandable one. This area has often provided privacy and refuge for other famous persons in the past.
>
> This newspaper welcomes Mrs. King, whose courage and dignity are to be admired, and we hope that people here will respect her wishes for privacy as we shall.

In connection with her visit, Stanley E. Stevens furnished this recollection to the author:[101]

> At that time...I was a young lieutenant. I never personally met Mrs. King, but was assigned to check the home where she was staying at least once each evening.
>
> I believe that Army Intelligence [alternatively, the Secret Service][102] may have been responsible for Mrs. King's protection..... My orders came directly from Chief Wentworth. During her stay Mrs. King resided at the Pennypacker Estate, an old farm on the Burwell Road. Although the house was in Wolfeboro, it could only be accessed from Brookfield. This road is the first on the left after passing the Cotton Mountain Church on the Stoneham Road.
>
> I was instructed to drive into the front drive, stop, activate the overhead blue light (back then we only had a single roof light), turn on the interior light so persons in the house could see me, and then, if no one came out (which they never did), turn off the lights and drive away....

### The Corson-Brooks Brouhaha

In 1969 John Corson and Richard Brooks, two of the three members of the Wolfeboro Police Commission, were arrested on charges of selling liquor without a license. The offense was said to have taken place on April 29 at Willey Brook on Route 109 when Corson and Brooks were manning a lunch cart set up by the Lions Club to provide food and refreshments to smelt fishermen. Offered for sale were hot dogs, coffee, and coffee royals (with liquor added), the same menu used on prior occasions dating back to 1962.

The third police commissioner, local pharmacist Louis A. Soucey, demanded the resignation of the two others, as did numerous townspeople and 100% of the mem-

The Basket Barn on the Smith River on Center Street, Wolfeboro Falls, as advertised October 30, 1964, in the *Granite State News.* The quaint-appearing shop with its decorative water wheel was a favorite tourist stop for many years.

bers of the local Police Department. The local paper commented:

> The situation presently confronting the town on the issue of police commissioners comes as an unpleasant and unwanted dilemma. The fact that two members of the Lions Club were arrested and fined for illegally selling liquor from the club's portable refreshment stand was regrettable; the fact that the two men involved also happen to be members of the Wolfeboro Police Commission was embarrassing to the town, and the fact that the two commissioners refuse to resign their office because the offense was "only a misdemeanor" is incomprehensible.
>
> What began as an unfortunate incident has now grown into a painful fissure in the community as petitions are being circulated in an effort to bring about the removal from office of the two men. The selectmen are being criticized for not acting while the local youth cite the case for an excuse for disrespect and disregard of the law....

In a letter to the paper, Tom W. Kane, of Massachusetts, commented:

> How absurd to admit publicly to breaking the law and excusing themselves because no personal gain was involved. I hope no one on the force picks me up this summer for speeding, etc., because according to your commissioners, all I need to say is "I didn't mean to, pardon me." These two men are showing your town a new kind of stupidity by rewriting the law.... All I can see is arrogance and irresponsibility every time they open their mouths. They should be laughed out of office.

Joseph P. Kennedy, a new resident in Wolfeboro and the father of nine children, suggested that the newspaper should publish "a list of laws that can be broken with impunity."

On June 4 the two confessed liquor sellers resigned. Chief Arnold H. Wentworth reminded townspeople that the Police Commission was a group of elected officials and that the Police Department was a separate entity. The actions of the former commissioners would affect in no way the Department's concern for enforcing the law. In a special election, the two Police Commission vacancies were filled by Alan Skelley and Frank Bickford.

In 1970 the federal government placed this advertisement in the local paper:

> "Is any part of your property used as a commercial establishment?" Wine-making isn't quite what the Census Bureau had in mind when it put this question on the census form. But, it you are making wine, the Bureau will keep it a secret. Your census form is just as confidential as your vote....

How this official government advertisement reconciled with the preceding year's discussion as to ethics on the part of public officials (the Lions Club liquor-selling incident) wasn't stated, but, obviously, there was a contradiction.[103]

## WIND, WAVES, WEATHER

### Freak Cold Wave

Saturday, December 29, 1962, began as a mild day. Around 4:00 in the afternoon, a heavy, wet snow began to fall, continuing throughout the evening. At intervals it would become slightly warmer, and the precipitation would change to rain. In the middle of the night an Arctic wind seemingly came from nowhere, and by 5:00 a.m. on the 30th the mercury registered 27° below zero. By three hours later, 8:00 a.m., the temperature rose to 0°. During the day the temperature remained very cold. At 8:36 in the evening, Wolfeboro Neck was raked by a terrific gale, possibly a small tornado, that tore down a large tree which took with it two utility poles and created a power outage. It was determined that the tornado (or whatever it was) had struck Centre Harbor about an hour earlier and had moved across Tuftonboro Neck on its way to Wolfeboro.

### Tornado!

On July 18, 1963, the *News* reported:

> Pleasant Valley was anything but "pleasant" for several minutes last Thursday morning. A driving rainstorm that drenched other areas of Wolfeboro turned up as a twister on the Hill School Camp property. The tornado struck at about 9:30 a.m., lasted for five or 10 minutes, and left behind a path of damage in the localized area of Rust Pond. Considerable timber and several camp tents were blown down. Three automobiles were demolished. Blankets, clothing, examination papers, and books littered the woods and clearings....

The Hill School Camp (today the Wolfeboro Camp School), established in 1910 for summer tutoring, was occupied at the time by 98 boys and a staff of 26.

### Memorable Waves

On August 24 of the same year several boaters who had stopped in Wolfeboro to shop were heading back to Moultonboro Neck and encountered waves estimated at eight feet in height between Parker Island and Wolfeboro Neck. Their 18-foot plywood craft split in the bottom and Mark Leopold of New York, age 66, was drowned; the others were rescued.

On November 30, 1963, winds reached hurricane proportions and:

> at times churned Lake Winnipesaukee into a raging ocean. Six- and eight-foot whitecaps hit the Town Docks area and set 20-foot sprays of water into the air. Many local people made trips to the docks during the high winds to get a glimpse of the angry "ocean" at the town's front door.

A year later, on the afternoon of Thanksgiving day, November 26, 1964, the town was pelted by hailstones as large as marbles. "A drift of them was still to be seen at the Wolfeboro Shopping Center on Friday morning."

Graduation exercises at Kingswood Regional High School on June 23, 1965, were not soon forgotten, especially by those who were in the path of a "baby tornado." Along parts of Main Street and Sewall Road, trees were damaged, power lines were downed, shingles were ripped from roofs, and pine cones flung about. In one yard, a bunch of lawn furniture was deposited in a conical heap. At the school, lights went out for a moment until auxiliary power kicked in.

Meanwhile, there had been a notable lack of rain, and in July the selectmen banned the use of water for outside purposes. Beach Pond, the town supply, was dangerously low.[104] During the drought a well-intentioned town employee dug up the end of the water line near the Libby Museum and used a fire pumper to take water from nearby Lake Winnipesaukee and force it through the system. The health authorities discovered the new source and quickly closed the operation down. The situation was hushed up as it was feared that it might reduce the number of tourists visiting Wolfeboro. However, no one became ill and, in fact, some "noticed a decided improvement in the quality of the water."[105]

### Ice and Snow

In March 1965 seasonal warming caused the ice on Wolfeboro Bay to expand considerably, threatening damage to the Town Docks. Curtis A. Pike, "Wolfeboro's dynamite expert," was hired. With a series of explosions, a channel was blasted, and the docks were saved. Meanwhile, onlookers were treated to a "spectacular show of sound supported by ice and water rising high into the air."

Beginning on February 23, 1967, snow fell to a depth of 22 inches within 24 hours, eventually depositing a total of 42 inches. Seven pieces of town highway equipment and 15 men plus mechanics worked around the clock for three days and nights to keep the roads open. Other notable snowstorms of the decade include those which began on November 7, 1968, and February 9, 1969, each recording 18 to 24 inches of accumulation.

Beginning on Tuesday, February 25, 1969, 30 inches of snow fell to add to what was already on the ground, making a whopping 68 inches. The load on the roof of Kingswood High School was so heavy that classes were canceled, while teams of student volunteers worked all day to clear the white stuff away. The town road crew reported drifts as high as 18 feet in some places.[106]

### Oil Slick

On June 3, 1970, high winds and a thunderstorm hit Wolfeboro, and for much of the day the water on Lake Winnipesaukee was very rough. For some time, oil had been seeping into the Smith River and coating the surface of Wolfeboro Bay. The wind blew much of this scum to the shore area extending from the Town Docks to Brewster Beach. Albert Powers, head of the Science Department at Brewster Academy, went down to water's edge and dipped a bottle into the lake. Upon viewing its contents, he saw it was half filled with "an ugly gray substance."

An investigation commenced, and it was found that one or more gas stations routinely dumped used oil and other petroleum substances down their drains. This was corrected by installing oil-catching basins.

On September 3, 1970, the local paper commented that "pollution is still the number one problem affecting everybody." The specter of mercury poisoning from fungicides and other contamination was raised. It was considered remarkable that local bathing beaches were able to remain open all summer.[107]

### Thump!

The April 18, 1968 *Granite State News* reported that a large meteor had recently streaked across the evening sky. It appeared to be quite spectacular, ablaze with a fiery tail. Apparently it hit the ground in or around town, causing a distinct thump which provoked the barking of dogs. The apparition was also seen in other parts of the state.

In his authoritative text, *Principles of Meteoritics*, E.L. Krinov wrote:[108]

> At the moment when a sufficiently large meteorite, weighing about 10 kilograms [22 pounds] or more, falls upon the ground, there resounds a dull detonation ("thump") which can be heard as far away as one or two kilometers [0.6 to 1.2 miles] from the place of fall.

The significance of this is that in all of recorded history, no meteorite among over 10,000 known worldwide falls and finds has ever been recovered within the boundaries of the state of New Hampshire. If, perchance, this "thump" did occur within Wolfeboro town limits, and *if* the meteorite is ever found, Wolfeboro will become world-famous in natural history circles! And, the finder will have something worth thousands of dollars to collectors and scientists.

## PRICES IN 1970

In the November 30, 1969 issue of the *Granite State News*, the editor noted that a selected list of groceries costing $3.37 in 1932 had risen in price to $5.15 in 1940. The editor took the list to a local market and found that the same items would cost $14.83 in autumn 1969. The average weekly wage in 1969 was $115.

The following prices are from advertisements in the *Granite State News*, 1970.

**All-terrain vehicle:** Passe Par Tout[109] vehicle suitable for swamp, woods, sand, snow or open country, at Albee GMC, Inc., $1,595.

**Appliances:** Philco-Ford two-door refrigerator-freezer, 14.2 cubic feet, $250. TV, Philco, 12" personal portable, black and white $100. TV, RCA color, 23" screen, $477. Washer, Whirlpool automatic, $200. Whirlpool clothes dryer, $150.

**Automobiles:** Chrysler Newport, two-door hardtop, $3,915.

Chrysler Town & Country station wagon, $4,515. Dodge Monaco, two-door, hardtop, $3,992. Ford Maverick, $1,995; fully equipped $2,366. Ford Pinto, $1,919. Plymouth Barracuda Grand Coupe, two-door, hardtop, $3,334. Plymouth Duster, basic, $2,172; fully equipped $2,456.75. Plymouth Sport Fury, two-door, hardtop, $3,851. Volkswagen Beetle III Sedan, 1971, $1,780 (plus other charges).

**Automobile tires:** 775 x 14 or 775 x 15 fiberglass belted, each $35. Full four-ply nylon 775 x 14 or 775 x 15, each $25.

**Beverages:** Coffee, Eight O'Clock brand, 1-pound bag, 59¢. Coffee, Maxim, freeze-dried, 8-ounce jar, $1.85. Milk, gallon, homogenized vitamin D, 99¢. Rum, Old Mr. Boston brand, half gallon, $7.70. Whiskey, Mr. Boston's Deluxe Blended, half gallon, $7.60.

**Book:** *Bartlett's Familiar Quotations*, $12. Rand McNally's *International Atlas*, $27.95.

**Cigarette lighter:** Zippo, $2.37.

**Dry cleaning:** Coin-operated, 8 pounds for $2.

**Food:** Meat: Bacon, sliced, pound, 79¢. Beef ribs, "cut from the first four ribs," pound, 98¢. Corned beef, thick cut, lean fancy brisket, pound, 69¢. Delmonico steak, pound, $1.98. New York sirloin steak, pound, 99¢. Tuna, Star-Kist, solid white, 7-ounce can, 35¢.

**Food:** Various: Apples, Cortland, 4-pound bag, 49¢. Bananas, Chiquita, pound, 15¢. Cauliflower, head, 49¢. Cereal, Wheaties, 18-ounce package, 39¢. Cookies, Nabisco, Chips Ahoy, 14.5-ounce package, 47¢. Eggs, large, dozen, brown, 45¢. Flour, Pillsbury's Best, 25-pound bag, $2.29. Ice cream, Marvel brand, A&P, 1/2 gallon, 69¢. Ketchup, Heinz, 20-ounce bottle, 29¢. Oranges, Florida, 5-pound bag, 49¢. Potatoes, 20-pound bag, 99¢. Spaghetti, Prince brand, 14-ounce package, 23¢.

**Furniture:** Mattress, two-piece Serta set, twin or full size, $120. Rug, polyester shag, 12x 20' red and olive, $175; 12x10' acrilan loop rug, $85.

**Haircut:** Adult, $2; child, $1.50.

**Household items:** Kleenex, 200 two-ply facial tissues, 3 packages for 89¢. Soap, 4-bar pack of personal-size Ivory soap, 29¢. Tide laundry detergent, 49-ounce package, 59¢.

**Interest on money:** 1970, February 5, First National Bank of Rochester announced 7.5% per year on certificates of deposit of $100,000 or more; on lower amounts, 5.75% per year on two-year certificates; 5.5% per year on one-year certificates; 5% on 39-day certificates, minimum $5,000.

**Medicine:** Aspirin, bottle of 250, 33¢. Bayer aspirin for children, bottle of 36, 25¢.

**Paint:** Kyanize floor and deck enamel, gallon, $9.50; latex sand-finish texture paint, gallon, $5.40; clear urethane finish, gallon, $12.30.

**Real estate:** Building lot, "finest in town, only two minutes to center of Wolfeboro, corner of North Main and Forest Road," $12,000. Five building lots on Forest Road, one minute from Carry Beach and three minutes to the center of Wolfeboro, $4,000 to $6,000. Jennie Sinclair estate in South Wolfeboro Bay; 12-room year-round home including eight bedrooms, three full and two half-bathrooms, 32-foot living room with fireplace, beautiful spacious dining room, two-bedroom guest cottage, greenhouse, available with 179 feet of lake frontage for $97,000 or 305 feet of frontage for $117,000. House, newly-built, three-bedrooms, at the end of Anagance Lane; attractively paneled living room, ceiling and walls, hot-water heat, $16,500. House on four acres near the top of Cotton Mountain, 12 rooms, $35,000. House, three-bedrooms, 156 feet of Lake Winnipesaukee frontage, central heat, insulated; 20-minute drive to downtown, $43,000.

**Recreation:** Cruise to Caribbean, eight days and seven nights including transportation from New York, $299 up. Skiing for a day, north of Wolfeboro in Jackson, including ski lesson, lift, lunch, and party, $6. Ticket to Saturday matinee at Hatch Theatre, 75¢; typical evening ticket prices, adult, $1.75; child, $1. Tour, 21-day guided European trip to 10 countries, departing from Maine, most meals included, $769.

**Restaurant food:** Dinner at restaurant with choice of roast beef, ham, turkey, etc., $2.95. Hamburger plate, 99¢. Sub sandwiches at Warren's Den: Salami 65¢, ham 80¢, Italian cold cuts 90¢, American cold cuts 75¢, roast beef $1.10, tuna 80¢. Pizza, 12", small, cheese and tomato $1.25, pepperoni and sausage $1.90, ham $1.90, mushroom $1.90, onion $1.65.

**Shoes:** Girls', $10 to $15.

**Snowmobile:** 1970 Sno-Jet, 634 cc engine, 36 h.p., $1,299.

**Tools:** Black & Decker radial arm saw, $99.95. Ladder, 16-foot flat-rung style, $16.88; 40-foot, $64.88; five-foot aluminum stepladder, $9.77.

**Watches:** Ladies' Gruen, 17 jewels, $35.88. Men's Waltham, colored dial, $18.88.

# CHAPTER 10
# WOLFEBORO 1971-1980

*Wolfeboro remains an unfortunately rare outpost of the kind of careful, alluring personal charm that American mythology has led us to expect of its small towns, but has more often left us disappointed.*
—Richard Hart, *Boston Globe,* August 13, 1978.[1]

## INTRODUCTION

Perhaps no better précis of the 1970s can be found than in the words of Bishop John Wesley Lord in an August 1975 talk to the Wolfeboro Rotary Club, in which he reviewed current dilemmas in American life, stating in part:

> In the next few years we will be, as a nation, laboring under great temptation toward hucksterism. By this we mean a day of small things and the absence of great ideals and excellence in human behavior. Trivia and trifles will usurp the great and the noble in our thoughts and actions. The mood of America already reflects this climate. There is hesitancy about our national goals. We are disenchanted because of events. The nation is in a mood of retrenchment, drawing back, of loss of vision....
>
> The family is in trouble. The voice of the church is uncertain. The government is floundering, looking for leadership. Education is being tempted to keep its enrollment in colleges and universities by resorting to gimmicks and lower standards. We are asked to meet vocational needs only rather than education for education's sake. Democracy is in trouble. It is being charged that the western democracy is devoid of ethical foundations and that the democracy there is simply a framework in which parties and social classes engage in the conflict of interest...
>
> If we succumb to hucksterism, we invade our capital, we forfeit our American heritage of inward happiness and world concern, we undermine the supports of religion and morality on which the foundation of our society was laid.

As will be seen, while Wolfeboro was not a direct reflection of the national scene during the decade, it could not help but be influenced by profound worldwide changes in politics, economics, sociology, and behavior.

Perhaps more so than any other decade, this 10-year period changed Wolfeboro from the old order to the new. Still, Wolfeboro "survived," and by 1980 the charm that has made our town so attractive to so many over the years was still intact.

## WAR AND POLITICS

### Vietnam

When Richard M. Nixon was elected president in November 1968, about 540,000 American ground troops were in combat in Vietnam. Following his campaign promises, Nixon gradually withdrew troops and trained and supplied South Vietnamese to do most of the ground fighting. As time went on, the plight of refugees and others in Cambodia and Laos became of increasing concern to the American people.

On October 25, 1971, the 26th Amendment to the Constitution lowered the voting age from 21 to 18. Now, many men and women who had placed their lives at risk in Vietnam could vote concerning their future.

By 1973 there were no American troops on the ground in Vietnam, although the United States continued to provide air cover. The military draft in America had ended. Meanwhile, many returning soldiers, especially those who had been physically or emotionally injured, had difficulty becoming adjusted to civilian life. There were no homecoming celebrations in Wolfeboro (or in most other places either), no victory rallies, no effusive congratulations for the sacrifices they had endured. However, the local Harriman-Hale Post of the American Legion did much to recognize its own. In 1975 the state of New Hampshire gave a $100 bonus to those who had been in active service between August 5, 1964, and August 15, 1973, among other qualifications.[2]

On November 11, Veterans' Day, 1976, the Wolfeboro Roll of Honor was dedicated near the Soldiers' Monument at Pickering Corner. Listed were the names of veterans who had served in World War II, the Korean War, and the Vietnam War.[3]

On January 21, 1977, President Jimmy Carter pardoned Vietnam War draft evaders, a highly controversial move. In 1979 numerous state and national government agencies belatedly accelerated the development of programs to assist veterans with emotional and adjustment problems.

### Those Who Served

The men and women who served in the Vietnam War, as listed on the Wolfeboro Roll of Honor, are given below. One, Carroll F. Hersey, gave his life.[4]

Geoffrey Adjutant, Frank R. Allen, Jr., Fred Antonucci, William Antonucci, Dennis Appleby, Albert F. Auderer III, Dean V. Austin, Allan E. Bailey, Jr., Howard Baker, Jr., Patricia A. Bean, Richard R. Bean, Scott E. Benson, Steven Benson, Gerald A. Bergeron, William S. Bodwell, Glenn A. Brewster, Walter F. Brothers, Robert G. Brown, Harold L. Brownell, Ralph W. Brownell, John T. Carr, Charles A. Chamberlin, Arthur J. Champagne, James Champagne, Roger O. Clark, Jr., James A. Clough, Daniel Clow, Arthur J. Copp, Harley P. Craigue, Richard M. Davis, Philip D. Day, Richard F. Delaney, Leonard Dodier, Ronald Dore, Ronald B. Dunbar, Forrest J. Durkee, Jr., Robert A. Durkee, William J.P. Durkee,

Everett A. Edmunds, Keith A. Elliott, Dennis Emack, Christopher Emerson, Richard A. Estes, Jr., Peter Reed Farrin, Roy Finniss, John Fisher, Robert Fisher, Richard Fogg, Wilbur Ford, Charles A. Foss, Walter C. Foss, Jr., Frederick R. Fraser, Richard L. Furfey, Ronald Gagnon, David C. Garner, Chester F. Gilman, Dennis Glidden, John Glidden, Lee C. Glidden, Mark Glidden, Ronald Glidden, Sandra J. Harris, Lawrence W. Hamm, Bruce N. Hatton, Frederick L. Hatton, Carroll F. Hersey, Dorothea L. Holmes, William S. Holmes, Jr., Allen E. Hooper, Lyford Hutchins, Stephen P. Jones, Wayne J. Kelloway, Michael Lord, Ronald S. Lord, Jeffrey Lynn, Douglas P. McKenzie,

Robert A. Michaud, Robert M. Moody, Harrison D. Moore, Donald M. Morgan, Sr., David S. Morrill, David W. Morrill, John L. Morrill, Jr., Philip H. Morrill, Jr., Timothy W. Morrill, Richard A. Monroe, Jr., James T. Nelson, Michael J. Niblett, David Parsons, Mark E. Pennell, Robert Penney, Chester H. Pike, Curtis A. Pike, Daniel R. Piper, Gary S. Piper, Ivan J. Piper III, Wayne R. Piper, Robert Pollini, Richard C. Reckmeyer, Jr., Reginald Ridlon, John E. Rines, Edward L. Roberge, William R. Rollins, Donald Savard, Carl F. Shannon, C. Stuart Shannon, Allen Shipman, John W. Shipman, Allen D. Simons, Lawrence L. Smart, John A. Staples, Charles E. Stead, John R. Stevens, Ralph P. Stevens, Lawrence A. Swinerton, Irving L. Thomas, David C. Tibbetts, Norman W. Turner, Jr., Fred B. White, Garry L. White, Michael Wilkes, Kevin Wilkins, Eliot U. Wyman, Malcolm L. Young, and Ralph E. Young.

### The Nixon Years

In 1971 the primary race for the November 1972 presidential contest began in a serious way. According to a poll the leading Democratic contender in New Hampshire in December 1971 was Sen. Edmund S. Muskie of Maine. The same survey showed that among Republicans, President Nixon was favored by 78% of the voters, while U.S. Congressman Paul N. McCloskey (from California) had 6%, Gov. Ronald Reagan (California) claimed 5.5%, and 9.5% of Republicans were undecided.[5]

On November 27, 1971, McCloskey visited Wolfeboro at a reception held with 50 people at the home of Warren Tickle on Lakeview Terrace.[6] While here, the candidate blasted President Nixon's war de-escalation policy and further stated that "under the Nixon administration the threat of concentrated wealth working secretively to influence governmental decision making has reached crisis proportions."[7]

By mid-January 1972, there were nine contenders in the presidential primary. On the Democratic side of the fence, Edmund Muskie, Los Angeles Mayor Sam Yorty, Indiana Sen. Vance Hartke, South Dakota Sen. George McGovern, and a man from Hartford, CT named Edward T. Coll "who heads an urban action group called the Revitalization Corps" had their hats in the ring. By this time, Republican hopefuls included Nixon, McCloskey, Ohio Congressman John Ashbrook, and, for good measure, comedian Pat Paulsen.[8]

On February 5, 1972, Billy Jo Clegg from Seminole, OK, visited town and greeted citizens at P.J. Lanes in Clarke Plaza. A registered Democrat, he had formed the Loyal USA Party, which claimed to have 100,000 members. In an interview on WASR Radio with Paul R. Hatch, Clegg stated that he would choose only Christians to be on his staff if he were elected president and that they were to "love and be loyal to the United States."[9]

Incumbents President Richard Nixon and Vice-President Spiro T. Agnew began strong efforts to stay in power. In town, the local office of "CREEP" (Committee for the Re-Election of the President) was located on the second floor of Black's Paper Store and had telephones manned by Mrs. Russell C. Chase, Mrs. "Lib" Coleman, Mrs. Virginia Phelps, Mrs. Winifred Miller, Mrs. Marian Larson, Mrs. Elfrida Hawkins, and Mrs. Bertha Harrison, "all of whom telephone all day long. They have made 400 calls, but more volunteers are needed."[10]

On February 26, 1972, in the midst of a snowstorm, Paul N. McCloskey revisited Wolfeboro, walked through the downtown streets, addressed an audience of 100 students and others at Brewster Academy and was interviewed by WASR Radio. He called Nixon's continued bombing of Vietnam indefensible and said it was only "to save the corrupt South Vietnam government, a police state and military dictatorship."[11]

On March 2, 1972, actress Shirley MacLaine, on the campaign trail on behalf of George McGovern, gave a talk at Bearce Hall at Brewster Academy.[12]

On March 7 the first-in-the-nation presidential primary election was held. In Wolfeboro, on the Republican ticket, Nixon swept the field with 747 votes, against 122 for McCloskey, 91 for Ashbrook, and just 5 for Paulsen. The Democratic contest was led by McGovern with 85 votes, followed by Muskie with 74, Yorty 9, Hartke 5, and Coll 1.[13]

From then on, it was Nixon vs. McGovern, with Nixon emphasizing his foreign policy achievements (better relations with the USSR, a cordial trip to hostile China in February 1972, reduction of the Vietnam War, etc.). The burglary of Democratic Headquarters in the Watergate Apartments in Washington on June 17, 1972, was a minor annoyance, but apparently had nothing to do with the White House. In the November election, the Nixon-Agnew ticket trampled McGovern, who won in only Massachusetts and the District of Columbia. In Wolfeboro the vote was 1,467 for Nixon and only 330 for McGovern.

However, the Watergate break-in would not go away. In January 1973 six people went on trial for the burglary, and on April 30, 1973, President Nixon announced that two of his top aides, H.R. Haldeman and John B. Ehrlichman, had resigned, and that White House Counsel John Dean III had been fired. Dean went on to become the primary witness at televised hearings of the Senate, which, as time went on, revealed massive lies and deception on the part of Nixon and his staff, the laundering of large sums of cash, and other illegal activities. As if that were not enough, on October 10, 1973, Vice-President Agnew resigned, pleading *nolo contendere* to federal charges of accepting bribes and evading income taxes. On December 6, 1973, Congress confirmed Nixon nominee Gerald R. Ford, Michigan congressman, to take Agnew's place as vice president.

Nixon, who had claimed innocence in the Watergate affair from the outset, became increasingly implicated as his former associates testified against him. On August 5, 1974, in response to a Supreme Court order, Nixon released secret tape recordings he had made of conversations in the Oval Office, which clearly indicated he was lying and obstructing justice. On August 9, 1974, Nixon resigned, becoming the first American president ever to do so. Gerald R. Ford automatically succeeded to the presidency, thus becoming the only person to attain that office without participating in a presidential election. He picked New York Gov. Nelson Rockefeller as his vice president. In a highly controversial move, Ford announced on September 8, 1974, that he had granted an unconditional pardon to Nixon, who went to his death (in 1994) still proclaiming his innocence and considering himself to be a distinguished elder statesman.

Concerning the new occupant of the White House, the editor of the *Granite State News* commented:

> President Ford says he is not a Lincoln but a Ford. Some view his stands on the Nixon pardon and amnesty for the Vietnam problem people as making him look more like an Edsel.[14]

### The 1976 Presidential Election

In July 1975 President Gerald R. Ford announced that he would run for election in the 1976 campaign. He was far from being the overwhelming choice of the Republican electorate. Ronald Reagan, for one, attacked Ford's ethics and record unmercifully. On January 5, 1976, Reagan toured Carroll County, but Wolfeboro was not on his itinerary. In the same month, other presidential aspirants including Birch Bayh, Morris Udall, Jimmy Carter, Sargent Shriver, and President Gerald Ford were in the state, but not in our town.[15] At primary time in February, 615 Wolfeboro citizens voted for incumbent Ford, and 399 for Reagan. Among the 14 Democrats on the ballot, Udall garnered the most votes.

As the final election drew close, Ford was viewed by many as being weak in character and devoid of major accomplishments. His challenger, Democrat Jimmy Carter, beat him handily nationwide on November 2. However, in Wolfeboro, 1,472 votes were cast for the Ford-Dole Republican ticket, and only 488 were tallied for the Carter-Mondale opposition.[16]

### The 1980 Presidential Contest

The next presidential campaign was well underway by November 30, 1979, when Barbara Pierce Bush, wife of Republican candidate George Bush, visited Wolfeboro and told listeners she was appalled at the idea of a Democrat remaining in the White House for the coming four years.[17] January 10, 1980, was George Bush Sticker Day, with Nancy C. Palmer in charge of posting Wolfeboro.[18] George himself was in Wolfeboro February 4 at the Masonic Temple, where he fielded questions. "Bush received much applause at his Wolfeboro appearance and looked very much the front-runner that many now predict him to be. He appeared far more confident and exuberant than in previous appearances," noted reporter Douglas Rooks.[19] He also spoke to the Wolfeboro Rotary Club and was favorably received.[20]

On February 13 and 14 Neil Bush, 24-year-old son of George, was in Carroll County on the campaign trail for his father and made a stop in Wolfeboro. On February 11 Sen. Howard Baker, another who had his hat in the ring, spoke to Brewster Academy students and a scattering of townspeople. On Sunday afternoon, February 17 a crowd of 500 crammed into the cafeteria at Kingswood High to see and hear Ronald Reagan, who was considered at the time to be the leading Republican hopeful. His wife Nancy was at his side.[21]

On the Republican ticket in the primary election in Wolfeboro on February 26, Reagan received 604 votes followed by George Bush 350, Howard H. Baker 155, John B. Anderson 66, Philip M. Crane 11, John B. Connally 10, and Robert Dole 5. On the Democratic ticket, Carter gained 115 votes, Edward Kennedy 88, Edmund G. Brown 29, and Lyndon LaRouche 4.

The election was held on November 4, 1980. In Wolfeboro, winning candidate Republican Ronald Reagan registered 1,536 votes, while Democrat Jimmy Carter captured 398, Independent J. Anderson polled 222, and Libertarian E. Clark had 6 supporters.[22]

### State and Local Politics

In November 1971 Gov. Walter Peterson noted that the Executive Council had approved funding for a computer to be used by certain state agencies. Such devices were somewhat of a novelty at the time. A few years later, it was noted that before the computer era one would walk into a Social Security office, fill out an application for a card, and receive one in a matter of minutes. "But then came computers which supposedly speeded up the whole process. Now all forms are sent to a central location, and the applicant is lucky to receive a card in six to eight weeks. The computer doesn't even smile pleasantly, either."

In May 1972 Brewster Academy considered buying a computer and told town officials that it would be available, "should the town decide to adopt a computerized bookkeeping system." The idea was ahead of its time. Finally, in 1976, a computer was used for the town payroll.

In 1972 Robert C. Smith, local realtor, entered politics and advertised:

> I am running for the office of selectman from Wolfeboro because I want to familiarize myself with *your* beliefs, problems and ideas. In a republic a leader is the elected representative of the people, but the people govern. Let me have the opportunity to be your voice in town affairs. Your comments and criticisms will be welcomed and they will be listened to! Vote for Robert C. Smith on March 7.

The winner in the five-way March race for selectman was local theatre owner Paul R. Hatch (who later, in 1980, ran unsuccessfully for the Republication nomination to the First NH Congressional District seat). Subsequently, Robert Smith was elected to the board of the Governor Wentworth Regional School District, then to Congress from NH District 1, then to the United States Senate. However, in the early 1970s he was busy with his Yankee Pedlar real estate agency.[23]

On March 12, 1973, Gov. Meldrim Thomson addressed the Chamber of Commerce at a dinner meeting at the Allen "A" Resort. Without a doubt, Thomson was the most talked-about governor of his era. For starters, he went against many in his own Republican party when he endorsed Reagan instead of incumbent Ford in the 1976 election. At one time, it was suggested that Thomson might run for the presidency himself, as a favorite son candidate. One always knew where he stood; his opinions and viewpoints were never in doubt and were always clearly stated. Thomson served three two-year terms, finally losing to Democratic contender Hugh Gallen in 1978.

### Selectmen in the News

On June 11, 1975, Selectman Paul R. Hatch resigned his post because of what he termed an "irreconcilable personal conflict" with Chairman Lawrence S. Toms. The two had scrapped bitterly at various meetings.[24] Paul A. Croteau, the next highest vote-getter in the most recent election, was appointed to fill the empty seat.

At the February 12, 1976 meeting of the selectmen, Hatch, sitting as a regular citizen in the audience, charged that the board had acted improperly in approving grants from the Josiah Brown Trust for scholarships, funds from which were given to the sons of selectmen Toms and Croteau. Moreover, the Brown will established the trusts for educational aid for the benefit, Hatch said, of the "poor and worthy" young men and women of the town. Neither Toms nor Croteau were in the poor category, he opined. The *Granite State News* reported the defense of the accused:

> The response of the selectmen, as condensed from individual statements by all three members of the board, was that they believed at the time and still believe that they had acted ethically and within the provisions of the will; that they are not trustees under the will but administrators of funds provided by that will; the same school of reasoning as to eligibility for grants applies to the applications filed by the two selectmen as is applied to all who apply under the will. It was further stated that at no time in the course of considering current applications had [other] applicants been refused...

Meanwhile, an election was in the offing on March 2, and it was past the filing date. In the third week of February, 1976, Paul R. Hatch declared that he was once again a candidate for selectman and solicited write-in votes for one of the seats. Hatch had many backers, including Robert Pralle, who wrote this letter to the local paper:

> For all their feeble attempts to justify a terrible breach of ethics, Wolfeboro selectmen missed the target miserably, because they simply cannot escape the language of the Brown will which states the money must be "used for the education of poor and worthy young ladies and men residents of said town." It does not say "poor or worthy" or even "poor and/or worthy."... The saddest comedy in the whole affair is that they actually believe they have done no wrong... I recommend that all three selectmen do the honorable thing and resign immediately, and that we elect three entirely new selectmen.

Write-in candidate Hatch won handily in the election. Not wishing to continue the controversy, the Lawrence Toms family returned $400 it had received under what it had considered proper circumstances from the Brown fund.[25] In the same contest, Lillian O. Brookes was elected selectman for a three-year term, the first woman in town history to hold the post.

## ECONOMY AND TOURISM

### Shortages in the Early 1970s

In the 1970s there were two main shortages: fuel and money. These concerns dominated political campaigns, dinner-table conversations, and everyday life. On August 15, 1971, President Nixon declared a 90-day wage and price freeze, tax cuts to combat rising unemployment, a temporary tariff of 10%, and reductions in government spending. On October 7, the second phase of restrictions was announced. Dr. Roger F. Murray II, former economist for a leading New York bank and later professor of banking and finance at Columbia University Graduate School of Business, stated:[26]

> The freeze is good news for Wolfeboro. People have been saving more and spending less of their incomes because they have been worried about the persistent rise in the cost of living as represented by necessities like groceries, rent, and health care. Now they feel at least something specific is being done to stop the inflationary spiral of prices. They are also more willing to believe that we are pulling out of the recession with the result that job opportunities will improve.

Despite nationwide economic difficulties, the town continued to draw tourists. In October the General Wolfe Inn had a special guest:[27]

> A celebrated writer and TV personality recently favored Wolfeboro with a recent visit when he stayed at the General Wolfe. Rod Serling and his charming wife had been visiting the New England states and chose our village whose quiet charm and hospitality more than pleased them with their choice. Pleasant evenings were spent in conversation with other guests in their comfortable living room at the Inn, and many pictures were taken.

Other favorite tourist accommodations of the era included the Wolfeboro Inn, Lakeview Inn, Lake Motel, Piping Rock Lodges, Berry Motel, Clearwater Lodges, and the Allen "A" Resort (which briefly called itself the Allen "A" Ranch), among other names. The Allen "A" had been sold by Allen H. Albee in 1968, and in the 1970s it experienced difficult economic times under its new owner, Norval H. ("Bud") Smith, who had acquired it with a Small Business Administration loan.

On December 24, 1971, a group of merchants treated kids to a free movie at the Hatch Theatre, while, presumably, their parents were spending money for last-minute gifts.[28]

In January 1972 retailers were required to post base prices for items that made up the bulk of their sales. In Wolfeboro, this primarily affected grocery and hardware stores.[29] In 1973 gas shortages, which had been very much in the news, worsened. The allocation for town departments, school buses, and other public entities was tightened, forcing reduced schedules.

### A New Bank

Ever since its founding in 1906, the Wolfeboro National Bank had enjoyed a monopoly. In 1973 the newly-opened Kingswood Bank and Trust Co., organized by regional investors in 1971, advertised itself as "The little bank with the big welcome" and enjoyed a rush of business. By July 1973 regular savings accounts in area banks paid 5% or more, and 7.5% could be earned on four-year certificates.[30]

Shortages spread, and in August 1973 beef was in short supply at price-freeze levels. Local groceries—including the A&P, First National Store, and Kent's Market—found it difficult to restock their shelves, and sirloin and tenderloin cuts were nearly impossible to find. However, at the Market Basket, Jim Clough, meat manager, had a good supply on hand, explaining that unlike other outlets, his store bought from three or four different wholesalers, not just one. A spate of meat extenders (Hamburger Helper, etc.) appeared in stores. In the same year, the Finast market (FIrst NAtional STore) in the Wolfeboro Shopping Center closed its doors, later to be replaced in the same site by Prescott Farms IGA Foodliner (one of multiple IGA franchises in town over the years).

### New Businesses

The Village Host, operated by George and Arlene Fair, the successor in 1974 to the decades-old Kent's Market, was a popular place to buy lunch meats, sandwiches, and beverages. In autumn 1978 grocery stores were given permission to sell wine by the State Legislature. Toward the end of the decade, the old-line A&P shut down and was quickly followed by Charlie Hunter's grocery, later best known as Hunter's IGA and Hunter's Farm Fresh Foods.[31]

Moods was founded by Carol Moody, and by 1980 she had two shops in town. Hampshire Pewter opened its doors on Route 28 next to Parsons Furniture and was staffed by master pewterers who came from England to teach locals the art. The Elk Shops, one for women and the other for men, operated by the Elkinton family, succeeded the former Mulvey's store and The Ballards. Peter D. Shulman and his wife Gaye opened the Wolfeboro Aquarium on Lehner Street, but its existence was brief. Harold F. Brown and his wife Ethelyn, who had operated Brown's Shoe and Clothing Store on South Main Street since 1937, sold to Edward and Patricia Ryan in 1972. The Ryans, who changed the store name to Mr. Ed's, pulled up stakes and moved to Colorado in 1978.

Over the years there have been numerous transportation companies in town. One of the shortest-lived was Don's Taxi Service, operated by Don Cronin of Dover, which began business on May 15, 1972, and collected its last fare less than three months later on August 8. With business ranging from $3.25 per day to a high of $40, the operation could not be made to pay. For a time, William Fluhr attracted press notices with his Metropolitan Taxi featuring a cab imported from London, which reckoned fares in shillings and pence (there was a handy chart posted for translation into dollars and cents). By 1980 Bodwell's Taxi was the only such service in town.

Charles Heard, an attorney from Massachusetts, decided to change his focus and was named superinten-

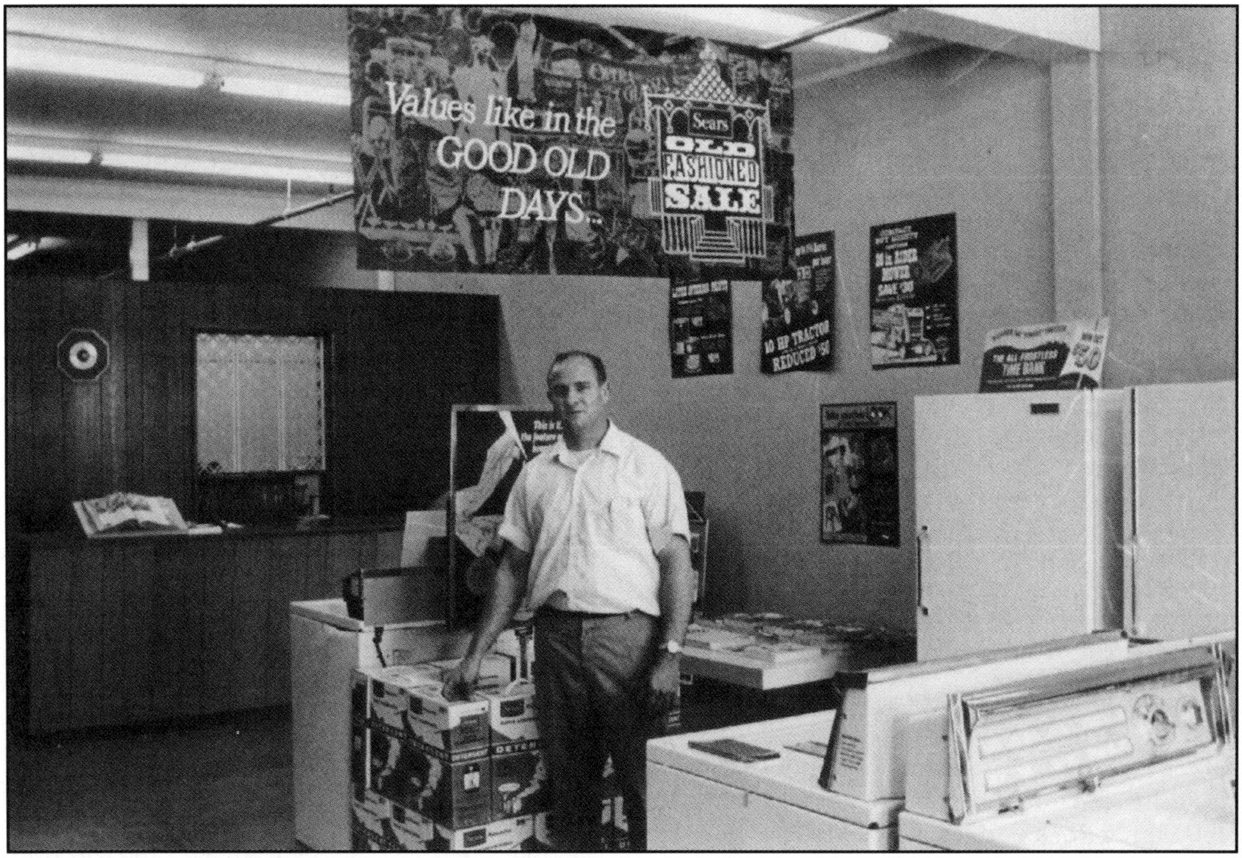


William ("Bill") Todesco, operator of the catalogue store for Sears & Roebuck in the Wolfeboro Shopping Center in the early 1970s. In 1976 the outlet was sold to Dennis and Dianne Sands. (Photograph by Bridgham)

In the late 1970s the former Camp Wyanoke, founded in 1909, was developed as Wyanoke Harbors, an area of fine homes on Wolfeboro Neck overlooking Winter Harbor.

dent of a newly-revived excelsior business using water power in the old Berry Mill in Wolfeboro Falls. The venture proved ephemeral, and soon Heard was back to lawyering, with Priscilla Porch later joining as a partner. Arguably, the best-known Wolfeboro attorney was James J. Kalled, who over a period of time had a number of partners who would later branch out on their own. Kalled, whose large office was upstairs in the Avery Building, was best known for his liability and tort cases and won a number of notable judgments for his clients. In 1980 he relocated to Center Ossipee.

A number of finely-made signs carved and painted by Craftsmen III, headed by Lee Gridley in Ossipee, were commissioned by downtown businesses and were much admired.

On River Street, the Wolfeboro Mills, owned by English investors, succeeded the Hewd Manufacturing Company and made Damart-brand thermal underwear.

### Environment, Ecology, Energy

*Environment* became a buzz-word in the 1970s, and *ecology* was another. Littering, trash dumping, industrial smoke, acid rain, cigarette smoking, and other environmentally unfriendly actions and situations commanded many columns of print. Economic realities were often ignored, and large sums of taxpayers' money were spent on poorly thought-out projects.

Natural foods became popular, and several local stores featured them, the Grist Mill (which later evolved into the Evergrain) being the most prominent. There was even a trend back in time to building log cabins, a number of which were erected locally.

In autumn 1973 gasoline remained in short supply, and some stations closed on Sundays. The town announced that to conserve electricity, outdoor Christmas trees would not be lighted this year. To conserve fuel Carpenter and Kingswood schools eliminated all field trips, reduced sports travel schedules, and extended the Christmas vacation by three days. By this time, the cost of living in NH had increased 7.9% for the year. At local agencies such as the Hart Motor Co. (Chevrolet, Buick) and Horne's Garage (Ford), buyers were ignoring "gas hogs" and buying small-size, fuel-efficient cars.

In January 1974 the selectmen mandated that piles of plowed snow not be removed from the downtown district, another fuel-saving measure. Newly designed versions of the old-fashioned woodstove achieved strong sales, mostly in the $400 to $800 range. At one point in the mid-1970s there were three stove shops in Wolfeboro (My Mother's Woodstove, Hanson Stove Co. which manufactured its own units, and New Hampshire Stove Co.), and one just across the town line in New Durham (Mountain Stove Shop). Even so, there were not enough stoves to meet the demand. In September 1979 President Jimmy Carter, as part of his fuel-saving program, accepted a New Hampshire woodstove to be used in the White House, if only on a ceremonial basis. Improperly installed and overheated stoves caused numerous fire calls.[32]

The antithesis of the ecology movement during the decade was the planning and construction of a nuclear power plant at Seabrook, NH, by the Public Service Co. of NH. In the early years, public sentiment, including that of many elected officials, was overwhelmingly against it. However, a massive advertising campaign by PSNH and rising fuel oil prices turned the tide, and most were in favor by 1980. The campaign to cast the atomic energy facility in a positive light included newspaper notices that if Seabrook were not built, citizens would have cold baths and uncooked food. The editorial integrity of the *Granite State News* was demonstrated by its printing letters and editorials denouncing Seabrook in certain of the same issues in which PSNH ran full-page advertisements.[33]

In January and February 1974 there were long lines of cars at gas pumps in Boston. During the first week of February, Wolfeboro had its own gas lines, but these proved temporary. The problem was "solved" locally in a curious way: although a gas station might be allotted only 80% of the gallonage it previously obtained, Wolfeboro outlets typically sold 25% to 30% of their gas to tourists. Now tourists were scarce, thus making the supply adequate for local use.

However, optimism was short-lived. By the third week of February, CLOSED and NO GAS signs were common in town as some stations ran short. By noon, Monday, February 18, not a single station in the downtown area was open. On Thursday, February 28, a photograph in the local paper had this caption:

> Gas-seeking motorists formed lines at Wolfeboro filling stations Tuesday morning and all stations were sold out before 9:00 a.m. This line extended down Route 28 from just below the Wolfeboro National Bank to a station in the shopping plaza. A shorter line extended part way up the hill north of the plaza.

Later, a state survey showed that 1973-1974 winter tourist traffic had been down over 30% from the year before.[34]

### The Mid-1970s

By May 1974 the gasoline crisis had abated somewhat, and it was expected that summer tourism would be at satisfactory levels. Kicking off events was the Wolfeboro Bay Aquatic Show sponsored by the Chamber of Commerce on May 17 and 18 at the Town Docks, with boat and equipment displays by regional marinas and organizations. The *Jacquelyn,* a classic wooden lake boat used in the highly-publicized motion picture *The Great Gatsby,* was a drawing card.

Increased interest rates and fuel shortages caused rising unemployment. On August 1, 1974, the state launched a food stamp program to assist those out of work or with low incomes. By August, NH gas prices averaged 56¢ per gallon for regular grade and 60¢ for premium. Supplies, while not generous, were sufficient in most areas. At season's end, Mildred A. Beach, spokesperson for the Lakes Region Association, stated that the summer tourist trade had been average.

In Wolfeboro, as across the nation, inflation was rampaging. "WIN" buttons were distributed by the government. (Whip Inflation Now, said to be the new, if unofficial, national motto.) On an airline flight to Palm Beach, a stewardess (as what we know today as flight attendants were then called) wore her button upside down, as NIM, for "Nation In a Mess."

At the December 11, 1974, selectmen's meeting, it was noted that in the past year the cost of living had increased 12.2%. Many local wage-earners were having trouble making ends meet. *Granite State News* columnist Helen Fetzer, quoting nineteenth century humorist Artemus Ward, suggested, "Let us all be happy and live within our means, even if we have to borrow money to do it."

In January 1975 gasoline continued to rise in price and hit 75¢ a gallon. While citizens were implored to save energy, the government was seen to be wasting it on several fronts. The Federal Energy Administration, whose avowed purpose was saving energy, sent not one but two copies of a news release to the *Granite State News,* using for each a large, heavy manila envelope to send a single thin sheet of paper. This prompted the editor to sarcastically comment, "We often wish that the federal government were run by 50 North Country types who have practiced conservation, penny-pinching and downright stinginess all their lives."[35]

Merchandise sold sluggishly locally, and even previously-scarce woodstoves were a drug on the market. Factory rebates were employed as a marketing scheme on big-ticket items such as automobiles. It was a buyers' market for many manufactured items and real estate. Notwithstanding this, the Memorial Day weekend tourist business surprised local merchants and hoteliers and was a blockbuster. The cause? The weak dollar overseas prompted the curtailment of many trips to Europe, and it was relatively inexpensive to drive up from Massachusetts or New York to spend a few days in America's Oldest Summer Resort.

Digital watches were the latest fad and ranged from a $39.95 Latronix at Hall's Pharmacy to an upscale stainless steel Pulsar model at Sawyer's Jewelry for $295. By early December, gas prices had slumped to 59¢ per gallon for regular. Other prices were "rolled back" (as the process was designated), with Wayne C. Wooley, manager of the Wolfeboro Inn, rescinding 75% of an increase put in place the preceding June.[36]

**Local Economy Rebounds**

In April 1976 twenty-six building permits were issued in Wolfeboro, a record for the period. Plumbers, electricians, carpenters, and masons were all busy at work. The popularity of circulating coinage changed. Kennedy half dollars, minted continuously since 1964, all but disappeared from pocket change, and the largest regularly seen denomination became the quarter dollar. The new $2 bills intended to economize on the use of $1 bills were a flop, noted Bob Fournier, president of the rapidly-expanding Kingswood Bank.

In 1977 among popular electronic devices were smoke detectors and beepers, and the town seriously considered equipping its employees with the latter. Microwave ovens and telephone answering machines racked up strong sales as well.

Local real estate agents of the time included:

Strout Realty, Henry S. Maxfield, Flying Eagle Farm Real Estate (Joseph I. Melanson, III), Richard I. Bowe, Inc., C.M. Mixer, Inc., Phyllis & the Major, Yankee Pedlar Real Estate, Kendall Real Estate, Inc., Hamel Realtors, George Waugh, Nedia Realty, and The Turners, Inc.

In November and December 1977 the following took part in the "Try Wolfeboro First" campaign to persuade people to do their holiday shopping in town:

Allen "A" Resort, Avery Insurance, Black's Paper Store and Gift Shop, Bradley's Hardware, C.M. Mixer Real Estate, Country Photo, Dandelion Florists, Deep Six, Diamond International, Dockside Hardware (until recently known as Wolfeboro Hardware), Father John's Pub, Gene's of Wolfeboro, Goodhue & Hawkins Navy Yard, Grist Mill, Hathcock Originals and Floral Studio, Hoyt's Tile and Carpet Company, Jerry's Restaurant, Kendall Insurance & Real Estate, Kingswood Bank, Kingswood Press, Kingswood Travel Agency, Ladies Elk Shop, Lakes Region Sports Shop, Lakeview Inn, Lakeview Oil Company, Little Red Hen's House, The Loft, Men's Elk Shop, Montgomery Ward, Mr. Ed's, My Mother's Woodstove, New Hampshire Woodstove Company, New York Life Insurance Co. (Richard Rollins), Nordic Skier, Norris Harriman-Contractor, Northeast Sail & Marina, Open Door Restaurant, Parsons Furniture, Prescott Farms, Radio Shack, Samaha's, Sawyer's Jewelry, Schillereff's Bovine, Scott's Pharmacy, Sears Catalog Store, Second Chance Closet, Shell Station, Stationery Shop, Sweaterville USA, Time Shop, Tobey's Pharmacy, Town Grocery, Varney Construction Company, Village Host Delicatessen, WASR Radio, Windrifter, Winnipesaukee Motorcraft Company, Wolfeboro Bowl, Inc. (Bowling in Clarke Plaza), Wolfeboro Building Materials, Wolfeboro National Bank, and Ye Olde Dime Store.

On May 21, 1978, the Kinville agency for Dodge and Chrysler automobiles had its grand opening on Route 28 after a prolonged legal scrap with neighbor Henry S. Maxfield, who insisted that part of the dealer's newly purchased tract was not zoned for commercial use. John Hall and Pete Stanard (Pete had operated a Mobil station earlier) were the salesmen, and Woody Elliot was manager of the service department. In the same month, the Kammler agency began business on Glendon Street, incorporating what was left of the Hart Motor Co. Offered for sale were the latest Chevrolet and Buick models. In autumn 1980 both Kinville and Kammler were sold to Jerry Lawless, who combined both into the Kinville location on Route 28. Meanwhile, the venerable Horne's Garage continued selling Fords on North Main Street.

In 1978 the merchants of Wolfeboro Falls sought to publicize themselves and ran advertisements with a map of their area. Participants included:

> Lauber's Carpet and Tile, Paul's Family Shoe Store, Ye Lantern Shoppe, The Clothes Inn, Barry Bishop, Ltd. (antiques and home accessories), Richard I. Bowe Real Estate, Shannon's Grocery, Little Red Hen's House, Basket Barn, and the Brick House Shop (antiques).

On May 29, 1978, the new rate of 15¢ for a one-ounce, first-class letter went into effect. The United Parcel Service (UPS) offered fast delivery service and was becoming a popular alternative to the U.S. mail.

Interest rates continued to rise, and a compounded eight-year certificate of deposit yielded a record 8.17% at the Kingswood Bank.[37]

### Activity in 1979

Interest rates rose even more, and in February 1979 a depositor could earn 10.2% yield on a six-month certificate of deposit. The writing of new mortgages slowed virtually to a standstill, adversely affecting the local construction trade. By December 1979 mortgages cost 13% to 14%, if you could find a lender. Treasury bills were paying 12% or more. Several firms (the long-established Fred E. Varney Co. among them) closed down, and numerous artisans moved out of town.

In the summer of 1979 there were extensive gas shortages throughout the state. Wolfeboro (and other) stations were required to post their open days and times. Some were open only six days a week, and some were open just a few hours each day. Gas stations within town limits at the time were the Amoco (Pickering Corner), Mobil (Pickering Corner), Texaco (Main and Union Streets), Tulsa (Lehner and Center Streets), Shell (Get-Mor Service; Clarke Plaza), Sunoco (North Main and Endicott Streets), and North Line Gulf (Route 28 at intersection with North Line Road) stations. Diesel fuel was available only at the Wolfeboro Oil Company on Lehner Street.

On Thursday, June 27, 1979, the local paper reported that "at various times Saturday and Monday there were short lines at stations which are pumping gasoline." The Mobil station had been out of gas since June 22 but expected delivery on June 28. The Texaco station ran out of gas on June 25, expected delivery on the 26th, and planned to open at that time with a $5 limit per customer. The Tulsa station was out of gas and did not expect any until Monday, July 1. The Shell station was out of gas and expected more on July 1. The Sunoco station was dry and expected none until the first allocation from its supplier in July. The North Line Gulf station had been out of gas since Saturday, and the next delivery was expected July 1 or 2.

Gov. Hugh Gallen published an advisory executive order on Monday, June 25, asking filling stations to demand $5 minimum purchases for four-cylinder cars and $7 for sixes and eights. This was an effort to halt the practice of "topping off" whereby motorists whose car tanks were nearly full kept adding fuel every time a few gallons were used, thus causing long lines at stations, not to mention wasting a lot of everyone's time. Boat traffic on the lake was a shadow of its former level. John O'Connell, who owned Northeast Marina off North Main Street, still had gas, but few boats were in operation to take advantage of it.

By the Labor Day weekend, there were "plentiful gas supplies" locally and much publicity about the abundance. Accordingly, tourists flocked into Wolfeboro, filled motels to capacity, formed waiting lines at restaurants, and created the best business of the season.

In October 1979 Town Manager Guy L. Krapp announced that a sheet-metal fabricating firm was considering building a plant in town to employ about 75 local residents. On November 15 the Brockhouse Corporation, based in England, disclosed plans to spend $1 million to erect facilities on an eight-acre site off Pine Hill Road near the old town dump, this being contingent upon the town's selling of the site for a reasonable price ($5,000) and rezoning it appropriately. It was stated that proposed wages would range from $3 to $7 an hour, with average hourly pay to be $4.50. Brockhouse proved to be of marginal profitability, eventually incurring losses, and was sold by leveraged buyout in 1988.[38]

### Closing the Decade (1980)

As if more problems in addition to fuel shortages, inflation, and high interest rates were needed, snowfall was very light in the winter of 1979-1980, causing losses at many local and regional tourist facilities. One motel posted a sign, "Super rooms at disaster rates."

Nationally, unemployment rates rose sharply. In Conway, about 35 miles from Wolfeboro, the rate was 7% in July 1980. However, fortune smiled on Wolfeboro, as it had done during the Great Depression of the 1930s, and the rate here was a paltry 2.7%.

In 1980 local construction slowed further. Several real estate developments remained largely unsold. Mortgage money continued to be virtually non-existent. A front-page article in the *Granite State News,* April 23, was headlined "Interest Rates, Funds Lack Halt Construction Activity." This precipitated a strong do-it-yourself trend toward converting seasonal residences to year-round housing. As few new structures were being built, rental units as well as houses for sale were scarce.

By spring 1980, certificates of deposit at both local banks were yielding over 15%. Gold and silver became popular for investment, and prices rose sharply in 1979-1980. Harry May of the Time Shop published gold and silver buying prices in the local paper.

Waterbeds accounted for about 15% of all bedding sales, heading toward 90% according to one prediction. Kerosene heaters and pot-bellied coal stoves were billed as a cheap alternative to other heating methods, and Kero-Sun and other brands became popular.[39]

### Museums

The Libby Museum continued to be a drawing card for tourists as well as residents. In 1971 the guest book was signed by 6,121 visitors. However, in 1980 just slightly over 3,000 came, due to restriction of travel during the gasoline crisis. In 1974 the exhibits were culled, and some mounted years ago by Dr. Henry F. Libby were now decrepit and were disposed of to provide space for new items. In 1975 and 1976, major redecoration and repairs were accomplished. Jackson H. Emery, Margaret J. Moody, Joan E. O'Connell, and Leanne Glidden were curators during the decade.[40]

In a 1971 break-in, two antique guns were taken from the Libby Museum. Years later in 1982 one of them, a French musket valued at $3,000, turned up in Pennsylvania and was returned to Wolfeboro in 1983.[41]

The town's other public museum, the Clark House, operated by the Wolfeboro Historical Society, drew fewer visitors. In 1972 and 1973, Hollis E. Brodrick, local collector of antiques, operated the Blacksmith Shop nearby and made reproductions of colonial era items. During the 1975-1976 bicentennial celebration, several special exhibits were shown.

## ENTERTAINMENT AND LIFE STYLES

### Entertainment

Each year the Winter Carnival sponsored by the Lions Club drew enthusiastic participation, and in the summer the annual Huggins Hospital Street Fair continued its popularity. The annual Rotary Marketplace also had its inception during the decade. First-run films were shown at the Hatch Theatre.

In Wolfeboro homes, color television, eight-track cartridge tapes, newly popular cassette tapes, and stereo offered entertainment. Slightly more than a third of the homes in Carroll County had at least one television set.[42] Amateur videotape recording was just beginning its popularity and was mostly used by schools and organizations. At decade's end, the selectmen held discussions concerning cable TV franchises.[43]

Among hobbies, the collecting of rocks and minerals became very popular, and several local talks and displays were given. Limited-edition collectors' plates were all the rage, and numerous citizens decorated their homes with them. Radio-controlled model boats and airplanes claimed many devotees.

### Stage Plays

Stage plays were produced regularly by Carpenter Elementary School, Kingswood High School, and Brewster Academy students. The Village Players, reactivated on October 21, 1977, grew to be a vital part of the community entertainment scene as years went on. H.E. ("Eric") Erickson was elected first president of the group.[44]

The Wolfeboro Playhouse, privately operated, presented several productions each summer toward the end of the decade, the first being Noel Coward's *Blithe Spirit,* which opened on August 13, 1974, produced by Carleton Davis and Richard Natkowski (director) of New York City. Fund raising proved difficult, and each of the next several seasons was begun with uncertainty.[45]

### Various Events

The following is a small sample of public entertainment and exhibition events of the decade:

**1971, January 17-19. Film:** *The Pink Panther,* with Peter Sellers, David Niven, Robert Wagner, Claudia Cardinale. Hatch Theatre.

**1971, March 26-27. Stage play:** *My Fair Lady,* given by Kingswood High students. Sandy Pace essayed the title role of Liza Doolittle, while Marshall Hewitt played Prof. Henry Higgins, and David Tibbetts was Col. Pickering. 131 people were involved in the production. Costumes by Nathalie Erickson.[46]

**1971, April 21. Stage play:** Carpenter School students presented *The Prince and the Pauper.* Players included Michael Lovett, Michael Decelle, Donald Shure, David Hayden, Jennifer Rose, Lynn Rollins, Heidi Stinchfield, and Steve Wood. "The acting was first rate, costumes were great, and the sets were substantial and beautiful to behold."[47]

**1971, May 8. WASR radio auction:** First annual Dollars for Scholars auction aired. Merchants contributed services and articles.[48]

**1971, June 30. Film:** *Love Story,* with Ryan O'Neal and Ali McGraw. Hatch Theatre.

**1971, July 24. All Saints' Fair:** Food, candy, arts and crafts, gifts, toys, books, etc. Lobster salad $2.50.

**1971, August 12. Stage play:** *Hansel and Gretel* by the Kingswood Summer Theatre for Children. 22 actors and actresses.

**1971, August 6-7. Huggins Hospital Street Fair:** Receipts totaled over $38,000. Fun, booths, entertainment.

**1971, August 28. Annual Art and Music Fest:** Allen "A" Resort. Over 20 exhibitors and more than a dozen performers.[49]

**1971, September. Films:** September 25: *Willard.* "Where your nightmares end." Followed on September 26-28, by George C. Scott in *The Last Run;* then on September 29-October 2, *Escape from the Planet of the Apes.* Hatch Theatre.

**1972, March 25. Rock concert:** James Montgomery Blues

Band and a group known as Park Street Under. Kingswood High. Selections included *Chicken Shack, Walking By Myself,* and *Mystery Train.*

**1972, April 14-15. Stage play:** *Kiss Me, Kate* by Kingswood students. Leads were Susan Lord and Eddie Doe.

**1972, June 8. Series announced:** Brewster Academy had made an arrangement with the Down East Players to house a musical theatre and drama school. Planned performances included *The Fantasticks, Man of LaMancha, You're A Good Man Charlie Brown, The Three Penny Opera,* and *I Do! I Do!*

**1972, July 17-22. Wolfeboro Fair:** Sponsored by the Lions Club. Fun, games, 10 carnival rides.[50]

**1972, July 25-26. "Floral Festival of Fashion":** Charlotte Baker, fashion commentator, led the proceedings at the Wolfeboro Inn to benefit Huggins Hospital.[51]

**1972, August 25. The Royal Wild West Circus:** "The largest Wild West circus in the world." Under canvas at the Allen "A" Resort.[52]

**1972, November 17-18. Stage play:** *Hello, Dolly* at Kingswood High, presented by the Governor Wentworth Education Association. The cast, mostly adults, included Bob Pralle, John Caneen, Johanna Schubert, Kent Lauber, Fred Fernald, and Judy Schaefer.

**1972, December 28. Film:** *Everything You Have Ever Wanted to Know About Sex, But Were Afraid to Ask* with Woody Allen. Hatch Theatre.

**1973, January 25-February 4. Lions Club Winter Carnival:** April Hlushuk, carnival queen, won a trip to Paris. Events included basketball games, ski races, the New England sled dog races, barbershop quartet, skiing, basketball, hockey, model train exhibit, snowmobile races, skating races, and carnival ball.[53]

**1973, July 9-21. Stage play:** Dinner Playhouse, a new private venture at Edwards-on-Wentworth, presented dinner, music by the Down East Players, plus the play *Jacques Brel is Alive and Well and Living in Paris.*[54]

**1973, July-August. Cate Park events:** July 20 and 27: 25-piece Bektash Temple Shrine band of Dover played concerts. August 31: Wolfeboro Wranglers held a square dance.[55]

**1973, October 6. Rotary Marketplace:** Kingswood High. Antique autos, model railroads, arts, crafts, sporting goods, etc., with lively piano playing as background music. Items for sale. Proceeds benefited local scholarships.[56] Became an annual event.

**1973, October 31. Hallowe'en haunted house:** Garage at the William Foote residence on Forest Road was rigged with tricks, under the direction of four Wolfeboro girls, Lorna Colquhoun, Debbie Foote, Jody Titus, and Hillary Hopewell. Admission by donation to UNICEF.[57]

**1973, December 7. Teens Singles Dance:** Kingswood High senior class.[58]

**1974, June 8. Antique automobile parade:** Profile Auto League members displayed such marques as Pierce-Arrow, Hudson, Reo, and Rickenbacker on North and South Main Streets.[59]

**1974, June 26-July 9. Film:** *The Sting,* Paul Newman and Robert Redford. Hatch Theatre.

**1974, July 4. New Maxfield novel:** "Because his son liked the manuscript of a book written by Henry S. Maxfield 16 years ago and in his files ever since, the Wolfeboro author-realtor is enjoying the experience this month of seeing publication by a major publisher of his second novel. *Another Spring,* a story set in a town easily recognizable locally as Wolfeboro, will [be published by Little, Brown & Co.] on July 12.... Maxfield will be on hand at Camelot Book Store...to autograph copies of the book."

**1974, August 24-25. Air show:** Acrobatic and comedy flying, sky-diving, and an exhibition of radio-controlled model aircraft held at the Wolfeboro Airport. Sponsored by the Wolfeboro Pilots Association to raise funds and to celebrate the recent completion of a 2,500-foot hard surface runway. Governor Meldrim Thomson, Jr., was on hand and cut a ribbon.[60]

**1974, October 12. Rotary Marketplace:** Kingswood High. On display was *Miss Bardahl,* a national racing champion (1963-1965) boat hull, 30 feet long, 13 feet wide, weighing 7,100 pounds, with a 3,000 h.p. Rolls-Royce engine which could drive it up to 170 mph. Sam Rogers of Wolfeboro was one of its owners.

**1974, December 31. New Year's Eve party:** Masonic Temple, sponsored by the Wolfeboro Snowmobile Club. Dancing to the Rita Weeks Quartet.[61]

**1975, February 7-17. Lions Club Winter Carnival:** Donna Shure crowned queen. Edward K. Roundy, first principal of Kingswood High School when it opened in 1964, was named Wolfeboro Citizen of the Year.

**1975, May 17-18. 2nd Annual Wolfeboro Bay Boat and Aquatic Show:** Sponsored by eight marinas displaying over 40 boats, plus diving, water skiing, sports gear, etc. The Wolfeboro Rescue Squad, Abenaki Water Ski Club, Red Cross, Winnipesaukee Power Squadron, the NH Department of Safety, and others had exhibits. "The newly outfitted Brewster Academy research boat...will offer free tests of water samples brought in by visitors to the show. The boat, a 38-foot Chris Craft Corinthian, was given to the school by William A. Dawson, Jr., of New York." Allan E. Bailey was commentator at the program. Waterskiing techniques were demonstrated, including pyramid building.[62]

**1975, June 7. Belly dancer:** At the Allen "A" Resort & Motor Lodge. Mid-Eastern Revue "featuring belly dancer Adonna plus the Bobby Spina Trio."[63]

**1975, June 20. Pageant:** *My Country 'Tis of Thee* by Carpenter School students traced the history of the United States.[64]

**1975, August 21. The New Hampshire Ballet Company:** At Brewster Academy.[65]

**1975, August. Film:** *Jaws* played three weeks and was the hit of the summer. Hatch Theatre.

**1975, November 1. Shaw Brothers concert:** Kingswood High.[66]

**1975, November 2. Second Annual Ski and Skate Swap:** Congregational Church. Sponsored by the Wolfeboro Day Care Center.[67]

**1976, April 23-24. Stage play:** *Oklahoma* by Kingswood High students. Directed by Ray Lord and with choreography by Merrill Rich. Orchestra directed by Robert Lauterbach. Cast members included Linda Corson, James Rines, Donald Stockman, Kathy Simpson, Tony Cass, Chris Warren, Tim Rankin, Donald Morgan, Sheryl Ellingwood, Bill McCullough, Jane Carville, Jennifer Rose, Lynne Wheeler, Debbie Erskine, Becky Ellingwood, Lynn Roome, Bethany Glidden, Rose Bourgeault, Julie Cloutier, George Stilphen, Michael Lovett, Wayne MacDougall, and others.[68]

**1976, July 5. Independence Day celebration:** Held Monday, the day after the 4th. "The longest and grandest parade Wolfeboro has ever seen." Carl Shannon, grand marshal. Over 80 units of marchers and floats. Fireworks displays on Saturday and Monday nights.[69]

**1976, August 16. Concert:** Kingswood Jazz Ensemble at Cate Park. Directed by Robert Lauterbach.

**1976, August 18. Piano concert:** Sponsored by the Friends of Music. William Stevens of Quebec, soloist. All Saints' Church.

**1977, April 14-15. Stage play:** *Fiddler on the Roof* presented by Kingswood High students. Players included Mike Lovett, Peter Capizzi, Susan Wheeler, Heidi Gruner, Cheryl Dumont, and Marshall Cram.[70]

**1977, June 14. Annual Plant Fair:** At the All Saints' Church. Wolfeboro Garden Club.[71]

**1977, July 20. Film:** *Star Wars*. Hatch Theatre.

**1977, August 24. Elvis Presley news:** The *Granite State News* noted that following the death the previous week of Elvis Presley, not a single Presley record was to be had in any area retail store—they were all sold out. Radio stations were deluged with requests for Presley tunes. However, "There were no calls at WASR in Wolfeboro, an 'easy listening station.' 'In fact, I haven't heard [an Elvis recording] since I have been here', said one employee, 'and that's over a year.'"

**1977, December 31. New Year's Eve parties:** Lakeview Inn, $25 per couple, featuring Mary Barkas at the organ, with sing-along. American Legion Hall, members and guests, $10 per couple. The Windrifter also had a party.[72]

**1978, March 16-18. Stage play:** Village Players' first production, *Yesteryears of Broadway* at Carpenter School, a musical revue. 700 attended. "Each night, as the curtain closed with full cast on stage, the audience arose as a body and cheered, whistled and applauded until the stage lights were dim and the house lights signaled the end of the show."[73]

**1978, April 27-28. Stage play:** Brewster Academy presented *A Thousand Clowns*, a comedy, produced and directed by Robert Reed. Six players were featured.[74]

**1978, November 16-18. Stage play:** Village Players presented the comedy, *You Can't Take it With You*, in the Carpenter School Auditorium. Leading roles were played by Robert Pralle, Sue Copeland, and Barbara Jackson. This was the first production in which the group designed and built its own sets. The cast included 19 people.

**1979, February 9-22. Wolfeboro Lions Winter Carnival:** Spread over many days. Included ski touring, pancake breakfasts, alpine races, carnival ball, broom hockey, snowmobile rides, sled-dog races (the first in many years and held on a mile-long course behind Kingswood High), cross-country races, and more. Edith DesMarais, founder of the Wolfeboro Area Children's Center, was named citizen of the year. "Carnival Queen Jennifer Douglass received congratulations from her mother, Keli Douglass. Jennifer was crowned queen during the carnival ball Saturday night. This was a particularly special event for mother and daughter because Keli Douglass was the first carnival queen, winning the crown 18 years ago."[75]

**1979, April 5-7. Stage play:** *The Sound of Music* at Kingswood High, directed by Ray Lord and Susan Wheeler. Debbie Foote played Maria. The children were portrayed by Sarah Whitten, Matthew Smith, Theresa Swanick, Mark Kagel, Denise DeChiaro, Pam Hall, and Gwen Shannon. Donald Stockman played Captain Von Trapp. Other important players included Todd Comstock, Elsa Schraeder, Debbie Pollini, Mark Milton, Julie Hahn, Gary Southard, Cynthia Bainton, Pat Russ, Terry DeWitt, Karen Rines, Carla Stock, Eric Sanborn, Sharon Massey, Bill Grace, Caren Pike, Marsha Morris, Rachael Hodgdon, Lee Davis, Cathy Harrington, and Lorna Colquhoun.

**1979, November 8-10. On stage:** An adaptation of Edgar Lee Masters' *Spoon River Anthology* at Kingswood High, featuring Fred Fernald, Keli Douglass, Susan Wheeler, and David Lineham, with Corrine Shannon providing guitar music. Ray Lord directed.[76]

**1980, March. Photographic exhibit:** At Brewster, "New Americans," featuring the works of Lewis W. Hine, who captured on film immigration scenes in New York City c.1903-1913. On loan from the George Eastman House, Rochester, NY.

**1980, May 10. Gymnastics Demonstration:** Masonic Temple. Given by students of Chris Widerstrom (who was also with the Wolfeboro School of Ballet).

**1980, May 17. Record hop:** American Legion Hall.

**1980, May 17. Ballet recital:** Masonic Temple. Students of Chris Widerstrom and Merrill Rich. Star performers included Patti Heard and Jennifer Douglass.[77]

**1980, summer. Stage plays:** Wolfeboro Playhouse Productions presented *You're A Good Man, Charlie Brown; Catch Me If You Can; Promenade All; Ten Little Indians;* and *Come Blow Your Horn*. Richard Natkowski, director. Funding assistance from the NH Commission on the Arts.

**1980, June 27-28. Carnival, etc.:** Gala affair included Boy Scout encampment, clowns, 39th Army Band concert, Wolfeboro Wranglers square dancing, banjo concert, golf championship, dog show, kite demonstrations, clowns, etc. Brewster Alumni Association, sponsor.[78]

**1980, July 20. Dixieland concert:** Cate Park. The Mink Brook Marching Society, a Dixieland band quite popular throughout the 1970s, featuring Doug Cady (piano and trombone), Peter Cole (trumpet and flugelhorn), Bill Swaffield (drums), Don Brookes (bass), George Hall (clarinet and saxophone), Ed Sutherland (banjo), and Chuck Churchill (trombone).[79]

**1980, August 23. Artists in the Park:** Art show on Brewster field. Sponsored by the Governor Wentworth Arts Council and the League of New Hampshire Craftsmen. Members of either group who wished to set up booths could do so by paying a $10 fee.[80]

**1980, August 30-31. Railroad hold-up:** The "Jaycees Gang" staged mock "Brazen Daylight Robbery of the Wolfeboro Rail Road" several times on Saturday and Sunday to benefit the Muscular Dystrophy Association.

## "Have a good day"

Life in the 1970s is reflected by numerous terms that originated or became especially popular during the decade, including the following.[81]

**Acid rain:** Precipitation containing traces of acid, usually from distant smoke stacks including in Canada. Caused pine trees to turn brown, fish to die.

**Aerobics:** A workout exercise regimen to lose weight and/or tone heart, lungs, muscles (in 1982, a videotape, *Jane Fonda's Workout*, was very successful).

**Animal rights:** Animals including seals and other fur-bearing creatures have rights and should not be mistreated in medical research or used to make coats for humans.

**Art glass:** Popularly but incorrectly called "Tiffany glass" (after Louis Comfort Tiffany of New York) was in great demand in hanging lampshades, window plaques, and other objects, and was made by many craftsmen who revived the old art. Locally the Schoolhouse Shop operated by the Wolfeboro Arts and Crafts Association had a nice selection.

**ATM:** Automatic teller machine on duty 24 hours a day. No friendly smile and no "Have a good day" (see below).

**Baby boomer:** A child born during or immediately after World War II and now an avid consumer of cars, houses, Rolex watches, etc.

**Bicentennial:** Spelled "buy-centennial" before the year 1976 ended.

**Big banking:** Why have small-town banks anymore? Bank mergers were going on all over America. Eventually, both

Wolfeboro banks were gobbled up.

**Biological clock:** A term used by certain women to describe their natural aging process, especially when they neared the end of their childbearing years.

**Bonding:** Establishing a close relationship with another human being, especially family members and romantic interests.

**Boom box:** A large portable radio, often with a cassette deck (popularized by Philips of Holland, and by decade's end, the replacement for eight-track tapes). Like as not, that boom box as well as that television set or other consumer electronic item was made in Japan.

**Burnout:** Too much work, and too little play. Time to get away, at least for a while, and do something different.

**Cable television:** Input of TV signals directly by means of special electrical circuits. Talked about in Wolfeboro in the 1970s but not a reality locally until the next decade.

**Cassette:** A newly popular music storage system that wrought havoc with other formats such as the eight-track tape and 33 rpm phonograph record.

**Ceiling fan:** Once thought of as an obsolete device remembered from years earlier, Casablanca (of Pasadena, CA, which started the modern fad) and other newly-made ceiling fans became wildly popular as a two-for-one device: to circulate air and thus help reduce heating and air conditioning bills, and as artistic and decorative items.

**Cellulite:** What a lot of people wanted to get rid of by performing aerobics (which see).

**Certificate of deposit:** What anyone who had $500 or more did with his/her money. All of a sudden, many people became financiers and paid attention to money market rates, interest rates, and all of that stuff that used to be only the purview of bankers.

**Chrysler:** An almost defunct car brand revived by Lee Iacocca, who for an encore refurbished the Statue of Liberty.

**Cigarette boat:** Beginning to appear on Lake Winnipesaukee, particularly at the other end near The Weirs (thank goodness). A lot of money would buy a lot of horsepower, a 70-mph ride, and a lot of noise.

**Civil defense:** It just faded away, bomb shelters grew cobwebs, etc. Where did those yellow-and-black signs go?

**Cluster development:** Group of houses nestled closely on a large lot to comply with zoning requirements and allow more jointly-owned "green space." Wolfeboro Common is an example.

**Codependent:** A newly popular term for what used to be called a clinging vine, a person who obsessively stays with another who is not good for him or her and becomes psychologically dependent in an unfavorable way.

**Coming out:** Voluntarily revealing that one is a homosexual or lesbian.

**Compact car:** A small car that gave many miles per gallon; antonym of gas-guzzler.

**Condominium:** A home built contiguous to another, or a bunch of others, but owned separately with group management.

**Credit card:** Visa card, MasterCard, American Express. Usable just about everywhere now. Veni, vidi, Visa = "I came, I saw, I shopped."

**Cuisinart:** A food-factory in your own kitchen. You could buy one at the Chrysanthemum shop operated by Fenton Friend.

**Designer jeans:** Levi's, Lees, and other jeans went from the barnyard to Fifth Avenue salons, with an according jump in price. Try The Loft, a popular downtown clothing store.

**Diesel cars:** Even Volkswagen came out with diesel models, said to save a lot of money because fuel was a lot cheaper than gasoline. Guess what? The oil companies raised the price of diesel, too. End of short-lived fad. Besides, only one place in town offered diesel fuel, the Wolfeboro Oil Co. on Lehner Street, and not everyone wanted a car that was hard to start and sounded like a teakettle.

**Disco:** Girls (usually, but sometimes men) on stage, usually two at a time, frantically performing steps to loud music. The Allen "A" offered disco dancing in 1976.

**Discount:** A newly popularized name for the regular sales price (OK, sometimes a bit cheaper) of an item, if sold in a warehouse-type of place (also see "factory outlet"). To fight such things, the Chamber of Commerce advised locals to "Try Wolfeboro First."

**Eating disorder:** Splurge and purge, anorexia nervosa, and other dysfunctions received much press and TV coverage.

**Factory outlet:** Popular merchandising trend, especially in North Conway. At first, many such places offered deep discounts on factory seconds, out-of-date items, and some current things. Later, prices inched up (profit margins must be maintained, you know). Although the "factory outlets" would seem to imply ownership by a factory, in practice, many were simply sales agents.

**FM radio:** Becoming popular, and Alan Severy (of WASR Wolfeboro Radio) said it was the (radio) wave of the future.

**Four-day workweek:** Talked about in 1979; never popular locally.

**Frozen yogurt:** Ice-cream-like dessert treat.

**Gas guzzler:** A very unpopular class of automobile once the Arab oil embargo got underway.

**Gasohol:** A mixture of 90% gasoline and 10% ethanol, said to be a weapon against the Arabs and their nasty embargo. However, at least one scientist said that ethanol cost more to make (gas to operate tractors to raise corn, from which it was made, etc.) than the money it saved. Besides, despite press-agentry, no one had any for sale in Wolfeboro.

**Good vibes:** A good feeling or "aura" about a person, place, situation, or thing. For example, "I had good vibes about my employment interview." Antonym: bad vibes. Perhaps the Beach Boys' song *Good Vibrations* is an expansion of the term.

**"Have a good day":** Popular substitute for the now old-fashioned "thank you" at check-out counters in stores and elsewhere.[82]

**Heimlich maneuver:** Henry Heimlich, a thoracic surgeon, developed this technique of compressing a victim's stomach upward to dislodge food stuck in a windpipe. Charts depicting this were posted in restaurants.

**Jogging:** Running a mile or two or three at regular intervals, for exercise, body toning, and health. Also see *Walkman*.

**Kerosene heaters:** Kero-Sun and other models were said to do a better job than that old oil burner.

**Midlife crisis:** A period of one's life, often in the forties and following a divorce, when one paused to take stock of one's direction. The future was getting shorter. Better have some fun *now*. Gail Sheehy's book, *Passages*, was the standard text on the subject.

**Murphy's Law:** Became very popular c.1974-1975 and was applied to various walks of life. Basically, Murphy's Law stated that if anything can go wrong, it will.

**Now Generation:** Today's younger set, particularly individuals in the 1970s who demand instant gratification. Under this term, for example, rather than waiting 20 years when one can afford a luxury car, one buys it now on credit. No waiting. Related term: Me Generation, meaning "I am first, and the interests of everyone else second."

**Palimony:** Alimony awarded to a lover at the end of a live-in relationship that did not result in marriage. (Its inception was a California court award on April 18, 1979, ordering actor Lee Marvin to pay palimony to a woman with whom he had lived out of wedlock for six years.) While palimony didn't make it to the Carroll County Courthouse, in Wolfeboro as elsewhere numerous romantic couples lived together without a marriage certificate hanging on the wall.

**Pasta salad:** Pasta with herbs and other things added was the center of attraction, replacing the fondue pot as the latest culinary novelty.

**Prenuptial agreement:** A supplement to the old-fashioned marriage certificate. Someone wanting to marry for love and money might now have to marry for love alone. Also see *palimony.*

**Pro-choice:** The right of a woman to have a safe, legal, medical abortion.

**Pro-life:** The assertion that women had no right to choose legal, medical abortion.

**Pump iron:** To lift weights as part of a body-building program.

**Quadraphasic:** Having four phases.[83]

**Quadraphonic sound:** Intended to render stereo obsolete, but it didn't catch on.

**Quality time:** A period specifically set aside to enjoy and interact with one's spouse, loved one, or family, to the exclusion of business and other pressing matters.

**Rehab:** Short for rehabilitate. 1. To recover from alcoholism or other dependence. 2. To refurbish a room or building to render it attractive for present use.

**Rollerblades:** In-line roller skates actually developed in the nineteenth century, but now introduced as a brand name without much competition at first. In the 1980s it would become a fad.

**Self-help:** Do-it-yourself therapy aided by a spate of how-to books, encounter groups, etc.

**Sexual harassment:** Unwanted sexual attention paid by one person to a member of the opposite sex, despite the recipient's request that the former desist.

**Shopping center:** Wolfeboro had two (Clarke Plaza and the Wolfeboro Shopping Center). Others, much larger, were rapidly springing up in the state, especially near the Massachusetts border where out-of-staters could escape sales tax (bumper sticker: "Taxachusetts, the Pay State").

**Significant other:** The most important other adult—a spouse or live-in—with whom one is romantically involved.

**Skateboard:** A piece of wood or fiberglass with four wheels, used by teenagers (especially) to travel from spot A to spot B on a road or sidewalk.

**Smoke detector:** electrical device, usually battery-powered, which detects ionization in the air and sounds an alarm when smoke above a certain level is indicated. Many lives have been saved by these devices.

**Stress:** Emotional (in particular) and physical pressure resulting from work, relationships, or simply everyday living. "Coping" (another popular word of the era) with stress was done by exercise, reading self-help books, listening to tapes ("white noise" was said to be soothing, as were whale grunts and other "nature sounds," flute music, etc.), or joining an "affinity group" (another popular phrase).

**Sunscreen:** In an about-face from the old days of Coppertone ads, suntans were not good for you. Lotion should contain sunscreen to help prevent skin cancer said to be caused by a depletion of the ozone layer in the upper atmosphere.

**Support group:** group, class, or gathering of several friends or perhaps others in the same situation as you are, who listen to problems and offer advice and suggestions.

**Trading stamps:** Now a promotional relic of the past, replaced by credit cards.

**Unleaded gas:** Just beginning to become popular at the pumps due to the increased use of the catalytic converter; most people still used gas with lead additives.

**Video arcade:** Successor to the pinball parlor. A TV screen was the medium.

**Videotapes:** Just becoming popular.

**Walkman:** A Sony-trademarked product whereby a cassette tape could be played just about anywhere, especially while jogging. No need to stay at home or even carry a boom box. Plural: Walkmans.

**Windmill:** Buy one to generate electricity (few people in Wolfeboro did; however, Public Service of NH put one up next to Seabrook, to see how it would do—it was quickly dismissed as a publicity stunt).

## SPORTS AND RECREATION

### On Snow and Ice

Skating and skiing were the town's most popular winter sports. The Abenaki Ski Area proved a magnet, as did various regional slopes. An exception was the 1973-1974 season when the ground was bare most of the time, in fact, the worst in 30 years, and Abenaki was open for skiing for just 12 days. The Lions Club Carnival was almost canceled that year, but was saved by some snow at the last minute.

In contrast, winter weekends of 1975-1976 saw about 160 to 235 or more skiers each day at Abenaki. Two new ski trails were laid out, and cross-country ski trails were maintained by a group of volunteers including Cal, Verna, and Steve Flagg, Howie and Jimmy Bean, and Peter and Judy Cole. Donald K. Brookes, director of recreation, was in charge.

During the summer of 1977 the Abenaki Ski Area was improved by building the Kehonka Trail, the Little Headwall, and the Estes Highway. These were cut with a chainsaw and made possible through a donation from the Kehonka Fund set up by Mr. and Mrs. A. Cooper Ballentine. In 1977 the Recreation Department also bought a powder machine which groomed trails into snow.

During the decade, Howie Bean captured several honors, including placing first in cross-country in the Class B-1 State Ski Meet in 1972, while at the same event the Kingswood High Boys' Ski Team were crowned state champions for the second year in a row. In 1974 Bean, a senior at Kingswood, won the Skimeister Award and was selected to represent the Eastern Ski Association at the National Junior Nordic Ski Championship in Steamboat Springs, CO. He was an athlete of many talents and was the 1970s equivalent of Archie A. Horne (who years earlier was described as the greatest athlete in Wolfeboro history).

In 1976 the Kingswood Girls Ski Team won for the first time the Class A State Championship in alpine events. Among those scoring well for Kingswood were Caryl Dow, Diane Brooks, Debbie Hale, Marianne Bean, Muzzy Smith, Carolyn Cole, and Debbie Foote. The final team score of Kingswood was 278.1, with Hanover at 277.8 next, trailed by Kearsarge, Gilford, Laconia, Kennett, and Berlin.

In 1978 Howie Bean, a student at UNH at the time, competed in the Senior North American Nordic American Championships at Lake Placid, NY. He placed in several events including third best U.S. skier in the 30-kilometer event.

Cross-country skiing continued its popularity, and trails were maintained by the Nordic Skier shop and others. Ski parties, moonlight tours, and other events were held from time to time. No snow? Not to worry. Practice skis with wheels at each end, for use in snowless seasons, were available.[84]

On Wolfeboro Bay ice boating and car racing were popular during the winter months. On February 27, 1972, a three-hour endurance race on a marked-off one-mile track was won by Roy Nixon of Manchester, who racked up 115 miles in a Lotus-powered Cortina.

Without a doubt, the most talked-about winter sport was snowmobiling, an activity which had begun in a big way in the 1960s. In February 1971 there were 124 machines entered in the Wolfeboro Snowmobile Club's races, with about 500 spectators turning out in a heavy snowstorm on Saturday and about 2,000 in clear weather on Sunday. The highly-prized Wolfeboro Cup went to a Maine contestant, Bruce Dunham, who was crowned NH state champion. On November 28, 1971, *Snowmobile Fun and Safety* was the theme of a show held at the Hatch Theatre. Color movies, guest speakers, a safety quiz, and a display of snowmobiles for sale all were sponsored by Goodhue & Hawkins, a dealer in Rupp snowmobiles. Other Wolfeboro area franchisees sold Ski-Doo, Arctic Cat, Yamaha, and other makes.

In view of the thousands that were drawn to the sport, David A. Senecal (president of the local club) and Cal Flagg (of the Nordic Skier) recommended to the Chamber of Commerce that if marked trails were set up, local tradespeople would get much additional business. In February 1973 the annual contest, titled the Wolfeboro Cup Grand Prix New Hampshire State Championship Snowmobile Races, drew 250 snow machines and strained the town's tourist facilities with 4,500 spectators, while local merchants' cash registers jingled merrily. Throughout the rest of the 1970s numerous other snowmobile events were held.[85]

### On the Water

On May 31, 1973, the annual Smith River Canoe Race was founded by Arthur Brunt, John Markowitz, and Barry N. Lougee. Brunt was in charge of the event, which began on Lake Wentworth at the Allen "A" beach and continued three and one-half miles down the Smith River, through Back Bay, ending at the Town Docks.

By 1975 contestants came from four of the six New England states. In that year the Class A event, with two adult male paddlers in a standard canoe, was won by Barry Lougee and Arthur Brunt of Wolfeboro, in 30 minutes, 5 seconds. In 1980 Jimmy and Howie Bean won in 24 minutes and 40 seconds. There were 160 contestants comprising several categories.

Another popular sport was sailing on Lake Winnipesaukee. In 1974 a reporter filed this story:

> The New Hampshire Invitational Laser Regatta, held for the second year in Wolfeboro, September 21-22, proved again to be the most strenuous test of men and boats encountered anywhere on the wide circuit of Laser events held throughout the United States and Canada. Many Olympic hopefuls were among the starters Saturday, as rain and light wind scattered the fleet across Winnipesaukee's east side... Rain poured on the shivering contenders as they were towed back into Wolfeboro Bay. A chicken dinner was held indoors Saturday night in Northeast Marina's new shed, and kegs of beer helped dispel the ominous roaring of heavy rain on the tin roof.
>
> Heavy northerlies whipped the lake into a froth on the second day. Sunday morning was bright and windy, and any discussion limiting the action to Wolfeboro Bay was dismissed by the top sailors who could see from top of the hill to continuous threads of whitecaps on The Broads. The wind was gusting over 30 knots as the committee boat, *Sea Mist,* obtained her station opposite Wolfeboro Neck. By the time the tacking Lasers had reached the starting area, some had already capsized more than once.
>
> The start itself was spectacular, with an especially heavy gust upending five boats simultaneously. However, the fleet settled to a hard slam to windward and the first marker at Parker Island. Rounding this mark the boats went into a spectacular three-mile plane across to Ship Island and back to Barndoor Island with a marker in the middle. Most boats tipped over an average of four times. Dr. John Chappell's fly-bridge cruiser, which was a stakeboat, was running at 20 knots to keep up with the screaming Lasers. Only eight boats survived, the rest limping back to Wolfeboro. Once again, Deems Buel [of Laconia] proved equal to the task, showing his superb physical conditioning as he won handily. Immediately after crossing the finish, he deliberately tipped his boat over, seating himself on the high gunwale to watch the rest of the show...

In 1977 Douglas Rooks, feature writer for the *Granite State News,* reported that while powerboating on Lake Winnipesaukee had remained unchanged for five years (primarily due to gasoline shortages), sailboating had registered a significant increase, per figures released by Safety Services Director John Bridges. John O'Connell, of the Northeast Sail and Motor Facility off North Main Street, commented, "A larger boat is actually easier to sail, and people feel more secure on one, especially those who have never sailed. You can afford to make a lot more mistakes on a large boat." Sunfish and Hobie Cats were also best

Ice boating on Wolfeboro Bay, 1971. Leigh Turner and other aficionados test the wind and ice. (Mildred A. Beach photograph)

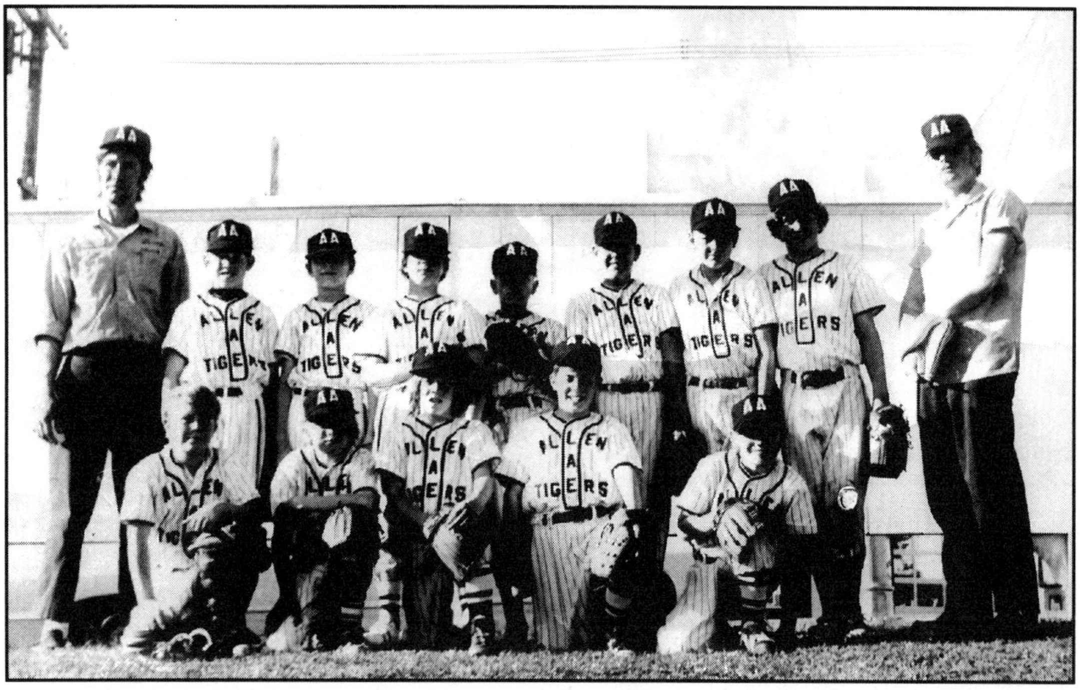

Coaches Pete Stanard (left) and Bill Hooper with the Allen "A" Tigers youth baseball team in the early 1970s. The Tigers had just won a championship game.

sellers. Among smaller boats, canoes were very popular.

The Abenaki Water Ski Club held shows each year. The August 13, 1972, event was highlighted by a pyramid including Peter Schillereff, Chip Maxfield, Bill Swaffield, and Bruce Love at the base, upon whom were standing Candy Love, Joy Pheeney, and Lucy Newall. About 15 members demonstrated tricks, slalom, jumping, barefoot skiing, speed skiing, doubles, and pyramids. Bill Swaffield won numerous state and regional trophies for his water-skiing prowess.

In the summer of 1980 Betsy McKenzie (sister of Alexander "Sandy" McKenzie IV of *Blue Ghost* mailboat fame) gave windsurfing demonstrations in Wolfeboro Bay and helped sign up people for lessons given by certified instructor John Barbary. Classes were given for three to six people.

In the same summer the Wolfeboro Swim Team successfully defended its Division III State Championship. Starring in the event was Melinda Eubanks, who "shocked the state with first place among all four divisions in the backstroke, making her the first Wolfeboro swimmer ever to get an overall first."[86]

### The Great Outdoors

Fishing, ever popular on lakes Wentworth and Winnipesaukee, continued to draw thousands of participants. Somewhat smaller in scale was the second annual Trout Fishing Derby sponsored for youngsters in 1971 by the Harriman-Hale American Legion Post 18. The brook running through the Allen "A" was stocked with 350 trout. The winner was Bobby McNally, who took a 14-inch trout, while Jimmy Pineo landed the smallest, a 4-1/2 incher.

In January 1974 Ronald Varney caught a 5-3/4 pound trout measuring 27-1/2 inches and was pictured with it on the front page of the *Granite State News*.

In the first week of August, 1980, Jill McCaffrey, 12 years of age, caught a 30-inch eel in Lake Wentworth, reportedly the first such creature found in that body of water since Mabel Foss caught one a quarter century earlier.

Hunting was also popular in season, particularly the quest for deer in autumn. The Lakes Region Sports & Photo Shop, run by George Elkins (who bought it from James Warner in 1975), was a favorite place to buy ammunition, get licenses, and swap tales about hunting or fishing. In 1982 Elkins sold out to Joey Melanson (J.I. Melanson IV).

In August 1972 the first annual Tour de King's Woods bicycle race was held. From the starting point at Bailey's Restaurant on South Main Street, bikers pedaled along Route 28 to Ossipee, taking Route 171 through Water Village, proceeding to Tuftonboro Corner, and returning to Wolfeboro on Route 109A, then back to Bailey's. In 1974 A.B. O'Leary was the winner with 1 hour, 14 minutes, 10 seconds, followed 39 seconds later by Howie Bean.

Other popular activities in season in the great outdoors included kite flying, frisbee throwing, jogging, and hiking.

Related to Wolfeboro were these two sporting items in the news:

In 1979 Gina Bovaird, wife of Tom Bovaird (son of Dr. and Mrs. James Bovaird of Wolfeboro), who lived out of town, was ranked as America's best professional woman motorcycle racer.

In 1980 William Jackson of Wolfeboro took the championship in the 15th annual Jaycees Daisy International BB Gun Matches in Bowling Green, KY. The selectmen voted him special recognition and congratulations.[87]

### Baseball

In 1975 the Wolfeboro town baseball team, the Royals, attracted modest support in its first year as a member of the Portland Twilight League. In 1976 the team fielded such players as Matt Hale, Howie and Jim Bean, and Chip Skelley, with Bob Dickerman as coach.

While there was interest in the Royals, more residents followed the achievements of their children and children's friends on the school teams. In 1980 the Minor League players wore shirts emblazoned with inscriptions for the Pirates, Cubs, Osgood Trucking, Black's Panthers, Bailey's, Mr. Ed's, Father John's Pub, and Corner Store Dodgers. In the Major League the teams were Market Basket, Wolfeboro Bankers, Allen "A," and Varney's.[88]

### Golf

Golf was as popular as ever at the sole town course, the Kingswood Golf Club. In September 1973 the Pro Days Golf Tournament saw Jim Pollini (father of Kingswood pro Dave Pollini) register a 72 for the lowest gross score in the top division (0 to 10 handicap). Finishing second and third were Jim Clough, Sr., with 75, and Ed Dadura with 78. "High winds made play difficult, and observers commented that scores could have been several shots lower on a calmer day."

In February 1974 Wolfeboro resident Ethel (Mrs. George) Black made a perfect shot with a 5-iron on the 122-yard over-the-water seventh hole at the Naples, Florida, Beach Club, the second hole-in-one in her 40 years at the game. That same summer, long-time golf enthusiast Joy Sweeney brought home the trophy for the Kingswood Golf Club Women's Championship.

In June 1977 this was printed:

> The first hole-in-one at the Kingswood Golf Club this season was shot recently by Tim Melanson, Kingswood High

School golfer. Using an 8-iron, he aced the 145-yard ninth hole. Tim will be playing his final year on the Kingswood High's golf team, having been a leading member of the team for the past four seasons.... Tim's playing partners when the hole-in-one was scored were his mother, Cindy Melanson, Dan Chase, and Chris Titus.[89]

### Track

During the decade, there were numerous track triumphs by Kingswood High School students. This October 31, 1974, account is representative:

> Kingswood's undefeated cross-country track team, with over 51 opponents, has its sights set on the state meet to be held November 2 in Durham. Runners who will represent the Knights Saturday are Doug Colquhoun, Scott Titus, Steve Rice, Dale Heath, Matty Toms, Captain Eric Heath, Dave Severance, and Coach Ed Roundy.
>
> In another impressive, record-setting performance the Kingswood cross-country team was victorious in the Invitational Race held Friday, October 25, on the home course with a final tally Kingswood 18, Merrimack Valley 53, Kennett 81, and St. Thomas 88. Coach Albert ("Duke") Southard served as meet director, Howard Bean was timer, and Chuck Robarts and Phil Decelle were on the sticks. Dave Severance broke the course record by three seconds with a pace of 12 minutes, 19 seconds...
>
> The 1974 season concluded with the cross-country team placing fifth in the New England Championship meet at Warwick, RI.

David Severance was the 2-mile champion in New England in both the Class I meet and the State Meet of Champions and followed these performances with a win in the same event in the New England Championships in June 1976. This accomplishment was one of the highlights on the track scene at Kingswood during the 1970s. David was a senior at the time and overcame a severe injury to his leg when struck with a thrown javelin in his sophomore year.[90]

### Football

In the 1970s football was the most watched sport at Kingswood High. In December 1971 Coach Tom Lovett announced that four Kingswood Knights players had been selected for the Division IV All-State Football Team: Keith Haney, Eric Roseen, Mike Jones, and Brian Ela.

This account appeared in print at season's end in 1976:

> "We're Number One!" That was the chant of the Kingswood High football fans after the Knights defeated Kennett 34-0 to end their regular season undefeated. It was a chant Saturday afternoon again when Kingswood out-defensed [Plymouth] 16-0 to take the Division III State title before what veteran fans said was the largest crowd ever to watch a Kingswood game....

Kingswood opponents for the year were Plymouth, Littleton, Hanover, Monadnock, St. Thomas, Fall Mountain, Franklin, Brady, and Kennett. Kingswood scored 281 points during the season against a total of only 48 registered by all of its competition. The team included the following:

> Coaches, *et al.*: Tim Corbin (manager), Phil Decelle (coach), Steve Durgan (coach), Gordon Harmon (tri-captain), Mike Lovett (tri-captain), Tom Lovett (coach), Rod Nelson (coach), Bill Pollini (manager), Robbie Pratt (manager), Chip Skelley (tri-captain), and Bill Wood (faculty manager).
>
> Players: Dave Alward, Gary Anderson, Fred Clifford, Matt Day, Mike Decelle, Peter Eckhoff, Dave Gouin, Bill Foster, Mark Frost, Caleb Johnson, Tim Jones, Bill Libby, Joe Lovett, Allen Margeson, Gary McGlinchey, Mark Merrow, Dave Orth, Steve Orth, Andy Parsons, Dan Richardson, Dan Russ, Steve Russ, Jerry Sanborn, Howie Shiebler, Rick Skelley, Glenn Stockbridge, Mike Stoneking, John Swedberg, Adam Tillinghast, Bruce Trottier, and Gary Ward.

On December 5, 1976, a special celebration was held at the Masonic Temple to honor the players, fans, friends, and families of the Kingswood victors.

In 1978 the Knights had their second best season in school history, ending the year with a 7-2 record. On November 4 they beat the Kennett Eagles 9-6 to capture the Carroll County Grid Crown.

In 1979 a 32-6 Knights victory over Kennett made Kingswood the highest scoring NH football team, with a season total of 236 points and a 7-2 record for the season.[91]

### Other Sports

In cooler months, candlepin bowling was popular at P.J. Lanes on Center Street, where several leagues played regularly. Results were given weekly in the *Granite State News*.

In 1972 the non-profit Karate Club operated at Brewster Academy, with 14 students training one hour per day, four days each week. The instructor was Nantge Alexander Tai, of West Germany, who had studied the art of Tae-Kwon-Do for six years.

Tennis attracted many devotees. In 1974 lessons and rental court space were available at Brewster Academy, Point Breeze, and the Wolfeboro Racquetball Club. In 1976 town tennis courts were opened at the Guy Foss Memorial Playground (dedicated to the memory of the former fire chief). There was no charge for their use. Foss Field, as it was popularly called, became a veritable beehive of recreational activity including outdoor basketball courts, a baseball diamond, and a children's playground.

On October 28, 1979, the Wolfeboro team won the first annual Southern Carroll County Soccer Tournament, which featured contenders from Wolfeboro, Moultonboro, Ossipee, Tamworth, and Wakefield. Star players for the locals included Robbie Fontaine with two goals and one goal each for Charlie Strater, Dewayne Waterhouse, and John Pollini. Headmaster David Smith of Brewster Academy made the school's facilities available to host the event, and Debbie Rankin assisted with the arrangements.

In October 1980 the Bay Village Racquetball Club opened on Varney Road. Various indoor sports activities were offered, and there was an upstairs lounge that served pizza, snacks, and refreshments.

Donald K. Brookes and Bonnie Rankin were among the people most active in town-sponsored sports during the decade, with the latter contributing numerous articles to the newspaper. In June 1978 Recreation Director Brookes announced that the summer program would include swimming lessons, tennis lessons, art, crafts, field trips, and more. In 1980 Rankin published a list of activities including a youth tennis program, girls' softball, morning tennis league, and even barbershop quartet singing instruction.

Skateboarding was quite popular with the younger set. At their meeting on July 29, 1977, the selectmen authorized a skateboard contest to be held in July on School Street to be sponsored by the Parks and Recreation Department.[92]

## TOWN

### Guy L. Krapp

In February 1971 Guy L. Krapp was hired at $16,500 per year as Wolfeboro's first town manager. A 1950 graduate of Bucknell University, he served with distinction as town manager of Mifflinburg and Quakertown, PA, and Williamstown, MA, before coming to New Hampshire. Guy L. Krapp reported for duty on April 5, "and spent the rest of the year mainly learning about the community, its people and town operations." Nearly from the outset, he had to dodge slings and arrows from the selectmen and several attempts to oust him and abolish his position. A reading of the minutes of the Board of Selectmen for the early 1970s reveals many rough edges as lines of authority were tried and tested.

In 1979 Selectman Edward W. Zulauf, prominent local resort owner and real estate agent, requested that the work of Guy L. Krapp be evaluated to see if the idea of having a town manager was working out as well as had been hoped when he had been hired. Mr. Krapp requested that said study be completed within four weeks. The Public and Non-Profit Management Service of Hallowell, ME, was hired to investigate. Subsequently, the firm stated that there were some improvements to be made and made 13 specific recommendations. Paramount was the suggestion that more authority be transferred from the selectmen to the town manager—such finding being just the opposite of what certain selectmen wanted. It was also noted that one selectman had two close family members who had been employed by the town for many years, and because of this "the potential for conflict is apparent, even with the best of intentions on the part of all parties."

Throughout the decade, Town Manager Guy L. Krapp remained one constant in a sea of change and accomplished much.[93]

### Goings-On Around Town

Reflective of growing interest in ecology, the first annual Wolfeboro Clean-Up Day, sponsored by Paul R. Hatch and the Hatch Theatre, took place on April 25, 1971, following Earth Week. A program of bottle recycling began in the state in 1971; however, in the absence of a so-called "bottle bill" providing cash for redemption, results fell short of expectations. Highways and byways continued to be littered with Budweiser, Miller, and Coca-Cola cans and bottles. Attention was focused on Back Bay, the bottom of which was lined with logs, sawdust, and refuse, and the area around the old Clow Mill used as a dumping ground for old refrigerators, tree stumps, and unwanted fill. By decade's end, Bayside Village arose on part of the Clow site, and much rehabilitation had been done.

At the March 6, 1973 annual town meeting, Russell C. Chase was at the podium as moderator, succeeding Robert F. Thurrell, who had presided over meetings for over a quarter century.

At the 1974 town meeting, voters established a framework for a Historic District Commission. After three years of study, the North Wolfeboro Historic District was approved at the 1977 meeting.

In February 1975 the selectmen met with Herbert Vinnicombe and John M. Ballard of the Rotary Club and set the wheels in motion that eventually led to the remodeling of the old fire station on Lehner Street into the Community Center. In 1976 it was rededicated.

At the selectmen's meeting of December 11, 1975, there was discussion as to whether plumbers and electricians working in town should be licensed. At various other times, the licensing of street vendors, door-to-door salesmen, and other tradesmen was considered.

Wolfeboro was growing in population. In autumn 1976 it was reported that the number of citizens had increased by 509, or 16.7%, since the 1970 census count and now stood at 3,545. The population of Carroll County increased 29% in the same period. The area was becoming increasingly attractive to out-of-staters, particularly "refugees" from Massachusetts—quite a few of whom found the NH tax structure and lower crime rate appealing. By autumn 1977 the number of citizens in Wolfeboro had increased to 3,697.[94]

In spring 1978 Lillian O. Brookes was named chairman of the Board of Selectmen. In autumn 1977 Selectman H.E. ("Eric") Erickson resigned and was replaced by Edward W. Zulauf, who had served in earlier years.

In 1977 citizens were told that by 1981 the United States was to be completely switched from the English system of weights and measures to the metric system to insure America's continued importance in the world economic community. While bottles of distilled spirits were changed over, as were a few other scattered products, by and large Wolfeboro and the rest of the nation successfully resisted "metrification."

One day in 1978 Mrs. Francis Libby bought a ticket for the New Hampshire Lottery at the Town Grocery in Clarke Plaza. Soon thereafter, she was watching television and saw her number drawn, became very excited, and contacted the Sweepstakes Commission to claim her winnings of $5,549. Her heart sank when she was told the state had no record of her ticket. At the time, all lottery agents of the state were required to telephone to Concord the numbers that had been selected by people buying tickets at their stores. Otherwise, people selling tickets could fill out numbers after the sweepstakes prize was drawn and there could be fraud. Inadvertently, the owner of the Town Grocery had forgotten to call Mrs. Libby's number in. Attorney Frederic L. Cox was retained by Mrs. Libby to help advance her case, which was finally settled in September when Gov. Meldrim Thomson and the State Council, realizing there was no indication of misdoing, voted to pay her in full.

In 1980 *Manning's Little Phone Book,* a mini-guide to area telephone numbers and merchants, was mailed free to local residents. The idea proved popular and was continued through the 1990s by various publishers.

In November 1979 town tax bills increased 16% over the previous year, now being $8.70 per $100 of property tax assessment. Town Clerk Rachel Jones noted that current assessments were at 21% of actual fair market value. This translated to $1,827 in yearly taxes for a property worth $100,000 retail.

In 1980 David A. Senecal was appointed town code enforcement officer, a position he retained through much of the ensuing decade.

On May 18, 1980, a team of 42 volunteer scuba divers from Cliff Simoneau's North Country Diving School spent the day underwater at the Town Docks cleaning up beer and soda cans, bottles, old tires, and other items that had fallen in the water over the years.

In May 1980 an advertisement was placed in the local paper by the Public Broadcasting System seeking movie extras for a documentary film titled *Labyrinthos* (later retitled to *The King of America,* and still later as *The Honor of Andreas Lambrakos*) to be shot in Wolfeboro June 11-18. Michael Welden was in the title role. Anyone interested was invited to contact talent scout Selia Costos, who was staying at the Lake Motel. The picture was filmed mainly along the Wolfeboro Rail Road (*sic;* it was spelled as two words) tracks and brought over $100,000 in business receipts to the Wolfeboro area. Around the same time, *On Golden Pond* (starring Henry Fonda and Katherine Hepburn) was filmed at Squam Lake about 30 miles from Wolfeboro and included some aerial footage of Wolfeboro Bay and Wolfeboro Neck.

The Wolfeboro Garden Club, long active in town beautification, recognized Miss Helen Forman in August 1980. Eleanor Bigelow, president of the group, placed a plaque at a small garden at the corner of Glendon and South Main Streets that had been tended for many years by the honoree.

In 1980 Mast Landing was the only public boat access to Lake Wentworth. Island and shore residents, most of whom were not voters (but were taxpayers), requested that the selectmen expand the docking and parking facilities. This was denied on the grounds there would be "increased risk of accidents, health problems, erosion, pollution of beaches," and other problems.

In December 1980 the town was given the opportunity to buy for $225,000 the Kammler Building on Glendon Street and the parking lot behind the Post Office, but declined.[95]

Wolfeboro, usually among the last on the New England Telephone Company's list when it came to telephone innovations, received direct dialing of long-distance station-to-station calls in the summer of 1973, long after most other towns in the southern part of the state had such service. Beginning September 15 the same year, computerized billing was instituted. In 1980 the company announced, "Touch-Tone phones are here, Wolfeboro."[96]

### Should Wolfeboro Be Changed?

No decade would be complete without its "master plan," and this one was no different, except that it was plural, as in master *plans.* It was felt by some citizens that many if not most municipal problems, and perhaps their own problems as well, would magically disappear if Wolfeboro were changed. Proposals ranged from bringing industry from out of town to having better movies at the local theatre.

In the summer of 1973 the Planning Board suggested that two years be spent to create a "current comprehensive plan for the town of Wolfeboro." Mildred A. Beach, who had been involved with the Lakes Region Association and other area and municipal activities since the 1930s, shared her wisdom in a talk to the Rotary Club, cautioning that in the past, "many assumptions were made without checking figures," and that those who desired industry were thinking in terms of days gone by. Further, "Wolfeboro has never liked to think of its largest industry as tourism. That never did set in their craws very well. But it has put a lot of kids into colleges and a lot of meat and potatoes on the tables in the region." She reminded listeners of the beauty of the lakes, trees, and town streets, and suggested that planning was worthwhile, if done carefully and with the right objectives. Somehow, the term *manufacturing* had a magic ring to it, and as regularly as summer follows winter, the town administrators seemed always willing to offer special privileges, concessions, etc., to industries, but not to tourist-based businesses.

In May 1974 the Planning Board announced it was going to mail a questionnaire to all local taxpayers to ask advice about the town's future. Chairman Warren D. Thompson suggested that about 60 citizens should be assigned to committees to study particular areas and submit recommendations. However, although some wanted change, perhaps the words of Marjorie Santulli, first-prize winner in the "Why I Like the Wolfeboro Area" contest sponsored by the Rotary Club, reflected the sentiment of the majority:

> This town of Wolfeboro snuggled in the foothills of the White Mountains holds us like a large family, safe and secure. Here our children can breathe the fresh mountain air and spread their arms in the freedom of space. They can reach out and grow as a child should develop, day by day, in an atmosphere of peace and God-given beauty. I pray this town remains as it is this day, without the development of modern day life. The high-rise apartments and condominiums, the smokestacks of industry, and the complex housing developments, the noisy freeways must never enter Wolfeboro. Progress here should be self-contained.
>
> This may well be accomplished with good civic leaders, schools that meet the requirements of a growing population, sports for our youngsters, perhaps a little more activity for our restless teenagers, our hospital, our police force, the churches in step with the times—this is my dream for my town. Sparkling clear lakes [must be cared for]. I want to remain a part of Wolfeboro after the tourists have left, to work among the people, to greet neighbors and friends downtown, to be included, this is indeed a rewarding life.
>
> Wolfeboro to me is home. My dream is to keep it safe and beautiful, warm and friendly, clean and fresh... My Shangri-La, my haven, the small town, nestled in the foothills of the White Mountains, a little place called Wolfeboro.

Indeed, the taxpayers *did* feel this way, for the Planning Board reported that the mailing of 2,200 questionnaires yielded 800 responses, and that:

> Wolfeboro residents, both year-round and seasonal, like their town the way it is and don't want to see any substantial changes. They prefer the semi-rural characteristics of the town... Tabulated returns indicated that people who live in Wolfeboro want it to continue primarily as a single home community. They don't want large apartment complexes nor do they wish to have large shopping centers.
>
> By strong majorities, both categories of residents want to see improvement in traffic flow. Both favor zoning which will tend to preserve open spaces and scenic areas... Encouragement of farming was widely favored by both groups as was home-based business. Retailing, service business and professional business offices drew strong approval from both groups. Residents favored restricting shopping centers.... Least popular with both groups was heavy industry and motels.

The account went on to say that underground placement of utilities was desired, as was a tough attitude by the planning board toward subdivision approval. Wetlands and other natural areas should be preserved.

Areas most favored for business expansion were various Route 28 locations including the Trotting Track Road, North Line Road, and Bourdon's Corner (Route 28 and Haines Hill Road). After much discussion, nothing permanent was accomplished.[97]

Fast forward to 1978: On September 6, the selectmen approved a request for yet another master plan.

In due course it was reported that the Planning Board had conducted another survey in 1979, and that, on balance and as before, citizens and taxpayers were happy with the status quo. In May 1980 the newspaper commented that this was the latest in a number of efforts over the years to endeavor to influence the town to adopt a master plan for its growth, none of which had been successful, although each one had portions which called attention to problems and eventually resulted in changes. At a public hearing on the subject in autumn 1980 only 45 people showed up. Henry S. ("Chip") Maxfield, Jr., and William Swaffield both suggested that cleaning up and dredging Back Bay would be money well spent, but the idea of creating a public walkway around the entire perimeter was not endorsed.

Current and earlier town surveys suggested that local landmarks worth preserving included Town Hall, Avery Block, Black's Paper Store, Brewster Academy main building, Wolfeboro Center Church, Wolfeborough Railroad Station, and the somewhat decrepit Monitor Hose Co. firehouse in South Wolfeboro. Some recommendations were made for a light industrial park, possibly next to the recently opened Brockhouse Corporation plant on 109A.[98]

Although great time and energy were spent by many citizens and town officials on master plans during the 1970s, once again, none was accepted.

### Electricity

The Municipal Electric Department was under the direction of H.E. ("Eric") Erickson from 1954 until his resignation in 1973 to become safety education director of the Northeast Public Power Association. He later resumed the Wolfeboro post. At the end of 1978, the town facility served 2,848 residential customers and 482 commercial accounts, supplying about 25 million kilowatt hours yearly.

In 1978 it was noted that the Municipal Electric Department was one of the smallest such facilities in the state, but "small size is not a hindrance to efficiency; it sells electricity to its customers at substantially lower rates than larger neighboring utilities such as Public Service Company and New Hampshire Electric Cooperative..." Further,

> A recently concluded rate study of the department conducted by A.E. Hodson Company of Waterville, Maine, concluded that the compactness of the system and careful management were the key elements in keeping Wolfeboro rates below that of its neighbors. Town Manager Guy L. Krapp, who has headed the department since 1974, agrees and notes, "Economy begins at the top. In a small town a public utility can share both manpower and equipment with other departments, and save money in the process."

Most day-to-day matters of the Electrical Department were taken care of by office manager Dennis E. Bean. In addition there were two full-time workers and one part-time administrative employee. Line crew workers included Ken Jordan, Warren Smith, John Lord, Dave Ridings, and Victor Cloutier, under the supervision of Steve Tufts.

In 1979 the town was invited to buy 1,289 shares in the Seabrook nuclear power plant for $5.8 million, to provide about 4,900 KWH of capacity. The selectmen took no action.[99]

### Youth Center Wanted

In the early 1970s the Wolfeboro Youth Center, Inc., operating in the old and somewhat shabby Boston & Maine Railroad Station, continued to provide a central meeting place for the Boy Scouts, Girl Scouts, Cooperative Kindergarten, Lakes Region Hobby Craft Association, and other groups. Soon the revived train line, the Wolfeboro Rail Road, became prominent, and the station was restored to its former grandeur. Another area was sought for activities for children and teenagers. In 1972 Wolfeboro Area Youth Services (WAYS) took the lead in the search, noting that while it was low on funds, "we're willing to work." In 1973 Patricia Vinnicombe, a Kingswood High senior and spokesperson for a group of her peers, commented that alcoholism and drug abuse among teens would be lessened if a facility for organized activities could be set up. The 1974 town warrant included a petition by the Kingswood Area Pastimes Association (KAPA) for an appropriation for a youth center of approximately 800 square feet, but voters defeated it.[100]

### New Public Safety Building

For many years the Police Department was housed in the Town Hall, and the Fire Department was in the old station on Lehner Street. On October 18, 1973, work began on a new facility, the Public Safety Building designed by Donald E.L. Hallock, to be erected on South Main Street.

When the structure was ready for occupancy in the summer of 1974, a tempest in a teapot arose when the selectmen (Raymond F. Pollini, chairman) sought to have keys to the facility, including areas in which confidential records of the Police Department were kept. Chief Arnold H. Wentworth stated that the integrity of the files would not be compromised in this manner, halted the move from Town Hall, and even threatened to resign if the selectmen persisted. Chairman Pollini stated, "No keys [for the selectmen], no move." The keys were returned to the builder (Beaver Corporation), and equipment already moved by the Police Department was returned to the Town Hall. Chief Wentworth reported that not even members of the independent Police Commission had ever requested keys to areas storing records.

Ultimately, the Police Commission intervened to make peace with the selectmen, and the Police Department was allowed to set up its own security system safe from prying eyes. On August 1, 1974, an open house was held, and citizens toured the new facility. In 1979 it developed that the roof on the building was faulty and carried no bond or guarantee. Voters coughed up $14,140 for repairs.[101]

### New Library

Another important municipal building had its inception in 1975, when taxpayers paid $40,000 for a lot of slightly over one acre upon which to build the new Wolfeboro Public Library. There was good news and bad news. On the positive side, it was learned that reallocation of Federal Economic Development Administration Funds would provide the full $600,000 cost for construction. On the negative side, the proposed flat-roofed modern design was roundly criticized by the majority of citizens who attended a meeting on the subject. Two shopping centers, the Public Safety Building and the architecturally out-of-place Kingswood High School had given residents their fill of what were widely considered to be tasteless designs. Most wanted colonial or traditional architecture. "It just isn't Wolfeboro," commented Mrs. Brenda McBride. John M. Ballard, who had headed a committee of volunteers to bring the project to fruition, was intolerant of this dissension and stated in no uncertain terms:

> The proposed design will be the one submitted with the application and will be the one built with federal funds if the application is approved. If Wolfeboro townspeople do not wish to build the proposed library of this present design, they may refuse to spend the federal money on the project. The town would then forfeit the federal funds and would have to raise money to build any other library design.

W.D. Flierl, an architect who was a long-time summer visitor and in the 1970s a full-time resident, commented that the design was a failure and on the exterior and interior was hardly conducive to the "joys of intellectual studies." Even more to the point, Roland C. Kimball stated that he observed that whoever drew the plans did not sign them and commented, "I wouldn't have signed them either if I had been the *student* who turned them in."

Town Moderator Robert C. Varney recalled the situation:[102]

Because it was to be built under a federal program, the design had to meet amazingly complex architectural specifications. Individual projects were authorized fiscal year to fiscal year. The result was that time spent satisfying the architectural specifications with a new design would have had the practical effect of delaying the project so long that the fiscal year would have ended and with it the authorization.

There were, however, a couple of generic pre-approved plans, including the one for our library. The town, therefore, was told it could get—for free—a library building, but it had to be *that* library building.

At that year's town meeting, general unhappiness with the design became so bound up with resentment over the idea that some fourth-tier Washington bureaucrat was telling us what *our* library would have to look like, that sentiment gathered to reject the approximately $600,000 grant from the government.

The efforts of widely respected community leaders like John W. McDermott, John M. Ballard, Doug Parsons, and Jeanne Harriman were clearly having no effect on the assembly. Let's face it, the building is ugly and the model we were looking at was even uglier. Something between a mutter and a growl followed every speech in favor. I remember thinking, "They're actually going to turn this down."

Just as sentiment was cresting, a slight, white-haired lady, Miss Wilma Paine, born and raised on Pleasant Valley Road, a retired school teacher and town librarian for many years, got up to speak. In a thin, wavering voice she said that she had attended town meetings for 50 years, that she had never once spoken before, but she now had to. She described the cramped stacks in the small Brewster Memorial Hall library, how children's books couldn't be displayed, the cold in the winter and the heat in the summer, how it had broken her heart to turn away children and to have to put away books that might otherwise be available because of lack of space.

As she went on, the crowd quieted and after some seconds became absolutely still. There wasn't a sound other than Miss Paine's thin voice, occasionally wavering nervously but describing with a librarian's precision the shortcomings of the old building and the advantages of the new one. She spoke in full grammatical sentences and did not embellish. She concluded by saying years of service and effort emboldened her to ask that we might agree that her dream of a new library—appearance notwithstanding—was a worthy one and announced her hope that she might live to see it. She spoke for no more than three minutes.

She sat down to absolute silence which, after a discernible pause, became loud, universal applause. There was no further debate, and the vote as I remember it was unanimous.

It is the one time in 20 years of being moderator that I have seen a single voice turn the meeting around 180 degrees on a matter of substance.

If she had remained silent there is no doubt—given the lack of local funds and recent changes in government programs—that there would be no new library. At least once at every meeting I think of the tiny, white-haired woman who waited 50 years to have her say.

An out-of-town contractor, Bonnet, Page & Stone, was hired to do the work. On May 24, 1979, the grand opening of the facility was held. Louise A. Gehman became the first full-time librarian on January 1, 1980, succeeding Gladys Tuttle, who had held the post for many years. A graduate of the University of Denver with an M.A. in Library Science, Mrs. Gehman had worked in a Denver library for three years, for six years in an Anchorage, AK library, and one year as a librarian in Millinocket, ME. In her new position she had four part-time assistants and 10 volunteers. On May 21, 1980, the Friends of the Wolfeboro Library group was organized and, as time went on, accomplished much for the facility. Once townspeople had a chance to experience the warm, cozy interior of the building, its amenities, and the friendly library staff, most opposition to the design was forgotten.[103]

### New Incinerator

Nearly all major municipal construction of the decade was fraught by problems, dissension, or both. The new town incinerator was no exception. Although the selectmen in 1975 and early 1976 had originally desired a large-capacity unit similar to that in Merrimack, new Board of Selectmen in 1976 opted to save money and purchase a smaller unit.[104] The lowest bid, $64,000, from a Concord firm, was accepted on January 12, 1977. On September 9, the facility began operating in conjunction with a voluntary separation and recycling program. As it turned out, huge piles of trash accumulated at the incinerator as incoming refuse had not been sorted and needed to be classified before being put through the burning process. "The backlog of material is assuming threatening proportions," it was observed. The incinerator crew was augmented by an extra shift, so the unit could be operated nearly around the clock.

By March 1978 the backlog had been reduced to a day-to-day supply of trash awaiting burning. After much thought, it was concluded that the incinerator, which was supposed to process 1,280 pounds per hour, was not sufficient for the job, and at the March 1978 town meeting $150,000 was approved for a new 2,500-pounds-per-hour unit. Trash separation by users was made mandatory. At first, glass was mixed, but effective July 15, 1980, it had to be separated into clear, green, and brown categories. After what a *Town Report* called a "trial and error period," the facility performed admirably.[105]

### New Sewage Treatment Plant

In 1974 under an Environmental Protection Agency grant and other funding, including $1.7 million on the 1973 and 1974 town warrants, a new municipal sewage plant was built off Beach Pond Road, serviced by a pumping station on Mill Street. Complications developed, and H. Fred Osgood, superintendent of the facility for the town, commented that while the installation crew did a fine job, some of the designs were faulty. In time, obstacles were overcome, and by 1976, it had processed 56 million gallons of sewage, thus ending the dumping of waste into Lake Winnipesaukee. This led to a re-evaluation of sewer lines in town and approval for $955,000 worth of new pipes and other feeders, with the federal, state, and town governments to pay for it on a 75-20-5 formula. In June 1979 H. Fred Osgood, who had seen the Water and Sewer Department through many years of change, turned in his resignation, which was accepted with regret.[106]

### Roads and Highways

In 1972 the uniform road signs of the styles used for years in Europe and now just beginning to be adopted in the United States, were installed in town. This type of sign had a line through an icon or word describing an action. For example, a line through a turn arrow indicated that the turn was prohibited. Standard DO NOT ENTER signs in red with white drop-out letters, and other new signs soon appeared.

In April of the same year the selectmen considered the confusing array of street numbers on buildings in town—there was no rhyme or reason to some designations—and considered adopting a set of rules. At it was, even and odd numbers were sometimes seen on the same side of the same street, and lower numbers would sometimes follow higher ones. However, it was not until more than 20 years later that a system was developed by which numbers had a logical sequence. In 1973 painted yellow lines in roads gradually replaced the old white ones throughout the state. In 1978 the state began a program of installing triangular signs to mark no-passing zones.

One of the greatest controversies in a decade filled with municipal challenges was a plan by the NH Department of Public Works and Highways to create a Route 28 limited-access bypass around the downtown district of Wolfeboro, in effect running a superhighway through the area. Two routes were proposed, one going west of Lake Wentworth and one going east, both starting on Pleasant Valley west of Rust Pond. The western route would go between Crescent Lake and Lake Wentworth and come out on Route 28 near North Line Road. The eastern route would go around the east side of Lake Wentworth and join Route 28 at the intersection of Haines Hill Road. A somewhat related idea had come up in 1964 and had been rejected.

An overflow crowd of 600 citizens attended a meeting held on January 16, 1973. Of the 30 or more who spoke out, not a single voice was in favor of either route. It was said that our town might turn into "another North Conway," that village being known for its strip of modern commercial buildings and frequent traffic snarls. The meeting achieved what its attendees hoped for; the state dropped the plan immediately.

Following the favorable resolution of the perceived threat of the Route 28 bypass, there was renewed appreciation of the roads already in place. At the March 1973 town meeting, Cotton Valley Road, Stoneham Road, and Pleasant Valley Road were designated as scenic roads under legislation which made them potentially available for funding from the state, "the purpose being to protect, enhance and maintain the scenic beauty of Wolfeboro." Soon thereafter, a committee comprised of Donald H. McBride, Allen Stevens, and Warren D. Thompson enlisted the Lakes Region Survey Service (Wayne J. Kelloway) to prepare a new tourist map showing town roads, points of scenic interest, and other features.

It was common practice in the 1970s, as it had been for decades, to spread used motor oil, a naturally biodegradable substance, on unpaved town roads to reduce dust.

In 1974 Gordon Kimball was placed in charge of the Road Department, where he served with distinction. In autumn 1979 self-employed local contractor Curtis A. Pike was named director of the Public Works Department and assumed his duties on October 1. Under his charge were placed the highway, water and sewer departments, the incinerator, treatment plant, and public works garage.[107]

### National Bicentennial

Like other towns and cities across the United States, Wolfeboro wanted to do its part to celebrate the 1776-1976 bicentennial of American independence. Starting in May 1974 the selectmen designated the Wolfeboro Historical Society to manage the event, with invitations extended to other groups to join the festivities. Edwin B. Goodall, M.D., prominent ophthalmologist and a resident since 1960, agreed to lead the Wolfeboro Bicentennial Committee. He was later succeeded by Russell C. Chase.

Eager to get started with the celebration, the committee announced that the "Bicentennial Year" was to begin early, on Memorial Day, May 30, 1975. On that day Robb Thomson, son of NH Governor Meldrim Thomson, Jr., whose engagement to Andrea Flagg of Wolfeboro had been recently announced (they were married on July 26), presented a historic flag to be flown during the bicentennial observance. Wolfeboro was not the only entity seeking a jump start; the government released 1976 bicentennial coins (quarters, half dollars, and dollars) in 1975, and by May they were on sale locally at Hall's Pharmacy and the Stationery Shop.

No sooner had the *real* bicentennial year begun in January 1976, than the editor of the *Granite State News* commented,

> We are being bicentennialed to death by reams of press releases and advertisements. Everything marketable seems to have a bicentennial motif right down to red, white and blue kitchen sponges which our neighbor found at a local store...

The Wolfeboro Chamber of Commerce sponsored the publication in 1976 of *Remember When,* a collection of photographs, captions, and narratives prepared by Kathy O'Meara, well-known feature writer for the *Granite State News*. Placed on sale at $3.50 (raised to $5.95 by decade's end), the book was enthusiastically acclaimed. Other activities included gathering old papers, research on grave markers (primarily done by Ida and Milton Pineo), and the organization of the Wolfeboro Militia, a group that marched in various regional parades.

Asked if the 1977 Fourth of July festivities would continue the same spirit, Allen Stevens, president of the Chamber of Commerce, stated succinctly, "Not really. People are pretty much fed up with the Bicentennial."[108]

### Developments

The real estate growth trend that started in the 1960s gained momentum in the 1970s. Numerous subdivisions were laid out. Popular developments included Cricket Hill Estates (by Joseph I. Melanson III), Old Mill Estates (Norris Harriman and others), and Wolfeboro Common (Bob Grott). In 1978 Wyanoke Harbors was platted by Herbert Pheeney (of Osterville, MA) with 33 lots on the site of venerable Camp Wyanoke, a Wolfeboro tradition, owned by the Bentley family since its founding in 1909.

On July 26, 1973, this appeared as a caption to a photograph in the *Granite State News:*

> Robin Acres Village on Route 109 in Wolfeboro is praised by the judges of SPARKS' (Spring Pick-Up and Repair Keeps [Wolfeboro] Sparkling) spring clean-up drive for the landscaping at the entrance to the development and for the tidy appearance of unsold lots in the development. This the judges found was in contrast to many developments where slash [tree limbs] and debris had been allowed to accumulate on unsold lots. Earlier this spring, Robin Acres received a Wolfeboro Chamber of Commerce Beautification Award for its landscaping effort.

In 1980 it was announced that Point Breeze, a vacation spot on Lake Wentworth that had been a drawing card since the late nineteenth century, was being sold by the Stevens family to out-of-staters who were going to build 51 (later reduced to 45) housing units, mostly condominiums.

Growth was not without its problems, and the Apple Hill subdivision, approved by the town in 1974, went bankrupt in 1976. A controversy arose when it was stated that persons intending to buy the struggling development wanted to acquire *one* shorefront lot in adjacent Port Wedeln and use it as "lake access" for 22 Apple Hill lots.

In 1980 the Wolfeboro selectmen agreed to accept Springfield Point Road as a town road, waiving the usual requirements of a 20-foot paved surface plus three-foot shoulders on each side. This prompted Joe ("Bucky") Melanson to threaten suit on behalf of himself and residents of Cricket Hill Estates, who had recently spent many thousands of dollars bringing their roads up to town standards.

In the late 1970s most of the acreage sold in the area went to out-of-staters. Within Wolfeboro, most buyers intended to build year-round or seasonal residences. However, elsewhere in the region, many distant investors put money into farms and forest tracts as an investment. The trend was nationwide.[109]

Just about anyone with a pickup truck and a few business cards could get into the subdividing game. Many new housing areas from two lots to a dozen or more were laid out in various parts of town. Numerous properties remained unsold because mortgage rates were 13% to 14% or more by 1980, and even at this level money was "tight." Many recently-bought investment parcels of real estate came back on the market, often with the owners willing to take a loss if buyers could be found.

Notable building and remodeling projects of the decade included the breaking up in 1973 of the former Colonial Arms Inn on North Main Street into 11 business and apartment units; the addition of a modern motel unit to the rear of the Windrifter Resort; and Richard Eaton's 1980 opening of a shop-office complex at the corner of North Main and Endicott Streets. Tenants at the latter facility included Mood's II Boutique (shoes and accessories), the Christmas Shop, the Chrysanthemum Shop (kitchenware), the Tannery (leather gift items), D.S.D.A., Inc. (food wholesaler), the Strawberry Patch sandwich shop, Phyllis & The Major Real Estate, and the local newspaper.

### The *Granite State News*

In April 1973 the business office of the *Granite State News* was moved from the Wolfeboro Shopping Center to South Main Street (where Merle Norman is in 1994), where it remained until near the end of the decade, when it moved to near the corner of Endicott and North Main Streets. Owner, editor, and publisher continued to be Jacob Burghardt of Ossipee, where the paper was printed. However, several correspondents, Helen L. Fetzer primary among them, contributed Wolfeboro social and church news. In May 1973 Kenneth Webb, formerly of the *Needham Times* in MA, was named managing editor, with an office in Wolfeboro, the first time in many years that the editor worked in our town. Chief photographer was Bruce W. Bedford of Ossipee, who was honored as Photographer of the Year in 1974 by the New England Press Association and won many other awards over the years.

On September 20, 1973, the first *Granite State News* issue printed by offset lithography set by Compugraphic equipment appeared, replacing the time-honored method of using metal type. Computer publishing was coming into its own. Before long, the Kingswood Press, Wolfeboro's commercial printer, would also install Compugraphic equipment.

In October 1976 a subscription to the paper cost $10. About 3,800 copies of each issue were printed, about evenly divided between mail subscriptions and newsstand and store sales. In the mid-1970s Mrs. Jourdan Houston and Kathy O'Meara wrote many feature articles on local people and businesses.[110]

## TRANSPORTATION

### The Wolfeboro Rail Road

The prime tourist attraction in Wolfeboro in the 1970s was the Wolfeboro Rail Road[111] under the direction of Donald E.L. Hallock, who had served as president of an antique steam railroad in Strasburg, PA. He and his wife Cay moved to Wolfeboro and became prominent citizens.

On December 19, 1972,[112] the Wolfeboro Rail Road Co., Inc., acquired from the Boston & Maine Railroad 12.1 miles of track from Wolfeboro to Sanbornville, plus the right of way (in general, 33 feet to each side of the track). President Hallock stated "the line would be a true common carrier operating under all federal regulations." Rolling stock consisted of two locomotives (a Plymouth industrial model and a 1926 Baldwin known as No. 250), four passenger cars (including two steel passenger cars from Jersey Central and a Laconia Car Co. wooden car with mahogany interior and kerosene chandeliers), four freight cars, a 70-year-old snowplow, and a caboose. Later two self-propelled rail cars were added, among other stock.

At the outset Richard Libby, local railroad historian and president of the Wolfeboro Branch Railroad Club, was deeply involved in the restoration and maintenance of the local station building, which had been chosen as the club's main project. The structure had fallen into disrepair, the ornate moldings and decorations of years earlier were long gone, and atop the building was an abandoned aircraft spotting station.

An arrangement between the club and the town was made whereby the restoration would be accomplished in phases, with each segment beginning no earlier than when complete funding for that phase was on deposit in a local bank. Club members of the Wolfeboro Branch Railroad Club—including Carol Furneé secretary, E. Fred Miller vice-president, and Virginia Berry treasurer—worked as part of an enthusiastic team.

From its first trial run on February 3, 1973, and continuing for the next five years, the railroad offered scenic rides, usually from the restored Wolfeborough Railroad Station to Sanbornville and return. Numerous civic events, parties, and other functions were held aboard the cars.

On August 21, 1973, the line was featured on the National Broadcasting Company's *Today Show.* The television segment opened with shots of modern trains in France then, for contrast, cut to the restored old equipment operating in Wolfeboro. Scenes included townspeople affiliated with the railroad, the station, the old Berry excelsior mill and nearby dam, and trackage. The coverage concluded with the song, *Down by the Station.*[113]

In the summer of 1974 twenty thousand revenue passengers were carried on a schedule of up to eight trains a day during the height of the season. In that year a round-trip ticket was $2.50 for an adult and $2.25 for a child under 12. The stock rolled along at a leisurely 15 to 20 miles per hour, with views of forests, lakes, causeways, streams, wetlands, and wildlife. On some trips food and refreshments were served at the Sanbornville end.

The following is excerpted from a February 1974 account by Ethelyn M. Brown:[114]

> I had a good time on the train. Mr. Hallock related a lot of history all along the route to Sanbornville, telling how they had brought back different stations and that they were going to do more building moving such as some of the old stations which are farther back on some old tracks, etc. Also, on the side tracks there are several passenger cars they had acquired and which they are fixing up with voluntary labor from the Railroad Club.
>
> He is the conductor aboard the train. He makes funny remarks along the way, too, to keep things lively. When we went across the stretch of track built across Crescent Lake or Crooked Pond, he told everyone to hold their feet up off the floor so as not to have so much weight while going across the bridge. He stood in the aisle and suspended himself in the aisle by holding himself up by his hands on the opposite row of seats near him....
>
> [On the return trip] we stopped just long enough to add a freight car with white spruce from the Pacific Northwest on its final run to Wolfeboro Falls....

Adding to revenue was a freight service which hauled 10 or more loads of lumber each year—the previously-quoted Ethelyn M. Brown account referred to such a shipment—to Diamond International in Wolfeboro Falls, and 15 to 18 cars of raw materials to the reactivated old Berry Mill (and carried finished excelsior from the facility). The line also hauled its own soft coal purchased wholesale in Boston from mines in Pennsylvania. In early 1976 a related railroad operation was run up the center of the state from Concord to Lincoln to serve a paper mill there. When the mill closed in June of the same year, revenues decreased dramatically.

By 1977 the cash flow of the local line had dropped considerably, and Donald E.L. Hallock put the business up for sale. The local Chamber of Commerce tried to find a buyer, a group of local businessmen endeavored to form a consortium, and other plans were discussed. Finally, on October 30, 1979, Hallock announced that New York City investors were going to buy the business, and that Dwight Hilson was to be the resident manager for the new owners, who were confident of success. A new corporation, the Wolfeboro Steam Railroad, was formed. The value of

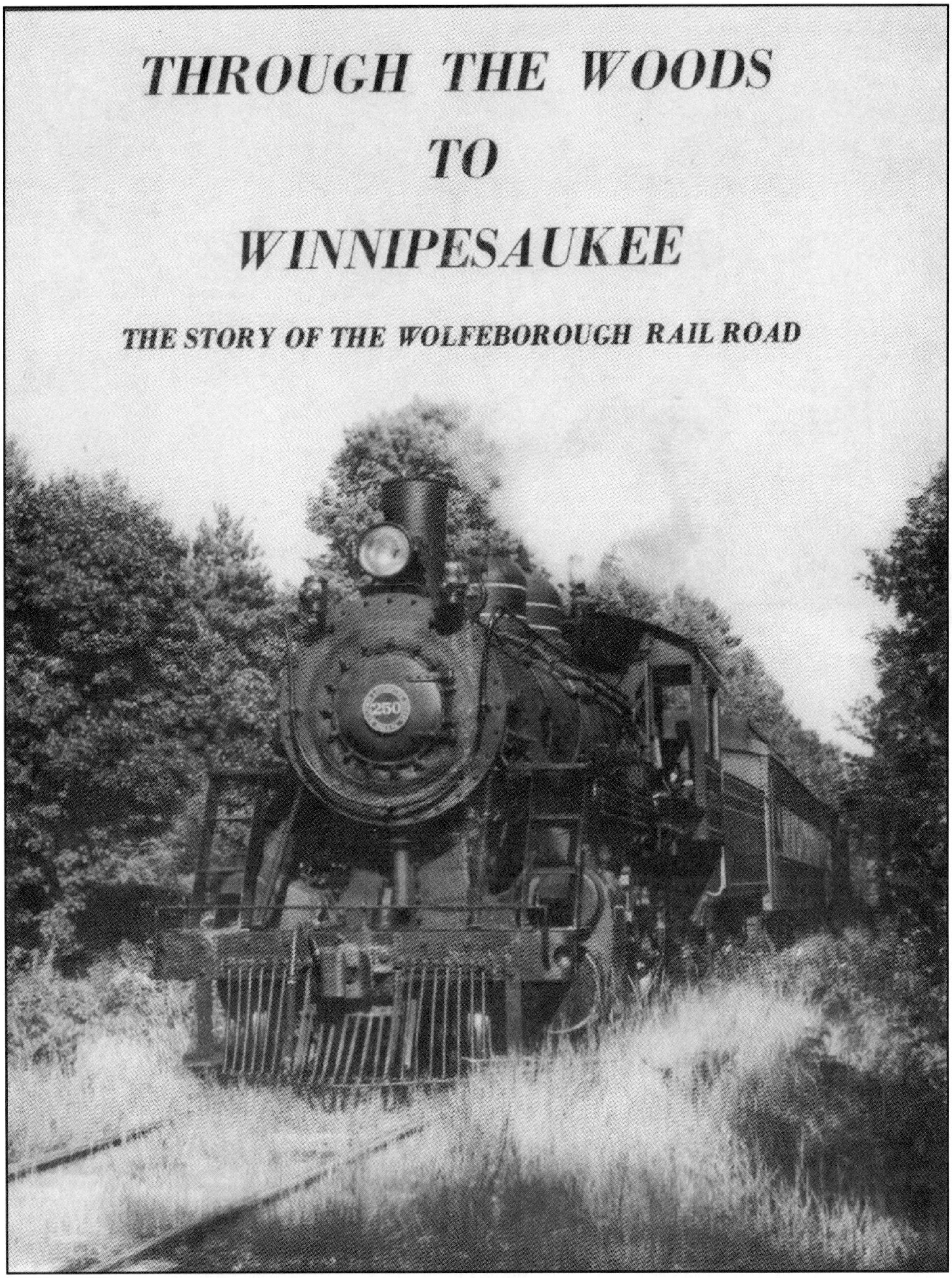

THROUGH THE WOODS
TO
WINNIPESAUKEE
THE STORY OF THE WOLFEBOROUGH RAIL ROAD


Cover of booklet written by Richard C. Libby and Carol M. Furneé and issued by the Wolfeboro Rail Road (here spelled "Wolfeborough"). Engine 250 was a familiar sight as it steamed along the 12 miles of tracks from Wolfeboro to Sanbornville.

It is February 7, 1975, and the Wolfeboro Rail Road line is being cleared for the "Railroad Days" celebration. Steam locomotive No. 250 is shoving hard on the line's 1902 Russell Snow Plow No. 450 as it hammers up Clows Hill north of Lake Wentworth. Steam and smoke billow, snow flies, and the whistle screams a warning as the train thunders toward Frost Crossing. Winter seems to bring out the best in the beast! (Dane H.G. Malcolm photograph; collection of the Remember the Iron Horse Museum)

During the 1970s and 1980s the Wolfeboro Rail Road played host to many special groups. Here excursionists from the New Hampshire Association for the Blind pose for lensman Steve Libby as the train waits on the Crescent Lake causeway. Having just had lunch at Edward's, the group will board the coaches for a trip to Sanbornville. (Steve Libby photograph; collection of the Remember the Iron Horse Museum)

It is August 19, 1972, and a crowd has gathered to celebrate 100 years of railroading on the Wolfeboro Branch of the Boston & Maine Railroad. Engineer Thad Berry rolls the Wolfeboro Rail Road's No. 9, a 25-ton Plymouth locomotive, through the weeds just east of the station. After a few speeches are given, short rides will be offered to Wolfeboro Falls and back. (Fred Miller photograph; collection of the Remember the Iron Horse Museum)

Two trains meet just east of the Wolfeborough (*sic*) Railroad Station. The steam train with Engine 250 is "in the clear" on the passing track. Westbound Railcar 10 occupies the main track as it rolls toward the depot on a summer day in the 1970s. This scene was repeated several times daily. (Steve Libby photograph; collection of the Remember the Iron Horse Museum)

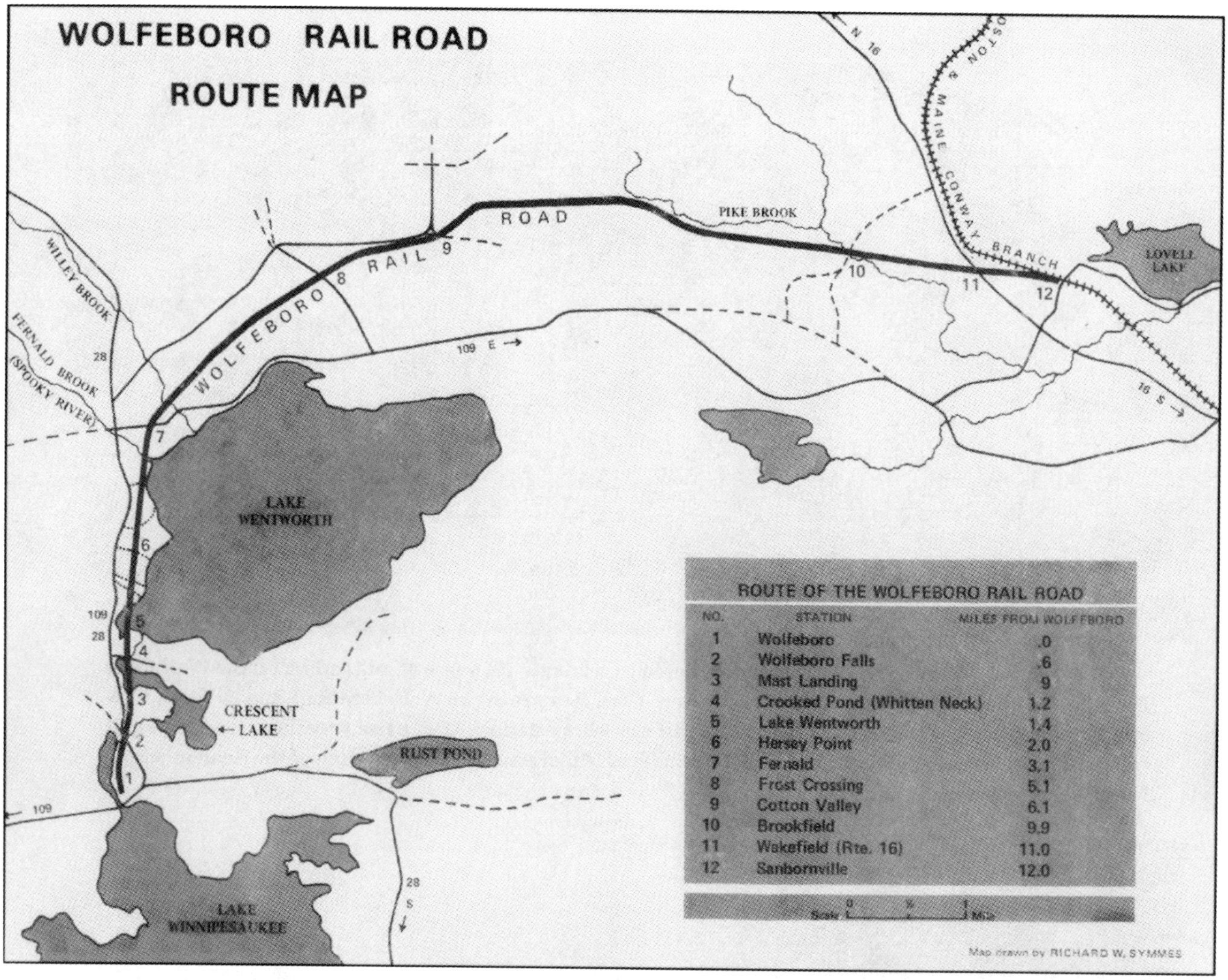


**Route map of the Wolfeboro Rail Road, which delighted tourists and townspeople during its years of operation 1972-1979.**

**The Smith River Canoe race, first held on May 31, 1973, quickly became an annual tradition. In this aerial view the start of the race on Lake Wentworth near the Allen "A" Resort is shown (not far from the No. 6 notation on the railroad map at the top of the page). (*Granite State News*)**

the transaction was not announced, but Hallock stated that if the line had been abandoned, the scrap value would be close to $275,000. Hallock remained with the line until 1980.

The new owners of the Wolfeboro Rail Road immediately began making the line ready for the 1980 season. To conform with federal regulations, steam locomotive No. 250 received a new set of boiler tubes and other improvements. Passenger cars were inspected to insure safe operation.

Due to more than a year of neglect and the effects of the harsh New England winter, several sections of track needed attention. By late spring all was in readiness.

As the steam engine was the only motive power left on the line, the company set out in search of a second locomotive to assist No. 250 in the daily operations. Otter Valley No. 1, an old Alco diesel switcher which had been running on a portion of the former Clarendon & Pittsford Railroad in Vermont, was leased for the season.

On opening day, due to some minor mechanical problems, No. 1 had not yet received "cab papers" and could not be operated. The company was sent scrambling for a replacement in order to meet the schedule. A diesel engine was leased from the Boston & Maine for the first few days. All seemed to go well, and local citizens and tourists alike were pleased that the scenic line would continue in business.[115]

### At the Airport

In 1974 and 1975, the Lakes Region Airpark (a.k.a. Wolfeboro Airport) expanded its main runway and announced that year-round air taxi service by twin-engine plane would come to town. Amphibair, Inc., quoted a fare from Wolfeboro to Boston of $26 per person for a group of five. However, charters did not materialize in the quantities hoped for, and the service ceased.

In March 1975 Jack R. Hildreth, in a letter published in the *Granite State News,* noted that with the prevailing gasoline shortage, travel by automobile was becoming difficult for many summer visitors. An improved local airport and passenger terminal, publicly supported, would bring many to the region, he suggested. As it was, "courageous pilots with their own money and labor have put in a hard-top runway at the Wolfeboro airport, make it possible now for light twins and limited airline commuter flights to operate for the convenience of travelers."

However, faced with inflation, reduced buying power, and ever-increasing local taxes, few local taxpayers wanted to add airport maintenance to their long and growing list of expenses.

On July 1, 1978, a single-engine Cessna carrying a New York couple and their three-year-old daughter crashed in the woods 200 feet short of the runway. Although the plane did not catch fire, much fuel was spread throughout the area.[116]

## HEALTH

### Huggins Hospital

On April 10, 1972, a ribbon was cut to dedicate the new Sinclair Patient Care Center at Huggins Hospital to recognize a donation of about $1 million from the Jennie H. Sinclair estate toward the $2.75 million addition. Administrator John F. Waters reported that about 1,500 people turned out to tour the new facility. Three years later, on July 7, 1975, another dedication took place with the unveiling of Mrs. Sinclair's portrait. In October 1976 the Sinclair Center received from Mr. and Mrs. Parker H. Rice of Tuftonboro 42 porcelain birds made by artist Edward Marshall Boehm, to be placed in a display cabinet where they have been an attraction ever since.[117]

In September 1973 the Telemed Corporation linked Huggins to a national computer network to transmit electrocardiograms for analysis. On October 15 the Meals-On-Wheels program was instituted by a group of volunteers operating from Huggins, who serviced shut-ins who paid a nominal $1 per meal.

At the annual meeting of the Huggins Hospital trustees, January 18, 1974, John F. Waters reported that the facility was financially sound and stable and that it was operating efficiently, although charging relatively low rates. However, it was a time of rampant inflation, and costs were rising in all sectors. Effective March 30, 1974, new rates went into effect whereby costs for room, meals, and nursing in the extended care unit increased from $33 per day to $39, and regular rates for acute hospital care went from $57 per day to $61.

Each summer, activity at Huggins swelled with the influx of tourists and visitors. During the weekend of July 4, 1977, over 200 people were treated at the Emergency Room. Spokesman David Oscarson noted:

> Minor cuts, bruises and burns were among injuries treated, along with the removal of fish hooks from nearly every imaginable part of the body, which is all quite normal for a big holiday weekend.[118]

By December 1978 Huggins Hospital employed 200 people who earned wages totaling over $1.5 million per year. Active physicians on the staff included: Frank R. Allen, Arthur E. Appleyard, James E. Bovaird, Gerard G. Bozuwa, Anne F. Collins, Philip M. Ellis, Edwin B. Goodall, Harold I.L. Loverud, Norman G.B. McLetchie, Robert H. Michaels, John C. Patten, Aleksander Ratsep, Harry M. Rose, Charles A. Shagoury, Charles S. Stevenson, Jr., and Donald C. Walsh. In addition, a number of other medical doctors were on the consulting staff,

**Views of Huggins Hospital before and after the 1972 addition (with three wings to the rear of the facility).**

and local dentists, doctors, and therapists were on the courtesy staff. John F. Waters continued as executive director, assisted by Carra Moore.

In late 1979, John F. Waters announced his retirement, and Roger S. Good was named as his replacement. In an interview, Good observed that "running a small hospital has its drawbacks." Referring to a stack of letters from state and federal agencies asking questions about compliance with regulations, reporting requirements, etc., the new director wryly observed that the government made very little distinction between Huggins and hospitals many times its size, and that Huggins had to "file the same reports in triplicate, answer the same questions, and appoint the same number of committees. The size of the apparatus surrounding all phases of hospital management has increased enormously; it seems like regulations run amok." Such paperwork, plus increasing lawsuits against hospitals and doctors, combined to sharply increase the cost of health care. As always, it was the citizenry who ultimately footed the bill.[119]

Huggins continued to expand its services as well as its physical plant. On June 7, 1980, the dedication was held of the $2.2 million Edward H.C. Bartsch facility comprising four additions totaling 23,000 square feet to the Sinclair Center. Included were expanded emergency and outpatient facilities and a new X-ray unit. To assist with financing, Huggins sold direct obligation notes due from 1981 to 1991, yielding 8% to 93/8%.

The retirement of John F. Waters, originally anticipated to be in 1979, was delayed until autumn 1980 so he could see the completion and utilization of the Bartsch addition. On October 23, 1980, more than 75 people attended ceremonies honoring the retired director, noting that he had joined the staff in June 1965, at which time it was a 56-bed institution. In the next 15 years, it increased to 82 beds, and much growth and many innovations were accomplished during his administration.[120]

### Health and Wellness

In the same decade, the Wolfeboro Home for the Aged, Inc., founded years earlier on June 22, 1946, completed its first project for the elderly—the 24-unit Christian Ridge complex on Crescent Lake Avenue which opened in 1978. This was followed in the 1980s by The Ledges off Center Street.

Throughout the 1970s there was great emphasis on physical fitness including exercise, proper weight, and healthful foods. Beginning in 1971 the Weight Watchers group—founded locally in 1969—met weekly at All Saints' Episcopal Church. The first session cost $6, after which rates were $2.50 per week. "Don't hide your size! Get wise" was their motto. Self-help groups were formed, including one conducted by Jackie (Mrs. Richard) House for "nervous people."[121]

James E. Bovaird, M.D., affectionately called "Dr. Jim," continued in the post of town health officer, a position he had held for many years. In each annual *Town Report* he gave a commentary on local conditions, noting in 1974, for example, that immunization had reduced the incidence of contagious diseases, and that venereal disease was not as prevalent in Wolfeboro as in urban areas. In 1976 Dr. Bovaird told of the swine flu scare, reporting that 604 people had been inoculated at a three-hour clinic at Huggins Hospital.

In 1976 the Public Health Nursing Association recorded 2,850 home visits by nurses and 450 by the physiotherapist. M. Virginia Dolan, registered nurse, was in charge.

In 1978 several cases of Type A infectious hepatitis broke out, but the big scare was an increase in venereal disease, especially herpes simplex II. A new awareness of the dangers of sexual promiscuity took place, primarily through nationwide publicity in print and on television.[122]

### Mental Health

In late summer 1972, the Carroll County Mental Health Services[123] (CCMHS) relocated from the Durgin block to Huggins Hospital. Clinical psychologist Frederick Ernst joined the staff and held office hours Monday through Friday, plus for any emergencies. The facility earned much acclaim, including a commentary by Dr. James Deykens, state director of community health services, who said that it was "three or four years ahead of the rest of the state," further noting that the organization "may be the first in the nation advancing a program of human services that put the citizen first rather than the bureaucracy."

Still, there were troubling signs, including the statistic that Carroll County had the highest suicide rate in the state. The most likely victim was a male in his 40s, recently divorced, living alone. Risk was greatest if alcohol was used. Locally the CCMHS and private psychologist Dr. Johr Chappell had full schedules. At one time, Dr. Chappell, who saw patients at his home-office on North Main Street, had an evening "hot line" through which free initial consultations could be secured.

By decade's end, Mimi Dye was the administrator of the local office of the CCMHS. The *Granite State News* told of progress in mental health and her contributions:

> During the past several years the Wolfeboro clinic, located in Huggins Hospital, has grown from a small branch office into a fully-staffed, comprehensive clinic delivering a wide range of services to adults and children. The growth of this office and high calibre of services delivered has been under the guidance and direction of Mimi Dye. Besides carrying a wide caseload and overseeing the operation of the clinic, she provides a consultation to the county nursing home, community groups, and other service organizations.

Dye, a Wolfeboro native, is the daughter of W.J. Paul Dye, a physician for many years in Wolfeboro who was greatly admired and respected by those who knew him, and the daughter of Mrs. George Black, who currently is an honorary trustee of Huggins Hospital.

In May 1977 Dayton Duncan, columnist for the *Granite State News,* wrote:

The *New York Times* recently had a front-page story headlined "Study Finds Urban Mental Health Better Than That in Rural Areas." The story quoted a Columbia University psychiatric sociologist who said residents of big cities, including New York, are mentally healthier than their counterparts in small towns in rural areas. Having spent all of my life in small towns, except for four years in the big city, I find it a little hard to believe that country folk are loonier than city folk. I'd always figured it the other way around. After all, we're here and they're there. What more proof is needed?...[124]

## FIRE DEPARTMENT

### Preserving History

In autumn 1971 the selectmen reported that there were four pieces of antique fire-fighting equipment held by the town, but their ownership was unknown. They expressed the hope that they could either be preserved by the town or donated to a public museum interested in such items. Nothing was done until July 1980, when Donald E.L. Hallock, who had restored the Wolfeboro Rail Road and recently sold his interest in it and was looking for a new project, told the selectmen he would like to participate in the restoration of the pieces. A plan was agreed upon, and work began.

Meanwhile, in South Wolfeboro, around the bend on the road to Alton, the old two-story Monitor Hose Co. fire station was in sad disrepair. Years earlier the downstairs had been used to store Fire Department equipment, and the upstairs had been utilized for dances, club meetings, and other social events. In 1974 the selectmen began an investigation of its status, stating that it should either be restored or sold so that it could be put on the tax rolls. During the next several years there was much discussion about saving it, but eventually the wooden structure was sold and demolished.[125]

### News and Events

In November 1971 the town announced that it had purchased from Miss Doris Butts 1.68 acres of land and an old house (subsequently razed) across from Huggins Hospital for $17,000 for use as the site for a new fire station.

On March 30, 1974, Chief Guy L. Foss resigned after 28 years of service. Wallace E. Keniston, a Wolfeboro native who had been a member of the department for 11 years, was named to replace him. Foss passed away on March 31, 1975. His loss was widely mourned.

An idea of fire activity for the year 1974 is gleaned from the *Town Report:* Types of fires: 48 structural, 15 gasoline spill, 4 car, 5 mutual aid to other towns, 5 brush, 3 dump, 23 grass, 4 LP gas leaks, 1 fireboat rescue, 1 boat fire, and 3 island fires. The crew worked 1,440 hours, traveled 619 miles, and spent 8 hours on the fireboat. Losses for fires where damage exceeded $100 totaled an estimated $1,024,350, but after insurance the net loss was only $50,950, with several claims still pending at year's end.

On July 27, 1974, the Fire Department moved into the new Public Safety Building. Fire equipment at the time consisted of: Ladder No. 1 (estimated current value $16,500; also called Engine No. 1 in some citations; however, it is believed that Engine No. 1 was inactive, on reserve status), Engine No. 2 ($2,000), Engine No. 3 ($100), Hose No. 2 ($2,250), Fireboat ($3,000), forest fire truck ($3,800), tank truck ($100), fire alarm and radio ($11,500), fire hose ($7,500), miscellaneous equipment and furniture ($7,250), for a total of $54,000.

In 1975 the department supplied oval "tot finder" stickers to residents to put on the windows of rooms occupied by children to facilitate their quick location by firemen in case of an emergency.

Effective February 20, 1976, Chief Keniston resigned due to lack of appreciation by two of the three selectmen, although he enjoyed his work, citing a statement made by one of them, Raymond Pollini, to the effect that if he did not like his job, Pollini knew of 10 people who would like to have it. Charles ("Zip") Foss, Jr., was named to the position of chief effective May 17, while Keniston was named fire captain (at $10,000 per year).[126]

### The Wolfeboro Rescue Squad

The Wolfeboro Rescue Squad, working closely with the fire and police departments, performed many valuable services during the decade. Peter D. Hayes, John Rines, and Peter A. Friend were among the top officials.

For the calendar year 1978, the crew responded to 79 calls involving 34 medical emergencies, 23 fires, 22 vehicular accidents, and was on standby for 9 civic events. In addition the Rescue Squad gave numerous first-aid demonstrations and public displays.

### Notable Fires

The following fires are from the records of Dr. W. Douglas Kipp and/or the *Granite State News* (latter cited in footnotes). Many of these fires were not reported in detail in the press.

**1971, January 21. Casselman workshop:** Sewall Road. Gutted.

**1971, March 31. R. Hale kitchen:** Wall and cupboard area burned.

**1971, May 31. Pleasant Valley Camp:** Main Lodge. Partition in ceiling burned.

**1971, June 15. Grey Shingles cottages:** South Wolfeboro. John Windhorst, owner. Four-unit cottage extensively damaged; two rooms gutted.

**1971, June 18. Grey Shingles cottages:** Motel destroyed. Firefighters were on the scene for two hours and 40 minutes. Second recent fire.

**1971, September 24. Keniston Island:** Ice house fire responded to by fireboat and crew. Out on arrival; building destroyed. Two juveniles had built a fire in the structure to dry their clothes and left without properly extinguishing it.[127]

**1972, February 27. Car fire:** Owned by "Bud" Bean; caught fire at the Wolfeboro Shopping Center. Extensive damage.[128]

**1972, May 12. Brewster Academy:** Brown Hall. Five fires were set by an arsonist. All were out by the arrival of the firemen.

**1972, May 19. Town Hall:** Fire started by defective wiring. Ceiling of courtroom, under stage, and walls on second floor damaged. Fire Department held damage to a minimum. Local youngsters helped the Police Department remove valuable records in time to prevent damage.[129] Two long-forgotten cases filled with unsold copies of Parker's now-scarce 1901 *History of Wolfeborough* came to light.[130]

**1972, October 18. Brewster Academy:** Main building. Three fires set by arsonist. Damage slight.

**1973, August 30. Gas oven explosion:** At the summer cottage of Barbara Haynes on Crescent Lake. Mrs. Haynes and her son suffered burns and were admitted to Huggins Hospital, and were released within the next two or three days.

**1973, August 31. Liquid propane gas explosion:** McNally home on Park Avenue in Wolfeboro Falls. Tom McNally, age 14, badly injured while trying to light a gas water heater, was transferred to the Maine Medical Center, then to the Shriners' Hospital for Children in Boston. Home extensively damaged. Local fund set up to help.

**1973, December 14. House gutted:** On Route 109.

**1974, January 19. Kingswood Regional High School:** Fire caused by defective wiring under the floor of portable classroom. Extensive damage.[131]

**1974, May 9. Kingswood Regional High School:** New wing. One room on fire; floor damaged.

**1974, May 15. Turtle Island Road:** East Wolfeboro. Outbuilding and grounds burned.

**1974, June 24. Windrifter:** Small flash fire in kitchen; George Turain, manager, suffered burns after throwing a glass of milk on the fire.[132]

**1974, June 28. Windrifter:** Another small fire.

**1974, June 28. Allen "A" Motel:** Attic and roof fire in Fireside Lounge; caused by defective ventilator in kitchen.[133]

**1974, May 11. Woods behind Highway Garage:** One acre burned.

**1974, August 13. Lyle Bickford house:** Park Avenue. Gutted despite a four-hour effort by firemen. Ruins became an eyesore and were removed by municipal order.

**1974, September 8. Boat fire:** 30-foot cabin cruiser caught fire in Wolfeboro Bay off Clark Point. The Wolfeboro Fire Department responded with its fire boat, but not in time to prevent a total loss to the vessel.[134]

**1974, December 21. Car fire:** Vehicle totally destroyed by fire on Route 109A in front of the Abenaki Ski Area.[135]

**1975, June 11. Brewster Academy:** Sargent Hall. Two rooms and corridor burned in major fire; loss: $20,000. Started by a kitchen stove accidentally left on in the apartment of teacher David Dubowik. Heat buildup was so intense that a large picture window on the back side of the dormitory blew out.[136]

**1975, June 12. House destroyed:** The so-called Leatherbee place, an unoccupied two and one-half story wood frame house owned by Russell Kelcourse on Clow's Hill. There was no nearby water line; thus, water was brought by tank truck from Lake Wentworth. Loss: $65,000.[137]

**1975, June 26. MacDonald garage:** Kingswood Road. Gutted.

**1975, June 27. Whitcomb bungalow:** Kingswood Road. Gutted. 2nd fire within two days on this road. Investigation underway.[138]

**1975, June 29. Three lightning-caused fires:** Dr. Martin Deutsch camp on Turtle Island Road completely destroyed. John H. McBride, Sr., house on Middleton Road: upstairs gutted; two minor injuries. Shed on William Simpson property, Cotton Mountain, destroyed. These fires started within a 27-minute period during a fierce storm accompanied by 60 mph winds.[139]

**1975, September 18. Huggins Hospital:** Fire in incinerator room caused smoke throughout building. Two people overcome by smoke.[140]

**1975, October 5. Furnace explosion:** In home of Mrs. James Douglas on North Main Street. No damage or injuries.[141]

**1975, October 8. Anderson house:** Cellar and first floor burned.

**1975, November 15. Huggins Hospital:** Another fire in the incinerator room. Smoke damage.

**1975, November 23. Huggins Hospital:** "Small fire in the blue wing of Huggins Hospital, 10:05 p.m. A patient, Henry Mountain, 63, tried to light a cigarette while in bed. Oxygen in the room was turned on, and a flash fire resulted. Burned patient around the face and damaged bedding."[142]

**1975, November 25. Paul Moore home:** Rocky Shore Road. Total loss, $50,000. Fireman Tom Morrill hospitalized for smoke inhalation. Structure fully involved when crew arrived.[143]

**1976, January 27. Brewster Academy:** Chemistry laboratory fire believed caused by spontaneous combustion.[144]

**1976, March 5. Brewster Academy:** Sargent Hall. Small fire in lounge.

**1976, March 10. Dr. and Mrs. Lawrence Hines residence:** On Highland Terrace; building owned by Mr. and Mrs. John Moore. Two rooms and attic burned, following malfunction of heating cable on water pipe in downstairs hall.[145]

**1976, March 21. Hitchcock house:** Kingswood Road. Loss: $12,000. Unoccupied.

**1976, March 24. Mrs. Conrad Lacaillade's guest house:** Kingswood Road. Unoccupied.

**1976, March 25. Hitchcock house (again):** Kingswood Road. Kitchen, bath and other parts of house burned. A firebug was on the loose on Kingswood Road. An investigation led to apprehending a nine-year-old boy who was later placed under a doctor's care.[146]

**1976, April 21. Lumber yard:** North Conway Lumber Company, Wolfeboro branch on Route 28, involved in spectacular blaze causing $150,000 damage. Fire started in furnace room, spread so quickly that the telephone was disabled; destroyed retail salesroom and paint storage facilities.[147]

**1976, June 21. Automobile fire:** Elm Street.

**1976, September 6. Henry Elliott residence:** Trotting Track Road. Small fire in attic, water damage to attic and kitchen.[148]

**1976, September 7. Melody Island:** Ground fire. Fire boat and crew on scene.

**1976, September 23. Hall residence:** Pork Hill Road. "Flashover, one room."[149] Firemen were on scene for one hour.

**1976, December 28. Lacaillade residence:** Kingswood

Road. Fire started in upstairs bedroom wiring. Several hundred dollars' damage.[150]

**1977, January 2. Mrs. Janet Berry home:** Center Street. Fire caused by overheated woodstove in cellar; $10,000 damage. The family dog died from smoke inhalation. Mrs. Berry, her daughter Lynn and two-year-old grandson Daniel Berry were in the house.[151]

**1977, January 8. Bittersweet Restaurant:** Fire gutted house. Barn was saved. Firemen could not reach buildings until Larry Hamm, who was driving by, cut a path in with his snowplow. Damage: $50,000 to $75,000. Larry Carville, fireman, was hospitalized overnight for smoke inhalation.[152]

**1977, January 28. Brewster Academy:** Fire caused $2,000 damage. A 17-year-old Tuftonboro youth was charged with arson.[153]

**1977, May 30. House on Lang Pond Road:** Two rooms and attic burned.

**1977, June 29. Robert Achorn shed and workshop:** Turtle Island Road. Total loss ($5,000) due to electrical overload causing a short circuit. "Noise caused by explosion of ammunition stored in the building called the family's attention to the fire."[154]

**1978, January 1. Bourdon's Store:** Route 28, near North Wolfeboro. Apartment and ell gutted; store smoke-damaged. Owned by Edgar Clauson, Newton Highlands, MA.

**1978, March 8. Former Radio Shack store and apartment:** Union Street. Gutted. Building owned by Sandy McKenzie. Fire started in mattress of apartment rented by Wes Fleur, who tried to drag it down the stairway. Mattress became wedged and had to be abandoned. Fire-fighting efforts were hampered by a frozen hydrant.[155]

**1978, April 18. Camp on Keniston Island:** Fire, believed to be of electrical origin, started in and destroyed cottage of Paul Gardent (of Weston, MA), loss $10,000 or more, and spread to cover four or five adjacent acres. "Several other camps, and perhaps the entire island, might have been lost, except for the efforts of three Wolfeboro firefighters. Captain Wallace Keniston and two volunteer firemen, Carl Shannon and Charles A. Foss, crossed the lake, [the ice on] which had begun to break up and put out the fire. Chief Foss said that because of the extreme danger involved in crossing the ice, he did not ask any men to try to reach the fire. The three who went volunteered. The men left the shore at the Warren Snyder residence in East Alton in an aluminum rowboat and traveled about three-quarters of a mile rowing in open water and dragged the boat across sections of honey-combed ice. Chief Foss estimated that it took the men about an hour to reach the island."[156]

**1979, February 10. Gary Warren house:** Rear part gutted.

**1979, March 11. Lamparter house:** North Main Street. Cellar and first floor burned.[157]

**1979, April 9. Gordon ("Lefty") Harris garage:** North Main Street. Substantial damage.

**1979, August 20. Kenneth and Ginny Perry house:** Dimon's Corner. Two rooms burned. Known as the Aaron Roberts-Hezekiah Willand house.[158]

**1979, September 7. Huggins Hospital:** Fire adjacent to incinerator.

**1979, November 9. Hugh Wallace house:** Pine Hill Road. Living room floor near fireplace and wall burned.

**1979, December 15. Mrs. Winifred Robie house:** Pleasant Valley. Nearly totally destroyed; personal effects of eight occupants lost. Caused by faulty pipe leading from woodstove. Nearest water was a mile away. Loss: $40,000. A relief fund to help the Robie family was set up at the Wolfeboro National Bank and directed by P. Scott Roberts.[159]

**1980, January 1. Cash Store:** Union Street. Upper floor apartment gutted. Four members of Richard Arthur family burned, Elizabeth (Mrs. Arthur) seriously. Apparently caused by a cigarette smoldering in living room sofa.[160]

**1980, February 3. White house:** Hidden Valley. Living room floor and cellar ceiling burned.

**1980, March 12. Furber house apartments:** South Main Street. Started by cigarette in sofa. Gutted. All 11 residents escaped without injury. Four firemen were treated at Huggins. Building owned by Richard J. Brown, earlier by Brewster Academy. Loss: $125,000.[161]

**1980, May 3. Warren Massey house:** Waumbeck Road. Fire started when water in a glass jug magnified sun's rays. Fire discovered before major damage was done.

**1980, August 27. Structure on Middleton Road:** Totally destroyed.

## LAW ENFORCEMENT

### With the Department

During the decade drug abuse accounted for numerous arrests in town, up sharply from the earlier 10-year period. In 1972 John D. McLaughlin, clerk of the Superior Court of Carroll County, estimated that drug-related cases in the area were 10 to 20 times greater than five to 10 years earlier. Motor vehicle infractions resulted in many arrests as well.[162]

In December 1971 the Wolfeboro Police Department, under Chief Arnold H. Wentworth, distributed over 550 gifts under the annual Christmas Fund, which had been established in 1967.

In 1971 the Police Department had four vehicles: 1968 Plymouth (13,548 miles driven during the year), 1969 Plymouth (34,036), 1970 Ford (48,755), and 1971 Plymouth (3,506).[163]

In the local court, cases were presented and tried before judges Philip Ganem and Jerry Thayer. The latter resigned in 1972 and was replaced by George W. Walker.[164]

In summer 1972 a cadet program was implemented for 10 weeks. Robert M. Blanchard, John P. Kalled, Pam Newhall, Thomas Norton, Alan Rines, and Jane Roundy signed up for duty.

On the weekend of November 25 of the same year, three 17-year-old boys from Massachusetts came to town—Barry O'Riordan, Richard Coleman, and Thomas Salvati—and stayed in the Lydiard cottage on Lake Wentworth. At midnight they took a canoe ride and disappeared. The police and others mounted a search to no avail. It was not until the next spring and summer that their bodies were found.[165]

In early 1974 no-fault divorces were instituted in New Hampshire, flooding the courts with cases. During one week in the spring, over 100 cases were heard in the Superior Court. In March the first woman officer was commissioned by the Department, Lorraine Lynn Wright. In May, Robert C. Varney, 29-year-old attorney with the local office of Cooper, Hall & Walker, was named special justice of the Wolfeboro District Court, where eventually he served for many years.

A new service, Project Good Morning, was set up by Chief Wentworth in December 1974, whereby people living alone could call the Department each day between 9:00 and 10:00 a.m. Those who did not call would receive an in-person visit to check on their welfare.[166]

In 1977 the Police Department had 10 full-time employees, plus nine special officers (four of whom worked full-time in the summer). That the Department offered attractive employment is evidenced by a vacancy that occurred in the summer of 1978, when Robert A. Tierney was selected from among 48 applicants.

On October 24, 1978, the resignation of Chief Arnold H. Wentworth was accepted by the selectmen. Lt. Stanley E. Stevens, who had turned in a stellar record in investigative matters, was appointed as the new chief, his duties to begin on January 1. Born in Concord, Stevens grew up in Penacook. He had worked for the State Police for two years, then for the Wolfeboro Police Department 1965-1968, then did a stint in the private sector with Lakes Region Survey Service, then, rejoined the Police Department in early 1971.[167]

In 1979 the new uniform patch worn by local police, the design of John Markowitz of the Graphic Arts Department of Kingswood High School, won first prize for its beauty in a national competition. The motif showed the *Lady of the Lake* steamer at the Town Docks in the nineteenth century and the inscription "The Oldest Summer Resort in America."

Radar was used for the first time in town to deter speeding, effectively it turned out, for vehicle accidents in town dropped from 187 in 1978 to just 144 in 1979, although the device had been in use only since June. At the end of the year, Chief Stevens reported that the Department had presented 469 adult and 49 juvenile cases to the court and had secured a 99% conviction rate, indicative of high quality work done by the officers.[168]

### Police Blotter

The following incidents and cases, crimes and accidents, are representative of the era.

**1971, March 30. Bomb threat:** Kingswood High School received a threat, and the facility was evacuated for 45 minutes. A young man, not a student at Kingswood, was picked up for questioning. Additional bomb threats occurred on December 17, 1975, and March 21 and 27, 1978.[169]

**1971, April 15. High school vandalism:** Principal Robert Morrison reported that at Kingswood destruction of property reached an all-time high, with ceiling tiles destroyed, lighting fixtures wrecked, bathrooms damaged, etc. In lieu of vandals being discovered, class treasuries would pay for any future losses.

**1971, April 23. Car theft:** Thomas O'Dowd's 1967 Chevrolet station wagon was stolen, but was soon recovered in Alton. A 31-year-old Wolfeboro man was later arrested and found guilty.[170]

**1971, May 27. "Laying rubber":** A local teenager was found guilty of doing this with a vehicle and fined $5.

**1971, June 17. "Pulling a wheelie":** *I.e.,* reckless driving on just one wheel of a motorcycle. A teenager was found guilty, fined $100, and lost his license for 60 days.

**1971, July 13. Marijuana:** An East Alton man was arrested in town and charged with possessing four pounds worth $1,500.[171]

**1971, August 16. Drug store break:** Hall's Pharmacy was burglarized of money, narcotics, and syringes.

**1971, November 6. Another drug theft:** Tobey's Pharmacy was hit, and "a large quantity of narcotics and controlled drugs was taken along with cash." Three youths saw the getaway vehicle and described it to police.[172]

**1972, March 9. Thefts solved:** The Police Department reported the arrest of two juveniles for thefts from the Lakes Region Sports Shop, Wolfeboro Hardware, and Schillereff's. Hugh Crowther of Stamford, CT, pleaded guilty to receiving stolen goods.[173]

**1973, April 2. Carjacking:** Warren Griffin of Grove Street was accosted by two men while visiting Rochester and was forced to drive back to his home in Wolfeboro, where he was beaten with a club, his home ransacked, and $8,200 in cash stolen. Griffin, seriously injured, was sent to a Boston hospital. Local citizens rallied to set up a fund to help with expenses. An arrest in Rochester was made soon thereafter, and the car was recovered.[174]

**1973, May 31. Marina hit:** Burglars broke into Winnipesaukee Motor Craft and absconded with 10 outboard motors valued at over $9,000, a company truck, and $500 cash.[175]

**1973, August 2. But who would want it?:** A privy was stolen in Cotton Valley.

**1973, August 15. Libby Museum:** Many old coins and antique buttons worth several thousands of dollars were stolen.[176]

**1973, August 18. Because of a purse:** In Bailey's Restaurant parking lot a heavy purse belonging to a lady from Laconia fell off the seat of her car and depressed the gas pedal, causing the car to strike a vehicle from Pennsylvania, which in turn hit another car, causing much damage.[177]

**1974, January 29. Gas theft:** Siphoned from a truck parked at Parsons' Furniture; representative of a newly popular crime evoked by the gasoline shortage. Such crimes continued apace as years went on. For example, in one week in June 1979 there were three incidents of gas siphoning and nonpayment at service stations.[178]

**1974, April 4. Ex cons in town:** Sgt. H. George Moody and Officer Guy Eldridge arrested a trio of burglars with drugs in their possession inside Tobey's Pharmacy at 8:40 p.m. Two were on furlough from a Massachusetts prison from which the third had recently been paroled. Stanley E. Stevens subsequently handled the prosecution, which landed each of the culprits in jail for three to seven years.[179]

**1974, June 4. Rash of burglaries:** Lt. Stanley E. Stevens and Sgt. H. George Moody solved two of four recent break-ins at the Wolfeboro Laundromat, Open Door Restaurant, Norm's Gulf, and Shannon's Grocery. The arrested man was from Massachusetts.

**1973, July 31. Antiques stolen:** Pewter, antique dolls, and lamps were stolen from the Clark House, operated by the Wolfeboro Historical Society, but were recovered on August 1. Two men from Massachusetts were arrested with the loot, plus $40,000 worth of glassware stolen in Meredith.[180] During the era criminals from the Bay State thought the Lakes Region of New Hampshire was easy pickings, but often learned otherwise.

**1974, August 15. Wolfeboro Rail Road hit:** Richard Libby, superintendent of the line, reported many instances of vandalism by youths who threw rocks, bottles, and other objects at trains, and placed boards, rocks, and other things on the rails.

**1974, October 31. Hallowe'en brawl:** Police assisted by a squad of firemen attempted to break up a rowdy group of 50 to 100 youths in the downtown district. Police officers and cruisers were pelted with eggs, insulted, and called obscene names. Police Commissioner Peter D. Shulman commented that the police acted with great restraint in view of extremely provocative circumstances. Three arrests were made. Eventually, the crowd dispersed. (Next year's Hallowe'en was quiet.)[181]

**1975, August 24. Open Door Restaurant:** $1,800 cash was taken during business hours.[182]

**1975, October 18-19. Wolfeboro Inn:** A police stake-out netted three Worcester, MA, residents who were charged with a series of thefts amounting to $3,800 in cash and checks.[183]

**1976, April 27. Hall's Pharmacy:** A break-in netted thieves $2,900 worth of drugs, watches, and cash.[184]

**1976, July 30. Cash crop:** Police discovered and uprooted 500 marijuana plants growing near Cotton Mountain Road.[185]

**1976, September 12. Teacher caught:** Tuftonboro police arrested James F. Taylor, 35, mathematics teacher at Kingswood High, after finding allegedly stolen merchandise at his house. He later pleaded guilty and was sentenced.[186]

**1976 *Town Report* commentary:** "A substantial increase in criminal cases is shown in the year 1976, especially in the area of juvenile cases, with 101 juveniles appearing before the juvenile court. Many of these cases involved major crimes. This increase should be of great concern to the Wolfeboro community." Many local citizens began installing silent alarms in their homes. By decade's end, the Knight Security Alarm Co. (Patrick O'Keefe) had a thriving business in electronic devices, as did the long-established Camp Patrol (Ned Bullock) with on-site inspections.

**1977, March 23. Tiffany glass:** $35,000 worth was stolen from the home of Robert Hebb, local businessman.[187]

**1977 *Town Report* commentary:** Noted that there were 29 driving while intoxicated (DWI; also called DUI for driving under the influence) cases and 27 drug cases in 1977. The number of juvenile cases in 1977 decreased 68% from the year before, and the number of adult cases decreased 6%.

**1977, September 17. Windrifter Yacht Club:** A break-in yielded $3,000 worth of items including electronic equipment. Within the week, Lt. Stanley E. Stevens reported all items had been recovered.[188]

**1979, June 20. Kung residence:** The summer residence of Col. Lin Chi Kung and his wife Debra Paget on Hopewell Road (which became incorrectly designated the "Chiang Kai-Shek mansion" in the next decade) was broken into, and Oriental rugs, lamps, clocks, dishes, candle holders, and a 12-gauge shotgun were taken.[189]

**1979, August 24. Chris Craft:** 19-foot boat valued at $4,000 was taken from the Town Docks.[190]

**1979, September 26. Boat vandalism:** Chief Stanley E. Stevens reported that 18 boats had been set adrift at the Northeast Marina, and there was a spate of other vandalism downtown.

**1980, January 19. Nutcracker statue:** A 24-year-old Wolfeboro man was arrested on a charge of damaging the papier maché Nutcracker statue in front of the Camelot Book Shop and moving it to the middle of North Main Street.[191]

**1980, April 26. Graveyard damaged:** Vandals injured more than 50 markers at the Pine Hill Cemetery, causing several thousand dollars' damage.[192]

**1980, June 25. Motorcycle madness:** Each June, "Motorcycle Weekend" held near Laconia caused a ruckus all around the lake, with loud noise, rowdyism, etc., including in Wolfeboro. Bruce Bedford, prize-winning photographer for the *Granite State News,* went to cover the motorcycle races and left in disgust after seeing live sex shows and the "tit tower" (upon which bare-breasted women cavorted).[193]

**1980, December 15. Shopkeeper assaulted:** Harry May, popular proprietor of the Time Shop on Railroad Avenue, and his wife and daughter were bound and gagged in their Center Ossipee home and forced to turn over the keys to the Wolfeboro store, which was subsequently broken into before May could free himself and notify police.[194]

During rapidly escalating crime on the national scene, the rebellion of many young people, a popular disregard for authority, and increasing drug use, the Wolfeboro Police Department did a very creditable job. It is worth noting that violent crimes were almost nonexistent locally.

## NATURAL PHENOMENA

### Weather

On Saturday afternoon, August 28, 1971, tropical storm Doria ripped through town with winds up to 68 miles per hour, leaving in its wake 2.29 inches of rainfall, about 25 downed trees, and about 110 power outages.

On August 25, 1972, what old-timers described as one of the worst electrical storms ever to hit the area took out power for 350 customers including Huggins Hospital, killed two dogs, and severely damaged a residence in the Port Wedeln development.

Summer 1973 saw extensive flooding. On June 29 and 30 about 3.5 inches of rain caused washouts on gravel roads and interruption of electrical service. More heavy rain in early August flooded the Wolfeboro Shopping Center and Clarke Plaza to a depth of a foot or more in certain spots and caused damage to the Kingswood Bank & Trust Co. and several stores. Federal and state officials visited on August 2 to determine eligibility for flood disaster funds. The owners of the shopping centers blamed the town for poor engineering and insufficient drainage, while old-timers recalled that both facilities had been built on filled-in bay and swamp areas, and what should the owners expect? From March 13 through

15, 1977, more than three inches of rain fell locally, flooding P.J. Lanes, Downeast Seafood, Second Chance Closet, Open Door Restaurant, and other Clarke Plaza businesses.[195]

On Sunday, June 29, 1975, a memorable electrical storm ignited three structural fires within 27 minutes. Winds were described as of savage ferocity.

January 1976 brought lots of snow combined with the lowest average temperature in 30 years, ideal for winter sports, but hard on residents' heating bills. A year later in January 1977 so much snow had fallen by the 10th of the month that most of the town's snow-removal budget for the year had been exhausted. On Monday and Tuesday, February 6 and 7, 1978, snowfall was so heavy that schools were closed, the Wolfeboro National Bank was locked all day Tuesday, the Kingswood Bank gave up at noon, and many residents were without transportation or open roads. However, employees at Town Hall made an effort to do business as usual.

In contrast, the winter of 1980 was notable for its lack of white stuff on the ground. Peter Cole commented, "It has been a disaster for my ski team at Kingswood." On the other hand, Ethel Tucker said, "Good! I can get out of the house."[196]

### Earthquakes, Comets, and Loons

Elm trees were becoming fewer and fewer in town due to the Dutch elm blight. For much of the decade, diseased elms were treated by the Main Line Tree Service (Kirk Titus) and others, under a program supervised by Tree Warden Bill Swaffield (better known as the proprietor of the Kingswood Press), but, eventually, all died, including more than 40 on North and South Main Streets and on the Brewster Academy campus. Among these was the Raymond J. Sanborn elm on South Main, measuring 15 feet in circumference, said to be the largest in the county.

At 9:30 in the evening, June 14, 1973, windows in town were rattled by tremors from a magnitude 5 earthquake centered near the Canadian border.

Skywatchers expected celestial fireworks in December 1973, when the great Comet Kohoutek was to put in an appearance. Sales of telescopes soared. *Time* magazine stated that it "may become the most spectacular comet of this century.... By early January its tail may stretch across one-sixth of the evening sky." However, it turned out to be a non-event, as the comet was hardly visible. Another contender, the relatively unpublicized Comet West, fared a bit better, and a photograph of it snapped by Phil Martin on March 7, 1976, appeared on the front page of the *Granite State News*.

America was in the midst of a flying saucer craze. In response to numerous unidentified flying object sightings in the area, in August 1974 the Nordic Skier advertised "U.F.O.s"—identified in smaller print as "Usual Fantastic Offers"—a summer sale of winter ski equipment.

Loons became a concern of the NH Audubon Society and others, as it was realized that relatively few of them remained locally. It was estimated that by 1976, only 15 adults were in Lake Winnipesaukee. Members of the Loon Preservation Society (in Centre Harbor) and other like-minded citizens sprang into action with dramatically successful results. By the end of the following decade, loons, while still considered an endangered species, were relatively plentiful on the local scene.

Meanwhile, there was no shortage of ducks in the vicinity. In the winter of 1976-1977 about 400 of the fowl decided it was better to remain in the Smith River and partake of the 100 pounds of grain put out each day by Mr. and Mrs. Russell Pinard (owners of the Sunshine Auction Gallery), than to fly south.

In the mid- and late 1970s the number of tent caterpillars increased each year, with resultant defoliation, especially of broad-leaf deciduous trees. Gypsy moths posed a threat in the summer of 1980, but not as severe as would occur the following year.

Other local items on the nature and ecology front at the end of the decade included a few hazy days from the cataclysmic explosion of Mt. St. Helens in Washington state, acid rain, and the proliferation of milfoil in Back Bay (an experimental harvest was conducted in 1980).[197]

## PRICES IN 1980

The following prices are from advertisements in the *Granite State News:*

**Appliances:** Dishwasher, Hotpoint, $339.95. Kerosene room heater, $100.95 to $268.95. Refrigerator, 21 cubic feet, frostless. $569.95. Smoke detector, Norelco, $13.99. Woodstove, typical, $400 to $800; some over $1,000.

**Automobile service:** Grease, oil and filter service, Bill's Auto Service, $10.95.

**Automobiles:** 1980 models. Buick Skyhawk, $5,467. Chevrolet Chevette, $4,894. Chrysler LeBaron, $6,600. Plymouth Volaré, $5,800.

**Beverages:** Coffee, Maxwell House instant, 10-ounce jar, $3.99. Milk, low-fat, gallon, $1.39. Diet Pepsi Cola, or Mountain Dew, 2-liter bottle, 99¢.

**Boat:** 16' Galaxy inboard-outboard with 120-hp Mercruiser engine, $5,730.

**Business opportunity:** Cheese Caboose, sold cheese and wine, Center Street, $15,000.

**Camera:** Minolta 35mm single lens reflex, $194.95.

**Ceiling fan:** Caribbean Breeze brand, $64.99.

**Clothing:** Pants, denim, men's, $13.50; boys', $11.

**Dog food:** Gaines Meal, 5-pound bag, $1.59.

**Food:** Meat: Haddock filets, pound, 99¢. Tuna, Geisha brand, solid white, 7-ounce can, 89¢. Chicken breast, pound, 99¢. Ground beef, pound, $1.39. Top round steak, pound, $2.68. Turkey, 18 to 20 pounds, per pound, 67¢. Frankfurters,

Schonland's, pound, $1.69.

**Food:** Various: Bananas, pound, 25¢. Cereal, Wheaties, 18-ounce box, 99¢. Flour, 5-pound bag, 85¢. Grapes, seedless green, pound, 79¢. Ice cream, Hood brand, 1/2 gallon, $1.39. Margarine, Mrs. Filbert's, pound, 50¢. Peanut butter, Skippy, 8-ounce jar, 99¢. Sugar, 5-pound bag, $2.59.

**Fuel:** Gasoline, regular, gallon in August, $1.25. Hardwood, cord, cut and split, 16-24" length, $70-$80.

**Furniture:** Mattress and springs, 3-piece Serta king-size set, $379.95. Water bed, $249.

**Hair styling:** Highlighting with blow-dry, Wolfeboro Clipper, $15.

**Laundry detergent:** Tide, giant size box, $1.69.

**Newspaper:** *Granite State News,* mail subscription $12.

**Paint:** Wall-Hide, Pittsburgh Paint, gallon, $10.99.

**Photography:** Children's portrait, one 8x10, two 5x7s, plus eight wallet size, studio or outdoor, Ned Bullock, photographer, $41.50.

**Real estate rentals:** Apartment, three rooms, bay window in living room, heated, fully applianced, new bath, per month, $350. Downtown store-office, 300+ square feet, $175 per month.

**Real estate:** House, Cricket Hill Estates, new cedar-shingled ranch, $87,500. House at Lake Wentworth, new year-round ranch with 150' of sandy shorefront, $97,000. Model home designed by Royal Barry Wills, Wyanoke Harbors, lake access, $165,000. Shorefront lot, 150' wide, Wyanoke Harbors, $75,000. Wooded five-acre parcel on town road with 290 feet of road frontage, $10,500.

**Recreation:** Cruise from Portland to Nova Scotia and return, private cabin, dancing, party, per couple, $139.95. Cruise, 55 miles on Lake Winnipesaukee with Capt. Sandy McKenzie on the mailboat *Blue Ghost,* adult, $7. Week time-sharing interval at Windrifter, lifetime membership, regular price $4,000, resale price $2,000.

**Restaurant food:** Complete prime rib dinner, $7.95; lasagna, all you can eat, $3.95; lobster dinner for two, $12.95. Lunch special, Cider Press, $1.95.

**Service:** Rototilling, per hour, $10.

**Sports:** Annual membership in new Bay Village Racquetball Club, $70. Bowling, P.J. Lanes, per line, 50¢. Skiing, lift ticket for day at Cannon Mountain, adult, $12, child $10. Skis, pair, $85 to $100.

**Toilet tissue:** Waldorf, 4 rolls for 85¢.

**Tool:** Power Shop by DeWalt, 10" blade, $249.95.

**Transportation:** Bodwell's taxi. First mile, $1.50; each additional, $1.10. Round-trip flight between Boston and Laconia, Precision Airlines, $46.

**Wages:** Grant writer, annual salary, $12,000-$14,000. Office staff, per hour, $4 to $5. U.S. census interviewer, per hour, $4.30.

# CHAPTER 11

# WOLFEBORO 1981-1990

*What a remarkable town – situated in a haven of beauty and populated by warm, friendly people.... Wolfeboro is a very special town!*

–Ruth and Dick Valentine, who had moved here from Beverly Hills, California. *Granite State News,* August 17, 1988.

**Introduction**

The 1980s are close enough in time that many readers will recall events first-hand.

The middle part of the decade saw a great real estate and economic boom with predictions by town officials that the town's population, which rose from 3,968 in the 1980 census to an estimated 5,300 in 1986 and 5,522 in 1987, would be 7,158 by 1990. This did not happen, and the 1990 census saw a pullback to 4,894.

Meanwhile, Wolfeboro was part of the big, wide world filled with crime, drugs, and changing society, not the least of the negatives being the AIDS epidemic.

As it had done for decades before, Wolfeboro came through, and in 1990 it remained a little gem of a community set in the Lakes Region of New Hampshire.

The 1980s will long be remembered as an era of economic and banking transitions and a decade when real estate development went wild. Many local events were influenced by these changes. Therefore, it seems appropriate to focus upon the economy as the introduction to the story of this period in Wolfeboro history.

## LOCAL ECONOMY

### Real Estate Market Afire

The Wolfeboro real estate market was sluggish in 1981, primarily because high interest rates paid by banks raised mortgage rates to over 15%. Home sales had dropped 30.3% in Carroll County in 1980 compared to the year before, and 1981 seemed to be no better. Few new homes were being built.[1]

After very quiet times the market became warm in 1983. Beginning about 1984 the market became hot. The *Town Report* in 1985 noted:

> New construction in the Wolfeboro area continues at an astonishing rate. Condominium projects such as Point Breeze, Pine Harbor, and Wolfeboro Common are progressing at a rapid rate. A period of growth puts a strain on all town departments since there are many capital projects while maintenance and repair are always present.

In 1986 the real estate market was in orbit. Throughout the Lakes Region – indeed, throughout much of New Hampshire generally – land prices escalated. While numerous private homes were constructed, emphasis was on cluster developments, condominiums, and time-sharing resorts. Such local firms as Henry S. Maxfield, Hamel, Dallas H. Edwards, Yankee Pedlar, George Waugh, and Century 21/Dockside literally did a land-office business. Banks gave easy credit to developers, and, in turn, developers offered low down payments and generous terms to buyers. Seemingly, nothing could go wrong.

But it did. After two or three years of frantic building, buying, and selling, the market stumbled in 1987 and crashed in 1988, and with it six of the seven leading banks in the state eventually collapsed, reorganized, or in one instance sold out. Fortunes were wiped out including nearly all of the stockholders' equity in the great BankEast debacle (about which more will be told).

In 1987 as the real estate market lost its balance and fell, asking prices of properties continued to *rise.* Speculators were slow to grasp reality. In messages published in the *Granite State News* in September 1987, Roy C. Ballentine of Consolidated Financial Planning, a local firm that was earning an outstanding reputation, reported that some local realtors had not had a closing in *six months* and others had cash flow problems. Wolfeboro closings for January through June were 19% below the comparable 1986 period. Ballentine endured some criticism from local real estate people for giving out "confidential information." He countered by stating that this was not so, and that the market was simply returning to normal.[2]

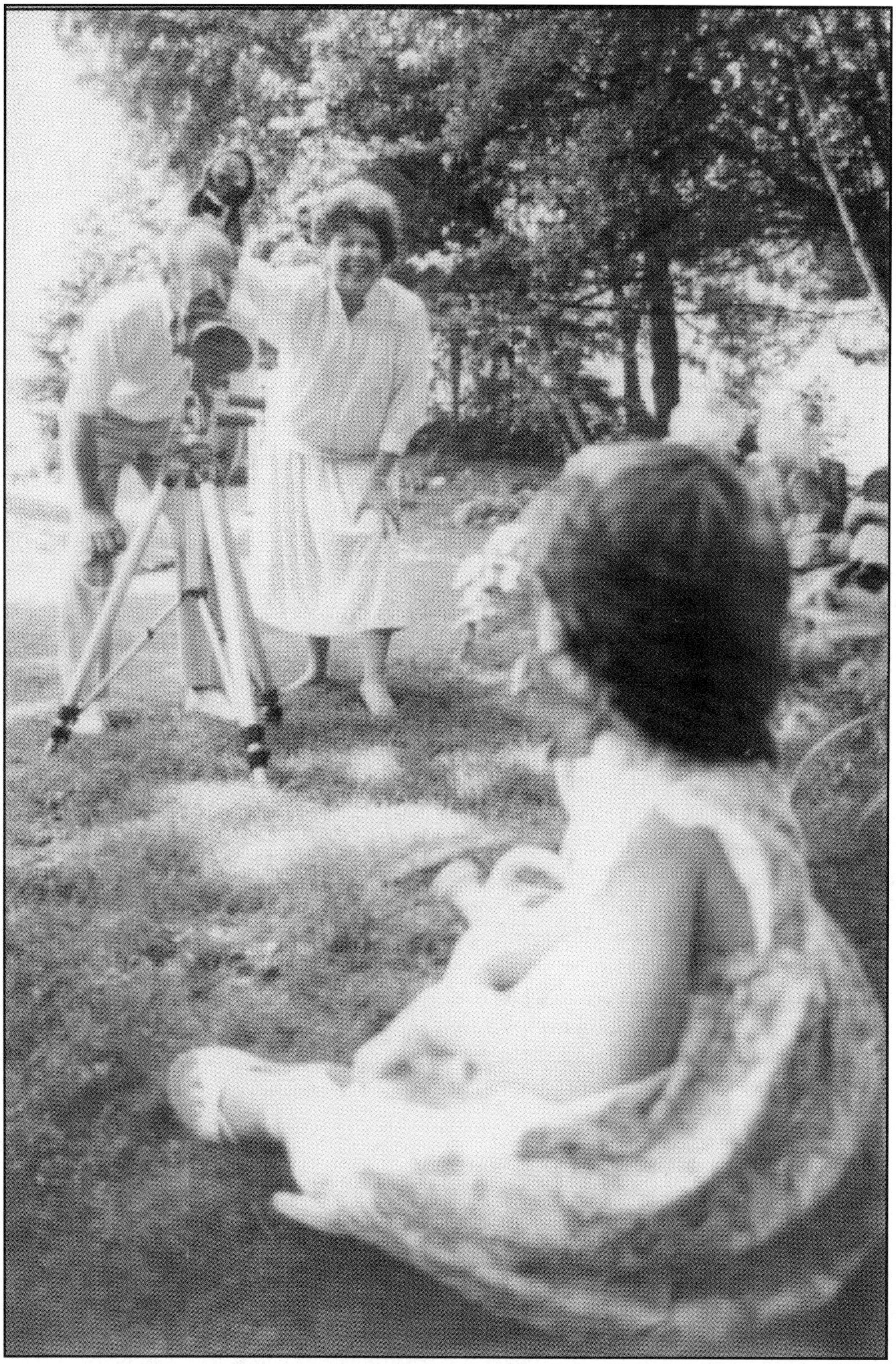

**Well-known local lens artist Ned Bullock and his wife Gloria take a photograph of a young client. (Sandy Martin photograph, 1990)**

Realtor Henry S. ("Chip") Maxfield, Jr., remembers the era:[3]

> My recollection of the 1985-1988 real estate market follows:
>
> The market took off in late 1985 and early 1986, and within 18 to 20 months prices on homes had doubled and on land had tripled. Example: two undeveloped lots in Wyanoke Harbors went under contract in January 1986 for $115,000 and $120,000. They closed to a third party two months later at $150,000 and $160,000. In 1987 the last undeveloped shorefront lot at Wyanoke sold for $375,000.
>
> I recall that 1987 was the peak year, but properties that got sold through 1988 also sold at peak prices. This occurred because in early and mid-1987 any property listed at that time was priced at about 20% over the peak. It only appeared as though sales prices were lower because people were comparing current high offering prices against actual sales prices which were lower. Although sales were usually below the asking prices, the net prices were still records compared to the levels of a few years earlier.
>
> Sales remained strong for our agency through 1987 as the more "moderately" priced or older listings were sold. By early 1988 almost 100% of all listings were overpriced by 20%, and the market stalled.
>
> The rest of the decade saw successively reduced prices and many foreclosures, although lakefront Wolfeboro property maintained a better value than did most listings in other Lakes Region communities.

Fortunately, most of the developmental excesses of the mid-1980s were elsewhere in the state including Gilford, Waterville Valley, Lincoln, and other places where time-sharing vacation condominiums were put up, often hastily and with little regard for quality. In contrast most Wolfeboro developments were laid out on larger lots and under stricter regulations that made the town somewhat unattractive for get-rich-quick promoters with jerry-built structures. A nod of appreciation for their foresight and wisdom in this regard is due Wolfeboro planners, selectmen, and voters. Sometimes things do not make sense until they are over and can be studied retrospectively at leisure.

When all was said and done several attractive new areas were created in Wolfeboro. However, the market peak of 1985-1986 was missed by several entrepreneurs. One project, Winnipesaukee Hill Estates, remained unbuilt for years thereafter, and the immense Collden Farm project never made it past the planning stage.

Perhaps no statistic is more poignant than that given in the 1990 *Town Report,* which showed that 175 building lots had been approved by the town in the frantic market of 1986, but in 1990 only 20 were approved.

Some of the more notable developments created, expanded, or substantially improved during the decade comprise a list unequaled in town history:[4]

500 Forest Road: Residential. Off Forest Road.

990 Sewall Road: Residential. Near intersection of Sewall and Forest Roads.

1000 Sewall Road: Residential. Near intersection of Sewall and Forest Roads.

2000 Centre Street: Business complex.

Abenaukee Estates: Residential. Begun in the 1970s. Off South Main Street.

Bayside Village: Business condominiums. Back Bay on site of old sawmill.

Central Square: Business condominiums. Refurbished Bradley's Hardware Building.

Centre at Wolfeboro: Business condominiums. Varney Road.

Clarke Plaza: Business rentals. Expanded, improved, landscaped.

Collden Farm: 310 acres with 60 homes in Wolfeboro but only accessible by automobile by going to Ossipee first; however, what would have been the largest development in town history was never built.

Crescent Point: Residential. Off Whitten Neck Road.

Cricket Hill: Residential. Development of area off Forest Road continued.

Depot Square: Business condominiums. Next to Wolfeborough Railroad Station.

Embassy Estates: Residential. Wolfeboro Neck.

Fairway View Estates: Residential. Off Clark Road.

Front Bay Professional Building (later occupied by the Community Bank & Trust Co.). Varney Road.

Greenleaf Estates: Residential. Off Clark Road.

Hidden Valley: Residential. Older development at Beach Pond re-advertised by the Patten Corporation.

Mountain West: Condominiums. Off South Main Street.

Narrows, The: Condominiums on Back Bay near the Wolfeborough Railroad Station.

Orchards, The: Residential. Pleasant Valley. Patten Corporation.[5]

Pine Harbor: Condominiums. Off North Main Street.

Piping Rock Lodges: Converted in part to condominium ownership.

Point Breeze: Condominiums. Project begun in the 1970s. Lake Wentworth.

Sewall Point: Residential. 15 lots off Sewall Road (later called Pointe Sewall).

Sky Ridge Farm: Condominiums. Off North Main Street.

Wasamegin Acres: Residential. Near Sargents Pond.

Wentworth Plaza: Strip mall of business condominiums. Route 28.

Westwood of Wolfeboro: Residential. 31-lot development off College Road.

Winnipesaukee Hill Estates: Residential. 43-lot development in South Wolfeboro on a large parcel of land used by the former Camp Kehonka. Unbuilt, this otherwise would have been Wolfeboro's second largest development (after Collden Farm).

Wolfeboro Common: Condominiums. Begun in the 1970s. Off North Main Street.

Wolfeboro Marketplace: Commercial complex. North Main Street.

Wolfeboro Shopping Center: Improved, name changed to Kingswood Plaza, then BankEast Plaza.

Wolfeborough Bay Manor: Durgin Block elegantly restored by Richard Eaton and Gorham W. Humphrey.

Wyanoke Harbors: Residential. Project begun in the 1970s. Wolfeboro Neck on the site of the former Camp Wyanoke on Winter Harbor.

### Age of the Discount

Elsewhere in the economy, the 1980s saw the word

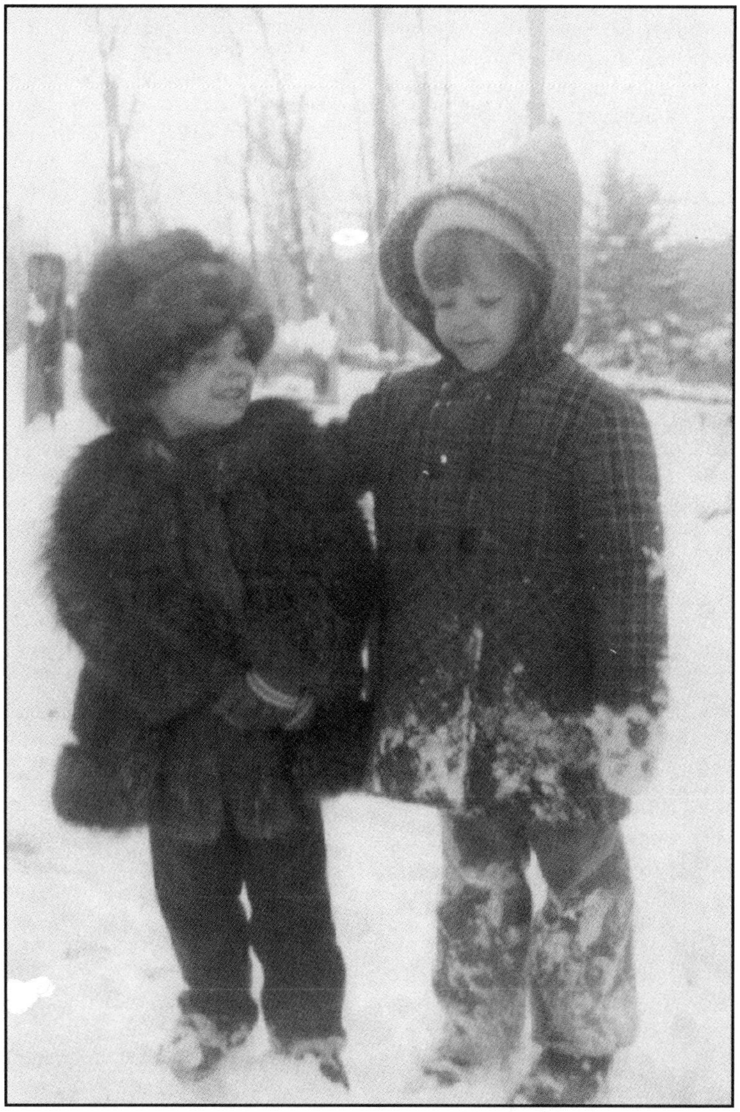

Fun on a snowy day in 1982. Youngsters Paige Foran (left) and Jenny Rines enjoy the white stuff. (Ruth Glidden Collection)

*discount* loom large in retailing circles. Not far from the Wolfeboro town line the Ames Department Store and Shop 'n Save grocery opened in Ossipee and advertised discount prices. In North Conway, 40 miles away, the main street was lined with stores calling themselves factory outlets (although some had no direct connection with any factory). To the south the Newington Mall was joined by the Fox Run Mall, while additional shopping plazas opened at other locations.

While discounts at some out-of-town stores proved to be less than bargains—especially if something needed service or personal attention—there is no doubt that a trip to the mall was a social as well as a shopping occasion. Times became tough for many Wolfeboro stores, especially those in the fields of clothing, gifts, and appliances. However, local merchants who concentrated on paying close attention to their clients did well and developed strong loyalties. There were several turnaround successes based upon service—one example being Charlie Hunter's acquisition of a failed grocery store, redecorating the premises, and opening Hunter's IGA, which emphasized attention to customers, courteous service, and fresh food. Hunter never claimed he was the *cheapest*, but eventually many thought he was the *best*.

During the decade probably more specialty retail shops opened in Wolfeboro than during any other 10-year period in its history. A generous number of these were located in the Wolfeboro Marketplace, a complex of buildings on North Main Street opened in 1984 next to the splendidly restored Durgin Block. Unfortunately, the layout of the area was such that the view from the street of nearly all of the shops was blocked by a large two-story wooden building set squarely in front of them. This, plus what were considered by many to be very high rents, created a remarkable turnover of tenants. These and other Wolfeboro Marketplace shops went out of business or moved from that location before decade's end:

Bookends, E. Motion & Co., Irish Tweed Shop, Cloud 9 Bed and Bath, Wolfeboro Bookshop (moved), Christmas Presence (moved), Classic Expression—All Cotton Outlet, Country Lady, The Magic Rose, Serendipity Fashions, Bridges' Hallmark Shop (moved), Nelson's Pet-Pourri, Canedy's Pendleton Shop, Panache Fashions, and Wreckless.

In contrast, Clarke Plaza was one of the success stories of the decade. Paul E. Zimmerman and his wife Deborah came to town from New Jersey and bought the complex of stores on Center Street owned by Richard and Marguerite Clarke. The new proprietors spent much money upgrading the facilities, adding attractive facades, landscaping, and on other improvements even including a decorative carved wooden moose. An unusual feature was The Office, a group of business suites offering shared telephone and secretarial facilities. Tenants in Clarke Plaza tended to remain for a relatively long time.

The Wolfeboro Shopping Center on Center Street went through several transformations mainly brought about by the Kingswood Bank and BankEast happenings. Most notable was an extensive and somewhat controversial remodeling of the bank building's exterior in 1990.

Another focal point of business activity was centered at the corner of North Main and Endicott Streets in the building owned by Richard Eaton. *The Laker* newspaper was founded there in 1984 by Richard Eaton and Kathy O'Meara (who later became Mrs. Eaton) and went on to achieve wide distribution throughout the region and to showcase recreational and shopping opportunities. The Strawberry Patch restaurant drew many patrons to its strawberry-motif premises, Congressman Bob Smith had his office in the building for six years; the Community Bank and Trust Company was founded there; Dallas H. Edwards, Jan Malcolm, and others sold real estate from that location; and many other businesses were operated from the site.

It should be said that no matter how a shopping complex might have been constructed or managed, there were always some enterprises that were formed by people with little practical business experience and with unrealistic expectations. The notion that one can escape from the big city (Boston, Providence, New York, etc.) and make a bundle by operating a small-town business in Wolfeboro or some other "backward but friendly town" is an enduring one. As has been stated in print numerous times, many Wolfeboro residents are just as savvy business-wise as their urban counterparts and on local matters might just be a bit smarter.

### Businesses Old and New

The era was one of changes. Robert and Gogi Adler moved into town with their Cornish Hill Pottery business in 1985 and went on to expand their clientele nationwide. Hampshire Pewter went through several transitions and was for a time owned by Joseph L. Santoro, local accountant and entrepreneur. Later, Andy and Jane Milligan owned the facility for a while, and then sold out and opened Milligan's Pendleton Shop on Railroad Avenue. Hampshire Pewter made ornaments for the New Hampshire state Christmas tree at the White House in Washington, and an item from this manufacturer always made a welcome gift for dignitaries and other visitors to town.

Among other local entrepreneurs, Joseph I. ("Bucky") Melanson III kept busy with a jewelry store, antiques business, and a real estate office. John Naramore was involved in several ventures including Wings Jet Ski, a bed-and-breakfast facility, a marina, real estate, and marketing programs for businesses. Charles Smith and Rick Kourian of Smith and Kourian were perhaps the most active of all entrepreneurs and owned nearly a dozen regional businesses—among them the Goodhue & Hawkins marina and boat facility—all operated from their command post at Plow Shares Trust on Route 28 across the street from their 2000 Centre Street complex.

The Lawless automobile agency on Route 28 changed ownership, became Auto Village, and was later sold to Gary R. Miller and his wife Bobbie, who emphasized customer service and made the dealership the most successful in the area. Chevrolet, Buick, Geo, Plymouth, Dodge, and Chrysler marques were sold and serviced. In 1983 Bradley's Hardware was bought by Gordon Hunt, who moved it across the street to expanded quarters. Dewey and Ginny Schou bought Wolfeboro Power Equipment near Frog Hollow (on Bay Street) and became the leading local supplier for Honda power mowers and Toro lawn equipment. Their clever advertisements on WASR 1420-AM radio included "ribbet" frog chirps in the background.

Meanwhile in the construction supply business, Diamond International on Center Street closed down, and Winnipesaukee Lumber Company opened and eventually built an impressive facility on Pine Hill Road. The Men's Elk Shop and the Ladies' Elk Shop operated by the Elkinton family closed, and the premises were sold, one becoming Miltner's Shoes and the other a restaurant (today Rumors Café is there).

Jeb Bradley operated Evergrain Natural Foods in the Colonial Arms Building on North Main Street. As if he did not have enough to do, he gave magic shows to Carpenter School kids and others, coached baseball, and found time to get himself elected to the State Legislature. Purveyors of tasty baked goods included Pop's Donuts (Ricky and Brenda LaPointe), Bread and Roses (Lovering family), Mum's Bakery (Ron and Nancy Ingham), and the venerable Yum Yum Shop (Kelly family).

John Bridges, son of the late Senator Styles Bridges, moved his Island Real Estate business to town from Alton and also set up the Sawmill Marina on Bay Street. His wife Barbara became proprietor of Bridges' Hallmark, first located in the Wolfeboro Marketplace and then on South Main Street next to Town Park. Robert Brokaw had his fingers in several business pies including Bookends (with JoEllen Scully—name later changed to the Wolfeboro Bookshop), The Gallery (featuring new art by Marcia Bush as well as antique paintings), and Wolfeboro VCR, the latter becoming the town's largest videocassette rental emporium. Elsewhere on the art scene Suzanne Bonin opened a gallery on the second floor of Black's Paper Store and offered her own work and that of others. Attracting quite a bit of attention were her pen-and-ink sketches of the Wolfeborough Railroad Station, the downtown area, and other local motifs. In 1989 local artist Jean Colquhoun, whose paintings achieved national recognition, illustrated a children's book, *Christmas in Water Village,* commissioned by Amina Roessiger, written by Christine Maxfield, and with text and pictures coordinated by Pat Hodder.[6] Charlene Lehto was among other local artists whose works were acclaimed.

North Country Scuba and WinnSports, operated by Cliff Simoneau, attracted divers and aquatic enthusiasts from all over the state. Simoneau's underwater exploration of shipwrecks and artifact sites provided interesting material for several feature stories and television documentaries. The *Lady Go-Diva,* familiarly known as the "dive boat," was custom built for Simoneau and was made to accommodate divers and their gear including cylinder tanks of compressed air.

Among businesses that lasted for only a short time were Mr. T. and Company (dermagraphic studio, *i.e.,* tattoo parlor) on Lehner Street, a North Main Street office for securities dealer Paine Webber, Harley Expressions (photographic studio), Tapestries of New England (at the Basket Barn in Wolfeboro Falls), The Wolfeboro Scrapbook (scenic photographs), JC Jewelry (John Cugno, Center Street), Wax 'n Facts (albums, rock concert souvenirs, etc.), Agape Knits, Skandic Antik (Scandinavian antiques and gifts), The Purple Unicorn (gifts), Wolfeboro Fun Company (balloon-o-grams), The Snow Goose, A Splash of Green (Deborah Kelloway's plant rental business set up as part of a Brewster senior project and intended to be ephemeral), and the Victorian Photo Parlour.

Meanwhile, the "old guard" retail and service businesses kept their customers happy, with some of the longest-established being Kingswood Press, Black's Paper Store, Norris Harriman Construction, Touchmark Antiques, Idle Hour beauty shop, the Hoyt and Lauber floor-covering businesses, J. Clifton Avery Insurance, Goodhue & Hawkins marina, Horne's Ford agency, Wolfeboro Oil, Osgood Trucking, Poisson Construction, Bradley's Hardware, Nordic Skier, Camelot gift shop, Hutchins' Antiques, and various restaurants, realtors, attorneys, craftsmen, and lodging places, among others.

These were trying years on the economic scene, and few businesses—old or new—had an easy time of it.

### The Banking Merry-Go-Round

A book—and a fairly lengthy one at that—could be written on the banking history of Wolfeboro. Anyone contemplating this would do well to set aside at least a chapter for somewhat improbable and certainly unpredictable events of the 1980s.

The Kingswood Bank & Trust Company on Center Street, which first opened for business on April 21, 1973, kept growing in size, and local investors with Kingswood shares in their portfolios had smiles on their faces. In October 1983, after a bitter fight that left long-lasting scars for many of the people involved, Kingswood was bought out by BankEast, a financial conglomerate headed by Walter N. ("Rink") DeWitt, a Melvin Village resident whose Wolfeboro connections included presidency of the Board of Trustees of Brewster Academy, his alma mater. Kingswood stockholders received $95 per share, far over the $35 to $37 that shares sold for on the open market a few months earlier. Stockholders' smiles grew wider. In the midst of the takeover bid, Bob Fournier, president of the Kingswood Bank, joined the ranks of BankEast, much to the dismay of certain stockholders who were against the merger.

BankEast dreamed of being a big player in the financial markets, not only NH banking but through such far-flung ventures as a mortgage company in New York and a brokerage firm in London. As events would later prove, millions of dollars were lost in the process.

In 1990 BankEast was in technical default of a major loan, but declared that this would in no way affect its banking subsidiaries. By this time Bob Fournier had resigned. In 1990 he took charge of still another Wolfeboro financial institution: a newly-formed branch of the Farmington National Bank, which set up facilities in Clarke Plaza and drew many customers to its attractive premises.

Meanwhile, the old-line Wolfeboro National Bank (established 1906), a member of the First NH Bancorp string of financial institutions, was gobbled up by the Bank of Ireland. Confusing matters after the acquisition was the merger of the Wolfeboro facility with the First Central Bank (Laconia), resulting in the local branch being named Central Bank in Wolfeboro for a short time. Later it was known as the First NH Bank, nomenclature continued to the present day.

Brad Gile, president of Wolfeboro National, turned in his resignation shortly after the Bank of Ireland takeover. He then enlisted local merchant Gregory Roark and other local talent to form the Community Bank & Trust Company which set up temporary offices at the corner of North Main and Endicott Streets, and later hung out its sign on Varney Road. Reminiscent of the growth of the Kingswood Bank and Trust Company in the early 1970s, the Community Bank went on to build equity and customer accounts faster than anyone could have imagined. Those who bought shares of common stock at the issue price of $10 soon wished they had acquired more.

The local banks and their officers—particularly Brad Gile and Bob Fournier—were strong financial donors to civic causes and projects.

**A Room for the Night**

During the 1980s the venerable Lakeview Inn on North Main Street was sold by the Jack Fallon family to Michelle Gerasin, who moved to town from Lincoln where she and her husband Fred had operated a motel. The Lakeview continued its popularity with the local crowd, many of whom came on weekend evenings to sing along to Mary Barkas' melodies on the electronic organ.

Clearwater Lodges and Piping Rock Lodges catered to out-of-state vacationers who often came to enjoy a week or more among the pines on the shore of Lake Winnipesaukee. Also popular was Allan E. Bailey, Jr.'s, attractive Lake Motel on Crescent Lake, which he managed while his wife Julie took care of the Wool Corner boutique downtown. The Berry Motel on Center Street drew tourists in season.

The Allen "A" Resort on Route 28 had a tough time during the 1980s. Norval H. ("Bud") Smith continued to operate it for a few years, but could not carve a profitable niche in the local tourist trade. In the mid-1980s it changed hands and was renamed the Wentworth Winds; then it changed ownership again and resumed the Allen "A" Resort title. Several different restaurants came and went at the Allen "A", but few drew sufficient patronage to remain open even a year. A grandiose plan to tear down the buildings and erect a $27 million, 180-unit condominium complex was nixed by town authorities.

Difficulties also attended the Wolfeboro Inn, which had been a popular local overnight accommodation and eatery since the early 1930s. In the 1980s it changed hands several times, the last time to a group of ambitious investors who sank millions of dollars into a vast expansion, much to the dismay of certain local residents who complained loudly about what was called the "monstrosity on Sewall Road," a take-off on the popular film title, *Nightmare on Elm Street.* An excursion boat, *The Judge David Sewall,* was launched, but sunk twice at its dock within its first year. Despite these and other travails, the Wolfeboro Inn went on to become a popular spot for local gatherings and functions, its modern, spacious rooms attracted an enthusiastic clientele, and along the way the American Automobile Association bestowed upon it the coveted Four Diamond Award for excellence.

**A Bite to Eat**

Many Wolfeboro restaurants opened with great expectations, only to close shortly thereafter for various reasons. By decade's end these names were but memories or were soon to be so:

Que Tacos, Adam's Rib, Abner's Seafood & Steaks, Soda Pups, Bailey's Dockside, Café-Deli, Father John's Pub, Botticelli's, Rines Seafood Restaurant, Victuals and Drafts, Snookers, The Greens, Ciani's, Back Bay Boathouse, Marketplace Café, Parsonage Fine Dining Inn, Courtroom Lounge,

Soho Bar and Grille, Hearty Colonial Restaurant, No-Name Pub, Jerry's Restaurant, Bay Village Restaurant, Mama Lisa's, KJ's, Riff's, Edwards, Maccherones, Dairy Bubble, Cracked Egg, Zip's Country Deli, Yellow Bird Lounge, Engine 250 Family Restaurant, Anzo's Old-Fashioned Subs, Down Under Lounge, Chatterbox, Aw Shucks!, The Copper Pot, Basic Tastes, Oyster Club, B.G.'s Sub Shop, and Dumont, Falls & Co.

In contrast, there were several success stories. Bob and Denise Earle bought the Cider Press Restaurant on Middleton Road near Rust Pond, and by dint of hard work and an appealing menu, built a dedicated clientele that at one point necessitated adding another dining room. West Lake Asian Cuisine on Route 28 opened on April 15, 1989, by Lin Ho, became so popular that within a year the proprietor established two out-of-town branches.

Bailey's Restaurant established on South Main Street in 1938 and East of Suez near the Alton town line continued to draw many patrons during the summer season. The Bittersweet out on Route 28 changed its restaurant name and managers a few times in the 1980s, but continued to go strong under the ownership of Gary Warren. The Village Host Deli moved from Railroad Avenue to Mill Street. The Mast Landing Restaurant remained a favorite spot for breakfast and lunch on North Main Street near the bridge.

New faces of the era such as Louis' Pizza, Katie's Kitchen, Vathally's Subs & Pizza, Cook's Corner Deli, Wolfe's Tavern, Strawberry Patch (opened in 1979), Rumors Café, PJ's Dockside, and Crossdeggers registered varying degrees of popularity and continued into the 1990s.

### Elsewhere on the Economic Scene

In April 1981 an office of the state Division of Employment Security was opened in Town Hall. During one week shortly thereafter, 104 people filed claims out of an estimated 150 local unemployed workers. The construction trades were slow at the time. Fortunately, the summer drew a good number of tourists, and a survey taken of 32 businesses in August 1981 showed that 22 found sales on an upward trend.

In 1982 gasoline prices, which had been falling, continued their decline, and in March a gallon of unleaded fuel cost about $1.35, about a dime more than a gallon of home heating oil.

Contrary to the trend of the 1970s, small farms in the state were increasing in number and prospering. In Pleasant Valley, Dennis DeVylder was busy renovating and updating the old Moore farm which he bought in 1978 and was growing apples, peaches, vegetables, and flowers for local markets. At the time his farm and King Hill Orchards (operated by Tom Hadley and his wife Shelley Gregoire) were the only significant agricultural businesses within town limits, a sharp contrast to the nineteenth century when farms were the town's mainstay. Certain other important businesses of yesteryear, including shoe manufacturing, poultry raising, and boat building, had long since disappeared by the 1980s. However, Wolfeboro Mills (knitwear) and Brockhouse (molded plastic items) were very active, although each eventually went through ownership changes.

The Chamber of Commerce helped stimulate the trade of local merchants with special events including sidewalk sales, such as the one held on June 25-26, 1982, when entertainment was provided by the Dockside Strutters Jazz Band and a performance by the Wolfeboro Wranglers. In the same month the unemployment rate in town was a low 3.7%. Despite jobs being plentiful, Carroll County had the lowest income per family in the entire state. At the same time the county had the state's highest property value per capita due to expensive lakefront and other vacation properties owned by nonresidents.

In 1984 tourism was barely satisfactory due to a very rainy summer and the falling of the Fourth of July on Wednesday (thus there was no long weekend holiday). The majority of out-of-state tourists that year were from Massachusetts, New York, Connecticut, New Jersey, Michigan, Pennsylvania, and Illinois, in that order.

By summer 1984 the local construction business had revived sharply, interest rates were lower, and in the month of August alone permits worth about $500,000 were issued. At year's end a gallon of unleaded gas cost about $1.16.[7]

Local manufacturer Brockhouse halved its payroll and laid off 40 workers in March 1985 due to a slowdown in the computer and electronics industry for which it produced cases and cabinets. Cottage rental units were scarce and demand was high, due to more vacationers combined with relatively few new units built—a contrast to the oversupply of vacation units in the northern part of the state. Helen Hayes, proprietor of the Deep Six Too Restaurant on Center Street, started advertising for a waitress in April 1985, and five weeks later she had not found one. "Help Wanted" signs were common. Local business thrived.

The real estate boom of 1984-1986 priced many local buyers out of the market. Local realtors had few residences listed for less than $80,000, except for a mobile home or two, and most were over $100,000, this compared to the average weekly wage in 1986 of $197 for a Carroll County resident, still the lowest in the state.

In 1986 the Fourth of July holiday brought mixed benefits to local merchants. Rain kept tourists away from marinas and beach areas, but restaurants and shops were crowded. At summer's end such local businesses as Bailey's Dockside, WinnSports, and marinas reported a slow season, but many other stores and shops were very

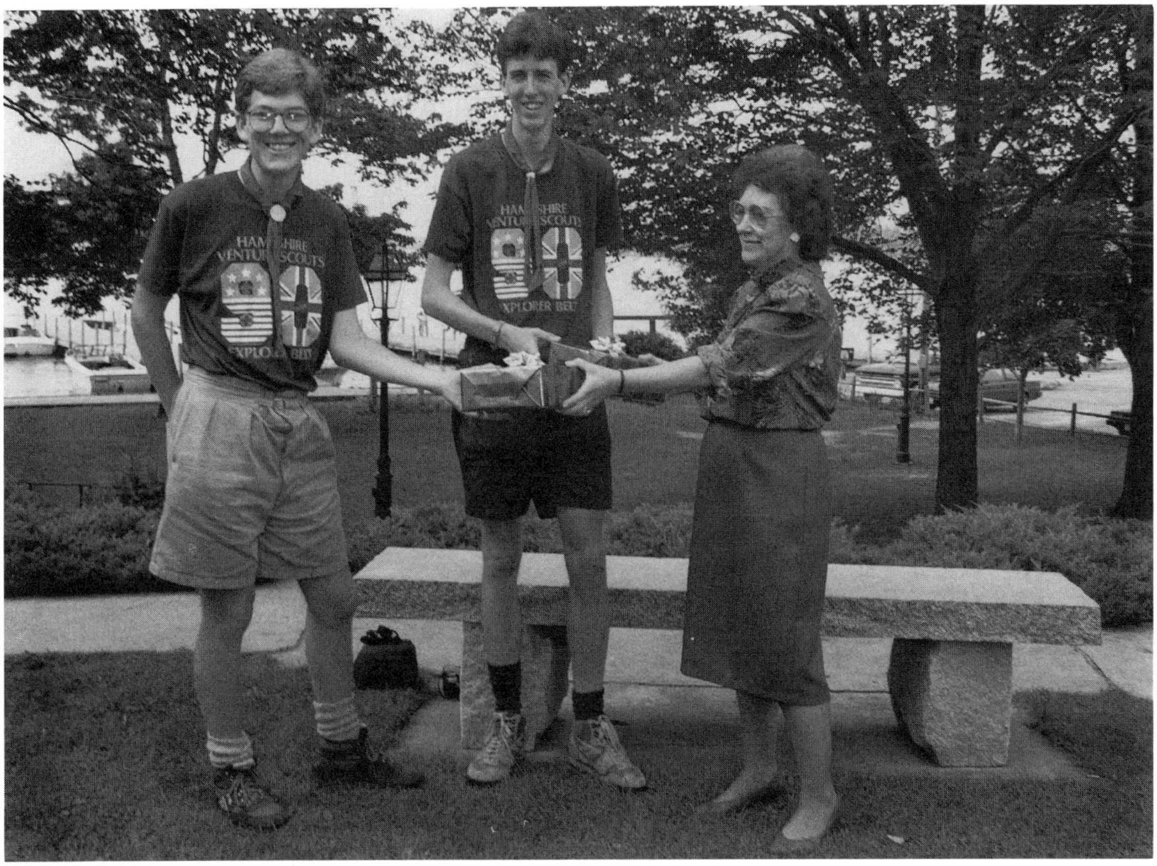

Town Clerk Pat Waterman presents gifts to two visiting Explorer Scouts from England who came to town in August 1990 to learn about local government. The picture was snapped in Town Park. (Sandy Martin photograph)

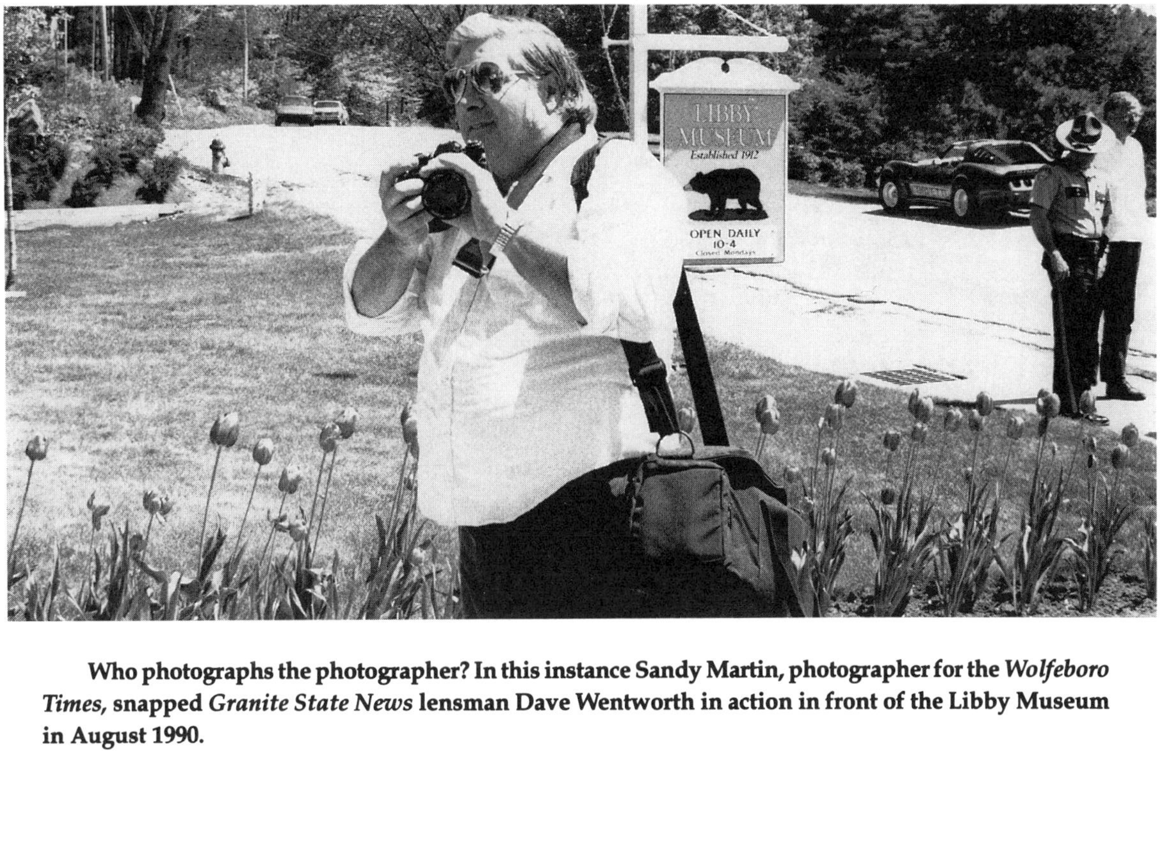


Who photographs the photographer? In this instance Sandy Martin, photographer for the *Wolfeboro Times,* snapped *Granite State News* lensman Dave Wentworth in action in front of the Libby Museum in August 1990.

Scene at the Town Docks one summer day in 1993. The car to the left went too far and had its front end dunked in Wolfeboro Bay. To the left is the Avery Building, built in 1890 as the Peavey Block, and to its right across the street in the distance is the venerable Bank Building, built in the mid-1850s, now with Moods clothing store on the ground floor. In the background to the right is Hall's Pharmacy. To the left of Hall's is the Stationery Shop housed in a building that would be demolished in September 1993 to make way for the Latchaw Building. (Ashton Woodhouse photograph)

pleased. The construction trade continued apace. In November 1986 the state unemployment rate, already the lowest in the nation, dropped to 2.6%.

In one dark day in October 1987 the Dow-Jones Industrial Average plummeted a record 508 points on the New York Stock Exchange, causing worldwide consternation. It was predicted that sales of durable items would fall due to investor uncertainty. Just the opposite happened. Many who contemplated putting funds in the securities market bought art, rare coins, vacation properties, and other tangible items instead. Wolfeboro seemed largely unaffected. Our town always marched to the beat of a different drummer, and many recalled that with the exception of the year 1933, the nationwide Depression of the 1930s was a time of relative prosperity locally.

Winter sports increased in popularity during the decade. The Wolfeboro Inn, Lakeview Inn, and other accommodations were often filled with eager cross-country skiers, ice-boaters, and snowmobilers. This combined with the growing trend of turning vacation homes into year-round homes brought predictions that the town would someday have a strong four-season retail economy. No longer were there abundant empty parking spaces downtown in January and February.

Economic growth in Wolfeboro probably peaked in 1987. As noted, for the real estate market, the zenith was probably in 1986, followed by a leveling and "grace period" in 1987, then a sharp fall in 1988. By the end of the latter year desirable houses were being offered once again for under $100,000. In early 1989 the median income of a Wolfeboro family was $30,000, which in banking terms meant that a home costing $90,000 (the three-times-annual-wage formula) would be affordable.

The winter sports economy of 1988-1989 was far below expectations due to sparse snowfall that by mid-January was only about 20% of normal. Times were tough in retail stores. Special discount promotions and increased use by customers of MasterCard, Visa, American Express and other credit cards (spend now, pay later) helped. The summer of 1989 was good for some, not so good for others. Hunter's IGA and Black's Paper Store reported better business than during the previous year. Real estate sales, especially for lakefront properties, rebounded sharply (counter to the trend in many other areas in the state).

Home heating oil prices rose, and Howard Bean, who had been in the business with his Wolfeboro Oil Company for 40 years, said he had never seen such a rapid increase. By the first week of January 1990 a gallon cost $1.50, up from just $1 six weeks earlier. Fortunately, the trend reversed itself, and by the end of February the price was below $1.

Money was becoming increasingly scarce for businessmen to obtain as banks that had been damaged by the runaway real estate market found themselves in reduced capital positions due to non-performing loans. Fewer new enterprises were being established in town. Retail rental spaces, once scarce enough to stimulate the building of new facilities, were becoming plentiful.

In the summer of 1990 Wolfeboro, a town of fewer than 5,000 year-round residents, had the distinction for a short time of having four weekly newspapers: the old-time *Granite State News*, the relatively new *Wolfeboro Times*, and the just-started and, as it turned out, short-lived *Wolfeboro Post*, all emphasized local news. In addition, *The Laker*, published in Wolfeboro, covered the entire Lakes Region.

The Chamber of Commerce continued in high gear with business promotions including Moonlight Madness, Olde Fashioned Sale Day (August 25, 1990), and sidewalk sale events during the summer. The November and December 1990 holiday promotions included Ladies' Night, Men's Night, Frantic Shoppers' Night, and more. Sales doubled at Sweaterville, but proprietor Carol Moody Bush said that customers were very careful, and all of her sales were under $100 per invoice.[8]

### Fads, Innovations, Necessities

The decade saw vast changes in office equipment. By 1990 the typewriter was on its way to becoming a museum piece in local businesses, having been replaced by the desktop computer. Such computer brands as IBM, Apple, Compac, and Leading Edge were found just about everywhere and proved much more popular than, and were only a fraction of the price of, the "heavy iron" mainframe units installed in earlier times by IBM, Digital Equipment Corporation, Burroughs, and others. Bar codes were common on products, and in a few stores an electronic "wand" replaced the hand-punching of keys on a cash register.

The Polaroid camera, once the mainstay of the real estate profession, was supplanted by the hand-held camcorder which made it possible to mail a videocassette to a prospective client in California and give him or her a tour of That Special Property on Sewall Road, Elm Street, Melody Island, North Line Road, or some other place in Wolfeboro. For those who wanted color prints, fast service was offered on premises by the aptly-named Spectrum 1-Hour Photo & Camera run by Grant and Lori Hatch.

The car telephone was becoming increasingly popular, not so much in Wolfeboro as in the southern part of the state, due to weak transmission in the Lakes Region. These could be plugged into cigarette lighters, an attachment with an uncertain future in automotive circles due to stepped-up government pressure against smoking during the decade. Increasingly, offices were supposed to be free of smoke, sexual harassment, and inequality. Restaurants set up smoking and non-smoking sections.

LIBBY
MUSEUM
ANNUAL RECEPTION
AUGUST 19, 1989
ROUTE 109, WOLFEBORO
4:00PM — 6:00PM
TICKETS AVAILABLE AT:
BLACK'S GIFT SHOP
CAMELOT BOOK/GIFT SHOP
THE STATIONERY SHOP
LIBBY MUSEUM
DESIGN & ILLUSTRATION BY P.M. HODDER

**LIBBY MUSEUM. Poster for the annual reception held by the Libby Museum, August 19, 1989. (Art by Pat M. Hodder)**

About 1986 local businessman Ray Merena installed a fax machine so that the Graphic Arts Department of Bowers and Merena Galleries could transmit copies of catalogue work to a printer in Virginia. An attorney for Ray's firm commented that he had heard of such devices but had never seen one in action, and wondered if he should get one. Change came fast. By decade's end the fax machine was almost as necessary as the drinking fountain or rest room in most local offices.

### Glory Years at the Libby Museum

During the first several years of the decade, the Libby Museum, founded in 1912, experienced the greatest period of growth and the largest attendance in its history. Much of this was due to Peter D. Shulman, an entrepreneur, sociologist, former dairy farmer, and movie actor, who came to town from Salem, NY, in 1973. Dr. Shulman soon became active in town offices and Police Commission, Planning Board, Zoning Board of Adjustment, and in local business.

As director of the Libby Museum in the summer of 1981, he instituted several new programs and aggressive publicity. The *Town Report* told the results:

> The 1981 season at the Libby Museum was a fantastic success. More than 8,000 visitors came to enjoy the exhibits, photo shows, sculpture classes, and evening slide shows. It is interesting to note that even though we had visitors from all 50 states and 12 foreign countries, over half our guests were from Wolfeboro and other nearby towns.

As it turned out, this was just a prelude. The 1982 season saw a record 11,836 visitors cross the threshold. Programs and events included eight special films (which drew a total of 2,000), slide shows (800 attended), and children's sculpture classes (400 students). Forty-two area artists and photographers displayed their work. The annual cocktail party included "everyone in local society from Elvira Avery on down" and drew 225.[9]

A crew from R.S. Painting (Robert Simmons, Jr.) repainted the facility in early summer 1983. The warmer months saw continued enthusiasm of the public, with 11,497 visitors stopping by. Special events included 15 National Geographic nature films, sponsored by BankEast, drawing over 2,500 people. To accommodate growth, the town appropriated $12,000 to build a mezzanine within the exhibit hall.

However, Curator Shulman left the museum and in October 1984 announced he was moving out of town. Interest waned, and in 1986 the unspent $12,000 was redirected toward the renovation of the Town Hall. By the summer of 1987 the annual visitor count had plummeted to just 3,700, increasing slightly to 4,062 in 1988. In the latter year Director Charles E. Campbell organized a group, The Friends of the Libby Museum. In 1990 Patricia F. Smith was named to the curatorship, a position she has retained through the 1990s.[10]

During the same years the Clark House, the Pleasant Valley Schoolhouse, and the Monitor Fire House Museum—all in Clark Park—were managed by the Wolfeboro Historical Society and were open in the summer.

### The *Granite State News*

During the decade the *Granite State News* remained the primary source for printed information concerning the town and its inhabitants. As always there was a bit of humor—often contributed by Editor Douglas Rooks—to be found among the more serious reports of crime, legislation, and other matters. In the issue of April 1, 1981 (important dateline here), readers were told that black flies, considered by some to be the bane of the late spring season, were actually very beneficial as they contributed to crowd control (prevented people from gathering in large groups outdoors), encouraged healthy exercise (swinging and swatting), provided a nice source of profit for those making or selling bug repellents, etc.

In another memorable piece Rooks suggested that as Wolfeboro was quite crowded in the summer, road maps could be redrawn so that there would be no way for strangers to find the place, thus maintaining tranquillity for local residents.

Throughout the decade "The Grunter," as some called the paper, carried home numerous awards from the New England Press Association. A brief list includes these honors:[11]

> David Isgur for a two-part series on the effect of 450 planned condominiums on the Wolfeboro area (1983).
>
> Community Service Award for reporting on the town water system (1983).
>
> MaryAnn Urquhardt for an illustration of the outdoors (1983).
>
> Bruce Bedford as "Photographer of the Year," the fourth time he was so honored by the New England Press Association (1984).
>
> Two second place awards for best community and public service reporting (1986).
>
> Dazzling sweep with four first-place awards and one third place. Editor Susan Slack received a first place award for best editorial; and the newspaper placed first for best editorial page, best educational reporting, and for community service (1987).
>
> General Excellence Award given by the New England Press Association for newspapers between 3,000 and 6,000 circulation (1989).

The *Granite State News* forgot that it had been established in 1860, and celebrated its 125th anniversary in 1984, rather than waiting until 1985. In the same year Kenneth Webb, contributor to the editorial page, retired after 52 years in the newspaper business including service locally in recent years. Douglas Rooks, who had joined the paper in 1976 and had been editor since 1980, resigned in October 1984. Wolfeboro's loss was the gain of the *Kennebec Journal* in Augusta, ME. Replacing him was Susan Slack, a graduate of Ohio State University who had signed on with the *Granite State News* staff in 1979.

With the first issue of 1985, the paper changed its format from six columns to seven. Lorna Colquhoun, local reporter and graduate of Kingswood High, left the paper in 1986 and joined the Haverhill *Gazette* (and later moved to the Manchester *Union Leader*).

Assigning specific people to write columns about local and area districts has been a long-time tradition. In late 1986 and early 1987 these bylines appeared:[12]

> Victoria Fogg (Cotton Valley), Bonnie Gagne (Mirror Lake; recent successor to Marion Bowles), Orissa Rines (South Wolfeboro and East Alton), Celia Harris (Wolfeboro Airport), Florence Ham (Tuftonboro), Theodore H. Brigden (North Wolfeboro), Maureen Borowski (Melvin Village), Eloise Bickford (New Durham), Mrs. Horace Richardson (Moultonboro), and Marion Howe Hansen (Sandwich).

The April 6, 1988, issue sported a new look. The masthead letters were bolder, and a new typeface was used in the body text, the result of a new computer typesetter at the office. For the first time in many years, the advertising and news layout was completely separate from its sister paper, the *Carroll County Independent*, although the *Granite* would still use some items of shared interest. "This week in the Lakes Region," a picture by photographer David Wentworth, was a new feature intended to capture the flavor of local life.

At decade's end Susan Zelek, who had joined the paper in 1978, was general advertising manager. The editor's chair was capably filled by Jeanne Tempest, who had edited the paper for a short time earlier, from August 1969 to November 1970.[13]

## ENTERTAINMENT

### Requiem for the Movies

The decade of the 1980s was to be the last for continuously scheduled movie shows at a town theatre, a tradition that had begun in the Masonic Temple in 1912 and had continued at the Town Hall (second floor) and, beginning in 1970, at the Hatch Theatre. In the second week of June 1987 the theatre rewound its last reel of film. Soon thereafter the Back Bay Construction Company began ripping out its interior. Certain parts of the structure were utilized for part of Depot Square, an eight-unit commercial facility put up on the site.[14]

The reason for the demise of movies was simple: insufficient patronage. It was not at all unusual to visit the theatre on a week night and see just a dozen or two patrons, if indeed that many. Competition was intense from television (including expanded selections made possible by cable and satellite dish antennas), videocassette rentals, multiplex movie theatres at shopping malls, FM radio (including expanded National Public Radio programs), video games at home and in arcades, compact disc players, and personal computers, among other things.

Theatre owner Paul R. Hatch turned his attention elsewhere including the operation of Sound Spectrum, a consumer electronics business with a well-stocked VCR rental section (if you can't lick 'em, join 'em).

The coming of cable television to Wolfeboro was no simple matter following approval of the idea at the 1980 town meeting. Newspaper columns in 1981 were filled with claims and counterclaims, accusations of conflicts of interest, and more. Commonwealth Cable Services, which offered service to areas in which there were 30 homes per mile of road, was given a contract by the selectmen on October 19, 1981. However, in November 1982 Commonwealth broke its agreement, citing financial difficulties, and eventually paid the town $50,000 in settlement. The town was back to square one.

In July 1983 Community TV of Laconia (later known as Lakes Cablevision) was chosen to provide local service, but a contract was not signed until January 18, 1984. Stringing of cable commenced in August 1985 in what was called a "rolling launch" with sections to be put in operation as soon as they were finished. By year's end many local residents had service. Regular network channels were offered as part of a standard "package." Others were available at extra cost—including New England Sports Network, Music TV, Nashville, Arts & Entertainment, Nickelodeon, Cable News Network, Lifetime, Home Box Office, and Cinemax. As years passed, the mix of channels offered varied. On March 1, 1987, the basic "package" rate increased from $9.95 to $15.90 a month.

People in other areas often bought satellite dishes for TV reception. Prices of the dishes and installation started at about $900 and went as high as $2,500 or more.[15]

Films shown at the Hatch Theatre during the decade included these titles among many others:

> **1981:** *Caddyshack, Any Which Way You Can, Nine to Five, Close Encounters of the Third Kind, Superman II, Raiders of the Lost Ark, The Great Muppet Caper,* and *Breaker Morant.*
>
> **1982:** *Neighbors, Sharky's Machine, Absence of Malice, On Golden Pond, Chariots of Fire, E.T., Star Trek II,* and *An Officer and a Gentleman.*
>
> **1983:** *Tootsie, Gandhi, Thunder, Return of the Jedi, Octopussy, War Games,* and *Flashdance.*
>
> **1984:** *Christine, Sudden Impact, The Man Who Loved Women, Terms of Endearment, Yentl, The Natural, Cannon Ball Run II, The Search for Spock, The Karate Kid, Indiana Jones and the Temple of Doom,* and *Ghostbusters.*
>
> **1985:** *Heavenly Bodies, Beverly Hills Cop, The Killing Fields, A Passage to India, Desperately Seeking Susan, Rambo: First Blood—Part II, Return of the Living Dead, Back to the Future,* and *Rocky IV.*
>
> **1986:** *Hannah and Her Sisters, Out of Africa, The Color Purple, Lucas, Down and Out in Beverly Hills, Top Gun, Ferris Bueller's Day Off, Club Paradise,* and *The Color of Money.*
>
> **1987:** *Star Trek IV – The Voyage Home, Crocodile Dundee, Children of a Lesser God, Outrageous Fortune,* and *Black Widow.*

The final advertisement for the Hatch Theatre appeared in the *Granite State News*, May 13, 1987: "*Tin Men,* a brand new comedy with Richard Dreyfuss, Danny DeVito and Barbara Hersey." The theatre remained open through the second week of June.

In the summer of 1990 it was announced that Wolfeboro would once again have a movie theatre. Chris Crowley, who had spent many summers on Keniston Island, and his brother-in-law Warren Shumway, proposed showing films in the old theatre on the second floor of the Town Hall. Tickets were $5 for adults and $4 for children and senior citizens. The first films were *Back to the Future II* and *Field of Dreams.* The idea proved short-lived.[16]

**Making Movies, Local Style**

In the summer of 1987 several days were spent by a crew from Van Dusen Films who utilized the facilities of the Abenaki Waterski Club on Back Bay and part of Wolfeboro Bay near Clark Point to film a commercial for Kellogg's Frosted Flakes cereal. Local stars of the film included Corey Schillereff on water skis, Scott Klemm who stood in for a male actor, and a high-performance Ski Nautique boat decked out in "Tony the Tiger" stripes. Mildred A. Beach handled the booking arrangements.[17]

In February 1990 Rust Pond in South Wolfeboro was the venue for the production company for the Hollywood film, *Once Around,* starring Richard Dreyfuss, Holly Hunter, and Danny Aiello. The story involved the charming Miss Hunter, who moves to Florida following the collapse of her wedding plans. There she meets and falls in love with Richard Dreyfuss, a real estate salesman from New York. The two move back to Hunter's home town of Boston.

Wolfeboro was chosen for its "New England charm," scenic beauty, and the availability of accommodations for the cast and crew of about 75 members. Filming was scheduled for February 27 through March 3.

Each day about 100 people went to Rust Pond to watch the filming out on the ice. Larry Ganem, son of Wolfeboro's Phil and Shirley Ganem, signed to be location assistant. Angela Anderson, another local figure, was a production assistant.

Photographs and captions in the *Granite State News* showed Kathy Rankin, a town employee (the crew rented her parents' home), making friends with Richard Dreyfuss and town clerk Pat Waterman reading a poem she had written for Dreyfuss.

Mr. Dreyfuss was given a pewter key to the town made by Hampshire Pewter from a mold supplied from Nathalie Erickson's costume collection. Tim Hutchins, Bryan Stanley, and Raymond Leslie skated and pushed around the dolly on which Holly Hunter sat as several scenes were being filmed and helped move various pieces of equipment. Allen Stevens and Irene Garvey were each paid $100 a day for having their ice boats available for background scenes. Fred Pflueger of Caretakers Plus cleared the snow from the ice. An emergency medical technician from Lakeside Ambulance was hired on standby each day. Local caterer and chef Leonard Martin provided breakfast and lunch for the cast and crew. One Thursday afternoon Governor Judd Gregg came by for a photo session with Dreyfuss.

The final report stated that more than $100,000 had been spent in Wolfeboro including $22,000 for lodging, $18,000 for meals, $5,000 for town services, $6,000 for location fees, and $50,000 for local business services and employment of extras. This did not include the money spent by the cast and crew for their own amusement and pleasure.[18]

In January 1991 Fred Pflueger and about a dozen other Wolfeboro residents were at the pre-screening of *Once Around* in Boston on the same night the country went to war with Iraq over the latter's invasion of Kuwait. The announcement of war was made at the beginning of the movie, which made everyone feel a little strange. Various terms used in the *Granite State News* account about the movie were "chaotic," "choppy," "unfocused," and "disappointing." Harrison D. Moore said that if he didn't know what Copple Crown looked like in the distance behind Rust Pond, he wouldn't know where the five or six minutes of Wolfeboro's shooting was done. Some liked the movie, but others said Holly Hunter was somewhat subdued by Richard Dreyfuss and Danny Aiello.[19]

**Many Entertainment Opportunities**

During the 1980s many stage plays, concerts, parades, festivals, exhibitions, shows, fairs, and other events crowded the calendar. The annual Huggins Hospital Street Fair offered a two-day program of booths with things for sale and entertainment, auction, snacks and drinks, evening sit-down dinners, raffle, rides, and other attractions, sponsored by the Hospital Aid Association.

The Wolfeboro Playhouse under the direction of Richard Natkowski of Manchester had begun summer performances in town in 1976 using recognized actors, but by 1981 it had a $12,000 annual deficit in its total budget of $45,000. In 1982 Bill Brooks was in charge of a resident company of amateurs who planned to offer five shows in what proved to be the group's final season.[20] Meanwhile, the Village Players staged numerous productions throughout the decade using local talent.

In September 1988 Darlene Williams moved to Wolfeboro from Utah. A lady of many talents, she soon had over 50 pupils taking lessons from her on the violin, viola, and cello. But, that was not all. She wrote music, poetry, and short stories, and—important to the present text—she wrote and presented three original stage plays through the not-for-profit company she di-

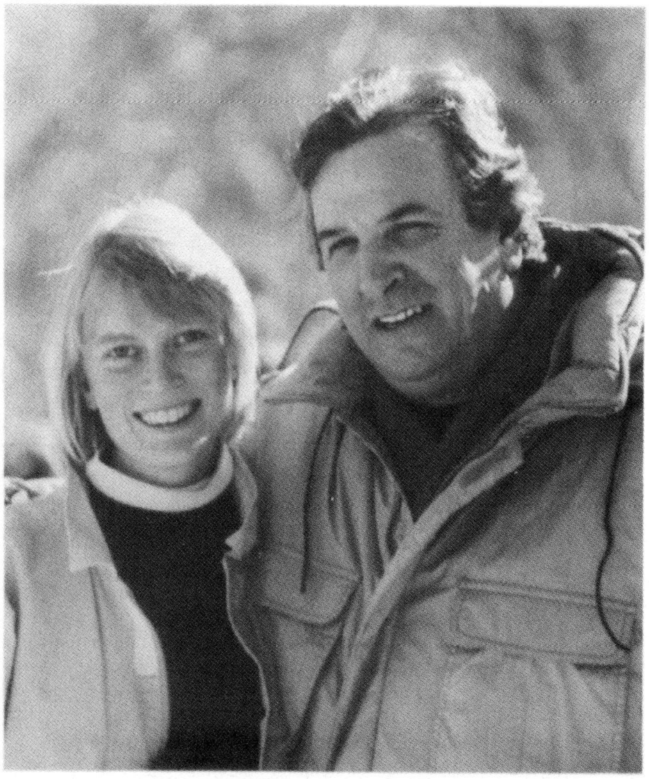

Scenes on Rust Pond, February 1990, during the filming of *Once Around*, starring Richard Dreyfuss, Holly Hunter, and Danny Aiello. Above: Wolfeboro's Sigrid Johannessen-Cameron with Danny Aiello. Mrs. Cameron visited the scene of the filming every day to watch the proceedings.

Richard Dreyfuss photographed with Rust Pond in the background.

Film crew and actors on the ice. (Photographs by Sigrid Johannessen-Cameron and Mike Gefers)

rected, Wolfeborough Historic Productions. The first, *Province*, was produced several times beginning with a memorable opening on July 4, 1989, and centered about the life of Gov. John Wentworth.[21] The next two were produced in the early 1990s (see Chapter 12).

The Lions Club Winter Carnival included an agenda of outdoor and indoor events, while on Wolfeboro Bay groups of little wooden "bob houses" were a smaller-scale reincarnation of Fisherville so popular in the 1940s.

At Kingswood High School, Brewster Gym, and under canvas on the Brewster athletic field, dozens of craft fairs, ski equipment sales, antiques shows, book fairs, and other events were often crowded. The Artists in the Park show sponsored each August by the Governor Wentworth Arts Council had become so popular that craftsmen and artists had to be selected by a jury in order to set up an exhibit. It often included music, a magic or puppet show, or other attraction.

In the 1980s karaoke (lip-sync singing to prerecorded musical videos) was popular at the All Stars Sports Pub, jukeboxes with compact discs were seen in several restaurants, and wide-screen television appeared in a few restaurants and many homes.

Any teenager with a pocketful of quarters was apt to spend them on arcade machines offering Pac Man, Donkey Kong, Tetris, and other electronic games. Meanwhile, youngsters—and the older set, too—played with Atari, Nintendo, and other game devices that could be hooked up to a television set at home. The electronic age of entertainment had arrived in a big way.

### Selected Entertainment Events

**1981, January 8-10. Stage play:** Kingswood students produced William Inge's 1953 play, *Picnic*, set in a small Kansas town.[22]

**1981, February. Lions Club Winter Carnival:** Theme: "A Family Affair." Pancake breakfast (at Father John's Pub), skating, obstacle course, broom hockey, downhill ski races, snow sculptures, sled dog races, Winter Carnival Ball (at the Masonic Temple).[23]

**1981, February 21. Firemen's Ball:** Masonic Temple.

**1981, February 7. Puppet show:** At the Hatch Theatre featuring Donna Marie performing for the benefit of Cub Scout Pack 165.[24]

**1981, March 11. Film and lecture:** *NH Writers and the Small Town*. Discussed attitudes of people toward the land, defense and cultivation of their property, and heroism when confronted with adversity. First NH Bank, sponsor. Wolfeboro Public Library.[25]

**1981, April-May. Crafts classes:** Wolfeboro Arts & Crafts Association. Schoolhouse Shop.[26]

**1981, April 22-23. Stage play at Carpenter School:** *Wizard of Oz*. Danielle DesMarais was Dorothy, Scott Good the scarecrow.[27]

**1981, May 22. Ballet and dance concert:** Wolfeboro School of Ballet students. Kingswood Auditorium. Featured the ballet from *Star Wars*.

**1981, June 17. Film crew in town:** Japanese actors and actresses were photographed aboard the Wolfeboro Rail Road as part of a 51/2-hour film, *Flags Over Portsmouth*, made for Japanese TV. Subject: The signing of the Treaty of Portsmouth, 1905, to end the Russo-Japanese War.[28]

**1981, July 19. Concert:** Cate Park. Featured Rocksalt & Nails, a local group made up of Peter Schillereff, Dave Winchester, J. Eastman, and Chris Meisner. Sponsored by the Wolfeboro Chamber of Commerce.[29]

**1981, July 25. Stage play:** *Sweeney Todd the Barber* by the Wolfeboro Playhouse.[30] Other performances this season included *The Owl and the Pussycat* (August 10-15) and *Let's Hear it for Love* (August 18-22).

**1981, August 5. Huggins Hospital Street Fair:** Brewster field. Games, booths, rides, contests, auction. Annual event set record gross of $64,000.[31]

**1981, August 12. Artists in the Park:** Annual fair in Cate and Town Parks sponsored by the Governor Wentworth Arts Council. (Then, as before, most people called this double facility simply Cate Park.)

**1981, October 23-24. Stage play:** *Oklahoma* by the Village Players.[32]

**1981, October 28-31. Hallowe'en haunted house:** Sponsored by Wolfeboro Area Jaycees at the former Wolfeboro Building Materials facility on Lehner Street. In darkness you stuck your hand in a bowl of cold, wet spaghetti noodles. Yuck![33]

**1981, December 3-5. Stage play:** *Our Town*. Kingswood High students.[34]

**1982, January 25. Artist's presentation:** Peter Ferber lecture and demonstration at the Wolfeboro Library where his art had been on view during the month. Sponsored by the Governor Wentworth Arts Council.[35]

**1982, February 18. Magic show:** Performed by Jeb Bradley at Brewster Academy during Seminar Day activities.[36]

**1982, March 6. Puppet show:** The Two-Headed Cow Puppet Theatre presented *Duffy and the Devil*, sponsored by the Governor Wentworth Arts Council.[37]

**1982, March 13. Dance:** St. Patrick's Day Leprechaun Hop. American Legion Hall. Sponsored by Wolfeboro Area Jaycees.[38]

**1982, April 8-10. Stage play:** *South Pacific* by Kingswood High students.[39]

**1982, April. Debbie Osgood to tour:** Selected to visit Europe for 26 days with the Sound of America Honor Band and Chorus.[40]

**1982, July 4. Parade:** Honoring veterans, POWs (prisoners of war), and MIAs (missing-in-action). Grand prize float by Lake Motel. The three category-winning floats were by Black's, Mood's Fashion Boutique, and the Stationery Shop.[41]

**1982, July 8. Renaissance music concert:** Fyre and Lightning, a Vermont group, sponsored by the Friends of Music. Wolfeboro Public Library.[42]

**1982, July 27. Pet show:** Best costume went to Bear, a German shepherd dressed in farmer garb. Wolfeboro Parks and Recreation Department.[43]

**1982, August. Concerts:** Mom & Pop's Band, formed in 1980, performed near the Town Docks and on a barge in Wolfeboro Bay. Steve Bush, Joe DeRose, Virginia Jackson, and Sandra Wentworth.[44]

**1982, November 11. Country and western music:** Singer, songwriter, and guitarist Tom Eslick at Brewster students' assembly at First Congregational Church.[45]

**1982, November 14. Concert:** Clearlakes Chorale at Huggins Hospital.[46]

**1983, February 7-20. Lions Club Winter Carnival:** Theme: "A Community at Work and Play." Citizens of the year: Dr.

**Models show holiday fashions from Moods clothing store at a fund raiser for the Miss Wolfeboro Scholarship Fund held at the Wolfeboro Inn.**

**Left to right: Erin Foran, Kathy Stone, Sabra Rines, Helen Swasey (in the rear with microphone), Amy Welsh (Miss Wolfeboro 1990-1991), Pat Bigelow, and Jane Foran. (Sandy Martin photograph, 1990)**

**The Don Austin residence on Lehner Street decorated for the holiday season with countless colored lights illuminating trees, scenes, and architectural outlines. (Sandy Martin photograph, December 1990)**

Local artistic talent among the younger set. Jennifer Meanley (left) and Paige Foran at work designing a totem pole as part of their Northwest Coast Native American Studies project at Carpenter School in Debbie Yurick's art class. Fifteen totem poles were constructed by students and placed on display at the Wolfeboro Public Library, (Sandy Martin photograph, 1990)

James and Dolly Bovaird.[47] Amusements included a laughing and screaming competition.

**1983, February 10. Stage play:** *Don Juan in Hell.* Village Players at Brewster. Sponsored by the Governor Wentworth Arts Council.[48]

**1983, April 20-21. Stage play:** *The Music Man.* Carpenter School. Cast included Marian Paroo, Hilary Gehman, Carolyn Plummer.[49]

**1983, May 14. Shaw Brothers concert:** KRHS auditorium. Well-known singing duo, Ron and Rick Shaw (their next performance in town was May 19, 1994; another on March 17, 1987). During the decade their song, *New Hampshire Naturally,* was a statewide hit.

**1983, May. Art exhibit:** Work of Wolfeboro artist Suzanne Bonin on display at the Wolfeboro Public Library. Pen and ink and dry brush watercolor art. Her picture of two loons was the new logo for the NH Audubon Society.[50]

**1983, May 7. Concert:** Lakes Region Symphony conducted by Joe DeRose (of Melvin Village). Sponsored by the Friends of Music, the event at the Brewster Gymnasium drew 400.[51]

**1983, May 21. Ballet concert**: Wolfeboro School of Ballet. *The Firebird Suite* and other numbers. Kingswood High.[52]

**1983, June 20. Musical trio:** Edith Sterns, pianist; Mark Churchill, cellist; Mary Lou Speaker Churchill, violinist. Sponsored by Friends of Music.

**1983, July 4. Independence Day:** 40 floats in parade with division prizes to Lee's Candy Kitchen and Huggins Hospital.[53]

**1983, July 15. Wolfeboro on TV:** Channel 4 (Boston) *Evening Magazine* program featured segments filmed in town aboard the Wolfeboro Rail Road and the *M/V Mount Washington.*[54]

**1983, July 26. Pet show:** Part of Wolfeboro Summer Activities Program. Leaders: Elinor Tasker, Kelly Colby-Little. 48 prize ribbons were given to children, many of whom went on a trip to Storyland the next day [55]

**1983, July 27-30. Stage play:** *6 RMS RIV VU* by Wolfeboro Playhouse. Cast included Keli Douglass, Wayne Gehman, Peg and Larry Hunter, Ruth Ann Stevens, Pete Kathan, Sandy Twyon, and Peter Oakes.[56]

**1983, July 30. Air show:** Lakes Region Airpark. Sponsored by the Lions Club. Allan E. Bailey, Jr., master of ceremonies; 500 attended. Stunt flyer Bob Weymouth, A-10 military jet aircraft, and other attractions. Music furnished by Dave Bowers' antique 53-note National air calliope mounted on a show trailer.[57]

**1983, August 20-21. Antique engine meet:** At the old Berry Mill, Wolfeboro Falls. Hosted by the Wolfeboro Rail Road.[58]

**1983, October 12. Male strippers:** Entertainment at first of four Ladies' Nights at Snookers Restaurant in a building earlier used by the Allen "A" Resort. Tonia Albee, manager. Caused some controversy and telephone calls of complaint to the selectmen (for not protesting such within the limits of Wolfeboro), but most who attended liked the show.[59]

**1983, October 31. St. Walpurga's Night Party:** Hallowe'en costume party. Wolfeboro Inn.[60]

**1983, December 3. Concert:** Buddy Rich Band. Kingswood High. Tickets: $10 adult, $8 student.[61]

**1984, February 10-19. Lions Club Winter Carnival:** Eleanor and Bud Bigelow were proclaimed citizens of the year at the Winter Carnival Ball. The king and queen of Kingswood High, Carolyn Toms and Sam Novotny, and the king and queen of Brewster Academy, James Fleming and Jennifer Scileppi, were crowned.[62]

**1984, April 18-19. Stage play:** *The Velveteen Rabbit.* Carpenter School students.[63]

**1984, May 31. Annual Book and Author Luncheon:** Back Bay Boathouse. Sponsored by Friends of the Wolfeboro Library. Tuftonboro resident Cecily Crowe was among four writers featured.[64]

**1984, May 25-26. Variety show:** "High Fever Frolics" presented by Huggins Hospital at Kingswood High. Ray Lord, director.[65]

**1984, July 25. Fashion show:** At Snookers Restaurant. Benefit for Huggins Hospital Street Fair.[66]

**1984, August 1-4. Stage play:** *Sly Fox.* Village Players for the Wolfeboro Playhouse.

**1984, October. Wolfeboro's Fourth Fall Festival:** Children's costume contest, pumpkin carving contest, underwater pumpkin hunt, etc. 40 people participated in two road races sponsored by the Wolfeboro Sports Gnome and the Wolfeboro Parks and Recreation Department. The 10-kilometer race winner was Howie Bean with a time of 35 minutes. Jennifer Caldwell was the winner in the women's category with 40:22. A two-mile "Fun Run" was won by Andrew Baird in the 12 and under age category with a time of 13:06, and the women's winner was Sonia Wisseman with 17:34.[67]

**1984, December. Gift-giving:** Trivial Pursuit was the board game hit of the holiday season, and supplies were short. By this time Cabbage Patch Kids dolls—which earlier in the year had been rationed to suppliers and sometimes caused near panic among buyers when supplies were put on sale at malls—were readily available. Pasta (newly popular word for noodles) makers were popular gifts in the appliance department.

**1984, December 31. New Year's Eve:** Charlie Dawson and Red Young entertained at the Cider Press Restaurant.[68]

**1985, April 11. Kingswood High Band concert:** Guest was saxophonist Sal Spicola from Boston, who had provided backup to Lionel Hampton, Boz Scaggs, and the Eagles.[69]

**1985, April 17-18. Stage play:** 80 Carpenter students in *The Emperor's New Clothes.* Jennifer St. Martin, empress; Brian Fuller, emperor; Heather Hudson, princess; Carter Gehman, prince; Steven Osgood, Dudley, the prince's servant; Rachel Hale, Millie.[70]

**1985, April 26-27. Stage play:** Village Players presented *Play It Again, Sam,* written by Woody Allen. Masonic Temple.[71]

**1985, May 2. Famous editor speaks:** *Yankee* magazine editor Judson Hale, Sr., entertained at Kingswood Auditorium with anecdotes and stories. Hale was no stranger to the Lakes Region. He had summered on a Winnipesaukee island, and his sons, Judson, Jr., Dan, and Chris, worked at local establishments including the Corinthian Yacht Club and the Wolfeboro Inn.[72]

**1985, September 15. Piano concert:** Featuring gifted local composer and pianist John W. Struble in a program of twentieth century piano masterpieces. Wolfeboro Public Library.[73]

**1985, October 18-19. Stage play:** Brewster Academy Drama Club presented the Broadway musical *West Side Story.*[74]

**1986, February 7-16. Lions Club Winter Carnival:** Jane Quimby was named citizen of the year. Carnival king and queen were T.J. Cogswell and Amy Babson of Kingswood High.[75]

**1986, March 27. Priscilla Berman presentation:** Two-part series titled "Monumental Brasses and Brass Rubbings," sponsored by the Friends of the Wolfeboro Library.[76]

**1986, May. Local artist's show:** Oil and watercolor paintings of Madelyn Albee were on exhibit at the Wolfeboro Public Library as the Governor Wentworth Arts Council's artist of the month.[77]

**1986, July 25. Storytelling and puppetry:** By Willy Claflin, Wolfeboro native, who had last appeared in town in 1964. He had recorded two albums. His son Brian performed with him in Cate Park.[78]

**1986, July 28-29. Stage play:** Kingswood Summer Theatre presented *Pinocchio.* Jim Foley, Pinocchio; Matthew Jones, Gepetto; Ericka Bailey, the Blue Fairy; Stephanie Miller, Mr. Cricket.[79]

**1986, September. Local quilts on display:** Wolfeboro Public Library. Made by Elissa Paquette, Deborah Strohbeen, and Valerie Schurer Christle, and works by Paquette's daughter Carrie.[80]

**1986, September. Local puppeteer on national TV:** Alison Mork of Wolfeboro, daughter of Phil and Willie Mork, performed as a puppeteer on the new Saturday morning children's series *Pee Wee Playhouse* on CBS. She graduated from Cornell University, majoring in art.[81]

**1986, October 5. Pottery demonstration:** Sally Cornwell Perkins at the Schoolhouse Shop. She had studied metalsmithing, lost wax casting, and pottery with Debbie Hopkins of Wolfeboro.[82]

**1986, December 13-14. Pops '86:** Kingswood Music Department presented the "Christmas Carousel" featuring the Clearlakes Chorale joining the Kingswood Vocal Ensemble and Symphonic Band in a performance of Handel's *Hallelujah Chorus* and other numbers.[83]

**1987, January. "A Parade of American Posters":** Exhibit at the Wolfeboro Public Library. Collection of Dave and Christine Bowers.

**1987, April 17. "Up With People" concert:** Multi-national players in a cast and band of 130 young people brought a message encouraging understanding among people of all nations. Played to a full house at Kingswood High.[84]

**1987, April 22-24. Stage play:** Wolfeboro students Marie Garland, Sarah Hayes, and Liz Scully starred in the Brewster Academy production of *You Can't Take it With You.*[85]

**1987, July 9. Concert:** Metropolitan Brass Quintet at Kingswood High. Sponsored by the Friends of Music.[86]

**1987, August 22. Diamond Jubilee reception:** At Libby Museum celebrating 75 years in Wolfeboro.[87]

**1987, September 10. Musical duo:** Friends of Music presented Stephanie Corcio, harpist, and Arlene Kies, pianist, in an evening of music for harp and keyboard at the Wolfeboro Public Library.[88]

**1987, December. Christmas festivities:** Activities sponsored by the Chamber of Commerce included the arrival of Santa Claus on a fire truck, two public Christmas trees, Clearlakes Chorale concert, and a giant bonfire (December 12).[89]

**1987, December 20. Ballet:** *The Nutcracker* at Kingswood High. Largest production ever staged by the Governor Wentworth Arts Council. Dana Hutchinson and Kathryn Stone were the reindeer.[90]

**1988, March 27. Famous jazz trumpeter:** Maynard Ferguson and his High Voltage Band packed the Kingswood High Auditorium.[91]

**1988, May 21. Spring Fair:** Carpenter School. White elephant sale, books, plants, games, clown, magic show, car wash, auction.[92]

**1988, May 28. Charity party:** The invitation read: "The pleasure of your company is requested for cocktails and hors d'oeuvres at Chiang Kai-Shek's family's former summer home on Hopewell Point, May 28, 1988. $25 per person to benefit the Southern Carroll County Chapter American Red Cross."[93]

**1988, June 1 to July 7. Silent film series:** Q. David Bowers presented the *Before Hollywood* film series created and sponsored by the American Federation of Arts and shown across America in different venues. The Wolfeboro Public Library's presentation marked the first time this six-part series was shown in New England. Arrangements were by Louise Gehman, librarian. The local presentation drew larger audiences than earlier appearances at the Smithsonian and Carnegie Hall.[94]

**1988, June 14. One-man show:** "Can I Speak for You, Brothers?" presented by Philip E. Walker, sponsored by the Governor Wentworth Arts Council. Dramatizations of the writings of black Americans including Martin Luther King, Jr., Booker T. Washington, *et al.* at Kingswood High.[95]

**1988, July 15. Stage play:** *Barefoot in the Park* by the Village Players. Wayne Gehman and Jen Ganem played newlyweds Paul and Corie Bratter. Dan Charlton played Victor Velasco.[96] Charlton, a well-known local personality, was also known as the "balloon man" at the Huggins Hospital Street Fair, was seen in many plays, and was cast in a memorable television advertisement for Green Mountain Furniture (of Ossipee) in which Dan lost his wife while shopping in what seemed like endless acres of furniture showrooms.

**1988, July 21. Roberts Bros. Circus:** Sponsored by the American Legion. Tickets: $6 adult, $4 child. Brewster Field.[97]

**1988, July 29-31. Stage play:** Wolfeboro Children's Summer Theatre presented *Alice in Wonderland* at Kingswood High. Heather Sands played Alice.[98]

**1988, September 13. Wolfeboro Senior Citizens Club trip:** To Quincy Market, Boston. Earlier, on August 10 and 11, forty-four members had gone to the Sugarbush Inn in Warren, VT.[99]

**1988, August 27. Air Force Band of New England:** Concert at Kingswood High sponsored by Friends of Music.[100]

**1988, September 25. Piano concert:** John W. Struble at the Wolfeboro Public Library.[101]

**1988, October 30. Ballet:** Boston Ballet's performance of *Snow White.*[102]

**1988, November 11-12. Stage play:** *Fiddler on the Roof* by the Village Players directed by Rosemary Flynn.[103]

**1988, December 10-11. Concert:** "The Pops Concert, A Christmas Festival," by the Kingswood High Music Department.[104]

**1989, February 10-19. Winter Carnival:** Sponsored by the Lions Club. Included the Ted Herbert Orchestra and the High Ryder Golden Oldies show 1950s sock hop, "Nitelite" wiffle ball game, spaghetti supper by the Boy Scouts, Carpenter School Valentine Brunch. Connie Thurrell was named Citizen of the Year.[105]

**1989, April 8. Spring fashion show:** Sponsored by Brewster Academy at the Pinckney Boathouse overlooking Wolfeboro Bay. Fashions featured were from such Wolfeboro stores as Kidding Around, The Loft, The Men's Hut, Merle Norman Boutique, Panache Fashions, Samaha's, Inc., Tender Times, and the Wool Corner.[106]

**1989, July 4. Historical play:** The annual Independence Day celebration included the evening premiere of *Province* by Darlene Williams' Wolfeborough Historic Productions, the first of a scheduled six-performance run on the grassy lot behind St. Cecilia's Church. In the words of Ms. Williams: "As the show was running about 15 minutes behind schedule that first night, we were given a great backdrop of brilliant and noisy fireworks about 15 minutes before the end. We had to wait for the pyrotechnics to finish so we could conclude our performance. It was a real testimony to either

1990 Independence Day parade: Bette Bourque (who later became Mrs. Richard Frazier) leads members of the Carpenter School Hot Peppers Jumprope Club. This view was taken from in front of the Avery Building and shows the Wool Corner in the distance (building with two dormers on the roof) and Black's Paper Store to the right.

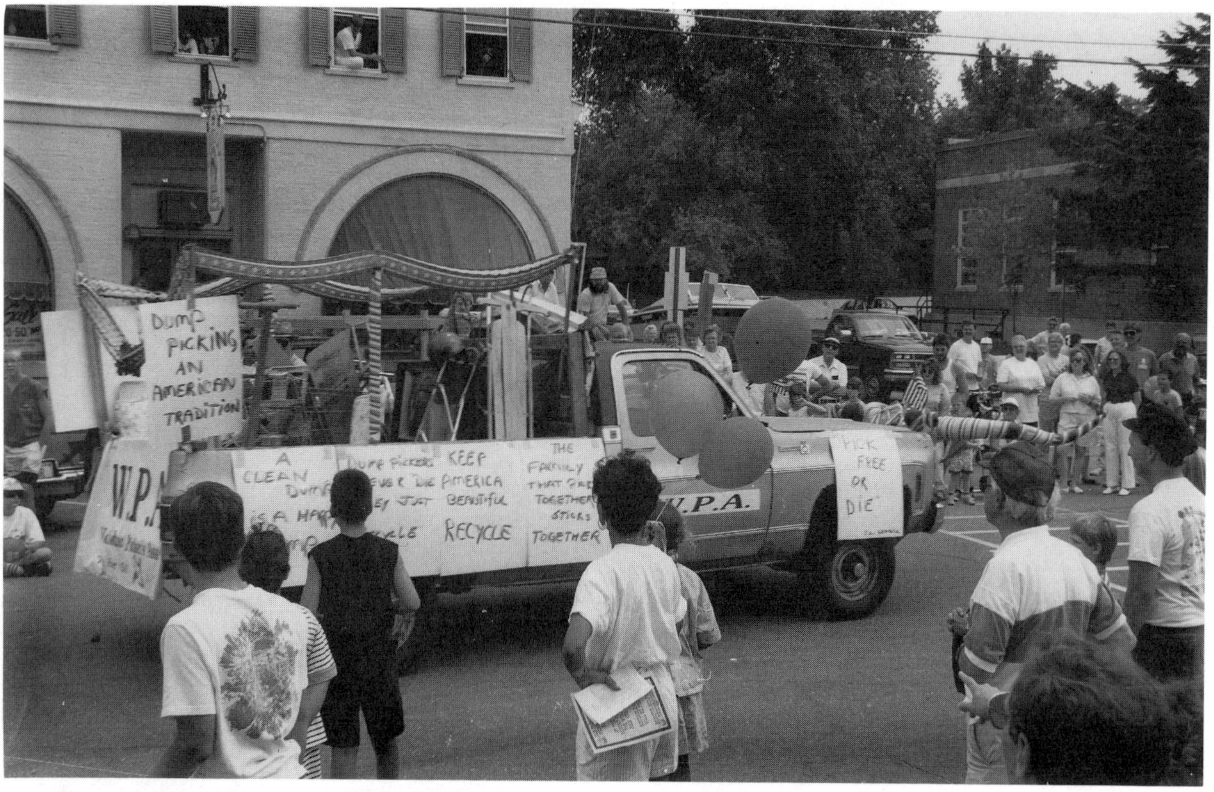


Wolfeboro Pickers Association float. The group, Jeff Badger, president, protested a town ordinance that prohibited "treasure hunting" at the dump and had as its slogan "Pick Free or Die." In the background is the Bank Building (with Moods clothing store on the ground floor) with the U.S. Post Office visible through trees to its right. (Sandy Martin photographs)

**Artists in the Park, held each August at Cate and Town Parks on South Main Street, has been a drawing card for tourists and residents for many years. At the 1990 event Nancy Piper paints the face of a young customer while visitors look on. (Sandy Martin photograph)**

**At the annual Artists in the Park various craftspeople—selected in advance by a jury of their peers—set up under white canvas tents. Visitors can browse, shop, and meet the artists who come from all over New England. (Sandy Martin photograph)**

Musical talent: The Wolfeboro Academy of Music and many of its students before their spring 1990 recital. The faculty includes those standing in the rear, Darlene Williams (to the left), and John Warthen Struble (right). (Sandy Martin photograph)

Student musicians from Kingswood Regional High School play tunes on South Main Street in front of Black's Paper Store during the arrival of Santa Claus. Left to right: Pat Sayers, Katie Roark, Becky Coolidge, Robin Bean, and Mark Roark. (Sandy Martin photograph, 1990)

Violin students of Darlene Williams play in Cate Park. Left to right: Jessica Mankus, Jennifer Williams, and Elizabeth Widmer. (Sandy Martin photograph, August 1990)

Bill Gibson leads the Girls' Chorus at Kingswood Regional High School's annual Christmas Pops Concert. (Sandy Martin photograph, December 1990)

The Wolfeboro School of Ballet, directed by Merrill Rich, showcases its students in a production of *Cinderella.* Jennifer Tibbetts (standing, center) looks down on Brenna Parsons (nearest camera) and Melissa Coffee. Kristen Spoelstra is shown standing to the right. (Sandy Martin photograph, 1990)

Heather Sands is on her toes as Jessica Blair looks on. (Sandy Martin photograph, 1990)

Nicole Black glides through the air while her ballet instructor, Merrill Rich, applauds. (Sandy Martin photograph, December 1990)

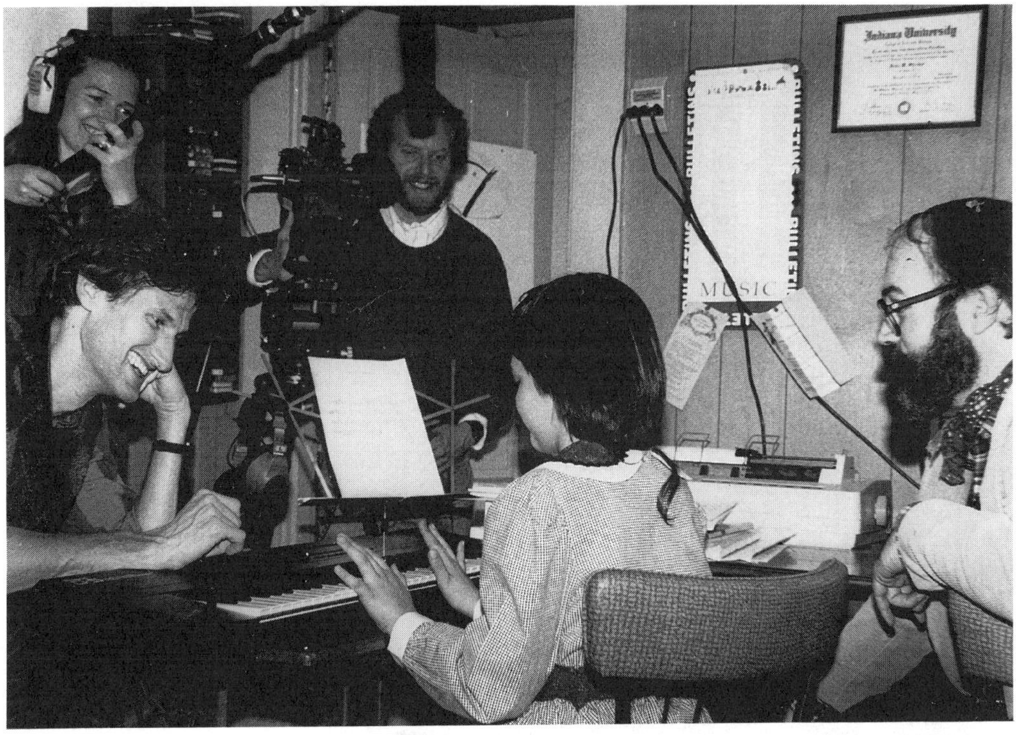

Director John Wackman and the crew of his *New Hampshire Crossroads* television program film Jackie Martin playing her original composition, *Asian Bananas,* as her music instructor, local composer John Warthen Struble, watches from behind her. (Sandy Martin photograph, 1990)

The children's brass band in the Village Players' production of *The Music Man,* November 15-17, 1990, directed by Holly Gardner with the assistance of Rosemary Flynn. Susan Olson was choreographer.

The title role of Prof. Harold Hill, a modern-day Pied Piper who hoodwinked the townspeople, was played by Wayne Gehman (left). (Sandy Martin photographs)

1990 production of *Wizard of Oz* at the Kingswood Summer Theatre for Children, Nathalie Erickson, director. Ballerinas Caitlyn Corson, Krista Carlson, Emily Copplestone, and Brittany Chick.

Lollipop boys Stewart Stone, Tim Sayers, Anthony DiFalco, and Derek Fletcher. Standing to the rear at the right are Doreen Allard and Aimee Frank. (Sandy Martin photographs)

Spooks and goblins: Hallowe'en fun at a party held for 100 Carpenter School students from grades 1 to 3 at the Kingswood Junior High School, October 1990. The event was sponsored by the Kingswood Junior High Homemakers' Club. (Sandy Martin photograph)

Hallowe'en party held in the former Hopewell house (so-called "Chiang Kai-shek estate") on Tips Cove, Wolfeboro Neck, sponsored by radio station WKLZ as a fund-raiser for the YMCA. (Sandy Martin photograph, October 1990)

Linda Roy (left) and Donna King Cooper purchase candles at the Wolfeboro Banking Office of the Farmington Bank, Clarke Plaza, December 1990. All proceeds from the candles, which were donated by WLKZ-FM radio, went to Harbor House. (Sandy Martin photograph)

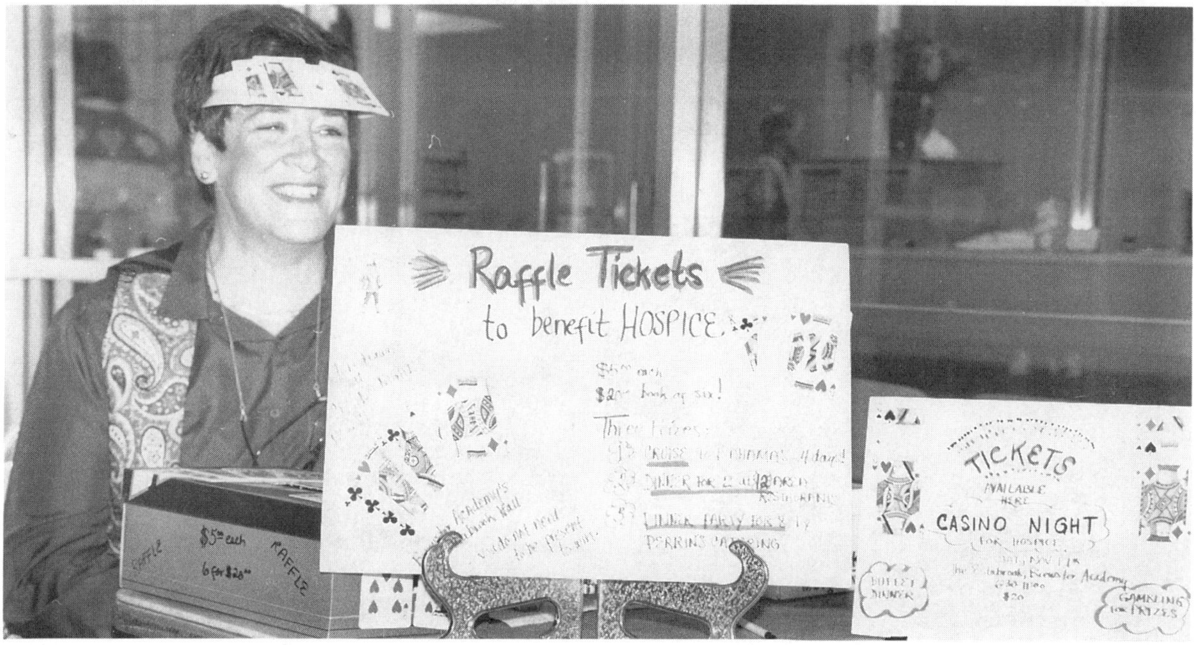


Casino night provided entertainment on the wheel of fortune, at blackjack, and at tables for craps and roulette, all for charity to benefit the Hospice of Southern Carroll County. Hume Gile is shown selling raffle tickets for the event at a table set up at the Rotary Marketplace at Kingswood High School. Casino Night was subsequently held at Estabrook Hall, Brewster Academy, on November 11, 1990. (Sandy Martin photograph)

Holiday fun: Wolfeboro residents enjoy a blazing bonfire on Center Street next to Clarke Plaza while sipping chocolate and singing carols, an annual event sponsored by the Chamber of Commerce.

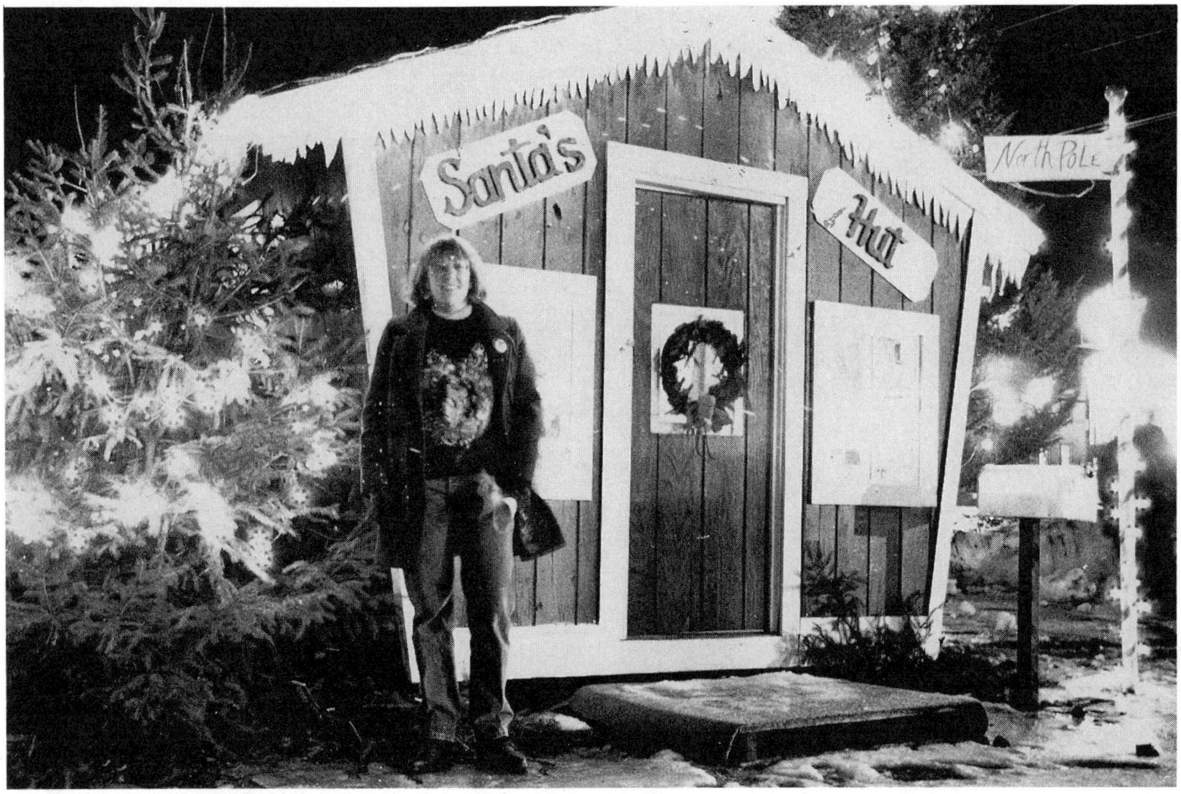


Selectman Sarah M. Silk near Santa's Hut during the same festivities. (Sandy Martin photographs, December 1990)

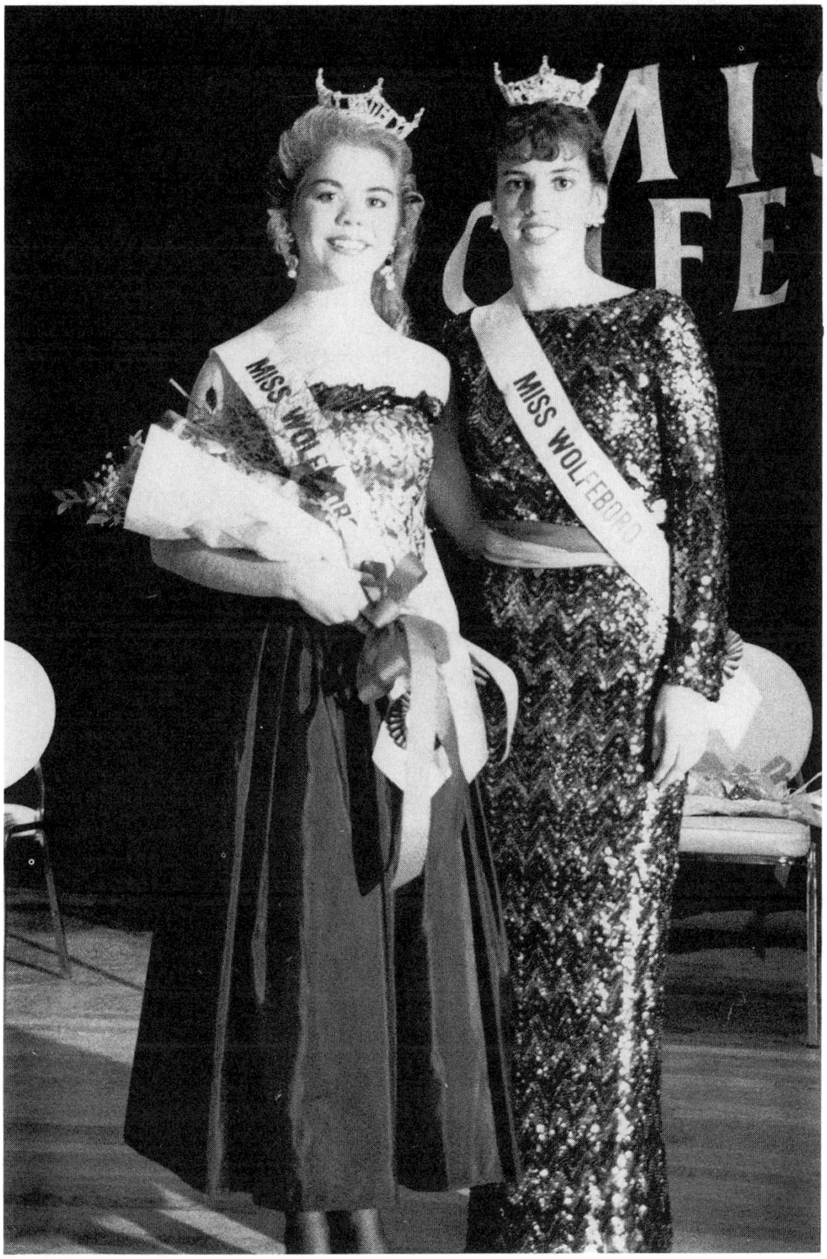


The new Miss Wolfeboro 1990-1991, Amy Welsh (left), after being crowned by last year's title holder, Kelly Grinnell. Kelly was able to attend Holy Cross from scholarship funds raised by the Miss Wolfeboro pageant. (Sandy Martin photograph, September 1990)

the endurance of our audience or the quality of the show—or both—that all but five of the 37 people attending that performance stayed to the end! The next year, 1990, we staged *Province* again, this time in the Brewster Gymnasium with an audience averaging 80 to 100 people per show, or more than double the turnout in 1989."[107]

**1989, August 16. Artists in the Park:** Cate Park. Poster designed by Pat Hodder, a local artist with many talents.[108]

**1989, October 14. First Miss Wolfeboro Pageant:** At the Allen "A" Resort. Kelly M. Grinnell, 16, won a $1,000 scholarship.[109]

**1989, December. Art exhibit:** Works of highly acclaimed local artist Jean Colquhoun, whose paintings had been used on wooden surfaces, reproduced on calendars and plastic bags, and featured in books.[110]

**1990, March 23-24. Stage play:** *Spring Quartet,* suite of four one-act plays—*Three on a Bench, The Still Alarm, The Actor's Nightmare,* and *Graceland*—by the Village Players. Carpenter School.[111]

**1990, April 22. Earth Day observance:** The Pinckney Boathouse was site for exhibits and displays of ecologically desirable products for sale (health foods, fitness items, chemical toilets, water purifiers, etc.). Entertainment by None of the Above, an octet headed by Cathy Marker, and the Anne, Eric and David trio. More than 1,000 attended.[112]

**1990, May 2. Bridge tournament:** Morgan Elmer and Neil Dollarhide, both of Wolfeboro, finished ahead of Pat Dugan and Kay Hamilton, also of Wolfeboro, by the razor-thin margin of 51 to 50-1/2 points. Dollarhide, well-known local accountant, garnered numerous mentions over the years for his bridge prowess.[113]

**1990, May 18. Summer Fashions Inn Style:** Dinner and fashion show at the Lakeview Inn sponsored by Michelle Gerasin (owner of the Lakeview) and Joy Sweeney of the Merle Norman Boutique.[114]

**1990, May 21. Bingo:** At the Masonic Temple, sponsored by the Lions Club. First of weekly Monday night games. $500 jackpot.[115]

**1990, July 25. Roberts Bros. Three Ring Circus:** In town for two performances. Sponsored by the American Legion.[116]

**1990, August 3-4, 10-11. Stage play:** Noel Coward's classic *Blithe Spirit* presented by the Village Players at the Carpenter School.[117]

**1990, August 15. Rock concert:** For teens. No alcohol served. Arranged by Jeff Badger and held at the Allen "A" Resort. Local band named KITE was featured; Scott Hopkins bassist, Greg Hopkins guitarist, and Michelle Roberts vocalist.[118]

**1990, October 21. Family Fun Day:** Sponsored by the Wolfeboro Parks and Recreation Department. Foss Field at 1 p.m. Events included volleyball, softball, horseshoes, three-legged race, water balloon toss, pumpkin carving, and executive briefcase throw. Food.[119]

**1990, November 15-17. Stage play:** *The Music Man* at KRHS Auditorium. Directed by Holly Gardner of Concord assisted by Rosemary Flynn of Wolfeboro. Adrith Sisson of Bartlett was the musical director, and Susan Olson of Wolfeboro did the choreography.[120] "Wayne Gehman played Harold Hill, the music man, and Robin MacDonald played Marian the librarian. The show had a very large cast with lots of children who were costumed in old band uniform jackets found in storage in the Carpenter School attic (they cut off the elastic off the bottoms of sweat pants and sewed stripes down the legs to complete the uniforms). The show had great music, a big chorus, wonderful improvised costumes, a great barber shop quartette." [121]

**1990, December 7. Bonfire and caroling:** Next to Clarke Plaza. Sponsored by the Wolfeboro Chamber of Commerce.[122]

## TOWN

### Running the Town

In March 1981 voters elected Planning Board members for the first time. Earlier the Board was appointed by the selectmen.

In the first election of the decade, theatre owner Paul R. Hatch won re-election as selectman over challenger Peter D. Shulman to join Edward W. Zulauf and Lillian O. Brookes on the ruling committee of three. Other selectmen during the decade included Peter D. Brewitt, H.E. Erickson, Shirley E. Ganem, and George W. Elkins. In 1986 there were no challengers to the incumbents. In 1990 the selectmen were George W. Elkins, Shirley E. Ganem, and Sarah M. Silk.[123] Being a selectman (there being no term for select*woman*) in the 1980s was a daunting task as the town government confronted more changes and challenges than in any other 10-year period in its history.

In 1984 Town Manager Guy L. Krapp made this comment:[124]

> The fact that I have announced my intent to retire at mid year will finalize 14 years as town manager of Wolfeboro. They were good years that left me with the feeling that I played a part in the many things that took place during that time. When my replacement is found, I hope you provide him with the many things you gave me—a wonderful place to work, fellow employees who were devoted to doing their best, and the ideal town to be a part of and live in.

Guy L. Krapp had helped guide the town through many transitions and difficult periods, and the consensus was that he had done a superb job. On August 5, 1985, Chester L. Spinney, town manager of North Reading, MA, was hired as his replacement.

Spinney remained for five years and announced his retirement to take place on May 4, 1990, at the age of 62. He noted that his greatest achievements while in office were improvements to the town water, sewer, and road systems. Notice of the impending vacancy spread, and by early April 1990 the town had over 130 applicants for the position, a field narrowed to 18 candidates by mid-month. In June the selectmen announced that James A. McSweeney had been hired. A native of Connecticut and now a resident of Merrimack, NH, McSweeney had served 22 years in municipal administrative posts and most recently had been employed by BankEast.

A man of action, one of McSweeney's first tasks was to visit various town facilities, meet with people, and draw up a list of 24 issues to discuss with the selectmen. He desired to set goals and time frames for implementing them.[125]

### Taking Care of Business

Town Hall was a busy place. Scarcely a month went by without changes, new regulations, or situations surfacing.

Compensation paid to municipal employees was a prime issue, especially in 1983-1985. Increases were given on several occasions, and in December 1983 a $250 bonus to each worker was recommended by the selectmen and the Wage Review Board. Certain employees sought to join a union, and in January 1984 thirty of them met with representatives of the American Federation of State, City and Municipal Employees (AFSCME) and signed up. By early May the town employees' unionization was approved, with the superintendent of the Electric Department, a secretary at the Town Hall, the director of Public Works, and the town manager excluded.

Separately, recognition was made of the extensive duties of Rachel Jones (who had been town clerk, tax collector, and secretary to the selectmen, among other duties; she resigned in June 1985 after 22 years of service) and the work done by Pat Waterman (secretary to the town manager, preparer of the *Town Report,* and more).

Relations between the union and town department heads and officials swirled with controversy in 1984 and 1985, beginning with an unfair labor practice suit filed in October 1984 against the town of Wolfeboro on behalf of its employees. The selectmen and town manager countered that the union was not bargaining in good faith. Finally, after nine months of arbitration and negotiation, the 30 employees who belonged to the AFSCME agreed to a new contract in July 1985.

Inflation was rampant, and it was becoming increasingly difficult for town employees or anyone else to pay higher costs for energy, housing, food, and other necessities of life.[126] However, despite occasional differences with the selectmen and others, the town employees remained a hard-working, dedicated, enthusiastic, and loyal group.

In 1982 Wolfeboro was one of just five NH towns to receive the Tree City U.S.A. Award for its outstanding program of urban forestry under the watchful eye of Tree Warden William H. Swaffield—who was perhaps better known for his water skiing prowess and his ownership of the largest print shop in town, the Kingswood Press. This award was earned in successive years as well, continuing into the 1990s.[127]

The town announced that on April 15, 1982, it would begin enforcing dog-control laws and would charge fines of $25 if a dog bit or snapped at a person, $10 if a dog were found running loose, and $15 if one caused damage. In practice, most dogs that were running loose on April 14 were still enjoying their liberty on the 16th.[128]

In 1983 the computer age officially arrived with the installation in the Wolfeboro town offices of a $52,000 Cado 20/24 mini computer and three terminals purchased from Northern Data Systems of Bedford.[129] In the same year Paul R. Hatch and JoEllen Scully announced they would be setting up their individual businesses—Sound Spectrum and Bookends—in a new commercial building to be erected behind the Post Office on land twice offered to the town for a parking lot and twice rejected.[130]

In 1985 a $10 million lawsuit brought against the town by David W. Walsh III of Somerville, MA, who had crashed his car into a culvert on Pleasant Valley Road and sustained injuries, was settled for $70,000 payable in seven annual installments.[131]

From 1986 to 1988 the town was involved in a landmark case involving Wolfeboro's taking from Charles I. White of 110 acres of land valued at $26,610 near Sargents Pond, because his taxes were delinquent for several years. It seems that White, who had moved to Durham, had let his tax bills accumulate, and notices mailed to an old address by the town were returned marked "Forwarding Order Expired." Following the seizure, White's attorney, George Walker, took the case to court, but the Carroll County Superior Court sided with the town. The verdict was appealed to the State Supreme Court, which ruled in White's favor, stating that it is illegal for a town to take property valued at a larger amount in exchange for a small percentage due on taxes. Instead, only part of the property can be taken, or the owner must be compensated for any extra amount above normal taxes and interest due to the town. The decision had far-reaching implications for all NH towns.[132]

During the decade the town received other and more potentially usable real estate by better means: donation and purchase. Included were Ellie's Woodland Walk near Lake Wentworth, the Russell C. Chase Bridge-Falls Path and certain former Wolfeboro Rail Road land, the Allen H. Albee Beach on Lake Wentworth, a large parcel of land on Lake Wentworth made available by Donald McBride, and 940 feet of Back Bay shorefront owned by Q. David Bowers and Raymond N. Merena, the latter two properties through donations by the owners and grants under the Trust for NH Lands. Final arrangements for and development of certain of these continued into the early 1990s.[133]

In June 1989 the town opened a new municipal parking lot at the end of the Glendon Street Extension. Michelle Gerasin, president of the Chamber of Commerce, cut a festive ribbon while dignitaries including selectmen Eric Erickson, Shirley Ganem, and George Elkins looked on.[134] There was a slight problem, however. It later developed that the parking lot was not quite as municipal as had been thought, and much of it had been paved on land belonging to a private citizen.

Robbie Karstedt (left) and Jimmy Lowry of Jane Walsh's class at Carpenter School enjoy a feast as part of their study of the Thanksgiving tradition with Pilgrims and Native Americans. (Sandy Martin photograph, November 30, 1990)

Carpenter principal Sumner Harris is flanked by Brendan Wyman and Ben Lord in the Thanksgiving feast. (Sandy Martin photograph, November 30, 1990)

At the 1989 town meeting citizens honored Edward W. Zulauf, who had served the town as selectman for many years. At the same gathering voters declared Wolfeboro to be a nuclear-free town. No nuclear weapons, fuel, or waste would be allowed to pass through the town or be stored in it, exceptions being material associated with licensed hospitals, pharmacies, and medical or dental practitioners.[135]

Parking for automobiles in the business district of town had been a problem for decades. In the 1980s various solutions—some them hardly new—were proposed including increased fines, parking meters (not adopted), and more regulations.

Perhaps the greatest parking hardships of all were endured by 35 families who owned island property on Lake Winnipesaukee and 18 on Lake Wentworth—most of whom lived out of town and could not vote, but who contributed tens of thousands of dollars in taxes to the community each year. These voteless taxpayers had to contend not only with limited-time automobile parking but restricted boat docking as well. In 1990 the selectmen decreed that anyone who parked a boat at a town dock for more than four hours would be subject to a $25 fine to be paid within 48 hours, or it would be increased to $50. This posed great difficulty for anyone who lived on an island and wanted to hold an eight-hour job in town or who wanted to spend more than four hours on the mainland. Several Lake Wentworth residents asked that Mast Landing be exempt, but this plea was rejected. An expensive alternative was paying up to $2,500 to rent a boat dock and car parking space at a private marina. As usual in the annals of Wolfeboro, the needs of islanders were ignored.[136]

### Planning Ahead

Each decade in recent history has been awash in controversy concerning planning for the town's future.

Should Wolfeboro be maintained as it is?

Should stricter zoning be put in place, and, if so, how and where?

What constitutes an "attractive" building, and what does not?

Should owners of certain property on Route 28 be allowed to use it for commercial purposes?

Should Wolfeboro continue to spend money to attract industry?

Is the most current Master Plan worthwhile, or should yet another one be drafted?

Dozens of suggestions were presented, many of them fervently, and in the process many experienced and well-intentioned citizens spent thousands of hours proposing ideas. However, for every point there seemed to be a counterpoint, and true progress was slow.

Forecasting for the future and planning for it was mainly done by the selectmen, who seemed to have the final say, the Planning Board, and from time to time, items placed on the annual town warrant for approval of the citizens. The Zoning Board of Adjustment (ZBA) and the town's code enforcement officers were charged with making decisions to implement the town's wishes.

In practice, much effort and energy were consumed heading off threatened lawsuits, answering actual legal actions, interpreting town regulations, and engaging in disputes with developers and land owners.

On February 24, 1981, the latest Master Plan for the town was accepted by the Planning Board and the Board of Selectmen. This sheaf of ideas had been prepared with the Lakes Region Planning Commission (LRPC) as consultant. On January 20, 1982, the plan was still being modified, and the selectmen met with David Morton of LRPC to discuss long-term capital improvements that would be incorporated into it.

Meanwhile, it was no easy task to keep current regulations enforced, as evidenced by the charge given to Code Enforcement Officer David A. Senecal to visit 19 local businesses which had been allowed to post 38 signs but which had put up 79. All of these surplus signs had to be removed or relocated.[137]

In January 1984 a committee was formed to help rewrite zoning ordinances and implement recommendations of the Master Plan. Planning Board Chairman Peter D. Shulman stated that he had no time for long-range planning as he was too busy with day-to-day issues. In June it was announced that the Planning Department was working on new ordinances that would almost entirely replace current zoning regulations. The composition of the Planning Board changed from time to time. In June 1985 local entrepreneur Richard Clarke was chairman but stepped down because of threats, pressure, and criticism.

These were hectic times on the development scene, and proposals for subdivisions and improvements arrived at Town Hall almost faster than they could be processed. The town code enforcement officer, formerly a part-time position, was now so busy that the selectmen considered raising building permit fees 100% to $3 per $1,000 of construction costs to help defray his costs. The pipeline for applications became so choked that the selectmen decreed that as of March 5, 1986, there would be a moratorium on receiving applications until the zoning ordinances could be reviewed and the Master Plan updated. Further, the Municipal Electric Department could not make electrical hookups as fast as new developments were approved. Arriving just before the deadline were proposals for 90 more lots to be developed.

With so much to be done, errors, omissions, and other problems arose. As an example, in April 1986 a zoning amendment intended to restrict mobile homes and mo-

Scene at the Carpenter School cafeteria. Andrew V. Bowers with his lunch tray. (Sandy Martin photograph, 1990)

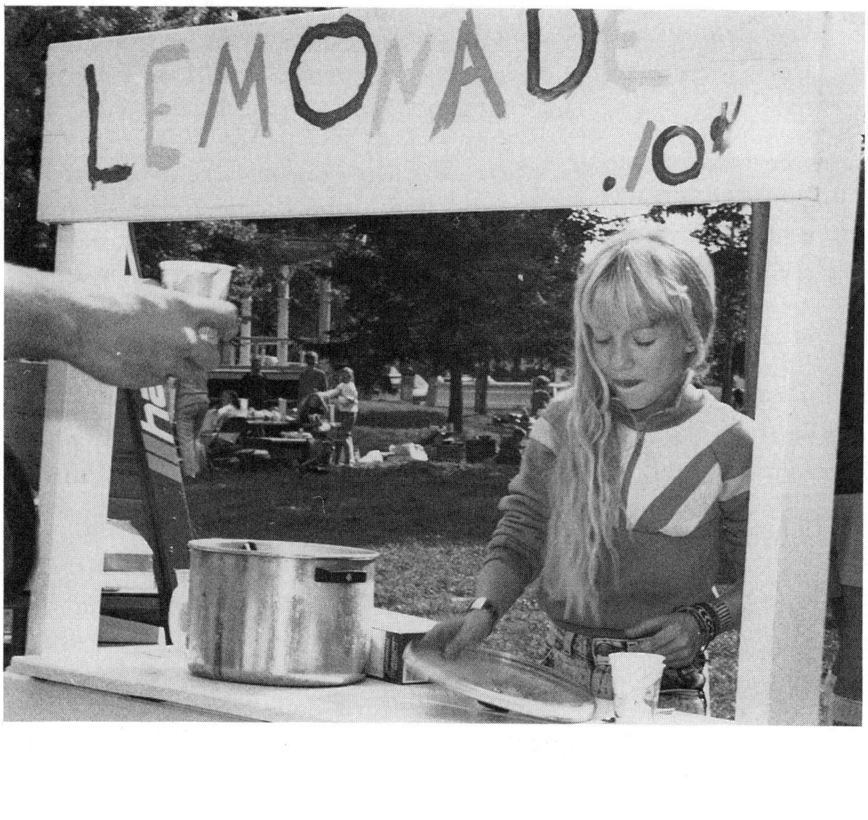


Molly Badger sells lemonade for 10¢ a cup at a yard sale set up on the front lawn of Carpenter School by students in Dr. Irene Ladd's Multi-Age Class. Proceeds were used to help send students to Space Camp the following spring. (Sandy Martin photograph, October 1990)

bile home parks could be interpreted as prohibiting hotels and motels in the commercial district.

In summer 1986 the town hired Peer Kraft-Lund as its first full-time town planner. Kraft-Lund was from Connecticut, but was no stranger to Wolfeboro as he had done his master's thesis on the town in 1984. An instructor at the University of New Hampshire, he was 52 and lived with his family in Center Barnstead.[138]

On November 22, 1986, members of the public attended a workshop titled "The Master Plan Revisited." One object was to redefine the town's major goals. It was suggested that efforts should be made to emphasize the town's tourist facilities and to promote more visitors. This was counter to long-term tradition—considered illogical by many—which had it that manufacturing businesses were ideal candidates for rent subsidies, electric rate discounts, grants and loans, and other concessions, while someone seeking financing for a store, tourist facility, or other recreation-oriented business received the cold-shoulder treatment. In December citizens were informed that a staggering 25 amendments were proposed for zoning regulations, to be put to the town warrant in March 1987. Eventually, all zoning changes endorsed by the Planning Board were passed while selected non-approved changes failed.

In 1987, seeking to make some order out of the situation, Town Planner Peer Kraft-Lund sent questionnaires to residents asking how they liked the quality of life in Wolfeboro, how growth should be handled, and how they rated town services. The big surprise to those in charge was that 96% of those who replied gave *historic preservation* as their number one priority. In other words, they liked the town for its present tradition. Other concerns included loss of open space and forested lands and fear of increased traffic congestion. *Virtually no one* wanted more industry, a fact that selectmen and "development" committees often have had great difficulty understanding.

In March 1987 David Scott, director of policy for the Office of State Planning, stated that using town master plans was an antique idea carried over from the 1930s and that too often they were thick summaries which ended up sitting forgotten on shelves. This commentary struck home, as multiple Wolfeboro master plans were quietly gathering dust at Town Hall.

In July 1987 the Planning Board continued to be overworked, and meetings often ran to four or five hours in length. Planner Kraft-Lund observed that the Board was charged with the immense and perhaps unrealistic responsibility of maintaining the quality of life that everyone wanted. In the same month Code Enforcement Officer Gordon A. Reade resigned his post amidst conflicts with certain members of the Planning Board.

In September 1987 Peer Kraft-Lund stated that as part of his revision of the Master Plan (which was to cover through the year 1995), the town should build a Fire Department substation and a parking garage and should institute public transportation. In December, Robert P. Hopewell was named to head a committee of two dozen citizens interested in orderly growth for the town.[139]

In April 1988 the planning situation became more complex when Kraft-Lund submitted his resignation to accept a position in Rochester. On March 27, 1989, Amanda L. Skinner (name later changed to her maiden name, Simpson) became the new town planner having left a similar position in Alton.[140] In April 1990 Joyce Davis was named new chairman of the Planning Board.

It was that time again, and in the summer of 1990 the town began work in earnest on yet another Master Plan using $23,000 in accumulated appropriations as a beginning. To be prepared were a set of land use maps to depict current developments and water and sewer lines, updated information on utilities and public services, a map showing environmentally-sensitive areas such as aquifers and wetlands, and a map identifying all excavation sites.[141]

During the decade requests to establish businesses or change from current zoning or use abounded, and each had to be considered. A short list of Planning Department, Zoning Board of Adjustment, code enforcement officer projects, and other related situations includes these representative examples:

Request for a pub at Shannon's Grocery (1982).

Major brouhaha involving the use of the former Conway Lumber Co. property on Center Street—which was eventually improved considerably and developed as 2000 Centre Street by Smith, Smith and Kourian—later known as Smith and Kourian (1983-1984).

What could and could not be done with gravel pits within town limits (1983-1987).

Nursing home regulations (1983).

Shorefront access requirements for condos (1984).

Mysterious disappearance from Town Hall of Planning Board documents including Racquetball Club plans and papers involving other major cases (1984).

Proposal for eliminating commercial zoning on Elm and Pine Streets and part of Center Street in Wolfeboro Falls (1984).

Suit involving non-approval of request for three business uses for property on Center Street and the construction of a 32,000 square-foot storage and repair facility (1984).

Expansion of Clarke Plaza.[142]

Many subdivision hearings (almost continuous).

Edward LeRoux proposal for pizza-sub shop (1985).

Wolfeboro Carriage House and Restaurant, Inc., proposal (1985).

What to do with street peddlers and vendors. Should they be limited in number? Licensed? Prohibited? Final decision (June 18, 1981): Only three allowed, and they must stay near the Town Docks.

Robert Emmel proposal for conversion of Baker house (formerly the Parshley house) into retail units; later proposal for addition and office, not retail use (1985).

Wolfeboro Citizens for Controlled Lakefront Development formed and placed a full-page advertisement in the *Granite State News* seeking to eliminate "overly restrictive zoning" (March 6, 1985).

Proposal by Alvin and Barbara White to set up RV (recreational vehicle) park on Route 28 (1986; this long-lived controversy was still alive in the 1990s).

Proposal for The Narrows at Back Bay, a 14-unit condo next to the Wolfeborough Railroad Station. This became a major controversy. Among other things, it was alleged that Gordon A. Reade, representing the town, twice issued and twice withdrew building permits (1986-1987).

Motel with 48 units on Bay Street with 500 feet of frontage on the water was proposed (1986).

Addition to Clipper Home (1986).

Proposal for bed and breakfast to accommodate 12 to 14 travelers in Lucas Nowell house at corner of Lucas and North Main Streets (1986).

Footbridge across Back Bay proposed by Leigh Turner (1986).

Noise level limits and permitted times on construction projects (1986).

Proposal to convert Stonelodge on Sewall Road to condos (1986).

People of Wolfeboro (POW) taxpayers' group forms to discuss growth and development issues (1987). Focus was on the next election, and it was intended to endorse specific candidates and proposals.

Commercial storage building erected by Steven Hunter on Route 109A without permit it was alleged; owner countered by saying the town had *twice* lost his file on the project, but that the town planner had said there would be no problem in any event (1987).

Proposal to establish "land bank" (1987).[143] This eventually became the Wolfeboro-Tuftonboro Land Bank.

### Property Assessments

The decade of the 1980s saw great increases in property values and two calls for reassessing real estate and buildings within town limits. On March 26, 1980, the selectmen signed an agreement with the United Appraisal Company to re-evaluate the town. By early July over 4,700 properties had been studied for a cost that ran $14,488.80 over the $63,900 budgeted for the work. "Numerous mistakes" were found in the appraisal work, and eventually United gave the town a $5,000 refund in compensation.

In 1987 another call was made for revaluation, but voters did not approve this item on the town warrant. Local resident Kathleen ("Kay") Moody felt that such work was long overdue in view of run-ups in real estate prices, and she took the lead in circulating a petition to force the town to reevaluate taxable property. In 1989 voters agreed to spend $230,000 to have the work done. It was stated that this should result in a drop in the tax *rate* (but not necessarily certain individual tax amounts). Avitar, a Chichester firm, was selected to do the work. New figures were to be derived from local real estate *sales* that had taken place between April 1988 and April 1990. In October the town announced that 5,400 properties had been studied, and the assessed value of property increased from $260 million to $723 million.

There was a small problem: By autumn 1990, many real estate prices had dropped sharply from highs of the 1988 period. Leigh Turner, Richard Eaton, and many others stated that certain reevaluations were far too high.[144] And, in some instances they were. For example, on July 22, 1990, four interior (not lakefront) properties in the Embassy Estates subdivision were publicly sold for $34,500, $34,500, $35,000, and $35,000 respectively. When the new owners received their tax bills in the autumn, these properties were assessed in the range of $61,000 to $62,000, although no *sales* of comparable Embassy Estates properties had ever taken place at such levels. A letter from the new owner of three of these properties addressed to Selectmen George Elkins, Shirley Ganem, and Sarah Silk did not receive the courtesy of a reply, nor was Avitar willing to discuss the problem or provide a cogent explanation of how the $61,000 to $62,000 figures were derived.[145]

"The power to tax is the power to destroy," it has been said,[146] and taxpayers' complaints were often ignored.

### Town Waste Disposal

In a decade in which environmental protection was an important issue nationwide, the town spent much time and money on rubbish and sewage disposal. Indeed, for many years efforts in this direction had met with great success, and by 1981 there were very few junk cars, trash piles, polluted lake areas, or other problems—in sharp contrast to the situation a few decades earlier.

On several occasions Cliff Simoneau and others from North Country Scuba worked with other divers and groups—including the Wolfeboro Lions Club, Boy Scout Troop 165, and the Abenaki Water Ski Club—to clean up litter on the bottom of Wolfeboro Bay at the Town Docks and, occasionally, Back Bay. A record was set in 1981 when three dump-truck loads of trash and logs were taken out of the water by 91 divers. Over a period of time North Country Scuba became very well known in New England and participated in many events including diving down to old wrecks in Lake Winnipesaukee, educating people about scuba diving, and effecting salvage and rescue operations.[147]

Removal of rubbish on land involved the effort of many people. In the private sector the Osgood and Morrill firms serviced residents and businesses, while many citizens acquired dump permits and hauled their own trash. Summer residents on islands in Lakes Winnipesaukee and Wentworth usually had to take care of their own waste removal, although in 1981 and 1982 discussions were held with two out-of-town entrepreneurs who wanted to start an over-the-water trash collection business. The selectmen were fearful that some trash might be collected from islands not in Wolfeboro (but in Alton, for example). Nothing was accomplished.

The town incinerator made news regularly. Either it was working very well as in February 1984, or was leaking "unhealthy elements" into a nearby brook as in April 1985, was seriously backlogged and had to be shut down as in July 1986, or in one serious (although it sounded somewhat comical) incident was incapacitated by a fire as in July 1987. In general, the operation of the facility seemed to cause a first-class headache.

Solid waste of another type made the news in 1984 and 1985 when Selectman Peter Brewitt proposed that duck droppings which whitened part of the Town Docks, the adjacent parking lot, and an occasional automobile—especially during the colder months—could be lessened or eliminated by prohibiting the feeding of such birds on town-owned property. As it was, mallard ducks found it more comfortable to spend winters near the docks and accept handouts than to fly south. The proposal was passed, citizens complied, and less fertilizer was generated on the waterfront.[148]

Maintenance, operation, and expansion of the town's sewage system and wastewater treatment plant involved much effort and millions of dollars' expense during the decade, but the results were quite worthwhile, and on balance most citizens were satisfied. In 1981 the quality of the treatment plant received high marks from the state Water Supply and Pollution Control Commission. In the same year work was begun on a $5 million project to triple the system's capacity. Waste water was rendered harmless and recycled by processing and spraying it onto about 100 acres of woods during the warmer seasons. In 1982 three 60 h.p. pumps processed about 122 million gallons of liquid. Gordon A. Reade was chief operator.

Major projects of the era included installing sewage lines on Sewall Road, Cricket Hill, and Forest Road—a project financed by the town ($4 million in bonds) and abutting property owners. In 1987 a new fee of $2,500 for existing homes and $1,500 per bedroom for new homes was instituted for a tie-in to the town water system. This would help fund new sewer line construction to carry the used water away.[149]

In 1990 the selectmen, expressing fears for safety and liability, prohibited citizens from picking through material deposited at the town dump and encouraged town employees to shoo away anyone engaging in the practice. For more years than anyone could remember, this dump-picking was considered to be a bonus for anyone seeking useable building material remnants, appliances and furniture sometimes in need of just slight repair, and other "goodies." On February 10, 1990, 20 protesters carrying signs with such slogans as "Pick Free or Die" and "The Family That Picks Together Sticks Together" braved chilly rain to make their position known. Jeff Badger, self-appointed president of the Wolfeboro Pickers' Association (WPA), acted as spokesman. Badger in one year had found so many valuable items that he declared an extra $2,700 profit on his income tax. Gary Warren, owner of the Bittersweet Restaurant, was another fan of treasure hunting at the dump and rented warehouse space to store what he found. The matter of eliminating picking later came up at town meeting for vote and was soundly defeated.[150]

**Electricity and Water**

In January 1981 the Municipal Electric Department's electricity rates were reported as being the second lowest in all of New England. During the next several years it became evident that the system needed major repairs in order to prevent such inconveniences as the January 17, 1983, outage (which originated in a Tuftonboro substation) said to be the longest in 20 years. Selectman H.E. Erickson, whose familiarity with the system was second to no one else's in town, drew up a list of improvements needed. It was debated whether the town should install a large diesel generating system or stay on line with Public Service of New Hampshire (PSNH) and possibly be a victim of its increasing rates prompted in part by the Seabrook nuclear generating plant debacle (vast cost overruns). Alexander ("Red") Parker chaired a committee that obtained estimates ranging from $5.5 to $10 million for building a new power station in Wolfeboro.

In summer 1986 a new substation was built at a cost of $160,000 on Filter Bed Road. In February 1987 the town announced that electricity rates would be reduced in view of a $440,000 surplus that had accumulated in the Department's bank account. The euphoria was short lived, as on May 1 the electric rate was increased by 1.27 cents per kilowatt hour due to a mandate by PSNH. The situation was to go from bad to worse, and rates were forecast as becoming "astronomical" once PSNH's Seabrook nuclear generating plant went on line. During the next several years costs increased on all fronts, including the purchase of power from PSNH, and con-

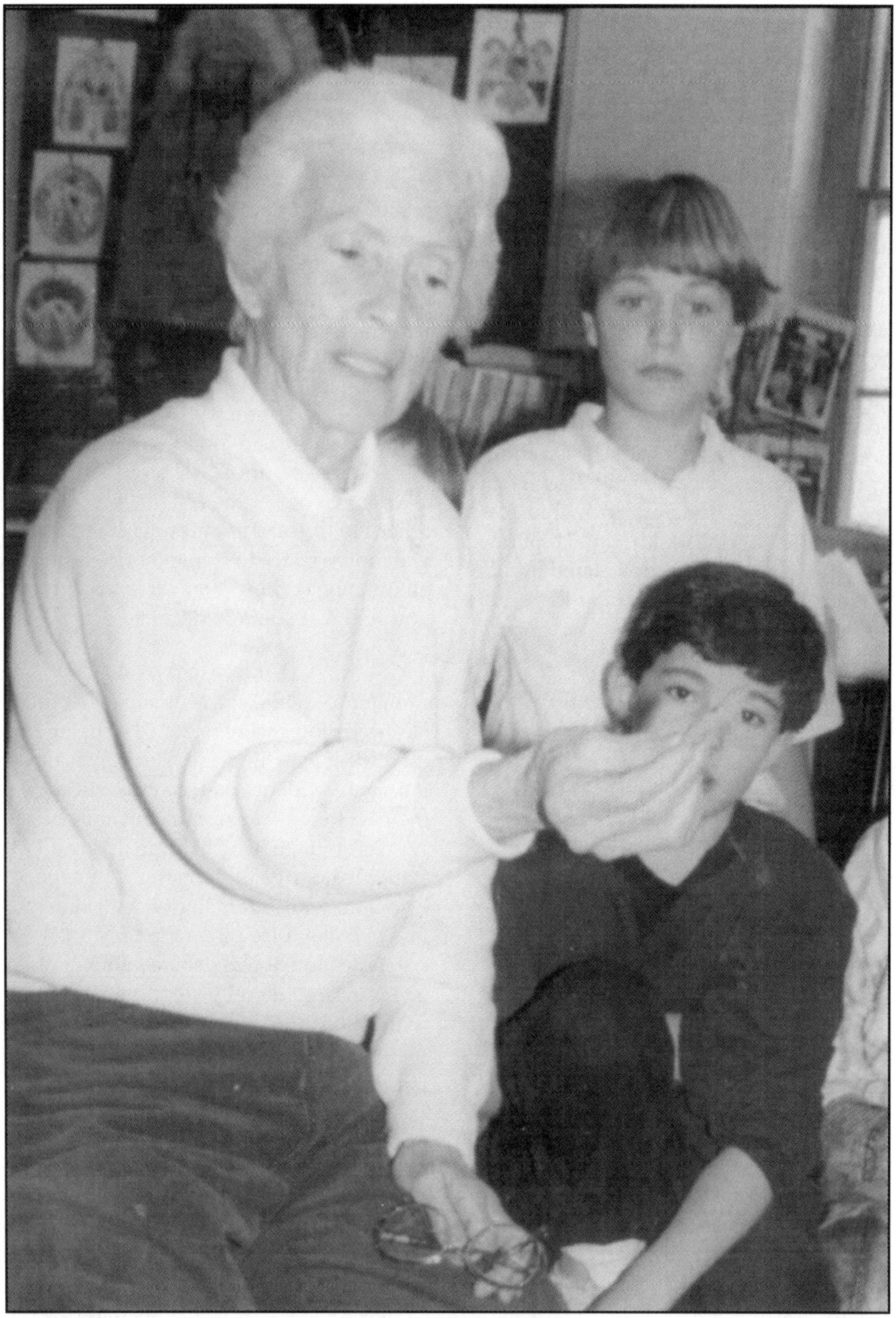

**Cay (Mrs. Donald) Hallock during a visit to Mrs. Marge Coupland's fourth grade class at Carpenter School. She displays an arrowhead from her collection, one of numerous Native American artifacts she found on property she owns near Lancaster, PA. (Sandy Martin photograph, 1990)**

sumers paid the highest rates in town history. Electricity was now a major part of just about everyone's monthly household budget.[151]

During the 1981-1990 period, major repairs were made to the town water system. Certain lines had been installed in the nineteenth century and now were clogged by rust and sediment. Public Works Director Curtis A. Pike said that some pipes were 75% filled with foreign matter. Annual use had grown to over 188,000,000 gallons by 1982. In 1983 certain pipes were cleaned by mechanical means, and work on a new 10-inch main was begun on South Main Street. Not all water went to consumers. On January 17, 1986, a huge leak was found in an 8-inch pipe on Pine Hill Road. It was estimated the water loss had been 45 million gallons—or a quarter of the town's supply—in the preceding year.

In 1988 the average house in town used about 300 gallons of water daily and had a bill of $15.40 per month.[152] Throughout the 1980s taxpayers had voted down several major capital projects for the water system, but still many improvements were made.

## TRANSPORTATION

### The Wolfeboro Steam Railroad

In 1981 the Wolfeboro Steam Railroad, successor to the Wolfeboro Rail Road, began its second season of operation.[153] The line had recently acquired two diesel locomotives. The main unit was Boston & Maine No. 1186, a retired Alco switcher. The second locomotive was purchased from the Guyon Pipe Company of Harrison, NJ, and was a 45-ton Whitcomb built in 1939 and formerly owned by the United States government. As it turned out, the latter was never used in regular service in Wolfeboro.

In 1981 "sunset dinner special" excursions were instituted, featuring lobster and corn-on-the cob at the Sanbornville end of the line.

The Victorian beauty of Wolfeboro's 1872 railroad depot was captured in a documentary about the Boston, Revere Beach & Lynn narrow gauge railroad. The intricate workings of the 1926 Baldwin steam locomotive, No. 250, were preserved on film and featured in a show titled "The Power of Steam," at the Knoxville World's Fair in 1982.

On the weekend of August 21-22, 1982, the line hosted a weekend for enthusiasts of railroad history ("railfans," as they are called). Many other events were held from time to time including promotions in conjunction with local clubs. For a time a "train robbery" was staged annually. In 1983 and 1984 an estimated 500,000 brochures were distributed each year to promote the attractions of the train. In July 1984 manager Brad Williamson stated that about 600 riders were accommodated each day during the busy part of the season.

By 1985 it was evident that the sagging national economy and rising gas prices had contributed to a significant cut in ridership. It was also felt that the town's growing lack of accommodations for overnight tourists was contributing to the problem. Faced with continuing losses the Wolfeboro Holding Company, parent of the Wolfeboro Steam Railroad, decided that the 1985 season would be its last. When the Columbus Day holiday festivities ended that year, so did an era of railroading on the Wolfeboro branch.

The company put the property and equipment up for sale through Henry S. Maxfield Real Estate. On January 7, 1986, the owners announced that a group of developers led by local entrepreneur Leigh Turner was going to buy the westernmost portion of the line between Wolfeboro and Wolfeboro Falls. However, due to a law which mandated that the state of New Hampshire had first right to purchase, and other technicalities, the sale never took place. Eventually the state purchased the 12-mile right-of-way in order to preserve the corridor for future use, matching the $575,000 offered by private bidders.

The last train over the line ran on June 15, 1986, when Locomotive No. 1186 moved all the coaches to Sanbornville where they were loaded aboard flat cars for the journey to their new home in California. The rest of the equipment also left the line for new homes, including steam engine No. 250, which traveled by truck to Lincoln, NH, where it was incorporated into the Hobo Railroad owned by Eddie and Brenda Clark. On November 13, 1986, a meeting was held with state and town officials and interested citizens. It was felt that most people wanted to see the right of way used as a linear park for biking, hiking, and other recreational opportunities. In December 1987 the state offered to sell the railroad property to the town for $507,925. Eventually it was purchased. Later the Trails Rails Action Committee (TRAC) was formed to improve and popularize the property. By the 1990s TRAC had several programs in place. Activities included walking, biking, snowmobiling, and horseback riding.[154]

### Molly the Trolley

In 1987, due to the efforts of local businessman Gregory Roark (who operated The Loft clothing store) and others, Molly the Trolley, a General Motors motor-home chassis styled to resemble an old-fashioned glass-windowed streetcar, made her debut and carried tourists on a narrated shuttle around the commercial district for 25¢ fare, with a turnaround at Kingswood High School. Aline ("Sis") Lee was the first driver.

Molly was a hit, carried about 200 to 250 riders each day, and became a permanent fixture of the summer season, even though one anticipated segment of riders—local office and shop workers traveling to their downtown posts after leaving their cars in remote parking lots—did not materialize in significant numbers.[155]

Other public transportation of the rubber-tired variety included intermittent bus service by Michaud-Trailways which picked up and dropped off passengers at Funspot on Center Street in the early 1980s. One schedule called for 9:00 a.m. and 3:30 p.m. stops in town, and another offered round-trip, same-day service to Boston at three times. In 1985 C&J Limo service of Dover, which ran a highly successful service from several NH towns to Boston's Logan Airport, added Wolfeboro to its itinerary. Again, there were not enough patrons to maintain the schedule.[156]

### The Airport

The Lakes Region Airpark—familiarly known as the Wolfeboro Airport—continued to provide a pleasant destination for aircraft owners, 94% of whom were said to use their planes for business rather than recreation purposes. Such craft made nice tax deductions. The owners of the facility, Merwin and Eleanor Horn, called it "the oldest air resort in America." In 1984 twenty members of the International Organization of Women Pilots helped to paint markings and a center stripe on the runway. At the time 19 aircraft called the Wolfeboro Airport their home base.

The aviation colony was saddened by the passing of Eleanor on November 8, 1988. With Merwin she had founded the fly-in facility in 1945 and before that had achieved local renown as a photographer. Observances in her memory included a flyover by vintage World War II military aircraft and in 1989 scenic rides for charity sponsored by the Eleanor Horn Memorial Flight to Fight Cancer.[157]

## SPORTS AND RECREATION

### Many Activities

From field hockey to water skiing, from fishing to ice boating, each season had a rich schedule of indoor and outdoor sports and recreational activities to offer. Carpenter, Kingswood High, and Brewster students competed with each other and with surrounding towns in team sports.

Throughout the decade the town Parks and Recreation Department had a full program of sports activities including skiing and skating at the Abenaki Recreation Area (a.k.a. Abenaki Ski Area), youth soccer, swimming, tennis, track and field sports, volleyball, and softball. By the winter of 1987-1988 it was not unusual for 2,500 people per week to use the Abenaki facility.

In 1981 Donald K. Brookes retired as director, a position he had held for 16 years, commenting:

> During that time I have seen the Back Bay transformed into a first-class outdoor recreational facility. I have seen the Abenaki Ski Area grow from one slope to four trails, ski jumps and 12 miles of cross-country trails, as well as having a Tucker Sno-Cat to groom all of these trails.... The new director of Parks and Recreation is Mr. Wade Lemmon, and he deserves your support and cooperation.[158]

In turn, Lemmon was succeeded as director in 1985 by Peter D. Brewitt, who in 1990 with his wife Peggy moved to Perkinsville, VT, to operate a store.[159] He was succeeded by Susan M. Glenn in 1990. Glenn had joined the department in 1987 and had done much to increase its outreach and services. Her energy seemed boundless.

The following listing in alphabetical order provides a very impressive glimpse at typical school, town, and private sports and recreational activities of the decade.

### Baseball

Baseball remained the town's number one outdoor, warm-weather team sport.

Kingswood High School had two divisions for girls, the Junior High softball team known as the Mini-Knights and the Kingswood Varsity softball team. Bonnie Rankin was coach in 1981. In 1983 star players on the Junior High team included April Wilson, Cindy Wilson, Sandy Stockbridge, J. Hansell, Staci Roberson, Heather Silva, Jen Douglass, Jane Haughey and Nan White.

For boys the Kingswood Knights and Kingswood Junior Varsity Baseball teams provided playing opportunities.

In May 1986 Kingswood's Junior High Knights baseball team after two close losses won a game with Kennett 20-5. Charlie Rogers had three hits and four stolen bases, and Chris Coolidge struck out six batters in four innings. In 1988 the Junior Knights had an outstanding season with 9 wins and 0 losses. Acclaimed players included Chris Martel, Andrew Cornwell, Jason Palmer, and Jeff Lynn.

In 1988 the Kingswood girls' softball team closed the season with an 11-8 record. In a 9-0 game against Oyster River winning pitcher Jill Richards became the first Kingswood player to hit a home run since 1984. She also stole six bases and struck out six batters.

On June 20, 1984, the Wolfeboro Babe Ruth All-Star team defeated North Conway 9-2. Notable Wolfeboro players from the Junior Baseball League included Kory Webster, Paul Doran, and John Pollini.

The 1987 season of the Wolfeboro-Tuftonboro Minor Baseball League came to an exciting conclusion on June 28 at Foss Field when the Bailey's Restaurant team defeated the WinnSports team 7-6 in the championship game. Notable performances were given by Tyler Dunbar, Joe Chellman, Ian Mullen, and Joy Ramsbotham.

In early June 1988 the Ben Franklin team was unbeaten in Little League baseball, having recently bested the Wolfeboro National Bankers 5-0 when winning hurler

Craig Johnson pitched a two-hitter and struck out 15 batters. Against the BankEast team Ben Franklin won 19-1 with the help of Mike Comperchio.

In 1989 the Hunter's IGA team took home the Wolfeboro-Tuftonboro Minor League championship by beating the Corner Store team 17-8. Brett Edmunds, who was one of the town's leading up-and-coming young sportsmen, had a three-run homer, and Frankie Mansfield and Jason Denver each hit doubles. On July 22, 1989, Lenny Beaulieu, age 12, pitched a no-hitter against Tilton amid much acclaim, as no-hitters were rare in Little League play. Even more remarkable was the fact that this was the first time he had ever pitched in a game!

In the summer of 1988 the Wolfeboro Parks and Recreation Department sponsored a softball team for girls in grades five and six.

In 1982 local adults played on the Wolfeboro Women's Softball Team sponsored by the accounting firm of Leone & Bigelow and the Wolfeboro Men's Softball Team sponsored by Shannon's Grocery. Toward the end of the decade ladies' teams fielded by Bowers and Merena Galleries (the "Griffins") and the Olympia Gym played against neighboring towns.[160]

**Basketball**

The Kingswood Junior Varsity basketball team played such opponents as Kennett, Franklin, Inter-Lakes, Tilton, Berwick Academy, and Calvary Christian. In January 1981 in a game against Bishop Brady, senior Greg Dollarhide, co-captain of the Kingswood High varsity team, became the first player in Kingswood history to reach a career total of 1,000 points. In the same year Kingswood's Jeri Southard was honored as Rookie of the Year and was named to the All-Lakes Region Girls' Team.

The Wolfeboro-Tuftonboro Youth Basketball League featured Carpenter School students in teams sponsored by local businesses. In a typical contest on March 13, 1982, the Wolfeboro National Bank Knicks took the number one spot by beating the WASR Warriors. On March 28, Doug Baker was given the Most Valuable Player award.

On November 26, 1983, the Kingswood varsity boys' basketball team defeated their alumni counterparts 90-86, with the adult players including Tony Kendall, John and Judd Lovering, and Matt Hale. Another team was composed of women students led by Jeri Southard and including Sue Martin, Jen and Liz Arlin, and Anita Nudd; they beat their women alumni opponents 54-53.

In representative 1985 games, in January the Kingswood girls' varsity basketball avenged an earlier loss with Pembroke, 58-34. Pam Southard scored 24 points and 17 rebounds, Lauren Douglass scored 14 and 10, and Tracy Ridings scored 14 and 11. In February the Kingswood boys' varsity basketball defeated Kennett 61-42 for their 11th win of the season. Leading shooters were Jim Klingensmith, Rob Fontaine, and Chris Downs.

In spring 1986 the Wolfeboro-Tuftonboro Youth Basketball League bestowed awards upon its most valuable players including Andrew Cornwell (Hunter's IGA team), Jesse Hooper (Loft Lakers), Corey Seymour (WASR Warriors), and Jeremy Osgood (Wolfeboro Oil). Osgood was also named the MVP in the entire league.

On December 4, 1989, the Kingswood girls' basketball squad pulled off an impressive 51-38 victory over Merrimack Valley. Freshman Nicole LaBelle—who went on to become one of the most acclaimed basketball players ever at Kingswood High—emerged with 22 points, and sophomores Michelle Hermann and Shauna Michaud contributed a combined 25 points. The team closed out the season by going 6-1 in its most recent seven games (out of a total of 18 games for the year).[161]

During the 1980s Brewster Academy fielded varsity A and B teams against other regional schools including Tilton, New Hampton, Bowdoin JV Polar Bears (Maine), Holderness, Hyde School (Bath, ME), Kimball Union, and others. By mid-January 1983 the Brewster Academy girls' basketball team was unbeaten with a 7-0 record.

The Brewster Academy girls' varsity basketball team took the 1985 Lakes Region championship with a 16-0 record. Holly Moulton, Lilly Dunlap, Liz Scully, Sair Goldenberg, Rachel Goldenberg, Joy Richards, Liz Engstrand, Sarah Hayes, Courtney Crane, Diana White, Julie Dabrowski, Marie Garland, and Renee Proulx were team members, with David Atwood as coach.

In 1988 the Brewster Academy men's varsity basketball team captured the Class B New England Prep School Tournament championship, March 5, beating Cushing Academy 73-67 for the title. Scott Webster from Salem, MA, and Chris Pottle from Wolfeboro were the keys to the win, with 21 combined points.

In 1989 the Brewster women's Bobcats basketball team won the New England Small Prep School Championship. Stars of the Brewster court included Julie Senecal, Emily Gile, Nancy Walsh, Kim Boyce, Kate Radley, and Deidre Magnifico. In 1990 the Bobcats scored many victories with some of the same notable players.[162]

Among exhibition games held in town a basketball contest between the New England Patriots professional *football* team and the Ossipee All-Stars basketball team held at Kingswood High on March 23, 1985, drew an overflow crowd estimated at 1,000, who watched the football players triumph 77-69.

On August 9, 1989, the Brewster All-Stars basketball team took on somewhat older (men in their 20s and 30s) members of the Soviet Union team, Sport Club "Sheksna," who were on a two-week American tour, and lost 92-76.[163]

### Bicycling

Bicycling was popular throughout the decade as a personal and family sport and also in competition. The Nordic Skier, local agent for Cannondale and other "mountain bikes," as rough-terrain models were called, experienced record sales. Piche's on Lehner Street, a newly-opened branch of a Laconia firm, also did well.

The premier event of the decade was the Tour de King's Wood bike race which had been originated by Bailey's Restaurant in 1972. On August 27, 1983, the event was won by Steve Sperry of Hampton, who pedaled 18 miles through Wolfeboro and Tuftonboro in 49 minutes and 22 seconds.

In September 1987 Steve Flagg of Wolfeboro, an owner of the local Nordic Skier sports shop, won the Top Cyclist Award in the senior men's group at the White Mountain Bicycle Races. In June 1988 he beat 174 contestants to win the 22-mile Waterboro, ME, bike race. On August 13 of the same year, he and a partner from Vermont won the VIP Health Club race in Maine. In 1989 he was the victor in the White Mountain series of bike races, and on July 29, 1990, he scored a multiple victory in a 25.6-mile time trial held in Plymouth, beating about 75 competitors and setting a course record of 58:24.[164]

### Bowling

Leagues and individual players competed in candlepin bowling at Fuller's Bowling and Games in the Clarke Plaza, a convivial gathering place that was also home to many electronic game machines, a fad of the decade.

### Canoeing

While canoeing on Lakes Wentworth and Winnipesaukee continued to draw many participants, it was the Smith River Canoe Race held each May, slightly renamed as the *Great* Smith River Canoe Race in 1989, that commanded the most attention. On May 15, 1982, the eighth annual event was won by brothers Howie and Jim Bean in 23 minutes and 27 seconds. The brothers Bean would go on to win multiple later contests (*e.g.*, 1983, 24:26; 1984, 25:22).

In the same sport Steve Flagg was well known, and in 1982 he was one of just eight canoe racers in America tapped to go to the World and International Canoe Championships in Switzerland.

Stan Kissell of Wolfeboro also established himself as one of America's best competitive canoeists, and in August 1988 he placed fourth in the Master's Division of the National Marathon Canoe-Kayak Championships sponsored by the U.S. Canoe Association. In 1988 he and Peter McAllister (of Belgrade Lakes, ME) won the Smith River Canoe Race. In 1989 the same duo took top honors among 203 paddlers at 23:37.

The 16th annual Great Smith River Canoe Race was held on May 19, 1990, with a film crew from the Public Broadcasting System's *New Hampshire Crossroads* on hand to record the event. The contest drew 205 participants—a record. Howard Bean was the recipient of the Barry Lougee Award presented annually to the person whose consistent and creative contributions to the race exemplified the spirit of race founder Lougee. Bean had been the timer for all 16 races. The fastest run of the day was Stan Kissell of Wolfeboro and Peter McAllister of Maine who took first place in the men's long racing class with a time of 23:41. Donna Day of Hillsboro and Karen Day of Durham had the fastest overall time for women with 33:53. Howie Bean and Jennifer Caldwell of Wolfeboro were the overall winners in the male-female category with a time of 24:35.[165]

### Darts

The Wolfeboro Dart Association was formed in 1983 and played games weekly at the Bittersweet Restaurant on Route 28. Darts were also popular at the Wolfeboro Inn, which expanded greatly during the decade and sought to offer a wider variety of services..[166]

### Field Hockey

Field hockey was a popular sport during the 1980s. In 1985 the Knights won the state Division AA championship for the first time in Kingswood High's history after defeating Dover 1-0. In 1990 the Knights had a record of 12-1-1 and were ranked number one in the state as they entered the championships, where they lost by only one goal. Among the leading Kingswood players of the decade were:[167]

Nikki Antonucci, Amy Babson, Shaun Brewitt, Julie Clough, Carolyn Cole, Maria DeChiaro, Theresa DeChiaro, Gina DeRose, Meghan Donovan, Nancy Doran, Jen Douglass, Deb Elkinton, Shannon Elliott, Michelle Fraser, Hilary Gehman, Rachel Hale, M.J. Harris, Jane Haughey, Kristie Hunter, Nickie Hunter, Heather Kinmond, Wendy Larrabee, Ann Lovett, Cindy Marden, Jen Marschner, Shayne Medico, Kate Oakes, Beth O'Dowd, Kate Phillips, Kathleen Rankin, Chris Richards, Katie Roark, Andrea Rollins, Gretchen Shannon, Barrie Twyon, and Pam Urda. Bonnie Rankin Lord was the coach 1980-1990 leading the Knights to the State Tournament nine times in 11 seasons.

In 1986 Brewster Academy registered the first year of play after a 10-year absence of a field hockey team. The players turned in a 4-1-1 record for the season and came in second in the Lakes Region League championships.[168]

### Fitness

Physical fitness was a popular objective during the 1980s. Running, jogging (often with a Sony Walkman), aerobic exercises, in-home track and exercise machines,

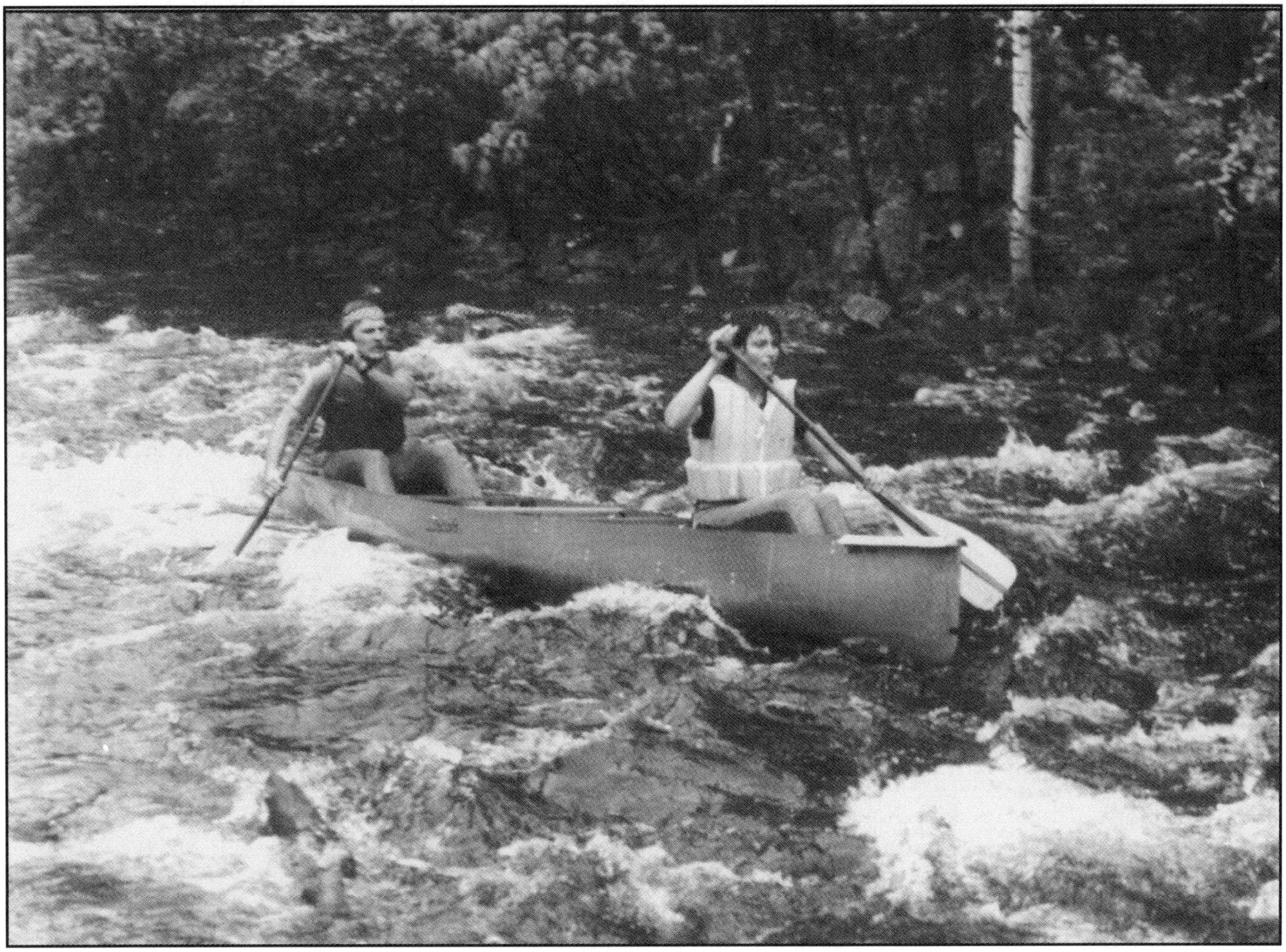

**Debbie and Stan Kissell in rapids along the course of the Smith River Canoe Race, May 19, 1984. This husband and wife team from Wolfeboro took first place with 25:34 in the Mixed Racing class. (Kissell Collection)**

and other disciplines and devices were popular. In 1987 BankEast took the lead in an effort, ultimately unsuccessful, in establishing a community indoor pool and exercise facility. The steering committee included Dr. Frank Allen, Dr. Winfield O. Kelley, Jr., Timothy Sullivan, Barbara and Larry Hull, Kit and Don Wright, Brewster Headmaster David M. Smith, Jeri Clarke, Charles Campbell, Dave Ford, Roberta Worrick, and Bonnie Lord.[169] During the decade there was also much discussion about establishing a YMCA branch in Wolfeboro, and Susan Campbell was for a time the leader in the movement, called at first the "YMCA without walls." Interest eventually lapsed.

**Football**

In 1981 Steven Durgan, who had been assistant coach for five years, was named coach of the Kingswood Knights football team. He was later followed in the position by Barry Tibbetts who served for most of the decade.

Kingswood Junior High and Senior High players making gridiron news throughout the decade included:

Dick Arthur, Charlie Beach, Lenny Beaulieu, Shawn Bernier, Matt Bogart, Justin Berkowitz, Corey Copp, Duane Davis, Paul Doran, Mike Fischer, Robbie Fontaine, Brian Gridley, John Hamblett, Randy Hunt, Woody Hutchins, Tony Hutchins, Robert Heald, Derek Jenner, Tony Kendall, David Keniston, Barry Kimball, Jim Klingensmith, Mark Labbe, John Lewis, David McBride, Tim Nash, Todd O'Dowd, Jared Olkkola, Mike Pollini, Peter Pollini, Matt Quirk, Rob Raven, Mike Ridings, Caleb Rudolph, Allen Schultz, Brennan Sheahan, Sean Sheahan, Dave Skelley, Doug Skelley, Mark Smart, Dave Smith, Karl Smith, John Swenson, Bob Tarbox, Adam Tasker, Cris Tibbetts, Rick Urda, Kory Webster, Dave Whitcomb, and Tim White.

Notable plays, games, and award recipients were many, including these:

On October 17, 1981, in a game in which the Knights trampled Plymouth, Robert ("Robbie") Fontaine had a 70-yard touchdown on the return of an opening kick-off.

In July 1982 Doug Skelley was the third member of his family to be named to the NH Shrine All-Star Team.

In 1984 six Knights were named to the All-State Football Team: David Keniston, Robert Fontaine, Duane Davis, Rick Urda, Jim Klingensmith, Dave Skelley.

In December 1987 Paul Doran and Kory Webster were named to the NH Football Coaches Association Division III All-State Team. Seniors Dave Whitcomb, Brennan Sheahan, and John Swenson, and junior Peter Pollini received honorable mentions.

In December 1989 Kingswood alumnus Dave Skelley, son of Alan and Virginia Skelley, received the Golden Helmet award for his play in a 23-19 win over Glassboro State and was named player of the week in the New England Divisions II and III. He had just completed his sophomore year as starting quarterback at Norwich University in Northfield, VT.

In July 1990 Matt McBride, captain of both KRHS's football and baseball teams, was chosen to play in the 37th Annual Shrine Maple Sugar Bowl game to be held August 11 at Dartmouth's Memorial Field.

In December 1990 the unbeaten 1990 Kingswood Regional Junior High football team was given jackets through the fundraising efforts of Wally Keniston, an avid sports fan.[170]

**Golf**

The Kingswood Golf Club's 18 holes were the focal point for many enjoyable times in private rounds as well as team play during the 1980s, with the Indian Mound (Ossipee) and the new 9-hole Perry Hollow (New Durham) courses attracting many Wolfeboro players as well.

Notable players on the Kingswood links in 1981 included Tom Newth (winner of the President's Cup); Cindy Melanson (Championship Flight winner in the Ladies' League); and youngsters Jay Pollini, age 10, and John Thurston, 11 (winners in the youth group with 29 and 27 respectively on a five-hole course).

In June 1982 a Wolfeboro team composed of club pro Dave Pollini in the company of Tim Melanson, Jerry Thayer, and Bill Antonucci finished tied for first with a 66 in the New England Pro Golfers Association Pro Am tournament at the White Mountain Golf Club. Melanson, whose grandfather Joseph I. Melanson, Jr., had been state golf champion several times, was well known as a collector of antique golf clubs and artifacts. In the same year he edged Bill Sweeney for the Kingswood Golf Club championship, one of several he was to win during the era. In 1983 Bill Antonucci claimed the club's top honor. In 1986 he set the official Kingswood course record for a game, a remarkable 63.

In 1985 the Kingswood High School Knights golf team posted its second undefeated season and had a 24-0 record, with especially close wins over Littleton and Gilford. Tri-captains were John Thurston, Sean O'Connor, and William Jackson. In September 1985 Jim Pollini earned the keys to a new Mercury Cougar automobile by dunking a hole-in-one in the Kingswood Golf Club's Pro Days competition. In the next year, Bill Sweeney's similar accomplishment won him a new car in the Lions Club Tournament.

In 1987 Jay Pollini led a team of Kingswood Knights golfers to win the high school's first State Division II title, a feat duplicated by the team in 1988 in a win over Hanover.

The first hole-in-one of the 1988 season at the Kingswood Golf Club was driven in by Salley Reynolds,

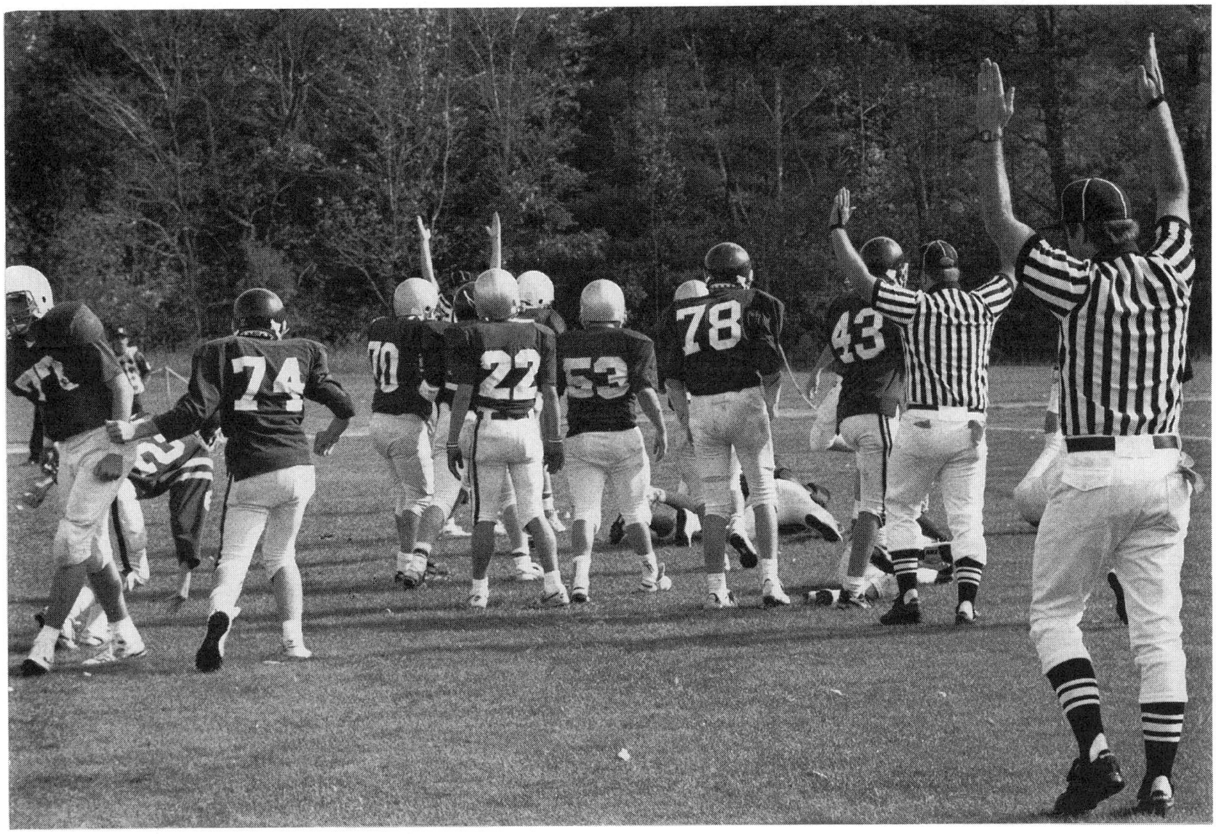


Kingswood Junior High School Knights football team in action under coach Mike Jones. (Sandy Martin photograph, 1990)

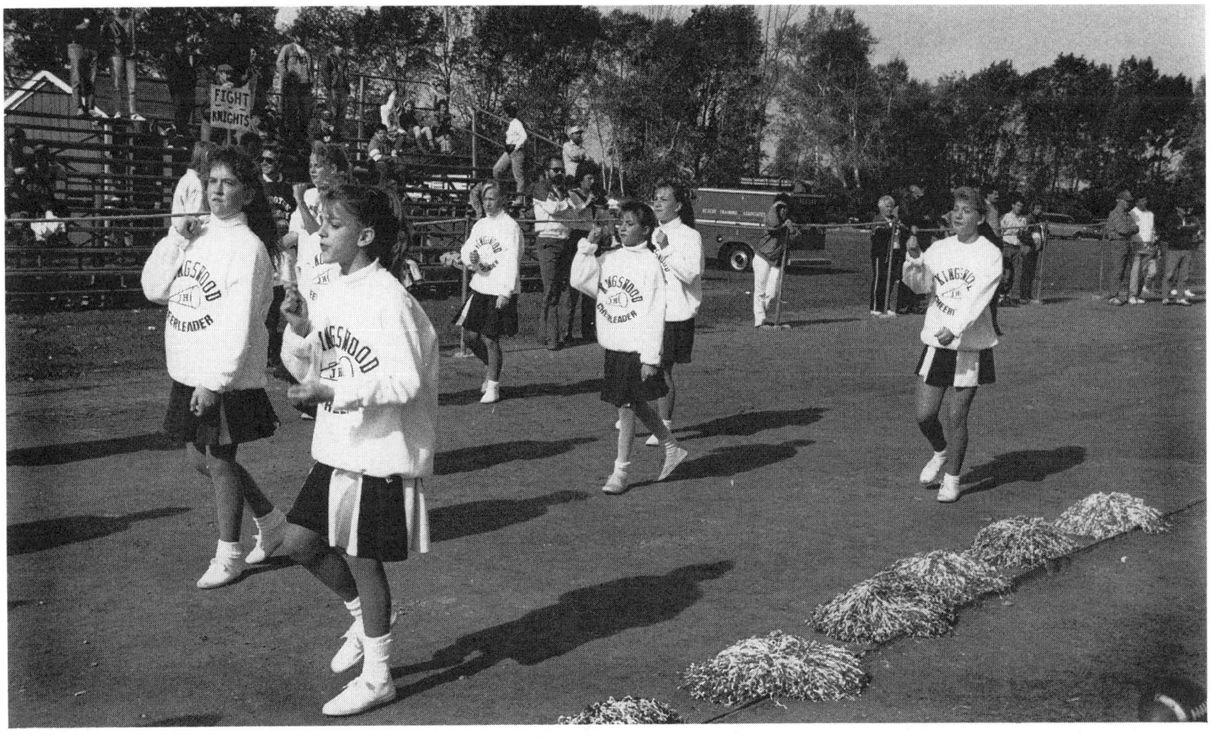


Kingswood Junior High School cheerleaders celebrate in formation. (Sandy Martin photograph, 1990)

Dedication of the Kingswood Memorial Athletic Fields at Kingswood Regional High School, October 20, 1990. Robert G. Hale was the first name on the plaque placed on a rock between fields. More names will be added as time goes on. To the far right is Gladys Stinchfield (Bob Hale's sister; in light quilted jacket) and next to her is Anita Hale (his wife; in dark quilted jacket). Four of his children—Gay Edmunds, Steve Hale, Matt Hale, and Debbie Skelley—are pictured with their families. Robert Hale maintained the fields and was a very strong supporter of the Kingswood athletic program over a long period of years. (Sandy Martin photograph)

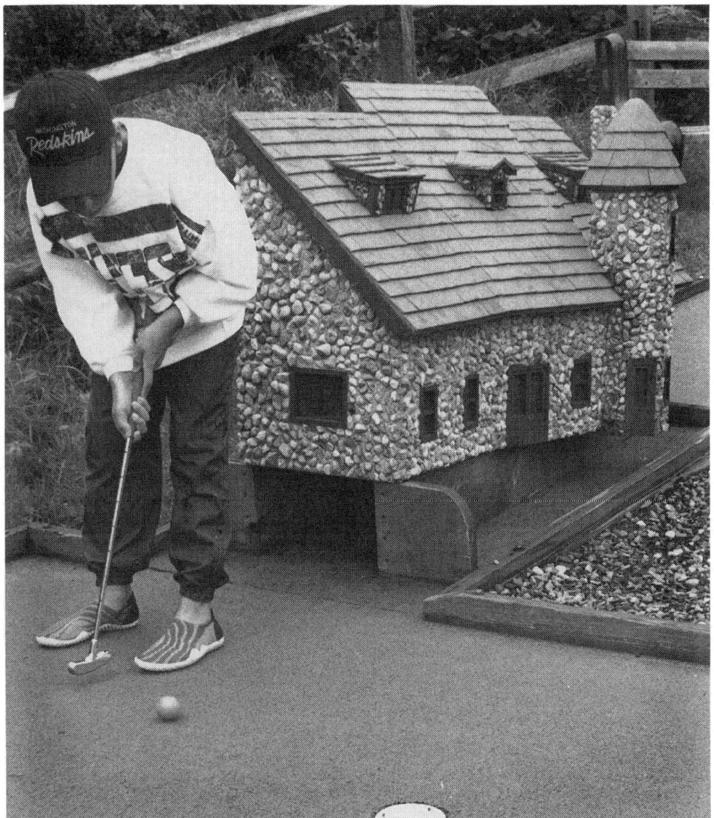


Playing a game of miniature golf at Putter's Village on Center Street downhill from and next to the First NH Bank. (Sandy Martin photograph, 1990)

a new member. In the same year Bob Hughes wrested the club championship away from long-time holder Bill Antonucci.

On September 21, 1990, Bill Sweeney accomplished one for the record books. While playing in a foursome with Babe Chagnon, Cy Hunter and Don Hughes, he scored a hole-in-one on a 250-yard par-4 hole, an accomplishment usually reserved for par-3 holes averaging 140 to 190 yards.[171]

During the decade there were several changes at Kingswood that did not involve golf play. In December 1981 a suit handled by attorney James Kalled was settled. Hilda H. Seaver, Phelps Wood II, and others claimed that certain actions by the Kingswood Corporation, formed on October 6, 1958 (name later changed to Kingswood Golf Club, Inc.), in an effort to revive the diminished fortunes of the Kingswood Golf Club, were improper and were not fair to certain beneficiaries of a property transfer to the club that took place years earlier in 1935. A settlement was made whereby 18 plaintiffs were given $35,200 in legal fees, one share of treasury stock, a 58.1% equity in real estate, dues-free lifetime memberships and other privileges.[172]

In 1989 a plan was announced for the reconfiguration of certain parts of the course to spread certain holes farther apart to avoid potential accidents and close calls. During the summer the course hosted about 320 rounds of golf daily, which amounted to a foursome teeing off about every eight minutes. Completion of the new layout was anticipated to occur in 1991.[173] Meanwhile, the course installed an improved irrigation system using lake rather than town water. In 1990 the Kingswood Golf Club, Inc., had 404 stockholders and 617 golf-playing members. Club pro was David Pollini, who had held the position since 1967, following Richard Thomas (1964-1966) and Frank Butler (1915-1963). At present the club is managed for the benefit of the community, and the public is welcome.

### Granite Man Triathlon

In 1981 the 1st annual Granite Man Triathlon was organized to feature a two-third mile swim, a 19-mile bicycle race, and a four-mile road run to benefit the Albert Dow III Scholarship Fund.[174] The 1984 event drew 450 athletes. Gary Mercer of Hampton took the laurels with a time of 1 hour, 29 minutes, and 37 seconds. Joan Blume of Concord crossed the finish line first in the women's category with 1:38:54.

The 1985 competition was won by Bruce McNichol of Nepean, Ontario, with 1:26:55, two minutes shorter than the previous record. Three Wolfeboro men won the team division in the 7th annual event held on August 27, 1988, when John Hammond ran; Dan Coons swam, and Steve Flagg bicycled to turn in a combined time of 1:31:23. The next year the Wolfeboro team of Tom Mack, Steve Flagg and John Hammond won the same event with 1:31:17. Brooks McQuade was the individual overall winner with a time of 1:33:17.[175] Howie Bean, Jennifer Caldwell, and other well-known local athletes figured in the record book in 1990.

### Gymnastics

In 1981 the Kingswood girls' gymnastic team was in the state championship and competed in two of four events.[176] Otherwise, this was not a school sport.

### Hiking and Walking

Climbing local hills and walking through woodlands was a popular pastime, but occasionally someone would venture farther afield. In the summer of 1981 David Severance of Wolfeboro hiked the Appalachian Trail from its beginning in Georgia to its end in Maine, punctuated by a brief return to town to recover from a case of food poisoning from a sandwich given to him by another hiker.[177]

### Horseback Riding

Classes were offered by Brewster Academy at Misty Meadows. In a competition held on April 30, 1988, members of the group took 11 ribbons home.[178] Many local residents, especially teenage girls, enjoyed horseback riding at Misty Meadows and Whispering Willows, both located a short distance out of town to the north.

### Hunting and Fishing

The Harriman-Hale Post of the American Legion sponsored fishing derbies for the younger set. Typical was the 1981 event held on June 14 at Tyler Brook at the Allen "A" Resort. Winner in the 7-12 age group was Ralph Carpenter with a 16-inch brook trout.

Due to overfishing and possibly other causes, catches in Lake Winnipesaukee declined during the decade. In January 1990 Carl Shannon organized a meeting between local fishermen and the NH Fish and Game Department. Wolfeboro sportsmen thought that Atlantic salmon recently introduced into the lake in quantity ate too many smelt, which were food fish for other species. The Fish and Game Department countered that 50 to 100 larger salmon stocked for the Winnipesaukee Derby would not make a significant difference in the smelt supply. Meanwhile, the smaller salmon stocked for general fishing purposes were expected to grow larger and in a year or two yield memorable specimens. Somehow, this did not happen, and the vast majority caught by anglers measured under 20 inches. Opening day of salmon season—April first—drew fewer Wolfeboro fishermen as the years went by.

Smelt—decades earlier so populous that catching them in brooks feeding into Lake Wentworth was a popular sport in itself—became much scarcer, as did crayfish, with resultant negative effects on the populations of larger fish that fed on them. Trout and cusk catches became smaller, and perch were seldom seen.[179]

Some suggested that Lake Winnipesaukee was becoming *too* popular as its fame spread due to television coverage broadcast in Boston, the hit film *On Golden Pond* (primarily filmed on Squam Lake, but with some Winnipesaukee scenes), and an increased interest in nature and the outdoors.

However, there was a bright spot: bass fishing. Popularity of this sport increased. Lake Wentworth was a popular venue as was Lake Winnipesaukee, particularly in the area near Springfield Point. More than a few local cars sported decals reading B.A.S.S. (Bass Anglers Sporting Society).

The 1980s saw a proliferation of moose in and around town including occasional sightings in the commercial district. By decade's end the visit of one or even a group of moose to one's backyard was no longer an item of news. Hunting them on a limited basis became legal in 1985, by which time it was estimated that there were 1,600 Moose in Coös, Carroll and parts of Grafton counties.[180] Black bears were occasionally reported, and wild turkeys were sometimes seen. Raccoon, deer, and skunk remained plentiful. No rattlesnakes had been reliably reported in town for decades, and even the once-aptly-named Rattlesnake Island had yielded no cousins of "Sweet Marie" for a long time.

The most popular big-game sport continued to be deer hunting, with Lakes Region Sports & Photo (Joe Melanson) being a popular supply depot and gathering place for participants.

### Ice Boating and Ice Surfing

Ice boating drew a small group of devotees throughout the 1980s. The sport was difficult to schedule due to widely varying ice conditions, snow accumulations, and temperatures.

On January 15, 1983, the Don Fellows Invitational Regatta, one of two major New England ice boating competitions, took place on Lake Wentworth. Wolfeboro enthusiast Leigh Turner was the only local entrant in a field of 11, a small turnout due to a snowstorm. Winner was Jeff Kent of Quincy, MA. From time to time the Great Lake Winnipesaukee Long Distance Ice Boat Race was held on a course from Wolfeboro to Centre Harbor and was more of an informal adventure than a speed contest. Typically, about 20 boats took part.[181]

In February 1986 Wolfeboro hosted the World Ice Surfing Championship, the first time the event was held outside of Europe (in 1985 it had been in Helsinki, Finland). Anticipation ran high that Wolfeboro would add a week of sports, festivity, and commercial activity to its winter season, for if the 1986 competition proved to be a success, others would be held. Cliff Simoneau, president of the Chamber of Commerce, helped with the planning. Unfortunately, the wind failed to cooperate, and neither the trials nor the final races were held. The 1986 *Town Report* contained this comment, curious inasmuch as it did not mention that the event never took place:

> The 1986 World Ice Surfing Championships brought hundreds of visitors. This event returns as the North American Championships.

In February 1987 hopes were raised again, and it was anticipated that the International Ice and Snow Sailing World Championships would bring up to 10,000 visitors to town. Sponsors were Michelob Light beer, Hamel Real Estate and Century 21-Dockside Realty. As the race days approached, Lake Winnipesaukee had only three to 10 inches of ice and was covered with nearly a foot of snow. The event was canceled. Souvenir posters, clothes, and other items, and a special postal cancellation remained as mute evidence of events that were hoped to be, but destined otherwise.[182]

### Ice Hockey

In 1981 Brian Hastings, science teacher at Kingswood Regional Junior High School, organized the Wolfeboro Youth Hockey League—known beginning in 1983 as the Back Bay Hockey Association—reintroducing a team sport that had not been active in town for many years. Participants were divided into four groups: grades 1-3, grades 4-6, junior high, and senior high. In the winter of 1982-1983, 80 boys and girls took part. A charge of $35 was levied to pay for ice time rented in a Gilford rink.

The first victory for the newly-formed Back Bay Hockey Association took place on January 15, 1984, when the Back Bay Indians (4th through 6th graders) played North Conway and won 7-2. The game included a hat trick (the scoring of three goals by a single player) by Billy Palm, two goals by Miles Barnard, with Rick Dearborn and Tyler Phillips each making one goal and one assist. Matt Rollins and Katy Phillips each had assists.

In 1986 the Back Bay Mites A team (age 8 and under) was undefeated for the season, finishing 21-0 in the Seacoast League. In the final game of the series—a contest with Laconia on February 22—scorers from Wolfeboro included Tony Hutchins, Caleb Rudolph, Danny Berry, P.J. Curran, and Robbie Newhall.

On December 6, 1987, the Back Bay Youth Hockey Midget players scored a 10-2 victory over Concord. Eric Assimakopoulos and Mike Hale scored three goals apiece, while John Swenson held his own in the net with help from Brandon Donovan, Jim Dearborn and Chris Laase on defense.

In 1988 the Squirt A team took the Seacoast League team with a 6-2 victory over Laconia, and the Squirt B team finished second in the league with a 5-4 triumph over Biddeford, ME.

On Feb. 3, 1989, the Mites upset York, ME, 11-1. Allie Skelley led the scoring with a hat trick, Chris MacLeod and Kevin Garrett got two goals, and Mal Hazeltine, Zach Antonucci, and Kris Newhall scored one goal.

In tournament play in Exeter in December 1989, the Back Bay Indians wiped out the Tritons from Cape Ann, MA, with Zach Antonucci scoring a remarkable six goals, Chris MacLeod delighting spectators with a hat trick, Brian Eaton and Eric Kaskiewicz registering two goals apiece, and single scores from Geordy Hutchinson, Mark Galloway, Matt Young and Dylan Pappas.

The newly-formed Men's All-Star Hockey Team improved its record to 3-1 on March 3, 1990, with a 5-4 win over North Conway. Local adult players included George Rogers, Bob Hughes, Rich Caples, Scott MacDonald, Greg Cefelo, Tim Heckman, Chris Pappas, Andy O'Shaughnessy, Dave Alessandroni, Tim Roy, Rick Eaton and goalies Dave O'Brien and Mike Hauser.

In spring 1990 the Pee Wee C team of the Back Bay Indians Youth Hockey Association won the three-day Dover Invitational Tournament. Players included: Keith Garrett, Peter McKenzie, Chris Swasey, Andy McLetchie, Scott MacLeod, George Stevens, Mike Kaskiewicz, Dan Chase, Eric True, Dan Peterson, Jesse Hale, Willy Laase, Ryan George, and Tom Antonucci.[183]

### Ice Skating

The biggest ice hockey news of the decade was the building and use of the indoor ice rink at the Abenaki Recreation Area. Paid for by a fund-raising campaign and named after Paul ("Pop") Whalen, athletic director at Brewster Academy from 1954 to 1971, the facility was dedicated on Saturday evening, January 7, 1989, when Whalen and his wife Winifred were honored by about 185 attendees. Sue Glenn was director.[184] On March 16-19, 1990, the rink hosted the first annual Pop Whalen Invitational Youth Hockey Tournament.

Figure skating became popular at the Abenaki Recreation Area, first on outdoor rinks and later under cover when the Pop Whalen Rink opened. The Abenaki Figure Skating Club was formed in 1985, and by 1986 there were 125 enrolled. Offered were lessons under the auspices of the United States Figure Skating Association.[185]

In 1986 Bonnie Varney, a U.S. Figure Skating Association certified instructor, offered figure skating lessons through the Wolfeboro Recreation Department.

In spring 1987 Hillary Palm, a sixth-grade student at Carpenter School, turned in fine performances at several skating competitions and brought home a bronze medal from the 22nd annual Worcester Open.

In 1990 Judith C. Breuninger of Wolfeboro was named publicity chairman of the first United States International Precision Skating Championship to be held in Boston. She had been well known in the field for many years.[186]

### Jet Skiing

Jet skiing became a popular and controversial activity. Wings Jet Ski, a commercial firm offering rentals, held a seven-event regatta on Rust Pond on July 25, 1982. As time went on, protests were raised against the noise and disruption said to be caused by jet skiers on various NH ponds and lakes. On June 6, 1989, the Legislature enacted new rules providing operators had to be 16 years old, could not go faster than headway speed (no wake) when leaving or approaching shore, had to go in a straight line at least 300 feet from shore before increasing speed, etc.

On July 8, 1989, supporters of a ban on jet skis on Lake Wentworth, Crescent Lake, and Rust Pond met in Town Hall to discuss the threat the sport posed to herons, loons, and the good times of others seeking to enjoy the lakes. Tod Blodget and Eric Arctander were among those giving commentaries. In August, State Safety Commissioner Robert Flynn issued a ban (effective October 1) against jet skis on these three lakes. In the same month the state held an informational meeting in Gilford that drew more jet ski defenders than opponents. As time went on, peace settled in, and one- and two-person sit-down craft such as the Sea-Doo began to replace the noisier jet skis.[187]

### Jumproping

Bette Bourque (who married Robert Frazier) formed and developed the Hot Peppers Jumprope Club. The name "Hot Peppers" was suggested by first-grader Kevin Bourque, while the team's logotype was from combined ideas of second-grader Kevin Bourque and third-grader Allie Skelley. The club began in autumn 1988 with 97 Carpenter School students from kindergarten through sixth grade, and by the early 1990s included about double that number.

Records of outstanding performers were posted in the Carpenter School gymnasium. In 1990 for the second year in a row Carpenter had five state jump-rope contest champions, the winners that year being Amy Kissell, Kristy Smith, Kevin Bourque, Heather Christle and Christopher Eckhoff. Among other demonstrations the Hot Peppers furnished entertainment at half-time during Kingswood High School Junior Varsity basketball games. The Jump Rope for Heart team is one of three NH teams representing the American Heart Association, and by 1995 the group had raised over $19,000 in donations for that group.[188]

Bette is one of the town's foremost "doers" and has led many recreational and fund-raising activities for school and church groups.

### Karate

This sport became very popular during the decade. Classes were held for a time at Brewster Academy. At the Centre at Wolfeboro on Varney Road, James Cameron conducted classes at Cameron's Uechiryu Karate Studio that attracted dozens of local residents from youngsters to adults who worked toward earning special achievement awards. On many occasions Jim Cameron gave demonstrations in local schools and at community events.

### Lacrosse

Lacrosse was a popular team sport at Brewster Academy where both men's and women's varsity and junior varsity teams were fielded. In 1989 the girls' varsity team beat such opponents in the Lakes Region League as New Hampton, Tilton, Kimball Union, and Derryfield. Head coach of the girls' varsity was Vicki Greenwald, and players included Julie Senecal, Fraser Lewis, Heather Vaillancourt, Noelle Lamperti, Deidre Magnifico, Sarah Larson, Carlene Sullivan, and Megan Boyle.[189]

### Racquetball

Played on indoor courts, this sport enjoyed popularity during the decade, especially during the brief (1980-1982) existence of the Bay Village Racquetball Club on Varney Road and succeeding activities in the same building including the Wolfeboro Racquet Club.

In another location at later date, men's and women's doubles champions were crowned on August 23, 1987, when Larry Hunter and Gary Morris won the men's title with a 6-3, 6-4 victory over Andre Lavoie and John Staples. Barbara Nordin and Noreen Pitts took the women's championship, beating Peg Hunter and Kathy Morris, 6-1, 6-1.[190]

### Rowing

Using the premise that the first intercollegiate contest of any kind was a crew race that took place in 1852 when teams from Harvard and Yale met on Wolfeboro Bay and at Centre Harbor, Brewster Academy decided to revive the "great crew tradition" on May 9, 1990, with a race against Derryfield School. Three races were held: men's first boat, men's second boat, and women's first boat. Local rowers included Bill Meehan of Alton; Peter Elkins, Gerald Holmberg, and Kate Radley of Wolfeboro; and Lauren Sheahan of Tuftonboro. Susan McLean of Wolfeboro was the coxswain. Brewster received two shells donated toward the end of the 1988-1989 school year by Mr. and Mrs. John Runstad, parents of Brewster alumna Stacey Runstad, Class of 1987.[191]

### Rugby

Brewster Academy hosted a Canadian team for international rugby matches on May 5-6, 1990. The teams met twice. The Huron Heights team scored 10-4 in the first tilt, but Brewster came back with a 4-0 victory. Rugby grew in popularity, but remained an unfamiliar sport to many Americans.[192]

### Sailing

Brewster Academy had an active sailing program during the decade and engaged in competition with Pingree School, Phillips Academy, and others. In 1984 the Brewster sailing team under Coach Whiteman Smith was named champion in the New England secondary school circuit following a competition at Harvard on May 6.

On July 11, 1981, the Lake Wentworth Kenney Shore Classic was held on a triangular, windswept course. Roger F. Murray III and Russ Schundler took first place, Al Cavalieri captured second, and Terry Conley and Alan Thompson came in third. On August 15 the Wolfeboro Regatta saw 13 yachts compete. The overall winner was Ralph Mosher, Clifton Park, NY. Wolfeboro participants included Andy Anderson, sixth; Carl Willgoose, eighth; and Tim Taussig, eleventh. On the next day, August 16, there were 200 entries in the Stamp Act Memorial Regatta held on Lake Wentworth. On August 6 and 7, 1983, the Wolfeboro Corinthian Yacht Club sponsored the third annual Wolfeboro Sailing Regatta in Lake Winnipesaukee near Little Barndoor Island. Twenty boats measuring from 22 to 32 feet long competed.[193]

Arguably, the most publicized sailing event of the decade was the 1990 championship race of the National Ensign Class Association held during the week of August 12 under the sponsorship of the Wolfeboro Corinthian Yacht Club, John O'Connell, director. The Association was comprised of 69 fleets throughout the country, with 1,775 boats. Twenty-three craft—including five from Wolfeboro—inaugurated the first national sailing competition of any kind to be based in Wolfeboro. Headquarters for brightly-colored vessels was the Pinckney Boathouse on the Brewster campus. Bill Faget, a dentist from New Orleans, was the winner.[194]

### Shooting

In July 1985 Arthur Jackson of Wolfeboro took second place in an international shooting competition held in England and received the Prince of Wales medal. He was the only member from NH on the U.S. Shooting Team. In the 1982 Olympics he had won a bronze medal for marksmanship.[195] In June 1990 in Indiana, two Wolfeboro children, brother and sister Jennifer Meanley, 12, and Brian Meanley, 8, took first and second place by beating 2,000 competitors in their divisions of the national championship competition of bench-rest muzzle-loader rifle shooting. Jennifer also placed first in the adult women's divisions and tied two national records. The entire Meanley family—the two youngsters and their father and stepmother—together walked away with 22 national awards and tied four national records.[196]

### Skiing

In cross-country skiing in the January 1981 Gilford Invitational Nordic Division I meeting, temperatures forced cancellation of cross-country events. In a contest held in North Conway, the girls' cross-country team won four of the five first places.[197]

In 1986 the Kingswood girls' cross-country team captured four of the first five places in a race against Kennett and Plymouth at Abenaki Recreation Area on January 14. Jen Douglass edged teammate Andrea Gagner. Other Kingswood finishers were Amy Babson, fourth; Kim Young, fifth; Theresa DeChiaro, eighth; Julie Fothergill, ninth; Julie Clough, 10th; Hilary Gehman, 12th; Andrea Rollins, 16th; and Stacey Kendall, 21st.

Soon thereafter Jen Douglass topped a field of 80 skiers in the Hanover High Interdivisional Cross-Country Ski Race on January 25, 1986, at the Hanover Country Club. Andrea Gagner came in third; Amy Babson, fifth; Kim Young, eighth; and Theresa DeChiaro, ninth. In the same year Douglass was tapped to participate in the Junior Olympics in California. In 1987 she went to Alaska for the Junior Nationals, one of seven skiers representing her age group in the Eastern Division. Douglass graduated from Kingswood High in 1987 and went to Middlebury College in Vermont, where she achieved further distinctions.[198]

In winter 1981-1982 Howie Bean shared a national title in team competition at Lake Placid, NY, was the only person from NH selected to participate in competition in Europe in January, and won the men's title in the National Nordic Skiing Championships at Bretton Woods. Bean, one of the most acclaimed athletes the town has ever known, won many other honors during the decade. Some wins—including the Presidential Ski Chase at Bretton Woods in 1984—were shared with Jennifer Caldwell of Putney, VT, who became his wife in 1988. Born in 1956, Howie Bean started cross-country skiing at age 14 in the ninth grade.[199]

The Wolfeboro Cross-Country Ski Association, open to all, was formed in time for the 1982-1983 season and maintained a ski course in the Sewall Point area. Much if not most of the trail grooming over the years has been done by Steve Flagg. He also gave ski lessons for the Nordic Skier shop, of which he was an owner, and, in fact, met his wife-to-be Beth in this way; she had received ski lessons as a gift from her sister Chris Karstedt.[200]

The slope at the Abenaki Recreation Area hosted much downhill skiing during the decade, but most competitions were held at the larger ski areas in New Hampshire and Vermont. On January 30, 1982, Becky Hatch outperformed 66 competitors to bring to Wolfeboro the second annual Lakes Region NASTAR (NAtional STAndard Race) Cup. In spring 1987 Jennifer Mynter of Wolfeboro represented the Eastern United States in the U.S. Telemark Skiing Championships in Aspen, CO.

In January 1988 Kingswood boys and girls receiving notice in a three-way meet against Gilford and Laconia at the Gunstock Ski Area included Brett Charvee, Ossie Babson, Todd Waterman, Justin Perry, Lauren Sheahan, Amanda Smith, Rachel Hale, and Stacy Hazeltine.

As part of the February 1988 Winter Festival, 13 skimeisters were named, representing some of the area's finest participants in the sport. Girls included Dana Hutchinson, Chris Sanford, Aimee Frank, Heidi Kendall, and Lindy Kilmer; while boys were Adam Grupp, Kyle Frank, Scott Hansen, Ryan George, Lance Durgan, Curt Grupp, Glen Moyer and Chris Pelletier.[201]

### Sled Dog Races

The New England Sled Dog Club races were held in the fields behind Kingswood High School on January 23, 1982, and drew 100 to 200 spectators.[202]

### Soccer

Top scorers on the Kingswood girls' 1986-1987 varsity soccer teams included tri-captains Jessica Daley and Charlotte Andrews who went on to state competitions.

In November 1990 the Wolfeboro-Tuftonboro team won the County Youth Soccer Tournament. Local team standings were: Wolfeboro Oil, 5-1-2; North Country Scuba Dudes, 5-2-1; True Value, 3-4-1; Bradley's 3-4-1, Avery's 1-6-1. The All-Star team consisted of Kyle Frank, Angela Hutchins, Rob Larson, Kris Newhall, Ted Newman, Ashley Hutchins, Alex Hunt, David DeNee, Jared Burke, Brett Edmunds, Mike Liedtke, Jon Button, Stephanie Hunter, Eric Patten, Todd MacLeod, Scott Hansen and John Foley.

Soccer was an important sport at Brewster Academy. Opponents included Berwick Academy, Hyde School, Holderness, Winchendon School, Kimball Union, Tilton, and Proctor Academy. In 1988 the Brewster men's varsity team captured the Lakes Region Championship title with a season record of 11-5-1.[203]

### Special Olympics

In August 1987 Becky Rich, age 13, was selected as one of two NH gymnasts to compete at the International Special Olympics in South Bend, IN. She brought home gold and bronze medals.[204]

### Swimming

In the summer Brewster Beach and Carry Beach, each supervised by the Wolfeboro Parks and Recreation Department, attracted many swimmers and sunbathers. In March 1989 the town voted to purchase shorefront on Lake Wentworth behind the Allen "A" Resort, where in due course the Allen H. Albee Beach was opened. The town lacked an indoor facility for off-season use by the public, but the Windrifter offered swimming memberships on a private basis, $127 being the charge for a family in 1981.

The Wolfeboro Swim Team comprised nearly 100 members from the Lakes Region and engaged in numerous competitions in the summer. In 1984 the team

Local sports heroine: Heather Sands, award-winning Wolfeboro track star, shown at the Hershey Meet in Pennsylvania in August 1990 when she won the national title with a standing long jump of 8'5", a record that remained unbroken as of the time the present book went to press. With her is Sue Glenn of the Wolfeboro Parks and Recreation Department.

Heather Sands with Joseph Mathes of Wolfeboro, both attending the Hershey Nationals in 1991, a year after Heather's world record. In the mid-1990s Sands was a champion field hockey player for Kingswood Regional High School.

observed its eighth season, having been founded by Howard Pride. Coach in 1984 was Dennis Benz. In August 1986 the team took two first-place finishes at the state meet held in Dover. Andy Benz won the 100-meter backstroke and took second in the 100-meter breaststroke in the boys' 15-18 age group, while Holly Wilson won the 50-meter breaststroke in the girls' 11-12 age group. In 1987 Evan Chapman placed first in the state in backstroke (age 8 and under), Robbie Schundler placed first in the state butterfly (ages 9-10), and Rusty Schundler placed first in the backstroke (ages 11-12). In the annual Fourth of July parade team members rode aboard a large float.[205]

### Tennis

Tennis was played at several different locations in town including Foss Field, Brewster Academy, private courses, and private clubs. In wintertime some local aficionados rented court time at Pick Point Lodges in Tuftonboro. Brewster Academy and Kingswood High organized tennis teams, and the Wolfeboro Parks and Recreation Department sponsored summer competition.

For two weeks in August 1982 the town held the Wolfeboro Open Tennis Tournament with 30 players. Rit Swain won the men's singles 6-4, 6-2 victory over Larry Hunter, and Kathy Why won the women's singles 4-6, 6-1, 6-2 over Trevis Kraft. In 1985 Sherrie Petro-Roy won the women's division and Mike Burke won the men's division of the Open Singles Tournament.

In South Wolfeboro the Springfield Point Tennis Tournament was started in 1982, and by 1987 it had raised more than $5,000 to benefit Huggins Hospital.

In 1988 and 1989 Kingswood High tennis players featured prominently in game accounts included Brooke Rice, Julie Goodrich, Cindi Bell, Jenn Rousseau, Mark Roark, Jason Santoro, Brian Nielsen, Patrick Rice, and Jim Cameron. In 1989 the top women's varsity squad player for Brewster was Kate Goldberg (of Weston, MA) followed by Susanna Maggard (Campbell Hall, NY).[206]

### Track

The Kingswood boys' varsity track team under the guidance of coach Barry Tibbetts won the 1981 Wilderness Track League championship held in Concord.

In May 1983 Eleanor Hogan of the Kingswood girls' track team became the Class I state champion in high jump, with a jump of 5'0". Lauren Douglass placed third overall in javelin with a throw of 99'0". Both went to the Meet of Champions in Concord.

On July 12, 1984, the Wolfeboro Recreation Department team competed in the Hershey State Track and Field Meet in Concord sponsored by the famous chocolate manufacturer. Matt Roberson took second in the softball throw and sixth in the standing long jump; Britt McLoy took fourth in the 800-meter and 400-meter runs; Jimmy Bennett took third in the 1600-meter run, and Jen Ladd placed sixth in the same event. The girls' relay team placed third and included Erin Heppe, Kate Radley, Julie Hansell, and Katie Roark. Kate Radley received third-place heat ribbon in the 100-meter dash. Julie Hansell and Katie Roark took second- and third-place heat ribbons in the 50-meter dash. Shauna Michaud received a ribbon for eighth place in the standing long jump.

In autumn 1984 Kingswood junior David Keslar achieved several recognitions for his cross-country running ability including leading the school team to victory over Inter-Lakes and Alton with a time of 16:23 for a three-mile course. Keslar made the news in succeeding years as well. In May 1985 the Kingswood girls' track team under coach Albert ("Duke") Southard ended the season undefeated for the first time in its history; the record was 17-0. The team also won the Wilderness Track League championship. Pam Urda became the state champion in javelin with a 123'3" throw. In 1989 Megan Donovan was state champion in the same event.

Each year it was usual for several Wolfeboro athletes to give the annual Boston Marathon a try. In 1988 local runners included Dr. John Hammond, Donna Kasianchuk, Becky Lougee, and Kim Young. They ran during cool, overcast and slightly rainy conditions. Hammond turned in a 3:21 performance for his seventh Boston marathon.

In any account of Wolfeboro athletics the name of Heather Sands must be prominent. In July 1988 she, Keri Edmunds, and Willie Swaffield excelled in the standing long jump competition at the NH Hershey Track and Field finals. Heather, 10 years old and about to enter the fifth grade, then went to Pennsylvania for the Hershey Finals, where on August 12 she finished second in nationwide competition with a jump of 6'11-3/4". On July 19, 1990, she jumped 8'5" at the NH State Finals, shattering both the state and *national* standing long jump records, the latter by one inch. A story about her accomplishment appeared on the first page of the *Granite State News*.[207] In the next several years she garnered numerous additional press clippings for her prowess at Hershey and other events. At later Hershey events she was given various honors during opening ceremonies including carrying the New Hampshire state flag one year and the American flag another year, and carrying the torch to light the flame. Heather commented:[208]

> My experiences competing in the national Hershey competition brought me new friends from across the United States along with giving me experiences that I shall always remember. The Hershey challenges have helped prepare me for future athletic competitions.

### Volleyball

Nine area teams gathered on Tuesday, June 12, 1990, at Kingswood High and Middle School gymnasiums to compete in a round-robin style coed adult volleyball tournament. After four hours of competition, the Wolfeboro "Red" team came out on top. Members of this team were: Jody Davis, Paul Harvey, Luanne Heald, Ken Podsen, and Jim and Nancy Thomas.[209]

### Water Skiing

The Abenaki Water Ski Club set up practice and competition courses in Back Bay during the decade. In August 1981 the group hosted the American Water Ski Association tournament, the first large-scale competition to be held in town since 1962. Local residents who achieved press notices in the sport included Bob Hughes, Dan Buttrick, Rick Finethy, Chip Jones, Bill Swaffield, John Jenkins, Skip Klemm, and Rick Jenkins.

In August 1983 an estimated 1,500 spectators gathered at the Town Docks to watch a show put on by the local group. On September 1, 1984, Bill Swaffield set a new men's state record in slalom competition. In 1986 several club members were among the top award winners in the East, per standings released by the American Water Ski Association. Rick Jenkins finished first in the boys' jumping standings with an average of 117.5 feet, and Skip Klemm was number one jumper in the men's veteran division, averaging 108.5 feet with a best of 109. Bill Swaffield in the men's 25-34 age group recorded the third best slalom run of the season in the East, 55 buoys, while breaking his own state record. During July and August 1986 Bill Swaffield was undefeated in his slalom category in New England tournaments, won his second Eastern Regional Slalom title, and went on to score 12th in the National Water Ski Championships in Florida. In August the Manchester *Union Leader / Sunday News* named him Athlete of the Month.

On June 17, 1989, the NH Slalom Open Water Ski Tournament was held on Back Bay. Skiers from all over New England competed. Local skiers Bob and Barbara Hughes and Bill Swaffield won the three divisions.

Wolfeboro skiers earned accolades in other venues as well. In June 1990 Jamie Beauchesne and Bill and Becky Swaffield won their respective divisions at the Vermont Slalom Derby held in Montpelier. Beauchesne skied in the junior boys' division and got 46 consecutive buoys. Bill Swaffield topped the men's 34 m.p.h. field with a score of 57 buoys. In the women's III-IV division, Becky Swaffield was the winner with 27 buoys. In September 1990 Bill Swaffield won his fifth consecutive men's III slalom title when he beat a large field of competitors to sweep all three rounds at the Connecticut Classic Water Ski Tournament in Avon. His 58 buoys broke his New Hampshire slalom record by one buoy and was the highest slalom total run in New England for the year.[210]

### Weightlifting

Two Wolfeboro athletes, Charlie Rogers and Steven Siegel, competed in their first weightlifting meet, under trainer Wayne McClay, on October 7, 1990, in Bellows Falls, VT. They both won fourth place in their weight divisions with totals of 810 pounds for Rogers and 1,210 for Siegel. At a second meet in Bellows Falls on November 10, Olympia Gym competitors Cheryl Parsons, Chris Downs and Ken Jones, in their first meet, and Jan Larson, a 9-year-old competitor, all brought home trophies.[211]

In March 1985 five Kingswood High students competed in a bench-press weightlifting competition at the Franklin Creative Gymnastic Health and Fitness Club. Dave Keniston took third place medal for personal best in the 184-pound weight class with 235 pounds, Jim Bean took second place for his 195-pound lift in the 145-pound weight class, and Adam Quinn and Jon Montgomery tied personal records with 220- and 210-pound lifts in their weight class.[212]

### Wrestling

Brewster Academy participated in wrestling matches with other schools. Notable participants included Ron Burt, Mark Nachman, and Stu Stinchfield.[213]

## FIRE AND RESCUE DEPARTMENTS

### Fire Museum

Donald E.L. Hallock, retired from his decade of work with the Wolfeboro Rail Road, volunteered his services to restore several pieces of antique fire-fighting equipment belonging to the town. Charlene Lehto assisted with painting and decorating. The 1845 Carroll County No. 2 hand pumper was finished in 1981 and was displayed at the Wolfeboro National Bank. Kingswood High School trades students built the Monitor Hose Co. Fire Museum next to the Clark House on South Main Street to provide a home for the apparatus restored by Don Hallock (the Monitor built in Boston by William Hanneman in 1842, Carroll No. 2, and the 1890 Monitor 2-horse hose wagon) and a cosmetically restored c.1875 Amoskeag steam-pumped fire engine and a fire-station signal device loaned to the town by Dave Bowers. Dedication of the facility was in early July 1982. Subsequently, an award was given by the American Association for State and Local History to the Wolfeboro Historical Society and Don Hallock.[214]

### With the Fire Department

In 1981 the Fire Department bought for $7,500 a used 23-foot Penn Yan Century fire boat to replace the old *H.W. Drury*, which was put out for bids.

In 1981 the popularity of woodstoves for home heating was riding the high wave begun in the preceding decade. Many units were improperly installed or were mistreated, resulting in 33 woodstove fire alarms during that year out of a department total of 141 alarms.

In 1982 various types of kerosene-fired heaters became popular. Until recent state legislation provided otherwise, it was illegal to use unvented heaters of this type in homes. Now they were allowed by permit in single-family dwellings. The town of Wolfeboro wanted to ban their use as unsafe, but several other New Hampshire towns were being sued by manufacturers whose units were prohibited. The manufacturers won the day in other places and Kero-Sun and other brands were allowed.[215] However, in Wolfeboro potential problems were averted when Fire Chief Charles ("Zip") Foss expressed great concern and, acting upon the legal opinion given by attorney Frederic L. Cox of the firm of Cox & Sullivan, the town allowed their use only in unoccupied structures.[216]

Firewood sales caused problems due to misleading advertising. It was against the law to use undefined terms such as "load" instead of precise measures such as cord (128 cubic feet). All deliveries were to be accompanied with a written invoice.[217] By 1986 it was estimated that 40.5% of New Hampshire homeowners used wood as their primary or secondary source of heat.[218]

At the 1987 town meeting $275,000 was appropriated for a new ladder truck for the Fire Department.[219] In 1988 Assistant Chief Dr. W. Douglas Kipp retired after 36 years of service with the department. He recalled that the biggest fire he had seen was that in the Central Block on January 1, 1958, and the most tragic situation was that occurring after the Rust Pond Inn fire in 1969 when Gene Lehner died after a fall from the hose tower.

On May 3, 1988, the State Legislature legalized Class C fireworks, but the selectmen outlawed their use in Wolfeboro.

In 1989 the historic old South Wolfeboro firehouse was torn down to make room for a parking lot for Leone and Bigelow, accountants. The owners suggested to the town and the Wolfeboro Historical Society that the two-story wooden structure be relocated and even offered to help pay for the move, but most agreed that the $50,000 to $80,000 needed to preserve it could not be raised.[220]

In the last year of the decade, 1990, the Department answered 215 alarms including 35 box alarms, 133 still alarms, and 7 engineer calls. In responding to the calls, 1,435 miles were traveled and 1,536 hours of labor were used.[221] Chief Charles ("Zip") Foss and the Fire Department were widely acclaimed for their fast response to alarms and the far more serious tragedies they helped prevent or reduce.

### Fire Log

Fires within Wolfeboro resulting in significant damage as reported in the *Granite State News* and in Dr. W. Douglas Kipp's fire log:[222]

**1981, March 5. Cressy residence:** Wentworth Park Road. Living room gutted. Fire caused by overheated fireplace.[223]

**1981, May 25. Clearwater Lodges:** North Main Street. Cottage gutted. Two visitors from New York lost all their belongings when they left a charcoal grill going overnight.[224]

**1981, June 5. Cider Press Restaurant:** Middleton Road. Cellar fire. Minor damage.[225]

**1981, June 28. Allen "A":** Wall and attic of cottage burned.

**1981, July 5. Ray Dumont residence:** Jiminy Drive. Electrical fire caused minor structural damage.[226]

**1981, August 12. Fire truck stolen, set afire, gutted:** A Wolfeboro teenager and his companion from New York were arrested, charged, and subsequently found guilty of stealing a 1978 pumper fire engine in Tuftonboro, driving it around Wolfeboro, and burning it near the Brockhouse plant on Route 109A.[227]

**1981, November 19. Velmore Collette house:** Endicott Street. Ell and shed burned. Dogs saved by fire crew. Intense smoke. Damage: $8,000.[228]

**1981, December 20. Norman Poisson residence:** Robin Acres. Structural fire. Minor damage.[229]

**1982, March 1. Log skidder fire:** Waumbeck Road. Skidder badly burned.[230]

**1982, March 31. Gene Head's store:** Lake Wentworth. Partitions burned. Caused by overheated chimney. Damage: $500.[231]

**1982, April 14.[232] Bruce Twyon residence:** Lakeview Drive. Upper bedroom gutted from electrical fire. No one at home at the time. One dog saved and one dog killed in fire. Extensive damage.

**1982, April 14. Brockhouse plant:** Shavings of steel, aluminum, and magnesium combined in a collection system ignited. Damage: $400.

**1982, August 19. Doug LeBlanc's trailer:** College Road. Destroyed by fire. Metal trailer and built-on wooden porch. Owned by Mary Warren; rented by Mr. and Mrs. LeBlanc. Two pet cats died. Only a wedding photo album was saved. On August 20, the fire flared up again.[233]

**1982, November 11. Truck fire:** Belonged to Jerry York. Route 28 and Trotting Track Road. Extensive damage.[234]

**1982, November 26. Douglas Keating cottage:** McCarthyanna Road, Museum Shores. Kitchen and living room burned. Extensive damage.[235]

**1983, April 12. Barry Caswell residence:** York Road. Destroyed. Fire due to greasy pan igniting on stove while owner slept. Firemen found road impassable due to mud.[236]

**1983, August 12. Car fire:** Mountain West Condominiums. Vehicle destroyed.[237]

**1983, September 17. Bell residence:** Center Street. Kitchen and contents burned.

**1983, November 3. Nicholas Skaterdas cottage:** A.k.a. Ashby Camp. Pleasant Valley Road. Walls and ceiling of two-room building burned. Damage: $1,000.[238]

**1983, December 30. Lawrence Essember residence:** Hopewell Point off Forest Road. Total loss by fire: $70,000.[239]

**1984, February 8. John Donnelly residence:** South Wolfeboro Bay. Total loss, $100,000. Road to house plowed but not sanded and was very icy; firemen could not reach the fire in time.[240]

Donald E.L. Hallock with two pieces of antique fire equipment he restored for the Fire Museum on South Main Street. Above is shown the Carroll County No. 2 hand pumper built in 1845, on display in 1981 in the lobby of the Wolfeboro National Bank.

Don works on the Monitor Hose No. 1 wagon in the driveway of his Clark Road home. Hallock did most of the restoration, and Charlene Lehto did much of the painting and decoration. (Donald Hallock Collection)

Restored Carroll No. 2 fire "tub" in the 1980s, shown on an out-of-town visit to Newburyport, MA. Personnel left to right: Arthur Brunt, Richard Goldthwait, Frank DeRamer, Allyn Perkins, and Charles Sturtevant. Restoration was under the direction of Donald Hallock. (Lee M. Stevens, Newburyport, photograph)

Interior of the Monitor Hose Co. reproduction fire house in Clark Park as exhibits were being put into place in July 1982. Shown to the left is the restored horse-drawn wagon, Monitor Hose 1, while in the background is a circa 1875 Amoskeag horse-drawn steam pumper made in Manchester, on loan from the collection of Dave and Christie Bowers. (Bruce Lorry photograph)

**1984, August 25. Boat fire:** At Melody (a.k.a. Varney) Island, handled by Safety Services Marine Patrol.[241]

**1984, August 28. Car fire:** Pleasant Valley Road. Vehicle owned by Mrs. Philip Petry. Total loss.[242]

**1984, October 7. Brush fire:** Cotton Valley Road. Caused by passing train.[243]

**1984, December 21. Alan Harding residence:** Oakwood Road. Gutted; total loss.[244]

**1985, February 7. Dwight Bickford residence:** Fire caused by improperly installed woodstove. $10,000 damage.[245]

**1985, April 2. Jet plane crash:** Air Force F-106 jet (all-weather interceptor, top speed 1,519 m.p.h., wingspan 38') on a training mission crashed in the woods off Tibbetts Road (off Route 28). Plane caught fire. Pilot John Anderson ejected and walked to Route 28 near the Center of Hope where he was picked up by Dennis Glidden. He had been on a training mission out of Otis Air Force Base. The wreckage was found later by Fish and Game officer David Beyer and Donald Meader who were searching the area in Meader's airplane. The press was not allowed any closer than 200 yards. TV crews were on hand from Manchester and Boston. Wreckage was cut up and removed.[246]

**1985, July 21. Falls Apartments:** Center Street. Four-apartment building. Second floor, attic and roof fire. Residents evacuated safely. Firefighter David Johnson was treated at Huggins Hospital for smoke inhalation. Residents including Karen Fontaine and daughter Crystal lost many possessions. Investigation revealed that despite state law, no smoke detectors had been installed. No charges were filed against the owner.[247]

**1985, August 29. Boat fire:** Winter Harbor, no injuries, boat total loss, responded together with the Tuftonboro Fire Department.[248]

**1985, September 14. Car fire:** In parking lot at Lauber Carpet, Wolfeboro Falls. Moderate damage.[249]

**1985, September 21. Berry Mill:** Center Street. Attic, roof, and side of building burned, despite there being sprinklers in working order in the mill. Fire began about 8 p.m. Firemen from five nearby communities assisted. A metal roof had been installed over an old wooden roof, thus enclosing the fire, encouraging its spread, and making it difficult for firemen to determine the best location to combat it.[250]

**1985, November 29. Car fire:** Central Avenue. Engine backfired through carburetor. Total loss.[251]

**1985, December 19. Brockhouse plant:** LP gas tank exploded on truck, causing damage. Roger Buford received minor burns.[252]

**1985, December 31. House on Bay Street:** Structure belonging to Apple Hill Trust gutted. Damage: $30,000. Caused by an improperly installed woodstove. Four occupants in the house were not injured.[253]

**1986, March 8. Douglas Meuse cabin:** Beach Pond Road. Destroyed.[254]

**1986, May 15. Tire fire at the tire dump:** Ignited by a brush fire near the town incinerator. 50 firemen responded including some from Ossipee and Tuftonboro. Brad Harriman, contractor, helped bury the fire with sand. It later rekindled and had to be put out again.[255]

**1986, May 15. Nyquist residence:** Oakwood Road. Put out with the help of the Alton Fire Department. Extensive damage.[256]

**1986, July 17. Boat fire:** Off Oakwood Road on South Wolfeboro Bay. Boat was total loss.[257]

**1986, September 4. Truck set on fire:** Outside of Down East Seafood on Lehner Street. Considerable damage.[258]

**1986, October 27. Scott house:** In this South Main Street building Nancy Elliott set her clothes on fire, was hospitalized, but later died from burns.[259]

**1987, May 30. Wolfeborough Railroad Station:** Lightning strike just after midnight caused extensive fire damage to roof, and during the course of firefighting, water damage occurred to the interior. Loss estimated at $179,000. Soon rebuilt.[260]

**1987, July 3. Car fire:** Route 28 near Ossipee line. Car found in flames when the Fire Department arrived. A driver had attempted a U-turn and was hit by another vehicle.[261]

**1987, July 25. Peter Brewitt house:** Bay Street. Fire destroyed barn and front of house. On October 25 the Fire Department had a controlled burn to level the remaining structure.[262]

**1988, April 17. Bruce Dawson residence:** Pleasant Valley. Approximately $50,000 damage from bedroom fire. The Fire Department was delayed about 10 minutes in responding while the owners of the house drove to the Police Station to report the blaze.[263]

**1988, June 25. Earle Steele residence:** Alpine Meadows. Small fire damaged vestibule and part of roof.[264]

**1988, July 31. Edna Nerney camp**: Lake Wentworth, Moose Point. Unoccupied for about a year. Heavily damaged. $45,000 loss.[265]

**1988, November 12. Truck fire:** In parking lot next to Odd Fellows Hall, Wolfeboro Falls. Vehicle belonged to the Hurd Roofing and Siding Co.[266]

**1989, February 8. Harvey Brown residence:** Trask Mountain Road. Unoccupied. Totally destroyed. Loss: $70,000 to $80,000.[267]

**1989, March 11. Gerald Hudson camp:** Nary Shores Road. Oil from french fries ignited and set kitchen afire.[268]

**1990, April 6. Tire fire:** 250 old tires caught fire at the town landfill. Firemen doused the blaze in 90 minutes.[269]

**1990, June 19. LaPointe home:** Lightning strike totally destroyed the Jennifer Circle home of Ricky and Brenda LaPointe and their three children, who were not home at the time. A fund was set up to help this popular family rebuild.[270]

**1990, October 9. Barry Caswell residence:** Totally consumed by flames by the time the Fire Department arrived.[271]

**1990, December 7. Carol McKeon residence:** Estabrook Road. Burned-out remains of structure found by painters in the morning; the fire had occurred at night without anyone noticing. Damage: $50,000.[272]

**1990, December 25. Tragedy averted:** An operating smoke detector roused Paul and Letitia Chiaravalle and their two children early Christmas morning when a fireplace ignited timbers in a wall. The Fire Department had 24 respondents to the alarm, and the blaze was quickly quelled, although not before extensive smoke damage resulted. Fortunately, no personal belongings—not even Christmas presents—were lost. The family spent Christmas in cheery surroundings at the Wolfeboro Inn.[273]

### The Wolfeboro Department of Rescue

Formed in 1965 the Wolfeboro Rescue Squad became the Department of Rescue under the authority of the selectmen in 1973 and was a town division staffed by volunteers. In 1977 Robert ("Peter") Friend was named captain, a position he filled capably until May 1985 when he was succeeded by Peter D. Hayes.

By 1987 it had accomplished much. In that year it had an annual operating budget of $7,000 plus help from various organizations and individuals. During the same year it was estimated that each member had donated about 350 hours in responding to calls, attending meetings, receiving instruction, and other activities, for a total of 4,100 hours of volunteer service. Each year at the Huggins Hospital Street Fair department personnel were on hand to show equipment, discuss operations, and to answer questions. In 1988 the selectmen voted to place the Rescue Squad under the direction of the Fire Department, but this did not meet with favor among members of the former. Soon the vote was rescinded.[274]

In 1990 the Department of Rescue answered 154 calls for assistance, which included 28 motor vehicle accidents (one of which was fatal), 101 medical calls, 25 fires, and 5 miscellaneous.[275]

One of the great rescues of the decade was made by a young boy. Lance Durgan, 10, of Wolfeboro, was operating a paddle boat on May 23, 1987, in Winter Harbor near the Piping Rock Motel. He saw a floating object in the water, thought it was a log, but upon drawing near realized it was a child. He pulled him out and called for help. The youth was rushed to Huggins Hospital and then to the Maine Medical Center, where he was listed in stable condition. Lance was commended by the Wolfeboro selectmen, given a plaque, and recognized nationally by a printed tribute in *The Congressional Record*.[276]

## LAW ENFORCEMENT

### It Can Happen Here

Crime proliferated during the decade. In the 1989 *Town Report*, Police Chief Stanley E. Stevens compared the current era with that of several decades earlier. In the 1940s the five major problems in local schools were talking in class, chewing gum, making noise, running in the halls, and getting out of turn in line. Now things were quite different, and heading the list of offenses were drug use, alcohol abuse, teenage pregnancy, teenage suicide, and rape—situations that although unfortunate were often far worse in larger towns and cities across America.

In 1989 there were 861 reportable incidents, or an average of more than two each day. ("A reportable incident is one serious enough to require a written report. It does not include accident reports or miscellaneous complaints.")[277]

The 1984 *Town Report* told of the Uniform Crime Report program in which:

> Seven offenses were chosen to serve as an index for gauging fluctuations in the overall volume and rate of crime. These were known jointly as the Crime Index and included the violent crimes of murder and non-negligent manslaughter, forcible rape, robbery and aggravated assault; and the property crimes of burglary, larceny-theft, and motor vehicle theft. By congressional mandate, arson was added as the eighth Index offense in 1979.

The rating was done on the Index crimes per 100,000 population adjusted for the fact that New Hampshire reporting entities did not have 100,000 people (the most populous entity was Manchester with 94,695). The crime rate per 100,000 in Wolfeboro for 1984 was 5,340, which was above average for the state. Of the reporting entities, Berlin had a rate of 1,809, Claremont 3,577, Concord 4,997, Derry 4,068, Dover 3,616, Durham 2,869, Nashua 4,102, Portsmouth 4,654, and Rochester 2,572. The only other reporting entities in the state with a crime rate exceeding 5,000 per 100,000 were Hampton 5,758, Keene 5,427, Laconia 6,946 (highest for the state), and Manchester 5,931.

Wolfeboro had the fifth highest crime rate of the state out of the 21 jurisdictions listed. Chief Stanley E. Stevens said that the local figure and its comparison to national averages was closer to what would be expected in a city with a population of about 25,000.

### Why?

What happened?

There was no easy answer. The world was changing and Wolfeboro with it. Drugs were a common problem and were said to be readily available in town, but dealers in drugs were seldom identified. Alcohol abuse played a part as it had for decades, and when combined with high-speed cars, was a formula that guaranteed disaster.

Mischievousness—starting trouble for the hell of it—dramatically increased. Bomb scares at Kingswood High were so common as to cause little comment after a while. On December 6, 1981, there was one, followed by another two days later on the 8th, the latter combined with two false fire alarms. On May 4, 1984, police were called to Kingswood for another threatened bombing, another five days later on May 9, one more on November 8, a further one on June 6, 1986, another on December 7, 1988—and this is just a *partial* list. Brewster Academy was not immune, and on Monday, October 23, 1989, a young female voice called in a bomb threat for Estabrook Hall, which was evacuated and later reopened when nothing was found. In an apparently unrelated situation employees and customers of seven Wolfeboro businesses including two inns were forced to evacuate their premises between midnight and 2:00 a.m. early Sunday morning, November 11, 1990, following telephoned bomb threats. No explosives were found. In this case the Wolfeboro Police Department was hot on the trail of a man who was seen at several of the establishments during the time in question. Detective Chris Walsh interviewed the 26-year-old resident, who made arrangements to turn himself in.[278]

Nationwide, things were not much better. The latest crime was to put poison in Tylenol capsules. Some said that intense media coverage given such incidents simply prompted other citizens to commit such acts. Dramas, documentaries, and other programs featuring violence, sex, and drugs were plentiful on the television screen, and quite a bit of it translated into actions on the local scene.[279]

Broken windows, vandalized cars, and damaged signs were reported frequently. Other crimes in the senseless category included booby-trapping a snowmobiler, damaging the Nutcracker statue in front of the Camelot Book Store (similar reports recur over the years), slashing car tires, destroying a mailbox, shooting out Christmas lights, cutting a telephone line, and hitching a truck to the town Christmas tree in front of Black's Paper Store and attempting to haul it off.

The vast majority of such offenses were committed by male teenagers and men in their twenties, although women occasionally appeared on the police blotter as well. Representative of the fairer sex is the case of a 23-year-old woman charged with 12 counts of criminal mischief including slashing screens at Carpenter School, uprooting flowers, and vandalizing automobiles in the downtown district. Women also comprised the majority of those arrested for shoplifting.

In September 1981 an 18-year-old was arrested three times in the course of a single night, a veritable one-man rampage. His alleged offenses included breaking a window at Black's Paper Store (cutting himself in the process), disorderly conduct upon arrival at Huggins Hospital, and upon release from there, the theft of a truck.

A particularly misguided 21-year-old man was found guilty in 1982 for vandalizing cars and buildings, breaking a large window in Schillereff's Bovine shop, and damaging an oil truck. This fellow received a 30-day jail sentence (20 days suspended), fined, and ordered to pay restitution and attend Alcoholics Anonymous meetings. In December 1987 a 15-year-old Wolfeboro boy was arrested and charged with breaking more than $4,000 worth of windows.

Almost in relief were occasional reports of non-destructive crimes such as one in July 1983 noting that two counterfeit $10 bills had been passed in town and had been detected by sharp-eyed tellers at the Kingswood Bank.[280]

In August 1988 about $30,000 worth of senseless vandalism was committed at Pine Hill Cemetery by damaging 30 headstones.[281]

In 1989 and 1990 the town received some publicity of the kind not wanted by the Chamber of Commerce when a fugitive who had lived here from 1963 to 1975 and again from 1985 to 1987 was featured in two separate shows on the Fox network TV program, *America's Most Wanted*. Earlier, the man had been arrested several times by Wolfeboro police and had served jail time, but allegedly went on to other localities to conduct scam operations, run prostitution rings, and engage in what was called "fantasy fraud" — including impersonating a State Police officer to gain access to a computer system and destroy his arrest record and warrants. At another time he was so successful in his police disguise that one town hired him as its police chief.[282]

### Sex, Abuse, Neglect, Discrimination

Child abuse, sexual crimes, and other offenses involving the intrusion of one person — often a family member — upon another's body or an adult upon a youngster, became endemic. Data showed that child abuse was up 250% between 1983 and 1985 and that one in four cases involved sexual abuse. 68% of the cases were substantiated or "founded."[283]

In a curious case a resident of Tamworth voluntarily confessed to authorities that he had raped his 12-year-old stepdaughter in Wolfeboro in January 1983. He claimed that a 1965 state law protected those who *reported* child abuse and that as he had done the reporting, he should be immune from prosecution. It was stated in the NH Supreme Court that the purpose of the immunity provision in the law is to protect someone from liability if a reported child abuse turned out to be false. Justice David Souter (who years later was named to the U.S. Supreme Court) disagreed that the clause's intent applies to those committing the act. Justice John King said those *committing* a child abuse act "can't *suspect* child abuse." The case dragged through the courts. In April 1987 the defendant agreed to plead guilty to aggravated felonious sexual assault, and in exchange he was sentenced to two to six years in NH State Prison with 20 months suspended. He was to be evaluated for participation in a sexual offender program.[284]

The public became increasingly aware of the problem. By 1987 Shirley Ganem, Wolfeboro selectman, had been the director of the NH Task Force on Child Abuse for five years. Effective local solutions included the August 1986 opening of Harbor House as a safe refuge for children experiencing difficulties with family situations including neglect, abuse, and in some instances, unavoidable problems.

Penny Hauser Warren, a divorced mother of two young sons and foster parent to four teenagers, was the driving force behind the establishment of Harbor House and a protective network to help children which began in summer 1984. Discussions with Detective Chris Walsh of the Wolfeboro Police Department and Selectman Shirley Ganem, early assistance from the Evangelical

Bible Church, and a loan facilitated by Bob Fournier at the Kingswood Bank made Harbor House a reality.[285]

On May 2, 1990, representatives of the Carroll County Against Domestic Violence and Rape organization came to Wolfeboro for the first time to enlist volunteers to add to their roster of 30.[286]

In 1981 a 23-year-old woman was employed for 34 hours a week as a clerk and stock person by the Stationery Shop (Mr. and Mrs. Raymond Sanborn were proprietors at the time; they later sold the business). According to testimony before the State Human Rights Committee, when the shop owners learned that the employee was pregnant and unmarried, her working hours were cut to 16 per week, then to zero. The young lady protested that this was illegal, whereupon she was told that she could leave immediately. The Sanborns were ordered to pay over $7,000 in fees, expenses, lost wages, and reimbursement.[287]

### The Barham Case

On August 14 or 15, 1981, Raymond Barham, 52, who had moved to Crescent City, CA, from Wolfeboro in 1978, called his former wife, who lived in town, to ask for money. Addicted to morphine from treatment received during wartime military service, he had been trying to make a new life for himself, and she was helping by sending monthly checks. He had run short and now wanted more. His request was denied.

Angered, he flew to New Hampshire on August 28, rented a car in Manchester, drove to Kittery, ME, to buy a gun and bullets, and then went to the Huggins Hospital Coffee Shop to watch and wait for his ex-wife and her boarder, Norman Walpole, age 56, to leave the Episcopal Church after Sunday morning services. He followed them to their home on North Main Street and shot and killed Walpole in the driveway. Barham was subsequently arrested, tried, convicted, and sentenced to life in prison without parole.[288]

### Burglaries, Thefts

In 1981 three men from Massachusetts spent part of a week in Wolfeboro and Alton planning burglaries. In the early hours of one morning they crept into three houses on Pleasant Street while the occupants were sleeping and stole an estimated $5,000 worth of sterling silver flatware from two homes and apparently found none in the other. Another burglary was accomplished in Alton. The three burglars were captured, and most of the loot was recovered.[289]

Not long thereafter a particularly patriotic thief—or one who hoped to be once he had the right equipment—absconded with an American flag and its staff from the Community Center on Lehner Street.[290]

The Back Bay Boathouse was the site of several burglaries and quite a few fights and rowdy incidents. In 1981 a 21-year-old Wolfeboro man used a key to enter and was caught by employees lying in wait inside. This apparently solved two previous burglaries amounting to about $2,000. Around the same time in an unrelated incident, a memorable fight at the bar started Saturday night, injured the participants and damaged the restaurant, was broken up by police, and then continued early Sunday morning necessitating a return call from the Police Department.[291]

On the morning of September 29, 1982, shoplifters struck the Wool Corner, Mood's, and the Ladies' Elk Shop and made off with over $600 in merchandise. Suspects were identified soon thereafter. On October 11, 1982, someone forcibly entered Mood's by prying open the front door and took $3,100 in women's clothing. In early August 1983 Carolyn Caplan of Florida, who had displayed jewelry at a fair at Kingswood High, stopped for dinner at the East of Suez Restaurant. A window in her car was broken, and $110,000 worth of merchandise was stolen.

In January 1984 a $42,000 Porsche 928S automobile was stolen from Lawless Buick-Chevrolet on Route 28. Two weeks later the vehicle was found abandoned in a parking garage in Portland, ME, apparently undamaged. In May 1985 $19,000 worth of items was stolen from a residence on Route 28. Two Wolfeboro men in their twenties were subsequently arrested.

A 66-year-old Wolfeboro woman was dragged several feet down Railroad Avenue after a male juvenile from Milton attempted to steal her purse. The suspect was chased away by local men and jumped into a car driven by another male found to be from West Newfield, ME. The two 17-year-olds were arrested shortly afterward.

In February 1989 burglars made off with a 400-pound safe from the Granite State Coin Company in Clarke Plaza after smashing the door with a sledge hammer. It contained life insurance policies, a marriage certificate, and citizenship papers in addition to inventory. Owner Melvin Chute offered a reward for its return.[292]

Two robbers held up the owner of the New England Craftsmen Association shop on North Main Street on June 25, 1990. Nearly $1,300 in cash and checks and a $400 necklace were reported taken. One robber ordered proprietor Monique DeBease to hand over her bank bag, claiming to have a gun in a paper bag he was carrying. His confederate threatened to shoot a woman customer. Police were frustrated in their investigation inasmuch as the customer had disappeared and could not be questioned.[293]

### Accidents

The decade of the 1980s was particularly unfortunate in its record number of deaths involving motor vehicles. Time and again funerals were held for Wolfeboro accident victims. Many more were injured or hospitalized. In 1985 the Police Department analyzed accident frequencies in terms of the days of the week they occurred and reported that more took place on a Wednesday than on any other day, followed by Tuesday, Saturday, Monday, Thursday, and then a tie between Friday and Sunday.[294]

On Wednesday afternoon, October 14, 1981, nine-year-old Nicole Jutras was in the crosswalk at North Main and Mill Streets and was struck by George Singleton, 76, who was cited for failure to yield. Nicole died a few days later.

Two weeks later on October 28, four lifelong Wolfeboro residents—Steven Osgood, 22; Kerry P. Hamlin, 23; Robert A. Newhall, 28; and Allen Evans, 24—were killed instantly when their high-performance car slammed into a row of mailboxes and a large tree on North Main Street near the intersection with Highland Terrace.

In October 1983 Jill Carlson, 18, a graduate of Brewster Academy, was pronounced dead after an accident on South Main Street near Walt's Lane in which car struck a telephone pole. In 1985 a Wolfeboro man, Scott Jones, 25, died after he jumped from a car driven by a local 19-year-old woman with whom he had been arguing. No charges were filed. Wolfeboro skidder operator, Robert Brown, 61, was killed when his machine rolled over in a logging area off Beach Pond Road. Other vehicular deaths continued to sadden the community.

On June 17, 1987, Howard Geer, 21, of Wolfeboro was injured in a motorcycle accident on North Main Street near the Lakeview Inn. Geer, who was not wearing a helmet, was not at fault, but his head injuries proved fatal, and he died at Huggins Hospital four days later. On November 6 of the same year, Jodi B. Stevens, 17, was killed when her car slid on "black ice" on Route 109 near Wentworth State Park and struck a utility pole. Jodi, an honor student and athlete at Kingswood High, was legally passing another car and was wearing a seat belt.

On Saturday night, May 27, 1989, Trey Whitfield, 18, a senior scheduled to graduate June 3 from Brewster Academy, drowned in Lower Beach Pond when he was with four companions in a boat that capsized. The four other Brewster students swam about 300 yards to shore before missing Whitfield, who apparently did not know how to swim.[295]

### Alcohol and Drugs

The implication of alcohol in automobile accidents was a familiar local scenario. In November 1983 town officials formed the Drunk Driving Task Force and asked citizens to help. However, problems continued. Within the next three years at least 11 alcohol-related deaths occurred in the Wolfeboro-Ossipee area.

On January 1, 1985, at 2:20 a.m., just after a New Year's Eve party, Jeffrey Labbe, 17, of Wolfeboro was killed when the red Mustang in which he was a passenger crashed into a tree on Waumbeck Road. The driver and another rider were injured. This case, which was said to have involved the use of alcohol by minors, became a *cause célèbre,* and soon thereafter resulted in the formation of a local chapter of SADD (Students Against Driving Drunk). Kingswood High School Principal Brian Berkowitz recommended that a list of telephone numbers be made available to teenagers to call if they needed a ride home or other help. An outpouring of sympathy inspired the Labbe family to write a poem which was published in the newspaper shortly thereafter. It later developed in testimony that Jeffrey's parents, who operated the Pronto Market, had sold kegs of beer to adults conducting the party which their son had attended, and that Jeff on the night of his death had repeatedly asked the driver to slow down. The 19-year-old driver from Melvin Village was sentenced to a 12-month jail term.[296]

In November of the same year Jeffrey C. Fothergill, 19, son of Sandra Fothergill Brown of Wolfeboro, was killed in a crash in a 1982 Dodge Omni driven by a 20-year-old who subsequently pleaded guilty to driving while under the influence of alcohol and cocaine and was sentenced to a year in jail. Both the driver and his passenger Jeffrey had been employed at Hunter's IGA. Jeffrey had never gotten over the loss of his father Robert and a sister who were killed in a head-on automobile accident in Ossipee three years earlier.

Students at Kingswood High sought community support in combating drunk driving. Sharre Connelly, a member of the Kingswood chapter of SADD, stated that there were "parties every weekend" because there was "nothing else to do." Kingswood students had 100 hours of drug and alcohol education in their four years at school, according to school officials. Three concerned SADD members met with the School Board to discuss ways to reduce the alcohol problem. Letters on the subject poured into the *Granite State News.* At an assembly at Kingswood High, 600 students heard about the potentially devastating effects of improper use of alcohol while seeing nine empty chairs representing students who had died in alcohol-related accidents since 1982. A positive note was that non-alcoholic beer was being marketed and was becoming popular.[297]

Reports of the illegal use of controlled substances—particularly marijuana—were plentiful and often involved the younger set, including a 13-year-old Kingswood student. Fortunately, such drugs did not seem to be a major factor in automobile or other accidents, with the aforementioned cocaine-related Fothergill death being an exception.

A notable entry in the drug reports included \$1.3 million dollars worth of marijuana that "went up in smoke" at the town incinerator on September 30, 1983, a cache including ten 80-pound bales seized in an August 27 drug bust plus 80 plants taken in Wakefield. Records are made to be broken, and more than a ton of marijuana was destroyed on August 30, 1985, at the town incinerator. However, this was from a drug raid in Effingham, not Wolfeboro. In the local schools the D.A.R.E. and other anti-drug programs were conducted.[298]

For two hours on Friday evening, September 1, 1988, a "sting" operation to catch those selling liquor to minors was conducted in eight stores in Wolfeboro and one in Wakefield. Two youths age 18 and 19 were paid by authorities to try to purchase liquor. All but two stores were willing to make sales. One of the offenders was the State Liquor Store. Nine salespeople were arrested and ordered to stand trial, and several were fined. Several stores lost their licenses for a time. The object was to raise awareness that stores should check identification. A different set of rules apparently applied to the State Liquor Store. It wasn't prosecuted.

In July 1989 the Wolfeboro Police Department joined a federally-funded crackdown on drunken driving (DWI) in view of the statistic that nationwide 50% of all serious accidents involved drinking. In August two boys about to enter Kingswood High were killed and another seriously injured in Laconia in an accident police said involved alcohol and excess speed. A cry was made to promote teen programs to provide recreational activities in town and to make counseling available. In the same month, two Wolfeboro men, ages 20 and 27, were charged with cocaine and marijuana sales respectively.

The lessons of history were soon forgotten, and in August 1989, when the Wolfeboro police conducted a liquor-sales sting on 10 stores, employees at The Yankee Rebel, Hunter's IGA, Camelot Bookstore, and Prescott Farms obligingly filled the request of a 19-year-old woman and sold her alcohol. Just one store asked for identification, and when she did not provide it, the store made the sale anyway.[299] However, yet another sting, this one conducted in 14 Wolfeboro and Tuftonboro stores in July 1990, resulted in only one citation for selling to a minor—an indication that the staffs of alcohol vendors were being trained properly.[300]

### With the Department

Despite the record number of reportable crimes and fatal accidents during the decade, most citizens continued to believe that Wolfeboro was a relatively safe place to live. Public aggravations and assaults were rare, and although there were many burglaries, there were few robberies involving force. The Wolfeboro Police Department, Stanley E. Stevens, chief, protected townspeople and visitors in a manner which most observers considered to be excellent.

In 1982 Francis X. Holt, local counselor and therapist and frequent contributor to the "letters" column of the paper, noted in an article that for a rural community Wolfeboro had a first-class alarm and dispatch system. However, with a cruise ship, seaplane base, regional high school, area hospital, and a population that tripled in the summer (estimates ranged up to 16,000 for the head count in July and August), there were many situations requiring attention.[301] Indeed, certain of these situations were responsible for giving Wolfeboro a statistical crime rating more typical of a town much larger than its year-round population of fewer than 5,000 would suggest. Clearly, Chief Stevens and his capable crew had their hands full during the warmer times of the year.

In 1983 the Department hired its first full-time female police officer, Janet Bergeron, who earlier had served as a clerk and special police officer. In 1984 Kimberly Kinmond, newly-hired dispatcher, took care of nine older people who were called each day as part of the continuing "Good Morning" Program. In November 1990 she was promoted to full-time police officer.[302]

In 1985 the Police Department's fleet consisted of a 1981 Chevrolet, 1982 Ford, 1983 Ford, 1984 Chevrolet, 1977 Volaré (traded in June), and 1984 Celebrity.[303]

The 20th anniversary of the Department's Wolfeboro Christmas Children's Fund was observed in 1987, and on December 24, Chief Stanley E. Stevens and his officers, each in uniform, made deliveries of clothing and toys to needy families in town. It was a happy time on July 25, 1988, when John Rechel, who had moved to town the year before, found a wallet containing $1,000 in cash and gave it to the police, who were able to locate its owner.[304]

Patrolman H. George Moody was honored by about 120 people at a surprise party at the Wolfeboro Inn in November 1989, upon retiring from 28 years of duty on the Wolfeboro Police force. He was the first Wolfeboro patrolman to be awarded the prestigious honor of Officer Emeritus by the Wolfeboro Police Commission.[305]

On Monday, December 4, 1989, an estimated 1,000 people, including Governor Judd Gregg and troopers from 23 states, attended the funeral at the First Congregational Church of Gary P. Parker, age 30, a well-liked town resident and state trooper who had earlier served with the Wolfeboro Police Department. Parker, fellow officer Joseph Gearty, and their passenger had been killed on November 29, when a lumber truck whose load had shifted slammed into their cruiser on a road in the northern part of the state. Two memorial funds were set up to benefit his widow Amy, their son Gregory, and their unborn child. In 1993 the portion of Route 28 passing through Wolfeboro was designated as the Gary Parker Memorial Highway.[306]

On June 25, 1990, Wolfeboro District Court Judge George Walker resigned after 17 years in office, citing health and pressing professional matters as reasons. Governor Judd Gregg subsequently appointed Robert Varney, prominent local attorney and long-time town moderator, to fill the position.[307]

At the end of the decade in 1990, Chief Stanley E. Stevens reported that for the year the town experienced a 25% decrease in accidents, but the statistics unfortunately included a fatality. Also reported were decreases in burglaries of 22%, theft 5%, and vandalism 30%. Reportable incidents totaled 812 in 1990, a decrease from 829 in 1989.

I believe these decreases are due in large part to the fact that the patrol force recorded a sizable increase in motor vehicle activity. Between the patrol force and the detectives, there was an increase in criminal arrests of 17%, motor vehicle arrests of 37%, summons of 36%, warnings of 61%, checkups of 19%, and [date expired] tags of 64%. I am sure this contributed to a reduction in accidents and criminal activity.[308]

## NATURAL PHENOMENA

### Snow

The winter of 1981-1982 brought with it much snow, and by the end of December many roofs were covered with 30 to 40 inches of the white stuff. Snow removal crews worked late into the night clearing an estimated 114 miles of town roads. For a time a bank of snow was plowed into the center of certain parts of South Main Street; in front of Town Hall a divided highway greeted onlookers. The snow continued to fall. And fall some more. A surprise snowstorm on April 6, 1982—just when everyone was set for warm spring weather—crippled much of New England. Several local buildings collapsed or were damaged by the snow weight including the barn at the Isaac Springfield house in South Wolfeboro and the carriage house behind the magnificent Victorian-style Hutchins mansion in Wolfeboro Falls. By the end of the month up to 121 inches of snow had been recorded for the season (the annual norm was 60 to 65 inches).[309]

### Wind, Rain, and Lack of Rain

On Wednesday, August 25, 1982, unexpected high winds raked the town, whipped waves up to six feet in Lake Winnipesaukee, damaged about a dozen boats, knocked out electrical service, and felled several trees. In August of the next year two more windstorms with 65 to 70 m.p.h. winds made the lake "look like an ocean." Another windstorm on November 25, 1983, uprooted many local trees. Lauren Douglass, 16, was driving on Middleton Road at 11 p.m. when a tree branch fell on her windshield, causing her car to hit a stone wall and turn on its side. Miss Douglass was treated at Huggins Hospital for minor bruises.

In the second week of June 1984 the water of Lake Winnipesaukee was at its highest level in 30 years, covering docks, flooding the parking lot behind the Avery Building downtown, and filling low-lying basements with water. The level was officially recorded at 505.55 feet above sea level, or about a foot and one-half above normal. Store owner Gregory Roark reported that The Loft, located on South Main Street near the Town Docks, sustained a loss of over $6,000 in inventory.

The next summer saw the opposite situation. Low snowfall (50 to 55 inches) the preceding winter and low rainfall combined to produce a severe drought. By early June 1986 the town water supply in Beach Pond was two feet below normal. Lawn watering and car washing were prohibited. Relief finally came in early August with a two-inch rainstorm. However, water levels remained low for the rest of year and were not restored until early 1986.[310]

### Gloria

On Friday, September 27, 1985, townspeople braced for Gloria, billed as one of the greatest hurricanes of the century, possibly even rivalling the great blow-out of 1938. This time there was ample warning, civil defense procedures were in place, school students were sent home, and boats were hauled ashore.

Happily, friction from the land mass slowed Gloria down, and by the time it arrived in Wolfeboro at 2:20 in the afternoon, winds had diminished to 45 m.p.h. or less. The main manifestations of what could have been a major disaster were downed trees, broken branches, and electrical power failures. Destruction was most intense at Lake Wentworth, Springfield Point, Clark Road, Sewall Road, and the shore along North Main Street to Carry Beach. Damage amounted to an estimated $25,000 to $30,000, primarily to the Municipal Electrical Department's facilities, these taking two weeks to restore to full service.[311]

### Wind, Lightning

On Monday, October 6, 1986, Bob Murphy, fleet captain for the Winnipesaukee Flagship Corporation, operator of the motor vessel *Mount Washington,* reported 10-foot waves on Lake Winnipesaukee, the roughest he had seen in 20 years. In fact, not since mid-December 1959 had waves of this height been observed by anyone. The same winds downed a large tree in front of the Windrifter on South Main Street and knocked out an important power line.

Multiple electrical storms caused destruction and even death in Wolfeboro in late spring 1986. On May 30, lightning struck the Wolfeborough Railroad Station, resulting in $179,000 fire and water damage. On June 8, an ancient pine on the Brewster Academy campus was hit. In the late afternoon of June 13 a bolt of lightning struck a 17-foot boat on Lake Wentworth, instantly killing Kevin J. Furlong, 29, of Somersworth, one of three in the craft, the first death of its kind in the state in 14 years.[312]

### Gypsy Moths

The greatest gypsy moth invasion in the town's history took place in the summer of 1981 when countless caterpillars covered leafy plants, trees, and anything else growing and green. By early July there were so many in overhead branches that their droppings falling on the ground sounded like raindrops. By month's end the majority of deciduous trees in town were bare, and many pines had been thinned. Nothing like it had happened before, nor has anything similar occurred since.

Theories and proposals abounded. Samples:

Gypsy moths like oak trees best (in the end it didn't matter; all trees fell victim).

Pine trees will not be harmed (reality: when the caterpillars had eaten everything else, they started on pine trees).

Spraying will kill caterpillars and solve the problem.

Spraying is expensive and will not help at all.

Spraying is environmentally hazardous.

New-type sprays are safe.

The town (or state or federal) government should take care of this.

No tourists will come to a leafless Wolfeboro this summer.

Tourists won't mind at all; the problem is just as bad in Massachusetts.

You ain't seen nuthin' yet; wait until the invasion of 1982 next year.

There was life after the 1981 defoliation. While some trees died from the experience, these were mostly in poor condition before the caterpillars started. Meanwhile, tourists seemed to be as plentiful as ever.

The following year most Wolfeboro trees were back to their full greenery. Statewide, about 2,000,000 acres had been stripped in the state in 1981, followed by a sharp decline to 400,000 to 500,000 acres in 1982.[313]

### Nature Notes

At 7:15 in the evening of Monday, January 18, 1982, Wolfeboro homes were shaken and dishes were rattled by a 4.4 Richter Scale earthquake centered in Franklin. Some reported a rushing noise sounding like a chimney fire.[314]

Halley's Comet, which had been a worldwide attraction during its last visit near earth in 1910 and had been viewed with interest at that time by many Wolfeboro residents, was scheduled to arrive again. Dedicated sky-watchers with binoculars could get an advance peek as early as November 1985, by December it would be visible to the naked eye, and early in 1986 Halley's would be a brilliant white banner across the night sky, a celestial apparition without equal in our lifetime. Or so the reasoning and announcements went. Telescope and binocular sales boomed. Reality was different. It was hardly visible at all, a "dud" as a reader of the local paper noted.[315]

On April 11, 1986, New England's tallest and New Hampshire's largest elm tree, on the Sanborn property on South Main Street, finally fell victim to the Dutch elm disease which had killed just about all other elms in America including Wolfeboro's venerable and quite famous "Feather Duster Elm" pictured on postcards after the turn of the century. A couple of pieces of the tree—which in one area showed 217 annual growth rings—were saved for the Libby Museum and the Wolfeboro Historical Society. The rest was hauled away.[316]

Loons became increasingly numerous and were often seen in Wolfeboro Bay, Winter Harbor, Lake Wentworth, and elsewhere. In the Varney Islands a loon preserve helped further the efforts of the Loon Preservation Committee, a Lakes Region group. Typically, loons would spend the warmer months in local waters and when the lakes were frozen go to salt-water bays along the seashore.[317]

## HEALTH AND WELLNESS

### On the Medical Scene

In the late 1970s and early 1980s Wolfeboro residents were warned about sexually transmitted herpes virus, but this soon paled in view of a more lethal threat, AIDS, which attacks the body's immune system and prevents it from effectively fighting other diseases. In the 1982 *Town Report,* John D. Foley, D.O., commented:

> The AIDS crisis looms on the horizon. Our area as yet has not been affected. However, it most certainly will be. Presently, there is no vaccine or cure for this lethal disease. The Acquired Immune Deficiency Syndrome will challenge all of us to develop fair and compassionate policies to help its victims.

By 1987 AIDS victims had been treated at Huggins Hospital. Medical workers were trained in handling afflicted patients and had two concerns: one was to treat AIDS patients with the dignity and confidentiality all patients deserve and, two, to treat them so that no one else contracted the highly contagious and always fatal disease.[318]

Another area of concern was cancer from smoking. In 1981 James E. Bovaird, M.D., town health officer, cautioned:[319]

I would be remiss if I did not end this report with a plea to everyone to stop smoking cigarettes. Hardly a day goes by without seeing the sad effects of tobacco in the form of lung cancer, emphysema, heart trouble and duodenal ulcers.

Less serious but still important was an outbreak of head lice that swept Carpenter School in 1982. Principal John Burnham and Registered Nurse Joan Frye in consultation with pediatrician Dr. Norman Kathan handled the situation by recommending prescription shampoo, advising against the sharing of brushes and combs, and raising the building temperature to 72°. The major infestation passed, but head lice remained a "low-grade problem" at Carpenter through early 1984, despite complete absence of the vermin during a check in mid-January 1983.[320]

In 1982 it was reported that in the Evergreen Park subdivision on Trotting Track Road the naturally-occurring fluoride content in wells was five to 10 times optimum recommended levels. This might be harmful to younger people exposed for 20 years or more.[321] Other natural hazards included radon gas accumulation in cellars and arsenic (a component of granite) in water supplies. For good measure, the press contained reports on acid rain damaging pine trees and polluting lakes, "swimmer's itch" caused by a cycle of minute larval organisms involving duck droppings and snails, giardiasis (carried in beaver feces), and coliform bacteria, not to overlook salmonella (found on poultry products, uncooked meat, and spoiled canned goods among other habitats). Just being outdoors could be quite dangerous, it seemed.[322] Not all was lost, for Charlie Hunter, proprietor of the local IGA market, reported in 1986 that he was selling about 200 gallons of bottled water a week to those who didn't want to drink the municipal product,[323] and Evergrain did a good business selling health foods, organically-grown items, and other items said to be purer than normal grocery store inventories.

Meanwhile, all of Lake Wentworth was rated by the state as a Class A lake (high quality, suitable for drinking), while Lake Winnipesaukee was Class B (slightly lower, but still potable).

In 1984 the Clipper Home opened off Clark Road, following nine months of construction. The attractively appointed facility had 72 beds and was intended for intermediate care for the elderly. In 1986 the Sherbourne Wing was added for congregate living.[324] The unit earned high marks for patient care, comforts, and cleanliness.

In October 1988 the Wolfeboro area Meals on Wheels program began its 16th year of operation. By this time its volunteer staff had served over 100,000 nutritionally-balanced hot meals to people who were ill, incapacitated, or elderly. This enabled people to stay in their own homes and other familiar surroundings, rather than go into nursing homes. The area served included Wolfeboro, Tuftonboro, Brookfield, and Wakefield.[325]

Lyme disease, a tick-borne disease common in coastal areas of southern New England and which derived its name for the place of its discovery, Lyme, CT, made its way to New Hampshire. The bacterium which causes Lyme Disease is transmitted by the bite of an infected deer tick, the adult being gray and 3/16-inch long, half the size of the more common "dog tick." Light-colored clothes made ticks easy to spot. The illness caused a rash and could be treated or even cured with antibiotics, but sometimes there were lingering effects.[326]

During the decade many fine physicians and medical specialists came to Wolfeboro to practice.[327] However, mention must be made of one physician—a long time resident of the town—who in 1986 advertised something virtually unknown in the modern medical profession: Donald C. Walsh, M.D., who made *house calls*.[328]

### At Huggins Hospital

There were many changes at Huggins Hospital during the 1980s. In January 1981 a nurse who had been on the staff for 35 years stated that her pay was $6.03 per hour, a figure considered low. Nurses had other grievances besides pay and formed a committee, Paul St. Martin in charge, to present their views to the Board of Trustees. Roger Good, executive director, and David Wanger, director of patient care, resigned. The following month there was a round of pay increases of 8% or more depending upon length of service. In June, Leslie MacLeod, executive director of Cambridge Hospital in Massachusetts and a member of the Harvard School of Public Health faculty, was named director of Huggins. His wife Nancy and their three sons moved to Wolfeboro in September.

Improvements and new equipment at the hospital during the decade included new ultrasound equipment, a new birthing center (with a birthing room, father's room, and birthing chair), a mammogram machine, a leased nuclear medicine X-ray machine, stress-testing devices, a Zeiss OPM operating microscope, and a C.A.T. (Computerized Axial Tomography) scanner, the latter requiring an addition to the building to accommodate it.[329]

In 1986 a gift shop at Huggins Hospital was opened with Kay Hudson and Barbara Sutherland as the volunteers in charge, while Ginny Gray took charge of the greeting card section. As of July 1, 1987, the hospital banned smoking (except on doctors' orders for certain patients).[330]

In 1987 David Garbacz, formerly clinical leader of the North Conway offices of Carroll County Mental Health Services, became clinical team leader at the Services' Wolfeboro office at Huggins. He replaced Mimi Dye, who continued as senior supervisor.[331] Mental health became an increasing concern during the decade, and

Politicking in the Wolfeboro tradition. Jeb Bradley (left), Ken MacDonald, and Bill Morrison watch a sign-carrying campaigner on the sidewalk in front of Town Hall. (Sandy Martin photograph, 1990)

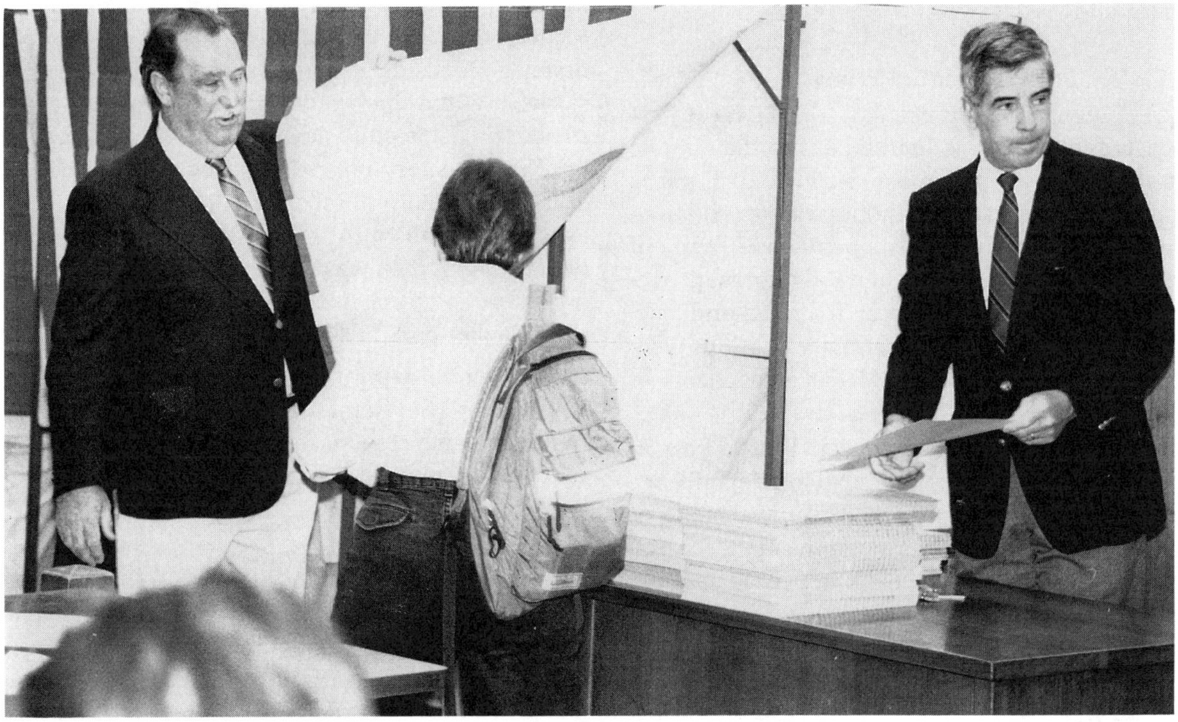

Voting in the Wolfeboro tradition. John Schillereff holds the curtain open for a voter at the Town Hall. Tom O'Dowd passes out ballots. (Sandy Martin photograph, 1990)

in the private sector several therapists and counselors opened offices in town.

In 1989 Huggins Hospital elected Carra Moore as Employee of the Year. She had been with the hospital since 1965.[332] In the same year the number of babies born at Huggins doubled from 1988 and was expected to triple in 1990. High insurance costs and a shortage of doctors willing to deliver babies threatened to permanently shut down the maternity ward. Two new doctors, Robert Mathes and Scott Johnson, had come to the hospital to practice obstetrics.[333] Dr. Johnson later moved to New York State, but Dr. Mathes remained to serve a growing clientele.

## POLITICS

### State Elections

In the 1982 gubernatorial election Republican John Sununu took 62% of the vote, unseating incumbent Democrat Hugh Gallen who was seeking a third term. Wolfeboro cast 1,087 votes for the winner and 594 for Gallen.[334] In 1984 and 1986 Sununu was reelected to second and third terms by wide margins. In 1988 he declined to run for a fourth term, stating that he could earn more in private business than his $56,000 annual stipend as governor. He and his wife Nancy had eight children, several of whom were of college age.[335] Later he went to Washington, DC, and was in charge of the White House staff under President George Bush. Judd Gregg was elected governor of the state in 1988 and re-elected by a wide margin in 1990.

### 1984 Presidential Primary

The campaigns for the presidential elections of 1984 and 1988 brought waves of candidates to the Granite State far in advance of November election day. Eager to establish their credentials and popularity for the first-in-the-nation primary, several hopefuls and many of their representatives came through town, perhaps creating situations that would be best described under *entertainment* in this book. However, their missions were serious. A primary winner in NH had a great chance of being the party's nominee for president.

In 1983 a rumor spread that President Ronald Reagan would come to Wolfeboro to review the Independence Day parade, and, indeed, a Republican official had contacted Selectman Paul R. Hatch about the matter. However, his appearance was canceled. In February of the next year, just before the primary election, Senator Robert Dole and his wife Elizabeth (who was secretary of transportation in President Ronald Reagan's Cabinet) held a Reagan-Bush re-election rally near the Town Docks. About 200 people attended to hear the Doles as well as Senator Howard Baker and congressional candidate Robert ("Bob") Smith.

There was not much local spark in the 1984 contest, as Reagan was viewed as a shoo-in for re-election, and the town had very few Democrats. February 28, primary election day, saw miserable weather including sleet, snow, and rain freezing as it hit the ground. Voter turnout was below 50%. Ronald Reagan was without competition on the Republican side and garnered 602 votes, while Democrats and others divided the rest of the pie which amounted to Gary Hart 86 votes, Walter Mondale 32, John Glenn 28, George McGovern 28, Jesse Jackson 15, Ernest Hollings 7, Alan Cranston 5, and Reuben Askew 3.[336]

In the November election Wolfeboro cast 1,811 votes for winner Reagan and 454 for Mondale.[337]

### 1988 Presidential Primary

Late in the afternoon of July 4, 1985, Vice-President George Bush arrived at the Town Docks aboard the *Mount Washington* as part of a fund-raising event for Bob Smith and Judd Gregg and, no doubt, to stir up some interest in what everyone expected to be Bush's run for the presidency a few years later. Planning had begun months earlier, and as the time approached Secret Service agents requested that the shades in the nearby Avery Building be pulled down. Scuba divers made a security sweep of the lake bottom near the Town Docks.

The vice-president and his entourage drew a spirited crowd of several hundred, many of whom had noisemakers and waved American flags, and all of whom had to pass through a metal detector set up outside of Bailey's Dockside Restaurant. Bush, dressed in gray slacks, a white shirt, and a baseball cap with the vice-presidential insignia, addressed onlookers following brief introductory remarks by Governor John Sununu and Representative Robert Smith. Bush then stepped ashore and walked through the crowd, shaking hands left and right, then was whisked off in a limousine, but not before accepting two goblets made locally by Hampshire Pewter and presented as a gift from the town.

Presidential aspirants were aplenty in Wolfeboro in 1987 as both the Republican and Democratic nominations were not yet settled, although Vice-President Bush was widely viewed as the leading contender for the Republican party.

Former Secretary of State Alexander M. Haig, Jr., spoke to a meeting of about 50 Carroll County Republicans at Bailey's Restaurant on June 17. Haig stated that he supported President Reagan's policies, but not "blindly," and that he disagreed with him on arms proposals. Taking a swipe at Sen. Robert J. Dole, he suggested that when Dole came to town, people would do well to ask why he and the Senate had allowed the deficit to double in the past five years.

Presidential candidate George Bush at the Kingswood Junior High School auditorium, February 13, 1988, a few days before his win in the primary election, after which he went on to win the national election in November. Bush is shown with Andrew V. Bowers, age 8, a Carpenter School student.

**Political personalities: Visitors to the annual open house held by the Friends of the Libby Museum in 1990. Pictured on the front sidewalk are, left to right: Ray Burton (of the Governor's Executive Council), Marge Webster (of the *Ossipee Times*), Scot McKay (WLKZ radio personality), Charles Campbell (Libby Museum curator), and Bill Zeliff (who was on the campaign trail for election as representative to Congress, and who arrived by helicopter with Ray Burton).**

**Another scene at the open house at the Libby Museum. Left to right: Roy Clark (county sheriff), Marge Webster, Bill Zeliff, Scot McKay, Charles Campbell, Jeb Bradley (representative to the State Legislature), and Ray Burton. (Sandy Martin photographs)**

U.S. Senate Majority Leader Robert J. Dole and his wife Elizabeth were here on July 4, 1987, and met with about 100 people for about an hour at the Wolfeboro Inn. Dole jokingly suggested that our town would be ideal for a summer retreat when he became president, a sort of Summer White House. In August Senator and Mrs. Dole were in Wolfeboro again—this time for a personal vacation. They greeted many well-wishers including shoppers at the Wolfeboro Marketplace.

Republican presidential hopeful Pierre duPont IV—who preferred to be called "Pete"—visited the office of the *Granite State News* on October 9, 1987, and commented that when voters made a choice at the primary election, they should consider the qualifications of the candidate (such as duPont) and not just vote for a familiar name (such as Bush or Dole). Contender duPont was in town again on the evening of December 14 to address Kingswood High students and others on the subject of drug-free schools.

On the afternoon of Monday, October 26, 1987, Democratic presidential candidate Paul Simon, a U.S. senator from Illinois, addressed Kingswood High students as part of his five-day "Octoberfest" campaign in the state.

Republican hopeful Jack Kemp visited Wolfeboro and was the guest at a reception held at the Yankee Pedlar real estate office by owner George Hutchinson. Among those in attendance was Wolfeboro resident Richard Valentine, who years earlier had been Kemp's athletic coach.

On Saturday afternoon, February 13, 1988, a few days before the primary election, George Bush was front row center at a colorful political rally in the gymnasium of Kingswood Junior High School. Against a backdrop of a 38-foot-wide American flag, he gave a speech attacking Bob Dole. Old-time Boston Red Sox baseball player Ted Williams joined him on the dais. There were limousines outside, Secret Service personnel inside, and state and local police along with fire and rescue squads.

On February 16 the first-in-the-nation presidential primary was held. Wolfeboro voted as follows: George Bush 658, Robert Dole 499, Pete duPont 161, Alexander Haig 3, Jack Kemp 138, Pat Robertson 69, Bruce Babbitt 33, Michael Dukakis 130, Richard Gephardt 55, Albert Gore, Jr., 26, Gary Hart 3, Jesse Jackson 58, and Paul Simon 82. Bush took the Republican nomination and Dukakis the Democratic.

In November Wolfeboro cast 2,075 votes for George Bush and 677 for Michael Dukakis.[338]

### Senator Bob Smith Comments

Robert C. Smith moved to Wolfeboro in 1970 and while here entered national politics. The following is edited from an interview with Senator Robert Smith ("Bob") and the author ("Dave") on January 24, 1994, in connection with the present book. Some of the author's questions have been omitted and just Senator Smith's answers given:

**Bob Smith:** How have you been?

**Dave Bowers:** Just fine, and your family?

**Bob:** We have been real well, the winters are long but I guess they are longer up there than they are here in Virginia [where the Smith family lives while the Senate is in session]. I don't get up to Wolfeboro enough but do when I can.

**Dave:** For the history of Wolfeboro project may I ask you some questions, and could you provide some biographical information?

**Bob:** I would be delighted to help.

After I served in the Navy I was discharged in Long Beach, California. I stayed a couple of years to do graduate work at Long Beach State College and then taught school there for about three years. My wife Mary Jo and I came to New Hampshire in the fall of 1970. It is a very interesting story how I came here:

We were both teachers, and we decided we wanted to move to New England. We applied to Maine, Vermont, and New Hampshire for positions on the condition that we both be hired by the same school district, so if one of us got a job the other would also. Otherwise no deal.

Maine never responded at all, Vermont said they didn't have any openings, and New Hampshire responded saying that there were openings in Colebrook, Somersworth and Wolfeboro. We looked at a map as we had never traveled New Hampshire extensively. We thought that Colebrook was probably too far to the north to allow us to easily visit Boston from time to time. I had never been to Wolfeboro either, but it seemed to be conveniently situated.

Shortly thereafter I was offered a teaching contract in Somersworth as was Mary Jo. We both signed the contracts and put them in the mail at four o'clock in the afternoon after we had come home from our teaching jobs. The next morning at seven o'clock we got a phone call from Bob Morrison, who was the principal of Kingswood Regional High School. He offered Mary Jo and me contracts—a contract for me in Wolfeboro at Kingswood High and one for Mary Jo in Alton in the elementary school [both Wolfeboro and Alton were part of the same supervisory union]. I don't recall there being any difference in the salary schedules between our Somersworth and Wolfeboro possibilities.

I said, "Well Bob, I have a problem here. Just yesterday afternoon I sent a signed contract to Somersworth, but I'm sure it hasn't gotten there yet."

He then asked, "Why are you coming to New Hampshire?"

I replied, "Because we like the country, the rural life, and the surroundings."

He commented, "Well you don't want to go to Somersworth, you want to go to Wolfeboro! That's what it's all about, rural and all that."

So, he talked me into it, and he hired me sight unseen. I'll never forget his quote: "I've read your application, and you are either the lousiest teacher they ever had and they want to get rid of you, or you're the best they ever had and they are giving you an outstanding recommendation."

I said, "Well, I'd like to think its the latter."

Anyway, he hired both of us on the spot. I sent a telegram and canceled my contract before they received it in Somersworth, and we wound up in Wolfeboro. That's how it happened.

I consider my conversation with Bob Morrison to have been the turning point in my career. If I had not come to Wolfeboro, I probably would have never entered politics.

**Dave:** What did you teach at Kingswood High School?

**Bob:** English and social studies. I taught there from 1970 through 1973. We rented Connie Nelson's home on Whitten Neck Road for a year. After that we bought a house in North Wolfeboro where we lived from 1971 to 1982. Then we moved to Tuftonboro.

**Dave:** How did you get involved with the Yankee Pedlar and C.M. Mixer businesses in Wolfeboro?

**Bob:** When Mary Jo and I came into town, we went to C.M. Mixer Realtors. John Mixer was running it at the time. When we negotiated the purchase of our home in North Wolfeboro, we had a terrible time with the transaction. The owners were in Florida, they were very hard to get hold of, they didn't respond quickly, and it seemed to me that they really didn't want to sell it. It took us several months to even get a contract. It was a very difficult purchase.

When we finally signed the agreement, I asked John Mixer, "Are all these transactions that difficult?"

He said, "No. Some of them are a lot easier."

I said, "I'm kind of fascinated by it. You don't need another salesman do you?"

He replied that I could work for him in the summer part-time if I wanted to. I obtained a real estate license and worked for Mixer in the summers when I got out of school and sometimes on weekends or evenings during the school year. When it got to the point that I was making twice as much selling real estate part-time as I did teaching full-time, I decided I might as well go into real estate full time, which I did in 1973. I ran Mixer's Ossipee office for a year and a half. The owner of C.M. Mixer at that time was Bill Sweeney. There were some pretty tough economic times, and he had to close the Ossipee office. Basically, I was out of a job. Mary Jo and I had a new baby; Jenni was born in '74 in November.

I visited my attorney friend Phil Ganem in Wolfeboro, who was also a friend of Al and Loucille Richardson who owned the Yankee Pedlar real estate agency. He said they wanted to sell Yankee Pedlar, which was right across the street from the C.M. Mixer agency.

As I didn't have a job, I had to borrow some money from my grandfather to pay my bills. I then met with the Richardsons and negotiated a deal to purchase Yankee Pedlar. That was in the spring of 1975. I did very well, and in the fall of 1977 I also purchased C.M. Mixer and merged the two firms. I bought Bill Sweeney's house as well. I kept the Yankee Pedlar-C.M. Mixer business active as a real estate firm until 1984 when I was elected to Congress. Then I sold the business to Mary Jo's brother, George Hutchinson (my brother-in-law).

**Dave:** Tell me about your career in public life.

**Bob:** Paul Hatch asked me if I would serve on the Wolfeboro Zoning Board of Adjustment. I was always interested in public activity, so I accepted and was on the board for about three years.

I then ran for the School Board in 1978. The impetus for this was a controversy over Tom Lovett, the assistant principal of Kingswood High—a good friend of mine who I thought was being maligned. He was the athletic director, and he was applying for the principal's job. His application was denied. Tom was one of those guys who was wonderful with kids and very inspirational—a good example for young people—and I felt that he had been treated unfairly. Because of this, I ran for election to the Board. I won and served for six years including three as chairman.

In Wolfeboro I coached junior high football, varsity baseball, and junior varsity baseball for a number of years. As a matter of fact, one year when they didn't have a coach for varsity baseball, I coached the sport while I was a member of the School Board. The School Board's attorney recommended against it, but I did it anyway. He said that I couldn't have two salaries. So I took the lesser of the two—the School Board salary—and coached for nothing because I really enjoyed it.

**Dave:** When did you decide to run for Congress for our district?

**Bob:** In late 1979 I made the decision to enter the Republican primary to be held in September 1980. That was a very interesting primary, as Paul Hatch ran also. Thus, two businessmen from the same town—Wolfeboro—with fewer than 1,500 people usually voting, were running for the same seat in a district that covered about half of the state. Out of seven contenders, I finished second. Marshall Cobleigh was the winner. It might have been different if voters in the region did not have to choose between Paul and me. I have no animosity about this, but that is the way it happened.

In 1982 I ran in the primary again. My office was in the Avery Building, as you remember—next to yours at the time. I won the primary, but lost the election to Norm d'Amours.

After the 1982 election, rolled up my sleeves and went back into my real estate business to make a living. Business was good. To be very candid, I had decided not to run for public office again. I had some debts from past campaigns, I had my real estate business to take care of, and I enjoyed being with my family.

In 1984 Norm d'Amours decided to run for the United States Senate against Senator Gordon Humphrey. This left his First District congressional seat open to all contenders. Mary Jo and I had a discussion about this new opportunity, and it seemed to both of us that I would have a good chance to win. I entered the contest, won the primary again, and in the election beat Democrat Dudley Dudley. I was re-elected to Congress in '86 and again in '88, and then was elected to the United States Senate in 1990.

**Dave:** Focusing on Wolfeboro, has our town ever played any part in any decisions you have made in the U.S. Congress or Senate?

**Bob:** During my time in Congress for six years I had an office in Wolfeboro, which has to be of historical significance as I am sure there was never one there before. I believe I'm the first congressman elected from Wolfeboro or Tuftonboro.

Our home is in Tuftonboro, and our family visits the area whenever we can. I remember the first year I came to Washington. My daughter Jenni's class at the Tuftonboro School came to Washington and stayed in our home—the entire class in our basement. Mary Jo gives tours of the United States Capitol, and from time to time she hosts our friends from Wolfeboro and Tuftonboro. A number of Wolfeboro people have worked in my office including Fran Madden, Stu Carmichael, my one-time legislative director Jim Cray, and others.

Wolfeboro was the launching pad for my political career. My business success in town made it possible to run for the School Board and Congress, which gave me experience with elective office and taught me much about organizing and campaigning.

The first "coffee" get-together I ever had during my campaigns was hosted by my good friends Fred and Marilyn Piehl just down from the Wolfeboro Inn on Sewall Road, who, when I asked, said they would be delighted to do it.

The rest is history.

## PRICES IN 1990

The following prices are from advertisements in the *Granite State News* in 1990.

**Appliances:** Dishwasher, Sears Kenmore, $318.85. Refrigerator, 11 cubic foot capacity, General Electric brand, $399.95. TV, 19" tabletop, Sears, $209.99. TV, 40" Projection monitor, Pioneer, $2,395. VHS video recorder, $204.99; 7-Lux hand-held camcorder, $699.77.

**Automobiles:** 1990 Buick LeSabre starting at $12,995. 1990 Ford Probe GT, air conditioning, sunroof, slightly used demonstrator, loaded, full warranty, list price $19,265, $16,600 with rebate.

**Automotive:** Service at Miller's, lube, oil, and filter, $16.95.

**Beverages:** Coca-Cola, 2-liter bottle, 88¢. Coffee, 12-13 ounce brick bag, $1.77. Can of soda from vending machine, 40¢ to 50¢.

**Camera:** Advanced autofocus, built-in flash with 28 mm lens, $389.95.

**Film developing:** 24 exposures, 35 mm. color, overnight service, $6.49.

**Food:** Meat: Tuna, Three Diamonds brand, chunk light, 6-1/2 ounces in water, can, 55¢. Bacon, sliced, Oscar Mayer, pound, $2.48. Beef, round roast, boneless bottom center cut, pound, $2.18. Chicken, boneless breasts, pound, $2.48. Pork chops, pound, $1.69.

**Food:** Various: Bananas, pound, 29¢. Butter, pound, $1.59. Cheese, Land O' Lakes, yellow or white, pound, $2.99. Flour, Gold Medal, 5-pound bag, 79¢. Grapes, red or green seedless, pound, $1.49. Oranges, navel, dozen, $1.99. Peanut butter, Skippy, 18-ounces, $1.99. Potatoes, Maine, 10-pound bag, 88¢. Squash, native, pound, 39¢. Sugar, granulated, 5-pound bag, $1.88. Vegetables, Del Monte, 16-17 ounce can, 40¢.

**Haircuts:** Men's regular, Pine Hill Stylist, $6. Woman's perm special with cut, $30. Wolfeboro Trim Tan, haircut, $10.

**Interest rates:** BankEast six-month certificate of deposit paid 8.10% annualized. Community Bank & Trust Company, interest paid on checking account with balance of $800 or more, 6%.

**Real estate:** House next to golf course and close to downtown; two-bedroom contemporary with fireplace in living room, cathedral ceilings, skylights, cobblestone flooring from Boston's Fanueil Hall, $99,000. House, four-bedroom cape in lovely neighborhood near town; living room with fireplace, deck overlooking mountains, air conditioning and two-car garage, $169,900. House, Lake Wentworth seasonal cottage, southwest views, sandy shore and adjacent waterfront lot, $245,000. New England log home, 3 bedrooms, 2 baths, fireplace, wraparound deck, and views; finish yourself or negotiate finished turnkey home with owner/builder. $130,000. Land, 30 acres with trout pond; building lot with privacy, to swim, fish or skate, with 3 bedroom septic approval, $75,000. Land, five acres on Pork Hill Road, $25,000. Waterfront, 101 feet on Wolfeboro Neck, $230,000.

**Restaurant food:** Dinner at The Wolfeboro Inn, soup, salad, entrée, dessert, and coffee or tea, $10.95. Dinner, all you can eat, Back Bay Boathouse, $9.95. Dinner, Thanksgiving Day, Bittersweet Restaurant, $13.95.

**Shoes:** Men's lined leather boot, Herman Survivors, $49.99. Sneakers, ladies' performance aerobic, Avia, $39.99.

**Sports equipment:** Ice skates, kids' figure, $29.95; adults' hockey, $53.95. Rollerblades, basic, $89.95. Snowshoes, youth, $24.95; adult, $39.95.

**Tanning:** Wolfeboro Trim Tan, unlimited use of tanning facility for one month, $49.95.

**Truck:** 1989 Ford Ranger 4x4 truck, demonstrator, XLT, 5-speed with bed liner, sliding rear window, and full warranty, list price $14,320, $11,200 with rebate.

# CHAPTER 12

# WOLFEBORO 1991-1994

*In order for the Board of Selectmen to guide the community into the next century, the participation and constructive input of its citizens are necessary. We not only welcome, but encourage your thoughts, ideas, and helpful hands to assist us in making Wolfeboro a thriving and vibrant community.*

—Board of Selectmen: Kenneth J. MacDonald, Paul R. Hatch, Shirley E. Ganem. 1994 *Town Report,* page 71.

### Introduction

The 1990s are our own time, and for many situations history is not much different from current news. "The more things change, the more they stay the same," it has been said—an aphorism echoed in "history repeats itself."

In the case of Wolfeboro it is evident that this is desirable. While from time to time some citizens still strive to make the town something else, surveys show again and again that what makes our town attractive is the way it is now.

As the historical chronicle that began with the formation of the town in 1770 now ends with 1994, the author cannot help but wonder if such topics as taxes, inflation, development, zoning, educational possibilities, activities for teenagers, and whether there are enough fish for all of the anglers will ever be resolved to everyone's satisfaction.

One can hope that Wolfeboro will prosper, endure, and maintain its personality. In the 1880s a problem in town was teenagers loitering on the Main Street bridge. Over a century later in 1994 the situation still existed, and hearings were held about it. If a century from now, in the 2090s (this date is hard to write, the "2000s" seem so distant), one of the most talked-about problems in town is still teenagers on the Main Street bridge, hopefully this will mean that the other problems of the intervening 100 years have been mostly small ones and that townspeople will have solved most of them.

A local Rip Van Winkle who fell asleep in Wolfeboro in the 1890s and awoke in the 1990s would scarcely recognize the town. Where are the Pavilion, Sheridan House, Belvue, and Glendon House? What happened to the Boston & Maine Railroad? Where are all of the horses? What are all of these motorized boats on the lake, and where did all of the shorefront cottages come from? What are those metal-and-glass four-wheeled things all over the place, and what is a service station? Why are the roads paved? Since when can people fly? My gosh, the telephone *did* become popular as predicted, but who ever heard of radios, television sets, and computers?

No one reading these words in the 1990s will be on the scene in 2095 to reflect upon the changes, but doubtless there will have been as many then as there have been in the century before.

## ECONOMY AND TOURISM

### The 1991 Recovery

During the early 1990s the Lakes Region Association and the Wolfeboro Chamber of Commerce continued to do much to bring tourists to the area. Habits were changing. In 1992 the average visitor to the state remained just two or three days, and very few came for a week or longer. Many were day-trippers who arrived after sunrise and were back in Massachusetts by sunset. There were 56 million visitor-days in the state, per one estimate.[1] Wolfeboro probably had less frequent turnover than many towns as many out-of-staters owned cottages on the lakes and often stayed for a month or two or more.

Summertime business was constant. If a day was rainy, people spent more time in local shops and stores. If the sun was shining, tourists bought more sports and recreation equipment. No matter what the weather might have been, they bought lots of food, dined in local restaurants, and quaffed beer in town pubs.

Winter was apt to be different. The 1990-1991 cold season was a "bust" according to David Lee, spokesman for the Lakes Region Association. Hardly any snow fell until winter was well underway, and icing-over of the lakes was slow in coming.

The real estate market continued to be sluggish and

Hampshire Pewter, a prominent local maker of pewter items sold nationwide, as seen across the water of Back Bay. (Sandy Martin photograph, April 8, 1994)

Traces of a bygone era: In the 1940s poultry raising was an important business in Wolfeboro. However, by the 1990s only a few scattered buildings remained as evidence, such as this abandoned structure on the old Moore farm on Pleasant Valley Road. (May 4, 1995 photograph)

was still reeling from the excesses of the preceding decade. However, there were signs of life, and the first quarter of 1991 saw sales at a rate double that of the comparable 1990 period. When properties changed hands they were often substantially below their assessed values, with the strongest sector being Winnipesaukee lakefront homes and lots.

There were numerous bright spots. Although construction money was reported as being virtually nonexistent and mortgage money was scarce, local builder Les Beckwith said that he was experiencing his best two-year period of the past seven, mostly from building high-end private homes. Often those commissioning a deluxe vacation home on the lake did their own financing.

Business continued to warm up, and by August 1991 permits had been issued for 39 new homes in Wolfeboro, triple the 1990 figure, this despite a *decline* in most other area towns. As has often been the case, Wolfeboro did not conform to typical regional, state, or national statistics.

In January 1991 the unemployment rate in Carroll County was 7.4%, dropping to 5.4% in August. No separate figure was given for Wolfeboro.

During the year the number of people using woodstoves as their primary heat source declined slightly. About 57% used oil, with wood being the second most popular fuel at 11.7%. However, the percentage of houses using wood as a supplementary fuel was much higher. Electric rates priced radiation heat out of the market, and public interest in solar heat had diminished.

In October 1991 the partnership of Smith and Kourian, real estate developers and entrepreneurs who were the town's largest taxpayers, filed for voluntary bankruptcy, an action said to have been precipitated by the First NH Bank calling a $3.6 million loan on their Embassy Estates real estate project. The filing specifically included the Road Stop Convenience Store, Goodhue and Hawkins Navy Yard, Embassy Estates, Melvin Village General Store, Village General Store in Tuftonboro, Plow Shares Trust, Kourian Investment Partnership, and Woodman Realty Trust. The partnership re-organized, sold off most assets, and co-owner Charles Smith became involved in the operation of a former division, the Goodhue and Hawkins marina.[2]

### The 1992-1993 Economic Scene

During the 1992 summer season the *M/V* [Motor Vessel] *Mount Washington* stopped in Wolfeboro twice a day, sometimes three times when special events were scheduled. Various innovative "theme" cruises were popular, mostly originating at Weirs Beach. One cruise might be "family night," while another was "big band night," and still others would have different themes. To facilitate ease of landing at the Wolfeboro Town Docks, a slowly-accumulating sandbar was removed from in front of the Dockside Restaurant.

In late summer 1993 the first of three Farmers' Markets scheduled for Clarke Plaza was held and featured a wide variety of freshly picked local vegetables, fruits, cut flowers, jellies, jams, and country crafts. David Hemenway, owner of Black's Paper Store on South Main Street, reported, "I've never seen so many people in Wolfeboro," but added that shoppers were still cautious with their money.

On July 6, 1994, the selectmen backed a proposal to secure from the state a $305,000 Community Development Block Grant to expand the manufacturing facility of Phoenix Custom Molders, Inc., on Pine Hill Road. Phoenix agreed to repay the loan, make capital improvements, and hire 31 more employees.[3] Meanwhile, Wickers Sportswear, Inc., founded in 1990, moved its manufacturing operation from an old wooden mill on River Street to a new 16,240 square-foot facility not far from Phoenix's plant. President Anthony Mazzenga and administrative manager Rosalie Triolo reported that business was good and that their impressive list of clients included such nationally-known firms as Lands' End, L.L. Bean, and Eastern Mountain Sports.[4]

The real estate market continued to improve, and in January 1994 Lisa Williams of the J. Malcolm Agency reported that a number of properties priced in the $1 million range had recently sold for cash. Other active real estate firms included Jeff Badger Real Estate & Insurance, Century 21-Dockside (the Century 21 franchise went to Malcolm later in the period), Chipmunk Realty, Hamel DeWolfe New England, Island Real Estate (specializing in Lake Winnipesaukee island properties), Lake Country Real Estate, Henry S. Maxfield Real Estate, Melanson Real Estate, Inc., Real Estate Options, Spencer-Hughes, Inc., Spiller Realty Services, and Yankee Pedlar.[5]

In particular demand were waterfront properties on Lake Winnipesaukee. All lakefront lots for sale in the Embassy Estates development had found buyers by 1994, there were no more Wyanoke Harbors shore lots on the market, and the supply of waterfront properties was very tight everywhere else as well. The Narrows, a group of condominiums on Back Bay near the Wolfeborough Railroad Station, had been stalled during the construction phase, changed hands, but in the 1990s was completed and sold out. Back Bay, an eyesore in 1974, was as pretty as the proverbial postcard 20 years later in 1994.

Most bank-owned foreclosure real estate parcels—typically inland (non-lakefront) residential and commercial properties—had found new buyers, often through the venue of a "caravan auction" held by Sanders-Mock (of Tamworth) whereby multiple parcels in several different towns would be sold in rotation in the same day.

One property might be auctioned at 10 a.m., then the auctioneer would move to another property in time for an 11 a.m. sale, and so on. Hilco, an affiliate of the First NH Bank, disposed of much of its non-performing loan portfolio in this manner.

While real estate brokers who sold $1 million worth of property in a year became increasingly numerous, not every business was in a position to sell big-ticket items. In South Wolfeboro the newly-formed Trish-Is-Pets store sold countless tiny tropical fish, and on Center Street Merrie Bushinger's Paw Prints shop offered frisky ferrets (recently made legal to own in the state) in addition to cats and dogs.[6]

### Food and Lodging

Quite possibly the biggest news on the local restaurant scene in the early 1990s was the controversy regarding the selectmen leasing the Dockside Restaurant at the Town Docks. The town had owned the property for many years, and at intervals the selectmen invited bids from prospective operators. Alan and Virginia Skelley had managed it as Bailey's Dockside since June 21, 1971, under two successive five-year leases. Now in 1991, there were 13 contenders for the contract. Many townspeople had become accustomed to the Bailey's Dockside tradition and felt they should be given an automatic renewal. The situation became heated, and the selectmen postponed their decision until 1992 by extending the Skelleys' lease on a temporary basis for one year. Meanwhile, offers—some of which were later revised—included these:

> Lisa and Nicholas Herder, a husband and wife team from Melvin Village, offered to run a Howard Johnson's Restaurant on the site, paying the town $250 per month for the first two years, $500 each month for the next six years, plus 1% of the gross sales during the colder months from October through April. They would also spend $100,000 on building improvements.
>
> The Skelleys, the current lessees, offered the larger of $21,000 or 6% of the annual gross sales, and agreed to make improvements.
>
> Paul and Joan Schalebaum, who operated PJ's in Ossipee and who had earlier run Adam's Rib in the Wolfeboro Marketplace, offered $1 per year plus 7.5% of the yearly gross, estimated to yield the town $22,000.

In 1992 the Schalebaums were given the nod, and in May the facility reopened as PJ's Dockside.[7] In 1994 the Schalebaums paid the town $34,538.95 (by contrast the town-owned Wolfeborough Railroad Station yielded $1,300 in rent).[8]

The Lakeview Inn and Motor Lodge, which had been operated by Michelle Gerasin since January 16, 1985, closed abruptly on March 14, 1993, when the First NH Banks foreclosed on the mortgage, much to the surprise of Gerasin, who believed that extended financing could be worked out, and who commented: "Everything looked as if it were going to pull together." Ironically, at about the same time she and the Lakeview Inn had been showcased as a happy bank client in *First Report*, a newsletter issued by First NH Banks. Five buyers were said to be interested in the property. In May the Cedrone family (Jay, Linda, Larry, and Jackie) of Massachusetts bought the Lakeview through Hamel Realty for a reported $560,000.[9] In June the Cedrones reopened the facility.

In the 1980s and early 1990s a great deal of commentary and letter-writing was directed toward the prevention of two fast-food franchises locating in Wolfeboro. At one time McDonald's apparently expressed interest in locating on the corner of Pine and Center Streets next to Clarke Plaza. To some vocal opponents the specter of this particular nationwide chain coming to town spelled the end of "old-time Wolfeboro tradition." McDonald's did not set up locally. The other franchise was Dunkin' Donuts sought by Edward ("Buddy") LeRoux, which after several years of negotiations, permit work, and other efforts, opened in August 1994 under the management of Sharon Walton. The facility featured both interior and drive-through service and attracted a large clientele from the outset.[10]

The Cider Press Restaurant on Middleton Road, operated by Bob and Denise Earle, offered a varied menu and continued to be a popular dining spot. In 1991 Crossdeggers Restaurant and Cocktails opened on Lehner Street. Owners Barry Edward Crossley and Brian Scheidegger offered a varied menu including roast beef carved from a tableside cart. In Clarke Plaza and across the street in the Wolfeboro Shopping Center eating places included Louis Pizza, Vathally's Subs and Pizza, and Katie's Kitchen. In warmer months I Scream (which spelled its name in lower case letters), Bailey's Bubble, the take-out windows at P.J.'s Dockside and at Bailey's Restaurant, and a street vendor or two offered ice cream sundaes, shakes, and cones.

On January 24, 1993, the Back Bay Club opened in Bayside Village off Mill Street in extensively redecorated premises used earlier by the Back Bay Boat House. James Kott was manager and Perrin Long was chef. In warmer months patrons could view the Wolfeborough Railroad Station across the water of Back Bay from a closed-in veranda. Often they would catch a glimpse of an antique "woody" cruiser—perhaps a Hacker Craft or Chris Craft meticulously restored by local craftsman George Johnson—that had departed the Saw Mill Marina a few hundred feet up the bay, and with a throaty chug-chug was on its way under the Main Street bridge to the "Big Lake."

At the Wolfeboro Inn on North Main Street, Wolfe's Tavern was a popular gathering place. As time went on, wooden pegs on the rafters were filled with mugs inscribed with the names of patrons who had sampled the selection including dozens of exotic beers, perhaps while playing the game of Trivial Pursuit in a competition staged there. The same establishment ran an excursion boat as described in these comments by Enda S. Slack in *The Laker:*[11]

> One of the best bargains of the 1993 season in the Lakes Region is a $6 per person cruise out of Wolfeboro Bay on Lake Winnipesaukee, aboard the *M/V Judge Sewall*. The 65-foot, 43-ton vessel carries a crew of four and up to 70 passengers. It is owned and operated by the historic Wolfeboro Inn for the entertainment of its guests as well as scores of area residents and tourists who have boarded at the Town Docks for daily cruises.
>
> Entertainment is a key word here. On a recent trip most passengers chose seats on the upper deck to enjoy the warm sun, cool lake breezes and an entertaining monologue by Captain Jodi Moser. Skippering *The Judge* up in the tiny but well equipped wheelhouse, Captain Moser kept her passengers' attention with a running commentary on such topics as the habits of careless boaters, the difference between the buoy system of Lake Winnipesaukee and ocean buoys, and how to remember the difference between "port" and "starboard." ("Port" means "left" and both words have four letters.) Jodi's friendly informality soon had passengers laughing and chatting, and the 90-minute cruise was the next-best thing to partying with friends on your own yacht....
>
> Leaving her berth at the Wolfeboro Town Docks, the sparkling white-and-green vessel sails at a leisurely nine-mile-an-hour speed, past the historic Goodhue & Hawkins Navy Yard. Rounding Sewall Point, Captain Moser also pointed out other notable sites, including The Carry, where the Abenaki Indians beached their canoes and carried them across a narrow strip of land between the bay and Winter Harbor to save them from canoeing all around Wolfeboro Neck; a large waterfront "cottage" where Jack Lemmon once lived; past Parker and Rattlesnake Islands with views of Mount Major and Gunstock Mountain ski runs in the distance....
>
> Back in Wolfeboro Bay, our captain waved a warning to several small children on the dock as she neatly nudged the *Sewall* into place. Her passengers applauded, and as we filed out everyone thanked her and [Second Mate Tap Jackson] for a most pleasant trip....

Among new entries in the restaurant field was the Sea Bird in Wolfeboro Falls featuring Chinese cuisine which was opened in March 1994 by Guy Pho and his wife Lan Sam who came to America from Vietnam. The large and impressive Latchaw Building featured Jo Greens, billed as "a garden café," which opened in 1994 on its second floor. The venerable Bittersweet Restaurant on Route 28 changed ownership in the same year.

Lest someone reading these words a century hence wonder which lodging places were active within the town limits of Wolfeboro in the autumn of 1994, the following listing represents those named in a brochure published by the Chamber of Commerce.[12]

Allen "A" Resort, Center Street.
Clearwater Lodges, North Main Street.
Grey Shingles, Middleton Road.
King's Pine Lodges, Whitten Neck Road.
Lake Motel, South Main Street.
Lakeview Inn, 120 North Main Street.
Piping Rock Resort, North Main Street.
Tuc' Me Inn Bed and Breakfast, North Main Street.
Wah Hoo Wah Inn, North Main Street.
Windrifter Resort Association, South Main Street.
Wolfeboro Inn, North Main Street.

### On the Retail Scene

The Loft, operated for over 15 years by Gregory Roark and Dick Elkinton on South Main Street, closed its doors in the summer of 1992. Roark had left the clothing retailer to become an executive of the Community Bank and Trust Company when it started in 1990, and in 1992 Elkinton was seeking new challenges. Its going-out-of-business sale in early July packed the downtown area with shoppers.[13]

Bridges' Hallmark, Black's Paper Store, Kokopelli's (Native American jewelry), the Turquoise Door, the Art Place, Country Corner Creations, Christmas Presence, Straw Cellar, and other stores catered to tourists seeking gifts and were favorites with local citizens as well. The town was well endowed with book stores including the Wolfeboro Bookshop on Glendon Street, Camelot on North Main Street, WordsWorth on Center Street, and the Country Bookseller on Railroad Avenue.

In 1993 Orient Expressions, operated in Wolfeboro by Viola Gabler since 1987, had its "End of an Era Sale" and closed its doors on North Main Street. The emporium had showcased many art objects, decorator items, and gifts from the other side of the globe.

In June 1992 Ann and Jim Clark opened Annie's Mercantile in the Wolfeboro Marketplace in the premises of the former Canedy's Pendleton shop. The interior was designed to resemble an old-fashioned country store and offered penny candy; a wide variety of soaps, candles, gifts, crafts including consignments from local artisans, clothing; and fashion accessories. The staff included Debbie McIntire and Janie Foran. Although it was a popular gathering spot, business did not materialize to the extent hoped, and it closed its doors on January 22, 1995, after which Cornish Hill Pottery (Robert and Gogi Adler) bought the building and moved there from premises on Mill Street.[14]

The Wolfeboro Marketplace merchants in 1994 included Made on Earth and Caffé Piccolo (both operated by Mary Beth Bryant), the popular Wolfeboro House of Pizza, an expanded two-story facility for Hamel-DeWolfe Real Estate, Best Kept Secret, Abigail's Closet, Wolfeboro Travel, and ReThreads.

The Avery Building, a cynosure since 1889 when it was opened as the Peavey Block, housed Avery Insurance in the left front side and Lakes Region Sports & Photo in the right. Square in the middle was Melanson's Many Facets, which had a virtual monopoly on fine jewelry sales in town and offered a wide selection of diamonds, silver and gold items, watches, and antique pieces.

**A scenic cruise: Eager passengers near the *Judge Sewall* at dock in Wolfeboro Bay.**

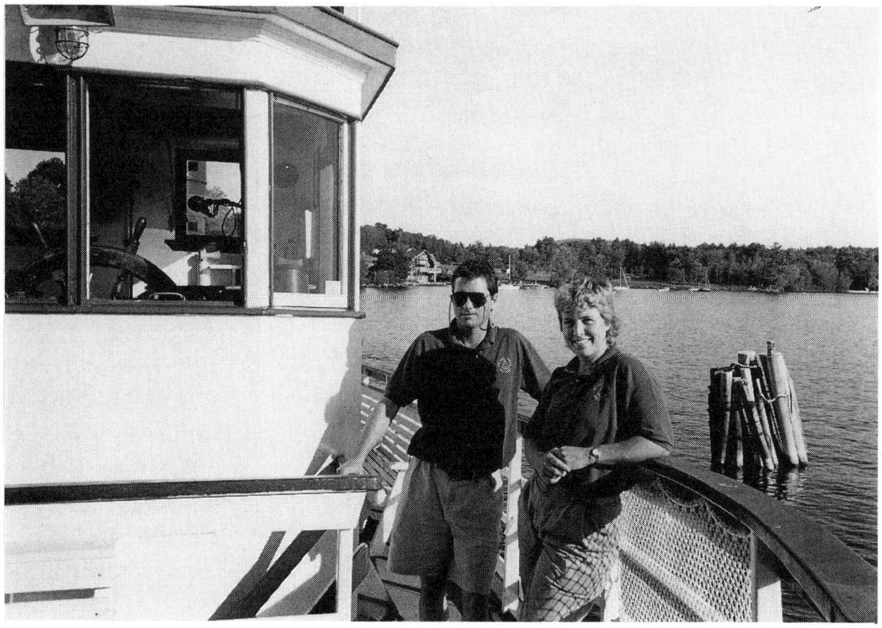

**Second Mate Tap Jackson and Captain Judi Moser on deck. (*The Laker,* September 6, 1993)**

In 1994 Rite-Aid Pharmacy opened in a new building on the site of the former Wolfeboro True Value Hardware on Glendon Street. The earlier structure, once the Glendon House stables, was demolished. Local sentiment was mostly against the opening of this national chain outlet in town, especially in view of there already being three pharmacies in town—Hall's, Tobey's, and the Medicine Shoppe.[15] Meanwhile, the hardware trade was carried on by Bradley's on Railroad Avenue (and its new annex, Bradley's Renter Center on Haley Court) and the new (May 1994) Bay Supply Hardware True Value franchise on Bay Street. Out on Pine Hill Road not far from the large showroom of Lauber Carpet and Tile, the extensive facilities of Winnipesaukee Lumber Company offered building materials. Heckman's Flooring did business at the 2000 Centre Street complex. Hoyt's Carpet & Tile on Bay Street offered a wide selection.

Clarke Plaza and the Wolfeboro Shopping Center, both on Center Street, were beehives of activity during the era, and offered the advantage of easy parking and access to shops, offices, and stores.

Hairdressers and beauty salons in 1994 included these:[16]

> Beauty Time Beauty Salon, Hair FX, Idle-Hour Beauty Shop, Katie-Did-It, Kingswood Klipper, Mirror Images, O-So-Good Barber-Stylist, Pine Hill Hair Stylist, Wolfeboro Clipper, Wolfeboro Hair Center, and Wolfeboro TrimTan.

Legal needs of the community were handled by these attorneys with offices within the town limits in 1994:[17]

> Diana Bolander, James J. Friedrichs, Philip Ganem, Jon S.B.C. Hanson, Charles W. Heard (of Cleveland, Waters & Bass), L. Bradley Helfer, Warren R. Lindsey, Roger F. Murray III, James R. Patten, Brian T. Stern, Timothy J. Sullivan, Robert C. Varney, Robert J. Waldron, George W. Walker, Thomas R. ("Randy") Walker, and Donald L. Wyatt, Jr.

### Banking

BankEast was having a tough time of it in the early 1990s, and reorganization was pending. Robert Sager, regional president, said that if and when the Federal Deposit Insurance Corporation took over there would be little or no advance warning. Meanwhile, those interested in picking up the pieces of BankEast were reported to include the Fleet/Norstar Financial Group based in Providence, RI, and KeyCorp of Albany, NY. Depositors would be protected by FDIC insurance up to $100,000. Town of Wolfeboro funds were safe, reported Carroll Piper, who managed municipal finances, as the total of all accounts amounted to less than this figure.

On October 11, 1991, BankEast customers at the facility on Center Street were greeted by a sign stating the branch was now owned by First NH Banks. Just one day before, First NH, a subsidiary of the Bank of Ireland, acquired a whole string of faltering state financial institutions including Amoskeag Bank, Bank Meridian, and the Nashua Trust Company. As it turned out, First NH Bank, which was also busy in town operating the former Wolfeboro National Bank a few hundred feet up Center Street, operated the former BankEast local branch briefly, then closed it down.[18]

Two new kids on the block were on the ascendancy—the Wolfeboro Banking Office (as it was called) of the Farmington National Bank, under the direction of Robert Fournier and located in facilities in Clarke Plaza; and the Community Bank and Trust Company, Bradford W. Gile, president. Community Bank and Trust Company achieved the fastest growth of any new financial institution in state history, offered an additional 150,000 shares to the public, and announced plans for a 4,000 square-foot addition to its premises. As of December 31, 1992, Community had over $57 million in assets and 16 full-time employees led by Brad Gile, Gregory Roark, Jackie Brackett, and Diane Hall. Stockholders at the 1994 annual meeting were shown plans for its first branch, a new facility to be opened in Exeter in 1995.[19]

In 1991 *Money* magazine reported that the Farmington National Bank was one of the two strongest banks in the state and had a B+ rating nationwide. By February 1993 the bank expanded under the direction of Robert Fournier to include branches in Alton and Melvin Village. On May 10, 1994, the Banknorth Group, Burlington, VT, agreed to buy the North American Bank Corporation and its sole subsidiary, Farmington National Bank, for $20.6 million in cash. Banknorth had $1.7 billion in assets, and the Farmington Bank had $162 million. During the same period Farmington's Wolfeboro Banking Office added a loan department in a separate facility in Clarke Plaza.[20]

### Media

During much of the early 1990s the *Wolfeboro Times* was operated by Kathryn Powell in a second-floor office in the Central Square business block. On the staff were Scot McKay, Mary M. McBride, and other local talent. In December 1993 the Powell Publishing Company sold the *Times* to the Journal Transcript Newspapers group of Revere, MA, and production was moved to Rochester, NH, under the publishing direction of Ms. Lou McGrew. The name of the paper was changed to the *Lakes Region Courier.* In early 1995, the *Courier* set up its Wolfeboro office in the old Scott house near Pickering Corner, which had been purchased and extensively renovated by John Pernokas in 1994. Mark Smith, formerly with the *Granite State News,* was named editor. Alan Pope, veteran newspaperman, continued to be a contributing editor, and Arthur F. Chamberlin, Mal Fuller, and other local personalities wrote feature columns.[21]

At the *Granite State News* there were notable changes and accomplishments. Susan Slack, editor for nearly eight years, turned over her desk to Jeanne Tempest on

Doris Toms at the Wolfeboro Animal Hospital grooms Judy Osgood's poodle, Jethro, who seems to be enjoying the procedure. Bottom: Dr. Lawrence S. Toms with another visitor to the Wolfeboro Animal Hospital on Keewaydin Road. (Sandy Martin photographs, September 17, 1994)

Susan and Mel Butsicaris at the counter of their popular Smith River Depot general store on Center Street in Wolfeboro Falls. (Sandy Martin photograph, September 21, 1994)

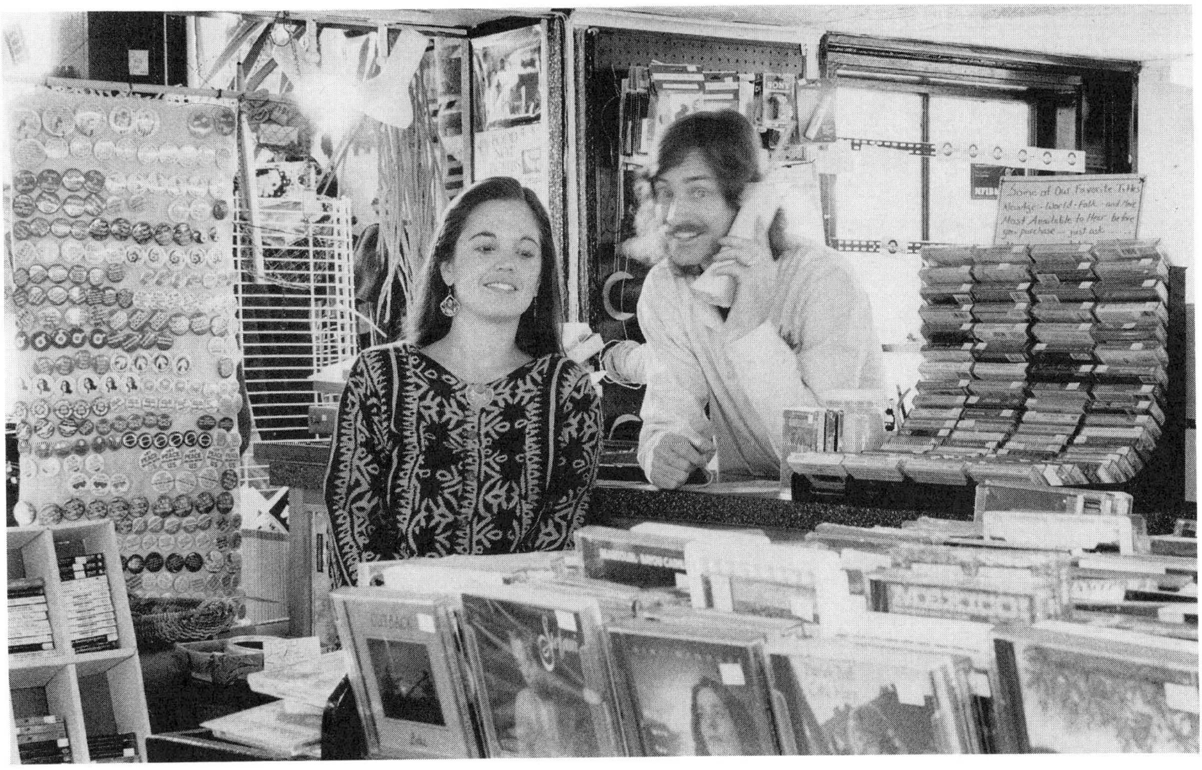

Stay Tuned was a popular shop for tourists and locals, particularly the younger set, in the 1990s. Items for sale included cassette and compact disc recordings, jewelry, and sportswear. Owners Mary Beth and Tom Bryant are shown. (Cathy Dumont Wilson photograph, March 16, 1994)

**The All Stars Sports Pub, located in The Depot business condominiums near the Wolfeborough Railroad Station, was founded in 1990 by Linda Jamieson (shown here) and Kim Madden. Drinks, refreshments, television, karaoke, and other entertainment were offered. The business was discontinued in 1995. (Sandy Martin photograph, September 9, 1994)**

Jodi and Bob Hughes in the office of Spencer-Hughes real estate and property management on Center Street, and their golden retriever, Spencer (who is memorialized in the name of the business). (Sandy Martin photograph, September 22, 1994)

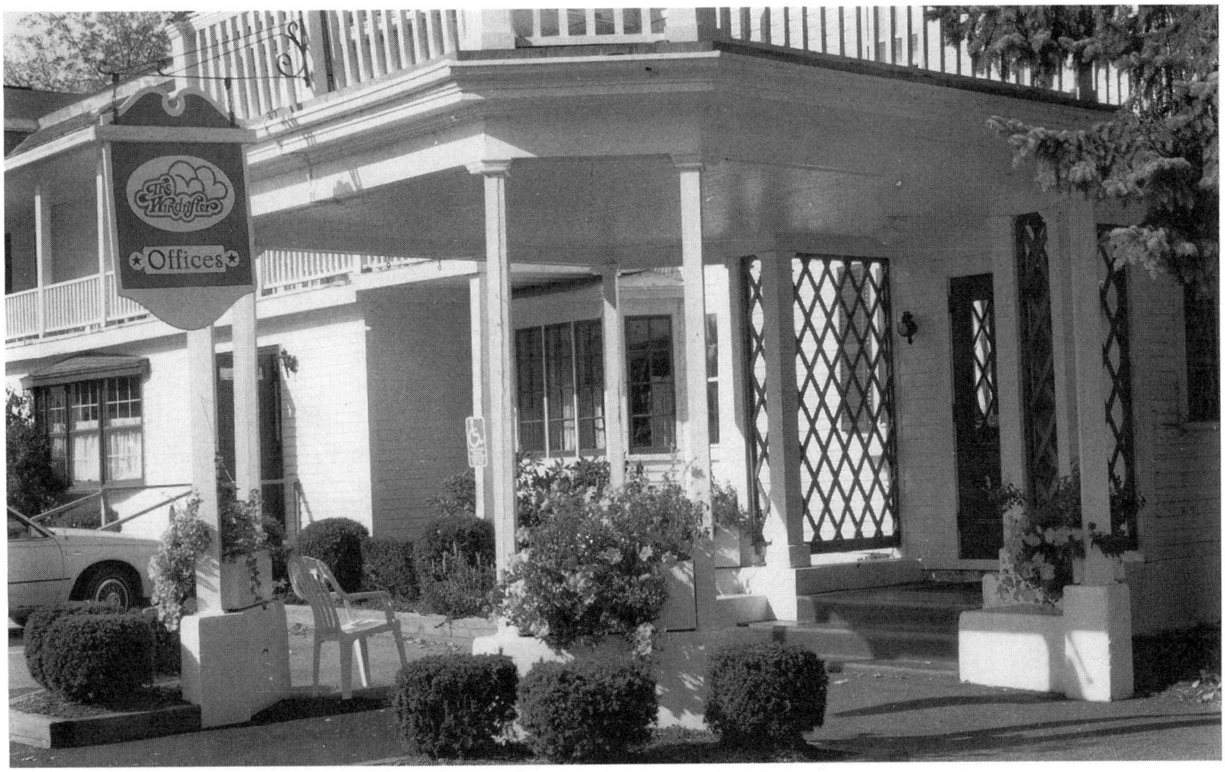


The Windrifter on South Main Street offers time-sharing condominiums as well as overnight stays and has the only indoor swimming pool available to the public (via membership) in town. The facility has operated under several different owners and names since the early part of the century. (Sandy Martin photograph, September 17, 1994)

Christy's convenience store, a popular stopping place at the corner of Route 28 (Center Street) and North Line Road. (May 4, 1994 photograph)

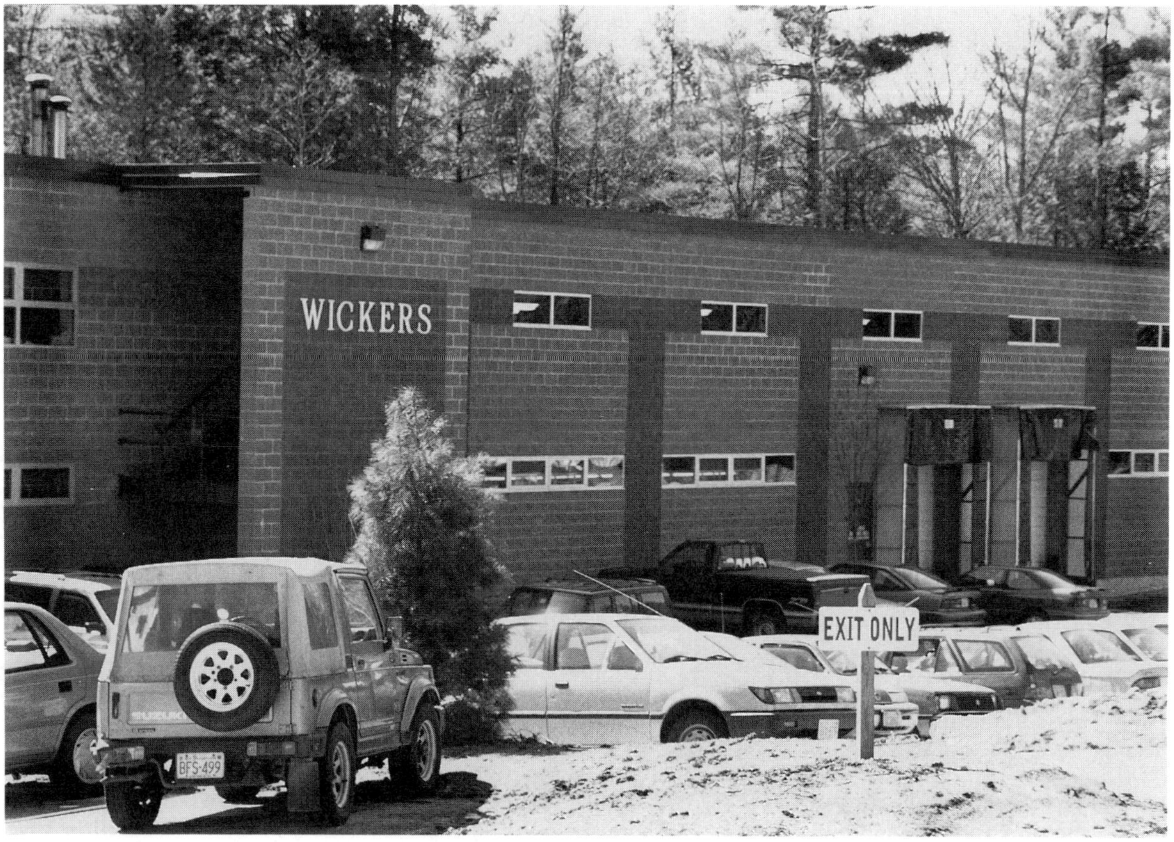


Wickers Sportswear, Inc., manufacturing plant off Pine Hill Road. The firm makes knitwear and other goods for several of the nation's leading sports clothing retailers and mail-order firms. (May 4, 1994 photograph)

Phoenix Custom Molders off Pine Hill Road not far from Wickers Sportswear. (May 4, 1994 photograph)

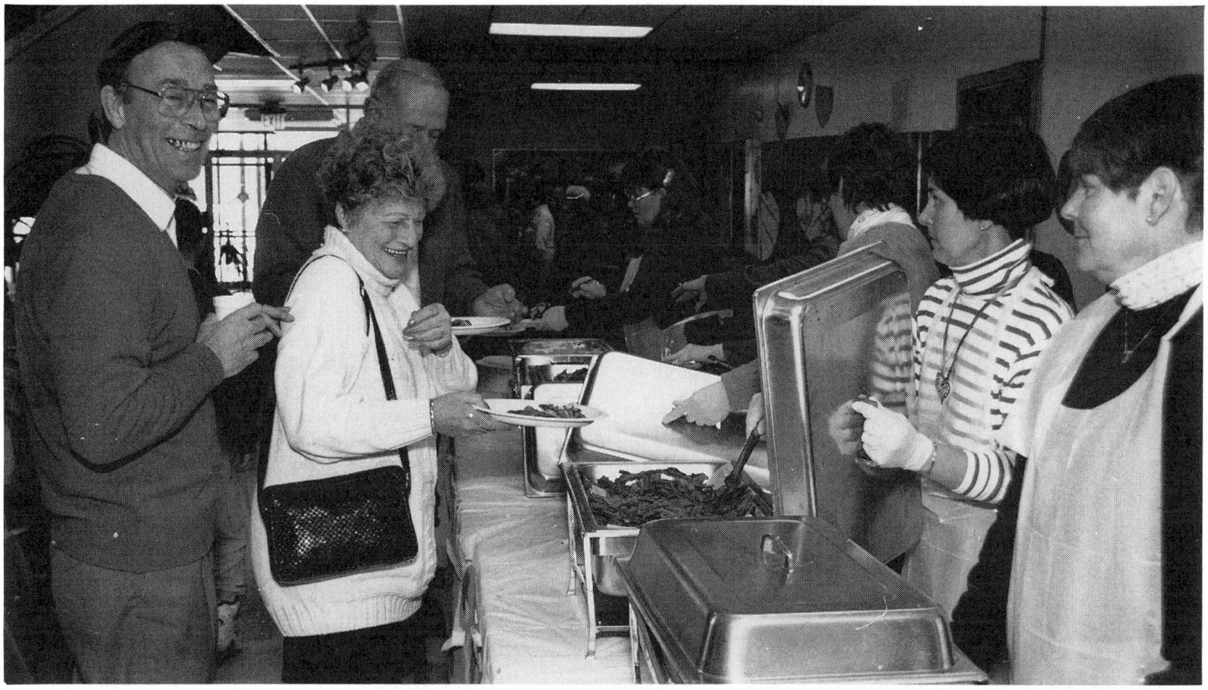

Food and beverages: Valentine's Day Brunch, February 1993, sponsored by Carpenter School and held at the Kingswood High School. Customers Paul Hatch (left) and Joan Frye are served by volunteers Karen DeVylder (holding lid) and Sue Astle (far right).

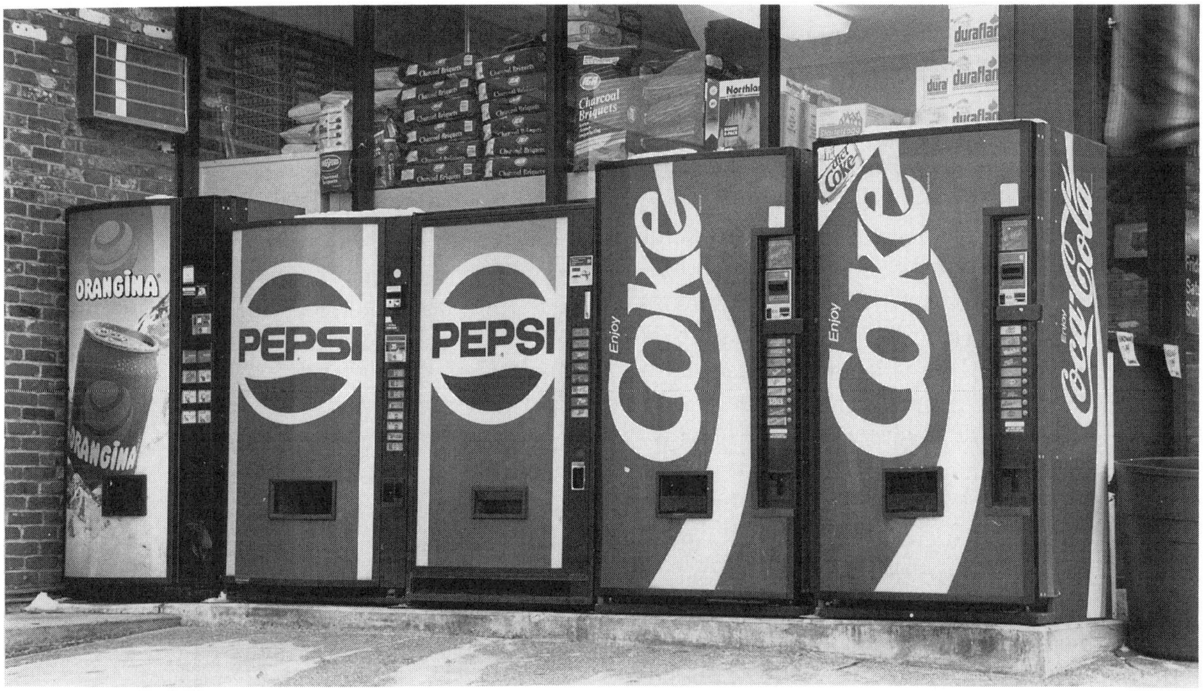


A row of soda vending machines outside Hunter's IGA. (February 1993 photograph)

August 5, 1992, and headed to Concord to enroll in the Franklin Pierce Law Center. Tempest had worked for the *Granite State News* as editor for part of 1969 and 1970 and most recently had come to town from the editorship of the *Newport Argus-Champion*. In 1992 Bruce Bedford, prize-winning photographer who had been with the paper since 1973, resigned.

In June 1993 staffers returned to town with a satchel full of awards from the NH Press Association. Mark Smith was named columnist of the year in the non-daily newspaper category. Smith and Editor Jeanne Tempest shared the second place award for community journalism. Tempest took second place for writer of the year, and Smith claimed two other awards including a second for spot news and a third for investigative reporting.

In January 1994 the newspaper won three first-place awards in the New England Press Association's Newspaper Contest. The special award for weekly newspapers was presented for "unique and outstanding journalistic accomplishment" in covering the Sarno case.[22]

Arguably, the Sarno case was the local judicial *cause célèbre* of the era. On August 22, 1992, Wolfeboro police arrested Stephen L. Sarno, age 40, of Massachusetts, following violence at Camp Ossipee in Wolfeboro. His alleged victims—his estranged wife Susan and a male companion—were treated at the emergency room at Huggins Hospital, Susan for severe injuries including what was described as a disfiguring laceration to the face, near the left eye, that required 17 stitches.

Stephen Sarno was charged with one count of simple assault and one count of second-degree assault, the latter a Class B felony. He was released from the Carroll County Jail after posting $5,000 bail. The case was to be presented in September 1992 to the Carroll County grand jury. In court, Judge William J. O'Neil accepted an arrangement whereby Stephen Sarno pleaded guilty to a misdemeanor, for which he was to serve 29 days in jail, plus 11 months deferred, possibly forever. Susan Sarno, local police, the Carroll County Against Domestic Violence and Rape group, and many citizens reacted with disappointment, frustration, and rage at what they considered to be a very light sentence.

The matter was made worse when County Attorney Maurice Geiger was alleged to have said "I can't conclude it [the attack on Susan] was completely unprovoked." He then added that Sarno could have limited his assault to just slapping the victim or to fighting the man she was with. He also said, "There's no doubt in my mind it was wrong." He made no apology for plea bargaining in this case and said he was not soft on domestic violence.

Wolfeboro police were praised for their stance, and many applauded Lt. Robert Tierney, who spoke against Geiger's and O'Neil's actions. On August 5, 1993, more than 100 people turned out for a rally at the Carroll County Court House to protest the decision and to call attention to domestic violence. Strong opinions concerning the case continued to appear in print for a long time thereafter.[23]

From the Panoramic Publishing Company office on North Main Street, Kathy Eaton and her husband Richard turned out *The Laker* newspaper at intervals more frequent during the tourist-laden summer months. Each issue was a cheery mixture of news about recreational and other pleasurable experiences, advertisements of regional merchants, photographs, and feature stories.

WASR-AM Radio 1420, owned by Alan and Sharon Severy, continued to offer a mix of old-time music with current news, signing on at sunrise and off at sunset. When the Persian Gulf War was in progress in January 1991, WASR went on the air round-the-clock with American Broadcasting Company coverage, but after 48 hours went back to regular scheduling.[24] Tom Zotti was news director.

Among many other activities, Sharon Severy was active with the Chamber of Commerce and in a publicity firm, while Alan was fond of leading cruises to Alaska. By dialing 569-LAKE (569-5253) listeners could hear the WASR Weatherphone Report 24 hours a day.

Elsewhere in the media, Scot McKay and Lois Segal formed Events Unlimited, name later changed to McSegal, Inc., and issued *The Community Phone Book* with listings of Ossipee, Wolfeboro, and Alton telephone subscribers plus a handy reverse-index. McSegal also put on events and promotions including for the Chamber of Commerce.

### Meanwhile, at Pronto Market

At Pronto Market in Clarke Plaza customers stream in and out morning, noon, and night to buy many things including snacks, coffee, soda, beer, and newspapers.

And Megabucks tickets—Megabucks tickets, as in two *winning* tickets bought for $1 each, one claimed in January 1991 by Aline and James Friedrichs which yielded $4.2 million at the rate of $212,000 per year for 20 years, and the other held by Paul W. Turner which beginning in 1993 paid out $2.8 million at $100,800 annually for the same period. Mr. and Mrs. Paul Labbe, owners of Pronto Market, received $30,000 and $28,000 for selling the two winning tickets.

### Museums and History

In 1994 Wolfeboro could boast at least four museums including one recently opened. Each acted as a drawing card for tourists.

The Clark House complex, with the nearby Pleasant Valley Schoolhouse and the Monitor Hose Company replica, all in Clark Park, continued to be operated in the summer season by the Wolfeboro Historical Society. From time to time special exhibits and lectures were featured. Under the guidance of Society President Joan Kimball and others, several members were involved in special projects. Harrison D. Moore and L. Winston Hamm announced in 1993 that they were going to videotape all of the important houses in town and record their past ownership, history, and stories. As a private venture, John Fipphen's book *Cemetery Inscriptions, Wolfeboro, New Hampshire,* was published as was Charles Campbell's book *Wolfeboro in Old Photographs* employing many old-time pictures borrowed from the Society. The Publications Committee under the direction of Chris Fipphen spent much time planning the three-volume set of Wolfeboro history books written by Q. David Bowers with major contributions by Chris Fipphen (education and schools section), Ted Brigden (churches and civic organizations), and many others, all of whom gave their time without compensation. At the 1994 town meeting, voters authorized $10,000 as a loan-grant to help fund the project. Meanwhile, many private and corporate donors helped.[25]

At the end of Main Street near the Tuftonboro line stood the Libby Museum, in operation since 1912, offering interesting exhibits from nature and history, plus occasional exhibits from artists and performers. Director Patricia F. Smith reported that during the warmer months of 1991 some 4,400 visitors crossed the threshold, a figure that went over the 5,000 mark in 1992, the year the museum celebrated its 80th anniversary (on August 22) with appetizers, refreshments, and music by the Wolfeboro Village Band. A 1912 Buick touring car—celebrating its own 80th anniversary—was another attraction on hand. Not so welcome were four or more raccoons that in October were found to have been holed up in the attic of the museum—apparently nesting for years—leaving behind 600 to 800 pounds of droppings that cost the town over $5,000 to clean up. Had the masked critters not tripped a burglar alarm, they might still be there.

In 1994 there were about 5,000 visitors to the Libby Museum, and 400 children participated in summer classes including nature classes by Sally Perkins, "Roots and Wings" by Susan Berry, and a bird-identification series conducted by June and Doug Dickinson.[26]

On Glendon Street, the Remember the Iron Horse Museum, operated by long-time railfan and historian Richard C. Libby, drew interested visitors to view railroad nostalgia in a decade in which real "iron horses" were absent from the Wolfeborough Railroad Station.

New on the local scene was the Wright Museum, a.k.a. the Wright Museum of American Enterprise 1939-1945, which opened in the summer of 1994 although construction continued to 1995. Passers-by on Center Street could not miss the World War II vintage tank appearing to burst through the front brick wall of the rectangular building. Various World War II equipment, artifacts, and other memorabilia were moved here by David M. Wright of Shrewsbury, MA, who established the facility as a non-profit enterprise. The vacant Diamond International warehouse-showroom was extensively and attractively remodeled, and new facilities were built in the back. Displays emphasized life on the home front during the war—production in factories, Red Cross activities, and other facets on the American scene. Eventually, a theatre, restaurant, and other amenities would be added according to announcements.[27] The Wright Museum soon gained nationwide notice.

## ENTERTAINMENT

### Many Activities

There was no lack of entertainment during the period, what with stage plays, concerts, exhibits, and many other attractions. Within homes, expanded cable program coverage, thousands of titles available for rental on videocassettes, and increased popularity of computers kept the eyes of people of all ages glued to the screen. In 1994 RCA announced a new satellite signal receiver that was not much larger than a cardboard pizza box. Costing about $800 to $1,000, the device challenged the more expensive large-diameter satellite dishes that had sprouted on the landscape during the past decade or so.

Darlene Williams and her Wolfeborough Historic Productions staged two plays in the early 1990s, both to great critical acclaim. *The Mill Race* dramatized life at the Amoskeag Mills (in Manchester) in the 1850s, while *Simple Gifts* described life in a New Hampshire Shaker village in the 1860s. In 1994 Darlene became Mrs. Ward Hanington and moved to Pennsylvania—a gain for the Keystone State and a loss for the Granite State.

After 1991 the Lions Club Winter Carnival was no more, and bob houses on the ice in Wolfeboro Bay were considerably fewer. In 1994 the Masonic Temple closed down, and in early 1995 it was sold to the Village Players, who planned to remodel and update its facilities. Other entertainment possibilities included a full plate of activities offered by the schools, a varied program under Susan Glenn of the Parks and Recreation Department, and more. Still, there was a call for a gathering spot in town that teenagers could call their own.

### Selected Events

**1991, January 30. Kitchensink Mime Theatre:** For preschool children. Wolfeboro Public Library.[28]

**1991, February. End of a tradition:** The 31st Annual Winter Carnival and the last of its kind. Sponsored by the Lions Club, the program spanned many days and included a dance, fishing derby, parade, spaghetti dinner, Valentine brunch (at

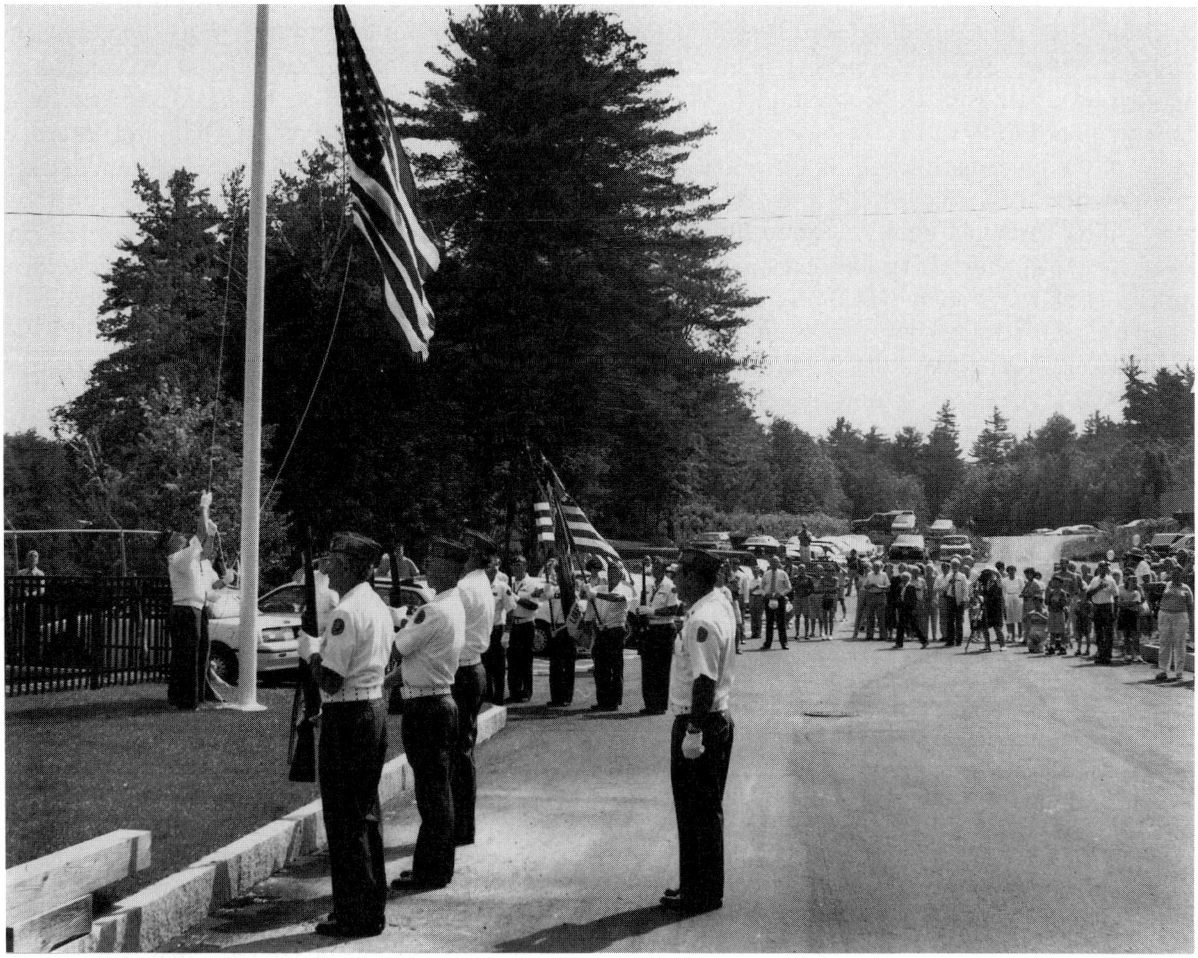

Flag raising at the opening ceremony for the Wright Museum. David Wright, a long-time summer resident of the area, moved his collection of World War II memorabilia to Wolfeboro in 1994 and set up an extensive and impressive museum on Center Street. (Sandy Martin photograph, July 16, 1994)

The Wright Museum under construction on Center Street. The gaping hole intentionally made in the front wall later framed a World War II tank seeming to burst through it. (Sandy Martin photograph, June 7, 1994)

Carpenter School), and winter sports. Attendance and interest had been declining in recent years due to expanded winter sports programs, home computers, video games, and other activities that helped pass the long winter hours.[29]

**1991, February 17. Chamber music concert:** Classical guitarist Mychal Gendron and violinist Steve Schuch. Sponsored by the Lakes Region Symphony Orchestra. Kingswood High.[30]

**1991, April 21. Eco-Fair:** Observance of Earth Day featured environmental displays, healthful products, children's activities, games, and food by Perrin's Catering.[31] At the Pinckney Boathouse on Brewster campus, a facility that hosted many functions.

**1991, April 25. Fashion show:** Second annual Spring Fashion Preview presented by WLKZ-FM Radio and Farmington National Bank to benefit the Wolfeboro Area Family YMCA. Wolfeboro Inn.[32]

**1991, May 1. Up With People concert:** At Kingswood High. Sponsored by the Wolfeboro Chamber of Commerce and WASR-AM Radio. This was the second appearance of this cosmopolitan group in town.[33]

**1991, May 3-4. Stage play:** Village Players presented *Death of a Salesman,* by Arthur Miller, directed by Michael Wilkes, at Carpenter School. Adults $5, children $3.[34]

**1991, June 22. Used book sale:** Wolfeboro Public Library.

**1991, July 4-6. Independence Day festivities:** The Brewster Academy field was not available due to its position in the path of the move of the Abbie H. Chamberlain house from the right side of the First Congregational Church to a new position several hundred feet down South Main Street. Accordingly, the carnival was held on the vacant lot on the corner of Pine and Center Streets next to Clarke Plaza. The July 4th parade, the theme of which was "Land of the Free, Home of the Brave," featured veterans from Operation Desert Storm, 80 floats, and many other attractions. Judges were George Elkins, Bert Wood, and Patricia Waterman. First-place prizes were won by Heckman's Flooring, Wolfeboro Area Children's Center, and the Wolfeboro Fireman's Relief Association and Auxiliary.[35]

**1991, July 12-13. Stage play:** Village Players presented *Saturday, the 14th,* at the Masonic Temple.

**1991, July 13-14. Arts & Crafts Festival:** Brewster athletic field. Over 125 exhibitors.[36]

**1991, July 14. Circus:** Roberts Bros. Three-Ring Circus under canvas at the Albee sand pit on Route 28 opposite the Allen "A".[37]

**1991, July 19-20. Antiques show:** Annual E.M.C. French Wolfeboro Antiques Show & Sale at Kingswood High. Sponsored this year by Goosefare Antiques & Promotions.[38]

**1991, July 20. All Saints' Summer Fair:** Annual event

**1991, July 25. Film and lecture:** *Legacy of a Loon* presented by Dan Evans, a marine biologist specializing in Lake Winnipesaukee. Held at the Public Library and sponsored by the Friends of the Library.[39] Beginning in the 1980s the loon became a prime symbol for ecology and wildlife preservation, and as area lakes have a generous quota of these large and beautiful birds, it wasn't long until many shops on Main Street in Wolfeboro had loon-motif T-shirts, napkins, postcards, calendars, sculptures, key chains, posters, jackets, books, caps, and sweaters in their windows.

**1991, August 4-18. Blockhaven at Brewster Summer Music Festival:** Five concerts featuring the Block Ensemble and other artists.[40]

**1991, August 14. Artists in the Park:** Annual exhibition under canvas of several dozen juried artisans held in Cate and Town Parks under the sponsorship of the Governor Wentworth Arts Council.[41]

**1991, August 17. Rock band concert:** Cate Park. Featured local rock bands Black Letter and KITE. Sponsored by the Governor Wentworth Arts Council.[42]

**1991, October 12. Ham and bean supper:** At the Fire Station. Sponsored by the Wolfeboro Firefighters Auxiliary.[43]

**1991, October 26. Pumpkin contest for kids:** At the JC Penney/Stinchfield's parking lot. Prizes, balloons, free cider from the Dow Farm.[44]

**1991, November 9. Pancake breakfast:** By Wolfeboro Area Boy Scout Troop 165 at the Kingswood Voc-Tech Dining Room. Followed by the annual Ski and Skate Swap (to benefit the Wolfeboro Area Childrens' Center).[45]

**1991, November 15-16. Two stage plays:** The Village Players presented A.T. Gurley's *The Dining Room* at the Masonic Temple on Glendon Street, while the Mask and Dagger Society of Kingswood High presented *Camelot* at the school.[46]

**1991, December. Tough time for Santa:** On Saturday, November 30, Santa Claus arrived in town on a horse-drawn carriage, to remain until Christmas to spread good cheer among the younger set. Santa's Hut was in a new location behind the Railroad Station, out of the way and, as it turned out, with both the hut and its electrical wiring in poor repair. Attendance was less than in previous years. Some non-believers made matters worse by shouting foul language at Santa and pelting him with snowballs.[47]

**1992, March 28. Concert:** Ha'Penny Theatre presented by the Wolfeboro Area Children's Center. Kingswood High.[48]

**1992, April 4. Stage play:** *January Thaw,* a comedy, was performed by Kingswood High School's Mask and Dagger Society.[49]

**1992, May 9. Walk-a-Thon:** Second annual Walk for Kids to benefit the Harbor House.

**1992, July 18. Radio auction:** Annual event sponsored by the Wolfeboro Rotary Club to benefit its many charitable activities. Donations by area merchants and others.

**1992, July 22. Band concert:** Performance by the newly-formed Cate Park Band, a "hometown summer band" under the direction of Jean Kemp. Included six flutes, two French horns, three trombones, a tuba, a snare drum, a bass drum and a clarinet or two. About 100 people gathered to listen.[50]

**1992, July 24-25. Antiques Fair, Antiquarian Book Fair:** Brewster Gymnasium. Sponsored by Water Village Promotions.[51]

**1992, August 13-15. Stage play:** Wolfeborough Historic Productions presented *The Mill Race* upstairs in the theatre in the Wolfeboro Town Hall. Music and lyrics were by Darlene Williams, Mary Paterno, and William Fluhr. Subsequent performances were given outdoors in Clark Park as well as in Bristol, Ossipee, and Wakefield.[52]

**1992, August 16. WinnipeDUCKee Race:** Numbered toy ducks afloat to benefit the Southern Carroll County Chapter of the American Cancer Society. Sandy Ballentine won the $500 cash prize donated by the First NH Bank.[53]

**1992, August 22. Mystery dinner theatre:** Presented by the Without a Clue Mystery Players, "Dances With Werewolves" was held at the American Legion to benefit the Appalachian Mountain Teen Project.[54]

**1992, September 18-20. Applefest '92:** Pony rides, pie-baking contest, etc., sponsored by the Chamber of Commerce and 18 local businesses.[55]

**1992, November 28. Crafts open house:** "A Gathering of Friends," a Christmas open house featuring artisans and their

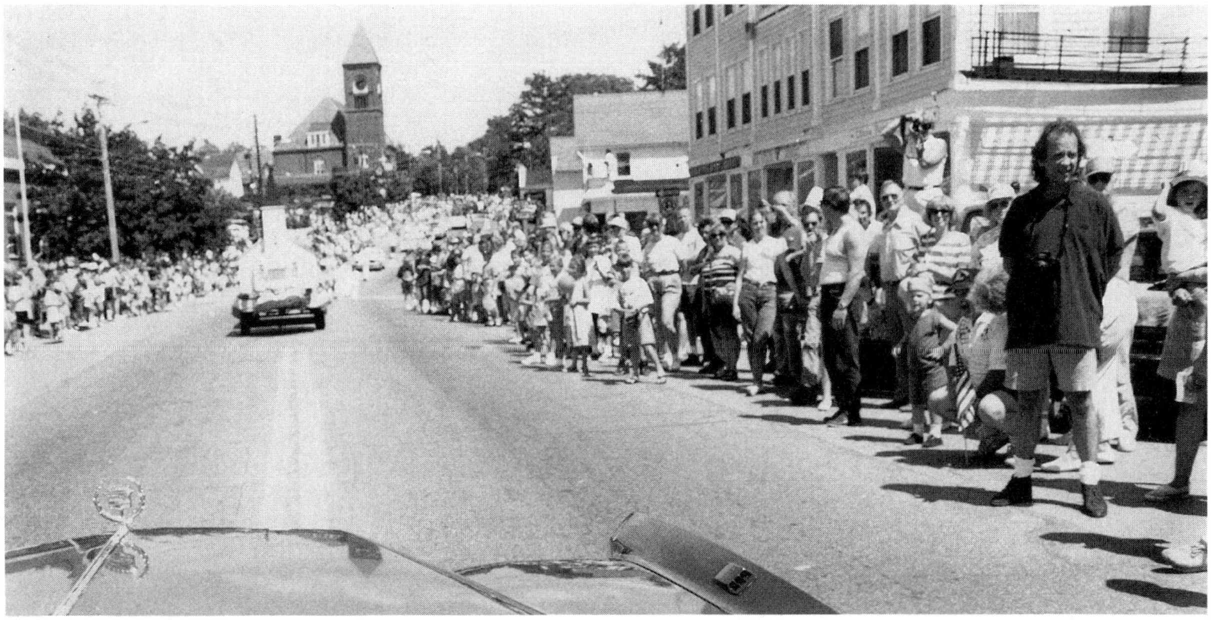

Independence Day 1993: A participant's eye view of the 1993 Independence Day parade as the floats and vehicles approach the Avery Building (right) with the Town Hall in the distance.

Independence Day 1994: By the rocket's red glare celebrants on Brewster Field watch the fireworks illuminate the sky on July 4, 1994. Thousands of spectators gathered at vantage points downtown and aboard several hundred boats in the lake. Each year in recent decades the American Legion has supervised a pyrotechnics display launched from near the shore of Wolfeboro Bay, usually at 10 p.m., continuing to about 10:25 or so, on the Fourth of July. (Sandy Martin photograph)

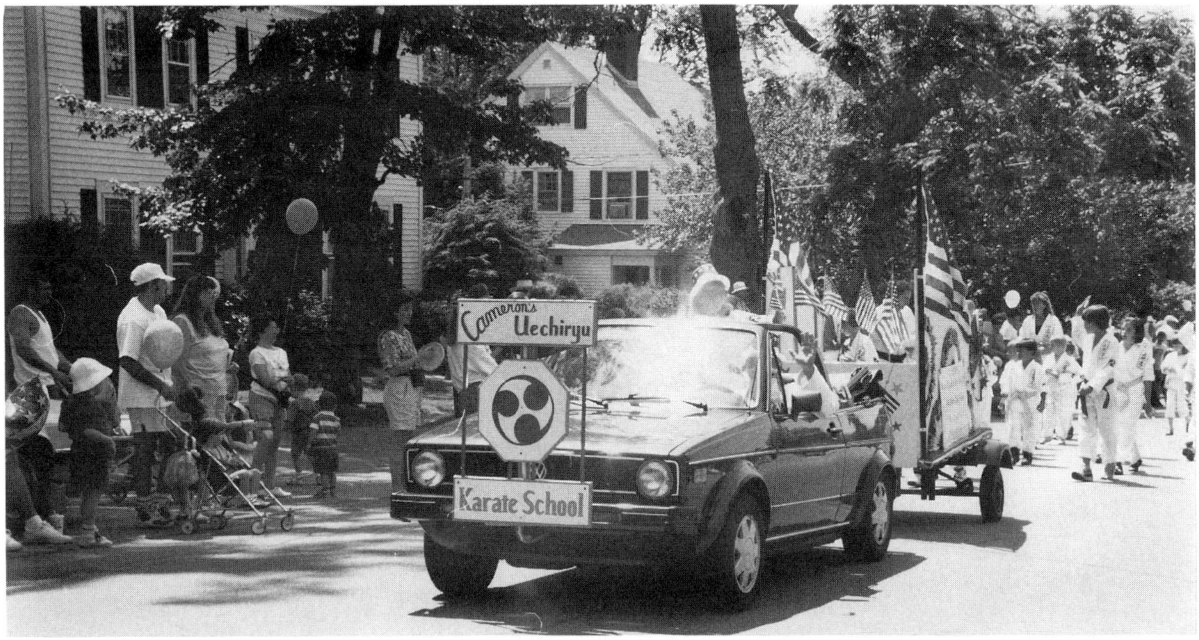


1994 Independence Day parade: Cameron's Uechiryu Karate School, James Cameron, owner, and some of his youthful students. The school offers classes for all ages and is located at The Centre on Varney Road.

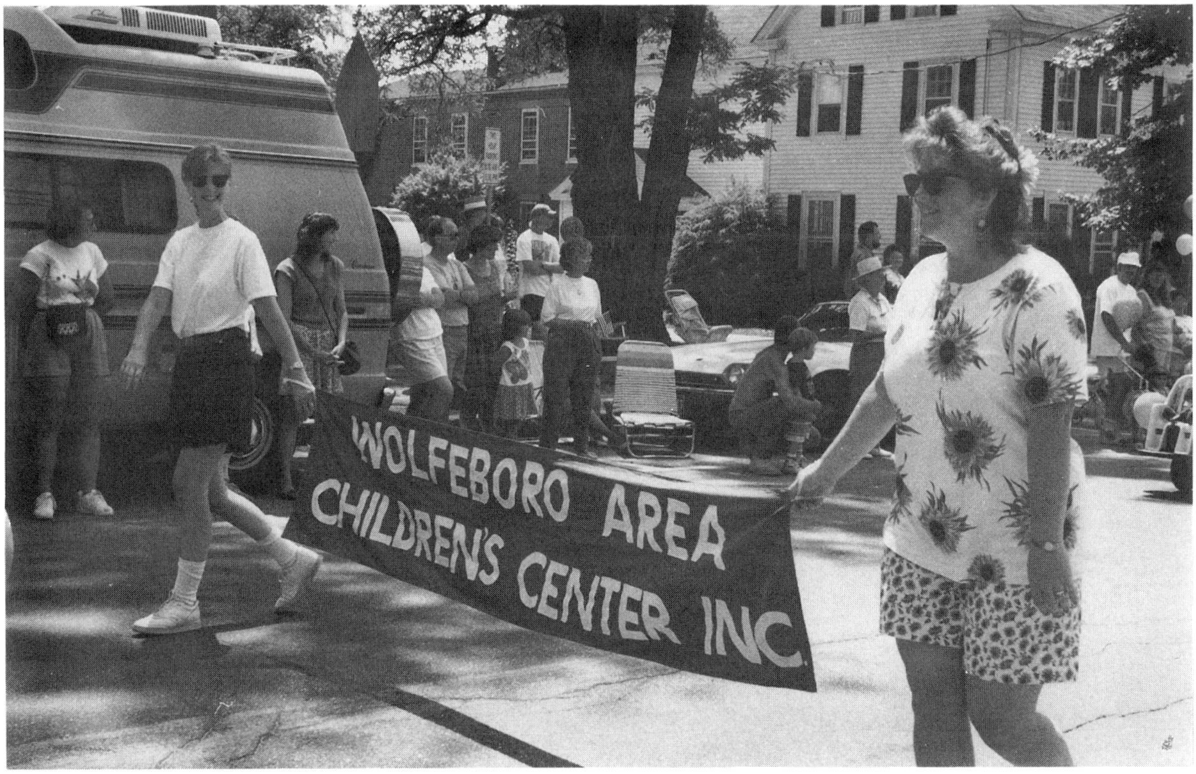


Wolfeboro Area Children's Center entry in the Fourth of July parade, 1994. (Sandy Martin photographs; views taken from in front of Town Hall looking toward the Avery House)

1994 Independence Day parade: Dave Bowers at the wheel of his 1972 Cadillac Eldorado convertible pulling a circa 1921 National air calliope with 53 brass whistles in the 1994 Independence Day parade. The calliope plays automatically from interchangeable perforated paper rolls each containing a program of 10 tunes. The poster on the side of the car is for the 1994 re-election campaign of Governor Steve Merrill.

Molly the Trolley. Advertisers whose notices appear on the side of the vehicle include Bailey's restaurant, Miller's automobile agency, Barnstormers (theatre in Tamworth), West Lake restaurant, and Kokopelli Native American crafts. Molly has been a summertime fixture in town since 1987. (Sandy Martin photographs)

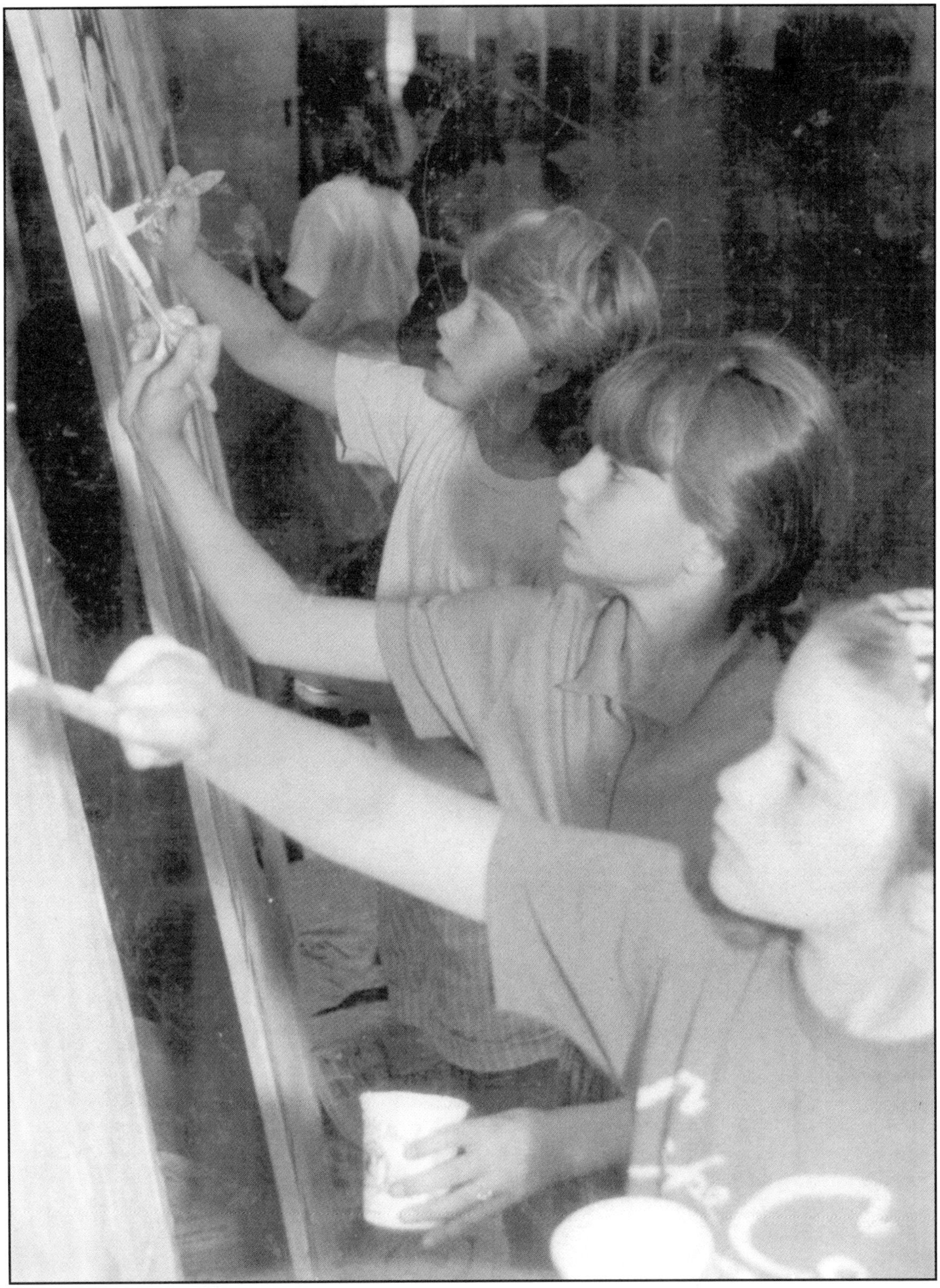

Behind the scenes at the Kingswood Summer Theatre for Children, 1992, painting the flats for *Oliver*. Front to back: Kim Martin, Caitlyn Corson, and Nicole Black. Directed by Nathalie Erickson, the play was staged on July 24, 27, and 28. (Ashton Woodhouse photograph for the *Granite State News*, July 15, 1992)

Entertainment by the younger set: The Carpenter School Christmas Concert chorus directed by Lisa Goodwin. Shown in the front row, left to right: Christine Hatch, Courtney Eckhoff, Alissa Leone, and Kim Martin. (Sandy Martin photograph, 1993)

**Music fills the air at Carpenter School: Robin McDonald, interim band leader, conducts students at a Memorial Day observance. (Sandy Martin photograph, 1993)**

**Richard Hatshorne, a chamber music player from southern New Hampshire, demonstrates instruments to youngsters gathered in the gymnasium. (Sandy Martin photograph, 1990)**

crafts, was held at the home of Amy and Eric Piper on South Main Street. Amy operated Creative Design Jewelry while Eric's business was Image Awnings. The open house was continued as an annual event.

**1993, March 30. First Annual Fashion Blast:** Held at the Back Bay Club, this event featured designs and techniques displayed by Annie's Mercantile, ReThreads, Stay Tuned, Trim Tan, and Hair FX.[56] As it turned out, this was also the one and only annual event.

**1993, May 15. Carpenter School Spring Fair:** Baked goods, children's games, silent auction, children's Chinese auction, refreshments, face painting, story telling, magic and more. Popular annual event.[57]

**1993, May 30. Memorial Day observance:** Featured the addition of nine new names to the plaques near the Soldiers' Monument at Pickering Corner. The names included one from World War II, three from the Vietnam War, plus five from the 1989 Panama invasion and the 1991 Persian Gulf War (Operation Desert Storm).[58]

**1993, June 5. Stage presentation:** The Miniature Theatre of Chester presented *Screaming For Trains,* by Mitchell Ganem, at Kingswood High. Ganem, a playwright, was a graduate of Kingswood High and the son of well-known local figures Philip and Shirley Ganem. The play opened to critical acclaim the week before at the Iron Horse Music Hall in Northampton, MA. Meghan Cary starred as Little Wing in the one-woman show. Featured the music of Jimi Hendrix, Bob Dylan, and Stephen Foster.[59]

**1993, July. Jaunts to Meredith:** Aboard Molly the Trolley on Tuesday and Saturday nights for dinner at Mame's Restaurant and a play at the Lakes Region Summer Theatre.[60] By this time Molly was a town fixture in the summer.

**1993, July 24. Airplane rides:** "A Flight to Fight Cancer" sponsored by the American Cancer Society at the Lakes Region Airpark. $10 was the cost of a 10- to 15-minute ride.[61]

**1993, July-August. Stage play:** *Nunsense,* a comedy about five little sisters of Hoboken, by the Village Players. Given on five different days.[62]

**1993, July 30, August 2-3. Stage play:** *Annie Get Your Gun,* presented by the Kingswood Summer Theatre for Children. Nathalie Erickson, director. Annie was played by Kathryn Stone, Allison McIntosh was Dolly, and Alec O'Meara took the part of Frank.[63]

**1993, August 6-7. Huggins Hospital Street Fair:** Annual fund-raising event exceeded even the $130,000 gross raised in 1992, according to coordinator Stephen Jones. After expenses this netted about $80,000 for the hospital. Booths, food, games, exhibits, and more.[64]

**1993, September 25. Male strippers:** "Men From Heaven," billed as "the sexiest male revue on the East Coast," was held at the Allen "A" Theatre.[65]

**1993, October 15-16. Stage play:** Wolfeborough Historic Productions presented *Simple Gifts,* a new musical by Darlene Williams, at the Town Hall. Featured players included Jenna Van Valen and James Williams. Others in the cast were Mark Dearborn, Marilyn McBride, Helen White, Angela Williams, Melissa Koda, Chris Tancrede, Betty Mata, Ward Hanington, Carol Cloutier, and Martha Peterson. The production was later staged at the Church of Jesus Christ of Latter Day Saints on North Main Street and at the Rochester Middle School.[66]

**1993, October 29. Hallowe'en dance:** 4th Annual Hallowe'en Masquerade Ball to benefit the Wolfeboro Area Children's Center Building Fund. Back Bay Club. Arranged by Events Unlimited.

**1993, November 20. Casino Night:** Las Vegas-style games to benefit the Hospice of Southern Carroll County. Brewster Academy. Similar events were held at other times in other locations by other sponsors including the Chamber of Commerce. Typical games of chance included blackjack, roulette, craps, and the wheel-of-fortune.[67]

**1993, December 12. Christmas pageant:** *Glad Tidings,* the story of the first Christmas, was staged at the Albee sand pit by the Evangelical Bible Church.[68]

**1993, December 31. Local talent goes to Portsmouth:** Melissa Koda, violinist, and James Williams, violist, both Kingswood students, had successfully auditioned for membership in the Portsmouth Youth String Ensemble. They performed with the group at Theatre by the Sea in Prescott Park the preceding summer and on New Year's Eve appeared in two concerts.[69]

**1993-1994. Pageant finalist:** Kristin J. Thurston, age 12 (in 1993), was featured on the radio and in the local press as a competitor and finalist in several contests including in 1993 the Miss New Hampshire Pre-Teen Pageant and National Pre-Teen Pageant.[70] In 1994 she was the second runner-up in the Miss National Pre-Teen Pageant in Orlando, FL, and won a $1,500 savings bond and other prizes.[71]

**1994, June 3-4. Clearlakes Chorale:** Annual Spring Concert at All Saints' Episcopal Church. Directed by Scott Lounsbury, accompanied by Cathy Marker.[72]

**1994, summer. WASR lake reports:** In season the local AM radio station broadcast reports of conditions on Lake Winnipesaukee from aboard the wheelhouse of the motor vessel *Mount Washington.* The typical commentary told of wave height, the availability of docking spaces at various ports, and the weather. Each morning in a separate feature John F. Bridges gave a special report from Little Barndoor Island, facing Wolfeboro Bay. Typically, John would arise very early, say at 5 a.m., and row around the islands including Little and Big Barndoor, Keniston, Melody, and the intermediate tiny islets, and would prepare a broadcast of what he had seen—a mother loon and her chicks, a moose on shore, a swimming squirrel, or whatever—often accompanied by an anecdote or two about lake lore and legend.

**1994, July 16. Hike:** TRAC-TREK, 2.7-mile hike from the Russell C. Chase Bridge-Falls Path to Lake Wentworth, culminating with a picnic.[73]

**1994, July 20. Abenaki Music Festival:** Abenaki Recreation Area. Second annual event co-sponsored by the Parks and Recreation Department to benefit the Appalachian Mountain Teen Project, a community-based prevention and intervention program.[74]

**1994, July 29-August 2. Stage play**: Kingswood Summer Theatre for Children presented *Annie* with Emily Copplestone in the title role. Kingswood High School. Nathalie Erickson, director.[75]

**1994, July 30. Family music festival:** Abenaki Ski Area. Music by David Colburn and Deborah Stuart; Positive Repercussions, a local band; The Blackwater Band (Carolyn Parrott, David Levine, and Bradshaw Nelson Dorsey); Unbroken Chain; and T.J. Wheeler and The Smokers.[76]

**1994, August 11-12. Stage play:** *Lend Me A Tenor* by the Village Players. Kingswood High.

**1994, August 26-27. Sidewalk Sale Days:** Sponsored by the Chamber of Commerce. The Chamber hit its stride during the era and staged many attention-getting promotions.

**1994, September 9. Poetry recital:** "Poetry Jam" in Wolfeboro Marketplace behind Made On Earth. First of a series.[77]

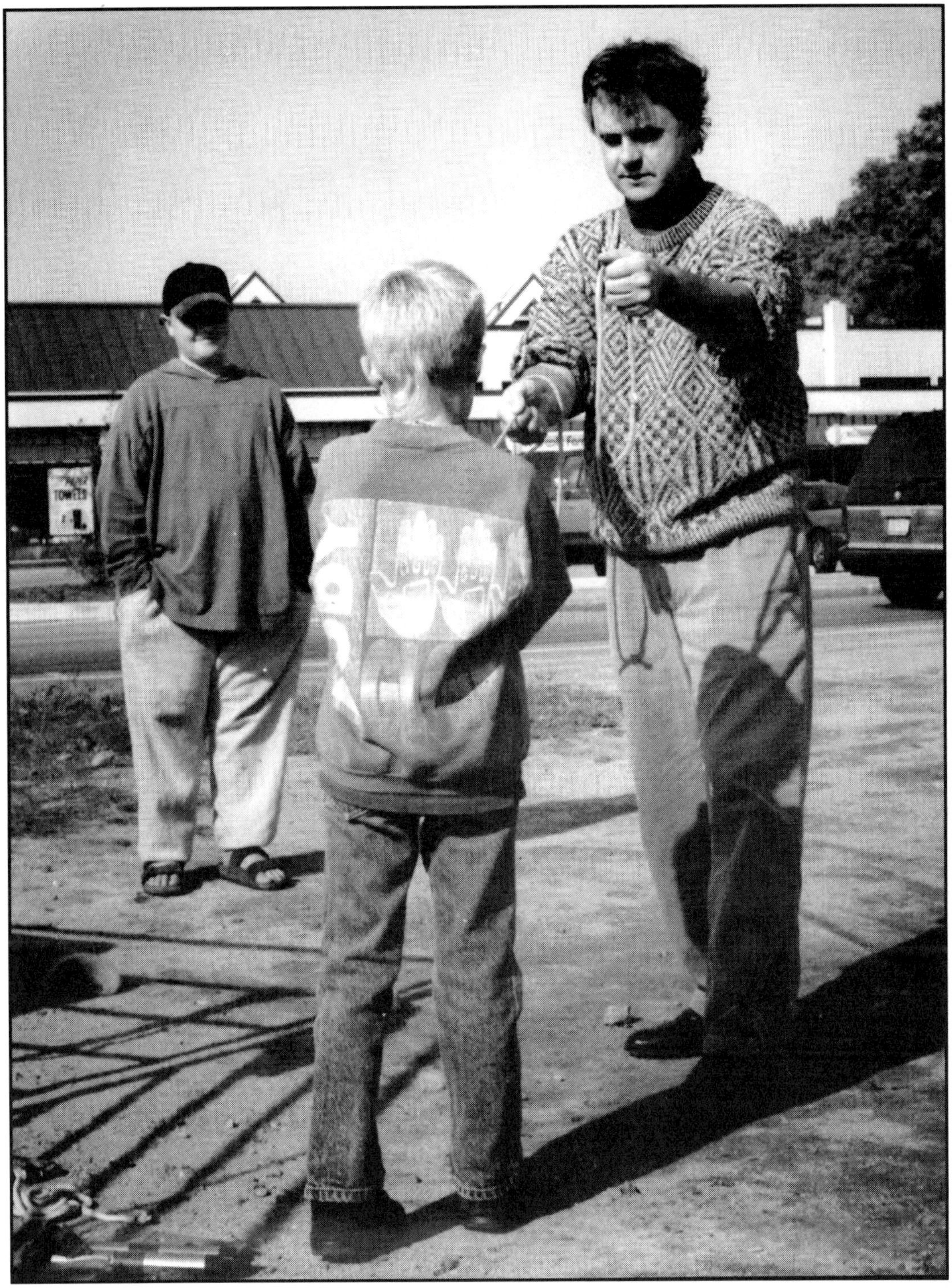

Jeb Bradley, representative to the State Legislature and owner of the Evergrain health food store, performs some magic tricks for youthful onlookers at Clarke Plaza during an Octoberfest celebration. The Wolfeboro Shopping Center is in the distance across Center Street. (Ashton Woodhouse photograph)

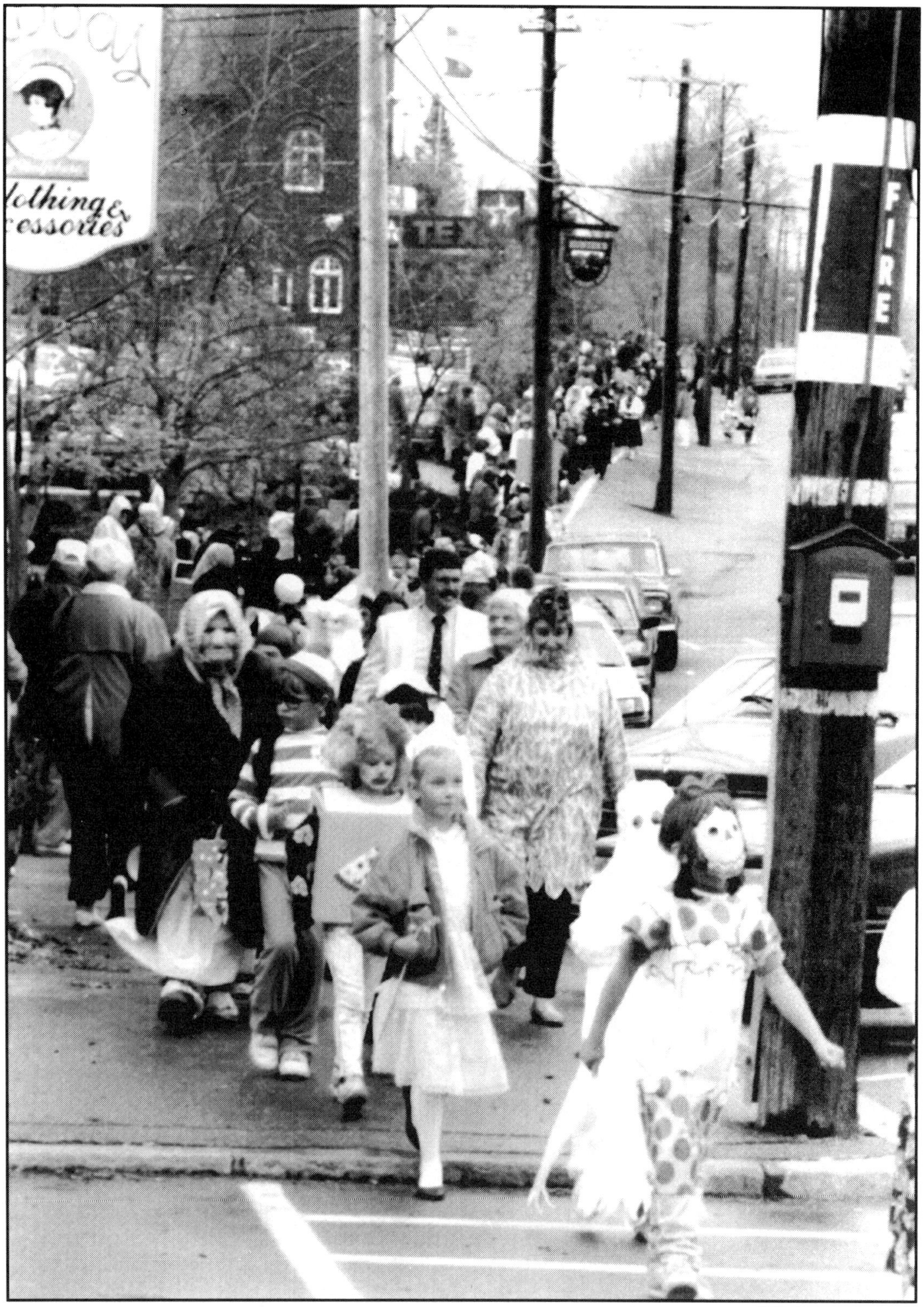


The Hallowe'en parade is an annual tradition for Carpenter School children. The route typically begins at the school, goes downhill on South Main Street to the business district, up North Main Street, across the street, and back down the other side. This view shows marchers on the sidewalk in front of the Post Office and crossing the street. The sign at upper left is for Moods clothing store in the Bank Building. (Ashton Woodhouse photograph, October 1991)

**1994, September 23-25. Applefest '94:** Events included an apple pie baking contest, supper at All Saints' Episcopal Church, a square dance and country line dancing on Railroad Avenue, the Shaw Brothers in concert at the Brewster Gym, apple-bobbing (at Tender Times), pancake breakfast (on the lawn of the Clipper Home), cider making (at Bridges' Hallmark and Sawmill Marina, courtesy of DeVylder Farms), and pony rides. Champion pie-makers were Cathy Kibbey (first prize), Betty Ann French, and Janet Maguire.[78] On September 25, rides in old-time wooden boats were given to benefit L.I.F.E. Ministries.

**1994, October 16. Fourth Annual Oktoberfest:** Wolfeboro Inn. Outdoor tent, German band, etc. Demonstration of "Sled Dogs" (shoes with snow ski bottoms) was held by Dive Winnipesaukee; interested attendees could "ski" downward on a rotating belt of carpeting while holding on to a handrail.[79]

**1994, December 9-10. Concert:** Clearlakes Chorale. Annual Christmas Concert at All Saints' Episcopal Church. Directed by Scott Lounsbury, accompanied by Cathy Marker.

**1994, December 10-11. Concert:** Kingswood High School Music Department presented its annual Christmas "Pops" Concert including a jazz-rock band and an 89-member symphonic band.[80]

**1994, December 31, New Year's Eve. First Night:** The year 1994, and with it the time period covered by this book, ended at midnight, December 31. It was a cold, but not bitter evening with most snow gone from the ground due to recent rain (the next snow would arrive on January 2). First Night was patterned after celebrations popularized in recent years in Concord, Portsmouth, and other large cities around New England and the nation. Several dozen citizens, firms, and others banded together to create a non-stop program from the afternoon of the 31st onward, culminated by a brilliant display of fireworks at midnight. Among the events were square dancing; ballads; an adult farce for "mature kids"; storytelling; puppet and marionette shows; clowns; Hot Peppers jump rope team demonstrations; Jim Cameron and his students in karate demonstrations; music by a harpist, pianists, guitarists, a flutist a barber shop quartet, folk singers, balladeers, organists, vocalists performing show tunes, and jazz performers; comedy classics of early film including Harold Lloyd, Charlie Chaplin, and Laurel & Hardy; a film festival for children; window displays; juggling and magic acts; a teenage dance; country line dancing; a lip-sync contest pitting teams from local real-estate firms against each other; snow and ice sculptures; a bonfire; and lots of snacks and refreshments including hot chocolate, coffee, and cookies. Gathering places included All Saints' Church, The Art Place, Avery Insurance, Brewster Gym, Carpenter School, Cate Park, Wolfeboro Area Children's Center, Church of the Nazarene, Clarke Plaza, Clipper Home, Country Bookseller, Dive Winnipesaukee, Estabrook Hall at Brewster Academy, First Christian Church, First Congregational Church, Hamel-DeWolfe Real Estate, Kingswood High School, Kingswood Middle School, The Ledges, Made on Earth, Moods, Pop Whalen Arena, Wolfeboro Public Library, and Stay Tuned. Joining Chairperson Jean S. Rowley (the initial force behind the project) were planners and committee members including Donna King Cooper, Ruth Glidden, Debbie Hopkins, Andy Milligan, Nancy Piper, Elli Tappan, Pam Tuttle, and many others including members of the sponsoring organizations, the Governor Wentworth Arts Council and the Wolfeboro Chamber of Commerce. By all accounts the celebration was a resounding success.[81]

## SPORTS

### Many Options

Sports continued to be a vital element in the local scene in the early 1990s. The Wolfeboro Parks and Recreation Department under Sue Glenn offered a wide selection of activities year-round, while Carpenter School, Kingswood Middle School, Kingswood High School, and Brewster Academy were active during the academic year.

The position of athletics in local schools is reflected by this comment in the Kingswood High yearbook, *Lance,* in 1993:

> Sports are a very important part of Kingswood. Sports gives you another way of reaching true teamwork, sportsmanship, and one's individual potential. From golf to softball, to the 1992 Girls' Basketball team winning the Class I Championship game, to Kingswood's own Stephanie Barbier being number three in the state in tennis and Jamie Hurtado being an All-State Golfer, to our own Girls' Field Hockey team being number one in the state.

And this from the 1994 edition:

> Athletics have always played a major role in the life of a Kingswood student. Sports have given many the chance to succeed both as an individual, but more importantly as a team member. The 1993-94 season was no exception. This year's soccer teams made impressive runs, narrowly missing the playoffs, and the golf team out-hit their expectations by far. The field hockey and football teams were by far the most impressive, though. The field hockey team made the Class I finals for the fifth year in a row and barely missed repeating their championship in a tough 1-0 double overtime loss. They also had four players make the New Hampshire AAU team which competed in California. The football team was equally impressive winning the most games in a season since 1985 and reaching the playoffs for the second year in a row.

A small sample of hundreds of contests and dozens of teams is given here.[82]

### Baseball

Baseball remained a popular warm-weather sport for all ages. The Wolfeboro-Tuftonboro Little League, popular with the younger set, was divided into the American League and National League and during the 1991-1994 years fielded teams with such designations as the Lawyers, Bankers, Lauber's, Carroll County Glass, Bradley's, Ben Franklin, Varney's, Bailey's, Wolfeboro Oilers, IGA, Loft, Albee's, Scuba Dudes, Corner Store, Osgood's, Miltner's, and Century 21—reflecting the names of their sponsors. In 1992 the Lawyers captured the league championship by edging the Scuba Dudes 17-16 in what was described as the most exciting game in league history. Mike Heald led the Lawyers with five hits and four runs, while Matthew Sheldon starred for the Scuba Dudes with six hits and five runs. Michael Hutchins slammed a notable home run, and Andrew Grupp tripled. In the 1993 championship playoff, the Community Bankers beat Bailey's 14-12 despite home runs hit for Bailey's by Brett Newcomb and Chris Helgerson.[83]

In 1991 the Kingswood boys' varsity baseball team played such opponents as Kennett, Sanborn, Timberlane, and Oyster River. In a notable encounter, Kingswood "ground Oyster River into the dirt" with a 23-7 win that featured a barrage of 18 hits. Frank Dodge got four runs, Brian Swinerton, three. Jesse Hooper, Andrew Cornwell, Gregg Walsh, and Josh Sciami hit two singles apiece, with Hooper, Cornwell, and Joel Hayford each bringing in three runners.[84]

In a representative vignette of Kingswood Knights varsity baseball activity for early May 1992, the team had a record of 10-2 at that point, having recently beat Timberland 4-2 (Jason Williams hit a spectacular three-run homer, and Rob Newhall singled to drive in Caleb Rudolph), lost to Goffstown 6-2, and beat Plymouth 6-5. In the last encounter Jason Williams was pitcher for the first three innings and struck out three, while Jesse Hooper finished the game with seven strikeouts.[85]

An account of the Kingswood Knights girls' softball game win against Oyster River 27-8 on May 13, 1993, noted:[86]

> Chris Richards hit two singles and scored three runs; Jill Hayford banged out two singles and a triple; Amy Floria hit another triple plus two singles and scored once; Shelley Libby tripled, singled twice, and scored three times. Kate Phillips hit three singles, doubled once and scored three runs; Jennifer Marschner doubled and scored four times; Shauna Michaud singled three times and scored three runs; Jessica Cornwell singled, doubled, scored three times, and stole three bases; Melanie Dufy singled twice, stole once and scored four runs.

In May 1993 the Kingswood girls' varsity softball team finished the season with a record of 11-5, the best in four years, enough to earn them a fifth-place finish in Class I. "This was the highest we've finished in the 15 years I've been here," said Coach Bonnie Lord.[87]

On April 19, 1994, in its opening game with Plymouth the Kingswood Middle School baseball team won 8-1. Allie Skelley struck out 13 batters and threw a no-hitter. In June senior Craig Johnson was named to the Class I All-State Team and the Granite State Team, the only Knight to receive either honor.[88]

### Basketball

In March 1991 four players from the Kingswood varsity boys' squad and three from the girls' team were named to the Granite I All-State teams: Craig Vezina (who in January had set a school career record by beating the 1,057 points achieved by Greg Dollarhide in 1981), John DiPaolo, Mark Roark, and Jeremy Osgood, Nicole LaBelle, Chris Richards, and Michelle Hermann. Boys' basketball coach Mike Rathgeber shared the honor of Coach of the Year along with the Timberlane head coach.[89]

The Wolfeboro-Tuftonboro Youth Girls' Basketball league included newsworthy players such as Jessica Bauer, Valerie Blais, Laura Buffa, Michelle Dumont, Christie Fluery, Karen Hadock, Susan Harrington, Stephanie Hunter, Angela Hutchins, Jennifer Jones, Jessica Kissell, Shannon Miller, Cory Milne, and Kristy Smith. The league had two divisions and many teams.[90]

The following sketch of the league's activities was provided by Frank X. Holt:[91]

> At the start of the 1990s the Wolfeboro-Tuftonboro Youth Girls Basketball League consisted of six teams in one division for fourth, fifth, and sixth grade girls. Under the guidance of Commissioner Frank Holt the league expanded enormously in the first half of the decade. In the 1992-1992 season, with greatly increased interest in girls' basketball in the community, the league grew to eight teams, still limited to grades 4 through 6. In the 1992-1993 season the league divided into Lower and Upper Divisions, with a new Upper Division consisting of four teams of girls in grades 7 through 9. Each division fielded an All-Star team which competed in area tournaments.
>
> In the 1993-1994 season a traveling team of seventh and eighth grade girls known as The Heat became a charter member of the newly-formed Great Eastern New Hampshire Basketball League. These girls play against seven other private school and community recreation teams throughout the lakes and seacoast areas. Over two years The Heat was built into a sturdy team which won a Great Eastern New Hampshire League Tournament championship on February 19, 1995, beating a previously undefeated Wakefield team. Kristy Smith of Wolfeboro scored 32 points in the championship game. Steve Marden, co-coach (with Frank Holt) of The Heat, made a promise that if the Heat won the League championship against Wakefield, the girls could shave his head. The Heat won, and for a while Steve was known as "Coach Baldie."
>
> The League provides organized competition for approximately 145 girls on 14 teams during the regular season. Throughout the course of a season 175 games are played, most at Kingswood Regional Middle School, but with occasional games at Brewster Academy. Additionally, All Star Teams and summer teams play another 50 ball games. There are so many teams needing practice time that the league is looking forward to the opening of the new gymnasium at Tuftonboro Central School. As a testimony to the increasing skills, speed, and number of schoolgirls participating, it is noted that the Carpenter School gym, once the home of the League, is now considered far too small for competition and severely limited for practice purposes.
>
> During the summer and autumn seasons the League runs basketball skills clinics. In the summer of 1995 in participation with Gilford, Upper Division girls played on a new AAU Club, the Mid-State Panthers, which plays for six weeks or so in June, July, and August.
>
> A benefit game that was initiated in 1992 is held each spring in which the members of the All-Star teams play against their coaches and parents. This is titled The Aging Hoopster Game, and it raises money for the league's summer basketball camp scholarship fund.
>
> Each year a league Awards Night is held in which the league participants and their families fill Estabrook Hall on the Brewster campus to receive awards for their achievements.
>
> The league maintains a good working relationship with the Women's Basketball Program at the University of New

The Kingswood Knights, Class I state basketball champions, as photographed after their February 29, 1992 win, the first such championship in Kingswood history.

Front row, left to right: Co-captains Shauna Michaud and Michelle Hermann.

Second row: Keri Edmunds, Jenni Spack, Tanya Lee, Maura Donovan, and Shelley Stevens.

Third row: Head Coach Bruce Hermann, Katie Roark, Amy Floria, Alicia Phillips, Nicole LaBelle, and Assistant Coach Larry Kimball. (*Granite State News* photograph)

Hampshire in Durham. Many players attend the UNH summer basketball camp, and UNH has often invited teams from the league to play games on "the big floor" at UNH during halftime of Women's Varsity games. A few players have had the excitement of being ball girls at these games as well.

As the league continues to grow, increasing community support is needed. Each team has continuing needs for uniforms and equipment, and the cost of insurance has skyrocketed. Local people and businesses have continued to provide not only dollars, but countless hours of service as coaches, referees, treasurers, and team drivers. The payoff has been that hundreds of girls have had thousands of hours of fun, made new friends, and have developed skill, confidence, and respect for their opponents. In several cases, alumnae of the WTYGBL have gone on to play in college with their tuition bills taken care of by full athletic scholarships. In all cases the community's investment in these girls pays off in some way.

In 1991 the Brewster Academy basketball team commanded attention under coach Dave Bolduc, and in three years under his direction the team had gained national attention when several of its alumni made good, including Troy Brown who starred on the Providence College team.[92]

On Leap Year's Day, February 29, 1992, the Kingswood girls' varsity basketball team beat Kennett to win the school's first Class I state championship. Those on the team included Jenny Spack, Alicia Phillips, Michelle Hermann, Shauna Michaud, Maura Donovan, Keri Edmunds, Amy Floria, Nicole LaBelle, Tanya Lee, Katie Roark, and Shelly Stevens. LaBelle scored 20 of the 40 points against Kennett, including all 6 overtime points. She also scored her 1,000th career point to become the most lauded female basketball player in Kingswood history. The win-loss record for the Kingswood girls' team that year was 24-1 including three defeats of Carroll County rival Kennett.[93]

Kingswood's Bruce Hermann was named Girls' Basketball Coach of the Year and inducted into its Hall of Fame in December 1992 by the NH Coaches Association. He began coaching in 1961 and in 1967 came to town to coach at Brewster Academy, moving to Kingswood High in 1970. First he coached boys' basketball at Kingswood. In 1977 he took time off from coaching. The next year he began coaching the girls' basketball team.[94]

During the 1993-1994 season co-captains of the girls' varsity team were Keri Edmunds and Nicole LaBelle, both of whom continued to win plaudits for their prowess, while Bruce Hermann was coach. Joy Ramsbotham was in the circle of Kingswood stars, as were Kristin Bley, Jaime Brulotte, Janis and Jessica Cornwell, Joni Deane, Maura Donovan, Amy Floria, Rachel Jenness, Michelle Kimball, Liza LaBelle, Kristen Rowe, and Jennie Spack, among others. In 1994 Jaime Brulotte of Kingswood was named the 12th grade girls' state championship foul shooter. In the next season, basketball coaches at Kingswood included Bruce Hermann (varsity girls' team) and Michael Desmarais (varsity boys').

The girls' junior varsity team was coached by Larry Kimball in 1993, while the boys' junior varsity coach was Richard Knapp. In the next year, 1994, players making the news included Missy Jackson, Shannon Miller, and Amy Vezina.[95]

In early 1994 the Brewster girls' basketball team under coach Tim Radley beat Providence 56-50 and advanced to a field of eight finalists in the New England Class B Tournament. Leading players in the game included Stephanie Hunter (9 points), Heather Arkwell and Dawn Rood (8 apiece), and Tier Morris (7). This was the sixth time in seven years that the Brewster team made it to the tournament. However, they lost to Suffield, CT, 55-45.[96]

### Biking

In 1991 Jeremiah Heilig, 13, a member of the Granite State Wheelmen, was one of 275 entrants in a bicycle tour of over 100 miles to benefit the NH Lung Association. Heilig alone raised several hundred dollars.

On July 26, 1992, Steve Flagg captured first place in his division in the Franconia 26-mile circuit race which included a three-quarter mile steep climb that had to be ascended five times. Eric Thomas, also of Wolfeboro, finished among the top 20.[97]

### Canoeing

Each year the Great Smith River Canoe Race sponsored by the Wolfeboro Lions Club was run from the Allen H. Albee Beach on Lake Wentworth, down the Smith River, through Back Bay, and across the finish line at the Dockside Restaurant on Wolfeboro Bay.

The May 18, 1991, contest saw a record 206 canoes entered in various categories, with the fastest time of the day registered by the team of Stan Kissell of Wolfeboro and Peter McAllister of Belgrade Lakes, ME, their fourth consecutive win.

On May 16, 1992, 186 boats competed. The fastest time of the day was posted at 24 minutes, 57 seconds by Bradley Helfer of Middleton and Dan Richardson of Wolfeboro. Lorrie Drake of Wolfeboro and Priscilla Reinertsen of Dunbarton clocked in the fastest women's time of 26:20. Michael and Peter McAllister of Belgrade Lakes, ME, set a new time of 25:13 in the family racing class, and Al Paradise of Pittsfield covered the course in a record 25:36 for singles. Stan Kissell and his daughter Jessica of Wolfeboro were the overall winners in the male/female category with a time of 26:47.

A couple of weeks later, on Memorial Day weekend, 1992, four canoeists from Wolfeboro—Bradley Helfer, Stan Kissell, Holly Manoogian and Donna San Antonio—joined 400 entrants in the 70-mile General Clinton Canoe Race in New York state. With the help of Sue Slack

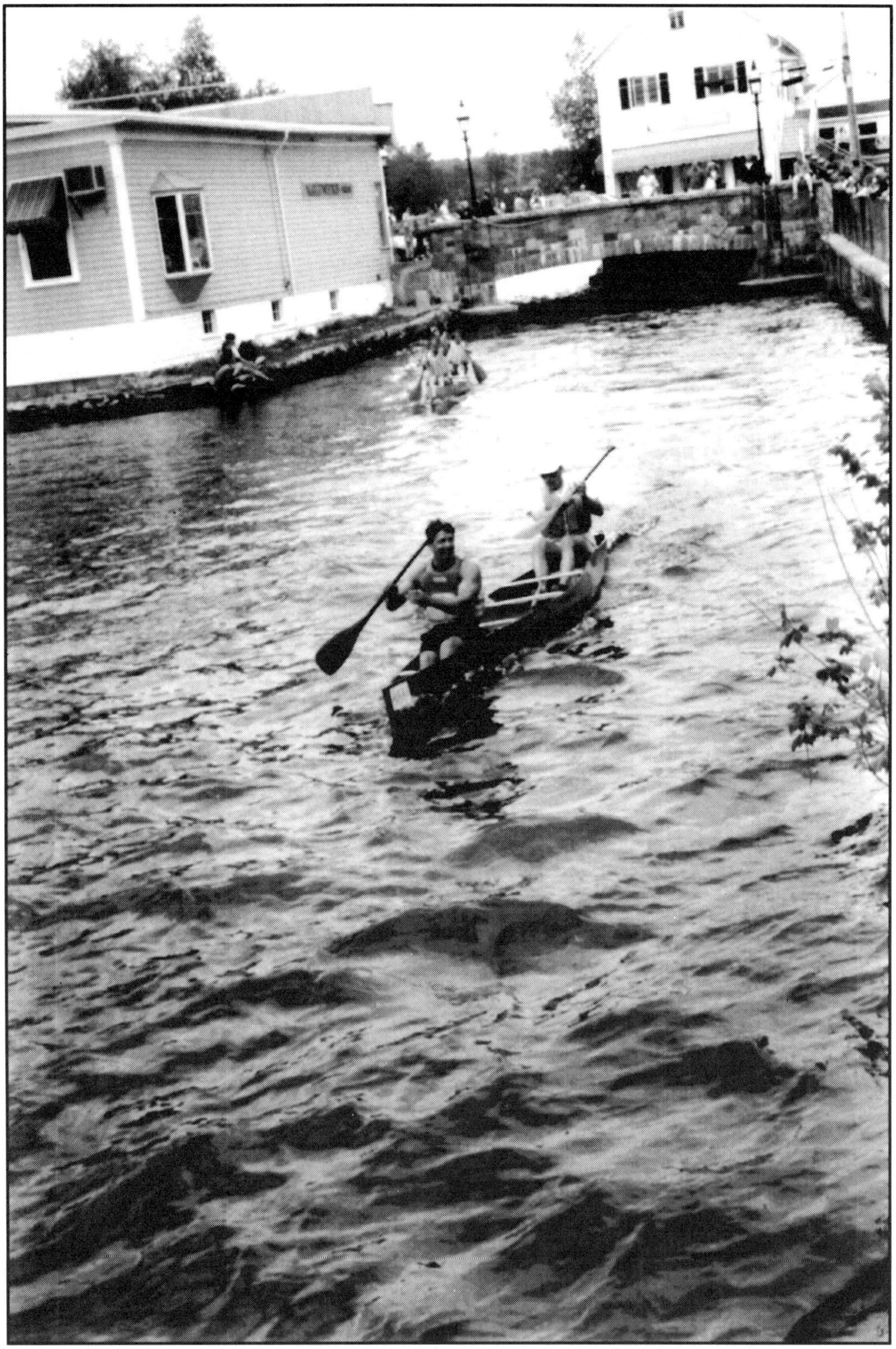

The first two canoes to cross the finish line in the Great Smith River Canoe Race, 1993. Bradley Helfer of Wolfeboro and Ron Keslar of Alton Bay are in the lead canoe. In the background are Miltner's Shoe Store, the Main Street Bridge, and the Wool Corner. (Ashton Woodhouse photograph, May 22, 1993)

as "pit crew" on the shore, Holly Manoogian and Donna San Antonio finished in 10 hours, 28 minutes, to claim second place for the women's division. Helfer placed in 10th place in 9:13; Stan Kissell and his partner Peter McAllister claimed third place in the Masters Amateur, finishing in 8:26.

In the May 22, 1993, running of the Great Smith River Canoe Race 175 competitors entered the various classes, the largest of which was the Two Men Conventional with 36 hopefuls, followed by the Family Conventional with 29. The fastest time of the day (25:19) was posted by the team of Bradley Helfer of Wolfeboro and Ron Keslar of Alton Bay. Jennifer Caldwell and Howie Bean of Wolfeboro were the overall winners in the male/female category with a time of 25:26. Lorrie Drake of Wolfeboro and Priscilla Reinertsen of Dunbarton had the fastest women's time, 27:53.

On Saturday, May 21, 1994, at the usual starting time of 1:15 p.m., the 20th annual Great River Canoe Race attracted 147 entrants. The lineup of winners included some familiar faces. The fastest time of the race was registered at 25:06 by Brad Helfer and Stan Kissell. Jennifer Caldwell and Howie Bean were winners in the male/female category with 25:08. Lorrie Drake of Wolfeboro and Priscilla Reinertsen of Dunbarton had the fastest women's time of 27:41. Kingswood Pewter produced a commemorative medallion for the 20th anniversary occasion featuring a design by the late Donald Clarke.[98]

### Croquet

Although the decidedly British game of croquet is mentioned infrequently in the annals of local sports, there was activity as on July 28, 1991, when the Croquet Society of Greater Wolfeboro held its second game of the season. Appropriate attire—including beribboned skimmers and bowlers, long skirts or white pants—was worn by members, creating a proper Victorian setting. The club, which included members from Alton, Tuftonboro, and Melvin Village in addition to the namesake town, was sufficiently popular that there was a long waiting list for membership.[99]

### Field Hockey

Five members of the 1990 Kingswood varsity field hockey team— Kate Phillips, Shayne Medico, Chris Richards, Meghan Donovan, and M.J. Harris—and their coach Bonnie Lord were invited in January 1991 to participate in the U.S. Field Hockey Association's Futures Program, designed to bring the best in the "field" together. Their "ultimate goal was to wear the Olympic Gold medal in 1996."[100]

In August 1992 sophomore Joy Ramsbotham and Kingswood coach Bonnie Lord went to the AAU Junior Olympic Games in Minnesota and returned as medalists.[101] On November 8, 1992, the Kingswood field hockey team captured the division championship and became Class I state champions by beating Sanborn 1-0 when Joy Ramsbotham scored. Kingswood's goalkeeper for the shutout was Christine Smith.[102]

On July 1, 1993, Kingswood participants in the 15 years and under Northeast National Futures Field Hockey Tournament included Janis Cornwell, Aimee Frank, Joy Ramsbotham, and Christine Smith. Ramsbotham went on to further honors including selection to the "A" camp of the U.S. Field Hockey Association Futures program.[103]

Joy Ramsbotham, a member of the varsity team for four years from 1991 to 1994, became the school's leading scorer with 84 career goals.

The year 1994 saw multiple triumphs for the Kingswood team and its members. At season's end they were the Class I state champions following a 2-0 shutout against Monadnock. Goals were scored by Joy Ramsbotham and Angela Hutchins, and Christine Smith defended the home cage. Kingswood's record of 17 wins, 0 losses, and 1 tie, made it the only undefeated field hockey team in the state. Goalkeeper Christine Smith had 14 shutout games for the 1994 season, duplicating her remarkable record of the season before.

In November 1994 Kingswood seniors Janis Cornwell, Joy Ramsbotham, and goalkeeper Christine Smith were nominated for All American status in field hockey. In the same month, Cornwell was selected as the most outstanding field hockey player in the state by the NH Field Hockey Association and the *Boston Globe*. In December, Ramsbotham was selected to the U.S. Field Hockey Association Under 18 National Squad. In the same month freshman Angela Hutchins was named to the group's Under 16 Women's Select Team and was tapped to tour England and the Netherlands in tournament play. Kingswood Head Coach Bonnie Rankin Lord was picked as head coach of the same team on its European trip and was also selected for induction into the New Agenda: Northeast Women's Hall of Fame for her 22 years of coaching high school sports.

In the 1994 season captains of the girls' varsity team were Joy Ramsbotham, Janis Cornwell, and Christine Smith under coaches Bonnie Lord and Cathy Smith.[104]

### Fishing

In 1991 the first day of fishing season saw few salmon catches and just a few rainbow trout, one about 15" long. The fish were surprisingly absent. There were signs that the fish were growing at a good rate, however.[105] Bass fishing continued its popularity in the early 1990s, and specially equipped bass boats were among the best selling items at regional marinas.

### Football

During the 1991-1992 period, the Kingswood Knights

Dave Parsons (left) and Bob Kepner, both of Wolfeboro, enjoy the facilities of the Kingswood Golf Club course. The Pro Shop is in the background to the right. (Ashton Woodhouse photograph, November 18, 1995)

Members of the Wolfeboro Swim Team at a family picnic at the Allen H. Albee Beach, August 10, 1991. (Stacy Kendall photograph for the *Granite State News*)

played regional opponents, and a number of team members made news. On October 17, 1992, the Knights beat Plymouth 8-7 for their first win against that team since 1979. Stars were Darrin Ladd and Matt Ridings.

On September 18, 1993, in a 24-21 win over Monadnock, Anthony Triolo took a throw from quarterback Nick Deleo and ran 76 yards for a touchdown. A few weeks later on October 16, Triolo scored the only touchdown, with just 1:27 left in the game, in the team's 6-0 victory over Plymouth.

In a memorable clash with Kennett on October 29, 1994, Kingswood came from behind to win 20-12 and bring the Carroll County Trophy back to Wolfeboro for the first time since 1985. Leading players in the game included Dicky Arthur, Peter Hayford, Mike Ridings, and Allie Skelley. Kingswood football coach Bill Lee had nine Knights selected to the 1994 All-State football squad: Mike Ridings, Dicky Arthur, Willie Laase, Peter Hayford, and Andy McLetchie among the first picks, with four receiving honorable mention: Sean Dunlap, Caleb Rudolph, Steve Morris, and Lance Durgan.[106]

In 1993 varsity captains were Darrin Ladd and Shane Nault under coaches Barry Tibbetts, Ralph Floria and Chip Skelley. In 1994 Dwight Armstrong, Anthony Triolo, and Erik Pelletier were captains.[107]

The Kingswood Middle School football team also had many successful contests, as on September 25, 1993, when the squad beat Plymouth 32-2 with points being scored by Mike Elliot, Kyle Frank, Shaun St. Onge, Allie Skelley, Josh Smart, and Willie Swaffield.

The Knights pasted visiting St. Thomas 31-0 in front of the homecoming crowd on a Saturday afternoon in October. Craig Johnson, who had never played football before and joined the team after the season had already started, ended up setting a record when he booted a school-record 43-yard field goal in the third quarter of the game.[108]

The head varsity football coach in 1993 was Ralph Floria, and in 1994 it was Bill Lee. Chip Skelley was an assistant under both, while Mike Jones was Middle School coach in 1993.

### Golf

Each summer the Kingswood Golf Club attracted hundreds of fans to its expansive 18-hole course. Holes-in-one were scored by Ann Pollini in May 1991 and by Blake Palmer in October 1993. In 1992 recognition was given to Ed Gascoigne, age 81, a retired Boston banker who lived in Wolfeboro, who during his lifetime had 12 holes-in-one and who had shot his age so many times that the Professional Golfers Association and *Golf Digest* stopped counting.

On June 27, 1991, fifteen members of the Ladies' Golf League turned in scores of under 74 in the Beat-the-Pro Tournament and were presented souvenir golf balls by club pro Dave Pollini. Turning in the lowest net scores were: Paula Garvey, Diane Clatur, Debbie Zimmerman, Margaret Thomson, Dot Churchill, Ding Puff, Nancy Palmer, Nancy Marshall, Barbara Waterhouse, Pauline Fallon, Margaret Lynch, Sally Maurer, Joan Klimm, Carolyn Sanborn, and Lee Todd. In August of the same year Cindy Melanson beat past winner Nancy Palmer to become ladies' champion of the club.[109]

In the 1992 season the Kingswood (High School) Knights golf team posted 16 wins, three forfeits, and 11 losses, and was led by Jamie Hurtado who was recognized as one of the state's top players.

On June 30, 1993, Joe and Tim Melanson won the Two-Man Best Ball Tournament, the Melanson name being one of the most familiar in Kingswood records. The team of Paul and Rita Stevens and Todd and Margaret Spiller combined for a 66 to take first place in the gross division at the Gross Scotch Golf Tournament held at the Kingswood Golf Club, June 19, 1994.[110]

Among the younger set, in 1994 Robbie Karstedt, age nine, was the NH Junior Golf Association's Pee Wee Division's Grand Prix winner and golf player of the year, based upon his first-place wins at the Kingswood Golf Club and Concord Country Club as well as close finishes in other contests.

On the lighter side, Allan E. ("Lanny") Bailey, Jr., arranged a fund-raising farcical "Crazy Golf" tournament held on downtown sidewalks and streets on March 26, 1994. Three divisions were set up, but only two had entrants (the third—for golfers "who know what they are doing"—drew no participants, a sign of what was to come). The Wolfeboro Police Department was a category winner as was a team called the Media Madams made up of *Granite State News* staffers and WASR Radio co-owner Sharon Severy. That the event was a success was attested to not only by the hilarity expressed but by the $7,500 raised for charitable purposes.[111]

### Granite Man Triathlon

Each year the Wolfeboro Parks and Recreation Department conducted the Granite Man Triathlon, a combination swim, bike, and road race held to benefit the Albert Dow III Scholarship Fund. The 10th annual event held in 1991 drew 296 men and women. Among Wolfeboro participants who were recognized for their accomplishments were:

Chip Martoccia (1st place in the elite category).
David Peters (2nd in men 17 years and under).
Jim Rankin (1st in men 50+).
Richard Johnson (2nd in men 50+).
Terri Moyer (4th in women 30-39).
Mary Ann Murray, Patty Cain, and Candy Crowell (3rd in women's team).
Don, Cassie and Kim Coons (1st in family team).
Dave and Pat McEachron (2nd in family team).

Brrrr! It's cold! Goodhue & Hawkins Navy Yard in the grip of winter. Wolfeboro Bay is in the background with the downtown district and Brewster Academy campus along the far shore.

Cross-country skiing on the vast snowy expanses of Lake Winnipesaukee near Sewall Point. (February 1993 photographs)

Dave Alessandroni, George Rogers, and Laura Ghirardiani (3rd in mixed team).

Kevin Bourque, age 9, John Foley, 12, and Robert Frazier, 14, were recognized as the youngest team ever to participate.

In the August 20, 1994, event the first Wolfeboro triathlete to cross the finish line was George Gaillardetz in 36th place with a time of 1:38:57. Brian Stanley placed close behind in the 38th position, and Robert Mathes was 53rd.

The three-event course was as follows:

1. Three-quarters of a mile swim at Carry Beach.

2. Bicycle race from Carry Beach up Forest Road to Route 109, to Nineteen Mile Bay in Tuftonboro, up Union Wharf Road to Route 109A, and back to Carry Beach.

3. Foot race from Carry Beach to the Lakes Region Air Park and back, 4.2 miles.[112]

### Hockey

The Pop Whalen Arena at the Abenaki Recreation Area was the focal point for many contests on the ice. The Back Bay Indians Youth Hockey team with such divisions as the Mites, Pee Wees, and Squirts played regional opponents. In the early 1990s such local players as Jay Anctil, Tom Antonucci, Brad Belcher, Justin Benes, Greg Bernier, Andy Carr, Ryan Foss, Mark Galloway, Kevin Garrett, Mal Hazeltine, Rob Larson, Seth Lovering, Guy Maloney, Jesse Mendenhall, Brett Newcomb, Kris Newhall, Eric Patten, Mike Pierro, Bart Rogers, Jeff Stevens, Eric True, Frankie Twitchell, and Wes Worthington were among the players who were reported in multiple news accounts.

From September 1991 through mid-April 1992 Matt Anctil, a fifth grader at Carpenter School, made ice hockey a major part of his life. With his family he traveled around New England and the eastern part of Canada with the Boston Elites, an all-star tournament team selected from the top 1% of New England players born in 1981. In June and July 1992 two other Wolfeboro players—Adam Carlson and Chris MacLeod—joined him in Canada at the Ottawa Invitational and the Toronto Tournament of Stars. In January 1993 Matt Anctil and Chris MacLeod, then both in sixth grade, played with the Elites in the 20th Anniversary International Hockey Tournament held in Germany. They lost the first game to Russia, 5-2, played to a 2-2 tie with Sweden, and prevailed over Austria and Switzerland with scores of 6-1 and 10-0, respectively.[113]

During the era Brewster's hockey team played regional prep school opponents.

On January 13, 1993, the Kingswood High varsity hockey team lost to Exeter 7-0. Head coach Fred Antonucci rallied his players, after which they flattened Oyster River, Portsmouth, and Somersworth in succession, with newsworthy scorers including Greg Shannon, Caleb Rudolph, Shane Lovering, and Danny Chase.[114]

In the summer of 1993 Parks and Recreation Department chief Sue Glenn revealed plans for a $160,000 four-phase addition to the Pop Whalen Arena to include a heated snack bar, larger locker rooms, a public viewing area, and new bathrooms accessible to the handicapped. At the time there were no restrooms, and the snack bar was unheated.[115]

### Sailing

In May 1991 Brewster's varsity team, sailing in a new fleet of 420-class sailboats, took first place in the NH State Sailing Championships against opponents including St. Paul's School, Dublin Academy, and Cardigan Mountain School.

Brewster's first-class sailing facility, headquartered at the Pinckney Boathouse, was open to tourists and others for boat rental and instruction during the summer.[116]

### Skiing

Skiing was of two main classes. Alpine or downhill skiing was mainly conducted at regional ski resorts including Gunstock (Gilford), King Pine, Attitash, and elsewhere. In February 1993 the slope was open at the Abenaki Recreation Area for the first time in four years, the facility having been hampered by lack of snow and by mechanical problems.[117] Cross-country or Nordic skiing was practiced many places in town including on the X-C Trail beginning on Clow Road and covering Sewall Point, and on the Kingswood Golf Course.

New equipment was mainly sold by Piche's (alpine) and Nordic Skier (cross-country). Each year a ski and skate sale of used equipment was conducted at Kingswood High to benefit the Wolfeboro Area Children's Center.

In alpine skiing in 1992, sixth-grader Willie Swaffield won the J-4 division for 11-12-year-olds at the Cannon Mountain Spring Slalom competition. This followed his wins in the giant slalom for the same division at Dartmouth and a silver medal in Attitash the month before. Swaffield, who had put his first snow skis on at age four and who was racing at King Pine when he was six, was also a champion on *water* skis. His sister Whitney was agile on snow skis as well, and in March 1993, then in fifth grade at Carpenter School, she placed second out of 60 entrants in the NH State Buddy Werner, Jr., V Girls' Team. At the time she was also a member of the Attitash Ski Team.[118]

On January 28, 1993, the Kingswood Alpine Ski Team won both the boys' and girls' divisions at Highlands, with the boys taking nine of the top 10 spots in the giant slalom course, and the girls winning in seven of the top 10. Finishing order was as follows for boys: Chad Helme (first), Josh Fischbein, Carter Gehman, Tom Hudson, Lance Durgan, Chris Phillips, Glen Moyer, Jason Williams, and Brendon George, while girls finished in this order: Rachel Hale (first), Carrie Bly, Gretchen Shannon, Michelle Hansen, Katja Liedtke, Lauren Perry, and Jessica Stimson.[119]

On January 14, 1994, at a meet in Gunstock in Gilford, Kingswood sophomore Carrie Bly finished first in the giant slalom. In the same year, the Kingswood boys' alpine team won the state championship under coach Kris Niiler. Making news were team members Martin dosSantos, Lance Durgan, Chad Helme, Josh Fischbein, Tom Hudson, and Alex Hunt.[120]

In 1991 Jen Douglass, a 1987 graduate of Kingswood High, was in her senior year at Middlebury College in Vermont and in the cross-country category was considered for the U.S. Olympic Ski Team. Unfortunately, she became ill and missed the next season. However, by January 1993 she was back in action training at Bend, OR, for future Olympics.[121]

In 1993 Jennifer Caldwell of Wolfeboro won the Masters Free-style United States Cross-Country Ski Championship for skiers age 30 and over, at Rumford, ME, by turning in a 26:04 time for the 10-kilometer event. She had started skiing as soon as she could walk. Her father, John Caldwell, was a former coach of the U.S. Ski Team.[122]

Josh Lanzetta, a freshman at Kingswood, did well on the cross-country ski team in 1993 and was selected for the NH J2 team.[123]

Kingswood cross-country skier Heidi Kendall won three medals in March 1993 in a week of competition at the Junior Olympics held in Biwabic, MN.[124] In January 1994 Josh Lanzetta took first place individual honors for the boys, followed by Chris Kelley and Dominic St. Martin in 6th and 13th places respectively, and the girls took seven of the top 10 spots to win first place team honors, as Kingswood participated in its first Nordic ski meet of the season at the Sandwich fairgrounds. Among the girls Michelle Judge finished third, followed by Julie Bowers, Kelly Bridges, Krista Marschner, Maria St. Martin and Hope Thornton. Heather Newcomb finished 10th and Kari Haddock 12th.[125]

### Soccer

In a representative scenario in September 1991, the Brewster Academy varsity women's soccer team defeated Tilton School 3-0 on goals scored by Sue Ballentine of Wolfeboro, Shea Purdy of Boulder, CO, and Beth Davies of Wolfeboro. The men's varsity soccer team lost to New Hampton, 2-3, in a close game. Senior Shaw Abrams of Pepper Pike, OH, and post-grad Steve Spangler of Newbury, MA, scored the two goals.[126]

At Kingswood High, Keri Edmunds was a "natural goal-scorer," according to her coach on the girls' varsity team, Steve Bell. She was his star offensive player in autumn 1991, scoring 12 out of the 18 goals by the Knights that year, making her the leading scorer two years in a row.[127]

### Special Olympics

In March 1991 ski teams from Carpenter School participated in the Special Olympics Games at Bretton Woods and came back with many awards. Second-grader Reuben Hebert captured a silver medal in the 50-meter race and a bronze medal in the 100-meter cross-country races. Andie Doerre returned with ribbons for her fourth, fifth and sixth places in downhill and slalom races. Terence Carroll won a gold medal for the beginning 10-meter ski glide and a silver medal for the beginning 10-meter ski walk. Third-grader Kristin Tower earned two gold medals, one for downhill and the other for slalom racing. Second grader Jenny Doe captured gold and silver medals for the 10 meter and 30-meter snowshoe races. Fifth-grader Tricia Mueller returned to Wolfeboro with fourth and fifth place ribbons in cross-country skiing.[128]

### Swimming

Swimming was enjoyed at many places including the three town-operated facilities: Carry Beach, Brewster Beach, and the new Allen H. Albee Beach. In addition, private beaches, swimming holes, coves, and even moored boats provided endless opportunities. Melissa Karstedt, a Wolfeboro resident who with her family spends much of her summers on Melody Island near Wolfeboro Bay, furnished this typical comment, "Lake Winnipesaukee is one of my favorite places to swim as the water is so clear and clean, and the scenery is so beautiful."[129]

The Wolfeboro Swim Team made news regularly during the era. First-place winners in different age-category and style swimming competition events in 1992, 1993, and 1994 included:[130]

> Margie Badman, Millie Badman, Toby Badman, Amy Bigelow, Gabe Bodwell, Anna Chesley, Martha Crootof, Anna DeVylder, Kurt DeVylder, Meg Ford, Kate Haskell, Rufus Hayes, Liz Hernandez, Chris Kehas, Ryan Kline, Matt Lubrano, Abby McCracken, Amanda McCracken, Aminah Mohammad, Michael Provenzale, Natalie Seibel, Megeen Simoneau, Andy Swan, Peter Ulrich, Claire Willscher, Garth Willscher, Gayle Willscher, and Steve Wood.
>
> In August 1993 Brendan Davey, Hilary Davey and Anthony Barbier were the first contestants from Wolfeboro in the NH American Red Cross Lifeguard Competition, and they won as a team.[131]

### Tennis

In 1992 the Kingswood girls' tennis team had its best year in 15 seasons with an 11-5 record. Among players cited in news accounts were Heather Andrade, Ericka Bailey, Stephanie Barbier, Katja Liedtke, Melissa Piehl, and Katie Roark. Opponents included Berlin, Laconia,

Clearing and excavating on the corner of Pine and Center Streets to make way for the new Dunkin Donuts shop and drive-through facility. View looking up Center Street toward Pickering Corner. (Sandy Martin photograph, May 17, 1994)

Somersworth, Oyster River, Moultonboro, Timberlane, and Kennett.[132]

On April 15, 1994, the Kingswood boys' tennis team went to Berlin to win its first match in two years, 7-1, with notable performances by Alvaro Rance, Mike Foley, Mike Liedtke, Ryan Jones, and Martin dosSantos.[133]

### Track

In track Heather Sands continued to make news with her accomplishments including at summer meets in Hershey, PA, in 1991 and 1992 and as a member of the Kingswood girls' track team.

Kingswood opened its 1992 track season on April 14 in Raymond against Raymond and Bishop Brady when the girls' team coached by Dianne Sands finished first against their competition and the boys finished second against theirs. Keri Edmunds placed first in the 100-meter dash, followed by Heather Sands in third, then Keri won the high jump with a 4-foot, 8-inch leap. Kris Anderson placed third in the high jump. Sands won and Edmunds finished second in the long jump. Kristin White took third in the triple jump. Meghan Donovan won the shotput, took second in the discus, then second in the javelin with a 96-foot, 5-inch throw. Caryn Augusta placed third in the discus. Aimee Frank placed second in the 200-meter run as did Brea Walters in the 400-meter competition, while Kelly Bridges claimed third in the latter event. In the 800-meter run Michelle Judge took first, Misty Durfee took second and Gina Fratantuono took third. In boys' track, Seth Hanley took second in the javelin, Darrin Ladd won the 400-meter run, and Chris Jones won the 200-meter run and took second in the long jump. In the high jump Jeff Phillips won with a 5-foot, 8-inch jump and Ryan Walsh placed second. Chris Tibbetts won both the one-mile and two-mile races.

In 1992 the girls' track team beat 17 other schools to win the Wilderness Championship, only the second time Kingswood captured this honor. The Kingswood girls were led by Captain Courtney Sands who placed first in the 100-meter high hurdles and the 300-meter low hurdles. Keri Edmunds placed second in the high jump, long jump, and 100-meter dash. Also placing were Meghan Donovan in javelin and discus and Heather Sands in long jump. In 1994 Kingswood runer Carrie Bly broke three distance records.[134]

In September 1992 Brewster Academy's cross-country team, in its first match against Proctor and White Mountain School, placed first with five of its runners placing in the top 12.[135]

### Water Skiing

Abenaki Water Ski Club members practiced and held exhibitions and tournaments on their course in Back Bay. Local members mentioned frequently in news accounts included Bob Hughes, Skip Klemm, Chip Maxfield, Bill Swaffield, and Bill's son Willie.

In June 1992 in the 4th Annual NH Jump and Slalom Open Water Ski Tournament, Wolfeboro's Bill Swaffield took his fourth consecutive first-place ribbon for the 34 m.p.h. group. In jumping, Jamie Beauchesne (from Canterbury; age 14) leaped 115 feet for the tournament's best distance, followed by Willie Swaffield with 85 feet. Skip Klemm won the men's jumping with a top leap of 111 feet.[136] In June 1993 Willie Swaffield won the Boys' II jump title at the Eastern Region Water Ski Championship held in Crabtree, PA. He also finished third in the slalom.[137]

Bill Swaffield won the Men's III slalom title at the 1993 Eastern championship contest, the third such win of his career. He broke his own record by rounding 59 consecutive buoys.

## POLITICS

### The Presidential Primary (1992)

On February 12, 1992, First Lady Barbara Bush visited Wolfeboro and greeted about 200 people at the Kingswood High cafeteria, where she accepted a Valentine card from six-year-old Emily Hastings, a student in Anita Hale's kindergarten class at Carpenter School, and urged listeners to vote for her husband in the first-in-the-nation presidential primary. The results at the Wolfeboro polls on February 18 were: Pat Buchanan (497 votes), incumbent George Bush (826; Republican winner); Edmund G. Brown (57), Bill Clinton (98), Tim Harkin (50), Bob Kerry (40), Paul Tsongas (218; Democratic winner). George Bush won his party's primary, with just under 60% of the Republican vote.

### The 1992 Presidential Campaign

As the year progressed, the campaign was lackluster. Even his supporters felt incumbent President George Bush campaigned half-heartedly. Perhaps he was tired from the rigors of having been in office for a term, or perhaps he felt that his election the second time around was a shoo-in.

A letter from Henry S. Maxfield to the editor encouraged people to vote for Texan H. Ross Perot for president, saying that it was a once-in-a-lifetime opportunity to vote for someone who was not being paid by Political Action Committee (PAC) funds, was not burdened with political baggage, and was someone who could get things done. Perot, who was a multi-billionaire from the electronics industry, essentially ran a one-man campaign featuring expensive television spots and even full program-length talks which he mostly paid for himself. H. Ross Perot's local popularity was evidenced by the results of a mock election held by Kingswood High students who chose him to be the nation's next president

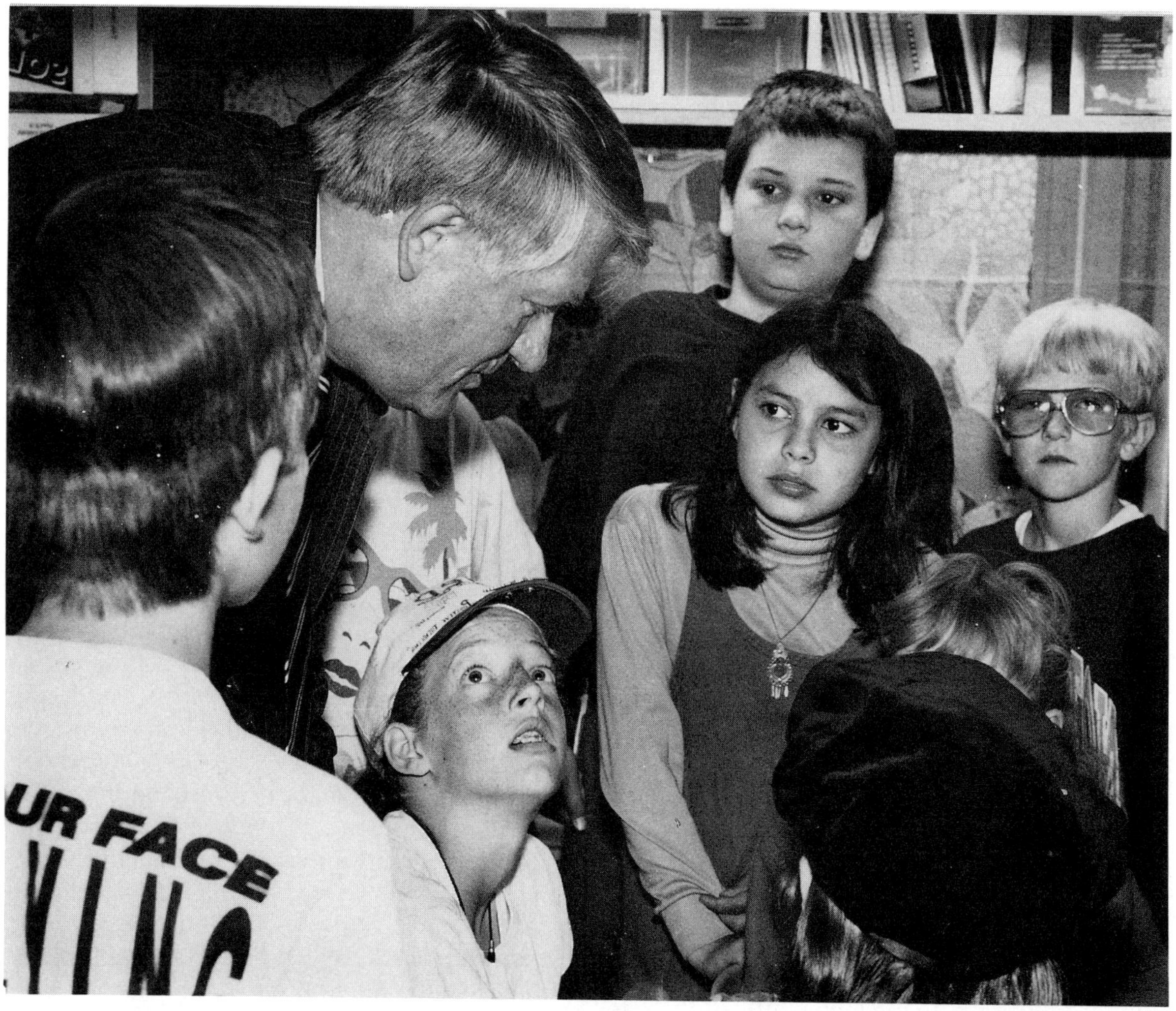


Congressman Bill Zeliff with Carpenter School students from Dr. Irene Ladd's multi-age class: Dennis Moran (right background), Kristy Smith (foreground, left of center), Alicia Childers, and John Murray. (Sandy Martin photograph, 1993)

with 146 votes to incumbent Bush's 66 and Libertarian Andre Marrou's 5.

### November 1992 Results

When election time rolled around on November 3, the winner nationwide was Democrat Bill Clinton, who had mounted an energetic campaign promising change. "A new season of American renewal has begun," he said.

In Wolfeboro ballots were cast for the first time in a new location at the rear of the Public Safety Building, a move from Town Hall. In Wolfeboro, George Bush had 1,485 votes, Bill Clinton 917, H. Ross Perot 753, and Andre Marrou 13. Although Bush was the state winner, in general his statewide vote tally was about 20% below fellow Republicans seeking other offices on the ticket.

Republican gubernatorial candidate Steve Merrill swept Wolfeboro with 2,036 votes, while Democrat "Arnie" Arnesen scored 985. Wolfeboro selectman Ken MacDonald achieved the District 3 seat in the State Senate with 65% of the votes. Locally, a three-way race for Wolfeboro's District 7 seat in the Legislature in Concord was won handily by incumbent Mildred A. Beach (1,985 votes) over Democrat Elaine Miller (848) and Libertarian David Skelley (203). Throughout the early 1990s Jeb Bradley was the other Wolfeboro representative to the State Legislature.

New Hampshire voters sent Governor Judd Gregg to the U.S. Senate to join Bob Smith (who was not running for re-election that year, nor would he until 1996).[138]

### Dole Returns to Town

On several occasions in the 1980s Senator Robert Dole, Republican presidential hopeful from Kansas, had expressed his admiration for Wolfeboro and stayed locally. In August 1993 he and his wife Elizabeth returned and stayed at a private home on Wolfeboro Neck and at the Wolfeboro Inn on North Main Street.

In 1994 and 1995 the state swarmed with early candidates for the 1996 Republican primary, including a visit to Wolfeboro by Richard Lugar who addressed Brewster Academy students, and a stroll around the downtown area by Arlen Specter. However, by summer 1995 campaigning was still casual, hardly serious.

## THE GULF WAR

### Operation Desert Storm

The short-lived Persian Gulf Crisis, later known as the Gulf War, was precipitated in 1990 by the invasion of oil-rich Kuwait by neighboring Iraq under its leader Saddam Hussein. The United States became concerned and initiated Operation Desert Shield whereby military forces were sent to the area.

On January 17, 1991, Operation Desert Storm (a slight renaming from Desert Shield), under the command of General Norman Schwarzkopf, commenced with bombing raids on Baghdad, Iraq. The small war was a media event in America with Schwarzkopf giving regular updates on the Cable News Network (CNN) and other television networks. The public watched as the scenario unfolded including the suspenseful events surrounding the stranding of news correspondents in a Baghdad hotel and the threat of Russian-built "Scud" ground-to-ground missiles deployed from within Iraq.

Soon after the start of the war several area churches opened their doors in the early evenings to people who wanted to offer prayer concerning the conflict, but few took advantage of the opportunity. In front of Carpenter School a yellow ribbon was tied around a tree, a traditional good wish that a soldier (or prisoner) would return safely.[139]

On February 28, the Gulf War was officially over, Kuwait was free, and vanquished Iraqi troops had retreated back across the border to their country. American forces did not invade Iraq, although many observers later stated that they should have.

### Wolfeboro's Involvement

American personnel losses were minimal. In Wolfeboro the situation affected several Wolfeboro area families with ties to the military. Wolfeboro accountant and entrepreneur Joseph Santoro, a lieutenant colonel in the Air Force reserves, went on duty at the Pentagon the day after Iraq invaded Kuwait. At the Logistics Readiness Center at the Pentagon he worked 14-hour shifts. George and Phyllis Gleason had sons George and John in the armed forces in the Persian Gulf. Lee C. Glidden, 40, an air transportation specialist for the 38th Aerial Port Squadron, Charleston Air Force Base, SC, son of Charles A. and Marjorie L. Glidden of Pleasant Valley Road, helped to bring troops home from the Persian Gulf.

Harriman-Hale Post 18 of the American Legion requested that all Wolfeboro residents display the stars and stripes on Memorial Day, that year also known as Welcome Home Day, May 30. A parade was formed and marched from the Wolfeborough Railroad Station to the Town Docks, then up to Pickering Corner for speeches and awards given to WASR-AM and WLKZ-FM radio for their war coverage. The Fourth of July parade also memorialized the Gulf War.[140]

## HEALTH

### Many Facilities

Wolfeboro continued to be blessed with multiple excellent facilities related to health, retirement, and care.

The non-profit Ledges and Christian Ridge housing areas for senior citizens and the private Clipper Home earned high marks from their residents. In addition many Wolfeboro retirees lived at the Mountain View

**Huggins Hospital Medical Arts Center, a modern facility attached to the west side of the hospital, was built in 1992. (Ashton Woodhouse photographs, November 18, 1995)**

**Huggins Hospital on South Main Street.**

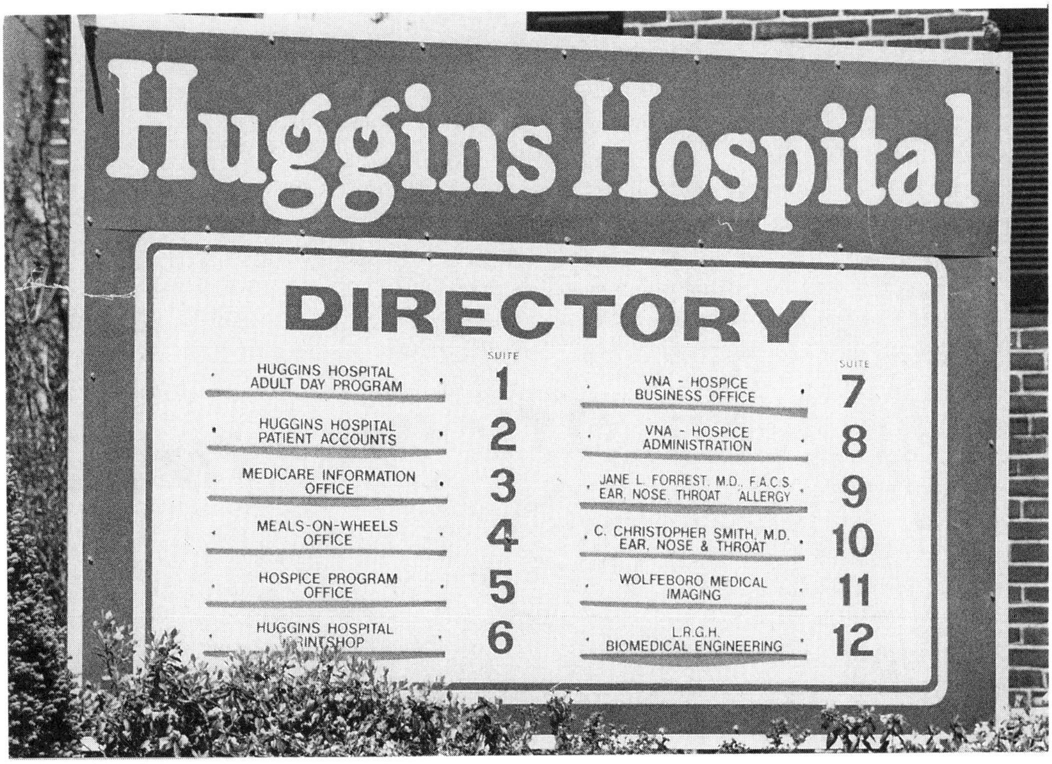


**Huggins Hospital directory. (1995 photographs)**

Nursing Home on Route 171 in Ossipee, not far from the Wolfeboro town line.

The Center of Hope on Route 28, Carroll County Mental Health Services on Bay Street, Harbor House, Caregivers, Red Cross, the Visiting Nurses' Association-Hospice, and private therapists and medical practitioners attended to the needs of local as well as regional citizens and visitors. Local churches also did much for the well-being of the community and provided a focal point for spirituality in an era in which morality and family values were subject to increasing challenges.[141]

In 1994 radon gas, a naturally occurring radioactive gas primarily emanating from granite rock, made the news on several occasions. There were no state standards on acceptable levels, nor did the state want to get involved, as it had no money for enforcement, and, as it was, many municipalities were having enough trouble keeping up with state and federal regulations in other areas such as waste disposal, water systems, and lead removal.

Rabies borne by foxes had been a concern for many years. In the early 1990s the state warned of a particularly virulent strain of the disease carried by raccoons. Area veterinarians sponsored vaccination clinics for cats and dogs.[142]

### Huggins Hospital

The big news of the era at Huggins Hospital was the New Medical Arts Center, a 36,000 square-foot addition designed by Frank Marinace of New Hampton and completed in autumn 1992 at a cost of about $1.8 million. The facility included eight medical suites of which six or seven were spoken for by the completion date. An open house was held on May 21, 1993.[143]

Among other news in 1991, the maternity ward was renovated to create safer and more homelike surroundings—including brighter birthing rooms and nursery. In 1992 and 1993 the hospital acquired three properties including the Church of the Nazarene contiguous to it on South Main Street from Crescent Lake Avenue to the hospital.

On April 21, 1993, more than 200 volunteers were honored in an awards ceremony. State Representative Robert W. Foster, chairman of the Board of Trustees, spoke of the important, continuing service role Huggins played in the community and the contributions made by everyone who helped. In 1993 the hospital upgraded its cardiac and pulmonary facilities so that patients could undergo procedures locally that would have required out-of-town trips earlier. John Murray was the manager of the Cardiopulmonary Department.[144]

In recent times, continuing in the 1990s, Huggins Hospital continued to attract many fine medical specialists. By 1994 most sophisticated procedures could be taken care of capably within the red brick facility on South Main Street, which continued under the leadership of its president, Leslie N.H. MacLeod.

## FIRE-RESCUE DEPARTMENT

### With the Department

Charles "Zip" Foss joined the Wolfeboro Fire Department in 1939, when he was 19 years old. He served continuously including as chief since 1976, except for service in the U.S. Army during World War II. On July 31, 1992, Chief Foss retired at age 72. In September 300 admirers turned out at a testimonial dinner to pay tribute to his accomplishments and service.[145] His replacement as of September 21, Chief Michael J. Howard, was selected from a field of 30 candidates and came to town from Nashua.

In spring 1993 the Wolfeboro fireboat, *H.W. Drury II,* received its first major overhaul since it was acquired 22 years earlier and was outfitted with a bow deck water gun, new hoses, updated medical equipment, and other refinements to the point at which it was as fully equipped as the town rescue truck.[146]

In December 1993 Steve Wood was promoted to captain of Rescue 1 from lieutenant of Ladder 1. Earl Keniston was promoted from firefighter with Tanker 1 to lieutenant of Tanker 1. Engine 3 firefighter Richard Greenwalt was named lieutenant of Engine 3.[147]

In late spring 1993, color-coded fire hydrants began to appear, as painters used different hues to indicate how much water flow was available to firemen. The system employed from that time onward is:[148]

Blue hydrant: Class AA, 1,500 gallons per minute or more.
Green: Class A, 1,000 to 1,499 g.p.m.
Orange: Class B, 500 to 999 g.p.m.
Red: Class C, less than 500 g.p.m.

In 1994 the Fire-Rescue Department took delivery of a 109-foot Aerial/Quint unit and a 4x4 midi pumper to enhance the response capability of firefighters. During the year 712 emergency calls were received including 75 box alarms, 262 still alarms, 354 rescue calls, and 21 requests by other communities for mutual aid. Rescue calls increased 67% from as recently as 1992.[149]

### Fire Log

**1991, January 26. Walker house:** Stoneham Road. Randy and Pat Walker's house caught fire about 5 a.m. around a chimney. The family of five escaped. The fire caused extensive damage to the ell of the house containing a first-floor kitchen and second-floor bedroom connecting the home to a barn.[150]

**1991, April 27. Glidden house:** North Main Street. Fire believed to have started in electrical wiring destroyed the house, barn and two cars belonging to Gordon and Ruth Glidden and extensively damaged another house nearby.[151]

**1991, August 17. Boat fire:** A blaze erupted when a gas leak ignited aboard a small boat about 250 feet offshore from Goodhue & Hawkins on Sewall Road. The two uninjured occupants jumped out and swam to shore. The Fire Department fire boat reached the scene quickly.[152]

**1991, August 28. Vacant house:** Park Avenue. Kitchen and back room of vacant house damaged by fire believed to have been ignited by lightning.[153]

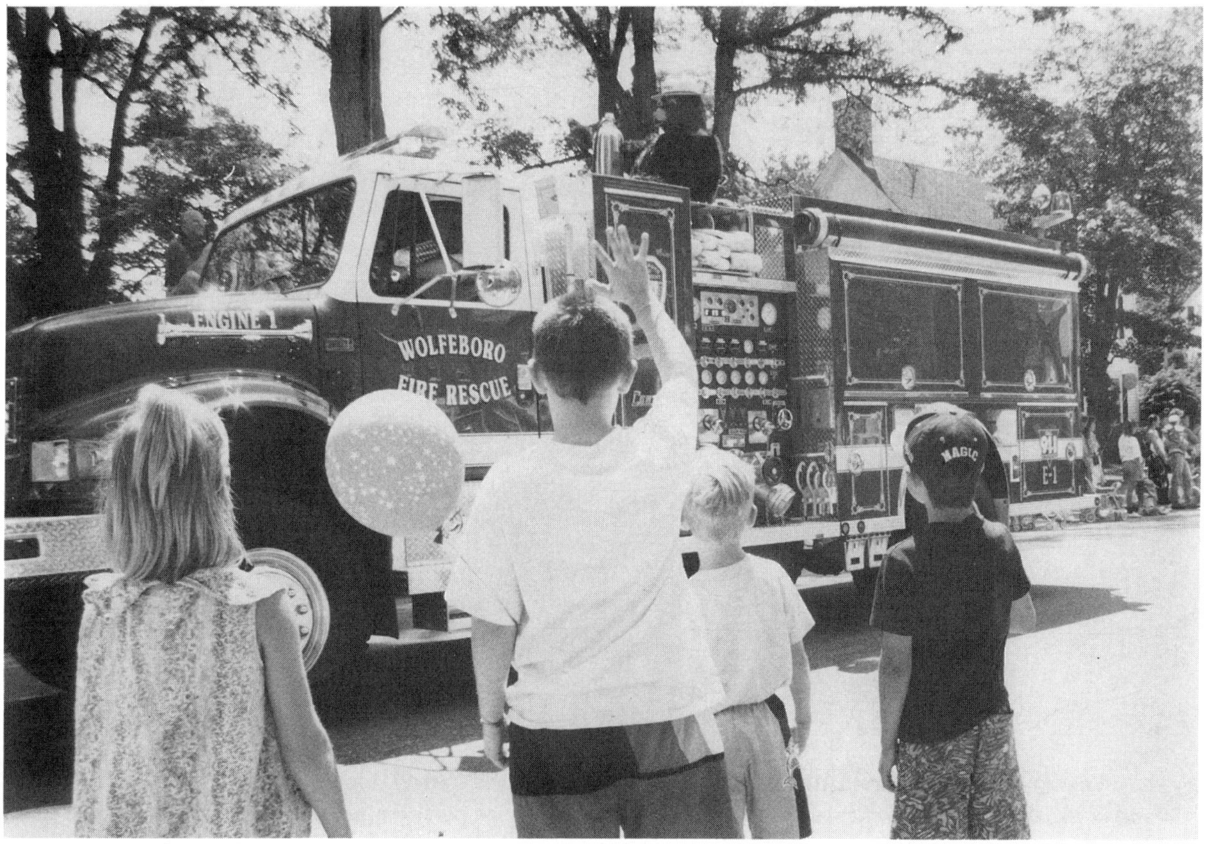


**1994 Independence Day parade: Wolfeboro Fire-Rescue Department's Engine No. 1 pumper truck. A figure representing Smokey the fire-fighting bear is shown atop the vehicle.**

**One of the Wolfeboro Police Department's patrol cruisers being driven by Sgt. Brian Black. The official decor is white with a blue stripe on the side. (Sandy Martin photographs)**

Therapy Dog Program at Huggins Hospital sponsored by the Carroll County Kennel Club. The trained and certified dogs visit patients in the extended care facility as part of a program that began in 1988. In addition, the dogs and their handlers visit nursing homes and schools. Left to right: Virginia Nichols with Tiffany and Kirby, Mary Holmes with Cassie, Sara Piper with Kelley and Tina, and Ruth Fraser with Copper. (Ashton Woodhouse photograph, 1993)

Engine No. 2 at the Wolfeboro Fire-Rescue Department, South Main Street behind the Public Safety Building, being attended to by Chris Ginter. (May 4, 1995 photograph)

**1991, December 29. Moody house:** King Street. Fire believed to have been caused by a short circuit severely damaged the home of George, Irene, and Fred Moody. No one was home, but a cat and dog were killed. The community quickly responded with clothing, cash, and furniture to help the family.[154]

**1992, March 9. Sunshine Trading Post:** Center Street antiques shop caught fire early in the morning. Contents a total loss. Owner Jerry McLellan made repairs and reopened.[155]

**1992, October 26. June Barstow residence:** Wentworth Park. Overheating of a chimney caused a fire that gutted the second floor and damaged the first floor.[156]

**1992, November 30. Wickers Sportswear:** Heavy fire, smoke, and water damage to the one-story office portion of the 24,000 square foot plant. Fire spotted at 9:50 p.m. by Chris Keaton of the Police Department. The Fire Department had it under control by 10:40.[157]

**1993, January 22. Hazeltine building:** Pine Hill Road. Storage building belonging to Malcolm Hazeltine, plumber and electrician, caught fire from a new LP gas heater. PVC pipe caused toxic smoke. Chevrolet van and other contents destroyed. Sixty firefighters were on the scene.[158]

**1993, February 9. Wolfeboro Inn:** Peter A. Friend, teacher at Brewster, saw a puff of smoke followed by a 30-foot burst of flame erupt from a chimney. An energetic response was called for, and firefighters arrived from several other towns including Rochester and Gilmanton, who quickly extinguished the fire. This struck some onlookers as over-response, but Chief Mike Howard said that given the nature of the blaze and its situation in a rambling wood-frame structure, a small fire could have easily blown up into something far more serious. Besides, Wolfeboro firefighters were already busy with a gas leak at the Pop Whalen Rink, and other area departments were battling a blaze in Granite (Ossipee district).[159]

**1993, April 25. Kitchen fire:** Patrick Macauley was heating food in an aluminum pan on his kitchen stove when he fell asleep. The pan melted, and his apartment was filled with smoke. Macauley was found unconscious and carried to safety by Fire Department and rescue personnel.[160]

**1993, July 1. Clipper Home:** Off Clark Road. A small but very smoky blaze in a dryer ignited some mop heads and forced the relocation of about 40 residents without injury.[161]

**1993, September 15. Child injured:** Six-year-old Raul Alexander Garcia was severely burned when a primitive "flame-thrower" made by an acquaintance erupted. After having skin grafts Alex made a remarkable recovery and was back in school within a month. A special fund sponsored by the Church of Jesus Christ of Latter Day Saints helped with expenses.[162]

**1993, November 8. House fire:** King Pine Road home owned by Frank Hammond, near Crescent Lake, that was rented by a family of four was moderately damaged by fire. Chief Mike Howard suggested it was caused by an inappropriately installed woodstove and a chimney with inadequate clearance from surrounding combustible material.[163]

**1994, March 18. Berry Mill:** The most spectacular local blaze in years turned night into day on Center Street when the old wooden excelsior mill erupted in flames. Susan Butsicaris, who lived above the nearby Smith River Depot store, called in the alarm at 8:42 p.m. Within minutes the entire large structure was involved, and soon the blazing ribs and joists of the roof, which remained after the attached boards burned away, collapsed. Eighteen pieces of firefighting equipment and about 100 personnel could do little for the old structure, but they averted greater loss by watering down nearby buildings including Smith River Depot, Mill Pond Place, the Adelman building (home of Duco Sales), and a multi-story apartment block. The intense heat melted vinyl siding on the Smith River Depot. Chief Michael J. Howard and the Fire Department received high praise for their preventive work.[164]

**1994, August 4. Car fire:** Volkswagen "beetle" gutted by fire in the Cider Press Restaurant parking lot. Caused by a mechanical problem.[165]

**1994, November 27. McKernan house:** Hopewell Point Road. Garage and overhead bedroom damaged by flames; smoke and water damage to the rest of the Richard McKernan house. "Chief Howard said hot ashes were placed in a trash bin too close to the garage portion of the home for safety's sake and apparently began the blaze."[166]

**1994, December 26. Vacant building:** Lehner Street. Firemen contained damage to basement and part of the first floor. Loss: $10,000.[167]

### A Memorable Rescue

Certainly the most publicized rescue of the era occurred Saturday afternoon, April 16, 1994, when Rochelle Juliano and three companions left Goodhue & Hawkins on Sewall Road in clear weather in their hovercraft and skimmed over the ice the short distance to her camp on Little Barndoor Island. The hovercraft was equipped with a whistle, lights, and other safety devices, but as the passengers were going over solid ice, they did not put life jackets aboard. On the afternoon on the way back, the hovercraft crew became lost in fog, went in the wrong direction, and became stranded in slushy ice 1,800 feet out from shore between Hopewell Point and Parker Island.

The four shouted for help, and soon the Rescue Department was on the scene. Reaching the hapless hovercraft was not easy, and Chief Michael Howard later reported that the rescue took four hours to accomplish, utilized 35 personnel, and required a long list of equipment including three rescue vehicles, three ambulances, a rescue hovercraft (from Alton), a private resident's aluminum boat, a winch, more than 3,000 feet of rope, six rescue suits, a 10-foot pike pole to break the ice, 35 blankets, 14 life vests, and six life preservers at a cost of $3,000 to $4,000. The four victims as well as rescuers Lt. Earl Keniston and Eric Finniss of Wolfeboro, Joseph Triolo and William Graham of Tuftonboro, and Stark Leidtke of Alton were taken to Huggins Hospital to check for hypothermia and were soon released.[168]

## LAW ENFORCEMENT, SAFETY

### Department Busy

The Wolfeboro Police Department under Chief Stanley E. Stevens was kept busy as usual attending to reports of burglaries, thefts, motor vehicle offenses, and other malfeasances. Loot taken ranged from a dealer's stock of sports cards (the greatest collecting fad of the era) to a red Amazonian parrot to a Corvette sports car.[169]

Among the more unusual situations—but, fortunately, one without injury to anyone—occurred on May 1, 1991, when a man and woman each about 30 years old came to the maple sugar products shop of retired Wolfeboro market owner Don Kent on North Main Street and told him they were setting up a mail order business to deal in syrup. The duo then asked him to change a $50 bill, which he did. At the same time, he received a telephone call requesting delivery of an order of maple syrup from an ice cream shop that had just opened for business in Clarke Plaza. Kent, a trusting soul, left his house unlocked and rushed off to help the new ice cream vendors, found that there was no such new shop in Clarke Plaza, and returned to North Main Street to find his home burgled.

Representative of petty theft is one which cost the perpetrator a ten-fold fine when he was caught: a 33-year-old man took a $10 bill from a donation basket at the Evangelical Bible Church and was fined $100 plus restitution. Chances are good that the church, which was well-known for its outreach, would have *given* him $10 had he asked. Perhaps in the same category was the theft (by a grinch?) a few weeks later of the Chamber of Commerce's Christmas tree from in front of its office.

Around two in the morning of August 19, 1991, nine revolvers and semi-automatic pistols were stolen from Lakes Region Sports by one or more thieves who broke the plate glass door in front, rushed in, and raced off before police could respond to the alarm they had activated. Early Sunday morning, December 15, 1991, one or more persons, believed to be drunken kids, drove by the Road Stop Convenience Store at the corner of Route 28 and North Line Road and shot out five large plate glass windows with eight to 10 bullets.[170]

Illegal drugs remained a problem, especially among the younger set, and it was said that marijuana was easily available locally to underage buyers, more so than alcohol. Some adults were upset that local law enforcement did not seem to be mounting much of an effort toward solving this problem, but the Police Department's request to add an officer in 1993 to help was cut from the budget. Meanwhile, in annual *Town Reports* Chief Stevens stated that alcohol was the worst "drug" of all in terms of the crime effects linked to it.

In late 1992 and early 1993, there was a spate of burglaries in the downtown area, prompting one store owner to declare that he might lie in wait at night with a loaded pistol for anyone who wanted to break into his shop. Maxfield Real Estate, Stay Tuned, Nordic Skier, Bittersweet Restaurant, Road Stop Convenience Store, and others were hit. At a hearing about the problem officers explained how the Police Department was organized and what its resources were. The town had approximately 5,000 residents, 50 miles of roads, and nine full-time policemen: the chief, a lieutenant, a detective sergeant, a patrol sergeant, and five patrolmen. Not long thereafter more than a half dozen suspects were arrested—none of them a Wolfeboro resident—and charged with most of the burglaries.

In April 1993 the police received a day of training and began utilizing a new weapon, a spicy spray of atomized red pepper called Punch II, to quell violent persons without harmful lasting effects. On September 5, 1993, Eric Borrin, the new bike patrol officer, went into action donning his outfit of uniform shirt, shorts, and bike helmet and mounting a new Cannondale M500 mountain bike donated to the community by the Flagg family, owners of the Nordic Skier shop. The bike patrol proved to be a very efficient way of monitoring the downtown area, especially when there was heavy traffic.

On September 30, 1993, a pipe-bomb blast destroyed a portable toilet near Foss Field, and shortly thereafter a suspicious fire caused about $20,000 worth of damage to a Municipal Electric Department pumphouse about a quarter mile away. Two 18-year-old men were subsequently charged with these and other crimes.[171]

In 1994 the Police Department logged 778 reportable incidents, up slightly from 765 in 1993. Criminal arrests totaled 252. Chief Stevens reported that during the year 649 cases were presented to the Wolfeboro District Court. "The vast majority were disposed of by guilty pleas, but we did conduct 46 trials in adult cases, resulting in conviction in about 60% of the cases." Chief Stevens noted that the workload was becoming more evenly spread over the year, whereas in earlier times it was mainly concentrated in the summer. "We're not investigating less in July, but more in January."[172]

## THE TOWN

### Selectmen and Town Managers

In 1991 the Board of Selectmen was composed of Shirley E. Ganem, George W. Elkins, and Sarah M. Silk. By 1995 the membership had changed to Shirley E. Ganem, Paul R. Hatch, and Roger F. Murray II. Meanwhile, Kenneth MacDonald, a former state representative, had been elected in 1992 and served through 1995 when he was replaced by Murray. MacDonald had not sought re-election.

James McSweeney, town manager since July 1990 when he replaced Chester Spinney, resigned his $55,000 per year post on August 1, 1993, to accept a similar position in Portsmouth paying an estimated $70,000 to $80,000. Among his Wolfeboro accomplishments, he was proud of his part in updating the town's budgetary system, municipal policies, and procedures.[173] His successor, chosen from among 83 applicants, was Paul Skowron, who had spent 22 years in the town manager

FAMILY ALBUM: The Peter Stanard family photographed in the Goodwin homestead on North Main Street in the 1990s. Left to right: Stephany Stanard, Joyce Goodwin Stanard, Jeff Goodwin (brother of Joyce), Peter Stanard, and Scott Stanard.

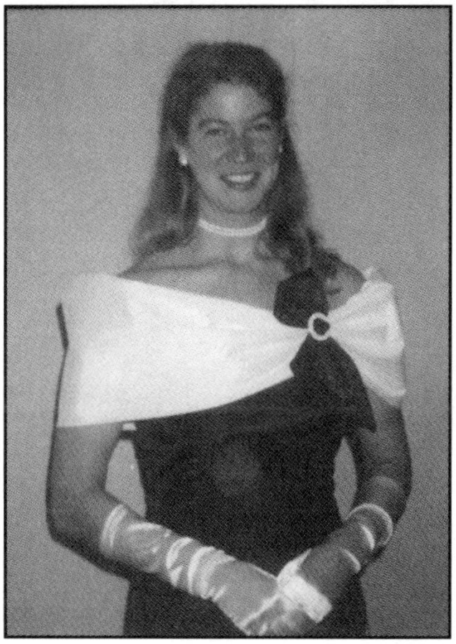

Stephany in 1995.

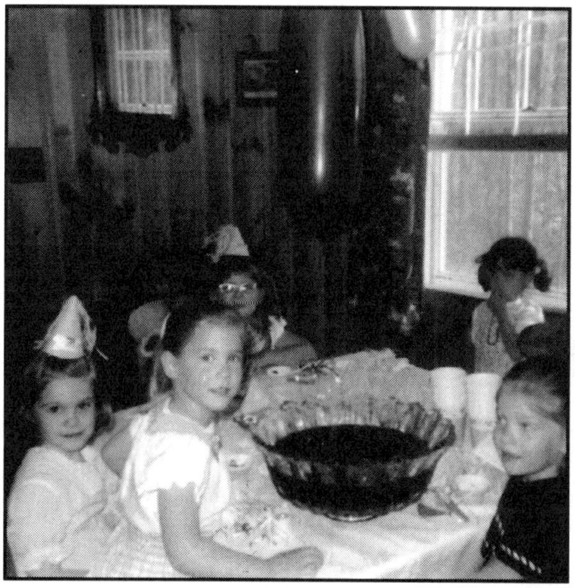

Stephany (closest to camera) at her birthday party circa 1970. Other celebrants include Heather Duncan, Heidi McBride, Kim Todesco, and Hilary Douglass.

Visiting the Municipal Electric Department plant: Dennis Bean (white shirt at tie, walking to the left) leads third graders from Carpenter School on a tour of the power plant on Lehner Street. )

Inside the building, students look on as plant operator Gerry Steimle explains how and when the large diesel engines supply electricity. (Sandy Martin photographs, October 8, 1993)

field in Enfield, CT (population 45,000), Newport, NH (6,500), and most recently in North Kingstown, RI (24,000), where he managed a budget of about $18 million and supervised 200 employees.[174]

### Amanda L. Simpson

In August 1990 the Planning Department sent out 4,052 surveys to town property owners to seek information useful for a new Master Plan to be prepared. Something unplanned happened: due to a computer error, all data were destroyed, and 97,000 keystrokes and a lot of written comments had to be re-entered. This was hardly an auspicious beginning for yet another Master Plan, since the Planning Board stated that the previous plan was gathering dust and had *no effect* on town planning decisions. Despite this, useful planning was done, and in 1993 the Wolfeboro Charrette (about which more will be said later) caused a lot of excitement.

Meanwhile, Town Planner Amanda L. Simpson was considered by some to be one of Wolfeboro's finest assets—a highly competent, well-trained, intelligent person with a great deal of energy—and by others to be an impediment. In particular, local surveyor and mapper Wayne J. Kelloway became upset when she awarded a mapping project to another firm, although he said his bid was lowest.

No one questioned Ms. Simpson's selfless dedication to the town or her statement on June 24, 1992, that the town needed to have a good Master Plan for "If we're not careful during the next boom, we could let it all run away from us."

On November 22, 1994, Ms. Simpson spent her last day at Town Hall before leaving for her new position as town planner of Laconia. Perhaps she thought unfortunate the statement made by several townspeople and even by Planning Board members that perhaps no new town planner was needed for Wolfeboro, and that the duties could be done on a part-time basis. But, surely she smiled when she later read the comment by Town Manager Paul Skowron that Wolfeboro might need to hire *two* people to replace her. This unhurried view of Simpson two months after her resignation may have been a classic manifestation of the old saying, "You don't appreciate what you have until you lose it." Many citizens appreciated her efforts and held a farewell party in her honor at the home of Erik H. Arctander.[175]

### Electricity

Time was when the Municipal Electric Department in Wolfeboro generated enough power for the town's needs, but no longer. In 1991 the primary supplier of current to the town was the Public Service Company of New Hampshire (PSNH) monopoly, which that year announced a monstrous 177.2% jump in rates that would nearly triple town electric bills. Dennis E. Bean, chief of Wolfeboro's department, said the rates were "unreasonable and unjust" and would put the town department out of business along with a lot of local enterprises. Following intervention by State Senators Wayne King and Roger Heath and by Governor Judd Gregg, PSNH modified its increase to about 7.5% annually for the next 10 years. The Seabrook nuclear generating facility, largely owned by PSNH, remained a financial disaster. Meanwhile, Quebec to the north had more hydro-electric power than it knew what to do with.

Notwithstanding all of the pressures from the outside, Business Manager Dennis E. Bean and the Municipal Electric Department crew continued to supply electricity for about 20% to 30% below what most other area communities charged their customers. For those who couldn't readily pay, Wolfeboro had its Gift of Warmth program to help with utility bills, with over $10,000 contributed in 1992 alone. Another program involved the sale at cost of low-energy, long-lasting, high-output bulbs that, for example, gave 75 watts of illumination with a consumption of only 11 watts. At Christmastime the department supplied decorative lighting to the downtown area.[176]

On January 27, 1994, the peak demand for electricity reached an all-time high of 13,267 kilowatts during a period of extreme cold.

### The Sugar Maple Community Playground

In December 1990 pennies began to accumulate at Carpenter School, and by February there were 50,000 on hand, plus $6,000 cash pledged by private donors, a foundation, and the Parent-Teachers Organization (PTO). The objective was to build a safe, challenging, and creative playground.

Recreation architect Bob Leathers was brought in from Ithaca, NY, to lead Design Day, April 10, 1991, in which the school children could help with the design and choose the features to be included. No stranger to the formula, Leathers had done the same thing in 500 other communities during the previous 20 years. Construction was to begin in October.

From April 5 to April 14 a donation of $1 to $2 was made in a diner's name for every lunch or dinner purchased at such local eateries as All Stars Sports Pub, Cider Press, Lakeview Inn, Papa John's Pub, Rumors Café and the Wolfeboro Inn. Local artist Pat Hodder designed a logo that was widely admired on those who wore special fund-raising T-shirts around town. Eventually, $50,000 was in the kitty including $8,500 in the form of 850,000 one-cent pieces.

Jim Bean, a master electrician, volunteered to be head foreman for the project. John Osgood, Ray Bernier, Bob Pollini, David O'Brien, and Brad Harriman—all prominent on the local building scene—offered equipment and

The new Sugar Maple Community Playground behind Carpenter School. Designed by Robert Leathers of Ithaca, NY, the facility cost about $50,000 and was built by over 400 local volunteers ranging in age from 5 to 70 years working in shifts for 14-hour days. Construction began on October 14, 1991, and was finished within a week. (Cathy Dumont Wilson photograph, 1994)

The Sugar Maple Community Playground under construction in October 1991. Debbie Skelley points to some work that needs to be done. Dr. Norman Kathan is in the left foreground, while to the right is John Rechel, a Carpenter School volunteer to whom the playground was dedicated.

Boards, wires, workers, ropes, and other elements of activity at the playground under construction behind Carpenter School. (Ashton Woodhouse photographs)

personnel. Fifty members of the Church of Jesus Christ of Latter Day Saints signed up to help with the playground, along with a dozen Girl Scouts, an athletic team, and a class of vocational students. Out at Steve Eckhoff's body shop in Ossipee, business slowed as Steve took off several days to be at the playground.

It was estimated that about 100 to 125 townspeople, including children, could work on the playground at any given time. Construction began on October 16, 1991. No beehive was ever more active than the once-empty space near the back fence behind Carpenter School. David O'Brien said, "I've never seen anything as well organized as this."

To keep spirits and energy at a high level, Jeb Bradley put on a magic show, Jim Cameron gave a karate demonstration, Beth Cobleigh was on hand with a cheerleading squad, Debbie Glazier demonstrated creative movements, Helen Fernald conducted an exercise class, Molly Leone and Sheila Brown painted kids' faces, George and Adam Kelly and the A-Team showed their gymnastics prowess, Sally Perkins told Indian stories, Denise Warren set up several sports events, Darlene Williams was on hand with several violinists, Ann Wyman and Donna Tilton showed how to make crafts, and clowns lent merriment. Dave Bowers' antique calliope filled the air with cheerful sounds, and one evening a dinner was provided gratis by Cook's Corner.

In five 14-hour days, the playground was completed. Elissa K. Paquette, one of the PTO leaders and an enthusiastic volunteer in the project, described the completed playground as a turreted network of tunnels, mazes, swings, and ramps for the handicapped access. There are surprises at every turn; a spider web of chains covered with rubber tubing and bolted into heavy poles, a bouncy bridge, a moving platform, an undulating slide and a circular slide (forming the tongue of a dragon or his fiery breath). It is a solid structure made of dense select structural lumber, cut, routed, sanded, sealed, lugged, hammered, and drilled into place entirely by volunteers—more than 400 ranging from age 5 through 70.

When all was said and done, Bob and Bev Davis, coordinators of the project, offered thanks to everyone and announced it would be called the Sugar Maple Community Playground, after a tree that stood on the site. The area was dedicated to John Rechel, who had volunteered many hours of his time working with Carpenter School children in their classrooms. The front page of the *Granite State News,* October 30, 1991, printed a full-color photograph of the seemingly countless volunteers who made the project a reality.[177]

**Town Notes (1991)**

On Monday, August 19, 1991, Hurricane Bob ripped through town blowing down trees and dropping branches on power lines, damaging several structures, and disrupting electrical service. Rob Kuel of the Municipal Electric Department was injured when he was hit by a falling tree limb. Nearly 300 children and staff members were evacuated from Camp Bernadette on Lake Wentworth and made comfortable at Kingswood High after falling trees damaged the camp office and chapel and destroyed a cabin. The Wolfeboro League Shop in its new headquarters on Center Street had an oak tree punch a hole in its roof. The town received $17,576 in disaster aid funds to help compensate in a small way for $35,000 in overtime paid to employees plus as much as $100,000 in damage to the town water pollution abatement facility and spray fields.[178]

Central Dispatch completed its first full year of operation in 1991 and coordinated the Police Department, the Fire Department, and the Rescue Squad. In 1994 Central Dispatch received 86,686 messages, 8,228 walk-in visitors. On the 911 line, which had been in operation since 1992, 458 emergency and 446 other calls were handled.

On May 31, 1991, Curtis A. Pike, Wolfeboro's first and to this point only director of Public Works, retired after 12 years of service. He had seen many changes during his tenure including the addition of 20 miles of roads and an increase in maintenance vehicles from 46 to 70. However, there were fewer employees in the Highway Department in 1991 than when he started. Marty Bilafer, a graduate of West Point who currently was serving as waste management superintendent in Plymouth, was chosen from 35 candidates as Pike's replacement and began his duties on June 5.[179]

In the same year Gordon A. Reade, who signed on with the town in 1965 as permit officer and from 1975 to 1977 was code enforcement officer, retired as chief operator of the wastewater facility, a position which he had held since May 1977. Reade passed away on January 9, 1994, and the 1993 *Town Report* was dedicated to him.[180]

On July 27, 1991, Wolfeboro participated for the third time in a special day-long collection program for hazardous wastes organized by the Lakes Region Planning Commission. Over 1,600 gallons of paint, drain and oven cleaners, pool chemicals, pesticides, solvents, thinners, etc., were brought in. Another effort involved the Wolfeboro Recycling Committee headed by Susan E. Campbell, who was also involved in an effort to establish a local YMCA, and who later became Christian education director at the First Congregational Church. The town was said to produce about 670 tons of recyclable trash annually, but very little of it was sorted and reclaimed. It was estimated that $13,500 could be saved if metals were sorted in accordance with existing town regulations, and another $4,000 could be realized from the sale of the metals. Selectman George Elkins commented that separating metals, especially aluminum and copper, made them easier to steal, and because these

Looking across Back Bay toward the Wolfeborough Railroad Station on the far shore. (Sandy Martin photograph, 1991)

The Wolfeborough Railroad Station in 1993 was home to the Chamber of Commerce office and the Wolfeboro Nursery School. The building was painted a dusty maroon with yellow trim. Trains had not called there for several years. (February 1993 photograph)

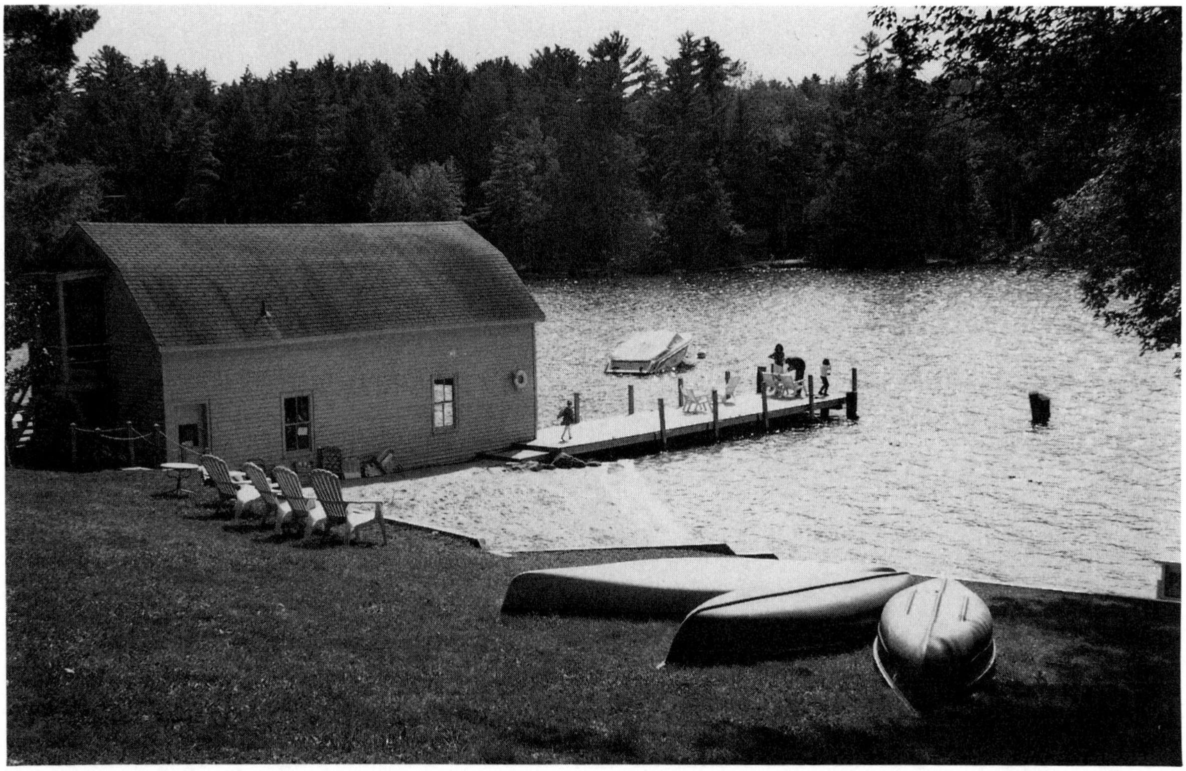

The shorefront on Winter Harbor at Piping Rock Lodges, North Main Street, a popular seasonal spot for tourists. (Sandy Martin photograph, September 7, 1994)

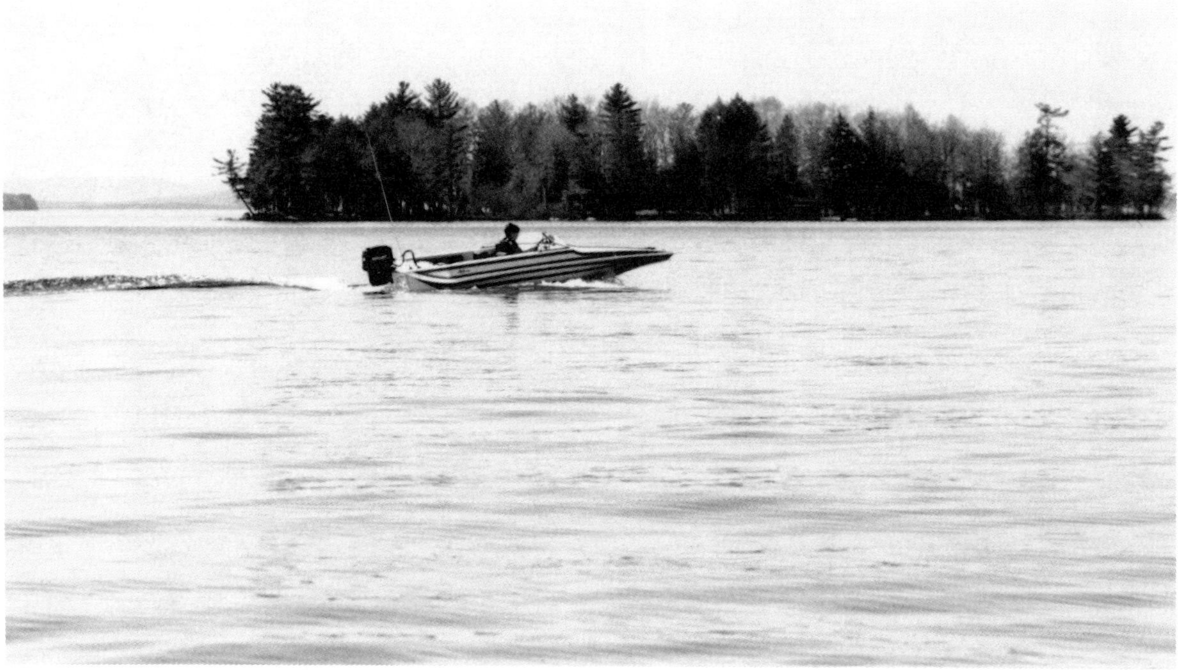

Pleasure boating in Wolfeboro Bay. Little Barndoor Island is in the background. (1994 photograph)

metals would mysteriously disappear, the town had abandoned a similar program years earlier.

In 1991 the town adopted a new logotype (featuring the Avery Building, Town Hall, and other landmarks as viewed from Wolfeboro Bay) designed by Kingswood High senior John Paterno.[181]

### A New Town Hall?

The 14-member Space Needs Study Committee began efforts in 1991 to determine whether a new Town Hall building was needed. It was felt by many that the Brewster Memorial Hall, in service for 100 years, was cramped and outmoded. The committee recommended a new facility, and an appropriate property was found upon which it could be built, but the selectmen rejected the idea. The thought would not go away, and in 1992 the Budget Committee added a $180,000 request for land acquisition to the town warrant which voters rejected by a two-thirds margin.

Meanwhile, there was agitation to merge the Wolfeboro District Court (which met in Town Hall) with that of Ossipee and relocate it to the Gateway Building in Wolfeboro, the bank-owned former Eastern Topographics site in Ossipee, or somewhere else. Wolfeboro Judge Robert Varney was solidly against the idea, and the selectmen voted unanimously in agreement with him.

The lack of space at the existing Town Hall became more acute. William Fluhr, welfare officer, had no office in which to meet clients, nor did Town Clerk Pat Waterman have a private facility in which to discuss personal issues such as adoption. In March 1993 the Town Hall Employee Renovation Investigation Group (THERIG) was formed to plan for better and more comfortable space, with Pat Waterman as chairman. Establishing one or more town department branches at other locations such as the Armory, the defunct Cosmos Yogurt Shop, or even Carpenter School (if the school district would sell it) was considered.

Eventually, the Wolfeboro District Court moved to the Carroll County Administration Building in Ossipee, not far from the Wolfeboro town line, which freed up Town Hall space. It was renamed the Southern Carroll County District Court, but was not merged with the court for the town of Ossipee. Robert Varney, well-known local attorney who also served as town moderator, continued as presiding judge.[182]

### A Mall at the Albee Sand Pit?

During the early 1990s continuing into 1995, there were many discussions about new uses for and zoning of property on Center Street. In 1991 Everett Albee proposed developing a shopping mall on the site of his sand pit across the street from the Allen "A" Resort, stating that a well-known regional mall developer, name not disclosed, was ready to go as soon as zoning was changed to permit it.

In 1994-1995 Alvin and Barbara White proposed once again the development of a recreational vehicle park at the Allen "A". The Lake Wentworth Association vehemently opposed the idea, and it was defeated in the March 1995 election. Many other ideas were proposed for the "Route 28 corridor" from the Allen "A" continuing to the Ossipee line, but no significant rezoning was done.

### Town Notes (1992)

"Fueled by a combination of the recession and cutbacks in federal programs, layoffs, and business failures," the Welfare Department had worked very hard, according to director William T. Fluhr, who noted that not one family that he was aware of had gone hungry or without shelter. During the year the number of welfare recipients increased by 50% to over 150 people.

In 1992 voters removed restrictions against "picking" at the town dump, voted not to abolish the Police Commission (a proposal made by Kay Moody), and struggled with continuing problems with the solid waste disposal facility and the impending closing of the landfill.

Town manager Jim McSweeney called upon town department heads to contribute toward making the processes through which developers must navigate easier to understand. "To many people, obtaining a permit of any kind is perceived as a costly, frustrating, and unpleasant experience," he commented.

In April 100,000 gallons or more of treated sewage accidentally flowed into Back Bay when a $40 sump pump failed, but it was said there was little or no health threat.

In 1992 the Street Numbering Committee began work in earnest to formulate name changes, starting in June with 33 streets whose titles were thought likely to be confused with others, such as Lakeview Terrace and Lakeview Drive. By early 1995, changes were still being made. New street numbers were assigned, and beginning in August 1994 they started appearing on mailboxes, buildings, and signs.[183]

### Town Notes (1993)

At the 1993 town meeting voters rejected a $7 million water system bond proposal, the highly-publicized new C-3 commercial zone, and municipal purchase of the Lakes Region Air Park on Wolfeboro Neck, but appropriated money toward the closure of the landfill. The $7 million water bond failure brought forth a threat that the Environmental Protection Agency could levy a $10,000 per *day* fine against the town if it did not work toward federal clean water standards. In August voters at a special meeting thus voted to comply at a cost which had risen to $8 million.[184]

Old mill building on Center Street, Wolfeboro Falls, as it appeared in the early 1990s. The benches and walkway in the foreground are part of the Russell C. Chase Bridge-Falls Path built on the former railroad right-of-way.

Girl Scouts Kim Martin (left) and Lindsay Fairtile accompany Doris Nyquist on a hike along the Wolfeboro Sanbornville Recreational Trail sponsored by TRAC (the Trails-Rails Action Committee), along the old railroad tracks. (Sandy Martin photograph)

In the spring of 1993 the Town Docks were damaged by wind-blown ice floes. Two docks were shortened by 15 feet, but remaining portions were considered safe. In 1994 the docks were completely reconstructed and expanded under the supervision of Public Works Director Marty Bilafer.[185]

Permits were no longer needed to conduct yard sales in town. Residents could hold up to four each year, lasting no longer than four days each with the items on sale coming from the residence on the same property.[186]

### Town Notes (1994)

Throughout the summers of 1992, 1993, and 1994, there were numerous complaints about "bridge people" – teenagers (mostly) who loitered on and near the Main Street bridge, blocked the sidewalk, and annoyed passers by. In one incident a boy was thrown through a plate-glass window at Tobey's Pharmacy next to the bridge. In another unfortunate circumstance a Kingswood High School football player was seriously injured when he did not complete a daring leap from the top of Tobey's into the Smith River, landing instead on the pavement. There was much discussion and even a proposal for an anti-loitering ordinance, but none was passed.[187]

In 1994 there were no "adult" bookstores or pornography shops in Wolfeboro, although they were common in most larger New England cities and towns. After much discussion, voters were told that they could not ban such a shop should someone wish to establish one, but they could regulate where it would be located. In 1995 an area in Wolfeboro Center near the intersection of North Line Road and Routes 28 and 109 was voted as being allowable for such, subject to certain restrictions. This brought forth many complaints that Wolfeboro should not be forced to admit offensive businesses. Henry S. Maxfield took the lead in a campaign against them. Meanwhile, there was no lack of sex-content films available at local videocassette rental outlets.[188]

Several prominent Wolfeboro landmarks were destroyed in 1993 and 1994. The Berry Mill in Wolfeboro Falls burned to the ground. A complex of small structures known as the Bell and Brummitt buildings, to the left of the Avery Block, was flattened in 1993, and in 1994 the Latchaw building arose on the site. Three stories high, the Latchaw building became home to several shops and a restaurant. On North Main Street, Horne's Garage was razed in November 1994, and developer John Pernokas began construction of a building on the site. The former Glendon House stables building, later the home of the Hart Motor Company and Kammler Chevrolet-Buick, on Glendon Street next to Hunter's IGA, was knocked down, and a Rite-Aid Pharmacy was erected in its place. Witnessing all of this demolition prompted Christina French, a pre-school girl, to ask her mother, "Will there be *any* buildings left in Wolfeboro?"[189]

### Guess Who Pays?

Indicative of government regulations run amok – in this instance federal rules – the cleanup of spilled diesel fuel from soil behind the Municipal Electric Department on Lehner Street was expected in 1991 to cost $250,000 for the first two years and $4,000 to $5,000 annually for several years after that. This was about the same amount of money that citizens thought it would cost to build a much-needed recreation center for town teenagers. Never mind that oil is a naturally biodegradable substance, that the spill was not near the lake, and that years earlier Wolfeboro and nearly every other town in America routinely spread thousands of gallons of oil on unpaved roads each year to keep the dust down.

Increasingly, the standard of living of Americans was dropping as taxes increased and expenses mounted to pay for inefficient waste disposal systems mandated by the federal government, for interest on the out-of-control national debt, for the right to sue doctors and others for large sums (medical bills escalated as insurance costs were passed on to patients), entitlement programs, bloated bureaucracies in Washington, and more.

On the local scene, building a dock, mooring a boat, or filling in a ditch was apt to require red tape involving months of waiting plus permit expenses, plans, and surveys costing large amounts of money.

Virtually every year local taxes went up-up-up and the state of NH cut back its services, while the federal government had long since abandoned financial reason. By the mid-1990s the national debt stood at $4.8 *trillion,* a figure equivalent to about $18,500 for every American citizen.[190]

In December 1994 the Wolfeboro Citizens and Taxpayers Association was formed. "Wolfeboro has had a very sharp increase in taxes over the past four years – about 25%. Our mission is to roll that back," stated Claude Roessiger, who was elected president of the group. John Rico was named vice president. It was further pointed out that from 1986 to 1994, the town population had increased from about 4,400 to 4,800, or 9%, while local taxes *figured net after inflation* jumped 46%. Within a few months of its formation, over 1,000 people had joined the association – indicative of widespread civil dissatisfaction with taxes and expenditures. No other group in town history had ever gained membership at such a rapid rate. It was pointed out that in Rochester just 25 miles away the mayor and the majority of the city council and school board were elected with the backing of that city's taxpayers' group.[191]

Doubtless, the ever-increasing flow of cash into town, state, and national coffers from Wolfeboro citizens' and landowners' paychecks sharply diminished the number of new Chevys sold by Miller's out on Route 28, spicy-flavored cheese at Camelot on North Main Street, carpets by Lauber, Hoyt, and Heckman at various showrooms around town, theorem paintings by Joey Thurston, custom wood items by Eric Lariviere, scuba masks by Dive Winnipesaukee, and apples by Dennis DeVylder. By 1994 many Americans were earning more but receiving less in terms of goods and services.

Notwithstanding the preceding, town employees put forth a great effort to serve the oldest resort in America. In the 1994 *Town Report,* Marty F. Bilafer, director of the Department of Public Works, emphasized the type of Town Hall-citizen cooperation that residents consider ideal:

> MISSION STATEMENT:
>
> To strive to provide outstanding Public Works' services, to emphasize cost effective results, to maintain efficient operations, and to have accountability in our divisions' operations, the Department of Public Works will implement and execute this mission by following these principles:
>
> Listen to our citizens, understanding their needs, keeping them informed, striving to exceed their expectations, and always meeting our commitments.
>
> Recognize that our citizens' opinions and feelings are important to our own success.
>
> Provide practical and economical solutions to citizens' concerns by the application of sound public works and engineering principles.
>
> Develop and maintain a talented work force and provide them the opportunity to maximize their personal and professional potential in the service of our citizens.
>
> Provide a safe working environment that emphasizes quality, teamwork, conservation, and career satisfaction.
>
> Maintain a leadership position in the New Hampshire public works field and continue to strive for excellence.

Despite the prevailing notion that the Wolfeboro selectmen had it in their power to turn the tide against increased spending and taxes, financial reality was that about 60% of local taxes went to the Governor Wentworth Regional School District, not to the Wolfeboro Town Hall. Neither the selectmen nor the town employees had any control over school expenses. Local government was mainly on a fiscally sound basis (no overhanging long-term debt without an asset base). Fortunately for those who live in town year-round, about 50% of local taxes are paid by seasonal residents who make very few demands upon town services and virtually none on the schools.

## PRICES IN 1994

The following prices are from advertisements of local and regional businesses in the *Granite State News* and the *Lakes Region Courier* in late 1994 and from other sources:

**Advertising rates:** Classified advertisement, 1 week, 4 lines, *Granite State News,* $4; each additional week, $2.40. Classified advertisement, 4 weeks, 4 lines, special price for private parties only, *Lakes Region Courier,* $10.

**Appliances:** Kirby vacuum cleaner, deluxe model with many attachments, $1,300; other brands, basic models, $200 to $400.

**Automobiles:** 1994 Oldsmobiles: Cutlass Ciera, $14,995; Cutlass Supreme, $17,995; Eighty-Eight Royale, $20,995. 1995 Dodge Caravan, basic model, $15,495. 1995 Jeep Grand Cherokee, manufacturer's standard retail price, $26,600, special price $24,887. 1995 Jeep Wrangler models, $12,259 and $14,539. 1995 Subaru Legacy, 4-wheel drive, standard transmission (automatic $750 more), $15,995.

**Beverages:** Beer, Budweiser, 6 pack of 12-ounce cans, $3.99. Champagne, Tott's Extra Dry, 750 ml. bottle, $7.49. Wine, Almaden light chablis, 1.5 liter bottle, $5.49. Coca-Cola, Pepsi, Mountain Dew, etc., single can from vending machine at most locations around town, 60¢ to 80¢; cardboard pack of 12 cans, Hunter's IGA, $3.89. Coffee, Maxwell House ground, 13-ounce can, $3.65. Coffee, premium quality Green Mountain brand, at Piccolo Caffé, cup, $1.50. Milk, homogenized, gallon, $2.29.

**Boats:** Glastron bow-rider, 23' model with many extras, at Goodhue & Hawkins, $32,000. Ski Nautique inboard-outboard, high performance, special limited-time winter offer, $21,619. Inflatable Sevylor paddle boat, small, one-person, $79.

**Carpeting:** Square yard, good quality, typical prices, $15 to $25.

**Cigarettes:** Merit brand, pack of 20, $1.85. Winston brand, pack, $1.95.

**Clothing:** Sweater, shaki wool, at Made On Earth, regularly $90, sale $50. T-shirt with scenic design or lettering, $8-$12.

**Computer software:** Typical entertainment program, $19 to $49. Business programs, typical, $39 to $99; Microsoft and other "office packages," list $300 to $500, widely discounted.

**Computers:** IBM clone, many models, price with monitor, 4 megabytes of RAM, 200 or more megabytes hard drive, basic software, $1,000 to $2,500.

**Federal Express:** Typical rate for overnight letter, $11.

**Food:** Meat: Beef, club steak, pound, $3.99. Beef, fresh ground chuck, pound, $2.19. Bacon, Armour brand, 1 pound, $2.19. Chicken breast, prepared and split, pound, $2.59. Tuna, 6 1/8-ounce can, Bumble Bee brand, $1.59.

**Food:** Staples: Bread, IGA brand, 1-pound loaf, 49¢. Butter, pound, $1.59. Carrots, cleaned and trimmed, 5-pound bag, $2.29. Cereal, Cheerios, 10-ounce box, $2.60. Flour, Gold Medal brand, 5-pound bag, $1.45. Onions, Spanish, pound, 49¢. Potatoes from Maine, 10-pound bag, $1.39.

**Food:** Sweet-tooth items: Cookies, Oreo brand, 1-pound package, $2.99. Gum, pack, 35¢ to 50¢. Hershey or other chocolate candy bar, small size, 35¢ to 50¢. Ice cream, Ben & Jerry's, various exotic flavors, pint, $2.59; Weeks brand ice cream, various flavors, quart, $2.39.

**Fuel:** Hardwood, dried and split and cut to stove length, delivered, cord, $110 to $120. Home heating oil, gallon, 82¢. Kerosene, gallon, $1.15. Unleaded gasoline, gallon, regular, $1.10; premium, $1.25.

**Greeting cards:** Hallmark or other popular brand at Bridges' Hallmark or Black's Paper Store, typical, $1 to $1.50; large or ornate cards, $3 to $5.

**Horse accommodations:** Stall rental, month, $75; rental with boarding and care, $150.

**Lottery ticket:** Tri-State Megabucks, pick 6 numbers from 1 to 40, numbers drawn Wednesday and Saturdays at 8 p.m. and shown on TV, typical payouts from $1 million to $4 million, ticket for one drawing, $1.

**Money:** Interest paid on certificates of deposit at Community Bank, First NH Bank, and Wolfeboro branch of Farmington Bank, slightly over 5.1%.

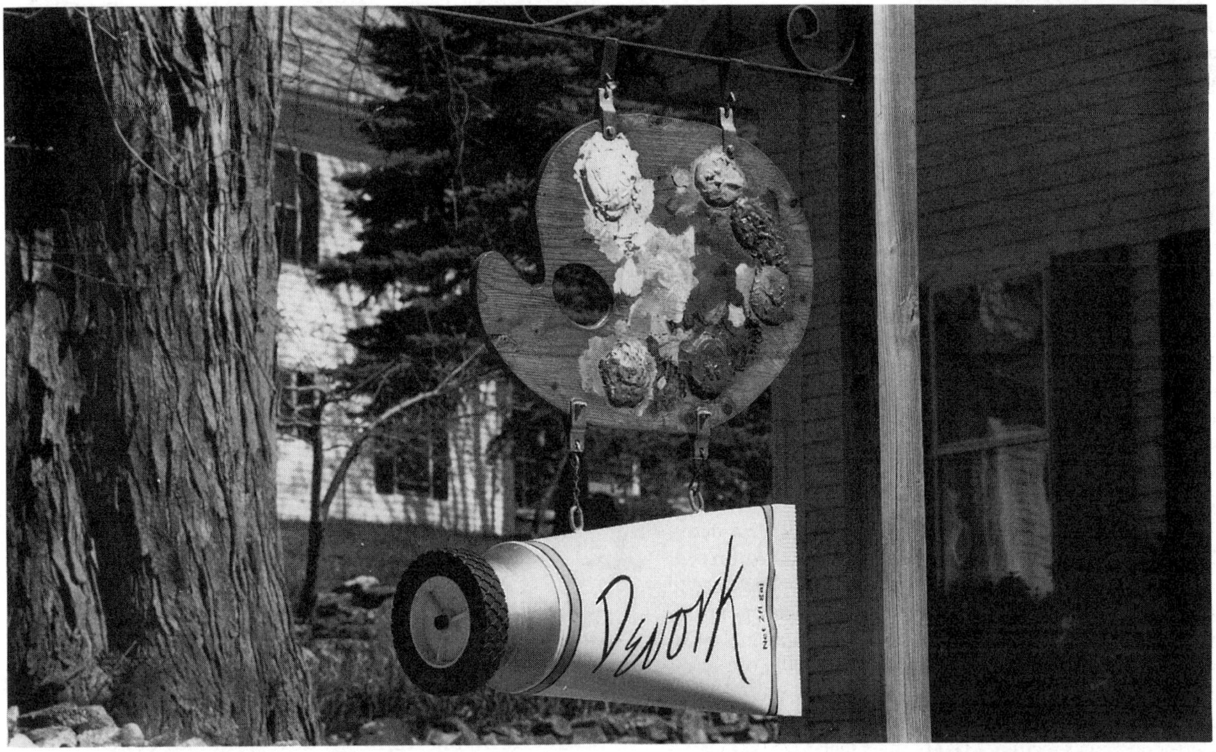


**Signs of the times on Elm Street (Devork studio) and its extension, Pine Hill Road (Pine Hill Shoe Repair). (May 4, 1994 photograph)**

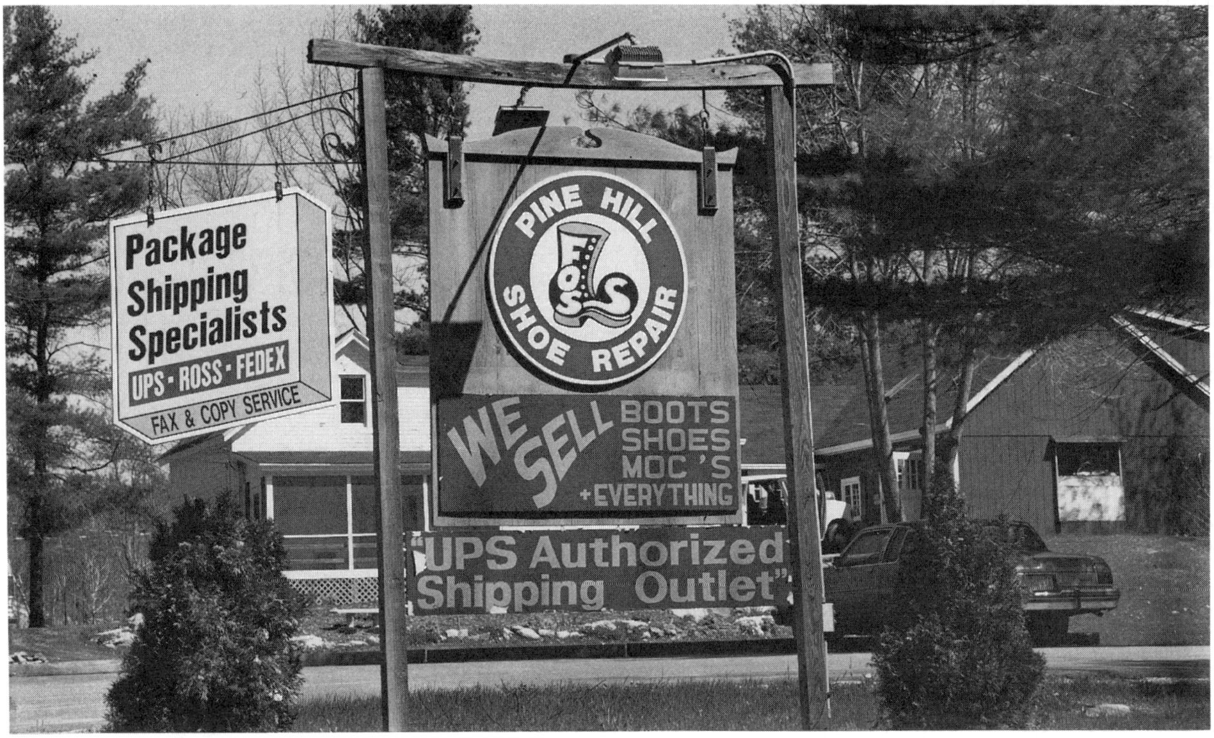

**Newspapers:** Copy of the *Granite State News*, 50¢; *Lakes Region Courier*, free, the *Laker*, free.

**Pewter items:** Made in Wolfeboro at Hampshire Pewter. Pair of "Hampshire" candlesticks $55. Pair of "Kingswood" candlesticks $52. Pair of "traditional" candlesticks $110. Colonial snuffer $17. Traditional tankard $82. Candlestick made into electrical lamp $89. Colonial napkin ring $8.50. 10" diameter dinner plate $78. Infant's cup $44.50. Large flower vase (7-1/2" tall) $84. Bud vase $26.50.

**Postage:** First-class letter rate, 29¢ (raised to 32¢ on January 1, 1995). Postcard, 19¢.

**Precious metals:** Gold, ounce, $380. Silver, ounce, $5.50. (Basic bullion prices; coins, small ingots, and retail transactions were at higher levels due to handling costs.)

**Real estate rentals:** 2-bedroom farmhouse, plus utilities, month, $600. 2- or 3-bedroom apartment with loft overlooking Back Bay, includes plowing and rubbish removal, plus utilities, month, $500. 3-bedroom house, ranch style, Robin Acres, plus utilities, month, $700. 3-room efficiency apartment, Center Street, plus heat, month, $295.

**Real estate:** Building lot, Cotton Valley Road, 3.5 acres, $17,500. House on Clark Road. 7 rooms, pine floors, tin ceilings, 4-car garage, etc., $154,900. Ranch-style house close to Carry Beach. 1.4 acre, 3,000 square feet, includes separate 3-room apartment, $129,000. Business condominium in the Colonial Arms Building, 1,300 square feet, $99,000. Cottage on Crescent Lake with 125 feet of waterfront, $149,900. Old mill building on Smith River, post and beam construction, steel exterior on newer section, 23,000 square feet, $225,000. Cape-style house on Winter Harbor, 3 or 4 bedrooms, 2 decks, 50-foot dock, $529,000.

**Recreation:** Night skiing season pass, King Pine, special offer, adult, $99, junior, $66. Typical day at regional ski area including lift ticket, food, and refreshments, $40-$50.

**Restaurant food:** Restaurant lunch, Back Bay Club or Wolfe's Tavern, not including beverage or tip, $4 to $9. Dinner at the Cider Press (spring 1993 menu), selections: Teriyaki steak $12; Kansas City strip sirloin $13.50; barbequed baby back ribs $11.95; scallops $11.95; chicken parmesan $8.95; Boston cream pie $2.50; carrot cake $2.50; New York cheesecake, $2.75.

**Snowmobile:** Ski-Doo, various models, $3,500 to $5,500.

**Supplies:** Batteries, pack of four Duracell AA batteries, $3.49. Toilet paper, Charmin brand, pack of 9, 450-sheet 1-ply rolls, $5.59.

**Tools:** Swiss Army knife, basic two-blade model, Bradley's Hardware, $7.95. Heavy-duty compound-action branch cutter, $37.

**Truck:** 1994 Ford Ranger XL, after rebate, special price, $8,995.

**Tuition:** Day student (living at home in region) at Brewster Academy, not including supplies and special fees, $10,600 (increased to $11,400 in 1995).

**Wages:** Construction trades, experienced worker, $15-$28 per hour. Clerk $4.25 (minimum wage) to $6 or so. Office worker $5-$7 up. Scuba diver for salvage operation, $75 or more per hour.

## LOOKING TO THE FUTURE

### Planning

Planning for the future continued to be a focal point for many people during the early 1990s. In the previous decade of the 1980s a small group of dedicated citizens worked with the Lakes Region Planning Commission to develop a 13-chapter, 482-page plan. In the early nineties a much larger group worked hard at updating the original chapters. Although there have been varying opinions as to the effectiveness of this and other plans, there is no doubt that certain branches of it have borne fruit, as in the restrictive zoning that prevented excessive commercialization and high-density condominium construction in the 1980s, the improvement in appearance of Back Bay, expansion and improvement of the Town Docks, and more.

However, Wolfeboro has historically resisted regulation or being told what to do. Thus, only a small percentage of the information compiled for various master plans has ever been used, and some master plans have been ignored virtually in their entirety.

As an interesting footnote in history, the yearly statement of the Board of Selectmen as printed in the 1994 *Town Report* didn't mention at all—not even in passing—what happened in 1994, but was devoted in its entirety to the future.

At the very least, planning for the future enables local citizens and officials to engage in introspection, to evaluate what we have, and, on balance, to appreciate that Wolfeboro is a special place in America.

### The Charrette

In 1992 Donald G. Hughes, a successful businessman who had retired to Wolfeboro and sought to contribute his management talents to the town, joined with Joyce Davis to co-chair the Wolfeboro 2000 project, "a collaboration of citizen committees, town staff and boards, and professional consultants working to develop a common vision of Wolfeboro."

In a related but really opposite situation the 1993 town warrant contained Article 2, Amendment 1, to create a new "Commercial District C-3" comprising about 250 acres of land located more or less in an interior area enclosed by Varney Road, Bay Street, Route 109A, and the town line with Tuftonboro. This significant increase in commercially zoned acreage was recommended by the selectmen because they felt it might bring new business in a recessionary time. However, it was opposed by the Planning Board, members of which felt that the area selected had more potential if used differently. At the annual town meeting on March 9, 1993, the vote was 689 for and 706 against, far short of the two-thirds majority required for passage. The Wolfeboro-Tuftonboro Land Bank, a non-profit organization founded in 1988 by Robert P. Hopewell, a significant owner of property in the proposed district, opposed the hastily-conceived zoning change. The Land Bank had not yet determined its own long-term objectives for the area and asked, in effect, "What's the rush?"

However, the large number of residents who seemed to favor increased commercial zoning did prompt the Land Bank to contact Town Planner Amanda L. Simpson and land consultant Rick Chellman to explore the most effective way to use this large tract of undeveloped land so close to town.

On March 16, 1993, Donald G. Hughes of the Wolfeboro 2000 project and representatives of the Land Bank met with the selectmen, who cautiously approved the idea of a "charrette," as it was called, later defined as "a relatively brief but intense working session to produce a set of design products by a given deadline." The term stuck, and Wolfeboro Charrette became the catch phrase of the year.

Land near Back Bay and additional acreage near the Abenaki Recreation Area was added to the tract under discussion. Eventually about 600 acres were studied. In addition it was decided to culminate and showcase at this event the work of the Wolfeboro 2000 committees who had been working on pieces of the Master Plan. The concept of residents working alongside professionals to add local knowledge to proven expertise gained considerable momentum, and on August 26-28, 1993, the Wolfeboro Charrette, subtitled the "Let's Do It Program," was held at the Kingswood Regional Middle School.

The event brought together members of the Wolfeboro Planning Board (Harold Parker, Joyce Davis, Shirley E. Ganem, Steve Hale, Donald G. Hughes, Paul A. Kimball, and William A. Rae), Town Planner Amanda L. Simpson, and committees consisting of over three dozen public-spirited local citizens.

Each committee had a display — typically accompanied by photographs and maps — and explanations were given of its proposals. For example, Roger F. Murray III, spokesman for the Parking and Docks Committee, stated that parking meters should not be a part of the town's future and that arriving in Wolfeboro by boat could be made much simpler by replacing and expanding the Town Docks.

The Pathways Committee graphically presented the concept of making Wolfeboro a more pedestrian town by developing trails and an effective sidewalk program. The Downtown Committee presented a simple design review ordinance to help retain the unique character of the town. The plan for the Charrette area was developed by the various professionals working on a series of long tables in the school cafeteria with members of the general public offering suggestions at planned intervals.

As promised, a 20-foot-long plan, pieced together on tracing paper, was finished and on hand at the crack of noon on August 28. Over 100 people braved a hot and humid hall to hear the results.

Even though wetlands made much of the land difficult to develop, the low-lying areas also provided a potential for beauty and the enjoyment of nature. It was suggested that one highlight of the area might be an upscale assisted-living area or a school. Another portion could be used for a village-type community consisting of apartments and small businesses. A new road parallel to Pine Hill Road could be built so that the latter could be returned to its original rural residential use. An industrial and commercial park could accommodate new and existing businesses that did not need a main road location. Further, a ball field could be built as well as a major walking-biking trail from the Pop Whalen Rink to the Russell C. Chase Bridge-Falls Path. In addition, a camping area was possible, and there would be land for a wildlife refuge.

It was estimated that about 400 people (equal to about 8% of the local population) came to learn about the Wolfeboro Charrette and add their input. Enthusiasm was intense. However, momentum to keep going to formalize the plan — and to complete both the Master Plan and the zoning recommendations — could not be sustained. The selectmen turned down a budget increase for an assistant to the town planner, and many volunteers had become exhausted.

In November the Wolfeboro Economic Development Committee and the Business Development Corporation suggested that their concept for a light industrial park on town-owned land on Route 109A opposite Beach Pond Road, that was already zoned commercial, could result in "the first fruits" of the Wolfeboro Charrette. Completely forgotten was the 1987 survey conducted by Town Planner Peer Kraft-Lund and paid for by the town that revealed that *virtually no one* wanted more industry! The fact that 96% of the citizens had stated that *historic preservation* was their number one priority was apparently ignored as well.

The Planning Board remained cautious about expanding commercial zoning in that area because they had bigger fish to fry. The Board announced that the 1994 town warrant would contain a very important proposal for a major zoning change to commercial covering a large amount of acreage along Route 28 north of Wolfeboro Falls, as developed over a two-year period by Planning Board members and the Economic Development Committee. However, public hearings resulted in mostly negative comments concerning the commercial zoning plan. Accordingly, the Planning Board decided not to recommend such a big change for that area of Route 28, and voters agreed.

In April 1994 the Wolfeboro Charrette won first prize in the "innovative projects" category in a ceremony held in Concord by the Office of State Planning. Former Planning Board chairman Donald G. Hughes, Town Planner

Amanda L. Simpson and current Planning Board Chairman Harold Parker were on hand to accept the award.[192]

**What Wolfeboro Wants**

On May 9, 1994, several dozen Wolfeboro residents gathered in the Pinckney Boathouse on the Brewster Academy campus to listen to Planning Board Chairman Harold Parker, Economic Development Committee Chairman Bill Wiebe, and others discuss the economic future of the town.

Wiebe commented that his committee's Economic Strategic Plan "will provide a strategy to take the town where it wants to go." Mark Smith, a reporter on hand from the *Granite State News*, later wrote that this brought forth a "chowder of ideas for the town's future." Kathryn Powell, editor of the *Lakes Region Courier*, was prompted to write a piece titled "Where is Wolfeboro Heading?"[193]

Town Planner Amanda L. Simpson asked the audience to define the quality of life in our town. Powell reported on what was expressed:

> The consensus was Wolfeboro is, and should remain, small, quiet, rural, quaint, with trees, beauty, mountains, lakes. It is charming, relaxing, clean, and safe, and never should smokestacks, parking meters, pornography or franchise architecture be allowed Also, Wolfeboro is multi-generational and should strive to maintain its open space.

Challenges included providing more facilities for the recreation and social lives of younger folk, upgrading the quality and service offered by local businesses, and making Town Hall more "user friendly," the latter from a popular phrase used to describe what a computer program should be. The possibility of dissolving the sprawling six-town Governor Wentworth Regional School District—which uses about 60% of the tax money collected in town—was discussed, with some longing for a return to the "good old days" when Wolfeboro controlled its own educational facilities and there was much less controversy.

Harold Parker, Selectman Paul R. Hatch, Donald G. Hughes, and some others suggested that Wolfeboro's current Master Plan be *used*. This seemingly basic proposal may have been made in light of comments such as that made subsequently by Kathryn Powell, "the amount of impact the *last* master plan has had on planning, has been, in a word, 'zip'." Further, "The old plan has been sitting on a shelf in someone's office collecting dust."

Powell reported that these questions were raised:

> Is the future of Wolfeboro in tourism or retirement?
>
> Can high-tech be quaint or can quaint be profitable?
>
> Are current planning regulations flexible enough to meet the needs of our children in 10 years? Do they meet our needs now?

Although just about everyone at the forum expressed in one form or another the sentiment "I love Wolfeboro," little else could be agreed upon.

The preceding forum could have been held in 1984 instead of 1994, or even a century earlier in 1894, and the sentiments would probably have been about the same.

**Possible Conclusion**

While Wolfeboro town officials and civic-minded citizens work hard at drawing up master plans that look to the future, and while many concede that such planning has had many valuable uses in the past and will probably continue to have value in the future, most people just cross their fingers and hope the town will stay the way it is.

# THE HISTORY OF WOLFEBORO,NH, 1770-1994, ENDNOTES

## NOTES FOR INTRODUCTION

[1] Suggested by Lawrence H. Conklin's book, *Letters to George F. Kunz*, 1986. Apropos of the present work the author issued numerous requests for contributions of information, such appearing in multiple issues of the *Granite State News*, *The Wellsweep*, and the *Wolfeboro Times*, as well as in letters, talks before local organizations, etc.

[2] Letters to the author, February 17 (first paragraph), November 1 (second paragraph), 1993.

[3] Letter, June 9, 1994.

## NOTES FOR CHAPTER 1

[1] Estimate, 1994 *Town Report*, p. 90.

[2] Data from 1969 federal report 701 by Edwards & Kelsey, Inc.

[3] Hitchcock, *The Geology of New Hampshire*, 1877, Vol. II, p. 606.

[4] Abbie Cotton Lang, "A Rich Traditional Heritage of Cotton Mountain," 1937. She stated this excavation of ore took place 65 years earlier.

[5] Richard P. Goldthwait, *Surficial Geology of the Wolfeboro-Winnipesaukee Area, NH*, 1968, p. 9: "An abandoned lead mine has been reported on the west shore of Crescent Lake."

## NOTES FOR CHAPTER 2

[1] The author has drawn upon Benjamin F. Parker's *The History of Wolfeborough* (1900) and his contribution to *The History of Carroll County* (1889) for selected information in this chapter. However, it is worth noting that Parker took certain wording *verbatim* from town records and included it, ostensibly as original text, in his 1900 work (per conversation of the author with Harrison D. Moore, February 23, 1993). Further, historian Dr. Robert F.W. Meader, no fan of Parker's book, commented in his monograph, *The Saga of a Palace*, that Parker engaged in a lot of guesswork. Certain information is from a manuscript created for the Wolfeboro Historical Society by Janet E. Macomber in the 1970s. Much additional information is also from the author's own research efforts.

[2] Bowman, p. 8, gives further details.

[3] *GSN*, July 29, 1955. Noted that on July 13 four campers from the Hill School Camp found two ancient Indian canoes underwater in Rust Pond.

[4] *GSN*, February 13, 1894.

[5] The 1907 legislation was House Bill No. 394. *GSN*, May 9, 1909: "The official spelling of our town is to be Wolfeboro, and the order goes into effect at once."

[6] Biographies are in Parker, Chap. VI.

[7] This house still stands and in 1994 is owned by Andrea F. Thomson; tax map 7-15-1 (cf. Harrison D. Moore).

[8] It was later stated that the fourth lot was sold to Thomas Taylor, not Thomas Piper (as stated by Benjamin F. Parker, *History of Wolfeborough*, p. 111). The bill was not paid, and two years later, on October 18, 1770, it was sold to Ebenezer Meder (Meader). Correction to Parker's text appeared in *GSN*, July 25, 1958.

[9] Deposition dated June 20, 1805; Strafford County Records, Book 48, pp. 244-245; orthography preserved. This is from a testimony taken to settle a land dispute. An individual stated that two mills had not been built on Smith River at a certain time; if so, the land would have gone to another party by default. Cf. Harrison D. Moore and Arthur F. Chamberlin.

[10] The information concerning the early years of the Clark House is not unequivocal. Benjamin F. Parker, *History of Wolfeborough*, p. 524, was confused and stated Joseph Clark built it; further, Enoch Clark was Joseph Clark's son. The present information is from the Strafford County records in Dover, researched by Harrison D. Moore.

[11] One of these, made by George Casebolt, is the property of the Wolfeboro Historical Society and has been exhibited widely.

[12] Robert F.W. Meader, *The Saga of a Palace*, published by the Wolfeboro Historical Society, 1962. Meader dismissed Benjamin F. Parker's information and sketches in *The History of Wolfeborough* as being largely inaccurate and poorly researched.

[13] The 1790 federal census recorded four slaves in towns which now constitute Carroll County. One was in Bartlett, another in Effingham (serving the John Costalow family), one in Moultonboro, and the fourth in Tamworth. None was in Wolfeboro.

[14] Quotation from auction advertisement, New Market, NH, March 29, 1780, published in the *Independent Chronicle and the Independent Advertiser*, April 20, 1770 (cited by Meader in *Saga of a Palace*, 1962).

[15] Stephen E. Clow (a descendant), letter to author, January 1994.

[16] Apparently in an untrained, inexperienced fashion and possibly "where they had not originally been," according to Robert F.W. Meader, *Saga of a Palace*, 1962.

[17] For detailed information see "So What's to Dig About at the Gov's Old Manse?" by Barbara Hobbie, *GSN*, August 20, 1986.

[18] This office was continued well into the 20th century; *e.g.*, *GSN*, November 9, 1911: "At a meeting of the selectmen, Saturday, November 4, Darius Ham, Charles H. Tibbetts, and Charles P. Moore were commissioned as fence viewers for this town until their successors are chosen or appointed."

[19] Prices reckoned in Continental Currency which at the time was slightly depreciated in value in terms of Spanish "dollars."

[20] Today in the 1990s the U.S. government still has not honored its first paper money.

[21] Libbey had exchanged his services with Tibbetts and certain others for goods. Thus, Tibbetts and others had labor credits with Libbey.

[22] In newspaper and other accounts, Whitton (as in the family of George Whitton) was sometimes spelled Whitten. Conversely, Whitten (as in the family of Jesse Whitten) was sometimes spelled Whitton. Arthur F. Chamberlin (letter, October 27, 1993) noted: "The heirs of the Whittons do not believe the Whittens to be any relation at all."

[23] Gertrude B. Hamm, "Wolfeboro's Contribution to the Civil War," p. 9.

[24] The term "gore" meant valley and was often used in connection with another place name, such as Alton Gore or Ossipee Gore (cf. Dr. Joyce E. Brown, letter, June 17, 1994).

[25] At the 1791 town meeting it was voted to raise more money to complete the New Bridge over Smith's River (information from Harrison D. Moore). At the time the lake level was 10 to 12 feet lower than it is now, and the Smith River was a rapidly-flowing stream (after the lake level was raised, Back Bay was largely created, on the same level as the main lake).

[26] Today The Weirs is usually referred to as Weirs Beach.

[27] Wolfboro Junction (as it was spelled on postal cancellations 1882-1895) was located in Sanborn's Mills (then a part of Wakefield), name later changed to Sanbornville. It was never a part of the town of Wolfeboro. The Wolfeborough part of the railroad name was shortened to Wolfeboro' (or simply Wolfeboro) in early 1872.

[28] Morgan's wife gave art lessons in Wolfeboro. Charles Morgan retired to Concord years later.

[29] *GSN*, January 24, 1893.

[30] Clayton M. Wallace notes preserved by the Wolfeboro Historical Society.

[31] *GSN*, September 18, 1871. For an overview of earthquakes in NH, see *Environmental Sheet*, Concord: NH Department of Environmental Services, 1933. The first temblor recorded in the state occurred October 29, 1727; the strongest in 1925. At least 262 quakes of magnitude 1.4 or greater and with epicenters within the state were felt between 1728 and 1993.

[32] Ledger in author's reference collection; obtained from an antique dealer who acquired it from a home in South Wolfeboro.

[33] Details in the *GSN*, April 15, 1911, at which time an update on the building's status was given. *GSN*, February 16, 1940, stated that the old factory was 36 windows long by 18 windows wide and was replaced on the same location by a factory of the same size having exactly half as many windows in each direction.

[34] Details of each bank will be found in Volume III. In the nineteenth century aper currency notes were issued by the Wolfborough Bank, Lake Bank, and Lake National Bank of Wolfborough. In the twentieth century the Wolfeboro National Bank issued currency.

[35] For a time it was suggested that the newspaper was founded in 1859. However, research established the date as November 1, 1860 (cf. *GSN*, March 1, 1919). An excellent history of the *GSN* appears in the August 28, 1931 issue; this includes the information about the paper being pre-printed on one side in the early days. *GSN*, August 17, 1934, stated Newell "bought out a little paper in Ossipee, and moved it to Wolfeboro"; no further details of the Ossipee periodical were given.

[36] Items under this heading were gathered by Janet E. Macomber in the 1970s; her commentary is given, lightly edited; the October 3, 1887, April 18, 1899, and law enforcement items were found by the author.

[37] Cf. Arthur F. Chamberlin, letter, October 27, 1993.

[38] *GSN*, January 11, 1886.

[39] The Free Soil Party had been especially prominent in the presidential election of 1848, when for advertising purposes it stamped coins with the inscription VOTE THE LAND FREE (meaning that the soil or land should be free from the slavery evil).

[40] Ms. owned by the University of Virginia.

[41] Known today as Sewall Point and Little Barndoor Island.

[42] *GSN*, April 7, 1915, as part of a history of the hotel. The 1860 map of Carroll County illustrates of the facility.

[43] This anecdote appears in numerous Wolfeboro accounts including Alta B. Meader's "Peripatetic Wolfeboro," 1955. Investigation into the matter is outlined in *GSN* November 28 and December 19, 1903, and the truth is revealed in an article dated January 23, 1904. An account of the wall's demolition was printed on October 10, 1914.

[44] Today the Brewster Academy soccer field is where the hotel stood.

[45] Dunton, earlier landlord of the Flume House in Franconia Notch, leased the Pavilion by 1859 (cf. Samuel C. Eastman, *White Mountain Guide Book*, 1859 edition, p. 142).

[46] *Chisholm's White Mountain Guide*, 1916, stated that the Kingswood Inn was owned by F.S. McLaughlin, accommodated 300 guests, was a half-mile from the railroad station, and charged rates of $8 to $15 per week. Obviously, this was outdated information.

[47] *GSN*, October 18, 1935; also the advertisement just quoted.

[48] Life dates: November 15, 1829-October 11, 1889.

[49] *GSN*, June 27, 1930.

[50] Information concerning libraries is largely from Benjamin F. Parker, *History of Wolfeborough*, pp. 413-416.

[51] *GSN*, May 15 and June 24, 1894, among others. Details are in Volume III under Wentworth, Hobbs & Rothwell's Uncle Tom's Cabin Co.

[52] Janet E. Macomber, undated ms. circa 1970s.

[53] *GSN*, November 20, 1894.

[54] *GSN*, August 28, 1894. Rattlesnake Island is in Alton.

55 *GSN*, September 29, 1896.

56 *GSN*, April 5, 1898. Subsequently, the April 12, 1898, *GSN* noted that the Wolfeboro showing realized a net income of $23.46.

57 A successor to the projection device made in France by the Lumière brothers. On December 28, 1895, Louis and Auguste Lumière projected films on their Cinématographe to Frenchmen who paid a franc apiece to gather before a screen in the basement of the Grand Café in Paris. Films used in these and other early performances were short subjects lasting only a minute or two or even less, and featured acrobats, dancers, vaudeville skits, trains, and other topics emphasizing rapid motion.

58 The observation had originated in 1681 by the Provincial Assembly to enable the citizens to pray for the recovery of Royal Governor John Cutt.

59 *History of Wolfeborough*, p. 527.

60 Certain remarks are adapted from Benjamin F. Parker, *History of Wolfeborough*.

61 *GSN*, November 25, 1889. Meader lived on a farm off North Main Street known as the Willow House, later as The Elms—a favorite lodging place for summer visitors (Skyridge Farm condominiums are on the site today).

62 Sources include Benjamin F. Parker's *History of Wolfeborough* and *GSN*, January 18, 1913, "Historical Fires." Parker was notoriously inaccurate in certain fire dates (see footnotes).

63 This citation is given here as it appears in Parker's *History of Wolfeborough*. However, so far as is known, John Taber had no pipe-making factory in Wolfeboro until later in the decade (see Taber entry in Volume III). In any event, the author has encountered no record of a Taber fire within town limits. Taber had a facility on Beaver Brook in East Alton, c. 1864-1868, that closed in the latter year; perhaps this burned. (Information from Paul Jung, conversation, December 29, 1993.)

64 Theodore H. Brigden, *Around Dimon's Corner*, p. 29.

65 *GSN*, October 19, 1864. As an example of how erroneous later recollections of dates can be, Benjamin F. Parker, in his *History of Wolfeborough* gave the date of this fire as 1887, an account of historical fires in *GSN*, January 18, 1913, said 1888, another *GSN* historical account, February 12, 1932, gave the date as 1867!

66 *GSN*, October 17, 1881.

67 Parker erroneously gave the fire date as August 10, 1887, perhaps excusable as the fire was not discovered until nearly 11 p.m. on the 9th. An account of the fire was printed in *GSN*, August 15.

68 *GSN*, November 7, 1887. Holton, who came to town seeking work but was turned away by several to whom he applied, pleaded guilty to arson.

69 Day date not known to author.

70 Day date not known to author.

71 *GSN*, December 30, 1889; also, historical account in *GSN*, December 26, 1893.

72 *GSN*, March 9, 1891. Nason's name appeared in other crime reports of the era.

73 *GSN*, November 13, 1891.

74 *GSN*, April 11, 1893.

75 *GSN*, June 6, 1893.

76 *GSN*, May 9, 1894 (insurance appraisers in town; fire date not given).

77 *GSN*, March 6, 1894.

78 *GSN*, July 24, 31, 1894.

79 *GSN*, October 23, 1894.

80 *GSN*, October 29, 1895.

81 *GSN*, January 7, 1896.

82 *GSN*, February 18, 1896. Another loss estimate was $6,000.

83 Date of account; fire was earlier.

84 *GSN*, September 22, 1896.

85 *GSN*, March 2, 1897.

86 *GSN*, November 23, 1897.

87 *GSN*, July 19, 1898.

88 *GSN*, May 30, 1899 (account paraphrased and condensed).

89 *GSN*, September 16, 1899.

90 *GSN*, September 21, October 19, 1897.

91 *GSN*, March 18, 1889 (proposal for cleaning lamps, furnishing with fuel, and lighting them solicited by town): February 12, 1892 (report of Precinct meeting of January 11, 1892).

92 *GSN*, May 11, August 17, 1897.

93 *GSN*, December 18, 1894.

94 To entice the firm the town offered incentives including exemption from taxes. Details will be found under Coburn, Gauss & Co. in Volume III.

95 In NH, Gov. Frank W. Rollins conceived the idea; a statewide Old Home Week Association was formed. Later, such events were held intermittently. (Cf. history in *GSN*, July 3, 1936.)

96 For additional information see *GSN*, August 18, 1900.

## NOTES FOR CHAPTER 3

1 This phrase appeared in print from time to time and was a local favorite. It appears to have been paraphrased from Isaak Walton's quoting Dr. Boteler on the desirability of the strawberry.

2 *GSN*, June 8, 1907.

3 *GSN*, June 6, 1908.

4 B.W. Parker died December 2, 1935; obituary in *GSN*, December 6, 1935, stated that he completed the unfinished town history.

5 Under "Unpaid Bills" on the *Town Report* of February 15, 1900, from open invoices of 1898 there is $193 due to Benjamin F. Parker for labor on the town history. *Town Report* of February 15, 1901, under "Miscellaneous Bills" states Parker was paid $237 for labor.

6 Edwin H. Lord, Albert B. Rust, and Frederick W. Prindle constituted the original committee of three who met with Parker in 1898 to initiate the project. As of February 15, 1908, the town had on hand 768 bound and 200 unbound copies of the book, carried on the records as costing $1,490 and $200 respectively. Thus, bound copies were valued at $1.94 each; apparently either the better bindings had been sold, or the cost was written down.

7 It is believed that Pianola was the first of the "ola" words, the predecessor of Victrola, Crayola, Motorola, payola, etc.

8 Meryl was an orphan girl who came to Wolfeboro and subsequently had many exciting adventures in the nearby Ossipee Mountains. Quite possibly, the large lodge mentioned in the novel was the inspiration a few years later for Thomas Plant's so-called (in a later era) "Castle in the Clouds." See Bibliography in Volume III for more information.

9 The *GSN*, January 23, 1894, noted: "Collecting stamps, especially of the Columbian issue, is now quite the rage among old and young."

10 Note: The word "trout" was often used at the time as a general term for lake fish, trout and otherwise.

11 Established in 1891 on Cow Island (a.k.a. Guernsey Island) in Tuftonboro.

12 Humorously spelled this way in the newspaper. Archie A. Horne was team captain for Wolfeboro and, quite possibly, the most acclaimed athlete in Wolfeboro history, although in modern times Howie Bean has mounted a strong challenge. Later, Horne became well known as a Ford automobile dealer.

13 Jared Alonzo Greene, Boston patent medicine king who marketed Nervura. A detailed, laudatory account of his business was given in the *GSN*, April 5, 1902. Greene professed to have "discovered" more than 40 remedies, of which Nervura was the best known. The business was located at 34 Temple Place in Boston. In addition to selling patent medicines, the versatile Dr. Greene advertised that people could be "treated successfully and scientifically for almost any disease through the mail." His brother, Dr. F.E. Greene, built a house in Moultonboro. Dr. J.A. Greene's son, Frank A. Greene, managed his father's poultry operation at Roxmont Castle, on Moultonboro Neck, where Geneva Point Camp is today. For additional information see *Belle of the Isles* entry in "Lake Winnipesaukee Boats with a Relationship to Wolfeboro," Volume II.

14 *GSN*, August 10, 1901. Advance billing.

15 Dates in this section represent newspaper publishing dates unless otherwise stated.

16 Event date, not newspaper article date.

17 The Angelus, made by Wilcox & White of Meriden, CT, was a push-up piano player cabinet. Selling for $250 to $400, the device was foot-pumped in the manner of the Pianola.

18 Babb managed the Woldcroft cottage colony (today known as Kehonka Hill) in South Wolfeboro near the Alton town line. For a time, he was also captain of the steamer *Brookline*. Annie Oakley was one of the most famous personalities to visit Wolfeboro during the decade.

19 Performance date, not newspaper date. Teddy bears were becoming a national fad.

20 Itinerant motion picture troupes did not advertise in the *GSN* but used handbills and posters put up around town by an advance man.

21 In the 1890s Edward J. Libbey, a partner in the Libbey Brothers lumber mill, was the leader of the original Wolfeboro Cornet Band. The group regularly met for practice sessions in the Boston & Maine Railroad Wharf Building until the structure was gutted by fire on May 28, 1899.

22 *GSN*, August 17, 1901, and other issues of the time gave details.

23 This structure was started in 1889 and completed in April 1890 by Alexander J. McDonald and J.A. Warren. It stands today and is the Dunau residence. Today Sewall Street is known as Sewall Road. *GSN*, October 14, 1889 and April 28, 1890 (Ferncliffe). *GSN*, October 11, 1892 (Dickinson installs windmill to pump lake water for use in drinking; first such windmill on lake).

24 The *Waveland* was jointly operated by residents of Waveland Island—better known as Keniston Island—facing Wolfeboro Bay. This picturesque across-the-water getaway had recently been developed by commercial interests from Lynn, MA, and several cottages had been built there.

25 *GSN*, August 16, 1902.

26 Cf. Arthur F. Chamberlin, letter, October 27, 1993.

27 Histories of specific camps are delineated in a separate chapter.

28 The publisher of the card was Frank W. Swallow of Exeter, NH. The correct title, as printed on the card, is: "Wolfboro, N.H., in the Future."

29 Edition of July 18, 1903.

30 A retrospective account in the *GSN* in 1956 moved the date back to 1896 and said that Libby brought it from *Bridgeport, Conn.* to Wolfeboro in the company of George E. Whitney, who built the first Locomobile under the name of the Whitney Steam Car. The steamer *Mohawk*, owned by Dr. Henry F. Libby, was sold, and in 1901, burned. The steamer *West Wind*, about 50 feet long, was built in 1891 for Dr. Henry F. *and* John H. Libby, who operated it as an excursion boat out of Winter Harbor until 1906, when it was sold to a man from Newmarket, who used it on the ocean. However, by 1920 it was seen locally once again and was operated out of Wolfeboro Bay by Capt. John Goodhue. Both the *Mohawk* and *West Wind* had steam-operated musical "chime whistles" aboard.

31 A September 28, 1897, follow-up article noted: "The Whitney Steam Carriage, the arrival here of which was noted in our last issue, took his departure on the steamer *Mount Washington* for Alton Bay on the morning trip of Saturday last. By courtesy of Mr. Libby, of course we mean Johnny. Many of their friends here residing were able to enjoy a trip over our highways during the days of last week, this gentleman controlling the motor power. All gave high praise to the thorough and complete working of the carriage, even on our highways, and gave the expression of the sincerity of sheer attainments on roads of better construction. The motor power is furnished by an engine using gasoline as fuel. Its weight is but 650 pounds. A distance of 30 miles can be traveled before requiring a new supply of water to be taken. It would seem those of a mechanical turn of mind that the Whitney steam carriage

would soon supply a very much desired want in road locomotion, and that the inventor is safely started on the road to fame and riches."

[32] Most information in this paragraph is from an article written for the Wolfeboro Historical Society in the 1960s by Florence Paine. Her sources included the *GSN*, Albert Auderer, Sr., and Rodney Haines.

[33] Calcium carbide, dripped on by a controlled flow of water, yields acetylene gas and calcium oxide. $CaC_2 + H_2O$ yields $C_2H_2 + CaO$. (Cf. Dr. Joyce E. Brown, letter, June 24, 1994)

[34] *GSN*, July 8, 1905.

[35] The same climb on Center Street up Brickyard Hill today is the incline from the Lehner Street junction to South Main Street.

[36] *GSN*, March 7, 1903.

[37] Unless stated otherwise the dates given are dates the fires occurred, not the publication dates in the *GSN* (which were generally within the next week). The descriptions are edited and adapted from accounts in the *GSN*.

[38] Date of the report in *GSN*, not the date of the fire.

[39] Date of *GSN* report; the fire date was not given.

[40] Per Arthur F. Chamberlin, letters to the author, February 17 and October 27, 1993. Name appears in at least one account as Mary Haines, but Alice was the owner.

[41] *GSN*, April 13, 1972 (historical account); also 1902 *Town Report*.

[42] *GSN*, October 26, 1901.

[43] *GSN*, April 24, 1909: Lamprey was to change the island's name to Samoset and divide it into 57 shore lots plus a forest reservation in the center.

[44] It is believed that the seven or eight residences built on Wolfeboro Neck earlier were either moved into the main part of town or destroyed by 1901.

[45] Wolfeboroite is the traditional name for a local resident; the term Wolfeboroean has been used occasionally in the late twentieth century.

[46] All were removed when the automobile eventually replaced the horse. Two of these old stone fountains have been preserved as historical artifacts. One is at the Libby Museum, and the other is in Clark Park. In the *GSN*, November 21, 1947, Mabel Fullerton Hatch remarked that the Goose Corner trough had been erected by Dr. Henry F. Libby years earlier and had recently disappeared. However, it was subsequently found in a nearby ditch, and in 1968 the town removed it to a new location in a grove of trees near the Libby Museum (cf. 1968 *Town Report* and *GSN*, July 18, 1968). Germs were not greatly feared at the turn of the century, and it was common practice to re-use drinking glasses in public places simply by refilling them for the next patron. Dishes and tableware in restaurants would be quickly rinsed in a container of sometimes not-too-clean water.

[47] Alta B. Meader, "Peripatetic Wolfeboro." Meader's comments are reproduced under the Cate Block entry in "Wolfeboro Place Names and Origins" in Volume II.

[48] Brochure published in 1902 from 1901 data, titled *Wolfeboro. What? When? Why?*

[49] Note: Actually, the larger one was called the Big Shop and the smaller one the Little Shop (or Clark Shop).

[50] The Village Precinct, also called the Village Fire Precinct or simply the Precinct, was a separate corporate entity serving the downtown (mainly) area that had its own funding and taxes for such functions as fire fighting and the generating of electricity.

[51] Note: It is not certain whether the "home flock" referred to Wolfeboro investors who were being "fleeced"!

[52] Made in Manchester, the 7-20-4 was the most widely advertised cigar in the state.

[53] Recollection of Dr. Scott in *GSN*, November 27, 1931.

[54] Veterinary practice noted by Barbara and Edward Zulauf, communication, September 1994. It was not uncommon for medical doctors to care for animals as well as humans.

[55] *GSN*, September 22, 1939. Biographical sketch of Dr. Clow, who credited Cotton with being there.

[56] Quoted from history in *GSN*, August 28, 1931; first names and occupations added by the present writer. Kent may have been Clarence E. Kent, local music teacher; not verified.

[57] Sources include: *GSN*, January 19, 1907 (area physicians meet at Getchell's); April 27, 1907 (trustees elected); January 14, 1928 (details of the January 9 meeting at Getchell's untold in the January 19, 1907 article).

[58] *GSN*, April 26, 1935: "Before the building was converted into a hospital it was the home of Mr. and Mrs. Edwin L. Furber. It was bought by Mrs. Furber and first husband, Rev. Theodore Jerome when he came here to assume the pastorate of the First Congregational Church, and named Fairview Sunnyside. Mr. Jerome was a great lover of the mountain and lake scenery of the country. He moved into his new home on top of King Hill.... All too brief was his enjoyment of it, however, for in about a year he and his oldest three children were drowned in Lake Winnipesaukee."

[59] Helen Keller (1880-1968) became world-famous as an author and lecturer. At the age of 19 months she lost her sight, speech, and hearing during an illness. Eventually, she consulted Alexander Graham Bell, who helped arrange a relationship between Keller and Anne Sullivan, who remained to work with her for 50 years. A syndicated serial by Keller, "My Religion," appeared in the *GSN* in early 1929.

## NOTES FOR CHAPTER 4:

[1] *GSN*, February 3, 1912 (Horne party); July 29, 1911 (DeRue); August 12, 1911 (Wyanoke); September 10, 1911 (Guy Bros.); February 16, 1912 (*Bridgit*); August 17, 1912 (publicity for Howe's), November 1, 1913 (12th NH Regiment); March 28, 1914 (4th Annual Concert); May 16, 1914 (Dixie's Comedians).

[2] *GSN*, July 18, 1914.

[3] The organ is believed to have been built by E. & G.G. Hook, Boston, Opus 154, 1853, for the Christian Baptist Church on Tyler Street in Boston. It had two manuals and pedal, and 20 registers which operated about 13 ranks of pipes. The instrument was junked c.1960. (Cf. Alan M. Laufman, Organ Historical Society; letter, November 1993.)

[4] *GSN*, June 9, 1917.

[5] *GSN*, November 1, 1913; January 24, 1914;

[6] A counterpart of sorts occurred in 1992 at a private party to which celebrants came in used clothing purchased that day at the Huggins Hospital Street Fair, no item of which was to have cost more than $1.

[7] Chautauqua information from *GSN*, April 22, 1916 (organizing); various July issues including July 29 (details of what happened); August 4, 1917 (1917 program); various June and July 1918 issues (1918 program).

[8] Most of the information concerning the sesquicentennial observance is paraphrased or quoted from *The Granite Monthly*, October 1920, "An Historic Event: Wolfeboro Celebrates Its 150th Anniversary."

[9] From this time forward, motion pictures were mentioned or advertised in nearly every issue of the *GSN*.

[10] By this time, film making had moved from Main Street to Wall Street, many small film-making operations had faded from the scene, and large corporations such as Paramount controlled much of the activity.

[11] *GSN*, October 7, 14, 1916.

[12] *GSN*, January 20, 1917.

[13] For the history of local Scouting see "Wolfeboro Civic Organizations, Groups, and Clubs" in Volume II.

[14] The Association was formed in March 1913. Baseball account in *GSN*, May 17, 1913.

[15] *GSN*, August 13, 1915.

[16] *GSN*, October 7, 1911.

[17] *GSN*, November 20, 1920 (team formation); November 27, 1920 (postponement); December 4, 1920 (first game); December 11, 1920 (Ossipee game); December 25, 1920 (Pittsfield game).

[18] *GSN*, September 26, 1914 (Lucas crew); July 10, 1915 (Kingswood Club links open); July 17, 1915 (tournament). Most other information is from *Kingswood Golf Club 75th Anniversary*, 1990, edited by Henry S. Maxfield, a booklet that also lists cup and tournament winners, club officials, etc.

[19] Years later Jennie Sinclair was a prime benefactor to Huggins Hospital.

[20] Probably related to George W. Armstrong (born 1836 in Boston), whose wife owned the 65-foot *Gilnockie*, berthed in Centre Harbor, the most palatial private craft on Lake Winnipesaukee. No print of this film is known to survive today.

[21] *GSN*, July 4, 1942, reprinted the 1912 automobile registration list from January 1 through June 20, 1912, listing 5,000 cars registered in the state, car owners and the brands they drove—a source for anyone wanting information beyond what is given here.

[22] Horne would buy a car wholesale, bring it to Wolfeboro, sell it, and then buy another.

[23] He bought another Pierce-Arrow in 1916.

[24] Civil War veterans were becoming fewer in number. The final national encampment of the Grand Army of the Republic was held in Indianapolis in the summer of 1949; six very old men attended (*GSN*, September 9, 1949).

[25] *Everybody* was getting into the automobile act. Libby was a laundryman, while Clow was a leading physician.

[26] *GSN*, April 5, 1913. Wolfeboro-Melvin Village report from *GSN*, April 19, 1913.

[27] *GSN*, June 20, 1914.

[28] *GSN*, October 10, 1914.

[29] Reported in the *GSN*, February 6, 1915.

[30] Dumping snow into the lake continued into the 1980s, when some ecologically (but not scientifically) minded government authority stated that this could no longer be done. Henceforth, snow had to be dumped away from the lake, so that road salt would somehow disappear without going into the water, never mind that other dumping places eventually drained into the lake anyway! However, there was the benefit that trash scraped with the snow from the roads no longer was put into Winnipesaukee.

[31] Ironically, in 1991 it was directed that a spill of low-grade heating oil in a storage facility on Lehner Street be cleaned up at a cost over $250,000. Apparently, ecologists were not aware that countless millions of gallons of oil were dumped on roads all over America for many years during the early twentieth century, with few if any apparent ill effects. Oil is an organic substance which degrades naturally over a period of time. (See details in Chapter 12.)

[32] A related monopolistic situation occurred decades later in the 1990s. By that time the Public Service Company of New Hampshire (PSNH), an electric utility, had a monopoly on electric service for much of the state and raised prices to what many felt were unconscionable levels. Gov. Stephen Merrill stated in June 1995 that he believed that competition in electric power was desirable, and comments were made to the effect that other suppliers might be allowed to compete with PSNH.

[33] *GSN* December 5, 1914; January 2, 1915; among other issues.

[34] *GSN*, August 16, 1919.

[35] *GSN*, October 7, 1911.

[36] Accounts of the economy in the *GSN*, January 20, February 17, June 1, 1912.

[37] *GSN*, June 22, 1912.

[38] GSN May 24 (Clow buildings) and April 19 (cigar factory), 1913. Note: In 1898, George W. Berry, a principal in the O.P. Berry Co., Wolfeboro Falls, manufactured cigars, apparently for just a short time.

[39] Accounts were printed in the *GSN* April 1, April 29, May 27, May 6 (poem), and September 2, 1911, among other issues.

[40] *GSN*, July 18, August 22, 1914.

[41] *GSN*, August 7, 1915.

[42] *GSN*, January 8, January 22, January 28, 1916. William J. Britton was president of the Wolfeboro Improvement Association, J. Clifton Avery was vice president, and Abel Haley was clerk.

[43] *GSN*, November 17, December 8, 1917; February 2, April 6, 1918.

[44] Hart later served in many civic capacities (including as first president of the Chamber of Commerce) and was a leading automobile dealer. In a letter to the author, September 1994, Barbara and Edward Zulauf noted, "He was labeled by some as impractical; he had visions for the town that were ahead of his time."

[45] *GSN*, September 22, 1917.

[46] *GSN*, December 29, 1917; April 27, 1918; December 21, 1918.

[47] *GSN*, June 19, 1920 editorial.

[48] *GSN*, July 31, 1920.

[49] September 18, 1920.

[50] *GSN*, January 7, February 4, 1911.

[51] New Hampshire's first public radio broadcasting license was acquired by WEAQ in Berlin in 1922, but, apparently, the station never functioned. The first commercial station to operate was Laconia, WKAV in 1922; it remained on the air for a decade, then went bankrupt.

[52] *GSN*, January 28, 1911 (expanded service); May 6, 1911 (new toll rates); August 19, 1911 (North Wolfeboro); May 30, 1914 (improved service); July 11, 1914 (toll rates listed; most of the toll rates were more then than they would be in the 1990s); June 26, 1915 (services).

[53] Note: Very few Wolfeboro homes actually had servants.

[54] Obituary in *GSN*, October 14, 1911.

[55] In the 1990s this fund is administered by attorney Philip Ganem. The principal has multiplied many times over.

[56] QDB note: A situation apparently considered by Doe to be advantageous.

[57] QDB note: This comment must have come as a surprise to many readers.

[58] *GSN*, June 3, 1911, "A company of Gypsies were seen in town Wednesday"; April 24, 1915: Numerous tramps in town.

[59] *GSN*, May 22, 1920, printed his obituary and biography. While his villa, Ferncliffe, was the first on Sewall Street, seasonal waterfront residences had been built elsewhere in the town earlier, including on Lake Wentworth.

[60] Now known as Bearce Hall on the campus of Brewster Academy, at the end of Green Street.

[61] Cf. *GSN*, April 5, 1916; May 13, 1916; May 20, 1916; June 10, 1916; December 2, 1916; etc.

[62] *GSN*, November 18, 1911.

[63] *World Almanac*, 1993, p. 521.

[64] *GSN*, November 23, 1918. This particular remedy was still being sold in the 1940s.

[65] *GSN* citations: March 25, 1911 (cold conditions); July 8, 1911 (high temperatures); July 15, 1911 (105°); August 30, 1913 (dry conditions); September 15, 1913 (heavy rain); October 25, 1913 (storm); June 23, 1917 (storm); August 4, 1917 (hot weather); January 12, 1918 (Auderer); February 28, 1920 (heavy snowfall); March 13 1920 ( snowfall).

[66] Such inconsistencies as recalling storm dates of 1873 1876, and 1893 while overlooking 1888 were common in the newspaper. The present writer has found printed editorial reminiscences and recollections to be very inaccurate in many instances, especially in reference to specific dates; many such errors plus new ones found their way into Benjamin F. Parker's *History of Wolfeborough*.

[67] *GSN* citations: February 4, 1911 (report of freak winds); December 7, 1912 (high winds of December 1); October 2, 1915 (windstorm).

[68] *GSN* citations: February 3, 1912 (moon rings); August 5, 1916 (yellow sky); March 27, 1920, (aurora).

[69] Unless noted otherwise, the date given is the date the fire occurred; these fires typically were reported in the next issue of the *GSN* (the following Saturday). In other instances, the *GSN* report date is given (and indicated); in these instances, the date of the fire was not stated in the paper.

[70] *GSN* report, September 20, 1919.

[71] Date of *GSN* article; the fire was earlier.

[72] *GSN*, April 27, November 30, 1912.

[73] Godfrey died in MA on February 11, 1925.

[74] *GSN*, May 3, 1913 (Heath); December 15, 1913 (Malloy); October 31, 1914 (Turtle Island); November 11, 1914 (Post Office); September 23, 1915 (Drew); September 23, 1915 (Sylvain); September 30, 1915 (Watson).

[75] *GSN*, November 15, 1913.

[76] *GSN*, June 26, 1920.

[77] Mrs. Ames was co-author (with John Livingstone Wright) of *Mr. Engle's U.S.A., as Seen in A Buggy Ride from Illinois to Boston*. Copies were on sale at the *GSN* office, October 18, 1898, for $1.25.

[78] In fact, the caribou was acquired later; cf. *GSN*, November 24, 1896: "Dr. H.F. Libby had a handsome large caribou arrive for his museum last week. This is a noble specimen and was shot by Dr. Libby last winter in the Maine woods. The first specimen set up ever brought into this section."

[79] *GSN*, September 7, 1912.

[80] *GSN*, November 10, 1919 (admission figures including 1912); October 12, 1912 (arboretum begun).

[81] *GSN*, March 31, 1917.

[82] *GSN*, May 29, 1920.

[83] Statement of Albert W. Noone, seeker of the nomination for senator, as quoted in *GSN*, September 4, 1920.

[84] *GSN*, December 5, 1914. "Germans Claim England to be Responsible."

[85] *GSN*, March 13, 1915.

[86] *GSN*, November 27, 1915.

[87] *GSN*, January 8, 1916.

[88] *GSN*, May 6, 1916 (alarmists active).

[89] *GSN*, July 8, 1916 (call for men); July 15, 1916 (4 men passed; relief help for Europe); December 16, 1917 (Summerbell sermon announced); February 22, 1917 (Summerbell letter to public officials); April 7, 1917 (Wolfeboro flags flying); April 21, 1917 (food production, conservation, etc.); April 22, 1917 (Red Cross); May 5, 1917 (German enslavement); May 12 (planting gardens, etc.); May 19, 1917 (First Liberty Loan); June 2, 1917 (registration for draft); August 25, 1917 (all about Charlotte, NC.).

[90] *GSN*, October 13, 1917; November 17, 1917; October 23, 1917.

[91] *GSN*, November 10, 1917.

[92] Published in the *GSN*, February 9, 1918.

[93] Harriman was born in Wolfeboro Falls on August 16, 1896. He was buried in the American Battle Area Cemetery in Bouresches, Ainse, France.

[94] *GSN*, January 26, 1918.

[95] *GSN*, April 13, 1918.

[96] Valley was killed in action on September 18, 1918, and buried overseas; his remains were later shipped to the U.S. Valley was from Sanford, ME, and had relatives in Wolfeboro.

[97] Pearson is listed on the monument as having been killed in the conflict; however, his name was not mentioned in this context in the appreciation ceremonies of August 22, 1919.

## NOTES FOR CHAPTER 5:

[1] In a reminiscence printed on January 6, 1925, Prindle said he could not remember when he was hired.

[2] *GSN*, January 1, 1921 and January 15, 1921 (news about the move to Railroad Avenue); October 15, 1921 (telephone).

[3] *GSN*, May 21, 1927.

[4] The staff at that time consisted of A.H. Beardsley, associate editor and publisher; and Miss Edna B. Castle (a.k.a. Edna Celeste), bookkeeper. During the year Earl Holden was added as stenographer. A Boston office in charge of W.A. French was maintained at 367 Boylston Street. Edna Celeste died on January 10, 1943. She had come to Wolfeboro in 1921 for the *Photo-Era Magazine* and later worked for the Thibodeau Construction Co. She was active in local social and church circles and never married.

[5] *GSN*, July 30, 1921 (car trip article described); January 22, 1921 (move to town noted), May 8, 1926 (office move).

[6] The Ouija name was derived by combining the French and German words for "yes." Mah jongg fever swept the country in 1923.

[7] *GSN*, June 17, 1922 (DAR chapter suggested), November 18, 1922 (chapter formed).

[8] *GSN*, March 28, 1925.

[9] *GSN*, March 3, 1929.

[10] Alan Douglas, *Radio Manufacturers of the 1920s*, Vol. 1, p. xxi, reprinted from *Radio Recording*, March 1928.

[11] Letter to the author, January 12, 1994. The Dempsey fight was on July 2, 1921. Allen Horne Albee later established the Allen "A" Resort on Route 28 (Center Street).

[12] A different organization from today's Lakes Region Association.

[13] Advertisement in *GSN*, July 22, 1922.

[14] *GSN*, June 28, 1926.

[15] Reviews are generally from the *GSN* on the Saturday after the event.

[16] Possibly, a Una-Fon system of electric tubular bells made in Chicago by the J.C. Deagan, Co., played from a keyboard and powered by a storage battery.

[17] The typical minstrel show of the era featured white (Caucasian) players in blackface.

[18] Roger Murray and his sister, who became Grace Murray Hopper, were among the most accomplished residents of Wolfeboro. Roger had an illustrious career in banking and finance, and in his retirement, was important in the oversight of the Governor Wentworth Regional School District and in 1995 was elected as a selectman. His local benefactions were numerous. Commodore Grace Murray Hopper, U.S.N., who earned her Ph.D. at Yale, invented COBOL (Commercial and Business-Oriented Language) for computers, which was adopted as the U.S. standard in 1968. Her accomplishments were legion and in part were recognized by 10 honorary degrees she received. A footnote in her biography is her invention of the computer term "bug." In 1945 when she was working at Harvard, a computer stopped, and upon inspection it was found that a moth had become stuck in a relay; the moth was removed by tweezers; later, if asked if she was accomplishing anything on the computer, she was fond of saying she was "debugging" it.

[19] Date of report in *GSN*.

[20] *GSN*, September 9 and November 4, 1922 (fish stocking); September 26, 1925 (Fish Rearing Station); April 13, 1929 (suckers); June 29, 1929 (bass in Wentworth).

[21] *GSN*, September 1, 8, 1928.

[22] *GSN*, July 7, 1928, and other accounts. Speed estimates varied from 70 to 80 miles per hour. In some mentions it was spelled as *Yeyee II*.

[23] *GSN*, February 2, 1929.

[24] Barbara and Edward Zulauf remember this building as being "cold, damp, derelict" (note, September 1994).

[25] *GSN*, December 29, 1928 (Clark remodeling); January 26, 1928 (account of January 22 game).

[26] *GSN*, August 13, 1921 (difficulty); September 19, 1925 (expands course).

[27] *GSN*, June 21, 1921.

[28] *GSN*, January 12, 1923 (250% increase); June 2, 1923 (Moore-Melrose); July 28, 1923, and other issues (guideboards).

[29] *GSN* citations include October 22 and December 12, 1925; February 13 and 26, and March 13, 1926.

[30] *GSN*, June 13, 1930.

[31] *GSN*, December 3, 1927 (Model A debut); December 10, 1927 (names of buyers; not quoted here); February 4, 1928 (number of buyers).

[32] *GSN*, March 10, 1928 (accident, etc.: March 24, 1928 (postcards).

[33] *GSN*, July 28, 1924 (two trains discontinued); August 2 and 9, 1924 (circus); December 6, 1924 (Wolfeboro Falls closing proposed).

[34] A retrospective in *GSN*, April 29, 1938, noted that in 1925 during August and through September 8, Fogg made 33 trips and was paid at the rate of $33 for each trip.

[35] Letter to the author, January 12, 1994.

[36] *GSN*, June 16, 1928 (Brewster field); September 1, 1928 (Hart & Hart).

[37] 1931 Annual Report covering fiscal year 1930. Doe was paid $224.69, and Clow received $251.01. Interest continued, and in 1933, $1,195.50 was paid for work on the town wharves and hydroplane landing.

[38] *GSN*, May 18, 1929.

[39] *GSN*, August 4, 1923.

[40] *GSN*, July 18, 1925.

[41] On September 25, 1925, it was announced that a real estate syndicate had an option on the Everett Banfield estate at Clark's Point and planned to erect a modern hotel with a commanding view of Lake Winnipesaukee.

[42] *GSN*, July 17, 1926 (trains bring visitors); September 17, 1926 (record breaker).

[43] *GSN*, July 22, 1922; Coolidge was born in Plymouth, VT, but spent much of his life in Northampton, MA.

[44] *GSN*, September 15, 1923.

[45] *GSN*, February 10, 1923.

[46] *GSN*, March 10, 1923.

[47] *GSN*, September 6, 1929. Goldthwait biographical information from *GSN*, January 1948: Born March 22, 1880. Received AB degree from Harvard in 1902 and doctorate in 1906. Taught at Harvard and Radcliffe and Northwestern before coming to Dartmouth in 1908. Internationally known geologist and scientist. Discoverer of the tilted shorelines of ice age lakes in the Great Lakes region. "His research indicated the manner in which glacial ice depressed the land, and how later, with the recession of the ice cap, the land had risen." Died December 31, 1947.

[48] Numerous *GSN* accounts include June 30, 1923 (feature story), April 18, 1925 (expansion plans); November 21, 1925 (feature article).

[49] *GSN*, June 25, 1921, there called the Moxie advertising car. The Horsemobile consisted of a model of a horse mounted on top of an automobile chassis.

[50] *GSN*, May 19, 1923 (labor scarce); June 16, 1923 (housing shortage); July 21, 1923 (sales vehicles).

[51] *GSN*, September 1, 1923.

[52] *GSN*,April 2, 1927; April 30, 1927.

[53] *GSN*, November 21, 1921 (many orders for Fox).

[54] *GSN*, July 21, 1923.

[55] *GSN*, April 15, April 22, April 29, and May 13, 1922.

[56] Note: The editor had forgotten that a similar incident had occurred at the Bell Brothers plant and had been reported in the issue of August 11, 1923.

[57] *GSN*, August 19, 1922 (description of products); August 26, 1922 (Profile blankets); September 13, 1924 (new line); October 4, 1924 (open again); April 11, 1925 (fire report); December 5, 1925 (sales room still open).

[58] *GSN*, August 12, 1922 (civics exam); December 3, 1927 (Hatch); January 14, 1928 (Glines). Note: In 1897, Glines purchased George F. Horn's summer camp on Wolfeboro Neck (*GSN*, June 29, 1897).

[59] Many items about this appeared in the press; *e.g.*, January 5, 1929 (problem of service); April 20, 1929 (new rates); April 27, 1929 (Lake Wentworth cottages being wired in anticipation of service); June 8 and June 15, 1929 (refrigerator installations); May 25, 1929 (new service progress report); March 28, 1930 (1929 customer count).

[60] June 14, 1924 (restroom); April 25, 1925 (wharf title); February 18, 1928, February 16 and March 11, 1929 (town manager).

[61] *GSN*, June 5, 9, and 23, and July 7, 1922 ("well goes dry").

[62] Reminiscent of the sentiment in the popular 1970s song, *Big Yellow Taxi*, which suggested that with municipal "improvements" such as parking lots one might have to go to a "tree museum" to "see 'em."

[63] *GSN*, July 30, August 6, 1924.

[64] *GSN*, November 20, 1926.

[65] Recollection of A.R. Friedman, conversation with the author, September 30, 1993. Friedman supervised many of Carpenter's business interests in Boston and was a frequent visitor to Wolfeboro. Similar recollection from Barbara and Edward Zulauf, note, September 1994.

[66] Example: *GSN*, January 5, 1924: Project for new Keith Theatre in Boston.

[67] Spelled Livonia in some accounts.

[68] Klinck was born in Jersey City, NJ. Information from *Town Reports* (there misspelled as Clink).

[69] *GSN*, March 9, 1927 (Board intervenes); March 19, 1927, April 23, 1927; September 3, 1927; October 8, 1927; November 12, 1927 (Foss worsens); November 19, 1927 (lengthy testimonial from a patient, George R. Field; not quoted here); November 19, 1927 (Foss dead).

[70] *GSN*, July 30, 1921 (Crabb gift); September 23, 1922 (new building needed); September 30, 1922 (fund-raising goal); November 8 and 15, 1924 (costs; dedication); April 26, 1935 (demolition).

[71] *GSN*, August 28, 1931 (historical account of transfusion).

[72] *GSN*, September 1, 1923.

[73] *GSN*, July 21, 1928 (Avery sale); December 8, 1928 (Jungalow). The Jungalow Camps property was later bought by Laura I. Mattoon and incorporated into Camp Kehonka.

[74] His son Archie, Jr., carried on the family sports tradition. On December 20, 1947, Beatrice became the bride of Charles Lewis French, Jr.

[75] Such comparisons of storms were very casual in the local paper and often contradictory. For example, in a description of the storm of March 6, 1920, Editor Prindle said this storm was worse than that of 1873; yet, the account of the January 1923 storm did not mention the storm of March 1920.

[76] *GSN*, September 24, 1921 (high winds); January 13 and 20, 1923 (snow); July 11, 1925 (flash downpour); August 15, 1925 (August downpour).

[77] *GSN*, July 9, 1927 (Foster); May 5, 1928 (South Main Street); September 13, 1929 (Wolfeboro Neck). Years later the Hopewell place was fancifully referred to as the "Chiang Kai-Shek estate" and developed as part of Embassy Estates.

[78] The epicenter was near LaMalbaie, Quebec, and there was magnitude 6.6 on the Richter Scale (*Environmental Sheet*, 1993).

[79] *GSN*, March 7, 1925; October 10, 1925.

[80] *GSN*, November 21, 1925 (meteor); April 13, 1926 (aurora borealis); September 19, 1930 (rainbow).

[81] 1926 *Town Report* (fiscal year).

[82] Wolfeboro Police Chief Stanley E. Stevens, comment to author, June 6, 1995, noted that Mitchell is not listing in Police Department records as ever having been chief.

[83] *GSN*, May 20, 1921; June 25, 1921; September 24, 1921 (chickens).

[84] *GSN*, ( July 28, 1923 (mail theft); *Concord Monitor*, June 7, 1924 (account of Welcome chase).

[85] *GSN*, October 17 and November 1, 1924 (Rogers); January 10, 1925; June 24, 1924 (four stores); August 1, 1930 (two youths).

[86] *GSN*, July 19, 1924 (arrest); September 13, 1924 (remain in jail).

[87] Letter, October 27, 1993. Additional information from Nute's obituary, *GSN*, March 31, 1950: Born May 25, 1889 in N. Wolfeboro. After settling his legal difficulties in Carroll County, Nute moved to ME, where he was involved in various legal actions. He died in the County Home in Ossipee, March 26, 1950.

[88] *GSN*, February 20, 1921 (Clows at inauguration); September 1, 1923 (have confidence); November 8, 1924 (good work); November 1, 1924 (Hatch runs).

[89] *GSN*, January 23, 1959. Recollection of an old-timer.

[90] *GSN*, January 24, 1925, letter signed E.E.C.

[91] *GSN*, October 3, 1925.

[92] Letter, October 27, 1993.

[93] *GSN*, October 22, 1921 (WCTU); October 22, 1921 (reckless driving); (cannot boast); April 30, 1925 (cider rules); November 21, 1925 (WCTU).

## NOTES FOR CHAPTER 6

[1] *GSN*, August 31, 1931.

[2] The craze peaked in February and March 1933. For an excellent discussion of the fad, see "Leisure in the Great Depression: The Many Pieces of the Jigsaw Puzzle Story," Anne D. Williams, essay in *The American Play Ethic, The Ephemera Journal*, Vol. 6, 1993.

[3] *GSN*, April 19, 1935 (subscribers); October 15, 1936 (Headley biography); December 17, 1937 (Linotype); May 20, 1938 (Linotype operator could set about eight columns per day. Setting began on Fridays, Mondays and Tuesdays when they were often short of news and might set items that would not otherwise be run. On Wednesdays and Thursdays the rush came for publication on Friday. This often necessitated holding important last minute news over to the next week so it could be typeset properly.). The subscription rate of $1.50 per year was raised to $2 on January 1, 1938. January 6, 1939 (First issue by Carpenter; announcement of new policies, more photos, etc.).

[4] *GSN*, January 29, 1937. Lavallee and the mailboat *Marshal Foch* were real; the other items are pure fiction. Epilogue (or, how soon we forget!): On January 29, 1976, *GSN* columnist Helen Fetzer commented: "One of the most intriguing newspaper clippings I have ever read was handed to me by Mrs. Herbert Tinker, Sunday after church, but she cannot find out in what copy of the *Granite State News* this was printed! The clipping has yellowed with age, and I almost fear to return it to her by mail so I guess I'd better take it to her." This was the article that told about the ship *Fearless*, and other "history." Rising to the challenge, historian Robert F.W. Meader, who, obviously, was not familiar with the clipping either, wrote to the *GSN*, February 12, 1976, stating that it was probably published as a joke on some long-ago April Fool's Day.

[5] *GSN*, January 8, 1932 (representatives in town); January 15, 1932 (Estabrook display and advertising); May 30 1932 (scheme revealed).

[6] *GSN*, October 23, 1937 (Porter); December 4, 1931 (road work); June 15, 1937 (First National); March 11, 1932 (American Legion; Sturgis would be appointed police chief the next month); June 10, 1932 (subsistence gardens); September 2 and 16, 1932 (state loan).

[7] Information concerning RFC and refinancing from Stephen E. Clow, letter to the author, January 12, 1994; Clow was an employee of the bank in the 1930s.

[8] *GSN*, December 22, 1933 (1932 labor statistics); February 3, 1933 (go fishing); March 10, 1933 (scrip); March 24, 1933 (Trickey).

[9] *GSN*, January 12, 1934 (barter).

[10] *GSN*, May 15, 1936 (rags and junk); February 4, 1938 (1937 report); February 25, 1938 (drugs); March 18, 1938 (Town Gardens); July 8, 1938 (refrigerators); December 30, 1938 (Christmas report).

[11] *GSN*, February 10, 1933 (name change recommended); March 10, 1933 (name change reported).

[12] A related commentary concerning this deception will be found in the reminisces of Harold F. Brown in Volume III. Brown noted that shoe trade publications carried warnings of con artists who went from place to place victimizing gullible towns.

[13] *GSN*, May 19, 1933 (impatience with long succession); April 10, 1931 (Holland); December 1, 1931 (Bell Shop closing threatened); March 3, 1933 (3 factories shift work to here); May 5, 1933 (Precinct meeting report); June 1, 1934 (Wolfeboro Shoe Co. prospers); April 8, 1935 (sheet factory); April 15 and 29, 1938 (factory sold); January 12, 1940 (open meeting); October 10, 1940 (Lyons-Patch plans).

[14] *GSN*, May 27, 1938. This organization was different from the Wolfeboro Woman's Club (organized 1894).

[15] *GSN*, January 16, 1931 (schedule cut); May 9, 1931 (RCA).

[16] Minutes of 1935 town meeting; *GSN*, March 6, 1936 and March 5, 1937 (Sanborn pleas); numerous other citations could be mentioned.

[17] *GSN*, July 17, 1935; announcement by Ansel Sanborn.

[18] Interview with the author, February 12, 1993.

[19] *GSN*, July 10, 1931.

[20] *GSN*, January 29, 1932 (report of organization of group); February 2, 1932 (officers elected); August 5, 1932 (concerts described; three towns represented). The Goodwin Block is the one-story, multiple-business block still standing to the right of the Avery Building. Over the years there have been several different buildings called the Goodwin Block.

[21] *GSN*, October 7 and 14, 1932.

[22] *GSN*, May 3 and 17, 1935.

[23] *GSN*, September 6, 1935.

[24] January 17, 1936 is date of report in *GSN*.

[25] The game of "beano" was very popular; after *bingo* was outlawed, innovative people simply came up with the word BEANO; otherwise, it was the same game. *38th Annual Old Home Week August 15-22, 1936 in New Hampshire*, a report of the State Old Home Week Association, tells of festivities in Wolfeboro during that time. The local event was held a week ahead of most other communities' celebrations.

[26] *GSN*, Friday, May 21, 1937; "Herbert 'Gebo' Bean always spelled his last name as Beane," noted Richard Marden, letter, November 10, 1994.

[27] *GSN*, October 16, 1936 (Franconia speaker); February 7, 1936 (formation; membership; Alton Carnival); October 11, 1940 (name change); November 19 and December 15, 1939 (new ski slope); December 27, 1940 (ski lodge dedication). In the 1940s "Wolfeboro" was dropped from the club's name.

[28] Over the years the designation Municipal Skating Rink was applied to different locations depending upon which particular site was maintained by the town in a given year.

[29] Mr. and Mrs. Wendell Carr were among the most active participants in the Wolfeboro Abenaki Outing Club and other winter activities. Their daughter, Judy Carr (married name: Judy Breuninger), in grade school at the time, later became a skating champion.

[30] *GSN*, January 10, 1893; also see January 3, 1893.

[31] *GSN*, January 27, 1939. Dusty's real name was Percy B. Rhodes. Born in Lawrence, MA, July 20, 1883, he moved to Wolfeboro c. 1931 and lived here until his death on September 4, 1964.

[32] Foster was a local fuel dealer and poultry raiser. The January 12, 1940 issue of *GSN* noted that he had been appointed "the summertime custodian of all fishing holes." The same issue observed that the Last Chance Saloon was managed by Joseph I. Melanson, and that Wendell Carr was all set to publish the *Fisherville News* from an office located on Shad Row.

[33] *GSN*, April 5, 1940 (election details). *The Laker*, February 1989, printed an article, "They Still Yarn About 'Old Perk'," by Barbara Hobbie, which described Perkins. Biographical data concerning Perkins, Allbee, Melanson, Foster, and certain other Fisherville personalities who owned local businesses will be found in Volume III.

[34] For example, in the summer of 1934, the federal government introduced 40,000 bass fry into Lake Wentworth followed by 32,000 the following summer (*GSN*, August 9, 1935).

[35] *GSN*, January 9, 1931 (Wolverines; details on Wolfeboro Arena).

[36] Recollection of Ethel (Mrs. George) Black in *Kingswood Golf Club 75th Anniversary*, p. 4.

[37] *GSN*, August 5, 1932 (cars).

[38] *Town Report*, 1938, for fiscal year 1937.

[39] *GSN*, November 20, 1931; 1941 *Town Report* for 1940 year (horses).

[40] *GSN*, January 27, 1939 (map of filled-in area; estimate of fill; three existing town docks were filled over).

[41] From June 1907 to 1914.

[42] *GSN*, May 22, 1931 (B&M bus service); September 20, 1935 (service discontinuation notice); October 4, 1935 and other issues (citizens protest, hearing held November 6, 1935 in town, etc.); May 1, 1936 (Wolfeboro Falls station); May 8, 1936 (freight trains to include a passenger car); May 15, 1935 (railcar service described); September 18, 1936 (sedan service); November 6, 1936 (petition to restore buses; Robert Thurrell, committee head); April 23, 1937 (B&M Modern Transportation; separately, notice of intent to end bus service to town); December 7, 1937 (buses to be discontinued January 4, 1938); December 17, 1937 (Hatch column).

[43] This rigid airship, LZ-126 (known in America as ZR-3, a.k.a. ZR-111), was built by the Luftschiffbau Zeppelin Company. It departed Friederichshafen, Germany, on October 12 under the command of Dr. Hugo Eckener and was delivered to the United States Navy on October 15, 1924. The craft was 658 feet in length, 92 feet in diameter, had a capacity of 2,472,000 cubic feet of hydrogen (or, in the U.S., helium, which has about 92.6% of the lifting capacity of hydrogen), was equipped with five Maybach 440-hp. engines, and could cruise at 79 miles per hour. On November 25, 1924, Mrs. Calvin Coolidge christened her the *Los Angeles*. The zeppelin was in active service, accumulating 4,320 flying hours, until decommissioning on June 30, 1932, after which she flew only occasionally through 1938. In 1940, she was dismantled.

[44] *GSN*, May 29, 1931 (overflight); October 9, 1931 (balloon); April 22, 1932 (*Los Angeles*); May 20, 1938 (Sikorsky).

[45] *GSN*, January 26, 1934 (airport proposed); February 9, 1934 (near Sandy Beach); February 16, 1934 (town meeting report); March 23, 1934 (proposal abandoned); December 11, 1936 (new WPA proposal not acted upon); February 13, 1940 (Merwin Horn); March 8, 1940 (Hopewell letter); March 15, 1940 (Ralph Horn's offer); March 29, 1940 (Wilkins letter); November 15 and 22, 1940 (Merwin Horn builds); November 29, 1940 (State Commission recommends Pleasant Valley site); December 13, 1940 (state investigates matter further, recommends Wolfeboro Neck site).

[46] Information from Madelyn Albee and the *GSN*. A detailed history of the Allen "A" Resort is given in Volume III.

[47] *GSN*, July 3, 1931 (Birchmont); June 24, 1932 (above normal season); May 22, 1931 (*National Geographic*); September 28, 1934 (quite prosperous season); August 30, 1935 (Point Breeze sets record); September 11, 1936 (not even a cot); September 18, 1936 (Information Booth); August 20, 1937 (another Point Breeze record); October 13, 1939 (round-up).

[48] Specific quotations (unless noted otherwise) for 1939 and 1940 are from yearly editions of *Where to – In the Lakes Region of New Hampshire*, a tourist guide with many advertisements.

[49] Letter to the author, April 2, 1993.

[50] *GSN*, March 24, 1939.

[51] *GSN*, March 8, 1935.

[52] *GSN*, March 24, 1939. William O. Douglas (1898-1980) was a justice of the United States Supreme Court from 1939 to 1975. His obituary in *GSN*, January 23, 1980, carried many reminiscences by local individuals.

[53] Reminiscence of Ethel (Mrs. George D.) Black to the author, February 19, 1992; also, mentions in *GSN*. In the 1940s the Fiedlers' young son Johann was also mentioned; later Fiedler citations include *GSN*, August 30, 1946. *GSN*, September 3, 1937: Announced that Mr. and Mrs. John U. Lemmon of Newton, MA, parents of the actor-to-be, purchased the Brooks Sargent property on Sewall Road through the office of Wentworth and Carpenter. *GSN*, March 3, 1939: "Mr. and Mrs. John U. Lemmon had three weeks' vacation at their home on Sewall Road and had as guests Mrs. Katherine Carver, of New York and Hollywood, former screen star—and several others." *GSN*, 1950, June 2: "A recent wedding of interest to a great many Wolfeboro people is that of John U. Lemmon III and Miss Cynthia Stone of Peoria, Illinois. Both young people are on radio and TV."

[54] *GSN*, July 19, 1935 (the cottage was owned by A.R. Crabb, of Newark, NJ). James Cash Penney began his career in Kemmerer, WY, 1902, with a general store. As he expanded, he called his outlets Golden Rule Stores. The 1939 Camp Wyanoke brochure listed Penney as a person to contact for references. Also, *GSN*, April 12, 1973 (historical account).

[55] *GSN*, December 27, 1935. Howard was later in *Gone With the Wind;* and, later, lost at sea in a flight from Europe.

[56] Reminiscence of Robert Hanson to the author.

[57] *GSN*, June 24, 1938. Born in Vienna in 1912, Rainer was a German actress brought to the U.S. by Metro-Goldwyn-Mayer in 1935. She won her first Oscar for *The Great Ziegfeld* (1936), followed by another for *The Good Earth* (1937).

[58] *GSN*, August 2, 1935 (boat registrations).

[59] *GSN*, December 29, 1939: Details of fire. Most successive issues through January 1940 carried additional information.

[60] Shea was a NY movie theatre operator through whom first-run films were often booked into Wolfeboro to be shown by Ansel N. Sanborn, with special showings for area camps. (Recollection of Stephen E. Clow, letter, January 12, 1994).

[61] *GSN*, August 26, 1932, reviewed the exhibit.

[62] *GSN*, August 14, 1931 (Clow, *et al.*, gifts); November 24 and December 22, 1933 (government interest); December 29, 1933 (Mayo gift); June 29, 1934 (28 at work); November 9, 1934 (excavations); February 21, 1936 (beach work completed); October 12, 1936 (foliage).

[63] *GSN*, July 3, 1931 (town planner needed; however, Dreier lived in Tuftonboro; what was to be done *there* was not stated); July 24, 1931 (zoning needed); November 6, 1931 (Nolen); August 5, 1931 (hearing planned); September 9, 1932 (fiasco); February 23, 1940 (new proposals).

[64] Nickname: "We Putter Around" (cf. Ted Brigden, note, January 6, 1994).

[65] *GSN*, January 8, 1932 (Back Bay mess); February 21, 1936 (start filling); in *1937*, WPA wages were about $5 per day; in *GSN*, April 16, 1937, Charles E. Stevens, of Point Breeze, noted that in New York City, WPA workers played ball in the streets, and that on another occasion he witnessed a crew of 20 men doing absolutely nothing, and one was asleep.

[66] One, a small cape, was moved to Pine Street. The other, two and one-half stories high, was demolished. (Cf. Harrison D. Moore.)

[67] *GSN*, February 3, 1933 (behind Peavey Block); May 10, 1935 (new bridge); December 22, 1933 (road signs); August 21, 1936 (Stop signs); December 24, 1937 and Jan 14, 1938 (Main Street excavations reveal old engineering methods; latter account by William J. Britton; the work was finished in the summer of 1938); July 21, 1939 (reptiles); July 15, 1938, etc. (entrance signs; a Wolfeboro Development Assn. project; Teague had designed wallpaper, vending machines, etc., and the Ford exhibit for the 1939 World's Fair). Teague died December 5, 1960. In 1929 he purchased the "Brick House" in Tuftonboro, later occupied by his daughter Cecily (a.k.a. Cecily Crowe, later Cecily Bentley), a nationally-known writer; January 2, 1959: Retrospective article about signs, "First" changed to "Oldest." From time to time over the years pranksters would alter the word "Oldest" to read "Coldest" or "Wildest."

[68] Italics not in original quotation. Apparently, the pun was unintentional.

[69] *GSN*, May 6, 1932 (Howard); May 13, 1932 (why Wolfeboro?); Oct 20, 1933 (not reasonable); October 27, 1933 (cost estimates); November 17, 1933 (self-liquidating); November 24, 1933 (more discussion, not quoted here); December 1, 1933 (meeting report); March 23, 1934 (suit); September 3, 1937 (yes vote; government help); October 20, 1939 (installation complete).

[70] *GSN*, March 15, 1935 (1935 meeting report); March 13, 1936 (1936 report). Sunday movies were legalized at the 1937 meeting.

[71] When an item was adjourned the selectmen had to call another meeting and go through the entire discussion and voting process again for that item. Many local citizens including Editor Frederick W. Prindle thought the typical adjourned meeting to be a waste of time.

[72] Local electrician and steamfitter; he did much wiring for the town Electric Department.

[73] Thurrell was manager of the Cotton Valley Farm poultry business, one of the most successful commercial enterprises in Wolfeboro. As did many successful people, he had his share of detractors.

[74] Local hardware dealer; a gentleman very interested in town history.

[75] *GSN*, July 27, 1934 (shortage); August 17, 1934 (Rust Pond water forbidden); April 26, 1935 (improvements).

[76] *GSN*, September 9, 1922 (Uncle Sam; report datelined Washington); September 6, 1935, told of offers of land made to the government for use as the site. The Sheridan House was offered for $10,000. The Ann Inn including extensive shore frontage was offered for $9,000. The Avery house on South Main Street (across from the present IGA in the 1990s) and the then-vacant lot to the right of it were offered for $10,000. The Hersey Block (née Pickering Block) was offered for $14,000. C.F. Pinkham offered his service station at the corner of South Main and Union Streets for $10,000. It seems that the government could have bought virtually the entire town if it had wished!

[77] *GSN*, January 21 and February 28, 1938 (murals; detailed biography of Winter, born in Estonia in 1893).

[78] *GSN*, June 7, 1935 (Daylight Savings Time a question); May 1, 1936 (test planned); May 8, 1936 (confusion); April 23, 1937 (Daylight Savings Time a certainty).

[79] *GSN*, November 23, 1934 (Carpenter obituary); December 21, 1934 (School Board tribute); October 14, 1932 (Carpenter quoted). Charlotte McDermott stated the Oakleigh-Oaklee name was taken from a golf course in MA (cf. conversation with the author, December 19, 1993). Oaklee, painted a dark color with white trim, illustrated the cover of the 1947 *Town Report*.

[80] *GSN*, February 5, 1937 (name change desired); March 12, 1937 (power plant); June 25, 1937 (only 10 houses); March 3, 1939 (new low rates); March 31, 1939 (meters).

[81] *GSN*, October 20, 1939 (no hand cranks); October 25, 1940 (new facilities described).

[82] *GSN*, May 22, 1931 (committee subsequently continued into the Roosevelt administration).

[83] The text stated: "Where the physician is in constant attendance upon a patient whose recovery depends upon the prescription for alcoholic liquor no charge will be made; the law and regulations of the prohibition authorities absolutely forbid the writing of prescriptions save for bonafide patients who are being actually attended by the physician issuing such prescriptions." From this it is not clear exactly when the $2 would be charged.

[84] *GSN*, October 6, 1939 (Pomeroy); February 9, 1940 (longevity); July 19, 1940 (Dr. Luke; hospital not otherwise described).

[85] However, Stephen E. Clow commented: "In 1921 and again in 1923, my dad, Dr. Fred E. Clow, spent a month or more taking refresher courses at London hospitals. On one of his trips back he brought an electrocardiograph (EKG) machine. The people at customs had no idea what it might be, could find nothing in their files to help, and so let the machine in duty free. Dad had a great time trying it out on us at home. It was messy, as the inking pen was crude and spilled ink on the charts." (Letter to the author, January 12, 1994)

[86] *GSN*, (electrocardiograph; the other was in Manchester); November 16, 1934 (history of facility); The September 1935 issue of *Modern Hospital* contained an illustrated article on Huggins (not cited here).

[87] Information in this paragraph from Ethel Black.

[88] Note: *GSN*, May 29, 1959, in a retrospective article, erroneously placed the first year as 1939.

[89] *GSN*, August 18 and 25, 1939 (1939 event); January 10, 1941 (financial report). Ethel Clow Dye (later, Ethel Clow Dye Black), daughter of Dr. Fred Clow, was the prime organizer of the Street Fair for many years.

[90] *GSN*, August 9, 1940.

[91] *GSN*, July 17, 1932. Further: In a letter to the author, January 12, 1994, Stephen E. Clow, grandson of Stephen W. Clow, recalled that his grandfather was sitting in the kitchen of his house atop Clow's Hill in East Wolfeboro. There was damage in the area, but, in his recollection, not to the extent the newspaper indicated. The Morrill house was moved about three feet off its foundation, and some trees were downed.

[92] *GSN*, July 6, 1934.

[93] *GSN*, March 20, 27 and April 3, 1936. The entire Northeastern U.S. suffered.

[94] Some information from Barbara Hobbie, "The Tiger's Claw That Ripped New England," article in *The Laker*, September 15, 1988. The *GSN* mentioned the hurricane in nearly every issue for many months thereafter. Selected citations: 1935: September 23 (first report), September 30 (more details), October 7 (about $10,000 damage to local power lines; statewide property damage estimated at $24 million), October 14 (WPA workers; all unpicked orchards wrecked locally), November 4 ("given labor a break"), November 18 (150,000 board feet of lumber down at the Frank Hopewell place on Wolfeboro Neck), December 9 (prices established at c. $12 per thousand board feet for salvaged lumber; 80% of this amount to be paid for white pine logs delivered to storage depots with possible additional payments later depending on the market), December 16 (trucks started filling Back Bay with logs; damage to loss of entire pine grove on Carpenter estate recounted), December 23 (Camp Birchmont losses given: 300,000 feet of timber). 1939: January 6 (about 400,000 feet of lumber delivered so far to Back Bay), January 13 (Wolfeboro Cove), January 20 (about a million feet in Back Bay so far; estimated that three sawmills would be needed to process the logs there), March 17 (21,030 feet in Wolfeboro Cove so far), March 24 (2 million feet in Back Bay, with possibly 6 million more on the way), April 21 (7,500,000 feet expected eventually in Wolfeboro Cove), June 9 (2,700,000 feet received in Wolfeboro Cove; new processing site set up on J. Clifton Avery's land on Crescent Lake behind Huggins Hospital), July 21 (269 million feet of lumber bought so far in state of NH by government, more than all of the rest of New England combined; 97 sawmills operating to cut it; owners averaged $11.77 per thousand board feet), August 11 (report on Wolfeboro Cove; opened December 7, 1938, closed on June 3, 1939, with 2,602,000 board feet of logs; later shipments were taken to Crescent Lake); April 18, 1941 (box company), October 31, 1941 (account of last log).

[95] Earthquake accounts: October 21, 1932; October 29, 1939; December 27, 1939; January 3, 1941. There were tremors and minor quakes on several other dates besides December 20 and 24.

[96] *GSN*, December 26, 1941, retrospective on the first anniversary. Also see *Environmental Sheet*, Concord, 1993, which noted that both December 20 and 24, 1940, quakes measured 5.8 on the Richter scale, and were the strongest ever measured with an epicenter within the state. The June 3, 1977, issue of *GSN* contained an analysis of the 1940 earthquakes, noting that the worst shock occurred at 2:27 a.m. on December 20, and that in the years since then, some $3 million had been spent investigating the event. The July 8, 1977 issue had a related article, "Origins of Ossipees of Geological Interest," by Richard J. Denison, Jr., which stated that a volcano towering 40,000 feet—two miles taller than Mount Everest—rose from a shallow sea and then exploded—creating the Ossipee ring dyke; Denison also discussed later earthquakes in the area.

[97] *GSN*, September 2 (main account) and 9 (Kehonka account), 1933.

[98] *GSN*, September 27, 1935 (sunflowers); February 28 and March 6, 1936 (dust); January 28, 1938 (aurora); February 11, 1938 (ice); September 8, 1938 (Snail Man).

[99] 1938 *Town Report*.

[100] *GSN*, September 29, 1939.

[101] *GSN*, March 17, 1940 (truck); May 24, 1940 (radio).

[102] Arthur F. Chamberlin (who was there), letter, February 22, 1994; this differs from a contemporary *GSN* report which gave the damage just as one barn.

[103] However, Harrison D. Moore, December 10, 1993, stated that it was his recollection the fire was started by blueberry pickers.

[104] *GSN*, May 18, 1934. This incident, with denials, charges, and counter-charges in the local press, reverberated for a long time.

[105] Arthur F. Chamberlin, letter, February 22, 1994; this differs from a contemporary *GSN* report which said the fire extended to the Grace Morgan and Herbert Chamberlain properties.

[106] Arthur F. Chamberlin, letter, February 22, 1994, giving information from Bruce MacBrien.

[107] *GSN*, November 1, 1935. The arsonist, if there was one, was never identified.

[108] *GSN*, August 28, 1936.

[109] *GSN*, November 20, 1936.

[110] *GSN*, January 15, 1937. Christian Science Society's rooms under the balcony were damaged by water; services moved to Carpenter School for a while. Town records in basement also damaged.

[111] *GSN*, July 23, 1937.

[112] *GSN*, November 30, 1994 (feature, "Wolfeboro's Historic Houses Carry a Rich Heritage of Changing Times," by Harrison D. Moore traced ownership since 1759).

[113] Arthur F. Chamberlin, letter, February 22, 1994. Also, *GSN*, June 10, 1938.

[114] *GSN*, July 21, 1939. Crowley was from Peabody, MA. In 1947, she married Dr. Lawrence Austin, who earlier had been a counselor at Camp DeWitt in Alton (*GSN*, July 4, 1947).

[115] Certain information from Dr. W. Douglas Kipp, note to the author, April 1994.

[116] *GSN*, July 12, 1940.

[117] *GSN*, March 6, 1931, and many other issues (Wentworth reward); summer resident Douglas, who later was named to the Supreme Court by President Franklin D. Roosevelt, became one of the town's most famous alumni.

[118] *GSN*, April 22, 1932 (Sturgis appointed chief); 1938 *Town Report* (chief's compensation); *GSN*, November 25, 1932 (Police Court in bank); letter from Stephen E. Clow to the author, January 12, 1994, noted that Ernest H. Trickey was at once CEO of the bank and judge of the Police Court. Further: "It seemed logical to have the court handy to him. The number of court cases during year was trivial." *GSN*, August 25, 1933 (new courtroom remodeled by Roscoe Clow).

[119] *GSN*, December 2 and 9, 1932 (Albee robbery); January 27 and February 3, 1933 (Hamel's); February 10, 1933 (Perry arrest); May 5 and September 15, 1933 (Copp).

[120] *GSN*, July 26 and August 2, 1935 (Dime Store awning); July 26, 1935 (Wolfeboro Laundry); December 20, 1935 (John Murray); December 27 (Auderer break-in).

[121] *GSN*, 1936: February 14 (over a dozen break-ins reported), March 4 (Rines solves the mystery), March 30 (sentences described); June 12, 1936 (Baker brothers); August 14 (Lovingheart); September 18, 1936 (account of police officers in town and county); November 6, 1936 (feud); January 28, 1937 (Rabin).

[122] *GSN*, July 9, 1937 (car theft of July 2), July 23, 1937 (Connor shop entered on July 17; loss: $12).

[123] *GSN*, April 14, 1939 (Libby camp); April 28 and July 7, 1939 (Young store); July 7, 1939 (Diamond Match, boat); November 10 and 17, 1939 (Shannon poultry); November 24, 1939 (church attendance); February 16, 1940 (brawl); August 23, 1940 (Hart's); September 20, 1940 (rug).

[124] *GSN*, May 22, 1931 (Stevens' account).

[125] *GSN*, April 29, 1932; a result of 347 yes votes to 101 no votes in the 1932 town meeting "to see if the town will authorize the selectmen to issue permits to local druggists to fill doctors' prescriptions for intoxicating liquor."

[126] *GSN*, October 14, 1932. Scott lived in the large brick house to the left of the Pickering Block on South Main Street to the left of where the Corner Store is in the 1990s. The building, constructed in 1836, was first used as a bank.

[127] *GSN*, May 26, 1933 (quoting *JAMA*, March 1928; also Hamel's report); May 26 and June 9, 1933 (additional commentary); June 30, 1933 (referendum); May 18, 1934 (state liquor stores).

[128] *GSN*, October 7 and November 4, 1932, among other issues.

[129] *GSN*, November 11, 1932, gave detailed election results and commentary.

[130] *GSN*, February 22, 1935.

[131] *GSN*, January 5, 1936, etc. (Coughlin); January 10 and 14, 1936, September 16 and 23, 1938, June 21, 1940 (Townsend).

[132] *GSN*, September 11, 1936 (liked Moses); November 6, 1936 (election report); in town, Landon and Knox won 910 votes, and Roosevelt and Garner picked up 404; April 28 and May 26, 1939 (Bridges for president); recollection of Styles' son John Bridges to the author ("Landon-Bridges"). Occasionally in local antique shops tiny blue ceramic elephants marked G.O.P. (Grand Old Party = Republican Party) and BRIDGES can be found—souvenirs produced during this ephemeral presidential bid.

[133] *GSN*, July 5, 1940 (phenomenon Willkie); November 8, 1940 (election results).

[134] Related note: In the *1934-1935 Wolfeboro, N.H. Directory*, p. 12, "Swastika Camp" (the swastika being the Nazi symbol; earlier, in American history it was a good-luck sign) is listed as being located at Wentworth Park. Several people have told the author that in the 1930s an entrance to a property along the road to Sanbornville (Route 109) had Nazi insignia, but it is not known whether this was simply a private seasonal camp or a local gathering spot for those having an interest in the German Nazis (whose misdeeds at the time were not known to the vast majority of Americans; such a gathering spot would not have been subversive in 1934).

[135] November 25, 1938: The editor of the *GSN* expressed his disgust with Lindbergh and railed against persecution of Jews by the Nazis; similar statements were made numerous other times in the local press c.1938-1941.

[136] *GSN*, December 10, 1937 (silk).

[137] *GSN*, August 19, 1938 (maneuvers).

# NOTES FOR CHAPTER 7

[1] *GSN*, January 10, 1941 (Red Cross at Dr. F.E. Meader's office); March 14, 1941 (Bundles).

[2] From a speech by M.F. Hatch, as reported in the *GSN*, June 29, 1941; none of the Miller group remained as permanent residents.

[3] *GSN*, July 11, 1941 (Savings Bonds; U.S.O.); August 15, 1941 (35 m.p.h.); November 21, 1941 (bombs).

[4] In the 1990s Brown Hall is a dormitory on the campus of Brewster Academy. When Brewster Academy became a private school in the 1960s it assumed ownership of the building, although a number of old-time citizens believed it was rightfully the property of the town of Wolfeboro. However, no action was taken to claim it. (Recollection of Dr. Lawrence S. Toms, note to author, April 1995.)

[5] *GSN*, December 19, 1941 (dog sleds); January 2, 1942 (sand); January 16, 1942 (aircraft markings; more money than goods).

[6] *GSN*, February 6, 1942 (tires rationed); March 6, 1942 (assembly lines dismantled); March 13 (sugar).

[7] *GSN*, March 27, 1942 (gas stations; speed); April 2, 1942 (bicycles); April 24, 1942 (blackout test report); May 1, 1942 (OPA registration).

[8] *GSN*, June 12, 1942 (insurance); July 31, 1942 (Bryant); September 11, 1942 (scrap).

[9] Honoring the first Wolfeboro residents to be killed in World Wars I (Harry A. Harriman) and II.

[10] *GSN*, March 5, 1943 (humorous editorial about bean rationing; not quoted here); March 12, 1943 (shortage of farm help; California visit; sliced bread; cartoon); May 7, 1942 (black market).

[11] *GSN*, May 14, 1943 (Tunisia, etc.); September 3, 1943 (driving ban lifted).

[12] *Town Report* for fiscal year ending January 31, 1944, with vital statistics for 1943.

[13] *GSN*, January 7, 1944 (Nary); March 31, 1944 (Jockey Cove); April 7, 1944 (hospitality thank-you letter from British Navy; not quoted here).

[14] *GSN*, April 14 (sugar); April 28, 1944 (cars); May 19 and 26, June 9, 1944 (tires; synthetic rubber was of two types, Buna S and Butyl rubber, made of styrene and butadiene).

[15] *GSN*, November 17, 1944 (Red Cross); November 10, 1944 (301 boxes); December 15, 1944 (milkweed; street lights); Jan 26, 1945 (lighting restrictions); November 24, 1944 (B-29s); December 15, 1944 (vapor trails).

[16] *GSN*, January 5, 1945 (counter-offensive); March 16, 1945 (editorial about raids on Japan).

[17] *GSN*, August 17, 1945. "Wolfeboro Goes Wild With Joy."

[18] *GSN*, December 29, 1946 and February 14, 1947 (VFW news).

[19] Sources include the Town Hall files and the names on the Honor Roll at the Soldiers' Monument. Some out-of-town people who enlisted in Wolfeboro may be included. * = Died in service.

[20] *GSN*, July 11, 1941 (40¢ per hour); July 25, 1941 (Allen "A"); November 14, 1941 (Furst).

[21] *GSN*, January 17, 24, 1941 (Wilson); April 25, 1941 (Factory Street).

[22] *GSN*, July 11, 1941 ("most successful"); ("the worst"; gold rush); June 26 and July 3, 1942 (local camps); July 31, 1942 (Point Breeze); September 18, 1942 (tourist numbers); November 7, 1942 (*Mount Washington*); August 3 and 17, 1945 (*Sophie C.*).

[23] *GSN*, September 4, 1942 (chickens, corn); February 12, 1942 (milk; prices varied town by town); January 28, February 4, February 11, April 21, May 12, June 2, 1944, and other issues (frozen food locker); June 9, 1944 (kindergartens).

[24] *GSN*, November 30, 1945 (labor shortage); February 15, 1946 (Hatch); February 22, 1946 (Merrow).

[25] *GSN*, March 8, 1946 (advance tourist bookings heavy); July 12, 1946 (greatest season ever), among other citations.

[26] Letter to the author, April 2, 1993.

[27] *GSN*, September 13, 1946.

[28] Instinct for trading, per conversation with his daughter, Judith Carr Breuninger, January 27, 1993. Real estate information from contemporary *GSN* issues.

[29] *GSN*, September 27, 1946 (Chevrolets); April 9, 1948 (butter); May 28, June 11, August 13, and October 4, 1948 (Belknap); June 18, 1948 (car styling).

[30] *GSN*, June 20, 1947 (Aeromarina); November 11, 1949 (Master Plan); July 11, 1947 (parking); September 12, 1947 (gripes); October 16, 1947 (Information Booth); August 20, 1947 (lack of spending).

[31] *GSN*, January 28, 1949 (mild depression); various May 1949 issues (slow around town); August 5, 1949 (Wolfeboro Industries); December 2, 1949, and January 27, 1950 (Santa).

[32] *GSN*, December 8, 1950 (shillings, etc.); August 25, 1950 (Ford); September 29, 1950 (years earlier in 1930 the Hart Motor Co. sold Austin Bantams); November 10, 1950 (insurance); November 12, 1943 (Haven).

[33] *GSN*, July 17, 1942 (empty roads); September 18, 1942, and June 26, 1943 (Melvin Village bus); January 28, 1944 (York).

[34] *GSN*, September 1, 1944 (Lakes Region Flying Service; the airport was never expanded to the extent of the runways anticipated); September 12, 1947 (CAB approval); June 23, 1950 (twin-engine Cessna); September 26, 1947 (P-51s); November 25, 1949 (Hudson advertising).

[35] *GSN*, March 30, 1942 (office move); November 29, 1946 (Walter Scott press; its July 1924 successor, the Cottrell press; etc.); July 16, 1948 (not quoted here but worthy of mention; portraits were published in the *GSN* of several dozen local children together with their parents' names and where they lived).

[36] *GSN*, January 11, 1946.

[37] *GSN*, September 26, 1952: "Senator and Mrs. H. Styles Bridges are selling their house on Sewall Road and building a log cabin style cottage on Forest Road near Camp Wyanoke and handy to the airport. A steady procession of trucks, all day, for several days, has been transporting gravel to build a road to the cottage."

[38] *GSN*, November 10, 1944 (November 7 election results); November 5, 1948 (November 2 election results); October 13, 1950 (health, etc.), among many others.

[39] *GSN*, November 21, 1942 (stamps); August 24, 1945 and notices in the summer of 1946 (coins); September 12, 1941 (cars).

[40] *GSN*, August 9, 1946.

[41] Ms. Parsons was born in 1927 and pursued a stage career. She later appeared in numerous films including *Bonnie and Clyde* (1967), *I Never Sang for My Father* (1969), *Don't Drink the Water* (1969), *I Walk the Line* (1970), *Watermelon Man* (1971), *Two People* (1973), *For Pete's Sake* (1974), *Foreplay* (1975).

[42] *GSN*, February 17, 1950.

[43] Dr. Joyce E. Brown (letter, June 9, 1994) recalled that there were others, such as *Esquire, Better Homes & Gardens, Popular Mechanics*, and *Field & Stream* (those listed here were the titles specifically advertised).

[44] Commentary in *GSN*, April 24, 1942.

[45] *GSN*, Aug 1, 1942.

[46] *GSN*, July 3, 1942 (instructions). The plaque was moved years later to near the Soldiers' Monument at Pickering Corner.

[47] *GSN*, August 28, 1942.

[48] Date of report.

[49] *GSN*, August 27, 1943.

[50] The founding of this club was made possible through a donation by Dr. Hamilton C. MacDowell of Wellesley, MA. Named for Edward MacDowell, born December 18, 1861, and who did most of his musical composing in a log cabin in Peterborough, NH, and whose widow founded the MacDowell Colony artists' retreat; he is remembered for his *Woodland Sketches* and other pieces.

[51] *GSN*, December 8, 1944; March 23, 1945 *GSN:* Discussion of the great success of the Teen-Age Canteen "from which our young people are deriving so much pleasure."

[52] *GSN*, July 20, 1945.

[53] Date of article.

[54] *GSN*, June 28, 1946.

[55] *GSN*, July 12, 1946.

[56] *GSN*, September 6, 1946.

[57] The school was conducted by Hedy Spielter on what is today known as Melody Island.

[58] Date of account.

[59] *GSN*, July 23, 1948.

[60] Date of account.

[61] Model CA-43 air-operated calliope, 43 notes, made by the Tangley Manufacturing Co., Muscatine, IA, and originally used by Ringling Brothers Circus. Sold second-hand to the Allen "A" where it remained until the 1980s when it was sold to a local collector who resold it to Harvey N. Roehl of Vestal, NY.

[62] *GSN*, 1943 and 1948 *Town Reports* (swimming); *GSN:* August 1 and 8, 1947 (Water Carnival). The sport of water skiing began in Florida in 1936.

[63] *GSN*, January 17, 1941 (Report of deer killed in Carroll County); November 15, 1946 (steaks, etc.); December 12, 1947 (problems).

[64] *GSN*, January 10, 1941 (Victrola); January 11, 1946 (hockey team, etc.); February 14, March 28, and December 5, 1947 (the Macombers; Mr. and Mrs. Clark Macomber purchased the Furbish farm in N. Wolfeboro in autumn 1940, per *GSN*, December 13, 1940); January 31, 1947 (ice boating).

[65] *GSN*, March 15, 1946 (baseball reactivated); 1948 *Town Report* (players shown).

[66] *GSN*, November 6, 1942 (Holderness); November 11, 1949 (Phillips Exeter); December 16, 1949 (banquet).

[67] *GSN*, August 1, 1941 (PGA scheduled); October 25, 1946, and November 15, 1946 (typical bowling accounts; not quoted here).

[68] L. Winston Hamm, letter to the *GSN*, February 6, 1994; copy to author.

[69] *GSN*, June 6, 1941, and January 31, 1947 (Planning Commission; zoning); June 21, 1946 (rubbish); May 30, 1947 (dumps); August 15 and 22, 1947 (parking; additional regulations were adopted on May 14, 1948).

[70] 1950 *Town Report*.

[71] *GSN*, January 24, 1941 (school closed); February 21, 1941 (Huggins full); August 10, 1945 (State Board); 1946 *Town Report*, p. 85 (2 cases); 1949 *Town Report* (measles, polio); *GSN*, August 12, 1949 (polio warning); September 9, 1949 (statistics).

[72] *GSN*, September 15, 1945 (Rounds appointment); August 12, 1949 (Burton); January 3, 1947 (Dye, Siefert); November 8, 1946 (diapers); June 13, 1947 (Gile); August 22 and 29, 1947 (campaign reports); April 8, 1949 (groundbreaking); 1950 *Town Report*, pp. 82, 84 (patient and financial data; outpatient data not quoted here); *GSN*, December 29, 1950 (fees).

[73] *GSN*, February 1, 1946 (Scott recalled early days).

[74] *GSN*, October 20, 1950 (obituary; editorial). October 27 (memorial services).

[75] *GSN*, July 21, 1944 (Dr. J.H. Clow); October 24, 1941 (Parshley obituary).

[76] *GSN*, October 2, 1942 (radio); September 20, 1946 (Foss new chief); June 18, 1948 (equipment illustrated; described in detail).

[77] *GSN*, June 20, 1941.

[78] *GSN*, September 26, 1941.

[79] *GSN*, July 24, 1942.

[80] *GSN*, November 20, 1942.

[81] *GSN*, December 3, 1943.

[82] *GSN*, Date of article; fire was earlier. During this decade, the paper was edited by Parker M. Merrow in Ossipee, and reports of fires in Wolfeboro were less detailed and precise than in earlier times. Undoubtedly, some were omitted. (The present-day Wolfeboro Fire Department lacks records of fires prior to 1964 and could not be used as a source.)

[83] Years later, on September 8, 1950, Fletcher placed an advertisement in the *GSN* alleging that the fire had been set and had been improperly investigated by authorities; he offered a reward for information.

[84] *GSN*, Date of article; fire was earlier.

[85] *GSN*, March 22, 1946.

[86] *GSN*, Date of article; fire was earlier.

[87] *GSN*, November 22, 1946.

[88] *GSN*, January 10, 1947.

[89] *GSN*, March 28, 1947.

[90] *GSN*, May 16, 1947.

[91] *GSN*, Date of article; fire was earlier.

[92] *GSN*, August 29, 1947.

[93] *GSN*, Date of article; fire was earlier.

[94] *GSN*, November 19, 1948.

[95] *GSN*, January 9, 1959. Account of second fire (on January 8, 1959) which killed the Allards.

[96] *GSN*, February 8, 1941 (slots); July 4 and 11, 1941 (crime ring); January 9, 1942 (Rossman); January 16, 1942 (slots); January 23 and October 23, 1942 (tires); August 3, 1945 (ration coupons); August 25, 1944 (Dime Store).

[97] Sturgis died December 29, 1969.

[98] *GSN*, February 21, 1947 (Johnson house); February 28, 1947 (Lillie); April 4, 1947 (Sturgis; he was born May 29, 1891 in Brockton, MA; worked in Wolfeboro as a blacksmith, and for six years for Goodwin & Doe as a plumber); July 18, 1947 (Moore); July 25, 1947 (Mayo); September 19, 1947 (Davis; no further report was printed).

[99] Herbert had other scrapes with the law and later lived in Union and Rochester. In 1959 he was back in jail, but escaped by threatening the jail keeper with a knife (*GSN*, March 22, 1959).

[100] *GSN*, October 10 and December 12, 1947 (Herbert); December 26, 1947 (trees); May 14, 1948 (Paper Store); August 13, 1948 (signs; camp name not specified); October 14 and December 23, 1949 (chief's health).

[101] *GSN*, June 27, 1941 (hail; date of storm not given); September 4, October 2, November 6, 1942 (drought), July 21, 1944 (storm); September 22, 1944 and other accounts (hurricane); October 20, 1944 (hail); February 16, 1945 (snow); April 27, 1945 (wind); May 18, 1945 (freak storm); October 24 and 27, November 14, 1947 (dry conditions, fires); November 14, 1947 (logs); September 1 and December 1, 1950 (rain storms).

[102] Typically, accounts from outlying areas were submitted earlier in the week; thus, "yesterday" was probably not April 13, 1944.

[103] *GSN*, March 10, 1944 (alarm sound); April 14, 1944 (earthquake; date of quake not stated; "yesterday" may have been the day before the column was written, whenever that was; Thurrell lived on Cotton Mountain Farm); November 17, 1944 (meteor); August 16, 1946 (peas); November 26, 1948 (meteor; Headley, a minister, was editor of the *GSN* briefly in the 1930s; the meteor probably fell farther away than Rochester—for information on estimating meteor fall distances see Harvey H. Nininger, *Find a Falling Star*, 1972).

[104] *GSN*, December 3, 1943; beginning and ending date of observation period not stated. As this observation point was in a mountainous area, there is a lack of water birds (loon, duck, etc.).

[105] *GSN*, September 30, 1949 (Russian bomb); November 11 and December 23, 1949 (National Guard); June 2, 1950 (recruiting); June 16, 1950 (activation); July 28, 1950 (Korea; hoarding); August 18, 1950 (why in Korea?); September 22 and December 22, 1950 (Winfield House); October 6, 1950 (Babson); October 13, 1950 (Civil Defense); October 27, 1950 (new name); November 17, 1950 (land).

## NOTES FOR CHAPTER 8

[1] *GSN*, February 16, 1951 (air raid signals explained); July 20, 1951 (war news, Nat'l Guard news, etc.; typical issue).

[2] *GSN*, January 11, June 27, July 11, 1952.

[3] The Korean situation was never a declared war and was often called the Korean Conflict at the time. Today it is known as the Korean War.

[4] * = Killed in service. This list was compiled for the Wolfeboro Historical Society by Ernest H. Swift and is from the W. H. S. archives.

[5] *GSN*, June 4, 1954 (70 men); April 9 and May 14, 1954 (hydrogen bomb); February 6, 1959 (new name).

[6] *GSN*, November 9, 1951.

[7] *GSN*, November 27 and December 4, 1953, May 7, 1954 (Communist scare).

[8] *GSN*, October 26, 1951 (direct primaries); March 14, 1952 (primary results).

[9] *GSN*, January 30, 1953.

[10] *GSN*, November 9, 1956 (election results); September 23, 1960 (Kennedy).

[11] *GSN*, February 20, 1959, etc.

[12] *GSN*, February 2, 1951 (price freeze); February 18, 1951 (unemployment office).

[13] *GSN*, August 24, 1951 (Festival of Fairs); March 14, 1952 (events planned by Chamber); June 12, 1953 (Gen. Wolfe Inn); January 14, 1955 (report on 1954 season); August 20, 1954 (Brendel); May 18, 1956 (Highway Robber).

[14] *GSN*, March 21, 1952 (Industrial Committee report); May 23, 1952 (Merit opens); October 31, 1952 (plant closed).

[15] *GSN*, January 14, 1955 (Chamber meeting proposed new industries; account not quoted here); February 17, 1956 (industrial brochure, not quoted here); October 11, 1957 (electronics); July 11, 1958 ("Progressive").

[16] *GSN*, September 9, 1955 (Federal Reserve reported on record July 1955 business); December 2, 1955 (Federal Reserve; national economy boom); July 20, 1956 (report of 1955 incomes); January 27, 1956 (Maxfield).

[17] These are the names of Wolfeboro residents having over 100 birds per the 1952 town tax list.

[18] *GSN*, October 28, 1955 (pet wife); September 9, 1955 (pay phones); April 8, 1955 (advertisement for new dial service).

[19] Henry S. Maxfield, letter, January 16, 1995.

[20] Trading stamps had been used in town for decades. This account is from the May 24, 1898 *GSN*: "The collecting of trading stamps is having quite a craze, as the cash purchaser thinks he sees a discount in his favor." This was two years after S&H (Sperry & Hutchinson) stamps made their debut.

[21] *GSN*, March 28, 1958 (illustration of projected center); December 18, 1959 (Fournier's Mobil advertisement with S&H stamps, for example); March 25, 1960 (bubblers).

[22] *GSN*, June 8 1956 (selectmen); July 6, 1956 (opening news); July 19, 26, 1957 (coins; Fonteyn had been connected with "the great museum in Brussels"); 1957-1960 *Town Reports* (attendance, etc.); August 19, 1960 (Davis).

[23] Not a *GSN* account. More information will be found under the Embassy Estates listing in the "Wolfeboro Place Names and Origins" section of Volume II. Factual data concerning Mme. Kai-Shek's presence in Wolfeboro is scant. The *GSN*, December 31, 1965, carried a mention by Gertrude B. Hamm. Neighbors (*e.g.*, John Bridges and John A. Graf) reported to the author that they had never seen Mme. Kai-Shek, although Paget was often in evidence. Debra Paget was born as Debralee Griffin in Denver, CO, in 1933. She entered the cinema as a teenager and spent 10 years on the screen in roles as a pretty but passive girl. Films include *Cry of the City, House of Strangers, Broken Arrow, Bird of Paradise, Fourteen Hours, Stripes Forever, Les Miserables, The Gambler from Natchez, Prince Valiant, Princess of the Nile, Seven Angry Men, The Last Hunt, Love Me Tender, White Feather, The River's Edge, From the Earth to the Moon, Tales of Terror*, and more. Benjamin Hoyt was caretaker of the Wolfeboro estate in the 1960s and 1970s.

[24] Part of notes to the author upon reading the manuscript.

[25] Rains (1889-1967) was born in London and was a stage actor until middle age, when he entered films. He specialized in lawyer, doctor and politician roles and was a frequent supporter of Bette Davis. After his first film, *The Invisible Man* (1933), he was seen in numerous others including *They Made Me a Criminal* (1939; played the detective); *Mr. Smith Goes to Washington* (1939; played Senator Payne); *The Lady With Red Hair* (1940; played playwright David Belasco); *Casablanca* (1943; played the police chief); *The Phantom of the Opera* (1943), *Notorious* (1946 Alfred Hitchcock film); *The Earth is Mine* (1959), *Lawrence of Arabia* (1962), and *The Greatest Story Ever Told* (1965; played King Herod).

[26] *GSN*, August 29, 1952; at the time, she lived with her family in Marblehead, MA.

[27] *GSN*, February 13, 1959, told of another visit to town.

[28] Donlevy (1899-1972) was born in County Armagh, Ireland. Usually cast as a villain in films. Pictures included *Barbary Coast* (1935), *Human Cargo* (1936), *High Tension* (1936), *Jesse James* (1939), *Beau Geste* (1939), *Destry Rides Again* (1939), *The Miracle of Morgan's Creek* (1940), *Birth of the Blues* (1941), *Billy the Kid*, (1942), *An American Romance* (1944), *Two Years Before the Mast*, (1946), *A Cry in the Night* (1956), *Never So Few* (1959), and many others.

[29] Brennan (1894-1974), was born in Swampscott, MA, and entered films in 1923 as a character actor. In 1932, an accident knocked out all of his front teeth, after which he became best known for playing parts of old men (in addition to toothless roles, he sometimes used false teeth for other parts). His list of movie and television credits is lengthy. One of his most famous parts was his Oscar-winning role as Judge Roy Bean in *The Westerner*, 1940. He also won Oscars for roles in *Come and Get It* (1936) and *Kentucky*(1938). Among other accounts of Brennan visits to town is one in the issue of July 14, 1961 (not quoted here).

[30] Stanislas Pascal Franchot Tone (1905-1968) was a leading man on stage and screen. Appeared in numerous films including *Moulin Rouge* (1934), *Mutiny on the Bounty* (1935; Academy Award nomination for best actor), *They Gave Him a Gun* (1937), *Phantom Lady* (1944), *Advise and Consent* (1962), and others. He was divorced from all of his wives who were actresses, including Joan Crawford, Jean Wallace, Delores Dorn-Heft, and Barbara Patten. Additional account in *GSN*, August 8, 1958. *GSN*, August 10, 1962, told of another visit.

[31] Kirk Douglas was born in 1916 as Issur Danielovitch Demsky. His film career began with *The Strange Love of Marsha Ivers* (1946), and continued to include *A Letter to Three Wives* (1948), *Ace in the Hole* (1951); *Young Man With a Horn* (1950), *The Glass Menagerie* (1951), *The Bad and the Beautiful* (1952); *The Story of Three Loves*(1953), *Lust for Life* (1956; played Vincent Van Gogh); *Gunfight at the OK Corral* (1957; played Doc Holliday); *Paths of Glory* (1957); *Town Without Pity* (1961); *Seven Days in May* (1964); *Cast a Giant Shadow*(1966); *Is Paris Burning?* (1966); *Once is Not Enough* (1975), and many others.

[32] The Cadillac fins originated when Harley Earl, chief stylist at General Motors, admired the tail of a Lockheed P-38 Lightning fighter plane (cf. "History of the Tailfin!" in *GSN*, March 15, 1957).

[33] *GSN*, September 16, 1955 (new Chevy); September 23, 1955 (editorial); August 1959 (various issues; accidents and editorials); September 11, 25, 1959 (Falcon, Corvair ads).

[34] *GSN*, August 1, 1952.

[35] *GSN*, August 10, 1956 (Chamberlain); August 30, 1957 (turnpikes).

[36] Althea Ballentine recollection, letter, April 1995: "Although regular passenger train

travel had ceased by this time, in the 1950s there were four trains that came into Wolfeboro during the summer time, two at the beginning and two at the end of the camping season. One was from New York City and the other came from Boston, carrying children for DeWitt, Kabeyun, Kehonka, and Wyanoke camps. They were always late arriving, sometimes several hours, since they were shunted onto sidings en route whenever anything else needed to get by on the track."

37 *GSN*, April 10 and November 13, 1959.

38 *GSN*, January 19, 1951 (Rust Pond); June 20, 1947 (Aeromarina set up by Northeast Equipment Co.); January 19, 1951 (B-36); January 20, 1956 (PBY acct. of preceding summer; during WWII the PBY was important in the Pacific theatre, esp. the Solomon Is.); April 1, 1955 (DC-6B); September 13, 1957 (Air Taxi); July 19, 1957 (Merrow); October 9, 1953 (computer).

39 *GSN*, 1961, August 11: Noted that John Fuller and his wife and three children were vacationing at Camp Ossipee and were visiting Wolfeboro friends; he had been a state employee for 11 years, including being New Hampshire state trooper for six years, and was stationed in Alton.

40 *GSN*, May 14, 1954 (to Brocky's); October 8, 1954 (statement of ownership, circulation); September 2, 1955 (Prescott); January 3, 1958 (fire; to Bullock home); the Hampshire Apts. were to the left of and behind where Walker & Varney is in the 1990s; August 26, 1960 (*Look* magazine item discussed; Betsy was the daughter of Mr. and Mrs. Chester Fernald of the Hotel Wawbeek, Melvin Village).

41 *GSN*, February 1, 1952.

42 *GSN*, October 15, 1954.

43 *GSN*, December 10, 1954.

44 The greatest period of building activity was 1953-1954.

45 *GSN*, July 11, 1953 (concert notice); July 31, 1953 (review); September 18, 1953 (NH Music Festival); numerous other accounts.

46 Quoted in the *GSN*, December 17, 1954.

47 1954 schedule: Island concerts on July 25, August 7 and 14; Town Hall on August 18.

48 *GSN*, July 22, 1955.

49 *GSN*, August 5, 1955; spent one week per *GSN*, 10 days per Emilie Tavel of the *Christian Science Monitor*, September 6, 1956 detailed feature. Leopold Stokowski (1882-1977) gained greatest fame as conductor of the Philadelphia Orchestra from 1912-1936; he was conducting the Houston Symphony Orchestra at the time he visited Melody Island.

50 Cf. Tavel, *Christian Science Monitor*. Conductor Maurice Bonney claimed kinship to Billy the Kid. The island's mascot was a dog, Traveler, a white pointer belonging to James Myers of the Atlanta Symphony Orchestra. The island's own shuttle boat was the somewhat dilapidated *Go-Go* (cf. John Bridges interview with the author).

51 *GSN*, February 14, 1951.

52 *GSN*, August 17, 1951.

53 Mr. and Mrs. H.E. Erickson were the originators of the Garden Club Players, which for a number of years presented plays. Account in *GSN*, March 7, 1952.

54 *GSN*, July 11, 1952.

55 Recollection of Althea Ballentine, letter, April 1995.

56 *GSN*, September 26 and October 17, 1952.

57 *GSN*, December 5, 12, 1952.

58 *GSN*, October 30, 1953.

59 *GSN*, June 1 (planning), July 2 (what happened, incl. spirited discussion of Communist China). Sen. Bridges passed away on November 27, 1961; for a time his widow, Deloris, sought reelection to his seat, but she was not nominated. *GSN*, December 1, 1961, printed a eulogy.

60 *GSN*, July 30, 1954. She was to return on July 31.

61 *GSN*, November 5, 1954.

62 *GSN*, February 4, 1955. Publicity.

63 *GSN*, March 11, 1955. Publicity.

64 *GSN*, July 16, 1956. Advance notice.

65 *GSN*, July 27, 1956.

66 *GSN*, February 8, 1957 (announcement).

67 Ned Bullock began his interest as a newscaster in the summer of 1951 when a TV scout heard him on a microphone during a boat carnival in Lake Winnipesaukee.

68 *GSN*, November 8, 1957. The parade was then and is today a long-standing Carpenter tradition.

69 *GSN*, February 28, 1958. At the following week's dance 55 were there.

70 Dr. Toms had come to town from Keene in June 1958, and established the Wolfeboro Animal Hospital.

71 *GSN*, June 3, 1960. Invitation.

72 *GSN*, August 3, 1951. *The Wild Duck* contained Mrs. Daniel Crowley (of Lynn, MA), her son Christopher, her granddaughter Holly Goodhue, and Peter Kimball. The Klinck boat carried Mrs. Klinck (of Concord, MA) and the couple's three sons, Christopher, Hoagie, and Jay, and their friend Martin Bartelt of Long Island.

73 *GSN*, August 24, 1951.

74 Editor Parker M. Merrow; *GSN*, September 13, 1957; Hardy letter, October 11, 1957.

75 SCUBA = Self-Contained Underwater Breathing Apparatus.

76 *GSN*, February 4, 1955 (not dangerous); February 11, 1955 (Abbott).

77 *GSN*, July 10, 1959 (club meeting to be held that same date); July 24, 1959 (ski jump).

78 *GSN*, August 26, 1960 (exhibition).

79 *GSN*, December 5, 1952 (moose; bobcats); April 10, 1953 (beavers); October 28, 1954 (game rules).

80 *GSN*, March 23, 1951 (smelt); August 31, 1951 (Pett); June 13, 1952 (Wyman; he also took 2nd prize; Fred Richardson came in third); February 29, 1952 (Elie).

81 *GSN*, August 6, 1954 (photo of Am. Legion Jr. League team); April 10, May 31, and June 5, 1959 (Little League); July 31, 1959 (history of youth baseball).

82 *GSN*, December 4, 1953 (1953 soccer champions; surnames of team members given); November 19, 1954 and others (1954 champions; Phillips canceled at the last minute); August 19, 1960 (town soccer team).

83 *GSN*, August 28, 1959.

84 *GSN*, September 19 and October 5, 1958 (Celtics); March 20, 1959 (Carpenter basketball); November 27, 1953 and various 1959 issues (bowling).

85 *GSN*, December 21, 1956 (Abenaki reopened); January 30, 1959 (Ned Bullock); December 22, 1959 (Parks and Recreation Comm.); February 5, 1960 (operating nicely); April 1, 1960 (season report); February 3, 1956 (airport).

86 *GSN*, June 15, 1951 (Melanson; zoning); December 3, 1955 (one of several Sunoco articles; over the years, the building of other gas stations evoked numerous letters of protest; November 2, 1956, and November 30, 1956 are examples); March 19, 1954 (town meeting; reassessment); April 23, 1954 (Lahti proposal); April 30, 1954 (voted out); February 25, 1955 (RR station); August 19, 1955 (lake fill); July 22, 1960 (Chas. French).

87 *GSN*, June 4, 1954 (rates); January 28, 1955 (mercury vapor); March 5, 1955 (outage); September 9, 1955 (chlorination).

88 *GSN*, June 3, 1955 (meter proposal); June 17, 1955 (voters reject); August 9, 1957 (yellow lights); November 12, 1958 (radio).

89 *GSN* Bicentennial items include June 26, July 3, July 10, July 17, July 24, 1959.

90 *GSN*, November 9, 1951 (polio cases to date); August 20, 1954 (new Salk vaccine affects March of Dimes); May 20, 1955 (first local clinic announced); August 12, 1955 (facilities closed); August 26, 1955 (17 cases); September 2, 9 (schools); January 10, 17, 1958 (Libby).

91 *GSN*, March 14, 1952.

92 *GSN*, May 28, 1954. The situation was most serious out of town in the Ossipee Mountain area.

93 *GSN*, February 23, 1951 (physiotherapy); December 11, 1953 (heart operation); September 20, 1957 (drive launched); October 11, 1957 (bids for construction solicited); June 6, 1958 (guests shown facility); May 29, 1959 (1958 Fair report); April 17 1959 (one of two institutions); October 9, 1959 (Adams and Bayer); October 23, 1959 (blood pressure).

94 *GSN*, April 26, 1957 (Bloodmobile history); April 1, 1955 (Ames announcement).

95 Numerous accounts in *GSN*, July 1953.

96 *GSN*, Apr 13, 1956.

97 *GSN*, November 15, 1957.

98 *GSN*, April 15, 1960.

99 Cf. *GSN*, February 15, 1952.

100 W. Douglas Kipp, fire journal.

101 Mt. Delight was called Mt. Pleasant in fire reports.

102 April 25 is date of *GSN* report; fire was the preceding week.

103 *GSN*, March 13, 1953.

104 W. Douglas Kipp, fire journal.

105 *Ibid.*

106 *GSN*, August 3, 1953. Robert was son of Lt. Col. and Mrs. Lyford Hutchins.

107 Date of *GSN* report; fire was earlier.

108 W. Douglas Kipp, fire journal.

109 *Ibid.*

110 *Ibid.*

111 Earlier this had belonged to the Leroy Brewster family of Scarsdale, NY. A new camp was planned to be built. Account in *GSN*, September 24, 1954. Photographs of the fire in progress were printed on the front page of *GSN*, October 1, 1954. All that remained was a chimney, which was pulled down by firemen to prevent injury. Apparently, the fire had been burning for several hours before it was detected.

112 W. Douglas Kipp, fire journal.

113 W. Douglas Kipp, fire journal; account in *GSN*.

114 *GSN*, August 12, 1955.

115 *GSN*, December 16, 1955; W. Douglas Kipp, fire journal.

116 W. Douglas Kipp, fire journal.

117 W. Douglas Kipp, fire journal; *GSN*, August 2, 1957.

118 *GSN*, July 5, 1957.

119 W. Douglas Kipp, fire journal; *GSN* account.

120 *GSN*, December 20, 1957. Fire time given as 1:30 a.m. on the night of December 13; here changed to December 14; W. Douglas Kipp, fire journal (as December 13).

121 *GSN*, January 3, 10, 1958. The Goodwin Block was owned by Martin F. Goodwin.

122 *GSN*, May 16, 1958. No one was in the area at the time, and the alarm was called in when flames were seen by someone a mile distant.

123 W. Douglas Kipp, fire journal (date of November 25 used); another account differs and was not used.

124 W. Douglas Kipp, fire journal. Donovan built another camp, which was destroyed on April 14, 1963.

125 *GSN*, January 9, 1959.

126 *GSN*, April 17, 1959.

127 W. Douglas Kipp, fire journal (his date of May 9 used); another account states May 8.

128 W. Douglas Kipp, fire journal.

129 *GSN*, March 11, 1960.

130 *GSN*, July 8, 1960.

131 *GSN*, November 18, 1960.

132 *GSN*, December 16, 1960. 1960 *Town Report* contained additional information; Colby had served the Fire Department about 19 yrs.

[133] Letter to *GSN*, January 28, 1955.

[134] *GSN*, July 1, 1955.

[135] *GSN*, June 8, 1951.

[136] *GSN*, March 27, 1953. Names of thieves not given.

[137] Date of *GSN* account.

[138] *GSN*, November 18, 1955.

[139] *GSN*, August 10, 1956.

[140] *GSN*, March 29, 1957.

[141] *GSN*, April 5, 1957.

[142] Date of *GSN* account.

[143] *GSN*, January 17, 1958. Names of criminals not given.

[144] Date of *GSN* report.

[145] *GSN*, November 21 and December 5, 1958. Lewis was stationed at the New London Submarine Base in CT.

[146] *GSN*, December 26, 1958.

[147] *GSN*, April 17, 1959.

[148] Date of *GSN* report.

[149] *GSN*, August 28, 1959.

[150] *GSN*, September 25, 1959 (aux. force proposed); the convicts were later captured in a manhunt; October 30, 1959 (molester); December 11, 1959 (typical crime report).

[151] *GSN*, February 19, 1960 (move); April 1, 1960 (election).

[152] *GSN*, July 8, 1960. Joy was a resident of Sanbornville and Farmington and had been in Wolfeboro only for a short time. Maynard was from Rochester. In the August 12, 1960 number it was reported that Joy had escaped from jail and was believed to be at large in the Wolfeboro area, committing more burglaries.

[153] 1957 *Town Report*, p. 12 (obscenity); 1958 *Town Report*, p. 11 (protection). Salaries of Police Department officers may be found in these and other reports.

[154] *GSN*, June 10, 1960.

[155] *GSN*, April 20, 1951 (freak winds); March 21, 1952, etc. (heavy snow conditions); September 26, 1952 (wind, rain, waves); April 17, 1953 (Carry Beach); June 11, 1954 (letter a year later from Jos. Melanson about the flooding of March-April 1953); December 25, 1953 (freak winds); May 14, 1954 (flooding); August 6, 1954 (tornado); September 3, 10, 17, 1954 (Carol); August 12, 1955 (Fuller); September 2, 1955 (high winds on the lake). Note: Camp Ossipee is described under "Wolfeboro Place Names and Origins" in Volume II.

[156] *GSN*, March 20 (snow); September 27, 1957 (low water); October 25, 1957 (old dam); January 24, 1958 (special appeal); March 20, 1959 (snow); November 20, 1959 (yellow houses explained).

[157] *GSN*, December 25, 1959 (waves); September 16, 1960 (Donna; also see 1960 *Town Report*, p. 101).

[158] *GSN*, October 5, 1951 (aurora); November 28, 1952 (meteor); November 27, 1957 (radiosonde).

[159] QDB note: The *GSN* indicated temblors occurring on October 25 and 26; the Harvard report mentioned another on October 27 (Monday).

[160] *GSN*, June 11, 1954 (albino); July 16, 1954 (eggs); July 23, 30, 1954 (gypsy moths); October 8, 29, 1954 (bears); October 22, 1954 (anomalous eggs); December 21, 1956 (elms; also August 28, 1959); October 25 (Sputnik); June 12, 1959 (bees).

[161] John A. Graf, age 58, senior partner in the law firm of McLane, Graf, Raulerson & Middleton in Manchester, died on January 31, 1994. This essay was contributed by him on February 2, 1993. From childhood until his passing he spent his summers in Wolfeboro in his family's cottage.

# NOTES FOR CHAPTER 9

[1] *GSN*, March 17, 1961 (Battery D); November 3, 1961 (fallout shelter financing; editorial on spreading Communism); September 18, 1964 (local public shelters); October 26, 1962 (Cuban crisis); November 29, 1963 (Kennedy death).

[2] *GSN*, January 24, 31, 1964 (Goldwater visit); March 13, 1964 (report of primary).

[3] *GSN*, February 4, 1966 (Tim Morrill).

[4] *GSN*, July 7, 1967 (Romney); November 3, 1967 (Wyman visit); January 11, 1968 (Oliver talk); February 8, 1968 (Evans talk); July 18, 1968 ( 1.5 million troops).

[5] *GSN*, October 9, 1969 (Red Cross); November 6, 1969 (American Citizens Fund advertisement); May 21, 1970 (Thomson, in that year, denied the Republican nomination, waged an unsuccessful campaign as the American Party nominee for governor); August 27, 1970 (editorial about Nixon).

[6] *GSN*, April 13, 1962 (bracelet); July 18, 1968 (stamps discontinued).

[7] 1963 *Town Report*, p. 13, and other sources.

[8] *GSN*, May 21 and June 18, 1965.

[9] *GSN*, June 26, 1969. William Watson of Marblehead, MA was the owner.

[10] *GSN*, September 4, 1970, and other sources. Also see listings under Giniewicz and Hewd Manufacturing in Volume III.

[11] *GSN*, March 22, 1963 (Wentworth Meadows); November 4, 11, 1966 (food price protest); March 24, 1967 (milk); October 8 and November 26, 1970 (new tax).

[12] *GSN*, September 8, 1961 (Information Booth); September 29, 1961 (turn-in sign).

[13] Some restaurants lasted for years; others just a season. A vignette of the restaurant scene for any other year would contain some different names.

[14] *GSN*, July 19, 1963, April 10, 1964, etc. (Colonial Arms).

[15] *GSN*, September 29, 1961 (Melody Island advertisement); August 17, 1964 (description of *Popular Boating* article; Bullock was best known as a photographer, but the illustrations were by Eric Sanford of Manchester); December 31, 1965 (Hamm article).

[16] Made by Nicholas Power, New York City, a leading manufacturer.

[17] *GSN*, May 18, 1962 (Brewster Museum); July 1, 1966 (commentary: Big W to open); February 11, 1966 (investors wanted); June 2, 1967 (26' sign).

[18] *GSN*, August 28, 1964 (art display).

[19] 1966 *Town Report* (repainting of building; artists' exhibit); *GSN*, August 1, 1968 (Libby dock); 1970 *Town Report* (Bicentennial medals; struck by V.H. Blackinton [incorrectly as "Blockingham" in at least one account] & Co., Attleboro Falls, MA; the local committee in charge included Charles Riley, Gerald Briggeman, and Donald McBride, details in *GSN*, March 26 and April 9, 1970).

[20] *GSN*, September 22, 1961 and April 17, 1964, etc. (Alan Pope); May 8, 1964 (Merrow succession plans); January 6, 1961 (Polaroid); June 5, 1964 ("Mrs." in listing); July 29, 1966 (Bowman); July 31, 1969 (Bullock resigns; Tempest becomes assoc. editor); November 19, 1970 (Tempest resignation).

[21] *GSN*, June 9, 1967.

[22] *GSN*, February 5, 1970. Editorial.

[23] Although it was not within the limits of Wolfeboro, we note that in the summer of 1964 Paul R. Hatch opened the North Country Drive-In near the junction of Routes 16 and 28 in Ossipee (cf. *GSN*, June 12, 1964, and other issues).

[24] *GSN*, April 23, 1970.

[25] *GSN*, April 30, 1970, illustrated and described the theatre; the Hatch family was shown with Estelle Parsons, who was currently in the film, *Don't Drink the Water*.

[26] *GSN*, July 24, 1969 (corporation formed); September 4, 1969 (construction permit granted); April 2, 1970 (planned programming); April 9, 1970 (account of debut).

[27] On December 20, 1961, she became Mrs. Kenneth Douglass. The couple subsequently had three children: Jennifer, Hilary, and Lauren.

[28] *GSN*, October 25, 1963 (announcement).

[29] *GSN*, February 7, 1964.

[30] *GSN*, June 15, 1964. Program.

[31] *GSN*, August 7, 1964. Publicity. In 1967, Ella Lord Gilbert, leading light of the club, died. The club struggled to survive (*GSN*, April 4, 1968). On June 17 1968, the club changed its name to the Friends of Music (*GSN*, June 20, 1968). Since that time it has flourished.

[32] *GSN*, January 29 and July 29, 1965. Additional information.

[33] *GSN*, June 4, 1965 (jazz band scheduled); August 27, 1965 (neighbors protest); September 3, 1965 (neighbors secure legal advice, etc.); see Volume III for additional details.

[34] *GSN*, December 10, 1965.

[35] *GSN*, March 4, 18, 1966.

[36] *GSN*, February 10, 1967. Notes: Owners of Copple Crown were Lee and Maurice Shibles of N. Berwick, ME, who began development in 1963 and opened the facility in 1965. Harriman Construction Co. developed 4,000 feet of road and parking for 600 cars on the 258-acre tract. In January 1967, the development was taken over by Locke Lake Development, of which Harry Hopewell and John Hopewell (president of Town & Country Homes) were partners. Additional information about Copple Crown is in *GSN* as follows, among other issues: July 19, 1963 (Copple Crown work begun); October 25, 1963 (Harriman; Copple Crown lifts; lodging); November 15, 1963 (equipment delayed); October 13 and December 10, 1965 (opening); January 21, 1966 (many skiers); January 13, 1967 (Hopewell, *et al*).

[37] *GSN*, April 14, 1967.

[38] *GSN*, March 10, 1967 (announcement).

[39] *GSN*, July 7, 1967.

[40] *GSN*, August 11, 1967.

[41] *GSN*, April 25, 1968.

[42] *GSN*, July 18, 1968.

[43] *GSN*, April 22, 1970 (announcement).

[44] *GSN*, August 13, 1970 (announcement).

[45] *GSN*, October 1, 1970 (schedule).

[46] *GSN*, November 5, 1970.

[47] *GSN*, December 7, 1970 (announcement). Ray Lord directed many stage events during this era.

[48] *GSN*, April 28, 1967 (Little League teams); December 16, 1966 (field hockey); November 17, 1961 (Brewster football); October 9, 1964 (Kingswood Knights); November 25, 1966 (Brewster football).

[49] *GSN*, September 6, 1963 (Ralph Stinchfield).

[50] *GSN*, August 22, 1968 (Racquet Club); June 4, 1970 (summer tennis programs).

[51] *GSN*, March 22, 1963 (Brewster j.v. basketball team photo and information); August 13, 1965 (PJ Lanes planned); October 24, 1968 (typical candlepin award notice). Pamela Jean Clarke was born in Wolfeboro, August 18, 1957, and died on October 13, 1962, at Children's Hospital in Boston. Her brother Donald, two years younger, also had the disease.

[52] *GSN*, May 11, 1962, etc. (Water Ski Club); July 27, 1962 (diving); August 7, 1964 (Briggs); November 11, 1966 (racing shell); June 19, 1969 (Sea-Doo; Armand Bombardier, of Quebec, had perfected a "power toboggan" in 1928 for use over snow).

[53] *GSN*, April 14 and May 5, 1961, and April 17, 1962 (Willey Brook); June 5, 1964 (salmon by plane); November 23, 1962 (moose).

[54] *GSN*, February 21 and March 6, 1964 (Bullock commentaries); February 28, 1964 (Abenaki for taxpayers only); March 13, 1964 (Parks and Playground Comm. reiterated its exclusionary policy); March 27, 1964 (Hersey statement); December 11, 1964 (new policies); February 15, 1968 (ski team).

[55] *GSN*, February 1, 1963 (Winter Carnival); November 20, 1964 (history of snowmobiles—not quoted here; January 29, 1970 contained history of the Snowmobile Co., Inc., once a prominent Ossipee business); December 28, 1967 (club formed); December 26, 1968 and February 20, 1969 (state championships); March 5, 1970 (championships); December 31, 1970 (editorial on safety).

[56] *GSN*, January 13, 1961 (school meeting; note: schools and education form a separate section of the present work in Volume II, by Chris Fipphen, and are not discussed at length here); January 20, 1961 (announcement of town meeting; new forms of town government to be discussed); March 17, 1961 (report of March 14 town meeting); July 14, 1961 (announcement of Summer Town Meeting); December 10, 1970 (town taxes and selectmen's comments).

[57] Note to author, April 1995.

[58] *GSN*, July 14 (new docks); October 12, 1962, May 3, 1963, etc. (eggs); April 26, 1963 (in a letter Cecily Crowe lamented the loss of elms); May 3, 1963 (Norway maples); June 28 1963 (zip codes); January 22, 1965 and others (by-pass; also see May 19, 1967 and July 16, 1970 issues of *GSN*, not quoted here, the latter with a letter from Henry S. Maxfield; also a letter from Maxfield to the author, January 16, 1995, was utilized); January 20, 1967 (1966 county survey); March 12, 1965, June 16, 1967, November 13, 1969, among others (Article X results. Follow-up: On May 20, 1994, a telephone call to the Town Offices resulted in the information that no one on hand at the time knew what happened to the report). In a note to the author, April 1995, former selectman Dr. Lawrence S. Toms that "there are several other succeeding 701 projects gathering dust in various filing cabinets at Town Hall."

[59] Recollection of Dr. Lawrence S. Toms, note to author, April 1994.

[60] *GSN*, March 8, 1963 (verdict; on July 28, 1967 a special town meeting was held to appropriate $35,000 to pay the settlement, representing the portion not covered by insurance, cf. 1967 *Town Report*); *GSN*, September 27 and October 18, 1963 (Public Service Co.); 1964 *Town Report* (Municipal Electric Department data); 1965 *Town Report* (microwave relay); May 23, 1968 (atomic power); March 31, 1967 (water meters); July 23, 1970 (Roger F. Murray's report); August 6, 1970 (sewage treatment plans).

[61] *GSN*, June 21, 1963 (new building planned); September 20, 1963 (illustration of building plan); September 18, 1964 (dial tone); September 25, 1965 (Zulauf-Hale); December 2, 1966 (history of tel. service in town); January 18, 1968 (911 nos.).

[62] *GSN*, June 19, 1969 (bus rates); June 30, 1961 (Buddliner cars); February 5, 1970 (abandon line); (October 2, 1962 (Sikorsky); July 29, 1966 (flight instruction); August 20, 1970 (Hart).

[63] *GSN*, November 19, 24, 1965 (McGee); 1968 *Town Report* (junk cars); *GSN*, June 23, 1967 (Clow apartments). The November 30, 1967 issue of *GSN* showed cars being crushed at the Wakefield Pit Dump; additional collection sites were in Pleasant Valley and East Wolfeboro.

[64] Details will be found in the Osseo listing in the "Wolfeboro Place Names and Origins" in Volume II.

[65] Letter, September 14, 1994. Hughes, with ties to the town dating back many years, was a leading figure in community planning in the 1990s.

[66] *GSN*, July 7, 1961 (Hooghkirk); February 11, 1966 (museum name change); September 1, 1961 (Sawyer estate); July 6, 1962 (Meader booklet); November 13, 1964 (Parker book); November 23, 1962 (new history); October 13, 1967 (bank ledger; however, the records of more than one bank were involved).

[67] *GSN*, March 16, 1962 (March 13 town meeting report); June 1, 1962 (Sabin vaccine); April 3, 1964 (Spence accident); July 29, 1966 (Attorney Walker); October 28, 1966 (local facility open); November 14, 1968 (Wolfeboro Knoll); December 19, 1968, and May 22, 1969 (Drs. Damm); July 10, 1969 (Weight Watchers); December 18, 1969 (pills).

[68] Comments received by the author from three prominent individuals who were associated with the hospital at the time but who requested anonymity.

[69] *GSN*, September 7, 1972 (portrait acquired); September 27, 1973 (protest)

[70] The painting was put in an area in which there were portraits of other doctors; apparently, the committee wanted it to be placed in a main passageway such as where Mrs. Jennie Sinclair's portrait was hung (per interview with Roberta French, October 1994, with a hospital staff member who recalled the incident).

[71] *GSN*, Dec 12, 1965 (Adams resignation discussed, after his death); December 3, 1965 (Adams obituary and eulogy); May 13, 1966 (Medicare); June 9, 1967 (1966 annual report); November 10, 1967 (TV); July 11, 1968 (new beds); May 22, 1969 (Dr. Goodall); July 24, August 21, and October 2, 1969, etc. (addition).

[72] 1961 *Town Report*.

[73] *GSN*, November 1, 1963.

[74] *GSN*, March 10, 1967.

[75] *GSN*, June 16, 1967 ("Dr. Drury's Fire Boat a Safety Asset for Lake," by Mildred A. Beach); January 8, 1970 (details of Drury's gift).

[76] *GSN*, February 17, 1961.

[77] *GSN*, February 17, 1961.

[78] *GSN*, April 6, 1962.

[79] Recollection of former selectman Dr. Lawrence S. Toms, note to author, March 1995.

[80] *GSN*, April 19, 1963.

[81] *GSN*, October 4, 1963.

[82] *GSN*, November 6, 1964 (Tumble Brook Fund).

[83] *GSN*, May 7, 1965.

[84] *GSN*, August 6, 1965.

[85] *GSN*, May 27, 1966. Kipp journal. She was the widow of Sen. H. Styles Bridges.

[86] *GSN*, January 20, 1967. Fire date not given. Not listed in Dr. Kipp's journal.

[87] *GSN*, July 21, 1967. Further (per a recollection of former selectman Dr. Lawrence S. Toms, note, March 1995): Stanley's scattered remains were gathered in a pail and taken to Huggins Hospital where they were shown to Dr. Dube (medical examiner), state troopers, and others. In Stanley's home on his bureau were found a sentimental ring which it is believed he never took off before, his wallet, and other personal things, suggesting the explosion may have been a suicide. Stanley was struggling with an alcoholism problem at the time.

[88] *GSN*, August 25, 1967 (accident); Boston *Herald Traveler*, January 23, 1971 (settlement).

[89] *GSN*, September 8, 1967.

[90] *GSN*, December 14, 1967.

[91] *GSN*, May 1, 1968 (Meffert charged with arson and three other crimes); June 6, 1968 (disposition of case). On June 2, 1970, Meffert, then of Northfield, was arrested and charged with burglary and malicious damage in Wolfeboro (*GSN*, June 11, 1970).

[92] *GSN*, May 2, 1968.

[93] *GSN*, January 30, 1969.

[94] Details of name change in 1969 *Town Report*, p. 21; *GSN*, March 12, 1970.

[95] Dr. Kipp indicated in his records that this fire, for which the firemen were on the scene for just 20 minutes, was not to be publicized.

[96] *GSN*, February 12, 1970.

[97] *GSN*, June 29, 1962 and June 18, 1970 (Brewster Beach); June 26, 1964 (golf course); July 10, 1964 (Kingswood High); February 12, 1965 (Post Office); February 14, 1964 (chase).

[98] *GSN*, February 19, 1965 (forum report); December 17, 1965 (Open Door); August 29, 1968 and August 7, 1969 (sign stealing); February 1, 1968 and November 20, 1969, etc. (narcotics); October 31, November 14, and December 12, 1965, etc. (Sports Shop); August 28, 1969 (First National); October 9, 1969 (bomb hoax); November 6, and December 11, 1969 (Bunnell); February 26, 1970 (Abenaki); March 12, 1970 (6 juveniles); April 2, 1970 (Libby Museum); April 2, 1970 (Lakes Region Survey Service); September 17 and October 15, 1970 (Cilley and Van Amburgh); December 3, 1970 (Huggins); December 3, 1970 (lights).

[99] The 1985 *Town Report*, p. 116, paid tribute to Harold E. Thompson (January 13, 1899-December 9, 1985); Thompson had joined the force in 1935.

[100] *GSN*, August 17, 1962 and October 3, 1968 (Troop E); July 17, 1964 (Chief Wentworth sworn in); May 15, 1965 (Beaulieu); October 29, 1965 and June 24, 1966 (Rescue Squad); November 5, 1965 (new Police Department headquarters); November 23, 1967 (District Court); January 1, 1970 (Sony). 1970 police cruiser information from 1970 *Town Report*.

[101] Letter, May 10, 1993, by which time Mr. Stevens was chief of police.

[102] Dr. Lawrence S. Toms, former selectmen, recalls it was the Secret Service (a branch of the Treasury Department); note to author, 1995.

[103] *GSN*, May 8, 15, 22, 29, June 5, and July 24, 1969 (Corson and Brooks); April 2, 1970 (census advertisement).

[104] *GSN*, January 4, 1963 (December 1962 cold snap and freak winds); July 26, 1963 (tornado); August 30, 1963 (waves); December 6, 1963 (waves); December 4, 1964 (hail); July 2, 1965 (tornado); July 23, 1965 (drought).

[105] Recollection of former selectman Dr. Lawrence S. Toms, note to author, 1995.

[106] *GSN*, March 19, 1965 (ice at docks); March 3, 1967 (snow); November 24, 1968 (snow); February 13, 27, and March 6, 1969 (snow).

[107] *GSN*, June 11, June 25, and October 15, 1970 (oil slick); September 3 and November 19, 1970 (mercury poisoning, pollution).

[108] English translation. Pergamon Press, 1960, p. 98.

[109] From the French, *passe partout*, a visa or item enabling one to have unrestricted travel.

# NOTES FOR CHAPTER 10

[1] Article, "Wolfeboro—a New Hampshire Resort With Charm That's Unique."

[2] *GSN*, August 17, 1975.

[3] *GSN*, November 17, 1976.

[4] As in previous listings of veterans, this compilation includes individuals who enlisted in Wolfeboro or who gave Wolfeboro as their mailing address; in some instances, citizens of other towns are included.

[5] *GSN*, December 2, 1971.

[6] Name later changed to the present Old Lakeview Terrace. Warren Tickle was a well-known teacher at Kingswood.

[7] *GSN*, November 25 and December 2, 1971.

[8] *GSN*, January 13, 1972.

[9] *GSN*, February 10, 1972. Paul R. Hatch was often on the radio, but was better known as the owner of the Hatch Theatre.

[10] *GSN*, February 17, 1972.

[11] *GSN*, February 24 and Mar 2, 1972.

[12] *GSN*, March 2, 1972 (schedule).

[13] *GSN*, March 9, 1972.

[14] *GSN*, October 3, 1974. "Problem people" were those who evaded the draft or protested against the war. Edsel = automobile marque introduced by Ford in the late 1950s and intended to become a major brand; it failed miserably, after which the Edsel became a synonym for failure, for a product gone wrong.

[15] *GSN*, January 1 and 8, and February 5, 1976.

[16] *GSN*, November 4, 1976.

[17] *GSN*, November 21 and December 5, 1979.

[18] *GSN*, January 9, 1980.

[19] *GSN*, January 23 and February 6, 1980.

[20] Robert Fournier, note to author, January 1995.

[21] *GSN*, February 6, 13, 20, 27, 1980.

[22] *GSN*, February 17, 1980 (primary); November 5, 1980 (presidential).

[23] *GSN*, July 10, 1975 (doesn't smile); May 4, 1972 and June 19, 1975 (computers in Wolfeboro); February 24, 1972 (Smith enters); March 19, 1980 (Hatch, 1st NH seat).

[24] Dr. Lawrence S. Toms later related (note to author, December 1994) that in his opinion, much of the conflict was caused by Selectman Hatch being so occupied with his work (for the state of NH) that he devoted little time outside of selectmen's meetings to other duties such as town taxes, property appraisal evaluation, etc.

[25] The Croteau family kept its $400. Dr. Toms (note to author, December 1994) stated that the situation arose when the director of charitable trusts wrote to the selectmen to state that too much money was being accumulated, and that disbursements should be acceler-

ated. "We doubled the award to $200 per semester, and gave it to all comers."

[26] *GSN*, September 2, 1971. The Roger F. Murray family summered in Wolfeboro for many years, later establishing permanent residence here.

[27] *GSN*, October 28, 1971.

[28] *GSN*, November 23, 1971.

[29] *GSN*, January 20, 1972.

[30] 1973 *Town Report*, p. 58 (fuel); *GSN*, July 12 (interest rates; Kingswood Bank slogan).

[31] *GSN*, August 16, 1973 (beef shortage); November 8, 1978 (wine).

[32] *GSN*, November 29, 1973 (energy conservation); November 7, 1974 (retrospective comment that the crisis began November 25, 1973), December 6, 1973 (school measures; cost of living); December 17, 1973 (gas hogs); January 24, 1974 (snow removal); January 31, 1974 (stoves); September 19, 1971 (White House).

[33] The Seabrook controversy evoked some of the most spirited commentary ever to appear in the pages of the local paper. However, as the facility is located outside of Wolfeboro, only brief mention is made of it here.

[34] *GSN*, February 7, 1974 (gas lines); February 21, 1974 (NO GAS); November 7, 1974 (30% down).

[35] *GSN*, May 16, 1974 (boat show); June 6, 1974 (food stamps announced); August 8, 1974 (gas prices); September 5, 1974 (Mildred A. Beach); December 5, 1974 (WIN); February 27, 1975 (NIM); January 16, 1975 (Fetzer); January 9, 1975 (75¢/gallon); June 24,1976 (manila envelope).

[36] *GSN*, March 13, 1975 (buyers' market); June 5, 1975 (Memorial Day); November 13, 1975 (watches); December 4, 1975 (59¢; Wooley).

[37] *GSN*, May 6, 1976 (26 permits); June 22, 1976 (coins); September 28, 1977 (electronics); July 5, 1978 (Wolfeboro Falls merchants); May 10, 1978, and other issues (Kinville); May 31, 1978 (new rate; stamps with the letter A were used until new stamps were ready); January 8, 1976 (UPS); June 7, 1978 (8.17%).

[38] *GSN*, December 19, 1979 (14%+ mortgage rates); December 26, 1979 (Treasury bills); June 20, 1979 (gas shortage); September 5, 1971 (Labor Day report); October 10, 1979 (Town Manager Krapp announcement); November 21, 1979 (Brockhouse identified).

[39] *GSN*, January 16, 1980 (no snow); July 16, 1980 (unemployment rate); April 30, 1980, do-it-yourself feature by Douglas Rooks); March 12 and April 2, 1980 (over 15%); April 30, 1980 (waterbeds); September 17, 1980 (kerosene).

[40] Issues of the *Town Report* for the decade give much information about the Libby Museum, including attendance, exhibits, expenses, etc.

[41] *GSN*, March 24 and April 14, 1982; February 6, 1983.

[42] Per 1970 census; quoted in *GSN*, May 11, 1972. There were 14,838 housing units in the county, and 5,651 had one or more TV sets.

[43] *GSN*, March 26, 1980, and other issues.

[44] *GSN*, October 26 and November 23, 1977. In the 1930s and again in 1947 performers banded together under the Village Players name; after the early 1950s interest lapsed until 1977.

[45] *GSN*, September 26, 1974; not quoted here: August 12, 1976 (finances); June 8, 15, 29, 1977; April 8, 1978; and numerous other issues discussed the Playhouse.

[46] *GSN*, March 25 and April 1, 1971.

[47] *GSN*, April 15, 1971 (announcement); April 29, 1971 (review).

[48] *GSN*, April 22, 1971 (notice).

[49] *GSN*, August 26, 1971 (announcement).

[50] *GSN*, June 22, 1972 (announcement). Similar events were held other years.

[51] *GSN*, July 13, 1972 (announcement).

[52] *GSN*, August 10, 1972 (announcement). It had been a long time since a circus had visited Wolfeboro.

[53] *GSN*, January 25 and February 1, 1973.

[54] *GSN*, June 28 and August 16, 1973 (advertisement).

[55] *GSN*, July 12, 1973 (notices).

[56] *GSN*, October 4, 1973 (announcement).

[57] *GSN*, October 25, 1973 (announcement).

[58] *GSN*, December 6, 1973 (announcement).

[59] *GSN*, June 13, 1974 (photo).

[60] *GSN*, August 19, 1974.

[61] *GSN*, December 26, 1974 (announcement).

[62] *GSN*, May 15, 1975 (announcement).

[63] *GSN*, June 5, 1975 (advertisement).

[64] *GSN*, June 12, 1975 (announcement).

[65] *GSN*, August 14, 1975 (announcement).

[66] *GSN*, October 30, 1975. The Shaw Brothers, singers, appeared in town several times over the years.

[67] *GSN*, November 6, 1975.

[68] *GSN*, April 19 (review).

[69] *GSN*, July 1 and July 8, 1976.

[70] *GSN*, April 20, 1977.

[71] *GSN*, June 8, 1977 (advertisement).

[72] *GSN*, December 15, 1977 (advertisements).

[73] *GSN*, March 15 (announcement) and 22 (review), 1978.

[74] *GSN*, April 19, 1978 (announcement).

[75] *GSN*, January 31 and February 14, 1979.

[76] *GSN*, November 7, 1979 (announcement).

[77] *GSN*, May 14 and 21 (photo), 1980.

[78] *GSN*, June 25, 1980 (program).

[79] *GSN*, July 16, 1980 (announcement).

[80] August 6, 1980 (announcement). In later years, exhibitors would be approved by a special jury.

[81] Certain terms are from the 20th Anniversary Issue of *People* magazine, 1994.

[82] *GSN*, September 11, 1975 (discussion of phrase). Also (especially in later years), "Have a nice day."

[83] *GSN*, March 30, 1975 (discussion of new terms used by the state of NH).

[84] 1974 *Town Report* (12 days only); *GSN*, February 14, 1974 (30 years); 1976 and 1977 *Town Reports* (Abenaki progress); February 22, 1972 and January 4, 1973 (Bean, ski team); February 28, 1974 (Bean); February 19, 1976 (girls win); March 15, 1978 (Bean); January 21, 1974 (moonlight ski tour announced); December 11, 1975 (snowless skiing).

[85] *GSN*, March 2, 1972 (Cortina wins); February 25, 1971 (snowmobile races); February 24, 1972 (Grand Prix; not quoted here); November 9, 1972 (town trails); 1973, February 22 (races).

[86] *GSN*, June 5, 1975, May 19, 1980, and other issues (Smith River Canoe Race); September 26, 1974 (Laser); August 17, 1977 (sailboats increase); August 3, 17, 1972 (ski show); July 13 and August 3, 1977 (Swaffield); July 16, 1980 (McKenzie); August 20, 1980 (Eubanks).

[87] *GSN*, June 10, 1971 (Derby); January 24, 1974 (Varney); August 13, 1980 (eel); July 13, 1972 (bike race announced for August 10, rain date August 11); August 15, 1974 (report of August 14 race); June 13, 1979 (Bovaird); July 16, 1980 (Jackson).

[88] *GSN*, May 13 and June 3, 1976 (Royals); May 28, 1980 (Minor and Major Leagues).

[89] *GSN*, September 13, 1973 (Pro Days); Feb 28, 1974 (Black); September 12, 1974 (Sweeney); June 22, 1977 (Melanson);

[90] Recollection of Albert ("Duke") Southard, letter, May 22, 1995.

[91] *GSN*, December 9, 1971 (All-State); November 17, 1976 (Number One!); December 1, 1976 (Masonic Hall); November 8, 1978 (2nd best season); November 7, 1979 (highest NH scores).

[92] *GSN*, February 28, 1974 (bowling); November 2, 1972 (karate); October 31, 1979 (soccer); October 1, 1980 (Bay Village); June 21, 1978 (Brookes); April 30, 1980 (Rankin); July 6, 1977 (skateboarding). Also *Town Reports*.

[93] GSN, February 18, 1971 (Krapp hired; biographical notes); 1971 *Town Report* (reported for duty); Also, *GSN*, April 25, 1979 (Zulauf request); May 16, 1979 (firm hired); June 13, 1979 (findings);

[94] *GSN*, April 22, 1971 (clean-up); May 1, 1971 (bottles); 1972 *Town Report* (Back Bay); 1973 *Town Report* (Thurrell-Chase); March 7, 1974 and March 9, 1977 (historic district); Feb 13, 1975 and other issues (Community Center). *GSN*, July 3, 1975; December 18, 1975 (plumbers, etc.); October 14, 1976 (population); September 21, 1977 (town population 3,697; not discussed here).

[95] *GSN*, September 20, 1978, and other issues (lottery); January 16, 1980 (Manning's); November 14, 1979 (tax rate); May 7, 21, 1980 (Simoneau); May 28, June 18, and Oct 1, 1980 (*Labyrinthos;* as *King of America* it was screened in Wolfeboro on January 23, 1982, cf. *GSN*, January 13, 1982 announcement); August 20, 1980 (Garden Club); November 26, 1980 (Mast Landing); December 24, 1980 (Kammler building, which was the old Glendon House Stable, Rite Aid was built on the site in 1994; behind the Post Office retail shops were later built).

[96] *GSN*, July 5, 1973 (direct dialing); September 13, 1973 (automatic billing); September 10, 1980 (touch tone).

[97] *GSN*, March 16, 1972 (citizens give opinions, including Nancy Schillereff, "I would like to see better movies here"); June 21, June 28, August 9, 1973 (comprehensive plan needed); September 13, 1973 (Mildred A. Beach); May 9 and 30, 1974 (questionnaire, etc.); July 4, 1974 (Santulli); September 26, 1974 (800 replies).

[98] *GSN*, September 6, 1978 (selectmen vote new plan); October 18, 1978 (details); 1979, December 9, 1979 (new survey); May 21, 1980 (none successful).

[99] *GSN*, May 17, 1973 (Erickson resigned); September 26, 1974 (rates, not quoted here, lowest was 1.8¢/KWH for volume); August 2, 1978 (1977 count; also 1978 about efficiency); March 28, 1979 (Seabrook).

[100] 1971 *Town Report* (central meeting place); *GSN*, March 9, 1972 (WAYS); November 1 and 8, 1973 (Vinnicombe); February 7, 1974 and other issues (KAPA).

[101] *GSN*, November 8, 1973 (Hallock); December 13, 1973 (work begun); July 4, 1974 (no keys, no move); July 25, 1974 (resolution); August 1, 1974 (open house announced); January 24, 1979 (roof).

[102] Letter to the author, December 2, 1994.

[103] *GSN*, January 16 and March 6, 1975 (land); July 27, 1977 (federal funds); October 21, 1976 (citizens' meeting; report by Kathy O'Meara); December 15, 1976 (Flierl); December 29, 1976 (Kimball); January 4, 1978 (contract); May 23, 1979 (announcement of opening); January 23, 1980 (Gehman biography); May 7 and September 17, 1980 (Friends). Also, note from Librarian Louise Gehman, January 10, 1995.

[104] Dr. Lawrence S. Toms, note to author, December 1994. "[The selectmen] were penny wise and pound foolish."

[105] *GSN*, January 19, August 31, October 19, October 26, and November 16, 1977; March 1, 15, July 12, 1978; June 11 and July 9, 1980; also *Town Report* issues of the era.

[106] *GSN*, January 3, 1974; September 19, 1974; December 22, 1976 (overhaul); June 30, 1979 (Osgood resignation). Also various *Town Reports*.

[107] *GSN*, December 30, 1971 (signs); April 17, 1972 (house numbering); April 27, 1972, January 11, 1973 (yellow lines); August 30, 1978 (no passing); January 18, 1973, January 25, 1973, and many other issues (bypass). North Conway was one of two regional towns often cited as an example of what Wolfeboro should not be; the other was The Weirs. At a later meeting of the state road commission held in Concord, a state commissioner said, "It will e a cold day in hell when the state spends a dime in Wolfeboro" (Dr. Lawrence S. Toms, note to author, December 1994). 1973 *Town Report* (scenic); *GSN*, August 10, 1977 (oil for Lang Pond Road); May 31, 1973 (map); July 18, 1974 (Kimball); September 12, December 10, 1979, and other issues (Pike).

[108] *GSN*, May 16, 1974 (W.H. Society); December 5, 1974 (Goodall); March 11, 1976 (Chase); May 22, 1975 (early start); June 5, 1975 (Thomson); January 22, 1976 (surfeit); June 17, 1976 (O'Meara); March 11, 1976 (Pineo research); June 29, 1977 (Stevens).

[109] *GSN*, August 19, 1976 (Apple Hill); October 15, 1980 (Springfield Point); February 21, 1979 (out-of-staters).

[110] *GSN*, April 19, 1973 (office moved); May 10, 1973 (Webb); August 13 and September 20, 1973 (new presses, etc.); October 14, 1976 (circulation).

[111] The Wolfeboro Rail Road spelled its name this way in its logo, but numerous various appeared in print including Wolfeboro Railroad, Wolfeborough Railroad, etc. Wolfeboro Rail Road is used here, although usage varied, as noted. To designate the depot, Wolfeborough Railroad Station nomenclature is used.

[112] Date supplied by R.C. Libby, Sr., letter, December 30, 1994; certain other accounts say December 17, 1972.

[113] Description of the television show by Ethelyn M. Brown, letter to her daughter Joyce on the day of the presentation, August 21, 1973 (copy furnished by Dr. Joyce E. Brown).

[114] Letter to her daughter Joyce, February 25, 1974 (copy provided by Dr. Joyce E. Brown).

[115] *GSN*, December 21, 1973 (track acquired); September 5, 1974 (20,000 carried); October 31, 1979 (sale announced); much information and some text is from a manuscript by Barbara Hobbie, "The Wolfeboro to Sanbornville Line: A 120-Year History of Local Motion"; Donald E.L. Hallock provided a scrapbook filled with illustrations and information. Information and some text concerning 1980 operations is from Richard Libby.

[116] *GSN*, October 24, 1974 (Amphibair); March 27, 1975 (Hildreth); July 5, 1978 (crash).

[117] *GSN*, April 6, 1972 (announcement); April 13, 1972 (special supplement featuring Huggins); April 20, 1972 (Waters commentary); July 10, 1975 (Sinclair biography; died in 1965 at age 97, had been a lifelong summer resident); November 4, 1976 (Boehm birds).

[118] *GSN*, September 27, 1973 (Telemed; Meals-On-Wheels); January 31, 1974 (finances); March 28, 1974 (new rates announced); July 6, 1977 (July 4th weekend).

[119] *GSN*, December 13, 1978; November 28, 1979 (Waters to retire; Good held a degree in hospital administration from Baylor University); January 16, 1980 (Good interview).

[120] *GSN*, September 28, 1977 ($2 million addition sought); June 18, 1978 and other issues (new addition; Bartsch was a former trustee who donated the land upon which the new facility was built); July 19, 1978 (ground-breaking); October 29, 1980 (Waters ceremony).

[121] *GSN*, May 27, 1971 (Weight Watchers); May 23, 1972 (nervous). Note: Mrs. House later changed the spelling of her first name to Jackie, then to Jacqui.

[122] *GSN*, May 24, 1978 (venereal disease); other information from *Town Reports*.

[123] Service (singular) in many citations; in 1994 listed as Services on the sign in front of its building on Bay Street.

[124] *GSN*, September 7, 1972 (CCMHS moved to Huggins); November 1, 1973 (Deykens); October 24, 1974 (suicide rate); November 26, 1980 (Mimi Dye; held degrees from Wellesley and Yale and had worked professionally at Yale before returning to Wolfeboro in March 1978); May 18, 1977 (urban vs. rural).

[125] *GSN*, October 7, 1971 (4 pieces of equipment); July 16, 1980 (Hallock); September 12, 26, 1974 (Monitor).

[126] *GSN*, November 11, 1971 (land); January 31, 1974 (Foss to resign); April 3, 1975 (Foss obituary); December 4, 1975 (stickers); February 5, 12, 1976 (Keniston resignation; also see 1976 *Town Report*); May 27 (chief, captain). Note: Ladder No. 1 was called Engine No. 1 in certain reports; however, Curtis A. Pike, letter, May 12, 1995, informed the author that "at the time we had no Engine No. 1; that should have been Ladder No. 1."

[127] *GSN*, September 30, 1971.

[128] *GSN*, March 2, 1972.

[129] 1972 *Town Report; GSN*, May 25, 1972. At first, it was believed that the fire was set as a diversionary tactic by bank burglars, as about the same time (c. 11:30 p.m.) a suspicious car was "flushed out" behind the Wolfeboro National Bank, given chase, but not captured.

[130] Dr. Lawrence S. Toms, note to author, December 1994.

[131] *GSN*, January 24, 1974.

[132] *GSN*, June 27, 1974. The Windrifter, earlier known as the General Wolfe, had just opened.

[133] *GSN*, July 4, 1974.

[134] *GSN*, September 12, 1974.

[135] *GSN*, January 2, 1975

[136] *GSN*, June 19, 1975.

[137] *Ibid.*

[138] *GSN*, June 27, 1975.

[139] *GSN*, July 3, 1975.

[140] *GSN*, September 18, 1975.

[141] *GSN*, October 9, 1975.

[142] *GSN*, November 27, 1975.

[143] *GSN*, December 4, 1975.

[144] *GSN*, February 19, 1976 (report of State Police Laboratory investigation).

[145] *GSN*, March 18, 1976.

[146] *GSN*, April 1, 1976 (report covered several fires).

[147] *GSN*, April 29, 1976.

[148] *GSN*, September 9, 1976.

[149] Dr. Kipp's notes.

[150] *GSN*, January 5, 1977.

[151] *Ibid.*

[152] L. Winston Hamm (father of Larry), letter, June 9, 1994; *GSN*, January 12, 1977.

[153] *GSN*, February 2, 1977.

[154] *GSN*, July 6, 1977.

[155] *GSN*, March 15, 1978.

[156] *GSN*, April 26, 1978. This heroic act received extensive praise from the citizenry.

[157] *GSN*, March 14, 1979.

[158] *GSN*, August 22, 1979.

[159] *GSN*, December 19, 1979.

[160] *GSN*, January 9, 1980.

[161] *GSN*, March 19, 1980.

[162] *GSN*, January 13, 1972 (McLaughlin);

[163] 1971 *Town Report*).

[164] *GSN*, September 21 and December 27, 1972.

[165] *GSN*, June 22, 1972 (cadets); July 12, 1973 and other issues (missing boys).

[166] *GSN*, April 25, 1974 (divorces); October 17, 1974 (Wright interview by Kathy O'Meara); May 9, 1974 (Varney); December 12, 1974 (Good Morning).

[167] *GSN*, August 20, 1977 (staff count); August 16, 1978 (Tierney); June 10, 1971 and November 1, 1978 (Stevens biography and appointment). Years later the 1988 *Town Report*, p. 142, told of Chief Wentworth's passing on October 18, 1988; he was born on May 1, 1915.

[168] *GSN*, May 16, 1979 (patch); *GSN*, June 5, 1979 and 1979 *Town Report* (radar).

[169] *GSN*, April 1, 1971; December 25, 1975; March 29, 1978.

[170] *GSN*, April 29 and June 3, 1971.

[171] *GSN*, July 15, 1971.

[172] *GSN*, November 11, 1971.

[173] *GSN*, March 23, 1972, and other issues.

[174] *GSN*, April 5, 12, 1973.

[175] *GSN*, June 7, 1973.

[176] *GSN*, August 23, 1973.

[177] *Ibid.*

[178] *GSN*, January 31, 1974; June 6, 1979.

[179] *GSN*, April 11, 1974 (arrest); October 17, 1974 (conviction).

[180] *GSN*, August 8, 1974.

[181] *GSN*, November 7, 1974 (detailed report of charges and counter-charges); November 6, 1975.

[182] *GSN*, September 11, 1975.

[183] *GSN*, October 23, 1975.

[184] *GSN*, April 19, 1976.

[185] August 5, 1976.

[186] *GSN*, September 16, 1976 (arrest); September 23, 1976 (indictment); November 17, 1976 (pleaded guilty, sentenced).

[187] *GSN*, March 30, 1977.

[188] *GSN*, September 21, 1977 (theft); September 28, 1977 (recovery).

[189] June 27, 1979.

[190] *GSN*, August 29, 1979.

[191] *GSN*, January 23, 1980.

[192] *GSN*, April 30, 1980.

[193] After the early 1980s Motorcycle Weekend became somewhat subdued and attracted a number of national sponsors. By that time it was viewed as a tourist draw rather than a civic nuisance.

[194] *GSN*, December 17, 1980. Years later in 1986, two brothers, one from Raymond, NH, and the other from Milford, CT, were indicted for the deed and later found guilty. Details in GSN, March 19, April 6, and November 18, 1986.

[195] *GSN*, September 2, 1971 (Doria; reports of outages and damage given by H.E. Erickson); August 31 (electrical storm); July 5, August 2 and August 16, 1973 (flooding); March 16, 1977 (more Clarke Plaza flooding).

[196] *GSN*, July 3, 1975 (electrical storm); January 22 and February 3, 1976 (lots of snow); January 12, 1977 (snow); February 8, 1978 (snow); February 6, 1980 (little snow); September 6, 1979 (hurricane David; did little damage; not quoted here; note for reference only).

[197] *GSN*, November 25, 1971, August 5, 26, 1976 (elms); January 29, 1976 (retrospective earthquake account); December 6, 1973 (Kohoutek); August 29, 1974 (UFOs); March 11, 1976 (West); August 8, 1974 and April 20 and June 15, 1977, and other issues (loons); February 23, 1977 (ducks); September 12, 1974 and June 4, 1980 (gypsy moths); May 28, 1980 (Mount St. Helens); August 13, 1980 (acid rain); September 17, 1980 (milfoil).

## NOTES FOR CHAPTER 11

[1] *GSN*, January 28, 1981 (mortgage rates; home sales slump).

[2] *GSN*, September 2, 9, 16, 1987 (Ballentine).

[3] Letter to the author, June 13, 1995.

[4] Information concerning dates, developers, number of units, etc., appears in Volume II under "Wolfeboro Place Names and Origins."

[5] *GSN*, January 14, 1987 (information about the Patten Corp., subdivider of over 800 acres in Carroll County; was 3rd best performing company on New York Stock Exchange in 1986).

[6] GSN, August 23, 1989. For background details see Barbara Hobbie's article in *The Laker*, July 1992, "Storybook Summons the Tone and Tenor of Christmas in the 1830s in Water Village."

[7] *GSN*, February 18, 1981 (unemployment); *GSN*, August 12, 1981 (upward trend); March 17, 1982 (gasoline); April 14, 1982 (DeVylder); June 16, 1982 (sidewalk sale); August 4, 1982 (June unemployment); August 8, 1984 (slow season); September 12, 1984 (building strong); January 2, 1985 (gasoline).

[8] *GSN*, April 3, 1985 (Brockhouse); April 24, 1985 (cottages); June 5, 1985 (Hayes); September 4, 1985 (summer business); April 9, 1986 (wages); July 9, 1986 (4th of July); September 10, 1986 (season report); *GSN*, November 4, 1987 (stock market, coins, etc.); August 31, 1988 (Maxfield); January 11, 1989 (incomes per Spiller Group statistics); January 25, 1989 (low snow); August 23, September 13, 1989 (real estate, rain); January 10, 1990 (Bean); February 28, 1990 (oil); May 30, 1990 (newspapers); November 28, 1990 (Sweaterville, etc.).

[9] Information from 1982 *Town Report;* Comment re: Mrs. Avery from remarks of the curator made at the time to the author.

[10] 1983-1990 *Town Reports; GSN*, May 25, 1983; March 14, 1984.

[11] *GSN*, January 26, 1983; February 1, 1984; January 29, 1986; January 28, 1987 (honors); January 25, 1989 (Excellence Award).

[12] *GSN*, June 6, 1984 (125th); June 20, 1984 (Webb); October 10, 1984 (Rooks); January 2, 1985 (Slack); December 26, 1984 (7 columns); April 23, 1986 (Colquhoun); December 17, 1986, January 14, 17, 1987 (local columnists).

[13] *GSN*, December 12, 1990 (Zelek appointed manager).

[14] *GSN*, April 29, May 13, June 10, 24, 1987.

[15] Cable TV items can be found in 1980-1984 *Town Report* issues as well as *GSN*, February 18, 25, March 4, 11, 18, April 8, May 6, 13, 20, July 8, 15, August 5, 19, September 23, October 28, November 25, 1981; February 10, March 17, 24, July 21, September 15, November 24, Dec, 1, 15, 1982; January 12, February 2, 16, March 16, 23, April 13, June 1, July 13, August 31, October 12, 26, December 7, 1983; January 25, April 18, July 25, November 14, 1984; April 17, July 24, August 14, 1985; January 8, 1986; February 25, 1987, and many other issues.

[16] *GSN*, June 20, 1990.

[17] *GSN*, August 5, 1987.

[18] *GSN*, February 21, March 7, 14, 1990.

[19] *GSN*, January 23, 1991 (pre-screening).

[20] *GSN*, May 6, 1981; April 21, May 5, June 23, 1982.

[21] Darlene Williams' musical and other accomplishments were detailed in a biographical article, "'Allegro' Best Describes the Tempo of Williams' Life," by Melissa Sauer, the *Granite Extra*, May 6, 1994.

[22] *GSN*, January 7, 1981.

[23] *GSN*, January 14, 21, 28; February 4, 1981.

[24] *GSN*, February 4, 1981.

[25] *GSN*, February 18, 1981.

[26] *GSN*, April 15, 1981.

[27] *GSN*, April 22, 1981 (these two players were pictured).

[28] *GSN*, May 20, June 17, 1981.

[29] *GSN*, July 15, 1981.

[30] *Ibid.*

[31] *GSN*, August 5, 12, 1981.

[32] *GSN*, October 21, 1981.

[33] *GSN*, October 28, 1981.

[34] *GSN*, December 2, 1981.

[35] *GSN*, January 6, 1982.

[36] *GSN*, February 24, 1982.

[37] *GSN*, March 3, 1982.

[38] *GSN*, March 10, 1982.

[39] *GSN*, March 31, 1982.

[40] *GSN*, April 28, 1982.

[41] *GSN*, July 7, 1982.

[42] *GSN*, June 30, 1982.

[43] *GSN*, August 4, 1982.

[44] *GSN*, August 25, 1982.

[45] *GSN*, November 10, 1982.

[46] *Ibid.*

[47] *GSN*, February 16, 23, 1983.

[48] *GSN*, February 2, 1983 (announcement).

[49] *GSN*, March 16, 1983.

[50] *GSN*, May 4, 1983.

[51] *GSN*, May 11, 1983.

[52] *GSN*, May 18, 1983 (announcement; photo of Jill Pralle).

[53] *GSN*, July 6, 1983.

[54] *GSN*, July 13, 1983 (filming had occurred on July 5).

[55] *GSN*, August 3, 1983.

[56] *GSN*, July 20, 1983.

[57] *GSN*, August 10, 1983. Storyland is in Glen, NH.

[58] *GSN*, August 17, 1983.

[59] *GSN*, November 9, 1983.

[60] *GSN*, October 19, 1983.

[61] *GSN*, November 23, 1983 (article).

[62] *GSN*, February 15, 1984.

[63] *GSN*, April 18, 1984.

[64] *GSN*, May 16, 1984.

[65] *GSN*, May 23, 1984.

[66] *GSN*, July 4, 1984.

[67] *GSN*, October 10, 1984.

[68] *GSN*, December 26, 1984.

[69] *GSN*, April 3, 1985.

[70] *GSN*, April 10, 1985.

[71] *GSN*, April 24, 1985.

[72] *GSN*, April 24, 1985; also Judson Hale, letter to author.

[73] *GSN*, September 11, 1985.

[74] *GSN*, October 23, 1985.

[75] *GSN*, February 5, 12, 1986.

[76] *GSN*, March 19, 1986.

[77] *GSN*, May 7, 1986.

[78] *GSN*, July 23, 1986.

[79] *Ibid.*

[80] *GSN*, September 10, 1986.

[81] *Ibid.*

[82] *GSN*, October 1, 1986.

[83] *GSN*, December 10, 1986.

[84] *GSN*, April 8, 1987.

[85] *GSN*, April 29, 1987.

[86] *GSN*, July 1, 1987.

[87] *GSN*, August 12, 1987.

[88] *GSN*, September 2, 1987.

[89] *GSN*, December 2, 1987.

[90] *GSN*, December 23, 1987.

[91] *GSN*, March 30, 1988.

[92] *GSN*, May 11, 1988.

[93] *Ibid.*

[94] *GSN*, May 25, 1988, and other issues; personal recollection of author.

[95] *GSN*, June 8, 1988.

[96] *GSN*, July 6, 1988.

[97] *GSN*, July 13, 1988.

[98] *GSN*, July 27, 1988.

[99] *GSN*, August 17, 1988.

[100] *GSN*, August 24, 1988.

[101] *GSN*, September 21, 1988.

[102] *GSN*, August 24, 1988.

[103] *GSN*, November 9, 1988.

[104] *GSN*, December 7, 1988.

[105] *GSN*, January 11, February 1, 8, 15, 1989.

[106] *GSN*, March 29, 1989.

[107] Letter from Darlene (Williams) Hanington to the author, June 20, 1995; here lightly edited.

[108] *GSN*, July 26, August 23, 1989.

[109] *GSN*, September 13, October 18, 1989.

[110] *GSN*, December 20, 1989.

[111] *GSN*, January 24, March 14 (new schedule), 1990.

[112] *GSN*, April 11, 18, 25, 1990.

[113] *GSN*, May 9, 1990.

[114] *GSN*, May 16, 1990.

[115] *Ibid.*

[116] *GSN*, June 27, 1990.

[117] *GSN*, July 25, 1990.

[118] *GSN*, August 22, 1990.

[119] *GSN*, October 3, 1990.

[120] *GSN*, August 29, 1990..

[121] Commentary to the author by Wilma ("Willie") Mork, July 1995, who considered this to be her favorite of the Village Players productions.

[122] *GSN*, November 28, 1990.

[123] *GSN*, January 28, March 11, 1981; March 21, 1984; March 6, 1985; February 5, 1986; February 25, 1987; town records (elections).

[124] 1984 *Town Report.*

[125] *GSN*, July 3, 1985 (search for Guy L. Krapp's replacement; hiring of Spinney); February 7, 1990 (Spinney to retire); April 4, 18, 25, May 23, 1990 (seeking a new town manager); June 13, 1990 (list of 24).

[126] *GSN*, January 4, 1984 (bonus); January 11, 1984 (union representatives); March 28, 1984 (union); May 9, 1984 (union); March 21, 1984 (Jones, Waterman); October 3, 1984 (unfair); October 17, 1984 (not good faith); January 23, May 1, July 10, 1985 (negotiations).

[127] 1982 *Town Report* and other sources.

[128] *GSN*, April 28, 1982 (dogs).

[129] *GSN*, January 12, February 2, April 27, June 8, 1983 (computer).

[130] *GSN*, July 13, 1983 (Hatch, Scully).

[131] 1985 *Town Report; GSN*, March 13, September 25, October 16, 1985 (Walsh).

[132] *GSN*, June 11, 30, 1986; April 1, July 1, 29, 1987; March 30, September 28, October 12, December 21, 1988.

133 Descriptions and details of these properties are found in Volume II under "Wolfeboro Place Names and Origins." Also see 1991 *Town Report.*

134 *GSN,* June 28, 1989.

135 1989 *Town Report.*

136 *GSN,* April 4, May 9, July 11, 1990.

137 1981 *Town Report* (1981 Master Plan); *GSN,* January 27, 1982 (capital improvement); July 14, 1982 (79 signs).

138 *GSN,* January 11, 1984 (re-write); June 13, 1984 (entirely replace); June 26, 1985 (Clarke); January 15, 1986 (fee increase); March 5, 1986 (moratorium); March 26, 1986 (errors, overload); April 9, 30, 1986 (hotels inadvertently banned); *GSN,* June 16, 1986, and 1986 *Town Report* (Kraft-Lund).

139 *GSN,* November 26, 1986 ("Revisited"); December 24, 1986 (25 amendments); March 11, 1987 (details of zoning election results); March 11, July 1, 1987 (questionnaire); April 1, 1987 (Scott); July 8, 1987 (overworked); January 29, August 19, 1987 (Reade); September 30, 1987 (Kraft-Lund's plan); December 16, 1987 (Hopewell).

140 *GSN,* February 22, 1989 (Skinner hired).

141 *GSN,* July 18, 1990.

142 *GSN,* October 27, 1982 (Shannon's); February 9, March 23, June 1, August 10, 1983; February 14, June 6, 1984, and many other issues (North Conway Lumber); April 13, 27, July 13, 1983, January 27, 1987, and other issues (gravel pits); February 15, 1984 (nursing homes); August 15, 1984 (condo shorefront); September 12, 1984 (missing plans); October 24, 1984 (eliminate commercial zoning); December 19, 1984, and other issues (32,000 square feet); March 13, 1985 (Clarke Plaza).

143 *GSN,* June 12, August 14, November 13, 1985 (pizza-sub shop); May 15, June 12, November 13, 1985 (Carriage House); April 24, May 22, 29, June 12, 26, July 10, 1985, and other issues (Baker); May 21, 28, October 15, 29, November 5, 1986, and many other issues (RV park); January 15, 1986, June 24, 1987, and other issues (Narrows); January 15, 29, February 5, 1986, and other issues (48 units); February 5, 1986 (Clipper); February 19, 1986 (Nowell); May 7, 1986 (footbridge); October 8, 1986 (noise); October 15, 1986 (Stonelodge); September 2, November 4, 1987 (POW); July 1, 1987 (Steven Hunter); November 18, 1987 (land bank).

144 *GSN,* April 2, 1980 (United Appraisal selected); April 22, 1981 (appraisal methods discussed); July 8, 1981 (4,700 properties); December 30, 1981 (mistakes); February 17, 1982 ($5,000 refund); February 25, 1987 (another call); March 16, 1988 (Moody); October 25, 1989 (Avitar; rate drop); August 22, 1990 (progress report; 85% completed); October 17, 1990 (final report); November 28, 1990 (Turner, Eaton).

145 Letter to selectmen dated October 26, 1990, in author's file.

146 By John Marshall (1745-1835) in McCulloch vs. Maryland, 1819.

147 *GSN,* May 20, 1981; May 12, 1982; May 18, 1983, and other issues (divers).

148 *GSN,* September 23, 1981; May 26, 1982 (island trash); February 8, 1984; May 1, 1985; July 16, 1986; July 22, 1987 (incinerator); September 26, 1984; January 9, 1985; October 23, 1985 (ducks).

149 *GSN,* January 21, 1981 (high marks); September 16, 1981 (triple); June 30, 1982 (more improvements); March 13, 1985, and other issues (Sewall Road); December 23, 1987 ($2,500); also various *Town Reports* of the decade.

150 *GSN,* February 14, 1990; also *New Hampshire Premier,* October 1992, "Haste Makes Waste: A Yankee Tale," by Elissa K. Paquette.

151 *GSN,* January 14, 1981 (2nd lowest); January 19, 1983 (outage); May 16, 1984 (Erickson); February 27, 1985, April 3, May 1, October 9, 1985 (planning for the future); July 8, 1987 (recollection of Parker effort); January 21, 1987 (substation); February 11, 1987 (reduction); April 22, 1987 (increase); August 19, 1987 (astronomical); other issues.

152 *GSN,* December 30, 1981 (old pipes); July 7, 1982 (Pike); 1982 *Town Report* (gallonage); *GSN,* March 9, April 27, August 31, October 26, 1983 (cleaning, etc.); January 29, 1986 (leak); 1988 *Town Report* (bills).

153 Much information concerning the line and certain text are from Richard C. Libby, Sr., local railroad historian.

154 *GSN,* May 26, 1982 (railfans scheduled); July 11, 1984 (600 riders, etc.); January 15, 22, February 6, March 5, June 25, 1986 (cessation of business; disposal of stock); November 19, 1986 (recreation); December 23, 1987 (state offer to sell).

155 *GSN,* April 22, 1987 (insurance, licensing, etc.); June 17, 1987 (plan in progress); June 24, 1987 (first service); July 29, 1987 (description of riders). Also 1987 *Town Report.*

156 *GSN,* February 4, June, 10, 1981, and other issues (Michaud); July 17, 1985, and other issues (C&J).

157 *GSN,* July 22, 1981 (air resort); November 16, 1988 (Eleanor Horn obituary); July 5, 1989 (94%; Eleanor Horn memorial); November 7, 1984 (paint stripe); December 19, 1984 (19 planes).

158 1981 *Town Report.*

159 *GSN,* May 16, 1990 (move to VT).

160 *GSN,* May 25, 1983 (stars); May 14, 1986 (vs. Kennett); June 8, 1988 (1988 season); June 1, 1988 (vs. Oyster River); June 27, 1984 (Babe Ruth); July 1, 1987 (1987 season); June 8, 1988 (Ben Franklin); August 2, 1989 (Beaulieu); July 5, 1989 (IGA); July 28, August 18, 1982 (W.W.S. Team).

161 *GSN,* January 14, 1981 (opponents listed); January 28, 1981 (G. Dollarhide); March 11, 1981 (J. Southard); March 17, 31, 1982 (W-T Y.B. League); November 30, 1983 (alumni); January 30, 1985 (vs. Pembroke); February 13, 1985 (vs. Kennett); April 2, 1986 (MVPs); December 6, 1989 (vs. Merrimack Valley).

162 *GSN,* April 17, 1985 (1985 L.R. championship); March 9, 1988 (Class B championship); February 15, 1989 and other issues (N.E.S.P.S. championship); February 14, March 7, 1990, and other issues (1990 season).

163 *GSN,* March 27, 1985 (Patriots); July 26, August 16, 1989 (Soviets).

164 *GSN,* August 31, 1983 (bike tour); September 23, 1987; June 29, August 13, 1988; September 6, 20, 1989; August 1, 1990 (Flagg victories).

165 *GSN,* May 19, 1982; May 23, 1984 (Bean brothers);July 21, 1982 (Flagg); May 18, September 21, 1988; May 24, 31, 1989 (Kissell); May 9, 23, 1990 (1990 race).

166 *GSN,* December 18, 1985.

167 Roster furnished by Bonnie Rankin Lord, letter, July 17, 1995. Listed alphabetically.

168 *GSN,* November 13, 1985 (Division AA); October 24, 1990 (12-1-1); October 1, November 5, 12, 1986 (Brewster).

169 *GSN,* February 4, 1987.

170 *GSN,* October 21, 1981 (Fontaine); July 21, 1982 (Doug Skelley); December 19, 1984 (6 Knights); December 23, 1987 (Doran, Webster); January 4, 1989 (David Skelley); July 18, 1990 (McBride); December 19, 1990 (jackets to victors).

171 *GSN,* July 15, 22, 1981 (Newth); August 26, 1981 (Cindy Melanson); September 2, 1981 (Jay Pollini, John Thurston); June 23, 1982 (Pollini, Melanson, Thayer, Antonucci); September 1, 1982 (Sweeney vs. Melanson); August 31, 1983 (Antonucci); July 25, 1985 (Kingswood High); September 11, 1985 (Jim Pollini); September 17, 1986 (Bill Sweeney hole-in-1); October 14, 1987 (state title); October 12, 1988 (2nd state title); June 15, 1988 (Salley Reynolds hole-in-1); August 31, 1988 (Antonucci vs. Hughes); October 12, 1988 (2nd state title); September 26, 1990 (Sweeney hole-in-1).

172 *GSN,* July 1, 22, 1981; additional information concerning the settlement and other Kingswood historical items is from the booklet, *Kingswood Golf Club 75th Anniversary,* p. 6.

173 *GSN,* August 16, 1989.

174 Dow, of Tuftonboro, had been killed during a winter rescue attempt on Mount Washington. This tragedy fueled a debate as to whether professionals such as Dow should risk their lives to try to save mountain climbers and others who often went up the peak in the winter without taking proper safety precautions.

175 *GSN,* September 12, 1984; September 11, 1985; August 31, 1988; August 30, 1989.

176 *GSN,* February 11, 1981.

177 *GSN,* August 12, 1981.

178 *GSN,* May 4, 1988.

179 *GSN,* June 3, 17, 1981 (derby); January 24, 1990 (salmon). Ronald Paquette provided information in a discussion with the author.

180 *GSN,* January 20, 1988; Fish and Game Commission estimate by Kristine Klein.

181 *GSN,* January 19, 1983 (Fellows); March 20, 1985, and March 9, 1989 (Long Distance).

182 *GSN,* July 31, 1985; December 11, 1985; January 15, February 5, 12, 19, 26, 1986; January 21, 1987; other issues.

183 *GSN,* December 16, 1981 (Hastings); March 2, November 9, 1983 (year's activities); January 18, 1984 (vs. North Conway); February 26, 1986 (Mites undefeated); December 9, 1987 (Midget win); March 2, 1988 (Squirt A and B teams); February 8, 1989 (vs. York); January 3, 1990 (vs. Tritons); March 7, 1990 (vs. North Conway).

184 *GSN,* December 28, 1988; January 4, March 22, 1989. The 1988 *Town Report* has additional information.

185 *GSN,* December 2, 1987.

186 *GSN,* January 15, 1986 (Varney); May 27, 1987 (Palm); October 17, 1990 (Breuninger).

187 *GSN,* July 28, 1982 (Rust Pond); June 28, 1989 (NH rules); July 12, 1989 (protesters meet); August 16, 1989 (banned); August 23, 1989 (defenders).

188 *GSN,* April 11, 1990. Historical information was provided by Bette Bourque, June 1995, especially for this volume.

189 *GSN,* April 26, May 10, 1989.

190 *GSN,* August 26, 1987.

191 *GSN,* May 16, 1990. Contemporary accounts of the Harvard-Yale contest encountered by the author mention Centre Harbor, but not Wolfeboro.

192 *GSN,* May 9, 1990.

193 *GSN,* May 20, 1981, May 9, 1984 (Brewster); *GSN,* July 15, 1981 (Kenney Shore); August 19, 1981 (Regatta; Stamp Act); August 17, 1983 (3rd annual).

194 *GSN,* September 20, 1989; July 4, August 1, 15, 22, 1990.

195 *GSN,* August 7, 1985.

196 *GSN,* July 25, 1990.

197 *GSN,* January 7, 14, 1981 (Gilford, North Conway).

198 *GSN,* January 22, 1986 (vs. Kennett, Plymouth); January 29, 1986 (Hanover); March 12, 1986 (Douglass to CA); March 4, 1987 (Douglass to AK); September 5, 1990 (Douglass at Middlebury).

199 *GSN,* February 11, 1981; December 30, 1981; February 10, March 10, 1982; March 23, 1983; February 1, 1984.

200 *GSN,* January 12, 1983 (X-C Association); January 22, 1986 (lessons in telemarking).

201 *GSN,* February 10, 1982 (Hatch); March 18, 1987 (Mynter); February 3, 1988 (Kingswood alpine skiers); March 2, 1988 (skimeisters; includes some from nearby towns).

202 *GSN,* January 20, 1982; personal attendance of author.

203 *GSN,* December 3, 1986 (Daley, Andrews); November 18, 1987 (Andrews); November 7, 1990 (W-T team); December 7, 1988 (Brewster).

204 *GSN,* August 19, 1987.

205 *GSN,* September 2, 1981 (Windrifter); July 25, 1984 (8th season); August 20, 1986 (Dover); August 19, 1987 (Dover); August 19, 1987 (Dover).

206 *GSN,* August 18, 1982 (Open); July 24, 1985 (Open); August 27, 1986 (Springfield); April 20, 1988; April 26, 1989 (Kingswood); May 17, 1989 (Brewster).

207 *GSN,* May 27, 1981 (championship); June 1, 1983 (Hogan); July 18, 1984 (Hershey); September 26, November 14, 1984 (Keslar); June 5, 1985 (Kingswood girls undefeated); May 31, 1989 (Donovan); May 4, 1988 (marathon); July 20, 1988; August 1, 22, 1990 (first page), and other issues (Sands).

208 Letter, July 31, 1995.

209 *GSN,* June 20, 1990.

210 *GSN,* February 4, July 22, August 5, 1981 (Back Bay); August 17, 1983 (show); September 5, 1984; June 18, 1986 (A.W.S.A.); June 21, 1989 (slalom); June 27, 1990 (Montpelier);

September 12, 1990 (Avon). In addition, certain information was supplied by William Swaffield, letter, June 23, 1995.

[211] *GSN*, November 28, 1990.

[212] *GSN*, March 14, 1984.

[213] *GSN*, January 21, 1981; March 14, 1984 (Burt, Nachman); February 15, 1989 (Stinchfield).

[214] 1982 *Town Report* (museum, etc.); *GSN*, March 18, 25, 1981 (Carroll County No. 2); July 7, 1982 (dedication).

[215] *GSN*, April 15, June 17, 1981 (fire boat); 1981 *Town Report* (wood stoves, alarms); *GSN*, September 1, October 27, December 15, 1982 (kerosene).

[216] From Fire Department records supplied by Philip H. Morrill, Jr.; copies of letters signed by Town Manager Guy L. Krapp and attorney Frederic L. Cox.

[217] *GSN*, September 26, 1984.

[218] *GSN*, December 10, 1986 (quoted Governor's Energy Office).

[219] 1987 *Town Report* ($275,000).

[220] *GSN*, March 30, 1988 (Kipp); May 18, 1988 (fireworks); October 4, 1989 (old firehouse).

[221] 1990 *Town Report* (activity).

[222] Dr. Kipp's log continued through 1985; entries used but not individually cited here.

[223] *GSN*, March 11, 1981.

[224] *GSN*, May 27, 1981.

[225] *GSN*, June 10, 1981.

[226] *GSN*, July 8, 1981.

[227] *GSN*, August 19, 26, November 4 (sentencing of one perpetrator), and December 16 (sentencing of the other perpetrator), 1981.

[228] *GSN*, November 25, 1981.

[229] *GSN*, December 30, 1981.

[230] *GSN*, March 10, 1982.

[231] *GSN*, April 7, 1982.

[232] *GSN*, April 14, 1982. Date of published account; date of fire was earlier.

[233] *GSN*, August 25, 1982.

[234] *GSN*, November 17, 1982.

[235] *GSN*, December 1, 1982.

[236] *GSN*, April 20, 1983. Also see later entry for October 9, 1990, fire at the Caswell residence.

[237] *GSN*, August 17, 1983.

[238] *GSN*, November 9, 1983 (there as Skaterdas cottage); Dr. W. Douglas Kipp fire journal (as Ashby Camp).

[239] *GSN*, January 4, 1984.

[240] *GSN*, February 15, 1984; Fire Department Records supplied by Lt. Philip H. Morrill, Jr.

[241] *GSN*, August 29, 1984.

[242] *GSN*, September 5, 1984.

[243] *GSN*, October 10, 1984.

[244] *GSN*, December 26, 1984.

[245] *GSN*, February 13, 1985.

[246] *GSN*, April 3, 10 (photo), 17, 1985.

[247] *GSN*, July 24 and August 14, 1985; also, Roberta French commentary to author.

[248] *GSN*, September 4, 1985.

[249] *GSN*, September 18, 1985.

[250] This is the last entry in Dr. W. Douglas Kipp's fire journal. Also *GSN*, September 25, 1985.

[251] *GSN*, December 4, 1985.

[252] *GSN*, December 25, 1985.

[253] Photo and caption, *GSN*, January 8, 1986.

[254] *GSN*, March 12, 1986.

[255] *GSN*, May 21, 1986.

[256] *Ibid.*

[257] *GSN*, July 23, 1986.

[258] *GSN*, September 10, 1986.

[259] From Fire Department records supplied by Philip H. Morrill, Jr.

[260] *GSN*, June 3, August 12, 1987.

[261] *GSN*, July 8, 1987.

[262] *GSN*, July 29, October 28, 1987.

[263] From Fire Department records supplied by Philip H. Morrill, Jr.

[264] *GSN*, June 29, 1988.

[265] *GSN*, August 3, 1988.

[266] *GSN*, November 16, 1988.

[267] *GSN*, February 15, 1989.

[268] *GSN*, March 15, 1989.

[269] *GSN*, April 11, 1990.

[270] *GSN*, June 20, 27, 1990.

[271] From Fire Department records supplied by Philip H. Morrill, Jr. Also see earlier listing for April 12, 1983, fire.

[272] From Fire Department records supplied by Philip H. Morrill, Jr.

[273] *GSN*, January 2, 1991.

[274] *GSN*, March 30, April 6, June 8, 1988.

[275] 1987, 1990, and other *Town Report* issues.

[276] *GSN*, June 3, 1987. Also conversation between the author and Lance Durgan.

[277] Definition quoted from 1983 *Town Report*, p. 78.

[278] *GSN*, November 14, 28, 1990 (more bomb threats).

[279] *GSN*, December 16, 30, 1981; May 9, 16, November 14, 1984; June 12, 1985; December 14, 1988; October 25, 1989—bomb scare reports. October 13, 1982 (Tylenol).

[280] *GSN*, July 20, 1983.

[281] *GSN*, September 7, 1988.

[282] *GSN*, February 28, 1990 (Fox TV).

[283] *GSN*, February 17, 1982 (cord across snow path); January 21, 1981 (Camelot); March 3, 1982 (tires slashed); August 18, 1982 (telephone line); January 12, 1983 (mailbox; Christmas lights); December 3, 17, 1986 (tree); August 27, 1986 (23-year-old); September 23, 1981 (18-year-old); December 16, 1987 ($4,000 worth of windows); June 23 and July 7, 1982 (21-year-old); November 5, 1986 (child abuse).

[284] *GSN*, April 6, July 6, 20, 27, November 16, 1983; April 4, October 3, 1984; April 22, 1987.

[285] *GSN*, May 20, 1987 (Task Force); also see history of the Harbor House separately in Volume II.

[286] *GSN*, May 2, 1990.

[287] *GSN*, October 30, 1985.

[288] *GSN*, September 2, October 28, November 4, 1981; January 19, 26, April 20, 27, June 8, August 3, September 25, 1983; January 4, 1984; September 25, 1985; and other issues including reports of unsuccessful appeals. An interview with Barham was printed in *GSN*, December 9, 1987. He had been a model prisoner and was a columnist for the "Monitor Forum."

[289] *GSN*, April 15, 22, May 13, 1981.

[290] *GSN*, June 3, 1981.

[291] *GSN*, November 25, 1981 ($2,000); September 2, 1981 (fight).

[292] *GSN*, October 6, 1982 (3 clothing shops); October 20, 1982 ($3,100); August 10, 1983 ($110,000); January 25 and February 1, 1984 (Porsche); May 22, 29, and July 17, 1985 ($19,000); February 15, 1984 (purse); February 8, 15, 1989 (Granite State).

[293] *GSN*, June 27, 1990.

[294] 1985 *Town Report.*

[295] *GSN*, October 21, 1981 (Jutras); November 4, 1981 (4 deaths); October 26, 1983 (Carlson); January 2, 16, 23, 1985, and June 5, 1985 (Jones); May 28, 1986 (Brown); June 24, 1987 (Geer); November 11, 1987 (Stevens); May 31, 1989 (Whitfield).

[296] *GSN*, January 2, 16, 23, 1985; January 8 and May 14, 1986 (Labbe and extensive follow-up including legal actions); November 23, 1983 (Task Force).

[297] *GSN*, November 6, 1985 (Fothergill); November 13 and November 20, December 18, 1985 (SADD).

[298] *GSN*, March 25, 1981 (13-yr.-old); October 5, 1983 (up in smoke); September 4, 1985 (Effingham).

[299] *GSN*, September 7, 21, October 5, 26, 1988 (sting); July 12, 1989 (DWI crackdown); August 2, 23, 1989 (2 killed); August 9, 1989 (drug arrests); August 30, September 27, 1989 (sting).

[300] *GSN*, August 1, 1990.

[301] *GSN*, February 10, 1982 ("Shared Dispatching in Wolfeboro"; included quotations from the magazine, *Emergency Communicator*). Other sources.

[302] *GSN*, November 7, 1990 (Kinmond).

[303] 1984-1985 *Town Reports.*

[304] *GSN*, December 2, 1987 (Christmas); September 14, 1988 ($1,000).

[305] *GSN*, November 22, 1989.

[306] *GSN*, December 6, 20, 1989.

[307] *GSN*, July 4, 1990, and other issues.

[308] 1990 *Town Report.*

[309] *GSN*, Dec 30, 1981; January 6, 13, 20, March 17, April 14, 1982. The ornate two-story Hutchins carriage house was subsequently replaced by a one-story version.

[310] *GSN*, September 1, 1982 (high winds); August 3, 24, 1983 (high winds); November 30, 1983 (Douglass); June 6, 13, 20, 27, 1984 (high water); May 1, 8, 15, June 12, July 3, 31, August 14, 1985 (drought).

[311] *GSN*, October 2, 23, 1985; 1985 *Town Report.*

[312] *GSN*, October 8, 1986 (waves); June 3, 10, 17, 1987 (lightning).

[313] *GSN*, May 27, June 10, 24, September 23, October 21, 1981; April 28, June 2, July 28, September 1, 1982.

[314] *GSN*, January 20, 1982.

[315] *GSN*, November 13, 1985; March 26, 1986.

[316] *GSN*, April 16, 1986.

[317] *GSN*, January 28, 1987 (rescue of an injured loon on Rust Pond by Rick Hesslein and Joyce Meck; one of many loon accounts of the era).

[318] *GSN*, April 22, 1987; June 8, 1988.

[319] 1981 *Town Report.*

[320] 1982 *Town Report* comment by John Foley, D.O.; December 1, 1982; January 26, 1983 (no head lice cases at Carpenter School, but two in New Durham); January 11, 1984 (low-grade problem at Carpenter).

[321] *GSN*, March 10, 1982.

[322] December 12, 1990 (giardiasis), and other issues. A later issue of *GSN*, June 26, 1991, gave extensive details of "swimmer's itch," a.k.a. "duck itch."

[323] *GSN*, March 5, 1986.

324 *GSN*, December 26, 1984; December 3, 1986; January 7, 1987.

325 *GSN*, October 26, 1988 (history); May 23, 1990.

326 *GSN*, June 8, 1988.

327 Names and biographical notes are given in Volume III.

328 *GSN*, April 2, 1986.

329 *GSN*, February 4, 1981 (nurse's pay; resignations); February 25, 1981 (raises); June 24, 1981 (MacLeod); March 16, 1983 (ultrasound); May 4, 1983 (birthing); February 1, 29, 1984 (new equipment); October 9, 1985 (Zeiss); October 7, 1987 (C.A.T.).

330 *GSN*, February 26, 1986 (gift shop); April 8, 1987 (no smoking).

331 *GSN*, November 4, 1987.

332 *GSN*, March 15, 1989.

333 *GSN*, October 11, 1989.

334 *GSN*, November 3, 1982.

335 *GSN*, June 1, 1988.

336 *GSN*, June 8, 1983 (4th of July); *GSN*, February 29, 1984 (primary results).

337 *GSN*, November 14, 1984.

338 *GSN*, January 23, 1985 (Bush visit planned); June 26, July 3, 1985 (Bush schedule given); July 10, 1985 (report of Bush visit); personal experience of author during Bush visit; June 10, 1987 (Haig schedule); July 1, 8, August 27, 1986 (Dole in town); October 21, 1987 (Simon schedule); October 14, December 9, 1987 (duPont); personal experience of author (Kemp reception); February 17, 1988 (Bush visit; final primary vote tally); November 8, 1988 (election results).

## NOTES FOR CHAPTER 12

1 Radio WEVO, 89.1 FM, Concord, July 24, 1993.

2 *GSN*, January 9, 1991 ("bust"); 1991 (life in real estate market); May 15, 1991 (money scarce); May 22, 1991 (Beckwith); August 7, 1991 (39 homes); October 16, 1991 (employment); November 6, 1991 (heat); November 6, 1991, and other issues (Smith & Kourian).

3 *GSN*, August 25, 1993 (Farmers' Market); September 15, 1993 (Hemenway); July 13, 1993 (Phoenix).

4 Cf. Enda S. Slack, *The Laker*, November 15, 1993.

5 This list represents advertisers in *The Community Phone Book*, 1994. In addition, many individuals held real estate licenses.

6 *GSN*, January 5, 1994 (Williams); March 3, 1993 (ferrets).

7 *GSN*, January 9, April 10, 1991; January 15, 22, April 1, 1992.

8 1994 *Town Report.*

9 *GSN*, March 24, 31, May 5, June 30, 1993; *Union Leader*, September 20, 1993.

10 *GSN*, January 30, March 27, April 10, June 26, November 6, December 25, 1991; September 23, October 21, 1992; October 13, 1993, and other issues; *Lakes Region Courier*, July 28, 1994, and other issues.

11 September 6, 1993; here excerpted.

12 Includes only members of the Chamber; other lodging places, rooming houses, etc., are not listed.

13 *GSN*, July 1, 1992 (feature article by Mark Smith detailed history of The Loft); other issues.

14 In 1995 Jim Clark set up Wolfe's Borough Coffee, a roasting facility on Lehner Street, which may provide a story for some future chronicler of the town. The same facility was used to make C. Atwood Coffee, packaged with a "Roasted in Wolfeboro" notation, a flavorful brew marketed by Christopher A(twood) Lomas and sold through regional stores.

15 *GSN*, May 11, 1994 (an example of an issue carrying letters for and against—mostly against—the new drug store). Follow-up note: Tobey's closed its doors in June 1995; its prescription business was bought by Rite Aid.

16 Listing from advertisers in *The Community Phone Book*, 1994, the NYNEX telephone directory, and other listings.

17 Listing from advertisers in *The Community Phone Book*, 1994. In addition there were many regional attorneys—including in Ossipee—who had clients in town.

18 *GSN*, October 2, 9, 16, 1991; January 2, 1992.

19 *GSN*, April 3, June 5, September 25, 1991; September 9, December 31, 1992; January 27, May 26, 1993; other issues; also annual stockholders' reports.

20 *GSN*, February 27, 1991; February 3, 1993; *Lakes Region Courier*, May 12, 1994.

21 *GSN*, January 5, 1994 (*Times* sold).

22 *GSN*, July 15, 1992 (Tempest); September 9, 1992 (Bedford); June 30, 1993 (awards); February 2, 1994 (NE awards).

23 *GSN*, August 26, 1992; June 2, 9, 16, August 11, September 1, 1993, and many other issues.

24 *GSN*, January 23, 1991.

25 1993 and 1994 *Town Reports*; *GSN*, February 16, March 2, March 16, April 6, 1994, and other issues. (Discussion of the book project is limited here as it is amply discussed in the introduction to the present volume.)

26 1991-1994 *Town Reports* (attendance, programs); *GSN*, August 19, 1992 (80th); October 28, 1992, and April 21, 1993 (raccoons).

27 *GSN*, December 15, 1993 (description of erroneous classification of the facility as a "place of public assembly," when it should have been called a museum under C-2 zoning; also, inscriptions on side of building were said to violate a sign ordinance); January 5, 1994 (special exception obtained); January 19, 1994 (heavy snow collapses one of the old Diamond International buildings).

28 *GSN*, January 23, 1991.

29 *GSN*, February 6, February 13, 1991. Also December 18, 1991 (noted that lack of interest forced cancellation of 1992 event).

30 *GSN*, February 6, 1991.

31 *GSN*, March 20, 1991.

32 *GSN*, April 10, 1991.

33 *GSN*, April 3, 1991.

34 *GSN*, April 24, 1991.

35 *GSN*, May 22, 29, June 5, 12, July 10, 1991.

36 *GSN*, July 10, 1991.

37 *GSN*, July 3, 1991.

38 *Ibid.*

39 *GSN*, July 17, 1991.

40 *GSN*, June 12, 1991.

41 *GSN*, July 3, 1991.

42 *GSN*, August 7, 1991.

43 *GSN*, October 9, 1991.

44 *GSN*, October 23, 1991.

45 *GSN*, November 6, 1991.

46 *GSN*, November 13, 1991.

47 *GSN*, November 20, 1991; January 1, 1992.

48 *GSN*, March 11, 1992.

49 *GSN*, April 1, 1992.

50 *GSN*, July 29, 1992.

51 *GSN*, July 1, 15, 1992.

52 *GSN*, August 5, 1992.

53 *GSN*, July 29, September 2, 1992; letter from Darlene (Williams) Hanington to the author, June 20, 1995.

54 *GSN*, August 5, 1992. "Dances With Werewolves" was a parody on the title of a popular film, *Dances With Wolves*, starring Kevin Costner.

55 *GSN*, September 16, 1992.

56 *GSN*, March 24, 1993.

57 *GSN*, May 5, 1993.

58 *GSN*, May 26, 1993.

59 *GSN*, May 26, June 2, 1993.

60 *GSN*, July 7, 1993.

61 *GSN*, July 21, 1993.

62 *GSN*, July 14, 1993.

63 *GSN*, July 21, 1993.

64 *GSN*, August 11, 1993; also Ethel Black, note, June 1994 (net receipts).

65 *GSN*, September 22, 1993.

66 *GSN*, October 6, 1993; letter from Darlene (Williams) Hanington to the author, June 20, 1995; play program.

67 *GSN*, October 6, 1993.

68 *GSN*, December 8, 1993.

69 *GSN*, December 22, 1993.

70 *GSN*, July 21, August 11, 1993, and other issues.

71 *GSN*, December 7, 1994.

72 *The Granite Extra*, May 20, 1994. Concert preview.

73 *GSN*, July 6, 1994.

74 *GSN*, June 1, 1994.

75 *GSN*, July 27, 1994.

76 *Ibid.*

77 *GSN*, September 7, 1994.

78 *GSN*, September 28, 1994.

79 *GSN*, October 5, 1994; other sources.

80 *GSN*, December 7, 1994.

81 Sources include December 1994 and January 1995 issues of the *GSN* and *Lakes Region Courier* and the printed First Night Program; experience of the author.

82 No attempt has been made to cover all accomplishments and notable players. During the four-year period 1991-1994 probably the number of participants in local athletics was well over 1,000. School yearbooks, the *Lakes Region Courier*, and the *Granite State News* are rich sources for further information.

83 *GSN*, July 1 (league standings), July 8 (Lawyers win), 1992; July 7, 1993 (Bankers win).

84 *GSN*, May 22, 1991.

85 *GSN*, May 13, 1992.

86 *GSN*, May 22, 1991 (here paraphrased).

87 *GSN*, June 2, 1993.

88 *GSN*, April 27, 1994 (Skelley); June 22, 1994 (Johnson).

89 *GSN*, March 27, 1991.

90 *GSN*, January 23, 1991, and other issues.

91 Submitted to the author in July 1995.

92 *GSN*, March 13, 1991.

93 *GSN*, March 4, 1992.

94 *GSN*, December 9, 1992.

[95] *GSN*, December 23, 1992; February 17, 1993; February 2, April 6, 1994; other issues. Thanks also to Everett Edmunds for a clarifying comment (letter, June 11, 1995).

[96] *GSN*, March 9, 1994.

[97] *GSN*, May 15, 1991 (Jeremiah Heilig); July 29, 1992 (Steve Flagg).

[98] *GSN*, May 22, 1991 (Smith River); May 20, 1992 (Smith River); June 24, 1992 (Clinton); April 21, May 26, 1993 (Smith River).

[99] *GSN*, July 31, 1991.

[100] *GSN*, January 23, 1991.

[101] *GSN*, August 19, 1992.

[102] *GSN*, November 11, 1992.

[103] *GSN*, July 14, 1993; October 19, December 21, 1994.

[104] Certain information concerning star players and team records is from Bonnie Rankin Lord, letter, July 17, 1995.

[105] *GSN*, April 3, 1991.

[106] *GSN*, November 2, 1994 (vs. Kennett); November 23, 1994 (All-State squad).

[107] *GSN*, October 21, 1992 (vs. Plymouth); September 15, 1993 (vs. Monadnock); October 20, 1993 (vs. Plymouth).

[108] *GSN*, September 29, 1993 (vs. Plymouth); October 13, 1993 (vs. St. Thomas).

[109] *GSN*, May 15, 1991 (Ann Pollini); November 3, 1993 (Blake Palmer); October 14, 1992 (Ed Gascoigne); July 3, 1991 (Beat-the-Pro); August 21, 1991 (Cindy Melanson).

[110] *GSN*, October 7, 1992 (Jamie Hurtado); July 14, 1993 (Melansons); June 29, 1994 (Gross Scotch).

[111] *GSN*, March 30, 1994.

[112] *GSN*, August 28, 1991; August 24, 1994.

[113] *GSN*, June 10, August 5, 1992; February 10, 1993.

[114] *GSN*, February 2, 1994.

[115] *GSN*, June 23, 1993.

[116] *GSN*, May 22, 1991 (NH State); June 26, 1991 (rentals).

[117] *GSN*, February 24, 1993 (Abenaki).

[118] *GSN*, April 8, 1992 (Willie Swaffield); March 17, 1993 (Whitney Swaffield).

[119] *GSN*, February 10, 1993 (Kingswood alpine team winners).

[120] *GSN*, February 23, 1994 (state champs).

[121] *GSN*, January 2, 1991; January 20, 1993.

[122] *GSN*, March 10, 1993.

[123] *GSN*, March 17, 1993.

[124] *Ibid.*

[125] *GSN*, January 12, 1994.

[126] *GSN*, September 25, 1991.

[127] *GSN*, November 6, 1991.

[128] *GSN*, March 20, 1991.

[129] Comment to author, July 24, 1995.

[130] *GSN*, July 22, 1992; July 7, 1993; August 10, 1994.

[131] *GSN*, August 18, 1993.

[132] *GSN*, April 22, May 20, 1992.

[133] *GSN*, April 20, 1994.

[134] *GSN*, April 22, 1992. Also, information from Dianne Sands, July 31, 1995.

[135] *GSN*, September 30, 1992.

[136] *GSN*, June 17, 1992 (most names of out-of-town winners not cited here).

[137] *GSN*, June 16, 1993.

[138] *GSN*, February 19, 1992 (Barbara Bush; primary election results); October 21, 1992 (Maxfield); November 4, 1992 (mock election; also actual election results).

[139] During the Civil War in the 1860s a popular song had these lines: "And in her hair she wore a yellow ribbon. She wore it in the springtime and in the month of May....for her sweetheart who was far, far away." In more recent times a popular song had lyrics including "Tie a yellow ribbon 'round the old oak tree" (based upon an anecdote about a returning prisoner published in *Reader's Digest*).

[140] *GSN*, August 29, 1990; various 1991 issues, especially January and February (overseas and at home); May 22, 1991 (Memorial Day; in NH this was celebrated on May 30 that year, later to change to a movable holiday to permit a three-day weekend as already adopted by many other states).

[141] Specific histories of churches and civic groups are given in Volume II of this work; Huggins Hospital activities are chronicled decade-by-decade in the present volume.

[142] *GSN*, March 30, April 6, 1994 (radon); April 29, 1992; March 31, June 23, 1993 (raccoons).

[143] *GSN*, May 29, July 24, 1991; February 12, March 25, November 25, 1992; May 12, 1993 (addition).

[144] *GSN*, October 2, 1991 (maternity); February 17, 1993 (properties bought); April 28, 1993 (200 volunteers); July 14, 1993 (cardiac).

[145] *GSN*, February 12, August 5, September 30, 1992 (Chief Foss).

[146] *GSN*, September 2, 16, 1992 (Chief Howard); May 5, 1993 (*Drury*).

[147] *GSN*, December 22, 1993.

[148] *Granite Extra*, June 4, 1993.

[149] 1994 *Town Report*. Chief Michael J. Howard commentary.

[150] *GSN*, January 30, 1991. Only significant fires are given in the Fire Log; the Fire Department received many calls for lesser blazes as well as for gas leaks (notable ones at the MacDonald residence and Clipper Home), inspections, etc.

[151] *GSN*, May 1, 1991.

[152] *GSN*, August 21, 1991.

[153] *GSN*, September 4, 1991.

[154] *GSN*, January 1, 1992.

[155] *GSN*, March 11, 1992.

[156] *GSN*, October 28, 1992.

[157] *GSN*, December 2, 1992.

[158] *GSN*, January 27, 1993.

[159] *GSN*, February 17, 1993.

[160] *GSN*, April 28, 1993.

[161] *GSN*, July 7, 1993.

[162] *GSN*, September 22, October 20, 1993.

[163] *GSN*, November 10, 1993.

[164] *GSN*, March 30, 1994. Also author's personal observation.

[165] *GSN*, August 10, 1994.

[166] *Lakes Region Courier*, December 1, 1994.

[167] *GSN*, December 28, 1994.

[168] *GSN*, April 20, 27, 1994, and other issues. Also, author's interview with Rochelle Juliano, May 21, 1994, from which the circumstances given here are somewhat different from those given in the media inasmuch as the journey was begun as a relatively simple short trip over ice, not a foolish, ill-prepared trip over soft ice, slush, and water as reported. Other over-ice vehicles such as snowmobiles do not customarily carry life preservers.

[169] *GSN*, August 19, 1992 (sports cards); October 2, 1991 (parrot); December 2, 1992 (Corvette).

[170] *GSN*, May 8, 1991 (Kent); November 27, 1991 ($10); December 25, 1991 (tree); August 21, 1991 (guns); December 18, 1991 (drive-by).

[171] *GSN*, November 11, 18, 1992, and other issues (drugs); November 18, December 2, 9, 23, 1992; January 13, February 10, 24, March 10, April 14, 1993 (burglaries, arrests); April 28, 1993 (pepper); September 8, 1993 (Cannondale); October 6, November 3, 1993; January 19, 1994 (bomb, fire).

[172] 1994 *Town Report*. Chief Stanley E. Stevens commentary.

[173] *The Times*, June 9, 1993.

[174] *GSN*, August 1, 1993.

[175] *GSN*, September 4, 1990 (questionnaire); January 15, 1992 (computer error); July 8, 1992 ("let it all run away"); *Union Leader*, November 8, 1994 (Simpson to Laconia); *GSN*, April 14, 21, 1993, and other issues (Kelloway); December 7, 1994, and other issues (is a new town planner necessary?).

[176] *GSN*, January 16, February 6, 13, 1991 (PSNH); 1992 *Town Report* (rates 20-30% below).

[177] *GSN*, February 13, 27, March 27, April 10, 17, May 15, July 10, July 24, August 7, 14, September 18, 25, October 2, 16, 23, 1991. Certain information is from an October 1991 manuscript by Elissa K. Paquette.

[178] *GSN*, August 21, October 2, December 18, 1991; 1991 *Town Report*.

[179] *GSN*, March 27, May 29, 1991.

[180] The 1993 *Town Report* was prepared after his death and was distributed in March 1994.

[181] *GSN*, February 13, 1991 (Campbell); March 13, 1991 (savings; Elkins); April 17, 1991 (logo). Additional 1991 notes from the *Town Report*.

[182] *GSN*, June 5, August 28, November 13, December 11, 25, 1991; January 1, 22, February 12, March 11, April 1, 1992; April 7, 14, July 7,1993. 1993 *Town Report*. Additional information provided by Judge Robert Varney.

[183] *GSN*, February 19, 1992 (Moody); March 11, 18, 1992 (voting); April 15, 1992 (permits; sewage); June 24, 1992, and many other issues through 1994 (street names; this topic is discussed in Volume II in the introduction to the "Wolfeboro Place Names and Origins" section).

[184] *GSN*, January 13, April 14, May 26, June 9, August 25, 1993.

[185] *GSN*, April 21, May 12, November 3, 1993, and other issues (docks).

[186] *GSN*, May 19, 1993.

[187] *GSN*, June 29, 1994.

[188] *GSN*, July 20, 29, 1994, and other issues.

[189] Anecdote related by Roberta French.

[190] *Union Leader*, June 2, 1985, p. A13.

[191] *GSN*, December 25, 1991 (oil); *Union Leader*, January 9, 1995, and numerous issues of *GSN* (Taxpayers Association). *GSN*, July 10, 1991, told of another oil spill, "neither toxic nor hazardous," beneath a 50-year-old tank on an old farm on South Main Street which the Department of Environmental Safety demand be excavated.

[192] *GSN*, March 14, 1990; October 21, 1992; other issues (W-T Land Bank); 1993 and 1994 *Town Reports*; *GSN*, March 24, 1993 (selectmen cautiously accept); July 28, August 18, September 8, 29, 1993, and other issues ("Let's Do It Program"); December 1, 1993 (first fruits); December 22, 1993 (special four-page supplement to the *GSN* prepared by Sarah James; included maps, plans, etc.), also vote to cancel Route 28 rezoning; April 27, 1994 (award).

[193] *Lakes Region Courier* May 12, 1994; *GSN*, May 11, 1994. Most quotations here are from the Powell text in the *Lakes Region Courier*.

# INDEX OF ILLUSTRATIONS

# INDEX

## C

## D

## E

## G

## H

## I



## J

## Q



## R

## S

## T

## U

## V



## W

## Y



## Z